Get Instant Access
to thousands of editors and agents

D0470628

WRITERSMARKET.COM

Register now and save $10!

Sure, you already know **Novel & Short Story Writer's Market** is the essential tool for selling your fiction. And now, to complement your trusty "writer's bible," subscribe to WritersMarket.com (see back for more information) for **$10 off the regular price!**

As a purchaser of **2006 Novel & Short Story Writer's Market**, get a $10 discount off the regular $29.99 subscription price for WritersMarket.com. Simply enter coupon code **WM6MB** on the subscription page at www.WritersMarket.com.

www.WritersMarket.com
The Ultimate Research Tool for Writers

Tear out your handy bookmark
for fast reference to symbols and abbreviations used in this book

NSS06

2006 NOVEL & SHORT ...RKET

...edition

 ...gented submissions only

 market is closed to submissions

 actively seeking new writers

 seeks both new and established writers

 prefers working with established writers, mostly referrals

 only handles specific types of work

 award-winning market

 Canadian market

 market is located outside of the U.S. and Canada

 imprint, subsidiary or division of major book publishing house (in book publishers section)

 $ market pays (in magazine sections)

 ● comment from the editor of *Novel & Short Story Writer's Market*

ms, mss manuscript(s)

SASE self-addressed, stamped envelope

SAE self-addressed envelope

IRC International Reply Coupon, for use in countries other than your own

(For definitions of words and expressions relating specifically to writing and publishing, see the Glossary in the back of this book.)

TEAR ALONG PERFORATION

2006 NOVEL & SHORT STORY WRITER'S MARKET
KEY TO SYMBOLS

 N market new to this edition

 publisher accepts agented submissions only

 market is closed to submissions

 actively seeking new writers

 seeks both new and established writers

 prefers working with established writers, mostly referrals

 only handles specific types of work

 award-winning market

 Canadian market

 market is located outside of the U.S. and Canada

 imprint, subsidiary or division of major book publishing house (in book publishers section)

 $ market pays (in magazine sections)

● comment from the editor of *Novel & Short Story Writer's Market*

ms, mss manuscript(s)

SASE self-addressed, stamped envelope

SAE self-addressed envelope

IRC International Reply Coupon, for use in countries other than your own

(For definitions of words and expressions relating specifically to writing and publishing, see the Glossary in the back of this book.)

TEAR ALONG PERFORATION

WRITERSMARKET.COM

Here's what you'll find at WritersMarket.com:

☀ **More than 5,700 listings** — At WritersMarket.com, you'll find thousands of listings that couldn't fit in the *2006 Writer's Market*! It's the most comprehensive database of verified markets available.

☀ **Easy-to-use searchable database** — Looking for a specific magazine or book publisher? Just type in the title or keyword for broad category results.

☀ **Listings updated daily** — It doesn't look good to address your query letter to the wrong editor or agent...and with WritersMarket.com, that will never happen. You'll be on top of all the industry developments...as soon as they happen!

☀ **Personalized for you** — Stay on top of your publishing contacts with **Submission Tracker**; store your best-bet markets in **Favorites Folders**; and get **updates** to your publishing areas of interest, every time you log in.

☀ **And so much more!**

Subscribe today and save $10!
(enter coupon code WM6MB)

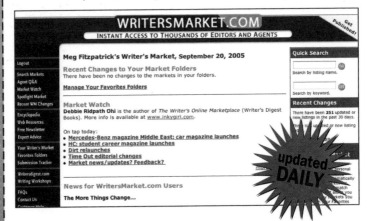

Tear out your handy bookmark
for fast reference to symbols and abbreviations used in this book

NSS06

2006
Novel & Short Story Writer's Market®

Lauren Mosko, Editor
Michael Schweer, Assistant Editor

WRITER'S DIGEST BOOKS
CINCINNATI, OH

Complaint Procedure

If you feel you have not been treated fairly by a listing in *Novel & Short Story Writer's Market*, we advise you to take the following steps:

- First try to contact the listing. Sometimes one phone call or a letter can quickly clear up the matter.
- Document all your correspondence with the listing. When you write to us with a complaint, provide the details of your submission, the date of your first contact with the listing, and the nature of your subsequent correspondence.

We will enter your letter into our files and attempt to contact the listing. The number and severity of complaints will be considered in our decision whether or not to delete the listing from the next edition.

If you are a publisher of fiction and would like to be considered for a listing in the next edition of *Novel & Short Story Writer's Market*, send a SASE (or SAE and IRC) with your request for a questionnaire to *Novel & Short Story Writer's Market*—QR, 4700 East Galbraith Road, Cincinnati OH 45236.

Managing Editor, Writer's Digest Market Books: Alice Pope
Senior Editor, Writer's Digest Market Books: Kathryn S. Brogan
Supervisory Editor, Writer's Digest Market Books: Donna Poehner
Technical Coordinator: Robert Lee Brewer

Writer's Digest Books website: www.writersdigest.com.
Writer's Market website: www.writersmarket.com.

2006 Novel & Short Story Writer's Market. Copyright © 2005 by Writer's Digest Books. Published by F+W Publications, 4700 East Galbraith Road, Cincinnati, Ohio 45236. Printed and bound in the United States of America. All rights reserved. No part of this book may be reproduced in any form or by any electronic or mechanical means including information storage and retrieval systems without written permission from the publisher, except by reviewers who may quote brief passages to be printed in a magazine or newspaper.

International Standard Serial Number 0897-9812
International Standard Book Number 1-58297-397-0

Cover design by Kelly Kofron

Interior design by Clare Finney

Production coordinated by Robin Richie

Attention Booksellers: This is an annual directory of F+W Publications. Return deadline for this edition is December 31, 2006.

Contents

CRAFT & TECHNIQUE

GETTING PUBLISHED

FOR MYSTERY WRITERS

FOR ROMANCE WRITERS

FOR SCIENCE FICTION/FANTASY & HORROR WRITERS

MARKETS

RESOURCES

From the Editor

© Tim Grondin

Have you ever met someone for the first time and been surprised when she volunteered an intimate personal detail, seemingly out of the blue? Say you dash to the deli around the corner for lunch. While waiting in line to order, you realize the new girl in the office is behind you. You politely say hello and then turn your attention back to the counter, where you settle on a turkey sandwich. "I used to have recurring turkey nightmares," volunteers your co-worker. "In grade school we had to sing this Thanksgiving song, and the recorded music that went with it had live turkeys gobbling in the background. The sound was unholy." You stammer something like, "Wow. Gosh. That's terrible," but you're really thinking, *why is she telling me this?*

Social psychologists call your co-worker's behavior "self-disclosure" and assert that self-disclosure creates connection and builds trust. Well, I'm the new girl in the office of *Novel & Short Story Writer's Market* and—in the spirit of revealing deep dark secrets to complete strangers—I have a confession to make: I've never published any fiction. In fact, I've never even submitted anything. More embarrassing for me to admit is that I'm scared to send out my stories. When I think of the great writers of the past and present and all the amazing talent being discovered every day, I am overwhelmed. Writing itself can be frightening for me because it requires a reckless abandon the editorial side of my brain often sabotages.

Why am I telling you this? Maybe you've never submitted fiction either, or maybe you're a seasoned submission-process veteran. Either way, we're in the same boat: We have a story to tell and we're searching for someone willing to listen. In fact, the only difference between us is it's my job to research the fiction market—and then share my findings with you. This year's edition is special to me, not only because it's my first as editor but also because it's the book's 25th anniversary. To celebrate, I've decided to take the plunge and send out my work. If you're ready, too, we can do it together.

Now that we're partners, I should mention that many social psychologists also support the "disclosure reciprocity effect," which basically means I've told you about myself so it's only fair you talk back. How has *Novel & Short Story Writer's Market* helped you publish your work? What could I do to make the next 25 editions even better than the first? Send me your success stories as well as your suggestions.

Best of luck with your writing this year. Let's check back with each other in 2007 and swap stories.

Lauren Mosko

Lauren Mosko
lauren.mosko@fwpubs.com

You've Got a Story

So What Now?

To make the most of *Novel & Short Story Writer's Market*, you need to know how to use it. And with more than 600 pages of fiction publishing markets and resources, a writer could easily get lost amid the information. This quick-start guide will help you wind your way through the pages of *Novel & Short Story Writer's Market*, as well as the fiction publishing process, and emerge with your dream accomplished—to see your fiction in print.

1. Read, read, read. Read numerous magazines, fiction collections and novels to determine if your fiction compares favorably with work currently being published. If your fiction is at least the same caliber as that you're reading, then move on to step two. If not, postpone submitting your work and spend your time polishing your fiction. Writing and reading the work of others are the best ways to improve craft.

For help with craft and critique of your work:

- You'll find advice and inspiration from best-selling authors and top fiction editors in the The Writing Life section, beginning on page 5.
- You'll find articles on the craft and business aspects of writing fiction in the Craft & Technique section, beginning on page 45, and in the Getting Published section, beginning on page 58.
- If you're a genre writer, you will find information in For Mystery Writers, beginning on page 75; For Romance Writers, beginning on page 83; and For Science Fiction/Fantasy & Horror Writers, beginning on page 95.
- You'll find Contest listings beginning on page 464.
- You'll find Conference & Workshop listings beginning on page 504.

2. Analyze your fiction. Determine the type of fiction you write to best target your submissions to markets most suitable to your work. Do you write literary, genre, mainstream or one of the many other categories of fiction? There are magazines and presses seeking specialized work in each of these areas as well as numerous others.

For editors and publishers with specialized interests, see the Category Index beginning on page 581.

3. Learn about the market. Read *Writer's Digest* magazine (F + W Publications, Inc.); *Publishers Weekly*, the trade magazine of the publishing industry; and *Independent Publisher*, which contains information about small- to medium-sized independent presses. And don't forget the Internet. The number of sites for writers seems to grow daily, and among them you'll find www.writersmarket.com and www.writersdigest.com.

4. Find markets for your work. There are a variety of ways to locate markets for fiction. The periodicals sections of bookstores and libraries are great places to discover new journals and magazines that might be open to your type of short stories. Read writing-related magazines and newsletters for information about new markets and publications seeking fiction submissions. Also, frequently browse bookstore shelves to see what novels and short story collections are being published and by whom. Check acknowledgment pages for names of editors and agents, too. Online journals often have links to the websites of other journals that may publish fiction. And last but certainly not least, read the listings found here in *Novel & Short Story Writer's Market*.

Also, don't forget to utilize the Category Indexes at the back of this book to help you target your fiction to the right market.

5. Send for guidelines. In the listings in this book, we try to include as much submission information as we can get from editors and publishers. Over the course of the year, however, editors' expectations and needs may change. Therefore, it is best to request submission guidelines by sending a self-addressed stamped envelope (SASE). You can also check each magazine's and press' website, which usually contains a page with guideline information. You can find updated guidelines of many of the markets listed here at www.writersdigest.com. And for an even more comprehensive and continually updated online markets list, you can obtain a subscription to www.writersmarket.com by visiting the site or calling 1-800-448-0915.

6. Begin your publishing efforts with journals and contests open to beginners. If this is your first attempt at publishing your work, your best bet is to begin with local publications or those you know are open to beginning writers. Then, after you have built a publication history, you can try the more prestigious and nationally distributed magazines. For markets open to beginners, look for the ☐ symbol preceding listing titles. Also, look for the ◪ symbol that identifies markets open to exceptional work from beginners as well as work from experienced, previously published writers.

7. Submit your fiction in a professional manner. Take the time to show editors that you care about your work and are serious about publishing. By following a publication's or book publisher's submission guidelines and practicing standard submission etiquette, you

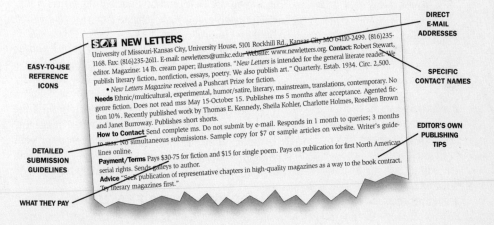

DIRECT
E-MAIL
ADDRESSES

EASY-TO-USE
REFERENCE
ICONS

SPECIFIC
CONTACT NAMES

EDITOR'S OWN
PUBLISHING
TIPS

DETAILED
SUBMISSION
GUIDELINES

WHAT THEY PAY

⑤◪ NEW LETTERS
University of Missouri-Kansas City, University House, 5101 Rockhill Rd., Kansas City MO 64110-2499. (816)235-1168. Fax: (816)235-2611. E-mail: newletters@umkc.edu. Website: www.newletters.org. **Contact:** Robert Stewart, editor. Magazine: 14 lb. cream paper; illustrations. "*New Letters* is intended for the general literate reader. We publish literary fiction, nonfiction, essays, poetry. We also publish art." Quarterly. Estab. 1934. Circ. 2,500.
• *New Letters Magazine* received a Pushcart Prize for fiction.
Needs Ethnic/multicultural, experimental, humor/satire, literary, mainstream, translations, contemporary. No genre fiction. Does not read mss May 15-October 15. Publishes ms 5 months after acceptance. Agented fiction 10%. Recently published work by Thomas E. Kennedy, Sheila Kohler, Charlotte Holmes, Rosellen Brown and Janet Burroway. Publishes short shorts.
How to Contact Send complete ms. Do not submit by e-mail. Responds in 1 month to queries; 3 months to mss. No simultaneous submissions. Sample copy for $7 or sample articles on website. Writer's guidelines online.
Payment/Terms Pays $30-75 for fiction and $15 for single poem. Pays on publication for first North American serial rights. Sends galleys to author.
Advice "Seek publication of representative chapters in high-quality magazines as a way to the book contract. Try literary magazines first."

Getting Started

2006 NOVEL & SHORT STORY WRITER'S MARKET KEY TO SYMBOLS

 market new to this edition

 publisher accepts agented submissions only

 market is closed to submissions

 actively seeking new writers

 seeks both new and established writers

 prefers working with established writers, mostly referrals

 only handles specific types of work

 award-winning market

 Canadian market

 market located outside of U.S. and Canada

imprint, subsidiary or division of larger book publishing house (in book publishers section)

$ market pays (in magazine sections)

● comment from the editor of *Novel & Short Story Writer's Market*

ms, mss manuscript(s)

SASE self-addressed, stamped envelope

SAE self-addressed envelope

IRC International Reply Coupon, for use in countries other than your own

(For definitions of words and expressions relating specifically to writing and publishing, see the Glossary in the back of this book.)

Find a handy pull-out bookmark, a quick reference to the icons used in this book, right inside the front cover.

can increase your chances that an editor will want to take the time to read your work and consider it for publication. Remember, first impressions last, and a carelessly assembled submission packet can jeopardize your chances before your story or novel manuscript has had a chance to speak for itself. For help with preparing submissions read "The Business of Fiction Writing," beginning on page 66.

8. Keep track of your submissions. Know when and where you have sent fiction and how long you need to wait before expecting a reply. If an editor does not respond by the time indicated in his market listing or guidelines, wait a few more weeks and then follow up with a letter (and SASE) asking when the editor anticipates making a decision. If you still do not receive a reply from the editor within a reasonable amount of time, send a letter withdrawing your work from consideration and move on to the next market on your list.

9. Learn from rejection. Rejection is the hardest part of the publication process. Unfortunately, rejection happens to every writer, and every writer needs to learn to deal with the negativity involved. On the other hand, rejection can be valuable when used as a teaching tool rather than a reason to doubt yourself and your work. If an editor offers suggestions with his or her rejection slip, take those comments into consideration. You don't have to automatically agree with an editor's opinion of your work. It may be that the editor has a different perspective on the piece than you do. Or, you may find that the editor's suggestions give you new insight into your work and help you improve your craft.

10. Don't give up. The best advice for you as you try to get published is be persistent and always believe in yourself and your work. By continually reading other writers' work, constantly working on the craft of fiction writing and relentlessly submitting your work, you will eventually find that magazine or book publisher that's the perfect match for your fiction. And, *Novel & Short Story Writer's Market* will be here to help you every step of the way.

GUIDE TO LISTING FEATURES

On page 3 you will find an example of the market listings contained in *Novel & Short Story Writer's Market*. Also included are call-outs identifying the various format features of the listings. (For an explanation of the symbols used, see the sidebar.)

Richard Ford

Pulitzer Winner Discusses His Writing Vocation

© Brigitte Friedrich

by Will Allison

n 1968, after dropping out of law school, receiving a medical discharge from the Marine Corps, and failing at several other vocational efforts, 24-year-old Richard Ford arrived at the University of California, Irvine to enroll in the MFA creative writing program.

For the unemployed Ford, pursuing fiction writing was not so much a career decision as a last attempt at discovering what he might do with his life. A few years earlier, in college, he'd written a piece of a story he carried around with him for a while. "I realized," he says, "that writing that bit of narrative, and the satisfaction of having written it, were about the only things I could think of I'd liked doing, had any respect for having done, and (most importantly) didn't already know I couldn't do."

Thirty-seven years later, Ford stands as one of America's most celebrated writers. The author of five novels and three story collections, he has been a Guggenheim fellow and two-time National Endowment for the Arts fellow. In 1987, his novel *The Sportswriter* (Random House) was a finalist for the PEN/Faulkner Award. Nine years later, his sequel to that novel, *Independence Day* (Knopf), became the first book to win both the Pulitzer Prize and the PEN/Faulkner Award.

In the following interview, Ford recalls his early efforts at writing and publishing and discusses the habits and attitudes that have helped him produce work of which he's proud.

When did you first get interested in writing fiction?

I don't really remember, which is to say it wasn't a Sistine Chapel moment. I wrote a piece of a story, something fictional, when I was in college and carried it around with me for two or three years. Eventually I tried to get it published when I was in law school, and that didn't work out. I say this because it seems to me I wrote something fiction-like—to take the question literally—*before* I actually got interested in writing fiction.

When I quit law school, that story fragment served me well because when I got to my mother's house in Little Rock I sat down and tried to think what I wanted to do with myself. I realized writing that bit of narrative, and the satisfaction of having written it, were about the only things I could think of I'd liked doing, had any respect for having done, and (most importantly) didn't already know I couldn't do. It wasn't an auspicious start, but I did choose

WILL ALLISON (www.willallison.com) is a staff member at the Squaw Valley Community of Writers and teaches creative writing at Indiana University-Purdue University at Indianapolis. His short stories have appeared in *Zoetrope: All-Story, Kenyon Review, One Story, Shenandoah, American Short Fiction, Atlanta, Florida Review* and *Kansas Quarterly/Arkansas Review*.

something my instincts led me to, rather than choosing something for merely practical reasons—or worse, for other people's reasons.

As a young writer, how did you handle rejection?

I think I handled rejection pretty well, although there are people who knew me then—in the late '60s—who'd say I wasn't crazy about having my stories disapproved of. But pure rejection—that is, magazines bouncing my submissions—I accommodated okay, without ever developing a true appetite for it. I'd already failed at lots of things before I started trying to write stories. I had little reason to think I had great aptitude for writing, which meant that being rejected, when it happened (and it happened often), wasn't a surprise. Beyond that, all I had to combat the woe of rejection was a high regard for literature and an intense doggedness based on habits I'd developed in college. I also had a frightened belief writing was my last chance (however unpromising) at doing anything worthwhile.

Do your stories get rejected now?

Yes. A magazine I publish in quite a lot rejected a story of mine two or three years ago. And since I don't write all that many stories, I had to work at not being bothered and discouraged by it. I managed okay. Not that it helps when the writer is oneself, but many great magazines reject the work of many greater writers. It happens. It isn't pleasant. One goes on. The hidden worry, of course, is rejection means you're no good, and that's always the background music to the whole vocation, as far as I'm concerned. One would like not to ''press on'' when it's hopeless, but find ways to be more useful in the world.

Probably a greater fear—if these are genuine fears and not just natural parts of the responsibility of being as good a writer as you can be—is the world will just go on giving you sanction long after you've ceased being any good. I once asked a publisher of mine, a dear friend, if he'd tell me if I wrote something really bad and seemed not to know it. He said, ''Absolutely not. That's *your* job.'' He was right.

Tell us about your first published story.

I really don't remember the first story I published. I know that sounds preposterous, but it's true. I know I had a story accepted (and probably published) by an utterly insignificant and ignoble college literary magazine. But I also had a story accepted and published by a much more reputable magazine in faraway New Zealand, and *that* might've been the first. It was a long time ago now. How I felt? Well, I was less excited than you might imagine, because in the case of the college literary magazine, I knew no one would read my story unless I handed that person a copy. Plus, the rest of the work in it was no good. So I had to wonder if my story was any good. In the case of the New Zealand publication, it was, after all, in New Zealand, a place I probably couldn't have found on the map then and couldn't imagine, although I still have copies of that magazine and remember being pleased in a sort of diluted way. I've since been to New Zealand and feel very good about having published a story there.

These experiences made me realize quite early in my writing life that 1) I didn't want to write stories only small groups of people would read; 2) I wanted to write stories Americans would read; and 3) getting published wasn't what writing was principally about—writing well was. If one wrote well, then satisfactory publication would take care of itself. I still believe that.

How did you decide where to send your stories?

At first, I had friends who were young writers and I sent my stories where they sent theirs. I probably looked in digests like this one. I hung around libraries and read their periodicals and either did or didn't send stories there. I never really had much luck getting quarterlies or so-called little magazines to publish my stories, and I forsook them pretty early. Finally, I had much better luck with much better magazines. The first bit of fiction I published that made me truly happy was in *The Paris Review*, and in that case Peter Matthiessen submitted it to George Plimpton, after having read the piece at the Squaw Valley Community of Writers in 1971. Nowadays, I have what's called a "first look" contract with a magazine, and so I send the few stories I write there. If they bounce a story, I talk to my agent about where else to send it.

You earned an MFA in creative writing at University of California, Irvine. How valuable was that experience, and do you recommend graduate writing programs in general?

Going to Irvine was great. For others, graduate school might not be great, and yet a writing life would come along. I arrived at Irvine in 1968, very motivated, having failed at several things. I was teachable, though I did not know very much. I had superb teachers both of literature and as workshop leaders there. Irvine stressed writing in a context of reading great literature, and the two have stayed joined in my mind ever since; i.e., I wanted to write great literature, not just write and get published so I could fill up a curriculum vitae or get a teaching job. I learned to read closely at Irvine. I learned to treat others' writing with respect. I learned that to write was to accept a high calling.

As to recommending graduate school, I'd rather not recommend anything—other than a good book—to anyone. I remember when I started at Irvine, we heard about one of our other incoming fellow-students arriving to Orange County, having a look around, being utterly demoralized by Southern California, and just getting back in his car with his family and driving straight back to Vermont. That was Howard Frank Mosher, an estimable writer in all ways.

Reprinted with permission.

Independence Day, winner of both the 1996 Pulitzer Prize and the PEN/Faulkner Award, is the sequel to Ford's *The Sportswriter*. This book continues the story of Frank Bascombe, a sportswriter-turned-real estate agent in the midst of midlife crisis, and recounts how the events over the fourth of July weekend transformed him.

Over the course of your career, do you find writing has gotten easier or harder?

I thought writing was hard to do when I was young. I didn't feel like a natural for it, and some people still agree with that assessment. Now that I'm not young, I don't think in terms of hard or easy. I choose to do it; whether it's hard or easy doesn't matter. And, I've never thought about my writing as a "career." I left "career" behind when I left law school. For me, writing's nearer to a vocation, something not separable from the everydayness of life, something without a staged progression, or a set of rules or protocols or skills. You make it up.

How long does it usually take you to write a story? A novel?

Stories can take a week to write or a month. Rarely longer. Novels are big clerical morasses. Of the five novels I've written—almost six—five have taken three years. One, *Wildlife*

The Writing Life

(Atlantic Monthly Press), which is pretty short, took about a year. I don't think this matters, though. Books and stories take whatever time you need to write them as well as possible. You know the old joke whose punch line is "What's time to a pig?" Well, what's time to a writer?

How much time do you spend on revision as compared to time spent on a first draft? Or do you revise as you go?

The entire notion of "drafts" has pretty much been left behind by me, except for the first draft of a story or novel, which I write in longhand with a (formerly 29¢) Bic pen. And even there I niggle around every morning with what I wrote the day before—makes for messy manuscripts. Then I type what I've written onto a laptop and revise things as I type. Then I read the typed paper pages, just like the old days, trying to improve one thing and then another, but not necessarily going through the whole thing start to finish—though I also do that eventually, of course. I'm dogged more than I'm terribly orderly in revising.

I've heard in order to get the words just right, you read all 700 pages of *Independence Day* aloud to your wife—*twice*. What's the value of reading one's work aloud?

I did read all of *Independence Day* aloud. Actually, I read it aloud twice to myself but not to my wife Kristina. We used to do that, but she got busy, and that book was pretty long, so I spared her. She did, of course, read it several times in manuscript and contributed to it immensely. Reading books aloud is an effort to authorize every word, every pause, every emphasis, to take complete control and responsibility for everything on the page. I can't seem to do it any other way. I call it "getting the whole book in my head," and that's the way it feels. It's a big job. But to me, this responsibility for everything is the heart of what it means to be a book's author. You authorize everything as much as possible; be sure you know—to the extent you can—how the reader will respond to every word. After all, you write them so somebody will read them.

Do you ever abandon stories or novels, or do you keep going back to them until they're finished?

I've yet to abandon a novel once I started it. So far, I've published the few novels I've started, and I've been pleased with every novel I wrote. And I haven't set aside more than four or five stories in my life. Why this is true is complicated and probably has to do with my personal psychology.

When I was beginning to write, I heard lots of stories about young writers, and not so young writers, who carried around with them like a curse "the unfinished novel." It was a sort of urban myth, though I'm sure it wasn't a myth. But it hung out there like a threat to me. Complicating this was the fact of my not fully completing, and even failing at, several vocational efforts before starting to write. Those failures, seen as unfinished efforts (law school, the Marine Corps, becoming a sportswriter, and others), frankly haunted me as I commenced to write fiction in my early 20s. It wasn't so much that I feared failure, but rather I feared not giving my all, not completing what I began. I didn't want that to be the final judgment on me. So I contrived ways to be sure I finished things. I planned. I collected voluminous raw material. I thought a lot about what I was intending to write before starting. I tried to anticipate impediments. I cleared out of my life things that would cause me to not finish my projects. I abolished the notion of writer's block. I dedicated myself to my vocation in, I suppose, the only way I understood. Which was fully.

What's the most useful piece of writing advice you've received?

My first writing teacher, a remarkable man named Carl Hartman, said to me when I was 20, "Richard, I think if you wanted to, you might make a go of this." He meant writing. It wasn't exactly full-throated encouragement, but it perfectly respected all the uncertainties of the writing life, and I understood that even when he said it.

Since then, I've heard lots of useful advice from lots of smart people. Book reviews don't usually teach one much, but once Walter Clemons, now sadly departed and then the chief book reviewer for *Newsweek*, wrote in that magazine that while he liked the book I'd just published (*The Ultimate Good Luck*), it was too bad that in writing it I ("Mr. Ford") had short-circuited my considerable sense of humor. That made an impression on me, and I've tried to remember it.

Later on, in the mid-'80s, I showed a story that wasn't entirely pleasing me to my friend Joyce Carol Oates, and she said, "Richard, what you need to do to this story is to start where it now seems to end, and just write some more." That made instant and great sense to me, and I've since then tried to write stories that contained all I could say, rather than stopping short for reason of effect. One can always take things out later, but (in my view, anyway) I want to be sure I've said it all. In my brain, that's the only way to get the best out of myself.

I assume you read a great many stories as guest editor for the 1990 edition of *Best American Short Stories*. Do you see any trends or changes in the stories being published today versus then?

I noticed only this, as I worked my way through a lot of stories in compiling *The Granta Book of the American Short Story, Volume 2*: American writers in 2004 seemed to be writing in every mode, every style, using every grasp on verisimilitude, in every humor, at varying lengths, using every conceit imaginable—all in the same country and at the same time—live and let live. What that says about the culture, I leave to others to assess.

When I was beginning, in the late '60s, American story writing aesthetics seemed to be balkanized and adversarial, the way the so-called poetry world seems to be to this day. In fiction, it was "antistory" practitioners versus traditionalists. Antistory loosely referred to ways of writing that distrusted and violated traditional formalities of character, temporal narrative, plot, structure—the unities—in favor of fictions that don't do that. The antistory writers, using vocabularies that implied moral laxity in their brother-traditionalists, had little good to say about the other. And the traditionalists rather tolerated the antistory writers, choosing—I thought at the time—simply to wait them out (although John Gardner rather heatedly wrote *On Moral Fiction* [Basic Books] to put the antistory writers in their place—unsuccessfully).

Perhaps this brief description is incorrect and owes to my youth, and to my lower-than-ground-level view of the fictional landscape of the time, but it seemed that way then. And the landscape seems notably *not* that way now. I don't know which is better. Years ago, there was a good deal of fecundity and felt tension in the air about fiction and how it ought—always "ought"—to be done. *TriQuarterly* was a vivid and exciting journal for thought and debate about these matters. I don't teach much, so it may be this is going on in universities and journals and I just don't hear about it. People seem just to be writing and not to be writing polemically about writing practice. I may be out of touch since I spend all my time writing and reading fiction rather than reading and writing about it.

What are you working on now?

Today, and for the past two years, I've been writing a novel titled *The Lay of the Land*, which—if I can finish it—will be the third in a short series of connected novels that includes *The Sportswriter* and *Independence Day*.

Jonathan Lethem

Finding His Way Home

© Sylvia Plachy

by Michael Schweer

J onathan Lethem came to a crossroads early in his writing career. He had to decide just what kind of writer he wanted to be. Would he allow the autobiographical to seep into his fiction or keep it wholly inventive? The answer seemed quite easy for him at the time: "I thought most of the writers I liked were on the side of inventors, so for me I've always been interested in disappearing from my work and producing fascinating characters who were not myself," the writer said during a public interview at the University of Cincinnati.

Lethem refused to write himself into his fiction. "I didn't value the autobiographical in my work," he says. "I validated my own imaginative work the most. I wanted people to marvel the way I did at Italo Calvino, Graham Greene, Franz Kafka and Patricia Highsmith." It's little surprise then that Lethem's early writings are alive with gun-toting kangaroos (*Gun, With Occasional Music* [Harcourt]), talking Bonsai trees (*Amnesia Moon* [Tor]), a black hole caught in a love triangle (*As She Climbed Across the Table* [Doubleday]), and telepathic travel (*Girl In Landscape* [Doubleday]).

But Lethem could only repress his own story for so long. In his best-selling novel *Motherless Brooklyn* (Doubleday), Lethem combined the fantastic world of a Tourettic detective and Zen-Buddhist gangsters with his own memories of childhood haunts and the characters who populated his borough.

Motherless Brooklyn marks a change in Lethem's writing, a point when he set aside his speculative fiction and began moving closer to familiar worlds. Lethem's next novel, *The Fortress of Solitude* (Doubleday), centered on a young boy who struggles against loneliness and discrimination after his family moves to Brooklyn; the story is threaded with similarities to Lethem's own bohemian upbringing there. His latest effort, *The Disappointment Artist* (Doubleday), is a collection of personal essays openly examining Lethem's adolescence through the lens of pop culture. If his early novels embody Lethem's aspirations of creating a world outside himself, then his newer work reflects his inability to ignore the world of his past.

The son of a painter and a storyteller, Lethem knew he was called to the creative life. "I can't remember a time when I didn't think I'd be an artist of some kind," he says. "In my family it would have been strange if I would've done something outside of the creative realm." He was the quintessential bohemian wunderkind, reading Kafka and going to Godard films. Skipping school to spend the day at the used bookstore seemed normal for the young

---

MICHAEL SCHWEER is the assistant editor of *Novel & Short Story Writer's Market* and *Songwriter's Market*.

Lethem. Hanging out in his father's studio every day, it was only natural Lethem's first identification with the artistic world was painting. He began following in the footsteps of his father—practicing and studying drawing and painting—but soon realized it was his mother's love of reading and her collection of books that truly called to him.

The first step in his (covert) evolution from painter to writer came when he was 14 and his mother gave him a typewriter. Wasting little time, Lethem wrote a 125-page story in one summer. In true romantic-writer form, the piece was written on loose-leaf paper, complete with blue lines and "hanging chads." Lethem admits the work wasn't anything special; it was the accumulation of his words and ideas on the page that made it special. "I was impressed with the fact that I wrote 125 pages. *I* created it," he reflects. "That was the starting point for me." From this moment on, he began to write more and more—almost as a secret addiction—all the while studying fine art.

Reprinted with permission.

When Lethem left for Vermont to attend Bennington College, he was still hanging onto his image as a visual artist and considered himself "a painter who wrote," despite the fact his room was overwhelmed with books. At the time, Bennington was a hotbed for future writers. On any day you might see Bret Easton Ellis, Jill Eisenstadt or Donna Tartt walking around campus. It was in this setting Lethem finally admitted to himself he was a writer. He began to paint less and write more. Before he knew it, he found himself questioning his stay at college. His answer was to go West. Lethem left Bennington his sophomore year and headed to the Bay Area to see what life outside of Brooklyn might hold for him.

Once in California, Lethem found his niche working in a used bookstore—a natural fit for the bibliophile. He read voraciously, cobbling together an education from out-of-print, first-edition books by vague authors most people would love to read but can't find. Not only did Lethem read them—he read them twice. He devoured works by Franz Kafka, Don DeLillo, Raymond Chandler, Italo Calvino, Patricia Highsmith, Philip K. Dick and just about any writer who ever put pen to paper. If Lethem liked an author, he was never satisfied reading just one book; he had to read everything the author ever wrote.

Lethem's appetite for reading was equaled by his passion for writing. It was during this time he seriously contemplated life as a writer. Lethem shed his fears of eeking out life as a used bookstore clerk/writer and willed himself to write. He thought back to his father's struggles as a painter: "My father never made a living as a painter, and that was okay, that didn't deem his work less important." Lethem accepted the idea of remaining at the bookstore and publishing when he could get a chance. This modest view of his work was soon turned on its head after his first novel, *Gun, With Occasional Music*, was published. The book was touted by *Publishers Weekly* as one of the best books of 1994 and by *Locus* as the best first novel of the year.

Never one to hesitate, Lethem quit his job as a book clerk after the success of his debut and took up writing full time. Ten books later, Lethem finds himself right back where he started—at home in Brooklyn doing what he loves best, writing. Here, Lethem shares his thoughts on his writing process.

The Writing Life

What was the first piece of work you had published?

I was 24 when I had my first piece published. It was a short story called "The Cave Beneath the Falls," which I sold to a magazine with the odd name *Aboriginal Science Fiction*. I had been sending stuff for a year or so—two years probably, which felt like 10 years at that point. I probably picked up 40 or 50 rejection slips because I was very assiduous in the early days. I would send the stories right back out the minute after they had been rejected. I probably only had a dozen stories, which I'd been using to harvest rejection slips very actively.

What did you do with the money you got from your first piece of published work?

I think I went out to dinner; it was a while ago. I was very eager to pay taxes. I wanted to be a professional writer. I had been gathering my receipts so I could claim some losses, but I was very happy to get paid.

You experienced success with your early work, but it seemed that *Motherless Brooklyn* was the work that really put you on the literary scene. How do you handle this success?

Reprinted with permission.

I think I'm a lucky writer in a funny way—for not having had an overnight success. The first few novels were well received in a smaller arena, and I built up sort of a cult success. By the time *Motherless Brooklyn* won the National Book Critics Award for Fiction in 1999 and became a minor best-seller, which was great fortune for me, I think I already felt like a writer. I knew I had many stories in me and I was going to do many different things, so rather than get knocked on my heels by *Motherless Brooklyn* and feel forced to try to repeat that formula, I took it as more of an opportunity, a vote of confidence for what I'd been doing all along.

Has your life changed as a result of more people reading your work?

I am hugely grateful for my readers. The most important differences for me—apart from the increased security I have from my publisher—are the number of side projects that come my way, the number of appearances I am asked to do personally, the number of silly journalistic possibilities that come along: the number of film stars I get asked to interview. All this is fine, but the privacy of my writing life is a delicate thing, and it has been more difficult to protect in the last couple of years.

Your early work had more of a science fiction bent to it, and your later work has more of a literary quality. What do you think caused this shift?

I had always loved a wide variety of novels, and I always wanted to be a writer who moved through a lot of different genres and approaches to the novel before I was done. The early work is specifically related to science fiction and hard-boiled detective fiction. It reflects the books I read throughout my teenage years. Those were the first type of stories I knew how to write because I had been reading those kinds of books so eagerly. As I became a reader with a much broader of range of influences, my capacity changed; I became able to write a wider variety of things.

Do you have any rituals you perform before, during or after writing a story?

Usually when I finish a novel I go on a binge of solitary movie going. I like to goof off for weeks at a time, going to the multiplex and sneaking into one film after the next.

Where do you normally write?

I like to write at home, but sometimes I need to shake it up, and so there are some cafés I like to sit in. I have been going to the Brooklyn Writers Space, which is basically a library without books where writers go to work. Anything I can do to keep myself from getting restless.

Do you write while on the road?

I do my best. I like to try to write when I travel. Of course you can't ever keep the same level of concentration, but I try.

When you start writing a novel, how do you begin, and what goals do you set for yourself? Do you make an outline, or do you just start writing?

No, I don't like outlines; I have a preference for holding the images and the ideas all in my head. The pleasurable tension of wanting to tell a story that hasn't been said on paper is what really motivates me to work every day. I will occasionally jot a note on a piece of paper for a specific idea for a line of dialogue or an image that comes to mind. But the majority of the storytelling I like to leave for the actual moment of work itself.

***The Disappointment Artist* is your collection of personal essays. Did you amass the essays over time, or were they byproducts of down time when working on other stories?**

The writing of the essays spanned the last six years, but the majority of them were written in the last two years. It was after I had written a couple of essays in this mode I realized there was a book in it. So in the last couple of years, since finishing *Fortress of Solitude,* I focused on writing the rest of the essays to complete the book. They're all cultural essays but they turn into confessional pieces. Memoir disguised as cultural commentary.

What do you do when you have writer's block? Do you go back to an old favorite book and read?

I do read a lot to nourish my writing. I like to keep books I love near. It's very much a part of my writing process. I'm lucky I'm not a writer who's prone to blocks. I'm mostly a pretty happy camper.

How do you deal with critics?

I went three or four books before I even got a slightly negative review because I was kind of a dark-horse author. People chose to rave about me—"Here is the great writer you never heard of''—or they ignored me because nobody was making any special big claims on my behalf. It was a long time before I began to get some bad reviews, and I always figured the fact that I did get a few was kind of a measure that I achieved something. I put them in an optimistic light.

Do you have any advice for new writers?

Don't stop writing because you've begun submitting or you're waiting for a response. For that matter, don't stop writing because you've sold a book. One of the most important things you can do, in the year or more it takes between placing a novel with a publisher and having it come out, is get deep into the next novel. You'll make yourself much more immune to the reviewers.

Want to Know More About Lethem?

Once Jonathan Lethem discovers a writer whose work he admires, he reads everything that writer ever published. This is by no means an exhaustive bibliography of Lethem's own work, but it's a great place for you to start.

- *The Disappointment Artist* (Doubleday, 2005)
- *Men and Cartoons: Stories* (Doubleday, 2004)
- *The Fortress of Solitude* (Doubleday, 2003)
- *This Shape We're In* (McSweeney's Books, 2001)
- *Motherless Brooklyn* (Doubleday, 1999)
- *Kafka Americana* with Carter Scholz (Subterranean Press, 1999)
- *Girl in Landscape* (Doubleday, 1998)
- *As She Climbed Across the Table* (Doubleday, 1997)
- *The Wall of the Sky, The Wall of the Eye* (Harcourt, 1996)
- *Amnesia Moon* (Harcourt, 1995)
- *Gun, With Occasional Music* (Harcourt, 1994)

Margot Livesey

Author and Teacher Discusses Creation of
'Fresh, Original Characters'

© Sigrid Estrada

by W.E. Reinka

On the one hand, Margot Livesey is flattered at being called a literary writer. On the other, she bristles at the label. "I fear the term literary has become a euphemism for not terribly fun and not terribly readable. I grew up reading those great Victorian novels which combined education and entertainment. I don't think the Brontës were aspiring to be literary. They were aspiring to write books people would read, and that's my aspiration."

Livesey read those Victorian novels in her childhood home in Scotland where her widowed father taught at a boy's school. "I grew up in the British tradition which seemed people were very much writing on their own and emerging fully formed into the world. It didn't occur to me until fairly late it could be helpful to study creative writing, to have a teacher, to have peers. I still feel considerable envy of my writing students for having people waiting for their work and ready to give thoughtful comments on it."

Livesey certainly did not spring fully formed into the writing world. After she came to North America, her jobs included stints as an incense packer, a flower seller in restaurants and, of course, a waitress. Once she discovered American writers did not necessarily emerge "fully formed" but often had been trained in college creative writing courses, Livesey began to study creative writing herself. She now teaches a graduate fiction seminar at Emerson College in Boston. While teaching has its demands, she still manages a few hours each day for her own work.

More than one critic has called her novels "quirky." Livesey laughs when asked about that. "It's not the first adjective I'd reach for to describe my work," she says in her precise British accent. "I like to tell myself that 'quirky' means I write fresh, original characters. Hopefully, there's a feeling when you read my work that you're discovering a landscape you haven't quite experienced before. That said, I'm interested in characters who see the world a little bit differently and who perhaps get into rather surprising situations as a result."

A bit differently indeed. In her latest novel *Banishing Verona* (Henry Holt & Co), Zeke, a housepainter with Asberger's Syndrome, falls passionately for Verona, a radio talk show host, after a somewhat anonymous one-night stand. Zeke's Asberger's Syndrome prevents him from reading facial expressions and other people's moods, but even so, he's puzzled when Verona disappears after a night of love. Unbeknownst to Zeke, Verona has been suddenly caught in the vortex of her unprincipled brother's problems with impatient loan sharks.

W.E. REINKA, who writes frequently about books and authors, contributes to newspapers and magazines nationwide.

The Writing Life

The plot description may sound convoluted but Livesey pulls it off because she succeeds in developing those ''fresh, original characters'' she talks about.

''My work consistently shows people with different perceptions and different versions of reality colliding. But at the same time, I would never say reality is absolutely a question of perception. There are completely obdurate and unnegotiable facts and very typically my characters come up against some of those facts. In *Eva Moves the Furniture* (Henry Holt & Co.) we see the main character having spirit companions who are visible only to her. This is a tremendous dilemma for her. She has a version of reality that doesn't coincide with other people's.'' In *The Missing World* (Knopf), Livesey follows the clever premise of a woman who's lost her memory and how her duplicitous boyfriend, with whom she actually had broken up, starts to reinvent their missing past.

Reprinted with permission.

Banishing Verona

a novel

MARGOT LIVESEY

the author of
EVA MOVES THE FURNITURE

One real-life conflict newer writers experience is the way they perceive their work versus how it's received by the publishing world. ''One of the big problems with writing is that, for the most part, young writers—and I was absolutely in this camp—have no idea how long it will take to learn to write fiction given they've been reading and writing fiction all their lives. Just because you read *Little Red Riding Hood* when you were five and wrote your first story when you were seven, does not mean anytime you decide to write a story or a novel you'll be able to any more than you'll be able to play Rachmaninov.''

The writing teacher who strives for ''fresh, original characters'' in her own work sees characterization as a frequent challenge in her students' works. Ironically, the problem usually lies with major characters, those fictional people writers think they know best. ''Often minor characters are quite vivid and major characters are missing in action. The reason for that is often the major character depends too heavily on the author. We're sometimes writing a version of ourselves, especially if we're writing in the first person. We're slow to realize how sketchy our main characters are because they are not necessarily autobiographical but too much connected to us. We don't realize how little we've put on the page until someone tells us.''

That's why Livesey extols searching for objective readers who aren't family members or friends. ''Readers who know us too well are doing the same thing we're doing when we're writing the characters: They're filling in the blanks.'' Livesey recalls how when she was a young writer, relying on first readers who were close to her proved to be a hidden stumbling block. ''Their support was vital to my continuing to write but their feedback was not necessarily as helpful as I perhaps imagined because they knew so much about me that wasn't on the page. One of the first things I learned as a young writer when I went to the Breadloaf Writers Conference in 1983 was that I really needed strangers to read my work. I needed to form alliances with people that were forged around writing and might grow into friendships but that didn't stem from friendships. That was immensely valuable to me.''

Now she recommends that writers—aspiring and otherwise—line up a few readers.

Livesey has long been privileged to have National Book Award winner Andrea Barrett as one of her readers. But for those of us who can't have a National Book Award winner for a reader, Livesey recommends using different readers at different stages of a project. "If you have writer friends who've read several revisions of a story, you might want to find fresh readers when you get to a more final stage. People who have read it several times may once again be bringing too much to the project."

Writers who are still lining up objective readers may benefit from an independent exercise Livesey gives her students. In order to mitigate problems with characterization, she has her students write at the bottom of their first page what the reader knows about the main character. For example, the first page might typically tell us the character's sex or profession. Then, Livesey has her students do the same thing with the second, third, fourth pages and so on. She wants students to see what readers learn "from the black marks on the page. It's very telling that often you know remarkably little about their main characters and that students are relying on their readers to fill in things like class, age, race, setting as well as tastes, occupation and the like."

Livesey has found one writer's critique of another writer's work can also be illuminating. She gathers her students' written critiques so they form a sort of on-going diary. "I make a list of the main things they criticize in other people's work and ask them to put that alongside the main things people criticize in their work. There's usually a substantial overlap in those two lists." In other words, the critic who asks for more clarity is, in turn, often asked by objective readers for more clarity. "Recognizing that overlap is the beginning of becoming a better reader for your own work. That's very helpful to overcoming the frustrating myopia that we all have facing our own pages."

Another disheartening fact Livesey gently reminds her students is that writers don't necessarily get steadily better. "Part of the frustration is we'll write one story or chapter that really seems to work and come together and the next thing we write will be dead on the page or disorganized and chaotic. Like most other things, developing our craft is a much more circumlocutious route than we would wish."

Still, the former waitress and incense packer sounds an encouraging note. "With more people on the planet reading and writing than ever before, there's sometimes a feeling of despair that it's remarkably hard to get one's work published. However, I do think good work eventually finds its way into the world. It usually doesn't happen as easily or as painlessly as we would wish, but in my experience, persistence very often does pay off."

Reprinted with permission.

Joanna Scott

The Unreliable Narrator and 'this
inability to tell the simple truth'

© Kathryn Longenbach

by Kelcey Parker

I will tell you exactly how it was . . ." begins the widower who narrates Joanna Scott's first novel, *Fading, My Parmacheene Belle* (Ticknor & Fields). But, as in all good literature, whether or not he gets it "exactly" right seems beside the point; it's the story itself that matters. In her five novels and short story collection published since then, Scott creates narrators and characters who delight in the telling of stories and—as in the case of her bee-keeper who studies the "language of bees"—the unlimited possibilities for interpreting them.

In Scott's fiction, there's often a fine line between genius and madness, and between the art of writing and the science of lens-grinding, taxidermy or medicine. Using historical figures as well as imaginary characters, Scott takes her readers around the globe—Vienna, Elba, New York, the Atlantic Ocean—and across the centuries to explore what she has called a "mathematical problem we have to deal with, the truth and the falsehood of fiction."

Scott's highly acclaimed works include the 1997 Pulitzer Prize finalist, *The Manikin* (Back Bay Books), and the story collection, *Various Antidotes* (Henry Holt & Co), which was a finalist for the 1995 PEN/Faulkner Award. Scott's most recent novel, *Liberation*, was published by Little, Brown in September. *Liberation* returns Scott's readers to the island of Elba, where Napoleon was once exiled, but this time her focus is on World War II. Scott has received a MacArthur Fellowship, and she lives and teaches in Rochester, New York.

Here, Scott discusses unreliable narrators and their relationship to "truth" in literature, and she explains how she utilizes historical facts to create imaginative fiction.

In a radio interview with the *Washington Post*, you said, "The relationship between the truth and the falsehood of fiction is something I keep wanting to write about in my work." You said that Defoe, for example, insists the fiction he's telling us is true. Is this still a concern? If so, how are you exploring this in your current writing projects?

Doesn't the spell cast by fiction have a lot to do with the contest between truth and falsehood? If a story is set in motion by a lie ("long ago, in a far away kingdom"), it's held in check by a commitment to truth. Anything can happen in the imaginary realm . . . until something happens. A good story enthralls with its twists and turns, but it also has an integral consistency. I think it's the consistency, the logic of a narrative, which becomes the measure of

KELCEY PARKER is a fiction writer and a Ph.D. student in Literature and Creative Writing at the University of Cincinnati. She is working on a novel, which will serve as her creative dissertation.

truth. We're held spellbound by fiction as it turns amorphous unreality into something powerfully logical—and therefore true.

What do you think is the source of this suspense—by which we're "held spellbound"—in fiction?

I think the most satisfying suspense in fiction occurs at the basic level of the sentence. Release words from the obligation to deliver information, and the connection between subjects and predicates is loosened. A fiction writer has the liberty to take every new sentence in an unexpected direction. "Gregor Samsa woke up one morning and . . .!" We read to find out what the writer will think of next. Yet at the same time we know there's a limit to imaginative expression. We're obliged to follow through and express a meaning that makes sense, from beginning to end. Suspense, then, is created by the tension between the wildness of imaginative invention and the sturdiness of logical meaning.

Who are some of your favorite narrators in literature? What makes them appealing? And, how reliable—or unreliable—would you say each is?

There's Vardamon in *As I Lay Dying*, whose mother is a fish. He's one of my favorites, along with his brother Darl. I remain in awe of Mouth and her blend of perilous sense and nonsense in Beckett's "Not I." Lear's Fool, if we can include him in the group of narrators, is exemplary. I find Virginia Woolf's narrators magical in their ability to convey the motion of thought. And now that I'm deep in my middle age, I've come to admire most those narrators who convince us their version is characterized by restraint. Wild invention can have more effect when it's communicated in a subdued form. I'm thinking in particular of the steady narrators in Chekhov's stories, like the one who tells us about a deaf man hanging his linen while an infant is shrieking.

At the end of your novel *Tourmaline*, Oliver concludes, "It's in my blood, this inability to tell the simple truth." Are all narrators inherently unreliable? What's the intended effect of having Oliver announce his unreliability? Does this make him somehow more reliable?

FINALIST FOR THE 1997 PULITZER PRIZE IN FICTION

The Manikin

A NOVEL

JOANNA SCOTT

AUTHOR OF *Tourmaline*

"One reads *The Manikin* in a kind of fever.... It is packed with extraordinary bounty." —*Newsday*

PICADOR USA

Reprinted with permission.

Since imaginative invention rather than available information is the predominant subject, the form of fiction itself is inherently unreliable. But that's not the point of the passage you quote. I'm concerned about the general way words can disguise opinion as fact. Readers are used to the unreality of fiction, which makes it a good arena to explore distortions of reality. By admitting his narrative isn't entirely true, Oliver is partly reacting to claims of authenticity that are used to bolster memoir and documentary. I don't know if he becomes more reliable by acknowledging there are embellishments or inaccuracies in his account, but at least he's offering fuel for healthy skepticism.

The Writing Life

The Writing Life

Is there a difference between an unreliable narrator and a narrator's unreliable memory? If so, what is it?

There are many reasons to account for a narrator's waywardness, but a faulty memory is a prime cause. Writers can make faulty memory really interesting. It's interesting to read about a character's attempt to match words with impressions. It's interesting to follow the struggle to make sense of a complicated situation. I like to think an unreliable narrator's unreliable memory is inherently interesting.

A haunting
success...
a dazzling
literary
performance."
— *The Washington Post
Book World*

A NOVEL

JOANNA SCOTT
AUTHOR OF *TOURMALINE*

ARROGANCE

(PICADOR)

Reprinted with permission.

I'll risk a little waywardness here and rant for a moment about the validity of "unreliable" narrative. A novel doesn't have to explain anything reliably to make itself worthy of our interest. Even the most information-filled fiction is blissfully propositional by nature, and when we're receptive readers, we gain insight into the made-up material—into Pip's lost past, Isabel Archer's imagination, Mrs. Dalloway's vitality. As I ponder this issue, I find myself thinking about how "unreliable fiction" can play an important role in expanding our potential for understanding. Whether or not we find ways to make use of this potential in our lives is another question, but I want to believe that fiction can share with all significant art the ability to make life more interesting, without explaining anything.

This reminds me of something Annie Dillard says in *Living By Fiction*: "When characters are telling the tale, and especially when they are telling it all cockeyed, the subject at hand may not be only the nature of art and the nature of narration, but also the nature of perception."

Annie Dillard's account of "perception" is full of her usual wisdom, and it's heartening to be reminded of how we can be returned to the world through fiction. It may make folks yawn to compare fiction with dreaming, but it's a comparison I find endlessly useful. The kind of understanding fiction can give us is similar to the reviving effect of dreams. It's not the effort of interpretation that revives us; it's the actual immersion in the dreams, the powerful experience of irresistibly logical mystery.

The Manikin begins with the owl's perspective; *Arrogance* contains occasional diary entries or letter snippets. How do you, as a writer, organize and structure the infinite possibilities of imaginary events to create some kind of inherent order within your work?

I've had too many promising ideas collapse on the page because I haven't been able to find a strong narrative structure to support them. I wish I knew a formula for matching every idea to a voice and every voice to a distinct structure. I can't even work from an outline or diagram, as some writers do. Or maybe I just don't want to begin that way. Even though it means I take the wrong turns sometimes, I love being in the uncertain midst of a fiction and discovering the order from within. In the early pages of an early draft, I blindly stumble along. I have to struggle to get my bearings. If I'm going to make it to the end of a story or novel, I have to create a design that accommodates ample variation but remains tightly ordered.

How does it complicate the narrator's—or narrators'—role when you choose to turn historical figures—like Egon Schiele (*Arrogance*) or Antonie Van Leeuwenhoek ("Concerning Mold Upon the Skin, etc.")—into fictional characters?

There's a bit of the graffiti enthusiast in me when it comes to history. I never intend to rewrite history, but I like to write upon it. Since I'm always in pursuit of secrets, I try to create characters whose surfaces hint at complex mysteries. When I turn to a historical figure, I mingle facts with presumption. Also, I should say the solidity of history can provide a good foundation for my rather undisciplined imagination. History can keep me from veering too far in the direction of wildness. Dates, names, addresses, guide books, old newspapers, even things like tide tables and ship diagrams—all the actual stuff of the past helps me figure out what belongs in the fiction, what might contribute to the meaning.

How do you find, select and research historical material?

I try to be selective about research, but sometimes I think the historical material selects me. I love wandering through the physical landscapes of my fictional settings, through city and countryside, around islands and mountain villages. My experience of a real place in the present always fundamentally changes my imagined version. A white horse grazing by a stream is enough to send my work-in-progress in a new direction. A book can do the same thing. When I have a topic in mind, I might head for the library stacks, but the most useful books I find are often unrelated to my search; they're the books that fate pushes off the shelf into the aisle in front of me, or at least they're the books I arbitrarily pick up. I've learned to accept the accidents of research, though often I don't recognize the implications of an accident until long after it has happened. Most recently, my new novel, *Liberation*, was prompted from conversations I had with people on the island of Elba when I was writing my last novel, *Tourmaline*. The stories I heard about World War II haunted me, but it took me two years before I could build a novel around the subject.

You've identified Virginia Woolf's *Orlando* as a favorite novel and Ovid's *Metamorphosis* as a book you wish you'd written. Both of these works are about transformation. What interests you about change?

One of the great subjects of art is the eternity implied by transformation. Echo will keep echoing forever. Niobe will always be a stone. Stories like these are as close as we'll ever come to imagining what we can't understand.

At the end of your short story, "Concerning Mold Upon the Skin, etc.," Antonie Van Leeuwenhoek, the mad lens grinder of Delft, is described as having "a success far more extraordinary, the freedom to tell the most amazing stories and to be believed." How might this idea inform our understanding of your narrators—or of you as a writer?

As a young writer, I found myself most interested in single points of view and tried to create distinct voices for my narrators—voices that express the complex work of the mind through the choices of words, syntax, rhythms. With my early novels, I tried to create a unique language for each of my narrators. Sometimes I think I can credit my whole career to this effort. Once I stopped trying to tell what I already knew and started imagining characters different from myself, I started writing! But by the time I began thinking about the novel that would become *Arrogance*, I felt a need to expand the cast. I wanted to bump different perspectives up against each other. I found myself creating narrators agile enough, or brazen enough, to slide between points of view.

Sometimes I feel that writing is as much a kind of mad science as it is an art. The experiments can fail. The inventions can spin out of control. Or they can be misread and misused. Luckily, fiction doesn't have much practical consequence. Usually the stories writers tell are no more than possibilities. It's a wonderful thing to become more aware of our potential to imagine possibilities—to follow a narrative wherever it might take us and, ultimately, to be convinced it all makes shocking sense.

In This Article

Works by Joanna Scott
- *Liberation* (Little, Brown, 2005)
- *Tourmaline* (Little, Brown, 2002)
- *Make Believe* (Little, Brown, 2000)
- *The Manikin* (Back Bay Books, 1996)
- *Various Antidotes* (Henry Holt & Co., 1994)
- *Arrogance* (Simon & Schuster, 1990)
- *The Closest Possible Union* (Ticknor & Fields, 1988)
- *Fading, My Parmacheene Belle* (Ticknor & Fields, 1987)

Other Works Mentioned
- "Not I" by Samuel Beckett (1963)
- *Great Expectations* by Charles Dickens (1860)
- *Living By Fiction* by Annie Dillard (Harper & Row, 1982)
- *As I Lay Dying* by William Faulkner (1930)
- *The Portrait of a Lady* by Henry James (1880)
- *The Metamorphosis* by Franz Kafka (1915)
- *Metamorphosis* by Publios Ovidios Naso (Ovid) (circa 1 AD)
- "King Lear" by William Shakespeare (circa 1604)
- *Mrs. Dalloway* by Virginia Woolf (1925)
- *Orlando* by Virginia Woolf (1928)

Daniel Wallace

From Refrigerator Magnets to Big Fish

© Dan Sears

by Brad Vice

I t never gets easier to write," warns multitalented Daniel Wallace, author, illustrator and off-beat entrepreneur. "Even though everybody tells you it never gets easier, you secretly think you're going to be the exception to the rule. But you're not."

These are humbling words coming from an author who has accomplished so much. After the phenomenal literary and cinematic success of *Big Fish* (Algonquin Books), the promise of hard labor strikes one as reassuring rather than discouraging coming from Wallace. Like *Big Fish*, Wallace's other novels *Ray in Reverse* (Penguin Books) and *The Watermelon King* (Houghton Mifflin) possess a strange, dreamlike confluence of the modern and the mythic. Too contemporary to be considered folk stories, too fantastic to be labeled realism, Wallace's novels transport the reader into a world resembling our own but ultimately shimmering with greater possibility—especially for those characters who aren't afraid to dream.

Like his fiction, Wallace is something of a contradiction as well. There's a Willie-Wonka-esque quality about the man who was willing to toil for 14 years in relative obscurity, eking out a living creating and distributing refrigerator magnets, never allowing himself to give into the temptation of getting a regular job. In fact, he doesn't seem bitter about the years of struggle; he seems proud of them. Wallace is an accomplished illustrator as well as an author, and this talent may explain the magical visual quality of his work. With his soon-to-be-published book *O Great Rosenfeld!* (Autrement [France], Tropea [Italy]), readers will get a chance to see the pictures as well as the words of an author who can only be described as visionary.

A lot of writers talk about paying their dues. You wrote five novels before you sold your first, *Big Fish*. When did you start writing, and what was your life like during the writing of those five novels?

I began writing in 1984. Before that, I'd tried to work in the business world, and I failed. I'd always wanted to write—why I don't know—but figured if I could be happy doing something else, I should. But I wasn't happy. I found a small apartment in Carrboro, North Carolina, and wrote in the morning, worked at bookstores in the afternoon, then came back and wrote

---

BRAD VICE was born and raised in Tuscaloosa, Alabama. His first collection of short stories, *The Bear Bryant Funeral Train*, won the Flannery O'Connor Award for Short Fiction and was published by the University of Georgia Press. His stories have appeared in many publications, including *The Georgia Review*, *The Southern Review*, *The Atlantic Monthly*, *New Stories from the South* (1997 and 2003), *Best New America Voices 2003*, and *Stories from the Blue Moon Café Vol III*. He teaches creative writing at Mississippi State University.

The Writing Life

Reprinted with permission.

Enjoy this self-portrait of Wallace each morning when you stumble sleepily to your fridge for the coffee grounds. Much of his art, especially the magnets, is available by e-mailing K. FLOYD at kfloyd2@nc.rr.com or visiting www.northshire.com/category/sub/kfloyd.

some more. It was hard, but I loved it. I thought I was great. I thought I must be great, anyway, based on how good it felt to write. But I wasn't. I wrote many stories and then many novels, and they were all admired in one way or another but then rejected. At the time, I felt misunderstood but later came to see I wasn't. The reason the novels didn't get published is because they were bad.

I persisted, in part because I knew learning how to do what I wanted to do, which was to write well, was hard, and then eventually because I had spent so much time learning and failing. As I got older and older, I realized to quit at that point would leave me with nothing, because I had absolutely no experience doing anything but what I had been doing: writing bad books and selling good ones—*some* good ones anyway. So I kept it up. I was afraid to quit. I didn't want to be *that guy*. As my father said, "if it was easy, everyone would be doing it." Fourteen years after I started learning to write, my first novel was published.

You mention your Dad. *Big Fish* is one of the most moving father/son stories in recent memory, and it's also a novel about dreamers. For you, are these subjects inextricably linked?

My father was a big dreamer and so am I, though in very different ways. His creativity and ambition he invested into his business, and mine goes into writing. But I think they're linked in a deeper way. My father was a mystery to me in so many ways, and the only way I could understand him was to place him in an imaginary context. Fathers show up in a lot of my fiction, and each time the father is reimagined, different, but all of them are my Dad. It's all such a mystery. I wish I understood all of this better, but on the other hand, I think this not-knowing is one of the most important aspects of being a writer. If you know everything already, why write at all?

Big Fish changed your life, but it took a while. Can you describe the process of supporting yourself while you wrote your second book, *Ray in Reverse*? How did the experience of publishing *Ray* differ from that of *Big Fish*?

I didn't really have to support myself writing *Ray*, as the movie money had just come in. But the publishing experience was interesting. First books are inherently exciting because they're the first; you don't know what to expect of second ones though. Deep down you hope it will be twice as successful, drawing twice the sales and twice the crowds at readings. Unfortunately, I had a little sophomore slump: Instead of twice as good, it was about half as good. The book disappeared down a dark well.

Was it hard to pick yourself up from the disappointment of *Ray*?

I gave myself a few days to wallow in disappointment, then I tried to forget about it and move on. There are lots of disappointments in the writing world and if you let them get to you, it's hard to begin the next project.

Did you find the making of the movie _Big Fish_ motivated you to write more or was it a distraction? How involved were you with the film?

The movie was a lot of fun, but it was a distraction from writing. There was so much to do, so many calls to take, and appearances . . . plus just the wonder of it all. I'd sit there for many minutes every day thinking, *a movie . . . a movie*. But it's over now, and I am happily back at work.

I had a small part in the film, and they kept me in the loop when things happened, actors attached, etc., but as far as having any real impact on the making of the movie . . . let's say zero. And that was fine with me.

You've gotten some of the best reviews of your career for *The Watermelon King*, a book that revisits the town of Ashland, Alabama, the setting for *Big Fish*. What did you learn from your first two books? How was the process of writing the third different?

What I learned from the first two books is over the past 20 years I've learned a few things about writing, and if I used those skills writing a story I liked, then I was much more likely to write something of value to me and also at the same time something others might want to read. But this was the hardest book to write. I really wasn't sure whether I had a story for a long time, and my friend Alan Shapiro had to keep talking me off the ledge of quitting.

You're an artist as well as a writer. Can you describe your career as an artist and what kind of influence it had on your prose?

I started drawing pictures a few years after I started writing, I guess around 1991. I'd never drawn before, but I started drawing little cartoons for my daughters who were waking up grumpy in those days. I always drew a talking rat for Lillian and a talking dog for Abby. At the same time, my first wife was looking for a way to have to not get a job—to become some sort of artist who also made money—and she thought by combining my charming lack of drawing skill with her very real skill of designing things, a product could be born. A product was born: We made refrigerator magnets. We sold a ton of them and still do. That's when I started drawing and, though it began sort of serendipitously, I love it and do more of it all the time.

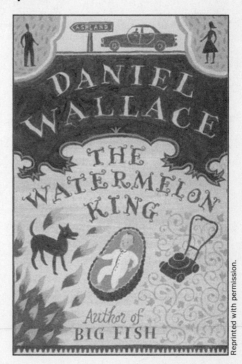

Reprinted with permission.

As far as the influence drawing has had on my writing, I don't know that it's had any at all. I've written stories and books that are illustrated, so in that case the drawings and the text work together to tell the story, but with my novels and most of my stories, the drawing—like the writing I do for movies—is in another world.

You are set to have *O Great Rosenfeld!* published overseas; it features your art as well as your words. Can you describe the book to us? Why did you choose to have it published overseas?

O Great Rosenfeld! is an odd little book, and this may be why it's the one closest to my heart. It takes place a few thousand years ago, when we are still tribal hunter-gatherers—when each member of the tribe had to contribute and produce or they were left behind or sacrificed to a god. The presumed writer of this book has no skills: He can't hunt, or gather, or fight, or build; he can only write. So he becomes the tribe's scribe and writes about their glorious leader, Rosenfeld, who's actually the worst possible leader. The drawings seem to complement rather than detract, so I have a lot of those. It's cool.

I would like to submit to you the reason I decided to publish it overseas was to object to the Bush Administration and its policies. And while I do object, this was not the reason. The reason is the first people to see what I see in the book happen to live in France and Italy. It will be published here as well, we've just yet to determine when. RCA recording artists FALCON have written a soundtrack to the book, the title song of which can be found at www.ogreatrosenfeld.com.

The link to the *O Great Rosenfeld!* website is also connected to DanielWallace. org. This website contains all kinds of information about you, your books, even your family. How did it come about? Do you run it yourself? How has it changed your relationship to the audience?

I thought it would be a good idea to establish some sort of Web presence after the movie came out, and so I got together with a friend named Holden Richards who works magic with HTML. Together we designed the site. I wanted it to reflect me as much as possible, so I used my drawings as links, and I occasionally post new ones. Most of the pages are pretty static, but I post news, events or whatever I want to in the blog section. It's fun.

Through the website I've been able to write to people from all over the world who have read the book and/or seen the movie, something I would never have been able to do without it. It's really been worth it.

Inman Majors

*Balancing Comedy and Commentary
to Keep It Fresh*

© Christy Majors

by Brad Vice

All those years of suffering and rejection had to be good for me somehow," says Tennessee poet and novelist Inman Majors, speaking of the virtues of being a late bloomer. "I think early and easy success might have ruined me for good. I know I would have been too arrogant for a really cool woman like my wife to want to go out with me. So when she met me, I was broke, unemployed, unpublished and living with my grandmother. And I was 32. What's not to like about that?"

Majors could be describing Dev Degraw, the protagonist of his latest novel *Wonderdog* (St. Martin's/Thomas Dunne Books). Like the author who created him, Degraw is something of a late bloomer. Degraw is the ne'er-do-well scion of a prominent Southern politician, a kind of modern-day version of Shakespeare's Prince Hal, a well-educated slacker who spends all his time and energy figuring out ways to avoid responsibility. Tapping into the comic wellspring that irrigates *Wonderdog*, Majors is only half joking when he speaks of his early years of struggle. He's a firm believer that "things work out for a reason—and I have no regrets about anything to do with my publishing history. I feel lucky and fortunate to have two presses who thought enough of my books to send them out for public consumption."

Though it is a common misconception, many writers believe publishing a book with a small or university press limits the publication options of their next book, but this is a fear Majors has proven to be unfounded. In fact, he sees his experience with a small press as an important stepping stone to building a readership, getting an agent and finding acceptance in the larger commercial world of publishing, a world that looks for mature talent and is unforgiving of ne'er-do-wells and slackers.

Your first novel *Swimming in the Sky* was published by Southern Methodist University (SMU) Press, a small but prestigious house. Most people think once you've published with a university press, no one at a commercial house will be interested in your work. How did *Wonderdog* get published by a large commercial press like St. Martin's? How was the experience of publishing with a big house different than a university press?

I guess I've been pretty fortunate in my ignorance of the marketplace and how it works, so I never considered the ramifications of publishing my first book with a university press. To

BRAD VICE was born and raised in Tuscaloosa, Alabama. His first collection of short stories, *The Bear Bryant Funeral Train*, won the Flannery O'Connor Award for Short Fiction and was published by the University of Georgia Press. His stories have appeared in many publications, including *The Georgia Review*, *The Southern Review*, *The Atlantic Monthly*, *New Stories from the South* (1997 and 2003), *Best New America Voices 2003*, and *Stories from the Blue Moon Café Vol III*. He teaches creative writing at Mississippi State University.

be honest, I was so grateful to have the book accepted in the first place I didn't see any downside, and I'm still unbelievably grateful to SMU for publishing the book. In my opinion, the university presses—not driven by commercial concerns—are one of the few places where a newcomer can get some daring, edgy material published. Thank God for the university presses; they, and the independent booksellers, are really doing yeoman's work when it comes to keeping a little artistic integrity in the literary world.

And, for those worried about such things, I'm convinced having the first book out from a university press was much better than having no book at all when it came time to querying agents. It just looked nice in the cover letter to say in the first sentence, "I am the author of a novel called *Swimming in Sky* (SMU Press, 2000) . . ." It was instant creditability. Trust me on this one—having the first book out was an advantage when it came time to get serious about finding an agent. So I am greatly indebted to SMU Press and my fine editor there, Kathie Lang.

Reprinted with permission.

I placed the first book without an agent. I didn't know what I was doing. I sent it to maybe three agents then got sick of how long it took them to reply, so I just started sending it over the transom. If I'd known then what I know now, I would have spent more time trying to get an agent for the first book. I still don't know why I didn't learn this stuff in graduate school. I guess I thought it somehow antiartistic to worry about the business side of things. Arrogance of youth, etc. At any rate, I had some near-acceptances and then SMU took it. The process of submission took about three years or so, but it felt longer. From the first page I wrote to having the book in my hand was eight years. So, as you can imagine, I was thrilled beyond belief to have the book taken at last—thrilled as well to be able to stop thinking and worrying and obsessing about the damn thing and whether it would ever get published at all.

For the second book, I spent about two weeks getting my cover letter just right. I worked on that letter and revised it as if it were a poem. I'd say I spent 20 hours writing it. By this point, obviously, I was more concerned with the business side of things—having a family will do that to you. So I ended up getting an agent, David McCormick, whom I really like. Luckily, it didn't take that long—a few months. After David and I hooked up, he gave me two or three really excellent editorial suggestions—my plot was too front-loaded in the original version—and I did a quick and relatively painless revision for him. Once he started sending the manuscript out, it took him about two weeks to place the book with St. Martin's. So there's a lesson to be learned here: Send your manuscript out yourself, and it takes three years to get a deal. Get yourself an agent, and it takes two weeks. At least that was my experience. But I don't have any regrets.

You are from Tennessee but *Wonderdog* is set in Tuscaloosa, Alabama. Why did you choose to set your novel there?

I went to graduate school in Tuscaloosa—spent four years at the University of Alabama getting my MFA. I just had the best time there. I loved the town, loved the people. Just being around so many good writers and fun people makes those four years some of the best of my life. It's in vogue now to put down the MFA and the whole concept of a creative writing concentration, but for me, it was nirvana: read cool books, teach, play basketball, and write and write and write.

I realized then I was experiencing something special. The best part, the most important part, of my education took place just hanging out with the other graduate students. We'd talk sports, movies, current events, etc., but eventually—inevitably—we ended up talking about books and writers and the writing process. You don't get that kind of intense concentration outside of grad school. Even when you're teaching at the university level, it's not the same obsessive need to talk about writing—talking writing just for the sake of talking writing— education at its purest form—love of the subject matter. So I guess *Wonderdog* was just a way to remember the town—reconnect with a place that meant so much to me then and now.

Since you first began your career as a poet, how do you think poetry has shaped your prose? Do you still write poems?
I still write poetry—will always write poetry. It just got to the point where ideas for novels kept coming to me, so I concentrated on that genre. But poetry absolutely influences my prose. It makes you concentrate on word choice and precision, imagery and, above all, rhythm. It don't mean a thing, if it ain't got that swing. I like a fast pace in my prose, like to get there quickly, say it once and move on. So I'd say my fiction is influenced by poetry in that it asks for a little work from the reader. I expect the reader to pay attention. I expect the reader's concentrated attention. So poetry, with its emphasis on concision and its refusal— I'm talking about good poetry here—to pander to the reader, has definitely influenced my aesthetic, style and, perhaps most importantly, my relationships with my readers.

Your protagonist is the ne'er-do-well son of the Alabama governor. You write about politics with great authority; is your family involved in politics? How did you research the novel? What was the impetus behind the book?
My father is a lobbyist in Nashville. When I was a kid, I'd go up there and run around the legislature and go to lunch with my dad and the legislators. So I was exposed to politics and the political arena for as long as I can remember. After graduate school, when I couldn't find a teaching position, I got a job as a bartender at Jimmy Kelly's Steakhouse in Nashville, which is the local hangout for all the politicos when the legislature is in session, so that was another good place to learn about the political arena. Of course, the politics in the book are rendered to comedic effect, so I'm not really going on real life people or events. Every thing and everyone is exaggerated just to get the cheap and easy laugh.

The main impetus for the political elements of the plot are my unvarnished love of Shakespeare's "Henry IV Part 1," with Prince Hal, the original and all-time best slacker, and Falstaff and the rest of the merry gang. I seem, at least in my fiction, to have an undue soft spot for the late bloomers and underachievers of

WONDERDOG

A NOVEL

INMAN MAJORS

"*Wonderdog* reads as if narrated by the ne'er-do-well, incorrigible, and brilliant wastrel cousin of W. Percy's Binx Bolling. But Inman Majors has a brilliant voice all his own—cockeyed, very funny, and deeply cognizant of this tender impasse. This book's a hell of a read. I loved it."
— BRAD WATSON, author of *The Heaven of Mercury*

Reprinted with permission.

The Writing Life

The Writing Life

the world. Dev Degraw, like Prince Hal, knows, without doubt, he has what it takes to make it in the political arena. He just chaffs at the notion his fate seems predetermined.

Strangely, the novel is textured and shaped by a mixture of politics and acting. The protagonist's days as a childhood actor in the second-rate television show "Bayou Dog" both haunt and define him, as does his father's political lineage. Did it take you a while to understand the parallel?

I'm not sure where the television angle came from, other than I always loved those old shows like *Gunsmoke* and often wondered what became of the bit actors and glorified stuntmen who populated them. Chad Kingston, the old cowboy in *Wonderdog*, is just my way of spending more time with those crusty looking cowpokes of my misspent youth. And again, another way to look at the strange phenomenon of minor fame.

Why did you decide to write a comic novel? How does comic prose differ from other kinds of writing?

I'd written my first book, a serious book, and was having a hard time getting it published. I knew I didn't want to quit writing despite the struggles to get published, but starting another serious book just seemed too depressing to even consider. So I said, "Okay, I'll just write something that is fun to write. It may not get published, *I* may never get published, but I'll at least make myself laugh while I'm working." And that's what I did.

As for how they differ, comedy might take a little more energy; good comedy should capture the mania of life. There should be nothing played safe in a comedy because comedy is about showing the ridiculous humanity we all share, something to balance the awful seriousness of being with which we are all burdened. The unfettered and unapologetic id is what I like in comedy. That's John Belushi, that's Michael Richards as Kramer. So much of life is about playing it safe. Comedy is about challenging that notion. Sticking it to the man. Just letting it absolutely rip.

The endings of comedies are tougher. A serious work seems to build to a natural close, the emotional pay-off for which we've been waiting. Comedies, on the other hand, even in the movies, seem to have disappointing endings: They feel more like an overt wrapping up of things, less innate, less natural and satisfying. I mean *Animal House* is one of the funniest movies ever made, but the ending, the big finale, does not have the comedic impact of the building scenes that precede it, the scenes that are more concerned with character than plot. Characters and scenes are funny because they are innate and spontaneous, or should seem so. Plot, the overtly premeditated aspect of prose, tends to show its warty and predetermined hand at the end of a comedy. So the challenge of comedy is to write one where the suspense is maintained until the end and the end has that same kind of logical but surprising close that the best books have.

What's next?

Back to the political arena I think. But a serious book this time. Maybe I'll alternate serious and comedy for a while—got to keep it fresh, you know.

Editors' Roundtable

Esquire, Harper's *and* The Atlantic

by I.J. Schecter

Known mainly for their social commentary and political reportage, glossy magazines seldom receive their due as outlets for worthy fiction. However, with steady readerships, established industry cachet and prominent spots on thousands of newsstands, these publications fill a vital commercial gap literary journals and annual prize anthologies can't. Here, three of today's top magazine editors—**Adrienne Miller** of *Esquire*, **Ben Metcalf** of *Harper's* and **C. Michael Curtis** of *The Atlantic*—talk about the importance of magazine fiction, the continually evolving craft of writing and the enduring magic of a great story.

What led you to your current role?
Metcalf: After growing up in Virginia, I chased a girl to New York. That didn't work out, but the job I landed at *Harper's* fortunately did. I liked the people and they liked me, and I just stayed.

Miller: I came to New York after graduating from college in Ohio. I was lucky enough to get a job at *GQ*, worked for a couple of years there as an assistant, then was even luckier to get the position as literary editor at *Esquire*. Luck and timing played undeniable roles in my career.

Curtis: I grew up in Arkansas and, after selling *The Atlantic* some poems while at the end of a PhD program in political science, accepted an invitation to join their staff.

What were the poems about?
Curtis: Bears. They've always inspired me. I was only intending to take a leave of absence from the graduate program to spend a year at the magazine. That was 42 years ago.

Are the others in the program wondering why you haven't returned?
Curtis: I doubt it. Most of them are dead.

How much collaboration do you have with other editors at your magazine?
Miller: I'm sort of the lone wolf, the weird fiction obsessive at the magazine who skulks around with a pile of short story manuscripts under her arm. The decisions about what stories to accept are mine, but I receive input from our editor-in-chief, David Granger.

I.J. SCHECTER (www.ijschecter.com) writes for leading magazines, newspapers and websites throughout the world, including *Condé Nast Brides, Golf Monthly, Men's Exercise, The Globe & Mail* and iParenting.com. He is also the author of a short story collection *The Bottom of the Mug* (Aegina Press Inc).

The Writing Life

Metcalf: I run everything by our editor, Lewis Lapham. It's a solid working relationship, since he takes a sincere interest in the stories the magazine publishes and also shows trust in my opinions.

How did you establish that trust?

Metcalf: I have no idea. I think I'm just lucky that we have similar tastes.

Is there ever a story you hate that your editor loves?

Metcalf: Sure. And it's also true the other editors can be involved. All I ask is they have a real love for the short story and know something about who's doing what.

Curtis: Our situation has changed a bit over the years, but for the past two decades or so, my job has been essentially to choose slightly more stories than we could accept and then send them to the managing editor, Cullen Murphy, with my ideas about their desirability. Few other of the editors on staff also read fiction. They probably could, but they're pretty busy in their own right.

Why is magazine fiction important?

Curtis: I think it speaks to the general culture. It may not increase our readership numbers, but it certainly does please those who read the magazine. It's hard to imagine someone with broad intellectual interests who doesn't also read fiction, or at least care about it. We've done some informal surveys to determine what proportion of our readers actually read the fiction [when it appeared in every issue]. Early figures indicated about 10 percent; more recent ones, 25 percent.

Metcalf: I think one of the things fiction does is help counter the modern notion that writing is meant only to convey facts. This is a growing trend today, in all areas of writing, but good fiction goes beyond. It expresses something. It's important to us that writers be allowed different voices and different modes of expression. Fiction is a way to fight the television-encouraged transmission-of-information trend that too much writing reflects today. People are always stopping me and wanting to discuss the latest short story in the magazine or the nature of the short story. That gives me continued hope.

Miller: *Esquire* does biannual focus groups with random subscribers, and we find readers tend to single out fiction among the top two or three things they look for in the magazine. Whether that's reality or just focus-group posturing, I'm not sure, but the magazine does draw both an enormous amount of fiction submissions as well as, perhaps more tellingly, plenty of letters in response to the stories we publish. I'm consistently impressed people care enough to send a letter. That isn't to say they're all positive but—especially for a magazine like ours, which isn't traditionally associated with the same kind of readership as *The Atlantic or Harper's*—it's a positive sign that people care to comment on fiction. I think

Adrienne Miller

Photo used with permission.

it's incredibly encouraging, in a world where people's energies are being pulled in so many different directions, so many are still enthusiastic—and often passionate—readers of short fiction in magazines.

Do you enjoy reading stories?

Curtis: Let's put it this way: I can't imagine anyone doing the job we do who didn't care an awful lot about fiction. I open every story with a kind of hopefulness, the anticipation of promise and excitement—especially via a story by someone who's never been published before. There's no greater gratification in this role than being allowed to take a hand in starting a career. It's been wonderful, over the course of my career, to see so many good writers come to the surface and thrive as a consequence of getting their work into print.

Miller: A great short story—one with guts, drama, tension—has to be the most perfect art form imaginable. The main pleasure in my job is finding emerging writers of real talent. There would be little interest in our jobs if we weren't looking for, and encouraged to find, talented writers with something to say. The mediocre story by a known author isn't really where our particular judgment as editors can be best applied; it's to a manuscript by someone you've never heard of who's been working in the shadows.

Is hope always the dominant feeling when you open a manuscript?

Miller: It has to be—immense hope. Otherwise, there's no reason to do it. Plus, the alternative is cynicism, and that doesn't belong in this role.

Metcalf: Hope is most certainly the word. You have to go into any text as not just a generous reader but also a fair one. You have to extend the proper amount of credit. There are times when you end up having to take some of that back and times when you have to take none back. And then there are times when you not only don't have to take any credit back, you in fact read and read and read and, in the end, realize you don't have enough credit to give. That's the experience I'm always seeking. I'm looking to be thrilled.

Curtis: We're not pleased we have to send back so many manuscripts with rejection slips. We realize it must make writers feel slapped in the face, especially if they've been around a while. But the sheer quantity of stories makes it impossible to respond to each one individually. We take no pleasure in rejection; it's simply a reality of the fiction world. The consideration is primarily one of time.

Miller: Writers should know we editors on the other side of the table are not sneering ogres looking to reject manuscript after manuscript. It's quite the contrary. As Ben [Metcalf] says, we're looking to be excited, not disappointed. With the number of submissions we receive, it's only inevitable that sometimes we'll be underwhelmed—but it's those other moments that keep us loving what we do.

How much of a manuscript do you have to get through before knowing whether it has legs?

Miller: A page. Sometimes less. You can often tell in a cover letter how the writer is representing himself. If it's written in crayon or includes a head shot, that tells you enough. But in terms of the actual writing, it's either alive or it's dead by the bottom of the first page. You know very quickly whether a story is authentic, whether it comes from a place of genuine inspiration.

Metcalf: I know after a paragraph, but, in the spirit of fairness I referred to, I'll read a page. The first sentence earns you a second sentence, that sentence earns you the one after, and so on. I think everyone will read a first paragraph, then maybe the first page to see if something merely went wrong in that first paragraph.

Curtis: Sometimes I don't need to go past the cover letter. One issue, I think, is many writers don't recognize what a truly good manuscript is because they've written one, and it's wonderful because it's theirs, it's a product of some spontaneous act of creation, but they've stopped short of self-evaluation. As a result, one encounters a number of red flags—too many adverbs and adjectives, misspellings or grammatical errors . . .

Metcalf: . . . clichéd prose, the same setups we've seen before, tired language . . .

Curtis: . . . clumsy expressions, sentences that don't end and detract from the story's potential merit. Having read thousands of submissions, I can safely predict that if I come across 10 of these mistakes on the first page, I'll come across a hundred before I'm done.

The Writing Life

Like Ben [Metcalf], I'm looking for a decent sentence. If that sentence contains a voice I think I'd like to hear from again, I'll read the next. Then I keep reading until I've been deeply engaged.

Miller: I agree. You start by asking yourself whether the person can write sentences, the individual units, the building blocks. Once they've passed that test, you consider whether the overall structure has an arc; whether the dialogue works; whether it has vitality, which is often more difficult to define; and, of course, whether it's appropriate for the magazine.

Metcalf: A well-constructed story, of course, doesn't have to be the perfect blend of plot and character in the traditional sense. I'm often looking for just a strong mood. The only thing I need to know to decide whether it succeeds is what the story is trying to be.

Curtis: I have a slightly different take, in the sense that I really like something to happen. I see a lot of stories that are wonderfully intelligent and well crafted and perceptive, but they're static. If I have to choose between a dynamic story and a static one, I'll choose the former every time. Atmosphere on its own won't normally do it for me.

C. Michael Curtis

Photo used with permission.

Miller: For *Esquire*, I'm generally looking for dramatic— some might say swaggering—short stories about men and by men. But by the same token, the writing should reflect whatever is going on at this particular cultural moment and should suggest a world outside of the story.

What is the number one thing a writer can do to get his story rejected?

Curtis: Include rejection slips from other magazines.

Miller: Omit the self-addressed, stamped envelope.

Metcalf: Tell me what the story is about in the cover letter.

What themes are dominating your submission pile?

Curtis: Recently I've received a great number of stories about protagonists with aging parents and all the practical and emotional issues and conflicts that go along with that. We've published a good number of these, but have had to turn away even more, some of them very impressively written.

Metcalf: I often see the kind of story that's been, for lack of a better description, overly workshopped in an MFA program. The story will be reviewed by the group, with the protagonist identified naturally as the writer, and whether the group likes the story depends on whether they like the writer. The result is a story in which most of the writer's energy seems to have gone into defending the protagonist. It's not a defense from some ideal reader but from the other members of the workshop.

Miller: I see a lot of the patently autobiographical, thinly veiled personal essay presented as a short story. Autobiographical fiction isn't necessarily interesting in itself; that is, something isn't interesting or important merely because it happened. For *Esquire*, of course, the type of piece I'm talking about more often involves impotence or lust, rather than aging parents, but the same principle applies.

Curtis: We've seen brilliant work in recent years by foreign writers—Asian writers, Russian writers, others—talking about their experiences caught between cultures. Some of these stories seem almost magical, perhaps because emigrants learn to use English in a way that is different from native English speakers.

What's your favorite activity that has nothing to do with writing?

Curtis: Playing basketball.

Metcalf: Playing my guitar.

Miller: Assembling the ideal protein shake.

What, in the final analysis, matters more: the story or the person telling it?

Curtis: You'll never accidentally find a good story from a bad writer, but you might find the occasional bad story from a good writer. Last year, I read an entire anthology of Chekhov's stories. Even his worst stories are pretty good, but, of course, some are better than others. To use another example, we've published over a dozen of Joyce Carol Oates' stories, but rejected many more than that.

Metcalf: Without a doubt, it's the writer that makes the story, not the other way around.

Miller: As both reader and editor, I'm more interested in the writer's individual sensibility than I am in the mechanics of plot. A genuine artist can give meaning to any story, and in so doing makes the world we inhabit seem like a bigger place.

Curtis: But there's no such thing as an inherently boring story. In the hands of a good writer, almost any experience can be made interesting.

What's the difference between a good writer and a great one?

Metcalf: Skill and perseverance. The latter is the person who can challenge himself to make every sentence perfect. When you see so many good stories, it's especially stirring to find a great one.

Miller: Often it's hard to identify that intangible element that vaults one story over another. The better one is just somehow greater than the sum of its parts. But you know when you've read something excellent; you melt right into it.

Metcalf: Most stories published by the better magazines are, let us say, at least the size of themselves. But we want something that makes the reader flip back through and say, "How did the writer do that? How did she pull it off?"

Curtis: Much of this is highly subjective. I've read stories that were technically impeccable yet boring. They just didn't convey that feeling of excitement or pleasure I'm always looking for. Often I can't explain it any better than that. I read 10 publishable stories for every one we can use.

All other things being equal, would you rather a story that warms your heart, kicks your guts out or makes you laugh?

Metcalf: One that makes me laugh.

Miller: Makes me laugh, or maybe a funny gut-kicking story.

Curtis: Some funny stories are only half-formed. Others are entertaining but exercises, not very well developed, and, in the end, not sufficiently ambitious.

Give me your top piece of advice for fiction writers wanting to break into magazines.

Miller: Read journals. Read the magazines to which you want to submit.

Ben Metcalf

Photo used with permission.

Metcalf: Reading is a big one. Even bigger is to revise. Don't just send in what you feel is your best story. Polish it. I remember a certain teacher once telling me a writer has to think about every single word. She was absolutely right.

Curtis: Don't take rejection personally. Understand magazines are seeing hundreds, or

The Writing Life

thousands, of stories for every one they can publish. We have to say no to a lot of very good work. You need to learn to just put it aside and move on.

Complete the following sentence. To publish fiction in magazines, you need:

Miller: Tenacity. Self-belief. Discipline.

Curtis: Perseverance combined with luck.

Metcalf: Talent, skill and, above all, time.

Are there really only a set number of basic storylines, or are stories, and the way they're told, continually evolving?

Curtis: Broadly speaking, there are actually only two storylines: the quest, and the new guy in town. But that matters little compared to how the story is told.

Metcalf: While you do see a lot of repetition, there are pockets of mode, style and voice always being mined. The culture always changes and the language always evolves, therefore there is always new territory being created for writers to explore.

Miller: Every reader reads for something different, so even the same story can be many things. For me, it's all about the way a story is told and the individual sensibility and style.

What compels us to tell stories to one another? Are we all just sitting around a big campfire waiting for the next tale to be told?

Metcalf: It's one of the things we can offer the aliens as justification for not destroying us. You look at a well-made short story like you look at a beautiful painting or wonderful piece of music. If a human being did this, the entire race can't be that bad.

Curtis: I think we tell stories because they teach us how to be. They give us examples of people making choices and discovering the consequences of those choices. Before we were ever able to write, storytelling provided explanations for things.

Miller: Fiction is essential for our emotional survival. Telling a good story is the most beautiful thing any person can do.

Première Voices

*Four Debut Authors Reflect on Their
Work and Their Publishing Experiences*

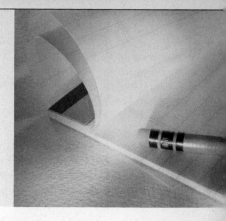

by Lauren Mosko

When publishing houses and literary magazines claim they're not looking for any particular style or type of work, many writers consider this the initiation of some sort of submission mindgame: *We're not going to tell you what we want. Guess.*

In truth, such an open-ended request should encourage writers, reinforcing that if your story is well conceived and well executed, you'll eventually find a home for it. The four debut works profiled here are an excellent illustration of the increasing diversity in the fiction market.

In terms of form, you'll find one "traditional" novel, one short story collection and two hybrid works—the tremendously popular novel-in-stories. (For more on novels-in-stories, see "The Novel-in-Stories: Break Into Print with Fresh Form" by Heather Sellers on page 62.)

Styles and tones range from Southern Gothic to social comedy, and the settings transport readers from New England to Middle America, through the Deep South and the Far East. Two of the books were published by commercial presses and two by smaller university presses.

You'll be hard-pressed to find anything that connects these books, other than they're all deeply sincere, well-crafted stories that draw readers in from the opening lines and refuse to let go, even after the final page has been turned.

Oh, and they're all authored by regular people—just like you—whose dedication, perseverance and belief in their own abilities finally earned them their first book.

Cathy Day, *The Circus in Winter*, Harcourt

Cathy Day keeps a bullhook—a sharp tool used to control elephants—in her English Department office at The University of Pittsburgh. The bullhook once belonged to her great-great-uncle Henry Hoffman who worked as an elephant trainer for the Hagenbeck-Wallace Circus. Upon the death of Day's Uncle Fred, Hoffman's son, she asked her Aunt Margaret to give the tool to her. "She couldn't figure out why I'd want such a strange thing instead of her china," says Day.

Why would a writer want an elephant prod? The short answer is, of course, research. But the real reason is much more personal.

© Sandy Carney

Cathy Day

LAUREN MOSKO is editor of *Novel & Short Story Writer's Market*. Of all the amazing things her job allows her to do, writing this feature is her favorite. If you would like to be considered for next year's "Première Voices," please e-mail her at lauren.mosko@fwpubs.com.

Day grew up in a small Indiana town, ordinary in most every way, except it once served as winter home to the Hagenbeck-Wallace Circus. "My childhood environment wasn't colorful or magical," Day says. "I knew some of my distant relatives were involved in that circus, but in Peru [Indiana], that certainly didn't make me special or unique. Lots of people I knew came from circus families."

While living in Peru, Day's heritage may have been typical, but once outside, the stories of her hometown history amazed her peers. "In Peru, it's not a big deal to say, 'My great-great-uncle was killed by an elephant,' but when I got to college and told that story, people stopped and listened. My family's historical connection to the circus is what prompted me to re-create Peru's past, but in the process, I realized that the boring, humdrum, post-circus town was worth writing about as well."

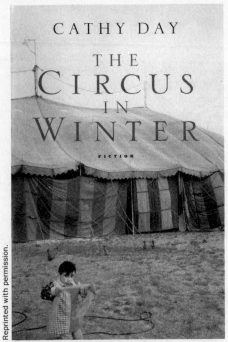

Reprinted with permission.

Explanations for the historic photographs that accompany each story in the collection can be found on Cathy Day's website, www.cathyday.com. *The Circus in Winter* was a finalist for The Story Prize in 2004.

Day's re-creations took the form of 11 linked stories, which she collected in her debut novel, *The Circus in Winter*. Through these stories, set in Lima, Indiana, Day spans four generations of lore surrounding the fictitious Great Porter Circus and its members. Readers become intimately familiar with the secrets of characters like Wallace Porter, who purchased the circus after the death of his wife and installed it in Lima; Jennie Dixianna, the beautiful and hardened acrobat whose famous Spin of Death seduces all who witness it; Bascomb Bowles, the son of Georgia slaves who is reinvented as a caricature of an African tribesman in order to escape his job emptying chamber pots on a steamboat; and Hans Hofstadter and Caesar, the former an elephant trainer (loosely based on Day's own great-great-uncle) and the latter the great beast responsible for the trainer's untimely death.

Don't be surprised by the unromantic descriptions; these stories focus not on circus grandeur but on its raw humanity. "I was trying to undercut the nostalgia," explains Day. "The more I researched the history of the American circus, the more I realized there was a dark underbelly to the greasepaint and spangles. That's why I deal with issues of racism, exploitation and animal cruelty in some stories."

The depth of the characters, the scope of the emotion and the precision of detail make one marvel at the amount of research Day must have conducted. It's no wonder the collection took her 13 years to complete. "At first, I simply devoured anything and everything on the American circus and about Peru's circus history," she said. Day believes she had the entire book—the town's past and present—in her head at once, but so much information and so many story threads began to hinder her work. Finally, John Keeble, her workshop leader at The University of Alabama, suggested she put the background material away and only research as each individual story demanded. She then tried starting at "the beginning," asking herself, "Why would a man buy a circus?" She wrote the first drafts of all the stories in roughly chronological order and then went back and finished them in whatever order time and research material allowed.

Day started sending out stories from the novel in 1994, but didn't start placing them until

1999. "The Circus House" was published first in *Story* and again in *New Stories from the South*, and it drew inquiries from a few agents, but, as her book was not completed, nothing came of the correspondence. Three years later, *The Southern Review* published the story "Wallace Porter," which caught the eye of agent Peter Steinberg (then of JCA Literary, now of Regal Literary). Steinberg agreed to represent the finished manuscript, so Day worked diligently on the remaining stories for the next two years. At a lunch meeting with Harcourt Executive Editor Ann Patty, Steinberg pitched the book. Serendipitously, Patty admitted she was also born in Indiana—not far from Peru—and agreed to read the manuscript. "A few weeks later, that was that," says Day, then adds, "I feel compelled to mention that the years in between 1991 and 2003 were very tough. I sent nine stories to *The Southern Review* before they accepted 'Wallace Porter.' I accumulated 200 rejection letters for the individual stories, and quite a few agents said, 'No thanks.' Publishing in great magazines like *Story*, *Shenandoah*, *The Antioch Review* and *The Gettysburg Review*—for me, that was the hard part."

Understanding and appreciating the true history of the American circus as she does now, it also couldn't have been easy for Day to hold that bullhook for the first time, acknowledging its connection to her great-great-uncle's tragic fate and the cruelty of life under the big top. She says she tried to describe the feeling in the story "The Bullhook." *A cold shiver tingled up Ollie's arm . . . its faint, almost electrical impulse seemed like a telegram that had waited 17 years to be delivered.* "Change the years to 96," she says, "and that's what it felt like."

Brad Vice, *The Bear Bryant Funeral Train*, University of Georgia Press

Brad Vice

One of the only times Brad Vice can recall being allowed to watch television in school was the day Bear Bryant, the legendary Alabama football coach, was buried. "About a million people gathered between Tuscaloosa and Birmingham to see his hearse drive by," Vice recalls. "After a while, it seemed the important thing was not that it happened but that I had watched it on TV, sitting on the floor with my entire third grade class. Our hometown was certified—and we collectively felt it—as we watched the whole world watch us bury our most famous citizen."

Watching Bryant's funeral procession influenced Vice so much it became the title of his debut collection of short stories, *The Bear Bryant Funeral Train*. However, the "Patron Saint of Tuscaloosa," as he calls the coach, isn't the only Southern figure readers encounter within the somber and visceral collection. Vice delivers indelible images of escaped mental patients and the KKK ("Tuscaloosa Knights"); Sissy Lynn, a little girl with no teeth and a vicious case of head lice ("Stalin"); Kurt Schaffer, a young farm boy who dreams of playing football under Coach Bryant but in reality spends his days shooting buzzards off the carcasses of water-starved cattle ("Report from Junction"); and an entourage of other beasts, including horses, mules, feral cats, chickensnakes, a voodoo farmer and a witchcraft-obsessed cookbook writer. This menagerie is no accident.

"On one level, the South is a mass cultural hallucination, but one I participate in with no small amount of joy. I really grew up with guns and mules and so that's a literal part of my world," explains Vice. "Most of my fiction I think of as 'blood and hay' realism, but that literal world can become sentimentalized and clichéd."

Conscious of this danger, Vice intentionally created the title story as one entirely different from the rest of the collection. "The Bear Bryant Funeral Train" is the tale of a Daimler-Chrysler concept engineer who has designed a secret mood-altering roller coaster based on

© Megan Bean

a post-modern interpretation of the aforementioned funeral procession. Where the other stories are physical and organic, the eponymous entry is a cold, cerebral and highly visual tale. "One of the reasons I wrote 'The Bear Bryant Funeral Train' was to write about Southern iconography *as* iconography, not as literal artifacts as I usually do," explains Vice. "I hoped titling the collection after that story would show I understand my stories in terms of a historical context that stretches back to [Flannery] O'Connor and [William] Faulkner and beyond."

Reprinted with permission.

Brad Vice calls the title story in his collection *The Bear Bryant Funeral Train* a "verbal collage," and the cover is a miniaturized, literal interpretation of that concept. What's the connection between these morbid images? Read the book to find out.

Vice's recognition of his literary and historical roots makes it fitting his collection received The Flannery O'Connor Award for Short Fiction, sponsored by the University of Georgia Press (UGAP). The acceptance of his manuscript and his path to publication were relatively serene. He gathered up the best stories he'd written over the last 10 years—several of which were previously published in journals like *The Southern Review*, *The Carolina Quarterly*, *Hayden's Ferry Review*, *Five Points*, *The Atlantic Monthly*, *New Stories from the South* and *Best New American Voices*—and submitted them to the contest. "I simply sent the manuscript off with a nominal reading fee like other hopeful writers. The process was all rather mysterious. I don't even know who the judges were," he says.

About five months passed and then the e-mail arrived. "I had been teaching at Mississippi State University all day and was very tired when I got the news, so I felt like I was dreaming. I kept reading the e-mail over and over to make sure it was authentic. I immediately printed it out and photocopied it to document the award in case somebody later said there was a mistake and they were going to take it back. In retrospect, I guess I could have just printed it out twice, but photocopying the letter made it seem real. It still doesn't feel quite real," he says.

Vice is thrilled about the opportunity to work with UGAP because he feels a university press will give his collection more attention than a commercial press, yet it won't stop printing the book if, ultimately, it isn't a best seller. Still, the publication process—rosy as it sounds—wasn't without a bit more work. "The press gave me a fantastic editor, David Walton, and he really pushed me to make the stories better. Many of them had been 'done' for years, and it was hard to crack them open again, but they have benefited greatly from the surgery," Vice acknowledges.

So what's next? "I wish I could tell you I was just about to finish a novel, but I can't. I've been focused almost solely on the collection. I've spent the better part of the last 12 years of my life in the dim glow of my computer or in the stacks of one university library or another," says Vice. "After I won the Flannery O'Connor Award, I called my friend Tim Parrish who was also my first creative writing teacher at Alabama. I told him I was terrified I had written out all the material of my childhood and I wouldn't have anything else to say. 'Dude,' he said. 'Just live your life.' I'm going to try and take his advice."

Vice must be living right; since this interview, *The Bear Bryant Funeral Train* earned the William Faulkner Foundation Award, sponsored by the University of Rennes in France. The Foundation will translate "Tuscaloosa Knights" into French and reissue it as a chapbook.

Trenton Lee Stewart, *Flood Summer*, Southern Methodist University Press

When it rains, it pours. Or, in the case of Trenton Lee Stewart, it floods. Stewart began submitting the manuscript for his first novel, *Flood Summer*, in 2001, all the while making notes for a children's book. "I didn't expect to write it anytime soon, but the ideas kept coming," Stewart reflects. "Eventually, I took the hint and got to work on it." Three years later, the children's book was finished, so Stewart sent it to an agent who had shown interest in some of his previous work. The agent responded immediately and, a few weeks later, *The Mysterious Benedict Society* sold to Little, Brown Books for

Trenton Lee Stewart

Photo courtesy of author

Young Readers. Southern Methodist University (SMU) Press accepted *Flood Summer* just six weeks after that. Stewart says the news "wasn't the least bit anticlimactic." He adds, "I'd spent a good deal of time contemplating my failure as a writer. Suddenly I had multiple publishing deadlines. A little disorienting, but as more than one person said to me that summer, 'Everyone should have such problems.'"

Though his work on and submission of both manuscripts overlapped, Stewart feels his literary fiction and his children's fiction are "fairly different enterprises." He explains, "Though I love to joke around, my literary fiction tends to be rather serious. Writing literary fiction is satisfying hard work, whereas writing the children's novel was more like satisfying hard play."

Calling *Flood Summer* "rather serious" is an understatement, as the novel, set in the fictitious town of Lockers Creek, Arkansas, follows two primary characters burdened by dark circumstances. Abe is a young man whose innocence is lost during an unrelenting rainstorm in which he is forced to fight for his own life and witness the loss of another. Similarly, as the novel unfolds, so does the identity of the initially mysterious Marie, a young woman who is tormented by memories of her childhood spent on the road with her drug-addled mother and her mother's abusive junkie friends. Guilt, shame and fear haunt both characters, affecting not only their perception of their own identities but also their perceptions of reality.

"I've long been interested in how intense experience can feel more real than mundane experience," says Stewart. "If your past is characterized by intense experience, then it's possible that your present, even though you're living it, might feel less real than your past. In the case of my characters, this contributes to their occasional, ridiculous sense of imposture and artifice. Abe and Marie instinctively look to their pasts as their reality, but they don't *want* to do this, and herein lies the tension. In other words, I've written another book about characters with haunted pasts—but mine has a flood in it."

Haunted pasts aside, *Flood Summer* distinguishes itself from other novels that explore similar ideas, with its crisp dialogue and acute description. When pressed to choose between the two, Stewart says, "I suppose dialogue comes easier to me, but it's also the most difficult to be satisfied with. Though I can somewhat easily shift details of geography, weather and architecture to suit my purposes, once characters have started breathing and talking, I can't change what they say without creating a ripple effect in their personalities and relationships, all of which must be given consideration and attended to. Readers are less inclined to doubt the description of a wire fence than they are the plausibility of a particular comment or conversation."

Stewart attributes his story's scenic realism to his personal experiences in Arkansas. The writer grew up in Hot Springs (not far from where he says Lockers Creek would be if it existed), attended college in Conway, and lived for a year in Little Rock. He drew on those memories when constructing the eponymous flood, the rural community and its inhabitants. "Like Marie's father, my own father has a small business in downtown Hot Springs. In fact, in an early draft of the novel I had Marie bump into him briefly in a café. He was very kind

The Writing Life

Reprinted with permission.

Flood Summer's cover features a painting by noted Arkansas artist Warren Criswell. Author Trenton Lee Stewart feels the art is fitting. "One of the reasons I like the painting is it depicts an actual exit in Benton, Arkansas, not far at all from where some of the dramatic scenes in the story take place," he says. To see more of Criswell's work, visit www.warrencriswell.com.

to her, as of course he would be, but I still had to yank him in the end," Stewart jokes.

As striking a story as he's composed and as lighthearted as Stewart seems now, it's hard to believe *Flood Summer's* path to publication began on such a slow foot. While revising the novel, Stewart contacted seven agents; only one read the entire manuscript. "This shouldn't have discouraged me," he admits. "I'd received some nice comments, and I knew plenty of writers who'd approached countless agents before finding one to represent them. I'm usually pretty stoic about rejection, but for some reason I developed the suspicion that my book was agent-proof. I stopped seeking representation for the book and turned instead to small presses, where agents fear to tread." For Stewart's first round of submissions, he chose four houses where he thought *Flood Summer* would fit. Two of them declined without elaboration, one politely declined with an invitation for future submission, and SMU Press requested the entire manuscript. "You know the rest," he says.

The aspect of working with SMU Press that most impressed Stewart was the level of input he had during the publishing process—not just on editorial matters but cover art and book design as well. In addition, Stewart received much positive feedback from the outside readers (all notable published authors) SMU Press' Senior Editor Kathryn Lang commissioned to review his manuscript prior to acceptance. "Reading their favorable comments was probably the most gratifying part of the whole publishing process," Stewart says. "The comments showed very clearly these writers understood and appreciated what I'd attempted. Up to that point, I'd never gotten any such indication from anyone."

Though Stewart must no doubt draw some confidence from these two victories, he's not showing any signs of slowing down. In addition to helping raise two little boys, Stewart is working on three literary novels and writing the follow-up to *The Mysterious Benedict Society*.

Paul Mandelbaum, *Garrett in Wedlock*, Berkley Books

One of the prompts in the reading guide at the end of Paul Mandelbaum's tender and comedic debut novel *Garrett in Wedlock* suggests the book is a portrait of "the new American family—a social dynamic redefined by multiple marriages, cultural diversity, global awareness and spiritual choices." However, the author did not create the family—which is made up of the protagonist, Garrett Hughes; his new wife, May-Annlouise; her two children from previous marriages; her two ex-husbands; and ex-husband No. 1's other wife— for the sake of either social commentary or comedy.

Photo courtesy of author

Paul Mandelbaum

"I constructed the family this way because I was living it," says Mandelbaum. "My wife at the time had been married twice before and had a daughter by an Indian businessman. I remember one afternoon my stepdaughter's first stepfather came by the house, and she insisted the three of us play croquet. It suddenly felt like I had married the entire world, an idea which I found fictionally interesting because it seemed like merely an exaggerated version of the 'new American family' so many people are experiencing now."

Driving the stories are triangles of conflict between the characters, which surface as each tries to establish or assert his or her identity in the family. In "The Explorers," the dynamic between Garrett, May-Annlouise and her ex-husband Tor is established when a terminally ill Tor shows up on Garrett's doorstep wanting to spend his last remaining days in the house with Turpin, his only son. In "Parni's Present," Garrett takes stepdaughter Lynn to visit her birthfather Parni in Bombay and struggles with the reality that Parni had been both husband to May-Annlouise and father to Lynn *first*. In "Changeling," readers recognize the maternal tensions between May-Annlouise and Parni's arranged-marriage partner Nazaar as both women exert claim to Lynn. However, Mandelbaum has created each character in such an endearing way that siding with any one seems absurd. "One of the points of the book is that sometimes people who we consider rivals really aren't," he says. "Tor and Parni aren't villains just because Garrett feels in conflict with them at times." The truth is there are no villains in this book; there are only members of one very extended family trying—sometimes desperately, sometimes awkwardly, sometimes touchingly—to find connection.

In addition to releasing the follow-up to *Garrett in Wedlock*, Paul Mandelbaum has also recently published his new anthology *12 Short Stories and Their Making* (Persea Books), featuring works by and his interviews with Sandra Cisneros, Ellen Gilchrist, Jhumpa Lahiri, Tobias Wolff and other luminaries. Visit Mandelbaum's website at www.paulmandelbaum.com.

Just as each individual member is undeniably connected to the family unit, so too are these 11 stories bound to the novel. It's true that all but the last two stories, "Lynn, Raving" and "Garrett in the Wild," functioned for a time on their own when they appeared in literary journals like *Glimmer Train Stories*, *The Southern Review*, *New England Review* and *Prairie Schooner*, but they clearly work best— even to the author—when gathered together. Mandelbaum believes creating each part of the novel as its own self-sustaining story "forced me to make each one feel satisfying and meaningful," while interlinking the stories (as a novel-in-stories, or what Mandelbaum refers to as a "stovel") enabled "the whole to feel greater than the sum of its parts."

Mandelbaum started the stories while a student at the Iowa Writers' Workshop and then attempted to convert them into a traditional novel. "I ended up with a few half-baked stories and some filler between," he reflects. "After putting it aside for a couple of years, I was emotionally ready to take a machete to it and isolate the elements that seemed like good

Reprinted with permission.

The Writing Life

ideas for stories in the first place." Finally, when the manuscript seemed ready, he contacted L.A.-based agent Betty Amster, whom he'd met through some friends.

While Amster and Mandelbaum were compiling a list of editors who should receive the manuscript, Mandelbaum happened to read a *New York Times* review of a novel by an author he admired, so he suggested Amster send his manuscript to the publisher of that novel, Berkley Books. Amster was already acquainted with Berkley's Senior Editor Allison McCabe, so the connection was made—but not without a little drama first. "Somewhere in the postal process, my manuscript got lost," recalls Mandelbaum. "We didn't know until Betsy e-mailed Allison to ask if it had arrived and was told it hadn't. The whole thing could so easily have fallen through the cracks without some follow up to make sure it got to its intended recipient." Finally, the manuscript surfaced and McCabe told Amster she'd take it home over the week-end. That Monday, McCabe called Amster to express her interest in adopting Garrett and the rest of the family.

"Betsy called with the good news while I was away teaching that day," says Mandelbaum. "My wife called the school and told me to call Betsy's cell phone right away because she was about to get on a plane. Betsy shared the delightful highlights, and we made a date to talk later. I exhaled and then returned to my class where I spent the rest of that meeting speaking in tongues."

Mandelbaum has an extensive editorial background—serving for a time as the managing editor of *Story Magazine* and editing the collection *First Words: Early Writings from Favorite Contemporary Authors* (Algonquin Books)—so the process of preparing the book for publication was relatively painless. The most valuable lesson he feels he's learned throughout the process is "publishing a book might be fun, but writing it is the real joy."

There's no shortage of fun or joy in Mandelbaum's house. Berkley has just published the follow-up to *Garrett in Wedlock*, another novel-in-stories titled *Adriane on the Edge* (after a tender and acerbic minor character who has a brief tryst with Garrett in the first book). Mandelbaum is also working on a novel. He remains tight-lipped regarding the particulars but does reveal it's "a novel-novel this time."

The Lowdown on Low-residency MFA Programs

by Will Allison

Many fiction writers who'd like to pursue an MFA in creative writing can't put their careers on hold, move to a new city and spend two years working toward a degree. For those writers, low-residency programs offer an intriguing alternative.

Here's how a typical low-residency program works: Students meet on campus twice a year for intensive residencies (usually seven or 10 days). In the interim, they work with faculty members via mail and e-mail, submitting work and receiving regular feedback. (Though low-residency MFA programs depend heavily upon correspondence, they're not to be confused with nonaccredited correspondence writing programs.)

Perhaps the best-known low-residency program is the one at Warren Wilson College (near Asheville, North Carolina), but low-residency programs are offered by a number of colleges and universities across the country, including Antioch University (Los Angeles); Bennington College (Vermont); Fairleigh Dickenson University (New Jersey); Goddard College (Vermont); Goucher College (Baltimore); University of New Orleans; University of Southern Maine/Stonecoast; Queens University of Charlotte (North Carolina) and many others.

To help writers who might consider enrolling in a low-residency program, *Novel & Short Story Writer's Market* asked graduates of five programs to discuss why they chose a low-residency program and how satisfied they were with the experience.

Anna Balint (Goddard College) is the author of *Horse Thief*, a collection of short stories (Curbstone Press); *Out of the Box*, poems (Poetry Around Press); and *spread them crimson sleeves like wings*, stories and poems (Poetry Around Press). She co-edited *Poets Against the War* (Three Poets Press), an anthology of poems protesting the Gulf War. Her poems and stories have appeared in numerous journals including *Calyx*, *Briar Cliff Review*, *Raven Chronicles*, *Stringtown* and *Clackamas Literary Review*. Balint received the 2001 Leading Voices Award for outstanding work with urban youth in the Puget Sound Region in the field of creative writing. In 2002, she received a Seattle Arts Commission literary

© Willie Pugh

Anna Balint

WILL ALLISON (www.willallison.com) is a staff member at the Squaw Valley Community of Writers and teaches creative writing at Indiana University-Purdue University at Indianapolis. His short stories have appeared in *Zoetrope: All-Story*, *Kenyon Review*, *One Story*, *Shenandoah*, *American Short Fiction*, *Atlanta*, *Florida Review* and *Kansas Quarterly/Arkansas Review*.

grant for the development of new work. She lives in Seattle where she teaches creative writing at Antioch University.

Jaime Clarke (Bennington College) is the author of the novel *We're So Famous* (Bloomsbury USA). His short stories have appeared in *Chelsea*, *Agni* and the *Mississippi Review*; he also served as guest editor for the *Mississippi Review* all-interview issue. He has twice been nominated for the Push-cart Prize. His website is www.weresofamous.com.

© P.S. Hausler

Jaime Clarke

Mary Cotton (University of Southern Maine/Stonecoast) is publisher and managing editor of *Post Road*, a biannual literary magazine based in New York and Boston (www.postr oadmag.com).

Anh Chi Pham (Antioch University) was born in Vietnam and grew up in California. She has been published in *Hunger Mountain*, *Nimrod International*, *Santa Monica Review* and *The Baltimore Review*. Her first published story, "Mandala," has been nominated for the Pushcart Prize. She will graduate from Antioch University's MFA program and attend Ragdale this winter.

Nona Martin Stuck (Queens University of Charlotte) lives and writes in Columbia, South Carolina. She was a winner of the 2000 South Carolina Fiction Project, and her work has appeared in *O, the Oprah Magazine*; *More Magazine* and the online magazine *Literary Mama*. She is completing her first novel.

Why did you choose a low-residency MFA program?

Balint: My life was so busy with parenting, work and health issues that attending a traditional program and having to run back and forth to classes all the time would have been extremely difficult, if not impossible. And I certainly wasn't in a position to move somewhere for two years. This immediately limited the traditional programs available to me. But most importantly, I learn best in an independent setting. So the structure of the low-residency model—and a program that allowed me to play a part in designing my own education—had great appeal.

One of the main things that attracted me to Goddard was the program didn't require me to apply in a specific genre. I write both fiction and poetry and wanted to keep open the possibility of pursuing either or both for my MFA. As it turned out, I ended up writing a collection of short stories. The makeup of the faculty was also important. I was looking for a good cultural/ethnic mix, as well as strong writers. Goddard had both.

Clarke: At the heart of the low-residency MFA program is the simple fact writers must be in the world to do what they do—not locked away in a laboratory—though in all honesty I applied to Bennington College on the strength of having wanted to go there as an undergraduate (but not being able to afford it) and the quality of the Bennington MFA faculty (the savior of my otherwise faulty decision-making apparatus). The format of the low-residency MFA primarily appealed to me because of the one-on-one mentorship each semester offered. Plus, I knew I wouldn't be wasting my time taking extraneous courses, as I had for my undergraduate degree in creative writing. I just wanted the occasion and opportunity to write (practice), write (practice), write (practice).

Cotton: I had just finished my undergraduate work a year before enrolling in an MFA program, and I wasn't looking for a program that required me to remain stationary.

Pham: I wanted to avoid the negatives of a regular program—the fishbowl environment, competitiveness, cold winters in the Heartland. Also, I thought the low-residency format would better prepare me for life after the MFA. I felt it was important to develop the habit of writing under real-life circumstances—juggling work, marriage and bills—yet at the same

Craft & Technique

time have the structure and community of a program. The theory is I'll be more prepared and more likely to keep writing when I'm on my own. Ask me how that goes in a year.

Stuck: I have two children still living at home, teenagers, and moving away for two years was not an option.

Tell us about your program.

Balint: Goddard is a four-semester/two-year program. Each semester begins with an eight-day residency in Vermont. These are wonderful, packed with workshops, readings and the luxury of ongoing discussion and dialogue with other writers. This is also the time to map out your study for the upcoming semester, a process that includes one-on-one meetings with your advisor, and the chance to begin forging the advisor/advisee relationship that's the core of the Goddard experience.

The heart of the program is the creative work. Other degree requirements are critical work (two short papers and a long one, as well as annotations) and a teaching practicum. I enjoyed all of it. Following the residency, the semester unfolds around "packets" sent in the mail to your advisor every three weeks: five in all. Each packet includes creative writing, critical writing and a process letter to reflect on your learning. Your advisor's response letters, supplemented by e-mails and phone calls as needed, shape and guide your work over the course of the semester. It wasn't until the end of the second semester that my creative thesis began to emerge and take shape. The first couple of semesters involved lots of discovery.

I worked with three very different advisors—Michael Klein, Marina Budhos (for two semesters) and Mariana Romo-Carmona—who all gave me something different and valuable. If I had to sum up in a word what I got from each it would be *voice* from Michael, *structure* from Marina, and *insight* from Mariana.

Clarke: The Bennington MFA is a two-year program with five, 10-day residencies on their beautiful Vermont campus. Each residency offers little chance for sleep: the days are filled with associate faculty lectures (Bennington brings two writers from outside the faculty, one for each five days, who give a series of lectures), workshops, faculty readings, graduate student readings, publishing panels (though Bennington eschews bringing agents on campus, offering instead an inside look at the publishing world), and general merriment which, for reasons that will become clear if you attend, I cannot go into here.

The Bennington MFA faculty includes: Douglas Bauer, April Bernard, Sven Birkerts, Martha Cooley, Betsy Cox, Susan Cheever, Amy Gerstler, Amy Hempel, Sheila Kohler, David Lehman, Philip Lopate, Alice Mattison, Askold Melnyczuk, E. Ethelbert Miller, Rick Moody, Liam Rector, Bob Shacochis and Jason Shinder.

Recent associate faculty include: Agha Shahid Ali, Lucie Brock-Broido, Robert Creeley, Mark Doty, Vivian Gornick, Barry Hannah, Edward Hoagland, Richard Howard, Marie Howe, Sue Miller, Jayne Anne Phillips, Robert Pinsky, Robert Polito, Mary Robison and Roger Shattuck, to name a few.

Cotton: The Stonecoast MFA is a two-year program. The 10-day residencies are held in mid-July and late December/early January. At the residency, you participate in two writing workshops of four days each. Workshops are usually scheduled for mornings and have between five and eight students and one faculty member; afternoons are spent at seminars given by faculty or graduating students. Each night several faculty members read. Near the end of the residency, you hand in a list of your top choices of faculty members to work with individually over the semester. Third-semester and final-semester students have priority.

© R. Leonard

Mary Cotton

Craft & Technique

Craft & Technique

After being assigned a mentor, you work with her to develop a reading list and a schedule for the next semester. The first two semesters, you must hand in five packets of 25 pages to your mentor; this includes several brief essays on your readings. The third semester is devoted to writing a critical thesis that focuses on some area of craft or theory. The final semester is spent working on your creative thesis, which is the culmination of the work you have done in the program and is supposed to consist of 120 pages of publishable writing.

At the final residency, graduating students must give both a seminar and a reading. I worked with Elizabeth Searle, Brad Barkley and Joan Connor, all fantastic writers and amazing teachers. Each residency, students have workshops with two different writers, with whom they may or may not choose to work over the semester. Either way, students get to "sample" the teaching styles of many of the faculty members and see how they fit with what their goals are. I had the chance to be in a workshop with Dennis Lehane, Ann Hood, Suzanne Strempek-Shea and many others.

Ahn Chi Pham

Photo courtesy of author

Pham: Antioch's structure is similar to other programs. Within two years, we complete four project periods and attend five residencies. During the 10-day residencies, we attend courses, workshops and readings. During the project period, we submit five packets to our mentors and read assigned books, which we discuss with fellow mentees online. Besides the final manuscript and readings, other requirements include a field study, an online translation seminar, two critical papers, teaching one seminar, and a senior reading.

The downside to the schedule is there's no break between project periods. Also, most mentors prefer snail mail when it comes to sending and critiquing work, so it takes one to two weeks on average to hear back. For some people, especially novelists, this delay affects their momentum, but we are learning (mostly) to work around it.

Speaking of mentors, I had romanticized notions—Robin Williams in *Dead Poets Society*—of what mentors would do for me. In a program like this, you get what you put in, and mentors are there to guide and support, but they don't assume responsibility for your development. It's not their job. Looking back, I got what I needed when I needed it from the mentors I worked with: Marcos McPeek Villatoro was the confidence builder; Brad Kessler was more craft-focused and analytical; Leonard Chang was tough-minded and blunt; and Jim Krusoe was the guru.

Stuck: The low-residency MFA program at Queens involves four semesters of coursework, each of which includes a seven-day, on-campus residency and, in the periods between residencies, an online workshop where the students share their writing with three or four other students and the assigned faculty mentor for that semester. At the end of two years, the graduating students return to campus for a fifth residency in which they each present a thesis, offer a public reading from their work, and lead fellow students in a craft seminar they've developed with a faculty advisor. In my time at Queens, I've worked directly with Pinckney Benedict, Fred Leebron, Jenny Offill, Elissa Schappell, Elizabeth Strout and Ashley Warlick. I've also attended courses led by J.D. Dolan, Jane Alison, Rebecca McClanahan, David Payne, Susan Perabo, Robert Polito, Patricia Powell, Cathy Smith-Bowers and Abigail Thomas.

Do you have any regrets about not attending a traditional program?

Balint: None. It wouldn't have suited me, and my learning experience at Goddard was exactly what I needed at exactly the right time.

Clarke: I never have a regret, but rather I have a hypothesis that could probably be proven: Traditional programs offer the chance to spend more time with those like-minded individuals whose energy and friendship can sustain you through severe periods of creative drought.

Cotton: Sure. Sometimes I feel that I would've benefited from a program of study that was more structured, with classes that met regularly. It can be easy to overestimate how much work you are doing when you do it all on your own. But a low-residency program really can become whatever the individual makes of it; there are plenty of opportunities for creating support systems with fellow students, and the faculty generally make every effort to be available for you to contact with questions and concerns throughout the semester.

Pham: Sometimes, I think I would have been more productive if I'd had to show my face in workshop every week. Having in-person critique pushes me to try harder, revise more. Without the regular classroom environment to push me, I've had to learn how to motivate myself, with varying degrees of success.

Stuck: As I never attended a traditional program, I don't know what I missed, so the answer is no.

What's your advice for writers considering a low-residency program?

Balint: Check in with yourself about your learning style and whether a self-directed model suits you or not. That's central. Other than that, shop around and enjoy. Having two years to put writing front and center is incomparable.

Clarke: Do your homework about the faculty. Low-residency MFA programs have become an easy way for a university to make a little extra change, so make sure you're not applying to a program that has nothing more to offer other than its good name.

© Mary Hollis Stuck

Nona Martin Stuck

Cotton: One of the main drawbacks of low-residency programs is that 10 days of ultra-intense study and discussion are followed by several months of much quieter work, where your only contact with your mentor might be via e-mail or letters. The residencies are thrilling but exhausting—make sure you're up for it.

Pham: You've got to be self-motivated: Know who you are and your priorities. Being in a low-residency program tests your commitment and puts strain on relationships. You're still at home, you're still working, so it's hard for friends, family and bosses to understand why your (and their) lifestyle has to change. Therefore, make sure you set expectations and boundaries with the people in your life.

Once you get into a program, reach out. It's easy to feel isolated during the project period. Antioch has a buddy system and local online conferences to create a sense of community, though virtual. Avoid working full-time, if you can. And do something—yoga, walking, basket weaving, whatever it takes—to stay sane.

Stuck: Visit the campus during one of the residency weeks if possible. Ask for addresses—e-mail and other—of current and former students and contact a few of them. I did this, and I got a lot of straight talk and helpful information.

Craft & Technique

Dulled at the Edges

Sharpen Your Secondary Characters

Photo courtesy of author

by I.J. Schecter

It's no surprise we often remember the scene-stealers in movies more than we remember the leads: Franck, Martin Short's bizarre-accented wedding consultant in *Father of the Bride*; Curly, Jack Palance's ornery cattle wrangler in *City Slickers*; cousin Jeffrey in your Uncle Stan's 50th birthday video.

So it is with great peripheral characters in fiction. For every Valjean imprinted in our minds, there is an equally memorable Javert; for every Scarlett, a Mammie. Astute writers, like skilled chefs accentuating their entrées with a sprig of parsley or a dash of thyme, maximize the impact of their secondary characters by making every word they say or act they perform significant. If Franck had appeared in every scene of *Father of the Bride*, we might have grown annoyed with him halfway through. (Why do you think half the country wanted to do away with Jar-Jar Binks after *The Phantom Menace*?) Instead, Short's character enhanced our enjoyment of the overall film and left us wanting more.

It can be difficult to evaluate the usefulness of your secondary characters within the entire panorama of your manuscript. Here's a helpful exercise. Imagine your protagonist walking along the street when he runs into a friend. With this friend is someone the protagonist has never met. Introductions are made and the friend proceeds to make small talk, asking about the protagonist's job, family, commenting on the weather, and so on.

Now, turn your attention to the stranger, visualizing her as a specific secondary character in your story. If, in your manuscript, you haven't clearly established her function, you'll find it difficult to picture her doing anything but shuffling her feet or gazing off into the distance as the protagonist talks to his friend.

On the other hand, if you know the specific reason this person exists, you should be able to envision her reaction to the protagonist automatically. Below are some examples of particular roles this secondary character might play.

Plot Generator

Perhaps the proudest role a secondary character can claim is that of the individual who, through a small or seemingly insignificant act, justifies the rest of the story. In Stephen King's novel *Gerald's Game* (Penguin Putnam), the main character makes an ignominious exit in the first several pages but launches the rest of the plot; in the movie *The Big Chill*, all of

I.J. SCHECTER (www.ijschecter.com) writes for leading magazines, newspapers and websites throughout the world, including *Condé Nast Brides*, *Golf Monthly*, *Men's Exercise*, *The Globe & Mail* and iParenting.com. He is also the author of a short story collection *The Bottom of the Mug* (Aegina Press Inc).

Kevin Costner's performance as the deceased man bringing together old friends was left on the cutting room floor save for a brief appearance of his hand—yet the rest of the story owes itself to his character; and in the novel I'm reading now, Jane Hamilton's *A Map of the World* (Doubleday), the unfortunate plot generator is a two-year-old girl named Lizzy who drowns in the protagonist's pond:

> When I came to the clearing I couldn't see past the single glaring point of sunlight, dancing on the water. I put my hand to my forehand, to make a visor, and still it took me a minute to find the pink seersucker bottom just beneath the surface, about fifteen feet from the beach.

Though Lizzy makes her departure before the end of the first chapter, her pivotal and tragic role sets the plot in motion, prompting another 370 pages of story.

Now think back to the street-corner conversation between your protagonist, the friend he's bumped into and the stranger. Does the stranger jump into a car that screeches to a stop at the curb before peeling away? Does she clutch her chest, drop to the ground and have a coronary? Does she internally combust? Perhaps—and perhaps it's this, or some similar act, that starts the wheels of your plot turning.

Antagonist

There are two types of foils for your protagonist: the subtle type and the one whose hostility is more in-your-face. Both types are present in *A Map of the World*, and, though given limited air time, each fulfills an important role. Here, we see the novel's protagonist, Alice—recently charged with sexual abuse—enduring the passive-aggressive humiliations of a classic adversary in literature, the mother-in-law:

> When the car started, the muffler sounding its call, Nellie cleared her throat and adjusted herself in her chair. She and Howard had planned this time for our little talk. I knew it, could see the pleasure of conspiracy in her big sincere face. "Alice, dear," she said, wiping her mouth with a napkin, "I can't help worrying about you. You're going to hurt yourself, sweetheart."

Later, having landed behind bars, Alice must deal with a far less restrained antagonist, a woman named Dyshett bent on clarifying just who rules the roost:

> She reached out and twisted my braid around hard in one hand, so hard my eyes smarted. "You probably think I should be showing you some respec', since you an old lady by now. But I don't take too kind to people who mess wid others. You sit and wait, Granny," she said, twisting harder. "You sit and wait for me."

If the secondary character whose value you're examining is an understated meanie, you might picture her making a snide, under-the-breath remark in response to something your protagonist says; if the in-your-face type, you might see her suddenly driving a heel into your protagonist's instep and then running off, leaving him confused—and, probably, more than a bit nervous.

Enigma

During the conversation on the street corner between your protagonist and his friend, perhaps the stranger appears all of a sudden to become angered, her features contorting severely, and then, in the next instance, perfectly serene. Your protagonist, understandably, doesn't quite know what to make of this.

Eventually, the significance of the stranger's mysterious behavior will be revealed—you owe that to the reader, otherwise it's a cheat—providing insight about the protagonist by the way he reacts or filling a retroactive, and deliberate, gap in the plot.

John Irving's classic *The Hotel New Hampshire* (Dutton Adult) begins with the following words:

> The summer my father bought the bear, none of us was born—we weren't even conceived: not Frank, the oldest; not Franny, the loudest; not me, the next; and not the youngest of us, Lilly and Egg. My father and mother were hometown kids who knew each other all their lives, but their "union," as Frank always called it, hadn't taken place when Father bought the bear.

Five Pitfalls of Secondary Characters

Tip

Because they have limited time to accomplish their purpose, secondary characters need to be handled deftly. Here are five ways in which those on the periphery are commonly misused.

1 Mistaking form for function. It's important to remember there's a difference between an inherently interesting character and one who serves to affect the plot. The guy who lives down the road from your protagonist might be a Russian spy moonlighting as a florist, but if you can't figure out what he does besides wave hello every morning, he needs to be turfed.

2 Casting Perry Mason. Secondary characters lose their potential impact if they seem plucked from an assembly line. The slick corporate lawyer, the tough-talking femme fatale, the unrefined-yet-wise hick—such stock characters, especially when they only appear sporadically, need something to distinguish them. Work hard to find that something.

3 Making false introductions. Injecting a character into a scene because the plot needs a catalyst at that particular point can be tempting; however, this move is counterproductive if that character disappears just as quickly and is never heard from again. Any character you introduce should have a valid reason for showing up—and sticking around (or being done away with).

4 Having fuzzy focus. It's important you know a secondary character's specific purpose before dropping him into your story. Readers are distracted—and, potentially, aggravated—by a character who seems not to know why he's there or, worse, who comes off as an indistinct amalgam of several unfinished characters.

5 Granting overexposure. If well drawn and judiciously placed, a secondary character should be able to establish her purpose in just a few appearances—or perhaps just one. Try to resist offering extra cameos; focus instead on doing more with less.

Besides grabbing our attention, Irving goes one better: He waits 12 pages before actually bringing the bear onstage, enveloping us in other elements of the plot while the question of the curious animal hangs in our minds.

Magnet

As objects of desire, secondary characters can have large plot implications—and reveal much about your lead's motivations, tendencies and moral fibre—by mere virtue of their presence. In *The English Patient* by Michael Ondaatje (Knopf), it's the moment the protagonist surrenders to his desire for the wife of a colleague that the story begins down a path from which it will never return:

> I sank to my knees in the mosaic-tiled hall, my face in the curtain of her gown, the salt taste of these fingers in her mouth. We were a strange statue, the two of us, before we began to unlock our hunger. Her fingers scratching against the sand in my thinning hair. Cairo and all her deserts around us.

Is your secondary character, the third wheel on the street corner, a magnet? In your vision, does the protagonist compulsively glance in her direction as he tries to maintain conversation with his friend? Does he inadvertently repeat a question he's asked three minutes before? Most important, does he continue thinking about her after she's left?

Soulmate

Sometimes, secondary characters can exert unforgettable impact on protagonists by affecting their souls rather than their loins—or, sometimes, both. Later in *The English Patient*, Ondaatje shows the principal's desire for his colleague's wife transcends mere physical yearning:

> Her life with others no longer interests him. He wants only her stalking beauty, her theatre of expressions. He wants the minute and secret reflection between them, the depth of field minimal, their foreignness intimate like two pages of a closed book.

Does your protagonist seem to connect, mysteriously but undeniably, with the new stranger on the street corner? Can you sense a spiritual energy flowing between them despite the fact they met only minutes ago? What sort of kinship bonds them? Will one or both acknowledge it? When? How?

Crusader

Secondary characters spearheading the pursuit of justice or redemption—which, after all, are at the heart of most stories—often play crucial roles, even if from the wings. As in real life, these crusaders are more compelling when nonstereotypical. Heck, they don't even have to be human. In H.G. Wells' *The War of the Worlds*, the pesky Martians who have unceremoniously laid waste to London are finally done in by a group of organisms much humbler than we:

> These germs of disease have taken toll of humanity since the beginning of things—taken toll of our prehuman ancestors since life began here. But by virtue of this natural selection of our kind we have developed resisting power; to no germs do we succumb without a struggle, and to many . . . our living frames are altogether immune. But there are no bacteria in Mars, and directly these invaders arrived, and directly they drank and fed, our microscopic allies began to work their overthrow. . . . By the toll of a million deaths man has bought his birthright of the earth, and it is his against all comers; it would still be his were the Martians ten times as mighty as they are.

In the conversation between the protagonist and his friend, does the stranger suddenly interject when the subject of furs comes up, railing against anyone who would wear a skin? Does she suddenly leave so as not to miss the meeting of her volunteer energy coalition? When she reaches into her bag for a lipstick, does the protagonist glimpse what might be an FBI badge?

Secondary characters can help round out the world of your story by encouraging, obstructing, adoring or despising your protagonist. If one of these characters keeps standing around without seeming to know what she's doing there, send her home. If, on the other hand, she's keen to get involved, it's up to you to help her figure out how.

An American Writer in Paris

Wooing Your Novel in the City of Lights

© Roccie Hill

by Eric Maisel

Editor's note: The following is an excerpt from Eric Maisel's latest book, *A Writer's Paris: A Guided Journey for the Creative Soul* (Writers Digest Books), released in October 2005. In this chapter, Maisel sets up the perfect six-month schedule for the writer abroad *en France*. Though he includes directives like ''Take a day trip to Monet's Giverny. Write on the métro to the commuter train. Write on the train to the bus. Write on the bus to Giverny. (Don't miss your stop!),'' you don't have to buy a plane ticket to benefit from this instruction. *Bon voyage, mes amis!* Don't forget to write!

P aris is a physical place defined by its beauty and its openness to strolling. It is also home to the intellectual history of the West, the place where modern art, modern writing and modern philosophy were born. Paris is the spot where artists gather, where a Czech filmmaker, a Russian choreographer, an African painter and a poet from Providence are most likely to collide. Above all, Paris is a place of associations: It moves the mind, stirs the heart and resonates forever.

Let's say you manage the miraculous and set yourself up with a six-month writing jaunt in Paris. The details and particulars of your jaunt aside, here is your perfect writing plan. It posits three writing stints a day separated and punctuated by strolling, socializing and general living. Your stints might include two hours in a park, two hours in a café and two hours on a bookstore sofa. Here we go!

Day 1. Arrive. Gather your wits. Collapse.

Day 2. Look for sublet (if you haven't arranged one from home). Walk everywhere. Savor.

Day 3. Look for sublet. Walk everywhere. In a café, pull out the notes for your novel. If you haven't begun your novel yet, entertain ideas. Massage your feet when you get back to your room.

ERIC MAISEL, author of *A Writer's Paris* (Writer's Digest Books), has sold hundreds of thousands of books to writers, painters and other creative and performing artists who respect his advice and love his style. His more than 20 works of fiction and nonfiction include *Affirmations for Artists*, named best book of the year for artists by *New Age Magazine*; *Fearless Creating*, currently in its 10th printing; *A Life in the Arts*, still in print since its appearance in 1990; and many others. In addition to Maisel's insight and advice, *A Writer's Paris* includes two-color art from Danny Gregory and Claudine Hellmuth. For more information, visit Writer's Digest Books online at www.writersdigest.com/store/books.asp.

Day 4. Secure your sublet for the first of the following month. Celebrate by writing. Have a splurge snack, perhaps a L'Opéra pastry and a really big cup of coffee. If you don't have an idea for a novel yet, ask for help from a passing American tourist. Say, ''Excuse me, I'm about to write a novel, and I need to choose among the following ideas. Which of these novels would you like to read?'' Ignore your respondent's advice but take careful note of your own reactions.

Day 5. Commence your writing routine of three writing stints a day. With luck this will amount to six pages a day (two pages a stint). Six pages a day is a novel in two months' time. You are well ahead of schedule!

Day 6. Write.

Day 7. Write.

Day 8. Write. Visit the Red Wheelbarrow bookstore in the Marais or some other Anglophone bookstore. Practice your English. Swap ''writing in Paris'' stories. Make a date with a stranger for coffee. Say to the bookstore owner, Penelope, if you find yourself at the Red Wheelbarrow, ''When my novel comes out two years from now, can I do a booksigning here?'' In this way, you'll have your first booksigning arranged.

Day 9. Write. Have coffee with that stranger. Write or make love or both.

Day 10. Write, unless you feel the need to read what you've written so far. Be careful! If you decide to read, be ready for a shock. You may have made a mess and may need to regroup. On the other hand, you may love what you've written. In that case, exult. Exult by writing.

Day 11. Take a day trip to Monet's Giverny. Write on the métro to the commuter train. Write on the train to the bus. Write on the bus to Giverny. (Don't miss your stop!) Write on a bench with a view of the Japanese Footbridge. Wander over to the Museum of American Impressionists just down the road, and use one of their excellent bathrooms. Write on the stone bench in front of the museum. (Don't miss the last bus! They stop running early.) Write on the bus to the commuter train. Etc.

Day 12. Maybe the blues have stuck. Splurge on a novel and read it all the way through in one sitting. Talk to someone. Fall in love. Don't worry about writing today. But plan to write tomorrow.

Day 13. Say *au revoir* to your lover. Back to work! Write, write, write.

Day 14. Two weeks in Paris! Catch up with your e-mail at an Internet cafe. Have a nice lunch, followed by a two-scoop Berthillon ice cream cone. Nap by the Seine.

Days 15 - 64. Write, write, write.

Day 65. You are practically a native. You can get around, you can get your hair cut. How are your finances? Better check and see. How are your emotions? If you're feeling too weird or blue, take a mental health day. Remind yourself writing in Paris is a brilliant way to make meaning and you are absolutely on track. Make this sales pitch work. If necessary, throw in chocolate. If you haven't been writing enough (or at all), release your guilt and embarrassment and start fresh. Consider it Day One.

Days 66 - 98. Write, write, write.

Day 99. Three months is a long time! If you've been writing on a daily basis, you will have thousands of words written. Should you read and revise or just keep writing? If it's been your habit to write without revising and that's gotten you into trouble before, bravely read what you've written. Weep for the parts that don't work and revel in the parts that do. If, on the other hand, it's been your habit to revise so tightly you end up with constipated nuggets, skip revising. Keep writing. You can read what you've written when you get back to Boise.

Days 100 - 134. Write, write, write.

Day 135. You've spent more than four months living in Paris. Hardly one in a million

Craft & Technique

writers pulls off that feat. Celebrate by buying a silly hat and taking a day trip to Chantilly or Fontainebleau, two forests-with-castles just outside of town. Picasso used to visit Fontainebleau to "gorge on green" and disgorge all that green when he got back to the studio. In the evening, buy a CD of Parisian cafe songs and play them at a friend's apartment.

Days 135 - 168. Write, write, write.

Days 169 - 180. Catch those last sights you missed by writing so much: the Rodin Museum, the Paris sewers, Voltaire memorabilia at the Musée Carnavalet. Pat yourself on the back. Get ready for the long flight home. Say *au revoir* to Paris but not goodbye. If you are braver than anyone I know, read your manuscript on the plane.

P.S. This routine also works in your own hometown. If you have a day job to manage, write first thing in the morning, during lunch and in the early evening. Let your town square be your *Place des Vosges*, your corner Starbucks your *Les Deux Magots*, your local Border's your Shakespeare & Company. It might be nicer if it were Paris—but it's the writing that counts.

Other Books by Eric Maisel

Eric Maisel is a prolific writer, creativity coach, teacher and counselor. For more information on him or his books, visit www.ericmaisel.com. In addition to *A Writer's Paris*, Maisel has written many other books on creativity, including

- *Coaching the Artist Within* (New World Library)
- *The Art of the Book Proposal* (Jeremy P. Tarcher)
- *Writers and Artists on Devotion*, Quotable Muse journal series (New World Library)
- *Writers and Artists on Love*, Quotable Muse journal series (New World Library)
- *The Van Gogh Blues* (Rodale Books)
- *Write Mind: 299 Things Writers Should Never Say to Themselves (And What They Should Say Instead)* (Jeremy P. Tarcher)
- *The Creativity Book* (Jeremy P. Tarcher)
- *Living the Writer's Life* (Watson-Guptill Publications)
- *Deep Writing: 7 Principles That Bring Ideas to Life* (Jeremy P. Tarcher)

Craft & Technique

Writer, Promote Thyself

Maximizing Your Novel's Visibility

by W.E. Reinka

Eager faces at writers' conferences cloud over whenever the editor or agent on the panel reminds the audience that writing their novel is only half the job. The other half is selling the novel—not to a publisher but to the book-buying public.

But doesn't the publisher do that?

Sadly, no, except for brand-name authors. In *Making a Literary Life* (Random House), Carolyn See writes, "After you write your book, you must sell it . . . Not your publisher or your agent or anyone else is going to do it for you." The first point John Kremer makes in *1001 Ways to Market Your Books* (Players Press) is "You will have to sell your books. No one else can do that for you."

Novelists can get discouraged in their drive to sell their books by reminders from experts that nonfiction books generally dovetail better with promotional angles, news hooks or organizations interested in a particular subject. But, before you scrap your dreams, stop, close your eyes and name five best-selling authors.

Chances are all five authors you named are novelists—and every one started their career as an unknown writer. It could be you haven't even read books by a couple of writers on your list but they're such brand names, they spring to mind anyway. Which brings up a fundamental advantage for fiction writers—novelists can build a brand name that transcends their individual titles.

Building a brand name

Robert S. Levinson, award-winning public relations authority whose thrillers include *Ask a Dead Man* (Five Star), says: "You stay in the marketplace by serving yourself, not the current title."

In *Guerilla Marketing for Writers* (Writer's Digest Books), authors Jay Conrad Levinson, Rick Frishman and Michael Larsen point out an indisputable fact of career building: "How well your first book sells helps determine the fate of succeeding books . . . You have more at stake than royalties. You're investing in your business." Romance author and literary agent Alice Orr encourages writers to promote themselves. In *No More Rejections: 50 Secrets to Writing a Manuscript that Sells* (Writer's Digest Books), she tells writers: "You always must be selling numbers, greater numbers with each book published under your name. And numbers are all about name recognition—not just title recognition, but name recognition."

It's never too early to start positioning yourself in the marketplace. Indeed, some experts

W.E. REINKA, who writes frequently about books and authors, contributes to newspapers and magazines nationwide.

would suggest you write your book to fit a marketing plan versus writing a marketing plan to fit your book. But most writers don't have a marketing plan when they face that first terrifyingly blank page of manuscript. Even without a formal marketing plan, there are steps you can take to increase visibility for your work and start building brand recognition.

Compiling lists for buyers & promoters

Some aspects of marketing should begin even before the manuscript is complete, starting with your mailing lists. You'll have one mailing list of people who may be interested in buying your book. See suggests the list include "your old professors and schoolmates, your carpet cleaner, the guy who fixed your roof. Before you say, 'Oh, I couldn't ask them,' think for a minute. If these people aren't going to buy your book, then who on earth is going to buy it?" She's right. Think how your interest would be piqued by a postcard or e-mail that an old classmate from Central High had just published a new novel.

Your second mailing list consists of people who will help promote your book. That list is as shameless as the first list and would include contacts from the media, writers' groups, bookstores and civic or professional organizations. For example, you're sitting in your dentist's waiting room when you notice the Rotary International plaque. Go home and add your dentist to the promotion list. Rotary International looks for speakers every week, and chances are your dentist will provide you contact information when you're ready to line up speaking gigs.

Another group of people who can help promote your book are booksellers. Schmooze the people at bookstores. "You want booksellers to think of you when they're recommending a book," says Naomi Epel, author of *The Observation Deck: A Toolkit for Writers* (Chronicle Books). "By being nice to them and appreciating their store, you'll get remembered, and they'll sell your book. They'll place it face out instead of spine out. They'll order a few more copies than they usually would."

Inventing imaginative news hooks & promotional angles

You may face a delicate challenge with the publicists at your publisher. On one hand, publicists usually devote their energy to front-list books. On the other, you may step on toes if you run roughshod over them. Linda McFall, publicity manager for St. Martin's Minotaur, recommends authors cultivate publicists' favor by saving them time. Promotion plans start months before publication, so demonstrate your willingness to cooperate and sensitivity to publicists' time by e-mailing them the various mailing lists you've compiled. Note especially if you have any out-of-town mailing lists (perhaps from your old hometown) of people likely to come to a book signing or publishing party if your publisher sends you to that city.

"Increasingly bookstores are requesting mailing lists," says Marie Coolman, director of publicity (West coast) for the Random House Publishing Group. "An author's local mailing list may persuade a store to host an event with an author they normally wouldn't be inclined to host."

Another way to help your publicist is by e-mailing (minimize precious phone time) talking points on your book or suggestions for news hooks to get you media interviews. Coolman recalls when historical romance writer Ciji Ware was promoting *Midnight on Julia Street* (Ivy Books), she and the author used the novel's subtext of historical preservation and Ware's personal expertise on preservation to garner more interviews. Those interviews, though ostensibly focused on historic preservation, gave Ware additional avenues to promote her novel.

If your novel or background dovetails with a specific angle like gardening, business or sports, contact editors of those newspaper sections and editors of trade or special interest magazines in that field. At the same time, be realistic; don't waste precious personal time or materials chasing far-fetched connections. No gardening editor cares about a sports book.

Part of running roughshod over your publicist is being unrealistic. Coolman laughs as she says, "I can't tell you how many authors have asked me about getting them on *Oprah*. Take a look at the *Today* show or *Oprah* to see what kinds of authors they have on."

Five years ago, Oline H. Cogdill, mystery columnist for the *South Florida Sun-Sentinel* would receive 10 or 20 review copies each week. Now she's deluged with up to 100. But since her reviews are syndicated in hundreds of newspapers worldwide, it's important to catch her eye. Guess what? A review copy with a note to please review your book isn't going to do it. Levinson advises "stand out from the pack." Don't just say your book is compelling. Everybody says that. Pitch a trend. Give it a news hook. Look for ways to make things easy for the book reviewer.

One way Cogdill says writers make things easy for reviewers is by putting downloadable color photos and book jackets on the writer's website. (But don't go ahead and e-mail them to the reviewer, the graphics take forever to download and you'll just upset reviewers by overloading their mailboxes.)

Michael Larsen, one of the *Guerilla Marketing* authors and San Francisco literary agent, suggests writers construct an online press kit with a news release, author photo, positive reviews, talking points, FAQs, author's bio, book jacket and information on classes the author might teach or other promotional information. In other words, the online press kit should include everything the author compiles for a hard copy press kit. And you'll want a press kit, not just review copies, to get people's attention.

Creating a website with personality

The world gets more electronic every day. So does book promotion. Epel declares, "Author websites are musts these days." But there are websites and then there are *websites*. Larsen points out, "Everybody has a book and everybody has a website. What makes creative websites unique comes out of personality." He advises authors set up their website while they're still compiling mailing lists, before the book appears in print, so it can be included on the back of the book. As with everything else related to book promotion, waiting until publication to set up a website is too late.

The easiest way to know what you want—and don't want—in a website is by examining existing author websites. Some are astoundingly clever; others cram too much on one page and look amateurish. Steal ideas. Adopt the trivia game Jeffery Deaver includes on his website. Borrow from Danielle Steel's website and award books or audio tapes as contest prizes. Think those mailing lists aren't important? Then why do brand names Stephen King, Nora Roberts and Fannie Flagg all use websites to expand their e-mail lists?

Preparing your public face

Just as you didn't send off your novel to a publisher or agent until you were convinced it was absolutely ready to go, don't line up promotional events without being ready to go yourself. Prepare answers in advance to common questions such as: Why did you write this book? What's your book about? What writers have influenced you? If you snagged the interview by tying your novel to a trend or news hook, know in advance how you'll tie in your book when your face the microphone.

Coolman begs writers, "Practice, practice, practice answers beforehand. Being on TV or radio looks and sounds like a normal conversation, but it isn't. In normal conversation we talk our way to our points. In TV, radio and even print media, we have to get to our points right off the bat." Likewise, Epel recalls how her media coach encouraged her to prepare three key points to help sell her book that she would make in every interview no matter what questions were asked.

Try to stand out from the pack at bookstore appearances. Lorna Landvik (*Patty Jane's House of Curl, Your Oasis on Flame Lake, Angry Housewives Eating Bon Bons* [Random House]), the comic chronicler of small-town life, throws a Hershey Kiss to any audience member who asks a question. One way Diane Mott Davidson (*Double Shot, Chopping Spree, Sticks & Scones* [Bantam]) climbs to the best-seller list is by giving away fresh-baked cookies at bookstores. (When she's on tour, her husband sends daily batches of cookies via FedEx to whatever city she's visiting.)

Some bookstores have a full-time events staff. Others don't have a clue how to host an event. Don't take chances. Two weeks before your appearance, send fliers to the store advertising your appearance. After the event, autograph leftover stock. It doesn't do you any good to sign a book unless potential buyers know it's signed. Print your own "autographed by author" stickers for those stores which don't supply their own. If this sounds cheesy, consider that Lawrence Block, named a "Grand Master" by the Mystery Writers of America, takes a roll of autograph stickers on every tour.

More and more authors participate in what are called "drive-by signings." They stop to sign stock at stores without hosting a formal event. Take your "autographed by author" stickers along to such signings. It also wouldn't hurt to take a copy of a letter from your publicist assuring stores that unsold signed stock can be returned in the normal fashion (if, in fact, this is your publisher's policy). A myth has built up over the years that signed books can't be returned. Not only is that not true but its perpetuation discourages stores from letting authors sign. If your book has limited distribution, phone the store in advance to suggest a future date for a stock signing, thus allowing the store time to bring in more copies of your book. Don't assume the store knows anything about marketing. Remember this book is your baby. As such, encourage stores to sprinkle signed stock on a display table, end cap or the front window, in addition to being face-out on the shelf. The more places your book is displayed, the more likely it is to attract attention.

Handling the merchandise

Bear in mind Kremer's advice in *1001 Ways to Market Your Books*: "There are two fundamental activities in marketing any product or service: 1) promotion and 2) distribution. In other words, you must get the word out and you must make sure that your product is available."

If you speak before the Rotary, take along a carton of books to sell. Use those months before publication to arrange to accept Visa and Mastercard. Half of today's purchases are not paid for by cash or check.

Publicize yourself by offering a copy of your novel for the PTA raffle. Give 10 copies to the local PBS station as premiums for their fundraiser provided they repeatedly describe your book. "The next 10 people who pledge at the $100 level will also get a copy of the compelling new medical thriller, *Bloody Scalpel*, by Springfield's own Kathy Martin."

Ingratiate yourself with a local bookseller by contracting to buy your author copies through them at a deep discount rather than taking advantage of the 40 percent author's discount with the publisher. Sales records are based on books sold through stores. Promotional and give-away copies you buy directly from the publisher won't count toward building your sales numbers.

Whether your novel remains half-formed in your mind or has already been bought by a publisher, it's time to start shaping your promotion plans. In the words of Levinson, "If you start today, you're already a day late."

The Novel-in-stories

Break into Print with Fresh Form

© Steve DeJong

by Heather Sellers

When I began my novel-in-stories, I desperately wanted to write a novel but had failed at three attempts. Frustrated, I redesigned my project and honed my craft; I wrote 30 short stories and selected the best 10 to interweave into a novel-in-stories. The form—a collection of independent yet related stories that together tell a larger story—is less intimidating than a novel. Instead of one large arc and a perfectly counter-pointed subplot or B story line, short stories depend on swift, manageable, singly-focused arcs and call for skills I already had developed: crisp dialogue, efficient character development and figurative language. If the tension flagged in a particular story, I could shore it up without having to send destabilizing aftershocks through my entire book. Working on one self-contained unit at a time let me build momentum and confidence. As I finished each story, I sent it out for publication; I submitted the manuscript to novel and short story manuscript contests and publishers. After 13 rejections, it was snatched up and went on to win a major national prize.

Sarah Gorham, editor-in-chief of Sarabande Books, who published my book, says anything that keeps the short story alive is vital. Other publishers are happy to see novels-in-stories because they are complete, polished and high quality from opening to end—many novels have weak middles and/or strained endings. The novel-in-stories suffers from neither of these drawbacks. It's a fresh, lively form that's extremely popular at the moment. Much interest in the form was garnered by Melissa Bank's *Girls Guide to Hunting and Fishing* (Viking Books). In 2004, Kate Walbert was nominated for the National Book Award for her novel-in-stories, *Our Kind* (Scribner), as was Joan Silbur for *Ideas of Heaven: A Ring of Stories* (W.W. Norton & Company).

What is a novel-in-stories and why should I write one?

A novel-in-stories is a book-length collection (250-350 manuscript pages) of related and interconnected stories. The novel-in-stories isn't new—*Canterbury Tales* is a novel-in-stories, as is *The Decameron*—but the form is currently experiencing a surge in popularity; it offers a terrific way for the new writer to publish.

Annie Dillard instructs new writers to avoid writing "pieces." Write books, she says. New writers are well served by thinking of their work in terms of a series, in terms of book-length

---

HEATHER SELLERS teaches writing workshops around the country. Her most recent book, *Page After Page* (Writer's Digest Books), presents a year-long writing course for writers of all levels. *Georgia Under Water* (Sarabande Books), her novel-in-stories, won a Barnes & Noble Discover Great New Writers Award in 2001. She is from Florida and currently is associate professor of creative writing at Hope College. (www.heathersellers.com)

projects. Too often, new writers are encouraged to develop their craft by working on a number of one-off, stand-alone stories. To what end? Why not get more out of your writing time by committing to a larger project at the outset of your writing year.

When thinking in terms of a series of short stories that connect, you are:

- more likely to keep writing every day instead of waiting for inspiration.
- delving into your subject more deeply and, therefore, are more likely to come upon original, interesting situations.
- building confidence: You are going to complete a book-length manuscript.
- more likely to publish stories than you are novel chapters, thus gaining the attention of editors and agents.

As the author of a novel-in-stories, you get to write that dream query letter: "Four of the stories from this manuscript appear in national literary magazines: *SuperReview*, *Great Stories R Us*, and the inaugural issue of *Wonder Story*." Most magazines don't consider novel chapters or excerpts from longer works. Magazines, and readers, thrive on pieces that take a short amount of time to read, that stand on their own, and when they want to read more by you, you have 10 *more* stories on deck, ready to go.

New writers who work on a series conceive of the larger connections, themes, patterns and shapes of their work. When you work in a series, you're forced to develop your characters much more fully. There's going to be more subtext in your stories. Layers will appear automatically. The individual stories are going to be healthier and more vibrant; they'll extend off the page. Additionally, a central problem beginning writers have is trying to do too much in a single story. Beginners, unsure of their material and its strengths, tend to overstuff the story. A series forces you to divide and conquer. You savor and save up your story moments, and you are forced to develop microstories, to look more closely. That state of mind is at the heart of the art of story-writing.

Thus, far from being too much to handle for a new writer, the novel-in-stories may actually prevent beginning writers from committing a number of errors:

- writing stories which are too long, padded, multifocused or unfocused;
- collapsing events, asking the story to do too much;
- improperly developing the Big Picture, the backdrop and backstory upon which the individual story must be firmly tethered;
- not writing enough stories.

Study the form

When writing in any new form, it's a good idea to read at least 100 book-length examples of that form before you put pen to page.

You'll want to choose half a dozen of your favorites to study, reread and map. Make an index card for each book you read and love. As you read to learn, focus on structure. What period of time is covered? How would this novel-in-stories be different from a collection of stories featuring the same characters, the same themes? How do the stories relate to each other? What is gained by reading them in order, and what is lost? While you write your book, you'll return to your touchstone books again and again to uncover the solutions to problems.

At the end of the novel-in-stories, the reader feels she has been taken through a significant series of events. However, the reader doesn't have to read the stories in a straight line, from first to last, in order to have this larger, more satisfying experience. If the short story, on its own, is like a light but nourishing tiny meal, the novel is a seven-course dinner. The novel-in-stories is Saturday night in your pajamas, snuggled in for the duration: You can start with dessert, nibble on salad later and then heat up lasagna. The order doesn't matter, and it can be fun, instructive and energizing to change up your routine.

For your focused reading, start with Sherwood Anderson's *Winesburg, Ohio*, a classic of the form, first published in 1919. George Willard's point of view is the cohesive thread that ties the stories together; the reader isn't in his head on every page, in every story, but we see the "key" players in the small town of Winesburg through his empathic vision, whether he is present or not.

Amy Tan's *Joy Luck Club* (G.P. Putnam's Sons) put the novel-in-stories on the map for a new generation in bookstores worldwide. Sandra Cisneros and Julia Alvarez came next with *House on Mango Street* (Knopf) and *How the Garcia Girls Lost Their Accents* (Algonquin Books). You may also want to consider Abigail Thomas's *Safekeeping* (Anchor), a memoir made of tiny one-paragraph stories. Consider Jennifer Lauck's memoir-in-stories for an excellent lesson in structuring the form. Look at Mavis Gallant's *Paris Stories* (New York Review of Books) and Hemingway's *In Our Time*.

From the spate of novels-in-stories that have just appeared, analyze the nature of the trend with a look at *Stop That Girl* (Random House) by Elizabeth McKenzie or *Woman Made of Sand* (Delphinium Books) by JoAnn Kobin.

The structure of your novel-in-stories

Like a good cook, tailor or teacher, you gather more materials than you need. You leave yourself room to grow. You'll begin by making lists of situations that could grow into stories. Some of these will be easy to write. Some will get messy. Some will die on the vine. Some will be almost there. You'll want to have stories to choose from. At first, simply generate stories—practicing your craft. One salient feature of the story is it's short—many readers would prefer to have a collection of 10-page stories to read rather than fewer, longer (more than 20 pages a piece) stories.

Your manuscript will be about 200-300 pages long. Short is good—keep in mind the operative word in short story, is *short*. Choices are good. Worry less about the "plot" of the whole book, and concentrate on writing a series of interesting stories. Give yourself room to move around, to write new stories, to try different directions and different orders.

Your stories can be from different points of view. And, at the beginning, the first six months of your writing year, don't worry about how they're going to work together. After you have some excellent pieces to choose from, you can see what kind of a line they indicate and write to fill in the necessary pieces. It's essential your stories stand on their own—readers of story collections are used to skipping around. Your book is going to be like a reversible jacket—it's going to work both ways.

First, make a plan. I suggest a story a month, with the idea that at the end of a year, the nine or so strongest stories can be submitted as a book manuscript while the individual pieces are circulating. (As you finish it, you'll send each story on its own to literary magazines.) If you're a new writer, you may want to allow two years to generate stories, so you have 24 to choose from when constructing your book-length manuscript.

Before you begin writing, you should have a focus of time and space from which you do not waver. You must work within the area you've decided to conquer. Your book needs to have a single unified setting (Paris, summer camp, a Florida condo, battlefields), and it needs to have a unity of time (one summer, one war, the July vacations, coming of age). Once you have your territory laid out, generate stories. You will order them later, based on the needs of your arc.

Use a simple arc to shape your book, and resist the urge to write stories to order. Instead, focus on writing good standalone stories, limiting the characters to those from your cast. Most novels-in-stories use a simple arc, a narrative "pre-set," if you will. Coming-of-age, the form I used when I wrote my novel-in-stories, *Georgia Under Water*, has a natural story shape—all you do is simply put the stories in age order. My book follows the character of Georgia from age 11 to age 16.

Be attuned to the natural story shapes in life. You're looking for experiences that have built-in beginnings, middles and ends. One year in Africa. A midlife crisis. Your year of getting pregnant—or not. College. The novel is baggier, roomier—it can sustain side trips, vacations, changes in locale. It can survive several locales, even decades can pass, side trips and subplots abound. A novel-in-stories can be enhanced by more tightly circumscribing time and place. Think of it this way. There's already enough looseness in a novel-in-stories; readers aren't getting that super crisp narrative throughline. The throughline is a dotted line. Keep your stories neatly tethered to a natural, real-life arc, and worry about order after you have your stories written. Instead of a plot, think in terms of a place.

A novel-in-stories must have a beginning story, where we are introduced to the main character (the person to whom the most will happen) and his or her most essential, most integral conflict (how to develop a moral self, how to fall in love, immigrant parents versus new generation, the tension between justice and passion). Alternatively you may decide to have your stories told through the eyes of two alternating characters: husband and wife, mother and daughter, ancestor and great-grandchild, etc., in which case you'll have a double beginning.

Your first story simply has to make us want to stay in the world of these characters. Your insights, your eye for detail, the charm, action and verve of your characters is what will keep us reading. We're less concerned with *what* happens and more concerned with *to whom* it's happening. When we read a novel-in-stories, we're patient. We aren't reading to find out if the virus escaped the lab, if the cops will get to the scene with the right hazmat suits. We commit to the book one story at a time. We can skip a story, return later, or not. We are not at a formal dinner, where nothing can be skipped or shuffled. This is a gathering, it's relaxed, we dip in and out of conversations and rooms, we retain the pleasure of wandering, unsupervised.

Your motives for choosing to work seriously in this form may stem from a desire to build a writing career step-by-step, using the marketplace to help you evaluate your story-writing skill as you amass a book-length manuscript. Perhaps you are intimidated by the time commitment a novel requires. Maybe, at least at this point in your learning curve, you may think more in terms of *short stories*—micromoments that indelibly alter the trajectory of a life—as opposed to more complex, intricate plots. Regardless, the novel-in-stories is a form that is currently thriving, open to newcomers, and replete with possibility. I kept attempting to push my material into the shape of a novel, and I kept failing. When I realized a coming-of-age tale is more like a series of loosely related stories and less like something that makes the perfect sense a novel does, I had my breakthrough, and the book finally started to write itself. Consider your material, study the form and write generously; make more stories than you'll need.

The novel-in-stories is like the middle diving board—not the short story low dive and not the scary novel high dive. You practice some of the moves of the novelist, but you don't have to have the whole book in your head at once. You can work one story at a time, practicing fiction technique, preparing for the novel you'll write next—or your second story cycle.

The Business of Fiction Writing

I t's true there are no substitutes for talent and hard work. A writer's first concern must always be attention to craft. No matter how well presented, a poorly written story or novel has little chance of being published. On the other hand, a well-written piece may be equally hard to sell in today's competitive publishing market. Talent alone is just not enough.

To be successful, writers need to study the field and pay careful attention to finding the right market. While the hours spent perfecting your writing are usually hours spent alone, you're not alone when it comes to developing your marketing plan. *Novel & Short Story Writer's Market* provides you with detailed listings containing the essential information you'll need to locate and contact the markets most suitable for your work.

Once you've determined where to send your work, you must turn your attention to presentation. We can help here, too. We've included the basics of manuscript preparation, along with information on submission procedures and how to approach markets. In addition, we provide information on setting up and giving readings. We also include tips on promoting your work. No matter where you're from or what level of experience you have, you'll find useful information here on everything from presentation to mailing to selling rights to promoting your work—the "business" of fiction.

APPROACHING MAGAZINE MARKETS

While it is essential for nonfiction markets, a query letter by itself is usually not needed by most magazine fiction editors. If you are approaching a magazine to find out if fiction is accepted, a query is fine, but editors looking for short fiction want to see *how* you write. A cover letter can be useful as a letter of introduction, but it must be accompanied by the actual piece. Include basic information in your cover letter—name, address, a brief list of previous publications if you have any—and two or three sentences about the piece (why you are sending it to *this* magazine or how your experience influenced your story). Keep it to one page and remember to include a self-addressed, stamped envelope (SASE) for reply. See the Sample Short Story Cover Letter on page 67.

APPROACHING BOOK PUBLISHERS

Some book publishers do ask for queries first, but most want a query plus sample chapters or an outline or, occasionally, the complete manuscript. Again, make your letter brief. Include the essentials about yourself—name, address, phone number and publishing experience. Include only the personal information related to your story. Show that you have researched the market with a few sentences about why you chose this publisher. See the Sample Book Query Cover Letter on page 68.

Short Story Cover Letter

Addresses letter to a specific editor and dates it ⟶

Italicizes the publication's title ⟶

Good intro. It succinctly states the title, word count, central characters and sets the hook ("grabber")

Mentions pertinent personal information and publishing credits

Editor knows his magazine gets first dibs on publishing this story, and how long he'll wait for a response

Offers disposal of manuscript and offers to send electronic version of story

Details enclosures

Stephen Cox
123 Chesterfield Lane
St. Augustine, FL 32086
Phone (904) 555-4444
Fax (904) 555-5556
cox@email.com

December 29, 2004   1 line
                                                                    1 line
Thomas Heffron
Thrills & Chills Magazine
782 Bridge St.
New York, NY 11000
                                                                    1 line
Dear Mr. Heffron: 1 line

Enclosed is my short story, "Spitfire Sunday" (2,500 words). It's
about Pastor Donald White, who spends every Sunday preaching   Story
hell, fire and brimstone. But his routine changes when atheist   title &
Katherine Condon comes into town. She doesn't just preach about   word
perpetual suffering—she delivers it. The target of her latest sadistic   count
crusade is none other than the preacher himself, as she kidnaps him
just before the clock strikes midnight on Easter Sunday.
                                                                    1 line
I am a full-time pastor by day and a part-time writer by night. My between
published stories have appeared in these mystery magazines: para-
Murderously Yours 12/02, *Crime Pays* 1/03 and *Mystery Times* 7/03.   graphs
You are the first editor I'm soliciting with this story, and I will wait
six weeks for your response before I approach another magazine. If
you are not interested in the story, feel free to dispose of the manuscript, but please notify me with the enclosed SASE. If, however, you   Single-
do want to publish it, I can send you an electronic version of the spaced
manuscript on disk, CD or via e-mail. Just let me know how you   text
would like it formatted.

Thank you for considering "Spitfire Sunday." I look forward to hearing from you.

Sincerely,

                                                                    Signature

Stephen Cox

Encl.: Short story, "Spitfire Sunday"
         SASE

Getting Published

Query to Publisher: Novel

Teresa McClain
273 Chesterfield Lane
Sacramento, CA 99999
(714)555-6262
teresawriter@email.com

November 20, 1996 ──────────────── 1 line

Addressed to specific editor ──── Steven T. Murray, Editor-in-Chief
Fjord Press
P.O. Box 16349
Seattle, WA 98116 ──────────── 1 line

Dear Mr. Murray: ──────────── 1 line

Single-spaced text ──── Please consider reviewing a novel that I have completed concerning the emotional struggles a thirteen-year-old African-American boy endures when his mother declares that he must leave his native Harlem and move ──── **Sounds good** down south (Florida) to live with a father he has never known. Entitled *Plenty Good Room*, the manuscript is written entirely from the viewpoint ──── **She got me here!** of the thirteen-year-old (a la *Catcher in the Rye*) and is a first-person account replete with emotion and stingingly blunt dialogue. This book is **Now I'm hooked— got to read this** ──── not a children's book. The language is contemporary and often raw and ──── **Got me again!** unrelenting. The book is, however, a timely exposé on a young black male growing up in a single-parent home where the parent is too young, too inexperienced, and too poor to adequately parent and where the father is not at all involved. ──────────── 1 line

Good that she gives a clear idea of the overall structure of the novel ──── The manuscript is divided into three stages of the young man's life: His life in New York and the events that subsequently lead to his mother's insistence that his father shoulder the remaining responsibility of rearing him; the not so clear-cut path he takes to become a part of his father's life; and his life with his father and the ultimate unraveling of a dream he thought had come true.

Details enclosures in the body of the letter— perfectly fine ──── I have enclosed the first twenty pages of my thirteen-chapter manuscript. Please notify me if you are interested in reviewing my complete text for possible publishing considerations. I have also enclosed an SASE for your prompt response.

Sincerely,

Signature ────

Teresa McClain

Comments provided by Steven Murray of Fjord Press.

A FEW WORDS ABOUT AGENTS

Agents are not usually needed for short fiction and most do not handle it unless they already have a working relationship with you. For novels, you may want to consider working with an agent, especially if you intend to market your book to publishers who do not look at unsolicited submissions. For more on approaching agents and to read listings of agents willing to work with beginning and established writers, see our Literary Agents section beginning on page 102.

THE SAMPLE COVER LETTER

A successful cover letter is no more than one page (20 lb. bond paper). It should be single spaced with a double space between paragraphs, proofread carefully and neatly typed in a standard typeface (not script or italic). The writer's name, address and phone number appear at the top, and the letter is addressed, ideally, to a specific editor. (If the editor's name is unavailable, address to "Fiction Editor.")

The body of a successful cover letter contains the name and word count of the story, the reason you are submitting to this particular publication and some brief biographical information, especially when relevant to your story. Mention that you have enclosed a self-addressed, stamped envelope or postcard for reply. Also let the editor know if you are sending a disposable manuscript that doesn't need to be returned. (More and more editors prefer disposable manuscripts that save them time and save you postage.) When sending a computer disk, identify the program you are using. Remember, however, that even editors who appreciate receiving your story on a disk usually also want a printed copy. Finally, don't forget to thank the editor for considering your story.

BOOK PROPOSALS

A book proposal is a package sent to a publisher that includes a cover letter and one or more of the following: sample chapters, outline, synopsis, author bio, publications list. When asked to send sample chapters, send up to three *consecutive* chapters. **An outline** covers the highlights of your book chapter by chapter. Be sure to include details on main characters, the plot and subplots. Outlines can run up to 30 pages, depending on the length of your novel. The object is to tell what happens in a concise, but clear, manner. **A synopsis** is a shorter summary of your novel, written in a way that expresses the emotion of the story in addition to just explaining the essential points. Evan Marshall, author of *The Marshall Plan for Getting Your Novel Published* (Writer's Digest Books), suggests you aim for a page of synopsis for every 25 pages of manuscript. Marshall also advises you write the synopsis as one unified narrative, without sections, subheads or chapters to break up the text. The terms synopsis and outline are sometimes used interchangeably, so be sure to find out exactly what each publisher wants.

MANUSCRIPT MECHANICS

A professionally presented manuscript will not guarantee publication. But a sloppy, hard-to-read manuscript will not be read; publishers simply do not have the time. Here's a list of suggested submission techniques for polished manuscript presentation.

• **Use white, 8½×11 bond paper,** preferably 16 or 20 lb. weight. The paper should be heavy enough so it will not show pages underneath it and strong enough to take handling by several people.

• **Type your manuscript** on a computer and print it out using a laser or ink jet printer, or use a typewriter with a new ribbon.

• **Proofread carefully.** An occasional white-out is okay, but don't send a marked-up manuscript with many typos. Keep a dictionary, thesaurus and stylebook handy and use the spellcheck function on your computer.

- **Always double space and leave a 1¼ inch margin** on all sides of the page.
- **For a short story manuscript,** your first page should include your name, address and phone number (single spaced) in the upper left corner. In the upper right, indicate an approximate word count. Center the name of your story about one-third of the way down, skip two or three lines and center your byline (byline is optional). Skip three lines and begin your story. On subsequent pages, put last name and page number in the upper right hand corner.
- **For book manuscripts,** use a separate cover sheet. Put your name, address and phone number in the upper left corner and word count in the upper right. Some writers list their agent's name and address in the upper right. (Word count is then placed at the bottom of the page.) Center your title and byline about halfway down the page. Start your first chapter on the next page. Center the chapter number and title (if there is one) one-third of the way down the page. Include your last name and page number in the upper right of this page and each page to follow. Start each chapter with a new page.
- **Include a word count.** If you work on a computer, chances are your word processing program can give you a word count. If you are using a typewriter, there are a number of ways to count the number of words in your piece. One way is to count the words in five lines and divide that number by five to find an average. Then count the number of lines and multiply to find the total words. For long pieces, you may want to count the words in the first three pages, divide by three and multiply by the number of pages you have.
- **Always keep a copy.** Manuscripts do get lost. To avoid expensive mailing costs, send only what is required. If you are including artwork or photos but you are not positive they will be used, send photocopies. Artwork is hard to replace.
- **Suggest art where applicable.** Most publishers do not expect you to provide artwork and some insist on selecting their own illustrators, but if you have suggestions, please let them know. Magazine publishers work in a very visual field and are usually open to ideas.
- **Enclose a self-addressed, stamped envelope (SASE)** if you want a reply or if you want your manuscript returned. For most letters, a business-size (#10) envelope will do. Avoid using any envelope too small for an 8½ × 11 sheet of paper. For manuscripts, be sure to include enough postage and an envelope large enough to contain it. If you are requesting a sample copy of a magazine or a book publisher's catalog, send an envelope big enough to fit.
- **Consider sending a disposable manuscript** that saves editors time and saves you money.
- **When sending electronic (disk or modem) submissions,** contact the publisher first for specific information and follow the directions carefully. Always include a printed copy with any disk submission. Fax or e-mail your submissions only with prior approval of the publisher.
- **Keep accurate records.** This can be done in a number of ways, but be sure to keep track of where your stories are and how long they have been ''out.'' Write down submission dates. If you do not hear about your submission for a long time—about three weeks to one month longer than the reporting time stated in the listing—you may want to contact the publisher. When you do, you will need an accurate record for reference.

MAILING TIPS

When mailing short correspondence or short manuscripts:

- Fold manuscripts under five pages into thirds and send in a business-size (#10) envelope.
- Mail manuscripts five pages or more unfolded in a 9 × 12 or 10 × 13 envelope.
- Mark envelopes in all caps, FIRST CLASS MAIL or SPECIAL FOURTH CLASS MANUSCRIPT RATE.
- For return envelope, fold it in half, address it to yourself and add a stamp or, if going to a foreign country, International Reply Coupons (available at the main branch of your local post office).

Getting Published

• Don't send by certified mail. This is a sign of an amateur, and publishers do not appreciate receiving unsolicited manuscripts this way.

• For the most current postage rates, visit the United States Postal Service online at www.usps.com.

When mailing book-length manuscripts:

First Class Mail over 11 ounces (about 65 8½×11 20 lb.-weight pages) automatically becomes **PRIORITY MAIL.**

Metered Mail may be dropped in any post office box, but meter strips on SASEs should not be dated.

The Postal Service provides, free of charge, tape, boxes and envelopes to hold up to two pounds for those using PRIORITY and EXPRESS MAIL. Requirements for mailing FOURTH CLASS and PARCEL POST have not changed.

Main branches of local banks will cash foreign checks, but keep in mind payment quoted in our listings by publishers in other countries is usually payment in their currency. Also note reporting time is longer in most overseas markets. To save time and money, you may want to include a return postcard (and IRC) with your submission and forgo asking for a manuscript to be returned. If you live in Canada, see "Canadian Writers Take Note" on page 550.

Important note about IRCs: Foreign editors sometimes find IRCs have been stamped incorrectly by the U.S. post office when purchased. This voids the IRCs and makes it impossible for foreign editors to exchange the coupons for return postage for your manuscript. When buying IRCs, make sure yours have been stamped correctly before you leave the counter. (Each IRC should be stamped on the bottom *left* side of the coupon, not the right.) More information about International Reply Coupons, including an image of a correctly stamped IRC, is available on the USPS website (www.usps.com).

RIGHTS

Know what rights you are selling. The Copyright Law states that writers are selling one-time rights (in almost all cases) unless they and the publisher have agreed otherwise. A list of various rights follows. Be sure you know exactly what rights you are selling before you agree to the sale.

• **Copyright** is the legal right to exclusive publication, sale or distribution of a literary work. As the writer or creator of a written work, you need simply to include your name, date and the copyright symbol © on your piece in order to copyright it. Be aware, however, that most editors today consider placing the copyright symbol on your work the sign of an amateur and many are even offended by it.

To get specific answers to questions about copyright (but not legal advice), you can call the Copyright Public Information Office at (202)707-3000 weekdays between 8:30 a.m. and 5 p.m. EST. Publications listed in *Novel & Short Story Writer's Market* are copyrighted *unless* otherwise stated. In the case of magazines that are not copyrighted, be sure to keep a copy of your manuscript with your notice printed on it. For more information on copyrighting your work see *The Copyright Handbook: How to Protect & Use Written Works*, 7th edition, by Stephen Fishman (Nolo Press, 2003).

Some people are under the mistaken impression that copyright is something they have to send away for and that their writing is not properly protected until they have "received" their copyright from the government. The fact is, you don't have to register your work with the Copyright Office in order for your work to be copyrighted; any piece of writing is copyrighted the moment it is put to paper. Registration of your work does, however, offer some additional protection (specifically, the possibility of recovering punitive damages in an infringement suit) as well as legal proof of the date of copyright.

Registration is a matter of filling out an application form (for writers, that's generally

Form TX) and sending the completed form, a nonreturnable copy of the work in question and a check for $30 to the Library of Congress, Copyright Office, Register of Copyrights, 101 Independence Ave. SE, Washington DC 20559-6000. If the thought of paying $30 each to register every piece you write does not appeal to you, you can cut costs by registering a group of your works with one form, under one title for one $30 fee.

Most magazines are registered with the Copyright Office as single collective entities themselves; that is, the individual works that make up the magazine are *not* copyrighted individually in the names of the authors. You'll need to register your article yourself if you wish to have the additional protection of copyright registration.

For more information, visit the United States Copyright Office online at www.copyright.gov.

• **First Serial Rights**—This means the writer offers a newspaper or magazine the right to publish the article, story or poem for the first time in a particular periodical. All other rights to the material remain with the writer. The qualifier "North American" is often added to this phrase to specify a geographical limit to the license.

When material is excerpted from a book scheduled to be published and it appears in a magazine or newspaper prior to book publication, this is also called first serial rights.

• **One-time Rights**—A periodical that licenses one-time rights to a work (also known as simultaneous rights) buys the *nonexclusive* right to publish the work once. That is, there's nothing to stop the author from selling the work to other publications at the same time. Simultaneous sales would typically be to periodicals without overlapping audiences.

• **Second Serial (Reprint) Rights**—This gives a newspaper or magazine the opportunity to print an article, poem or story after it has already appeared in another newspaper or magazine. Second serial rights are nonexclusive; that is, they can be licensed to more than one market.

• **All Rights**—This is just what it sounds like. All rights means a publisher may use the manuscript anywhere and in any form, including movie and book club sales, without further payment to the writer (although such a transfer, or *assignment*, of rights will terminate after 35 years). If you think you'll want to use the material later, you must avoid submitting to such markets or refuse payment and withdraw your material. Ask the editor whether he is willing to buy first rights instead of all rights before you agree to an assignment or sale. Some editors will reassign rights to a writer after a given period, such as one year. It's worth an inquiry in writing.

• **Subsidiary Rights**—These are the rights, other than book publication rights, that should be covered in a book contract. These may include various serial rights; movie, television, audiotape and other electronic rights; translation rights, etc. The book contract should specify who controls these rights (author or publisher) and what percentage of sales from the licensing of these sub rights goes to the author.

• **Dramatic, Television and Motion Picture Rights**—This means the writer is selling his material for use on the stage, in television or in the movies. Often a one-year option to buy such rights is offered (generally for 10 percent of the total price). The interested party then tries to sell the idea to other people—actors, directors, studios or television networks, etc. Some properties are optioned over and over again, but most fail to become dramatic productions. In such cases, the writer can sell his rights again and again—as long as there is interest in the material. Though dramatic, television and motion picture rights are more important to the fiction writer than the nonfiction writer, producers today are increasingly interested in nonfiction material; many biographies, topical books and true stories are being dramatized.

• **Electronic Rights**—These rights cover usage in a broad range of electronic media, from online magazines and databases to CD-ROM magazine anthologies and interactive games.

The editor should specify in writing if—and which—electronic rights are being requested. The presumption is that unspecified rights are kept by the writer.

Compensation for electronic rights is a major source of conflict between writers and publishers, as many book publishers seek control of them and many magazines routinely include electronic rights in the purchase of print rights, often with no additional payment. Alternative ways of handling this issue include an additional 15 percent added to the amount to purchase first rights and a royalty system based on the number of times an article is accessed from an electronic database.

About Our Policies

Important

We occasionally receive letters asking why a certain magazine, publisher or contest is not in the book. Sometimes when we contact a listing, the editor does not want to be listed because they:

- do not use very much fiction.
- are overwhelmed with submissions.
- are having financial difficulty or have been recently sold.
- use only solicited material.
- accept work from a select group of writers only.
- do not have the staff or time for the many unsolicited submissions a listing may bring.

Some of the listings do not appear because we have chosen not to list them. We investigate complaints of unprofessional conduct in editors' dealings with writers and misrepresentation of information provided to us by editors and publishers. If we find these reports to be true, after a thorough investigation, we will delete the listing from future editions. See Important Listing Information on the copyright page for more about our listing policies.

There is no charge to the companies that list in this book. Listings appearing in *Novel & Short Story Writer's Market* are compiled from detailed questionnaires, phone interviews and information provided by editors, publishers, and awards and conference directors. The publishing industry is volatile and changes of address, editor, policies and needs happen frequently. To keep up with the changes between editions of the book, we suggest you check the monthly Markets columns in *Writer's Digest*. Also check the market information on the *Writer's Market* website at www.writersmarket.com or on the *Writer's Digest* website at www.writersdigest.com. Many magazine and book publishers offer updated information for writers on their websites. Check individual listings for those website addresses.

Club newsletters and small magazines devoted to helping writers also list market information. For those writers with access to online services, several offer writers' bulletin boards, message centers and chat lines with up-to-the-minute changes and happenings in the writing community.

We rely on our readers, as well, for new markets and information about market conditions. Write us if you have any new information or if you have suggestions on how to improve our listings to better suit your writing needs.

PROMOTION TIPS

Everyone agrees writing is hard work whether you are published or not. Yet once you arrive at the published side of the equation the work changes. Most published authors will tell you the work is still hard but it is different. Now, not only do you continue working on your next project, you must also concern yourself with getting your book into the hands of readers. It becomes time to switch hats from artist to salesperson.

While even best-selling authors whose publishers have committed big bucks to promotion are asked to help in promoting their books, new authors may have to take it upon themselves to plan and initiate some of their own promotion, sometimes dipping into their own pockets. While this does not mean that every author is expected to go on tour, sometimes at their own expense, it does mean authors should be prepared to offer suggestions for promoting their books.

Depending on the time, money and personal preferences of the author and publisher, a promotional campaign could mean anything from mailing out press releases to setting up book signings to hitting the talk-show circuit. Most writers can contribute to their own promotion by providing contact names—reviewers, hometown newspapers, civic groups, organizations—that might have a special interest in the book or the writer.

Above all, when it comes to promotion, be creative. What is your book about? Try to capitalize on it. For example, if you've written a mystery whose protagonist is a wine connoisseur, you might give a reading at a local wine-tasting or try to set something up at one of the national wine events. For more promotional tips, see the article titled "Writer, Promote Thyself" by W.E. Reinka on page 58.

Important Listing Information

- Listings are not advertisements. Although the information here is as accurate as possible, the listings are not endorsed or guaranteed by the editor of *Novel & Short Story Writer's Market*.

- *Novel & Short Story Writer's Market* reserves the right to exclude any listing that does not meet its requirements.

Getting Published

Anne Perry

*Research with Precision but Write
Like You're Riding a Tiger*

Photo courtesy of Random House

by W.E. Reinka

Anne Perry doesn't write hard-boiled mysteries but she does keep an egg timer on her desk. The egg timer helps her capture stolen moments most other writers blow off, such as those 20 minutes before the hairdresser's appointment. The egg timer lets her get absorbed in her work without fear she'll forget the time.

Time is precious to a writer under contract to produce two full-length mysteries a year for Ballantine Books. The last couple of years she's added a Christmas novella and sometimes edits anthologies. On top of that, she travels more months than not. From her remote home base in Scotland, lectures and book tours take Perry as far afield as Singapore, France and Chicago.

Not that she stops writing when she travels. "Paper is highly portable," she says with a laugh. "One of my pages of tiny scrawl can produce two and a half pages of typewritten copy."

With 40-some books to her credit, all of them still in print so far as she knows, some readers might expect the 60-something author to rest on her oars. Quite the opposite—she keeps setting new challenges for herself.

After decades of alternating between two mystery series set in different periods of the Victorian era, Perry embarked on a five-book series set in World War I. Each of the World War I novels is an individual mystery, while an overall mystery spans the five books and will be resolved in the final installment.

Her first Victorian series features Thomas Pitt, a London police inspector, and his wife Charlotte. The other, set earlier in the era, focuses on William Monk, a policeman whose memory of his past is wiped out in a carriage accident. In order to keep the two series from getting stale, Perry reassigned her protagonists in recent years, moving Pitt to Special Branch and Monk over to the River Police. "Otherwise, you're just doing more of the same. I think the readers would get bored and I know would. If it isn't stretching you, it isn't worth doing."

She plans to stretch herself with new projects once the World War I series is complete but remains tight-lipped about her plans. Meantime, Perry has always stretched herself in painstaking historical research. Every time one of her characters stops for a bite or buys a necktie, Perry pores over sources to make certain her descriptions and costs are accurate and time appropriate. No wonder she relies on her egg timer to milk every minute despite a working schedule that stretches to six days a week, 12 hours per day.

"Say I need to take a train journey. The year is 1892 and I'm going from London to Dover. Which of the main line stations will I depart from? How much will it cost? How long will it

W.E. REINKA, who writes frequently about books and authors, contributes to newspapers and magazines nationwide.

take? Do I have to change trains? Because if something happens on the train journey that's important, I'm going to look stupid if I send them from the wrong railway station or it would cost more than they'd be likely to have in their pockets or if I made them change when they wouldn't or not when they would.''

Researching World War I not only brought her to an entirely new era but also into the realm of existing memories. "I was very very afraid of tackling something as recent as World War I because there are people still alive who remember and certainly children of people who remember. Not only was I concerned about tiny inaccuracies—giving someone a hard helmet when they still had soft hats or making the weather wrong on a very important day—but as a woman who has never actually been to war trying to say what it was like for men in the trenches, there were times I asked myself, 'Who do you think you are?'"

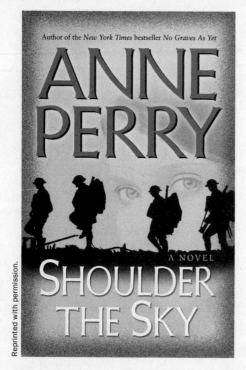

Reprinted with permission.

Typical of Perry, she actually walked the remaining trenches in Ypres, Belgium, where two massive armies faced off in miserable stalemate. It shows. The most gripping parts of *Shoulder the Sky* (Ballantine Books), the second in the World War I series, come as the men in the trenches fight off lice, rats and mud as well as the enemy that is dug in just hundreds of yards away across "no man's land."

"Shoulder the sky" is a phrase from a poem by A.E. Housman. Just out is *Angels in the Gloom* (Ballantine Books), which gets its title from a phrase in the war poetry of Siegfried Sassoon. All five of the World War I titles are poetic phrases. Although she is not a poet herself, Perry can't remember a time when she didn't love poetry. She can quote memorized stanzas at length. "Poetry is part of who I am. It roots me back in what matters. In the perfection of form, it's like a perfect gem." She is especially fond of the poems of G.K. Chesterton. "He's the one I don't memorize because I carry his poetry around with me."

Though Perry seems now to be the epitome of a successful mystery writer, hers wasn't an overnight success. In her 20s, she wrote in anonymity while she toiled at day jobs that ranged from household domestic to limousine dispatcher. She can't remember exactly how many never-published novels she wrote but knows that it was "several." Finally in her 30s, she published *The Cater Street Hangman* (St. Martin's), the first Pitt mystery.

Why didn't she just give up?

She laughs at such a silly question. Because she is a writer, that's why. "When people say to me, 'Should I be a writer?' I ask if there's anything I can say that will make a difference. Because if there is, then no, they shouldn't. If you're going to be a writer, nothing anybody says is going to make any difference. You're going to do it because that's who you are."

She once joked she writes mysteries because "that's what they published first." Now that she is able to look back from the vantage point of success, she understands why her early novels were not published.

"It tended to be historical stuff because I love history. I would get my heroes into various events I thought were marvelous. I wrote one that wound up with the signing of the Magna

Carta. But it was 'this happened and then this happened and then that happened.' It's got to be 'this happened so that had to happen so that, of course, that had to happen.' Plotting is the most difficult thing. It must be tight and compulsive. Everybody does something for a reason and, given their character and circumstances, there's nothing else they really could have done."

She thinks a lot about characters and character motivations. "The choices have to be between good and better or bad and worse, not between good and bad. The choice between good and bad is not interesting—take the good and that's the end of it. Nobody deliberately does what they know to be bad. Back when I started writing, I didn't know the interesting choices are where everything is bad and doing nothing is even worse."

In *Shoulder the Sky*, she intentionally backs Army chaplain Joseph Reavley into a tough fix where he must decide whether to keep a dangerous man alive and risk the danger the man's continued life poses to humankind or stand by and let him die.

Likewise, human motivation is at the heart of her advice to writers just starting out. "Remember your protagonists have to care about whatever it is because your readers won't care if the protagonist doesn't care. Be prepared to write it several times. And try to write honestly. By that, I don't mean anybody writes dishonestly, but try to explore your own heart and your own reason for doing things. There's a tremendous difference between writing what you think people want to hear and writing what you really feel. It's like the difference between a musical instrument that's in tune and one that's out of tune. You can feel it when a person is exploring their own heart."

Perry keeps things tight by outlining every book in advance. "Not everybody plots before they start writing. It can be a very useful exercise," she says with wry understatement. She finds outlines "much tougher" to write than the novels themselves. "If you have the outline, you've done most of the difficult stuff. After that, it's a matter of applying yourself and getting on with it. Twenty pages or thirty pages of outline. For every chapter your outline must show where you are, when you are, who's present and why, along with a thumbnail sketch of your main characters—half a page maybe for each. If nothing can be tweaked and pulled and poked out of that, it's pretty tight."

While in the thick of invention, Perry shoots for "the feeling I'm on a tiger and I can't get off. If you're on a horse, you can get off anytime you want."

Ace Atkins

Music and Mystery in the Dirty South

Photo courtesy of Harper Collins

by Brad Vice

The hardest thing about reading an Ace Atkins novel is suspending your disbelief concerning his Southern sleuth Nicks Travers who, on the surface, appears a little too good to be true. Travers is an ex-pro football player for the New Orleans Saints turned Tulane professor and an Alan Lomax-style musicologist with a special talent for hunting down old Bluesmen. But one can only shrug with admiration when you flip over the book jacket and learn that Atkins himself played college ball for Auburn University and was a Pulitzer Prize-nominated crime reporter in Tampa, Florida, before he settled in Oxford, Mississippi, to teach journalism at the University of Mississippi and write novels. Now in his early 30s—an age when most writers are just getting started—Atkins has published four novels and was recently awarded his alma mater's first Arts Advancement Award.

In Atkins' previous novels *Crossroad Blues* (St. Martin's), *Leavin' Trunk Blues* (St. Martin's/Minotaur) and *Dark End of the Street* (William Morrow), Travers used his detective skills to unearth mysteries long-swallowed by the past. With Atkins' latest novel, *Dirty South* (William Morrow), both Travers and crime are dragged kicking and screaming into the 21st century. Though his love for the Blues is still intact, Atkins' multitalented detective submerges himself in the syncopated beats of the New Orleans' projects when one of his old teammates asks him to protect a teenage Hip Hop star from the glitter of Big Easy thug life.

The plot of *Dirty South* is an evolution of Atkins' own growing interest in popular music, which he sees as an extension of the music Delta Bluesmen used to sing in juke joints in the '20s and '30s. The gritty realism of Atkins' street-tough prose matches the simple but drumming rhythms of his subject matter. Despite the fact Travers seems to be a little larger than life, Atkins' readers won't doubt this athlete-turned-academic-turned-gumshoe has his feet planted firmly in the dirt of the Delta or on the mean streets of New Orleans. Oh, and if you're wondering if the description of *Dirty South*'s author is a little too good to be true, the book jacket testifies: "And yes, Ace is his real name."

BRAD VICE was born and raised in Tuscaloosa, Alabama. His first collection of short stories, *The Bear Bryant Funeral Train*, won the Flannery O'Connor Award for Short Fiction and was published by the University of Georgia Press. His stories have appeared in many publications, including *The Georgia Review*, *The Southern Review*, *The Atlantic Monthly*, *New Stories from the South* (1997 and 2003), *Best New America Voices 2003*, and *Stories from the Blue Moon Café Vol III*. He teaches creative writing at Mississippi State University.

Your protagonist Nick Travers is a former pro football player for the New Orleans Saints. You played college ball for Auburn. What did athletics teach you about writing?

I don't think athletics taught me much about writing. Maybe discipline, if, on some days, I actually have it.

But the overall experience of being in the dorm with a diverse bunch of kids taught me a lot about people. You had rich kids and poor kids. Black and white. From the country and from the city. I find myself mining character traits all the time from people I knew back then. It was much better than just knowing the standard folks in a fraternity or club from college. I did get a lot of crap from my position coach. He just couldn't understand anyone wanting to be a writer and a serious football player. I earned the nickname, "The Poet." Of course, I never tried to explain to him that I wrote prose.

But even in college I wanted to be a writer. I had a recent experience of being in a restaurant with both Elmore Leonard and Archie Manning. I thought, "In 40 years would I rather be an ex-jock or a writer at the top of his game?" I knew I'd rather be Leonard. I'd hate to think my best work was behind me.

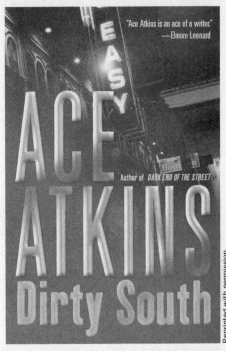

"Ace Atkins is an ace of a writer."
—Elmore Leonard

Author of *DARK END OF THE STREET*

Reprinted with permission.

You're now a professor of journalism at the University of Mississippi, but once you were a crime reporter. How has that influenced your writing? Did you always want to write mystery novels even when you were training to be a journalist?

I've always loved crime novels. [Raymond] Chandler and [Dashiell] Hammett were my entry into books and writing. I'm a strong believer in the crime novel as absolute serious fiction. And the real critics—the good ones—know a book is about the way it's executed, not its subject matter. I'm not standing up for my books when I say this. I just find it pretty ridiculous when someone says, "I won't read a crime novel or a mystery. I only read literary books." What is literary? Is that a genre? To discount writers like Elmore Leonard, Dennis Lehane, George Pelecanos or James Lee Burke doesn't make a lot of sense. Those guys are the bar any serious crime novelist wants to reach. And to do that, you have to know what the hell you're talking about. Those guys make a serious effort to get it right; those little-old-lady mysteries or that light-weight kind of stuff doesn't make the cut. Crime is not pretty or fun or neat; it's messy and violent and mean. Many of the writers I admired had worked as reporters—from Hemingway to Julie Smith in New Orleans. I figured that's where I needed to start.

Nick Travers is a musicologist who is obsessed with the Blues and has a special talent for hunting down old Bluesmen. How did you become interested in the Blues? Why do you feel compelled to write about music?

I got into Blues when I was about 14 after buying Muddy Waters' *Hard Again* album. It was unlike anything I'd ever heard. Raw and full of emotion, certainly more than the electronic pop that was popular in the early '80s. From Muddy, I learned about Son House and from Son House to Robert Johnson, and from there it just kind of spread out. I'm into all kinds of music from Punk Rock to Old Country to Soul. But Blues has such a fantastic backstory that makes it an excellent path for fiction, crime novels to be specific.

For me, the Blues and the Bluesmen and women's stories were always peppered with violence and self-destruction. There was murder and double crosses and wonderful gritty tales. So, for four novels—the Nick Travers' stories—I got to explore early Blues in the '30s to modern-day Rap in New Orleans, but my new novel is completely separate from the music. I think I'm done with those stories for now.

Your latest novel *Dirty South* isn't about the Blues but Hip Hop. Is Dirty South music a break with the Blues or is there a natural confluence?

Dirty South is *the* style of Rap in the South. It basically started in New Orleans and has become the dominant style of Rap throughout the country. Once again, the South has lead the way in music as it did with Blues, Jazz and Rock 'n' Roll. But Dirty South Rap is just today's Blues. In the same way that Muddy Waters sang lyrics his audience would understand and appreciate, today's rappers make a connection with their world.

The reason I wanted to write about the Dirty South came from the basic premise of writing a book taking place in today's world. All my other novels centered on past sins playing out generations later—from the murder of Robert Johnson to the disappearance of Soul music. This was also the last novel in the Nick Travers stories, with a backstory running from early Delta Blues to Rap and from New Orleans up to Chicago. The Dirty South world was just too great to pass up, too. Incredible wealth coming from great poverty. Guys from the projects now riding in Bentleys with women and champagne. This is just the great American story playing out over and over. It's just Elvis.

So you're not only done writing about music, you're also retiring Nick Travers? What are you working on next?

I think I've done about all I can working within the Chandler model of crime novels. Anyone who writes detective fiction is under that huge shadow of style, and I wanted to do something on my own. Even though I write about the South and music, I was still putting a hell of a lot of Chandler into my work. My new work is a true story and has more in common with Truman Capote than Chandler.

In a crime novel, plot is as important as style. Chandler and Hammet have lasted because of their breakthrough hard-boiled style. It's easy to see how you're influenced by them, but how do you piece together a plot? What rules of thumb do you use to help you navigate your way through a book?

Plotting is very important in a crime novel, but I would argue it's just as important in any novel. I see a lot of young writers pushing their plotless works and bragging on its lack of story arc. It's really a pretty ridiculous thing and an excuse for not knowing a damned thing about construction. The finest writers know how to construct a work in great detail without you seeing that construction. Hemingway, Steinbeck, Faulkner—I don't think we have that class of writer anymore. And here in Oxford, with the passing of Larry Brown, that writer-craftsman is becoming extinct. I believe writing is a trade just like being a plumber or a carpenter, and honing a strong story is your skill. A plotless novel is a waste of time. But to clarify, it takes a great writer to make [a great book] seem so random and plotless. Not a lot of people can do that. Only the greats. The rest of us just pretend we can.

Resources

Where to Look for More Information

Below is a list of invaluable resources specifically for mystery writers. To order any of the Writer's Digest Books titles or to get a consumer book catalog, call (800)448-0915. You may also order Writer's Digest Books selections through www.writersdiges t.com, Amazon.com or www.barnesandnoble.com.

MAGAZINES

- *Mystery Readers Journal*, Mystery Readers International, P.O. Box 8116, Berkeley CA 94707. Website: www.mysteryreaders.org.
- *Mystery News*, Black Raven Press, PMB 152, 105 E. Townline Rd., Vernon Hills IL 60061-1424. Website: www.blackravenpress.com.
- *Mystery Scene*, 331 W. 57th St., Suite 148, New York NY 10019. Website: www.mysterys cenemag.com.

BOOKS

Howdunit series (Writer's Digest Books)

- *Private Eyes: A Writer's Guide to Private Investigators*, by Hal Blythe, Charlie Sweet and John Landreth
- *Missing Persons: A Writer's Guide to Finding the Lost, the Abducted and the Escaped*, by Fay Faron
- *Deadly Doses: A Writer's Guide to Poisons*, by Serita Deborah Stevens and Anne Klarner
- *Cause of Death: A Writer's Guide to Death, Murder & Forensic Medicine*, by Keith D. Wilson, M.D.
- *Scene of the Crime: A Writer's Guide to Crime Scene Investigation*, by Anne Wingate, Ph.D.
- *Just the Facts, Ma'am: A Writer's Guide to Investigators and Investigation Techniques*, by Greg Fallis
- *Rip-off: A Writer's Guide to Crimes of Deception*, by Fay Faron

Other Writer's Digest Books for mystery writers

- *The Criminal Mind, A Writer's Guide to Forensic Psychology*, by Katherine Ramsland
- *Howdunit: How Crimes are Committed and Solved*, by John Boertlein
- *Urge to Kill: How Police Take Homicide from Case to Court*, by Martin Edwards
- *Writing Mysteries: A Handbook by the Mystery Writers of America*, edited by Sue Grafton
- *Writing and Selling Your Mystery Novel: How to Knock 'em Dead With Style*, by Hallie Ephron
- *You Can Write a Mystery*, by Gillian Roberts

ORGANIZATIONS & ONLINE

- Crime Writers of Canada. Website: www.crimewriterscanada.com.
- Crime Writers' Association. Website: www.thecwa.co.uk.
- Mystery Writers of America, 17 E. 47th St., 6th Floor, New York NY 10017. Website: www.mysterywriters.org.
- The Private Eye Writers of America, 4342 Forest DeVille Dr., Apt. H, St. Louis MO 63129. Website: http://hometown.aol.com/rrandisi/myhomepage/writing.html.
- Sisters in Crime, P.O. Box 442124, Lawrence KS 66044-8933. Website: www.sistersincrime.org.
- Writer's Market Online. Website: www.writersmarket.com.
- Writer's Digest Online. Website: www.writersdigest.com.

© Stanley Studios, Melbourne, FL

FOR ROMANCE WRITERS

Writing Erotic Scenes

Finding Your Comfort Level

by Leslie Kelly

Picture this: You're at your spouse's holiday cocktail party, surrounded by semi-strangers talking budgets and forecasts. You're nursing a white wine spritzer when you'd rather be sucking down a dirty martini, but the job is too important to risk any lampshade-on-the-head incidents. You mingle, you pick at the cold hors d'oeuvres that should be hot (or the warm ones that should be cold). You keep a fake smile on your lips while shooting your hubby looks that say, "I'd better get jewelry in exchange for this."

And then it happens. From several feet away, in a voice loud enough to warn of an impending iceberg, someone says, "Hey, aren't you the one who writes those *sex* books?"

You instinctively look around the room, wondering if Larry Flynt has crashed the party. Then the truth dawns. The half-tanked loser from accounting was talking to you, the smut queen of the group. You know, the one who writes romance novels.

Sound familiar? If you're a romance writer, I'm sure it does. If you want to be a romance writer, prepare yourself . . . it *will* happen. While no one at an office cocktail party would dare ask a surgeon if he's amputated the wrong limb lately or an attorney if he's gotten a murderer off the hook this week, for some reason people have no problem asking obnoxious questions about one aspect of the romance writing profession: the sex.

Sex sells, of course. We all know that. Unfortunately, however, some people think sex is the only thing romance novels contain—and that we live what we write. While at first your husband might not mind everyone believing your sex scenes are based on your own life, you will both, eventually, get tired of the lewd comments and the lascivious looks. So before you find yourself in this situation—where you can respond by asking the obnoxious guy if he's the one who has half a brain and one-third an ounce of common courtesy—you need to think about and define your own comfort level when it comes to writing romance.

SEX! SEX! SEX!

First things first: Not all romance novels contain sex. There are subgenres beneath the romance umbrella where there is either no sex or it takes place behind closed doors. An immediate example is the inspirational romance. These faith-based novels have experienced a huge

---

LESLIE KELLY, since selling her first book to Harlequin in 1999, has become known for writing sassy, sexy and sometimes irreverent stories filled with strong heroines and playful heroes. A National Reader's Choice Award winning author, Kelly has twice been nominated for the highest award in romance, the RWA Rita Award, and is a four-time nominee for the Romantic Times (RT) Bookclub Award. Kelly resides in Florida with her husband, three daughters, and a fuzzy little dog who hasn't yet been informed she's not a human.

For Romance Writers

surge in popularity and the subgenre has exploded into new areas like chick lit, historical sagas and sassy contemporaries. Powerhouse publisher Harlequin has achieved such success with their Steeple Hill line that they've recently expanded it.

For those unfamiliar with them, inspirational romances have all the drama and emotion of any other romance novel, but they also incorporate the characters' religious beliefs into their romantic journey. While not preachy, the message of faith is an integral part of the story. And because of the inherent promise to the inspirational reader, there usually won't be graphic sex in the pages of those books.

Among traditional romance novels, there are plenty of books where the sex is a minor part of the story, or is nonexistent. Physical attraction is there, but the big payoff may take place after the book ends, or at least off the page. Think of *Star Trek*'s Captain Kirk kissing some green alien chick in his cabin. After fading to commercial, we return to see him sitting on his bunk pulling his boots on. We know what happened . . . but it's behind closed doors.

Reprinted with permission.

You might see this kind of sex in some of the "sweet" romance novels, though it's usually only between couples who are already committed to one another. As an aside, the term "sweet" seems a misnomer, since it implies "insipid." In actuality, the sweeter romance novels have all the emotional depth, drama and angst of any other romance, they simply keep the action above the belt.

If you've examined these options and have decided you're comfortable writing a sexy romance, you still have a wide variety of opportunities. Whether you're writing light contemporary novels or long historicals, there is a broad range in which to work. Some authors have become known for their hot, intense love scenes, and their readers fully expect them. Others who may write the same length book for the same publisher prefer to keep the sex shorter and less erotic. The audience will expect that, too. Be warned, however. You may get the occasional hate letter from a reader who picks up your steamy novel by mistake, when she was looking for a kisses-only story. Being consigned to the fiery pit by a little old lady from the Midwest won't be the highlight of your career.

Leslie Kelly loves adding extra spice to her novels, as evidenced by her Harlequin Temptation title *Wickedly Hot: Heat*, a story of revenge, desire and a little voodoo magic, set in Savannah, Georgia.

Still, it's safe to say readers will seek out authors whose books continue to satisfy their own demands in terms of sexual content. So while your own comfort level dictates the original level of sensuality in your books, quite often your readership will be the ones reinforcing that decision as your career progresses.

Hot or not?

Some publishers or category "lines" are, by definition, hotter than others. Harlequin Blaze novels, as well as Kensington Brava, Red Sage and Ellora's Cave, all promise a sexy reading experience. Choosing to write in one of these more erotic venues comes back to that comfort level question: How will you respond to the jerk at the cocktail party? Is the letter from the little old lady going to haunt you? Does the thought of your child's kindergarten teacher reading your book make your heart stop?

Essentially, what's the line you will not cross and how, exactly, do you figure out where that line is?

You *could* start with trial and error. If you find yourself blushing as you try to come up with another word for a certain part of the male anatomy, you're probably not an erotica writer. Conversely, if you love cranking-up the volume of a hot rock 'n' roll song that sets a pulsing rhythm for your characters to rip each other's clothes off, you'd likely be okay aiming for Blaze or Brava.

There is, of course, one obvious problem with trying to write books with completely different levels of sensuality. Remember those readers who buy your books based on how sexy—or nonsexy—your last one was? Unless you want to publish under a pseudonym, you're really going to tick them off if they expect a few kisses but get a three-alarm fire.

In considering this topic, I solicited the opinions of other authors of romance. They all, it seemed, had their own ways of finding—and maintaining—their comfort level.

New York Times best-selling author Vicki Lewis Thompson, who was the launch author for the hot and sexy Harlequin Blaze line, finds herself able to write sexy stories by making them funny. She also, however, has one more litmus test, saying, "My comfort level is also controlled by the commitment of the two characters. If they're emotionally attached and the encounter feels safe for both of them, I can pull out all the stops."

Others had varied perspectives on how much, how far and how detailed to make their love scenes. Authors Katherine Garbera and Toni Blake believe sex to be another human attribute, and an important part of any realistic relationship. They'd feel guilty leaving it out. Amusingly, successful authors Jill Shalvis and Heidi Betts both said they base sexual content on their own personal "ick factor," while *New York Times* best-selling author Patricia Rice seeks to avoid boredom. Rice says, "These days, I can conjure up no new ways of creating an exciting sexual experience for me or my reader, so I've been gradually reducing sex scenes to the romantic and emotional tension between the couple."

Some authors who write very hot romance simply enjoy the challenge and the excitement of their craft. Erotica author Vella Munn has found writing her Ellora's Cave novels under a pseudonym to be freeing and she likes that "fantasy is given free rein." Downtown Press author Julie Elizabeth Leto constantly pushes herself, saying, "To stir things up, I like to write outside my comfort zone, so with each book I try to pick at least one thing that pushes me farther than I've ever gone before."

Leslie Kelly is perfectly comfortable trading steamy scenes for "sass and class," as she does in *She's Got the Look* (HQN).

Reprinted with permission.

From all the authors who spoke about this topic, there seemed to be one common theme. Whether spicy or sweet, erotic or innocent, fleshed-out or quietly implied, sex is an important part of the romance novel, but it's not *the* most important part. The relationship between the hero and heroine is the most important part. Author Julia Ross puts it best: "The sex must serve the novel, not the other way around."

With that in mind, take some time to explore the different subgenres and think long and hard about how you'll face those rude party guests or shocked kindergarten teachers. Finding your own level of comfort is the first—and often most important—step on the road to becoming a published romance writer.

By the way . . . what's my comfort level? Well, I'm the one who likes to crank up the rock 'n' roll song and let the driving beat carry me—and my characters—away. And if I can throw in a few laughs while I'm at it, I have a simply marvelous time doing my job. How do I answer the party jerk? Originally when someone would hit me with one of those obnoxious questions, I'd get all indignant and snap back about how there's absolutely nothing wrong with sex between two committed, monogomous adults and they needed to get their facts straight about what romance was really all about. Now I say, "Sure. Don't you like sex?" That usually hushes people right up.

Spice Up Your Research

To help you find your own comfort level, check out these romance novels written by authors mentioned in this article.

- *Naturally Naughty* (Blaze), by Leslie Kelly
- *She Drives Me Crazy* (HQN), by Leslie Kelly
- *She's Got the Look* (HQN), by Leslie Kelly
- *Make Me Over* (Temptation), by Leslie Kelly
- *Wickedly Hot: Heat* (Temptation), by Leslie Kelly
- *Killing Time* (Harlequin), by Leslie Kelly
- *Every Woman's Fantasy* (Harlequin), by Vicki Lewis Thompson
- *Night Life* (Silhouette), by Katherine Garbera
- *The Red Diary* (Warner Forever), by Toni Blake
- *Much Ado About Magic* (Signet Eclipse), by Patricia Rice
- *Free Fall* (Temptation), by Jill Shalvis
- *Blame It On the Blackout* (Desire), by Heidi Betts
- *Cheyenne Summer* (Forge), by Vella Munn
- *Line of Fire* (Harlequin Code Red), by Julie Elizabeth Leto
- *The Seduction* (Berkley Sensation), by Julia Ross

Jennifer Blake

Living Legend of Romance Reflects on Her Career and Offers Insight into Craft

© Bryan Rockett

by Deborah Bouziden

I n 1977, Jennifer Blake reached *The New York Times* best-seller list for the first time with her book, *Love's Wild Desire* (U.S.A. Popular Library). In her 35-year career, she's been called "a legend in romance," and fans of the genre today hail her as "the best writer of all time."

"The reactions of fans have been one of the most unexpected things I've found about being a writer," Blake says. "The closeness readers can feel based on your work—they think they know you personally, and maybe they do since it's impossible to hide your true nature over the course of many books."

With more than 50 books published, titles released in 19 languages, and an estimated 30 million copies in print worldwide, Blake continues to pen stories about dashing rogues and daring ladies. Writing from the second-floor office of her Key West-style home in Louisiana, she holds regular office hours. Inspired by the view of weeping willows and maple trees and the aroma of roses from her garden, she creates worlds to which her readers can escape.

Blake has won numerous awards over the years including the Holt Medallion for Outstanding Literary Talent, the Frank Waters Award for Excellence in Fiction, and the Golden Treasure RITA for Lifetime Achievement from Romance Writers of America.

"I'm extremely grateful for all the recognition I've received, but the award I value most is the Lifetime Achievement," she says. "Nothing is quite as meaningful as the accolades of one's peers, the people who know exactly what it takes to do the job."

Her current project, the Master At Arms series, promises to be another award-winning and timeless adventure.

"The idea for the Master At Arms series came to me over a decade ago, when I first ran across mention of the *maitres d'armes*, sword masters of old New Orleans in Herbert Asbury's *French Quarter*. They were such a fascinating group, men of fearsome athletic power and dangerous reputation who were idolized by society in much the same way as sports heroes are today.

"I began to gather research until I had reams of detail on everyday life. My ambition then became to re-create this society for readers much as Georgette Heyer had done for Regency England."

Blake's first book of the series, *Challenge to Honor* (MIRA), hit the stands in January 2005,

DEBORAH BOUZIDEN, since 1985, has had hundreds of articles published and has authored or co-authored seven books, including *In Their Name*, *The Journal Wheel and Guidebook*, and *Oklahoma: Off The Beaten Path*, her latest project. To learn more about Bouziden, visit her website at www.deborahbouziden.com.

and she will have fulfilled her contract for book No. 6 of the series by 2008. This venture ensures that fans will be able to enjoy Blake's new work for years and her legendary status will continue.

Did you have any goals when you started writing?

My first writing goal was to make enough money to be able to travel. Later, I wrote $1,000,000 in huge print on a sheet of paper and tacked it on the bulletin board above my desk. If you're going to have a goal, it might as well be a big one! As important as these goals were, they came about some three or four years after I started. I decided to be an author because it was something I could do while being a stay-at-home mom and for the pleasure of seeing my words and thoughts on paper.

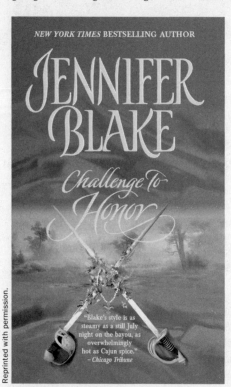

NEW YORK TIMES BESTSELLING AUTHOR

JENNIFER BLAKE

Challenge To Honor

"Blake's style is as steamy as a still July night on the bayou, as overwhelmingly hot as Cajun spice."
– Chicago Tribune

Reprinted with permission.

Do you think goal setting is important for writers?

During my early 20s, I picked up from my husband's nightstand a book called *Think and Grow Rich* (High Roads Media) by Napoleon Hill, now the standard for goal setting and how the process works to help achieve success. My first goal was formed after reading it. I believe every writer should have her heart's desire pinned in plain sight.

How do you plot your books and keep track of the plot? Do you make outlines before you begin working or keep notes as you go?

My first act in plotting is to sit down with a legal pad and pen and brainstorm every dramatic crisis that can be derived using the situation and characters I've constructed. From this list, I choose the best seven or eight crises and place them in order of occurrence, spacing them fairly evenly over the 20 or so chapters in the story. These basic plot points are then transferred to a computer file, labeled "Chapter Chart," which is saved within the book's story folder. I then play with the crises I've placed there, adding ideas and possibilities until I have the basis for two or three scenes per chapter. Additional ideas that occur during the actual writing of the story are noted in this chapter file as well. When I begin the text for each chapter, the lists of events and notes for it are copied and pasted into the master book file and carried along below the text as handy working references. As I put the events down in text form, I delete the ideas I've used, and those leftover are carried forward to the next chapter.

How do you know when your manuscripts are ready? Do you review your work after it's published and wish you could change things?

I don't think I've ever read one of my books from cover to cover after it was published—except *Royal Seduction* (Fawcett Books) that I revised for electronic format. Too, too traumatic!

Regardless of all the polishing I do, the rule of thumb I go by is simple: When I start changing the revised version back to the way I had it in the beginning, then it's time to leave it alone.

What books on writing would you recommend to writers? Why?

Dwight Swain's *Techniques of the Selling Writer* (University of Oklahoma Press) is a classic for craft; *The Artist's Way* (Jeremy P. Tarcher) by Julia Cameron is a great source for inspiration; *Writing the Breakout Novel* (Writer's Digest Books) by Donald Maass is worth the price for his exposition on characterization, plus his ideas for taking your work to a new level; and Albert Zuckerman's *Writing the Blockbuster Novel* (Writer's Digest Books) has good insight into the making of a best-seller.

You garden, quilt and paint. Does the creative process in these activities help you with your writing? Would you recommend using other art mediums? Why?

Most of my hobbies have a right brain, creative aspect. Gardening, quilting and painting are as much about color and design as they are hoes, needles or paintbrushes. They're also relaxing in their execution, and anything that relaxes the body allows the brain to function better on a subconscious level. All creative pursuits tend to reinforce each other then. It's important for writers to have other interests because it's fatally easy to become so focused on your work you lose perspective. The result is burn out. Anything that recharges the batteries is a valuable addition.

How has romance writing changed in the last decade? Do you think these changes have helped the genre or hindered it?

The main change is the proliferation of niche-market romance categories, from chick lit and erotica at one end of the spectrum to inspirationals on the other. Since romance continues to outsell other types of fiction, it doesn't seem to have hurt the genre. On the other hand, I'm not sure it's helped romance authors since the pie has been, and continues to be, sliced into smaller and smaller pieces.

With the changes in technology, where do you see publishing and the romance field in the future? Do you think these changes will help authors or cause problems?

I'm tremendously excited about the future of electronic publishing and handheld readers and can't wait to see how it plays out. Where is it going? It may take 20 years to get there, but I think we'll eventually see books released in electronic format as the primary outlet, with print copies as an option. We'll have graphics and sound included as enrichment, so the release becomes a multifaceted piece of entertainment. Romance novels will continue to dominate the market because they are the primary escapism for working women and reflect their deepest joys, needs and strengths. Writers will exercise more control over the content and the future of their books because they will have the option to self-publish without the old stigma attached to that process. The downside is the current trend of authors being forced to become their own editors may get worse. This will likely lead to a decline in quality—not because they can't do the job but because no one can be that objective.

What's the best piece of advice you've ever received from another writer (or editor)?

"Write the book you would like to read." I'd been doing that for years when I came across it in a book on writing, but it was very freeing to know the approach wasn't my personal ego trip.

How does it feel to be considered a romance legend?

A little like a person must feel who reaches the 100-year mark, as if it's something that happened while I was busy with other things. Still, it's grand to have the title while I'm here to enjoy it.

For Romance Writers

© Dick Stanley

FOR ROMANCE WRITERS

Genre-hopping Your Way Out of the Midlist

by Roxanne St. Claire

The Midlist. You know where that is, don't you? Technically, it's the section of a publisher's catalog stuffed with books written by authors who are neither debut nor best-sellers. For new writers of commercial genre fiction, especially romance, this is a well-defined destination. No longer a newbie, a midlister has a decent, if not magnificent, print run. A midlist writer probably has a good agent, a fairly attentive editor, and a growing audience. Life in the midlist is *fine*—not the fanciest house on the street but, heck, it's in an exclusive neighborhood. The lure of "lead" is out there—the next destination, the next move up.

That is, unless you linger in the midlist too long. A few too many books that don't inch their way up in the sales catalog, and a writer can face something much worse than languishing on the midlist: life without contracts. This can happen after just a few years or a few books, primarily because one or two books sell only moderately well, causing booksellers to reduce orders for the next book, resulting in lower print runs. This is not an uncommon situation but it's one that can either cause your publisher not to offer a new contract or force a writer to "relaunch" herself with a name booksellers don't recognize.

Another danger with an extended stay in the midlist is publishing infrequency. A writer at a major house may be delighted to be playing with the "big guys and girls" only to find the lead and best-selling authors get the first and most slots—often with reissues—while a newer midlist author is published once a year, if that.

One of the ways to avoid both low-to-no print runs and a paucity of pub dates is to create a "safety net" by publishing in multiple subgenres, such as paranormal, women's fiction, historical, contemporary, chick lit, comedy or young adult. Publishing within more than one subgenre, or moving from one subgenre to another, offers a number of benefits, including:

- An increased base of readers
- More frequent releases
- Enhanced career security with two publishers
- Fresh opportunities for creativity
- Additional income from advances and royalty checks
- Delighted publishers who see an increase in orders

ROXANNE ST. CLAIRE is a best-selling author of romantic suspense for Pocket Books, chick lit for Downtown Press and contemporary romance for Silhouette Books. Prior to launching a full-time career as a novelist in 2000, she spent nearly two decades in marketing and business management. A serial genre-hopper since her first book was published in 2003, she has sold 12 novels in three subgenres under two slightly different names.

For Romance Writers

Of course, the technique is not without its detractors. Some say genre-hopping can dilute a writer's audience, increase her marketing budget and, worst of all, infuriate her publishing house. However, if you choose two or three subgenres that share readers, handle the issue of marketing and names properly, and work with your publisher(s) to time releases for the most impact on sales, genre-hopping can be a godsend to a midlist writer.

Genre-hopping is best done on a voluntary, planned basis. Several authors interviewed for this article stated they were forced to switch genres because of dried up contracts, a new editor or a failed line. This "imposed genre-hopping" has given the practice a bad name, inducing stern warnings that writers should "pick their niche" and stay with it.

While that is often wise advice, niche-picking and niche-staying can be frustrating to prolific, ambitious, creative writers who not only are able to write in multiple subgenres but also want and need to for financial and artistic reasons. In talking to a number of highly productive and motivated genre-hoppers, a few key pieces of advice emerged that will help ensure success in moving between and among multiple genres.

Analyze your personality.

Genre-hopping is not for the faint of heart. You'll need to juggle multiple projects, deadlines, editors, personalities and, most importantly, writing styles. Your voice is your voice, and it will shine through regardless of the subgenre. But category romance requires a different pacing than single title, historical demands phrasing true to the time period, and paranormal readers like their prose dark. To accomplish this juggling act, you'll need to be organized and flexible. If you're neither, genre-hopping may not be your ticket out of midlist.

Gauge subgenres' appeal to your muse.

There are some obvious differences at first glance: category is shorter than single title; erotica is, well, more erotic than mainstream romance; romantic suspense requires a dead body contemporary romance can do without.

Killer Curves (Pocket Books), a romantic suspense set in the turbo-charged world of auto racing, is an example of one of Roxanne St. Claire's many subgenre projects. For more on St. Claire, visit her website at www.roxannestclaire.com.

But there are also much more subtle differences in tone, language, audience expectations, character types and taboos. To know them, you need to read within each subgenre, communicate with other writers in the subgenre, and follow the reviews, where you'll get a sense of the story premises and themes. Once you know the subgenres well, you'll recognize the opportunity to feed your muse by trying your hand at different types of romance. For many writers, this is a stronger impetus for genre-hopping than any business or financial reason.

Multipublished author Melanie Jackson hopped from the historical subgenre to the paranormal because she "wanted to write in a broader universe." She explains the actual historical events and people confined the reality in which she could write, "but in a world of time-travel and magic, one can do anything and explain it away." At the time she wanted to make the switch, paranormals were "still looked at with suspicion" and historicals were a known market. Her approach was to write both until her readers and her editor recognized her success in paranormal, and today she's happier writing in the wildly popular subgenre of paranormal and enjoying a much wider audience.

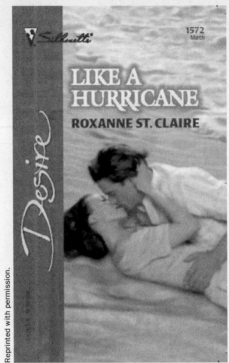

Reprinted with permission.

St. Claire turns up the heat with the contemporary romance *Like a Hurricane* (Silhouette Desire), the first in the three-book McGrath brothers series.

Choose subgenres that will support each other.

The most effective genre-hopping occurs where the crossover audience is built-in, such as mystery and romantic suspense; light comedy and chick lit; erotica and dark paranormal; or contemporary romance and women's fiction.

Award-winning author Brenda Novak writes romantic suspense single-title and long contemporary romance. Novak recommends writers select their subgenres with the same care and consideration they would in investing their money. "Writing for series (category romance) is like investing in bonds," she says. "They're safer, more secure. Single titles are like investing in stocks. They're a little riskier, but they have greater earning potential because they can hit a list and stay on the shelf longer." The only downside for Brenda is "the work load." She notes that in writing for two subgenres "you have to be pretty prolific, and it's not always easy to turn out that many books in a year."

Play the name game.

You have three choices when you genre-hop regarding your pen name(s). You can keep one name for all subgenres. The benefit is a reduction of marketing costs; it does take an investment to build a brand, run a website, produce collateral, or increase name recognition. The downside, of course, is the possibility of diluting that brand so readers don't know what to expect. Many authors have written in multiple subgenres under one name. Julie Garwood, Linda Lael Miller and Karen Robards, for example, are writers who have fairly well-established "brands" and legions of readers who opt to buy by author, not genre. Their publishers wisely alter covers, cover copy and advertising to promote the "different" versions of the brand.

Another option is to create a completely separate name, such as Rachel Lee and Sue Civil Brown; or Jayne Ann Krentz and Amanda Quick; or Nora Roberts and J.D. Robb. This completely eliminates the worry about diluting an audience, but it does increase the cost of marketing and brand-building. Most authors are open about their duel identities and encourage readers to give their other "self" a chance. If the two subgenres have little crossover audience (young adult and erotica, for instance), then this is a recommended avenue. It might not get you out of the midlist as quickly as having one name, but it will build overall sales and spread your talent around.

The final option is a "similar" name. Meggin and Meg Cabot, writing chick lit and young adult, or Nicole and Niki Burnham, writing romance and young adult, are examples. The goal is to bring along established readers, but make it clear (along with entirely different covers and even formats) they should not expect a similar "read" from these books.

Explore category romance.

Category, or series romance, published primarily by Harlequin/Silhouette, is one of the great training grounds for genre-hopping. Writers who sell to one "line" (such as Silhouette Desire or Harlequin Intrigue) have an easier time sliding from one type of category romance to another. In addition, the move to single title is encouraged with the HQN and Mira imprints, and authors who find they're able to write a longer book with multiple sub-plots and points of view have the opportunity to do so for their own house or for others.

Moving into category *after* selling a single title to a mainstream publisher is a far less common career choice, but can be a wise one for a prolific, disciplined writer. I made that move in 2004 for a number of strategic reasons. Category romance does not require a great deal of marketing investment and the readers tend to be loyal line buyers, so the need to establish a name is less pressing than it is in single title. In addition, the high print runs ensure a large, new audience will discover your work—an audience that many believe does cross over to single title when they like a particular author.

Reprinted with permission.

St. Claire adds chick lit to her repertoire with *Hit Reply* (Downtown Press), the story of three girlfriends who navigate love and cyberspace with hilarious and heartwarming results.

The timing of category releases can also have a powerful impact on the sales of a single title. My agent recommends releasing a category book a month after a single title, to give the single title a sales boost from readers who enjoy the category and then seek more from the same author. This kind of carefully planned timing requires open and regular communication with your editors, but they want your sales to be as high as possible and will usually work to schedule releases for the greatest benefit to everyone.

Beware the option clause.

If you are inclined to genre-hop, the biggest impediment to doing so for more than one publishing house will be the option clause in your contract. Be certain your agent or literary attorney limits the wording of this clause to precisely the subgenre you've sold. For example, the publisher should have a right of first refusal on your next "100,000 word contemporary romantic comedy"—thereby allowing you to write category, paranormal, suspense or women's fiction for another publishing house.

If the clause is general, open-ended or requires the house have first refusal on something as vague as "the writer's next work," you may have a difficult time moving to another house or another genre. If you succeed, you need to keep both or all editors apprised of your schedule and meet all your deadlines, remembering they are, in a sense, competitors for your time. Like any smart business person, never let one "customer" think they are less valuable to you than another.

If you've recently entered the midlist, congratulations. The arrival is a tremendous accomplishment. But if you'd like your stay to be brief, you might consider hopping right out of that bulging middle and into the lead spot in your publisher's catalog.

FOR ROMANCE WRITERS

Resources

Where to Look for More Information

Below is a list of invaluable resources specifically for romance writers. To order any of the Writer's Digest Books titles or to get a consumer book catalog, call (800)448-0915. You may also order Writer's Digest Books selections through www.writersdigest.com, Amazon.com or www.barnesandnoble.com.

MAGAZINES

- *Romance Writers Report*, Romance Writers of America, 16000 Stuebner Airline Rd., Suite 140, Spring TX 77379. (832)717-5200. Fax: (832)717-5201. E-mail: info@rwanational.org.
- *Romantic Times Bookclub Magazine*, 55 Bergen St., Brooklyn NY 11201. (718)237-1097. Website: www.romantictimes.com.

BOOKS

- *How To Write Romances (Revised and Updated)**, by Phyllis Taylor Pianka
- *Keys to Success: The Professional Writer's Career Handbook*, Romance Writers of America
- *Writing Romances: A Handbook by the Romance Writers of America*, edited by Rita Clay Estrada and Rita Gallagher
- *You Can Write a Romance*, by Rita Clay Estrada and Rita Gallagher (Writer's Digest Books)

ORGANIZATIONS & ONLINE

- Canadian Romance Authors' Network. Website: www.canadianromanceauthors.com.
- Romance Writers of America, Inc. (RWA), 16000 Stuebner Airline Rd., Suite 140, Spring TX 77379. (832)717-5200. Fax: (832)717-5201. E-mail: info@rwanational.org. Website: www.rwanational.org.
- Romance Writers of America regional chapters. Contact National Office (address above) for information on the chapter nearest you.
- The Romance Club. Website: http://theromanceclub.com.
- Romance Central. Website: www.romance-central.com. Offers workshops and forum where romance writers share ideas and exchange advice about romance writing.
- Writer's Market Online. Website: www.writersmarket.com.
- Writer's Digest Online. Website: www.writersdigest.com.

* Out of print. Check your local library.

Gordon Van Gelder

Editor Seeks 'Laudable Speculative Fiction'

© Al Bogdan

by I.J. Schecter

For Gordon Van Gelder, editor and publisher of *The Magazine of Fantasy & Science Fiction*, the search for laudable speculative fiction is more than a stimulating challenge; it's also a genuine labor of love. Here Van Gelder talks about everything from his early aspiration to be a paleontologist to the enduring magic of great stories.

What's your greatest asset as an editor and publisher?

The only thing an editor really has is his or her taste. You can border on incompetence in every other aspect of the business, but if you've got taste readers respond to, you'll do fine. I've been lucky enough people like my taste in fiction.

After four years as a publisher, I'm still not sure. A good work ethic, I suppose.

What's your most counterproductive trait?

I'm lousy at delegating work.

What are you thinking when you pick up an unopened manuscript?

My answer differs on any given day (What time is it? Did I remember to feed the cats? How did they solve Fermat's Last Theorem?), but my basic condition is a blank slate. That is, I'm not thinking anything in particular.

Does a story have to follow certain conventions to be publishable?

I stay away from the word "publishable." As far as conventions are concerned, we ran one story a few years ago that consisted entirely of footnotes. But to answer your question from a different direction, a common flaw I see is stories that are fragments—pieces in which the feeling or mood is the highest priority, and once that emotion is evoked, the author drops the rest of the story. There's no interest in completing the narrative arc as long as the epiphany is deeply felt. That doesn't often work for me.

What was your childhood like?

The best comparison I can make is to the kids in *The Royal Tenenbaums*—that kind of crazy, interesting environment. My father was a museum curator, and my parents exposed us to a

I.J. SCHECTER (www.ijschecter.com) writes for leading magazines, newspapers and websites throughout the world, including *Condé Nast Brides*, *Golf Monthly*, *Men's Exercise*, *The Globe & Mail* and iParenting.com. He is also the author of a short story collection The Bottom of the Mug (Aegina Press Inc).

Sci Fi/Fantasy/Horror

lot of unusual experiences. We spent four weeks in Mozambique when I was six years old, for instance. For the most part, it was a fairly typical suburban childhood, but things like the fact we regularly had animal specimens in our freezer made it exceptional.

Reprinted with permission.

What did you want to be growing up?
Being a paleontologist was tops on my list until age seven or eight. Then I don't recall thinking much more about it until I was 12 and decided I wanted to be a writer. The bug bit me hard.

How do your parents, or family, perceive your job? Do they connect with your passion for writing?
Both sides of my family are word-oriented; both my parents published children's fiction, my uncle is a reporter, and almost everyone in the family writes. About five years ago, I was contacted out of the blue by a guy who had just turned 40, grew up in foster homes, and wanted to get in touch with his biological family. He turned out to be a second cousin of mine. His occupation? Investigative journalist.

The stories of mine you've rejected (no hard feelings) have always been accompanied by thoughtful, personal notes. How do you do this when virtually no others in your position do? Is it that you care more?
It's not a matter of caring more. Virtually every editor I know cares as much about submissions as I do. It's more a matter of systems. I came from book publishing and basically brought over some of the systems I used for handling book submissions. When you have to make a decision on a full novel in just an hour or so, you learn how to evaluate quickly.

If you were allowed to write just one short story, where would you set it?
Earth. Glib answer, but there's an awful lot of stuff on this planet, and science fiction writers sometimes forget that.

Do you have assistants who are delegated to sifting through the slush pile these days, or do you still try to see every manuscript that comes in?
I'm no longer able to read every submission. My current assistant, John Joseph Adams, handles the bulk of submissions nowadays.

Please describe the experience of reading a story online versus in your hands.
Personally, I hate reading fiction online. I know some who don't mind it, and I hear from more people all the time who are finding it palatable to read on handheld devices, but the printed word is an old and well-developed technology, and I still favor it.

Does this influence your vision for the future of the magazine?
We do offer electronic editions and they're growing in sales, but I doubt a day will ever come when we go 100 percent electric. Too many of our readers got hooked when they found Dad's box of old magazines in the attic.

You come across a typo on page one of a manuscript. Do you keep reading?

There's an anecdote I've told for years about a story that came in with a handwritten cover letter and had two or three typos on the first page, including misuse of "lay" versus "laid." But the writer's voice made me forget the little glitches, and I wound up buying that story— and several more—from the writer. So yes, I'll overlook typos in a manuscript, but they do have the effect of throwing me out of the story.

In your opinion, are writers writing better or worse now than, say, 50 years ago?

I think the best writing today is as good as the best writing of the 1950s, and the worst writing of the 21st century is just as bad as the worst writing of 50 years ago. Writing today is more heavily influenced by media newscasting than it was 50 years ago; there are more neologisms and popular clichés in today's prose. The other big change in writing, in general, is that it's supersized. Fifty years ago, most writers used as little typing paper as possible to tell a story. Computers have made it harder to find lean writing.

How would you compare your job to that of someone in a noncreative position?

I've known plenty of people working what they consider dead-end jobs who've said to me, "It must be great getting paid to read all day." It is, and it isn't. There are days when I'd love to work at McDonald's, do my shift, and know when I clock out my work is done. But most days, I view the job the way parents view child rearing: Sometimes it's great, sometimes it's a pain in the butt, but you wouldn't give it up for anything.

What do you love most about the written word?

As much as I love music, art and movies, there's nothing that rivals the experience of getting caught up in a good story. When the magic happens, that direct connection, it's exhilarating. The story doesn't have to be upbeat, but the whole experience of reading a great story is tremendously uplifting.

I won't ask the standard "Give me three pieces of advice for fiction writers" question. Give me two instead.

One, prune your stories. As I said, the computer has created an epidemic of prose obesity. If I'm reading a story and I start to skim, I'm almost certainly not going to buy it. Two, study your market. This one may sound obvious, but I still get submissions that are completely inappropriate for the magazine. For instance, people see the words "Science Fiction" in our title, and they fire off a proposal for an article about the Bermuda Triangle or crop circles, without ever bothering to note we're a fiction magazine.

What are your top two submission peeves?

Number one is electronic submissions. Yes, I know it's vastly easier to hit Send and bypass the whole process of putting a hard copy in the mail. I even believe the editors who say they prefer electronic submissions. But with the quantity of submissions we receive and the logistics of our office, electronic submissions just don't work for me. My real peeve on this count is all the people who query me asking if I can pretty-please make an exception for them. I already know I'm a meanie for not taking your e-mail submission; get over it and mail the story already. Number two is stories accompanied by handwritten cover letters with misused words.

What would be your ideal epitaph?

"STET" has a nice quality to it.

Sci FI/Fantasy/Horror

Mel Odom

*Jack of All Genres
a 'Constant Student' of Craft*

Photo courtesy of author

by Deborah Bouziden

Mel Odom has been described as a regular guy, but to his legion of fans and the many publishing companies who acquire his work, he's anything but ordinary. This prolific author of 17 game strategy guides and more than 89 books—including series and single titles in every genre and movie and television novelizations of such well-loved characters as Buffy, Sabrina the Teenage Witch, Blade, and Lara Croft: Tomb Raider—began training for his career in third grade.

"I grew up in several small towns that didn't have much in the way of television," Odom said. "My mom only took me to the public library once every two weeks, and I could only check out five books. After two days, I'd read them all and had to start writing my own books to fill in the additional 12 days till the next trip."

Living in Oklahoma and coming from a small town, Odom never really felt he could write professionally until his big break in 1988, when he sold his first book to Gold Eagle Books. It was then that Odom took the leap and began writing professionally. A year later, Lynx Books released *Stranded*, a volume in their Time Police Series. Since then, Odom has published mystery, suspense, science fiction, fantasy, western, horror and romance books, as well as movie novelizations, computer strategy guides and comics.

Today, Odom still lives in Oklahoma with his wife and five children. On any given day, you can find him coaching Little League at the local park, doing laundry and running errands with his children, then heading to his small, windowless office to travel to other worlds and create magic for himself and his readers.

One of your projects is the Rover series (Tor), a trilogy of fantasy stories about books. How did the idea for this type of work come to you?
The idea for *The Rover* came about by mixing *The Lord of the Rings* elements with *How the Irish Saved Civilization*. The Lord Of The Rings movies had come out, and I'd recently read the nonfiction book. I was fascinated by the latter and saw a way to wed it to fantasy. I've always been a fan of JRR Tolkien's work but wanted to do my riff on that kind of story. As I worked on the story outline, [my protagonist] Wick kind of took over (he has a habit of doing that) and whispered the tale to me. I've always felt that libraries were magical places. Where else in the world can you go and be everywhere else in the world at the same time?

DEBORAH BOUZIDEN, since 1985, has had hundreds of articles published and has authored or co-authored seven books, including *In Their Name*, *The Journal Wheel and Guidebook*, and *Oklahoma: Off The Beaten Path*, her latest project. To learn more about Bouziden, visit her website at www.deborahbouziden.com.

Plus, readers have a tendency to love books and I (and my wise editor Brian Thomsen at Tor Books) felt those readers would understand completely Wick's love of a tale well told.

You've worked on so many projects. What challenges you today?

I am still very much challenged by my writing. Reading tastes seem to change on a daily basis. Readers want the same thing from a writer, but at the same time they want something different. Figuring out how to put together the same but different is a challenge. Also, I want to get better at what I'm doing and how I do it. Sometimes I frustrate myself while working on a book by trying to reinvent the wheel, but when I have those moments that everything comes together, it's worth it.

Do you prefer single titles or series?

Both have pluses and minuses. I love the idea of doing single titles because I can put the characters and places in a box and be done with them and never have to worry about orphaning a potential sequel. Single titles are cleaner writing without having to worry about past history or possibly doing a book that conflicts with canon set forth in earlier volumes. On the other hand, I've rarely written a book about characters that I didn't end up with a handful of ideas (and usually more!) for other books. Writing series is nice, though, because you usually get a multibook deal and you're selling a familiar character or world that the publisher and readers have faith in.

You've written in many different genres; which do you prefer?

Of the seven genres that I recognize (mystery, suspense, science fiction, fantasy, western, horror and romance—everything will fit into one of those categories, trust me), I don't have a true favorite. Each has something to offer the writer, and each has stumbling blocks.

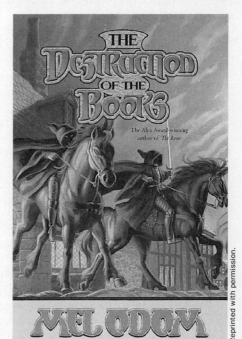

Reprinted with permission.

The Destruction of Books (Tor) is the second in Odom's fantasy Rover series.

Mysteries offer chances to hone characterization (motives) and structure (clues, timelines and killer) but don't allow major action scenes or heavy exploration of side stories. Suspense offers a chance to work on action writing, backgrounding and dialogue but doesn't allow for leisurely pacing to build worlds or characters that deflect from the marathon run for the finish line.

Science fiction space opera gives the writer the chance to play in a far larger universe but requires adequate grounding in a world everyone understands; tech science fiction gives the writer the opportunity to explore what might possibly happen with cutting-edge technology but requires so much introduction of the science a lot of readers get information overload.

Fantasy is great because a writer can make up *everything*; however, if the writer continues writing these books, attention must be paid to what has gone before, which can be a wake-up call to writers who pull everything out of the toy box and don't keep notes on what's used.

Western is a great genre for writing strong characters and background. But I question how writers can do anything new readers will accept.

Horror offers a chance to use setting and atmosphere, but the downside is following conventional terror-building tactics everyone has seen before that will bore more writers.

Romance, at present, offers the broadest palette, which is why I've started writing in that genre lately under a pen name. Anything goes in romance as long as the writer brings the lovers together. The downside is the lovers *have* to be brought together, so it isn't a surprise.

I like all the genres because each offers me a chance to hone different writer's skills, bring in different material, and spin the story in different ways.

How has publishing changed since you started writing, and what lessons have you learned along the way?

Publishing has changed a lot since I got into the business. The midlist is gone. The backlist is hard to find unless you're a major player. Thankfully the online bookstores like Amazon and Barnes & Noble have stepped in to fill those gaps. Publishers and authors have settled for lower numbers these days because the market is so fragmented, but they still keep an eye on them to exploit a trend. The major rule I've learned, and one I've always lived by, is to remember I'm a constant student in this craft. God forbid I should ever learn it all. I have ADHD, and doing the same thing over and over again would probably kill me. However, with the way publishing and the market moves, I successfully re-create myself often. I love the hustle of selling books and the chance to meet readers.

How do you think new technology will change publishing?

Technology has already changed a lot of publishing with the print-on-demand availability. Microsoft Reader and other handhelds are vying for part of the market as well. Certainly a few e-publishers (like Ellora's Cave) have made a go of it. I think we can expect that trend to continue, but people will always love books they can hold in their hands.

What advice can you give to other writers?

Read! So many people come to my writing classes and don't read. There's no way to learn how to do something without immersing yourself in it. Sure, writing can be taught, but what to write? How to write it? What's selling right now? Why? All these things come to the writer who is an on-going aggressive reader. I read heavily in all the genres. I know the best-sellers and I know more than a few of the practitioners who toil without ever making the big lists. I take time to figure out what skills they're best at and learn from them, and I learn to spot their weaknesses so I can find them in my own manuscripts when I'm proofreading. You can learn story from movies and television, but you can't learn how to put those stories down in prose. Many screenwriters are great at what they do, but they'll never be book writers unless they spend time with that craft. Despite the story-telling similarities, the work is different. Read in the genre you want to write in, and read out of it as well. Maybe you're fated to write science fiction, but you're going to have to learn your chops from mystery and suspense to do it.

Of all the worlds you've created, which one do you like the best?

I love my own world the best. I get to spend time with my kids, coach them in baseball and basketball, play video games on a regular basis, watch sports, argue over inane things, and go to movies. And have the occasional long conversation with my wonderful wife about absolutely nothing at all.

Resources

Where to Look for More Information

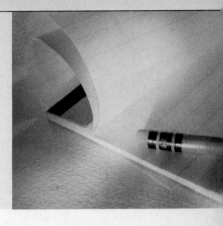

Below is a list of invaluable resources specifically for science fiction, fantasy and horror writers. To order any of the Writer's Digest Books titles or to get a consumer book catalog, call (800)448-0915. You may also order Writer's Digest Books selections through www.writersdigest.com, Amazon.com or www.barnesandnoble.com.

MAGAZINES
- *Locus*, P.O. Box 13305, Oakland CA 94661. E-mail: locus@locusmag.com.
- *Science Fiction Chronicle*, P.O. Box 022730, Brooklyn NY 11202-0056. (718)643-9011. Fax: (718)522-3308. E-mail: sfchronicle@dnapublications.com.
- SPECFICME! (bi-monthly PDF newsletter). Website: www.specficworld.com.

BOOKS (by Writer's Digest Books)
- *Aliens and Alien Societies: A Writer's Guide to Creating Extraterrestrial Life-forms*, by Stanley Schmidt
- *Worlds of Wonder, How to Write Science Fiction and Fantasy**, by David Gerrold
- *How to Write Science Fiction & Fantasy*, by Orson Scott Card
- *The Writer's Complete Fantasy Reference*, from the editors of Writer's Digest Books
- *Writing Horror**, edited by Mort Castle

ORGANIZATIONS & ONLINE
- Fantasy-Writers.org. Website: www.fantasy-writers.org.
- Horror Writers Association, P.O. Box 50577, Palo Alto CA 94303. Website: www.horror.org.
- Science Fiction & Fantasy Writers of America, Inc., P.O. Box 877, Chestertown MD 21620. E-mail: execdir@sfwa.org. Website: www.sfwa.org/.
- SF Canada, 303-2333 Scarth St., Regina SK S4P 2J8. Website: www.sfcanada.ca.
- SpecFicWorld. Website: www.specficworld.com. Covers all 3 speculative genres (science fiction, fantasy and horror).
- Books and Writing Online. Website: www.interzone.com/Books/books.html.
- Writer's Market Online. Website: www.writersmarket.com.
- Locus Magazine Online. Website: www.locusmag.com.

* Out of print. Check your local library.

Literary Agents

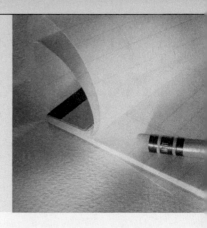

Many publishers are willing to look at unsolicited submissions but most feel having an agent is in the writer's best interest. In this section, we include agents who specialize in or represent fiction. These agents were also selected because of their openness to submissions from writers.

The commercial fiction field is intensely competitive. Many publishers have small staffs and little time. For that reason, many book publishers rely on agents for new talent. Some publishers are even relying on agents as "first readers" who must wade through the deluge of submissions from writers to find the very best. For writers, a good agent can be a foot in the door—someone willing to do the necessary work to put your manuscript in the right editor's hands.

It would seem today that finding a good agent is as hard as finding a good publisher. Yet those writers who have agents say they are invaluable. Not only can a good agent help you make your work more marketable, an agent also acts as your business manager and adviser, protecting your interests during and after contract negotiations.

Still, finding an agent can be very difficult for a new writer. If you are already published in magazines, you have a better chance than someone with no publishing credits. (Many agents routinely read periodicals searching for new writers.) Although many agents do read queries and manuscripts from unpublished authors without introduction, referrals from their writer clients can be a big help. If you don't know any published authors with agents, attending a conference is a good way to meet agents. Some agents even set aside time at conferences to meet new writers.

Almost all the agents listed here have said they are open to working with new, previously unpublished writers as well as published writers. Most do not charge a fee to cover the time and effort involved in reviewing a manuscript or a synopsis and chapters.

USING THE LISTINGS

It is especially important that you read individual listings carefully before contacting these busy agents. The first information after the company name includes the address and phone, fax, e-mail address (when available) and website. **Member Agents** gives the names of individual agents working at that company. (Specific types of fiction an agent handles are indicated in parenthesis after that agent's name.) The **Represents** section lists the types of fiction the agency works with. Reading the **Recent Sales** gives you the names of writers an agent is currently working with and, very importantly, publishers the agent has placed manuscripts with. **Writers' Conferences** identifies conferences an agent attends (and where you might possibly meet that agent). **Tips** presents advice directly from the agent to authors.

Also, look closely at the openness to submissions icons that precede most listings. They will indicate to you how willing an agency is to take on new writers.

DOMINICK ABEL LITERARY AGENCY, INC.

146 W. 82nd St., #1B, New York NY 10024. Fax: (212)595-3133. E-mail: agency@dalainc.com. Estab. 1975. Member of AAR. Represents 100 clients. Currently handles: adult nonfiction books; adult novels.

How to Contact Query with SASE by mail.

Terms Agent receives 15% commission on domestic sales; 20% commission on foreign sales.

☒ ☑ ACACIA HOUSE PUBLISHING SERVICES, LTD.

51 Acacia Rd., Toronto ON M4S 2K6 Canada. (416)484-8356. Fax: (416)484-8356. E-mail: fhanna.acacia@rogers.com. **Contact:** (Ms.) Frances Hanna. Estab. 1985. Represents 100 clients. Currently handles: 30% nonfiction books; 70% novels.

- Ms. Hanna has been in the publishing business for 30 years, first in London (UK) as a fiction editor with Barrie & Jenkins and Pan Books, and as a senior editor with a packager of mainly illustrated books. She was condensed books editor for 6 years for *Reader's Digest* in Montreal, senior editor and foreign rights manager for (the then) William Collins & Sons (now HarperCollins) in Toronto. Her husband, vice president Bill Hanna, has over 40 years experience in the publishing business.

Member Agents Bill Hanna, vice president (business, self-help, modern history).

Represents Nonfiction books, novels. **Considers these nonfiction areas:** Animals; biography/autobiography; language/literature/criticism; memoirs; military/war; music/dance; nature/environment; theater/film; travel. **Considers these fiction areas:** Action/adventure; detective/police/crime; literary; mainstream/contemporary; mystery/suspense; thriller.

- ⊙¬ This agency specializes in contemporary fiction: literary or commercial. Actively seeking "outstanding first novels with literary merit." Does not want to receive horror, occult, science fiction.

How to Contact Query with outline and SASE. *No unsolicited mss.* No e-mail or fax queries. Responds in 6 weeks to queries. Returns materials only with SASE.

Recent Sales Sold over 75 titles in the last year. Also made numerous international rights sales. This agency prefers not to share information on specific sales or clients.

Terms Agent receives 15% commission on English language sales, 20% on dramatic sales, 25% commission on foreign sales. Charges clients for photocopying, postage, and courier, as necessary.

Tips "We prefer that writers be previously published, with at least a few short stories or articles to their credit. Strongest consideration will be given to those with 3 or more published books. However, we would take on an unpublished writer of outstanding talent."

☑ THE AHEARN AGENCY, INC.

2021 Pine St., New Orleans LA 70118-5456. (504)861-8395. Fax: (504)866-6434. E-mail: pahearn@aol.com. **Contact:** Pamela G. Ahearn. Estab. 1992. Member of MWA. Represents 25 clients. 20% of clients are new/unpublished writers. Currently handles: 10% nonfiction books; 90% novels.

- Prior to opening her agency, Ms. Ahearn was an agent for 8 years and an editor with Bantam Books.

Represents Nonfiction books, novels, short story collections (if stories previously published). **Considers these nonfiction areas:** Animals; child guidance/parenting; current affairs; ethnic/cultural interests; gay/lesbian issues; health/medicine; history; music/dance; popular culture; self-help/personal improvement; theater/film; true crime/investigative; women's issues/studies. **Considers these fiction areas:** Action/adventure; contemporary issues; detective/police/crime; ethnic; family saga; feminist; gay/lesbian; glitz; historical; humor/satire; literary; mainstream/contemporary; mystery/suspense; psychic/supernatural; regional; romance; thriller.

- ⊙¬ This agency specializes in historical romance and is also very interested in mysteries and suspense fiction. Does not want to receive category romance, science fiction or fantasy.

How to Contact Query with SASE. Accepts e-mail queries, no attachments. Considers simultaneous queries. Responds in 8 weeks to queries; 10 weeks to mss. Obtains most new clients through recommendations from others, solicitations, conferences.

Recent Sales *The Perfumed Sleeve*, by Laura Joh Rowland (St. Martin's); *To Pleasure a Prince*, by Sabrina Jeffries (Pocket).

Terms Agent receives 15% commission on domestic sales; 20% commission on foreign sales. Offers written contract, binding for 1 year; renewable by mutual consent.

Writers' Conferences Moonlight & Magnolias; RWA National Conference (Orlando); Virginia Romance Writers (Williamsburg VA); Florida Romance Writers (Ft. Lauderdale FL); Golden Triangle Writers Conference; Bouchercon (Monterey, November); Malice Domestic (DC, May).

Tips "Be professional! Always send in exactly what an agent/editor asks for, no more, no less. Keep query letters brief and to the point, giving your writing credentials and a very brief summary of your book. If one agent rejects you, keep trying—there are a lot of us out there!''

ALIVE COMMUNICATIONS, INC.

7680 Goddard St., Suite 200, Colorado Springs CO 80920. (719)260-7080. Fax: (719)260-8223. Website: www.alivecom.com. Estab. 1989. Member of CBA, Authors Guild. Represents 200+ clients. 5% of clients are new/unpublished writers. Currently handles: 50% nonfiction books; 35% novels; 5% novellas; 10% juvenile books.

Member Agents Rick Christian, president (blockbusters, bestsellers); Jerry ''Chip'' MacGregor (popular/commercial nonfiction and fiction, new authors with breakout potential); Beth Jusino (thoughtful/inspirational nonfiction, women's fiction/nonfiction, Christian living); Lee Hough (popular/commercial nonfiction and fiction, thoughtful spirituality, children's).

Represents Nonfiction books, novels, short story collections, novellas. **Considers these nonfiction areas:** Biography/autobiography; business/economics; child guidance/parenting; how-to; memoirs; religious/inspirational; self-help/personal improvement; women's issues/studies. **Considers these fiction areas:** Action/adventure; contemporary issues; detective/police/crime; family saga; historical; humor/satire; literary; mainstream/contemporary; mystery/suspense; religious/inspirational; thriller.

    ⊶ This agency specializes in fiction, Christian living, how-to, and commercial nonfiction. Actively seeking inspirational/literary/mainstream fiction and work from authors with established track record and platforms. Does not want poetry, young adult paperback, scripts, dark themes.

How to Contact Works primarily with well-established, bestselling, and career authors. Returns materials only with SASE. Obtains most new clients through recommendations from others. ''On rare occasions accepts new clients through referrals.''

Recent Sales Sold 300+ titles in the last year. Left Behind series, by Tim LaHaye and Jerry B. Jenkins (Tyndale); *Let's Roll*, by Lisa Beamer (Tyndale); *The Message*, by Eugene Peterson (NavPress); Every Man series, by Stephen Arterburn (Waterbrook); *One Tuesday Morning*, by Karen Kingsbury (Zondervan).

Terms Agent receives 15% commission on domestic sales; 15% commission on foreign sales. Offers written contract; 2-month written notice must be given to terminate contract.

Tips ''Rewrite and polish until the words on the page shine. Endorsements and great connections may help, provided you can write with power and passion. Network with publishing professionals by making contacts, joining critique groups, and attending writers' conferences in order to make personal connections in publishing and to get feedback. Alive Communications, Inc., has established itself as a premiere literary agency. Based in Colorado Springs, we serve an elite group of authors who are critically acclaimed and commercially successful in both Christian and general markets.''

ALTAIR LITERARY AGENCY, LLC

P.O. Box 11656, Washington DC 20008. (202)237-8282. Website: www.altairliteraryagency.com. Estab. 1996. Member of AAR. Represents 50 clients. 20% of clients are new/unpublished writers. Currently handles: 95% nonfiction books; 5% novels.

Member Agents Andrea Pedolsky, partner; Nicholas Smith, partner.

Represents Nonfiction books. **Considers these nonfiction areas:** History; popular culture; sports; science (history of); illustrated; current events/contemporary issues; museum; organization; corporate-brand books. **Considers these fiction areas:** Historical (pre-20th century mysteries only).

    ⊶ This agency specializes in nonfiction with an emphasis on authors who have credentials and professional recognition for their topic, and a high level of public exposure. Actively seeking solid, well-informed authors who have a public platform for the subject specialty.

How to Contact Query with SASE; or see website for more specific query information and to send an online query. Considers simultaneous queries. Responds in 2-4 weeks to queries; 1 month to mss. Obtains most new clients through recommendations from others, solicitations, author queries.

Recent Sales *Performance Nutrition for Runners*, by Matt Fitzgerald (Rodale); *Online Roots*, by Pamela Porter, CGRS, CGL and Amy Johnson Crow (Rutledge Hill Press); *How Herbs Work*, by Suzette Holly Phaneuf (Marlowe/Avalon Publshing); *You Can Sell It!*, by Frank McNair (Sourcebooks); *That Might Be Useful*, by Naton Leslie (Lyons Press); *Good Catholic Girls*, by Angela Bonavoglia (ReganBooks/HarperCollins); *Life's a Bitch and Then You Change Careers*, by Andrea Kay (Stewart/Tabori & Chang).

Terms Agent receives 15% commission on domestic sales; 20% commission on foreign sales. Offers written contract, binding for 1 year; 2-month notice must be given to terminate contract. Charges clients for postage, copying, messengers and FedEx and UPS.

MIRIAM ALTSHULER LITERARY AGENCY

53 Old Post Rd. N., Red Hook NY 12571. (845)758-9408. **Contact:** Miriam Altshuler. Estab. 1994. Member of AAR. Represents 40 clients. Currently handles: 45% nonfiction books; 45% novels; 5% story collections; 5% juvenile books.

- Ms. Altshuler has been an agent since 1982.

Represents Nonfiction books, novels, short story collections, juvenile books. **Considers these nonfiction areas:** Biography/autobiography; ethnic/cultural interests; history; language/literature/criticism; memoirs; multicultural; music/dance; nature/environment; popular culture; psychology; sociology; theater/film; women's issues/studies. **Considers these fiction areas:** Literary; mainstream/contemporary; multicultural.

O— Does not want self-help, mystery, how-to, romance, horror, spiritual, fantasy, poetry, screenplays, science fiction, techno-thriller.

How to Contact Query with SASE. Prefers to read materials exclusively. If no SASE is included, no response will be sent. *No unsolicited mss.* No e-mail or fax queries. Considers simultaneous queries. Responds in 2 weeks to queries; 3 weeks to mss. Returns materials only with SASE. Obtains most new clients through recommendations from others.

Terms Agent receives 15% commission on domestic sales; 20% commission on foreign sales. Charges clients for overseas mailing, photocopies, overnight mail when requested by author.

Writers' Conferences Bread Loaf Writers' Conference (Middlebury VT, August); Washington Independent Writers Conference (Washington DC, June), North Carolina Writers Network Conference (Carrboro NC, October).

☑ BETSY AMSTER LITERARY ENTERPRISES

P.O. Box 27788, Los Angeles CA 90027-0788. **Contact:** Betsy Amster. Estab. 1992. Member of AAR. Represents over 65 clients. 35% of clients are new/unpublished writers. Currently handles: 65% nonfiction books; 35% novels.

- Prior to opening her agency, Ms. Amster was an editor at Pantheon and Vintage for 10 years, and served as editorial director for the Globe Pequot Press for 2 years. "This experience gives me a wider perspective on the business and the ability to give focused editorial feedback to my clients."

Represents Nonfiction books, novels. **Considers these nonfiction areas:** Biography/autobiography; child guidance/parenting; ethnic/cultural interests; gardening; health/medicine; history; money/finance; psychology; sociology; women's issues/studies; Career. **Considers these fiction areas:** Ethnic; literary; mystery/suspense (quirky); thriller (quirky); women's (high quality).

O— Actively seeking "strong narrative nonfiction, particularly by journalists; outstanding literary fiction (the next Michael Chabon or Jhumpa Lahiri); witty, intelligent, commercial women's fiction (the next Elinor Lipman or Jennifer Weiner); and high-profile self-help and psychology, preferably research based." Does not want to receive poetry, children's books, romances, westerns, science fiction, action/adventure.

How to Contact For fiction, send query, first 3 pages, and SASE. For nonfiction, send query or proposal with SASE. No e-mail or fax queries. Considers simultaneous queries. Responds in 1 month to queries; 2 months to mss. Obtains most new clients through recommendations from others, solicitations, conferences.

Recent Sales *González & Daughter Trucking Co.*, by María Amparo Escandón (Crown); *The Modern Jewish Girl's Guide to Guilt*, edited by Ruth Andrew Ellenson (Dutton); *Rejuvenile: How a New Species of Reluctant Adults is Redefining Maturity*, by Christopher Nixon (Crown); *The Reluctant Tuscan*, by Phil Doran (Gotham). Other clients include Dwight Allen, Dr. Elaine N. Aron, Barbara DeMarco-Barrett, Dr. Helene Brenner, Robin Chotzinoff, Frank Clifford, Rob Cohen & David Wollock, Jan DeBlieu, Margaret Lobenstine, Paul Mandelbaum, Wendy Mogel, Sharon Montrose, Joy Nicholson, Katie Singer, R.J. Smith, Louise Steinman.

Terms Agent receives 15% commission on domestic sales; 20% commission on foreign sales. Offers written contract, binding for 1 year; 3-month notice must be given to terminate contract. Charges for photocopying, postage, long distance phone calls, messengers, and galleys and books used in submissions to foreign and film agents and to magazines for first serial rights.

Writers' Conferences Squaw Valley; San Diego Writers Conference; UCLA Extension Writer's Program; The Loft Literary Center (Minneapolis).

☑ MARCIA AMSTERDAM AGENCY

41 W. 82nd St., New York NY 10024-5613. (212)873-4945. **Contact:** Marcia Amsterdam. Estab. 1970. Signatory of WGA. Currently handles: 15% nonfiction books; 70% novels; 5% movie scripts; 10% TV scripts.

- Prior to opening her agency, Ms. Amsterdam was an editor.

Represents Novels, feature film, TV movie of the week, sitcom. **Considers these fiction areas:** Action/adventure; detective/police/crime; horror; mainstream/contemporary; mystery/suspense; romance (contemporary, historical); science fiction; thriller; young adult. **Considers these script subject areas:** Comedy; mainstream; mystery/suspense; romantic comedy; romantic drama.

How to Contact Submit outline, 3 sample chapters, SASE. Responds in 1 month to queries.

Recent Sales *Rosey in the Present Tense*, by Louise Hawes (Walker); *Flash Factor*, by William H. Lovejoy (Kensington); *Lucky Leonardo*, by Jonathan Canter (Landmark); *Hidden Child*, by Isaac Millman (Frances Foster Books, FSG).

Terms Agent receives 15% commission on domestic sales; 20% commission on foreign sales; 10% commission on dramatic rights sales. Offers written contract, binding for 1 year. Charges clients for extra office expenses, foreign postage, copying, legal fees (when agreed upon).
Tips "We are always looking for interesting literary voices."

☑ APPLESEEDS MANAGEMENT
200 E. 30th St., Suite 302, San Bernardino CA 92404. (909)882-1667. **Contact:** S. James Foiles. Estab. 1988. 40% of clients are new/unpublished writers. Currently handles: 15% nonfiction books; 85% novels.
Represents Nonfiction books, novels. **Considers these nonfiction areas:** True crime/investigative. **Considers these fiction areas:** Detective/police/crime; mystery/suspense.
How to Contact Query with SASE. Responds in 2 weeks to queries; 2 months to mss.
Recent Sales This agency prefers not to share information on specific sales.
Terms Agent receives 10-15% commission on domestic sales; 20% commission on foreign sales. Offers written contract, binding for 1-7 years.
Tips "Appleseeds specializes in mysteries with a detective who could be in a continuing series because readership of mysteries is expanding."

☑ ARCADIA
31 Lake Place N., Danbury CT 06810. E-mail: arcadialit@att.net. **Contact:** Victoria Gould Pryor. Member of AAR.
Represents Nonfiction books (readable, serious), literary and commercial fiction. **Considers these nonfiction areas:** Biography/autobiography; business/economics; current affairs; history; memoirs; psychology; science/technology; true crime/investigative; women's issues/studies; medicine; investigative journalism; culture; classical music; life transforming self-help.
> ⚷ "I'm a very hands-on agent, necessary in this competitive marketplace. I work with authors on revisions until whatever we present to publishers is as perfect as it can be. I represent talented, dedicated, intelligent, and ambitious writers who are looking for a long-term relationship based on professional success and mutual respect." No science fiction/fantasy or children's/YA. "We are only able to read fiction submissions from previously published authors."
How to Contact Query with SASE. E-mail queries accepted without attachments.
Recent Sales This agency prefers not to share information on specific sales.

☑ AUTHENTIC CREATIONS LITERARY AGENCY
875 Lawrenceville-Suwanee Rd., Suite 310-306, Lawrenceville GA 30043. (770)339-3774. Fax: (770)339-7126. E-mail: ron@authenticcreations.com. Website: www.authenticcreations.com. **Contact:** Mary Lee Laitsch. Estab. 1993. Member of AAR, Authors Guild. Represents 70 clients. 30% of clients are new/unpublished writers. Currently handles: 60% nonfiction books; 40% novels.
● Prior to becoming an agent, Ms. Laitsch was a librarian and elementary school teacher; Mr. Laitsch was an attorney and a writer.
Member Agents Mary Lee Laitsch; Ronald Laitsch; Jason Laitsch.
Represents Nonfiction books, novels, scholarly books. **Considers these nonfiction areas:** Anthropology/archaeology; biography/autobiography; child guidance/parenting; crafts/hobbies; current affairs; history; how-to; science/technology; self-help/personal improvement; sports; true crime/investigative; women's issues/studies. **Considers these fiction areas:** Action/adventure; contemporary issues; detective/police/crime; family saga; literary; mainstream/contemporary; mystery/suspense; romance; sports; thriller.
How to Contact Query with SASE. No e-mail or fax queries. Considers simultaneous queries. Responds in 2 weeks to queries; 2 months to mss.
Recent Sales Sold 20 titles in the last year. *Secret Agent*, by Robyn Spizman and Mark Johnston (Simon & Schuster); *Beauchamp Beseiged*, by Elaine Knighton (Harlequin); *Visible Differences*, by Dominic Pulera (Continuum).
Terms Agent receives 15% commission on domestic sales; 15% commission on foreign sales. Charges clients for photocopying.
Tips "We thoroughly enjoy what we do. What makes being an agent so satisfying for us is having the opportunity to work with authors who are as excited about the works they write as we are about representing them."

☑ THE AXELROD AGENCY
55 Main St., P.O. Box 357, Chatham NY 12037. (518)392-2100. Fax: (518)392-2944. E-mail: steve@axelrodagency.com. **Contact:** Steven Axelrod. Estab. 1983. Member of AAR. Represents 20-30 clients. 1% of clients are new/unpublished writers. Currently handles: 5% nonfiction books; 95% novels.

• Prior to becoming an agent, Mr. Axelrod was a book club editor.

Represents Nonfiction books, novels. **Considers these fiction areas:** Mystery/suspense; romance; women's.

How to Contact Query with SASE. Considers simultaneous queries. Responds in 3 weeks to queries; 6 weeks to mss. Returns materials only with SASE. Obtains most new clients through recommendations from others.

Recent Sales This agency prefers not to share information on specific sales.

Terms Agent receives 15% commission on domestic sales; 20% commission on foreign sales. No written contract.

Writers' Conferences Romance Writers of America (July).

⚅ LORETTA BARRETT BOOKS, INC.

101 Fifth Ave., New York NY 10003. (212)242-3420. Fax: (212)807-9579. E-mail: mail@lorettabarrettbooks.com. **Contact:** Loretta A. Barrett or Nick Mullendore. Estab. 1990. Member of AAR. Currently handles: 60% nonfiction books; 40% novels.

• Prior to opening her agency, Ms. Barrett was vice president and executive editor at Doubleday and editor-in-chief of Anchor Books.

Represents Nonfiction books, novels. **Considers these nonfiction areas:** Biography/autobiography; business/economics; child guidance/parenting; creative nonfiction; current affairs; ethnic/cultural interests; gay/lesbian issues; government/politics/law; health/medicine; history; language/literature/criticism; memoirs; money/finance; multicultural; nature/environment; philosophy; popular culture; psychology; religious/inspirational; science/technology; self-help/personal improvement; sociology; spirituality; sports; women's issues/studies; nutrition. **Considers these fiction areas:** Action/adventure; contemporary issues; detective/police/crime; ethnic; family saga; historical; literary; mainstream/contemporary; mystery/suspense; psychic/supernatural; thriller.

○⟶ This agency specializes in general interest books. No children's, juvenile, science fiction or fantasy.

How to Contact Query with SASE. No e-mail or fax queries. Considers simultaneous queries. Responds in 6 weeks to queries. Returns materials only with SASE.

Recent Sales *Fantastic Voyage*, by Ray Kurzweil and Terry Grossman (Rodale); *The Singularity Is Near*, by Ray Kurzweil (Viking); *Invisible Heroes*, by Belleruth Naparstek (Bantam); *Islands of the Mind*, by John Gillis (Palgrave); *Letters to a Young Catholic* and *Cathedral and the Cube*, by George Weigel (Basic Books); *Talk to the Mirror*, by Florine Mark (John Wiley & Co.); *The Meaning of the 21st Century*, by James Martin (Riverhead); *Unattended Sorrow*, by Steve Levine (Rodale).

Terms Agent receives 15% commission on domestic sales; 20% commission on foreign sales. Offers written contract. Charges clients for shipping and photocopying.

Writers' Conferences San Diego State University Writer's Conference; Pacific Northwest Writer's Association; SEAK Medical Writer's Conference.

⚅ MEREDITH BERNSTEIN LITERARY AGENCY

2112 Broadway, Suite 503A, New York NY 10023. (212)799-1007. Fax: (212)799-1145. Estab. 1981. Member of AAR. Represents 85 clients. 20% of clients are new/unpublished writers. Currently handles: 50% nonfiction books; 50% fiction.

• Prior to opening her agency, Ms. Bernstein served in another agency for 5 years.

Member Agents Meredith Bernstein, Elizabeth Cavanaugh.

Represents Nonfiction books, fiction of all kinds. **Considers these nonfiction areas:** Any area of nonfiction in which the author has an established platform. **Considers these fiction areas:** Literary; mystery/suspense; romance; thriller; women's.

○⟶ This agency does not specialize. It is "very eclectic."

How to Contact Query with SASE. No e-mail or fax queries. Considers simultaneous queries. Obtains most new clients through recommendations from others, conferences, also develops and packages own ideas.

Recent Sales *Tripping the Prom Queen: Envy, Competition & Jealousy Among Women*, by Susan Shepiro Barash (St. Martin's Press); *Sleep on It*, by Carol Gordon (Hyperion); 3-book deal of contemporary romances by Sandra Hill to Warner Books; 6-book deal by *The New York Times* best-selling romance writer Sharon Sala (aka Dinah McCall) to Mira Books/Harlequin.

Terms Agent receives 15% commission on domestic sales; 20% commission on foreign sales. Charges clients $75 disbursement fee/year.

Writers' Conferences SouthWest Writers Conference (Albuquereque, August); Rocky Moutnain Writers' Conference (Denver, September); Golden Triangle (Beaumont TX, October); Pacific Northwest Writers Conference; Austin League Writers Conference; Willamette Writers Conference (Portland OR); Lafayette Writers Conference (Lafayette LA); Surrey Writers Conference (Surrey BC); San Diego State University Writers Conference (San Diego CA).

◑ DANIEL BIAL AGENCY

41 W. 83rd St., Suite 5-C, New York NY 10024-5246. (212)721-1786. Fax: (309)213-0230. E-mail: dbialagency @juno.com. **Contact:** Daniel Bial. Estab. 1992. Represents under 50 clients. 15% of clients are new/unpublished writers. Currently handles: 95% nonfiction books; 5% novels.

● Prior to opening his agency, Mr. Bial was an editor for 15 years.

Represents Nonfiction books, novels. **Considers these nonfiction areas:** Animals; anthropology/archaeology; biography/autobiography; business/economics; child guidance/parenting; cooking/foods/nutrition; current affairs; ethnic/cultural interests; government/politics/law; history; how-to; humor/satire; language/literature/criticism; memoirs; military/war; money/finance; music/dance; nature/environment; New Age/metaphysics; popular culture; psychology; religious/inspirational; science/technology; self-help/personal improvement; sociology; spirituality; sports; theater/film; travel; true crime/investigative; women's issues/studies. **Considers these fiction areas:** Action/adventure; contemporary issues; detective/police/crime; erotica; ethnic; humor/satire; literary.

How to Contact Submit proposal package, outline. Responds in 2 weeks to queries. Returns materials only with SASE. Obtains most new clients through recommendations from others, solicitations, "good rolodex."

Recent Sales This agency recently had a No. 1 *New York Times* bestseller with *Osama Bin Ladin: The Man Who Delcared War on America*, by Yossef Bodansky.

Terms Agent receives 15% commission on domestic sales; 25% commission on foreign sales. Offers written contract, binding for 1 year with cancellation clause. Charges clients for overseas calls, overnight mailing, photocopying, messenger expenses.

Tips "Publishers want their authors to have platforms. In other words, they want the authors to have the ability to sell their work or get themselves in the media even before the book comes out. And successful agents get publishers what they want."

◑ BIGSCORE PRODUCTIONS, INC.

P.O. Box 4575, Lancaster PA 17604. (717)293-0247. Fax: (717)293-1945. E-mail: bigscore@bigscoreproductions. com. Website: www.bigscoreproductions.com. **Contact:** David A. Robie, agent. Estab. 1995. Represents 50-75 clients. 25% of clients are new/unpublished writers.

Represents Nonfiction and fiction (see website for categories of interest).

○┐ This agency specializes in inspirational and self-help nonfiction and fiction, and has over 20 years in the publishing and agenting business.

How to Contact See website for submission guidelines. Query by e-mail or mail. No fax queries. Considers simultaneous queries. Responds in 2 months to proposals.

Terms Agent receives 15% commission on domestic sales. Offers written contract, binding for 6 months. Charges clients for expedited shipping, ms photocopying and preparation, and books for subsidiary rights submissions.

Tips "Very open to taking on new clients. Submit a well-prepared proposal that will take minimal fine-tuning for presentation to publishers. Nonfiction writers must be highly marketable and media savvy—the more established in speaking or in your profession, the better. Bigscore Productions works with all major general and Christian publishers"

◐ DAVID BLACK LITERARY AGENCY

156 Fifth Ave., Suite 608, New York NY 10010-7002. (212)242-5080. Fax: (212)924-6609. **Contact:** David Black, owner. Estab. 1990. Member of AAR. Represents 150 clients. Currently handles: 90% nonfiction books; 10% novels.

Member Agents David Black; Susan Raihofer (general nonfiction to literary fiction); Gary Morris (commercial fiction to psychology); Joy E. Tutela (general nonfiction to literary fiction); Leigh Ann Eliseo.

Represents Nonfiction books, novels. **Considers these nonfiction areas:** Biography/autobiography; business/economics; government/politics/law; history; memoirs; military/war; money/finance; multicultural; sports. **Considers these fiction areas:** Literary; mainstream/contemporary; commercial.

○┐ This agency specializes in business, sports, politics and novels.

How to Contact Query with SASE, outline. No e-mail or fax queries. Considers simultaneous queries. Responds in 2 months to queries. Returns materials only with SASE.

Recent Sales *Body for Life*, by Bill Phillips with Mike D'Orso (HarperCollins); *Devil in the White City*, by Erik Carson; The Don't Know Much About series by Ken Davis.

Terms Agent receives 15% commission on domestic sales. Charges clients for photocopying and books purchased for sale of foreign rights.

◐ BLEECKER STREET ASSOCIATES, INC.

532 LaGuardia Place, #617, New York NY 10012. (212)677-4492. Fax: (212)388-0001. **Contact:** Agnes Birnbaum. Estab. 1984. Member of AAR, RWA, MWA. Represents 60 clients. 20% of clients are new/unpublished writers. Currently handles: 75% nonfiction books; 25% novels.

- Prior to becoming an agent, Ms. Birnbaum was a senior editor at Simon & Schuster, Dutton/Signet, and other publishing houses.

Represents Nonfiction books, novels. **Considers these nonfiction areas:** Animals; biography/autobiography; business/economics; child guidance/parenting; computers/electronic; cooking/foods/nutrition; current affairs; ethnic/cultural interests; government/politics/law; health/medicine; history; how-to; memoirs; military/war; money/finance; nature/environment; New Age/metaphysics; popular culture; psychology; religious/inspirational; science/technology; self-help/personal improvement; sociology; sports; true crime/investigative; women's issues/studies. **Considers these fiction areas:** Ethnic; historical; literary; mystery/suspense; romance; thriller; women's interest.

> **O→** "We're very hands-on and accessible. We try to be truly creative in our submission approaches. We've had especially good luck with first-time authors." Does not want to receive science fiction, westerns, poetry, children's books, academic/scholarly/professional books, plays, scripts, short stories.

How to Contact Query with SASE. No e-mail, phone, or fax queries. Considers simultaneous queries. Responds in 2 weeks to queries; 1 month to mss. Returns materials only with SASE. Obtains most new clients through recommendations from others, solicitations, conferences, "plus, I will approach someone with a letter if his/her work impresses me."

Recent Sales Sold 20 titles in the last year. *How America Got It Right*, by Bevin Alexander (Crown); *The Dim Sum of All Things*, by Kim Wong Keltner (Morrow/Avon); *American Bee*, by James Maguire (Rodale); *Guide to the Galaxy*, by Pat Barnes-Svarney (Sterling); *Deal Breakers*, by Maia Dunkel (Doubleday).

Terms Agent receives 15% commission on domestic sales; 25% commission on foreign sales. Offers written contract; 1-month notice must be given to terminate contract. Charges for postage, long distance, fax, messengers, photocopies, not to exceed $200.

Tips "Keep query letters short and to the point; include only information pertaining to book or background as writer. Try to avoid superlatives in description. Work needs to stand on its own, so how much editing it may have received has no place in a query letter."

THE BLUMER LITERARY AGENCY, INC.

350 Seventh Ave., Suite 2003, New York NY 10001-5013. (212)947-3040. **Contact:** Ms. Olivia B. Blumer. Estab. 2002; Board member of AAR. Represents 34 clients. 60% of clients are new/unpublished writers. Currently handles: 67% nonfiction books; 33% novels.

- Prior to becoming an agent, Ms. Blumer spent 25 years in publishing—subsidiary rights, publicity, editorial.

Represents Nonfiction and fiction. **Considers these nonfiction areas:** Agriculture/horticulture; animals; anthropology/archaeology; art/architecture/design; biography/autobiography; business/economics; cooking/foods/nutrition; ethnic/cultural interests; health/medicine; how-to; humor/satire; language/literature/criticism; memoirs; money/finance; nature/environment; photography; popular culture; psychology; religious/inspirational; self-help/personal improvement; true crime/investigative; women's issues/studies; crafts/hobbies, interior design/decorating, New Age/metaphysics. **Considers these fiction areas:** Detective/police/crime; ethnic; family saga; feminist; historical; humor/satire; literary; mainstream/contemporary; mystery/suspense; regional; thriller.

> **O→** Actively seeking quality fiction, practical nonfiction, memoir with a larger purpose.

How to Contact Query with SASE. No e-mail or fax queries. Responds in 2 weeks to queries; 4-6 weeks to mss. Returns materials only with SASE. Obtains most new clients through recommendations from others, but significant exceptions have come from slush pile.

Recent Sales *Almost French*, by Sarah Turnbull (Gotham/Penguin); *What Happened to Henry*, by Sharon Pywell (Putnam). Other clients include Joan Anderson, Marialisa Calta, Ellen Rolfes, Mark Forstater, Laura Karr, Liz McGregor, Constance Snow, Lauri Ward, Michelle Curry Wright, Susann Cokal, Dennis L. Smith.

Terms Agent receives 15% commission on domestic sales; 20% commission on foreign sales. Charges for photocopying, overseas shipping, and Fed Ex/UPS.

◖ BOOK DEALS, INC.

244 Fifth Ave., Suite 2164, New York NY 10001-7604. (212)252-2701. Fax: (212)591-6211. **Contact:** Caroline Francis Carney. Estab. 1996. Member of AAR. Represents 40 clients. 15% of clients are new/unpublished writers. Currently handles: 85% nonfiction books; 15% novels.

- Prior to opening her agency, Ms. Carney was editorial director for a consumer book imprint within Times Mirror and held senior editorial positions in McGraw-Hill and NYIF/Simon & Schuster.

Represents Nonfiction books, novels (commercial and literary). **Considers these nonfiction areas:** Business/economics; child guidance/parenting; ethnic/cultural interests; health/medicine (nutrition); history; how-to; money/finance; multicultural; popular culture; psychology (popular); religious/inspirational; science/technology; self-help/personal improvement; spirituality. **Considers these fiction areas:** Ethnic; literary; mainstream/contemporary; women's (contemporary); urban literature.

> ⌖ This agency specializes in highly commercial nonfiction and books for African-American readers and women. Actively seeking well-crafted fiction and nonfiction from authors with engaging voices and impeccable credentials.

How to Contact Query with SASE. Considers simultaneous queries.

Recent Sales *Eat Right for Your Personality Type*, by Dr. Robert Kushner & Nancy Kushner (St. Martin's Press); *Self-Proclaimed*, by Rochelle Shapiro (Simon & Schuster); *Par for the Course*, by Alice Dye and Mark Shaw (HarperCollins).

Terms Agent receives 15% commission on domestic sales; 20% commission on foreign sales. Offers written contract. Charges clients for photocopying and postage.

BOOKENDS, LLC

136 Long Hill Rd., Gillette NJ 07933. (908)362-0090. E-mail: editor@bookends-inc.com. Website: www.bookends-inc.com. **Contact:** Jessica Faust, Jacky Sach or Kim Lionetti. Estab. 1999. Represents 50+ clients. 20% of clients are new/unpublished writers. Currently handles: 50% nonfiction books; 50% novels.

> • "Please review submission guidelines on our website before sending anything to BookEnds." Fiction areas of interest include mystery, romance, chick lit, suspense, women's fiction. Current nonfiction areas of interest include parenting, spirituality, business, finance, true crime, general self-help.

Represents Nonfiction books, novels. **Considers these nonfiction areas:** Business/economics; child guidance/parenting; ethnic/cultural interests; gay/lesbian issues; health/medicine; how-to; money/finance; New Age/metaphysics; psychology; religious/inspirational; self-help/personal improvement; women's issues/studies. **Considers these fiction areas:** Mainstream/contemporary; mystery/suspense; romance; thriller; detective/police/crime/cozies.

> ⌖ BookEnds does not want to receive children's books, screenplays, science fiction, poetry, technical/military thrillers.

How to Contact Submit outline, 3 sample chapters (but no more than 50 pages).

◎ BOOKS & SUCH

4788 Carissa Ave., Santa Rosa CA 95405. (707)538-4184. Fax: (707)538-3937. E-mail: janet@janetgrant.com. Website: janetgrant.com. **Contact:** Janet Kobobel Grant. Estab. 1996. Member of CBA (associate). Represents 60 clients. 5% of clients are new/unpublished writers. Currently handles: 49% nonfiction books; 50% novels; 1% children's picture books.

> • Prior to becoming an agent, Ms. Grant was an editor for Zondervan and managing editor for *Focus on the Family*.

Represents Nonfiction books, novels, children's picture books. **Considers these nonfiction areas:** Child guidance/parenting; humor/satire; juvenile nonfiction; religious/inspirational; self-help/personal improvement; women's issues/studies. **Considers these fiction areas:** Contemporary issues; family saga; historical; juvenile; mainstream/contemporary; picture books; religious/inspirational; romance; African-American adult.

> ⌖ This agency specializes in "general and inspirational fiction, romance, and in the Christian booksellers market." Actively seeking "material appropriate to the Christian market."

How to Contact Query with SASE. Considers simultaneous queries. Responds in 1 month to queries; 2 months to mss. Returns materials only with SASE. Obtains most new clients through recommendations from others, conferences.

Recent Sales Sold 60 titles in the last year. *Boo Hiss*, by Renee Gutterridge; *Mozart's Sister*, by Nancy Moser; *The Fine China Plate*, by Robin Jones Gunn. Other clients include Joanna Weaver, Janet McHenry, Jane Orcutt, Gayle Roper, Stephanie Grace Whitson.

Terms Agent receives 15% commission on domestic sales; 15% commission on foreign sales. Offers written contract; 2-month notice must be given to terminate contract. Charges clients for postage, photocopying, telephone calls, fax, and express mail.

Writers' Conferences Mt. Hermon Writers Conference (Mt. Hermon CA, March); Wrangling Writers (Tucson AZ, January); Glorieta Writer's Conference (Glorieta NM, October).

Tips "The heart of my motivation is to develop relationships with the authors I serve, to do what I can to shine the light of success on them, and to help be a caretaker of their gifts and time."

◎ GEORGES BORCHARDT, INC.

136 E. 57th St., New York NY 10022. (212)753-5785. Fax: (212)838-6518. Estab. 1967. Member of AAR. Represents 200 clients. 10% of clients are new/unpublished writers. Currently handles: 60% nonfiction books; 37% novels; 1% novellas; 1% juvenile books; 1% poetry.

Member Agents Anne Borchardt; Georges Borchardt; Valerie Borchardt.

Represents Nonfiction books, novels. **Considers these nonfiction areas:** Anthropology/archaeology; biography/autobiography; current affairs; history; memoirs; travel; women's issues/studies. **Considers these fiction areas:** Literary.

O→ This agency specializes in literary fiction and outstanding nonfiction.

How to Contact Responds in 1 week to queries; 1 month to mss. Obtains most new clients through recommendations from others.

Recent Sales Sold 80 titles in the last year. *Tooth and Claw*, by T. Coraghessan Boyle (Viking/Penguin); *Saturday*, by Ian McEwan (Nan Talese/Doubleday); *Where Shall I Wander*, by John Ashbery (HarperCollins); *Anti-Intellectual Tradition*, by Susan Jacoby (Pantheon); *Anti Civilization*, by Anne Applebaum (Doubleday).

Terms Agent receives 15% commission on domestic sales; 20% commission on foreign sales. Offers written contract. "We charge clients cost of outside photocopying and shipping manuscripts or books overseas."

◑ THE BARBARA BOVA LITERARY AGENCY

3951 Gulfshore Blvd. N., PH1-B, Naples FL 34103. (941)649-7237. Fax: (239)649-7263. Website: www.barbara bovaliteraryagency.com. **Contact:** Barbara Bova. Estab. 1976. Represents 30 clients. Currently handles: 20% nonfiction books; 80% novels.

Represents Nonfiction books, novels. **Considers these nonfiction areas:** Biography/autobiography; science/technology; self-help/personal improvement; true crime/investigative; women's issues/studies; social sciences. **Considers these fiction areas:** Action/adventure; detective/police/crime; glitz; mystery/suspense; science fiction; thriller; women's; chick lit; teen lit.

O→ This agency specializes in fiction and nonfiction, hard and soft science.

How to Contact Query through website. Obtains most new clients through recommendations from others.

Recent Sales Sold 6 titles in the last year. *Mercury*, by Ben Bova; *Magic Street*, by Orson Scott Card; *Malpractice*, by Aaron Johnston; *Walks on Shadows*, by Joyce Henderson; *Inuit*, by M. Shayne Bell.

Terms Agent receives 15% commission on domestic sales; 20% commission on foreign sales.

Tips This agency also handles foreign rights, movies, television, audio.

◐ BRANDT & HOCHMAN LITERARY AGENTS, INC.

1501 Broadway, Suite 2310, New York NY 10036. (212)840-5760. Fax: (212)840-5776. **Contact:** Carl Brandt; Gail Hochman; Marianne Merola; Charles Schlessiger. Estab. 1913. Member of AAR. Represents 200 clients.

Represents Nonfiction books, novels, short story collections, juvenile books, journalism. **Considers these nonfiction areas:** Biography/autobiography; current affairs; ethnic/cultural interests; government/politics/law; history; women's issues/studies. **Considers these fiction areas:** Contemporary issues; ethnic; historical; literary; mainstream/contemporary; mystery/suspense; romance; thriller; young adult.

How to Contact Query with SASE. No e-mail or fax queries. Considers simultaneous queries. Responds in 1 month to queries. Returns materials only with SASE. Obtains most new clients through recommendations from others.

Recent Sales This agency prefers not to share information on specific sales. Clients include Scott Turow, Carlos Fuentes, Ursula Hegi, Michael Cunningham, Mary Pope Osborne, Julia Glass.

Terms Agent receives 15% commission on domestic sales; 20% commission on foreign sales. Charges clients for "manuscript duplication or other special expenses agreed to in advance."

Tips "Write a letter which will give the agent a sense of you as a professional writer, your long-term interests as well as a short description of the work at hand."

◑ BARBARA BRAUN ASSOCIATES, INC.

104 Fifth Ave., 7th Floor, New York NY 10011. Fax: (212)604-9041. E-mail: barbarabraun@earthlink.net. Website: www.barbarabraunagency.com. **Contact:** Barbara Braun. Member of AAR.

Member Agents Barbara Braun; John F. Baker.

Represents Nonfiction books, novels.

O→ "Our fiction is strong on stories for women, historical and multicultural stories, as well as mysteries and thrillers. We're interested in narrative nonfiction and books by journalists. We do not represent poetry, science fiction, fantasy, horror or screenplays." Look online for more details.

How to Contact Query with SASE. Accepts e-mail queries.

Recent Sales *The Forest Lover*, by Susan Vreeland (Viking/Penguin); *The Lost Van Gogh*, by A.J. Zerries (Tor/Forge); *Sakharov: Science and Freedom*, by Gennady Gorelik and Antonina Bouis (Oxford University Press).

Terms Agent receives 15% commission on domestic sales; 20% commission on foreign sales.

Ⓝ ◐ RICK BROADHEAD & ASSOCIATES LITERARY AGENCY

501-47 St. Clair Ave. W., Toronto ON M4V 3A5 Canada. (416)929-0516. Fax: (416)927-8732. E-mail: rickb@rba literary.com. Website: www.rbaliterary.com. **Contact:** Rick Broadhead, president. Estab. 2002. Member of

The Authors Guild. Represents 20 clients. 50% of clients are new/unpublished writers. Currently handles: 85% nonfiction books; 5% novels; 10% juvenile books.

• Mr. Broadhead discovered his passion for books when he co-authored his first bestseller at the age of 23. His vast knowledge of the publishing industry, both as an author and an agent, and his relationships with American publishers have allowed the agency to consistently negotiate excellent deals for its clients. Mr. Broadhead brings a passion, tenacity and energy to agenting that his clients love.

Member Agents Rick Broadhead (all genres, primarily nonfiction).

Represents Nonfiction books, novels, juvenile books. **Considers these nonfiction areas:** Animals; anthropology/archaeology; art/architecture/design; biography/autobiography; business/economics; child guidance/parenting; computers/electronic; cooking/foods/nutrition; crafts/hobbies; current affairs; education; ethnic/cultural interests; government/politics/law; health/medicine; history; how-to; humor/satire; language/literature/criticism; memoirs; military/war; money/finance; music/dance; nature/environment; popular culture; psychology; religious/inspirational; science/technology; self-help/personal improvement; sociology; sports; true crime/investigative; women's issues/studies; interior design/decorating, juvenile nonfiction. **Considers these fiction areas:** Action/adventure; detective/police/crime; humor/satire; juvenile; literary; mainstream/contemporary; mystery/suspense; picture books; thriller.

O→ This established agency represents American authors to American and foreign publishers in a wide vareity of genres, including business, self-help, gift books, parenting, memoir, reference, history/politics, current affairs, health/medicine, pop culture, and humor. The agency is deliberately small, which allows clients to receive personalized service to maximize the success of their book projects and brands. The agency sells projects to foreign publishers (United Kingdom, Australia/New Zealand) directly and in partnership with co-agents. Actively seeking compelling nonfiction proposals, especially from authors with an established media platform (television, radio, print exposure). Does not want television or movie scripts or poetry.

How to Contact If sending by mail, include a complete proposal and 1-2 sample chapters. Agency will reply only to projects of interest. E-mail queries preferred. Considers simultaneous queries. Responds in 1-2 weeks to queries; 4 weeks to mss. Obtains most new clients through solicitations, e-mail queries, referrals from existing clients.

Recent Sales Sold 9 titles in the last year. *Confessions of a Military Housewife*, by Sarah Smiley (Penguin); *The Full-Flavor Diet*, by David Katz, MD (Rodale); *Corporate Canaries: How to Avoid Business Disasters with a Coalminer's Secrets*, by Gary Sutton (Thomas Nelson Business Books). Other clients include Mat Connolley, Marianne Szymanski, Michelle Schoffro Cook, Al Heavens, Terence Denman, George Lorenzo, Kim Danger.

Terms Agent receives 15% commission on domestic sales; 20-25% commission on foreign sales. Offers written contract.

Tips ''The agency has excellent relationships with New York publishers and most of the agency's clients are American authors. The agency welcomes queries by e-mail.''

◪ CURTIS BROWN, LTD.

10 Astor Place, New York NY 10003-6935. (212)473-5400. Also Peter Ginsberg, President at CBEF: 1750 Montgomery St., San Fancisco CA 94111. (415)954-8566. Member of AAR; signatory of WGA.

Member Agents Laura Blake Peterson; Ellen Geiger; Emilie Jacobson, senior vice president; Maureen Walters, senior vice president; Ginger Knowlton, vice president (adult, children's); Timothy Knowlton, CEO (film, screenplays); Ed Wintle; Mitchell Waters; Elizabeth Harding; Kirsten Manges; Dave Barbor (translation rights).

Represents Nonfiction books, novels, short story collections, novellas, juvenile books, poetry books, movie scripts, feature film, TV movie of the week. **Considers these nonfiction areas:** Agriculture/horticulture; americana; animals; anthropology/archaeology; art/architecture/design; biography/autobiography; business/economics; child guidance/parenting; computers/electronic; cooking/foods/nutrition; crafts/hobbies; creative nonfiction; current affairs; education; ethnic/cultural interests; gardening; gay/lesbian issues; government/politics/law; health/medicine; history; how-to; humor/satire; interior design/decorating; juvenile nonfiction; language/literature/criticism; memoirs; military/war; money/finance; multicultural; music/dance; nature/environment; New Age/metaphysics; philosophy; photography; popular culture; psychology; recreation; regional; religious/inspirational; science/technology; self-help/personal improvement; sex; sociology; software; spirituality; sports; theater/film; translation; travel; true crime/investigative; women's issues/studies; young adult. **Considers these fiction areas:** Action/adventure; comic books/cartoon; confession; contemporary issues; detective/police/crime; erotica; ethnic; experimental; family saga; fantasy; feminist; gay/lesbian; glitz; gothic; hi-lo; historical; horror; humor/satire; juvenile; literary; mainstream/contemporary; military/war; multicultural; multimedia; mystery/suspense; New Age; occult; picture books; plays; poetry; poetry in translation; psychic/supernatural; regional; religious/inspirational; romance; science fiction; short story collections; spiritual; sports; thriller; translation; westerns/frontier; young adult; women's.

How to Contact Query individual agent with SASE. Prefers to read materials exclusively. *No unsolicited mss.*

No e-mail or fax queries. Responds in 3 weeks to queries; 5 weeks to mss. Obtains most new clients through recommendations from others, solicitations, conferences.

Recent Sales This agency prefers not to share information on specific sales.

Terms Offers written contract. Charges for photocopying, some postage.

☑ BROWNE & MILLER LITERARY ASSOCIATES

410 S. Michigan Ave., Suite 460, Chicago IL 60605-1465. (312)922-3063. E-mail: mail@browneandmiller.com. **Contact:** Danielle Egan-Miller. Estab. 1971. Member of AAR, RWA, MWA, Author's Guild. Represents 150 clients. 2% of clients are new/unpublished writers. Currently handles: 40% nonfiction books; 60% novels.

Member Agents Danielle Egan-Miller.

Represents Nonfiction books, novels. **Considers these nonfiction areas:** Agriculture/horticulture; animals; anthropology/archaeology; biography/autobiography; business/economics; child guidance/parenting; cooking/foods/nutrition; crafts/hobbies; creative nonfiction; current affairs; ethnic/cultural interests; health/medicine; how-to; humor/satire; juvenile nonfiction; memoirs; money/finance; nature/environment; popular culture; psychology; religious/inspirational; science/technology; self-help/personal improvement; sociology; sports; true crime/investigative; women's issues/studies. **Considers these fiction areas:** Contemporary issues; detective/police/crime; ethnic; family saga; glitz; historical; juvenile; literary; mainstream/contemporary; mystery/suspense; religious/inspirational; romance (contemporary, gothic, historical, regency); sports; thriller.

> ⚡ "We are generalists looking for professional writers with finely honed skills in writing. We are partial to authors with promotion savvy. We work closely with our authors through the whole publishing process, from proposal to after publication." Actively seeking highly commercial mainstream fiction and nonfiction. Does not represent poetry, short stories, plays, screenplays, articles, children's books.

How to Contact Query by mail, SASE required. *No unsolicited mss.* Prefers to read material exclusively. Responds in 1 month to queries. Returns materials only with SASE. Obtains most new clients through "referrals, queries by professional, marketable authors."

Terms Agent receives 15% commission on domestic sales; 20% commission on foreign sales. Offers written contract, binding for 2 years. Charges clients for photocopying, overseas postage, faxes, phone calls.

Writers' Conferences BEA (June); Frankfurt Book Fair (October); RWA (July); CBA (July); London International Book Fair (March); Boucheron (October).

Tips "If interested in agency representation, be well informed."

Ⓝ ☑ PEMA BROWNE, LTD.

11 Tena Place, Valley Cottage NY 10989. Website: www.pemabrowneltd.com. **Contact:** Perry Browne or Pema Browne. Estab. 1966. Signatory of WGA. Represents 30 clients. Currently handles: 40% nonfiction books; 30% novels & romance novels; 25% juvenile books.

> • Prior to opening their agency, Mr. Browne was a radio and TV performer; Ms. Browne was a fine artist and art buyer.

Member Agents Pema Browne (children's fiction and nonfiction, adult fiction and nonfiction).

Represents Nonfiction books, novels, juvenile books, reference books. **Considers these nonfiction areas:** Business/economics; child guidance/parenting; cooking/foods/nutrition; ethnic/cultural interests; gay/lesbian issues; health/medicine; how-to; juvenile nonfiction; military/war; money/finance; nature/environment; New Age/metaphysics; popular culture; psychology; religious/inspirational; self-help/personal improvement; spirituality; sports; true crime/investigative; women's issues/studies; reference. **Considers these fiction areas:** Action/adventure; contemporary issues; detective/police/crime; feminist; gay/lesbian; glitz; historical; humor/satire; juvenile; literary; mainstream/contemporary (commercial); mystery/suspense; picture books; psychic/supernatural; religious/inspirational; romance (contemporary, gothic, historical, regency); young adult.

> ⚡ "We are not accepting any new projects or authors until further notice." Seeking adult nonfiction, romance, juvenile, middle grade, some young adult, picture books, novelty books.

How to Contact Query with SASE. No e-mail or fax queries. Responds in 6 weeks to queries; 6-8 weeks to mss. Returns materials only with SASE. Obtains most new clients through "editors, authors, *LMP, Guide to Literary Agents* and as a result of longevity!"

Recent Sales *The Savior*, by Faye Snowden (Dafina/Kensington); *Salvation*, by Susan Scott Cora (Verlag); *Point Horror-Dark I and II*, by Linda Cargill (Scholastic UK).

Terms Agent receives 15% commission on domestic sales; 20% commission on foreign sales.

Tips "We do not review manuscripts that have been sent out to publishers. If writing romance, be sure to receive guidelines from various romance publishers. In nonfiction, one must have credentials to lend credence to a proposal. Make sure of margins, double-space and use clean, dark type."

⊘ SHEREE BYKOFSKY ASSOCIATES, INC.

16 W. 36th St., 13th Floor, New York NY 10018. E-mail: shereebee@aol.com. Website: www.shereebee.com. **Contact:** Sheree Bykofsky. Estab. 1984, incorporated 1991. Member of AAR, ASJA, WNBA. Currently handles: 80% nonfiction books; 20% novels.

- Prior to opening her agency, Ms. Bykofsky served as executive editor of The Stonesong Press and managing editor of Chiron Press. She is also the author or co-author of more than 17 books, including *The Complete Idiot's Guide to Getting Published.* Ms. Bykofsky teaches publishing at NYU and The 92nd St. Y.

Member Agents Janet Rosen, associate; Megan Buckley, associate.

Represents Nonfiction books, novels. **Considers these nonfiction areas:** Americana; animals; art/architecture/ design; biography/autobiography; business/economics; child guidance/parenting; cooking/foods/nutrition; crafts/hobbies; creative nonfiction; current affairs; education; ethnic/cultural interests; gardening; gay/lesbian issues; government/politics/law; health/medicine; history; how-to; humor/satire; interior design/decorating; language/literature/criticism; memoirs; military/war; money/finance (personal finance); multicultural; music/ dance; nature/environment; New Age/metaphysics; philosophy; photography; popular culture; psychology; recreation; regional; religious/inspirational; science/technology; self-help/personal improvement; sex; sociology; spirituality; sports; theater/film; translation; travel; true crime/investigative; women's issues/studies; anthropolgy. **Considers these fiction areas:** Literary; mainstream/contemporary; mystery/suspense.

- O→ This agency specializes in popular reference nonfiction, commercial fiction with a literary quality, and mysteries. "I have wide-ranging interests, but it really depends on quality of writing, originality, and how a particular project appeals to me (or not). I take on fiction when I completely love it—it doesn't matter what area or genre." Does not want to receive poetry, material for children, screenplays, westerns, horror, science fiction, or fantasy.

How to Contact Query with SASE. *No unsolicited mss or phone calls.* Considers simultaneous queries. Responds in 1 week to queries with SASE. Responds in 1 month to requested mss. Returns materials only with SASE. Obtains most new clients through recommendations from others.

Recent Sales Sold 100 titles in the last year. *10 Sure Signs a Movie Character Is Doomed and Other Surprising Movie Lists*, by Richard Roeper (Hyperion); *What Is Love?*, by Taro Gold (Andrews & McMeel); *How to Make Someone Love You in 90 Minutes or Less—And Make it Last Forever*, by Nick Boothman.

Terms Agent receives 15% commission on domestic sales; 20% commission on foreign sales. Offers written contract, binding for 1 year. Charges for postage, photocopying and fax.

Writers' Conferences ASJA (New York City); Asilomar (Pacific Grove CA); St. Petersburg; Whidbey Island; Jacksonville; Albuquerque; Austin; Columbus; Southwestern Writers; Willamette (Portland); Dorothy Canfield Fisher (San Diego); Writers Union (Maui); Pacific NW; IWWG; and many others.

Tips "Read the agent listing carefully, and comply with guidelines."

⊘ THE JOHN CAMPBELL AGENCY

11 Island Ave., Suite 1107, Miami Beach FL 33139. E-mail: litraryagt@aol.com. **Contact:** John Campbell. Estab. 1985. Currently handles: 90% nonfiction books; 10% novels.

Represents Nonfiction books, novels. **Considers these nonfiction areas:** Art/architecture/design; biography/ autobiography; ethnic/cultural interests; health/medicine; history; how-to; interior design/decorating; language/literature/criticism; photography; popular culture; psychology; self-help/personal improvement. **Considers these fiction areas:** Action/adventure; literary; thriller.

- O→ This agency specializes in high-quality nonfiction, illustrated, reference, how-to and entertainment books. Does not want to receive poetry, memoir, children's fiction, category fiction, romance, science fiction or horror.

How to Contact Submit proposal package, outline, SASE. Prefers to read materials exclusively. Accepts e-mail queries. No fax queries. Responds in 5 days to queries; 2 weeks to mss. Obtains most new clients through recommendations from others, solicitations.

Recent Sales Sold 38 titles in the last year. *In Character*, by Howard Schatz (Bulfinch); *The Essential Dale Chihuly* (Abrams); *Faces of Africa*, by Angela Carol/Fisher Beckwith (National Geographic); *Line of Beauty* (Rizzoli); *The New Garden Paradise* (Norton/House & Garden).

Terms Agent receives 15% commission on domestic sales. Offers written contract; 1- to 2-month notice must be given to terminate contract. Offers criticism service, included in 15% commission. Charges clients for photocopying, long-distance telephone, overnight express-mail, messengering.

Tips "We welcome submissions from new authors, but proposals must be unique, of high commercial interest, and well written. Follow your talent. Write with passion. Know your market. Submit polished work instead of apologizing for its mistakes, typos, incompleteness, etc. We want to see your best work."

⊘ MARIA CARVAINIS AGENCY, INC.

1350 Avenue of the Americas, Suite 2905, New York NY 10019. (212)245-6365. Fax: (212)245-7196. E-mail: mca@mariacarvainisagency.com. **Contact:** Maria Carvainis, president; Donna Bagdasarian, literary agent. Estab. 1977. Member of AAR, Authors Guild, Women's Media Group, ABA, MWA, RWA; signatory of WGA. Represents 75 clients. 10% of clients are new/unpublished writers. Currently handles: 34% nonfiction books; 65% novels; 1% poetry.

• Prior to opening her agency, Ms. Carvainis spent more than 10 years in the publishing industry as a senior editor with Macmillan Publishing, Basic Books, Avon Books and Crown Publishers. Ms. Carvainis has served as a member of the AAR Board of Directors and AAR Treasurer, as well as serving as chair of the AAR Contracts Committee. She presently serves on the AAR Royalty Committee. Donna Bagdasarian began her career as an academic at Boston University, then spent 5 years with Addison Wesley Longman as an acquisitions editor before joining the William Morris Agency in 1998. She has represented a breadth of projects, ranging from literary fiction to celebrity memoir.

Member Agents Moira Sullivan, literary associate; Daniel Listwa, literary associate; Anna Parrinello, contracts manager.

Represents Nonfiction books, novels. **Considers these nonfiction areas:** Biography/autobiography; business/economics; history; memoirs; science/technology (pop science); women's issues/studies. **Considers these fiction areas:** Historical; literary; mainstream/contemporary; mystery/suspense; thriller; women's; middle grade and young adult.

O— Does not want to receive science fiction or children's picture books.

How to Contact Query with SASE. Responds in 1 week to queries; 3 months to mss. Obtains most new clients through recommendations from others, conferences; 60% from conferences/referrals, 40% from query letters.

Recent Sales *Simply Unforgettable*, by Mary Balogh (Delacorte); *The Mourning Sexton*, by Michael Baron (Doubleday); *In the Shadow of Fame*, by Sue Erikson Bloland (Viking); *Chill Factor*, by Sandra Brown (Simon & Schuster); *An Unexpected Pleasure*, by Candace Camp (MIRA); *The Grail Bird*, by Tim Gallagher (Houghton Mifflin); *The Edge & The Limit*, by Cindy Gerard (St. Martin's Press); *The Perfect Hero*, by Samantha Jones (Avon); *A Killing Rain*, by P.J. Parrish (Kensington); *To Kingdom Come*, by Will Thomas (Touchstone Fireside). Other clients include Elisabeth Brink, Greg Chandler, Pam Conrad, Tim Cummings, S.V. Date, Michael G. Downs, Phillip DePoy, Carlos Dews, Tyler Dilts, John Faunce, Stan Goldberg, Kristan Higgins, Dorothy Love, Staton Rabin, Kristine Rolofson, Christine Sneed.

Terms Agent receives 15% commission on domestic sales; 20% commission on foreign sales. Offers written contract, binding for 2 years on a book-by-book basis. Charges clients for foreign postage, bulk copying.

Writers' Conferences BEA; Frankfurt Book Fair; London Book Fair.

CASTIGLIA LITERARY AGENCY

1155 Camino Del Mar, Suite 510, Del Mar CA 92014. (858)755-8761. Fax: (858)755-7063. **Contact:** All agents. Estab. 1993. Member of AAR, PEN. Represents 50 clients. Currently handles: 55% nonfiction books; 45% novels.

Member Agents Julie Castiglia, Winifred Golden, Sally Van Haitsma.

Represents Nonfiction books, novels. **Considers these nonfiction areas:** Animals; anthropology/archaeology; biography/autobiography; business/economics; child guidance/parenting; cooking/foods/nutrition; current affairs; ethnic/cultural interests; health/medicine; history; language/literature/criticism; money/finance; nature/environment; New Age/metaphysics; psychology; religious/inspirational; science/technology; self-help/personal improvement; sociology; women's issues/studies. **Considers these fiction areas:** Contemporary issues; ethnic; literary; mainstream/contemporary; mystery/suspense; women's (especially).

O— Does not want to receive horror, screenplays or academic nonfiction.

How to Contact Query with SASE. No fax queries. Responds in 2 months to mss. Returns materials only with SASE. Obtains most new clients through recommendations from others, solicitations, conferences.

Recent Sales Sold 25 titles in the last year. *Imaginary Men*, by Anjali Banerjee (Pocket Books/Simon & Schuster); *Courtyards*, by Douglas Keister (Gibbs Smith); *Historic English Arts & Crafts Homes*, by Brian Coleman (Gibbs Smith); *The New Vegan: Fresh, Fabulous and Fun*, by Janet Hudson (Thorsons/HarperCollins); *Will He Really Leave Her for Me*, by Rona Subotnik (Adams Media).

Terms Agent receives 15% commission on domestic sales; 25% commission on foreign sales. Offers written contract; 6-week notice must be given to terminate contract. Charges clients for Fed Ex or Messenger.

Writers' Conferences Southwestern Writers Conference (Albuquerque NM, August); National Writers Conference; Willamette Writers Conference (OR); San Diego State University (CA); Writers at Work (UT); Austin Conference (TX).

Tips "Be professional with submissions. Attend workshops and conferences before you approach an agent."

JANE CHELIUS LITERARY AGENCY

548 Second St., Brooklyn NY 11215. Website: www.janechelius.com. Member of AAR.

O— "We accept all genres except for young adult, children's, scripts/screenplays and poetry."

How to Contact Query first with the first 3 chapters and synopsis. No unsolicted mss.

⚉ WM CLARK ASSOCIATES

355 W. 22nd St., New York NY 10011. (212)675-2784. Fax: (646)349-1658. E-mail: query@wmclark.com. Website: www.wmclark.com. Estab. 1997. Member of AAR. 50% of clients are new/unpublished writers. Currently handles: 50% nonfiction books; 50% novels.

 • Prior to opening WCA, Mr. Clark was an agent at the William Morris Agency.

Represents Nonfiction books, novels. **Considers these nonfiction areas:** Art/architecture/design; biography/autobiography; current affairs; ethnic/cultural interests; history; memoirs; music/dance; popular culture; religious/inspirational (Eastern philosophy only); science/technology; sociology; theater/film; translation. **Considers these fiction areas:** Contemporary issues; ethnic; historical; literary; mainstream/contemporary; Southern fiction.

 ○ "Building on a reputation for moving quickly and strategically on behalf of his clients, and offering individual focus and a global presence, William Clark practices an agressive, innovative and broad-ranged approach to the representation of content and the talent that creates it, ranging from authors of first fiction and award-winning bestselling narrative nonfiction to international authors in translation, as well as musicians and artists."

How to Contact E-mail queries only. Prefers to read requested materials exclusively. Responds in 1-2 months to queries.

Recent Sales Sold 25 titles in the last year. *Fallingwater Rising: E.J. Kaufman and Frank Lloyd Wright Create the Most Exciting House in the World*, by Franklin Toker (Alfred A. Knopf); *The Balthazar Cookbook*, by Riad Nasr, Lee Hanson and Keith McNally (Clarkson Potter); *The Book of 'Exodus': The Making and Meaning of Bob Marley's Album of the Century*, by Vivien Goldman (Crown/Three Rivers Press); *Hungry Ghost*, by Keith Kachtick (HarperCollins). Other clients include Russell Martin, Daye Haddon, Bjork, Mian Mian, Jonathan Stone, Jocko Weyland, Peter Hessler, Rev. Billy (aka Billy Talen).

Terms Agent receives 15% commission on domestic sales; 20% commission on foreign sales. Offers written contract.

Tips "WCA works on a reciprocal basis with Ed Victor Ltd. (UK) in representing select properties to the U.S. market and vice versa. Translation rights are sold directly in the German, Italian, Spanish, Portuguese, Latin American, French, Dutch and Scandinavian territories in association with Andrew Nurnberg Associates Ltd. (UK); through offices in China, Bulgaria, Czech Republic, Latvia, Poland, Hungary and Russia; and through corresponding agents in Japan, Greece, Israel, Turkey, Korea, Taiwan and Thailand."

COLLINS MCCORMICK LITERARY AGENCY

30 Bond St., New York NY 10012. (212)219-2894. Fax: (212)219-2895. E-mail: info@collinsmccormick.com. Website: www.collinsmccormick.com. **Contact:** David McCormick or Nina Collins. Estab. 2002. Member of AAR. Represents 150 clients. 60% of clients are new/unpublished writers. Currently handles: 60% nonfiction books; 30% novels; 5% story collections; 5% poetry.

 • Prior to becoming an agent, Mr. McCormick was an editor at *The New Yorker* and *Texas Monthly*; Ms. Collins was a book scout for foreign publishers and film and TV companies.

Member Agents Leslie Falk (literary fiction, narrative nonfiction); Matthew Elblonk (literary fiction, narrative nonfiction, pop culture); Amy Williams (literary fiction, narrative nonfiction); PJ Mark (literary fiction, narrative nonfiction, pop culture).

⚉ DON CONGDON ASSOCIATES INC.

156 Fifth Ave., Suite 625, New York NY 10010-7002. (212)645-1229. Fax: (212)727-2688. E-mail: dca@doncongdon.com. **Contact:** Don Congdon, Michael Congdon, Susan Ramer, Cristina Concepcion. Estab. 1983. Member of AAR. Represents 100 clients. Currently handles: 60% nonfiction books; 40% fiction.

Represents Nonfiction books, fiction. **Considers these nonfiction areas:** Anthropology/archaeology; biography/autobiography; child guidance/parenting; cooking/foods/nutrition; creative nonfiction; current affairs; ethnic/cultural interests; government/politics/law; health/medicine; history; humor/satire; language/literature/criticism; memoirs; military/war; multicultural; music/dance; nature/environment; popular culture; psychology; science/technology; sociology; theater/film; travel; true crime/investigative; women's issues/studies. **Considers these fiction areas:** Action/adventure; detective/police/crime; horror; humor/satire; literary (especially); mainstream/contemporary; multicultural; mystery/suspense; short story collections; thriller; women's.

How to Contact Query with SASE or via e-mail (material should be copied and pasted into e-mail). Responds in 1 week to queries; 1 month to mss. Obtains most new clients through recommendations from others.

Terms Agent receives 15% commission on domestic sales; 19% commission on foreign sales. Charges client for extra shipping costs, photocopying, copyright fees and book purchases.

Tips "Writing a query letter with a self-addressed stamped envelope is a must. No phone calls. We never download attachments to e-mail queries for security reasons, so please copy and paste material into your e-mail."

N ⊘ CONNOR LITERARY AGENCY

2911 W. 71st St., Minneapolis MN 55423. Phone/Fax: (612)866-1486. E-mail: coolmkc@aol.com. **Contact:** Marlene Connor Lynch. Estab. 1985. Represents 50 clients. 30% of clients are new/unpublished writers. Currently handles: 50% nonfiction books; 50% novels.

- Prior to opening her agency, Ms. Connor served at the Literary Guild of America, Simon & Schuster and Random House. She is author of *What is Cool: Understanding Black Manhood in America* (Crown).

Member Agents Deborah Coker (children's books).

Represents Nonfiction books, novels, especially with a minority slant. **Considers these nonfiction areas:** Child guidance/parenting; cooking/foods/nutrition; crafts/hobbies; current affairs; ethnic/cultural interests; government/politics/law; health/medicine; how-to; humor/satire; interior design/decorating; language/literature/criticism; money/finance; photography; popular culture; self-help/personal improvement; sports; true crime/investigative; women's issues/studies; relationships. **Considers these fiction areas:** Historical; horror; literary; mainstream/contemporary; multicultural; thriller; women's; suspense.

How to Contact All unsolicited mss returned unopened. Obtains most new clients through recommendations from others, conferences, grapevine.

Recent Sales *Outrageous Commitments*, by Dr. Ronn Elmore (HarperCollins); *Seductions*, by Snow Starborn (Sourcebooks); *Simplicitys Simply the Best Sewing Book, Revised Edition*.

Terms Agent receives 15% commission on domestic sales; 25% commission on foreign sales. Offers written contract, binding for 1 year.

Writers' Conferences National Writers Union, Midwest Chapter; Agents, Agents, Agents; Texas Writer's Conference; Detroit Writer's Conference.

Tips "Seeking previously published writers with good sales records and new writers with real talent."

N ⊘ THE COOKE AGENCY

278 Bloor St. E., Suite 305, Toronto ON M4W 3M4 Canada. (416)406-3390. Fax: (416)406-3389. E-mail: agents@ cookeagency.ca. Website: www.cookeagency.ca. **Contact:** Elizabeth Griffin. Estab. 1992. Represents 60 clients. 30% of clients are new/unpublished writers. Currently handles: 50% nonfiction books; 50% novels.

Represents Nonfiction books, literary novels. **Considers these nonfiction areas:** Biography/autobiography; business/economics; child guidance/parenting; current affairs; gay/lesbian issues; health/medicine; popular culture; science/technology; young adult. **Considers these fiction areas:** Literary.

- The Cooke Agency represents some of the best Canadian writers in the world. "Through our contacts and sub-agents, we have built an international reputation for quality. Curtis Brown Canada is jointly owned by Dean Cooke and Curtis Brown New York. It represents Curtis Brown New York authors in Canada." Does not want to receive how-to, self-help, spirituality, genre fiction (science fiction, fantasy, mystery, thriller, horror).

How to Contact Query with SASE. Accepts e-mail and fax queries. Considers simultaneous queries. Responds in 6-8 weeks to queries. Returns materials only with SASE. Obtains most new clients through recommendations from others.

Recent Sales Sold 20 titles and sold 4 scripts in the last year. *Last Crossing*, by Guy Vanderhaeghe (Grove/Atlantic); *Adultery*, by Richard B. Wright (HarperCollins Canada, HarperAustralia, De Geus Holland); *Story House*, by Timothy Taylor (Knopf Canada); *Wrong Way; The Fall of Conrad Black*, by Jacque McNish & Sinclair Stewart (Penguin); *Possessing Genius: The Bizarre Odyssey of Einstein's Brain*, by Carolyn Abraham (Penguin Canada, St. Martin's Press, Icon Books UK). Other clients include Lauren B. Davis, Doug Hunter, Andrew Podnieks, Steven Hayward, Robertson Davies.

Terms Agent receives 15% commission on domestic sales; 20% commission on foreign sales. Offers written contract. Charges clients for postage, photocopying, courier.

Tips "Check our website for complete guidelines rather than calling for them."

⊘ THE DOE COOVER AGENCY

P.O. Box 668, Winchester MA 01890. (781)721-6000. Fax: (781)721-6727. Estab. 1985. Represents more than 100 clients. Currently handles: 80% nonfiction books; 20% novels.

Member Agents Doe Coover (general nonfiction, cooking); Colleen Mohyde (literary and commercial fiction, general and narrative nonfiction); Amanda Lewis (children's books); Frances Kennedy, associate.

- This agency specializes in nonfiction, particularly books on history, biography, social issues and narrative nonfiction, as well as cooking and gardening and literary and commercial fiction. Does not want romance, fantasy, science fiction, poetry.

How to Contact Query with SASE, outline. No e-mail or fax queries. Considers simultaneous queries. Returns materials only with SASE. Obtains most new clients through recommendations from others, solicitations.

Recent Sales Sold 25-30 titles in the last year. *The Gourmet Cookbook*, by Gourmet Magazine (Houghton Mifflin); *Fast Food My Way*, by Jacques Pepin (Houghton Mifflin); *Seven Things Your Teenager Doesn't Want*

You to Know, by Jennifer Lippincott and Robin Deutsch (Ballantine); *The Art of Civilized Conversation*, by Margaret Shepherd and Sharon Hogan (Broadway Books); *Portrait of My Mother Who Posed Nude in Wartime*, by Marjorie Sandor (Sarabande Books). Movie/TV MOW script optioned/sold: *Drinking: A Love Story*, by Caroline Knapp. Other clients include WGBH, Blue Balliett, Deborah Madison, Rick Bayless, Adria Bernardi, Suzanne Berne.

Terms Agent receives 15% commission on domestic sales; 10% on original advance commission on foreign sales.

CORNERSTONE LITERARY, INC.

4500 Wilshire Blvd., 3rd Floor, Los Angeles CA 90010. (323)930-6037. Fax: (323)930-0407. Website: www.corne rstoneliterary.com. **Contact:** Helen Breitwieser. Estab. 1998. Member of AAR; Author's Guild; MWA; RWA. Represents 40 clients. 30% of clients are new/unpublished writers.

- • Prior to founding her own boutique agency, Ms. Breitwieser was a literary agent at The William Morris Agency.

Represents Nonfiction books, novels. **Considers these fiction areas:** Detective/police/crime; erotica; ethnic; family saga; glitz; historical; literary; mainstream/contemporary; multicultural; mystery/suspense; romance; thriller; women's.

- O—¬ Actively seeking first fiction, literary. Does not want to receive science fiction, westerns, children's books, poetry, screenplays, fantasy, gay/lesbian, horror, self-help, psychology, business or diet.

How to Contact Query with SASE. Responds in 6-8 weeks to queries; 2 months to mss. Returns materials only with SASE. Obtains most new clients through recommendations from others.

Recent Sales Sold 38 titles in the last year. *How Was It For You*, by Carmen Reid (Pocket); *Sisters in Pink*, by Kayla Perrin (St. Martin's Press); *What Angels Fear*, by Candice Proctor (NAL). Other clients include Stan Diehl, Elaine Coffman, Danielle Girard, Rachel Lee, Marilyn Jaye Lewis, Carole Matthews.

Terms Agent receives 15% commission on domestic sales; 20% commission on foreign sales. Offers written contract, binding for 1 year; 2-month notice must be given to terminate contract.

Tips "Don't query about more than 1 manuscript. Do not e-mail queries/submissions."

CRAWFORD LITERARY AGENCY

92 Evans Rd., Barnstead NH 03218. (603)269-5851. Fax: (603)269-2533. E-mail: crawfordlit@att.net. Winter Office: 3920 Bayside Rd., Fort Myers Beach FL 33931. (239)463-4651. Fax: (239)463-0125. **Contact:** Susan Crawford. Estab. 1988. Represents 45 clients. 10% of clients are new/unpublished writers. Currently handles: 50% nonfiction books; 50% novels.

Member Agents Susan Crawford; Lorne Crawford (commercial fiction and nonfiction); Scott Neister (scientific/techno thrillers).

Represents Nonfiction books, novels. **Considers these nonfiction areas:** Psychology; religious/inspirational; self-help/personal improvement; women's issues/studies; celebrity/media. **Considers these fiction areas:** Action/adventure; mystery/suspense; thriller (medical).

- O—¬ This agency specializes in celebrity and/or media-based books and authors. Actively seeking action/adventure stories, medical thrillers, self-help, inspirational, how-to and women's issues. Does not want to receive short stories, poetry.

How to Contact Query with SASE. Considers simultaneous queries. Responds in 3 weeks to queries. Returns materials only with SASE. Obtains most new clients through recommendations from others, solicitations, conferences.

Recent Sales Sold 44 titles in the last year. *The Soul of a Butterfly*, by Muhammad Ali with Hana Ali (Simon & Schuster); *John Travolta's Autobiography* (Hyperion); *The Hormonally Vulnerable Woman*, by Geoffrey Redmond, MD (Regan Books); *Flashback*, by Gary Braver (Tor/Forge); *The Xeno Solution*, by Dr. Nelson Erlick (Tor/Forge); *What's a Parent to Do?*, by Henry Abraham, MD (New Horizon).

Terms Agent receives 15% commission on domestic sales; 20% commission on foreign sales. Offers written contract, binding for 3 months; 100% of business is derived from commissions on ms sales.

Writers' Conferences International Film & Television Workshops (Rockport ME); Maui Writers Conference.

Tips "Keep learning to improve your craft. Attend conferences and network."

N CREATIVE MEDIA AGENCY, INC.

240 W. 35th St., Suite 500, New York NY 10001. (212)560-0909. E-mail: assistantcma@aol.com. Website: www.thecmagency.com. **Contact:** Paige Wheeler, Lisa VanAuken, Nadia Cornier. Estab. 1998. Represents approximately 60 clients. 50% of clients are new/unpublished writers. Currently handles: 25% nonfiction books; 70% novels; 5% juvenile books.

- • Paige Wheeler, president of Creative Media Agency, has worked as an agent in both a literary and entertainment capacity over the course of her career. She was an editor for Harlequin/Silhouette and for Euromoney Publications in London, and is an active member of Women in Publishing. Before becoming an agent, Lisa

VanAuken fell into the real estate industry as both a title searcher and an acquisitions agent at an investment company. Before joining CMA, Nadia Cornier worked with award-winning and bestselling authors through her public relations firm Cornier & Associates.

Member Agents Paige Wheeler (romance, mysteries, thrillers, adventure, nonfiction); Lisa Van Auken (romance, thrillers, adventure, erotica, nonfiction); Nadia Cornier (young adult/juvenile, science fiction, fantasy).

Represents Nonfiction books, novels, novellas, juvenile books, scholarly books. **Considers these nonfiction areas:** Agriculture/horticulture; animals; anthropology/archaeology; art/architecture/design; biography/autobiography; business/economics; child guidance/parenting; cooking/foods/nutrition; crafts/hobbies; current affairs; education; ethnic/cultural interests; gay/lesbian issues; government/politics/law; health/medicine; history; how-to; juvenile nonfiction; language/literature/criticism; memoirs; military/war; money/finance; music/dance; nature/environment; New Age/metaphysics; popular culture; psychology; religious/inspirational; science/technology; self-help/personal improvement; sociology; sports; true crime/investigative; women's issues/studies. **Considers these fiction areas:** Action/adventure; confession; erotica; ethnic; experimental; family saga; feminist; gay/lesbian; historical; humor/satire; juvenile; literary; mainstream/contemporary; mystery/suspense; psychic/supernatural; regional; religious/inspirational; romance; sports; thriller; young adult.

○╍ CMA is committed to nurturing an open, communicative relationship with its clients. "We represent authors, not projects. We are enthusiastic about what we do. In other words, we strive never to become disenchanted, cynical or closed-minded about new writers. We love books as much as you do, and we enjoy helping our clients make a living doing what they love to do."

How to Contact For snail mail only, send query, synopsis, first 50 pages. Accepts e-mail submissions (no attachments). Considers simultaneous queries. Responds in 2-4 weeks to queries; 3-8 weeks to mss.

Recent Sales Sold 60 titles in the last year.

Terms Agent receives 15% commission on domestic sales; 20% commission on foreign sales. Offers written contract. Charges for postage, copying.

Writers' Conferences RWA (Reno NV, July).

Tips "Whether your subject is small-town life or medieval Paris, or a man who runs a bakery, or a woman who strives to cure cancer, you must be able write about your subject as easily and comfortably as if you lived it. I'm eager to find talented writers who are scrupulously informed about their subject matter and who fascinate and captivate readers using that knowledge."

ⓦ RICHARD CURTIS ASSOCIATES, INC.

171 E. 74th St., New York NY 10021. (212)772-7363. Fax: (212)772-7393. Website: www.curtisagency.com. Estab. 1979. Member of RWA; MWA; WWA; SFWA; signatory of WGA. Represents 100 clients. 1% of clients are new/unpublished writers. Currently handles: 70% nonfiction books; 20% genre fiction, 10% fiction.

• Prior to opening his agency, Mr. Curtis was an agent with the Scott Meredith Literary Agency for 7 years and has authored over 50 published books.

Member Agents Richard Curtis; Pamela Valvera.

Represents Commercial nonfiction and fiction. **Considers these nonfiction areas:** Health/medicine; history; science/technology.

How to Contact One-page query letter, plus no more than a 1-page synopsis of proposed submission. No submission of ms unless specifically requested. If reply requested, submission must be accompanied by a SASE. No e-mail or fax queries. Returns materials only with SASE.

Recent Sales Sold 150 titles in the last year. *Olympos*, by Dan Simmons; *The Side-Effects Solution*, by Dr. Frederic Vagnini and Barry Fox; *Quantico*, by Greg Bear. Other clients include Janet Dailey, Jennifer Blake, Leonard Maltin, D.J. MacHale, John Altman, Beverly Barton, Earl Mindell, Barbara Parker.

Terms Agent receives 15% commission on domestic sales; 25% commission on foreign sales. Offers written contract, binding for book-by-book basis. Charges for photocopying, express, international freight, book orders.

Writers' Conferences Science Fiction Writers of America; Horror Writers of America; Romance Writers of America; World Fantasy Conference.

ⓦ DARHANSOFF, VERRILL, FELDMAN LITERARY AGENTS

236 W. 26th St., Suite 802, New York NY 10001. (917)305-1300. Fax: (917)305-1400. Estab. 1975. Member of AAR. Represents 120 clients. 10% of clients are new/unpublished writers. Currently handles: 25% nonfiction books; 60% novels; 15% story collections.

Member Agents Liz Darhansoff, Charles Verrill, Leigh Feldman.

Represents Nonfiction books, novels, short story collections.

How to Contact Obtains most new clients through recommendations from others.

◐ LIZA DAWSON ASSOCIATES

240 W. 35th St., Suite 500, New York NY 10001. (212)465-9071. **Contact:** Liza Dawson, Caitlin Blasdell. Member of AAR, MWA, Women's Media Group. Represents 50 clients. 15% of clients are new/unpublished writers. Currently handles: 60% nonfiction books; 40% novels.

• Prior to becoming an agent, Ms. Dawson was an editor for 20 years, spending 11 years at William Morrow as vice president and 2 at Putnam as executive editor. Ms. Blasdell was a senior editor at HarperCollins and Avon. Read our Insider Report with Liza Dawson on page 122.

Member Agents Liza Dawson, Caitlin Blasdell.

Represents Nonfiction books, novels. **Considers these nonfiction areas:** Biography/autobiography; health/medicine; history; memoirs; psychology; sociology; women's issues/studies; politics; business; parenting. **Considers these fiction areas:** Ethnic; family saga; historical; literary; mystery/suspense; regional; science fiction (Blasdell only); thriller.

O→ This agency specializes in readable literary fiction, thrillers, mainstream historicals, women's fiction, academic, history, business, journalism and psychology. Does not want to receive westerns, sports, computers, juvenile.

How to Contact Query with SASE. Responds in 3 weeks to queries; 6 weeks to mss. Obtains most new clients through recommendations from others, conferences.

Recent Sales Sold 40 titles in the last year. *Going for It*, by Karen E. Quinones Miller (Warner); *Mayada: Daughter of Iraq*, by Jean Sasson (Dutton); *It's So Much Work to Be Your Friend: Social Skill Problems at Home and at School*, by Richard Lavoie (Touchstone); *WORDCRAFT: How to Write Like a Professional*, by Jack Hart (Pantheon); . . . *And a Time to Die: How Hospitals Shape the End of Life Experience*, by Dr. Sharon Kaufman (Scribner); *Zeus: A Biography*, by Tom Stone (Bloomsbury).

Terms Agent receives 15% commission on domestic sales; 20% commission on foreign sales. Offers written contract. Charges clients for photocopying and overseas postage.

◐ DEFIORE & CO.

72 Spring St., Suite 304, New York NY 10012. (212)925-7744. Fax: (212)925-9803. E-mail: info@defioreandco.com. Website: www.defioreandco.com. **Contact:** Brian DeFiore. Estab. 1999. Represents 55 clients. 50% of clients are new/unpublished writers. Currently handles: 70% nonfiction books; 30% novels.

• Prior to becoming an agent, Mr. DeFiore was publisher of Villard Books 1997-1998; editor-in-chief of Hyperion 1992-1997; editorial director of Delacorte Press 1988-1992.

Member Agents Brian DeFiore (popular nonfiction, business, pop culture, parenting, commercial fiction); Laurie Abkemeier (nonfiction only—memoir, health, parenting, business, how-to/self-help, cooking, spirituality, popular science); Kate Garrick (literary fiction, crime, pop culture, politics, history, psychology, narrative nonfiction).

Represents Nonfiction books, novels. **Considers these nonfiction areas:** Biography/autobiography; business/economics; child guidance/parenting; cooking/foods/nutrition; health/medicine; money/finance; multicultural; popular culture; psychology; religious/inspirational; self-help/personal improvement; sports. **Considers these fiction areas:** Ethnic; literary; mainstream/contemporary; mystery/suspense; thriller.

How to Contact Query with SASE. Considers simultaneous queries. Responds in 3 weeks to queries; 2 months to mss. Returns materials only with SASE. Obtains most new clients through recommendations from others.

Recent Sales Sold 20 titles in the last year. *Food Forensics*, by Steve Ettlinger; *Marley and Me*, by John Grogan; *She's Got Issues*, by Stephanie Lessing; *This Is My Future*, by David Goodwillie; *All for a Few Perfect Waves*, by David Rensin. Other clients include Loretta LaRoche, Jason Starr, Joel Engel, Christopher Keane, Robin McMillan, Jessica Teich, Ronna Lichtenberg, Fran Sorin, Jimmy Lerner, Lou Manfredini, Bally's Total Fitness, Hilary Devries, Norm Green, Lisa Kusel.

Terms Agent receives 15% commission on domestic sales; 20% commission on foreign sales. Offers written contract; 10-day notice must be given to terminate contract. Charges clients for photocopying, overnight delivery (deducted only after a sale is made).

Writers' Conferences Maui Writers Conference (Maui HI, September); Pacific Northwest Writers Association Conference; North Carolina Writer's Network Conference.

◑ DHS LITERARY, INC.

10711 Preston Rd., Suite 100, Dallas TX 75230. (214)363-4422. Fax: (214)363-4423. E-mail: submissions@dhsliterary.com. Website: www.dhsliterary.com. **Contact:** David Hale Smith, president. Estab. 1994. Represents 35 clients. 15% of clients are new/unpublished writers. Currently handles: 60% nonfiction books; 40% novels.

• Prior to opening his agency, Mr. Smith was an editor at a newswire service.

Represents Nonfiction books, novels. **Considers these nonfiction areas:** Biography/autobiography; business/economics; child guidance/parenting; cooking/foods/nutrition; current affairs; ethnic/cultural interests; popular culture; sports; true crime/investigative. **Considers these fiction areas:** Detective/police/crime; ethnic; literary; mainstream/contemporary; mystery/suspense; thriller; westerns/frontier.

    ○╌ This agency specializes in commercial fiction and nonfiction for the adult trade market. Actively seeking thrillers, mysteries, suspense, etc., and narrative nonfiction. Does not want to receive poetry, short fiction, children's books.

How to Contact Accepts new material by referral only. *No unsolicited mss.* Considers simultaneous queries. Responds in 1 month to queries. Obtains most new clients through recommendations from others.

Recent Sales Sold 35 titles in the last year. *The Curve of the World*, by Marcus Stevens (Algonquin); *No Mountain High Enough: Raising Lance, Raising Me*, by Linda Armstrong Kelly (Broadway).

Terms Agent receives 15% commission on domestic sales; 25% commission on foreign sales. Offers written contract; 10-day notice must be given to terminate contract. Charges for client expenses, i.e., postage, photocopying. 100% of business is derived from commissions on sales.

Tips "Remember to be courteous and professional and to treat marketing your work and approaching an agent as you would any formal business matter. When in doubt, always query first via e-mail. Visit our website for more information."

⊘ SANDRA DIJKSTRA LITERARY AGENCY

1155 Camino del Mar, PMB 515, Del Mar CA 92014. (858)755-3115. Fax: (858)794-2822. E-mail: sdla@dijkstraagency.com. **Contact:** Elise Capron. Estab. 1981. Member of AAR, Authors Guild, PEN West, Poets and Editors, MWA. Represents 200 clients. 30% of clients are new/unpublished writers. Currently handles: 50% nonfiction books; 45% novels; 5% juvenile books.

    ● We specialize in a number of fields.

Member Agents Sandra Dijkstra.

Represents Nonfiction books, novels. **Considers these nonfiction areas:** Anthropology/archaeology; business/economics; child guidance/parenting; cooking/foods/nutrition; ethnic/cultural interests; government/politics/law; health/medicine; history; language/literature/criticism; military/war; money/finance; nature/environment; psychology; science/technology; sociology; women's issues/studies. **Considers these fiction areas:** Ethnic; literary; mainstream/contemporary; mystery/suspense; thriller.

How to Contact Submit proposal package, outline, sample chapters, author bio, SASE. No e-mail or fax queries. Responds in 1 month to queries; 6 weeks to mss. Obtains most new clients through recommendations from others, solicitations, conferences.

Recent Sales *The Hottentot Venus*, by Barbara Chase-Riboud (Doubleday); *The Lady, the Chef and the Lover*, by Marisol Konczal (Harper Collins); *End of Adolescence*, by Robert Epstein (Harcourt).

Terms Agent receives 15% commission on domestic sales; 20% commission on foreign sales. Offers written contract. Charges clients for expenses "to cover domestic costs so that we can spend time selling books instead of accounting expenses. We also charge for the photocopying of the full manuscript or nonfiction proposal and for foreign postage."

Writers' Conferences "Have attended Squaw Valley, Santa Barbara, Asilomar, Southern California Writers Conference, Rocky Mountain Fiction Writers, to name a few. We also speak regularly for writers groups such as PEN West and the Independent Writers Association."

Tips "Be professional and learn the standard procedures for submitting your work. Give full biographical information on yourself, especially for a nonfiction project. Send no more than 50 pages of your manuscript, a very brief synopsis, detailed author bio (awards, publications, accomplishments) and a SASE. We will not respond to submissions without a SASE. Nine-page letters telling us your life story, or your book's, are unprofessional and usually not read. Tell us about your book and write your query well. It's our first introduction to who you are and what you can do. Call if you don't hear within 6 weeks. Be a regular patron of bookstores, and study what kind of books are being published. Read. Check out your local library and bookstores—you'll find lots of books on writing and the publishing industry that will help you. At conferences, ask published writers about their agents. Don't believe the myth that an agent has to be in New York to be successful—we've already disproved it!"

⊘ THE JONATHAN DOLGER AGENCY

49 E. 96th St., Suite 9B, New York NY 10128. (212)427-1853. **Contact:** Herbert Erinmore; President: Jonathan Dolger. Estab. 1980. Member of AAR. Represents 70 clients. 25% of clients are new/unpublished writers.

    ● Query before submitting.

Represents Nonfiction books, novels, illustrated books.

    ○╌ This agency specializes in adult trade fiction and nonfiction, and illustrated books.

How to Contact Query with SASE.

Recent Sales This agency prefers not to share information on specific sales.

Liza Dawson

The hows and whys of getting an agent

Photo used with permission

Y ou've submitted your manuscript. You've waited for months in quiet desperation for some acknowledgement of its existence, but you know it's been relegated to a six-foot-tall slush pile beside some over-worked editorial assistant's desk. So you debate: Should I get an agent? According to literary agent Liza Dawson of Liza Dawson Associates, obtaining an agent's services is essential. Having formerly served as executive editor at Putnam and vice-president at William Morrow, Dawson should know: "An agent is the point person for your literary career. Her job is to know all the major and many of the minor publishing houses and their editors. You're paying for this expertise."

Then again, you could just as easily flip through this book and get several names for yourself; why go through the laborious process of finding the right agent for you? For one, as Dawson attests, not only do agents have better access to editors but they also significantly increase the chances of getting your work into the right hands and getting it published. Since publishers are inundated with query letters and manuscripts from all over the world, most publishers encourage writers to get an agent, and they often look to these agents to find the "next great talent," as Viking did with one of Dawson's clients, Tawni O'Dell, whose *Back Roads* was an Oprah selection. Before you scoff at the notion of someone's obtaining a commission off your life's work, consider that finding the right agent with the determination to see your work on bookshelves can be a major asset in your quest to get published.

So what can an agent do for you? Their knowledge of what editors are looking for helps get you into a publishing house, but a good agent will also make sure you're treated well once you're there. Dawson explains, "You're paying the agent to anticipate problems and to explain when a problem is serious and when it is just business as usual." In other words, if a writer feels he isn't getting enough publicity or isn't getting paid on time, an agent can be the heavy and make the calls. On the other hand, during her publishing tenure, Dawson had occasions when authors refused to get agents. In those cases, "I sent them to publishing lawyers, knowing at least they'd get a good contract but knowing a lawyer is not paid to fight to get the best jacket and marketing plan for a book." Not to mention the hand-holding and requisite pep talks writers might need during the anxious six weeks prior to publication that your friends and family would prefer an agent handle.

Having an agent does not automatically insure you'll get published (Dawson sells about 80 percent of what she takes on), and Dawson admits from experience "it's harder for an author to get an agent than it is to find a publisher for the book." However, "if you have the right agent, you have a good chance of finding a publisher." The process of finding this person may seem daunting since there are numerous agents with varying degrees of success. Since this person represents you and your work, you need to feel confident she has your best interest in mind, before and after you sign with a publisher. Dawson advises authors not to look for "any" agent but "to look for the agent whose background and expertise fit with your accomplishments. A friend of mine, who got an agent after nine months of searching [for a publisher], just sold her book—two weeks after that agent submitted it. What happened? My friend found an agent who loved the book, had sold books like it before, and knew instantly which editors to send it to. Because that agent had a good track record and submitted it with great enthusiasm, editors read it immediately—and had a bidding war over it. The right agent is someone who loves your book and whose voice sounds excited when she talks about it."

If you think getting an agent might be best for your career, before you begin your search, Dawson first suggests that writers read Michael Larsen's *How to Write a Book Proposal, 3rd Edition* (Writer's Digest Books) and Susan Rabiner's *Thinking Like Your Editor* (WW Norton). Next, Dawson recommends looking at the names of agents on the acknowledgements pages in your favorite books and at Publishers Lunch (www.publisherslunch.com).

In addition, "Look for agents who have sold to [or worked at] the major publishers. It means the agent knows how decisions are made in the house." Dawson says don't be deterred by an agent who is new to the field because "younger agents can be appealing if they work at a more established agency and so have a wealth of expertise to draw on." Finally, if you know someone who knows an agent, pick up the phone. From Dawson's experience, "the best way to get an agent is from a referral, because the agent will [probably] read your material more quickly and thoughtfully."

Dawson maintains all agents are taking on new writers—even if they say they are not—so before submitting, look at the agents listed in this book to see what they need and then note their submission guidelines. (For more information on agents and additional listings, check out *2006 Guide to Literary Agents* [Writer's Digest Books].) She suggests you submit a query letter with a SASE and "mention friends in common if you've got them; mention books the agent has represented that seem similar." But, she encourages you to try to make each submission personal; avoid the mass-produced and generic-sounding letter. Once a submission comes in to her office, Dawson's assistant "sorts through everything and gives me any queries or manuscripts she feels I should look at," particularly referrals since that's where Dawson gets most of her clients.

If an agent passes on your manuscript, "we're not telling you your book is unpublishable. We're telling you, at this time, you're not what we're looking for," says Dawson. Keep in mind: Like many agents, Dawson receives about 200 letters a week, about 50 proposals, and about two dozen manuscripts. Though she asks to see material from about one in a hundred query letters, she only takes on about ten new writers a year. But there is hope. "Last year, four of the new writers I took on were from the slush pile," Dawson says.

Finding the right agent is only half the battle. Dawson emphasizes that "once you are ready to sign a contract, avoid a contract that is difficult to get out of and that gives the agent a couple of years to sit on the work without doing anything." The most important advice Dawson offers is something many writers fail to do: Ask questions. "When you sign with an agent, come with a list of 20 questions, such as, 'What happens after the contract with a publishing house is signed? Who handles your foreign rights, your movie rights? How many manuscripts are you sending out in your first round of submissions? Will there be a second and a third round if it doesn't sell? Is there a time when you'll give up? Will you send me the rejection letters?' And after the book is acquired: 'Have you worked with this editor before? How much editorial work will the editor want me to do? Should I hire a freelance publicist? What can I do to make this book a success?' ''

According to Dawson, agents share a common goal: ''Selling books is how we make money. Our goal is not to pass judgment on the literary merit of your book; it's to decide whether we think it is worth an investment of our time to take you on.'' Therefore, Dawson recommends you think of the process of finding the right agent as a job search because ''you're seeking a position in the publishing industry for your manuscript; this task needs to be approached with the same kind of research and diligence that any job hunt requires.'' In order to attain that position, Dawson recommends ''educating yourself in the lingo, customs and needs of agents and editors.''

—Marian Montgomery

Terms Agent receives 15% commission on domestic sales; 25% commission on foreign sales. Charges clients for ''standard expenses.''

Tips ''Writer must have been previously published if submitting fiction. Prefers to work with published/established authors; works with a small number of new/previously unpublished writers.''

JIM DONOVAN LITERARY

4515 Prentice St., Suite 109, Dallas TX 75206. **Contact:** Jim Donovan, president; Kathryn Lindsey. Estab. 1993. Represents 30 clients. 20% of clients are new/unpublished writers. Currently handles: 65% nonfiction books; 35% novels.

Member Agents Jim Donovan (president); Kathryn Lindsey.

Represents Nonfiction books, novels. **Considers these nonfiction areas:** Biography/autobiography; business/economics; child guidance/parenting; current affairs; health/medicine; history; military/war; money/finance; music/dance; nature/environment; popular culture; sports; true crime/investigative. **Considers these fiction areas:** Action/adventure; detective/police/crime; historical; horror; literary; mainstream/contemporary; mystery/suspense; sports; thriller; westerns/frontier.

    ⊙⊶ This agency specializes in commercial fiction and nonfiction. Does not want to receive poetry, humor, short stories, juvenile, romance or religious work.

How to Contact Query with SASE. For nonfiction, send query letter. For fiction, send 2- to 5-page outline and 3 sample chapters. No e-mail or fax queries. Considers simultaneous queries. Responds in 1 month to queries; 1 month to mss. Obtains most new clients through recommendations from others, solicitations.

Recent Sales Sold 24 titles in the last year. *Brotherhood of Heroes*, by Bill Sloan (Simon & Schuster); *Halfbreed*, by David Halaas and Andy Masich (Da Capo); *Given Up for Dead*, by Bill Sloan (Bantam); *Slam*, by Curt Sampson (Da Capo); *Streetcar: Blanche Dubois, Marlon Brando, and the Movie that Outraged America*, by Sam Staggs (St. Martin's); *Sea of Bones*, by Ron Faust (Bantam); *How Mrs. Claus Saved Christmas*, by Jeff Guinn (Tarcher).

Terms Agent receives 15% commission on domestic sales; 20% commission on foreign sales. Offers written contract, binding for 1 year; written notice must be given to terminate contract.

Tips ''The vast majority of material I receive, particularly fiction, is not ready for publication. Do everything you can to get your fiction work in top shape before you try to find an agent. I've been in the book business since 1981, in retail (as a chain buyer), as an editor, and as a published author. I'm open to working with new writers if they're serious about their writing and are prepared to put in the work necessary—the rewriting—to become publishable.''

DUNHAM LITERARY, INC.

156 Fifth Ave., Suite 625, New York NY 10010-7002. (212)929-0994. Website: www.dunhamlit.com. **Contact:** Jennie Dunham. Estab. 2000. Member of AAR. Represents 50 clients. 15% of clients are new/unpublished writers. Currently handles: 25% nonfiction books; 25% novels; 50% juvenile books.

    ● Prior to opening her agency, Ms. Dunham worked as a literary agent for Russell & Volkening. The Rhoda Weyr Agency is now a division of Dunham Literary, Inc.

Represents Nonfiction books, novels, short story collections, juvenile books. **Considers these nonfiction areas:** Anthropology/archaeology; biography/autobiography; ethnic/cultural interests; government/politics/law; health/medicine; history; language/literature/criticism; nature/environment; popular culture; psychology; science/technology; women's issues/studies. **Considers these fiction areas:** Ethnic; juvenile; literary; mainstream/contemporary; picture books; young adult.

How to Contact Query with SASE. No e-mail or fax queries. Responds in 1 week to queries; 2 months to mss. Obtains most new clients through recommendations from others, solicitations.

Recent Sales *America the Beautiful*, by Robert Sabuda; *Dahlia*, by Barbara McClintock; *Living Dead Girl*, by Tod Goldberg; *In My Mother's House*, by Margaret McMulla; *Black Hawk Down*, by Mark Bowden; *Look Back All the Green Valley*, by Fred Chappell; *Under a Wing*, by Reeve Lindbergh; *I Am Madame X*, by Gioia Diliberto.

Terms Agent receives 15% commission on domestic sales; 20% commission on foreign sales.

DUPREE/MILLER AND ASSOCIATES INC. LITERARY

100 Highland Park Village, Suite 350, Dallas TX 75205. (214)559-BOOK. Fax: (214)559-PAGE. E-mail: dmabook @aol.com. **Contact:** Submissions Department. President: Jan Miller. Estab. 1984. Member of ABA. Represents 200 clients. 20% of clients are new/unpublished writers. Currently handles: 90% nonfiction books; 10% novels.

Member Agents Jan Miller; Michael Broussard; Shannon Miser-Marven (business affairs); Kym Wilson; Jennifer Holder; Annabelle Baxter (assistant to Jan Miller).

Represents Nonfiction books, novels, scholarly books, syndicated material. **Considers these nonfiction areas:** Americana; animals; anthropology/archaeology; art/architecture/design; biography/autobiography; business/economics; child guidance/parenting; cooking/foods/nutrition; crafts/hobbies; creative nonfiction; current affairs; education; ethnic/cultural interests; gardening; gay/lesbian issues; government/politics/law; health/medicine; history; how-to; humor/satire; interior design/decorating; language/literature/criticism; memoirs; money/finance; multicultural; music/dance; nature/environment; New Age/metaphysics; philosophy; photography; popular culture; psychology; recreation; regional; religious/inspirational; science/technology; self-help/personal improvement; sex; sociology; spirituality; sports; theater/film; translation; travel; true crime/investigative; women's issues/studies. **Considers these fiction areas:** Action/adventure; contemporary issues; detective/police/crime; ethnic; experimental; family saga; feminist; gay/lesbian; glitz; historical; humor/satire; literary; mainstream/contemporary; mystery/suspense; picture books; psychic/supernatural; religious/inspirational; sports; thriller.

O→ This agency specializes in commercial fiction, nonfiction.

How to Contact Query with SASE, outline. Considers simultaneous queries. Responds in 3 months to mss. Obtains most new clients through recommendations from others, conferences, lectures and "very frequently through publisher's referrals."

Recent Sales Sold 30 titles in the last year. *Family First*, by Dr. Phil McGraw (Simon & Schuster); *The 8th Habit*, by Stephen Covey; *Kitchen Life*, by Art Smith; *Crucial Confrontations*, by Joseph Grenny. Other clients include Fantasia Barrino, Nicole Richie, Anthony Robbins.

Terms Agent receives 15% commission on domestic sales. Offers written contract.

Writers' Conferences Aspen Writers Foundation (Aspen CO).

Tips If interested in agency representation, "it is vital to have the material in the proper working format. As agents' policies differ, it is important to follow their guidelines. The best advice I can give is to work on establishing a strong proposal that provides sample chapters, an overall synopsis (fairly detailed), and some bio information on yourself. Do not send your proposal in pieces; it should be complete upon submission. Remember you are trying to sell your work, and it should be in its best condition."

DYSTEL & GODERICH LITERARY MANAGEMENT

1 Union Square W., Suite 904, New York NY 10003. (212)627-9100. Fax: (212)627-9313. E-mail: miriam@dystel. com. Website: www.dystel.com. **Contact:** Miriam Goderich. Estab. 1994. Member of AAR. Represents 300 clients. 50% of clients are new/unpublished writers. Currently handles: 65% nonfiction books; 25% novels; 10% cookbooks.

● Dystel & Goderich Literary Management recently acquired the client list of Bedford Book Works.

Member Agents Stacey Glick; Jane Dystel; Miriam Goderich; Michael Bourret; Leslie Josephs; Jim McCarthy.

Represents Nonfiction books, novels, cookbooks. **Considers these nonfiction areas:** Animals; anthropology/archaeology; biography/autobiography; business/economics; child guidance/parenting; cooking/foods/nutrition; current affairs; education; ethnic/cultural interests; gay/lesbian issues; government/politics/law; health/medicine; history; humor/satire; military/war; money/finance; New Age/metaphysics; popular culture; psychology; religious/inspirational; science/technology; true crime/investigative; women's issues/studies. **Considers these fiction areas:** Action/adventure; contemporary issues; detective/police/crime; ethnic; family saga; gay/lesbian; literary; mainstream/contemporary; mystery/suspense; thriller (especially).

O→ This agency specializes in commercial and literary fiction and nonfiction, plus cookbooks.

How to Contact Query with SASE. Considers simultaneous queries. Responds in 1 month to queries; 6 weeks to mss. Obtains most new clients through recommendations from others, solicitations, conferences.

Terms Agent receives 15% commission on domestic sales; 19% commission on foreign sales. Offers written contract, binding for book-to-book basis. Charges for photocopying. Galley charges and book charges from the publisher are passed on to the author.

Writers' Conferences West Coast Writers Conference (Whidbey Island WA, Columbus Day weekend); University of Iowa Writer's Conference; Pacific Northwest Writer's Conference; Pike's Peak Writer's Conference; Santa Barbara Writer's Conference; Harriette Austin's Writer's Conference; Sandhills Writers Conference; ASU Writers Conference.

Tips "Work on sending professional, well-written queries that are concise and addressed to the specific agent the author is contacting. No dear Sirs/Madam."

ETHAN ELLENBERG LITERARY AGENCY

548 Broadway, #5-E, New York NY 10012. (212)431-4554. Fax: (212)941-4652. E-mail: agent@ethanellenberg.com. Website: www.ethanellenberg.com. **Contact:** Ethan Ellenberg. Estab. 1983. Represents 80 clients. 10% of clients are new/unpublished writers. Currently handles: 25% nonfiction books; 75% novels.

- Prior to opening his agency, Mr. Ellenberg was contracts manager of Berkley/Jove and associate contracts manager for Bantam.

Member Agents Ethan Ellenberg.

Represents Nonfiction books, novels. **Considers these nonfiction areas:** Biography/autobiography; health/medicine; history; military/war; New Age/metaphysics; religious/inspirational; science/technology. **Considers these fiction areas:** Fantasy; romance; science fiction; thriller; women's.

- This agency specializes in commercial fiction, especially thrillers, romance/women's fiction and specialized nonfiction. "We also do a lot of children's books." Actively seeking commercial and literary fiction, children's books, break-through nonfiction. Does not want to receive poetry, short stories, westerns, autobiographies, screenplays.

How to Contact For fiction, send introductory letter (with credits, if any), outline, first 3 chapters, and SASE (stamps only, post office will not accept metered mail). For nonfiction, send query letter and/or proposal, 1 sample chapter, if written, and SASE. For children's books: Send introductory letter (with credits, if any), up to 3 picture book mss, outline, first 3 chapters for longer projects, SASE. No fax queries. Accepts e-mail queries, no attachments. Will only respond to e-mail queries if interested. Considers simultaneous queries. Responds in 4-6 weeks to mss. Returns materials only with SASE.

Recent Sales Has sold over 100 titles in the last 3 years. *The Aide*, by Ward Carroll (Dutton); *The Lord of the Libraries*, by Mel Odom (Tor); *Mystic and Rider* and *The Thirteenth House*, by Sharon Shinn (Berkley); *Lethal Lies*, by Laurie Breton (Mira); *She, Myself and I,*, by Whitney Gaskell (Bantam); *I Hunger for You*, by Susan Sizemore (Pocket); *What Einstein Told His Cook 2*, by Robert Wolke (Norton); *Clara and Asha*, by Eric Rohmann (Roaring Book Press).

Terms Agent receives 15% commission on domestic sales; 10% commission on foreign sales. Offers written contract. Charges clients for "direct expenses only limited to photocopying, postage, by writer's consent only."

Writers' Conferences RWA National; Novelists, Inc; and other regional conferences.

Tips "We do consider new material from unsolicited authors. Write a good, clear letter with a succinct description of your book. We prefer the first 3 chapters when we consider fiction. For all submissions you must include a SASE for return or the material is discarded. It's always hard to break in, but talent will find a home. Check our website for complete submission guidelines. We continue to see natural storytellers and nonfiction writers with important books."

NICHOLAS ELLISON, INC.

affiliated with Sanford J. Greenburger Associates, 55 Fifth Ave., 15th Floor, New York NY 10003. (212)206-6050. Fax: (212)463-8718. Website: www.greenburger.com. **Contact:** Nicholas Ellison. Estab. 1983. Represents 70 clients. Currently handles: 50% nonfiction books; 50% novels.

- Prior to becoming an agent, Mr. Ellison was an editor at Minerva Editions, Harper & Row, and editor-in-chief at Delacorte.

Member Agents Nicholas Ellison, Jennifer Cayea, Abigail Koons.

Represents Nonfiction books, novels. **Considers these nonfiction areas:** Considers most nonfiction areas. **Considers these fiction areas:** Literary; mainstream/contemporary.

How to Contact Query with SASE. Responds in 6 weeks to queries.

Recent Sales *Night Fall*, by Nelson DeMille (Warner); *The Big Love*, by Sarah Dunn (Little, Brown); *The Stupidest Angel*, by Christopher Moore (HarperCollins). Other clients include Olivia Goldsmith, P.T. Deutermann, Nancy Geary, Jeff Lindsay, Lee Gruenfeld, Thomas Christopher Greene, Bill Mason.

Terms Agent receives 15% commission on domestic sales; 20% commission on foreign sales.

ANN ELMO AGENCY, INC.

60 E. 42nd St., New York NY 10165. (212)661-2880, 2881. Fax: (212)661-2883. **Contact:** Lettie Lee. Estab. 1959. Member of AAR, MWA, Authors Guild.

Member Agents Lettie Lee; Mari Cronin (plays); A.L. Abecassis (nonfiction).

Represents Nonfiction books, novels. **Considers these nonfiction areas:** Biography/autobiography; current affairs; health/medicine; history; how-to; money/finance; music/dance; popular culture; psychology; science/technology; self-help/personal improvement; theater/film. **Considers these fiction areas:** Contemporary issues; ethnic; family saga; mainstream/contemporary; romance (contemporary, gothic, historical, regency); thriller; women's.

How to Contact Letter queries only with SASE. No fax queries. Responds in 3 months to queries. Obtains most new clients through recommendations from others.

Recent Sales This agency prefers not to share information on specific sales.

Terms Agent receives 15% commission on domestic sales; 20% commission on foreign sales. Offers written contract. Charges clients for "special mailings or shipping considerations or multiple international calls. No charge for usual cost of doing business."

Tips "Query first and, when asked only, please send properly prepared manuscript. A double-spaced, readable manuscript is the best recommendation. Include SASE, of course."

▢ ELAINE P. ENGLISH

Graybill & English, LLC, 1875 Connecticut Ave. NW, Suite 712, Washington DC 20009. (202)588-9798, ext. 143. Fax: (202)457-0662. E-mail: elaineengl@aol.com. Website: www.graybillandenglish.com. **Contact:** Elaine English. Member of AAR. Represents 18 clients. 50% of clients are new/unpublished writers. Currently handles: 100% novels.

  ● Ms. English is also an attorney specializing in media and publishing law.

Member Agents Elaine English (fiction, including women's fiction, romance, thrillers and mysteries).

Represents Novels. **Considers these fiction areas:** Historical; mainstream/contemporary; multicultural; mystery/suspense; romance (including single titles, historical, contemporary, romantic, suspense, chick lit, erotic); thriller; women's.

  ⚮ "While not as an agent per se, I have been working in publishing for over 15 years. Also, I'm affiliated with other agents who represent a broad spectrum of projects." Actively seeking women's fiction, including single-title romances. Does not want to receive any science fiction or time travel.

How to Contact Submit synopsis and first 3 chapters, SASE. Responds in 6-12 weeks to queries; 6 months to requested ms. Returns materials only with SASE. Obtains most new clients through recommendations from others, solicitations, conferences.

Terms Agent receives 15% commission on domestic sales; 20% commission on foreign sales. Offers written contract; 30-day notice must be given to terminate contract. Charges only for expenses directly related to sales of manuscript (long distance, postage, copying).

Writers' Conferences RWA Nationals (July); SEAK Medical Fiction Writing for Physcians (Cape Cod, September); Emerald City (Seattle WA, October); Novelists, Inc. (New York, April).

▣ FARBER LITERARY AGENCY, INC.

14 E. 75th St., #2E, New York NY 10021. (212)861-7075. Fax: (212)861-7076. E-mail: farberlit@aol.com. Website: www.donaldfarber.com. **Contact:** Ann Farber; Dr. Seth Farber. Estab. 1989. Represents 40 clients. 50% of clients are new/unpublished writers. Currently handles: 25% nonfiction books; 15% scholarly books; 25% stage plays; 35% fiction books.

Member Agents Ann Farber (novels); Seth Farber (plays, scholarly books, novels); Donald C. Farber (attorney, all entertainment media).

Represents Nonfiction books, novels, juvenile books, textbooks, stage plays. **Considers these nonfiction areas:** Child guidance/parenting; cooking/foods/nutrition; music/dance; psychology; theater/film. **Considers these fiction areas:** Action/adventure; contemporary issues; humor/satire; juvenile; literary; mainstream/contemporary; mystery/suspense; thriller; young adult.

How to Contact Submit outline, 3 sample chapters, SASE. Prefers to read materials exclusively. Responds in 1 month to queries; 2 month to mss. Obtains most new clients through recommendations from others.

Terms Agent receives 15% commission on domestic sales; 20% commission on foreign sales. Offers written contract, binding for 1 year. Client must furnish copies of ms, treatments, and any other items for submission.

Tips "Our attorney, Donald C. Farber, is the author of many books. His services are available to the agency's clients as part of the agency service at no additional charge."

▣ ▣ FARRIS LITERARY AGENCY, INC.

P.O. Box 570069, Dallas TX 75357. (972)203-8804. E-mail: agent@farrisliterary.com. Website: www.farrisliterary.com. **Contact:** Mike Farris or Susan Morgan Farris. Estab. 2002. Represents 30 clients. 60% of clients are new/unpublished writers.

  ● Both Mike and Susan are attorneys.

Member Agents "We specialize in both fiction and nonfiction books. We are particularly interested in discovering unpublished authors. We adhere to AAR guidelines."

Represents Nonfiction books, novels. **Considers these nonfiction areas:** Biography/autobiography; business/economics; child guidance/parenting; cooking/foods/nutrition; current affairs; government/politics/law; health/medicine; history; how-to; humor/satire; memoirs; military/war; music/dance; popular culture; religious/inspirational; self-help/personal improvement; sports; women's issues/studies. **Considers these fiction areas:** Action/adventure; detective/police/crime; historical; humor/satire; literary; mainstream/contemporary; mystery/suspense; religious/inspirational; romance; sports; thriller; westerns/frontier.

○ Does not consider science fiction, fantasy, gay and lesbian, erotica, young adult, children's.

How to Contact Query with SASE. Considers simultaneous queries. Responds in 2-3 weeks to queries; 4-8 weeks to mss. Returns materials only with SASE. Obtains most new clients through recommendations from others, solicitations, conferences.

Recent Sales Sold 4 titles in the last year. *Detachment Fault*, by Susan Cummins Miller (Berkley); Untitled, by Susan Cummins Miller (Berkley); *Creed*, by Sheldon Russell (Oklahoma University Press); *How to Understand Autism: The Easy Way*, by Dr. Alexander Durig (Jessica Kingsley Publishers Ltd.). Agent receives 15% commission on domestic sales; 20% commission on foreign sales. Offers written contract, 30-day notice must be given to terminate contract. Postage and photocopying.

Writers' Conferences Oklahoma Writers Federation, Inc. (Oklahoma City OK); The Screenwriting Conference at Santa Fe (Sante Fe NM); Pikes Peak Writers Conference; Women Writing the West.

○ DIANA FINCH LITERARY AGENCY

116 W. 23rd St., Suite 500, New York NY 10011. (646)375-2081. E-mail: diana.finch@verizon.net. **Contact:** Diana Finch. Estab. 2003. Member of AAR. Represents 45 clients. 20% of clients are new/unpublished writers. Currently handles: 65% nonfiction books; 25% novels; 5% juvenile books; 5% multimedia.

• Prior to opening her agency, Ms. Finch was an agent with Ellen Levine Literary Agency for 18 years.

Represents Nonfiction books, novels, scholarly books. **Considers these nonfiction areas:** Biography/autobiography; business/economics; child guidance/parenting; computers/electronic; current affairs; ethnic/cultural interests; government/politics/law; health/medicine; history; how-to; humor/satire; memoirs; military/war; money/finance; music/dance; nature/environment; photography; popular culture; psychology; science/technology; self-help/personal improvement; sports; theater/film; translation; true crime/investigative; women's issues/studies; juvenile. **Considers these fiction areas:** Action/adventure; detective/police/crime; ethnic; historical; literary; mainstream/contemporary; thriller; young adult.

○ Actively seeking narrative nonfiction, popular science and health topics. Does not want romance, mysteries or children's picture books.

How to Contact Query with SASE, or by e-mail (no attachments). No phone or fax queries. Considers simultaneous queries. Returns materials only with SASE. Obtains most new clients through recommendations from others.

Recent Sales Untitled nonfiction, by Greg Palast (Penguin US and UK); *Journey of the Magi*, by Tudor Parfitt (Farrar, Straus, & Giroux); *Sixth Grade*, by Susie Morgenstern (Viking Children's); *We Were There: African-American Vets*, by Yvonne Latty and Ron Tarver (HarperCollins); *Lipstick Jihad*, by Azadeh Moaveni (Public Affairs). Other clients include Keith Devlin, Daniel Duane, Thomas Goltz, Hugh Pope, Sebastian Matthews, Joan Lambert, Dr. Robert Marion.

Terms Agent receives 15% commission on domestic sales; 20% commission on foreign sales. Offers written contract. "I charge for photocopying, overseas postage, galleys and books purchased and try to recap these costs from earnings received for a client, rather than charging outright."

Tips "Do as much research as you can on agents before you query. Have someone critique your query letter before you send it. It should be only 1 page and describe your book clearly—and why you are writing it—but also demonstrate creativity and a sense of your writing style."

◐ THE FOGELMAN LITERARY AGENCY

7515 Greenville, Suite 712, Dallas TX 75231. (214)361-9956. Fax: (214)361-9553. E-mail: info@fogelman.com. Website: www.fogelman.com. Also: 415 Park Ave., New York NY 10022. (212)836-4803. **Contact:** Evan Fogelman. Estab. 1990. Member of AAR. Represents 100 clients. 2% of clients are new/unpublished writers. Currently handles: 40% nonfiction books; 40% novels; 10% scholarly books; 10% TV scripts.

• Prior to opening his agency, Mr. Fogelman was an entertainment lawyer. He is still active in the field and serves as chairman of the Texas Entertainment and Sports Lawyers Association.

Member Agents Evan Fogelman (nonfiction, women's fiction); Linda Kruger (women's fiction, nonfiction); Helen Brown (literary fiction/nonfiction).

Represents Nonfiction books, novels. **Considers these nonfiction areas:** Biography/autobiography; business/economics; child guidance/parenting; current affairs; education; ethnic/cultural interests; government/politics/law; health/medicine; popular culture; psychology; sports; true crime/investigative; women's issues/studies. **Considers these fiction areas:** Historical; literary; mainstream/contemporary; romance (all sub-genres).

Literary Agents

O⊸ This agency specializes in women's fiction and nonfiction. "Zealous advocacy" makes this agency stand apart from others. Actively seeking "nonfiction of all types; romance fiction." Does not want to receive children's/juvenile.

How to Contact Query with SASE. Considers simultaneous queries. Responds in 3 months to mss. Returns materials only with SASE. Obtains most new clients through recommendations from others.

Recent Sales Sold 60 titles in the last year. *A Little Secret Between Friends*, by C.J. Carmichael (Harlequin Superromance); *The Good, the Bad and the Ugly Men I've Dated*, by Shane Bolks (Avon); *Caught in the Act*, by Pam McCutcheon (Kensington). Other clients include Caroline Hunt, Katherine Sutcliffe, Crystal Stovall.

Terms Agent receives 15% commission on domestic sales; 10% commission on foreign sales. Offers written contract, binding for project to project.

Writers' Conferences Romance Writers of America; Novelists, Inc.

Tips "Finish your manuscript, and see our website."

Ⓝ Ⓞ THE FOLEY LITERARY AGENCY

34 E. 38th St., New York NY 10016-2508. (212)686-6930. **Contact:** Joan Foley or Joseph Foley. Estab. 1961. Represents 10 clients. Currently handles: 75% nonfiction books; 25% novels.

Member Agents ICM (Ron Bernstein) handles TV/film rights.

Represents Nonfiction books, novels.

How to Contact Query with letter, brief outline, SASE. Responds promptly to queries. Obtains most new clients through recommendations from others, rarely taking on new clients.

Recent Sales This agency prefers not to share information on specific sales.

Terms Agent receives 10% commission on domestic sales; 15% commission on foreign sales. 100% of business is derived from commissions on ms sales.

Tips Desires brevity in querying.

⊕ Ⓜ FORT ROSS, INC., RUSSIAN-AMERICAN PUBLISHING PROJECTS

26 Arthur Place, Yonkers NY 10701-1703. (914)375-6448. Fax: (914)375-6439. E-mail: fort.ross@verizon.net. Website: www.fortross.net. **Contact:** Dr. Vladimir P. Kartsev. Estab. 1992. Represents about 100 clients. 2% of clients are new/unpublished writers. Currently handles: 50% nonfiction books; 40% novels; 10% juvenile books.

Member Agents Ms. Olga Borodyanskaya, St. Petersburg, Russia, phone: 7-812-1738607 (fiction, nonfiction); Mr. Konstantin Paltchikov, Moscow, Russia, phone: 7-095-2388272 (romance, science fiction, fantasy, thriller).

Represents Nonfiction books, novels, juvenile books. **Considers these nonfiction areas:** Biography/autobiography; history; memoirs; psychology; self-help/personal improvement; true crime/investigative. **Considers these fiction areas:** Action/adventure; detective/police/crime; fantasy; horror; juvenile; mystery/suspense; romance (contemporary, gothic, historical, regency); science fiction; thriller; young adult.

O⊸ This agency specializes in selling rights for Russian books and illustrations (covers) to American publishers; American books and illustrations for Europe; and Russian-English and English-Russian translations. Actively seeking adventure, fiction, mystery, romance, science fiction, thriller from established authors and illustrators for Russian and European markets.

How to Contact Send published book or galleys. Accepts e-mail and fax queries. Considers simultaneous queries. Returns materials only with SASE.

Recent Sales Sold 12 titles in the last year. *Mastering Judo with Vladimir Putin*, by Vladimir Putin et al (North Atlantic Books [USA]); *Max*, by Howard Fast (Baronet [Czech Republic]); *Kiss of Midas*, by George Vainer (Neri [Italy]); *Redemption*, by Howard Fast (Oram [Israel]); *A Suitcase*, by Sergey Doveatov (Amber [Poland]).

Terms Agent receives 10% commission on domestic sales; 20% commission on foreign sales. Offers written contract, binding for 2 years; 2-month notice must be given to terminate contract.

Tips "Established authors and book illustrators (especially cover art) are welcome for the following genres: romance, fantasy, science fiction, mystery and adventure."

CANDICE FUHRMAN LITERARY AGENCY

60 Greenwood Way, Mill Valley CA 94941. (415)383-6081. Fax: (415)384-0739. E-mail: candicef@pacbell.net. **Contact:** Candice Fuhrman. Estab. 1987. Member of AAR.

Member Agents Elsa Hurley.

Represents Nonfiction books (adult), novels (adult). **Considers these nonfiction areas:** Current affairs; health/medicine; popular culture; psychology; women's issues/studies; adventure, mind/body/spirit, lifestyle. **Considers these fiction areas:** Literary.

O⊸ No children's category, no genre.

How to Contact *No unsolicited mss.* Please query first. Query with SASE and include e-mail address.

Terms Agent receives 15% commission on domestic sales; 20-30% commission on foreign sales.

◨ GELFMAN, SCHNEIDER, LITERARY AGENTS, INC.

250 W. 57th St., Suite 2515, New York NY 10107. (212)245-1993. Fax: (212)245-8678. **Contact:** Jane Gelfman, Deborah Schneider. Estab. 1981. Member of AAR. Represents 300+ clients. 10% of clients are new/unpublished writers.

Represents Nonfiction books, novels. **Considers these fiction areas:** Literary; mainstream/contemporary; mystery/suspense.

O─ Does not want to receive romances, science fiction, westerns or children's books.

How to Contact Query with SASE. No e-mail queries accepted. Responds in 1 month to queries; 2 months to mss. Obtains most new clients through recommendations from others.

Terms Agent receives 15% commission on domestic sales; 20% commission on foreign sales. Offers written contract. Charges clients for photocopying, messengers and couriers.

◨ THE GISLASON AGENCY

219 Main St. SE, Suite 506, Minneapolis MN 55414-2160. (612)331-8033. Fax: (612)331-8115. E-mail: gislasonbj @aol.com. Website: www.thegislasonagency.com. **Contact:** Barbara J. Gislason, literary agent. Estab. 1992. Member of Minnesota State Bar Association, American Bar Association, Art & Entertainment Law Section (former chair), Animal Law (section chair), Internet Committee, Minnesota Intellectual Property Law Association Copyright Committee (former chair); also a member of SFWA, MWA, Sisters in Crime, Icelandic Association of Minnesota (former president) and American Academy of Acupuncture and Oriental Medicine (advisory board member). 80% of clients are new/unpublished writers. Currently handles: 10% nonfiction books; 90% novels.

• Ms. Gislason became an attorney in 1980, and continues to practice Art & Entertainment Law. She has been nationally recognized as a Leading American Attorney and a Super Lawyer. She is also the owner of Blue Raven Press, which publishes fiction and nonfiction about animals.

Member Agents Deborah Sweeney (fantasy, science fiction); Kellie Hultgren (fantasy, science fiction); Lisa Higgs (mystery, literary fiction); Kris Olson (mystery); Kevin Hedman (fantasy, science fiction, mystery, literary fiction).

Represents Nonfiction books, novels. **Considers these nonfiction areas:** Animals (behavior/communications). **Considers these fiction areas:** Fantasy; literary; mystery/suspense; science fiction; thriller (legal).

O─ Do not send personal memoirs, poetry, short stories, screenplays or children's books.

How to Contact For fiction, query with synopsis, first 3 chapters, and SASE. For nonfiction, query with proposal and sample chapters; published authors may submit complete ms. No e-mail or fax queries. Responds in 2 months to queries; 3 months to mss. Obtains most new clients through recommendations from others, conferences, *Guide to Literary Agents, Literary Market Place,* and other reference books.

Recent Sales *Historical Romance #4,* by Linda Cook (Kensington); *Dancing Dead,* by Deborah Woodworth (HarperCollins); *Owen Keane's Lonely Journey,* by Terence Faherty (Harlequin).

Terms Agent receives 15% commission on domestic sales; 20% commission on foreign sales. Offers written contract, binding for 1 year with option to renew. Charges clients for photocopying and postage.

Writers' Conferences SouthWest Writers; Willamette Writers; Wrangling with Writing. Also attends other state and regional writers conferences.

Tips "Cover letter should be well written and include a detailed synopsis (if fiction) or proposal (if nonfiction), the first 3 chapters, and author bio. Appropriate SASE required. We are looking for a great writer with a poetic, lyrical or quirky writing style who can create intriguing ambiguities. We expect a well-researched, imaginative and fresh plot that reflects a familiarity with the applicable genre. If submitting nonfiction work, explain how the submission differs from and adds to previously published works in the field. Scenes with sex and violence must be intrinsic to the plot. Remember to proofread. If the work was written with a specific publisher in mind, this should be communicated. In addition to owning an agency, Ms. Gislason practices law in the area of art and entertainment and has a broad spectrum of entertainment industry contacts."

◨ GOLDFARB & ASSOCIATES

721 Gibbon St., Alexandria VA 22314. (202)466-3030. Fax: (703)836-5644. E-mail: rglawlit@aol.com. Website: www.ronaldgoldfarb.com. **Contact:** Ronald Goldfarb. Estab. 1966. Currently handles: 75% nonfiction books; 25% novels; roster of TV and movie projects is rapidly growing (works closely with MainStreet Media, a production company owned by Mr. Goldfarb).

Member Agents Ronald Goldfarb is an experienced trial lawyer and a veteran literary agent, as well as the author of 10 books and over 230 articles. Robbie Anna Hare, a native Australian currently residing in both Israel and the U.S., is a literary agent with experience as a reporter, writer and radio and television producer. Louise Wheatley, whose background is teaching English literature, is an editor who also works with new authors.

Represents Nonfiction books, novels, movie scripts, TV scripts.

○━ "Serious nonfiction is our most active area (with all publishing houses and editors), though we do handle fiction selectively. Our location in the nation's capital enables us to represent many well-known print journalists, TV correspondents, politicians and policymakers in both fiction and nonfiction fields. But many of our clients come from all over this country and some from abroad."

How to Contact The firm is accepting select new projects, usually on the basis of personal referrals or from existing clients.

Tips "We are a law firm and a literary agency. Through our work with writers' organizations, we are constantly adding new and talented writers to our list of literary clients and matching collaborators with projects in need of authors or editors. We have found writers to develop book ideas at the request of publishers."

◙ FRANCES GOLDIN LITERARY AGENCY, INC.

57 E. 11th St., Suite 5B, New York NY 10003. (212)777-0047. Fax: (212)228-1660. E-mail: agency@goldinlit.com. Website: www.goldinlit.com. Estab. 1977. Member of AAR. Represents over 100 clients.

Member Agents Francis Goldin, principal/agent; Sydelle Kramer, agent (works with established academics and young writers interested in breaking into mainstream); Matt McGowan, agent/rights director (innovative works of fiction and nonfiction); Sam Stoloff, agent (literary fiction, memoir, history, accessible sociology and philosophy, cultural studies, serious journalism, narrative and topical nonfiction with a progressive orientation); David Csontos, agent/office manager (literary fiction, biography, memoir, psychology, spirituality, gay and social studies and the arts).

Represents Nonfiction books, novels. **Considers these nonfiction areas:** Serious, controversial nonfiction with a progressive political orientation. **Considers these fiction areas:** Adult literary.

○━ "We are hands-on, and we work intensively with clients on proposal and manuscript development." Does not want anything that is racist, sexist, agist, homophobic or pornographic. No screenplays, children's books, art books, cookbooks, business books, diet books, self-help or genre fiction.

How to Contact Query with SASE. *No unsolicited mss* or work previously submitted to publishers. No e-mail or fax queries. Responds in 4-6 weeks to queries.

Recent Sales *Skin Deep*, by Dalton Conley (Pantheon); *Conned: How Millions Have Lost the Right to Vote*, by Sasha Abramsky (New Press); *Wake-Up Calls*, by Bruce Grierson (Bloomsbury USA).

◙ GOODMAN ASSOCIATES

500 West End Ave., New York NY 10024-4317. (212)873-4806. **Contact:** Elise Simon Goodman. Estab. 1976. Member of AAR. Represents 50 clients.

● Arnold Goodman is the former chair of the AAR Ethics Committee.

Member Agents Elise Simon Goodman; Arnold P. Goodman.

Represents Nonfiction books, novels. **Considers these nonfiction areas:** Americana; animals; anthropology/archaeology; biography/autobiography; business/economics; child guidance/parenting; cooking/foods/nutrition; creative nonfiction; current affairs; education; ethnic/cultural interests; government/politics/law; health/medicine; history; language/literature/criticism; memoirs; military/war; money/finance; multicultural; music/dance; nature/environment; philosophy; popular culture; psychology; recreation; regional; science/technology; sex; sociology; sports; theater/film; translation; travel; true crime/investigative; women's issues/studies. **Considers these fiction areas:** Action/adventure; contemporary issues; detective/police/crime; erotica; ethnic; family saga; historical; literary; mainstream/contemporary; military/war; multicultural; multimedia; mystery/suspense; regional; sports; thriller; translation.

○━ Accepting new clients by recommendation only. Does not want to receive poetry, articles, individual stories, children's or YA material.

How to Contact Query with SASE. Responds in 10 days to queries; 1 month to mss.

Terms Agent receives 15% commission on domestic sales; 20% commission on foreign sales. Charges clients for certain expenses: faxes, toll calls, overseas postage, photocopying, book purchases.

◙ THE THOMAS GRADY AGENCY

209 Bassett St., Petaluma CA 94952-2668. (707)765-6229. Fax: (707)765-6810. E-mail: tom@tgrady.com. Website: www.tgrady.com. **Contact:** Thomas Grady. Member of AAR. 10% of clients are new/unpublished writers.

How to Contact E-mail queries preferred.

◙ ASHLEY GRAYSON LITERARY AGENCY

1342 18th St., San Pedro CA 90732. Fax: (310)514-1148. E-mail: graysonagent@earthlink.net. Member of AAR. Represents 100 clients. 5% of clients are new/unpublished writers. Currently handles: 20% nonfiction books; 50% novels; 30% juvenile books.

Member Agents Ashley Grayson (commercial and literary fiction, historical novels, mysteries, science fiction, thrillers, young adult); Carolyn Grayson (mainstream commercial fiction, mainstream women's fiction, romance, crime fiction, suspense, thrillers, horror, true crime, young adult, science, medical, health, self-help, how-to, pop culture, creative nonfiction); Dan Hooker (commercial fiction, mysteries, thrillers, suspense, hard science fiction, contemporary and dark fantasy, horror, young adult and middle grade, popular subjects and treatment with high commercial potential, New Age by published professionals).

> ○━ "We prefer to work with published (traditional print publishing), established authors. We will give first consideration to authors who come recommended to us by our clients or other publishing professionals. We accept a very small number of new, previously unpublished authors."

How to Contact Submit query by regular post plus first 3 pages of ms or overview of the nonfiction proposal.
Recent Sales Sold more than 100 titles in the last year. *Dreaming Pachinko*, by Isaac Adamson (HarperCollins); *The Sky So Big and Black*, by John Barnes (Tor); *Move Your Stuff, Change Your Life*, by Karen Rauch Carter (Simon & Schuster).
Terms Agent receives 15% commission on domestic sales; 20% commission on foreign sales.

○ SANFORD J. GREENBURGER ASSOCIATES, INC.
55 Fifth Ave., New York NY 10003. (212)206-5600. Fax: (212)463-8718. Website: www.greenburger.com. **Contact:** Heide Lange. Estab. 1945. Member of AAR. Represents 500 clients.
Member Agents Heide Lange, Faith Hamlin, Dan Mandel, Peter McGuigan, Matthew Bialer.
Represents Nonfiction books, novels. **Considers these nonfiction areas:** Agriculture/horticulture; americana; animals; anthropology/archaeology; art/architecture/design; biography/autobiography; business/economics; child guidance/parenting; computers/electronic; cooking/foods/nutrition; crafts/hobbies; current affairs; education; ethnic/cultural interests; gardening; gay/lesbian issues; government/politics/law; health/medicine; history; how-to; humor/satire; interior design/decorating; juvenile nonfiction; language/literature/criticism; memoirs; military/war; money/finance; multicultural; music/dance; nature/environment; New Age/metaphysics; philosophy; photography; popular culture; psychology; recreation; regional; religious/inspirational; science/technology; self-help/personal improvement; sex; sociology; software; sports; theater/film; translation; travel; true crime/investigative; women's issues/studies; young adult. **Considers these fiction areas:** Action/adventure; contemporary issues; detective/police/crime; ethnic; family saga; feminist; gay/lesbian; glitz; historical; humor/satire; literary; mainstream/contemporary; mystery/suspense; psychic/supernatural; regional; sports; thriller.

> ○━ Does not want to receive romances or westerns.

How to Contact Submit query, first 3 chapters, synopsis, brief bio, SASE. Considers simultaneous queries. Responds in 2 months to queries; 2 months to mss.
Recent Sales Sold 200 titles in the last year. This agency prefers not to share information on specific sales. Clients include Andrew Ross, Margaret Cuthbert, Nicholas Sparks, Mary Kurcinka, Linda Nichols, Edy Clarke, Brad Thor, Dan Brown, Sallie Bissell.
Terms Agent receives 15% commission on domestic sales; 20% commission on foreign sales. Charges for photocopying, books for foreign and subsidiary rights submissions.

○ GREGORY & CO. AUTHORS' AGENTS
3 Barb Mews, London W6 7PA England. 020-7610-4676. Fax: 020-7610-4686. E-mail: info@gregoryandcompany.co.uk. Website: www.gregoryandcompany.co.uk. **Contact:** Jane Gregory, sales; Anna Valdinger, editorial; Claire Morris, rights. Estab. 1987. Member of Association of Authors' Agents. Represents 60 clients. Currently handles: 10% nonfiction books; 90% novels.

> ● Prior to becoming an agent, Ms. Gregory was Rights Director for Chatto & Windus.

Represents Nonfiction books and fiction books. **Considers these nonfiction areas:** Biography/autobiography; history. **Considers these fiction areas:** Detective/police/crime; historical; literary; mainstream/contemporary; thriller; contemporary women's fiction.

> ○━ "Jane Gregory is successful at selling rights all over the world, including film and television rights. As a British agency we do not generally take on American authors." Actively seeking well-written, accessible modern novels. Does not want to receive horror, science fiction, fantasy, mind/body/spirit, children's books, screenplays and plays, short stories, poetry.

How to Contact Query with SASE, submit outline, 3 sample chapters, SASE. Considers simultaneous queries. Returns materials only with SASE. Obtains most new clients through recommendations from others, conferences.
Recent Sales Sold 100 titles in the last year. *Tokyo*, by Mo Hayder (Bantam UK/Gove Atlantic); *The Torment of Others*, by Val McDermid (HarperCollins UK/St. Martin's Press NY); *Disordered Minds*, by Minette Walters (MacMillan UK/Putnam USA); *The Lover*, by Laura Wilson (Orion UK/Bantam USA); *Gagged & Bound*, by Natasha Cooper (Simon & Schuster UK/St. Martin's Press USA); *Demon of the Air*, by Simon Levack (Simon & Schuster/St. Martin's USA).
Terms Agent receives 15% commission on domestic sales; 20% commission on foreign sales. Offers written

contract; 3-month notice must be given to terminate contract. Charges clients for photocopying of whole type-scripts and copies of book for submissions.
Writers' Conferences CWA Conference (United Kingdom, Spring); Dead on Deansgate (Manchester, Autumn); Harrogate Literary Festival (United Kingdom, Summer); Bouchercon (location varies, Autumn).

JILL GROSJEAN LITERARY AGENCY
1390 Millstone Rd., Sag Harbor NY 11963-2214. (631)725-7419. Fax: (631)725-8632. E-mail: jill6981@aol.com. Website: www.hometown.aol.com/jill6981/myhomepage/index.html. **Contact:** Jill Grosjean. Estab. 1999. Represents 27 clients. 100% of clients are new/unpublished writers. Currently handles: 100% novels.
- Prior to becoming an agent, Ms. Grosjean was manager of an independent bookstore. She also worked in publishing and advertising.
Represents Novels (exclusively). **Considers these fiction areas:** Contemporary issues; historical; literary; mainstream/contemporary; mystery/suspense; regional; romance.
- This agency offers some editorial assistance (ie, line-by-line edits). Actively seeking literary novels and mysteries.
How to Contact Query with SASE. No cold calls, please. Considers simultaneous queries. Responds in 1 week to queries; 1 month to mss. Returns materials only with SASE. Obtains most new clients through recommendations from others, solicitations.
Recent Sales *I Love You Like a Tomato*, by Marie Giordano (Forge Books); *Nectar*, by David C. Fickett (Forge Books); *Cycling* (Kensington), *Crooked Lines* (NavPress) and *Sanctuary* (Kensington), by Greg Garrett; *The Smoke*, by Tony Broadbent (St. Martin's/Minotaur); *Flights of Joy*, by Marie Bostwick (Kensington).
Terms Agent receives 15% commission on domestic sales; 20% commission on foreign sales. No written contract. Charges clients for photocopying, mailing expenses.
Writers' Conferences Book Passages Mystery Writer's Conference (Corte Madera CA, July); Writers' League of Texas Conference (Austin TX, July).

THE GROSVENOR LITERARY AGENCY
5510 Grosvenor Lane, Bethesda MD 20814. Fax: (301)581-9401. E-mail: dcgrosveno@aol.com. **Contact:** Deborah C. Grosvenor. Estab. 1996. Member of National Press Club. Represents 30 clients. 10% of clients are new/unpublished writers. Currently handles: 80% nonfiction books; 20% novels.
- Prior to opening her agency, Ms. Grosvenor was a book editor for 16 years.
Represents Nonfiction books, novels. **Considers these nonfiction areas:** Animals; anthropology/archaeology; art/architecture/design; biography/autobiography; business/economics; child guidance/parenting; current affairs; government/politics/law; health/medicine; history; how-to; language/literature/criticism; military/war; money/finance; music/dance; nature/environment; photography; popular culture; psychology; religious/inspirational; science/technology; self-help/personal improvement; sociology; spirituality; theater/film; translation; true crime/investigative; women's issues/studies. **Considers these fiction areas:** Contemporary issues; detective/police/crime; family saga; historical; literary; mainstream/contemporary; mystery/suspense; romance (contemporary, gothic, historical); thriller.
How to Contact Send outline/proposal for nonfiction; send query and 3 sample chapters for fiction. No fax queries. Responds in 1 month to queries; 2 months to mss. Returns materials only with SASE. Obtains most new clients through recommendations from others.
Terms Agent receives 15% commission on domestic sales; 20% commission on foreign sales. Offers written contract; 10-day notice must be given to terminate contract.

REECE HALSEY NORTH
98 Main St., Tiburon CA 94920. Fax: (310)652-7595. E-mail: info@reecehalseynorth.com. Website: www.reece halseynorth.com. **Contact:** Kimberley Cameron (all queries) at Reece Halsey North. Estab. 1957 (Reece Halsey Agency); 1993 (Reech Halsey North). Member of AAR. Represents 40 clients. 30% of clients are new/unpublished writers. Currently handles: 25% nonfiction books; 75% fiction.
- The Reece Halsey Agency has an illustrious client list largely of established writers, including the estate of Aldous Huxley, and has represented Upton Sinclair, William Faulkner and Henry Miller.
Member Agents Dorris Halsey, Reece Halsey Agency (Los Angeles); Kimberley Cameron, Reece Halsey North.
Represents Nonfiction books, novels. **Considers these nonfiction areas:** Biography/autobiography; current affairs; history; language/literature/criticism; popular culture; science/technology; true crime/investigative; women's issues/studies. **Considers these fiction areas:** Action/adventure; contemporary issues; detective/police/crime; ethnic; family saga; historical; literary; mainstream/contemporary; mystery/suspense; science fiction; thriller; women's.
- "We are looking for a unique and heartfelt voice."
How to Contact Query with SASE, submit first 10 pages of novel. Please do not fax queries. Responds in 3-6

weeks to queries; 3 months to mss. Obtains most new clients through recommendations from others, solicitations.

Terms Agent receives 15% commission on domestic sales; 10% commission on dramatic rights sales. Offers written contract, binding for 1 year. Requests 6 copies of ms if representing an author.

Writers' Conferences Maui Writers Conference; Aspen; Willamette.

Tips "Always send a well-written query and include a SASE with it."

☑ THE MITCHELL J. HAMILBURG AGENCY

149 S. Barrington Ave., #732, Los Angeles CA 90049-2930. (310)471-4024. Fax: (310)471-9588. **Contact:** Michael Hamilburg. Estab. 1937. Signatory of WGA. Represents 70 clients. Currently handles: 70% nonfiction books; 30% novels.

Represents Nonfiction books, novels. **Considers these nonfiction areas:** Anthropology/archaeology; biography/autobiography; business/economics; child guidance/parenting; cooking/foods/nutrition; creative nonfiction; current affairs; education; government/politics/law; health/medicine; history; memoirs; military/war; money/finance; psychology; recreation; regional; self-help/personal improvement; sex; sociology; spirituality; sports; travel; women's issues/studies; romance; architecture; inspirational; true crime. **Considers these fiction areas:** Action/adventure; experimental; feminist; glitz; humor/satire; military/war; mystery/suspense; New Age; occult; regional; religious/inspirational; romance; sports; thriller; crime; mainstream; psychic.

How to Contact Query with SASE, submit outline, 2 sample chapters. Responds in 1 month to mss. Obtains most new clients through recommendations from others, conferences, personal search.

Terms Agent receives 10-15% commission on domestic sales.

☑ THE JOY HARRIS LITERARY AGENCY, INC.

156 Fifth Ave., Suite 617, New York NY 10010. (212)924-6269. Fax: (212)924-6609. E-mail: gen.office@jhlitagent.com. **Contact:** Joy Harris. Member of AAR. Represents over 100 clients. Currently handles: 50% nonfiction books; 50% novels.

Member Agents Leslie Daniels; Stéphanie Abou; Sara Lustg.

Represents Nonfiction books, novels. **Considers these fiction areas:** Contemporary issues; ethnic; experimental; family saga; feminist; gay/lesbian; glitz; hi-lo; historical; humor/satire; literary; mainstream/contemporary; multicultural; multimedia; mystery/suspense; picture books; regional; short story collections; spiritual; translation; women's.

    ○➡ Does not want to receive screenplays.

How to Contact Query with sample chapter, outline/proposal, SASE. Considers simultaneous queries. Responds in 2 months to queries. Obtains most new clients through recommendations from clients and editors.

Recent Sales This agency prefers not to share information on specific sales.

Terms Agent receives 15% commission on domestic sales; 20% commission on foreign sales. Charges clients for some office expenses.

☑ HARTLINE LITERARY AGENCY

123 Queenston Dr., Pittsburgh PA 15235-5429. (412)829-2495 or 2483. Fax: (412)829-2450. E-mail: joyce@hartlineliterary.com. Website: www.hartlineliterary.com. **Contact:** Joyce A. Hart. Estab. 1990. Represents 40 clients. 30% of clients are new/unpublished writers. Currently handles: 40% nonfiction books; 60% novels.

Member Agents Joyce A. Hart, principal agent; Janet Benrey; Tamela Hancock Murray; Andrea Boeshaar and James D. Hart.

Represents Nonfiction books, novels. **Considers these nonfiction areas:** Business/economics; child guidance/parenting; cooking/foods/nutrition; money/finance; religious/inspirational; self-help/personal improvement; women's issues/studies. **Considers these fiction areas:** Action/adventure; contemporary issues; family saga; historical; literary; mystery/suspense (amateur sleuth, cozy); regional; religious/inspirational; romance (contemporary, gothic, historical, regency); thriller.

    ○➡ This agency specializes in the Christian bookseller market. Actively seeking adult fiction, self-help, nutritional books, devotional, business. Does not want to receive science fiction, erotica, gay/lesbian, fantasy, horror, etc.

How to Contact Submit outline, 3 sample chapters. Accepts e-mail and fax queries. Considers simultaneous queries. Responds in 2 months to queries; 3 months to mss. Returns materials only with SASE. Obtains most new clients through recommendations from others.

Recent Sales *Vanished*, by Ward Tanneberg (Kregel); *Hosea's Bride, Unless Two Agree, Beauty for Ashes* and *Joy for Mourning*, by Dorothy Clark (Steeple Hill); *Dead as a Scone* and *The Final Crumpet*, by Ron and Janet Benrey (Barbour Publishing); *Overcoming the Top Ten Reasons Singles Stay Single*, by Drs. Tom and Beverly Rodgers (NavPress); *A Land of Sheltered Promise* and *Homestead*, by Jane Kirkpatrick (Waterbrook); *An Act of Murder*, by Linda Rosencrance (Kensington); *When Skylarks Fall*, by John Robinson (Riveroak); *Some Wel-*

come Home, by Sharon Wildwind (Five Star); *Beauty Queens and Front Porch Princesses*, by Kathryn Springer (Steeple Hill); *Sahm I Am*, by Meredith Efken (Steeple Hill); *Disturbing Behavior*, by Lee Virkich and Steve Vandergriff.

Terms Agent receives 15% commission on domestic sales. Offers written contract.

JOHN HAWKINS & ASSOCIATES, INC.

71 W. 23rd St., Suite 1600, New York NY 10010. (212)807-7040. Fax: (212)807-9555. E-mail: jha@jhalit.com. Website: jhaliterary.com. **Contact:** John Hawkins, William Reiss. Estab. 1893. Member of AAR. Represents over 100 clients. 5-10% of clients are new/unpublished writers. Currently handles: 40% nonfiction books; 40% novels; 20% juvenile books.

Member Agents Moses Cardona; Warren Frazier; Anne Hawkins; John Hawkins; William Reiss.

Represents Nonfiction books, novels, juvenile books. **Considers these nonfiction areas:** Agriculture/horticulture; americana; anthropology/archaeology; art/architecture/design; biography/autobiography; business/economics; creative nonfiction; current affairs; education; ethnic/cultural interests; gardening; gay/lesbian issues; government/politics/law; health/medicine; history; how-to; interior design/decorating; language/literature/criticism; memoirs; money/finance; multicultural; nature/environment; philosophy; popular culture; psychology; recreation; science/technology; self-help/personal improvement; sex; sociology; software; theater/film; travel; true crime/investigative; young adult; music. **Considers these fiction areas:** Action/adventure; contemporary issues; detective/police/crime; ethnic; experimental; family saga; feminist; gay/lesbian; glitz; gothic; hi-lo; historical; literary; mainstream/contemporary; military/war; multicultural; multimedia; mystery/suspense; psychic/supernatural; religious/inspirational; short story collections; sports; thriller; translation; westerns/frontier; young adult; women's.

How to Contact Query with SASE, submit proposal package, outline. Considers simultaneous queries. Responds in 1 month to queries. Returns materials only with SASE. Obtains most new clients through recommendations from others.

Recent Sales *The Last Shot*, by Lynn Schooler; *Joplin's Ghost*, by Tananarive Due.

Terms Agent receives 15% commission on domestic sales; 20% commission on foreign sales. Charges clients for photocopying.

RICHARD HENSHAW GROUP

127 W. 24th St., 4th Floor, New York NY 10011. (212)414-1172. Fax: (212)414-1182. E-mail: submissions@henshaw.com. Website: www.rich.henshaw.com. **Contact:** Rich Henshaw. Estab. 1995. Member of AAR, SinC, MWA, HWA, SFWA, RWA. Represents 35 clients. 20% of clients are new/unpublished writers. Currently handles: 30% nonfiction books; 70% novels.

● Prior to opening his agency, Mr. Henshaw served as an agent with Richard Curtis Associates, Inc.

Represents Nonfiction books, novels. **Considers these nonfiction areas:** Animals; biography/autobiography; business/economics; child guidance/parenting; computers/electronic; cooking/foods/nutrition; current affairs; gay/lesbian issues; government/politics/law; health/medicine; how-to; humor/satire; military/war; money/finance; music/dance; nature/environment; New Age/metaphysics; popular culture; psychology; science/technology; self-help/personal improvement; sociology; sports; true crime/investigative; women's issues/studies. **Considers these fiction areas:** Action/adventure; detective/police/crime; ethnic; family saga; fantasy; glitz; historical; horror; humor/satire; literary; mainstream/contemporary; mystery/suspense; psychic/supernatural; romance; science fiction; sports; thriller.

○━ This agency specializes in thrillers, mysteries, science fiction, fantasy and horror.

How to Contact Query with SASE. Responds in 3 weeks to queries; 6 weeks to mss. Obtains most new clients through recommendations from others, solicitations, conferences.

Recent Sales *A Taint in the Blood*, by Dana Stabenow (St. Martin's); *Wife of Moon*, by Margaret Coel (Berkely); *The Well-Educated Mind*, by Susan Wise Bauer (Norton); *The Witch's Tongue*, by James D. Doss (St. Martin's); *How to Box Like the Pros*, by Joe Frazier & William Dettloff (HarperCollins). Other clients include Jessie Wise, Peter van Dijk, Jay Caselberg, Judith Laik.

Terms Agent receives 15% commission on domestic sales; 20% commission on foreign sales. No written contract. 100% of business is derived from commissions on ms sales. Charges clients for photocopying mss and book orders.

Tips "While we do not have any reason to believe that our submission guidelines will change in the near future, writers can find up-to-date submission policy information on our website. Always include a SASE with correct return postage."

SUSAN HERNER RIGHTS AGENCY

P.O. Box 57, Pound Ridge NY 10576. (914)234-2864. Fax: (914)234-2866. E-mail: sherneragency@optonline.net. **Contact:** Susan Herner. Estab. 1987. Represents 100 clients. 30% of clients are new/unpublished writers. Currently handles: 60% nonfiction books; 40% novels.

Member Agents Susan Herner, president (nonfiction, thriller, mystery, strong women's fiction).
Represents Nonfiction books (adult), novels (adult). **Considers these nonfiction areas:** Anthropology/archaeology; child guidance/parenting; current affairs; ethnic/cultural interests; gay/lesbian issues; government/politics/law; health/medicine; history; how-to; language/literature/criticism; nature/environment; New Age/metaphysics; popular culture; psychology; religious/inspirational; science/technology; self-help/personal improvement; sociology; spirituality; true crime/investigative; women's issues/studies; biography. **Considers these fiction areas:** Action/adventure; contemporary issues; detective/police/crime; ethnic; feminist; glitz; literary; mainstream/contemporary; mystery/suspense; thriller.

> ◯ᴛ "I'm particularly looking for strong women's fiction and thrillers. I'm particularly interested in women's issues, popular science and feminist spirituality."

How to Contact Query with SASE, outline, sample chapters, or query by e-mail (no attachments). Considers simultaneous queries. Responds in 1 month to queries. Returns materials only with SASE.
Recent Sales *Heartwood*, by Barbara Campbell (Daw Books); *Our Improbable Universe*, by Michael Mallary (4 Walls 8 Windows); *Everything You Need to Know About Latino History*, by Himilce Novas (Plume).
Terms Agent receives 15% commission on domestic sales; 20% commission on foreign sales; 20% commission on dramatic rights sales. Charges clients for extraordinary postage and photocopying. "Agency has 2 divisions: one represents writers on a commission-only basis; the other represents the rights for small publishers and packagers who do not have in-house subsidiary rights representation. Percentage of income derived from each division is currently 80-20."

◙ FREDERICK HILL BONNIE NADELL, INC.

1842 Union St., San Francisco CA 94123. (415)921-2910. Fax: (415)921-2802. **Contact:** Irene Moore. Estab. 1979. Represents 100 clients.
Member Agents Fred Hill (president); Bonnie Nadell (vice president); Irene Moore (associate).
Represents Nonfiction books, novels. **Considers these nonfiction areas:** Current affairs; language/literature/criticism; nature/environment; biography; government/politics. **Considers these fiction areas:** Literary; mainstream/contemporary.
How to Contact Query with SASE. No e-mail or fax queries. Considers simultaneous queries. Returns materials only with SASE.
Recent Sales *Field Guide to Getting Lost*, by Rebecca Solnit; *All That Matters*, by Senator Barbara Boxer; *Cancer Made Me a Shallower Person*, by Miriam Enjelberg.
Terms Agent receives 15% commission on domestic sales; 20% commission on foreign sales; 15% commission on dramatic rights sales. Charges clients for photocopying.

◙ HOPKINS LITERARY ASSOCIATES

2117 Buffalo Rd., Suite 327, Rochester NY 14624-1507. (585)352-6268. **Contact:** Pam Hopkins. Estab. 1996. Member of AAR, RWA. Represents 30 clients. 5% of clients are new/unpublished writers. Currently handles: 100% novels.
Represents Novels. **Considers these fiction areas:** Historical; mainstream/contemporary; romance; women's.

> ◯ᴛ This agency specializes in women's fiction, particularly historical, contemporary and category romance, as well as mainstream work.

How to Contact Submit outline, 3 sample chapters. No e-mail or fax queries. Considers simultaneous queries. Responds in 2 weeks to queries; 1 month to mss. Returns materials only with SASE. Obtains most new clients through recommendations from others, solicitations, conferences.
Recent Sales Sold 50 titles in the last year. *The First Mistake*, by Merline Lovelace (Mira); *The Romantic*, by Madeline Hunter (Bantam); *The Damsel in this Dress*, by Marianne Stillings (Avon).
Terms Agent receives 15% commission on domestic sales; 20% commission on foreign sales. No written contract.
Writers' Conferences Romance Writers of America.

Ⓝ INKWELL MANAGEMENT, LLC

521 Fifth Ave., 26th Floor, New York NY 10175. (212)922-3500. Fax: (212)922-0535. E-mail: contact@inkwellmanagement.com. Estab. 2004. Represents 500 clients. Currently handles: 60% nonfiction books; 40% novels.
Member Agents Michael Carlisle; Richard Pine; Kimberly Witherspoon; George Lucas; Catherine Drayton; Matthew Guma.
Represents Nonfiction books, novels. **Considers these nonfiction areas:** Business/economics; current affairs; health/medicine; money/finance; psychology; self-help/personal improvement. **Considers these fiction areas:** Detective/police/crime; family saga; historical; literary; mainstream/contemporary; thriller.
How to Contact Query with SASE. Prefers to read materials exclusively. No e-mail or fax queries. Responds in 1 month to queries. Obtains most new clients through recommendations from others.

Recent Sales Sold 100 titles in the last year.

Terms Agent receives 15% commission on domestic sales; 15% commission on foreign sales. Offers written contract.

Tips "Our agency will consider exclusive submissions only. All submissions must be accompanied by postage or SASE. We will not read manuscripts before receiving a letter of inquiry."

🌀 J DE S ASSOCIATES, INC.

9 Shagbark Rd., Wilson Point, South Norwalk CT 06854. (203)838-7571. **Contact:** Jacques de Spoelberch. Estab. 1975. Represents 50 clients. Currently handles: 50% nonfiction books; 50% novels.

● Prior to opening his agency, Mr. de Spoelberch was an editor with Houghton Mifflin.

Represents Nonfiction books, novels. **Considers these nonfiction areas:** Biography/autobiography; business/economics; current affairs; ethnic/cultural interests; government/politics/law; health/medicine; history; military/war; New Age/metaphysics; self-help/personal improvement; sociology; sports; translation. **Considers these fiction areas:** Detective/police/crime; historical; juvenile; literary; mainstream/contemporary; mystery/suspense; New Age; westerns/frontier; young adult.

How to Contact Query with SASE. Responds in 2 months to queries. Obtains most new clients through recommendations from authors and other clients.

Terms Agent receives 15% commission on domestic sales; 20% commission on foreign sales. Charges clients for foreign postage and photocopying.

🌀 JABBERWOCKY LITERARY AGENCY

P.O. Box 4558, Sunnyside NY 11104-0558. (718)392-5985. Website: awfulagent.com. **Contact:** Joshua Bilmes. Estab. 1994. Member of SFWA. Represents 40 clients. 15% of clients are new/unpublished writers. Currently handles: 15% nonfiction books; 75% novels; 5% scholarly books; 5% other.

Represents Nonfiction books, novels, scholarly books. **Considers these nonfiction areas:** Biography/autobiography; business/economics; cooking/foods/nutrition; current affairs; gay/lesbian issues; government/politics/law; health/medicine; history; humor/satire; language/literature/criticism; military/war; money/finance; nature/environment; popular culture; science/technology; sociology; sports; theater/film; true crime/investigative; women's issues/studies. **Considers these fiction areas:** Action/adventure; contemporary issues; detective/police/crime; ethnic; family saga; fantasy; gay/lesbian; glitz; historical; horror; humor/satire; literary; mainstream/contemporary; psychic/supernatural; regional; science fiction; sports; thriller.

⚿ This agency represents quite a lot of genre fiction and is actively seeking to increase the amount of nonfiction projects. It does not handle juvenile or young adult. Book-length material only; no poetry, articles or short fiction.

How to Contact Query with SASE. No mss unless requested. No e-mail or fax queries. Considers simultaneous queries. Responds in 2 weeks to queries. Returns materials only with SASE. Obtains most new clients through solicitations, recommendation by current clients.

Recent Sales Sold 20 titles in the last year. *Dead as a Doornail*, by Charlaine Harris (ACE); *Marque & Reprisal*, by Elizabeth Moon (Del Rey); *Elantris*, by Brandon Sanderson (Tor). Other clients include Simon Green, Tanya Huff and "Hot Blood and "Dark Delicacies" anthology series.

Terms Agent receives 15% commission on domestic sales; 20% commission on foreign sales. Offers written contract, binding for 1 year. Charges clients for book purchases, photocopying, international book/ms mailing.

Writers' Conferences Malice Domestic (Washington DC, May); World SF Convention (Los Angeles, August); Icon (Stony Brook NY, April).

Tips "In approaching with a query, the most important things to me are your credits and your biographical background to the extent it's relevant to your work. I (and most agents) will ignore the adjectives you may choose to describe your own work."

JCA LITERARY AGENCY

174 Sullivan St., New York NY 10012. (212)807-0888. E-mail: tom@jcalit.com. Website: www.jcalit.com. **Contact:** Tom Cushman. Estab. 1978. Member of AAR. Represents 100 clients. 10% of clients are new/unpublished writers. Currently handles: 20% nonfiction books; 75% novels; 5% scholarly books.

Member Agents Tom Cushman, Melanie Meyers Cushman, Tony Outhwaite.

Represents Nonfiction books, novels. **Considers these nonfiction areas:** Biography/autobiography; business/economics; current affairs; government/politics/law; history; language/literature/criticism; memoirs; military/war; money/finance; nature/environment; popular culture; science/technology; sociology; sports; theater/film; translation; true crime/investigative. **Considers these fiction areas:** Action/adventure; contemporary issues; detective/police/crime; family saga; historical; literary; mainstream/contemporary; mystery/suspense; sports; thriller.

O— Does not want to receive screenplays, poetry, children's books, science fiction/fantasy, genre romance.

How to Contact Query with SASE. No e-mail or fax queries. Considers simultaneous queries. Responds in 2 weeks to queries; 10 weeks to mss. Returns materials only with SASE. Obtains most new clients through recommendations from others, solicitations, conferences.

Recent Sales *Jury of One*, by David Ellis (Putnam); *The Heaven of Mercury*, by Brad Watson (Norton); *The Rope Eater*, by Ben Jones; *The Circus in Winter*, by Cathy Day. Other clients include Ernest J. Gaines, Gwen Hunter.

Terms Agent receives 15% commission on domestic sales; 20% commission on foreign sales. No written contract. "We work with our clients on a handshake basis." Charges for postage on overseas submissions, photocopying, mss for submission, books purchased for subrights submission, and bank charges, where applicable. "We deduct the cost from payments received from publishers."

Tips "We do not ourselves provide legal, accounting or public relations services for our clients, although some of the advice we give falls somewhat into these realms. In cases where it seems necessary we will recommend obtaining outside advice or assistance in these areas from professionals who are not in any way connected to the agency."

▣ ◪ JELLINEK & MURRAY LITERARY AGENCY

2024 Muana Place, Honolulu HI 96822. (808)521-4057. Fax: (808)521-4058. E-mail: jellinek@lava.net. **Contact:** Roger Jellinek. Estab. 1995. Represents 75 clients. 90% of clients are new/unpublished writers. Currently handles: 70% nonfiction books; 30% novels.

• Prior to becoming an agent, Mr. Jellinek was deputy editor, *New York Times Book Review* (1966-74); editor-in-chief, New York Times Book Co. (1975-1981); editor/packager book/TV projects (1981-1995); editorial director, Inner Ocean Publishing (2000-2003).

Member Agents Roger Jellinek (general fiction, nonfiction); Eden Lee Murray (general fiction, nonfiction).

Represents Nonfiction books, novels, textbooks, movie scripts (from book clients), TV scripts (from book clients). **Considers these nonfiction areas:** Animals; anthropology/archaeology; art/architecture/design; biography/autobiography; business/economics; child guidance/parenting; computers/electronic; cooking/foods/nutrition; current affairs; ethnic/cultural interests; gay/lesbian issues; government/politics/law; health/medicine; history; how-to; memoirs; military/war; money/finance; nature/environment; New Age/metaphysics; popular culture; psychology; religious/inspirational; science/technology; self-help/personal improvement; travel; true crime/investigative; women's issues/studies. **Considers these fiction areas:** Action/adventure; confession; contemporary issues; detective/police/crime; erotica; ethnic; family saga; feminist; gay/lesbian; glitz; historical; horror; humor/satire; literary; mainstream/contemporary; multicultural; mystery/suspense; New Age; picture books; psychic/supernatural; regional (specific to Hawaii); thriller.

O— This agency is the only literary agency in Hawaii. "Half our clients are based in Hawaii; half from all over the world. We prefer submissions (after query) via e-mail attachment. We only send out fully-edited proposals and manuscripts." Actively seeking first-rate writing.

How to Contact Query with SASE, submit outline, 2 sample chapters, author bio, credentials/platform. Accepts e-mail and fax queries. Considers simultaneous queries. Responds in 2-3 weeks to queries; 2 months to mss. Returns materials only with SASE. Obtains most new clients through recommendations from others, solicitations, conferences.

Recent Sales Sold 10 titles and sold 1 script in the last year.

Terms Agent receives 15% commission on domestic sales; 25% commission on foreign sales. Offers written contract, binding for indefinite period; 30-day notice must be given to terminate contract. Charges clients for photocopies and postage. May refer to editing services occasionally, if author asks for recommendation. "We have no income deriving from our referrals. Referrals to editors do not imply representation."

Writers' Conferences Mr. Jellinek manages the publishing program at the Maui Writers Conference.

Tips "Would-be authors should be well read and knowledgeable about their field and genre."

◪ NATASHA KERN LITERARY AGENCY

P.O. Box 2908, Portland OR 97208-2908. (503)297-6190. Website: www.natashakern.com. **Contact:** Natasha Kern. Estab. 1986. Member of RWA, MWA, SinC.

• Prior to opening her agency, Ms. Kern worked as an editor and publicist for New York publishers (Simon & Schuster, Bantam, Ballantine). "This agency has sold over 600 books."

Represents Adult commercial nonfiction and fiction. **Considers these nonfiction areas:** Animals; anthropology/archaeology; business/economics; child guidance/parenting; current affairs; ethnic/cultural interests; gardening; health/medicine; nature/environment; New Age/metaphysics; popular culture; psychology; religious/inspirational; science/technology; self-help/personal improvement; spirituality; women's issues/studies; investigative journalism. **Considers these fiction areas:** Historical; mainstream/contemporary; multicultural;

mystery/suspense; religious/inspirational; romance (contemporary, historical); thriller (medical, scientific, historical); chick lit; lady lit.

> ⊶ This agency specializes in commercial fiction and nonfiction for adults. "We are a full-service agency." Does not represent sports, true crime, scholarly works, coffee table books, war memoirs, software, scripts, literary fiction, photography, poetry, short stories, children's, horror, fantasy, genre science fiction, stage plays or traditional Westerns.

How to Contact Query with SASE, include submission history, writing credits, length of ms. Considers simultaneous queries. Responds in 3 weeks to queries.

Recent Sales Sold 53 titles in the last year. *Beyond the Shadows*, by Robin Lee Hatcher (Tyndale); *The Waiting Child*, by Cindy Champnella; *Perfect Killer*, by Lewis Perdue (TOR); *The Secret Lives of the Sushi Club*, by Christy Yorke; *Ride the Fire*, by Pamela Clare (Leisure).

Terms Agent receives 15% commission on domestic sales; 20% commission on foreign sales; 15% commission on dramatic rights sales.

Writers' Conferences RWA National Conference; MWA National Conference; and many regional conferences.

Tips "Your chances of being accepted for representation will be greatly enhanced by going to our website first. Our idea of a dream client is someone who participates in a mutually respectful business relationship, is clear about needs and goals, and communicates about career planning. If we know what you need and want, we can help you achieve it. A dream client has a storytelling gift, a commitment to a writing career, a desire to learn and grow, and a passion for excellence. We want clients who are expressing their own unique voice and truly have something of their own to communicate. This client understands that many people have to work together for a book to succeed and that everything in publishing takes far longer than one imagines. Trust and communication are truly essential."

⬭ KISSED PUBLICATIONS & LITERARY AGENCY

P.O. Box 9819, Hampton VA 23670. (757)722-3031. Fax: (757)722-1301. E-mail: kissed@kissedpublications.com. Website: www.kissedpublications.com. **Contact:** Kimberly T. Matthews. Estab. 2003. Member of Better Business Bureau. Currently handles: 10% nonfiction books; 90% novels.

> • Prior to becoming an agent, Ms. Matthews was an author and speaker.

Represents Nonfiction books, novels, short story collections. **Considers these nonfiction areas:** Religious/inspirational. **Considers these fiction areas:** Ethnic; mainstream/contemporary; religious/inspirational; young adult.

> ⊶ This agency specializes in African-American mainstream fiction and inspirational nonfiction. Actively seeking new, unpublished authors/clients.

How to Contact Query with SASE. Accepts e-mail queries. No fax queries. Considers simultaneous queries. Responds in 2 weeks to queries; 8 weeks to mss. Returns materials only with SASE.

Terms Agent receives 15% commission on domestic sales; 20% commission on foreign sales. Offers written contract. Charges authors for postage and photocopying.

HARVEY KLINGER, INC.

301 W. 53rd St., Suite 21-A, New York NY 10019. (212)581-7068. Fax: (212)315-3823. E-mail: queries@harveyklinger.com. Website: www.harveyklinger.com. **Contact:** Harvey Klinger. Estab. 1977. Member of AAR. Represents 100 clients. 25% of clients are new/unpublished writers. Currently handles: 50% nonfiction books; 50% novels.

Member Agents David Dunton (popular culture, with a speciality in music-related books; literary fiction; crime novels; thrillers); Wendy Silbert (narrative nonfiction; historical narrative nonfiction; politics; history; biographies; memoir; literary ficiton; business books; culinary narratives); Sara Crowe (children's and young adult authors, some adult authors, foreign rights sales).

Represents Nonfiction books, novels. **Considers these nonfiction areas:** Biography/autobiography; cooking/foods/nutrition; health/medicine; psychology; science/technology; self-help/personal improvement; spirituality; sports; true crime/investigative; women's issues/studies. **Considers these fiction areas:** Action/adventure; detective/police/crime; family saga; glitz; literary; mainstream/contemporary; mystery/suspense; thriller.

> ⊶ This agency specializes in "big, mainstream, contemporary fiction and nonfiction."

How to Contact Query with SASE. No phone queries. Accepts e-mail queries. No fax queries. Responds in 2 months to queries; 2 months to mss. Obtains most new clients through recommendations from others.

Recent Sales *The Red Hat Society: Fun & Friendship After Fifty*, by Sue Ellen Cooper; *Wilco: Learning How to Die*, by Greg Kot; *A Window Across the River*, by Brian Morton; *The Sweet Potato Queen's Field Guide to Men: Every Man I Love Is Either Gay, Married, or Dead*, by Jill Conner Browne; *Get Your Share: A Guide to Striking it Rich in the Stock Market*, by Julie Stav; *Wink: The Incredible Life & Epic Journey of Jimmy Winkfield*, by Ed Hotaling. Other clients include Barbara Wood, Terry Kay, Barbara De Angelis, Jeremy Jackson.

Terms Agent receives 15% commission on domestic sales; 25% commission on foreign sales. Offers written contract. Charges for photocopying mss, overseas postage for mss.

THE KNIGHT AGENCY

577 S. Main St., Madison GA 30650. E-mail: submissions@knightagency.net. Website: www.knightagency.net. **Contact:** Judson Knight, ms coordinator. Estab. 1996. Member of AAR, RWA, Authors Guild. Represents 65 clients. 40% of clients are new/unpublished writers. Currently handles: 50% nonfiction books; 50% novels.
Member Agents Deidre Knight (president, agent); Pamela Harty (agent); Nephele Tempest.
Represents Nonfiction books, novels. **Considers these nonfiction areas:** Business/economics; child guidance/parenting; current affairs; ethnic/cultural interests; health/medicine; history; how-to; money/finance; popular culture; psychology; religious/inspirational; self-help/personal improvement; theater/film. **Considers these fiction areas:** Literary; mainstream/contemporary (commercial); romance (contemporary, paranormal, romantic suspense, historical, inspirational); women's.

> O— "We are looking for a wide variety of fiction and nonfiction. In the nonfiction area, we're particularly eager to find personal finance, business investment, pop culture, self-help/motivational and popular reference books. In fiction, we're always looking for romance; women's fiction; commercial fiction; literary and multicultural fiction." Does not want science fiction/fantasy, mysteries, action/adventure, horror, short story or poetry collections.

How to Contact Query with SASE. Accepts e-mail queries; no attachments. No phone queries, please. Considers simultaneous queries. Responds in 1-3 weeks to queries; 3 months to mss.
Recent Sales Sold approximately 65 titles in the last year. *Soul Journey*, by Jacquelin Thomas (BET/New Spirit); *Heart Duel*, by Robin Owens (Berkley); *Pink Slip Party*, by Cara Lockwood (Pocket Books/Downtown Press).
Terms Agent receives 15% commission on domestic sales; 20-25% commission on foreign sales. Offers written contract, binding for 1 year; 1-month notice must be given to terminate contract. Charges clients for photocopying, postage, overnight courier expenses. "These are deducted from the sale of the work, not billed upfront."
Tips "At the Knight Agency, a client usually ends up becoming a friend."

☑ ELAINE KOSTER LITERARY AGENCY, LLC

55 Central Park W., Suite 6, New York NY 10023. (212)362-9488. Fax: (212)712-0164. **Contact:** Elaine Koster, Stephanie Lehmann. Member of AAR, MWA. Represents 40 clients. 10% of clients are new/unpublished writers. Currently handles: 30% nonfiction books; 70% novels.

• Prior to opening her agency in 1998, Ms. Koster was president and publisher of Dutton NAL.
Represents Nonfiction books, novels. **Considers these nonfiction areas:** Biography/autobiography; business/economics; child guidance/parenting; cooking/foods/nutrition; current affairs; ethnic/cultural interests; health/medicine; history; how-to; money/finance; nature/environment; popular culture; psychology; self-help/personal improvement; spirituality; women's issues/studies. **Considers these fiction areas:** Contemporary issues; detective/police/crime; ethnic; family saga; feminist; historical; literary; mainstream/contemporary; mystery/suspense (amateur sleuth, cozy, culinary, malice domestic); regional; thriller; chick lit.

> O— This agency specializes in quality fiction and nonfiction. Does not want to receive juvenile, screenplays, or science fiction.

How to Contact Query with SASE, outline, 3 sample chapters. Prefers to read materials exclusively. No e-mail or fax queries. Responds in 3 weeks to queries; 1 month to mss. Returns materials only with SASE. Obtains most new clients through recommendations from others.
Recent Sales Sold 42 titles in the last year. *Dreaming in Titanic City*, by Khaled Hosseini (Riverhead); *The Nineteenth Wife*, by David Ebershoff (Random House); *Run the Risk*, by Scott Frost (Putnam).
Terms Agent receives 15% commission on domestic sales. Bills back specific expenses incurred doing business for a client.
Tips "We prefer exclusive submissions. Don't e-mail or fax submissions. Please include biographical information and publishing history."

☑ KRAAS LITERARY AGENCY

13514 Winter Creek Ct., Houston TX 77077. (281)870-9770. Fax: (281)679-1655. **Contact:** Irene Kraas. Address Other: 3447 NE 23rd Ave., Portland OR 97212. (503)319-0900. **Contact:** Ashley Kraas. Estab. 1990. Represents 40 clients. 75% of clients are new/unpublished writers. Currently handles: 5% nonfiction books; 95% novels.
Member Agents Irene Kraas, principal (psychological thrillers, medical thrillers, mysteries, literary fiction); Ashley Kraas, associate (romance, women's fiction, historical fiction, memoirs, biographies, self-help, spiritual). Please send appropriate submissions to the correct address.
Represents Nonfiction books, novels, young adult.

> O— This agency specializes in adult fiction. Actively seeking "books that are well written with commercial potential." Does not want to receive short stories, plays or poetry.

How to Contact Submit cover letter, first 50 pages of a completed ms, SASE; must include return postage and/or SASE. No e-mail or fax queries. Considers simultaneous queries. Returns materials only with SASE.
Recent Sales *Words to Die By*, by Kyra Davis (Harlequin); St. Germain Series (17&18), by Chelsea Quinn Yarbro (Tor); *Shriker*, by Janet Lee Carey (Atheneum); *Crazy Quilt*, by Paula Paul (UNH Pres); *The Sword, the Shield & the Crown*, a trilogy by Hilari Bell (Simon & Schuster).
Terms Agent receives 15% commission on domestic sales. Offers written contract. Charges clients for photocopying and postage.
Writers' Conferences *Irene:* Southwest Writers Conference (Albuquerque NM); Durango Writers Conference (Durango CO); Wrangling with Writing (Tucson AZ); *Ashley:* Surrey Writers Conference (Surrey BC); Wrangling with Writing (Tucson AZ); Schwap Writers Conference (Schuwap BC); Willamette Writers Group (Portland OR).
Tips "Material by unpublished authors will be accepted in the above areas only. Published authors seeking representation may contact us regarding any material in any area except children's picture books and chapter books."

PETER LAMPACK AGENCY, INC.
551 Fifth Ave., Suite 1613, New York NY 10176-0187. (212)687-9106. Fax: (212)687-9109. E-mail: alampack@verizon.net. **Contact:** Andrew Lampack. Estab. 1977. Represents 50 clients. 10% of clients are new/unpublished writers. Currently handles: 20% nonfiction books; 80% novels.
Member Agents Peter Lampack (psychological suspense, action/adventure, literary fiction, nonfiction, contemporary relationships); Rema Delanyan (foreign rights); Andrew Lampack (new writers).
Represents Nonfiction books, novels. **Considers these fiction areas:** Action/adventure; detective/police/crime; family saga; historical; literary; mainstream/contemporary; mystery/suspense; thriller; contemporary relationships.
  ○→ This agency specializes in commercial fiction and nonfiction by recognized experts. Actively seeking literary and commercial fiction, thrillers, mysteries, suspense, psychological thrillers. Does not want to receive horror, romance, science fiction, western, academic material.
How to Contact Query with SASE. *No unsolicited mss.* Accepts e-mail queries. No fax queries. Considers simultaneous queries. Responds in 2 months. Obtains most new clients through referrals made by clients.
Recent Sales *Slow Man*, by J.M. Coetzee; *Black Wind*, by Clive and Dirk Cussler; *Sacred Stone*, by Clive Cussler and Craig Dirgo; *Lost City*, by Clive Cussler with Paul Kemprecos.
Terms Agent receives 15% commission on domestic sales; 20% commission on foreign sales.
Writers' Conferences BEA (June).
Tips "Submit only your best work for consideration. Have a very specific agenda of goals you wish your prospective agent to accomplish for you. Provide the agent with a comprehensive statement of your credentials: educational and professional."

MICHAEL LARSEN/ELIZABETH POMADA, LITERARY AGENTS
1029 Jones St., San Francisco CA 94109-5023. (415)673-0939. E-mail: larsenpoma@aol.com. Website: www.larsen-pomada.com. **Contact:** Mike Larsen or Elizabeth Pomada. Estab. 1972. Member of AAR, Authors Guild, ASJA, PEN, WNBA, California Writers Club, National Speakers Association. Represents 100 clients. 40-45% of clients are new/unpublished writers. Currently handles: 70% nonfiction books; 30% novels.
  • Prior to opening their agency, Mr. Larsen and Ms. Pomada were promotion executives for major publishing houses. Mr. Larsen worked for Morrow, Bantam and Pyramid (now part of Berkley). Ms. Pomada worked at Holt, David McKay and The Dial Press.
Member Agents Michael Larsen (nonfiction); Elizabeth Pomada (fiction, narrative nonfiction, nonfiction for women).
Represents Adult book-length fiction and nonfiction that will interest New York publishers or are so irresistibly written or conceived that it doesn't matter. **Considers these nonfiction areas:** Anthropology/archaeology; art/architecture/design; biography/autobiography; business/economics; cooking/foods/nutrition; current affairs; ethnic/cultural interests; gay/lesbian issues; government/politics/law; health/medicine; history; how-to; humor/satire; memoirs; money/finance; music/dance; nature/environment; New Age/metaphysics; popular culture; psychology; religious/inspirational; science/technology; self-help/personal improvement; sociology; sports; theater/film; travel; true crime/investigative; women's issues/studies; futurism. **Considers these fiction areas:** Action/adventure; contemporary issues; detective/police/crime; ethnic; experimental; family saga; fantasy; feminist; gay/lesbian; glitz; historical; humor/satire; literary; mainstream/contemporary; mystery/suspense; religious/inspirational; romance (contemporary, gothic, historical); chick lit.
  ○→ "We have diverse tastes. We look for fresh voices and new ideas. We handle literary, commercial and genre fiction and the full range of nonfiction books." Actively seeking commercial and literary fiction.

Does not want to receive children's books, plays, short stories, screenplays, pornography, poetry or stories of abuse.

How to Contact Query with SASE, first 10 pages of completed novel, 2-page synopsis. For nonfiction, send title, promotion plan and proposal done according to our plan. (Please see our website.) No e-mail or fax queries. Responds in 2 days to queries; 2 months to mss.

Recent Sales Sold at least 15 titles in the last year. *If Life Is a Game, These Are the Stories*; *How to Sleep With a Movie Star*; *To Love a Thief*; *Guerilla Marketing for Consultants*.

Terms Agent receives 15% commission on domestic sales; 20% (30% for Asia) commission on foreign sales. May charge for printing, postage for multiple submissions, foreign mail, foreign phone calls, galleys, books and legal fees.

Writers' Conferences Book Expo America; Santa Barbara Writers Conference (Santa Barbara); Founders of the San Francisco Writers Conference (www.sanfranciscowritersconference.com).

Tips "If you can write books that meet the needs of the marketplace and you can promote your books, now is the best time ever to be a writer. We must find new writers to make a living, so we are very eager to hear from new writers whose work will interest large houses and nonfiction writers who can promote their books. For a list of recent sales, helpful info and three ways to make yourself irresistible to any publisher, please visit our website."

Ⓝ ▢ THE STEVE LAUBE AGENCY

5501 N. 7th Ave., #502, Phoenix AZ 85013. (602)336-8910. Fax: (602)532-7123. E-mail: krichards@stevelaube.com. Website: www.stevelaube.com. **Contact:** Steve Laube. Estab. 2004. Member of CBA. Represents 50 clients. 20% of clients are new/unpublished writers. Currently handles: 48% nonfiction books; 48% novels; 2% novellas; 2% scholarly books.

● Prior to becoming an agent, Mr. Laube worked 11 years as a bookseller and 11 years as an editor with Bethany House Publishers as editorial director of nonfiction.

Represents Nonfiction books, novels. **Considers these nonfiction areas:** Biography/autobiography; business/ economics; child guidance/parenting; current affairs; education; how-to; humor/satire; military/war; money/ finance; music/dance; popular culture; psychology; religious/inspirational; self-help/personal improvement; sports; theater/film; true crime/investigative; women's issues/studies; juvenile nonfiction. **Considers these fiction areas:** Action/adventure; detective/police/crime; fantasy; historical; humor/satire; literary; main-stream/contemporary; mystery/suspense; religious/inspirational; romance; science fiction; thriller; westerns/ frontier.

○⇥ "We primarily serve the Christian market (CBA). However, we have had success representing books in a variety of fields." Actively seeking fiction, nonfiction religious. Does not want children's picture books, poetry or cookbooks.

How to Contact Submit proposal package, outline, 3 sample chapters, SASE. Considers simultaneous queries. Responds in 1 month to mss. Responds in 6-8 weeks. Returns materials only with SASE. Obtains most new clients through recommendations from others, solicitations, conferences.

Recent Sales Sold 50 titles in the last year. Clients include Deborah Raney, Bright Media, Allison Bottke, H. Norman Wright, Ellie Kay, Jack Cavanaugh, Karen Ball, Tracey Bateman and Clint Kelly.

Terms Agent receives 15% commission on domestic sales; 20% commission on foreign sales. Offers written contract; 30-day notice must be given to terminate contract.

Writers' Conferences Mt. Hermon Christian Writers (Mt. Hermon CA); American Christian Fiction Writers; Glorieta Christian Writers Conference (Glorieta NM).

Ⓝ ▢ LAZEAR AGENCY, INC.

431 2nd St., Suite 300, Hudson WI 54016. (715)531-0012. Fax: (715)531-0016. E-mail: info@lazear.com. Website: www.lazear.com. **Contact:** Editorial Board. Estab. 1984. Represents 250 clients. Currently handles: 60% nonfiction books; 30% novels; 10% juvenile books.

● The Lazear Agency opened a New York Office in September 1997.

Member Agents Jonathon Lazear; Christi Cardenas; Julie Mayo; Anne Blackstone.

Represents Nonfiction books, novels, juvenile books, licensing; new media with connection to book project. **Considers these nonfiction areas:** Agriculture/horticulture; americana; animals; anthropology/archaeology; art/architecture/design; biography/autobiography; business/economics; child guidance/parenting; computers/ electronic; cooking/foods/nutrition; crafts/hobbies; creative nonfiction; current affairs; education; ethnic/cultural interests; gardening; gay/lesbian issues; government/politics/law; health/medicine; history; how-to; humor/satire; interior design/decorating; juvenile nonfiction; language/literature/criticism; memoirs; military/ war; money/finance; multicultural; music/dance; nature/environment; New Age/metaphysics; philosophy; photography; popular culture; psychology; recreation; regional; religious/inspirational; science/technology; self-help/personal improvement; sex; sociology; software; spirituality; sports; theater/film; translation; travel;

true crime/investigative; women's issues/studies; young adult. **Considers these fiction areas:** Action/adventure; comic books/cartoon; confession; contemporary issues; detective/police/crime; erotica; ethnic; experimental; family saga; fantasy; feminist; gay/lesbian; glitz; gothic; hi-lo; historical; horror; humor/satire; juvenile; literary; mainstream/contemporary; military/war; multicultural; multimedia; mystery/suspense; New Age; occult; picture books; plays; poetry; poetry in translation; psychic/supernatural; regional; religious/inspirational; romance; science fiction; short story collections; spiritual; sports; thriller; translation; westerns/frontier; young adult; women's.

How to Contact Query with SASE, outline/proposal. Highly selective. No phone calls or faxes. Responds in 3 weeks to queries; 1 month to mss. Returns materials only with SASE. Obtains most new clients through recommendations from others, "through the best-seller lists, word of mouth."

Recent Sales Sold over 50 titles in the last year. *Lies and the Lying Liars Who Tell Them*, by Al Franken (Dutton); *All I Did Was Ask*, by Terry Gross (Hyperion); *We Got Fired and It Was the Best Thing that Ever Happened to Us*, by Harvey Mackay (Ballantine); *Father Joe*, by Tony Hendra (Random House); *You Ain't Got No Easter Clothes*, by Laura Love (Hyperion).

Terms Agent receives 15% commission on domestic sales; 20% commission on foreign sales. Offers written contract. Charges clients for photocopying, international express mail, bound galleys and finished books used for subsidiary rights sales. "No fees charged if book is not sold."

Tips "The writer should first view himself as a salesperson in order to obtain an agent. Sell yourself, your idea, your concept. Do your homework. Notice what is in the marketplace. Be sophisticated about the arena in which you are writing."

LESCHER & LESCHER, LTD.

47 E. 19th St., New York NY 10003. (212)529-1790. Fax: (212)529-2716. **Contact:** Robert Lescher, Susan Lescher. Estab. 1966. Member of AAR. Represents 150 clients. Currently handles: 80% nonfiction books; 20% novels.

Represents Nonfiction books, novels. **Considers these nonfiction areas:** Current affairs; history; memoirs; popular culture; biography; cookbooks and wines; law; contemporary issues; narrative nonfiction. **Considers these fiction areas:** Literary; mystery/suspense; commercial fiction.

O─ Does not want to receive screenplays, science fiction or romance.

How to Contact Query with SASE. Obtains most new clients through recommendations from others.

Recent Sales Sold 35 titles in the last year. This agency prefers not to share information on specific sales. Clients include Neil Sheehan, Madeleine L'Engle, Calvin Trillin, Judith Viorst, Thomas Perry, Anne Fadiman, Frances FitzGerald, Paula Fox and Robert M. Parker, Jr.

Terms Agent receives 15% commission on domestic sales; 20-25% commission on foreign sales.

LEVINE GREENBERG LITERARY AGENCY, INC.

307 7th Ave., Suite 1906, New York NY 10001. (212)337-0934. Fax: (212)337-0948. Website: www.levinegreenberg. com. Estab. 1989. Member of AAR. Represents 250 clients. 33% of clients are new/unpublished writers. Currently handles: 70% nonfiction books; 30% novels.

● Prior to opening his agency, Mr. Levine served as vice president of the Bank Street College of Education.

Member Agents James Levine; Arielle Eckstut; Daniel Greenberg; Stephanie Kip Roston; Jenoyne Adams.

Represents Nonfiction books, novels. **Considers these nonfiction areas:** Animals; art/architecture/design; biography/autobiography; business/economics; child guidance/parenting; computers/electronic; cooking/foods/nutrition; gardening; gay/lesbian issues; health/medicine; money/finance; nature/environment; New Age/metaphysics; psychology; religious/inspirational; science/technology; self-help/personal improvement; sociology; spirituality; sports; women's issues/studies. **Considers these fiction areas:** Contemporary issues; literary; mainstream/contemporary; mystery/suspense; thriller (psychological); women's.

O─ This agency specializes in business, psychology, parenting, health/medicine, narrative nonfiction, spirituality, religion, women's issues and commercial fiction.

How to Contact See website for full submission procedure. Prefers e-mail queries. Obtains most new clients through recommendations from others.

Recent Sales *The Onion: Our Dumb Century*; *Alternadad*, by Neal Pollack; *The Opposite of Death Is Love*, by Nando Parrado.

Terms Agent receives 15% commission on domestic sales; 20% commission on foreign sales. Offers written contract, binding for variable length of time. Charges clients for out-of-pocket expenses—telephone, fax, postage and photocopying—directly connected to the project.

Writers' Conferences ASJA Annual Conference (New York City, May).

Tips "We work closely with clients on editorial development and promotion. We work to place our clients as magazine columnists and have created columnists for *McCall's* (renamed *Rosie's*) and *Child*. We work with clients to develop their projects across various media—video, software and audio."

PAUL S. LEVINE LITERARY AGENCY

1054 Superba Ave., Venice CA 90291-3940. (310)450-6711. Fax: (310)450-0181. E-mail: pslevine@ix.netcom.com. Website: home.netcom.com/ ~ pslevine/lawliterary.html. **Contact:** Paul S. Levine. Estab. 1996. Member of the State Bar of California. Represents over 100 clients. 75% of clients are new/unpublished writers. Currently handles: 30% nonfiction books; 30% novels; 10% movie scripts; 30% TV scripts.

Represents Nonfiction books, novels, movie scripts, feature film, TV scripts, TV movie of the week, episodic drama, sitcom, animation, documentary, miniseries, syndicated material. **Considers these nonfiction areas:** Art/architecture/design; biography/autobiography; business/economics; child guidance/parenting; computers/electronic; cooking/foods/nutrition; crafts/hobbies; creative nonfiction; current affairs; education; ethnic/cultural interests; gay/lesbian issues; government/politics/law; health/medicine; history; how-to; humor/satire; interior design/decorating; language/literature/criticism; memoirs; military/war; money/finance; music/dance; nature/environment; New Age/metaphysics; photography; popular culture; psychology; religious/inspirational; science/technology; self-help/personal improvement; sociology; sports; theater/film; true crime/investigative; women's issues/studies. **Considers these fiction areas:** Action/adventure; comic books/cartoon; confession; contemporary issues; detective/police/crime; erotica; ethnic; experimental; family saga; feminist; gay/lesbian; glitz; historical; humor/satire; literary; mainstream/contemporary; mystery/suspense; regional; religious/inspirational; romance; sports; thriller; westerns/frontier. **Considers these script subject areas:** Action/adventure; biography/autobiography; cartoon/animation; comedy; contemporary issues; detective/police/crime; erotica; ethnic; experimental; family saga; feminist; gay/lesbian; glitz; historical; horror; juvenile; mainstream; multimedia; mystery/suspense; religious/inspirational; romantic comedy; romantic drama; sports; teen; thriller; western/frontier.

O── Actively seeking commercial fiction and nonfiction. Also handles children's and young adult fiction and nonfiction. Does not want to receive science fiction, fantasy or horror.

How to Contact Query with SASE. Accepts e-mail and fax queries. Considers simultaneous queries. Responds in 1 day to queries; 2 months to mss. Returns materials only with SASE. Obtains most new clients through conferences, referrals, listings on various websites and through listings in directories.

Recent Sales Sold 25 titles in the last year. This agency prefers not to share information on specific sales.

Terms Agent receives 15% commission on domestic sales; 20% commission on foreign sales. Offers written contract. Charges clients for messengers, long distance, postage. "Only when incurred. No advance payment necessary."

Writers' Conferences California Lawyers for the Arts (Los Angeles CA); National Writers Club (Los Angeles CA); "Selling to Hollywood" Writer's Connection (Glendale CA); "Spotlight on Craft" Willamette Writers Conference (Portland OR); Women in Animation (Los Angeles CA); and many others.

LINDSEY'S LITERARY SERVICES

7502 Greenville Ave., Suite 500, Dallas TX 75231. (214)890-9262. Fax: (214)890-9295. E-mail: bonedges001@aol.com. **Contact:** Bonnie James; Emily Armenta. Estab. 2002. Represents 14 clients. 60% of clients are new/unpublished writers. Currently handles: 70% nonfiction books; 30% novels.

● Prior to becoming an agent, Ms. James was a drama instructor and magazine editor and Ms. Armenta was an independent film editor and magazine editor.

Member Agents Bonnie James (nonfiction: New Age/metaphysics, self-help, psychology, women's issues; fiction: mystery/suspense, thriller, horror, literary, mainstream, romance); Emily Armenta (nonfiction: New Age/metaphysics, self-help, psychology, women's issues; fiction: mystery/suspense, thriller, horror, literary, mainstream, romance).

Represents Nonfiction books, novels. **Considers these nonfiction areas:** Animals; biography/autobiography; ethnic/cultural interests; gay/lesbian issues; health/medicine; history; memoirs; multicultural; New Age/metaphysics; psychology; self-help/personal improvement; true crime/investigative; women's issues/studies. **Considers these fiction areas:** Action/adventure; detective/police/crime; ethnic; historical; horror; literary; mainstream/contemporary; multicultural; mystery/suspense; New Age; religious/inspirational; romance; science fiction; thriller.

O── "We are a new agency with a clear vision and will aggressively represent our clients." Actively seeking nonfiction self-help, metaphysical, psychology and women's issues; for fiction, seeking exceptionally written books. Does not want poetry, children's books, text books.

How to Contact Query with SASE or by e-mail. For nonfiction, submit proposal package, writing sample and brief bio (list credentials and platform details). For fiction, include first 3 chapters, synopsis and brief bio. No phone calls, please. Considers simultaneous queries. Responds in 4-6 weeks to queries; 2-3 months to mss. Returns materials only with SASE. Obtains most new clients through recommendations from others, solicitations.

Recent Sales Sold 5 titles in the last year. *Crisis Pending*, by Stephen Cornell (Durban House); *Horizon's End*, by Andrew Lazarus (Gladden Books); *No Ordinary Terror*, by J. Brooks Van Dyke (Durban House).

Terms Agent receives 15% commission on domestic sales; 20% commission on foreign sales. Offers written contract, binding for 1 year; cancelable by either party with 1-month written notice.
Tips "Write a clear, concise query describing your project. Pay attention to the craft of writing. Provide complete package, including education, profession, writing credits and what you want to accomplish."

THE LITERARY GROUP
270 Lafayette St., 1505, New York NY 10012. (212)274-1616. Fax: (212)274-9876. E-mail: fweimann@theliterary group.com. Website: www.theliterarygroup.com. **Contact:** Frank Weimann. Estab. 1985. 65% of clients are new/unpublished writers. Currently handles: 50% nonfiction books; 50% fiction.
Member Agents Frank Weimann (fiction, nonfiction); Ian Kleinert (fiction, nonfiction).
Represents Nonfiction books and fiction books. **Considers these nonfiction areas:** Animals; anthropology/archaeology; biography/autobiography; business/economics; child guidance/parenting; crafts/hobbies; creative nonfiction; current affairs; education; ethnic/cultural interests; government/politics/law; health/medicine; history; how-to; humor/satire; juvenile nonfiction; language/literature/criticism; memoirs; military/war; money/finance; multicultural; music/dance; nature/environment; popular culture; psychology; religious/inspirational; science/technology; self-help/personal improvement; sociology; sports; theater/film; true crime/investigative; women's issues/studies. **Considers these fiction areas:** Action/adventure; contemporary issues; detective/police/crime; ethnic; family saga; fantasy; feminist; horror; humor/satire; mystery/suspense; psychic/supernatural; romance (contemporary, gothic, historical, regency); sports; thriller; westerns/frontier.
   ○─ This agency specializes in nonfiction (memoir, military, history, biography, sports, how-to).
How to Contact Query with SASE, outline, 3 sample chapters. Prefers to read materials exclusively. Responds in 1 week to queries; 1 month to mss. Returns materials only with SASE. Obtains most new clients through referrals, writers' conferences, query letters.
Recent Sales Sold 150 titles in the last year. *There and Back Again: An Actor's Tale*, by Sean Astin; *The Ambassador's Son*, by Homer Hickam; *Idiot*, by Johnny Damon; *Lemons Are Not Red*, by Laura Vaccaro Seeger; *The Good Guys*, by Bill Bonanno & Joe Pistone. Other clients include Robert Anderson, Michael Reagan and J.L. King.
Terms Agent receives 15% commission on domestic sales; 20% commission on foreign sales. Offers written contract; 30-day notice must be given to terminate contract.
Writers' Conferences Detroit Women's Writers (MI); Kent State University (OH); San Diego Writers Conference (CA); Maui Writers Conference (HI); Austin Writers' Conference (TX).

NANCY LOVE LITERARY AGENCY
250 E. 65th St., New York NY 10021-6614. (212)980-3499. Fax: (212)308-6405. E-mail: nloveag@aol.com. **Contact:** Nancy Love. Estab. 1984. Member of AAR. Represents 60-80 clients. 25% of clients are new/unpublished writers. Currently handles: 90% nonfiction books; 10% novels.
Member Agents Nancy Love; Miriam Tager.
Represents Nonfiction books, fiction. **Considers these nonfiction areas:** Biography/autobiography; child guidance/parenting; cooking/foods/nutrition; current affairs; ethnic/cultural interests; government/politics/law; health/medicine; history; how-to; nature/environment; New Age/metaphysics; popular culture; psychology; religious/inspirational; science/technology; self-help/personal improvement; sociology; spirituality; travel (armchair only, no how-to travel); true crime/investigative; women's issues/studies. **Considers these fiction areas:** Mystery/suspense; thriller.
   ○─ This agency specializes in adult nonfiction and mysteries. Actively seeking narrative nonfiction. Does not want to receive novels other than mysteries and thrillers.
How to Contact For nonfiction, send a proposal, chapter summary and sample chapter. For fiction, query first. No e-mail or fax queries. Considers simultaneous queries. Responds in 3 weeks to queries; 6 weeks to mss. Returns materials only with SASE. Obtains most new clients through recommendations from others, solicitations.
Recent Sales Sold 18 titles in the last year. Book 5 in Blanco County Mystery Series, by Ben Rehder (St. Martin's Press); *Cutter Vaccine Incident*, by Paul Offit, M.D. (Yale U. Press); *Don't Panic*, by Stanton Peele, Ph.D. (Crown); *Regime Change*, by Steven Kinzer (Henry Holt).
Terms Agent receives 15% commission on domestic sales; 20% commission on foreign sales. Offers written contract. Charges clients for photocopying "if it runs over $20."
Tips "Nonfiction author and/or collaborator must be an authority in subject area and have a platform. Send a SASE if you want a response."

LOWENSTEIN-YOST ASSOCIATES
121 W. 27th St., Suite 601, New York NY 10001. (212)206-1630. Fax: (212)727-0280. **Contact:** Barbara Lowenstein. Estab. 1976. Member of AAR. Represents 150 clients. 20% of clients are new/unpublished writers. Currently handles: 60% nonfiction books; 40% novels.

Literary Agents

Member Agents Barbara Lowenstein (president); Nancy Yost (vice president); Eileen Cope (agent); Norman Kurz (business affairs); Dorian Karchmar (agent); Julie Culver (foreign rights manager).

Represents Nonfiction books, novels. **Considers these nonfiction areas:** Animals; anthropology/archaeology; biography/autobiography; business/economics; child guidance/parenting; creative nonfiction; current affairs; education; ethnic/cultural interests; government/politics/law; health/medicine; history; how-to; language/literature/criticism; memoirs; money/finance; multicultural; nature/environment; popular culture; psychology; self-help/personal improvement; sociology; travel; women's issues/studies; music; narrative nonfiction; science; film. **Considers these fiction areas:** Contemporary issues; detective/police/crime; erotica; ethnic; feminist; historical; literary; mainstream/contemporary; mystery/suspense; romance (contemporary, historical, regency); thriller.

> This agency specializes in health, business, creative nonfiction, literary fiction, commercial fiction—especially suspense, crime and women's issues. "We are a full-service agency, handling domestic and foreign rights, film rights and audio rights to all of our books."

How to Contact Query with SASE. Prefers to read materials exclusively. For fiction, send outline and first chapter. No unsolicited mss. Responds in 6 weeks to queries. Returns materials only with SASE. Obtains most new clients through recommendations from others, solicitations, conferences.

Recent Sales Sold 75 titles in the last year. *6 Day Body Makeover*, by Michael Thurmond (Warner); *Hot Ice*, by Cherry Adair. Other clients include Ishmael Reed, Deborah Crombie, Leslie Glass, Jennifer Haigh, Stephanie Laurens, Grace Edwards, Kuwana Hausley, Perri O'Shaughnessy, Tim Cahill, Kevin Young.

Terms Agent receives 15% commission on domestic sales; 20% commission on foreign sales. Offers written contract. Charges for large photocopy batches, messenger service and international postage.

Writers' Conferences Malice Domestic; Bouchercon.

Tips "Know the genre you are working in and read!"

◙ DONALD MAASS LITERARY AGENCY

160 W. 95th St., Suite 1B, New York NY 10025. (212)866-8200. Website: www.maassagency.com. **Contact:** Donald Maass, Jennifer Jackson, Rachel Vater, Cameron McClure. Estab. 1980. Member of AAR, SFWA, MWA, RWA. Represents over 100 clients. 5% of clients are new/unpublished writers. Currently handles: 100% novels.

• Prior to opening his agency, Mr. Maass served as an editor at Dell Publishing (New York) and as a reader at Gollancz (London). He also served as the president of AAR.

Member Agents Donald Maass (mainstream, literary, mystery/suspense, science fiction); Jennifer Jackson (commercial fiction, especially romance, science fiction, fantasy, mystery/suspense); Rachel Vater (chick lit, mystery, thriller, fantasy, commercial, literary); Cameron McClure (literary, historical, mystery/suspense, fantasy, women's fiction, narrative nonfiction and projects with multicultural, international and environmental themes).

Represents Novels. **Considers these fiction areas:** Detective/police/crime; fantasy; historical; horror; literary; mainstream/contemporary; mystery/suspense; psychic/supernatural; romance (historical, paranormal, time travel); science fiction; thriller; women's.

> This agency specializes in commercial fiction, especially science fiction, fantasy, romance and suspense. Actively seeking "to expand the literary portion of our list and expand in women's fiction." Does not want to receive nonfiction, children's or poetry.

How to Contact Query with SASE, synopsis or first 5 pages. Returns material only with SASE. Considers simultaneous queries. Responds in 2 weeks to queries; 3 months to mss.

Recent Sales Sold over 100 titles in the last year. *The Shifting Tide*, by Anne Perry (Ballantine); *The Longest Night*, by Gregg Keizer (G.P. Putnam's Sons).

Terms Agent receives 15% commission on domestic sales; 20% commission on foreign sales.

Writers' Conferences *Donald Maass:* World Science Fiction Convention; Frankfurt Book Fair; Pacific Northwest Writers Conference; Bouchercon and others; *Jennifer Jackson:* World Science Fiction and Fantasy Convention; RWA National and others; *Rachel Vater:* Pacific Northwest Writer's Conference, Pennwriters and others.

Tips "We are fiction specialists, also noted for our innovative approach to career planning. Few new clients are accepted, but interested authors should query with SASE. Subagents in all principle foreign countries and Hollywood. No nonfiction or juvenile works considered."

◖ GINA MACCOBY LITERARY AGENCY

P.O. Box 60, Chappaqua NY 10514. (914)238-5630. **Contact:** Gina Maccoby. Estab. 1986. Represents 25 clients. Currently handles: 33% nonfiction books; 33% novels; 33% juvenile books; Represents illustrators of children's books.

Represents Nonfiction books, novels, juvenile books. **Considers these nonfiction areas:** Biography/autobiography; current affairs; ethnic/cultural interests; history; juvenile nonfiction; popular culture; women's issues/

studies. **Considers these fiction areas:** Juvenile; literary; mainstream/contemporary; mystery/suspense; thriller; young adult.

How to Contact Query with SASE. Considers simultaneous queries. Responds in 3 months to queries. Returns materials only with SASE. Obtains most new clients through recommendations from own clients and publishers.

Recent Sales Sold 21 titles in the last year.

Terms Agent receives 15% commission on domestic sales; 25% commission on foreign sales. Charges clients for photocopying. May recover certain costs such as the cost of shipping books by air to Europe or Japan or legal fees.

MANUS & ASSOCIATES LITERARY AGENCY, INC.

425 Sherman Ave., Suite 200, Palo Alto CA 94306. (650)470-5151. Fax: (650)470-5159. E-mail: manuslit@manus lit.com. Website: www.manuslit.com. **Contact:** Jillian Manus, Jandy Nelson, Stephanie Lee, Donna Levin, Penny Nelson. Also: 445 Park Ave., New York NY 10022. (212)644-8020. Fax (212)644-3374. **Contact**: Janet Manus. Estab. 1985. Member of AAR. Represents 75 clients. 30% of clients are new/unpublished writers. Currently handles: 70% nonfiction books; 30% novels.

  • Prior to becoming an agent, Jillian Manus was associate publisher of two national magazines and director of development at Warner Bros. and Universal Studios; Janet Manus has been a literary agent for 20 years.

Member Agents Jandy Nelson (self-help, health, memoirs, narrative nonfiction, women's fiction, literary fiction, multicultural fiction, thrillers); Stephanie Lee (self-help, narrative nonfiction, commercial literary fiction, quirky/edgy fiction, pop culture, pop science); Jillian Manus (political, memoirs, self-help, history, sports, women's issues, Latin fiction and nonfiction, thrillers); Donna Levin (mysteries, memoirs, self-help, nonfiction); Penny Nelson (memoirs, self-help, sports, nonfiction).

Represents Nonfiction books, novels. **Considers these nonfiction areas:** Biography/autobiography; business/economics; child guidance/parenting; creative nonfiction; current affairs; ethnic/cultural interests; health/medicine; how-to; memoirs; money/finance; nature/environment; popular culture; psychology; science/technology; self-help/personal improvement; women's issues/studies; Gen X and Gen Y issues. **Considers these fiction areas:** Literary; mainstream/contemporary; multicultural; mystery/suspense; thriller; women's; quirky/edgy fiction.

  ⊶ This agency specializes in commercial literary fiction, narrative nonfiction, thrillers, health, pop psychology, women's empowerment. "Our agency is unique in the way that we not only sell the material but we edit, develop concepts, and participate in the marketing effort. We specialize in large, conceptual fiction and nonfiction and always value a project that can be sold in the TV/feature film market." Actively seeking high-concept thrillers, commercial literary fiction, women's fiction, celebrity biographies, memoirs, multicultural fiction, popular health, women's empowerment, mysteries. Does not want to receive horror, romance, science fiction/fantasy, westerns, young adult, children's, poetry, cookbooks, magazine articles. Usually obtains new clients through recommendations from editors, clients and others; conferences; and unsolicited materials.

How to Contact Query with SASE. If requested, submit outline, 2-3 sample chapters. No faxes, please. All queries should be sent to California office. Accepts e-mail queries. Considers simultaneous queries. Responds in 3 months to queries; 3 months to mss. Returns materials only with SASE. Obtains most new clients through recommendations from others, solicitations, conferences.

Recent Sales *Nothing Down for the 2000's* and *Multiple Streams of Income for the 2000's*, by Robert Allen; *Missed Fortune* and *Missed Fortune 101*, by Doug Andrew; *Cracking the Millionaire Code*, by Mark Victor Hansen and Robert Allen; *Stress Free for Good*, by Dr. Fred Luskin and Dr. Ken Pelletier; *The Mercy of Thin Air*, by Ronlyn Domangue; *The Fine Art of Small Talk*, by Debra Fine; *Bone Man of Bonares*, by Terry Tarnoff. Other clients include Dr. Lorraine Zappart, Marcus Allen, Carlton Stowers, Alan Jacobson, Ann Brandt, Dr. Richard Marrs, Mary LoVerde, Lisa Huang Fleishman, Judy Carter, Daryl Ott Underhill, Glen Kleier, Andrew X. Pham, Alexander Sanger, Lalita Tademy, Frank Baldwin, Katy Robinson, K.M. Soehnlein, Joelle Fraser, James Rogan, Jim Schutze, Deborah Santana, Karen Neuburger, Mira Tweti, Newt Gingrich, William Forstchen, Ken Walsh, Doug Wead, Nadine Schiff, Deborah Santana, Tom Dolby, Laurie Lynn Drummond, Christine Wicker, Wendy Dale, Mineko Iwasaki, Dorothy Ferebee.

Terms Agent receives 15% commission on domestic sales; 20-25% commission on foreign sales. Offers written contract, binding for 2 years; 60 days notice must be given to terminate contract. Charges for photocopying and postage/UPS.

Writers' Conferences Maui Writers Conference (Maui HI, Labor Day); San Diego Writer's Conference (San Diego CA, January); Willamette Writers Conference (Willamette OR, July); BEA; MEGA Book Marketing University.

Tips "Research agents using a variety of sources, including *LMP*, guides, *Publishers Weekly*, conferences and even acknowledgements in books similar in tone to yours."

◻ MARCH TENTH, INC.

4 Myrtle St., Haworth NJ 07641-1740. (201)387-6551. Fax: (201)387-6552. E-mail: hchoron@aol.com. Website: www.marchtenthinc.com. **Contact:** Harry Choron, vice president. Estab. 1982. Represents 40 clients. 30% of clients are new/unpublished writers. Currently handles: 75% nonfiction books; 25% novels.

Represents Nonfiction books, novels. **Considers these nonfiction areas:** Biography/autobiography; current affairs; health/medicine; history; humor/satire; language/literature/criticism; music/dance; popular culture; theater/film. **Considers these fiction areas:** Confession; ethnic; family saga; historical; humor/satire; literary; mainstream/contemporary.

   ⊶ Writers must have professional expertise in their field. "We prefer to work with published/established writers."

How to Contact Query with SASE. Considers simultaneous queries. Responds in 1 month to queries. Returns materials only with SASE.

Recent Sales Sold 12 titles in the last year. *The Case for Zionism*, by Rabbi Arthur Hertzberg; *Learning Sickness*, by James Lang; *The 100 Simple Secrets of Happy Families*, by David Niven.

Terms Agent receives 15% commission on domestic sales; 20% commission on foreign sales; 20% commission on dramatic rights sales. Charges clients for postage, photocopying, overseas phone expenses. "Does not require expense money upfront."

◻ THE DENISE MARCIL LITERARY AGENCY, INC.

156 Fifth Ave., Suite 625, New York NY 10010. (212)337-3402. Fax: (212)727-2688. **Contact:** Denise Marcil, president; Maura Kye, agent. Estab. 1977. Member of AAR. Represents 50 clients. 10% of clients are new/unpublished writers. Currently handles: Commercial fiction and nonfiction.

   • Prior to opening her agency, Ms. Marcil served as an editorial assistant with Avon Books and as an assistant editor with Simon & Schuster.

Represents Commercial fiction and nonfiction books.

   ⊶ Denise Marcil specializes in thrillers, suspense, women's commercial fiction, popular reference, how-to, self-help, health, business and parenting. "I am looking for fresh, new voices in commercial women's fiction: chick lit, mom lit, stories that capture women's experiences today—as well as historical fiction." Maura Kye is seeking narrative nonfiction (adventure, women's issues, humor and memoir) and fiction (multicultural, paranormal, suspense, chick lit, and well-written novels with an edgy voice, quirky characters and/or unique plots and settings. "I'm particularly interested in representing books that would appeal to 20- and 30-year-olds."

How to Contact Query with SASE.

Recent Sales Sold 43 titles in the last year. *Fatal Flaw*, by Ginna Gray (Mira); *The Back-Up Plan*, by Sherryl Woods (Mira); *Silent Wager*, by Anita Bunkley (Dafina/Kensington); *10 Questions Every Leader Should Ask to Stay on Top of the Game*, by Graham Alexander (Nelson Business); *Going Visual: Using Images to Enhance Productivity and Profit*, by Alexis Gerard and Robert Goldstein (Wiley); *The Complete Book of Women Saints*, by Sarah Gallick (Harper San Francisco); *When Someone You Love is Angry*, by W. Doyle Gentry, PhD (Berkley); *You Want Me to Work With Who?*, by Julie Janson (Penguin); *Death's Little Helpers*, by Peter Spiegelman (Knopf); *Lost: A Photo Expedition's Desperate Battle for Survival in the Amazon Jungle*, by Marlo and Stephen Kirkpatrick (W).

Terms Agent receives 15% commission on domestic sales; 20% commission on foreign sales. Offers written contract, binding for 2 years; 100% of business is derived from commissions on ms sales. Charges $100/year for postage, photocopying, long-distance calls, etc.

Writers' Conferences Pacific Northwest Writers Conference; RWA.

◻ THE EVAN MARSHALL AGENCY

Six Tristam Place, Pine Brook NJ 07058-9445. (973)882-1122. Fax: (973)882-3099. E-mail: evanmarshall@thenovelist.com. Website: www.publishersmarketplace.com/members/evanmarshall/. **Contact:** Evan Marshall. Estab. 1987. Member of AAR, MWA, RWA, Sisters in Crime, American Crime Writers League. Currently handles: 100% novels.

   • Prior to opening his agency, Mr. Marshall served as an editor with Houghton Mifflin, New American Library, Everest House and Dodd, Mead & Co. and then worked as a literary agent at The Sterling Lord Agency.

Represents Novels. **Considers these fiction areas:** Action/adventure; erotica; ethnic; historical; horror; humor/satire; literary; mainstream/contemporary; mystery/suspense; religious/inspirational; romance (contemporary, gothic, historical, Regency); science fiction; westerns/frontier.

How to Contact Query first with SASE; do not enclose material. No e-mail queries. Responds in 1 week to queries; 3 months to mss. Obtains most new clients through recommendations from others.

Recent Sales *Killer Take All*, by Erica Spindler (Mira); *Flaming Luau of Death*, by Jerrilyn Farmer (Morrow); *Haven*, by Bobbi Smith (Dorchester).
Terms Agent receives 15% commission on domestic sales; 20% commission on foreign sales. Offers written contract.

◐ HELEN MCGRATH

1406 Idaho Ct., Concord CA 94521. (925)672-6211. Fax: (925)672-6383. E-mail: hmcgrath_lit@yahoo.com. **Contact:** Helen McGrath. Estab. 1977. Currently handles: 50% nonfiction books; 50% novels.
Represents Nonfiction books, novels. **Considers these nonfiction areas:** Biography/autobiography; business/economics; current affairs; health/medicine; history; how-to; military/war; psychology; self-help/personal improvement; sports; women's issues/studies. **Considers these fiction areas:** Contemporary issues; detective/police/crime; literary; mainstream/contemporary; mystery/suspense; psychic/supernatural; romance; science fiction; thriller.
How to Contact Submit proposal with SASE. *No unsolicited mss.* Responds in 2 months to queries. Obtains most new clients through recommendations from others.
Terms Agent receives 15% commission on domestic sales. Offers written contract. Charges clients for photocopying.

◑ MCHUGH LITERARY AGENCY

1033 Lyon Rd., Moscow ID 83843-9167. (208)882-0107. Fax: (603)688-6437. E-mail: elisabetmch@turbonet.com. **Contact:** Elisabet McHugh. Estab. 1994. Represents 42 clients. 30% of clients are new/unpublished writers. Currently handles: 30% nonfiction books; 70% fiction. **Considers these nonfiction areas:** Open to most subjects, except business. **Considers these fiction areas:** Historical; mainstream/contemporary; mystery/suspense; romance; thriller (psychological).
○→ Does not handle children's books, poetry, science fiction, fantasy, horror, westerns.
How to Contact Query first by e-mail. Do not send material unless asked for. Returns materials only with SASE.
Recent Sales *The Complete RV Handbook: Making the Most of Your Life on the Road* (Ragged Mountain Press/McGraw-Hill); *Dead Wrong* (Bantam); *Puppy Love* (Harlequin).
Terms Agent receives 15% commission on domestic sales; 20% commission on foreign sales. Does not charge any upfront fees. Offers written contract. "Client must provide all copies needed for submissions."

◑ MENZA-BARRON AGENCY

(formerly Claudia Menza Literary Agency), 1170 Broadway, Suite 807, New York NY 10001. (212)889-6850. **Contact:** Claudia Menza, Manie Barron. Estab. 1983. Member of AAR. Represents 100 clients. 50% of clients are new/unpublished writers.
Represents Nonfiction books, novels. **Considers these nonfiction areas:** Current affairs; education; ethnic/cultural interests (especially African-American); health/medicine; history; multicultural; music/dance; photography; psychology; theater/film.
○→ This agency specializes in African-American fiction and nonfiction and editorial assistance.
How to Contact Query with SASE. Responds in 2-4 weeks to queries; 2-4 months to mss. Returns materials only with SASE.
Recent Sales This agency prefers not to share information on specific sales.
Terms Agent receives 15% commission on domestic sales; 20% (if co-agent is used) commission on foreign sales; 20% commission on dramatic rights sales. Offers written contract.

◐ DORIS S. MICHAELS LITERARY AGENCY, INC.

1841 Broadway, Suite 903, New York NY 10023. (212)265-9474. Fax: (212)265-9480. E-mail: query@dsmagency.com. Website: www.dsmagency.com. **Contact:** Doris S. Michaels, president. Estab. 1994. Member of AAR, WNBA.
Represents Novels. **Considers these fiction areas:** Literary (with commercial appeal and strong screen potential).
How to Contact Query by e-mail; see submission guidelines on website. Obtains most new clients through recommendations from others, conferences.
Recent Sales Sold over 30 titles in the last year. *Cycles: How We'll Live, Work and Buy*, by Maddy Dychtwald (The Free Press); *In the River Sweet*, by Patricia Henley (Knopf); *Healing Conversations: What to Say When You Don't Know What to Say*, by Nance Guilmartin (Jossey-Bass); *The Mushroom Man*, by Sophie Powell (Peguin Putnam); *How to Become a Marketing Superstar*, by Jeff Fox (Hyperion).
Terms Agent receives 15% commission on domestic sales; 20% commission on foreign sales. Offers written contract, binding for 1 year; 1-month notice must be given to terminate contract. 100% of business is derived

from commissions on ms sales. Charges clients for office expenses, not to exceed $150 without written permission.

Writers' Conferences BEA; Frankfurt Book Fair (Germany, October); London Book Fair; Maui Writers Conference.

MARTHA MILLARD LITERARY AGENCY

50 W. 67th St., #1G, New York NY 10023. (212)787-7769. Fax: (212)787-7867. E-mail: marmillink@aol.com. **Contact:** Martha Millard. Estab. 1980. Member of AAR, SFWA. Represents 50 clients. Currently handles: 25% nonfiction books; 65% novels; 10% story collections.

- Prior to becoming an agent, Ms. Millard worked in editorial departments of several publishers and was vice president at another agency for four and a half years.

Represents Nonfiction books, novels. **Considers these nonfiction areas:** Art/architecture/design; biography/ autobiography; business/economics; child guidance/parenting; cooking/foods/nutrition; current affairs; education; ethnic/cultural interests; health/medicine; history; how-to; juvenile nonfiction; memoirs; money/finance; music/dance; New Age/metaphysics; photography; popular culture; psychology; self-help/personal improvement; theater/film; true crime/investigative; women's issues/studies. **Considers these fiction areas:** Considers fiction depending on writer's credits and skills.

How to Contact No unsolicited queries. No e-mail or fax queries. Returns materials only with SASE. Obtains most new clients through recommendations from others.

Recent Sales *Backfire*, by Peter Burrows (Wiley); *Fallen Star*, by Nancy Herkness (Berkley Sensation); *The Rosetta Codex*, by Richard Paul Russ (Penguin).

Terms Agent receives 15% commission on domestic sales; 20% commission on foreign sales. Offers written contract.

MAUREEN MORAN AGENCY

P.O. Box 20191, Park West Station, New York NY 10025-1518. (212)222-3838. Fax: (212)531-3464. E-mail: maureenm@erols.com. **Contact:** Maureen Moran. Represents 30 clients. Currently handles: 100% novels.

Represents Novels. **Considers these fiction areas:** Women's.

- This agency specializes in women's fiction, principally romance and mystery. Does not want to receive science fiction, fantasy or juvenile books.

How to Contact Query with SASE. Will accept e-mail query without attachments. *No unsolicited mss.* Considers simultaneous queries. Responds in 1 week to queries. Returns materials only with SASE.

Recent Sales *Alpine Quilt*, by Mary Daheim; *Death By Thunder*, by Gretchen Sprague; *Jeremy's Daddy*, by Julianna Morris.

Terms Agent receives 10% commission on domestic sales; 15-20% commission on foreign sales. Charges clients for extraordinary expenses such as courier, messenger and bank wire fees by prior arrangement.

Tips "This agency does not handle unpublished writers."

HENRY MORRISON, INC.

105 S. Bedford Rd., Suite 306A, Mt. Kisco NY 10549. (914)666-3500. Fax: (914)241-7846. **Contact:** Henry Morrison. Estab. 1965. Signatory of WGA. Represents 51 clients. 5% of clients are new/unpublished writers. Currently handles: 5% nonfiction books; 95% novels.

Represents Nonfiction books, novels. **Considers these nonfiction areas:** Anthropology/archaeology; biography/autobiography; government/politics/law; history. **Considers these fiction areas:** Action/adventure; detective/police/crime; family saga; historical.

How to Contact Query with SASE. Responds in 2 weeks to queries; 3 months to mss. Obtains most new clients through recommendations from others.

Recent Sales Sold 18 titles in the last year. *The Moscow Vector*, by Robert Ludlum and Patrick Larkin (St. Martin's Press); *The Bourne Legacy*, by Eric Van Lustbader (St. Martin's Press); *Doublecross Blind*, by Joel Ross (Doubleday); *Michelangelo's Notebook*, by Christopher Hyde (Signet Books); *The Last Spymaster*, by Gayle Lynds (St. Martin's Press); *Office Superman*, by Alan Axelrod (Running Press); *The Glass Tiger*, by Joe Gores (Penzler Books/Harcourt); *Native Sons*, by James Baldwin and Sol Stein (Ballantine Books); *Enemy of My Enemy*, by Allan Topol (Signet Books); *Kingdom Come*, by Beverly Swerling (Simon & Schuster); *The Coil*, by Gayle Lynds (St. Martin's Press). Other clients include Samuel R. Delany, Molly Katz, Daniel Cohen, Brian Garfield, Joe Gores.

Terms Agent receives 15% commission on domestic sales; 25% commission on foreign sales. Charges clients for ms copies, bound galleys, and finished books for submissions to publishers, movie producers, foreign publishers.

DEE MURA LITERARY

269 West Shore Dr., Massapequa NY 11758-8225. (516)795-1616. Fax: (516)795-8797. E-mail: samurai5@ix.netcom. com. **Contact:** Dee Mura, Karen Roberts, Frank Nakamura, Brian Hertler, Kimiko Nakamura. Estab. 1987. Signatory of WGA. 50% of clients are new/unpublished writers.

- Prior to opening her agency, Ms. Mura was a public relations executive with a roster of film and entertainment clients and worked in editorial for major weekly news magazines.

Represents Nonfiction books, juvenile books, scholarly books, feature film, TV scripts, episodic drama, sitcom, animation, documentary, miniseries, variety show, fiction books. **Considers these nonfiction areas:** Agriculture/horticulture; animals; anthropology/archaeology; biography/autobiography; business/economics; child guidance/parenting; computers/electronic; current affairs; education; ethnic/cultural interests; gay/lesbian issues; government/politics/law; health/medicine; history; how-to; humor/satire; juvenile nonfiction; memoirs; military/war; money/finance; nature/environment; science/technology; self-help/personal improvement; sociology; sports; travel; true crime/investigative; women's issues/studies. **Considers these fiction areas:** Action/adventure; contemporary issues; detective/police/crime; ethnic; experimental; family saga; fantasy; feminist; gay/lesbian; glitz; historical; humor/satire; juvenile; literary; mainstream/contemporary; mystery/suspense; psychic/supernatural; regional; romance (contemporary, gothic, historical, regency); science fiction; sports; thriller; westerns/frontier; young adult; espionage; political. **Considers these script subject areas:** Action/adventure; cartoon/animation; comedy; contemporary issues; detective/police/crime; family saga; fantasy; feminist; gay/lesbian; glitz; historical; horror; juvenile; mainstream; mystery/suspense; psychic/supernatural; religious/inspirational; romantic comedy; romantic drama; science fiction; sports; teen; thriller; western/frontier.

- ⌐ "We work on everything but are especially interested in literary fiction, commercial fiction and nonfiction, thrillers and espionage, humor and drama (we love to laugh and cry), self-help, inspirational, medical, scholarly, true life stories, true crime, women's stories and issues." Actively seeking "unique nonfiction manuscripts and proposals; novelists who are great storytellers; contemporary writers with distinct voices and passion." Does not want to receive "ideas for sitcoms, novels, films, etc., or queries without SASEs."

How to Contact Query with SASE. No fax queries. Accepts queries by e-mail without attachments. Considers simultaneous queries. Responds in 2 weeks to queries (depending on mail load). Returns materials only with SASE. Obtains most new clients through recommendations from others and queries.

Recent Sales Sold over 40 titles and sold 35 scripts in the last year.

Terms Agent receives 15% commission on domestic sales; 20% commission on foreign sales. Offers written contract. Charges clients for photocopying, mailing expenses, overseas and long distance phone calls and faxes.

Tips "Please include a paragraph on the writer's background, even if the writer has no literary background, and a brief synopsis of the project. We enjoy well-written query letters that tell us about the project and the author."

JEAN V. NAGGAR LITERARY AGENCY, INC.

216 E. 75th St., Suite 1E, New York NY 10021. (212)794-1082. **Contact:** Jean Naggar. Estab. 1978. Member of AAR, PEN, Women's Media Group and Women's Forum. Represents 80 clients. 20% of clients are new/unpublished writers. Currently handles: 35% nonfiction books; 45% novels; 15% juvenile books; 5% scholarly books.

- Ms. Naggar served as president of AAR.

Member Agents Alice Tasman, senior agent (narrative nonfiction, commercial/literary fiction, thrillers); Anne Engel (academic-based nonfiction for general readership); Jennifer Weltz, director, subsidiary rights (also represents children's books and YA); Mollie Glick, agent (serious nonfiction, literary and commercial fiction).

Represents Nonfiction books, novels. **Considers these nonfiction areas:** Biography/autobiography; child guidance/parenting; current affairs; government/politics/law; health/medicine; history; juvenile nonfiction; memoirs; New Age/metaphysics; psychology; religious/inspirational; self-help/personal improvement; sociology; travel; women's issues/studies. **Considers these fiction areas:** Action/adventure; contemporary issues; detective/police/crime; ethnic; family saga; feminist; historical; literary; mainstream/contemporary; mystery/suspense; psychic/supernatural; thriller.

- ⌐ This agency specializes in mainstream fiction and nonfiction and literary fiction with commercial potential.

How to Contact Query with SASE. Prefers to read materials exclusively. No e-mail or fax queries. Responds in 1 day to queries; 2 months to mss. Returns materials only with SASE. Obtains most new clients through recommendations from others, solicitations, conferences.

Recent Sales *Leaving Ireland*, by Ann Moore (NAL); *The Associate*, by Phillip Margolin (HarperCollins); *Quantico Rules*, by Gene Riehl (St. Martin's Press). Other clients include Jean M. Auel, Robert Pollack, Mary McGarry Morris, Lily Prior, Susan Fromberg Schaeffer, David Ball, Elizabeth Crane, Maud Casey.

Terms Agent receives 15% commission on domestic sales; 20% commission on foreign sales. Offers written contract. Charges for overseas mailing; messenger services; book purchases; long-distance telephone; photocopying. "These are deductible from royalties received."

Writers' Conferences Willamette Writers Conference; Pacific Northwest Writers Conference; Breadloaf Writers Conference; Virginia Women's Press Conference (Richmond VA); Marymount Manhattan Writers Conference; SEAK Conference, New York is Book Country: Get Published.

Tips "Use a professional presentation. Because of the avalanche of unsolicited queries that flood the agency every week, we have had to modify our policy. We will now only guarantee to read and respond to queries from writers who come recommended by someone we know. Our areas are general fiction and nonfiction, no children's books by unpublished writers, no multimedia, no screenplays, no formula fiction, no mysteries by unpublished writers. We recommend patience and fortitude: the courage to be true to your own vision, the fortitude to finish a novel and polish and polish again before sending it out, and the patience to accept rejection gracefully and wait for the stars to align themselves appropriately for success."

NEW BRAND AGENCY GROUP, LLC

E-mail: mark@literaryagent.net. Website: www.literaryagent.net. **Contact:** Mark Ryan. Estab. 1994. Currently handles: 33% nonfiction books; 33% novels; 33% juvenile books.

● New Brand Agency is currently closed to submissions. Check website for more details.

Member Agents Mark Ryan handles fiction and nonfiction with bestseller and/or high commercial potential.

Represents Nonfiction books, novels, juvenile books (books for younger readers). **Considers these nonfiction areas:** Biography/autobiography; business/economics; juvenile nonfiction; memoirs; popular culture; psychology; religious/inspirational; self-help/personal improvement; sex; spirituality; women's issues/studies; body and soul, health, humor, family, finance, fitness, gift/novelty, leadership, men's issues, parenting, relationships, success. **Considers these fiction areas:** Fantasy; historical; horror; juvenile; literary; mainstream/contemporary; romance (mainstream); science fiction; thriller; cross-genre, mystery, magical realism, supernatural, suspense.

   ⊶ "We only work with authors we are passionate about." Actively seeking the story and voice that no one else can share but you.

How to Contact Accepts e-mail queries only; submit electronic query online at website. Responds in 1 week to mss. Responds in 48 hours to queries if interested. Obtains most new clients through queries.

Recent Sales *Black Valley*, by Jim Brown (Ballantine); *The Marriage Plan*, by Aggie Jordan, Ph.D. (Broadway/Bantam); *Mother to Daughter*, by Harry Harrison (Workman); *The She*, by Carol Plum-Ucci (Harcourt).

Terms Agent receives 15% commission on domestic sales. Offers written contract, binding for 6 months; 1-month notice must be given to terminate contract. 20% commission for subsidiary rights. Charges for postage and phone costs after sale of the project.

☑ NINE MUSES AND APOLLO, INC.

525 Broadway, Suite 201, New York NY 10012. (212)431-2665. **Contact:** Ling Lucas. Estab. 1991. Represents 50 clients. 10% of clients are new/unpublished writers. Currently handles: 90% nonfiction books; 10% novels.

● Ms. Lucas formerly served as vice president, sales & marketing director, and associate publisher of Warner Books.

Represents Nonfiction books. **Considers these nonfiction areas:** Animals; biography/autobiography; business/economics; current affairs; ethnic/cultural interests; health/medicine; language/literature/criticism; psychology; spirituality; women's issues/studies. **Considers these fiction areas:** Ethnic; literary; mainstream/contemporary (commercial).

   ⊶ This agency specializes in nonfiction. Does not want to receive children's and young adult material.

How to Contact Submit outline, 2 sample chapters, SASE. Prefers to read materials exclusively. Responds in 1 month to mss.

Recent Sales *My Daddy Is a Pretzel*, by Baron Baptiste (Barefoot Books); *The Twelve Gifts of Healing*, by Charlene Costanzo (HarperCollins); *The Twelve Gifts of Marriage*, by C. Costanzo (HarperCollins); *Once Upon a Time in China*, by Jeff Yang (Atria).

Terms Agent receives 15% commission on domestic sales; 20-25% commission on foreign sales. Offers written contract. Charges clients for photocopying, postage.

Tips "Your outline should already be well developed, cogent, and reveal clarity of thought about the general structure and direction of your project."

☑ HAROLD OBER ASSOCIATES

425 Madison Ave., New York NY 10017. (212)759-8600. Fax: (212)759-9428. Estab. 1929. Member of AAR. Represents 250 clients. 10% of clients are new/unpublished writers. Currently handles: 35% nonfiction books; 50% novels; 15% juvenile books.

Member Agents Phyllis Westberg; Pamela Malpas; Emma Sweeney; Knox Burger; Craig Tenney (not accepting new clients).

Represents Nonfiction books, novels, juvenile books. **Considers these nonfiction areas:** Considers all nonfiction areas. **Considers these fiction areas:** Considers all fiction subjects.

How to Contact Query letter only with SASE. No e-mail or fax queries. Responds as promptly as possible. Obtains most new clients through recommendations from others.

Terms Agent receives 15% commission on domestic sales; 20% commission on foreign sales. Charges clients for photocopying and express mail or package services.

THE RICHARD PARKS AGENCY

Box 693, Salem NY 12865. Website: www.richardparksagency.com. **Contact:** Richard Parks. Estab. 1988. Member of AAR. Currently handles: 55% nonfiction books; 40% novels; 5% story collections.

Represents Nonfiction books, novels. **Considers these nonfiction areas:** Animals; anthropology/archaeology; art/architecture/design; biography/autobiography; business/economics; child guidance/parenting; cooking/foods/nutrition; crafts/hobbies; current affairs; ethnic/cultural interests; gardening; gay/lesbian issues; government/politics/law; health/medicine; history; how-to; humor/satire; language/literature/criticism; memoirs; military/war; money/finance; music/dance; nature/environment; popular culture; psychology; science/technology; self-help/personal improvement; sociology; theater/film; travel; women's issues/studies. **Considers these fiction areas:** Considers fiction by referral only.

⚬— Actively seeking nonfiction. Does not want to receive unsolicited material.

How to Contact Query by mail only with SASE. No e-mail or fax queries. Considers simultaneous queries. Responds in 2 weeks to queries. Returns materials only with SASE. Obtains most new clients through recommendations and referrals.

Terms Agent receives 15% commission on domestic sales; 20% commission on foreign sales. Charges clients for photocopying or any unusual expense incurred at the writer's request.

KATHI J. PATON LITERARY AGENCY

19 W. 55th St., New York NY 10019-4907. (908)647-2117. E-mail: kjplitbiz@optonline.net. **Contact:** Kathi Paton. Estab. 1987. Currently handles: 65% nonfiction books; 35% fiction.

Represents Nonfiction books, novels, short story collections, book-based film rights. **Considers these nonfiction areas:** Business/economics; child guidance/parenting; money/finance (personal investing); nature/environment; psychology; religious/inspirational; women's issues/studies. **Considers these fiction areas:** Literary; mainstream/contemporary; short story collections.

⚬— This agency specializes in adult nonfiction.

How to Contact Accepts e-mail queries. For nonfiction, send proposal, sample chapter and SASE. For fiction, send first 40 pages and plot summary or 3 short stories and SASE. Considers simultaneous queries. Obtains most new clients through recommendations from other clients.

Recent Sales *Future Wealth*, by McInerney and White (St. Martin's Press); *Unraveling the Mystery of Autism*, by Karyn Seroussi (Simon & Schuster).

Terms Agent receives 15% commission on domestic sales; 20% commission on foreign sales. Offers written contract. Charges clients for photocopying.

Writers' Conferences Attends major regional panels, seminars and conferences.

L. PERKINS ASSOCIATES

16 W. 36 St., New York NY 10018. (212)279-6418. Fax: (718)543-5354. E-mail: lperkinsagency@yahoo.com. **Contact:** Lori Perkins or Amy Stout (astoutlperkinsagency@yahoo.com). Estab. 1990. Member of AAR. Represents 50 clients. 10% of clients are new/unpublished writers.

• Ms. Perkins has been an agent for 18 years. Her agency has an affiliate agency, Southern Literary Group. She is also the author of *The Insider's Guide to Getting an Agent* (Writer's Digest Books).

Represents Nonfiction books, novels. **Considers these nonfiction areas:** Popular culture. **Considers these fiction areas:** Fantasy; horror; literary (dark); science fiction.

⚬— Most of Ms. Perkins' clients write both fiction and nonfiction. "This combination keeps my clients publishing for years. I am also a published author, so I know what it takes to write a good book." Actively seeking a Latino *Gone With the Wind* and *Waiting to Exhale* and urban ethnic horror. Does not want to receive "anything outside of the above categories, i.e., westerns, romance."

How to Contact Query with SASE. Considers simultaneous queries. Responds in 6 weeks to queries; 3 months to mss. Returns materials only with SASE. Obtains most new clients through recommendations from others, solicitations, conferences.

Recent Sales Sold 100 titles in the last year. *How to Make Love Like a Porn Star: A Cautionary Tale*, by Jenna Jameson (Reagan Books); *Dear Mom, I Always Wanted You to Know*, by Lisa Delman (Perigee Books); *The*

Illustrated Ray Bradbury, by Jerry Weist (Avon); *The Poet in Exile*, by Ray Manzarek (Avalon); *Behind Sad Eyes: The Life of George Harrison*, (St. Martin's Press).

Terms Agent receives 15% commission on domestic sales; 20% commission on foreign sales. No written contract. Charges clients for photocopying.

Writers' Conferences San Diego Writer's Conference; NECON; BEA; World Fantasy.

Tips "Research your field and contact professional writers' organizations to see who is looking for what. Finish your novel before querying agents. Read my book, *An Insider's Guide to Getting an Agent*, to get a sense of how agents operate."

STEPHEN PEVNER, INC.

382 Lafayette St., 8th Floor, New York NY 10003. (212)674-8403. Fax: (212)529-3692. E-mail: spevner@aol.com. **Contact:** Stephen Pevner.

Represents Nonfiction books, novels, feature film, TV scripts, TV movie of the week, episodic drama, animation, documentary, miniseries. **Considers these nonfiction areas:** Biography/autobiography; ethnic/cultural interests; gay/lesbian issues; history; humor/satire; language/literature/criticism; memoirs; music/dance; New Age/metaphysics; photography; popular culture; religious/inspirational; sociology; travel. **Considers these fiction areas:** Comic books/cartoon; contemporary issues; erotica; ethnic; experimental; gay/lesbian; glitz; horror; humor/satire; literary; mainstream/contemporary; psychic/supernatural; thriller; urban. **Considers these script subject areas:** Comedy; contemporary issues; detective/police/crime; gay/lesbian; glitz; horror; romantic comedy; romantic drama; thriller.

    O➡ This agency specializes in motion pictures, novels, humor, pop culture, urban fiction, independent filmmakers. Actively seeking urban fiction, popular culture, screenplays and film proposals.

How to Contact Query with SASE, outline/proposal. Prefers to read materials exclusively. No e-mail or fax queries. Responds in 2 weeks to queries; 1 month to mss. Obtains most new clients through recommendations from others.

Recent Sales *In the Company of Men* and *Bash: Latterday Plays*, by Neil Labute; *The Vagina Monologues*, by Eve Ensler; *Guide to Life*, by The Five Lesbian Brothers; *Noise From Underground*, by Michael Levine. Other clients include Richard Linklater, Gregg Araki, Tom DiCillo, Genvieve Turner/Rose Troche, Todd Solondz, Neil LaBute.

Terms Agent receives 15% commission on domestic sales; 20% commission on foreign sales. Offers written contract, binding for 1 year; 6-week notice must be given to terminate contract. 100% of business is derived from commissions on ms sales.

Tips "Be persistent, but civilized."

ALISON J. PICARD, LITERARY AGENT

P.O. Box 2000, Cotuit MA 02635. (508)477-7192. Fax: (508)477-7192 (Please contact before faxing.). E-mail: ajpicard@aol.com. **Contact:** Alison Picard. Estab. 1985. Represents 48 clients. 30% of clients are new/unpublished writers. Currently handles: 40% nonfiction books; 40% novels; 20% juvenile books.

    • Prior to becoming an agent, Ms. Picard was an assistant at an NYC literary agency.

Member Agents Alison Picard (mysteries/suspense/thriller, romance, literary fiction, adult nonfiction, juvenile books).

Represents Nonfiction books, novels, short story collections, novellas, juvenile books. **Considers these nonfiction areas:** Animals; anthropology/archaeology; art/architecture/design; biography/autobiography; business/economics; child guidance/parenting; cooking/foods/nutrition; current affairs; education; ethnic/cultural interests; gay/lesbian issues; government/politics/law; health/medicine; history; how-to; humor/satire; juvenile nonfiction; memoirs; military/war; money/finance; multicultural; music/dance; nature/environment; New Age/metaphysics; popular culture; psychology; religious/inspirational; science/technology; self-help/personal improvement; translation; travel; true crime/investigative; women's issues/studies; young adult. **Considers these fiction areas:** Action/adventure; contemporary issues; detective/police/crime; erotica; ethnic; experimental; family saga; feminist; gay/lesbian; glitz; historical; horror; humor/satire; juvenile; literary; mainstream/contemporary; multicultural; mystery/suspense; New Age; picture books; psychic/supernatural; regional; religious/inspirational; romance; sports; thriller; young adult.

    O➡ "Many of my clients have come to me from big agencies, where they felt overlooked or ignored. I communicate freely with my clients and offer a lot of career advice, suggestions for revising manuscripts, etc. If I believe in a project, I will submit it to a dozen or more publishers, unlike some agents who give up after four or five rejections." Actively seeking commercial adult fiction and nonfiction, middle grade juvenile fiction. Does not want to receive science fiction/fantasy, westerns, poetry, plays, articles.

How to Contact Query with SASE. Considers simultaneous queries. Responds in 2 weeks to queries; 4 months to mss. Returns materials only with SASE. Obtains most new clients through recommendations from others, solicitations.

Recent Sales Sold 32 titles in the last year. *A Hard Ticket Home*, by David Housewright (St. Martin's Press); *Indigo Rose*, by Susan Miller (Bantam Books/Random House); *Fly Fishing & Funerals*, by Mary Bartek (Henry Holt & Co.); *Stage Fright*, by Dina Friedman (Farrar Straus & Giroux); *Fashion Slaves*, by Louise de Teliga (Kensington). Other clients include Osha Gray Davidson, Amy Dean, Nancy Means Wright.

Terms Agent receives 15% commission on domestic sales; 20% commission on foreign sales. Offers written contract, binding for 1 year; 1-week notice must be given to terminate contract.

Tips "Please don't send material without sending a query first via mail or e-mail. I don't accept phone or fax queries. Always enclose a SASE with a query."

🖉 PINDER LANE & GARON-BROOKE ASSOCIATES, LTD.

159 W. 53rd St., Suite 14C, New York NY 10019-6005. (212)489-0880. E-mail: pinderl@interport.net. **Contact:** Robert Thixton. Member of AAR; signatory of WGA. Represents 30 clients. 20% of clients are new/unpublished writers. Currently handles: 25% nonfiction books; 75% novels.

Member Agents Dick Duane, Robert Thixton.

Represents Nonfiction books, novels. **Considers these fiction areas:** Contemporary issues; detective/police/crime; family saga; fantasy; gay/lesbian; literary; mainstream/contemporary; mystery/suspense; romance; science fiction.

  O⇥ This agency specializes in mainstream fiction and nonfiction. Does not want to receive screenplays, TV series teleplays or dramatic plays.

How to Contact Query with SASE. *No unsolicited mss.* Responds in 3 weeks to queries; 2 months to mss. Obtains most new clients through referrals, queries.

Recent Sales Sold 20 titles in the last year. *Diana & Jackie—Maidens, Mothers & Myths*, by Jay Mulvaney (St. Martin's Press); The Sixth Fleet series, by David Meadows (Berkley); *Dark Fires*, by Rosemary Rogers (Mira Books).

Terms Agent receives 15% commission on domestic sales; 30% commission on foreign sales. Offers written contract, binding for 3-5 years.

Tips "With our literary and media experience, our agency is uniquely positioned for the current and future direction publishing is taking. Send query letter first giving the essence of the manuscript and a personal or career bio with SASE."

AARON M. PRIEST LITERARY AGENCY

708 Third Ave., 23rd Floor, New York NY 10017-4103. (212)818-0344. Fax: (212)573-9417. E-mail: lchilds@aaron priest.com. **Contact:** Aaron Priest or Molly Friedrich. Estab. 1974. Member of AAR. Currently handles: 25% nonfiction books; 75% novels.

Member Agents Lisa Erbach Vance; Paul Cirone; Aaron Priest; Molly Friedrich; Lucy Childs.

Represents Nonfiction books, novels.

How to Contact No e-mail or fax queries. Considers simultaneous queries. If interested, will respond within 2 weeks.

Recent Sales *She is Me*, by Kathleen Schine; *Killer Smile*, by Lisa Scottoline.

Terms Agent receives 15% commission on domestic sales. Charges for photocopying, foreign-postage expenses.

🌙 SUSAN ANN PROTTER, LITERARY AGENT

110 W. 40th St., Suite 1408, New York NY 10018. (212)840-0480. **Contact:** Susan Protter. Estab. 1971. Member of AAR, Authors' Guild. Represents 40 clients. 5% of clients are new/unpublished writers. Currently handles: 50% nonfiction books; 50% novels; occasional magazine article or short story (for established clients only).

  ● Prior to opening her agency, Ms. Protter was associate director of subsidiary rights at Harper & Row Publishers.

Represents Nonfiction books, novels. **Considers these nonfiction areas:** Biography/autobiography; current affairs; health/medicine; science/technology; international and Middle Eastern issues. **Considers these fiction areas:** Fantasy; mystery/suspense; science fiction; thriller; crime.

  O⇥ Writers must have book-length project or ms that is ready to sell. Does not want westerns, romance, fantasy, children's books, young adult novels, screenplays, plays, poetry, Star Wars or Star Trek.

How to Contact Currently looking for limited number of new clients. Send short query by mail with SASE. *No unsolicited mss.* Responds in 3 weeks to queries; 2 months to mss.

Recent Sales *Beyond the Mirage: America's Fragile Partnership with Saudi Arabia*, by Thomas W. Lippman (Westview); *House of Storms*, by Ian R. MacLeod (Ace); *Einstein for Dummies*, by Carlos Calle, Ph.D. (Wiley).

Terms Agent receives 15% commission on domestic sales; 15% commission on dramatic rights sales. "If, after seeing your query, we request to see your manuscript, there will be a small shipping and handling fee requested to cover cost of returning materials should they not be suitable." Charges clients for photocopying, messenger, express mail, airmail and overseas shipping expenses.

Tips "Please send neat and professionally organized queries. Make sure to include a SASE, or we cannot reply. We receive approximately 200 queries a week and read them in the order they arrive. We usually reply within 2 weeks to any query. Please, do not call or e-mail queries. If you are sending a multiple query, make sure to note that in your letter. I am looking for work that stands out in a highly competitive and difficult market."

QUICKSILVER BOOKS—LITERARY AGENTS

508 Central Park Ave., #5101, Scarsdale NY 10583. (914)722-4664. Fax: (914)722-4664. Website: www.quicksilverbooks.com. **Contact:** Bob Silverstein. Estab. 1973 as packager; 1987 as literary agency. Represents 50 clients. 50% of clients are new/unpublished writers. Currently handles: 75% nonfiction books; 25% novels.

• Prior to opening his agency, Mr. Silverstein served as senior editor at Bantam Books and Dell Books/Delacorte Press.

Represents Nonfiction books, novels. **Considers these nonfiction areas:** Anthropology/archaeology; biography/autobiography; business/economics; child guidance/parenting; cooking/foods/nutrition; current affairs; ethnic/cultural interests; health/medicine; history; how-to; language/literature/criticism; memoirs; nature/environment; New Age/metaphysics; popular culture; psychology; religious/inspirational; science/technology; self-help/personal improvement; sociology; sports; true crime/investigative; women's issues/studies. **Considers these fiction areas:** Action/adventure; glitz; mystery/suspense; thriller.

○➡ This agency specializes in literary and commercial mainstream fiction and nonfiction (especially psychology, New Age, holistic healing, consciousness, ecology, environment, spirituality, reference, cookbooks, narrative nonfiction). Actively seeking commercial mainstream fiction and nonfiction in most categories. Does not want to receive science fiction, pornography, poetry or single-spaced mss.

How to Contact Query with SASE. Authors are expected to supply SASE for return of ms and for query letter responses. No e-mail or fax queries. Considers simultaneous queries. Responds in 2 weeks to queries; 1 month to mss. Returns materials only with SASE. Obtains most new clients through recommendations, listings in sourcebooks, solicitations, workshop participation.

Recent Sales Sold over 20 titles in the last year. *Nice Girls Don't Get Rich*, by Lois P. Frankel, Ph.D. (Warner Books); *The Young Patriots*, by Charles Cerami (Sourcebooks); *The Coming of the Beatles*, by Martin Goldsmith (Wiley); *The Real Food Daily Cookbook*, by Ann Gentry (Ten Speed Press); *The Complete Book of Vinyasa Yoga*, by Srivatsa Ramaswami (Marlow & Co.).

Terms Agent receives 15% commission on domestic sales; 20% commission on foreign sales. Offers written contract.

Writers' Conferences National Writers Union Conference (Dobbs Ferry NY, April).

Tips "Write what you know. Write from the heart. Publishers print, authors sell."

HELEN REES LITERARY AGENCY

376 North St., Boston MA 02113-2013. (617)227-9014. Fax: (617)227-8762. E-mail: reesagency@reesagency.com (no unsolicited e-mail submissions). **Contact:** Joan Mazmanian, Ann Collette, Helen Rees or Lorin Rees. Estab. 1983. Member of AAR, PEN. Represents 80 clients. 50% of clients are new/unpublished writers. Currently handles: 60% nonfiction books; 40% novels.

Member Agents Ann Collette (literary fiction, women's studies, health, biography, history); Helen Rees (business, money/finance/economics, government/politics/law, contemporary issues, literary fiction); Lorin Rees (business, money, finance, management, history, narrative nonfiction, science, literary fiction, memoir).

Represents Nonfiction books, novels. **Considers these nonfiction areas:** Biography/autobiography; business/economics; current affairs; government/politics/law; health/medicine; history; money/finance; women's issues/studies. **Considers these fiction areas:** Contemporary issues; historical; literary; mainstream/contemporary; mystery/suspense; thriller.

How to Contact Query with SASE, outline, 2 sample chapters. No e-mail or fax queries. Responds in 2-3 weeks to queries. Obtains most new clients through recommendations from others, solicitations, conferences.

Recent Sales Sold 30 titles in the last year. *Get Your Ship Together*, by Capt. D. Michael Abrashoff; *Overpromise and Overdeliver*, by Rick Berrara; *MBA in a Box*, by Joel Kurtzman; *America the Broke*, by Gerald Swanson; *Murder at the B-School*, by Jeffrey Cruikshank; *Skin River*, by Steven Sidor; *Father Said*, by Hal Sirowitz.

Terms Agent receives 15% commission on domestic sales; 20% commission on foreign sales.

REGAL LITERARY AGENCY

1140 Broadway, Penthouse, New York NY 10001. (212)684-7900. Fax: (212)684-7906. E-mail: office@regal-literary.com. Website: www.regal-literary.com. **Contact:** Bess Reed, Lauren Schott. Estab. 2002. Member of AAR. Represents 70 clients. 20% of clients are new/unpublished writers. Currently handles: 48% nonfiction books; 46% novels; 2% story collections; 2% novellas; 2% poetry.

• Prior to becoming agents, Gordon Kato was a psychologist, Jospeph Regal was a musician, and Peter Steinberg and Lauren Schott were magazine editors.

Member Agents Gordon Kato (literary fiction, commercial fiction, pop culture); Joseph Regal (literary fiction, science, history, memoir); Peter Steinberg (literary and commercial fiction, history, humor, memoir, narrative nonfiction); Bess Reed (literary fiction, narrative nonfiction, self-help); Lauren Schott (literary fiction, commercial fiction, memoir, narrative nonfiction, thrillers, mysteries).

Represents Nonfiction books, novels, short story collections, novellas. **Considers these nonfiction areas:** Anthropology/archaeology; art/architecture/design; biography/autobiography; business/economics; cooking/foods/nutrition; current affairs; ethnic/cultural interests; gay/lesbian issues; government/politics/law; history; humor/satire; language/literature/criticism; memoirs; military/war; music/dance; nature/environment; photography; popular culture; psychology; religious/inspirational (includes inspirational); science/technology (includes technology); sports; translation; true crime/investigative; women's issues/studies. **Considers these fiction areas:** Comic books/cartoon; detective/police/crime; ethnic; historical; literary; mystery/suspense; thriller; contemporary.

O➤ "We have discovered more than a dozen successful literary novelists in the last 5 years. We are small but are extraordinarily responsive to our writers. We are more like managers than agents, with an eye toward every aspect of our writers' careers, including publicity and other media." Actively seeking literary fiction and narrative nonfiction. Does not want romance, science fiction, horror, screenplays or children's books.

How to Contact Query with SASE, submit 5-15 sample pages. No e-mail or fax queries. Considers simultaneous queries. Responds in 2-3 weeks to queries; 4-12 to mss. Returns materials only with SASE. Obtains most new clients through recommendations from others, unsolicited submissions.

Recent Sales Sold 30 titles in the last year. Clients include James Reston, Jr., Tim Winton, Tony Earley, Dennie Hughes, Mark Lee, Jake Page, Cheryl Bernard, Daniel Wallace, John Marks, Keith Scribner, Alex Abella, Audrey Niffenegger, Cathy Day, Alicia Erian, Gergory David Roberts, Dallas Hudgens, John Twelve Hawks.

Terms Agent receives 15% commission on domestic sales; 20% commission on foreign sales. No written contract. Charges clients for typical, major office expenses, such as photocopying and foreign postage.

◑ JODY REIN BOOKS, INC.

7741 S. Ash Court, Centennial CO 80122. (303)694-4430. Fax: (303)694-0687. Website: www.jodyreinbooks.com. **Contact:** Winnefred Dollar. Estab. 1994. Member of AAR, Authors' Guild. Currently handles: 70% nonfiction books; 30% novels.

• Prior to opening her agency, Jody Rein worked for 13 years as an acquisitions editor for Contemporary Books, Bantam/Doubleday/Dell (executive editor), and Morrow/Avon (executive editor).

Member Agents Jody Rein; Johnna Hietala.

Represents Nonfiction books (primarily narrative and commercial nonfiction), novels (select literary novels, commercial mainstream). **Considers these nonfiction areas:** Business/economics; child guidance/parenting; current affairs; ethnic/cultural interests; government/politics/law; history; humor/satire; music/dance; nature/environment; popular culture; psychology; science/technology; sociology; theater/film; women's issues/studies. **Considers these fiction areas:** Literary; mainstream/contemporary.

O➤ This agency specializes in commercial and narrative nonfiction and literary/commercial fiction.

How to Contact Query with SASE. No e-mail or fax queries. Considers simultaneous queries. Responds in 6 weeks to queries; 2 months to mss. Obtains most new clients through recommendations from others, solicitations.

Recent Sales *8 Simple Rules for Dating My Teenage Daughter*, by Bruce Cameron (ABC/Disney); *Skeletons on the Zahara*, by Dean King (Little, Brown); *The Big Year*, by Mark Obmascik (The Free Press).

Terms Agent receives 15% commission on domestic sales; 25% commission on foreign sales; 20% commission on dramatic rights sales. Offers written contract. Charges clients for express mail, overseas expenses, photocopying ms.

Tips "Do your homework before submitting. Make sure you have a marketable topic and the credentials to write about it. Well-written books on fresh and original nonfiction topics that have broad appeal. Novels written by authors who have spent years developing their craft. Authors must be well established in their fields and have strong media experience."

◑ JODIE RHODES LITERARY AGENCY

8840 Villa La Jolla Dr., Suite 315, La Jolla CA 92037-1957. **Contact:** Jodie Rhodes, president. Estab. 1998. Member of AAR. Represents 50 clients. 60% of clients are new/unpublished writers. Currently handles: 60% nonfiction books; 35% novels; 5% middle to young adult books.

• Prior to opening her agency, Ms. Rhodes was a university-level creative writing teacher, workshop director, published novelist, and vice president media director at the N.W. Ayer Advertising Agency.

Member Agents Jodie Rhodes, president; Clark McCutcheon (fiction); Bob McCarter (nonfiction).

Represents Nonfiction books, novels, juvenile books. **Considers these nonfiction areas:** Biography/autobiography; child guidance/parenting; ethnic/cultural interests; government/politics/law; health/medicine; history;

Literary Agents

memoirs; military/war; science/technology; women's issues/studies. **Considers these fiction areas:** Contemporary issues; ethnic; family saga; historical; juvenile; literary; mainstream/contemporary; mystery/suspense; thriller; young adult; women's.

> O— Actively seeking "writers passionate about their books with a talent for richly textured narrative, an eye for details, and a nose for research." Nonfiction writers must have recognized credentials and expert knowledge of their subject matter. Does not want to receive erotica, horror, fantasy, romance, science fiction, children's books, religious or inspirational books.

How to Contact Query with brief synopsis, first 30-50 pages, and SASE. No e-mail or fax queries. Considers simultaneous queries. Responds in 10 days to queries. Returns materials only with SASE. Obtains most new clients through recommendations from others, agent sourcebooks.

Recent Sales Sold 32 titles in the last year. *The Village Bride in Beverly Hills*, by Kavita Daswani (Putnam U.S./HarperCollins UK); *Memory Matters*, by Scott Hagwood (Simon & Schuster); *Raising Healthy Eaters*, by Dr. Henry Legeres (Perseus/Da Capo Press); *The Anorexia Diaries*, by Linda and Tara Rio (Rodale); *Memoirs of a Dwarf in the Sun King's Court*, by Paul Weidner (University of Wisconsin Press); *Becoming Japanese*, by Karin Muller (Rodale); *Free Your Child from Asthma*, by Dr. Gary Rachelefsky (McGraw-Hill); *The Potty Myth*, by Jill Lekovic (Crown/3 Rivers Press); *Intimate Partner Violence*, by Dr. Connie Mitchell (Oxford University Press); *Our Fragile Planet*, by Dana Desonie (Facts on File); *Modern Babies*, by Dr. Daniel Potter (Marlowe & Co.); *Biology for a New Century*, by Dr. Stan Rice (John Wiley & Sons); *A Writer's Paris*, by Eric Maisel (Writer's Digest Books); *Post Adoption Blues*, by Karen Foli (Rodale).

Terms Agent receives 15% commission on domestic sales; 20% commission on foreign sales. Offers written contract; 1-month notice must be given to terminate contract. Charges clients for fax, photocopying, phone calls and postage. "Charges are itemized and approved by writers upfront."

Tips "Think your book out before you write it. Do your research, know your subject matter intimately, write vivid specifics, not bland generalities. Care deeply about your book. Don't imitate other writers. Find your own voice. We never take on a book we don't believe in, and we go the extra mile for our writers. We welcome talented, new writers."

ANGELA RINALDI LITERARY AGENCY

P.O. Box 7877, Beverly Hills CA 90212-7877. (310)842-7665. Fax: (310)837-8143. E-mail: mail@rinaldiliterary.com. Estab. 1994. Member of AAR. Represents 50 clients. Currently handles: 30% nonfiction books; 70% novels.

> ● Prior to opening her agency, Ms. Rinaldi was an editor at NAL/Signet, Pocket Books and Bantam and the manager of book development for *The Los Angeles Times*.

Represents Nonfiction books, novels, TV and motion picture rights for clients only. **Considers these nonfiction areas:** Biography/autobiography; business/economics; health/medicine; money/finance; self-help/personal improvement; true crime/investigative; women's issues/studies; books by journalists and academics. **Considers these fiction areas:** Literary; commercial; upmarket women's fiction; suspense.

> O— Actively seeking commercial and literary fiction. Does not want to receive scripts, poetry, category romances, children's books, westerns, science fiction/fantasy, technothrillers or cookbooks.

How to Contact For fiction, send the first 3 chapters, brief synopsis, SASE. For nonfiction, query with SASE first or send outline/proposal, SASE. Do not send certified mail. Do not send metered mail as SASE. Brief e-mail inquiries OK, no attachments. Considers simultaneous queries. Please advise if this is a multiple submission. Responds in 6 weeks to queries. Returns materials only with SASE.

Recent Sales *My First Crush*, by Linda Kaplan (Lyons Press); *Rescue Me*, by Megan Clark (Kensington); *The Blood Orange Tree*, by Drusilla Campbell (Kensington); *Some Writers Deserve to Starve: 31 Brutal Truths About the Publishing Industry*, by Elaura Niles (Writer's Digest Books); *Indivisible by Two: Great Tales of Twins, Triplets and Quads*, by Dr. Nancy Segal (Harvard University Press).

Terms Agent receives 15% commission on domestic sales; 20% commission on foreign sales. Offers written contract. Charges clients for photocopying if not provided by client.

☑ ANN RITTENBERG LITERARY AGENCY, INC.

1201 Broadway, Suite 708, New York NY 10001. (212)684-6936. **Contact:** Ann Rittenberg, president. Estab. 1992. Member of AAR. Represents 35 clients. 40% of clients are new/unpublished writers. Currently handles: 50% nonfiction books; 50% novels.

Member Agents Ann Rittenberg, Ted Gideonse.

Represents Nonfiction books, novels. **Considers these nonfiction areas:** Biography/autobiography; gay/lesbian issues; history (social/cultural); memoirs; women's issues/studies. **Considers these fiction areas:** Literary.

> O— This agent specializes in literary fiction and literary nonfiction.

How to Contact Submit outline, 3 sample chapters, SASE. Considers simultaneous queries. Responds in 6 weeks to queries; 2 months to mss. Obtains most new clients through referrals from established writers and editors.

Recent Sales Sold 20 titles in the last year. *Bad Cat*, by Jim Edgar (Workman); *A Certain Slant of Light*, by Laura Whitcomb (Houghton Mifflin); *Cities of Weather*, by Matthew Fox (Cormorant Books); *Late & Soon*, by Bob Hughes (Carroll & Graf).

Terms Agent receives 15% commission on domestic sales; 20% commission on foreign sales. Offers written contract. Charges clients for photocopying only.

☑ RLR ASSOCIATES, LTD.

Literary Department, 7 W. 51st St., New York NY 10019. (212)541-8641. Fax: (212)541-6052. Website: www.rlrli terary.net. **Contact:** Jennifer Unter, Tara Mark. Represents 50 clients. 25% of clients are new/unpublished writers. Currently handles: 70% nonfiction books; 25% novels; 5% story collections.

Member Agents Jennifer Unter, Tara Mark.

Represents Nonfiction books, novels, short story collections, scholarly books. **Considers these nonfiction areas:** Animals; anthropology/archaeology; art/architecture/design; biography/autobiography; business/economics; child guidance/parenting; cooking/foods/nutrition; current affairs; education; ethnic/cultural interests; gay/lesbian issues; government/politics/law; health/medicine; history; humor/satire; interior design/decorating; language/literature/criticism; memoirs; money/finance; multicultural; music/dance; nature/environment; photography; popular culture; psychology; religious/inspirational; science/technology; self-help/personal improvement; sociology; sports; translation; travel; true crime/investigative; women's issues/studies. **Considers these fiction areas:** Action/adventure; comic books/cartoon; contemporary issues; detective/police/crime; ethnic; experimental; family saga; feminist; gay/lesbian; historical; horror; humor/satire; literary; mainstream/contemporary; multicultural; mystery/suspense; sports; thriller.

> **O—** "We provide a lot of editorial assistance to our clients and have connections." Actively seeking fiction (all types except for romance and fantasy), current affairs, history, art, popular culture, health, business. Does not want to receive screenplays.

How to Contact Query with SASE. Considers simultaneous queries. Responds in 5 weeks. Returns materials only with SASE. Obtains most new clients through recommendations from others.

Recent Sales Sold 20 titles in the last year. Clients include Shelby Foote, The Grief Recovery Institute, Don Wade, Don Zimmer, The Knot.com, David Plowden, PGA of America, Danny Peary, Goerge Kalinsky and Peter Hyman.

Terms Agent receives 15% commission on domestic sales; 20% commission on foreign sales. Offers written contract.

Tips "Please check out our website for more details on our agency. No e-mail submissions, please."

☑ B.J. ROBBINS LITERARY AGENCY

5130 Bellaire Ave., North Hollywood CA 91607-2908. (818)760-6602. Fax: (818)760-6616. E-mail: robbinsliterary@aol.com. **Contact:** (Ms.) B.J. Robbins. Estab. 1992. Member of AAR. Represents 40 clients. 50% of clients are new/unpublished writers. Currently handles: 50% nonfiction books; 50% novels.

Member Agents Missy Pontious (YA).

Represents Nonfiction books, novels. **Considers these nonfiction areas:** Biography/autobiography; child guidance/parenting; current affairs; ethnic/cultural interests; health/medicine; how-to; humor/satire; memoirs; music/dance; popular culture; psychology; self-help/personal improvement; sociology; sports; theater/film; travel; true crime/investigative; women's issues/studies. **Considers these fiction areas:** Contemporary issues; detective/police/crime; ethnic; literary; mainstream/contemporary; mystery/suspense; sports; thriller; young adult.

How to Contact Submit 3 sample chapters, outline/proposal, SASE. E-mail queries OK; no attachments. No fax queries. Considers simultaneous queries. Responds in 2 weeks to queries; 6 weeks to mss. Returns materials only with SASE. Obtains most new clients through conferences, referrals.

Recent Sales Sold 15 titles in the last year. *The Sex Lives of Cannibals*, by J. Maarten Troost (Broadway); *Quickening*, by Laura Catherine Brown (Random House/Ballantine); *Snow Mountain Passage*, by James D. Houston (Knopf); *The Last Summer*, by John Hough, Jr. (Simon & Schuster); *Last Stand on the Little Bighorn*, by James M. Donovan (Little, Brown).

Terms Agent receives 15% commission on domestic sales; 20% commission on foreign sales. Offers written contract; 3-month notice must be given to terminate contract. 100% of business is derived from commissions on ms sales. Charges clients for postage and photocopying only. Writers charged for fees only after the sale of ms.

Writers' Conferences Squaw Valley Fiction Writers Workshop (Squaw Valley CA, August); SDSU Writers Conference (San Diego CA, January).

☑ THE ROBBINS OFFICE, INC.

405 Park Ave., New York NY 10022. (212)223-0720. Fax: (212)223-2535. **Contact:** Kathy P. Robbins, owner.

Member Agents David Halpern, Teri Tobias (foreign rights).

Represents Nonfiction books, novels. **Considers these nonfiction areas:** Biography/autobiography; government/politics/law (political commentary); language/literature/criticism (criticism); memoirs; Investigative journalism. **Considers these fiction areas:** Literary; mainstream/contemporary (commercial); poetry.

    O⊸ This agency specializes in selling serious nonfiction, commercial and literary fiction.

How to Contact Accepts submissions by referral only.

Recent Sales *Ask Not*, by Thurston Clarke (Holt); *The Sleeper*, by Christopher Dickey (Simon & Schuster); *Entering Hades*, by John Leake (Farrar Straus & Giroux); *Garlic and Sapphires*, by Ruth Reichl (Penguin); *French Women Don't Get Fat*, by Mireille Guiliano (Knopf).

Terms Agent receives 15% commission on domestic sales; 15% commission on foreign sales; 15% commission on dramatic rights sales. Bills back specific expenses incurred in doing business for a client.

◢ LINDA ROGHAAR LITERARY AGENCY, INC.

133 High Point Dr., Amherst MA 01002. (413)256-1921. Fax: (413)256-2636. E-mail: contact@lindaroghaar.com. Website: www.lindaroghaar.com. **Contact:** Linda L. Roghaar. Estab. 1996. Represents 50 clients. 40% of clients are new/unpublished writers. Currently handles: 90% nonfiction books; 10% novels.

    • Prior to opening her agency, Ms. Roghaar worked in retail bookselling for 5 years and as a publishers' sales rep for 15 years.

Represents Nonfiction books, novels. **Considers these nonfiction areas:** Animals; anthropology/archaeology; biography/autobiography; education; history; nature/environment; popular culture; religious/inspirational; self-help/personal improvement; women's issues/studies. **Considers these fiction areas:** Mystery/suspense (amateur sleuth, cozy, culinary, malice domestic).

How to Contact Query with SASE. Accepts e-mail queries. No fax queries. Considers simultaneous queries. Responds in 2 months to queries; 4 months to mss.

Recent Sales *Thieves Break In*, by Cristina Summers (Bantam); *Mindful Knitting*, by Tara Jon Manning (Tuttle).

Terms Agent receives 15% commission on domestic sales; negotiable commission on foreign sales. Offers written contract, binding for negotiable time.

◢ THE ROSENBERG GROUP

23 Lincoln Ave., Marblehead MA 01945. (781)990-1341. Fax: (781)990-1344. Website: www.rosenberggroup.com. **Contact:** Barbara Collins Rosenberg. Estab. 1998. Member of AAR, recognized agent of the RWA. Represents 32 clients. 25% of clients are new/unpublished writers. Currently handles: 30% nonfiction books; 30% novels; 10% scholarly books; 30% textbooks.

    • Prior to becoming an agent, Ms. Rosenberg was a senior editor for Harcourt.

Member Agents Barbara Collins Rosenberg.

Represents Nonfiction books, novels, textbooks. **Considers these nonfiction areas:** Current affairs; popular culture; psychology; sports; women's issues/studies; women's health; food/wine/beverages. **Considers these fiction areas:** Literary; romance; women's.

    O⊸ Ms. Rosenberg is well-versed in the romance market (both category and single title). She is a frequent speaker at romance conferences. Actively seeking romance category or single title in contemporary chick lit, romantic suspense and the historical sub-genres. Does not want to receive time-travel, paranormal or inspirational/spiritual romances.

How to Contact Query with SASE. No e-mail or fax queries. Responds in 2 weeks to queries; 4-6 weeks to mss. Returns materials only with SASE. Obtains most new clients through recommendations from others, solicitations, conferences.

Recent Sales Sold 27 titles in the last year.

Terms Agent receives 15% commission on domestic sales; 15% commission on foreign sales. Offers written contract; 1-month notice must be given to terminate contract. Postage and photocopying limit of $350/year.

Writers' Conferences RWA Annual Conference (Reno NV); RT Booklovers Convention (St. Louis MO); BEA (New York).

◢ JANE ROTROSEN AGENCY LLC

318 E. 51st St., New York NY 10022. (212)593-4330. Fax: (212)935-6985. E-mail: firstinitiallastname@janerotrosen.com. Estab. 1974. Member of AAR, Authors Guild. Represents over 100 clients. Currently handles: 30% nonfiction books; 70% novels.

Member Agents Jane R. Berkey, Andrea Cirillo, Annelise Robey, Margaret Ruley, Perry Gordijn (director of translation rights).

Represents Nonfiction books, novels. **Considers these nonfiction areas:** Biography/autobiography; business/economics; child guidance/parenting; cooking/foods/nutrition; current affairs; health/medicine; how-to; humor/satire; money/finance; nature/environment; popular culture; psychology; self-help/personal improvement; sports; true crime/investigative; women's issues/studies. **Considers these fiction areas:** Action/adventure; detective/police/crime; family saga; historical; horror; mainstream/contemporary; mystery/suspense; romance; thriller; women's.

How to Contact Query with SASE. By referral only. No e-mail or fax queries. Responds in 2 months to mss. Responds in 2 weeks to writers who have been referred by a client or colleague. Returns materials only with SASE.

Recent Sales This agency prefers not to share information on specific sales.

Terms Agent receives 15% commission on domestic sales; 20% commission on foreign sales. Offers written contract, binding for 3-5 years; 2-month notice must be given to terminate contract. Charges clients for photocopying, express mail, overseas postage, book purchase.

THE DAMARIS ROWLAND AGENCY

5 Cooper Rd., Apt. 13H, New York NY 10010. (212)475-8942. Fax: (212)358-9411. **Contact:** Damaris Rowland or Steve Axelrod. Estab. 1994. Member of AAR. Represents 50 clients. 10% of clients are new/unpublished writers. Currently handles: novels.

Represents Novels. **Considers these fiction areas:** Historical; literary; mainstream/contemporary; romance (contemporary, gothic, historical, regency); commercial.

  0-¬ This agency specializes in women's fiction. Submit query with SASE.

How to Contact Responds in 6 weeks to queries. Obtains most new clients through recommendations from others, solicitations, conferences.

Recent Sales *The Next Accident*, by Lisa Gardner; *To Trust a Stranger*, by Karen Robard; *Nursing Homes*, by Peter Silin.

Terms Agent receives 15% commission on domestic sales; 20% commission on foreign sales. Offers written contract; 1-month notice must be given to terminate contract. Charges only if extraordinary expenses have been incurred, e.g., photocopying and mailing 15 mss to Europe for a foreign sale.

Writers' Conferences Novelists, Inc. (Denver, October); RWA National (Texas, July); Pacific Northwest Writers Conference.

THE PETER RUBIE LITERARY AGENCY

240 W. 35th St., Suite 500, New York NY 10001. (212)279-1776. Fax: (212)279-0927. E-mail: peterrubie@prlit.com. Website: www.prlit.com. **Contact:** Peter Rubie or June Clark (pralit@aol.com). Estab. 2000. Member of AAR. Represents 130 clients. 20% of clients are new/unpublished writers.

  • Prior to opening his agency, Mr. Rubie was a founding partner of another literary agency (Perkins, Rubie & Associates) and the fiction editor at Walker and Co. Ms. Clark is the author of several books and plays and previously worked in cable TV marketing and promotion.

Member Agents Peter Rubie (crime, science fiction, fantasy, literary fiction, thrillers, narrative/serious nonfiction, business, self-help, how-to, popular, food/wine, history, commercial science, music, education, parenting); June Clark (nonfiction consisting of celebrity biographies, parenting, pets, women's issues, teen nonfiction, how-to, self-help, offbeat business, food/wine, commercial New Age, pop culture, entertainment); Caren Johnson, assistant; Hanna Rubin, agent-at-large (hanna.rubin@prlit.com); Jodi Weiss, agent-at-large.

Represents Nonfiction books, novels. **Considers these nonfiction areas:** Business/economics; creative nonfiction; current affairs; ethnic/cultural interests; how-to; popular culture; science/technology; self-help/personal improvement; health/nutrition; cooking/food/wine; music; theater/film/television; prescriptive New Age; parenting/education; pets; commercial academic material; TV. **Considers these fiction areas:** Fantasy; historical; literary; science fiction; thriller.

How to Contact For fiction, submit short synopsis and first 30-40 pages. For nonfiction, submit 1-page overview of the book, TOC, outline, 1-2 sample chapters. Accepts e-mail queries. Responds in 2 months to queries; 3 months to mss. Returns materials only with SASE. Obtains most new clients through recommendations from others.

Recent Sales Sold 50 titles in the last year. *Walking Money*, by James Born (Putnam); *Finishing Business*, by Harlan Ullman (Naval Institute Press); *The Nouvelle Creole Cookbook*, by Joseph Carey (Taylor).

Terms Agent receives 15% commission on domestic sales; 20% commission on foreign sales. Offers written contract. Charges clients for photocopying and some foreign mailings.

Tips "We look for professional writers and writers who are experts, have a strong platform and reputation in their field, and have an outstanding prose style. Be professional and open-minded. Know your market and learn your craft. Go to our website for up-to-date information on clients and sales."

RUSSELL & VOLKENING

50 W. 29th St., #7E, New York NY 10001. (212)684-6050. Fax: (212)889-3026. **Contact:** Timothy Seldes, Kirsten Ringer. Estab. 1940. Member of AAR. Represents 140 clients. 20% of clients are new/unpublished writers. Currently handles: 45% nonfiction books; 50% novels; 3% story collections; 2% novellas.

Member Agents Timothy Seldes (nonfiction, literary fiction).

Represents Nonfiction books, novels, short story collections. **Considers these nonfiction areas:** Anthropology/archaeology; art/architecture/design; biography/autobiography; business/economics; cooking/foods/nutrition; creative nonfiction; current affairs; education; ethnic/cultural interests; gay/lesbian issues; government/politics/law; health/medicine; history; language/literature/criticism; military/war; money/finance; music/dance; nature/environment; photography; popular culture; psychology; science/technology; sociology; sports; theater/film; true crime/investigative; women's issues/studies. **Considers these fiction areas:** Action/adventure; detective/police/crime; ethnic; literary; mainstream/contemporary; mystery/suspense; picture books; sports; thriller.

   ○━ This agency specializes in literary fiction and narrative nonfiction.

Recent Sales *The Amateur Marriage*, by Anne Tyler (Knopf); *Loot*, by Nadine Gardiner; *Flying Crows*, by Jim Lehrer (Random House).

Terms Agent receives 15% commission on domestic sales; 20% commission on foreign sales. Charges clients for "standard office expenses relating to the submission of materials of an author we represent, e.g., photocopying, postage."

Tips "If the query is cogent, well written, well presented, and is the type of book we'd represent, we'll ask to see the manuscript. From there, it depends purely on the quality of the work."

VICTORIA SANDERS & ASSOCIATES

241 Ave. of the Americas, Suite 11 H, New York NY 10014. (212)633-8811. Fax: (212)633-0525. E-mail: queriesvsa@hotmail.com. Website: www.victoriasanders.com. **Contact:** Victoria Sanders or Diane Dickensheid. Estab. 1993. Member of AAR; signatory of WGA. Represents 75 clients. 25% of clients are new/unpublished writers. Currently handles: 50% nonfiction books; 50% novels.

Member Agents Benee Knauer, assistant literary agent.

Represents Nonfiction books, novels. **Considers these nonfiction areas:** Biography/autobiography; current affairs; ethnic/cultural interests; gay/lesbian issues; government/politics/law; history; humor/satire; language/literature/criticism; music/dance; popular culture; psychology; theater/film; translation; women's issues/studies. **Considers these fiction areas:** Action/adventure; contemporary issues; ethnic; family saga; feminist; gay/lesbian; literary; thriller.

How to Contact Query by e-mail only.

Recent Sales Sold 20 titles in the last year. *Indelible*, by Karin Slaughter (Morrow); *When Love Calls, You Better Answer*, by Bertice Berry (Doubleday).

Terms Agent receives 15% commission on domestic sales; 20% commission on foreign sales. Offers written contract. Charges for photocopying, ms, messenger, express mail, and extraordinary fees. If in excess of $100, client approval is required.

Tips "Limit query to letter, no calls, and give it your best shot. A good query is going to get a good response."

SCHIAVONE LITERARY AGENCY, INC.

236 Trails End, West Palm Beach FL 33413-2135. (561)966-9294. Fax: (561)966-9294. E-mail: profschia@aol.com. Website: www.publishersmarketplace.com/members/profschia. **Contact:** James Schiavone, Ed.D. Estab. 1996. Member of National Education Association. Represents 60 clients. 2% of clients are new/unpublished writers. Currently handles: 50% nonfiction books; 49% novels; 1% textbooks.

   • Prior to opening his agency, Dr. Schiavone was a full professor of developmental skills at the City University of New York and author of 5 trade books and 3 textbooks.

Represents Nonfiction books, novels, juvenile books, scholarly books, textbooks. **Considers these nonfiction areas:** Animals; anthropology/archaeology; biography/autobiography; child guidance/parenting; current affairs; education; ethnic/cultural interests; gay/lesbian issues; government/politics/law; health/medicine; history; how-to; humor/satire; juvenile nonfiction; language/literature/criticism; military/war; nature/environment; popular culture; psychology; science/technology; self-help/personal improvement; sociology; true crime/investigative. **Considers these fiction areas:** Contemporary issues; ethnic; family saga; historical; horror; humor/satire; juvenile; literary; mainstream/contemporary; science fiction; young adult.

   ○━ This agency specializes in celebrity biography and autobiography. Actively seeking serious nonfiction, literary fiction and celebrity biography. Does not want to receive poetry.

How to Contact Query by letter only with SASE. One page e-mail queries with no attachments are accepted and encouraged for fastest response. Does not accept phone or fax queries. Considers simultaneous queries. Responds in 2 weeks to queries; 6 weeks to mss. Returns materials only with SASE. Obtains most new clients through recommendations from others, solicitations, conferences.

Terms Agent receives 15% commission on domestic sales; 20% commission on foreign sales. Offers written contract. Charges clients only for postage.

Literary Agents

Writers' Conferences Key West Literary Seminar (Key West FL, January); South Florida Writer's Conference (Miami FL, May).

Tips ''I prefer to work with established authors published by major houses in New York. I will consider marketable proposals from new/previously unpublished writers.''

⚫ WENDY SCHMALZ AGENCY

Box 831, Hudson NY 12534. (518)672-7697. Fax: (518)672-7662. E-mail: wendy@schmalzagency.com. **Contact:** Wendy Schmalz. Estab. 2002. Member of AAR. Represents 35 clients. 10% of clients are new/unpublished writers. Currently handles: 25% nonfiction books; 25% novels; 50% juvenile books.

Represents Nonfiction books, novels, YA novels. **Considers these nonfiction areas:** Biography/autobiography; current affairs; gay/lesbian issues; popular culture; juvenile nonfiction. **Considers these fiction areas:** Gay/lesbian; juvenile; literary; young adult; contemporary issues.

   ○⇥ No picture book texts, science fiction or fantasy.

How to Contact Query with SASE. Accepts e-mail queries. No fax queries. Responds in 2 weeks to queries; 6 weeks to mss. Returns materials only with SASE. Obtains most new clients through recommendations from others.

Terms Agent receives 15% commission on domestic sales; 20% commission on foreign sales. No written contract. Charges authors actual expenses incurred by agent for photocopying and Fed Ex charges incurred for Fed Ex mss.

⚫ SUSAN SCHULMAN, A LITERARY AGENCY

454 W. 44th St., New York NY 10036-5205. (212)713-1633. Fax: (212)581-8830. E-mail: schulman@aol.com. Website: www.schulmanagency.com. **Contact:** Susan Schulman, president. Estab. 1979. Member of AAR, Dramatists Guild, Women's Media Group; signatory of WGA—East. 10-15% of clients are new/unpublished writers. Currently handles: 70% nonfiction books; 20% novels; 10% stage plays.

Member Agents Susan Schulman (books for, by and about women and women's issues/interests, including self-help, health, business and spirituality); Linda Migalti (children's books, ecology, natural sciences and business books); Emily Uhry (plays and pitches for films).

Represents Nonfiction books, novels. **Considers these nonfiction areas:** Anthropology/archaeology; biography/autobiography; child guidance/parenting; current affairs; education; ethnic/cultural interests; gay/lesbian issues; government/politics/law; health/medicine; history; how-to; juvenile nonfiction; money/finance; music/dance; nature/environment; popular culture; psychology; self-help/personal improvement; sociology; theater/film; translation; true crime/investigative; women's issues/studies. **Considers these fiction areas:** Contemporary issues; detective/police/crime; gay/lesbian; historical; literary; mainstream/contemporary; mystery/suspense; young adult. **Considers these script subject areas:** Comedy; contemporary issues; detective/police/crime; feminist; historical; mainstream; mystery/suspense; psychic/supernatural; teen.

   ○⇥ This agency specializes in books for, by and about women's issues, including family, careers, health and spiritual development, business, sociology, history and economics. Emphasizing contemporary women's fiction and nonfiction books of interest to women.

How to Contact Query with SASE, outline/proposal, SASE. Accepts e-mail and fax queries. Considers simultaneous queries. Responds in 1 week to queries; 6 weeks to mss. Returns materials only with SASE.

Recent Sales Sold 30 titles in the last year. *Prayers for a Non-Believer*, by Julia Cameron (Putnam); *The Half-Empty Heart*, by Alan Downs (St. Martin's Press); *The Walls Around Us*, by David Owen (Simon & Schuster); *Rise of the Creative Class*, by Richard Florida (Basic Books). Movie/TV MOW scripts optioned/sold: *In the Skin of a Lion*, by Michael Ondaatje (Serendipity Point Productions); *Holes*, by Louis Sachar (Disney); *Sideways Stories from Wayside School*, by Louis Sachar (Lin Oliver Productions); *Twirling at Ole Miss*, by Terry Southern (Blue Magic Pictures).

Terms Agent receives 15% commission on domestic sales; 7$^1\!/_2$-10% (plus 7$^1\!/_2$-10% to co-agent) commission on foreign sales; 10-20% commission on dramatic rights sales. Charges client for special messenger or copying services, foreign mail and any other service requested by client.

⚫ LAURENS R. SCHWARTZ AGENCY

5 E. 22nd St., Suite 15D, New York NY 10010-5325. (212)228-2614. **Contact:** Laurens R. Schwartz. Estab. 1984. Signatory of WGA. Represents 100 clients.

Represents Nonfiction books, novels, general mix of nonfiction and fiction. Also handles movie and TV tie-ins, licensing and merchandising.

How to Contact Query with SASE. *No unsolicited mss.* Responds in 1 month to queries. ''Have had 18 bestsellers.''

Terms Agent receives 15% commission on domestic sales; 25% (WGA rates where applicable) commission on foreign sales. ''No client fees except for photocopying, and that fee is avoided by an author providing necessary copies or, in certain instances, transferring files on diskette or by e-mail attachment." Where necessary to bring a project into publishing form, editorial work and some rewriting provided as part of service. Works with authors on long-term career goals and promotion.

Tips "I do not like receiving mass mailings sent to all agents. I am extremely selective—only take on 1-3 new clients a year. Do not send everything you have ever written. Choose 1 work and promote that. Always include an SASE. Never send your only copy. Always include a background sheet on yourself and a 1-page synopsis of the work (too many summaries end up being as long as the work)."

SCOVIL CHICHAK GALEN LITERARY AGENCY

381 Park Ave. S., Suite 1020, New York NY 10016. (212)679-8686. Fax: (212)679-6710. E-mail: mailroom@scglit. com. Website: www.scglit.com. **Contact:** Russell Galen. Estab. 1993. Member of AAR. Represents 300 clients. Currently handles: 70% nonfiction books; 30% novels.

Member Agents Russell Galen, Jack Scovil, Anna Ghosh.

How to Contact Accepts e-mail and fax queries. Considers simultaneous queries.

Recent Sales Sold 100 titles in the last year. *Across the Black Waters*, by Minai Hajratwala (Houghton Mifflin); *The Secret*, by Walter Anderson (HarperCollins); *Chainfire*, by Terry Goodkinf (Tor); *Lord John and the Private Matter*, by Diana Gabaldon; *The King of the Jews*, by Nick Tosches (Little, Brown).

Terms Charges clients for photocopying and postage.

N ✉ SCRIBBLERS HOUSE LLC LITERARY AGENCY

(formerly part of Clausen, Mays & Tahan), P.O. Box 1007, Cooper Station, New York NY 10276-1007. E-mail: query@scribblershouse.net. Website: www.scribblershouse.net. **Contact:** Stedman Mays, Garrett Gambino. Estab. 2003. 25% of clients are new/unpublished writers.

● Stedman Mays cofounded Clausen, Mays & Tahan in 1976.

Represents Mostly nonfiction and an occasional novel. **Considers these nonfiction areas:** Business/economics; health/medicine; history; how-to; language/literature/criticism; memoirs; popular culture; psychology; self-help/personal improvement; sex; spirituality; diet/nutrition; the brain; personal finance; biography; politics; writing books; relationships; gender issues; parenting. **Considers these fiction areas:** Historical; literary; women's; suspense; crime; thrillers.

How to Contact Query by e-mail. Put Nonfiction Query or Fiction Query in the subject line followed by the title of your project. Considers simultaneous queries. Responds in up to 1 month to queries.

Recent Sales *Perfect Balance: Dr. Robert Greene's Breakthrough Program for Getting the Hormone Health You Deserve*, by Robert Greene, MD, and Leah Feldon (Clarkson Potter/Random House); *Age-Proof Your Mind*, by Zaldy Tan, MD (Warner); *The Okinawa Program* and *The Okinawa Diet Plan*, by Bradley Willcox, MD, Craig Willcox, PhD, and Makoto Suzuki, MD (Clarkson Potter/Random House); *The Emotionally Abusive Relationship*, by Beverly Engel (Wiley); *Help Your Baby Talk*, by Dr. Robert Owens with Leah Feldon (Perigee).

Terms Agent receives 15% commission on domestic sales. Charges clients for postage, shipping and copying.

Tips "We prefer e-mail queries, but if you must send by snail mail, we will return material or respond to United States Postal Service-accepted SASE. (No international coupons or outdated mal strips, please.) Presentation means a lot. A well-written query letter with a brief author bio and your credentials is important. For query letter models, go to the bookstore or online and look at the cover copy and flap copy on other books in your general area of interest. Emulate what's best. Have an idea of other notable books that will be perceived as being in the same vein as yours. Know what's fresh or 'hooky' about your project and articulate it in as few words as possible. Consult our website for the most up-to-date information on submitting."

N ☐ SCRIBE AGENCY, LLC

5508 Joylynne Dr., Madison WI 53716. (608)249-0491. E-mail: queries@scribeagency.com. Website: www.scribe agency.com. **Contact:** Kris O'Higgins. Estab. 2004. Represents 1 client. 100% of clients are new/unpublished writers. Currently handles: 100% novels.

● "We worked as agency assitants at a literary agency, editorial assistants for a publishing company, and a copywriter in two marketing departments. Not only do we have previous experience working at a literary agency, but we also have editorial and marketing experience. We also love books as much or more than anyone you know."

Member Agents Kris O'Higgins and Jesse Vogel.

Represents Nonfiction books, novels, short story collections, novellas, juvenile books, poetry books. **Considers these nonfiction areas:** Cooking/foods/nutrition; crafts/hobbies; ethnic/cultural interests; gay/lesbian issues; how-to; humor/satire; memoirs; music/dance; New Age/metaphysics; photography; popular culture; science/technology; self-help/personal improvement; true crime/investigative; women's issues/studies. **Considers these fiction areas:** Action/adventure; comic books/cartoon; confession; detective/police/crime; erotica; ethnic; experimental; family saga; fantasy; feminist; gay/lesbian; historical; horror; humor/satire; juvenile; literary;

mainstream/contemporary; mystery/suspense; picture books; regional; science fiction; thriller; young adult; psychic/supernatural.

    O━ Actively seeking excellent writers with ideas and stories to tell. Does not want cat mysteries and anything not listed above.

How to Contact Query with SASE. Responds in 2 weeks to queries; 1-2 months to mss. Returns materials only with SASE.

Recent Sales Sold 2 titles in the last year.

Terms Agent receives 17% commission on domestic sales; 25% commission on foreign sales. Offers written contract. Charges for postage and photocopying.

Writers' Conferences WisCon, Wisconsin Book Festival, World Fantasy Convention (all in Madison WI).

◪ SEDGEBAND LITERARY ASSOCIATES, INC.

7312 Martha Lane, Fort Worth TX 76112. (817)496-3652. Fax: (425)952-9518. E-mail: queries@sedgeband.com. Website: www.sedgeband.com. **Contact:** David Duperre. Estab. 1997. 50% of clients are new/unpublished writers. Currently handles: 50% nonfiction books; 50% fiction novels.

Member Agents David Duperre (literary, scripts, mystery, suspense); Ginger Norton (romance, horror, nonfiction, mainstream/contemporary).

Represents Nonfiction books, novels. **Considers these nonfiction areas:** Biography/autobiography; ethnic/cultural interests; history; true crime/investigative. **Considers these fiction areas:** Action/adventure; fantasy; literary; mainstream/contemporary; mystery/suspense; romance; science fiction.

    O━ This agency is looking for talented writers who have patience and are willing to work hard. Actively seeking new nonfiction writers, query for fiction.

How to Contact Use the online submission form on our website. Prefers queries via e-mail. No phone queries accepted. No full mss unless requested. Accepts e-mail queries with no attachments; repsonds in 2-4 weeks. Paper response in 2-3 months to written queries. Responds in 4 months to requested mss. Returns materials only with SASE. Obtains most new clients through queries, the Internet, referrals.

Recent Sales Sold 8 titles in the last year.

Terms Agent receives 15% commission on domestic sales; 20% commission on foreign sales. Offers written contract, binding for 1 year; 30-day written notice must be given to terminate contract. Charges clients for postage, photocopies, long-distance calls, etc. "We do not charge any reading or retainer fees."

Tips "We care about writers and books, not just money, but we care about the industry as well. We will not represent anyone who might hurt our clients or our reputation. We expect our writers to work hard and to be patient. Do not send a rude query; it will get you nowhere. If we ask to see your book, don't wait around to send it or ask a bunch of irrelevant questions about movie rights and so forth *(at this point we haven't even offered to represent you!)*. If you can't write a synopsis, don't bother to query us. The industry is based on the synopsis; sometimes it is all the editor ever sees. Don't handwrite your query or send us samples of your writing that are handwritten—we won't read them. Be professional and follow our guidelines when submitting. And don't believe everything you hear on the Internet about editors and publishers—it isn't always true."

◪ LYNN SELIGMAN, LITERARY AGENT

400 Highland Ave., Upper Montclair NJ 07043. (973)783-3631. **Contact:** Lynn Seligman. Estab. 1985. Member of Women's Media Group. Represents 32 clients. 15% of clients are new/unpublished writers. Currently handles: 70% nonfiction books; 30% novels.

    ● Prior to opening her agency, Ms. Seligman worked in the subsidiary rights department of Doubleday and Simon & Schuster and served as an agent with Julian Bach Literary Agency (now IMG Literary Agency).

Represents Nonfiction books, novels. **Considers these nonfiction areas:** Anthropology/archaeology; art/architecture/design; biography/autobiography; business/economics; child guidance/parenting; cooking/foods/nutrition; current affairs; education; ethnic/cultural interests; government/politics/law; health/medicine; history; how-to; humor/satire; interior design/decorating; language/literature/criticism; money/finance; music/dance; nature/environment; photography; popular culture; psychology; science/technology; self-help/personal improvement; sociology; theater/film; true crime/investigative; women's issues/studies. **Considers these fiction areas:** Detective/police/crime; ethnic; fantasy; feminist; gay/lesbian; historical; horror; humor/satire; literary; mainstream/contemporary; mystery/suspense; romance (contemporary, gothic, historical, regency); science fiction.

    O━ This agency specializes in "general nonfiction and fiction. I also do illustrated and photography books and have represented several photographers for books." This agency does not handle children or young adult books.

How to Contact Query with SASE, sample chapters, outline/proposal. Prefers to read materials exclusively. No e-mail or fax queries. Considers simultaneous queries. Responds in 2 weeks to queries; 2 months to mss. Returns materials only with SASE. Obtains most new clients through referrals from other writers or editors.

Recent Sales Sold 15 titles in the last year. *My Father Before Me*, by Dr. Michael Diamond with Roberta Israeloff; *Grave Intent*, by Deborah Le Blanc.

Terms Agent receives 15% commission on domestic sales; 25% commission on foreign sales. Charges clients for photocopying, unusual postage or telephone expenses (checking first with the author), express mail.

☐ SERENDIPITY LITERARY AGENCY, LLC

732 Fulton St., Suite 3, Brooklyn NY 11238. (718)230-7689. Fax: (718)230-7829. E-mail: rbrooks@serendipitylit. com. Website: www.serendipitylit.com. **Contact:** Regina Brooks. Estab. 2000. Represents 30 clients. 20% of clients are new/unpublished writers. Currently handles: 60% nonfiction books; 40% novels.

- Prior to becoming an agent, Ms. Brooks was an acquisitions editor for John Wiley & Sons, Inc. and McGraw-Hill Companies.

Represents Nonfiction books, novels, juvenile books, scholarly books, textbooks, children's. **Considers these nonfiction areas:** Business/economics; computers/electronic; education; ethnic/cultural interests; how-to; juvenile nonfiction; memoirs; money/finance; multicultural; New Age/metaphysics; popular culture; psychology; religious/inspirational; science/technology; self-help/personal improvement; sports; women's issues/studies. **Considers these fiction areas:** Action/adventure; confession; ethnic; historical; juvenile; literary; multicultural; mystery/suspense; picture books; romance; thriller. **Considers these script subject areas:** Ethnic; fantasy; juvenile; multimedia; also interested in children's CD/video projects.

- ☐ Serendipity provides developmental editing. "We help build marketing plans for nontraditional outlets." Actively seeking African-American nonfiction, commercial fiction, computer books (nonfiction), YA novels with an urban flair, juvenile books. Does not want to receive poetry.

How to Contact Prefers to read materials exclusively. Nonfiction, submit outline, 1 sample chapter, SASE. Responds in 2 months to queries; 3 months to mss. Obtains most new clients through conferences, referrals.

Recent Sales This agency prefers not to share information on specific sales. Recent sales available upon request by prospective client.

Terms Agent receives 15% commission on domestic sales; 20% commission on foreign sales. Offers written contract; 2-month notice must be given to terminate contract. Charges clients $200 upon signing for office fees, or office fees will be taken from any advance. Does not make referrals to editing services. "If author requests editing services, I can offer a list of potential services." 0% of business is derived from referral to editing services.

Tips "Looking for African-American children's and teen novels. We also represent illustrators."

☑ THE SEYMOUR AGENCY

475 Miner St., Canton NY 13617. (315)386-1831. Fax: (315)386-1037. E-mail: marysue@slic.com. Website: www.theseymouragency.com. **Contact:** Mary Sue Seymour. Estab. 1992. Member of AAR, CBA, RWA and The Author's Guild. Represents 75 clients. 5% of clients are new/unpublished writers. Currently handles: 50% nonfiction books; 50% fiction.

- Ms. Seymour is a retired New York State certified teacher.

Represents Nonfiction books, novels (romance). **Considers these nonfiction areas:** Business/economics; health/medicine; how-to; self-help/personal improvement; Christian books; cookbooks; any well-written nonfiction that includes a proposal in standard format and 1 sample chapter. **Considers these fiction areas:** Literary; religious/inspirational (Christian books); romance (any type); westerns/frontier.

How to Contact Query with SASE, synopsis, first 50 pages for romance. Accepts e-mail queries. No fax queries. Considers simultaneous queries. Responds in 1 month to queries; 3 months to mss. Returns materials only with SASE.

Recent Sales Penny McCusker's 3 books to Harlequin/Silhouette; Emilee Hines' 2-book deal to Warner Books; Dr. Val Dmitriev's vocabulary book to Adams Media Corp.

Terms Agent receives 12% (from authors' material whose books the agency sold) and 15% (on new clients) commission on domestic sales.

Writers' Conferences Desert Rose (Scottsdale AZ); Mountain Laurel (Knoxville TN); Romantic Times Convention (New York City); RWA National (Dallas); CBA (Atlanta); Put Your Heart in a Book (New Jersey).

☑ WENDY SHERMAN ASSOCIATES, INC.

450 Seventh Ave., Suite 3004, New York NY 10123. (212)279-9027. Fax: (212)279-8863. Website: www.wsherm an.com. **Contact:** Wendy Sherman. Estab. 1999. Member of AAR. Represents 50 clients. 30% of clients are new/unpublished writers. Currently handles: 50% nonfiction books; 50% novels.

- Prior to opening the agency, Ms. Sherman worked for The Aaron Priest agency and was vice president, executive director of Henry Holt, associate publisher, subsidary rights director, sales and marketing director.

Member Agents Tracy Brown, Wendy Sherman.

Represents Nonfiction books, novels. **Considers these nonfiction areas:** Psychology; narrative nonfiction, practical. **Considers these fiction areas:** Literary; women's (suspense).

    0— ''We specialize in developing new writers as well as working with more established writers. My experience as a publisher has proven to be a great asset to my clients.''

How to Contact Query with SASE or send outline/proposal, 1 sample chapter. No e-mail queries. Considers simultaneous queries. Responds in 1 month to queries. Returns materials only with SASE. Obtains most new clients through recommendations from others.

Recent Sales Clients include *Fiction*: William Lashner, Nani Power, DW Buffa, Howard Bahr, Suzanne Chazin, Sarah Stonich, Ad Hudler, Mary Sharratt, Libby Street, Heather Estay, Darri Stephens, Megan Desales; *Nonfiction*: Rabbi Mark Borovitz, Alan Eisenstock, Esther Perel, Clifton Leaf, Maggie Estep, Greg Baer, Martin Friedman, Lundy Bancroft, Alvin Ailey Dance, Lise Friedman, Liz Landers, Vicky Mainzer.

Terms Agent receives 15% commission on domestic sales; 20% commission on foreign sales. Offers written contract.

JEFFREY SIMMONS LITERARY AGENCY

15 Penn House, Mallory St., London NW8 8SX England. (020)7224 8917. E-mail: jas@london-inc.com. **Contact:** Jeffrey Simmons. Estab. 1978. Represents 43 clients. 40% of clients are new/unpublished writers. Currently handles: 60% nonfiction books; 40% novels.

    • Prior to becoming an agent, Mr. Simmons was a publisher, and he is also an author.

Represents Nonfiction books, novels. **Considers these nonfiction areas:** Biography/autobiography; current affairs; government/politics/law; history; language/literature/criticism; memoirs; music/dance; popular culture; sociology; sports; theater/film; translation; true crime/investigative. **Considers these fiction areas:** Action/adventure; confession; detective/police/crime; family saga; literary; mainstream/contemporary; mystery/suspense; thriller.

    0— This agency seeks to handle good books and promising young writers. ''My long experience in publishing and as an author and ghostwriter means I can offer an excellent service all around, especially in terms of editorial experience where appropriate.'' Actively seeking quality fiction, biography, autobiography, showbiz, personality books, law, crime, politics, world affairs. Does not want to receive science fiction, horror, fantasy, juvenile, academic books, specialist subjects (i.e., cooking, gardening, religious).

How to Contact Submit sample chapter, outline/proposal, IRCs if necessary, SASE. Prefers to read materials exclusively. Responds in 1 week to queries; 1 month to mss. Obtains most new clients through recommendations from others, solicitations.

Recent Sales Sold 18 titles in the last year. *Decoding Sion*, by Picknett & Prince (Time Warner UK, Simon & Schuster US); *Complete Carry On*, by Webber (Random House).

Terms Agent receives 10-15% commission on domestic sales; 15% commission on foreign sales. Offers written contract, binding for lifetime of book in question or until it becomes out of print.

Tips ''When contacting us with an outline/proposal, include a brief biographical note (listing any previous publications, with publishers and dates). Preferably tell us if the book has already been offered elsewhere.''

BEVERLEY SLOPEN LITERARY AGENCY

131 Bloor St. W., Suite 711, Toronto ON M5S 1S3 Canada. (416)964-9598. Fax: (416)921-7726. E-mail: beverly@slopenagency.ca. Website: www.slopenagency.ca. **Contact:** Beverley Slopen. Estab. 1974. Represents 60 clients. 40% of clients are new/unpublished writers. Currently handles: 60% nonfiction books; 40% novels.

    • Prior to opening her agency, Ms. Slopen worked in publishing and as a journalist.

Represents Nonfiction books, novels, scholarly books, textbooks (college). **Considers these nonfiction areas:** Anthropology/archaeology; biography/autobiography; business/economics; current affairs; psychology; sociology; true crime/investigative; women's issues/studies. **Considers these fiction areas:** Literary; mystery/suspense.

    0— This agency has a ''strong bent towards Canadian writers.'' Actively seeking ''serious nonfiction that is accessible and appealing to the general reader.'' Does not want to receive fantasy, science fiction or children's.

How to Contact Query with SAE and IRCs. Returns materials only with SASE (Canadian postage). Accepts short e-mail queries. Considers simultaneous queries. Responds in 2 months to queries.

Recent Sales Sold over 40 titles in the last year. *Court Lady* and *Country Wife*, by Lita-Rose Betcherman (HarperCollins Canada/Morrow/Wiley UK); *Vermeer's Hat*, by Timothy Brook (HarperCollins Canada); *Midnight Cab*, by James W. Nichol (Canongate US/Droemer/Germany); *Fatal Passage* and *Ancient Mariner*, by Ken McGoogan (Carroll & Graf US/Bantam Press UK); *Understanding Uncertainty*, by Jeffrey Rosenthal (HarperCollins Canada); *Damaged Angels*, by Bonnie Buxton (Carroll & Graf US); *Sea of Dreams*, by Adam Mayers (McClelland & Stewart Canada); *Hair Hat*, by Carrie Snyder (Penguin Canada). Other clients include Modris Eksteins,

Michael Marrus, Robert Fulford, Donna Morrissey, Howard Engel, Morley Torgov, Elliott Leyton, Don Gutteridge, Joanna Goodman, Roberta Rich, Jennifer Welsh, Margaret Wente, Frank Wydra.
Terms Agent receives 15% commission on domestic sales; 10% commission on foreign sales. Offers written contract, binding for 2 years; 3-month notice must be given to terminate contract.
Tips "Please, no unsolicited manuscripts."

SPECTRUM LITERARY AGENCY

320 Central Park W., Suite 1-D, New York NY 10025. Website: www.spectrumliteraryagency.com. **Contact:** Eleanor Wood, president. Represents 90 clients. Currently handles: 10% nonfiction books; 90% novels.
Member Agents Lucienne Diver.
Represents Nonfiction books, novels. **Considers these nonfiction areas:** Considers select nonfiction. **Considers these fiction areas:** Contemporary issues; fantasy; historical; mainstream/contemporary; mystery/suspense; romance; science fiction.
How to Contact Query with SASE, include publishing credits and background information. No phone, e-mail or fax queries. Responds in 1-3 months to queries. Obtains most new clients through recommendations from authors and others.
Recent Sales Sold over 100 titles in the last year. This agency prefers not to share information on specific sales.
Terms Agent receives 15% commission on domestic sales. Deducts for photocopying and book orders.

SPENCERHILL ASSOCIATES

P.O. Box 374, Chatham NY 12032. (518)392-9293. Fax: (518)392-9554. E-mail: ksolem@klsbooks.com. **Contact:** Karen Solem. Estab. 2001. Member of AAR. Represents 40 clients. 5% of clients are new/unpublished writers. Currently handles: 5% nonfiction books; 90% novels; 5% novellas.
- Ms. Solem is not taking on many new clients at the present time. Prior to becoming an agent, Ms. Solem was editor-in-chief at HarperCollins and associate publisher.
Represents Nonfiction books (Christian), novels. **Considers these nonfiction areas:** Animals; religious/inspirational. **Considers these fiction areas:** Detective/police/crime; historical; mainstream/contemporary; religious/inspirational; romance; thriller.
- "I handle mostly commercial women's fiction, romance, thrillers and mysteries. I also represent Christian fiction and nonfiction." No poetry, science fiction, juvenile or scripts.
How to Contact Query with SASE, submit proposal package, outline. Responds in 1 month to queries. Returns materials only with SASE.
Recent Sales Sold 110 titles in the last year.
Terms Agent receives 15% commission on domestic sales; 20% commission on foreign sales. Offers written contract; 3-months notice must be given to terminate contract.

THE SPIELER AGENCY

154 W. 57th St., 13th Floor, Room 135, New York NY 10019. **Contact:** Katya Balter. Estab. 1981. Represents 160 clients. 2% of clients are new/unpublished writers.
- Prior to opening his agency, Mr. Spieler was a magazine editor.
Member Agents Joe Spieler; John Thornton (nonfiction); Lisa M. Ross (fiction/nonfiction); Deirdre Mullane (nonfiction/fiction); Eric Myers (nonfiction/fiction). Spieler Agency West (Oakland, CA): Victoria Shoemaker.
Represents Nonfiction books, literary fiction, children's books. **Considers these nonfiction areas:** Biography/autobiography; business/economics; child guidance/parenting; current affairs; gay/lesbian issues; government/politics/law; history; memoirs; money/finance; music/dance; nature/environment (environmental issues); religious/inspirational; sociology; spirituality; theater/film; travel; women's issues/studies. **Considers these fiction areas:** Experimental; feminist; gay/lesbian; literary.
How to Contact Query with SASE. Prefers to read materials exclusively. Returns materials only with SASE; otherwise materials are discarded when rejected. No fax queries. Considers simultaneous queries. Responds in 2 weeks to queries; 5 weeks to mss. Obtains most new clients through recommendations and occasionally through listing in *Guide to Literary Agents.*
Recent Sales *What's the Matter with Kansas*, by Thomas Frank (Metropolitan/Holt); *Natural History of the Rich*, by Richard Conniff (W.W. Norton).
Terms Agent receives 15% commission on domestic sales. Charges clients for messenger bills, photocopying, postage.
Writers' Conferences London Bookfair.

NANCY STAUFFER ASSOCIATES

P.O. Box 1203, Darien CT 06820. (203)655-3717. Fax: (203)655-3704. E-mail: nanstauf@optonline.net. **Contact:** Nancy Stauffer Cahoon. Estab. 1989. Member of the Authors Guild. 5% of clients are new/unpublished writers. Currently handles: 15% nonfiction books; 85% novels.

Represents Nonfiction books, novels. **Considers these nonfiction areas:** Creative nonfiction; current affairs; ethnic/cultural interests. **Considers these fiction areas:** Contemporary issues; literary; regional.

How to Contact Obtains most new clients through referrals from existing clients.

Recent Sales Untitled nonfiction and Richard Pryor biography by Sherman Alexie; *No Enemy But Time*, by William C. Harris (St. Martin's Press); *An Unfinished Life*, by Mark Spragg.

Terms Agent receives 15% commission on domestic sales; 20% commission on foreign sales; 15% commission on dramatic rights sales.

✪ STEELE-PERKINS LITERARY AGENCY

26 Island Lane, Canandaigua NY 14424. (585)396-9290. Fax: (585)396-3579. E-mail: pattiesp@aol.com. **Contact:** Pattie Steele-Perkins. Member of AAR, RWA. Currently handles: 100% romance and mainstream women's fiction.

Represents Novels. **Considers these fiction areas:** Mainstream/contemporary; multicultural; romance (inspirational); women's.

　Oᴙ Actively seeking inspirational, romance, women's fiction and multicultural works.

How to Contact Submit outline, 3 sample chapters, SASE. Considers simultaneous queries. Responds in 6 weeks to queries. Returns materials only with SASE. Obtains most new clients through recommendations from others, queries/solicitations.

Recent Sales This agency prefers not to share information on specific sales.

Terms Agent receives 15% commission on domestic sales. Offers written contract, binding for 1 year; 1-month notice must be given to terminate contract.

Writers' Conferences National Conference of Romance Writers of America; BookExpo America Writers' Conferences; CBA; Romance Slam Jam.

Tips ''Be patient. E-mail rather than call. Make sure what you are sending is the best it can be.''

✪ STERLING LORD LITERISTIC, INC.

65 Bleecker St., 12th Floor, New York NY 10012. (212)780-6050. Fax: (212)780-6095. E-mail: info@sll.com. Website: www.sll.com. Estab. 1952. Member of AAR; signatory of WGA. Represents 600 clients. Currently handles: 50% nonfiction books; 50% novels.

Member Agents Philippa Brophy, Laurie Liss, Chris Calhoun, Peter Matson, Sterling Lord, Claudia Cross, Neeti Madan, George Nicholson, Jim Rutman, Charlotte Sheedy (affiliate); Douglas Stewart; Manuel Stoeckl; Paul Rodeen; Robert Guinsler.

Represents Nonfiction books, novels, literary value considered first.

How to Contact Query with SASE. Responds in 1 month to mss. Obtains most new clients through recommendations from others.

Recent Sales This agency prefers not to share information on specific sales. Clients include Kent Haruf, Dick Fancis, Mary Gordon, Sen. John McCain, Simon Winchester, James McBride, Billy Collins, Richard Paul Evans, Dave Pelzer.

Terms Agent receives 15% commission on domestic sales; 20% commission on foreign sales. Offers written contract. Charges clients for photocopying.

🌐 ✪ THE SUSIJN AGENCY

3rd Floor, 64 Great Titchfield St., London W1W 7QH England. 0044 (207)580-6341. Fax: 0044 (207)580-8626. E-mail: info@thesusijnagency.com. Website: www.thesusijnagency.com. **Contact:** Laura Susijn, Charles Buchau. Estab. 1998. Currently handles: 15% nonfiction books; 85% novels.

　● Prior to becoming an agent, Ms. Susijn was a rights director at Sheil Land Associates and at Fourth Estate, Ltd.

Member Agents Laura Susijn.

Represents Nonfiction books, novels. **Considers these nonfiction areas:** Biography/autobiography; memoirs; multicultural; popular culture; science/technology; travel. **Considers these fiction areas:** Literary.

　Oᴙ This agency specializes in international works, selling world rights, representing non-English language writing as well as English. Emphasis on cross-cultural subjects. Does not want self-help, romance, sagas, science fiction, screenplays.

How to Contact Submit outline, 2 sample chapters. Considers simultaneous queries. Responds in 2 months to queries. Returns materials only with SASE. Obtains most new clients through recommendations from others, via publishers in Europe and beyond.

Recent Sales Sold 120 titles in the last year. *Trespassing*, by Uzma Aslam Khan (Flamingo UK); *Gone*, by Helena Echlin (Secker and Warburg, UK); *Daalder*, by Philibert Schogt (4 Walls 8 Windows); *The Memory Artists*, by Jeffrey Moore (Weidenfeld & Nicholson). Other clients include Vassallucci, Podium, Atlas, De Arbeiderspers, Tiderne Skifter, MB Agency, Van Oorschot.

Terms Agent receives 15% commission on domestic sales; 15-20% commission on foreign sales. Offers written contract; 6 weeks notice must be given to terminate contract. Charges clients for photocopying, buying copies only if sale is made.

☻ PATRICIA TEAL LITERARY AGENCY

2036 Vista Del Rosa, Fullerton CA 92831-1336. Phone/Fax: (714)738-8333. **Contact:** Patricia Teal. Estab. 1978. Member of AAR. Represents 20 clients. 10% of clients are new/unpublished writers. Currently handles: 10% nonfiction books; 90% fiction.

Represents Nonfiction books, novels. **Considers these nonfiction areas:** Animals; biography/autobiography; child guidance/parenting; health/medicine; how-to; psychology; self-help/personal improvement; true crime/investigative; women's issues/studies. **Considers these fiction areas:** Glitz; mainstream/contemporary; mystery/suspense; romance (contemporary, historical).

> O→ This agency specializes in women's fiction and commercial how-to and self-help nonfiction. Does not want to receive poetry, short stories, articles, science fiction, fantasy, regency romance.

How to Contact *Published authors only.* Query with SASE. No e-mail or fax queries. Considers simultaneous queries. Responds in 10 days to queries; 6 weeks to mss. Returns materials only with SASE. Obtains most new clients through conferences, recommendations from authors and editors.

Recent Sales Sold 20 titles in the last year. *Texas Rose*, by Marie Ferrarella (Silhouette); *Watch Your Language*, by Sterling Johnson (St. Martin's); *The Black Sheep's Baby*, by Kathleen Creighton (Silhouette); *Man with a Message*, by Muriel Jensen (Harlequin).

Terms Agent receives 10-15% commission on domestic sales; 20% commission on foreign sales. Offers written contract, binding for 1 year. Charges clients for postage.

Writers' Conferences Romance Writers of America conferences; Asilomar (California Writers Club); BEA; Bouchercon; Hawaii Writers Conference (Maui).

Tips "Include SASE with all correspondence. Taking on very few authors."

☻ 3 SEAS LITERARY AGENCY

P.O. Box 7038, Madison WI 53708. (608)221-4306. E-mail: threeseaslit@aol.com. Website: www.threeseaslit.com. **Contact:** Michelle Grajkowski. Estab. 2000. Member of Romance Writers of America, Chicago Women in Publishing. Represents 40 clients. 15% of clients are new/unpublished writers. Currently handles: 5% nonfiction books; 80% novels; 15% juvenile books.

- Prior to becoming an agent, Ms. Grajkowski worked in both sales and in purchasing for a medical facility. She has a degree in journalism from the University of Wisconsin-Madison.

Represents Nonfiction books, novels, juvenile books, scholarly books.

> O→ 3 Seas focuses on romance (including category, historicals, regencies, westerns, romantic suspense, paranormal), women's fiction, mysteries, nonfiction, young adult and children's stories. Does not want to receive poetry, screenplays or short stories.

How to Contact For fiction, please query with first 3 chapters, a synopsis, your bio and SASE. For nonfiction, please query with your complete proposal, first 3 chapters, number of words, a bio and SASE. Considers simultaneous queries. Responds in 1 month to queries. Responds in 3 months to partials. Returns materials only with SASE. Obtains most new clients through recommendations from others, conferences.

Recent Sales Sold 75 titles in the last year. *Fire Me Up, Sex, Lies & Vampires* and *Hard Day's Knight*, by Katie MacAlister; *Calendar Girl*, by Naomi Neale; *To Die For*, by Stephanie Rowe; *The Phantom in the Bathtub*, by Eugenia Riley; *The Unknown Daughter*, by Anna DeStefano. Other clients include Winnie Griggs, Diane Amos, Pat Pritchard, Barbara Jean Hicks, Carrie Weaver, Robin Popp, Kerrelyn Sparks, Sandra Madden.

Terms Agent receives 15% commission on domestic sales; 20% commission on foreign sales. Offers written contract, binding for 1 month.

Writers' Conferences RWA National Conference (July).

☻ VAN DER LEUN & ASSOCIATES

40 E. 89th St., New York NY 10128. (212)477-2033. E-mail: pvanderleun@earthlink.net. Website: www.publishersmarketplace.com/members/pvanderleun. **Contact:** Patricia Van der Leun, president. Estab. 1984. Represents 30 clients. Currently handles: 75% nonfiction books; 25% novels.

- Prior to becoming an agent, Ms. Van der Leun was a professor of Art History.

Represents Nonfiction books, novels, illustrated books. **Considers these nonfiction areas:** Art/architecture/design (art history); biography/autobiography; cooking/foods/nutrition (food and wine, cookbooks); creative nonfiction; current affairs; ethnic/cultural interests; gardening; history; memoirs; religious/inspirational; spirituality; sports; travel. **Considers these fiction areas:** Comic books/cartoon; contemporary issues; humor/satire; literary; mainstream/contemporary; multicultural; multimedia; picture books; short story collections; translation; women's.

O← This agency specializes in fiction, art history, food and wine, gardening, biography.
How to Contact Query with letter only, include author bio and SASE. Considers simultaneous queries. Responds in 2 weeks to queries.
Recent Sales Sold 15 titles in the last year. *De Kooning's Bicycle*, by Robert Long (Farrar, Straus & Giroux, Inc.); *The Perfect $100,000 House*, by Karrie Jacobs (Viking); *Buddhist Meditation Straight Up*, by Alan Wallace (John Wiley).
Terms Agent receives 15% commission on domestic sales; 25% commission on foreign sales. Offers written contract. Charges clients for postage and photocopying of ms.

☑ THE VINES AGENCY, INC.

648 Broadway, Suite 901, New York NY 10012. (212)777-5522. Fax: (212)777-5978. E-mail: jv@vinesagency.com. Website: www.vinesagency.com. **Contact:** James C. Vines, Ali Ryan, Gary Neuwirth, Alexis Caldwell. Estab. 1995. Signatory of WGA; Author's Guild. Represents 52 clients. 20% of clients are new/unpublished writers. Currently handles: 50% nonfiction books; 50% novels.
• Prior to opening his agency, Mr. Vines served as an agent with the Virginia Barber Literary Agency.
Member Agents James C. Vines (quality and commercial fiction and nonfiction); Gary Neuwirth; Alexis Caldwell (women's fiction, ethnic fiction, quality nonfiction); Ali Ryan (women's fiction and nonfiction, mainstream).
Represents Nonfiction books, novels, feature film. **Considers these nonfiction areas:** Biography/autobiography; business/economics; current affairs; ethnic/cultural interests; history; how-to; humor/satire; memoirs; military/war; money/finance; nature/environment; New Age/metaphysics; photography; popular culture; psychology; religious/inspirational; science/technology; self-help/personal improvement; sociology; spirituality; sports; translation; travel; true crime/investigative; women's issues/studies. **Considers these fiction areas:** Action/adventure; contemporary issues; detective/police/crime; ethnic; experimental; family saga; feminist; gay/lesbian; historical; horror; humor/satire; literary; mainstream/contemporary; mystery/suspense; occult; psychic/supernatural; regional; romance (contemporary, historical); science fiction; sports; thriller; westerns/frontier; women's. **Considers these script subject areas:** Action/adventure; comedy; detective/police/crime; ethnic; experimental; feminist; gay/lesbian; historical; horror; mainstream; mystery/suspense; romantic comedy; romantic drama; science fiction; teen; thriller; western/frontier.
O← This agency specializes in mystery, suspense, science fiction, women's fiction, ethnic fiction, mainstream novels, screenplays, teleplays.
How to Contact Submit outline, 3 sample chapters, SASE. Considers simultaneous queries. Responds in 2 weeks to queries; 1 month to mss. Returns materials only with SASE. Obtains most new clients through query letters, recommendations from others, reading short stories in magazines, soliciting conferences.
Recent Sales Sold 48 titles and sold 5 scripts in the last year. *Sunset and Sawdust*, by Joe R. Lansdale; *Camilla's Rose*, by Bernice McFadden; *Ecstasy*, by Beth Saulnier.
Terms Agent receives 15% commission on domestic sales; 25% commission on foreign sales. Offers written contract, binding for 1 year; 1-month notice must be given to terminate contract. 100% of business is derived from commissions on ms sales. Charges clients for foreign postage, messenger services, photocopying.
Writers' Conferences Maui Writer's Conference.
Tips "Do not follow up on submissions with phone calls to the agency. The agency will read and respond by mail only. Do not pack your manuscript in plastic 'peanuts' that will make us have to vacuum the office after opening the package containing your manuscript. Always enclose return postage."

☑ MARY JACK WALD ASSOCIATES, INC.

111 E. 14th St., New York NY 10003. (212)254-7842. **Contact:** Danis Sher. Estab. 1985. Member of AAR, Authors' Guild, SCBWI. Represents 35 clients. 5% of clients are new/unpublished writers. Currently handles: nonfiction books; novels; story collections; novellas; juvenile books.
• This agency is not accepting mss at this time.
Member Agents Mary Jack Wald, Danis Sher, Lynne Rabinoff Agency (association who represents foreign rights); Alvin Wald.
Represents Nonfiction books, novels, short story collections, novellas, juvenile books, movie and TV scripts by our authors. **Considers these nonfiction areas:** Biography/autobiography; current affairs; ethnic/cultural interests; history; juvenile nonfiction; language/literature/criticism; music/dance; nature/environment; photography; sociology; theater/film; translation; true crime/investigative. **Considers these fiction areas:** Action/adventure; contemporary issues; detective/police/crime; ethnic; experimental; family saga; feminist; gay/lesbian; glitz; historical; juvenile; literary; mainstream/contemporary; mystery/suspense; picture books; thriller; young adult; satire.
O← This agency specializes in literary works and juvenile works.
How to Contact Not accepting new clients at this time.

Recent Sales *The Secret of Castle Cant*, by K.P. Bath; *Summer at Ma Dear's House*, by Denise Lewis Patnick.
Terms Agent receives 15% commission on domestic sales; 15-30% commission on foreign sales. Offers written contract, binding for 1 year.

WALES LITERARY AGENCY, INC.
P.O. Box 9428, Seattle WA 98109-0428. (206)284-7114. E-mail: waleslit@waleslit.com. Website: www.waleslit.com. **Contact:** Elizabeth Wales, Josie di Bernardo. Estab. 1988. Member of AAR, Book Publishers' Northwest, Pacific Northwest Booksellers Association, PEN. Represents 65 clients. 10% of clients are new/unpublished writers. Currently handles: 60% nonfiction books; 40% fiction.
• Prior to becoming an agent, Ms. Wales worked at Oxford University Press and Viking Penguin.
Member Agents Elizabeth Wales, Adrienne Reed.
○➡ This agency specializes in narrative nonfiction and quality mainstream and literary fiction. Does not handle screenplays, children's literature, genre fiction or most category nonfiction.
How to Contact Query with cover letter, writing sample (approx. 30 pages) and SASE. No phone or fax queries. Prefers regular mail queries but accepts 1-page e-mail queries with no attachments. Considers simultaneous queries. Responds in 3 weeks to queries; 6 weeks to mss. Returns materials only with SASE.
Recent Sales *Breaking Ranks*, by Norman H. Stamper (Nation Books); *Birds of Central Park*, photographs by Cal Vornberger (Abrams); *Against Gravity*, by Farnoosh Moshiri (Penguin).
Terms Agent receives 15% commission on domestic sales; 20% commission on foreign sales.
Writers' Conferences Pacific NW Writers Conference (Seattle); Writers at Work (Salt Lake City); Writing Rendezvous (Anchorage); Willamette Writers (Portland).
Tips "Especially interested in work that espouses a progressive cultural or political view, projects a new voice, or simply shares an important, compelling story. Encourages writers living in the Pacific Northwest, West Coast, Alaska and Pacific Rim countries and writers from historically underrepresented groups, such as gay and lesbian writers and writers of color, to submit work (but does not discourage writers outside these areas). Most importantly, whether in fiction or nonfiction, the agency is looking for talented storytellers."

JOHN A. WARE LITERARY AGENCY
392 Central Park W., New York NY 10025-5801. (212)866-4733. Fax: (212)866-4734. **Contact:** John Ware. Estab. 1978. Represents 60 clients. 40% of clients are new/unpublished writers. Currently handles: 75% nonfiction books; 25% novels.
• Prior to opening his agency, Mr. Ware served as a literary agent with James Brown Associates/Curtis Brown, Ltd., and as an editor for Doubleday & Co.
Represents Nonfiction books, novels. **Considers these nonfiction areas:** Anthropology/archaeology; biography/autobiography; current affairs; health/medicine (academic credentials required); history (including oral history, Americana and folklore); language/literature/criticism; music/dance; nature/environment; popular culture; psychology (academic credentials required); science/technology; sports; true crime/investigative; women's issues/studies; social commentary; investigative journalism; 'bird's eye' views of phenomena. **Considers these fiction areas:** Detective/police/crime; mystery/suspense; thriller; accessible literary noncategory fiction.
○➡ Does not want personal memoirs.
How to Contact Query first by letter only, including SASE. No e-mail or fax queries. Considers simultaneous queries. Responds in 2 weeks to queries.
Recent Sales *Hawking the Empire: Inside the National Security Syndicate*, by Tim Shorrock (Simon & Schuster); *The Pledge (of Allegiance)*, by Jeffrey Owen Jones (Thomas Dunne Books/St. Martin's); *Rise of the Cajun Mariner: The Race for Big Oil*, by Woody Falgoux (Pelican); *Jedburgh: The Mobilization of the French Resistance*, by Will Irwin (PublicAffairs); *Chain Lightning: The True Legend of Man o' War*, by Dorothy Ours (St. Martin's); *The Traveller: A Biography of John Ledyard*, by Bill Gifford (Harcourt).
Terms Agent receives 15% commission on domestic sales; 20% commission on foreign sales; 15% commission on dramatic rights sales. Charges clients for messenger service, photocopying.
Tips "Writers must have appropriate credentials for authorship of proposal (nonfiction) or manuscript (fiction); no publishing track record required. Open to good writing and interesting ideas by new or veteran writers."

WAXMAN LITERARY AGENCY, INC.
80 Fifth Ave., Suite 1101, New York NY 10011. Website: www.waxmanagency.com. Estab. 1997. Represents 60 clients. 50% of clients are new/unpublished writers. Currently handles: 60% nonfiction books; 40% novels.
• Prior to opening his agency, Mr. Waxman was editor for five years at HarperCollins.
Member Agents Scott Waxman (all categories of nonfiction, commercial fiction).
Represents Nonfiction books, novels. **Considers these nonfiction areas:** Narrative nonfiction. **Considers these fiction areas:** Literary.

O→ "Looking for serious journalists and novelists with published works."
How to Contact Query through website. All unsolicited mss returned unopened. Considers simultaneous queries. Responds in 2 weeks to queries; 6 weeks to mss. Returns materials only with SASE. Obtains most new clients through recommendations from others, solicitations, conferences.
Terms Agent receives 15% commission on domestic sales; 25% commission on foreign sales. Offers written contract; 2-month notice must be given to terminate contract.

⊘ CHERRY WEINER LITERARY AGENCY

28 Kipling Way, Manalapan NJ 07726-3711. (732)446-2096. Fax: (732)792-0506. E-mail: cherry8486@aol.com. **Contact:** Cherry Weiner. Estab. 1977. Represents 40 clients. 10% of clients are new/unpublished writers. Currently handles: 10-20% nonfiction books; 80-90% novels.
• This agency is currently not looking for new clients except by referral or by personal contact at writers' conferences.
Represents Nonfiction books, novels. **Considers these nonfiction areas:** Self-help/personal improvement. **Considers these fiction areas:** Action/adventure; contemporary issues; detective/police/crime; family saga; fantasy; historical; mainstream/contemporary; mystery/suspense; psychic/supernatural; romance; science fiction; thriller; westerns/frontier.
O→ This agency specializes in fantasy, science fiction, westerns, mysteries (both contemporary and historical), historical novels, Native American works, mainstream, all genre romances.
How to Contact Query with SASE. Prefers to read materials exclusively. No fax queries. Responds in 1 week to queries; 2 months to mss. Returns materials only with SASE.
Recent Sales Sold 75 titles in the last year.
Terms Agent receives 15% commission on domestic sales; 15% commission on foreign sales. Offers written contract. Charges clients for extra copies of mss "but would prefer author do it"; 1st-class postage for author's copies of books; Express Mail for important document/mss.
Writers' Conferences Western writers conventions; science fiction conventions; fantasy conventions; romance conventions.
Tips "Meet agents and publishers at conferences. Establish a relationship, then get in touch with them reminding them of meetings and conference."

◖ THE WEINGEL-FIDEL AGENCY

310 E. 46th St., 21E, New York NY 10017. (212)599-2959. **Contact:** Loretta Weingel-Fidel. Estab. 1989. Currently handles: 75% nonfiction books; 25% novels.
• Prior to opening her agency, Ms. Weingel-Fidel was a psychoeducational diagnostician.
Represents Nonfiction books, novels. **Considers these nonfiction areas:** Art/architecture/design; biography/autobiography; memoirs; music/dance; psychology; science/technology; sociology; women's issues/studies; investigative. **Considers these fiction areas:** Literary; mainstream/contemporary.
O→ This agency specializes in commercial, literary fiction and nonfiction. Actively seeking investigative journalism. Does not want to receive genre fiction, self-help, science fiction, fantasy.
How to Contact Referred writers only. *No unsolicited mss.* Obtains most new clients through referrals.
Terms Agent receives 15% commission on domestic sales; 20% commission on foreign sales. Offers written contract, binding for 1 year; automatic renewal. Bills sent back to clients all reasonable expenses such as UPS, express mail, photocopying, etc.
Tips "A very small, selective list enables me to work very closely with my clients to develop and nurture talent. I only take on projects and writers about which I am extremely enthusiastic."

◖ LYNN WHITTAKER, LITERARY AGENT

Graybill & English, LLC, 1875 Connecticut Ave. NW, Suite 712, Washington DC 20009. (202)588-9798, ext. 127. Fax: (202)457-0662. E-mail: lynnwhittaker@aol.com. Website: www.graybillandenglish.com. **Contact:** Lynn Whittaker. Estab. 1998. Member of AAR. Represents 24 clients. 10% of clients are new/unpublished writers. Currently handles: 80% nonfiction books; 20% novels.
• Prior to becoming an agent, Ms. Whittaker was an editor, owner of a small press, and taught at the college level.
Represents Nonfiction books, novels. **Considers these nonfiction areas:** Animals; biography/autobiography; current affairs; ethnic/cultural interests; health/medicine; history; memoirs; money/finance; multicultural; nature/environment; popular culture; science/technology; sports; women's issues/studies. **Considers these fiction areas:** Detective/police/crime; ethnic; historical; literary; multicultural; mystery/suspense; sports.
O→ "As a former editor, I especially enjoy working closely with writers to polish their proposals and manuscripts." Actively seeking literary fiction, sports, history, mystery/suspense. Does not want to receive romance/women's commercial fiction, children's/young adult, religious, fantasy/horror.

How to Contact Query with SASE. Responds in 2 weeks to queries; 1 month to mss. Returns materials only with SASE. Obtains most new clients through recommendations from others.

Terms Agent receives 15% commission on domestic sales; 20% commission on foreign sales. Offers written contract; 1-month notice must be given to terminate contract. Direct expenses for photocopying of proposals and mss, UPS/FedEx.

⬤ WIESER & ELWELL, INC.

80 Fifth Ave., Suite 1101, New York NY 10011. (212)260-0860. **Contact:** Jake Elwell. Estab. 1975. 30% of clients are new/unpublished writers. Currently handles: 50% nonfiction books; 50% novels.

Member Agents Jake Elwell (history, military, mysteries, romance, sports, thrillers, psychology, fiction, pop medical).

Represents Nonfiction books, novels. **Considers these nonfiction areas:** Business/economics; cooking/foods/ nutrition; current affairs; health/medicine; history; money/finance; nature/environment; psychology; sports; true crime/investigative. **Considers these fiction areas:** Contemporary issues; detective/police/crime; historical; literary; mainstream/contemporary; mystery/suspense; romance; thriller.

 ⌐ This agency specializes in mainstream fiction and nonfiction.

How to Contact Query with outline/proposal and SASE. Responds in 2 weeks to queries. Obtains most new clients through queries, authors' recommendations and industry professionals.

Recent Sales *Honored*, by Roberta Kells Dorr (Revell); *History's Greatest Conspiracies*, by H. Paul Jeffers (Lyons); *Havoc's Sword*, by Dewey Lambdin (St. Martin's Press); *The Voyage of the Hunley*, by Edwin P. Hoyt (Burford Books); *Threat Level Black*, by Jim DeFelice (Pocket); *Street Hungry*, by Bill Kent.

Terms Agent receives 15% commission on domestic sales; 20% commission on foreign sales. Offers written contract. Charges clients for photocopying and overseas mailing.

Writers' Conferences BEA; Frankfurt Book Fair.

Ⓝ ⬤ WORDSERVE LITERARY GROUP

10152 S. Knoll Circle, Highlands Ranch CO 80130. (303)471-6675. Fax: (303)471-1297. E-mail: greg@wordserve literary.com. Website: www.wordserveliterary.com. **Contact:** Greg Johnson. Estab. 2003. Represents 20 clients. 25% of clients are new/unpublished writers. Currently handles: 30% nonfiction books; 40% novels; 10% story collections; 5% novellas; 10% juvenile books; 5% multimedia.

 • Prior to becoming an agent in 1994, Mr. Johnson was a magazine editor and freelance writer of more than 20 books and 200 articles.

Represents Primarily religious books in these categories: nonfiction books, novels, short story collections, novellas, juvenile books. **Considers these nonfiction areas:** Biography/autobiography; business/economics; child guidance/parenting; current affairs; how-to; humor/satire; memoirs; religious/inspirational; self-help/ personal improvement; sports. **Considers these fiction areas:** Action/adventure; detective/police/crime; family saga; historical; humor/satire; juvenile; religious/inspirational; romance; sports; thriller.

How to Contact Query with SASE, submit proposal package, outline, 2-3 sample chapters. Considers simultaneous queries. Responds in 1 week to queries; 1 month to mss. Returns materials only with SASE. Obtains most new clients through recommendations from others, solicitations.

Recent Sales Sold 1,300 titles in the last 10 years. Clients include Gilbert Morris, Calvin Miller, Robert Wise, Jim Burns, Ed Young Sr., Wayne Cordeiro, Denise George, Jordan Robin, Susie Shellenberger, Tim Smith, Joe Wheeler.

Terms Agent receives 15% commission on domestic sales; 10-15% commission on foreign sales. Offers written contract; 30-60 days notice must be given to terminate contract.

Tips "We are looking for good proposals, great writing, and authors willing to market their books, as appropriate."

⬤ WRITERS HOUSE

21 W. 26th St., New York NY 10010. (212)685-2400. Fax: (212)685-1781. Estab. 1974. Member of AAR. Represents 440 clients. 50% of clients are new/unpublished writers. Currently handles: 25% nonfiction books; 40% novels; 35% juvenile books.

Member Agents Albert Zuckerman (major novels, thrillers, women's fiction, important nonfiction); Amy Berkower (major juvenile authors, women's fiction, art and decorating, psychology); Merrilee Heifetz (quality children's fiction, science fiction and fantasy, popular culture, literary fiction); Susan Cohen (juvenile and YA fiction and nonfiction, Judaism, women's issues); Susan Ginsburg (serious and popular fiction, true crime, narrative nonfiction, personality books, cookbooks); Michele Rubin (serious nonfiction); Robin Rue (commercial fiction and nonfiction, YA fiction); Jennifer Lyons (literary, commercial fiction, international fiction, nonfiction, and illustrated); Jodi Reamer (juvenile and YA fiction and nonfiction, adult commercial fiction, popular

culture); Simon Lipskar (literary and commercial fiction, narrative nonfiction); Nicole Pitesa (juvenile and YA fiction, literary fiction); Steven Malk (juvenile and YA fiction and nonfiction).
Represents Nonfiction books, novels, juvenile books. **Considers these nonfiction areas:** Animals; art/architecture/design; biography/autobiography; business/economics; child guidance/parenting; cooking/foods/nutrition; health/medicine; history; interior design/decorating; juvenile nonfiction; military/war; money/finance; music/dance; nature/environment; psychology; science/technology; self-help/personal improvement; theater/film; true crime/investigative; women's issues/studies. **Considers these fiction areas:** Action/adventure; contemporary issues; detective/police/crime; erotica; ethnic; family saga; fantasy; feminist; gay/lesbian; gothic; hi-lo; historical; horror; humor/satire; juvenile; literary; mainstream/contemporary; military/war; multicultural; mystery/suspense; New Age; occult; picture books; psychic/supernatural; regional; romance; science fiction; short story collections; spiritual; sports; thriller; translation; westerns/frontier; young adult; women's; cartoon.

O— This agency specializes in all types of popular fiction and nonfiction. Does not want to receive scholarly, professional, poetry, plays or screenplays.

How to Contact Query with SASE. No e-mail or fax queries. Responds in 1 month to queries. Obtains most new clients through recommendations from others.
Recent Sales Sold 200-300 titles in the last year. *Moneyball*, by Michael Lewis (Norton); *Cut and Run*, by Ridley Pearson (Hyperion); *Report from Ground Zero*, by Dennis Smith (Viking); *Northern Lights*, by Nora Roberts (Penguin/Putnam); Captain Underpants series, by Dav Pilkey (Scholastic); Junie B. Jones series, by Barbara Park (Random House). Other clients include Francine Pascal, Ken Follett, Stephen Hawking, Linda Howard, F. Paul Wilson, Neil Gaiman, Laurel Hamilton, V.C. Andrews, Lisa Jackson, Michael Fruber, Chris Paolini, Barbara Delinsky, Ann Martin.
Terms Agent receives 15% commission on domestic sales; 20% commission on foreign sales. Offers written contract, binding for 1 year. Agency charges fees for copying mss and proposals and overseas airmail of books.
Tips "Do not send manuscripts. Write a compelling letter. If you do, we'll ask to see your work."

☑ WRITERS' REPRESENTATIVES, INC.

116 W. 14th St., 11th Floor, New York NY 10011-7305. Phone/Fax: (212)620-0023. E-mail: transom@writersreps .com. Website: www.writersreps.com. **Contact:** Glen Hartley or Lynn Chu. Estab. 1985. Represents 130 clients. 5% of clients are new/unpublished writers. Currently handles: 90% nonfiction books; 10% novels.

• Prior to becoming agents, Ms. Chu was a lawyer and Mr. Hartley worked at Simon & Schuster, Harper & Row and Cornell University Press.

Member Agents Lynn Chu, Glen Hartley, Catharine Sprinkel.
Represents Nonfiction books, novels. **Considers these fiction areas:** Literary.

O— This agency specializes in serious nonfiction. Actively seeking serious nonfiction and quality fiction. Does not want to receive motion picture/television screenplays.

How to Contact Query with SASE. Prefers to read materials exclusively. Considers simultaneous queries, but must be informed at time of submission. Obtains most new clients through "reading."
Recent Sales Sold 30 titles in the last year. *Where Shall Wisdom Be Found?*, by Harold Bloom; *War Like No Other*, by Victor Davis Hanson; *Call of the Mall*, by Paco Underhill; *The Language of Police*, by Diane Ravitch.
Terms Agent receives 15% commission on domestic sales; 20% commission on foreign sales.
Tips "Always include a SASE—that will ensure a response from the agent and the return of material submitted."

☑ WYLIE-MERRICK LITERARY AGENCY

1138 S. Webster St., Kokomo IN 46902-6357. (765)459-8258. E-mail: smartin@wylie-merrick.com; rbrown@wy lie-merrick.com. Website: www.wylie-merrick.com. **Contact:** S.A. Martin, Robert Brown. Estab. 1999. Member of SCBWI. Currently handles: 10% nonfiction books; 50% novels; 40% juvenile books.

• Ms. Martin holds a master's degree in Language Education and is a writing and technology curriculum specialist.

Member Agents S.A. Martin (juvenile/picture books/young adult); Robert Brown (adult fiction/nonfiction, young adult).
Represents Nonfiction books (adult and juvenile), novels (adult and juvenile), juvenile books. **Considers these nonfiction areas:** Biography/autobiography; juvenile nonfiction. **Considers these fiction areas:** Mystery/suspense; picture books; religious/inspirational; romance; young adult; women's; chick lit, high-level mainstream.

O— This agency specializes in children's and young adult literary as well as genre adult fiction.

How to Contact Obtains most new clients through recommendations from others, conferences.
Recent Sales *How I Fell in Love and Learned to Shoot Free Throws*, by Jon Ripslinger (Roaring Brook); *Red Polka Dot in a World Full of Plaid*, by Varian Johnson; *Death for Dessert*, by Dawn Richard; *Secret War*, by Regina Silsby.
Terms Agent receives 15% commission on domestic sales; 20% commission on foreign sales; 20% commission

on dramatic rights sales. Offers written contract. Charges clients for postage, photocopying, handling.

Writers' Conferences Pike's Peak (CO); Willamette (Portland OR).

Tips "We no longer accept queries from writers unless we have met with them at a writing conference or they've been referred to us by an editor or another agent we've worked with in the past. Any queries we receive that don't meet these criteria will be deleted or recycled unread."

☑ ZACHARY SHUSTER HARMSWORTH

1776 Broadway, Suite 1405, New York NY 10019. (212)765-6900. Fax: (212)765-6490. E-mail: sshagat@zshlitera ry.com. Website: www.zshliterary.com. Boston Office: 535 Boylston St., 11th Floor. (617)262-2400. Fax: (617)262-2468. **Contact:** Sandra Shagat. Estab. 1996. Represents 125 clients. 20% of clients are new/unpublished writers. Currently handles: 45% nonfiction books; 45% novels; 5% story collections; 5% scholarly books.
- "Our principals include 2 former publishing and entertainment lawyers, a journalist and an editor/agent." Lane Zachary was an editor at Random House before becoming an agent.

Member Agents Esmond Harmsworth (commercial mysteries and literary fiction, history, science, adventure, business); Todd Shuster (narrative and prescriptive nonfiction, biography, memoirs); Lane Zachary (biography, memoirs, literary fiction); Jennifer Gates (literary fiction, nonfiction).

Represents Nonfiction books, novels. **Considers these nonfiction areas:** Animals; biography/autobiography; business/economics; current affairs; gay/lesbian issues; government/politics/law; health/medicine; history; how-to; language/literature/criticism; memoirs; money/finance; music/dance; psychology; science/technology; self-help/personal improvement; sports; true crime/investigative; women's issues/studies. **Considers these fiction areas:** Contemporary issues; detective/police/crime; ethnic; feminist; gay/lesbian; historical; literary; mainstream/contemporary; mystery/suspense; thriller.
- This agency specializes in journalist-driven narrative nonfiction, literary and commercial fiction. Actively seeking narrative nonfiction, mystery, commercial and literary fiction, memoirs, history, biographies. Does not want to receive poetry.

How to Contact For fiction, submit query letter with 1-page synopsis, SASE. For nonfiction, submit letter explaining topic of proposed book, along with analysis of why book is needed and will be a commercial success for publisher. No e-mail or fax queries. Considers simultaneous queries. Responds in 3 months to mss. Obtains most new clients through recommendations from others, solicitations, conferences.

Recent Sales Sold 40-50 titles in the last year. *The Pentagon's New Map*, by Thomas Barnett (Putnam's); *A Carnivore's Inquiry*, by Sabina Murray (Grove); *War Trash*, by Ha Jin (Pantheon); *The Pennington Plan*, by Dr. Andrea Pennington (Avery); *Choke Point*, by James S. Mitchell (St. Martin's). Other clients include Leslie Epstein, David Mixner.

Terms Agent receives 15% commission on domestic sales; 20% commission on foreign sales. Offers written contract, binding for 1 work only; 30-days notice must be given to terminate contract. Charges clients for postage, copying, courier, telephone. "We only charge expenses if the manuscript is sold."

Tips "We work closely with all our clients on all editorial and promotional aspects of their works."

☑ SUSAN ZECKENDORF ASSOC., INC.

171 W. 57th St., New York NY 10019. (212)245-2928. **Contact:** Susan Zeckendorf. Estab. 1979. Member of AAR. Represents 15 clients. 25% of clients are new/unpublished writers. Currently handles: 50% nonfiction books; 50% novels.
- Prior to opening her agency, Ms. Zeckendorf was a counseling psychologist.

Represents Nonfiction books, novels. **Considers these nonfiction areas:** Biography/autobiography; child guidance/parenting; health/medicine; history; music/dance; psychology; science/technology; sociology; women's issues/studies. **Considers these fiction areas:** Detective/police/crime; ethnic; historical; literary; mainstream/contemporary; mystery/suspense; thriller.
- Actively seeking mysteries, literary fiction, mainstream fiction, thrillers, social history, parenting, classical music, biography. Does not want to receive science fiction, romance. "No children's books."

How to Contact Query with SASE. No e-mail or fax queries. Considers simultaneous queries. Responds in 10 days to queries; 3 weeks to mss. Returns materials only with SASE.

Recent Sales *How to Write a Damn Good Mystery*, by James N. Frey (St. Martin's); *Moment of Madness*, by Una-Mary Parker (Headline); *The Handscrabble Chronicles* (Berkley); *Something to Live For (The Susan McCorkle Story)* (Northeastern University Press).

Terms Agent receives 15% commission on domestic sales; 20% commission on foreign sales. Charges for photocopying, messenger services.

Writers' Conferences Central Valley Writers Conference; The Tucson Publishers Association Conference; Writer's Connection; Frontiers in Writing Conference (Amarillo TX); Golden Triangle Writers Conference (Beaumont TX); Oklahoma Festival of Books (Claremont OK); SMU Writers Conference (NYC).

Tips "We are a small agency giving lots of individual attention. We respond quickly to submissions."

Literary Magazines

This section contains markets for your literary short fiction. Although definitions of what constitutes "literary" writing vary, editors of literary journals agree they want to publish the "best" fiction they can acquire. Qualities they look for in fiction include creativity, style, flawless mechanics and careful attention to detail in content and manuscript preparation. Most of the authors writing such fiction are well read and well educated, and many are students and graduates of university creative writing programs.

Please also review our Online Markets section, page 313, for electronic literary magazines. At a time when paper and publishing costs rise while funding to university presses continues to be cut or eliminated, electronic literary magazines are helping generate a publishing renaissance for experimental as well as more traditional literary fiction. These electronic outlets for literary fiction also benefit writers by eliminating copying and postage costs and providing the opportunity for much quicker responses to submissions. Also notice that some magazines with websites give specific information about what they offer on their websites, including updated writer's guidelines and sample fiction from their publications.

STEPPING STONES TO RECOGNITION

Some well-established literary journals pay several hundred or even several thousand dollars for a short story. Most, though, can only pay with contributor's copies or a subscription to their publication. However, being published in literary journals offers the important benefits of experience, exposure and prestige. Agents and major book publishers regularly read literary magazines in search of new writers. Work from among these journals is also selected for inclusion in annual prize anthologies such as *The Best American Short Stories*, *Prize Stories: The O. Henry Awards*, *Pushcart Prize: Best of the Small Presses* and *New Stories from the South: The Year's Best*.

You'll find most of the well-known prestigious literary journals listed here. Many, including *Carolina Quarterly* and *Ploughshares*, are associated with universities, while others like *The Paris Review* are independently published.

SELECTING THE RIGHT LITERARY JOURNAL

Once you have browsed through this section and have a list of journals you might like to submit to, read those listings again carefully. Remember this is information editors present to help you in submitting work that fits their needs. You've Got a Story, starting on page 2, will guide you through the process of finding markets for your fiction.

This is the only section in which you will find magazines that do not read submissions all year long. Whether limited reading periods are tied to a university schedule or meant to

Literary Magazines

accommodate the capabilities of a very small staff, those periods are noted within listings (when the editors notify us). The staffs of university journals are usually made up of student editors and a managing editor who is also a faculty member. These staffs often change every year. Whenever possible, we indicate this in listings and give the name of the current editor and the length of that editor's term. Also be aware that the schedule of a university journal usually coincides with that university's academic year, meaning that the editors of most university publications are difficult or impossible to reach during the summer.

FURTHERING YOUR SEARCH

It cannot be stressed enough that reading the listings for literary journals is only the first part of developing your marketing plan. The second part, equally important, is to obtain fiction guidelines and read with great care the actual journal you'd like to submit to. Reading copies of these journals helps you determine the fine points of each magazine's publishing style and sensibility. There is no substitute for this type of hands-on research.

Unlike commercial periodicals available at most newsstands and bookstores, it requires a little more effort to obtain some of the magazines listed here. The super chain bookstores are doing a better job these days of stocking literaries, and you can find some in independent and college bookstores, especially those published in your area. The Internet is an invaluable resource for submission guidelines, as more and more journals establish an online presence. You may, however, need to send for a sample copy. We include sample copy prices in the listings whenever possible. In addition to reading your sample copies, pay close attention to the **Advice** section of each listing. There you'll often find a very specific description of the style of fiction that editors at that publication prefer.

Another way to find out more about literary magazines is to check out the various prize anthologies and take note of journals whose fiction is being selected for publication there. Studying prize anthologies not only lets you know which magazines are publishing award-winning work but it also provides a valuable overview of what is considered to be the best fiction published today. Those anthologies include:

- *Best American Short Stories*, published by Houghton Mifflin.
- *New Stories from the South: The Year's Best*, published by Algonquin Books of Chapel Hill.
- *Prize Stories: The O. Henry Awards*, published by Doubleday/Anchor.
- *Pushcart Prize: Best of the Small Presses*, published by Pushcart Press.

At the beginnings of listings, we include symbols to help you narrow your search. Keys to those symbols can be found on the inside covers of this book.

▣ ACM (ANOTHER CHICAGO MAGAZINE)

Left Field Press, 3709 N. Kenmore, Chicago IL 60613. E-mail: editors@anotherchicagomag.com. Website: www. anotherchicagomag.com. **Contact:** Sharon Solwitz, fiction editor. Magazine: $5^{1}/_{2} \times 8^{1}/_{2}$; 200-220 pages; "art folio each issue." Biannual. Estab. 1977. Circ. 2,000.

Needs Ethnic/multicultural, experimental, feminist, gay, lesbian, literary, translations, contemporary, prose poem. No religious, strictly genre or editorial. Receives 300 unsolicited mss/month. Reads mss from February 1-August 31. Publishes ms 6-12 months after acceptance. **Publishes 10 new writers/year.** Recently published work by Stuart Dybek and Steve Almond.

How to Contact Responds in 3 months to queries; 6 months to mss. Accepts simultaneous, multiple submissions. Sample copy for $8 ppd. Writer's guidelines online.

Payment/Terms Pays small honorarium when possible, contributor's copies and 1 year subscription. Acquires first North American serial rights.

Advice "Support literary publishing by subscribing to at least one literary journal—if not ours, another. Get used to rejection slips, and don't get discouraged. Keep introductory letters short. Make sure manuscript has name and address on every page, and that it is clean, neat and proofread. We are looking for stories with freshness and originality in subject angle and style and work that encounters the world and is not stuck in its own navel."

▣ ADVOCATE, PKA'S PUBLICATION

PKA Publications, 1881 Little Westkill Rd. CO2, Prattsville NY 12468. (518)299-3103. Tabloid: $9^{3}/_{8} \times 12^{1}/_{4}$; 32 pages; newsprint paper; line drawings; color and b&w photographs. "Eclectic for a general audience." Bimonthly. Estab. 1987. Circ. 12,000.

Needs Adventure, children's/juvenile (5-9 years), ethnic/multicultural, experimental, fantasy, feminist, historical, humor/satire, literary, mainstream, mystery/suspense, regional, romance, science fiction, western, young adult/teen (10-18 years), contemporary, prose poem, senior ctizen/retirement, sports. "Nothing religious, pornographic, violent, erotic, pro-drug or anti-enviroment. Currently looking for equine (horses) stories, poetry, art, photos and cartoons. The *Gaited Horse Newsletter* is currently published within the pages of PKA's *Advocate.*" Receives 60 unsolicited mss/month. Accepts 6-8 mss/issue; 34-48 mss/year. Publishes ms 4 months to 1 year after acceptance. Also publishes poetry. Sometimes comments on rejected mss.

How to Contact Send a complete ms with cover letter. Responds in 2 months to mss. No simultaneous submissions "no work that has appeared on the Internet." Sample copy for $4 (US currency for inside US; $5.25 US currency for Canada). Writer's guidelines with purchase of sample copy.

Payment/Terms Pays contributor copies. Acquires first rights.

Advice "The highest criterion in selecting a work is its entertainment value. It must first be enjoyable reading. It must, of course, be orginal. To stand out, it must be thought provoking or strongly emotive or very cleverly plotted. Will consider only previously unpublished works by writers who do not earn their living principally through writing. We are currently very backed-up on short stories. We are mostly looking for art, photos and poetry."

$▣ AFRICAN AMERICAN REVIEW

Saint Louis University, Humanities 317, 3800 Lindell Boulevard, St. Louis MO 63108-3414. (314)977-3703. Fax: (314)977-1514. E-mail: keenanam@slu.edu. Website: aar.slu.edu. **Contact:** Joycelyn Moody, editor. Magazine: 7×10; 176 pages; 60 lb., acid-free paper; 100 lb. skid stock cover; illustrations; photos. "Essays on African-American literature, theater, film, art and culture generally; interviews; poetry and fiction by African-American authors; book reviews." Quarterly. Estab. 1967. Circ. 2,067.

- *African American Review* is the official publication of the Division of Black American Literature and Culture of the Modern Language Association. The magazine received American Literary Magazine Awards in 1994 and 1995.

Needs Ethnic/multicultural, experimental, feminist, literary, mainstream. "No children's/juvenile/young adult/teen." Receives 50 unsolicited mss/month. Accepts 40 mss/issue. Publishes ms 1-2 years after acceptance. Agented fiction 10%. Recently published work by Solon Timothy Woodward, Eugenia Collier, Jeffery Renard Allen, Patrick Lohier, Raki Jones, Olympia Vernon. Length: 2,500-5,000 words; average length: 3,000 words. Also publishes literary essays, literary criticism, poetry. Sometimes comments on rejected mss.

How to Contact Responds in 1 month to queries; 6 months to mss. Sample copy for $12. Writer's guidelines online. Reviews fiction.

Payment/Terms Pays $25-100, 3 contributor's copies and 10 offprints. Pays on publication for first North American serial rights. Sends galleys to author.

Literary Magazines

$ ☑ ☒ AGNI

Boston University, 236 Bay State Rd., Boston MA 02215. (617)353-7135. Fax: (617)353-7134. E-mail: agni@bu.e du. Website: www.agnimagazine.org. **Contact:** Sven Birkerts, editor. Magazine: $5^3/_8 \times 8^1/_2$; 240 pages; 55 lb. booktext paper; art portfolios. "Eclectic literary magazine publishing first-rate poems, essays, translations and stories." Biannual. Estab. 1972. Circ. 4,000.

● Founding editor Askold Melnyczuk won the 2001 Nora Magid Award for Magazine Editing. Work from *AGNI* has been included and cited regularly in the *Pushcart Prize* and *Best American* anthologies.

Needs Translations, stories, prose poems. "No science fiction or romance." Receives 500 unsolicited mss/ month. Accepts 3-5 mss/issue; 6-10 mss/year. Reading period September 1 through May 31 only. Publishes ms 6 months after acceptance. **Publishes 30 new writers/year.** Recently published work by Chitra Divakaruni, Ilan Stavans, Jack Pulaski, David Foster Wallace, Lise Haines, Patrick Tobin and Nicholas Montemarano.

How to Contact Responds in 2 weeks to queries; 4 months to mss. Accepts simultaneous submissions. Sample copy for $10 or online. Writer's guidelines for #10 SASE, or online.

Payment/Terms Pays $10/page up to $150, 2 contributor's copies, 1-year subscription, and 4 gift copies. Pays on publication for first North American serial rights. Rights to reprint in *AGNI* anthology (with author's consent). Sends galleys to author.

Advice "Read *AGNI* and other literary magazines carefully to understand the kinds of stories we do and do not publish. It's also important for artists to support the arts."

$ ☑ ALASKA QUARTERLY REVIEW

ESB 208, University of Alaska-Anchorage, 3211 Providence Dr., Anchorage AK 99508. (907)786-6916. E-mail: ayaqr@uaa.alaska.edu. Website: www.uaa.alaska.edu/aqr. **Contact:** Ronald Spatz, fiction editor. Magazine: 6×9; 232-300 pages; 60 lb. Glatfelter paper; 12 pt. C15 black ink or 4-color; varnish cover stock; photos on cover only. *AQR* "publishes fiction, poetry, literary nonfiction and short plays in traditional and experimental styles." Semiannual. Estab. 1982. Circ. 3,500.

● Two stories selected for inclusion in the 2004 *Prize Stories: The O'Henry Awards*.

Needs Experimental, literary, translations, contemporary, prose poem. "If the works in *Alaska Quarterly Review* have certain characteristics, they are these: freshness, honesty and a compelling subject. What makes a piece stand out from the multitude of other submissions? The voice of the piece must be strong—idiosyncratic enough to create a unique persona. We look for the demonstration of craft, making the situation palpable and putting it in a form where it becomes emotionally and intellectually complex. One could look through our pages over time and see that many of the pieces published in the *Alaska Quarterly Review* concern everyday life. We're not asking our writers to go outside themselves and their experiences to the absolute exotic to catch our interest. We look for the experiential and revelatory qualities of the work. We will, without hesitation, champion a piece that may be less polished or stylistically sophisticated, if it engages me, surprises me, and resonates for me. The joy in reading such a work is in discovering something true. Moreover, in keeping with our mission to publish new writers, we are looking for voices our readers do not know, voices that may not always be reflected in the dominant culture and that, in all instances, have something important to convey." Receives 200 unsolicited mss/month. Accepts 7-18 mss/issue; 15-30 mss/year. Does not read mss May 10-August 25. Publishes ms 6 months after acceptance. **Publishes 6 new writers/year.** Recently published work by Howard Norman, Douglas Light, Courtney Angela Brkic, Nicholas Montemarano, Edna Ziesk and Edith Pearlman. Publishes short shorts.

How to Contact Responds in 4 months to queries; 4 months to mss. Simultaneous submissions "undesirable, but will accept if indicated." Sample copy for $6. Writer's guidelines online.

Payment/Terms Pays $50-200 subject to funding; pays in contributor's copies and subscriptions when funding is limited. Honorariums on publication when funding permits. Acquires first North American serial rights. Upon request, rights will be transferred back to author after publication.

Advice "Professionalism, patience and persistence are essential. One needs to do one's homework and know the market. The competition is very intense, and funding for the front-line journals is generally inadequate, so staffing is low. It takes time to get a response, and rejections are a fact of life. It is important not to take the rejections personally and also to know that editors make decisions for better or worse, and they make mistakes too. Fortunately there are many gatekeepers. *Alaska Quarterly Review* has published many pieces that had been turned down by other journals—including pieces that then went on to win national awards. We also know of instances in which pieces *Alaska Quarterly Review* rejected later appeared in other magazines. We haven't regretted that we didn't take those pieces. Rather, we're happy that the authors have made a good match. Disappointment should *never* stop anyone. Will counts as much as talent, and new writers need to have confidence in themselves and stick to it."

☒ ◎ ALBERTAVIEWS, The Magazine About Alberta for Albertans

Local Perspectives Publishing, Inc., Suite 208-320 23rd Ave. SW, Calgary AB T2S 0J2 Canada. (403)243-5334. Fax: (403)243-8599. E-mail: editor@albertaviews.ab.ca. Website: www.albertaviews.ab.ca. "We are a regional magazine providing thoughtful commentary and background information on issues of concern to Albertans. Most of our writers are Albertans." Published 8 times per year. Estab. 1997. Circ. 30,000.

Needs Only fiction by Alberta writers. Publishes ms 3 months after acceptance.

How to Contact Send complete ms. Accepts submissions by e-mail. Responds in 6 weeks to queries; 2 months to mss. Sample copy free. Writer's guidelines online.

Payment/Terms Pays $1,000 maximum. Pays on publication for first North American serial, electronic rights.

THE ALLEGHENY REVIEW, A National Journal of Undergraduate Literature

Thomson-Shore, Inc., Box 32 Allegheny College, Meadville PA 16335. E-mail: review@allegheny.edu. Website: http://review.allegheny.edu. **Contact:** Senior editor. Magazine: 6×9; 100 pages; illustrations; photos. "*The Allegheny Review* is one of America's only nationwide literary magazines exclusively for undergraduate works of poetry, fiction and nonfiction. Our intended audience is persons interested in quality literature." Annual. Estab. 1983.

Needs Adventure, ethnic/multicultural, experimental, family saga, fantasy, feminist, gay, historical, horror, humor/satire, lesbian, literary, mainstream, military/war, mystery/suspense, New Age, psychic/supernatural/occult, religious/inspirational (general), romance, science fiction, western. "We accept nothing but fiction by currently enrolled undergraduate students. We consider anything catering to an intellectual audience." Receives 50 unsolicited mss/month. Accepts 3 mss/issue. Publishes ms 2 months after deadline. **Publishes roughly 90% new writers/year.** Recently published work by Dianne Page, Monica Stahl and DJ Kinney. Publishes short shorts. Also publishes literary essays, literary criticism, poetry. Sometimes comments on rejected mss.

How to Contact Send complete mss with a cover letter. Accepts submissions on disk. Responds in 2 weeks to queries; 4 months to mss. Send disposable copy of ms and #10 SASE for reply. Sample copy for $4. SASE, by e-mail or on website.

Payment/Terms Pays 1 contributor's copy; additional copies $3. Sponsors awards/contests.

Advice "We look for quality work that has been thoroughly revised. What stands out includes: unique voice, interesting topic and playfullness with the English language. Revise, revise, revise! And be careful how you send it—the cover letter says a lot. We definitely look for diversity in the pieces we publish."

THE AMERICAN DRIVEL REVIEW, A Unified Field Theory of Wit

1425, Stuart Street #1, Longmont CO 80501. (720)494-8719. E-mail: info@americandrivelreview.com. Website: www.americandrivelreview.com. **Contact:** Tara Blaine and David Wester, editors. Magazine: 6×9; 60-80 pages; illustrations; photos. *The American Drivel Review* is a journal of literary humor dedicated to formulating a Unified Field Theory of Wit. Estab. 2004. Circ. 200.

Needs "We are delighted to consider any categories, styles, forms or genres—real or imagined. We are interested in quality humorous writing in every conceivable form." Receives 20-30 unsolicited mss/month. Accepts 10-12 mss/issue; 40-48 mss/year. Publishes ms 2 months after acceptance. **Publishes 10-15 new writers/year.** Recently published work by Willie Smith, Laird Hunt, Junior Burke, Jack Collom, Richard Froude, Takashi Kendrick and Howard Muggins. Publishes short shorts. Also publishes literary essays, literary criticism, poetry.

How to Contact Send complete ms. Accepts submissions by e-mail, disk. Send SASE for return of ms. Responds in 2-3 months to queries. Accepts multiple submissions. No simultaneous submissions. Sample copy for $4.50. Writer's guidelines for #10 SASE, online or by e-mail.

Payment/Terms Pays 2 contributor's copies. Pays on publication for one-time rights.

Advice "We look primarily for sublime, funny, brilliant writing and a unique or experimental voice."

AMERICAN LITERARY REVIEW

University of North Texas, P.O. Box 311307, Denton TX 76203-1307. (940)565-2755. Fax: (940)565-4355. E-mail: americanliteraryreview@yahoo.com. Website: www.engl.unt.edu/alr/. **Contact:** John Tait, fiction editor. Magazine: 6×9; 128 pages; 70 lb. Mohawk paper; 67 lb. Wausau Vellum cover. "Publishes quality, contemporary poems and stories." Semiannual. Estab. 1990. Circ. 900.

Needs Literary, mainstream. "No genre works." Receives 150-200 unsolicited mss/month. Accepts 4-6 mss/issue; 8-16 mss/year. Reading period: September 1-May 1. Publishes ms within 2 years after acceptance. Recently published work by Dana Johnson, Bill Roorbach, Cynthia Shearer, Mark Jacobs and Sylvia Wantanabe. Also publishes literary essays, poetry. Critiques or comments on rejected mss.

How to Contact Send complete ms with cover letter. Responds in 2-4 months to mss. Accepts simultaneous submissions. Sample copy for $6. Writer's guidelines for #10 SASE.

Payment/Terms Pays in contributor's copies. Acquires one-time rights.

Advice "We would like to see more short shorts and stylisically innovative and risk-taking fiction. We like to see stories that illuminate the various layers of characters and their situations with great artistry. Give us distinctive character-driven stories that explore the complexities of human existence." Looks for "the small

Literary Magazines

moments that contain more than at first possible, that surprise us with more truth than we thought we had a right to expect."

ANCIENT PATHS, A Journal of Christian Art and Literature

P.O. Box 7505, Fairfax Station VA 22039. Website: www.literatureclassics.com/ancientpaths/magazine/table.ht ml. **Contact:** Skylar H. Burris, editor. Magazine: digest size; 48 pages; 20 lb. plain white paper; cardstock cover; perfect bound; illustrations. "*Ancient Paths* publishes quality fiction and creative nonfiction for a literate Christian audience. Religious themes are usually subtle, and the magazine has non-Christian readers as well as some content by non-Christian authors. However, writers should be comfortable appearing in a Christian magazine." Annual. Estab. 1998. Circ. 175-200.

Needs Historical, humor/satire, literary, mainstream, novel excerpts, religious/inspirational (general religious/literary), science fiction (Christian), slice-of-life vignettes. No retelling of Bible stories. Literary fiction favored over genre fiction. Receives 5-10 unsolicited mss/month. Accepts 4-8 mss/issue. Publishes ms 2-4 months after acceptance. Recently published work by Larry Marshall Sams, Erin Tocknell, Maureen Stirsman and Chris Williams. Length: 250-2,500 words; average length: 1,500 words. Publishes short shorts. Often comments on rejected mss.

How to Contact Send complete ms. Accepts submissions by e-mail (skylar.burris@gte.net [only international submissions]). Include estimated word count. Send SASE for return of ms or send a disposable copy of ms and #10 SASE for reply only. Responds in 1 week to queries; 4-5 weeks to mss. Accepts simultaneous and reprints, multiple submissions. Sample copy for $3.50; make checks payable to Skylar Burris *not* to *Ancient Paths*. Writer's guidelines online. Reviews fiction.

Payment/Terms Pays $2, 1 copy, and discount on additional copies. Pays on publication for one-time rights. Not copyrighted.

Advice "We look for fluid prose, intriguing characters and substantial themes in fiction manuscripts."

ANTHOLOGY MAGAZINE

Anthology Inc., P.O. Box 4411, Mesa AZ 85211-4411. (480)461-8200. E-mail: lisa@anthology.org. Website: www.anthology.org. **Contact:** Elissa Harris, prose editor. Magazine: $8\frac{1}{2} \times 11$; 32 pages; 20 lb. paper; 60-100 lb. cover stock; illustrations; photos. "Our intended audience is anyone who likes to read good fiction." Not accepting unsolicited manuscripts. Quarterly. Estab. 1994. Circ. 1,000.

Needs Adventure, fantasy (science fantasy, sword and sorcery), humor/satire, literary, mystery/suspense (amateur sleuth, police procedural, private eye/hard-boiled), science fiction (hard science, soft/sociological). "No graphic horror or erotica." Receives 70-80 unsolicited mss/month. Accepts 2-4 mss/issue; 8-16 mss/year. Publishes ms 10-12 months after acceptance. **Publishes 8-10 new writers/year.** Recently published work by Elisha Porat, Kent Robinson and Sarah Mlynowski. Average length: 3,000-5,000 words. Publishes short shorts. Also publishes poetry.

How to Contact Send complete ms with cover letter. Include estimated word count. Send SASE for reply, return of ms or send disposable copy of ms. Responds in 2-4 months to mss. No simultaneous submissions. Sample copy for 4.95. Writer's guidelines for #10 SASE. Reviews fiction.

Payment/Terms Pays in contributor's copies; additional copies $2. Acquires first North American serial, one-time, electronic rights.

Advice "Is there passion in writing? Is there forethought? Will the story make an emotional connection to the reader? Send for guidelines and a sample issue. If you see that your work would not only fit into, but add something to *Anthology*, then send it."

ANTIETAM REVIEW

Washington County Arts Council, 41 S. Potomac St., Hagerstown MD 21740-5512. (301)791-3132. Fax: (240)420-1754. E-mail: antietamreview@washingtoncountyarts.com. Website: www.washingtoncountyarts.com. **Contact:** Mary Jo Vincent, managing editor. Magazine: $8\frac{1}{2} \times 11$; 75-90 pages; glossy paper; light card cover. A literary magazine of short fiction, poetry and black-and-white photography. Annual. Estab. 1982. Circ. 1,000.

Needs Condensed novels, ethnic/multicultural, experimental, literary ("short stories of a literary quality"), novel excerpts ("if works as an independent piece"), creative nonfiction, interviews, memoirs and book reviews. No religious, romance, erotic, confession or horror. Accepts 8-10 mss/year. Publishes ms 3-4 months after acceptance. **Publishes 2-3 new writers/year.** Recently published work by Stephen Dixon, Pinckney Benedict, Brad Barkley, Ellyn Bache, Joyce Kornblatt.

How to Contact Send complete ms. "Reading period September 1-December 1, annually. Queries accepted by mail, e-mail and phone. No electronic submissions. Manuscripts are not returned unless requested and sufficient postage and SASE is enclosed. #10 SASE for response only." Sample copy for $8.40 (current issue), $6.30 (back issue).

Payment/Terms Pays $50 and 2 contributor's copies. Pays on publication for first North American serial rights.

Advice "We seek high-quality, well-crafted work with significant character development and shift. No specific theme. We look for work that is interesting, involves the reader, and teaches us a new way to view the world. A manuscript stands out because of its energy and flow. Most of our submissions reflect the times more than industry trends. We also seek a compelling voice, originality, magic." Contributors are encouraged to review past issues before submitting.

⚡ $⃠ THE ANTIGONISH REVIEW

St. Francis Xavier University, P.O. Box 5000, Antigonish NS B2G 2W5 Canada. (902)867-3962. Fax: (902)867-5563. Website: www.antigonishreview.com. **Contact:** Bonnie McIsaac, office manager. Literary magazine for educated and creative readers. Quarterly. Estab. 1970. Circ. 1,000.

Needs Literary, translations, contemporary, prose poem. No erotica. Receives 50 unsolicited mss/month. Accepts 6 mss/issue. Publishes ms 4 months after acceptance. **Publishes some new writers/year.** Recently published work by Arnold Bloch, Richard Butts and Helen Barolini. Sometimes comments on rejected mss.

How to Contact Send complete ms. Accepts submissions by fax. Accepts electronic (disk compatible with WordPerfect/IBM and Windows) submissions. Prefers hard copy with disk submission. Responds in 1 month to queries; 6 months to mss. No simultaneous submissions. Sample copy for $7 or online. Writer's guidelines for #10 SASE or online.

Payment/Terms Pays $50 for stories. Pays on publication. Rights retained by author.

Advice "Learn the fundamentals and do not deluge an editor."

$⃠ ANTIOCH REVIEW

P.O. Box 148, Yellow Springs OH 45387-0148. E-mail: review@antiock.edu. Website: www.review.antioch.edu. **Contact:** Fiction editor. Magazine: 6×9; 200 pages; 50 lb. book offset paper; coated cover stock; illustrations "seldom." "Literary and cultural review of contemporary issues, and literature for general readership." Quarterly. Estab. 1941. Circ. 5,100.

Needs Experimental, literary, translations, contemporary. No science fiction, fantasy or confessions. Receives 275 unsolicited mss/month. Accepts 5-6 mss/issue; 20-24 mss/year. Reading period: June 1-September 1. Publishes ms 10 months after acceptance. Agented fiction 1-2%. **Publishes 1-2 new writers/year.** Recently published work by Gordon Lish, Jean Ross Justice, Patricia Lear, William Cobb, Leon Rooke, Valerie Leff, Stephanie Koven, Andrew Porter and Liza Ward.

How to Contact Send complete ms with SASE, preferably mailed flat. Responds in 2 months to mss. Sample copy for $7. Writer's guidelines online.

Payment/Terms Pays $10/printed page. Pays on publication for first, one-time rights.

Advice "Our best advice is to always *read* the *Antioch Review* to see what type of material we publish. Quality fiction requires an engagement of the reader's intellectual interest supported by mature emotional relevance, written in a style that is rich and rewarding without being freaky. The great number of stories submitted to us indicates that fiction still has great appeal. We assume that if so many are writing fiction, many must be reading it."

⃠ ◎ APPALACHIAN HERITAGE

CPO 2166, Berea KY 40404. (859)985-3699. Fax: (859)985-3903. E-mail: george-brosi@berea.edu. Website: http://community/berea.edu/appalachianheritage/. **Contact:** George Brosi. Magazine: 6×9; 104 pages; 60 lb. stock; 10 pt. Warrenflo cover; drawings; b&w photos. "*Appalachian Heritage* is a Southern Appalachian literary magazine. We try to keep a balance of fiction, poetry, essays, scholarly works, etc., for a general audience and/or those interested in the Appalachian mountains." Quarterly. Estab. 1973. Circ. 750.

Needs Historical, literary, regional. "We do not want to see fiction that has no ties to Southern Appalachia." Receives 60-80 unsolicited mss/month. Accepts 2-3 mss/issue; 12-15 mss/year. Publishes ms 3-6 months after acceptance. **Publishes 8 new writers/year.** Recently published work by Meridith Sue Willis, Lee Maynard, Bo Ball, Fred Chappell, Silas House, Ron Rash and Lee Smith. Publishes short shorts. Occasionally comments on rejected mss.

How to Contact Send complete ms. Send SASE for reply, return of ms or send a disposable copy of ms. Responds in 1 month to queries; 6 weeks to mss. Sample copy for $6. Writer's guidelines free.

Payment/Terms Pays 3 contributor's copies; $6 charge for extras. Acquires first North American serial rights.

Advice "Get acquainted with *Appalachian Heritage*, as you should with any publication before submitting your work."

🌐 AQUARIUS

Flat 4, Room-B, 116 Sutherland Ave., Maida-Vale, London W92QP England. 0171-289-4338. **Contact:** Eddie Linden, editor. Semiannual. Estab. 1969. Circ. 3,000.

Literary Magazines

Needs Humor/satire, literary, novel excerpts, serialized novels, prose poem. Receives 1,000 unsolicited mss/month. Recently published work by W.S. Graham and George Baker.

How to Contact Sample copy in UK £6 plus postage and packing; in US $18 plus $3 postage.

Payment/Terms Payment is by agreement.

N. ☑ ARABLE, A Literary Journal

514 Washburn Avenue, Louisville KY 40222. (502)802-2786. E-mail: arable@insightbb.com. **Contact:** Edmund August. Magazine: 6×9; 100 pages; 60 lb. paper; 10 pt. cover stock. "*Arable* is dedicated to the fundamental belief that creativity in literature (as well as in all arts and sciences) needs room in which to grow. Our hope is that this journal will serve as one plot of nurturing land for that growth." Triannual. Estab. 2004. Circ. 300.

Needs Ethnic/multicultural, experimental, feminist, gay, historical, literary, mainstream. Receives 50-60 unsolicited mss/month. Accepts 4-12 mss/issue; 12-36 mss/year. Publishes ms 3 months after acceptance. **Publishes 8 new writers/year.** Recently published work by Annette Allen, Reid Bush, Erin Keanem, W. Loran Smith, Amelia Blossom and Pamela Steele. Length: 500-6,000 words; average length: 2,500 words. Publishes short shorts. Also publishes literary essays, poetry. Sometimes comments on rejected mss.

How to Contact Send complete ms. Accepts submissions by e-mail. Responds in 1-4 months to mss. Accepts simultaneous, multiple submissions. Sample copy for $10. Writer's guidelines by e-mail.

Payment/Terms Pays one contributor's copy. Acquires one-time rights.

Advice "*Arable* looks for stories with consistent narrative voice, one I can hear inside my head, one that makes me stop thinking as an editor and allows me to sit back and enjoy being taken on a jouney."

☑ ARKANSAS REVIEW, A Journal of Delta Studies

Department of English and Philosophy, P.O. Box 1890, Arkansas State University, State University AR 72467-1890. (501)972-3043. Fax: (501)972-3045. E-mail: tswillia@astate.edu. Website: www.clt.astate.edu/arkreview. **Contact:** Eric Miles Williamson, fiction editor. Magazine: 8¼×11; 64-100 pages; coated, matte paper; matte, 4-color cover stock; illustrations; photos. Publishes articles, fiction, poetry, essays, interviews, reviews, visual art evocative of or responsive to the Mississippi River Delta. Triannual. Estab. 1996. Circ. 700.

Needs Literary (essays and criticism), regional (short stories). "No genre fiction. Must have a Delta focus." Receives 30-50 unsolicited mss/month. Accepts 2-3 mss/issue; 5-7 mss/year. Publishes ms 6-12 months after acceptance. Agented fiction 1%. **Publishes 3-4 new writers/year.** Recently published work by Eric Miles Williams, George Singleton and Anne Dyer Stuart. Also publishes literary essays, poetry. Sometimes comments on rejected mss.

How to Contact Accepts submissions by e-mail, fax. Send SASE for reply, return of ms or send a disposable copy of ms. Responds in 1 week to queries; 4 months to mss. Sample copy for $7.50. Writer's guidelines for #10 SASE.

Payment/Terms Pays 5 contributor's copies; additional copies for $5. Acquires first North American serial rights.

Advice "We see a lot of stories set in New Orleans but prefer fiction that takes place in other parts of the Delta. We'd love more innovative and experimental fiction too, but adhere primarily to the criterion of stories that involve and engage the reader and evoke or respond to the Delta natural and/or cultural experience."

☑ THE ARMCHAIR AESTHETE

Pickle Gas Press, 31 Rolling Meadows Way, Penfield NY 14526. (585)388-6968. E-mail: bypaul@netacc.net. **Contact:** Paul Agosto, editor. Magazine: 5½×8½; 60-75 pages; 20 lb. paper; 110 lb. card stock color cover. "*The Armchair Aesthete* seeks quality writing that enlightens and entertains a thoughtful audience (ages 9-90) with a 'good read.'" Quarterly. Estab. 1996. Circ. 100.

Needs Adventure, fantasy (science fantasy, sword and sorcery), historical (general), horror, humor/satire (satire), mainstream (contemporary), mystery/suspense (amateur sleuth, cozy, police procedural, private eye/hard-boiled, romantic suspense), science fiction (soft/sociological), western (frontier, traditional). "No racist, pornographic, overt gore; no religious or material intended for or written by children. Receives 90 unsolicited mss/month. Accepts 13-18 mss/issue; 60-80 mss/year. Publishes ms 3-9 months after acceptance. Agented fiction 5%. **Publishes 15-25 new writers/year.** Recently published work by Don Stockard, Frank Andreotti, Joyce G. Bradshaw, Daniel Roozen and John Sunseri. Average length: 3,000 words. Publishes short shorts. Also publishes poetry. Sometimes comments on rejected mss.

How to Contact Accepts submissions by e-mail. Send SASE for reply, return of ms or send a disposable copy of ms. Responds in 2-3 weeks to queries; 3-6 months to mss. Accepts simultaneous and reprints, multiple submissions. Sample copy for $3 (paid to P. Agosto, Ed.) and 3 first-class stamps. Writer's guidelines for #10 SASE. Reviews fiction.

Payment/Terms Pays 1 contributor's copy; additional copies for $3 (pay to P. Agosto, editor). Pays on publication for one-time rights.

Advice "Clever, compelling storytelling has a good chance here. We look for a clever plot, thought-out characters, something that surprises or catches us off guard. Write on innovative subjects and situations. Submissions should be professionally presented and technically sound."

$⬤ ARTFUL DODGE

Dept. of English, College of Wooster, Wooster OH 44691. (330)263-2577. Website: www.wooster.edu/artfuldodge/home.htm. **Contact:** Editor. Magazine: 180 pages; illustrations; photos. "There is no theme in this magazine, except literary power. We also have an ongoing interest in translations from Central/Eastern Europe and elsewhere." Annual. Estab. 1979. Circ. 1,000.

Needs Experimental, literary, translations, prose poem. "We judge by literary quality, not by genre. We are especially interested in fine English translations of significant prose writers. Translations should be submitted with original texts." Receives 50 unsolicited mss/month. Accepts 5 mss/year. **Publishes 1 new writer/year.** Recently published work by Dan Chaon, Lynne Sharon Schwartz, Robert Mooney, Joan Connor and Sarah Willis; and interviews with Tim O'Brien, Lee Smith, Michael Dorris and Stuart Dybek. Average length: 2,500 words. Also publishes literary essays, literary criticism, poetry. Occasionally comments on rejected mss.

How to Contact Send complete ms with SASE. Do not send more than 30 pages at a time. Responds in 1 year to mss. Accepts simultaneous submissions if contacted immediately after being accepted elsewhere. Sample copy for $7. Writer's guidelines for #10 SASE.

Payment/Terms Pays 2 contributor's copies and honorarium of $5/page, "thanks to funding from the Ohio Arts Council." Acquires first North American serial rights.

Advice "If we take time to offer criticism, do not subsequently flood us with other stories no better than the first. If starting out, get as many *good* readers as possible. Above all, read contemporary fiction and the magazine you are trying to publish in."

$ ARTS & LETTERS, Journal of Contemporary Culture

Georgia College & State University, Campus Box 89, Milledgeville GA 31061. E-mail: al@gcsu.edu. Website: al.gcsu.edu. **Contact:** Allen Gee, fiction editor. Literary magazine: 7×10; 200 pages; 60 lb. joy white; some photos. "The journal features the mentors interview series, the world poetry translation series, and color reproductions of original artistic prints. Also, it is the only journal nationwide to feature authors and artists that represent such an eclectic range of creative work." Semiannual. Estab. 1999. Circ. 1,500.

Needs Literary. No genre fiction. Receives 50 unsolicited mss/month. Accepts 5 mss/issue; 10 mss/year. Reads mss September 1-April 1. Publishes ms 6-12 months after acceptance. **Publishes 1-2 new writers/year.** Recently published work by Bret Lott, Heather Sellers, Edith Pearlman and Austin Ratner. Length: 3,000-7,500 words; average length: 6,000 words. Sometimes comments on rejected mss.

How to Contact Send complete ms with cover letter. Include estimated word count, brief bio and list of publications. Send disposable copy of ms and #10 SASE for reply only. Responds in 4-8 weeks to mss. Sample copy for $5, plus $1 for postage. Writer's guidelines online.

Payment/Terms Pays $10 minimum or $50/published page. Pays on publication. Rights revert to author after publication. Sends galleys to author.

Advice "An obvious, but not gimmicky, attention to and fresh usage of language. A solid grasp of the craft of story writing. Fully realized work."

⬤ AXE FACTORY REVIEW

Cynic Press, P.O. Box 40691, Philadelphia PA 19107. **Contact:** Joseph Farley, editor. Magazine: 11×17 folded to 8½×11; 30-60 pages; 20 lb. stock paper; 70 lb. stock cover; illustrations; photos on occasion. "We firmly believe that literature is a form of (and/or expression/manifestation of) madness. We seek to spread the disease called literature. We will look at any genre. But, we search for the quirky, the off-center, the offensive, the annoying, but always the well-written story, poem, essay." Biannual. Estab. 1986. Circ. 200.

Needs Adventure, comics/graphic novels, erotica, ethnic/multicultural (Asian), experimental, fantasy (space fantasy, sword and sorcery), feminist, gay, historical, horror (dark fantasy, futuristic, psychological, supernatural), humor/satire, lesbian, literary, mainstream, military/war, mystery/suspense, New Age, psychic/supernatural/occult, regional (Philadelphia area), religious/inspirational (general religious, inspirational, religious mystery/suspense), romance, science fiction (hard science/technological, soft/sociological, cross genre), thriller/espionage, translations, western (frontier saga, traditional). "We would like to see more hybrid genres, literary/science fiction, Beat writing. No genteel professional gibberish." Receives 20 unsolicited mss/month. Accepts 1-2 mss/issue; 3 mss/year. Publishes ms 6-12 months after acceptance. Recently published work by Tim Gavin and Michael Hafer. Length: 500-5,000 words; average length: 3,000 words. Publishes short shorts. Also publishes literary essays, literary criticism, poetry. Often comments on rejected mss.

How to Contact Send SASE (or IRC) for return of ms. Responds in 6 weeks to mss. Accepts simultaneous and reprints, multiple submissions. Sample copy for $8. Current issue $9. Reviews fiction.

Payment/Terms Pays 1-2 contributor's copies; additional copies $8. Pays on publication for one-time rights, anthology rights.

Advice ''In fiction we look for a strong beginning, strong middle, strong end; memorable characters; and most importantly language, language, language.''

◢ THE BALTIMORE REVIEW

P.O. Box 36418, Towson MD 21286. E-mail: susanmd@e-global.com. Website: www.baltimorereview.org. **Contact:** Susan Muaddi Darraj, managing editor. Magazine: 6×9; 128 pages; 60 lb. paper; 10 pt. CS1 gloss film cover. Showcase for the best short stories, creative nonfiction and poetry by writers in the Baltimore area and beyond. Semiannual. Estab. 1996.

Needs Ethnic/multicultural, literary, mainstream. ''No science fiction, westerns, children's, romance, etc.'' Accepts 8-12 mss/issue; 16-24 mss/year. Publishes ms 1-9 months after acceptance. **Publishes ''at least a few'' new writers/year.** Average length: 3,000 words. Publishes short shorts. Also publishes poetry.

How to Contact Send SASE for reply, return of ms or send a disposable copy of ms. Responds in 3-4 months to mss. Accepts simultaneous submissions; no e-mail or fax submissions. Sample copy online.

Payment/Terms Pays 2 contributor's copies. Acquires first North American serial rights.

Advice ''We look for compelling stories and a masterful use of the English language. We want to feel that we have never heard this story, or this voice, before. Read the kinds of publications you want your work to appear in. Make your reader believe—and care.''

◢ BARBARIC YAWP

Bone World Publishing, 3700 County Rt. 24, Russell NY 13684-3198. (315)347-2609. **Contact:** Nancy Berbrich, fiction editor. Magazine: digest-size; 60 pages; 24lb. paper; matte cover stock. ''We publish what we like. Fiction should include some bounce and surprise. Our publication is intended for the intelligent, open-minded reader.'' Quarterly. Estab. 1997. Circ. 120.

Needs Adventure, experimental, fantasy (science, sword and sorcery), historical, horror, literary, mainstream, psychic/supernatural/occult, regional, religious/inspirational, science fiction (hard, soft/sociological). ''We don't want any pornography, gratuitous violence or whining.'' Wants more suspense and philosophical work. Receives 30-40 unsolicited mss/month. Accepts 10-12 mss/issue; 40-48 mss/year. Publishes ms up to 6 months after acceptance. **Publishes 4-6 new writers/year.** Recently published work by Michael Fowler, Jeff Grimshaw, Robert Layden and Holly Interlandi. Length:1,500 words; average length: 600 words. Publishes short shorts. Also publishes literary essays, literary criticism, poetry. Often comments on rejected mss.

How to Contact Send SASE for reply, return of ms or send a disposable copy of ms. Responds in 2 weeks to queries; 4 months to mss. Accepts simultaneous and reprints, multiple submissions. Sample copy for $4. Writer's guidelines for #10 SASE.

Payment/Terms Pays 1 contributor's copy; additional copies $3. Acquires one-time rights.

Advice ''Don't give up. Read much, write much, submit much. Observe closely the world around you. Don't borrow ideas from TV or films. Revision is often necessary—grit your teeth and do it. Never fear rejection.''

◢ BATHTUB GIN

Pathwise Press, P.O. Box 2392, Bloomington IN 47402. (812)339-7298. E-mail: charter@bluemarble.net. Website: www.bluemarble.net/~charter/btgin.htm. **Contact:** Fiction Editor. Magazine: 8½×5½; 60 pages; recycled 20-lb. paper; 80-lb. card cover; illustrations; photos. ''*Bathtub Gin* is looking for work that has some kick to it. We are very eclectic and publish a wide range of styles. Audience is anyone interested in new writing and art that is not being presented in larger magazines.'' Semiannual. Estab. 1997. Circ. 250.

Needs Condensed novels, experimental, humor/satire, literary. ''No horror, science fiction, historical unless they go beyond the usual formula. We want more experimental fiction.'' Receives 20 unsolicited mss/month. Accepts 2-3 mss/issue. Reads mss for two issues June 1st-September 15th. ''We publish in mid-October and mid-April.'' **Publishes 10 new writers/year.** Recently published work by Karen Dione and Eileen Cruz-Coleman. Publishes short shorts. Also publishes literary essays, literary criticism, poetry. Often comments on rejected mss.

How to Contact Accepts submissions by e-mail. Send SASE for reply, return of ms or send a disposable copy of ms. Responds in 1-2 months to queries. Accepts simultaneous and reprints, multiple submissions. Sample copy for $5. Writer's guidelines for #10 SASE. Reviews fiction.

Payment/Terms Pays 2 contributor's copies; discount on additional copies. Rights revert to author upon publication.

Advice ''We are looking for writing that contains strong imagery, is complex, and is willing to take a chance with form and structure.''

N 🖊 **BAYOU**

English Dept. University of New Orleans, 2000 Lakeshore Drive, New Orleans LA 70148. (504)280-6144 ext. 3133. E-mail: bayou@uno.edu. Website: www.uno.edu/%7Ecww/bayou.htm. **Contact:** Joanna Leake, editor (Winter); Laurie O'Brien, editor (Spring). Magazine: 6×9; 128 pages; matte cover stock; photographs. Semiannual. Estab. 2001. Circ. 500.

- Send submissions for Spring issue to: English Dept. University of West Florida, 11000 University Parkway, Penscola FL 32514.

Needs ''We are looking for good work: short stories, may be novel or an essay excerpt. There is not a limit to theme or the audience targeted.'' Winter, University of New Orleans reads from September 1-November 7. Spring, University of West Florida reads from November 8-February 15. Publishes ms 2-3 months after acceptance. Recently published work by Philip Cioffari, Chimamanda and Ngozi Adichie. Also publishes literary essays, poetry. Sometimes comments on rejected mss.

How to Contact Send complete ms. Send disposable copy of the ms and #10 SASE for reply only. Responds in 3-4 months to mss. Accepts simultaneous submissions. Sample copy for $5.

Payment/Terms Pays 2 contributor's copies. Pays on publication for first North American serial rights. Not copyrighted.

Advice ''We look for good work. Of course this is a subjective thing—good. Sometimes a piece will stand out in its subject matter, voice, style, time travel, point of view, arc—just send us your best work.''

🖊 **BEGINNINGS PUBLISHING INC., A Magazine for the Novice Writer**

Beginnings Publishing, P.O. Box 214, Bayport NJ 11705. (631)645-3846. E-mail: jenineb@optonline.net. Website: www.scbeginnings.com. **Contact:** Jenine Killoran, fiction editor. Magazine: 8½×11; 54 pages; matte; glossy cover; illustrations; photographs. ''*Beginnings* publishes only beginner/novice writers. We do accept articles by professionals pertaining to the craft of writing. We have had many new writers go on to be published elsewhere after being featured in our magazine.'' Triannual. Estab. 1999. Circ. 2,500.

Needs Adventure, family saga, literary, mainstream, mystery/suspense (amateur slueth), romance (contemporary), science fiction (soft/sociological), western. ''No erotica, horror.'' Receives 425 unsolicited mss/month. Accepts 10 mss/issue; 20 mss/year. Does not read mss during January and April. Publishes ms 3-4 months after acceptance. **Publishes 100 percent new writers/year.** Recently published work by Harvey Stanbrough, Sue Guiney, Tom Cooper and Stephen Wallace. Average length: 2,500 words. Publishes short shorts. Also publishes poetry. Sometimes comments on rejected mss.

How to Contact Send complete ms. Send disposable copy of ms and #10 SASE for reply only; however, will accept SASE for return of ms. Responds in 3 weeks to queries; 10-13 weeks to mss. Accepts simultaneous and reprints submissions. Sample copy for $4. Writer's guidelines for SASE, e-mail or on website.

Payment/Terms Pays one contributor's copy; additional copies $4. Pays on publication for first North American serial, first rights.

Advice ''Originality, presentation, proper grammar and spelling a must. Non-predictable endings. Many new writers confuse showing vs. telling. Writers who have that mastered stand out. Study the magazine. Check and double check your work. Original storylines, well thought out, keep up a good pace. Presentation is important, too! Rewrite, rewrite!''

🖊 **BELLEVUE LITERARY REVIEW, A Journal of Humanity and Human Experience**

Dept. of Medicine, NYU School of Medicine, 550 First Avenue, OBV-A612, New York NY 10016. (212)263-3973. Fax: (212)263-3206. E-mail: info@blreview.org. Website: www.blreview.org. **Contact:** Ronna Wineberg, fiction editor. Magazine: 6×9; 160 pages. ''The *BLR* is a literary journal that examines human existence through the prism of health and healing, illness and disease. We encourage creative interpretations of these themes.'' Semiannual. Estab. 2001. Member, CLMP.

Needs Literary. No genre fiction. Receives 85 unsolicited mss/month. Accepts 9 mss/issue; 18 mss/year. Publishes ms 3-6 months after acceptance. Agented fiction 1%. **Publishes 3-6 new writers/year.** Recently published work by Sheila Kohler, Abraham Verghese, Stephen Dixon and Susan Dworkin. Length: 5,000 words; average length: 2,500 words. Publishes short shorts. Also publishes literary essays, poetry. Sometimes comments on rejected mss.

How to Contact Send complete ms. Send SASE (or IRC) for return of ms or disposable copy of the ms and #10 SASE for reply only. Online submissions now accepted, www.blreview.org. Responds in 3-6 months to mss. Accepts simultaneous submissions. Sample copy for $7. Writer's guidelines for SASE, e-mail or on website.

Payment/Terms Pays 2 contributor's copies; additional copies $5. Pays on publication for first North American serial rights. Sends galleys to author.

🖊 **BELLINGHAM REVIEW**

Mail Stop 9053, Western Washington University, Bellingham WA 98225. (360)650-4863. E-mail: bhreview@cc. wwu.edu. Website: www.wwu.edu/~bhreview. **Contact:** Fiction Editor. Magazine: 6×8¼; 150 pages; 60 lb.

Literary Magazines

Literary Magazines

white paper; four color cover.'' *Bellingham Review* seeks literature of palpable quality; stories, essays, and poems that nudge the limits of form or execute traditional forms exquisitely. Semiannual. Estab. 1977. Circ. 1,600.

● The editors are actively seeking submissions of creative nonfiction, as well as stories that push the boundaries of the form. The Tobias Wolff Award in Fiction Contest runs December 1-March 15; see website for guidelines or send SASE.

Needs Experimental, humor/satire, literary, regional (Northwest). Does not want anything nonliterary. Accepts 3-4 mss/issue. Does not read ms February 2-September 30. Publishes ms 6 months after acceptance. Agented fiction 10%. **Publishes 10 new writers/year.** Recently published work by Christie Hodgen, Robert Van Wagoner and Joan Leegeant. Publishes short shorts. Also publishes poetry.

How to Contact Send complete ms. Responds in 3 months to mss. Accepts simultaneous submissions. Sample copy for $7. Writer's guidelines online. Reviews fiction.

Payment/Terms Pays on publication when funding allows. Acquires first North American serial rights.

Advice ''We look for work that is ambitious, vital and challenging both to the spirit and the intellect.''

☑ ⚇ BELLOWING ARK, A Literary Tabloid

P.O. Box 55564, Shoreline WA 98155. E-mail: bellowingark@bellowingark.org. **Contact:** Fiction Editor. Tabloid: 11½×17½; 28 pages; electro-brite paper and cover stock; illustrations; photos. ''We publish material which we feel addresses the human situation in an affirmative way. We do not publish academic fiction.'' Bimonthly. Estab. 1984. Circ. 650.

● Work from *Bellowing Ark* appeared in the *Pushcart Prize* anthology.

Needs Literary, mainstream, serialized novels. ''No science fiction or fantasy.'' Receives 10-20 unsolicited mss/month. Accepts 2-5 mss/issue; 700-1,000 mss/year. Publishes ms 6 months after acceptance. **Publishes 10-50 new writers/year.** Recently published work by Larsen Bowker, Nancy Corson Carter, Shelley Uva, Tanyo Ravicz, Susan Montag and E.R. Romaine. Publishes short shorts. Also publishes literary essays, literary criticism, poetry. Sometimes comments on rejected mss.

How to Contact SASE. Responds in 6 weeks to mss. No simultaneous submissions. Sample copy for $4, 9½×12½ SAE and $1.43 postage.

Payment/Terms Pays in contributor's copies. Acquires one-time rights.

Advice ''*Bellowing Ark* began as (and remains) an alternative to the despair and negativity of the workshop/academic literary scene. We believe that life has meaning and is worth living; the work we publish reflects that belief. Learn how to tell a story before submitting. Avoid 'trick' endings; they have all been done before and better. *Bellowing Ark* is interested in publishing writers who will develop with the magazine, as in an extended community. We find *good* writers and stick with them. This is why the magazine has grown from 12 to 32 pages.''

☑ ⚇ BELOIT FICTION JOURNAL

Box 11, 700 College St., Beloit College WI 53511. (608)363-2577. E-mail: skylerh@beloit.edu. Editor-in-chief: Clint McCowan. **Contact:** Heather Skyler, managing editor. Literary magazine: 6×9; 250 pages; 60 lb. paper; 10 pt. C1S cover stock; illustrations; photos on cover; ad-free. ''We are interested in publishing the best contemporary fiction and are open to all themes except those involving pornographic, religiously dogmatic or politically propagandistic representations. Our magazine is for general readership, though most of our readers will probably have a specific interest in literary magazines.'' Annual. Estab. 1985.

● Work first appearing in *Beloit Fiction Journal* has been reprinted in award-winning collections, including the *Flannery O'Connor* and the *Milkweed Fiction Prize* collections, and has won the Iowa Short Fiction award.

Needs Literary, mainstream, contemporary. Wants more experimental and short shorts. Would like to see more ''stories with a focus on both language and plot, unusual metaphors and vivid characters. No pornography, religious dogma, science fiction, horror, political propaganda or genre fiction.'' Receives 200 unsolicited mss/month. Accepts 20 mss/year. Reads mss August 1-December 1. Replies take longer in summer. Publishes ms 9 months after acceptance. **Publishes 3 new writers/year.** Recently published work by Dennis Lehane, Silas Houlse and David Harris Ebenbach. Length: 250-10,000 words; average length: 5,000 words. Sometimes comments on rejected mss.

How to Contact SASE for ms. No fax, e-mail or disk submissions. Responds in 2 weeks to queries; 2 months to mss. Accepts simultaneous submissions if identified as such. Sample copy for $15 for double issue; $7 for single issue. Writer's guidelines for #10 SASE.

Advice ''Many of our contributors are writers whose work we had previously rejected. Don't let one rejection slip turn you away from our—or any—magazine.''

⬛ BERKELEY FICTION REVIEW

10 Eshleman Hall, University of California, Berkeley CA 94720. (510)642-2892. E-mail: smh@uclink.berkeley.e du. Website: www.OCF.Berkeley.EDU/~bfr/. **Contact:** Sarah Haufrect and Julia Simon, editors. Magazine: 5½×8½; 180 pages; perfect-bound; glossy cover; some b&w art; photographs. "The mission of *Berkeley Fiction Review* is to provide a forum for new and emerging writers as well as writers already established. We publish a wide variety of contemporary short fiction for a literary audience." Annual. Estab. 1981. Circ. 1,000.

Needs Experimental, literary, mainstream. "Quality, inventive short fiction. No poetry or formula fiction." Receives 60 unsolicited mss/month. Accepts 10-20 mss/issue. **Publishes 15-20 new writers/year.** Publishes short shorts. Occasionally comments on rejected mss.

How to Contact Responds in 6-7 months to mss. Accepts simultaneous, multiple submissions. Sample copy for $9.50. Writer's guidelines for SASE.

Payment/Terms Pays one contributor's copy. Acquires first rights. Sponsors awards/contests.

Advice "Our criteria is fiction that resonates. Voices that are strong and move a reader. Clear, powerful prose (either voice or rendering of subject) with a point. Unique ways of telling stories—these capture the editors. Work hard; don't give up. Don't let your friends or family critique your work. Get someone honest to point out your writing weaknesses, and then work on them. Don't submit thinly veiled autobiographical stories; it's been done before—and better. With the proliferation of computers, everyone thinks they're a writer. Not true, unfortunately. The plus side though is ease of transmission and layout and diversity and range of new work."

$⬛ BIBLIOPHILOS, A Journal of History, Literature, and the Liberal Arts

The Bibliophile Publishing Co., Inc., 200 Security Building, Fairmont WV 26554. (304)366-8107. **Contact:** Gerald J. Bobango, editor. Literary magazine: 5½×8; 68-72 pages; white glossy paper; illustrations; photos. "We see ourself as a forum for new and unpublished writers, historians, philosophers, literary critics and reviewers, and those who love animals. Audience is academic-oriented, college graduate, who believes in traditional Aristotelian-Thomistic thought and education, and has a fair streak of the Luddite in him/her. Our ideal reader owns no television, has never sent nor received e-mail, and avoids shopping malls at any cost. He loves books." Quarterly. Estab. 1981. Circ. 400.

Needs Adventure, ethnic/multicultural, family saga, historical (general, US, Eastern Europe), horror (psychological, supernatural), humor/satire, literary, mainstream, military/war, mystery/suspense (police procedural, private eye/hard-boiled, courtroom), novel excerpts, regional (New England, Middle Atlantic), romance (gothic, historical, regency period), slice-of-life vignettes, suspense, thriller/espionage, translations, western (frontier saga, traditional), utopian, Orwellian. "No 'I found Jesus and it turned my life around'; no 'I remember Mama, who was a saint and I miss her terribly'; no gay or lesbian topics; no drug culture material; nothing harping on political correctness; nothing to do with healthy living, HMOs, medical programs or the welfare state, unless it is against statism in these areas." No unsolicited submissions. Accepts 5-6 mss/issue; 25-30 mss/year. Publishes ms 12-18 months after acceptance. **Publishes 2-6 new writers/year.** Recently published work by Mardelle Fortier, Clevenger Kehmeier, Gwen Williams, Manuel Sanchez-Lopez, Janet Tyson, Andrea C. Poe, Norman Nathan. Also publishes literary essays, literary criticism, poetry. Often comments on rejected mss.

How to Contact Query with clips of published work. Include bio, SASE and $5.25 for sample issue. Responds in 2 weeks to queries; 1 month to mss. Sample copy for $5.25. Writer's guidelines for 9½×4 SAE and 2 first-class stamps.

Payment/Terms Pays $15-40. Pays on publication for first North American serial rights.

Advice "Write for specifications, send for a sample issue, then *read* the thing, study the formatting, and follow the instructions, which say query first, before sending anything. We shall not respond to unsolicited material. We don't want touchy-feely maudlin stuff where hugging kids solves all of life's problems, and we want no references anywhere in the story to e-mail, the Internet or computers, unless it's to berate them."

⬛ 🏴 BIG MUDDY: A JOURNAL OF THE MISSISSIPPI RIVER VALLEY

Southeast Missouri State University Press, MS2650 English Dept., Southeast MO State University, Cape Girardeau MO 63701. E-mail: sswartwout@semo.edu. Website: www6.semo.edu/universitypress/. **Contact:** Susan Swartwout, editor. Magazine: 8½×5½ perfect-bound; 150 pages; acid-free paper; color cover stock; layflat lamination; illustrations; photos. "*Big Muddy* explores multidisciplinary, multicultural issues, people, and events mainly concerning the ten-state area that borders the Mississippi River, by people who have lived here, who have an interest in the area, or who know the River Basin. We publish fiction, poetry, historical essays, creative nonfiction, environmental essays, biography, regional events, photography, art, etc." Semiannual. Estab. 2001. Circ. 500.

● *Big Muddy* was *Small Press Review's* "Best Pick" in magazines in 2001.

Needs Adventure, ethnic/multicultural, experimental, family saga, feminist, historical, humor/satire, literary, mainstream, military/war, mystery/suspense, regional (Mississippi River Valley; Midwest), translations. "No romance, fantasy or children's." Receives 50 unsolicited mss/month. Accepts 2-4 mss/issue. Publishes ms 6 months after acceptance. Recently published work by Philip Kolin, Virgil Suarez, John Cantey Knight and Joan Connor.

How to Contact Send SASE for return of ms or send a disposable copy of ms and #10 SASE for reply only. Responds in 10 weeks to mss. Accepts multiple submissions. Sample copy for $6. Writer's guidelines for SASE, e-mail, fax or on website. Reviews fiction.

Payment/Terms Pays 2 contributor's copies; additional copies $5. Acquires first North American serial rights.

Advice "In fiction manuscripts we look for clear language, avoidance of clichés except in necessary dialogue, a *fresh* vision of the theme or issue. Find some excellent and honest readers to comment on your work-in-progress and final draft. Consider their viewpoints carefully. Revise."

Ⓝ $Ⓓ BIGnews, The Art and Literary Monthly

Grand Central Neighborhood, 211 E. 43rd. St. Suite 1003, New York NY 10017. (212)867-7204 ext. 304. Fax: (212)883-0672. E-mail: BIGnewsmag@aol.com. Website: www.mainchance.org. **Contact:** Ron Grunberg, editor. Magazine: 11×17; 16 pages; tabloid paper; 50 lb. cover stock; illustrations; photos. Monthly. Estab. 2000. Circ. 30,000.

  • Received the 2002 North American Street Newspaper Association (NASNA) Awards for Best Editorial or Essay, Best Art, Best Poetry.

Needs Literary, mainstream. "Generally, no genre fiction." Receives 25 unsolicited mss/month. Accepts 10 mss/year. Publishes ms 2-3 months after acceptance. **Publishes 5 new writers/year.** Recently published work by Robert Sheckley, John Ray, JR., J.L. Navarro and Tim Hall. Length: 200-5,000 words; average length: 2,700 words. Publishes short shorts. Also publishes literary essays. Sometimes comments on rejected mss.

How to Contact Send complete ms. Accepts submissions by e-mail, fax. Send disposable copy of the ms and #10 SASE for reply only. Responds in 1 month to queries; 1 month to mss. Accepts simultaneous, multiple submissions. Sample copy free. Writer's guidelines online.

Payment/Terms Pays $50-75; 5 contributor's copies and a free subscription to the magazine. Pays on publication for one-time rights.

Advice "A very busy editor has to want to read the whole thing through. Avoid clever. Take risks. Don't write knowingly. Make it an effort of discovery."

Ⓓ ◎ BILINGUAL REVIEW

Hispanic Research Center, Arizona State University, Box 872702, Tempe AZ 85287-2702. (480)965-3867. E-mail: brp@asu.edu. Website: www.asu.edu/brp/brp.html. **Contact:** Gary D. Keller, editor-in-chief. Magazine: 7×10; 96 pages; 55 lb. acid-free paper; coated cover stock. Scholarly/literary journal of US Hispanic life: poetry, short stories, other prose and short theater. 3 times/year. Estab. 1974. Circ. 2,000.

Needs US Hispanic creative literature. "We accept material in English or Spanish. We publish orginal work only—no translations." US Hispanic themes only. Receives 50 unsolicited mss/month. Accepts 3 mss/issue; 9 mss/year. Publishes ms 1 year after acceptance. Recently published work by Daniel Olivas, Virgil Suárez and Ibis Gomez-Vega. Also publishes literary criticism, poetry. Often comments on rejected mss.

How to Contact Accepts submissions by e-mail. Responds in 1-2 months to queries. Accepts simultaneous submissions and high-quality photocopied submissions. Sample copy for $8. Reviews fiction.

Payment/Terms Pays 2 contributor's copies; 30% discount for extras. Acquires 50% of reprint permission fee given to author as matter of policy rights.

Advice "We do not publish literature about tourists in Latin America and their perceptions of the 'native culture'. We do not publish fiction about Latin America unless there is a clear tie to the United States (characters, theme, etc.)."

Ⓓ THE BITTER OLEANDER

4983 Tall Oaks Dr., Fayetteville NY 13066-9776. (315)637-3047. Fax: (315)637-5056. E-mail: info@bitteroleander. com. Website: www.bitteroleander.com. **Contact:** Paul B. Roth. Zine specializing in poetry and fiction: 6×9; 128 pages; 55 lb. paper; 12 pt. CIS cover stock; photos. "We're interested in the surreal; deep image particularization of natural experiences." Semiannual. Estab. 1974. Circ. 2,000.

Needs Experimental, translations. "No pornography; no confessional; no romance." Receives 100 unsolicited mss/month. Accepts 1-2 mss/issue; 2-4 mss/year. Does not read in July. Publishes ms 4-6 months after acceptance. Recently published work by Tom Stoner, John Michael Cummings, Sara Leslie. Average length: 2,500 words. Publishes short shorts. Also publishes literary essays, poetry. Always comments on rejected mss.

How to Contact Send SASE for reply, return of ms. Responds in 1 week to queries; 1 month to mss. Accepts multiple submissions. Sample copy for $8. Writer's guidelines for #10 SASE.

Payment/Terms Pays 1 contributor's copy; additional copies $8. Acquires first rights.

Advice "If within the first 100 words my mind drifts, the rest rarely makes it. Be yourself and listen to no one but yourself."

☒ $☐ ◎ BLACK LACE

BLK Publishing Co., P.O. Box 83912, Los Angeles CA 90083-0912. (310)410-0808. Fax: (310)410-9250. E-mail: newsroom@blk.com. Website: www.blacklace.org. **Contact:** Fiction Editor. Magazine: $8^1/_8 \times 10^5/_8$; 48 pages; book stock; color glossy cover; illustrations; photos. *"Black Lace* is a lifestyle magazine for African-American lesbians. Its content ranges from erotic imagery to political commentary." Quarterly. Estab. 1991.

Needs Ethnic/multicultural, lesbian. "Avoid interracial stories of idealized pornography." Accepts 4 mss/year. Recently published work by Nicole King, Wanda Thompson, Lynn K. Pannell, Sheree Ann Slaughter, Lyn Lifshin, JoJo and Drew Alise Timmens. Publishes short shorts. Also publishes literary essays, literary criticism, poetry.

How to Contact Query with published clips or send complete ms. Send a disposable copy of ms. No simultaneous submissions. Accepts electronic submissions. Sample copy for $7. Writer's guidelines free.

Payment/Terms Pays $50 and 2 contributor's copies. Acquires first North American serial rights. Right to anthologize.

Advice *Black Lace* seeks erotic material of the highest quality. The most important thing is that the work be erotic and that it feature black lesbians or themes. Study the magazine to see what we do and how we do it. Some fiction is very romantic, other is highly sexual. Most articles in *Black Lace* cater to black lesbians between two extremes."

☒ ◪ ◉ THE BLACK MOUNTAIN REVIEW

Black Mountain Press, P.O. Box 9, Ballyclare Co Antrim BT390JW N. Ireland. E-mail: info@blackmountainrevie w.com. Website: www.blackmountainreview.com. **Contact:** Editor. Magazine: A5; approximately 100 pages. "We publish short fiction with a contemporary flavour for an international audience." Semiannual. Estab. 1999.

Needs Ethnic/multicultural (general), experimental, historical (literary), literary, regional (Irish), religious/inspirational (general religious, inspirational), romance (literary), science fiction (literary), translations. Publishes ms 5 months after acceptance. **Publishes many new writers/year.** Recently published work by Cathal O Searcaigh, Michael Longley and Brian Keenan. Average length: 1,500-3,000 words. Publishes short shorts. Also publishes literary essays, literary criticism, poetry. Sometimes comments on rejected mss.

How to Contact Send SASE (or IRC) for return of ms or send a disposable copy of ms and #10 SASE for reply. Material should be supplied on $3^1/_2$ inch floppy disk or by e-mail (word.txt format, preferably not attachments) with paper typescript by snail mail. Submissions *must* be accompanied with an e-mail or disk version. Responds in 2 months to queries; 4 months to mss. Accepts simultaneous submissions. Sample copy for $4.50. Writer's guidelines for SASE or by e-mail. Reviews fiction.

Payment/Terms Pays 1 contributor's copy; additional copies $4.50. Pays on publication for one-time rights.

Advice "We look for literary quality. Write well."

$◪ ▨ BLACK WARRIOR REVIEW

P.O. Box 862936, Tuscaloosa AL 35486-0027. (205)348-4518. E-mail: bwr@ua.edu. Website: www.webdelsol. com/bwr. **Contact:** Sarah Blackman, fiction editor. Magazine: 6×9; 160 pages; color artwork. "We publish contemporary fiction, poetry, reviews, essays and art for a literary audience. We publish the freshest work we can find." Semiannual. Estab. 1974. Circ. 2,000.

• Work that appeared in the *Black Warrior Review* has been included in the *Pushcart Prize* anthology, *Harper's Magazine, Best American Short Stories, Best American Poetry* and *New Stories from the South.*

Needs Literary, contemporary, short and short-short fiction. Want "work that is conscious of form and well-crafted. We are open to good experimental writing and short-short fiction. No genre fiction please." Receives 300 unsolicited mss/month. Accepts 5 mss/issue; 10 mss/year. Unsolicited novel excerpts are not considered unless the novel is already contracted for publication. Publishes ms 6 months after acceptance. **Publishes 5 new writers/year.** Recently published work by Gary Fincke, Anthony Varallo, Wayne Johnson, Jim Ruland, Elizabeth Wetmore, Bret Anthony Johnston, Rick Bass and Sherri Flick. Length: 7,500 words; average length: 2,000-5,000 words. Occasionally comments on rejected mss.

How to Contact Send complete ms with SASE (1 story per submission). Responds in 4 months to mss. Accepts simultaneous submissions if noted. Sample copy for $8. Writer's guidelines online.

Payment/Terms Pays up to $100, copies, and a 1-year subscription. Pays on publication for first rights.

Advice "We look for attention to language, freshness, honesty, a convincing and sharp voice. Send us a clean, well-printed, proofread manuscript. Become familiar with the magazine prior to submission."

☐ ◎ BLUE MESA REVIEW

University of New Mexico, MSC03 2170, 1 University of New Mexico, Alburquerque NM 87131-0001. (505)277-6155. Fax: (505)277-5573. E-mail: bluemesa@unm.edu. Website: www.unm.edu/~bluemesa. **Contact:** Julie

Literary Magazines

Literary Magazines

Shigekuni. Magazine: 6×9; 300 pages; 55 lb. paper; 10 pt CS1 photos. *"Blue Mesa Review* publishes the best/most current creative writing on the market." Annual. Estab. 1989. Circ. 1,200.

Needs Adventure, ethnic/multicultural, experimental, feminist, gay, historical, humor/satire, lesbian, literary, mainstream, regional, western. Receives 25 unsolicited mss/month. Accepts 100 mss/year. Accepts mss July 1-October 1; all submissions must be post marked by October 1; reads mss November-December; responds in January. Publishes mss 5-6 months after acceptance. Recently published work by Kathleen Spivack, Roberta Swann and Tony Mares. Publishes short shorts. Also publishes literary essays, poetry.

How to Contact Send SASE for reply. Sample copy for $12. Writer's guidelines online. Reviews fiction.

Payment/Terms Pays 1 contributor's copy. Acquires first North American serial rights.

Advice "Contact us for complete guidelines. All submissions must follow our guidelines."

⊘ ◎ BLUELINE

125 Morey Hall, Department of English and Communication, SUNY Potsdam, Postdam NY 13676. (315)267-2043. E-mail: blueline@postdam.edu. Website: www.potsdam.edu/ENGL/Blueline/blue.html. **Contact:** Fiction Editor. Magazine: 6×9; 200 pages; 70 lb. white stock paper; 65 lb. smooth cover stock; illustrations; photos. *"Blueline* is interested in quality writing about the Adirondacks or other places similar in geography and spirit. We publish fiction, poetry, personal essays, book reviews and oral history for those interested in Adirondacks, nature in general, and well-crafted writing." Annual. Estab. 1979. Circ. 400.

Needs Adventure, humor/satire, literary, regional, contemporary, prose poem, reminiscences, oral history, nature/outdoors. No urban stories or erotica. Receives 8-10 unsolicited mss/month. Accepts 6-8 mss/issue. Does not read January-August. Publishes ms 3-6 after acceptance. **Publishes 2 new writers/year.** Recently published work by Joan Connor, Laura Rodley and Ann Mohin. Length: 500-3,000 words; average length: 2,500 words. Also publishes literary essays, poetry. Occasionally comments on rejected mss.

How to Contact Accepts simultaneous submissions. Sample copy for $6.

Payment/Terms Pays 1 contributor's copy; charges $7 each for 3 or more copies. Acquires first rights.

Advice "We look for concise, clear, concrete prose that tells a story and touches upon a universal theme or situation. We prefer realism to romanticism but will consider nostalgia if well done. Pay attention to grammar and syntax. Avoid murky language, sentimentality, cuteness or folkiness. We would like to see more good fiction related to the Adirondacks and more literary fiction and prose poems. If manuscript has potential, we work with author to improve and reconsider for publication. Our readers prefer fiction to poetry (in general) or reviews. Write from your own experience, be specific and factual (within the bounds of your story) and if you write about universal features such as love, death, change, etc., write about them in a fresh way. Triteness and mediocrity are the hallmarks of the majority of stories seen today."

⊘ BOGG, Journal of Contemporary Writing

Bogg Publications, 422 N. Cleveland St., Arlington VA 22201-1424. E-mail: boggmag@aol.com. **Contact:** John Elsberg, US editor. Magazine: 6×9; 56 pages; 70 lb. white paper; 70 lb. cover stock; line illustrations. "American and British poetry, prose poems, experimental short 'fictions,' reviews, and essays on small press." Published 2 or 3 times a year. Estab. 1968. Circ. 850.

Needs Very short experimental fiction and prose poems. "We are always looking for work with British/Commonwealth themes and/or references." Receives 25 unsolicited mss/month. Accepts 1-2 mss/issue; 3-6 mss/year. Publishes ms 3-18 after acceptance. **Publishes 25-50 new writers/year.** Recently published work by Linda Bosson, Brian Johnson, Pamela Gay, Art Stein and Hugh Fox. Also publishes literary essays, literary criticism. Occasionally comments on rejected mss.

How to Contact Responds in 1 week to queries; 2 weeks to mss. Sample copy for $4 or $5 (current issue). Reviews fiction.

Payment/Terms Pays 2 contributor's copies; reduced charge for extras. Acquires one-time rights.

Advice "We look for voice and originality. Read magazine first. We are most interested in prose work of experimental or wry nature to supplement poetry and are always looking for innovative/imaginative uses of British themes and references."

ℕ ◻ ⊛ BOOK WORLD MAGAZINE

Christ Church Publishers Ltd., 2 Caversham Street, London SW3 4AH United Kingdom. 0207 351 4995. Fax: 0207 3514995. E-mail: leonard.holdsworth@btopenworld.com. **Contact:** James Hughes. Magazine: 64 pages; illustrations; photos. "Subscription magazine for serious book lovers, book collectors, librarians and academics." Monthly. Estab. 1971. Circ. 6,000.

Needs Also publishes literary essays, literary criticism.

How to Contact Query. Send IRC (International Reply Coupon) for return of ms. Responds in 3 months to queries; 3 months to mss. Accepts simultaneous submissions. Sample copy for $7.50. Writer's guidelines for IRC.

Payment/Terms Pays on publication for one-time rights.

Advice "Always write to us before sending any mss."

$✍ BOULEVARD

Opojaz, Inc., 6614 Clayton Rd., PMB 325, Richmond Heights MO 63117. (314)862-2643. Fax: (314)862-2982. E-mail: ballymon@hotmail.com. Website: www.boulevardmagazine.com. **Contact:** Richard Burgin, editor. Magazine: $5^{1}/_{2} \times 8^{1}/_{2}$; 150-250 pages; excellent paper; high-quality cover stock; illustrations; photos. "*Boulevard* is a diverse literary magazine presenting original creative work by well-known authors, as well as by writers of exciting promise." Triannual. Estab. 1985. Circ. 11,000.

Needs Confessions, experimental, literary, mainstream, novel excerpts. "We do not want erotica, science fiction, romance, western or children's stories." Receives over 600 unsolicited mss/month. Accepts about 10 mss/issue. Does not accept manuscripts between May 1 and October 1. Publishes ms 9 months after acceptance. Agented fiction 25-33%. **Publishes 10 new writers/year.** Recently published work by Joyce Carol Oates, Floyd Skloot, Alice Hoffman, Stephen Dixon and Frederick Busch. Length: 9,000 words maximum; average length: 5,000 words. Publishes short shorts. Also publishes literary essays, literary criticism, poetry. Sometimes comments on rejected mss.

How to Contact Send complete ms. Accepts submissions by disk. Accepts mss on disk. SASE for reply. Responds in 2 weeks to queries; 3 months to mss. Accepts multiple submissions. No simultaneous submissions. Sample copy for $8. Writer's guidelines online.

Payment/Terms Pays $50-700. Pays on publication for first North American serial rights.

Advice "We pick the stories that move us the most emotionally, stimulate us the most intellectually, are the best written and thought out. Don't write to get published—write to express your experience and vision of the world."

✍ THE BRIAR CLIFF REVIEW

Briar Cliff University, 3303 Rebecca St., Sioux City IA 51104-0100. (712)279-5477. E-mail: curranst@briarcliff.edu. Website: www.briarcliff.edu/bcreview. **Contact:** Phil Hey or Tricia Currans-Sheehan, fiction editors. Magazine: $8^{1}/_{2} \times 11$; 88 pages; 70 lb. Finch Opaque cover stock; illustrations; photos. "*The Briar Cliff Review* is an eclectic literary and cultural magazine focusing on (but not limited to) Siouxland writers and subjects. We are happy to proclaim ourselves a regional publication. It doesn't diminish us; it enhances us." Annual. Estab. 1989. Circ. 750.

Needs Ethnic/multicultural, feminist, historical, humor/satire, literary, mainstream, regional. "No romance, horror or alien stories. Accepts 15 mss/year. Reads mss only between August 1 and November 1. Publishes ms 3-4 months after acceptance. **Publishes 10-14 new writers/year.** Recently published work by Jenna Blum, Brian Bedard, Constance Squires, Andrew Schultz, Paul Crenshaw and Josip Novakovich. Length: 2,500-5,000 words; average length: 3,000 words. Also publishes literary essays, literary criticism, poetry. Sometimes comments on rejected mss.

How to Contact Send SASE for return of ms. Accepts electronic submissions (disk). Responds in 4-5 months to mss. Accepts simultaneous submissions. Sample copy for $12 and 9×12 SAE. Writer's guidelines for #10 SASE. Reviews fiction.

Payment/Terms Pays 2 contributor's copies; additional copies available for $9. Acquires first rights.

Advice "So many stories are just telling. We want some action. It has to move. We prefer stories in which there is no gimmick, no mechanical turn of events, no moral except the one we would draw privately."

✍ BRILLANT CORNERS, A Journal of Jazz & Literature

Lycoming College, Williamsport PA 17701. (570)321-4279. Fax: (570)321-4090. E-mail: feinstei@lycoming.edu. **Contact:** Sascha Feinstein, editor. Journal: 6×9; 100 pages; 70 lb. Cougar opaque, vellum, natural paper; photographs. "We publish jazz-related literature—fiction, poetry and nonfiction." Semiannual. Estab. 1996. Circ. 1,200.

Needs Condensed novels, ethnic/multicultural, experimental, literary, mainstream, romance (contemporary). Receives 10-15 unsolicited mss/month. Accepts 1-2 mss/issue; 2-3 mss/year. Does not read mss May 15-September 1. Publishes ms 4-12 after acceptance. Publishes short shorts. Also publishes literary essays, literary criticism, poetry. Rarely comments on rejected mss.

How to Contact SASE for return of ms or send a disposable copy of ms. Accepts unpublished work only. Responds in 2 weeks to queries; 1-2 months to mss. Sample copy for $7. Reviews fiction.

Payment/Terms Acquires first North American serial rights, sends galleys to author when possible.

Advice "We look for clear, moving prose that demonstrates a love of both writing and jazz. We primarily publish established writers, but we read all submissions carefully and welcome work by outstanding young writers."

BRYANT LITERARY REVIEW

Bryant University, 1150 Douglas Pike, Faculty Suite F, Smithfield RI 02917. (401)232-6802. Fax: (401)232-6270. E-mail: blr@bryant.edu. Website: http://web.bryant.edu/ ~ blr. **Contact:** M.J. Kim. Magazine: 6×9; 125 pages; photos. Annual. Estab. 2000. Circ. 2,400. CLMP.

Needs Adventure, ethnic/multicultural, experimental, family saga, fantasy, feminist, historical, humor/satire, literary, mainstream, military/war, mystery/suspense, New Age, psychic/supernatural/occult, regional, science fiction, thriller/espionage, translations, western. "No novellas or serialized novels; only short stories." Receives 100 unsolicited mss/month. Accepts approx. 7 mss/issue. Does not read January through August. Publishes ms 4-5 months after acceptance. **Publishes 1-2 new writers/year.** Recently published work by Lyzette Wanzer, K.S. Phillips and Richard N. Bentley. Publishes short shorts. Also publishes poetry.

How to Contact Send a disposable copy of ms and #10 SASE for reply only. Responds in 2 weeks to queries; 12 weeks to mss. No simultaneous submissions. Sample copy for $8. Writer's guidelines by e-mail or on website.

Payment/Terms Pays 2 contributor's copies; additional copies $8. Pays on publication.

$ BYLINE

Box 5240, Edmond OK 73083-5240. (405)348-5591. E-mail: mpreston@bylinemag.com. Website: www.bylinemag.com. **Contact:** Marcia Preston, fiction editor. Magazine "aimed at encouraging and motivating all writers toward success, with special information to help new writers. Articles center on how to write better, market smarter, sell your work." Monthly. Estab. 1981.

Needs Literary, genre, general fiction. "Does not want to see erotica or explicit graphic content. No science fiction or fantasy." Receives 100-200 unsolicited mss/month. Accepts 1 mss/issue; 11 mss/year. Publishes ms 3 months after acceptance. **Publishes many new writers/year.** Recently published work by Connie Harrington, Leann Keenan and Jimmy Caral Harris. Also publishes poetry.

How to Contact No cover letter needed. Responds in 6-12 weeks to mss. Accepts simultaneous submissions "if notified." Writer's guidelines for #10 SASE or online.

Payment/Terms Pays $100 and 3 contributor's copies. Pays on acceptance for first North American serial rights.

Advice "We look for good writing that draws the reader in; conflict and character movement by story's end. We're very open to new writers. Submit a well-written, professionally prepared ms with SASE. No erotica or senseless violence; otherwise, we'll consider most any theme. We also sponsor short story and poetry contests. Read what's being published. Find a good story, not just a narrative reflection. Keep submitting."

CALLALOO, A Journal of African-American and African Diaspora Arts and Letters

Dept. of English, TAMU 4227, Texas A&M University, College Station TX 77843-4227. (979)458-3108. Fax: (979)458-3275. E-mail: callaloo@tamu.edu. Website: http://xroads.virginia.edu/ ~ public/callaloo/home/calla loohome.htm. **Contact:** Charles H. Rowell, editor. Magazine: 7×10; 250 pages. "Devoted to publishing fiction, poetry, drama of the African diaspora, including North, Central and South America, the Caribbean, Europe and Africa. Visually beautiful and well edited, the journal publishes 3-5 short stories in all forms and styles in each issue." Quarterly. Estab. 1976. Circ. 2,000.

• One of the leading voices in African-American literature, *Callaloo* has recieved NEA literature grants. Several pieces every year are chosen for collections of the year's best stories, such as *Beacon's Best*. John Wideman's "Weight" from *Callaloo* won the 2000 O. Henry Award.

Needs Ethnic/multicultural (black culture), feminist, historical, humor/satire, literary, regional, science fiction, serialized novels, translations, contemporary, prose poem. "No romance, confessional. Would like to see more experimental fiction, science fiction and well-crafted literary fiction particularly dealing with the black middle class, immigrant communities and/or the black South." Accepts 3-5 mss/issue; 10-20 mss/year. **Publishes 5-10 new writers/year.** Recently published work by Charles Johnson, Edwidge Danticat, Thomas Glave, Nallo Hopkinson, John Edgar Wideman, Jamaica Kincaid, Percival Everett and Patricia Powell. Also publishes poetry.

How to Contact Generally accepts unpublished work, rarely accepts reprints. Responds in 2 weeks to queries; 6 months to mss. Accepts multiple submissions. Sample copy for $12. Writer's guidelines online.

Payment/Terms Pays in contributor's copies. Acquires some rights. Sends galleys to author.

Advice "We look for freshness of both writing and plot, strength of characterization, plausibilty of plot. Read what's being written and published, especially in journals such as *Callaloo*."

CALYX, A Journal of Art & Literature by Women

Calyx, Inc., P.O. Box B, Corvallis OR 97339. (541)753-9384. Fax: (541)753-0515. E-mail: calyx@proaxis.com. Website: www.proaxis.com/ ~ calyx. **Contact:** Editor. Magazine: 6×8; 128 pages per single issue; 60 lb. coated matte stock paper; 10 pt. chrome coat cover; original art. Publishes prose, poetry, art, essays, interviews and critical and review articles. "*Calyx* exists to publish fine literature and art by women and is committed to publishing the work of all women, including women of color, older women, working class women and other voices that need to be heard. We are committed to discovering and nurturing beginning writers." Biannual. Estab. 1976. Circ. 6,000.

Needs Receives approximately 1,000 unsolicited prose and poetry mss when open. Accepts 4-8 prose mss/ issue; 9-15 mss/year. Reads mss October 1-December 31; submit only during this period. Mss received when not reading will be returned. Publishes ms 4-12 months after acceptance. **Publishes 10-20 new writers/year.** Recently published work by M. Evelina Galang, Chitrita Banerji, Diana Ma and Catherine Brady. Also publishes literary essays, literary criticism, poetry.

How to Contact Responds in 4-12 months to mss. Accepts simultaneous submissions. Sample copy for $9.50 plus $2 postage. SASE. Reviews fiction.

Payment/Terms "Combination of free issues and 1 volume subscription.

Advice Most mss are rejected because "The writers are not familiar with *Calyx*. Writers should read *Calyx* and be familar with the publication. We look for good writing, imagination and important/interesting subject matter."

$ THE CAPILANO REVIEW

2055 Purcell Way, North Vancouver BC V7J 3H5 Canada. Website: www.capcollege.bc.ca/about/publications/ capilano-review/tcr/index.html. Magazine: 6×9; 90-120 pages; book paper; glossy cover; perfect-bound; visual art. "Triannual visual and literary arts magazine that publishes only what the editors consider to be the very best fiction, poetry, drama or visual art being produced. *TCR* editors are interested in fresh, original work that stimulates and challenges readers. Over the years, the magazine has developed a reputation for pushing beyond the boundaries of traditional art and writing. We are interested in work that is new in concept and in execution." Estab. 1972. Circ. 900.

Needs Experimental, novel excerpts (previously unpublished only), literary. "No traditional, conventional fiction. Want to see more innovative, genre-blurring work." Receives 80 unsolicited mss/month. Accepts 1 mss/ issue; 3-5 mss/year. Publishes ms 2-4 months after acceptance. **Publishes some new writers/year.** Recently published work by Michael Turner, Lewis Buzbee and George Bowering. Also publishes literary essays, poetry.

How to Contact Include 2- to 3-sentence bio and brief list of publications. Send Canadian SASE or IRCs for reply of ms. Responds in 1 month to queries; 4 months to mss. No simultaneous submissions. Sample copy for $9. Writer's guidelines for #10 SASE with IRC or Canadian stamps or online.

Payment/Terms Pays $50-200. Pays on publication for first North American serial rights.

Advice "Do not send conventional realist fiction. Read the magazine before submitting and ensure your work is technically perfect."

THE CARIBBEAN WRITER

The University of the Virgin Islands, RR 02, Box 10,000-Kinghill, St. Croix Virgin Islands 00850. (340)692-4152. Fax: (340)692-4026. E-mail: qmars@uvi.edu. Website: www.CaribbeanWriter.com. **Contact:** Quilin B. Mars, managing editor. Magazine: 6×9; 304 pages; 60 lb. paper; glossy cover stock; illustrations; photos. "*The Caribbean Writer* is an international magazine with a Caribbean focus. The Caribbean should be central to the work, or the work should reflect a Caribbean heritage, experience or perspective." Annual. Estab. 1987. Circ. 1,500.

● Work published in *The Caribbean Writer* has received a Pushcart Prize and Quenepon Award.

Needs Historical (general), humor/satire, literary, mainstream, translations, contemporary and prose poem. Receives 65 unsolicited mss/month. Accepts 60 mss/issue. **Publishes approximately 20% new writers/year.** Recently published work by Cecil Gray, Virgil Suarez and Opal Palmer Adisa. Also publishes literary essays, poetry.

How to Contact Accepts submissions by e-mail. "Blind submissions only. Send name, address and title of manuscript on separate sheet. Title only on manuscript. Manuscripts will not be returned unless this procedure is followed." SASE (or IRC). Accepts simultaneous, multiple submissions. Sample copy for $7 and $4 postage.

Payment/Terms Pays 2 contributor's copies. Annual prizes for best story ($400); for best poem ($300); $200 for first-time publication; best work by Caribbean Author ($500); best work by Virgin Islands author ($200). Acquires one-time rights.

Advice Looks for "work which reflects a Caribbean heritage, experience or perspective."

CAROLINA QUARTERLY

Greenlaw Hall CB #3520, University of North Carolina, Chapel Hill NC 27599-3520. (919)962-0244. Fax: (919)962-3520. E-mail: cquarter@unc.edu. Website: www.unc.edu/depts/cqonline. **Contact:** Tessa Joseph, editor-in-chief. Literary journal: 80-100 pages; illustrations. Publishes fiction for a "general literary audience." Triannual. Estab. 1948. Circ. 900-1,000.

● Work published in *Carolina Quarterly* has been selected for inclusion in *Best American Short Stories* and *New Stories from the South: The Year's Best.*

Needs Literary. "We would like to see more short/micro-fiction and more stories by minority/ethnic writers."

Literary Magazines

Receives 150-200 unsolicited mss/month. Accepts 4-5 mss/issue; 14-16 mss/year. Does not read mss May-August. Publishes ms 4 months after acceptance. **Publishes 5-6 new writers/year.** Recently published work by Pam Durban, Elizabeth Spencer, Brad Vice, Wendy Brenner and Nanci Kincaid. Publishes short shorts. Also publishes literary essays, poetry. Occasionally comments on rejected mss.

How to Contact Responds in 3 months to queries; 6 months to mss. No simultaneous submissions. Sample copy for $6. Writer's guidelines for SASE.

Payment/Terms Pays in contributor's copies. Acquires first rights.

⬛ CENTER, A Journal of the Literary Arts

University of Missouri, 202 Tate Hall, Columbia MO 65211. (573)882-4971. E-mail: cla@missouri.edu. Website: www.missouri.edu/~center. **Contact:** Fiction editor. Magazine: 6×9; 125-200 pages; perfect bound, with 4-color card cover. *Center's* goal is to publish the best in literary fiction, poetry and creative nonfiction by previously unpublished and emerging writers, as well as more established writers. Annual. Estab. 2000. Circ. 500.

Needs Ethnic/multicultural, experimental, humor/satire, literary. Receives 30-50 unsolicited mss/month. Accepts 3-5 mss/year. Reads mss from July 1-December 1 only. Publishes ms 6 months after acceptance. **Publishes 25% new writers/year.** Recently published work by Lisa Glatt and Robert Root. Publishes short shorts. Also publishes literary essays, poetry. Sometimes comments on rejected mss.

How to Contact Send SASE (or IRC) for return of ms or send a disposable copy of ms and #10 SASE for reply only. Responds in 1 month to queries; 3-4 months to mss. Accepts simultaneous, multiple submissions. Sample copy for $3, current copy $6. Writer's guidelines for SASE.

Payment/Terms Pays 1 contributor's copy; additional copies $3. Pays on publication for one-time rights.

⬛ CHAFFIN JOURNAL

English Department, Eastern Kentucky University, Case Annex 467, Richmond KY 40475-3102. (859)622-3080. E-mail: robert.witt@eku.edu. Website: www.english.eku.edu/chaffin_journal. **Contact:** Robert Witt, editor. Magazine: 8×5½; 120-130 pages; 70 lb. paper; 80 lb. cover. "We publish fiction on any subject; our only consideration is the quality." Annual. Estab. 1998. Circ. 150.

Needs Ethnic/multicultural, historical, humor/satire, literary, mainstream, regional (Appalachia). "No erotica, fantasy." Receives 20 unsolicited mss/month. Accepts 6-8 mss/year. Does not read mss October 1 through May 31. Publishes ms 6 months after acceptance. **Publishes 2-3 new writers/year.** Recently published work by Meridith Sue Willis, Marie Manilla, Raymond Abbott, Marjorie Bixler and Chris Helvey. Length: 10,000 words; average length: 5,000 words.

How to Contact Send SASE for return of ms. Responds in 1 week to queries; 3 months to mss. Accepts simultaneous, multiple submissions. Sample copy for $6. Writer's guidelines for SASE, by e-mail or online.

Payment/Terms Pays 1 contributor's copy; additional copies $6. Pays on publication for one-time rights.

Advice "All manuscripts submitted are considered."

N: ⬛ CHAPMAN

Chapman Publishing, 4 Broughton Place, Edinburgh EH1 3RX Scotland. (+44)131 557 2207. Fax: (+44)131 556 9565. E-mail: chapman-pub@blueyounder.co.uk. Website: www.chapman-pub.co.uk. **Contact:** Joy Hendry, fiction editor. "*Chapman*, Scotland's quality literary magazine, is a dynamic force in Scotland, publishing poetry, fiction, criticism, reviews; articles on theatre, politics, language and the arts. Our philosophy is to publish new work, from known and unknown writers, mainly Scottish, but also worldwide." Quarterly. Estab. 1970. Circ. 2,000.

Needs Experimental, historical, humor/satire, literary, Scottish/ international. "No horror, science fiction." Accepts 4-6 mss/issue. Publishes ms 3 months after acceptance. **Publishes 50 new writers/year.**

How to Contact No simultaneous submissions. Writer's guidelines by e-mail.

Payment/Terms Pays by negotiation. Pays on publication for first rights.

Advice "Keep your stories for six months and edit carefully. We seek challenging work which attempts to explore difficult/new territory in content and form, but lighter work, if original enough, is welcome."

$⬛ THE CHARITON REVIEW

English Dept., Brigham Young University, Provo UT 84602. (660)785-4499. Fax: (660)785-7486. **Contact:** Jim Barnes. Magazine: 6×9; approximately 100 pages; 60 lb. paper; 65 lb. cover stock; photographs on cover. "We demand only excellence in fiction and fiction translation for a general and college readership." Estab. 1975. Circ. 600.

Needs Ethnic/multicultural, experimental, literary, mainstream, novel excerpts (if they can stand alone), translations, traditional. "We are not interested in slick or sick material." Accepts 3-5 mss/issue; 6-10 mss/year. Publishes ms 6 months after acceptance. **Publishes some new writers/year.** Recently published work by Ann

Townsend, Glenn DelGrosso, Paul Ruffin and X.J. Kennedy. Also publishes literary essays, poetry. Sometimes comments on rejected mss.

How to Contact Send complete ms. No book-length mss. Responds in 1 week to queries; 1 month to mss. No simultaneous submissions. Sample copy for $5 and 7x10 SAE with 4 first-class stamps. Reviews fiction.

Payment/Terms Pays $5/page (up to $50). Pays on publication for first North American serial rights.

Advice "Do not ask us for guidelines; the only guidelines are excellence in all matters. Write well and study the publication you are submitting to. We are interested only in the very best fiction and fiction translation. We are not interested in slick material. We do not read photocopies, dot-matrix, or carbon copies. Know the simple mechanics of submission—SASE, no paper clips, no odd-sized SASE, etc. Know the genre (short story, novella, etc.). Know the unwritten laws. There is too much manufactured fiction; assembly-lined, ego-centered personal essays offered as fiction."

$⬛ ⬛ THE CHATTAHOOCHEE REVIEW

Georgia Perimeter College, 2101 Womack Rd., Dunwoody GA 30338-4497. (770)551-3019. Website: www.chattahoochee-review.org. **Contact:** Lawrence Hetrick, editor. Magazine: 6×9; 150 pages; 70 lb. paper; 80 lb. cover stock; illustrations; photos. "We publish a number of Southern writers, but *Chattahoochee Review* is not by design a regional magazine. All themes, forms and styles are considered as long as they impact the whole person: heart, mind, intuition and imagination." Quarterly. Estab. 1980. Circ. 1,350.

• Fiction from *The Chattahoochee Review* has been included in *New Stories from the South* and was a 2003 winner of a Governor's Award in Humanities.

Needs "No juvenile, romance, science fiction." Accepts 5 mss/issue. Does not read ms June 1-August 31. Publishes ms 3 months after acceptance. **Publishes 5 new writers/year.** Recently published work by Philip Lee Williams, Martin Lammon, Mary Ann Taylor-Hall, Anthony Grooms and Greg Johnson. Length: 6,000 words maximum; average length: 2,500 words. Sometimes comments on rejected mss.

How to Contact Send complete ms. SASE. Responds in 2 weeks to queries; 4 months to mss. Accepts simultaneous submissions. Sample copy for $6. Writer's guidelines online. Reviews fiction.

Payment/Terms Pays $20/page, $250 max and 2 contributor's copies. Pays on publication for first rights.

Advice "Arrange to read magazine before you submit to it."

CHELSEA

Chelsea Associates, P.O. Box 773 Cooper Station, New York NY 10276-0773. "We stress style, variety, originality. No special biases or requirements. Flexible attitudes, eclectic material. We take an active interest, as always, in cross-cultural exchanges and superior translations, and are leaning toward cosmopolitan, interdisciplinary techniques, but maintain no strictures against traditional modes." Semiannual. Estab. 1958. Circ. 2,200.

Needs Mainstream, novel excerpts, literary. Publishes ms 6 months after acceptance.

How to Contact Send complete ms. Responds in 3-5 months to mss. Sample copy for $6. Writer's guidelines and contest guidelines available for #10 SASE.

Payment/Terms Pays $15/page. Pays on publication for first North American serial rights.

⬛ CHICAGO QUARTERLY REVIEW

Monadnock Group Publishers, 517 Sherman Ave., Evanston IL 60202-2815. (719)633-9794. E-mail: lawlaw58@aol.com. **Contact:** Syed Haider, Jane Lawrence and Lisa McKenaie, editors. Magazine: 6×9; 125 pages; illustrations; photos. Annual. Estab. 1994. Circ. 300.

Needs Literary. Receives 20-30 unsolicited mss/month. Accepts 6-8 mss/issue; 8-16 mss/year. Reading period September-February. Does not read March-August. Publishes ms 1 year after acceptance. Agented fiction 10%. **Publishes 3 new writers/year.** Length: 5,000 words; average length: 2,500 words. Publishes short shorts. Also publishes literary essays, poetry. Sometimes comments on rejected mss.

How to Contact Send a disposable copy of ms and #10 SASE for reply only. Responds in 2 months to queries; 6 months to mss. Accepts simultaneous submissions. Sample copy for $9.

Payment/Terms Pays 1 contributor's copy; additional copies $6. Pays on publication for one-time rights.

Advice "The writer's voice ought to be clear and unique and should explain something of what it means to be human. We want well-written stories that reflect an appreciation for the rhythm and music of language; work that shows passion and commitment to the art of writing."

⬛ ⬛ CHICAGO REVIEW

5801 S. Kenwood Ave., Chicago IL 60637. (773)702-0887. E-mail: chicago-review@uchicago.edu. Website: humanities.uchicago.edu/orgs/review. **Contact:** Joshua Kotin, editor. Magazine for a highly literate general audience: 6×9; 128 pages; offset white 60 lb. paper; illustrations; photos. Quarterly. Estab. 1946. Circ. 3,500.

Needs Experimental, literary, contemporary. Receives 200 unsolicited mss/month. Accepts 2 mss/issue; 8 mss/

Literary Magazines

year. Recently published work by Harry Mathews, Tom House, Viet Dinh and Doris Dörrie. Also publishes literary essays, literary criticism, poetry.
How to Contact SASE. Responds in 2-4 months to mss. No simultaneous submissions. Sample copy for $10. Guidelines via website or SASE.
Payment/Terms Pays 3 contributor's copies and subscription.
Advice "We look for innovative fiction that avoids cliché."

CIMARRON REVIEW

Oklahoma State University, 205 Morrill Hall, OSU, Stillwater OK 74078-0135. (405)744-9476. Website: cimarronr eview.okstate.edu. **Contact:** Toni Graham, Andrea Koenig, fiction editors. Magazine: 6×9; 110 pages. "Poetry and fiction on contemporary themes; personal essays on contemporary issues that cope with life in the 20th and 21st century. We are eager to receive manuscripts from both established and less experienced writers who intrigue us with their unusual perspective, language, imagery and character." Quarterly. Estab. 1967. Circ. 600.
Needs Literary-quality short stories and novel excerpts. No juvenile or genre fiction. Accepts 3-5 mss/issue; 12-15 mss/year. Publishes ms 2-6 months after acceptance. **Publishes 2-4 new writers/year.** Recently published work by Adam Braver, Gary Fincke, Catherine Brady, Nona Caspers and David Ryan. Also publishes literary essays, literary criticism, poetry.
How to Contact Send complete ms. SASE. Responds in 2-6 months to mss. Accepts simultaneous submissions. Sample copy for $7. Reviews fiction.
Payment/Terms Pays 2 contributor's copies plus a year's subscription. Acquires first North American serial rights.
Advice "In order to get a feel for the kind of work we publish, please read an issue or two before submitting."

THE CINCINNATI REVIEW

P.O. Box 210069, Cincinnati OH 45221-0069. (513)556-3954. E-mail: editors@cincinnatireview.com. Website: www.cincinnatireview.com. **Contact:** Brock Clarke, fiction editor. Magazine: 6×9; 180-200 pages; 50 lb. Glatfelter antique paper. "A journal devoted to publishing the best new literary fiction and poetry as well as book reviews, essays and interviews." Semiannual. Estab. 2003.
Needs Literary. Does not want genre fiction. Accepts 13 mss/year. Reads submissins September 1-May 31. Word length should be under 40 double-spaced pages.
How to Contact Send complete ms. Include name and contact info at beginning of work. Send SASE. Responds in 2 weeks to queries; 1 month to mss. Accepts simultaneous submissions with notice. Sample copy for $7, subscription $12. Writer's guidelines online, or by e-mail.
Payment/Terms Pays $25/page. Pays on publication for first North American serial, electronic rights. All rights revert to author upon publication.

THE CLAREMONT REVIEW, The Contemporary Magazine of Young Adult Writers

The Claremont Review Publishers, 4980 Wesley Rd., Victoria British Columbia V8Y 1Y9. (250)658-5221. Fax: (250)658-5387. E-mail: editor@theClaremontReview.ca. Website: www.theClaremontReview.ca. **Contact:** Susan Field (business manager), Janice McCachen, editors. Magazine: 6×9; 110-120 pages; book paper; soft gloss cover; b&w illustrations. "We are dedicated to publishing emerging young writers aged 13-19 from anywhere in the English-speaking world, but primarily Canada and the U.S." Biannual. Estab. 1992. Circ. 700.
Needs Young adult/teen ("their writing, not writing for them"). "No science fiction, fanatasy." Receives 20-30 unsolicited mss/month. Accepts 10-12 mss/issue; 20-24 mss/year. Publishes ms 3 months after acceptance. **Publishes 100 new writers/year.** Recently published work by Alissan Chan, Laura Ishiguro and Jason Tsai. Length: 5,000 words; average length: 1,500-3,000 words. Publishes short shorts. Also publishes poetry. Always comments on rejected mss.
How to Contact Responds in 3 months to mss. Accepts multiple submissions. Sample copy for $10.
Payment/Terms Pays 1 contributor's copy. Additional copies for $6. Acquires first North American serial, one-time rights. Sponsors awards/contests.
Advice Looking for "good concrete narratives with credible dialogue and solid use of original detail. It must be unique, honest and a glimpse of some truth. Send an error-free final draft with a short cover letter and bio. Read us first to see what we publish."

COLORADO REVIEW

Center for Literary Publishing, Department of English, Colorado State University, Fort Collins CO 80523. (970)491-5449. E-mail: creview@colostate.edu. Website: http://coloradoreview.colostate.edu. **Contact:** Stephanie G'Schwind, editor. Literary journal: 224 pages; 60 lb. book weight paper. Estab. 1956. Circ. 1,300.
Needs Ethnic/multicultural, experimental, literary, mainstream, contemporary. "No genre fiction." Receives 600 unsolicited mss/month. Accepts 4-5 mss/issue. Does not read mss May-August. Publishes ms within 1 year

after acceptance. Recently published work by Robert Boswell, Kent Haruf, Jonis Agee and Jacob Appel. Also publishes poetry.

How to Contact Send complete ms. Responds in 2 months to mss. Sample copy for $10. Writer's guidelines online. Reviews fiction.

Payment/Terms Pays $5/page plus two contributor's copies. Pays on publication for first North American serial rights. Rights revert to author upon publication. Sends galleys to author.

Advice "We are interested in manuscripts that show craft, imagination and a convincing voice. If a story has reached a level of technical competence, we are receptive to the fiction working on its own terms. The oldest advice is still the best: persistence. Approach every aspect of the writing process with pride, conscientiousness— from word choice to manuscript appearance. Be familiar with the *Colorado Review*; read a couple of issues before submitting your manuscript."

COLUMBIA, A Journal of Literature and Art

415 Dodge Hall, New York NY 10027. Fax: (212)854-7704. E-mail: columbiajournal@columbia.edu. Website: www.columbia.edu/cu/arts/journal. **Contact:** Editor-in-Chief. Magazine: 6×9; 176 pages; glossy cover; illustrations; photos. "We publish the very best contemporary poetry, fiction and creative nonfiction from emerging and established writers." Annual. Estab. 1977. Circ. 2,000.

Needs Ethnic/multicultural, experimental, historical, humor/satire, literary, translations. "We are not interested in children's literature or genre pieces, unless they can be considered to transcend the genre and be of interest to the general reader." Receives 50+ unsolicited mss/month. Publishes ms 1-12 months after acceptance. Agented fiction 70%. **Publishes 2-4 new writers/year.** Recently published work by Gary Lutz, Mary Gordon, Jonathan Lethem and Jonathan Safran Foer. Length: 5,000 words; average length: 3,000 words. Publishes short shorts. Rarely comments on rejected mss.

How to Contact Send complete ms. Responds in 3 months to queries. Accepts simultaneous, multiple submissions. Sample copy for $8. Writer's guidelines online.

Payment/Terms Acquires first North American serial rights. Sponsors awards/contests.

N CONCHO RIVER REVIEW

Angelo State University, English Dept., Box 10894 ASU Station, San Angelo TX 76904. (325)942-2269, ext. 230. Fax: (325)942-2208. E-mail: me.hartje@angelo.edu. **Contact:** Charlie McMurtry, fiction editor. Magazine: 6½×9; 100-125 pages; 60 lb. Ardor offset paper; Classic Laid Color cover stock; b&w drawings. "We publish any fiction of high quality—no thematic specialties." Semiannual. Estab. 1987. Circ. 300.

Needs Ethnic/multicultural, historical, humor/satire, literary, regional, western. Also publishes poetry, nonfiction, book reviews. "No erotica; no science fiction." Receives 10-15 unsolicited mss/month. Accepts 3-6 mss/issue; 8-10 mss/year. Publishes ms 4-6 months after acceptance. **Publishes 4 new writers/year.** Recently published work by Gordon Alexander, Riley Froh, Gretchen Geralds and Kimberly Willis Holt. Length: 1,500-5,000 words; average length: 3,500 words.

How to Contact Send disk copy upon acceptance. Responds in 3 weeks to queries. Accepts simultaneous submissions (if noted). Sample copy for $4. Writer's guidelines for #10 SASE. Reviews fiction.

Payment/Terms Pays in contributor's copies; $5 charge for extras. Acquires first rights.

Advice "We prefer a clear sense of conflict, strong characterization and effective dialogue."

CONFLUENCE

Ohio Valley Literary Group Inc., P.O. Box 336, Belpre OH 45714-0336. (304)295-6599. E-mail: confluence1989@ yahoo.com. Website: www.marietta.edu/%7Eengl/confluence.html. **Contact:** Dr. Beverly Hogue or Sandra Tritt. Magazine: 6×9; 128 pages; 60 lb. paper; card stock cover; illustrations. "We publish quality short stories, essays and poetry in collabroration with Marietta College." Annual. Estab. 1989. Circ. 1,000.

Needs Ethnic/multicultural, literary, mainstream, regional. "No children's/juvenile or young adult." Receives 12 unsolicited mss/month. Accepts 4 mss/year. "We'd accept more if we recieved more quality fiction." Does not read mss February through August. Publishes ms 9 months after acceptance. **Publishes 6 new writers/year.** Recently published work by T.M. Bemis, Deidre Woolard and Pearl Cannick Solomon. Length: 5,000 words; average length: 3,000 words. Publishes short shorts. Also publishes literary essays, poetry. Often comments on rejected mss.

How to Contact Send SASE for reply, return of ms or send disposable copy of ms. Responds in 3 weeks to queries; 7 months to mss. Sample copy for $6.50. Writer's guidelines for SASE or by e-mail.

Payment/Terms Pays 3 contributor's copies; additional copies $4.50. Pays on publication for one-time rights. Sponsors awards/contests.

Advice "We consider overall quality. We look for well-rounded characters, consistent point of view, precise wording, setting integrated into plot, dialogue that moves the plot forward, and so on. Read current short stories, avoid clichés and passive voice, and join a critique group which offers honest evaluation."

Literary Magazines

☐ ☒ CONFRONTATION, A Literary Journal

Long Island University, Brookville NY 11548. (516)299-2720. Fax: (516)299-2735. **Contact:** Jonna Semeiks. Magazine: 6×9; 250-350 pages; 70 lb. paper; 80 lb. cover; illustrations; photos. "We are eclectic in our taste. Excellence of style is our dominant concern." Semiannual. Estab. 1968. Circ. 2,000.

- *Confrontation* has garnered a long list of awards and honors, including the Editor's Award for Distinguished Achievement from CCLP and NEA grants. Work from the magazine has appeared in numerous anthologies including the *Pushcart Prize, Best Short Stories* and *O. Henry Prize Stories.*

Needs Experimental, literary, mainstream, novel excerpts (if they are self -contained stories), regional, slice-of-life vignettes, contemporary, prose poem. "No 'proselytizing' literature or genre fiction." Receives 400 unsolicited mss/month. Accepts 30 mss/issue; 60 mss/year. Does not read June-September. Publishes ms 6 months after acceptance. Agented fiction approximately 10-15%. **Publishes 20-30 new writers/year.** Recently published work by Susan Vreeland, Lanford Wilson, Tom Stacey, Elizabeth Swados and Sallie Bingham. Publishes short shorts. Also publishes literary essays, poetry.

How to Contact Send complete ms. Accepts submissions by disk. "Cover letters acceptable, not necessary. We accept simultaneous submissions but do not prefer them." Accepts diskettes if accompanied by computer printout submissions. Responds in 3 weeks to queries; 2 months to mss. Accepts simultaneous submissions. Sample copy for $3. Writer's guidelines not available. Reviews fiction.

Payment/Terms Pays $25-250. Pays on publication for first North American serial, first, one-time rights.

Advice "We look for literary merit. Keep trying."

☑ ☒ CONNECTICUT REVIEW

Connecticut State University System, 39 Woodland St., Hartford CT 06105-2337. (203)392-6737. Fax: (203)248-5007. E-mail: ctreview@southernct.edu. **Contact:** John Briggs, senior editor. Magazine: 6×9; 208 pages; white/heavy paper; glossy/heavy cover; color and b&w illustrations and photos; artwork. "*Connecticut Review* presents a wide range of cultural interests that cross disciplinary lines. The editors invite the submission of academic articles of general interest, thesis-oriented essays, translations, short stories, plays, poems and interviews." Semiannual. Estab. 1968. Circ. 4,000. CELJ, CLMJ.

- Work published in *Connecticut Review* has won the *Pushcart Prize* and inclusion in *Best American Poetry, Best American Short Stories 2000. CR* has also recieved the Phoenix Award for Significant Editorial Achievement and 2001 National Public Radio's Award for Literary Excellence.

Needs Literary. "Content must be under 4,000 words and suitable for circulation to libraries and high schools." Receives 250 unsolicited mss/month. Accepts 6 mss/issue; 12 mss/year. Does not read mss June-August. Publishes ms 1 year after acceptance. **Publishes 6-8 new writers/year.** Recently published work by John Searles, Michael Schiavone, Norman German, Tom Williams and Paul Ruffin. Publishes short shorts. Also publishes literary essays, poetry.

How to Contact Send two disposable copies of ms and #10 SASE for reply only. Responds in 4 months to queries. Accepts simultaneous submissions. Sample copy for $8. Writer's guidelines for SASE.

Payment/Terms Pays 2 contributor's copies; additional copies $6. Pays on publication for first rights. Rights revert to author on publication. Sends galleys to author.

☑ CONVERGENCE

P.O. Box 1127, Magalia CA 95954. E-mail: editor@convergence-journal.com. Website: www.convergence-journ al.com. **Contact:** Lara Gularte, editor. *Convergence* seeks to unify the literary and visual arts and draw new interpretations of the written word by pairing poems and flash fiction with complementary art. Quarterly. Estab. 2003. Circ. 400.

Needs Ethnic/multicultural, experimental, feminist, gay, lesbian, literary, regional, translations. Accepts 10 mss/issue. Publishes ms 3 weeks after acceptance. Recently published work by Andrena Zawinski, Grace Cavalieri, Lola Haskins, Molly Fisk and Renato Rosaldo. Publishes short shorts. Also publishes poetry. Sometimes comments on rejected mss.

How to Contact Send complete ms. E-mail submissions only. Responds in 2 weeks to queries; 4 months to mss. Accepts reprints, multiple submissions. Writer's guidelines online.

Payment/Terms Acquires electronic rights.

Advice "We look for freshness and originality and a mastery of the craft of flash fiction."

☑ COTTONWOOD

Box J, 400 Kansas Union, University of Kansas, Lawrence KS 66045-2115. (785)864-2516. Fax: (785)864-4298. E-mail: tlorenz@ku.edu. **Contact:** Tom Lorenz, fiction editor. Magazine: 6×9; 100 pages; illustrations; photos. "*Cottonwood* publishes high quality prose, poetry and artwork and is aimed at an audience that appreciates the same. We have a national scope and reputation while maintaining a strong regional flavor." Semiannual. Estab. 1965. Circ. 500.

Needs "We publish literary prose and poetry." Receives 25-50 unsolicited mss/month. Accepts 5-6 mss/issue; 10-12 mss/year. Publishes ms 6-18 months after acceptance. Agented fiction 10%. **Publishes 1-3 new writers/ year.** Recently published work by Connie May Fowler, Oakley Hall and Cris Mazza. Length: 1,000-8,000 words; average length: 2,000-5,000 words. Publishes short shorts. Also publishes literary essays, literary criticism, poetry.

How to Contact SASE for return of ms. Responds in 6 months to mss. Accepts simultaneous submissions. Sample copy for $8.50, 9×12 SAE and $1.90. Reviews fiction.

Payment/Terms Acquires one-time rights.

Advice "We're looking for depth and/or originality of subject matter, engaging voice and style, emotional honesty, command of the material and the structure. *Cottonwood* publishes high quality literary fiction, but we are very open to the work of talented new writers. Write something honest and that you care about and write it as well as you can. Don't hesitate to keep trying us. We sometimes take a piece from a writer we've rejected a number of times. We generally don't like clever, gimmicky writing. The style should be engaging but not claim all the the attention itself."

$◨ ◪ CRAB ORCHARD REVIEW, A Journal of Creative Works

Southern Illinois University at Carbondale, English Department, Faner Hall, Carbondale IL 62901-4503. (618)453-6833. Fax: (618)453-8224. Website: www.siu.edu/~crborchd. **Contact:** Jon Tribble, managing editor. Magazine: 5½×8½; 275 pages; 55 lb. recycled paper, card cover; photo on cover. "We are a general interest literary journal published twice/year. We strive to be a journal that writers admire and readers enjoy. We publish fiction, poetry, creative nonfiction, fiction translations, interviews and reviews." Estab. 1995. Circ. 2,500.

• *Crab Orchard Review* has won an Illinois Arts Council Literary Award and a 2005 Program Grant from the Illinois Arts Council.

Needs Ethnic/multicultural, literary, translations, excerpted novel. No science fiction, romance, western, horror, gothic or children's. Wants more novel excerpts that also stand alone as pieces. List of upcoming themes available on website. Receives 600 unsolicited mss/month. Accepts 15-20 mss/issue; 20-40 mss/year. Reads during summer only for special issues. Publishes ms 9-12 months after acceptance. Agented fiction 1%. **Publishes 2 new writers/year.** Recently published work by Sefi Atta, Danit Brown, Paula Nangle and Linda Manheim. Length: 1,000-6,500 words; average length: 2,500 words. Also publishes literary essays, poetry. Rarely comments on rejected mss.

How to Contact Send SASE for reply, return of ms. Responds in 3 weeks to queries; 9 months to mss. Accepts simultaneous submissions. Sample copy for $8. Writer's guidelines for #10 SASE.

Payment/Terms Pays $100 minimum; $20/page maximum, 2 contributor's copies and a year subscription. Acquires first North American serial rights.

Advice "We look for well-written, provocative, fully realized fiction that seeks to engage both the reader's senses and intellect. Don't submit too often to the same market, and don't send manuscripts that you haven't read over carefully. Writers can't rely on spell checkers to catch all errors. Always include a SASE. Read and support the journals you admire so they can continue to survive."

CRAZYHORSE

College of Charleston, Dept. of English, 66 George St., Charleston SC 29424. (843)953-7740. E-mail: crazyhorse@ cofc.edu. Website: crazyhorse.cofc.edu. **Contact:** Editors. Literary magazine: 8¾×8¼; 150 pages; illustrations; photos. "*Crazyhorse* publishes writing of fine quality regardless of style, predilection, subject. Editors are especially interested in original writing that engages in the work of honest communication." Raymond Carver called *Crazyhorse* "an indispensable literary magazine of the first order." Semiannual. Estab. 1961. Circ. 2,000.

• Richard Jackson's "This" won a 2004 *Pushcart Prize* for *Crazyhorse*.

Needs All fiction of fine quality. Receives 100 unsolicited mss/month. Accepts 8-10 mss/issue; 16-20 mss/year. Publishes ms 6-12 months after acceptance. Recently published work by W.D. Wetherell, T.M. McNally, Lia Purpura, Elizabeth Weld and Steven Schwarz. Length: 35 pages; average length: 15 pages words. Publishes short shorts. Also publishes literary essays, poetry.

How to Contact Send SASE for return of ms or disposable copy of ms and #10 SASE for reply only. Responds in 1 week to queries; 3 months to mss. Accepts simultaneous submissions. Sample copy for $5. Writer's guidelines for SASE or by e-mail.

Payment/Terms Pays 2 contributor's copies; additional copies $5. Acquires first North American serial rights. Sends galleys to author. Sponsors awards/contests.

Advice "Write to explore subjects you care about. Clarity of language; subject is one in which something is at stake."

Literary Magazines

☑ ☒ THE CRESCENT REVIEW

The Crescent Review, Inc., P.O. Box 7959, Shallotte NC 28470-7959. E-mail: review@mindspring.com. Website: www.crescentreview.org. **Contact:** Editor. Magazine: 6×9; 160 pages. Triannual. Estab. 1982.

• Work appearing in *The Crescent Review* has been included in *O. Henry Prize Stories*, *Best American Short Stories*, *Pushcart Prize*, *Sudden Fiction* and *Black Southern Writers* anthologies and in *New Stories from the South.*

Needs "Well-crafted stories." Wants shorter-length pieces (though will publish stories in the 6,000-8,000 word range). Wants stories where choice has consequences. Does not read submissions May-June and November-December. **Publishes 20-25% new writers/year.** Recently published work by Madison Smartt Bell, Melinda Haynes and Julia Slavin.

How to Contact SASE. Responds in 3 months to mss. Sample copy for $9.40 plus postage. Writer's guidelines online.

Payment/Terms Pays 2 contributor's copies; discount for additional copies. Acquires first North American serial rights. Sponsors awards/contests.

Advice "We are looking for stories told in compelling voices that capture readers' attention. We especially appreciate a light touch or humor that leavens the serious."

⊕ $☑ ◎ CRIMEWAVE

TTA Press, 5 Martins Lane, Witcham Ely Cambs CB6 2LB, Great Britain. E-mail: ttapress@aol.com. Website: www.ttapress.com. **Contact:** Andy Cox, fiction editor. Magazine: 176 pages; lithographed, color; perfect bound. Magazine publishes "modern crime fiction from across the waterfront, from the misnamed cozy to the deceptively subtle hard-boiled." Biannual. Published in June and December.

Needs Mystery/suspense (amateur sleuth, cozy, police procedural, private eye/hard-boiled), thriller/espionage. Accepts 15-20 mss/issue. Recently published work by Chaz Brenchley, Ian Rankin, Muriel Gray, James Sallis, James Lovegrove and Christopher Fowler.

How to Contact "Send one story at a time plus adequate return postage, or disposable ms plus 2 IRC's or e-mail address—but no e-mail submissions. No reprints." No simultaneous submissions. Sample copy for $12 US or for 4 issues: $40. Writer's guidelines online.

Payment/Terms "Relatively modest flat fee, but constantly increasing." Acquires first North American serial rights. Contract on acceptance, payment on publication.

☑ CRUCIBLE

English Dept., Barton College, College Station, Wilson NC 27893. (252)399-6343. Editor: Terrence L. Grimes. **Contact:** Fiction Editor. Magazine of fiction and poetry for a general, literary audience. Annual. Estab. 1964. Circ. 500.

Needs Ethnic/multicultural, experimental, feminist, literary, regional. Would like to see more short shorts. Receives 20 unsolicited mss/month. Accepts 5-6 mss/year. Does not normally read mss from April 30 to December 1. Publishes ms 4-5 months after acceptance. **Publishes 5 new writers/year.** Recently published work by Sally Buckner.

How to Contact Send 3 complete copies of ms unsigned with cover letter which should include a brief biography, "in case we publish." Responds in 6 weeks to queries; 4 months to mss. Sample copy for $7. Writer's guidelines free.

Payment/Terms Pays in contributor's copies. Acquires first rights.

Advice "Write about what you know. Experimentation is fine as long as the experiences portrayed come across as authentic, that is to say, plausible."

☑ CUTBANK

English Dept., University of Montana, Missoula MT 59812. (406)243-6156. E-mail: cutbank@umontana.edu. Website: www.umt.edu/cutbank. **Contact:** Fiction Editor. Magazine: 5½×8½; 115-230 pages. "Publishes serious-minded and innovative fiction and poetry from both well-known and up-and-coming authors." Semiannual. Estab. 1973. Circ. 1,000.

Needs No "science fiction, fantasy or unproofed manuscripts." "Innovative, challenging, well-written stories." Receives 200 unsolicited mss/month. Accepts 6-12 mss/year. Does not read mss April 15-August 15. Publishes ms 6 months after acceptance. **Publishes 4 new writers/year.** Recently published work by Padgett Powell and William Kittredge. Occasionally comments on rejected mss.

How to Contact SASE. Responds in 4 months to mss. Accepts simultaneous submissions. Sample copy for $4 (current issue $6.95). Writer's guidelines for SASE.

Payment/Terms Pays 2 contributor's copies. Rights revert to author upon publication, with provision *Cutbank* receives publication credit.

Advice "Strongly suggest contributors read an issue. We have published stories by Kevin Canty, Chris Offutt and Pam Houston in recent issues and like to feature new writers alongside more well-known names. Send only your best work."

THE DALHOUSIE REVIEW
Dalhousie University, Halifax NS B3H 4R2 Canada. (902)494-2541. Fax: (902)494-3561. E-mail: dalhousie.revie w@dal.ca. Website: http://dalhousiereview.dal.ca. **Contact:** Dr. Robert Martin, editor. Magazine: 15cmX23cm; approximately 140 pages; photographs sometimes. Publishes articles, book reviews, short stories and poetry. Published 3 times a year. Circ. 400.
Needs Literary. Publishes essays on history, philosophy, literature, etc. Recently published work by Melissa Hardy, Kim Bridgford, Eugene Dubnov and Shalom Camenietzki.
How to Contact SASE (Canadian stamps or IRCs). Sample copy for $15 (Canadian) including postage. Reviews fiction.
Payment/Terms Pays 10 offprints and 2 complimentary copies.

DAN RIVER ANTHOLOGY
Conservatory of American Letters., P.O. Box 298, Thomaston ME 04861. (207)354-0998. Fax: (207)354-8953. Website: www.americanletters.org. **Contact:** R.S. Danbury III, editor. Book: 6×9; 192 pages; 60 lb. paper; gloss 10 pt. full-color cover. Deadline every year is March 31, with acceptance/rejection by May 15, proofs out by May 15, and book released December 7. Annual. Estab. 1984. Circ. 750.
Needs Adventure, ethnic/multicultural, experimental, fantasy, historical, horror, humor/satire, literary, mainstream, psychic/supernatural/occult, regional, romance (contemporary and historical), science fiction, suspense, western, contemporary, prose poem, senior citizen/retirement. "Virtually anything but porn, evangelical, juvenile. Would like to see more first-person adventure." Reads "mostly in April." Length: 800-3,500 words; average length: 2,000-2,400 words. Also publishes poetry.
How to Contact Send complete ms. No simultaneous submissions. Sample copy for $15.95 paperback, $39.95 cloth, plus $3.25 shipping. Writer's guidelines available for #10 SASE or online.
Payment/Terms Payment "depends on your experience with us, as it is a nonrefundable advance against royalties on all sales that we can attribute to your influence. For first-timers, the advance is about 1¢/word." Pays on acceptance for first rights.
Advice "Read an issue or two, know the market. Don't submit without reading guidelines."

DELMAR, A Literary Annual
Delmar, Inc., 215 Reedway, St. Louis MO 63122-2614. E-mail: editorial@delmarmag.org. Website: www.delmar mag.org. **Contact:** Jeff Hamilton, executive editor. Magazine: 6½×8½; 80-100 pages; 20 lb. white paper; coated cover stock. "*Delmar* is a St. Louis literary magazine with a national reputation for excellence and careful presentation of the highest quality of work. We publish literary fiction, poetry that fits the categories reductively named experimental and mainstream, and literary work that fits none of these descriptions. We are committed to a local scene but are always looking for ways to extend beyond it." Annual. Estab. 1989. Circ. 500.
Needs Adventure, comics/graphic novels, erotica, ethnic/multicultural, experimental, fantasy (psychological/ mythographical), feminist, gay, historical, humor/satire, lesbian, literary, mainstream, science fiction (soft/ sociological), translations. Receives 2 unsolicited mss/month. Accepts 1-3 mss/issue. **Publishes 1 new writers/ year.** Recently published work by Ken Dixon. Average length: 2,200 words. Publishes short shorts. Also publishes literary essays, literary criticism, poetry. Always comments on rejected mss.
How to Contact Send complete ms. Send SASE for return of the ms or send disposable copy of the ms and #10 SASE for reply only. Responds in 2-3 months to mss. Accepts multiple submissions. No simultaneous submissions. Sample copy for $6 ($7.50 with postage). Writer's guidelines online.
Payment/Terms Pays 2 contributor's copies. Pays on publication for first, electronic, reprint rights.
Advice "Write about what you know."

DESERT VOICES
Palo Verde College, One College Drive, Blythe CA 92225. (760)921-5449. E-mail: aminyard@paloverde.edu. **Contact:** Applewhite Minyard, editor. Magazine: 6×9; 48-60 pages; illustrations; photos. "Our magazine is intended to be a showcase for our college and local/regional writers to express themselves in a creative manner, or for other writers with experiences with our area." Semiannual. Estab. 2003. Circ. 1,500.
Needs Adventure, ethnic/multicultural, feminist, humor/satire, literary, mainstream, regional (desert Southwest), science fiction, western. "No erotica, though sexual/sensual content is acceptable if essential to the story/poem." Receives 10-15 unsolicited mss/month. Accepts 4-5 mss/issue. Does not read during Summer. Publishes ms 6 months after acceptance. **Publishes 5-10 new writers/year.** Average length: 2,000 words. Publishes short shorts. Also publishes literary essays, poetry.
How to Contact Send complete ms. Accepts submissions by e-mail. Include estimated word count. Send SASE

Literary Magazines

(or IRC) for return of ms or disposable copy of ms and #10 SASE for reply only. Responds in 4 weeks to queries; 3 months to mss. Accepts reprints, multiple submissions. Writer's guidelines by e-mail. Reviews fiction.
Payment/Terms Pays on publication for one-time rights. Not copyrighted.
Advice "Write what you feel, write what you know, write what you know you feel, write clearly, write with emotion. Write and you will be heard. We are looking for good quality fiction with a regional theme. Writers should be familiar with life in the desert Southwest, though we are not interested in romanticized westerns. Poetry or artwork should meet generally accepted stylistic considerations, as well as having heart."

DICEY BROWN MAGAZINE, poetry, fiction, photography
Dicey Books, 1226 Old US 421, Lillington NC 27546. E-mail: diceybrown@yahoo.com. Website: www.diceybrown.com. **Contact:** Karen ashburner, general editor; Lydia Copeland, fiction editor. Magazine: 8½×5; 50 pages; illustrations; photos. *Dicey Brown* is urban, gritty, raw, funny and heartbreaking. Quarterly. Estab. 2001.
Needs Comics/graphic novels, ethnic/multicultural, feminist, humor/satire, literary. Does not want western, fantasy, sci-fi, children's or religious material. Accepts 10 mss/issue; 40 mss/year. Publishes ms 3 months after acceptance. Agented fiction 1%. **Publishes 30 new writers/year.** Length: 100-2,000 words; average length: 1,500 words. Publishes short shorts. Also publishes poetry. Sometimes comments on rejected mss.
How to Contact Accepts submissions by e-mail. Does not accept submissions by regular mail. Responds in 2 months to mss. Accepts simultaneous, multiple submissions. Sample copy for $3. Writer's guidelines by e-mail.
Payment/Terms Pays on publication for first, electronic rights.

DOWNSTATE STORY
1825 Maple Ridge, Peoria IL 61614. (309)688-1409. Website: www.wiu.edu/users/mfgeh/dss. **Contact:** Elaine Hopkins, editor. Magazine: includes illustrations. "Short fiction—some connection with Illinois or the Midwest." Annual. Estab. 1992. Circ. 250.
• Fiction received the Best of Illinois Stories Award.
Needs Adventure, ethnic/multicultural, experimental, historical, horror, humor/satire, literary, mainstream, mystery/suspense, psychic/supernatural/occult, regional, romance, science fiction, suspense, western. No porn. Accepts 10 mss/issue. Publishes ms 1 year after acceptance. Publishes short shorts. Also publishes literary essays.
How to Contact Send complete ms with a cover letter. SASE for return of ms. Responds "ASAP" to mss. Accepts simultaneous submissions. Sample copy for $8. Writer's guidelines online.
Payment/Terms Pays $50. Pays on acceptance for first rights.

ECLIPSE, A Literary Journal
Glendale College, 1500 N. Verdugo Rd., Glendale CA 91208. (818)240-1000. Fax: (818)549-9436. E-mail: eclipse@glendale.edu. **Contact:** Michael Ritterbrown, fiction editor. Magazine: 8½×5½; 150-200 pages; 60 lb. paper. "*Eclipse* is committed to publishing outstanding fiction and poetry. We look for compelling characters and stories executed in ways that provoke our readers and allow them to understand the world in new ways." Annual. Circ. 1,800. CLMP.
Needs Ethnic/multicultural, experimental, literary. "Does not want horror, religious, science fiction or thriller mss." Receives 50-100 unsolicited mss/month. Accepts 10 mss/year. Publishes ms 6-12 months after acceptance. **Publishes 5 new writers/year.** Recently published work by Amy Sage Webb, Ira Sukrungruang, Richard Schmitt and George Rabasa. Length: 6,000 words; average length: 4,000 words. Publishes short shorts. Also publishes poetry. Sometimes comments on rejected mss.
How to Contact Send complete ms. Responds in 2 weeks to queries; 4-6 weeks to mss. Accepts simultaneous submissions. Sample copy for $5. Writer's guidelines for #10 SASE or by e-mail.
Payment/Terms Pays 2 contributor's copies; additional copies $4. Pays on publication for first North American serial rights.
Advice "We look for well-crafted fiction, experimental or traditional, with a clear unity of elements. A good story is important, but the writing must transcend the simple act of conveying the story."

THE EDGE CITY REVIEW
Reston Review, Inc., 10912 Harpers Square Court, Reston VA 20191. E-mail: ecreds@earthlink.net. Website: www.edge-city.com. **Contact:** T.L. Ponick, editor. Magazine: 8½×11; 44-52 pages; 60 lb. paper; 65 lb. color cover. "We publish Formalist poetry, well-plotted artistic or literary fiction, literary essays and book reviews. No left-wing screeds, please." Triannual. Estab. 1994. Circ. 500.
Needs Humor/satire, literary, serialized novels. "We see too much fiction that's riddled with four-letter words and needless vulgarity." Receives 20 unsolicited mss/month. Accepts 1-2 mss/issue; 3-6 mss/year. Publishes ms 6-8 months after acceptance. Length: 1,500-3,000 words; average length: 2,000 words. Also publishes literary essays, literary criticism, poetry. Sometimes comments on rejected mss.

How to Contact Send SASE for reply, return of ms or send a disposable copy of ms. Responds in 1 month to queries; 4-6 months to mss. Sample copy for $6. Reviews fiction.

Payment/Terms Pays 2 contributor's copies; additional copies $5. Acquires first North American serial rights. Sponsors awards/contests.

Advice "We are looking for character-based fiction. Most fiction we receive does not grow out of its characters, but finely wrought characters, fully realized, are what we want to see."

$🖵 ELLIPSIS MAGAZINE

Westminster College of Salt Lake City, 1840 S. 1300 E., Salt Lake City UT 84105. (801)832-2321. Website: www.westminstercollege.edu/ellipsis. **Contact:** Rachel McDonald (revolving editor; changes every year). Magazine: 6×9; 110-120 pages; 60 lb. paper; 15 pt. cover stock; illustrations; photos. *Ellipsis Magazine* needs good literary poetry, fiction, essays, plays and visual art. Annual. Estab. 1967. Circ. 2,500.

Needs Receives 110 unsolicited mss/month. Accepts 4 mss/issue. Does not read mss November 1-July 31. Publishes ms 3 months after acceptance. **Publishes 2 new writers/year.** Length: 6,000 words; average length: 4,000 words. Also publishes poetry. Rarely comments on rejected mss.

How to Contact Send complete ms. Send SASE (or IRC) for return of ms or send disposable copy of the ms and #10 SASE for reply only. Responds in 6 months to mss. Accepts simultaneous submissions. Sample copy for $7.50. Writer's guidelines online.

Payment/Terms Pays $50 per story and one contributor's copy; additional copies $3.50. Pays on publication for first North American serial rights. Not copyrighted.

Advice "Have friends or mentors read your story first and make suggestions to improve it."

Ⓝ 🖸 EMRYS JOURNAL

The Emrys Foundation, P.O. Box 8813, Greenville SC 29604. (864)455-4652. Fax: (864)235-0084. E-mail: ldishman@charter.net. Website: www.emrys.org. **Contact:** L.B. Dishman. Catalog: 9×9¾; 120 pages; 80 lb. paper. "We publish short fiction, poetry and creative nonfiction. We are particularly interested in hearing from women and other minorities." Annual. Estab. 1984. Circ. 400.

Needs Literary, contemporary. No religious, sexually explicit or science fiction mss. Accepts 18 mss/issue. Reading period: August 15-December 1. Publishes mss in April. **Publishes several new writers/year.** Recently published work by Jessica Goodfellow and Ron Rash. Length: 5,000 words; average length: 3,500 words. Publishes short shorts.

How to Contact Send complete ms. SASE. Responds in 6 weeks to mss. Accepts multiple submissions. Sample copy for $15 and 7×10 SAE with 4 first-class stamps. Writer's guidelines for #10 SASE.

Payment/Terms Pays in contributor's copies. Acquires first rights.

Advice Looks for previously unpublished literary fiction.

$🖸 🖾 EPOCH

Cornell University, 251 Goldwin Smith Hall, Cornell University, Ithaca NY 14853. (607)255-3385. Fax: (607)255-6661. **Contact:** Joseph Martin, senior editor. Magazine: 6×9; 128 pages; good quality paper; good cover stock. "Well-written literary fiction, poetry, personal essays. Newcomers always welcome. Open to mainstream and avant-garde writing." Estab. 1947. Circ. 1,000.

● Work originally appearing in this quality literary journal has appeared in numerous anthologies including *Best American Short Stories*, *Best American Poetry*, *Pushcart Prize*, *The O. Henry Prize Stories*, *Best of the West* and *New Stories from the South*.

Needs Ethnic/multicultural, experimental, literary, mainstream, novel excerpts, literary short stories. "No genre fiction. Would like to see more Southern fiction (Southern US)." Receives 500 unsolicited mss/month. Accepts 15-20 mss/issue. Does not read in summer (April 15-September 15). Publishes ms an average of 6 months after acceptance. **Publishes 3-4 new writers/year.** Recently published work by Antonya Nelson, Doris Betts and Heidi Jon Schmidt. Also publishes poetry. Sometimes comments on rejected mss.

How to Contact Send complete ms. Responds in 2 weeks to queries; 6 weeks to mss. No simultaneous submissions. Sample copy for $5. Writer's guidelines for #10 SASE.

Payment/Terms Pays $5 and up/printed page. Pays on publication for first North American serial rights.

Advice "Read the journals you're sending work to."

Ⓝ 🖸 ◎ ERASED, SIGH, SIGH., A Journal of Death Poets and Suicide Writers

Via Dolorosa Press, 701 East Schaaf Road, Cleveland OH 44131. E-mail: viadolorosapress@aol.com. Website: www.angelfire.com/oh2/dolorosa/index.html. **Contact:** Hyacinthe L. Raven, editor. Magazine: 5½×8½; 48 pages; parchment paper; parchment cover stock; illustrations. "We only publish writing with an existential slant whose subject is death or suicide. We print mostly poetry, but that's only because the majority of our submissions have been poems. Our audience is 18-40 year-olds, college-educated, and primarily members of the punk and goth subculture.'' Semiannual. Estab. 1994. Circ. 500.

Needs Experimental, literary, mainstream. "No genre fiction. Also, no humor as our theme is of a serious tone and no children/juvenile/teen fiction as our audience is college-aged." Receives 10 unsolicited mss/month. Accepts 1-2 mss/issue; 2-4 mss/year. Publishes ms 6-12 months after acceptance. **Publishes 10 new writers/year.** Recently published work by John Sweet, John Grey, David Stone, Giovanni Malito, Lyn Lifshin. Length: 1,500 words; average length: 1,000 words. Publishes short shorts. Also publishes poetry. Sometimes comments on rejected mss.

How to Contact Send complete ms. Send disposable copy of the ms and #10 SASE for reply only. Responds in 1-2 months to queries; 1-2 months to mss. Accepts simultaneous and reprints, multiple submissions. Sample copy for $4 payable to Via Dolorosa Press. Writer's guidelines for SASE and on website.

Payment/Terms Pays 1 contributor's copy. Pays on publication for one-time rights.

Advice "Be familiar with our theme and the style of the poets we print—we're more likely to print fiction that has the same feel as the poetry of our regulars like John Sweet and Giovanni Malito."

☑ EUREKA LITERARY MAGAZINE

300 E. College Ave., Eureka College, Eureka IL 61530-1500. (309)467-6591. E-mail: vperry@eureka.edu. **Contact:** Val Perry, fiction editor. Magazine: 6×9; 120 pages; 70 lb. white offset paper; 80 lb. gloss cover; photographs (occasionally). "We seek to be open to the best stories that are submitted to us. Our audience is a combination of professors/writers, students of writing and literature, and general readers." Semiannual. Estab. 1992. Circ. 500.

Needs Adventure, ethnic/multicultural, experimental, fantasy (science), feminist, historical, humor/satire, literary, mainstream, mystery/suspense (private eye/hard-boiled, romantic), psychic/supernatural/occult, regional, romance (historical), science fiction (soft/sociological), translations. Would like to see more "good literary fiction stories, good magical realism, historical fiction. We try to achieve a balance between the traditional and the experimental. We look for the well-crafted story, but essentially any type of story that has depth and substance to it is welcome." Receives 50 unsolicited mss/month. Accepts 8-10 mss/issue; 15-20 mss/year. Does not read mss in summer (May-August). **Publishes 5-6 new writers/year.** Recently published work by Jane Guill, Forrest Robinson, Ray Bradbury, Earl Coleman, Virgil Suarez, Cynthia Gallaher and Wendell Mayo. Length: 7,000-8,000 words; average length: 4,500 words. Publishes short shorts. Also publishes poetry.

How to Contact Accepts submissions by e-mail. Send SASE for reply, return of ms or send disposable copy of ms. Responds in 1 week to queries; 4 months to mss. Accepts simultaneous, multiple submissions. Sample copy for $7.50.

Payment/Terms Pays free subscription to the magazine and 2 contributor's copies. Acquires first, one-time rights.

Advice "We look for expert storytelling technique; a powerful statement about the human condition; eloquent or effective use of language—metaphor, imagery, description. Find a copy of the magazine and read it before submitting your work. Order a copy if you can."

☑ $☑ ☑ EVENT

Douglas College, P.O. Box 2503, New Westminster BC V3L 5B2 Canada. (604)527-5293. Fax: (604)527-5095. Website: event.douglas.bc.ca. **Contact:** Christine Dewar, fiction editor. Magazine: 6×9; 136 pages; quality paper and cover stock. "We are eclectic and always open to content that invites involvement. Generally, we like strong narrative." Estab. 1971. Circ. 1,250.

● Fiction originally published in *Event* has been included in *The Journey Anthology* and *Best Canadian Stories*, and work published in *Event* has been nominated for numerous awards over the years.

Needs Feminist, humor/satire, literary, regional, contemporary. "No technically poor or unoriginal pieces." Receives 100 unsolicited mss/month. Accepts 3-5 mss/issue. Publishes ms 8 months after acceptance. **Publishes 2-3 new writers/year.** Recently published work by Bill Gaston, Gary Geddes and Elisabeth Harvor. Also publishes poetry.

How to Contact Send complete ms. Accepts submissions by fax. Responds in 1 month to queries; 6 months to mss. Accepts simultaneous submissions. Sample copy for $5. Writer's guidelines online.

Payment/Terms Pays $22/page to $500. Pays on publication for first North American serial rights.

Advice "We're looking for a strong, effective point of view; well-handled and engaging characters, attention to language and strong details."

☑ ☑ FAT TUESDAY

Manada Gap Rd., Grantville PA 17028. (717)469-7517. E-mail: cotolo@excite.com. **Contact:** F.M. Cotolo, editor-in-chief. Journal: 8½×11 or 5×8; 27-36 pages; bond paper; heavy cover stock; saddle-stiched; b&w illustrations; photos. "Generally, we are an eclectic journal of fiction, poetry and visual treats. Our issues to date have featured artists like Patricia Kelly, Charles Bukowski, Gerald Locklin, Chunk Taylor and many more who have focused on an individualistic nature of fiery elements. We are a literary mardi gras—as the title indicates—and irreverancy is as acceptable to us as profundity as long as there is fire! Our audience is anyone who can praise literature and condemn it at the same time. Anyone too serious about it on either level will not like *Fat Tuesday*.'' Annual. Estab. 1981. Circ. 700.

Needs Comics/graphic novels, erotica, experimental, humor/satire, literary, psychic/supernatural/occult, serialized novels, prose poem and dada. Does not want to see sci-fi, romance, mystery, mainstream in general. ''Although we list categories, we are open to feeling out various fields if they are delivered with the mark of an individual and not just in the format of the particular field.'' Receives 20 unsolicited mss/month. Accepts 4-5 mss/issue. Publishes ms 3-10 months after acceptance. **Publishes 40 new writers/year.** Publishes short shorts. Occasionally comments on rejected mss.

How to Contact Responds in 1 month to mss. No simultaneous submissions. Sample copy for $10 in print or audio.

Payment/Terms Pays 1 contributor's copy. Acquires one-time rights.

Advice ''As *Fat Tuesday* crawls through its third decade, we find publishing small press editions more difficult than ever. Money remains a problem, mostly because small press seems to play to the very people who wish to be published in it. In other words, the cast is the audience, and more people want to be in *Fat Tuesday* than want to buy it. It is through sales that magazine supports itself. This is why we emphasize buying a sample issue ($10) before submitting. Please specify in-print or audio issue. As far as what we want to publish—send us shorter works that are 'crystals of thought and emotion which reflect your individual experiences—dig into your guts and pull out pieces of yourself. Your work is signature; like time itself, it should emerge from the penetralia of your being and recede into the infinite region of the cosomos,' to coin a phrase, and remember *Fat Tuesday* is mardi gras—so fill up before you fast. Bon soir.''

◪ FAULTLINE, Journal of Art and Literature

Dept. of English and Comparitive Literature, University of California, Irvine, Irvine CA 92697-2650. (949)824-1573. E-mail: faultline@uci.edu. Website: www.humanities.uci.edu/faultline. **Contact:** Editors change in September each year. Literary magazine: 6×9; 200 pages; illustrations; photos. ''We publish the very best of what we recieve. Our interest is quality and literary merit.'' Annual. Estab. 1992.

Needs Translations, literary fiction up to 20 pages. ''Novel excerpts are fine, but they should be self-contained. No sci-fi, mystery, horror, westerns or romance.'' Receives 150 unsolicited mss/month. Accepts 6-9 mss/year. Does not read mss April-September. Publishes ms 9 months after acceptance. Agented fiction 10-20%. **Publishes 30-40% new writers/year.** Recently published work by Maile Meloy, Aimee Bender, David Benioff, Helena Maria Viramontes and Thomas Keneally. Publishes short shorts. Also publishes literary essays, poetry.

How to Contact Send SASE for reply, return of ms or send a disposable copy of ms. Responds in 2 weeks to queries; 4 months to mss. Accepts simultaneous submissions. Sample copy for $5. Writer's guidelines for business-size envelope.

Payment/Terms Pays 2 contributor's copies. Pays on publication for one-time rights.

Advice ''Our commitment is to publish the best work possible from well-known and emerging authors as well as those who have been affiliated with UCI's esteemed graduate studies program.''

◪ ◎ FEMINIST STUDIES

0103 Taliaferro, University of Maryland, College Park MD 20742. (301)405-7415. Fax: (301)405-8395. E-mail: info@feministstudies.org. Website: www.feministstudies.org. **Contact:** Shirley Lim, fiction editor. Magazine: journal-sized; about 200 pages; photographs. ''Scholarly manuscripts, fiction, book review, essays for professors, graduate/doctoral students; scholarly interdisciplinary feminist journal.'' Triannual. Estab. 1974. Circ. 7,500.

Needs Ethnic/multicultural, feminist, gay, lesbian, contemporary. Receives 20 unsolicited mss/month. Accepts 2-3 mss/issue. ''We review fiction twice a year. Deadline dates are May 1 and December 1. Authors will recieve notice of the board's decision by July 15 and February 15, respectively.'' Recently published work by Bell Chevigny, Betsy Gould Gibson and Joan Jacobson. Sometimes comments on rejected mss.

How to Contact No simultaneous submissions. Sample copy for $15. Writer's guidelines free.

Payment/Terms Pays 2 contributor's copies and 10 tearsheets. Sends galleys to authors.

$ ◪ ▣ FICTION

% Department of English, The City College of New York, 138th St. & Convent Ave., New York NY 10031. (212)650-6319. E-mail: fictionmagazine@yahoo.com. Website: www.fictioninc.com. **Contact:** Mark J. Mirsky, editor. Magazine: 6×9; 150-250 pages; illustrations; occasionally photos. ''As the name implies, we publish only fiction; we are looking for the best new writing available, leaning toward the unconventional. *Fiction* has traditionally attempted to make accessible the unaccessible, to bring the experimental to a broader audience." Semiannual. Estab. 1972. Circ. 4,000.

• Stories first published in *Fiction* have been selected for inclusion in the *Pushcart Prize* and *Best of the Small Presses* anthologies.

Needs Experimental, humor/satire (satire), literary, translations, contemporary. No romance, science fiction, etc. Receives 200 unsolicited mss/month. Accepts 12-20 mss/issue; 24-40 mss/year. Reads mss September 15-April 15. Publishes ms 1 year after acceptance. Agented fiction 10-20%. Recently published work by Joyce Carol Oates, Robert Musil and Romulus Linney. Publishes short shorts. Sometimes comments on rejected mss.

How to Contact Send complete ms with cover letter. SASE. No e-mail submissions. Responds in 3 months to mss. Accepts simultaneous submissions. Sample copy for $5. Writer's guidelines online.

Payment/Terms Pays $114. Acquires first rights.

Advice "The guiding principle of *Fiction* has always been to go to *terra incognita* in the writing of the imagination and to ask that modern fiction set itself serious questions, if often in absurd and comical voices, interrogating the nature of the real and the fantastic. It represents no particular school of fiction, except the innovative. Its pages have often been a harbor for writers at odds with each other. As a result of its willingness to publish the difficult, experimental, unusual, while not excluding the well known, *Fiction* has a unique reputation in the U.S. and abroad as a journal of future directions."

FIRST CLASS, Four-Sep Publications

P.O. Box 86, Friendship IN 47021. E-mail: christopherm@four-sep.com. Website: www.four-sep.com. **Contact:** Christopher M, editor. Magazine: 4¼×11; 60+ pages; 24 lb./60 lb. offset paper; craft cover; illustrations; photos. "*First Class* features short fiction and poetics from the cream of the small press and killer unknowns—mingling before your very hungry eyes. I publish plays, too." Biannual. Estab. 1995. Circ. 200-400.

Needs Erotica, literary, science fiction (soft/sociological), satire, drama. "No religious or traditional poetry, or 'boomer angst'—therapy-driven self-loathing." Receives 50-70 unsolicited mss/month. Accepts 4-6 mss/issue; 10-12 mss/year. Publishes ms 1 month after acceptance. **Publishes 10-15 new writers/year.** Recently published work by Gerald Locklin, John Bennnet and B.Z. Niditch. Length: 5,000-8,000; average length: 2,000-3,000 words. Publishes short shorts. Also publishes poetry. Sometimes comments on rejected mss.

How to Contact Send SASE and #10 SASE for reply only or send a disposable copy of ms. Responds in 1 week to queries. Accepts simultaneous and reprints submissions. Sample copy for $6. Writer's guidelines for #10 SASE. Reviews fiction.

Payment/Terms Pays 1 contributor's copy; additional copies $5. Acquires one-time rights.

Advice "Don't bore me with puppy dogs and the morose/sappy feeling you have about death. Belt out a good, short, thought-provoking, graphic, uncommon piece."

$ ☯ FIVE POINTS, A Journal of Literature and Art

MSC 8R0318 Georgia State University, 33 Gilmer St. SE, Unit 8, Atlanta GA 30303-3083. (404)463-9484. Fax: (404)651-3167. E-mail: msexton@gsu.edu. Website: www.webdelsol.com/Five_Points. **Contact:** Megan Sexton, associate editor. Magazine: 6×9; 200 pages; cotton paper; glossy cover; and photos. *Five Points* is "committed to publishing work that compels the imagination through the use of fresh and convincing language." Triannual. Estab. 1996. Circ. 2,000.

• Fiction first appearing in *Five Points* has been anthologized in *Best American Fiction*, *Pushcart* anthologies, and *New Stories from the South*.

Needs List of upcoming themes available for SASE. Receives 250 unsolicited mss/month. Accepts 4 mss/issue; 15-20 mss/year. Does not read mss April 30-September 1. Publishes ms 6 months after acceptance. **Publishes 1 new writer/year.** Recently published work by Frederick Busch, Ursula Hegi and Melanie Rae Thon. Average length: 7,500 words. Publishes short shorts. Also publishes literary essays, poetry. Sometimes comments on rejected mss.

How to Contact Send SASE for reply to query. No simultaneous submissions. Sample copy for $7.

Payment/Terms Pays $15/page minimum; $250 maximum, free subscription to magazine and 2 contributor's copies; additional copies $4. Acquires first North American serial rights. Sends galleys to author. Sponsors awards/contests.

Advice "We place no limitations on style or content. Our only criteria is excellence. If your writing has an original voice, substance and significance, send it to us. We will publish distinctive, intelligent writing that has something to say and says it in a way that captures and maintains our attention."

FLORIDA REVIEW

Dept. of English, University of Central Florida, P.O. Box 161346, Orlando FL 32816-1346. (407)823-2038. E-mail: flreview@mail.ucf.edu. Website: www.english.ucf.edu/~flreview. **Contact:** Jeanne Leiby, editor. Magazine: 6×9; 144 pages; semi-gloss full color cover, perfect bound. "We publish fiction of high "literary" quality—

stories that delight, instruct and take risks. Our audience consists of avid readers of fiction, poetry and creative nonfiction." Semiannual. Estab. 1972. Circ. 1,500.

Needs Experimental, literary. "We aren't particularly interested in genre fiction (sci-fi, romance, adventure, etc.) but a good story can transcend any genre." Receives 250 unsolicited mss/month. Accepts 5-7 mss/issue; 10-14 mss/year. Publishes ms 3 months after acceptance. **Publishes 2-4 new writers/year.** Recently published work by Philip Dearer, Chris Chambers and Gina Ochsner. Length: 2,000-7,000 words; average length: 5,000 words. Publishes short shorts. Also publishes literary essays, poetry. Rarely comments on rejected mss.

How to Contact Send complete ms. Send SASE (or IRC) for return of the ms or send disposable copy of the ms and #10 SASE for reply only. Responds in 2 weeks to queries; 2 months to mss. Accepts simultaneous submissions. Sample copy for $6. Writer's guidelines for #10 SASE or online.

Payment/Terms Rights held by UCF, revert to author after publication. Sends galleys to author.

Advice "We're looking for writers with fresh voices and original stories. We like risk."

FOLIO, A Literary Journal at American University

Doyle, Department of Literature, American University, Washington DC 20016. (202)885-2971. E-mail: folio_editors@yahoo.com. Website: www.foliojournal.org. **Contact:** Amina Hafiz. Magazine: about 70 pages; illustrations; photos. "*Folio* is a journal of poetry, fiction and creative nonfiction. We look for work that ignites and endures, is artful and natural, daring and elegant." Semiannual. Estab. 1984. Circ. 300.

Needs Literary. Does not want anything that is sexually offensive. Receives 50-60 unsolicited mss/month. Accepts 2-3 mss/issue; 5-8 mss/year. Does not read mss May-August. **Publishes 2-3 new writers/year.** Length: 3,500 words; average length: 2,500 words. Publishes short shorts. Also publishes poetry. Sometimes comments on rejected mss.

How to Contact Send complete ms. Send a SASE (or IRC) for return of the ms or send a disposable copy of the ms and #10 SASE for reply only. Responds in 3-4 months to mss. Accepts simultaneous, multiple submissions. Sample copy for $6. Writer's guidelines for #10 SASE or online.

Payment/Terms Pays 2 contributor's copies. Pays on publication for first North American serial rights.

Advice "Visit our website and/or read the journal to get a sense of *Folio* style."

FOURTEEN HILLS, The SFSU Review

Dept. of Creative Writing, San Francisco State University, 1600 Holloway Ave., San Francisco CA 94132. (415)338-3083. E-mail: hills@sfsu.edu. Website: www.14hills.net. **Contact:** Editors change each year. Magazine: 6×9; 200 pages; 60 lb. paper; 10 point C15 cover. "*Fourteen Hills* publishes the highest quality innovative fiction and poetry for a literary auduience." Semiannual. Estab. 1994. Circ. 700.

Needs Ethnic/multicultural, experimental, gay, humor/satire, lesbian, literary, mainstream, translations. Receives 300 unsolicited mss/month. Accepts 8-10 mss/issue; 16-20 mss/year. Does not usually read mss during the summer. Publishes ms 2-4 months after acceptance. Recently published work by Terese Svoboda, Peter Rock and Stephen Dixon. Publishes short shorts. Also publishes literary essays, poetry. Sometimes comments on rejected mss.

How to Contact SASE for return of ms. Responds in 5 months to mss. Sample copy for $9. Writer's guidelines for #10 SASE.

Payment/Terms Pays 2 contributor's copies. Acquires one-time rights. Sends galleys to author.

Advice "Please read an isssue of *Fourteen Hills* before submitting."

$ FRANK, An International Journal of Contemporary Writing & Art

Association Frank, 32 rue Edouard Vaillant, Montreuil, France. (33)(1)48596658. Fax: (33)(1)48596668. E-mail: submissions@readfrank.com. Website: www.readfrank.com or www.frank.ly. **Contact:** David Applefield. "Writing that takes risks and isn't ethnocentric is looked upon favorably." Published twice/year. Estab. 1983. Circ. 4,000.

Needs Experimental, novel excerpts, international. "At *Frank*, we publish fiction, poetry, literary and art interviews, and translations. We like work that falls between existing genres and has social or political consciousness." Accepts 20 mss/issue. Publishes ms 1 year after acceptance.

How to Contact Send complete ms. Send IRC or $5 cash. Must be previously unpublished in English (world). E-mail submissions as Word attachments are welcome and should be saved in RTF. Responds in 1 month to queries; 2 months to mss. Sample copy for $10. Writer's guidelines online.

Payment/Terms Pays $10/printed page. Pays on publication for one-time rights.

Advice "Send your most daring and original work. At *Frank*, we like work that is not too parochial or insular, however, don't try to write for a 'French' market."

$ FREEFALL MAGAZINE

The Alexandra Writers' Centre Society, 922 Ninth Ave. SE, Calgary Alberta T2G 0S4 Canada. (403)264-4730. E-mail: awcs@telusplanet.net. Website: www.alexandrawriters.org. **Contact:** Vivian Hansen, editor. Magazine:

Literary Magazines

$8^{1}/_{2} \times 11$; 40 pages; bond paper; bond stock; illustrations; photos. *"FreeFall* features the best of new, emerging writers and gives them the chance to get into print along with established writers. Now in its fourteenth year, *FreeFall* seeks to attract readers looking for well-crafted stories, poetry and artwork." Semiannual. Estab. 1990. Circ. Under 500. Alberta Magazine Publishers Association (AMPA).

Needs "No science fiction, horror." Wants to see more well-crafted literary fiction. Accepts 3-5 mss/issue; 6-10 mss/year. Does not read mss January-February, June-August. Publishes ms 6 months after acceptance.
Publishes 40% new writers/year. Recently published work by Thomas Robert Barnes, J.L. Bond, Shirley Black, Judy Gayford, Elizabeth Lindgre-Kubitz, Renee Norman, Cheryl Sikomas, Rebecca Marshall-Courtois and Diane Stuart. Length: 500-3,000 words; average length: 2,500 words. Publishes short shorts. Also publishes poetry. Sometimes comments on rejected mss.
How to Contact Send SASE (or IRC) for return of ms or send a disposable copy of ms with #10 SASE for reply only, or include e-mail address for reply. Responds in 3 months to mss. Accepts reprints submissions. Sample copy for $6.50 (US). Writer's guidelines for SASE, e-mail or on website.
Payment/Terms Pays $5 (Canadian)/printed page and 1 contributor's copy; additional copies $8.50 (US). Acquires first North American serial, one-time rights.
Advice "We look for thoughtful word usage that conveys clear images and encourages further exploration of the story's idea and neat, clean presentation of work. Carefully read *FreeFall* guidelines before submitting. Do not fold manuscript and submit 9×11 envelope. Include SASE/IRC for reply and/or return of manuscript. You may contact us by e-mail after initial hardcopy submission. For accepted pieces a request is made for disk or e-mail copy. Web presence attracts submissions from writers all over the world."

FRESH BOILED PEANUTS

P.O. Box 43194, Cincinnati OH 45243-0194. E-mail: contact@freshboiledpeanuts.com. Website: www.freshboiledpeanuts.com. "We embrace the fact that literary magazines are a dime a dozen. We have no grand illusions of money or fame. We publish for the sake of the work itself. So it better be good." Semiannual. Estab. 2004.
Needs "Open to all fiction categories." Also publishes literary essays, literary criticism, poetry. Sometimes comments on rejected mss.
How to Contact Send complete ms. Accepts submissions by e-mail (must be a doc file or txt file). Send SASE (or IRC) for return of the ms. Responds in 6-8 weeks to mss. Accepts simultaneous, multiple submissions. Sample copy online. Writer's guidelines online.
Payment/Terms Pays 1 contributor's copy. Acquires one-time rights.
Advice "Write like you mean it, but don't quit your day job."

FRONT & CENTRE

Black Bile Press, 573 Gainsborough Ave., Ottawa ON K2A 2Y6 Canada. (613)729-8973. E-mail: firth@istar.ca. Website: www.blackbilepress.com. **Contact:** Matthew Firth, editor. Magazine: half letter-size; 40-50 pages; illustrations; photos. "We look for new fiction from Canadian and international writers—bold, aggressive work that does not compromise quality." Three issues per year. Estab. 1998. Circ. 500.
Needs Literary ("contemporary realism/gritty urban"). "No science fiction, horror, mainstream, romance or religious." Receives 30-40 unsolicited mss/month. Accepts 6-7 mss/issue; 10-20 mss/year. Publishes ms 6 months after acceptance. Agented fiction 10%. **Publishes 4-5 new writers/year.** Recently published work by Kenneth J. Harvey, David Rose, Laura Hird, Jon Boillard, Nichole McGill and John Swan. Length: 50-4,000 words; average length: 2,500 words. Publishes short shorts. Always comments on rejected mss.
How to Contact Send SASE (or IRC) for return of ms or send a disposable copy of ms with #10 SASE for reply only. Responds in 2 weeks to queries; 4 months to mss. Accepts multiple submissions. Sample copy for $6. Writer's guidelines for SASE or by e-mail. Reviews fiction.
Payment/Terms Acquires first rights. Not copyrighted.
Advice "We look for attention to detail; unique voice; not overtly derivative; bold writing; not pretentious. We should like to see more realism. Read the magazine first—simple as that!"

FUGUE

200 Brink Hall, University of Idaho P.O. Box 441102, Moscow ID 83844-1102. (208)885-6156. Fax: (208)885-5944. E-mail: fugue@uidaho.edu. Website: www.uidaho.edu/fugue. **Contact:** Fiction editor. Magazine: 6×9; 175 pages; 70 lb. stock paper. By allowing the voices of established writers to lend their authority to new and emerging writers, *Fugue* strives to provide its readers with the most compelling stories, poems, essays, interviews and literary criticism possible. Semiannual. Estab. 1990. Circ. 1,400.
• Work published in *Fugue* has won the *Pushcart Prize* and has been cited in *Best American Essays*.
Needs Ethnic/multicultural, experimental, humor/satire, literary. Receives 80 unsolicited mss/month. Accepts 6-8 mss/issue; 12-15 mss/year. Does not read mss May 1-August 31. Publishes ms 6 months after acceptance.
Publishes 4-6 new writers/year. Recently published work by Kent Nelson, Marilyn Krysl, Cary Holladay,

Literary Magazines

Padgett Powell and Matthew Vollmer. Publishes short shorts. Also publishes literary essays, literary criticism, poetry. Sometimes comments on rejected mss.

How to Contact Send complete ms. Send SASE (or IRC) for return of the ms or disposable copy of the ms and #10 SASE for reply only. Responds in 3-4 months to mss. Accepts simultaneous submissions. Sample copy for $8. Writer's guidelines for SASE or on website.

Payment/Terms Pays $10 minimum and 1 contributor copy, as well as a one-year subscription to the magazine; additional copies $5. Pays on publication for first North American serial, electronic rights.

Advice "The best way, of course, to determine what we're looking for is to read the journal. As the name *Fugue* indicates, our goal is to present a wide range of literary perspectives. We like stories that satisfy us both intellectually and emotionally, with fresh language and characters so captivating that they stick with us and invite a second reading. We are also seeking creative literary criticism which illuminates a piece of literature or a specific writer by examining that writer's personal experience."

GARGOYLE

P.O. Box 6216, Arlington VA 22206-0216. (703)525-9296. E-mail: atticus@atticusbooks.com. Website: www.atticusbooks.com. **Contact:** Richard Peabody and Lucinda Ebersole, editors. Literary magazine: 6×9; 200 pages; illustrations; photos. "*Gargoyle* began in 1976 with twin goals: to discover new voices and to rediscover overlooked talent. These days we publish a lot of fictional efforts written by poets. We have always been more interested in how a writer tells a story than in plot or story per se." Annual. Estab. 1976. Circ. 2,000.

Needs Erotica, ethnic/multicultural, experimental, gay, lesbian, literary, mainstream, translations. "No romance, horror, science fiction." Wants "good short stories with sports and music backgrounds." Wants to see more Canadian, British, Australian and Third World fiction. Receives 50-200 unsolicited mss/month. Accepts 10-15 mss/issue. Accepts submissions from Memorial Day until Labor Day. Publishes ms 6-12 months after acceptance. Agented fiction 5%. **Publishes 2-3 new writers/year.** Recently published work by Rebecca Brown, Kenneth Carroll, Wanda Coleman and Doug Rice. Length: 30 pages maximum; average length: 5-10 pages. Publishes short shorts. Also publishes literary essays, literary criticism, poetry. Sometimes comments on rejected mss.

How to Contact Send SASE for reply, return of ms or send a disposable copy of ms. Responds in 2 weeks to queries; 3 months to mss. Accepts simultaneous submissions. Sample copy for $12.95.

Payment/Terms Pays 1 contributor's copy; additional copies for ½ price. Acquires first North American serial, first, first British rights. Sends galleys to author.

Advice "We have to fall in love with a particular fiction."

A GATHERING OF THE TRIBES

A Gathering of the Tribes, Inc., P.O. Box 20693, Tompkins Square Station, New York NY 10009. (212)674-3778. Fax: (212)388-9813. E-mail: info@tribes.org. Website: www.tribes.org. **Contact:** Steve Cannon. Magazine: 8½×10; 130 pages; glossy paper and cover; illustrations; photos. A "multicultural and multigenerational publication featuring poetry, fiction, interviews, essays, visual art, musical scores. Audience is anyone interested in the arts from a diverse perspective." Estab. 1992. Circ. 2,000-3,000.

Needs Erotica, ethnic/multicultural, experimental, fantasy (science), feminist, gay, historical, horror, humor/satire, lesbian, literary, mainstream, romance (futuristic/time travel, gothic), science fiction (soft/sociological), translations, senior citizen/retirement. "Would like to see more satire/humor. We are open to all; just no poor writing/grammar/syntax." Receives 20 unsolicited mss/month. Publishes ms 3-6 months after acceptance. **Publishes 40% new writers/year.** Recently published work by Carl Watson, Ishle Park, Wang Pang and Hanif Kureishi. Publishes short shorts. Also publishes literary essays, literary criticism, poetry.

How to Contact Send complete ms. Send SASE for reply, return of ms or send a disposable copy of ms. Accepts simultaneous and reprints submissions. Sample copy for $15. Reviews fiction.

Payment/Terms Pays 1 contributor's copy; additional copies $12-50. Sponsors awards/contests.

Advice "Make sure your work has substance."

$ THE GEORGIA REVIEW

The University of Georgia, 012 Gilbert Hall, University of Georgia, Athens GA 30602-9009. (706)542-3481. Fax: (706)542-0047. Website: www.uga.edu/garev. **Contact:** T.R. Hummer, editor. Journal: 7×10; 208 pages (average); 50 lb. woven old-style paper; 80 lb. cover stock; illustrations; photos. "Our readers are educated, inquisitive people who read a lot of work in the areas we feature, so they expect only the best in our pages. All work submitted should show evidence that the writer is at least as well educated and well read as our readers. Essays should be authoritative but accessible to a range of readers." Quarterly. Estab. 1947. Circ. 5,000.

- Stories first published in *The Georgia Review* have been anthologized in *Best American Short Stories*, *Best American Mystery Stories*, *New Stories from the South* and the *Pushcart Prize Collection*. *The Georgia Review* was a finalist for the National Magazine Award in Fiction in 2003.

Literary Magazines

Needs ''Ordinarily we do not publish novel excerpts or works translated into English, and we strongly discourage authors from submitting these.'' Receives 300 unsolicited mss/month. Accepts 3-4 mss/issue; 12-15 mss/year. Does not read unsolicited mss May 15-August 15. Publishes ms 6 months after acceptance. **Publishes some new writers/year.** Recently published work by Brock Clarke, Christie Hodgen, Liza Ward, Robert Olen Butler, Joyce Carol Oates, Guy Davenport and Carrie Brown. Also publishes literary essays, literary criticism, poetry. Occasionally comments on rejected mss.

How to Contact Send complete ms. Responds in 2 weeks to queries; 3-6 months to mss. No simultaneous submissions. Sample copy for $7. Writer's guidelines online. Reviews fiction.

Payment/Terms Pays $40/published page. Pays on publication for first North American serial rights. Sends galleys to author.

GERTRUDE, A Journal of Voice & Vision

Gertrude % Eric Delehoy, 7957 N. Wayland Ave., Portland OR 97203. **Contact:** Eric Delehoy, editor. Magazine: 5×8½; 64-72 pages; perfect bound; 60 lb. paper; glossy card cover; illustrations; photos. *Gertrude* is an ''annual publication featuring the voices and visions of the gay, lesbian, bisexual, transgender and supportive community.'' Estab. 1999. Circ. 400.

Needs Ethnic/multicultural, feminist, gay, humor/satire, lesbian, literary, mainstream. ''No romance, pornography or mystery.'' Wants more multicultural fiction. ''We'd like to publish more humor and positive portrayals of gays—steer away from victim roles, pity.'' Receives 15-20 unsolicited mss/month. Accepts 4-8 mss/issue; 4-8 mss/year. Publishes ms 1-2 months after acceptance. **Publishes 4-5 new writers/year.** Recently published work by Carol Guess, Demrie Alonzo, Henry Alley and Scott Pomfret. Length: 200-3,000 words; average length: 1,800 words. Publishes short shorts. Also publishes poetry.

How to Contact Send SASE for reply to query and a disposable copy of ms. Responds in 4 months to mss. Accepts multiple submissions. No simultaneous submissions. Sample copy for $5, 6×9 SAE and 4 1st-class stamps. Writer's guidelines for #10 SASE.

Payment/Terms Pays 1-2 contributor's copies; additional copies $4. Pays on publication. Author retains rights upon publication. Not copyrighted.

Advice ''We look for strong characterization, imagery and new, unique ways of writing about universal experiences. Follow the construction of your work until the ending. Many stories start out with zest, then flipper and die. Show us, don't tell us.''

$ THE GETTYSBURG REVIEW

Gettysburg College, Gettysburg PA 17325. (717)337-6770. Fax: (717)337-6775. Website: www.gettysburgreview.com. **Contact:** Mark Drew, assisant editor. Magazine: 6¼×10; 170 pages; acid free paper; full color illustrations. ''Our concern is quality. Manuscripts submitted here should be extremely well written.'' Reading period September-May. Quarterly. Estab. 1988. Circ. 4,000.

• Work appearing in *The Gettysburg Review* has also been included in *Prize Stories: The O. Henry Awards*, *Pushcart Prize* anthology, *Best American Fiction*, *New Stories from the South*, *Harper's* and elsewhere. It is also the recipient of a Lila Wallace-Reader's Digest grant and NEA grants.

Needs Experimental, historical, humor/satire, literary, mainstream, novel excerpts, regional, serialized novels, contemporary. ''We require that fiction be intelligent and esthetically written.'' Receives 350 unsolicited mss/month. Accepts 15-20 mss/issue; 60-80 mss/year. Publishes ms within 1 year after acceptance. **Publishes 1-5 new writers/year.** Recently published work by Robert Olen Butler, Joyce Carol Oates, Naeem Murr, Tom Perrotta, Alison Baker and Peter Baida. Length: 2,000-7,000 words; average length: 3,000 words. Publishes short shorts. Also publishes literary essays, literary criticism, poetry. Sometimes comments on rejected mss.

How to Contact Send complete ms. Accepts submissions by fax. SASE. Responds in 1 month to queries; 3-6 months to mss. Accepts simultaneous submissions. Sample copy for $7. Writer's guidelines online.

Payment/Terms Pays $30/page. Pays on publication for first North American serial rights.

Advice ''Reporting time can take more than three months. It is helpful to look at a sample copy of *The Gettysburg Review* to see what kinds of fiction we publish before submitting.''

GINOSKO

P.O. Box 246, Fairfax CA 94978. (415)785-2802. E-mail: ginoskoeditor@aol.com. **Contact:** Robert Cesaretti, editor. Magazine: 4×6; 50-60 pages; standard paper; photo glossy cover; b&w art and photos. Ghin-*oce*-koe: to perceive, understand, come to know; knowledge that has an inception, an attainment; the recognition of truth by personal experience. ''We are looking for writing that reflects religious intensity and truth yet without being too ethereal or intangible; is imagistic, poetic, stylized, mythic; that lifts up the beauty and grace of human frailty and apprehensions yet carries with it the strength and veracity of humility, compassion and belief.'' Published ''when material permits.'' Estab. 2003. Circ. 500.

Needs Experimental, literary, mainstream, stylized; ''consider 'Pagan Night' by Kate Braverman, 'Driving the

Heart' by Jason Brown, 'Customs of the Country' by Madison Smartt Bell.'' Does not want stylized, strong on theme, imagistic writing. Receives 10-20 unsolicited mss/month. **Publishes 4 new writers/year.** Recently published work by Ritchie Swanson and D.L. Olsen.

How to Contact Send complete ms. Accepts submissions by e-mail (ginoskoeditor@aol.com). SASE for return of ms. Responds in 1-3 months to mss. Accepts simultaneous and reprints submissions. Sample copy free.

Payment/Terms Pays one contributor's copy. Pays on publication for one-time rights. Not copyrighted.

Advice ''I am looking for a style that conveys spiritual hunger and yearning, yet avoids religiosity and convention—*between literary vision and spiritual realities.*''

$⬚ ⬚ GLIMMER TRAIN STORIES

Glimmer Train Press, Inc., 1211 NW Glisan St. #207, Portland OR 97209. (503)221-0836. Fax: (503)221-0837. Website: www.glimmertrain.com. **Contact:** Susan Burmeister-Brown and Linda Swanson-Davies. Magazine: 7¼×9¼; 260 pages; recycled; acid-free paper; 12 photographs. ''We are interested in well-written, emotionally-moving short stories published by unknown, as well as known, writers.'' Quarterly. Estab. 1991. Circ. 16,000.

• The magazine also sponsors an annual short story contest for new writers and a very short fiction contest.

Needs Literary. Receives 4,000 unsolicited mss/month. Accepts 10 mss/issue; 40 mss/year. Reads in January, April, July, October. Publishes ms up to 2 years after acceptance. Agented fiction 10%. **Publishes 12 new writers/year.** Recently published work by Judy Budnitz, Nancy Reisman, Herman Carrillo, Andre Dubus III, William Trevor, Alberto Rios and Alice Mattison. Sometimes comments on rejected mss.

How to Contact Submit work online at www.glimmertrain.com. Accepted work published in *Glimmer Train Stories*. Responds in 3 months to mss. No simultaneous submissions. Sample copy for $9.95 on website. Writer's guidelines online.

Payment/Terms Pays $500. Pays on acceptance for first rights.

Advice ''When a story stays with us after the first reading, it gets another reading. Those stories that simply don't let us set them aside, get published. Read good fiction. It will often improve the quality of your own writing.''

⬚ $⬚ GRAIN LITERARY MAGAZINE

Saskatchewan Writers Guild, P.O. Box 67, Saskatoon SK S7K 3K1 Canada. (306)244-2828. Fax: (306)244-0255. Website: www.grainmagazine.ca. **Contact:** Kent Bruyneel, editor. Literary magazine: 6×9; 128 pages; Chinook offset printing; chrome-coated stock; some photos. ''*Grain* publishes writing of the highest quality, both traditional and innovative in nature. *Grain* aim: To publish work that challenges readers; to encourage promising new writers; and to produce a well-designed, visually interesting magazine.'' Quarterly. Estab. 1973. Circ. 1,500.

Needs Experimental, literary, mainstream, contemporary, prose poem and poetry. ''No romance, confession, science fiction, vignettes, mystery.'' Receives 80 unsolicited mss/month. Accepts 8-12 mss/issue; 32-48 mss/year. Publishes ms 11 months after acceptance. Recently published work by J. Jill Robinson, Curtis Gillespi, John Laven. Also publishes poetry. Occasionally comments on rejected mss.

How to Contact Send complete ms with SASE (or IRC) and brief letter. Accepts queries by e-mail, mail, fax and phone. Responds in 1 month to queries; 4 months to mss. No simultaneous submissions. Sample copy for $13 or online. Writer's guidelines for #10 SASE or online.

Payment/Terms Pays $40-175. Pays on publication for first, Canadian serial rights.

Advice ''Submit a story to us that will deepen the imaginative experience of our readers. *Grain* has established itself as a first-class magazine of serious fiction. We receive submissions from around the world. If Canada is a foreign country to you, we ask that you *do not* use U.S. postage stamps on your return envelope. If you live outside Canada and neglect the International Reply Coupons, we *will not* read or reply to your submission. We look for attention to detail, credibility, lucid use of language and metaphor and a confident, convincing voice. Make sure you have researched your piece, that the literal and metaphorical support one another.''

⬚ GRANTA, The Magazine of New Writing

Granta Publications, 2-3 Hanover Yard, Noel Rd., London NI 8BE United Kingdom. (44)(0)20 7704 9776. E-mail: editorial@granta.com. Website: www.granta.com. **Contact:** Ian Jack, editor. Magazine: paperback, 256 pages approx; photos. ''*Granta* magazine publishes fiction, reportage, biography and autobiography, history, travel and documentary photography. It does not publish 'writing about writing.' The realistic narrative—the story—is its primary form.'' Quarterly. Estab. 1979. Circ. 80,000.

Needs Literary, novel excerpts. No genre fiction. Themes decided as deadline approaches. Receives 100 unsolicited mss/month. Accepts 0-1 mss/issue; 1-2 mss/year. **Publishes 1-2 new writers/year.**

How to Contact Send SAE and IRCs for reply, return of ms or send a disposable copy of ms. Responds in 3 months to mss. Accepts simultaneous submissions. Sample copy for $14.95. Writer's guidelines online.

Literary Magazines

Payment/Terms Payment varies. Pays on publication. Buys world English language rights, first serial rights (minimum). ''We hold more rights in pieces we commission.'' Sends galleys to author.

Advice ''We are looking for the best in realistic stories; originality of voice; without jargon, connivance or self-conscious 'performance'—writing that endures.''

GRASSLANDS REVIEW

P.O. Box 626, Berea OH 44017-0626. E-mail: grasslandsreview@aol.com. Website: hometown.aol.com/glreview/oldindex.html. **Contact:** Laura B. Kennelly, editor. Magazine: 6×9; 80 pages. *Grasslands Review* prints creative witing of all types; poetry, fiction, essay for a general audience. ''Designed as a place for new writers to publish.'' Semiannual. Estab. 1989. Circ. 300.

Needs Ethnic/multicultural, experimental, fantasy, horror, humor/satire, literary, regional, science fiction, western, contemporary, prose poem. ''Nothing pornographic or overtly political or religious.'' Accepts 1-3 mss/issue. Reads work post marked October or March. Publishes ms 6 months after acceptance. **Publishes 5 new writers/year.** Recently published work by J.L. Schneider, Toiya Smith and Thérèse Halscheid. Length: 100-3,500 words; average length: 1,000 words. Publishes short shorts. Also publishes poetry. Sometimes comments on rejected mss.

How to Contact SASE. Responds in 3 months to mss. No simultaneous submissions. Sample copy for $5 old copy; $6 for most recent copy.

Payment/Terms Pays in contributor's copies. Acquires one-time rights. Not copyrighted.

Advice ''A fresh approach, imagined by a reader for other readers, pleases our audience. We are looking for fiction which leaves a strong feeling or impression—or a new perspective on life. The *Review* began as an in-class exercise to allow experienced creative writing students to learn how a little magazine is produced. It now serves as an independant publication, attracting authors from as far away as the Ivory Coast, but its primary mission is to give unknown writers a start.''

THE GREEN HILLS LITERARY LANTERN

Published by Truman State University, Division of Language & Literature, Kirksville MO 63501. (660)785-4487. E-mail: adavis@truman.edu. Website: http://ll.truman.edu/ghllweb. **Contact:** Fiction editor. Magazine: 6×9; 200-300 pages; good quality paper with glossy 4-color cover. ''The mission of *GHLL* is to provide a literary market for quality fiction writers, both established and beginners, and to provide quality literature for readers from diverse backgrounds. We also see ourselves as cultural resource for North Missouri. Our publication works to publish the highest quality fiction—dense, layered, subtle and, at the same time, fiction which grabs the ordinary reader. We tend to publish traditional short stories, but we are open to experimental forms.'' Annual. Estab. 1990. Circ. 500.

Needs Ethnic/multicultural, experimental, feminist, humor/satire, literary, mainstream, regional. ''Our main requirement is literary merit. Wants more quality fiction about rural culture. No adventure, crime, erotica, horror, inspirational, mystery/suspense, romance.'' Receives 40 unsolicited mss/month. Accepts 15-17 mss/issue. Publishes ms 6-12 months after acceptance. **Publishes 0-3 new writers/year.** Recently published work by Karl Harshbarger, Mark Jacobs, J. Morris, Gary Fincke and Dennis Vannatta. Length: 7,000 words; average length: 3,000 words. Publishes short shorts. Also publishes poetry. Sometimes comments on rejected mss.

How to Contact SASE for return of ms. Responds in 4 months to mss. Accepts simultaneous, multiple submissions. Sample copy for $10 (includes envelope and postage).

Payment/Terms Pays 2 contributor's copies. Acquires one-time rights.

Advice ''We look for strong character development, substantive plot and theme, visual and forceful language within a multilayered story. Make sure your work has the flavor of life, a sense of reality. A good story, well crafted, will eventually get published. Find the right market for it, and above all, don't give up.''

GREEN MOUNTAINS REVIEW

Johnson State College, Box A-58, Johnson VT 05656. (802)635-1350. E-mail: greenmountainsreview@jsc.vsc.edu. **Contact:** Tony Whedon, fiction editor. Magazine: digest-sized; 160-200 pages. Semiannual. Estab. 1975. Circ. 1,700.

- *Green Mountain Review* has received a *Pushcart Prize* and Editors Choice Award.

Needs Adventure, experimental, humor/satire, literary, mainstream, serialized novels, translations. Receives 100 unsolicited mss/month. Accepts 6 mss/issue; 12 mss/year. ''Manuscripts will not be read and will be returned between March 1 and September 1.'' Publishes ms 6-12 months after acceptance. **Publishes 0-4 new writers/year.** Recently published work by Howard Norman, Debra Spark, Valerie Miner and Peter LaSalle. Publishes short shorts. Also publishes literary criticism, poetry. Sometimes comments on rejected mss.

How to Contact SASE. Responds in 1 month to queries; 6 months to mss. Accepts simultaneous submissions if advised. Sample copy for $7.

Payment/Terms Pays contributor's copies, 1-year subscription and small honorarium, depending on grants. Acquires first North American serial rights. Rights revert to author upon request.
Advice "We're looking for more rich, textured, original fiction with cross-cultural themes. The editors are open to a wide spectrum of styles and subject matter as is apparent from a look at the list of fiction writers who have published in its pages. One issue was devoted to Vermont fiction, another issue filled with new writing from the People's Republic of China, and a recent issue devoted to literary ethnography."

⬤ ▼ THE GREENSBORO REVIEW

English Dept., 134 McIver Bldg., UNC Greensboro, P.O. Box 26170, Greensboro NC 27402-6170. (336)334-5459. E-mail: jlclark@uncg.edu. Website: www.greensbororeview.com. **Contact:** Jim Clark, editor. Magazine: 6×9; approximately 128 pages; 60 lb. paper; 80 lb. cover. Literary magazine featuring fiction and poetry for readers interested in contemporary literature. Semiannual. Circ. 800.

  • Stories from *The Greensboro Review* have been included in *Best American Short Stories, Prize Stories: The O. Henry Awards, New Stories from the South* and *Pushcart Prize.*

Needs Accepts 6-8 mss/issue; 12-16 mss/year. Unsolicited manuscripts must arrive by September 15 to be considered for the spring issue and by February 15 to be considered for the fall issue. Manuscripts arriving after those dates may be held for the next consideration. **Publishes 10% new writers/year.** Recently published work by Robert Morgan, George Singleton, Robert Olmstead, Brock Clarke, Dale Ray Phillips and Kelly Cherry.
How to Contact Responds in 4 months to mss. Accepts multiple submissions. No simultaneous submissions. Sample copy for $5.
Payment/Terms Pays in contributor's copies. Acquires first North American serial rights.
Advice "We want to see the best being written regardless of theme, subject or style."

THE GRIFFIN

Gwynedd-Mercy College, P.O. Box 901, 1325 Sumneytown Pike, Gwynedd Valley PA 19437-0901. (215)641-5518. Fax: (215)641-5552. E-mail: fazzini.j@gmc.edu or allego.d@gmc.edu. **Contact:** Donna Allego and Jill Fazzini, editors. Literary magazine: 8½×5½; 112 pages. "*The Griffin* is a literary journal sponsored by Gwynedd-Mercy College. Its mission is to enrich society by nurturing and promoting creative writing that demonstrates a unique and intelligent voice. We seek writing which accurately reflects the human condition with all its intellectual, emotional and ethical challenges." Annual. Estab. 1999. Circ. 500.
Needs Short stories, essays and poetry. Open to genre work. "No slasher, graphic violence or sex." Accepts mss depending on the quality of work submitted. Receives 10-12 unsolicited mss/month. Publishes ms 6 months after acceptance. **Publishes 10-15 new writers/year.** Length: 2,500 words; average length: 2,000 words. Publishes short shorts. Also publishes literary essays, poetry.
How to Contact Send complete ms. Send SASE for return of ms or send disposable copy of ms and #10 SASE for reply only. Responds in 2-3 months to queries; 6 months to mss. Accepts simultaneous submissions "if notified." Sample copy for $6.
Payment/Terms Pays in 2 contributor's copies; additional copies for $6.
Advice "Looking for well-constructed works that explore universal qualities, respect for the individual and community, justice and integrity. Check our description and criteria. Rewrite until you're sure every word counts. We publish the best work we find regardless of industry needs."

⬤ THE GSU REVIEW

Georgia State University, Campus P.O. Box 1894, MSC 8R0322 Unit 8, Atlanta GA 30303-3083. (404)651-4804. Fax: (404)651-1710. E-mail: martah@mindspring.com. Website: www2.gsu.edu/~wwwrev/. **Contact:** Jody Brooks, fiction editor. Magazine. "*The GSU Review* us a biannual literary magazine publishing poetry, fiction, creative nonfiction and artwork. We want orginal voices searching to rise above the ordinary. No subject or form biases." Semiannual.
Needs Literary, novel excerpts. "No pornography." Receives 200 unsolicited mss/month. Publishes short shorts.
How to Contact Accepts submissions by e-mail. SASE for notification. Responds in 1 month to queries; 1-2 months to mss. Sample copy for $5. Writer's guidelines for SASE or on website.
Payment/Terms Pays in contributor's copy. Acquires one-time rights.

$⬤ ▼ GULF COAST, A Journal of Literature & Fine Arts

Dept. of English, University of Houston, Houston TX 77204-3013. (713)743-3223. Fax: (713)743-3215. Website: www.gulfcoast.uh.edu. **Contact:** Tiphanie Yanique Galiber, fiction editor. Magazine: 7×9; approx. 300 pages; stock paper, gloss cover; illustrations; photos. "Innovative fiction for the literary-minded." Estab. 1987. Circ. 1,500.

• Work published in *Gulf Coast* has been selected for inclusion in the *Pushcart Prize* anthology, *O'Henry Prize* anthology and *Best American Short Stories*.

Needs Ethnic/multicultural, experimental, literary, regional, translations, contemporary. "No children's, genre, religious/inspirational." Wants more "cutting-edge, experimental" fiction. Receives 150 unsolicited mss/month. Accepts 4-8 mss/issue; 12-16 mss/year. Publishes ms 6 months-1 year after acceptance. Agented fiction 5%. **Publishes 2-8 new writers/year.** Recently published work by Justin Cronin, Cary Holladay, Ellen Litman, Michael Marfone, Joe Meno and Mishelle Wildgen. Publishes short shorts. Sometimes comments on rejected mss.

How to Contact Responds in 6 months to mss. Accepts simultaneous submissions. Back issue for $6, 7×10 SAE and 4 first-class stamps. Writer's guidelines for #10 SASE or on website.

Payment/Terms Pays $50-100. Acquires one-time rights.

Advice "Rotating editorship, so please be patient with replies. As always, please send one story at a time."

ℕ ◖ GULF STREAM MAGAZINE

Florida International University, English Dept., Biscayne Bay Campus, 3000 N.E. 151st St., N. Miami FL 33181-3000. (305)919-5599. E-mail: gulfstreamfiu@yahoo.com. Editor: John Dufresne. **Contact:** Fiction Editor. Magazine: 5½×8½; 96 pages; recycled paper; 80 lb. glossy cover; cover illustrations." "We publish *good qualty*—fiction, nonfiction and poetry for a predominately literary market." Semiannual. Estab. 1989. Circ. 1,000.

Needs Literary, mainstream, contemporary. Does not want romance, historical, juvenile or religious work. Receives 250 unsolicited mss/month. Accepts 5 mss/issue; 10 mss/year. Does not read mss during the summer. Publishes ms 3-6 months after acceptance. **Publishes 2-5 new writers/year.** Recently published work by Marureen Seaton, Charles Harper Webb, Lise Saffran, Janice Eidus, Susan Neville. Length: 7,500 words; average length: 5,000 words. Publishes short shorts. Also publishes poetry.

How to Contact Send complete ms. SASE. Responds in 3 months to mss. Accepts simultaneous submissions "if noted." Sample copy for $5. Writer's guidelines for #10 SASE.

Payment/Terms Pays in gift subscriptions and contributor's copies. Acquires first North American serial rights.

Advice "Looks for good concise writing—well plotted with interesting characters. Usually longer stories do not get accepted. There are exceptions, however."

$ ◖ HAPPY

240 E. 35th St., Suite 11A, New York NY 10016. E-mail: bayard@aol.com. **Contact:** Bayard, fiction editor. Magazine: 5½×8; 150-200 pages; 60 lb. text paper; 150 lb. cover; perfect-bound; illustrations; photos. Quarterly. Estab. 1995. Circ. 500.

Needs Erotica, ethnic/multicultural, experimental, fantasy, feminist, gay, horror, humor/satire, lesbian, literary, novel excerpts, psychic/supernatural/occult, science fiction, short stories. No "television rehash or religious nonsense." Want more work that is "strong, angry, empowering, intelligent, God-like, expressive." Receives 300-500 unsolicited mss/month. Accepts 30-40 mss/issue; 100-150 mss/year. Publishes ms 6-12 months after acceptance. **Publishes 25-30 new writers/year.** Length: 6,000 words maximum; average length: 1,000-3,500 words. Publishes short shorts. Often comments on rejected mss.

How to Contact Send complete ms. Include estimated word count. Send SASE for reply, return of ms or send a disposable copy of ms. Responds in 1 month to queries. Accepts simultaneous submissions. Sample copy for $20. Writer's guidelines for #10 SASE.

Payment/Terms Pays 1-5¢/word. Pays on publication for one-time rights.

Advice "Excite me!"

◖ ◎ HARD ROW TO HOE

Potato Eyes Foundation, P.O. Box 541-I, Healdsburg CA 95448. (707)433-9786. **Contact:** Joe E. Armstrong, editor. Magazine: 8½×12; 12 pages; 60 lb. white paper; illustrations; photos. "We look for literature of rural life, including environmental, Native American and foreign (English only) subjects. Book reviews, short story, poetry and a regular column. So far as we know, we are the only literary newsletter that features rural subjects." Triannual. Estab. 1982. Circ. 200.

Needs Rural, enviromental, Native American, foreign (English only). "No urban subjects. We would like to see more fiction on current rural lifestyles." Receives 5-10 unsolicited mss/month. Accepts 2-3 mss/issue; 6-8 mss/year. Publishes ms 10 months after acceptance. **Publishes 2 new writers/year.** Recently published work by Gary Every, Victoria Gorton and Jane Bradbury. Average length: 1,200 words. Publishes short shorts. Also publishes literary essays, poetry. Often comments on rejected mss.

How to Contact Send complete ms. Send SASE for return of ms or send a disposable copy of ms and #10 SASE for reply only. Responds in 2 weeks to queries; 6 weeks to mss. Accepts multiple submissions. Sample copy for $3. Writer's guidelines for SASE. Reviews fiction.

Payment/Terms Pays 2 contributor's copies; additional copies $3. Pays on publication for one-time rights. **Advice** "Work must exhibit authentic setting and dialogue."

HARPUR PALATE, A Literary Journal at Binghamton University

English Department, P.O. Box 6000, Binghamton University, Binghamton NY 13902-6000. E-mail: hpfiction@ho tmail.com. Website: harpurpalate.binghamton.edu. **Contact:** Letitia Moffitt, fiction editor. Magazine: 5½×8; 80-120 pages; coated or uncoated paper; 90 lb. coated or uncoated cover; illustrations; photos. "We have no restrictions on subject matter or form. Quite simply, send us your highest-quality fiction and poetry." Semiannual. Estab. 2000. Circ. 500.

- Stories published in *Harpur Palate* have been chosen for *Best American Mystery Stories 2003* and *Best of the Rest 3*.

Needs Adventure, ethnic/multicultural, experimental, fantasy, historical, horror, humor/satire, mainstream, mystery/suspense, novel excerpts, science fiction, suspense, literary, fabulism, magical realism, metafiction, slipstream (genre blending). Receives 150 unsolicited mss/month. Accepts 5-10 mss/issue; 12-20 mss/year. Publishes ms 1-2 months after acceptance. **Publishes 5 new writers/year.** Recently published work by Hugh Cook, Scott Wolven, Lydia Davis, M. Evelina Galang and Bruce Holland Rogers. Length: 250-8,000 words; average length: 2,000-4,000 words. Publishes short shorts. Also publishes poetry. Sometimes comments on rejected mss.

How to Contact Send complete ms with a cover letter. Include e-mail address on cover. Include estimated word count, brief bio, list of publications. Send a disposable copy of ms and #10 SASE for reply only. Responds in 1-3 week to queries; 4-6 months to mss. Accepts simultaneous submissions if stated in the cover letter. Sample copy for $8. Writer's guidelines online.

Payment/Terms Pays 2 copies. Pays on publication for first North American serial, electronic rights. Sponsors awards/contests.

Advice "*Harpur Palate* now accepts submissions all year; deadline for the Winter issue is October 15, for the Summer issue March 15. *Harpur Palate* also sponsors a fiction contest for the Summer issue. Due to concerns about computer viruses, we no longer accept submissions via e-mail. Also, due to the large number of submissions we receive, we cannot answer queries about the status of a particular story. Almost every literary magazine already says this, but it bears repeating: look at a copy of our publication (and other publications as well) to get an idea of the kind of writing published. Do an honest (perhaps even ruthless) assessment of your work to see if it's indeed ready to be submitted."

HARVARD REVIEW

Harvard University, Lamont Library, Level 5, Cambridge MA 02138. (617)495-9775. E-mail: harvrev@fas.harvar d.edu. Website: http://hcl.harvard.edu/harvardreview. **Contact:** Christina Thompson, editor. Magazine: 6×9; 192-240 pages; illustrations; photographs. Semiannual. Estab. 1992. Circ. 2,000.

Needs Literary. Receives 80-100 unsolicited mss/month. Accepts 4 mss/issue; 8 mss/year. Publishes ms 3-6 months after acceptance. **Publishes 3-4 new writers/year.** Recently published work by John Updike, Alice Hoffman, Thomas McGuane and Jess Row. Length: 1,000-7,000 words; average length: 3,000-5,000 words. Publishes short shorts. Also publishes literary essays, literary criticism, poetry. Sometimes comments on rejected mss.

How to Contact Send SASE for return of ms or disposable copy of ms and SASE for reply only. Responds in 2 months to queries; 3-6 months to mss. Accepts simultaneous submissions. Writer's guidelines online.

Payment/Terms Pays 2 contributor's copies; additional copies $6. Pays on publication for first North American serial rights. Sends galleys to author.

HAWAI'I PACIFIC REVIEW

Hawai'i Pacific University, 1060 Bishop St., Honolulu HI 96813. (808)544-1108. Fax: (808)544-0862. E-mail: pwilson@hpu.edu. Website: www.hpu.edu. **Contact:** Patrice M. Wilson, editor. Magazine: 6×9; 100 pages; glossy coated cover. "*Hawai'i Pacific Review* is looking for poetry, short fiction and personal essays that speak with a powerful and unique voice. We encourage experimental narrative techniques and poetic styles, and we welcome works in translation." Annual.

Needs Ethnic/multicultural (general), experimental, fantasy, feminist, historical (general), humor/satire, literary, mainstream, regional (Pacific), translations. "Open to all types as long as they're well done. Our audience is adults, so nothing for children/teens." Receives 25-40 unsolicited mss/month. Accepts 5-10 mss/year. Does not read mss January-August each year. Publishes ms 10 months after acceptance. **Publishes 1-2 new writers/ year.** Recently published work by Wendell Mayo, Elizabeth Crowell and Janet Flora. Publishes short shorts. Also publishes literary essays, poetry. Sometimes comments on rejected mss.

How to Contact Send SASE for return of ms or send a disposable copy of ms and SASE for reply only. Responds

Literary Magazines

in 2 weeks to queries; 15 weeks to mss. Accepts simultaneous submissions—must be cited in the cover letter. Sample copy for $5.

Payment/Terms Pays 2 contributor's copies; additional copies $5. Pays on publication for first North American serial rights.

Advice "We look for the unusual or original plot; prose with the texture and nuance of poetry. Character development or portrayal must be unusual/original; humanity shown in an original insightful way (or characters); sense of humor where applicable. Be sure it's a draft that has gone through substantial changes, with supervision from a more experienced writer, if you're a beginner. Write about intense emotion and feeling, not just about someone's divorce or shaky relationship. No soap-opera-like fiction."

$⬛⬛⬛ HAYDEN'S FERRY REVIEW

The Virginia G. Piper Center for Creative Writing at Arizona State University, Box 875002, Arizona State University, Tempe AZ 85287-1502. (480)965-1243. E-mail: hfr@asu.edu. Website: www.haydensferryreview.org. **Contact:** Fiction editor. Editors change every 1-2 years. Magazine: 7×9¾; 128 pages; fine paper; illustrations; photos. "*Hayden's Ferry Review* publishes best quality fiction, poetry and creative nonfiction from new, emerging and established writers." Semiannual. Estab. 1986. Circ. 1,300.

• Work from *Hayden's Ferry Review* has been selected for inclusion in *Pushcart Prize* anthologies.

Needs Ethnic/multicultural, experimental, humor/satire, literary, regional, slice-of-life vignettes, contemporary, prose poem. Possible special fiction issue. Receives 250 unsolicited mss/month. Accepts 5 mss/issue; 10 mss/year. Publishes ms 6 months after acceptance. Recently published work by T.C. Boyle, Raymond Carver, Ken Kesey, Rita Dove, Chuck Rosenthal and Rick Bass. Publishes short shorts. Also publishes literary criticism.

How to Contact Send complete ms. SASE. Responds in 2 weeks to queries; 3 months to mss. Accepts simultaneous submissions. Sample copy for $7.50. Writer's guidelines online.

Payment/Terms Pays $25-100. Pays on publication for first North American serial rights. Sends galleys to author.

$⬛⬛ HEARTLANDS, A Magazine of Midwest Life and Art

(formerly *The Heartlands Today*)The Firelands Writing Center, Firelands College of BGSU, Huron OH 44839. (419)433-5560. E-mail: lsmithdog@aol.com. Website: www.theheartlandstoday.net. **Contact:** Fiction editor. Magazine: 8½×11; perfect bound; 160 pages; b&w illustrations; 15 photos. *Material must be set in the Midwest.* "We prefer material that reveals life in the Midwest today for a general, literate audience." Biannual. Estab. 1991.

Needs Ethnic/multicultural, humor/satire, literary, mainstream, regional (Midwest). Receives 15 unsolicited mss/month. Accepts 6 mss/issue. Does not read August-December. "We edit between January 1 and May 15." Submit then. Publishes ms 6 months after acceptance. Recently published work by Wendell Mayo, Tony Tomassi, Gloria Bowman. Also publishes literary essays, poetry. Sometimes comments on rejected mss.

How to Contact Send SASE for ms, not needed for query. Responds in 2 months to mss. Accepts simultaneous submissions, if noted. Sample copy for $5.

Payment/Terms Pays $10-20 and 2 contributor's copies. Pays on publication for first rights.

Advice "We look for writing that connects on a human level, that moves us with its truth and opens our vision of the world. If writing is a great escape for you, don't bother with us. We're in it for the joy, beauty or truth of the art. We look for a straight, honest voice dealing with human experiences. We do not define the Midwest, we hope to be a document of the Midwest. If you feel you are writing from the Midwest, send your work to us. We look first at the quality of the writing."

⬛⬛⬛ HEAVEN BONE

Heaven Bone Press, Box 486, Chester NY 10918. (845)469-2326. E-mail: heavenbone@aol.com. **Contact:** Steven Hirsch and Kirpal Gordon, editors. Magazine: 8½×11; 96-116 pages; 60 lb. recycled offset paper; full color cover; computer clip art, graphics, line art, cartoons, halftones and photos scanned in tiff format. "Expansive, fine surrealist and experimental literary, earth and nature, spiritual path. We use current reviews, essays on spiritual and esoteric topics, creative stories. Also: reviews of current poetry releases and expansive literature." Readers are "scholars, surrealists, poets, artists, muscians, students." Annual. Estab. 1987. Circ. 2,500.

Needs Experimental, fantasy, regional, esoteric/scholarly, spiritual. "No violent, thoughtless, exploitive or religious fiction." Receives 45-110 unsolicited mss/month. Accepts 5-15 mss/issue; 12-30 mss/year. Publishes ms 2 weeks-10 months after acceptance. **Publishes 3-4 new writers/year.** Recently published work by Keith Abbot and Stephen-Paul Martin. Length: 1,200-5,000 words; average length: 3,500 words. Publishes short shorts. Also publishes literary essays, literary criticism, poetry. Sometimes comments on rejected mss.

How to Contact Send SASE for reply or return of ms. Responds in 3 weeks to queries; 10 months to mss. Accepts reprints submissions. Sample copy for $10. Writer's guidelines for SASE. Reviews fiction.

Payment/Terms Pays in contributor's copies; charges for extras. Acquires first North American serial rights. Sends galleys to author.

Advice "Read a sample issue first. Our fiction needs are temperamental, so please query first before submitting. We prefer shorter fiction. Do not send first drafts to test them on us. Please refine and polish your work before sending. Always include SASE. We are looking for the unique, unusual and excellent."

ⓃⒺⓈ HOME PLANET NEWS

Home Planet Publications, P.O. Box 455, High Falls NY 12440. (845)687-4084. **Contact:** Donald Lev, editor. Tabloid: $11^{1}/_{2} \times 16$; 24 pages; newsprint; illustrations; photos. "*Home Planet News* publishes mainly poetry along with some fiction, as well as reviews (books, theater and art), and articles of literary interest. We see *HPN* as a quality literary journal in an eminently readable format and with content that is urban, urbane and politically aware." Triannual. Estab. 1979. Circ. 1,000.

● *HPN* has received a small grant from the Puffin Foundation for its focus on AIDS issues.

Needs Ethnic/multicultural, experimental, feminist, gay, historical, lesbian, literary, mainstream, science fiction (soft/sociological). No "children's or genre stories (except rarely some science fiction)." Upcoming themes: "Midrash." Publishes special fiction issue or anthology. Receives 12 unsolicited mss/month. Accepts 1 mss/issue; 3 mss/year. Publishes ms 1 year after acceptance. Recently published work by Maureen McNeil, Eugene Stein, Hugh Fox, Walter Jackman and Layle Silbert. Length: 500-2,500 words; average length: 2,000 words. Publishes short shorts. Also publishes literary criticism.

How to Contact Send complete ms. Send SASE for reply, return of ms or send a disposable copy of the ms. Responds in 6 months to mss. Sample copy for $4. Writer's guidelines for SASE.

Payment/Terms Pays 3 contributor's copies; additional copies $1. Acquires one-time rights.

Advice "We use very little fiction, and a story we accept just has to grab us. We need short pieces of some complexity, stories about complex people facing situations which resist simple resolutions."

Ⓔ HOTEL AMERIKA

English Department, 360 Ellis Hall, Ohio University, Athens OH 45701. (740)597-1360. E-mail: editors@hotelam erika.net. Website: www.hotelamerika.net. **Contact:** David Lazar, editor. Magazine: 130 pages; cardstock cover stock; photos. *Hotel Amerika* is a literary journal open to all genres and schools of writing, from the most formalistic to the most avant garde. Biannual. Estab. 2002. Circ. 2,000.

● Work published in *Hotel Amerika* was selected for the 2003 *Pushcart Prize* anthology.

Needs Literary. Receives 30-40 unsolicited mss/month. Accepts 3-5 mss/issue; 6-10 mss/year. Does not read mss May 1-August 31. Publishes ms 4-12 months after acceptance. Recently published work by Louise Wareham, Edith Pearlman and William Black. Publishes short shorts. Also publishes literary essays, poetry. Sometimes comments on rejected mss.

How to Contact Send complete ms. Send SASE (or IRC) for return of the ms or send disposable copy of the ms and #10 SASE for reply only. Responds in 3 months to mss. Accepts multiple submissions. Writer's guidelines for #10 SASE or online. No simultaneous submissions.

Payment/Terms Pays contributor's copies. Pays on publication for first North American serial rights. Sends galleys to author.

$ THE HUDSON REVIEW, A magazine of literature and the arts

The Hudson Review, Inc., 684 Park Ave., New York NY 10021. (212)650-0020. Fax: (212)774-1911. E-mail: info@hudsonreview.com. Website: www.hudsonreview.com. **Contact:** Ronald Koury. Quarterly. Estab. 1948. Circ. 5,000.

Needs Reads between September 1 and November 30 only. Publishes ms 6 months after acceptance.

How to Contact Responds in 2 months to queries; 3 months to mss. Sample copy for $9. Writer's guidelines for #10 SASE.

Payment/Terms Pays $2^{1}/_{2}$¢/word. Pays on publication. Only assigned reviews are copyrighted.

$Ⓔ THE ICONOCLAST

1675 Amazon Rd., Mohegan Lake NY 10547-1804. **Contact:** Phil Wagner, editor. Journal: $8^{1}/_{2} \times 5^{1}/_{2}$; 44-96 pages; 20 lb. white paper; 50 lb. cover stock; illustrations. "Aimed for a literate general audience with interests in fine (but accessible) fiction and poetry." Bimonthly. Estab. 1992. Circ. 700.

Needs Adventure, ethnic/multicultural, experimental, humor/satire, literary, mainstream, novel excerpts, science fiction, literary. No character studies, slice-of-life, pieces strong on attitude/weak on plot. Receives 150 unsolicited mss/month. Accepts 3-6 mss/issue; 25-30 mss/year. Publishes ms 9-12 months after acceptance. **Publishes 8-10 new writers/year.** Recently published work by Sandra Novack, Harold R. Larmer and Karl Harshbarger. Publishes short shorts. Also publishes literary essays, poetry. Sometimes comments on rejected mss.

Literary Magazines

How to Contact Send complete ms. Send SASE for reply, return of ms or send a disposable copy of the ms labeled as such. Responds in 2 weeks to queries; 5 months to mss. No simultaneous submissions. Sample copy for $2.50. Writer's guidelines for #10 SASE. Reviews fiction.

Payment/Terms Pays 1¢/word. Pays on publication for first North American serial rights.

Advice "We like fiction that has something to say (and not about its author). We hope for work that is observant, intense and multi-leveled. Follow Pound's advice—'make it new.' Write what you want in whatever style you want without being gross, sensational or needlessly explicit—then pray there's someone who can appreciate your sensibility. Read good fiction. It's as fundamental as learning how to hit, throw and catch is to baseball. With the increasing American disinclination towards literature, stories must insist on being heard. Read what is being published—then write something better—and different. Do all rewrites before sending a story out. Few editors have time to work with writers on promising stories; only polished."

$ ⊘ ▩ THE IDAHO REVIEW

Boise State University, English Dept., 1910 University Dr., Boise ID 83725. (208)426-1002. Fax: (208)426-4373. E-mail: mwieland@boisestate.edu. **Contact:** Mitch Wieland, editor. Magazine: 6×9; 180-200 pages; acid-free accent opaque paper; coated cover stock; photos. "A literary journal for anyone who enjoys good fiction." Annual. Estab. 1998. Circ. 1,000. CLMP.

* Two stories chosen for 2003 *Prize Stories: The O. Henry Awards*, plus one story listed as "special mention" in 2003 *Puchcart Prize*.

Needs Experimental, literary. "No genre fiction of any type." Receives 150 unsolicited mss/month. Accepts 5-7 mss/issue; 5-7 mss/year. "We do not read from December 16-August 31." Publishes ms 1 year after acceptance. Agented fiction 5%. **Publishes 1 new writer/year.** Recently published work by Rick Bass, Melanie Rae Thon, Ron Carlson, Joy Williams, Frederick Busch, Alyson Hagy and Edith Pearlman. Length: open; average length: 7,000 words. Publishes short shorts. Also publishes literary essays, poetry. Sometimes comments on rejected mss.

How to Contact Send SASE for return of ms or send a disposable copy of ms and #10 SASE for reply only. Responds in 3-5 months to mss. Accepts simultaneous, multiple submissions. Sample copy for $8.95. Writer's guidelines for SASE. Reviews fiction.

Payment/Terms Pays $100 when funds are available plus 2 contributor's copies; additional copies $5. Pays on publication for first North American serial rights. Sends galleys to author.

Advice "We look for strongly crafted work that tells a story that needs to be told. We demand vision, intelligence and mystery in the fiction we publish."

⊘ THE IDIOT

Anarchaos Press, P.O. Box 69163, Los Angeles CA 90069. E-mail: idiotsubmission@yahoo.com. Website: www.theidiotmagazine.com. **Contact:** Brian Campbell and Toni Plummer, lackeys. Magazine: 5½×8½; 48 pages; 20 lb. white paper; cardboard glossy cover; illustrations. "For people who enjoy Triumph The Insult Comic Dog, *The Daily Show*, *South Park*, *Ali G*, Louis Black, old Woody Allen, S.J. Perelman, James Thurber and Albert Camus. We're looking for black comedy. Death, disease, God, religion and micronauts are all potential subjects of comedy. Nothing is sacred, but it needs to be funny. I don't want whimsical, I don't want amusing, I don't want some fanciful anecdote about a trip you took with your uncle when you were eight. I want laugh-out-loud-fall-on-the-floor-funny. If it's cute, give it to your mom, your sweetheart, or your puppy dog. Length doesn't matter, but most comedy is like soup. It's an appetizer, not a meal. Short is often better. Bizarre, obscure, referential and literary are all appreciated. My audience is mostly comprised of bitter misanthropes who play Russian Roulette between airings of *The Simpsons* each day. I want dark." Annual. Estab. 1993. Circ. 1,000.

Needs Humor/satire. Wants more short, dark humor. Publishes ms 6-12 after acceptance. **Publishes 1-3 new writers/year.** Recently published work by Judd Trichter, Freud Pachenko, Brad Hufford and Johnny "John-John" Kearns. Length: 2,000 words; average length: 500 words. Publishes short shorts. Also publishes poetry. Sometimes comments on rejected mss.

How to Contact Accepts submissions by e-mail. Send SASE for reply, return of ms or send a disposable copy of ms. Responds in 1-12 months to mss. Accepts simultaneous and reprints submissions. Sample copy for $5, subscription $10.

Payment/Terms Pays 1 contributor's copy. Acquires one-time rights. Sends galleys to author.

Advice "We almost never use anything over 1,500 words, but if it's really funny I'll take a look at it."

⊘ ILLUMINATIONS, An International Magazine of Contemporary Writing

℅ Dept. of English, College of Charleston, 66 George St., Charleston SC 29424-0001. (843)953-1920. Fax: (843)953-1924. E-mail: lewiss@cofc.edu. Website: www.cofc.edu/illuminations. **Contact:** Simon Lewis, editor. Magazine: 5×8; 80 pages; illustrations. "*Illuminations* is one of the most challengingly eclectic little literary magazines around, having featured writers from the United States, Britain and Romania as well as Southern Africa.'' Annual. Estab. 1982. Circ. 400.

Needs Literary. Receives 5 unsolicited mss/month. Accepts 1 mss/year. **Publishes 1 new writer/year.** Recently published work by John Michael Cummings. Also publishes poetry. Sometimes comments on rejected mss.

How to Contact Send SASE for reply, return of ms or send a disposable copy of ms. Responds in 2 weeks to queries; 2 months to mss. No simultaneous submissions. Sample copy for $10 and 6×9 envelope. Writer's guidelines free.

Payment/Terms Pays 2 contributor's copies of current issue; 1 of subsequent issue. Acquires one-time rights.

☾ ILLYA'S HONEY

The Dallas Poets Community, A non-profit corportation, P.O. Box 700865, Dallas TX 75370. E-mail: info@dallas poets.org. Website: www.dallaspoets.org. **Contact:** Ann Howells, editor. Magazine: 5½×8½; 34 pages; 24 lb. paper; glossy cover; photos. ''We publish poetry and flash fiction under 200 words. We try to present quality work by writers who take time to learn technique—aimed at anyone who appreciates good literature.'' Quarterly. Estab. 1994. Circ. 125.

Needs Ethnic/multicultural, experimental, feminist, gay, historical, humor/satire, lesbian, literary, mainstream, regional, flash fiction. ''We accept only flash (also known as micro) fiction.'' Receives 10 unsolicited mss/ month. Accepts 2-8 mss/issue. Publishes ms 3-5 months after acceptance. **Publishes 2-3 new writers/year.** Recently published work by Paul Sampson, Susanne Bowers and Denworthy. Also publishes poetry. Sometimes comments on rejected mss.

How to Contact Send complete ms. Send SASE for return of ms or send a disposable copy of ms and #10 SASE for reply only. Responds in 6 months to mss. Sample copy for $4. Writer's guidelines for SASE.

Payment/Terms Pays 1 contributor's copy; additional copies $6. Pays on publication for first North American serial rights.

Advice ''We would like to see more character studies, humor.''

$☑ IMAGE, Art, Faith, Mystery

3307 Third Ave. W, Seattle WA 98119. (206)281-2988. E-mail: image@imagejournal.org. Website: www.imagej ournal.org. **Contact:** Gregory Wolfe. Magazine: 7×10; 136 pages; glossy cover stock; illustrations; photos. ''*Image* is a showcase for the encounter between religious faith and world-class contemporary art. Each issue features fiction, poetry, essays, memoirs, an in-depth interview and articles about visual artists, film, music, etc. and glossy 4-color plates of contemporary visual art.'' Quarterly. Estab. 1989. Circ. 6,000. CLMP.

Needs Literary, translations. Receives 100 unsolicited mss/month. Accepts 2 mss/issue; 8 mss/year. Publishes ms 1 year after acceptance. Agented fiction 5%. Recently published work by Annie Dillard, David James Duncan, Robert Olen Butler, Bret Lott and Melanie Rae Thon. Length: 4,000-6,000 words; average length: 5,000 words. Also publishes literary essays, poetry.

How to Contact Send SASE for reply, return of ms or send disposable copy of ms. Responds in 1 month to queries; 3 months to mss. Sample copy for $12. Reviews fiction.

Payment/Terms Pays $10/page and 4 contributor's copies; additional copies for $5. Pays on acceptance. Sends galleys to author.

Advice ''Fiction must grapple with religious faith, though the settings and subjects need not be overtly religious.''

$☑ ⛾ INDIANA REVIEW

Indiana University, Ballantine Hall 465, 1020 E. Kirkwood, Bloomington IN 47405-7103. (812)855-3439. Website: www.indiana.edu/~inreview. **Contact:** Fiction editor. Magazine: 6×9; 160 pages; 50 lb. paper; Glatfelter cover stock. ''*Indiana Review*, a nonprofit organization run by IU graduate students, is a journal of previously unpublished poetry and fiction. Literary interviews and essays also considered. We publish innovative fiction and poetry. We're interested in energy, originality and careful attention to craft. While we publish many well-known writers, we also welcome new and emerging poets and fiction writers.'' Semiannual. Estab. 1976. Circ. 2,000.·

    ● Work published in *Indiana Review* received a *Pushcart Prize* (2001) and was included in *Best New American Voices* (2001). *IR* also received an Indiana Arts Council Grant and a National Endowment In the Arts grant.

Needs Ethnic/multicultural, experimental, literary, mainstream, novel excerpts, regional, translations, literary, short fictions, translations. No genre fiction. Receives 300 unsolicited mss/month. Accepts 7-9 mss/issue. Does not read mss mid-December-mid-January. Publishes ms an average of 3-6 months after acceptance. **Publishes 6-8 new writers/year.** Recently published work by Stuart Dybek, Marilyn Chin, Ray Gonzalez and Abby Frucht. Also publishes literary essays, poetry.

How to Contact Send complete ms. Accepts submissions by e-mail. Cover letters should be *brief* and demonstrate specific familiarity with the content of a recent issue of *Indiana Review*. SASE. Responds in 4 months to

Literary Magazines

Literary Magazines

mss. Accepts simultaneous submissions if notified *immediately* of other publication. Sample copy for $9. Writer's guidelines online.

Payment/Terms Pays $5/page, plus 2 contributor's copies. Pays on publication for first North American serial rights. Sponsors awards/contests.

Advice "Because our editors change each year, so do our literary preferences. It's important that potential contributors are familiar with our most recent issue of *Indiana Review* via library, sample copy or subscription. Beyond that, we look for prose that is well crafted and socially relevant. Dig deep. Don't accept your first choice descriptions when you are revising. Cliché and easy images sink 90% of the stories we reject. Understand the magazines you send to—investigate!"

INKWELL MAGAZINE

Manhattanville College, 2900 Purchase St., Purchase NY 10577. (914)323-7239. Fax: (914)323-3122. E-mail: inkwell@mville.edu. Website: www.inkwelljournal.org. **Contact:** Jeremy Church, editor. Literary Journal: $5\frac{1}{2} \times 7\frac{1}{2}$; 120-170 pages; 60 lb. paper; 10 pt C1S, 4/c cover; illustrations; photos. "*Inkwell Magazine* is committed to presenting top quality poetry, prose and artwork in a high quality publication. *Inkwell* is dedicated to discovering new talent and to encouraging and bringing talents of working writers and artists to a wider audience. We encourage diverse voices and have an open submission policy for both art and literature." Annual. Estab. 1995. Circ. 1,000. CLMP.

Needs Experimental, humor/satire, literary. "No erotica, children's literature, romance, religious." Receives 120 unsolicited mss/month. Accepts 45 mss/issue. Does not read mss December-July. Publishes ms 2 months after acceptance. **Publishes 3-5 new writers/year.** Recently published work by Alice Quinn, Margaret Gibson and Benjamin Cheever. Length: 5,000 words; average length: 3,000 words. Publishes short shorts. Also publishes poetry.

How to Contact Send a disposable copy of ms and #10 SASE for reply only. Responds in 1 month to queries; 4-6 months to mss. Sample copy for $6. Writer's guidelines for SASE.

Payment/Terms Pays 2 contributor's copies; additional copies $8. Acquires first North American serial, first rights. Sponsors awards/contests.

Advice "We look for well-crafted original stories with a strong voice."

$ THE IOWA REVIEW

308 EPB, The University of Iowa, Iowa City IA 52242. (319)335-0462. Fax: (319)335-2535. Website: www.uiowa.edu/~iareview/. **Contact:** Fiction Editor. Magazine: $5\frac{1}{2} \times 8\frac{1}{2}$; 200 pages; first-grade offset paper; Carolina CS1 10-pt. cover stock. "Stories, essays, poems for a general readership interested in contemporary literature." Triannual magazine. Estab. 1970. Circ. 2,500.

Needs "We are open to a range of styles and voices and always hope to be surprised by work we then feel we need." Receives 600 unsolicited mss/month. Accepts 4-6 mss/issue; 12-18 mss/year. Does not read mss January-August. Publishes ms an average of 12-18 months after acceptance. Agented fiction less than 2%. **Publishes some new writers/year.** Recently published work by Joshua Harmon, Katherine Vaz, Mary Helen Stefaniak and Steve Tomasula. Also publishes literary essays, literary criticism, poetry.

How to Contact Send complete ms with cover letter. "Don't bother with queries." SASE for return of ms. Responds in 3 months to queries; 3 months to mss. "We discourage simultaneous submissions." Sample copy for $7 and online. Writer's guidelines online. Reviews fiction.

Payment/Terms Pays $25 for the first page and $15 for each additional page, plus 2 contributor's copies; additional copies 30% off cover price. Pays on publication for first North American serial, nonexclusive anthology, classroom, and online serial rights.

Advice "We have no set guidelines as to content or length; we look for what we consider to be the best writing available to us and are pleased when writers we believe we have discovered catch on with a wider range of readers. It is never a bad idea to look through an issue or two of the magazine prior to a submission."

IRIS, A Journal About Women

P.O. Box 800588, University of Virginia, Charlottesville VA 22908. (434)924-4500. E-mail: iris@virginia.edu. **Contact:** Fiction Editor. Magazine: $8\frac{1}{2} \times 11$; 80 pages; glossy paper; heavy cover; illustrations; artwork; photos. "Material of particular interest to women. For a feminist audience, college educated and above." Semiannual. Estab. 1980. Circ. 3,500.

Needs Experimental, feminist, lesbian, literary, mainstream. "We're just looking for well-written stories of interest to women (particularly feminist women)." Receives 25 unsolicited mss/month. Accepts 5 mss/year. Publishes ms 1 year after acceptance. **Publishes 1-2 new writers/year.** Recently published work by Sheila Thorne, Lizette Wanzer, Marsha Recknagel and Denise Laughlin. Average length: 2,500-4,000 words. Sometimes comments on rejected mss.

How to Contact Accepts submissions by e-mail. SASE. Responds in 3 months to mss. Accepts simultaneous submissions. Sample copy for $5. Writer's guidelines for SASE. Label: Fiction Editor.

Payment/Terms Pays in contributor's copies and 1 year subscription. Acquires one-time rights.

Advice "My major complaint is with stories that don't elevate the language above the bland sameness we hear on the television everyday. Read the work of the outstanding women writers, such as Alice Munro and Louise Erdrich."

$⟐ THE JOURNAL

The Ohio State University, 164 W. 17th Ave., Columbus OH 43210. (614)292-4076. Fax: (614)292-7816. E-mail: thejournal@osu.edu. Website: english.osu.edu/journals/the_journal/. **Contact:** Kathy Fagan (poetry); Michelle Herman (fiction). Magazine: 6×9; 150 pages. "We're open to all forms; we tend to favor work that gives evidence of a mature and sophisticated sense of the language." Semiannual. Estab. 1972. Circ. 1,500.

Needs Novel excerpts, literary short stories. No romance, science fiction or religious/devotional. Receives 100 unsolicited mss/month. Accepts 2 mss/issue. Publishes ms 1 year after acceptance. Agented fiction 10%. **Publishes some new writers/year.** Recently published work by Michael Martone, Gregory Spatz and Stephen Graham Jones. Sometimes comments on rejected mss.

How to Contact Send complete ms with cover letter. SASE. Responds in 2 weeks to queries; 2 months to mss. Accepts simultaneous submissions; no electronic submissions. Sample copy for $7 or online. Writer's guidelines online.

Payment/Terms Pays $25. Pays on publication for first North American serial rights. Sends galleys to author.

Advice Mss are rejected because of "lack of understanding of the short story form, shallow plots, undeveloped characters. Cure: read as much well-written fiction as possible. Our readers prefer 'psychological' fiction rather than stories with intricate plots. Take care to present a clean, well-typed submission."

$⟐ ◎ ▨ KALEIDOSCOPE, Exploring the Experience of Disability Through Literature and the Fine Arts

Kaleidoscope Press, 701 S. Main St., Akron OH 44311-1019. (330)762-9755. Fax: (330)762-0912. Website: www. udsakron.org. **Contact:** Gail Willmott, editor-in-chief. Magazine: 8½×11; 56-64 pages; non-coated paper; coated cover stock; illustrations (all media); photos. Subscribers include individuals, agencies and organizations that assist people with disabilities and many university and public libraries. Appreciates work by established writers as well. Especially interested in work by writers with a disability, but features writers both with and without disabilities. "Writers without a disability must limit themselves to our focus, while those with a disability may explore any topic (although we prefer original perspectives about experiences with disability)." Semiannual. Estab. 1979. Circ. 1,000.

• *Kaleidoscope* has received awards from the American Heart Association, the Great Lakes Awards Competition and Ohio Public Images.

Needs "We look for well-developed plots, engaging characters and realistic dialogue. We lean toward fiction that emphasizes character and emotions rather than action-oriented narratives. No fiction that is stereotypical, patronizing, sentimental, erotic or maudlin. No romance, religious or dogmatic fiction; no children's literature." Upcoming theme: "Portrayals of Disability in the Media" (deadline March 2006). Receives 20-25 unsolicited mss/month. Accepts 10 mss/year. Agented fiction 1%. **Publishes 1 new writer/year.** Recently published work by Mark Wellman, Tamara B. Titus and Elizabeth Cohen. Also publishes poetry.

How to Contact Accepts submissions by fax. Query first or send complete ms and cover letter. Include author's education and writing background and if author has a disability, how it influenced the writing. SASE. Responds in 3 weeks to queries; 6 months to mss. Accepts simultaneous and reprints, multiple submissions. Sample copy for $6 prepaid. Writer's guidelines online.

Payment/Terms Pays $10-125, and 2 contributor's copies; additional copies $6. Pays on publication for first rights, reprints permitted with credit given to original publication. Rights return to author upon publication.

Advice "Read the magazine and get submission guidelines. We prefer that writers with a disability offer original perspectives about their experiences; writers without disabilities should limit themselves to our focus in order to solidify a connection to our magazine's purpose. Do not use stereotypical, patronizing and sentimental attitudes about disability."

⟐ KALLIOPE, a journal of women's literature & art

Florida Community College at Jacksonville, 11901 Beach Blvd., Jacksonville FL 32246. (904)646-2081. E-mail: skoeppl@fccj.edu. Website: www.fccj.org/kalliope. **Contact:** Fiction Editor. Magazine: 7¼×8¼; 120 pages; 70 lb. coated matte paper; Bristol cover; 16-18 halftones per issue. "*Kalliope* publishes poetry, short fiction, reviews and b&w art, usually by women artists. We look for artistic excellence." Estab. 1978. Circ. 1,600.

Needs Ethnic/multicultural, experimental, novel excerpts, literary. "Quality short fiction by women writers. No science fiction or fantasy. Would like to see more experimental fiction." Receives approximately 100 unsolic-

Literary Magazines

ited mss/month. Accepts up to 10 mss/issue. Does not read mss May-August. Publishes ms 3 months after acceptance. **Publishes 3 new writers/year.** Recently published work by Edith Pearlman, Bette Howland, Ruth Knafo Setton and Leslea Newman. Publishes short shorts. Also publishes poetry. Sometimes comments on rejected mss.

How to Contact Send complete ms. Responds in 1 week to queries; 3 months to mss. No simultaneous submissions. Sample copy for $9 (recent issue) or $4 (back copy), or see sample issues on website. Writer's guidelines online. Reviews fiction.

Payment/Terms Pays $10 honorarium if funds are available, otherwise 2 copies or subscription. Pays on publication for first rights. "We accept only unpublished work. Copyright returned to author upon request."

Advice "Read our magazine. The work we consider for publication will be well written and the characters and dialogue will be convincing. We like a fresh approach and are interested in new or unusual forms. Make us believe your characters; give readers an insight which they might not have had if they had not read you. We would like to publish more work by minority writers." Manuscripts are rejected because "1) nothing *happens!*, 2) it is thinly disguised autobiography (richly disguised autobiography is OK), 3) ending is either too pat or else just trails off, 4) characterization is not developed, and 5) point of view falters."

KARAMU

English Dept., Eastern Illinois University, 600 Lincoln Ave., Charleston IL 61920. (217)581-6297. E-mail: cfoxa@ eiu.edu. **Contact:** Fiction Editor. Literary magazine: 5×8; 132-136 pages; illustrations; photos. "*Karamu* is a literary magazine of ideas and artistic expression independently produced by the faculty members and associates of Eastern Illinois University. We publish writing that captures something essential about life, which goes beyond superficial, and which develops voice genuinely. Contributions of creative nonfiction, fiction, poetry and artwork of interest to a broadly eduactated audience are welcome." Annual. Estab. 1969. Circ. 500.

• *Karamu* has received two Illinois Arts Council Awards.

Needs Adventure, ethnic/multicultural, experimental, feminist, gay, historical, humor/satire, lesbian, literary, mainstream, regional. "No pornographic, science fiction, religious, political or didactic stories—no dogma or proselytizing." List of upcoming editorial themes available for SASE. Receives 80-90 unsolicited mss/month. Accepts 10-15 mss/issue. Does not read February 16-September 1. Publishes ms 1 year after acceptance. **Publishes 3-6 new writers/year.** Recently published work by Denise Seibert, Stephanie Dickinson, Laura Albritton, Bill Embly, Judi Goldenberg and Daniel North. Publishes short shorts. Also publishes poetry. Sometimes comments on rejected mss.

How to Contact Send SASE for reply. Responds in 1 week to queries. Accepts simultaneous, multiple submissions. Sample copy for $8 or $6 for back issues. Writer's guidelines for SASE.

Payment/Terms Pays 1 contributor's copy; additional copies at discount. Acquires one-time rights.

Advice Looks for "convincing, well-developed characters and plots expressing aspects of human nature or relationships in a perceptive, believable and carefully considered and written way."

KELSEY REVIEW

Mercer County College, P.O. Box B, Trenton NJ 08690. (609)586-4800. Fax: (609)586-2318. E-mail: kelsey.revie w@mccc.edu. Website: www.mccc.edu. **Contact:** Robin Schore. Magazine: 7×14; 98 pages; glossy paper; soft cover. "Must live or work in Mercer County, NJ." Annual. Estab. 1988. Circ. 1,900.

Needs Regional (Mercer County only), open. Receives 10 unsolicited mss/month. Accepts 24 mss/issue. Reads mss only in May. **Publishes 10 new writers/year.** Recently published work by Janet Kirk, Jamie McCulloch and William T. Vandegrift, Jr. Publishes short shorts. Also publishes literary essays, poetry. Always comments on rejected mss.

How to Contact SASE for return of ms. Responds in June to mss. Accepts multiple submissions. Sample copy free.

Payment/Terms 5 contributor's copies. Rights revert to author on publication.

Advice Look for "quality, intellect, grace and guts. Avoid sentimentality, overwriting and self-indulgence. Work on clarity, depth and originality."

$ THE KENYON REVIEW

Walton House, 104 College Dr., Gambier OH 43022. (740)427-5208. Fax: (740)427-5417. Website: www.kenyonr eview.org. **Contact:** Fiction Editor. An international journal of literature, culture and the arts dedicated to an inclusive representation of the best in new writing (fiction, poetry, essays, interviews, criticism) from established and emerging writers. Estab. 1939. Circ. 6,000.

• Work published in the *Kenyon Review* has been selected for inclusion in *Pushcart Prize* anthologies, *Best American Short Stories*, and *Best American Poetry*.

Needs Condensed novels, ethnic/multicultural, experimental, feminist, gay, historical, humor/satire, lesbian, literary, mainstream, translations, contemporary. Receives 400 unsolicited mss/month. Unsolicited mss typically read only from September 1 through March 31. Publishes ms 1 year after acceptance. Recently published work by Alice Hoffman, Beth Ann Fennelly, Romulus Linney, John Koethe, Albert Goldbarth and Erin McGraw. **How to Contact** Now accepting mss via online submissions program. Please visit website for instructions. Do not submit ms via e-mail. No simultaneous submissions. Sample copy $12 single issue, includes postage and handling. Please call or e-mail to order. Writer's guidelines online.

Payment/Terms Pays $15-40/page. Pays on publication for first rights.

Advice "We look for strong voice, unusual perspective, and power in the writing."

KEREM, Creative Explorations in Judaism

Jewish Study Center Press, Inc., 3035 Porter St. NW, Washington DC 20008. (202)364-3006. E-mail: langner@erols.com. Website: www.kerem.org. **Contact:** Sara R. Horowitz and Gilah Langner, editors. Magazine: 6×9; 128 pages; 60 lb. offset paper; glossy cover; illustrations; photos. "*Kerem* publishes Jewish religious, creative, literary material—short stories, poetry, personal reflections, text study, prayers, rituals, etc." Estab. 1992. Circ. 2,000.

Needs Jewish: feminist, humor/satire, literary, religious/inspirational. Receives 10-12 unsolicited mss/month. Accepts 1-2 mss/issue. Publishes ms 2-10 months after acceptance. **Publishes 2 new writers/year.** Also publishes literary essays, poetry.

How to Contact Accepts submissions by e-mail. Send SASE for reply, return of ms or send disposable copy of ms. Responds in 2 months to queries; 5 months to mss. Accepts simultaneous, multiple submissions. Sample copy for $8.50. Writer's guidelines online.

Payment/Terms Pays free subscription and 2-10 contributor's copies. Acquires one-time rights.

Advice "Should have a strong Jewish content. We want to be moved by reading the manuscript!"

KIMERA, A Journal of Fine Writing

N. 1316 Hollis, Spokane WA 99201. E-mail: kimera@js.spokane.wa.us. Website: www.js.spokane.wa.us/kimera. **Contact:** Jan Strever, editor. Electronic and print magazine. "*Kimera* attempts to meet John Locke's challenge: Where is the head with no chimeras? We seek fiction that pushes the edge in terms of language use and craft." Semiannual online; annual print version. Estab. 1995. Circ. 2,000 (online), 300 (print).

Needs Eclectic, energetic fiction. "Nothing badly conceived; attention to the muscularity of language." No erotica. Receives 50 unsolicited mss/month. Accepts 5 mss/issue. Publishes ms 1 year after acceptance. **Publishes some new writers/year.** Recently published work by L. Lynch and G. Thomas. Publishes short shorts. Also publishes literary essays, poetry. Sometimes comments on rejected mss.

How to Contact Send SASE for return of ms, SASE for reply only, or disposable copy of ms. Responds in 3 weeks to queries; 3 months to mss. Accepts simultaneous submissions. Sample copy for $5. Writer's guidelines free.

Payment/Terms Pays 1 contributor's copy. Pays on publication for first rights. Sponsors awards/contests.

Advice "We look for clarity of language. Read other writers and previous issues."

$ THE KIT-CAT REVIEW

244 Halstead Ave., Harrison NY 10528. (914)835-4833. **Contact:** Claudia Fletcher, editor. Magazine: 8½×5½; 75 pages; laser paper; colored card cover stock; illustrations. "*The Kit-Cat Review* is named after the 18th Century Kit-Cat Club, whose members included Addison, Steele, Congreve, Vanbrugh and Garth. Its purpose is to promote/discover excellence and originality." *The Kit-Kat Review* is part of the collections of the University of Wisconsin (Madison) and State University of New York (Buffalo). Quarterly. Estab. 1998. Circ. 500.

Needs Ethnic/multicultural, experimental, literary, novel excerpts, slice-of-life vignettes. No stories with "O. Henry-type formula endings. Shorter pieces stand a better chance of publication." No science fiction, fantasy, romance, horror or new age. Receives 40 unsolicited mss/month. Accepts 6 mss/issue; 24 mss/year. Publishes ms 6-12 months after acceptance. **Publishes 14 new writers/year.** Recently published work by Chayym Zeldis, Michael Fedo, Louis Phillips. Length: 5,000 words maximum; average length: 2,000 words. Publishes short shorts. Also publishes literary essays, literary criticism, poetry.

How to Contact Send complete ms. Accepts submissions by disk. Send SASE (or IRC) for return of ms, or send disposable copy of ms and #10 SASE for reply only. Responds in 1 week to queries; 2 months to mss. Accepts simultaneous, multiple submissions. Sample copy for $7 (payable to Claudia Fletcher). Writer's guidelines not available.

Payment/Terms Pays $25-200 and 2 contributor's copies; additional copies $5. Pays on publication for first rights.

LA KANCERKLINIKO

162 rue Paradis, P.O. Box 174, 13444 Marseille Cantini Cedex, France. (33)2-48-61-81-98. Fax: (33)2-48-61-81-98. E-mail: a.lazarus-1.septier@wanadoo.fr. **Contact:** Laurent Septier. "An Esperanto magazine which appears

Literary Magazines

4 times annually. Each issue contains 32 pages. *La Kancerkliniko* is a political and cultural magazine." Quarterly. Circ. 300.

Needs Science fiction, short stories or very short novels. "The short story (or the very short novel) must be written only in Esperanto, either original or translation from any other language." Wants more science fiction. **Publishes 2-3 new writers/year.** Recently published work by Mao Zifu, Manuel de Sabrea, Peter Brown and Aldo de'Giorgi.

How to Contact Accepts submissions by e-mail, fax. Accepts disk submissions. Accepts multiple submissions. Sample copy for 3 IRCs from Universal Postal Union.

Payment/Terms Pays in contributor's copies.

✪ LAKE EFFECT, A Journal of the Literary Arts

Penn State Erie, Humanities and Social Sciences, 5091 Station Rd., Erie PA 16563-1501. (814)898-6281. Fax: (814)898-6032. E-mail: goL1@psu.edu. **Contact:** George Looney, editor-in-chief. Magazine: 5½×8½; 136-150 pages; 55lb. natural paper; 12 pt. C1S cover. "In addition to seeking strong, traditional stories, *Lake Effect* is open to more experimental, language-centered fiction as well." Annual. Estab. as *Lake Effect*, 2001; as *Tempest*, 1978. Circ. 500. CLMP.

Needs Experimental, literary, mainstream. "No children's/juvenile, fantasy, science fiction, romance or young adult/teen." Receives 50 unsolicited mss/month. Accepts 5-9 mss/issue. Publishes ms 1 year after acceptance. **Publishes 6 new writers/year.** Recently published work by Edith Pearlman, Abby Frucht, Cris Mazza, Michael Czyzniejewski and Joanna Howard. Length: 4,500 words; average length: 2,600 words. Publishes short shorts. Also publishes literary essays, poetry.

How to Contact Send SASE for return of ms or send a disposable copy of ms and #10 SASE for reply only. Responds in 3 weeks to queries; 4-6 months to mss. Accepts simultaneous submissions. Sample copy for $6. Writer's guidelines for SASE.

Payment/Terms Pays 2 contributor's copies; additional copies $2. Acquires first, one-time rights. Not copyrighted.

Advice "We're looking for strong, well-crafted stories that emerge from character and language more than plot. The language is what makes a story stand out (and a strong sense of voice). Be sure to let us know immediately should a submitted story be accepted elsewhere."

ⓃⒶⓄ THE LAMP-POST, of the Southern California C.S. Lewis Society

1106 W. 16th St., Santa Ana CA 92706. (714)836-5257. E-mail: dgclark@adelphia.com. **Contact:** David G. Clark, editor. Magazine: 5½×8½; 34 pages; 7 lb. paper; 8 lb. cover; illustrations. "We are a literary review focused on C.S. Lewis and like writers." Quarterly. Estab. 1977. Circ. 200.

Needs "Literary fantasy and science fiction for children to adults." Publishes ms 3-12 months after acceptance. **Publishes 3-5 new writers/year.** Length: 1,000-5,000 words; average length: 2,500 words. Also publishes literary essays, literary criticism, poetry. Sometimes comments on rejected mss.

How to Contact Send via e-mail as Word file or rich text format. Send SASE for reply, return of ms or send a disposable copy of ms. Responds in 2 weeks to mss. Accepts reprints submissions. No simultaneous submissions. Sample copy for $3. Writer's guidelines for #10 SASE. Reviews fiction.

Payment/Terms Pays 2 contributor's copies; additional copies $3. Acquires first North American serial, one-time rights.

Advice "We look for fiction with the supernatural, mythic feel or the fiction of C.S. Lewis and Charles Williams. Our slant is Christian but we want work of literary quality. No inspirational. Is it the sort of thing Lewis, Tolkien and Williams would like—subtle, crafted fiction? If so, send it. Don't be too obvious or facile. Our readers aren't stupid."

Ⓝ▣ LANDFALL/UNIVERSITY OF OTAGO PRESS

University of Otago Press, P.O. Box 56, Dunedin New Zealand. Fax: (643)479-8385. E-mail: landfall@otago.ac.nz. **Contact:** Fiction Editor.

Needs Publishes fiction, poetry, commentary and reviews of New Zealand books.

How to Contact Send copy of ms with SASE. Sample copy not available.

Advice "We concentrate on publishing work by New Zealand writers, but occasionally accept work from elsewhere."

◗ THE LAUREL REVIEW

Northwest Missouri State University, Dept. of English, Maryville MO 64468. (660)562-1739. E-mail: nmayer@mail.nwmissouri.edu. Website: http://info.nwmissouri.edu/~m500025/laurel. **Contact:** Nancy Mayer, Rebeca Aaronsen, John Gallaher. Magazine: 6×9; 124-128 pages; good quality paper. "We publish poetry and fiction of high qulity, from the traditional to the avant-garde. We are eclectic, open and flexible. Good writing is all we seek.'' Biannual. Estab. 1960. Circ. 900.

Needs Literary, contemporary. ''No genre or politically polemical fiction.'' Receives 120 unsolicited mss/month. Accepts 3-5 mss/issue; 6-10 mss/year. Reading period: September 1-May 1. Publishes ms 1-12 months after acceptance. Agented fiction 1%. **Publishes 1-2 new writers/year.** Recently published work by Christine Sneed, Judith Kitchen and Joan Connor. Also publishes literary essays, poetry.

How to Contact Responds in 4 months to mss. No simultaneous submissions. Sample copy for $5.

Payment/Terms Pays 2 contributor's copies and 1 year subscription. Acquires first rights. Copyright reverts to author upon request.

Advice ''Nothing really matters to us except our perception that the story presents something powerfully felt by the writer and communicated intensely to a serious reader. (We believe, incidentally, that comedy is just as serious a matter as tragedy, and we don't mind a bit if something makes us laugh out loud; we get too little that makes us laugh, in fact.) We try to reply promptly, though we don't always manage that. In short, we want good poems and good stories. We hope to be able to recognize them, and we print what we believe to be the best work submitted.''

N 🖉 ◎ LE FORUM, Supplement Littéraire

Franco-American Research Opportunity Group, University of Maine, Franco American Center, Orono ME 04469-5719. (207)581-3764. Fax: (207)581-1455. E-mail: lisa_michaud@umit.maine.edu. Website: www.francomaine. org. **Contact:** Lisa Michaud, managing editor. Magazine format: 60 pages; illustrations; photos. Publication was founded to stimulate and recognize creative expression among Franco-Americans, all types of readers, including literary and working class. This publication is used in classrooms. Circulated internationally. Quarterly. Estab. 1986. Circ. 5,000.

Needs ''We will consider any type of short fiction, poetry and critical essays having to with Franco-American experience. They must be of good quality in French or English. We are also looking for Canadian writers with French-North American experiences.'' Receives 10 unsolicited mss/month. Accepts 2-4 mss/issue. **Publishes some new writers/year.** Length: 750-2,500 words; average length: 1,000 words. Occasionally comments on rejected mss.

How to Contact SASE. Responds in 3 weeks to queries; 1 month to mss. Accepts simultaneous and reprints submissions. Sample copy not available.

Payment/Terms Pays 3 copies. Acquires one-time rights.

Advice ''Write honestly. Start with a strongly felt personal Franco-American experience. If you make us feel what you have felt, we will publish it. We stress that this publication deals specifically with the Franco-American experience.''

✉ 🖉 LICHEN, Art & Letter Preview

234-701 Rossland Road East, Whitby ON L1N 9K3 Canada. E-mail: info@lichenjournal.ca. Website: www.lichen journal.ca. **Contact:** Ruth E. Walker and Gwynn Scheltema, fiction editors. Magazine: $5^1/_4 \times 8^1/_4$; 144 pages; text/illustrations black ink on Rolland Opaque, Natural 60 lb. 8 page photos black on 80 lb. Coated White paper. ''*Lichen* publishes fiction, poetry, plays, essays, reviews, interviews, black & white art and photography by local, Canadian and international writers and artists. We present a unique mix of city and country, of innovation and tradition to a broad spectrum of readers.'' Semiannual. Estab. 1999. Circ. 1,000.

 • *Lichen* was named runner-up for ''Favourite Literary Magazine'' in *Write Magazine*'s National 2000 Reader Poll.

Needs Literary. ''No work that is obtuse, bigotted, banal or hate-mongering. We will consider almost any subject or style if the work shows clarity and attention to craft.'' Receives 12-24 unsolicited mss/month. Accepts 5-8 mss/issue; 10-16 mss/year. Publishes ms 2-12 months after acceptance. **Publishes 4-7 new writers/year.** Recently published work by Nancy Holmes, Stan Rogal, J.J. Steinfeld, Brad Smith, George Elliott Clarke. Length: 250-3,000 words; average length: 1,000-2,500 words. Publishes short shorts. Also publishes literary essays, literary criticism, poetry. Sometimes comments on rejected mss.

How to Contact Send complete ms. Accepts submissions by e-mail. Include estimated word count, brief bio and list of publications. Send SASE for return of ms or disposable copy of ms and #10 SASE for reply only. For submissions outside Canada, include IRC with SASE. Responds in 1-4 weeks to queries; 3-6 months to mss. Sample copy for $12. Writer's guidelines online.

Payment/Terms 1 contributor's copy and a 1-year subscription. Pays on publication for first North American serial rights.

Advice ''We look for exceptional writing that engages the reader, professional presentation in standard ms format, and an indication of knowledge of the type of writing we publish, as well as knowledge of our submission guidelines. Keep your cover letter brief, not cute.''

Literary Magazines

✪ THE LISTENING EYE

Kent State University Geauga Campus, 14111 Claridon-Troy Rd., Burton OH 44021. (440)286-3840. E-mail: grace_butcher@msn.com. **Contact:** Grace Butcher, editor. Magazine: $5^1/_2 \times 8^1/_2$; 60 pages; photographs. "We publish the occasional very short stories (750 words/3 pages double spaced), in any subject and any style, but the language must be strong, unusual, free from cliché and vagueness. We are a shoestring operation from a small campus but we publish high-quality work." Annual. Estab. 1970. Circ. 250.

Needs Literary. "Pretty much anything will be considered except porn." Does not read mss April 15 through January 1. Publishes ms 3-4 months after acceptance. Recently published work by Elizabeth Scott, Sam Ruddick and H.E. Wright. Publishes short shorts. Also publishes poetry. Sometimes comments on rejected mss.

How to Contact Send SASE for return of ms or disposable copy of ms with SASE for reply only. Responds in 4 weeks to queries; 4 months to mss. Accepts reprints submissions. Sample copy for $3 and $1 postage. Writer's guidelines for SASE.

Payment/Terms Pays 2 contributor's copies; additional copies $3 with $1 postage. Pays on publication for one-time rights.

Advice "We look for powerful, unusual imagery, content and plot. Short, short."

◯ LITERAL LATTÉ, Mind Stimulating Stories, Poems & Essays

Word Sci, Inc., 200 East 10th Street Suite 240, New York NY 10003. (212)260-5532. E-mail: litlatte@aol.com. Website: www.literal-latte.com. **Contact:** Jeff Bockman, editor. Magazine: illustrations; photos. "Publishes great writing in many flavors and styles. *Literal Latté* expands the readership for literary magazines by offering free copies in New York coffeehouses and bookstores." Bimonthly. Estab. 1994. CLMP.

Needs Experimental, fantasy, literary, science fiction. Receives 4,000 unsolicited mss/month. Accepts 5-8 mss/issue; 40 mss/year. Agented fiction 5%. **Publishes 6 new writers/year.** Length: 500-6,000 words; average length: 4,000 words. Publishes short shorts. Often comments on rejected mss.

How to Contact Send SASE for return of mss or send a disposable copy of ms and #10 SASE for reply only or include e-mail for reply only. Responds in 6 months to mss. Accepts simultaneous, multiple submissions. Sample copy for $3. Writer's guidelines for SASE, e-mail or check website. Reviews fiction.

Payment/Terms Pays 10 contributor's copies, a free subscription to the magazine and 2 gift certificates; additional copies $1. Pays on publication for first, one-time rights. Sponsors awards/contests.

Advice "Keeping free thought free and challenging entertainment are not mutually exclusive. Words make a manuscript stand out, words beautifully woven together in striking and memorable patterns."

✪ 🗹 THE LITERARY REVIEW, An International Journal of Contemporary Writing

Fairleigh Dickinson University, 285 Madison Ave., Madison NJ 07940. (973)443-8564. Fax: (973)443-8364. E-mail: tlr@fdu.edu. Website: www.theliteraryreview.org. **Contact:** René Steinke, editor-in-chief. Magazine: 6×9; 160 pages; professionally printed on textpaper; semigloss card cover; perfect-bound. "Literary magazine specializing in fiction, poetry and essays with an international focus. Our audience is general with a leaning toward scholars, libraries and schools." Quarterly. Estab. 1957. Circ. 2,000.

  • Work published in *The Literary Review* has been included in *Editor's Choice, Best American Short Stories* and *Pushcart Prize* anthologies.

Needs Works of high literary quality only. Does not want to see "overused subject matter or pat resolutions to conflicts." Receives 90-100 unsolicited mss/month. Accepts 20-25 mss/year. Does not read submissions during June, July and August. Publishes ms $1^1/_2$-2 years after acceptance. Agented fiction 1-2%. **Publishes 80% new writers/year.** Recently published work by Irvin Faust, Todd James Pierce, Joshua Shapiro and Susan Schwartz Senstadt. Also publishes literary essays, literary criticism, poetry. Occasionally comments on rejected mss.

How to Contact Responds in 3-4 months to mss. Accepts multiple submissions. Sample copy for $7. Writer's guidelines for SASE. Reviews fiction.

Payment/Terms Pays 2 contributor's copies; $3 discount for extras. Acquires first rights.

Advice "We want original dramatic situations with complex moral and intellectual resonance and vivid prose. We don't want versions of familiar plots and relationships. Too much of what we are seeing today is openly derivative in subject, plot and prose style. We pride ourselves on spotting new writers with fresh insight and approach."

✪ THE LONG STORY

18 Eaton St., Lawrence MA 01843. (978)686-7638. E-mail: rpburnham@mac.com. Website: http://homepage.mac.com/rpburnham/longstory.html. **Contact:** R.P. Burnham. Magazine: $5^1/_2 \times 8^1/_2$; 150-200 pages; 60 lb. cover stock; illustrations (b&w graphics). For serious, educated, literary people. Annual. Estab. 1983. Circ. 1,200.

Needs Ethnic/multicultural, feminist, literary, contemporary. "No science fiction, adventure, romance, etc. We publish high literary quality of any kind but especially look for stories that have difficulty getting published elsewhere—committed fiction, working class settings, left-wing themes, etc." Receives 30-40 unsolicited mss/month. Accepts 6-7 mss/issue. Publishes ms 3 months to 1 year after acceptance. **Publishes 90% new writers/year.** Length: 8,000-20,000 words; average length: 8,000-12,000 words.

How to Contact SASE. Responds in 2 months to mss. Accepts simultaneous submissions "but not wild about it." Sample copy for $7.

Payment/Terms Pays 2 contributor's copies; $5 charge for extras. Acquires first rights.

Advice "Read us first and make sure submitted material is the kind we're interested in. Send clear, legible manuscripts. We're not interested in commercial success; rather we want to provide a place for long stories, the most difficult literary form to publish in our country."

☑ ◎ LOST AND FOUND TIMES

Luna Bisonte Prods, 137 Leland Ave., Columbus OH 43214. **Contact:** John M. Bennett, editor. Magazine: $5^1/2 \times 8^1/2$; 60 pages; good quality paper; good cover stock; illustrations; photos. Theme: experimental, avant-garde and folk literature, art. Twice yearly. Estab. 1975. Circ. 300.

Needs Experimental, literary, contemporary, prose poem. "No 'creative writing' workshop stories." The editor would like to see more short, extremely experimental pieces. Accepts 2 mss/issue. **Publishes some new writers/year.** Recently published work by Spryszak, Steve McComas, Willie Smith, Rupert Wondolowski, Al Ackerman. Publishes short shorts. Also publishes poetry.

How to Contact Query with published clips. SASE. Responds in 1 week to queries; 2 weeks to mss. No simultaneous submissions. Sample copy for $7.

Payment/Terms Pays 1 contributor's copy. Rights revert to authors after publication.

☑ ◎ LOUISIANA LITERATURE, A Review of Literature and Humanities

Southeastern Louisiana University, SLU 792, Hammond LA 70402. (504)549-5783. Fax: (504)549-5021. E-mail: ngerman@selu.edu. Website: www.selu.edu. **Contact:** Norman German, fiction editor. Magazine: $6^3/4 \times 9^3/4$; 150 pages; 70 lb. paper; card cover; illustrations. "Essays should be about Louisiana material; preference is given to fiction and poetry with Louisiana and Southern themes, but creative work can be set anywhere." Semiannual. Estab. 1984. Circ. 400 paid; 500-700 printed.

Needs Literary, mainstream, regional. "No sloppy, ungrammatical manuscripts." Receives 100 unsolicited mss/month. May not read mss June through July. Publishes ms 6-12 months after acceptance. **Publishes 4 new writers/year.** Recently published work by Anthony Bukowski, Tim Parrish, Robert Phillips and Andrew Otis Haschemeyer. Length: 1,000-6,000 words; average length: 3,500 words. Also publishes literary essays, literary criticism, poetry. Sometimes comments on rejected mss.

How to Contact SASE. Responds in 3 months to mss. Sample copy for $8. Reviews fiction.

Payment/Terms Pays usually in contributor's copies. Acquires one-time rights.

Advice "Cut out everything that is not a functioning part of the story. Make sure your manuscript is professionally presented. Use relevant, specific detail in every scene. We love detail, local color, voice and craft. Any professional manuscript stands out."

◎ THE LOUISIANA REVIEW

% Division of Liberal Arts, Louisiana State University at Eunice, P.O. Box 1129, Eunice LA 70535. (337)550-1315. E-mail: bfonteno@lsue.edu. **Contact:** Dr. Jason Ambrosiano and Dr. Billy Fontenot, editors. Magazine: $7^1/2 \times 11$; 124 pages; glossy cover; illustrations; photos. "While we will accept some of the better works submitted by our own students, we prefer excellent work by Louisiana writers as well as those outside the state who tell us their connection to it." Annual. Estab. 1999. Circ. 500-700.

Needs Ethnic/multicultural (Cajun or Louisiana culture), historical (Louisiana-related or setting), regional (Louisiana), romance (gothic). Receives 25 unsolicited mss/month. Accepts 5-7 mss/issue. Does not read mss April-December. Publishes ms 11 months after acceptance. Recently published work by Tom Bonner, Laura Cario and Sheryl St. Germaine. Length: 1,000-3,000 words; average length: 2,000 words. Publishes short shorts. Also publishes comments on rejected mss.

How to Contact Send SASE (or IRC) for return of ms. Responds in 5 weeks to queries; 10 weeks to mss. Accepts reprints, multiple submissions. Sample copy for $3. Reviews fiction.

Payment/Terms Pays 1-2 contributor's copies; additional copies $3. Pays on publication for one-time rights. Not copyrighted but has an ISSN number.

Advice "We do like to have fiction play out visually as a film would rather than static and undramatic."

☑ THE LOUISVILLE REVIEW

College of Arts and Sciences, Spalding University, 851 S. Fourth St., Louisville KY 40203. (502)585-9911, ext. 2777. E-mail: louisvillereview@spalding.edu. Website: www.louisvillereview.org. **Contact:** Sena Jeter Naslund,

Literary Magazines

editor. Literary magazine. "We are a literary journal seeking original stories with fresh imagery and vivid language." Semiannual. Estab. 1976.

Needs Literary. Receives 200+ unsolicited mss/month. Accepts 4-6 mss/issue; 8-12 mss/year. Publishes ms 6 months after acceptance. **Publishes 8-10 new writers/year.** Recently published work by Maura Stanton, Ursula Hegi, Silas House, Neela Vaswani, Jane Mayhall, Robin Lippincott, Jhumpa Lahiri. Publishes short shorts. Also publishes literary essays, poetry. Sometimes comments on rejected mss.

How to Contact Send SASE for return of ms or send a disposable copy of ms and #10 SASE for reply only. Responds in 6 months to queries; 6 months to mss. Accepts multiple submissions. Sample copy not available.

Payment/Terms Pays 2 contributor's copies.

LULLWATER REVIEW

Emory University, P.O. Box 22036, Atlanta GA 30322. (404)727-6184. E-mail: lullwaterreview@yahoo.com. **Contact:** Hannah Morril, fiction editor. Magazine: 6×9; 100 pages; 60 lb. paper; photos. "*Lullwater Review* seeks submissions that are strong and original. We require no specific genre or subject." Semiannual. Estab. 1990. Circ. 2,000. Member, Council of Literary Magazines and Presses.

Needs Adventure, condensed novels, ethnic/multicultural, experimental, fantasy, historical, humor/satire, mainstream, mystery/suspense, novel excerpts, religious/inspirational, science fiction, slice-of-life vignettes, suspense, western. "No romance or science fiction, please." Receives 75-115 unsolicited mss/month. Accepts 3-7 mss/issue; 6-14 mss/year. Does not read mss in June, July, August. Publishes ms 1-2 months after acceptance. **Publishes 25% new writers/year.** Recently published work by Greg Jenkins, Thomas Juvik, Jimmy Gleacher, Carla Vissers and Judith Sudnolt. Also publishes poetry.

How to Contact Send complete ms. Accepts submissions by postal mail only. Responds in 1-3 months to queries; 3-6 months to mss. Accepts simultaneous submissions. Sample copy for $5. Writer's guidelines for #10 SASE.

Payment/Terms Pays 3 contributor copies. Pays on publication for first North American serial rights. Sponsors awards/contests.

Advice "We at the *Lullwater Review* look for clear cogent writing, strong character development and an engaging approach to the story in our fiction submissions. Stories with particularly strong voices and well-developed central themes are especially encouraged. Be sure that your manuscript is ready before mailing it off to us. Revise, revise, revise!"

$ LYNX EYE

ScribbleFest Literary Group, 581 Woodland Drive, Los Osos CA 93402. (805)528-8146. **Contact:** Pam McCully. Magazine: 5½×8½; 120 pages; 60 lb. book paper; varied cover stock. "Each issue of *Lynx Eye* offers thoughtful and thought-provoking reading." Quarterly. Estab. 1994. Circ. 500.

Needs Adventure, condensed novels, erotica, ethnic/multicultural, experimental, fantasy (science), feminist, gay, historical, horror, humor/satire, literary, mainstream, mystery/suspense, novel excerpts, romance, science fiction, serialized novels, translations, western. "No horror with gratuitous violence or YA stories." Receives 500 unsolicited mss/month. Accepts 30 mss/issue; 120 mss/year. Publishes ms 6 months after acceptance. **Publishes 30 new writers/year.** Recently published work by Anjali Banerjee, Jean Ryan, Karen Wendy Gilbert, Jack Random and Robert R. Gass. Length: 500-5,000 words; average length: 2,500 words. Also publishes literary essays, poetry.

How to Contact Send complete ms. Include name and address on page one; name on *all* other pages. Send SASE for reply, return of ms or send a disposable copy of ms. Responds in 3 weeks to queries; 4 months to mss. Accepts simultaneous, multiple submissions. Sample copy for $7.95. Writer's guidelines for #10 SASE.

Payment/Terms Pays $10. Pays on acceptance for first North American serial rights.

Advice "We consider any well-written manuscript. Characters who speak naturally and who act or are acted upon are greatly appreciated. Your high school English teacher was correct. Basics matter. Imaginative, interesting ideas are sabotaged by lack of good grammar, spelling and punctuation skills. Most submissions are contemporary/mainstream. We could use some variety. Please do not confuse confessional autobiographies with fiction."

THE MACGUFFIN

Schoolcraft College, Department of English, 18600 Haggerty Rd., Livonia MI 48152-2696. (734)462-4400, ext 5327. Fax: (734)462-4679. E-mail: macguffin@schoolcraft.edu. Website: www.macguffin.org. **Contact:** Steven A. Dolgin, editor; Nausheen S. Khan, managing editor; Elizabeth Kircos, fiction editor; Carol Was, poetry editor. Magazine: 6×9; 164+ pages; 60 lb. paper; 110 lb. cover; b&w illustrations; photos. "The *MacGuffin* is a literary magazine which publishes a range of material including poetry, creative nonfiction and fiction. Material ranges from traditional to experimental. We hope our periodical attracts a variety of people with many different interests." Biannual. Estab. 1984. Circ. 600.

Needs Adventure, ethnic/multicultural, experimental, historical (general), humor/satire, literary, mainstream, translations, contemporary, prose poem. "No religious, inspirational, juvenile, romance, horror, pornography." Future themes TBA. Receives 35-50 unsolicited mss/month. Accepts 10-15 mss/issue; 30-50 mss/year. Does not read mss between July 1-August 15. Publishes ms 6 months to 2 years after acceptance. Agented fiction 10-15%. **Publishes 30 new writers/year.** Recently published work by Gerry LaFemina, Margaret Karmazin, Linda Nemec Foster and Conrad Hilberry. Length: 100-5,000 words; average length: 2,000-2,500 words. Publishes short shorts. Also publishes literary essays. Occasionally comments on rejected mss.
How to Contact SASE. Responds in 4 months to mss. Sample copy for $6; current issue for $15. Writer's guidelines free.
Payment/Terms Pays 2 contributor's copies. Acquires one-time rights.
Advice "We want to give promising new fiction writers the opportunity to publish alongside recognized writers. Be persistent. If a story is rejected, try to send it somewhere else. When we reject a story, we may accept the next one you send us. When we make suggestions for a rewrite, we may accept the revision. There seems to be a great number of good authors of fiction, but there are far too few places for publication. However, this is changing. Make your characters come to life. Even the most ordinary people become fascinating if they live for your readers."

◙ THE MADISON REVIEW

Department of English, Helen C. White Hall, 600 N. Park St., University of Wisconsin, Madison WI 53706. (608)263-0566. E-mail: madisonreview@yahoo.com. **Contact:** Lynda Phung and Sonya Larson, fiction editors. Magazine: 6×9; 180 pages. "Magazine for fiction and poetry with special emphasis on literary stories and some emphasis on Midwestern writers." Semiannual. Estab. 1978. Circ. 1,000.
Needs Experimental, literary, novel excerpts, translations, prose poems. "We would like to see more contemporary fiction; however, we accept fiction of any creative form and content. No historical fiction." Receives 10-50 unsolicited mss/month. Accepts 6 mss/issue. Does not read May-September. Publishes ms 4 months after acceptance. **Publishes 4 new writers/year.** Recently published work by Maurice Glenn Taylor and John McNally. Average length: 4,000 words. Also publishes poetry.
How to Contact Responds in 4 months to mss. Accepts multiple submissions. Sample copy for $3 via postal service or e-mail.
Payment/Terms Pays 2 contributor's copies; $2.50 charge for extras. Acquires first North American serial rights.

◙ $◙ ◙ THE MALAHAT REVIEW

The University of Victoria, P.O. Box 1700, STN CSC, Victoria BC V8W 2Y2 Canada. (250)721-8524. E-mail: malahat@uvic.ca. Website: www.malahatreview.ca. **Contact:** John Barton, editor. "We try to achieve a balance of views and styles in each issue. We strive for a mix of the best writing by both established and new writers." Quarterly. Estab. 1967. Circ. 1,000.
• *The Malahat Review* has received the National Magazine Award for poetry and fiction.
Needs "General ficton and poetry." Accepts 3-4 mss/issue. Publishes ms 6 months after acceptance. **Publishes 4-5 new writers/year.** Recently published work by Michael Kenyon, Elise Levine, Bill Gaston and Marilyn Bowering.
How to Contact Send complete ms. "Enclose proper postage on the SASE (or send IRC)." Responds in 2 weeks to queries; 3 months to mss. No simultaneous submissions. Sample copy for $15 (US). Writer's guidelines online.
Payment/Terms Pays $30/magazine page. Pays on acceptance for second serial (reprint), first world rights.
Advice "We do encourage new writers to submit. Read the magazines you want to be published in, ask for their guidelines and follow them. Write for information on *Malahat*'s novella competition."

◙ MANGROVE, University of Miami's Literary Magazine

University of Miami, Dept. of English, Mangrove P.O. Box 248145, Coral Gables FL 33124-4632. (305)284-2182. E-mail: mangrove@miami.edu. **Contact:** fiction editor. Magazine: 120 pages. Annual. Estab. 1992. Circ. 400.
Needs *Mangrove* is a annual literary journal devoted to publishing work that is provacative and challenging yet written with heart and intelligence. We are looking for fierce language, not greeting card sentimentality. Send us your most existentially urgent fiction, flash fiction, prose and/or lineated poetry, creative nonfiction, memoir, interviews and drama. We appreciate work that challenges traditional forms, themes and style. Receives 10-20 unsolicited mss/month. Accepts 3-4 mss/issue. Reads ms August-December. Recently published work by Terese Svoboda, Denise Duhamel, Jim Elledge, Richard Grayson and M. Nourbese Philip. Publishes short shorts. Also publishes poetry. Comments on rejected mss.
How to Contact SASE for reply. Accepts simultaneous, multiple submissions. Sample copy for $10, SASE. Writer's guidelines for SASE.

Payment/Terms Pays 2 contributor's copies. Acquires one-time rights.
Advice "Send only one story at a time and send us your best."

$⬚ ⬚ MANOA, A Pacific Journal of International Writing

English Dept., University of Hawaii, Honolulu HI 96822. (808)956-3070. Fax: (808)956-3083. E-mail: mjournal-l@hawaii.edu. Website: http://www.hawaii.edu/mjournal/. Editor: Frank Stewart. Magazine: 7×10; 240 pages. "High quality literary fiction, poetry, essays, personal narrative, reviews. Most of each issue devoted to new work from Pacific and Asian nations. Our audience is primarily in the U.S., although expanding in Pacific countries. U.S. writing need not be confined to Pacific settings or subjects." Semiannual. Estab. 1989. Circ. 2,500.

• *Manoa* has received numerous awards, and work published in the magazine has been selected for prize anthologies.

Needs Literary, mainstream, translations (from U.S. and nations in or bordering on the Pacific), contemporary, excerpted novel. No Pacific exotica. Accepts 1-2 mss/issue. Agented fiction 10%. **Publishes 1-2 new writers/year.** Recently published work by Ha Jin, Catherine Ryan Hyde, Samrat Upadhyay and Josip Novakovich. Also publishes poetry.

How to Contact Send complete ms. SASE. Does not accept submissions by e-mail. Responds in 3 weeks to queries; 1 month to poetry mss; 6 months to fiction to mss. Accepts simultaneous submissions. Sample copy for $10 (US). Writer's guidelines online. Reviews fiction.

Payment/Terms Pays $100-500 normally ($25/printed page). Pays on publication for first North American serial, non-exclusive, one-time print rights. Sends galleys to author.

⬚ ⬚ MANY MOUNTAINS MOVING, a literary journal of diverse contemporary voices

420 22nd St., Boulder CO 80302-7909. (303)641-4459. Fax: (303)444-6510. E-mail: mmm@mmminc.org. Website: www.mmminc.org. **Contact:** Naom Horii, editor. Magazine: 6×8¾; 300 pages; recycled paper; color/heavy cover; illustrations; photos. "We publish fiction, poetry, general-interest essays and art. We try to seek contributors from all cultures." Semiannual. Estab. 1994. Circ. 2,500.

• Work from *Many Mountains Moving* has been reprinted in *Pushcart* anthology and *Best American Poetry*.

Needs Ethnic/multicultural, experimental, feminist, gay, historical, humor/satire, lesbian, literary, mainstream, translations. "No genre fiction. Plans special fiction issue or anthology." Receives 400 unsolicited mss/month. Accepts 4-6 mss/issue; 12-18 mss/year. Publishes ms 2-8 months after acceptance. Agented fiction 1%. **Publishes some new writers/year.** Recently published work by Stephen Dobyns, Steven Huff, Rahna Reiko Rizzuto and Matthew Chacko. Publishes short shorts. Also publishes literary essays, poetry. Sometimes comments on rejected mss.

How to Contact Send SASE for reply, return of ms or send a disposable copy of ms. Responds in 2 weeks to queries; 3 months to mss. Accepts simultaneous submissions. Sample copy for $6.50 and enough IRCs for 1 pound of airmail/printed matter. Writer's guidelines for #10 SASE.

Payment/Terms Pays 2 contributor's copies; additional copies $3. Acquires first North American serial rights. Sends galleys to author "if requested." Sponsors awards/contests.

Advice "We look for top-quality fiction with fresh voices and verve. We would like to see more humorous literary stories. Read at least one issue of journal to get a feel for what kind of fiction we generally publish."

⬚ ⬚ THE MARLBORO REVIEW

The Marlboro Review Inc., P.O. Box 243, Marlboro VT 05344-0243. (802)254-4938. E-mail: marlboro@marlbororeview.com. Website: www.marlbororeview.com. **Contact:** Helen Fremont, fiction editor. Magazine: 6×9; 80-120 pages; 60 lb. paper; photos. "We are interested in cultural, philosophical, scientific and literary issues approached from a writer's sensibility. Our only criterion for publication is strength of work." Semiannual. Estab. 1996. Circ. 600. CLMP, AWP.

• Works published in *The Marlboro Review* have received *Pushcart Prizes*.

Needs Literary, translations. Receives 400-500 unsolicited mss/month. Accepts 2-3 mss/issue; 4-6 mss/year. "Accepts manuscripts September through May." Publishes ms 1 year after acceptance. Recently published work by Stephen Dobyns, Jean Valentine, Joseph Shuster, Chana Bloch, William Matthews and Alberto Rios. Length: 500-12,000 words; average length: 7,000 words. Publishes short shorts. Also publishes literary essays, literary criticism, poetry.

How to Contact Send SASE for return of ms or send a disposable copy of ms and #10 SASE for reply only. No summer or e-mail submissions. Responds in 3 months to queries; 4 months to mss. Accepts simultaneous, multiple submissions. Sample copy for $10. Writer's guidelines for SASE or on website. Reviews fiction.

Payment/Terms Pays 2 contributor's copies; additional copies $5. All rights revert to author on publication. Sends galleys to author.

Advice "We're looking for work with a strong voice and sense of control. Do your apprenticeship first. The minimalist impulse seems to be passing and for that we are grateful. We love to see great, sprawling, musical, chance-taking fiction.''

$⦿✉ THE MASSACHUSETTS REVIEW

South College, University of Massachusetts, Amherst MA 01003-9934. (413)545-2689. Fax: (413)577-0740. E-mail: massrev@external.umass.edu. Website: www.massreview.org. **Contact:** Fiction Editor. Magazine: 6×9; 172 pages; 52 lb. paper; 65 lb. vellum cover; illustrations; photos. Quarterly. Estab. 1959. Circ. 1,200.

• Stories from *The Massachusetts Review* has been anthologized in the *100 Best American Short Stories of the Century* and the *Pushcart Prize* anthology.

Needs Short stories. Wants more prose less than 30 pages. Does not read fiction mss June 1—October 1. Publishes ms 18 months after acceptance. Agented fiction approximately 5%. **Publishes 3-5 new writers/year.** Recently published work by Ahdaf Soueif, Elizabeth Denton and Nicholas Montemarano. Also publishes poetry. Sometimes comments on rejected mss.

How to Contact Send complete ms. No returned ms without SASE. Responds in 3 months to mss. Accepts simultaneous, multiple submissions. Sample copy for $7. Writer's guidelines online.

Payment/Terms Pays $50. Pays on publication for first North American serial rights.

Advice ''Shorter rather than longer stories preferred (up to 28-30 pages).'' Looks for works that ''stop us in our tracks.'' Manuscripts that stand out use ''unexpected language, idiosyncrasy of outlook and are the opposite of ordinary.''

⦿ MATRIACH'S WAY, Journal of Female Supremacy

Artemis Creations Publishing, 100 Chatham E, West Palm Beach FL 33417. E-mail: artemispub@hotmail.com. Website: www.artemiscreations.com. **Contact:** Fiction editor. Magazine: e-book format; illustrations; photos. *Matriach's Way* is a ''matriarchal feminist'' publication. Estab. 1996.

Needs Condensed novels, erotica (quality), experimental, fantasy (science, sword and sorcery), horror, humor/satire, literary, psychic/supernatural/occult, religious/inspirational (pagan), romance (futuristic/time travel, gothic, historical), science fiction (soft/sociological), serialized novels. ''No Christian anything.'' Want more ''femme dominant erotica and sci-fi.'' Upcoming themes: ''Science of Matriachy'' and ''What it Means to be a Female 'Other.''' Receives 40 unsolicited mss/month. **Publishes 50% new writers/year.** Often comments on rejected mss.

How to Contact Accepts submissions by e-mail (and disk). SASE for reply or send a disposable copy of ms. Responds in 1 week to queries; 6 weeks to mss. Reviews fiction.

Payment/Terms Acquires one-time rights.

Advice Looks for ''a knowledge of subject, originality and good writing style.'' Looks for ''professional writing—equates with our purpose/vision—brave and outspoken.''

⦿ MEDICINAL PURPOSES, Literary Review

Poet to Poet Inc., 75-05 210 St. #6 N., Bayside NY 11364. (718)776-8853. Fax: (718)847-2150. **Contact:** Robert Dunn, editor. Magazine: 8½×11; 40 pages; illustrations. ''*Medinal Purposes* publishes quality work that will benefit the world, though not necessarily through obvious means.'' Semiannual. Estab. 1995. Circ. 1,000.

Needs Adventure, ethnic/multicultural, experimental, fantasy, feminist, gay, historical, humor/satire, lesbian, literary, mainstream, mystery/suspense, psychic/supernatural/occult, regional, romance, science fiction, western, young adult/teen, senior citizen/retirement, sports. ''Please no pornography or hatemongering.'' Receives 15 unsolicited mss/month. Accepts 2-3 mss/issue; 8 mss/year. Publishes ms 4-24 months after acceptance. **Publishes 24 new writers/year.** Recently published work by Charles E. Brooks and Bernadette Miller. Length: 50-3,000 words; average length: 2,000 words. Publishes short shorts. Also publishes literary essays, poetry. Sometimes comments on rejected mss.

How to Contact SASE. Responds in 6 weeks to queries; 8 weeks to mss. Sample copy for $9, 6×9 SAE and 4 first-class stamps. Writer's guidelines for #10 SASE.

Payment/Terms Pays 2 contributor's copies. Acquires first rights.

Advice ''Writers should know how to write. This occurs less often than you expect. Try to be entertaining, and write a story that was worth the effort in the first place. Avoid confusing the general with the universal. Read guidelines first!''

$⬜◎✉ MERLYN'S PEN, Fiction, Essays and Poems by America's Teens

Merlyn's Pen Inc., P.O. Box 2550, Providence RI 02906. (401)751-3766. Fax: (401)274-1541. E-mail: merlyn@merlynspen.org. Website: www.merlynspen.org. **Contact:** R. Jim Stahl, publisher. Magazine: 8⅜×10⅞; 100 pages; 70 lb. paper; 12 pt. glossy cover; illustrations; photos. ''We publish fiction, essays and poems by America's teen writers, age 11-19 exclusively.'' Each November. Estab. 1985. Circ. 5,000.

• Winner of the Paul A. Witty Short Story Award and selection on the New York Public Library's Book List of Recommended Reading. *Merlyn's Pen* has also received a Parent's Choice Gold Award.

Needs Adventure, experimental, fantasy, historical, horror, humor/satire, literary, mainstream, mystery/suspense, romance, science fiction, slice-of-life vignettes, suspense, western, young adult/teen, one-act plays and dramatic monologue. "Would like to see more humor." Must be written by students in grades 6-12. Receives 1,200 unsolicited mss/month. Accepts 50 mss/issue; 50 mss/year. Publishes ms 6 months after acceptance. **Publishes 50 new writers/year.** Length: 100-5,000 words; average length: 1,500 words. Publishes short shorts. Also publishes poetry.

How to Contact Send complete ms. Send for cover-sheet template. Submissions via website only. Responds in 3 months to queries; 3 months to mss. Accepts multiple submissions. Sample articles and writer's guidelines available on website.

Payment/Terms Pays $20-250. Pays on publication. Published works become the property of Merlyn's Pen, Inc.

Advice "Write what you *know*; write where you are. We look for authentic voice and experience of young adults."

METAL SCRATCHES

9251 Lake Drive NE, Forest Lake MN 55025. E-mail: metalscratches@aol.com. **Contact:** Kim Mark, editor. Magazine: $5^{1}/_{2} \times 8^{1}/_{2}$; 35 pages; heavy cover-stock. "*Metal Scratches* focuses on literary fiction that examines the dark side of humanity. We are not looking for anything that is 'cute' or 'sweet'." Semiannual. Estab. 2000.

Needs Erotica, experimental, horror (psychological), literary. "No poetry, science fiction, rape, murder or horror as in gore." Receives 20 unsolicited mss/month. Accepts 5-6 mss/issue; 20 mss/year. Publishes ms 6 months after acceptance. **Publishes 3 new writers/year.** Length: 3,500 words; average length: 3,000 words. Publishes short shorts. Sometimes comments on rejected mss.

How to Contact Send complete ms. Accepts submissions by e-mail (no attachments). Send disposable copy of the ms and #10 SASE for reply only. Responds in 1 month to mss. Accepts simultaneous, multiple submissions. Sample copy for $3. Writer's guidelines for SASE or by e-mail.

Payment/Terms Pays 2 contributor's copies; additional copies for $2.50. Pays on publication for one-time rights. Not copyrighted.

Advice "Clean manuscripts prepared according to guidelines are a must. Send us something new and inventive. Don't let rejections from any editor scare you. Keep writing and keep submitting."

$ MICHIGAN QUARTERLY REVIEW

3574 Rackham Bldg., 915 E. Washington, University of Michigan, Ann Arbor MI 48109-1070. (734)764-9265. E-mail: mqr@umich.edu. Website: www.umich.edu/~mqr. **Contact:** Fiction Editor. "An interdisciplinary journal which publishes mainly essays and reviews, with some high-quality fiction and poetry, for an intellectual, widely read audience." Quarterly. Estab. 1962. Circ. 1,500.

• Stories from *Michigan Quarterly Review* have been selected for inclusion in *The Best American Short Stories*, *O. Henry* and *Pushcart Prize* volumes.

Needs Literary. "No genre fiction written for a market. Would like to see more fiction about social, political, cultural matters, not just centered on a love relationship or dysfunctional family." Receives 200 unsolicited mss/month. Accepts 2 mss/issue; 8 mss/year. Publishes ms 1 year after acceptance. **Publishes 1-2 new writers/ year.** Recently published work by Nicholas Delbanco, Clarke Blaise, Elizabeth Searle, Marian Thurm and Lucy Ferriss. Length: 1,500-7,000 words; average length: 5,000 words. Also publishes literary essays, poetry.

How to Contact Send complete ms. "I like to know if a writer is at the beginning, or further along, in his or her career. Don't offer plot summaries of the story, though a background comment is welcome." SASE. Responds in 2 months to queries; 2 months to mss. No simultaneous submissions. Sample copy for $4. Writer's guidelines online.

Payment/Terms Pays $10/published page. Pays on publication. Buys first serial rights. Sponsors awards/ contests.

Advice "There's no beating a good plot and interesting characters and a fresh use of the English language. (Most stories fail because they're written in such a bland manner, or in TV-speak.) Be ambitious, try to involve the social world in the personal one, be aware of what the best writing of today is doing, don't be satisfied with a small slice-of-life narrative but think how to go beyond the ordinary."

$ MID-AMERICAN REVIEW

Department of English Box W, Bowling Green State University, Bowling Green OH 43403. (419)372-2725. Fax: (419)372-6805. Website: www.bgsu.edu/midamericanreview. **Contact:** Michael Czyzniejewski, fiction editor. Magazine: 6×9; 192 pages; 60 lb. bond paper; coated cover stock. "We try to put the best possible work in front of the biggest possible audience. We publish serious fiction and poetry, as well as critical studies in contemporary literature, translations and book reviews." Semiannual. Estab. 1981.

- Work published in *Mid-American Review* has received the *Pushcart Prize*.

Needs Experimental, literary, translations, Memoir, prose poem, traditional. "No genre fiction. Would like to see more short shorts." Receives 500 unsolicited mss/month. Accepts 6-8 mss/issue. Publishes ms 6 months after acceptance. Agented fiction 5%. **Publishes 4-8 new writers/year.** Recently published work by Dan Chaon, Steve Almond and Robert Olmstead. Also publishes literary essays, poetry. Occasionally comments on rejected mss.

How to Contact Accepts submissions by disk. Send complete ms with SASE. Responds in 4 months to mss. Sample copy for $7 (current issue), $5 (back issue); rare back issues $10. Writer's guidelines online. Reviews fiction.

Payment/Terms Pays $10/page up to $50, pending funding. Pays on publication when funding is available. Acquires first North American serial, one-time rights. Sponsors awards/contests.

Advice "We look for well-written stories that make the reader want to read on past the first line and page. Cliché themes and sloppy writing turn us off immediately. Read literary journals to see what's being published in today's market. We tend to publish work that is more non-traditional in style and subject, but are open to all literary non-genre submissions."

MINDPRINTS, A Literary Journal

Learning Assistance Program, Allan Hancock College, 800 S. College Dr., Santa Maria CA 93454-6399. (805)922-6966, ext. 3274. Fax: (805)922-3556. E-mail: pafahey@hancockcollege.edu. Website: www.imindprints.com. **Contact:** Paul Fahey, editor. Magazine: 6×9; 125-150 pages; 70 lb. matte coated paper; glossy cover; illustrations; photos. "*Mindprints, A Literary Journal* is one of a very few college publications created as a forum for writers and artists with disabilities or for those with an interest in the field. The emphasis on flash fiction and the fact that we are a national journal as well puts us on the cutting edge of today's market." Annual. Estab. 2000. Circ. 600.

Needs Literary, mainstream. Receives 20-30 unsolicited mss/month. Accepts 75 mss/year. Does not read mss June-August. Publishes ms 6 months after acceptance. **Publishes 25-30 new writers/year.** Recently published work by Susan Rolston, Eldonna Edwards, Christine Beebe and Gina Kokes. Length: 250-750 words; average length: 500 words. Publishes short shorts. Also publishes poetry. Often comments on rejected mss.

How to Contact Accepts submissions by e-mail (only from outside of the United States). Send a disposable copy of ms and cover letter and #10 SASE for reply only. Responds in 1 week to queries; 4 months to mss. Accepts simultaneous and reprints, multiple submissions. Sample copy for $6 and $2 postage or IRCs. Writer's guidelines for SASE, by e-mail or fax.

Payment/Terms Pays 1 contributor's copy; additional copies $5. Pays on publication for one-time rights. Not copyrighted.

Advice "We look for a great hook; a story that grabs us from the beginning; fiction and memoir with a strong voice and unusual themes; stories with a narrowness of focus yet broad in their appeal. We would like to see more flash or very short fiction. Read and study the flash fiction genre. Revise, revise, revise. Do not send manuscripts that have not been proofed. Our mission is to showcase as many voices and world views as possible. We want our readers to sample creative talent from a national and international group of published and unpublished writers and artists."

THE MINNESOTA REVIEW, A Journal of Committed Writing

Dept. of English, Carnegie Mellon University, Pittsburgh PA 15213. (412)268-1977. E-mail: jwill@audrew.cmu.edu. Website: http://theminnesotareview.org. **Contact:** Jeffrey Williams, editor. Magazine: 5¼×7½; approximately 200 pages; some illustrations; occasional photos. "We emphasize socially and politically engaged work." Semiannual. Estab. 1960. Circ. 1,500.

Needs Experimental, feminist, gay, historical, lesbian, literary. Receives 50-75 unsolicited mss/month. Accepts 3-4 mss/issue; 6-8 mss/year. Publishes ms 6-12 months after acceptance. **Publishes 3-5 new writers/year.** Recently published work by E. Shaskan Bumas, Carlos Fuentes, Maggie Jaffe and James Hughes. Publishes short shorts. Also publishes literary essays, literary criticism, poetry. Occasionally comments on rejected mss.

How to Contact SASE. Responds in 3 weeks to queries; 3 months to mss. Accepts simultaneous, multiple submissions. Sample copy for $12. Reviews fiction.

Payment/Terms Pays in contributor's copies. Charge for additional copies. Acquires first rights.

Advice "We look for socially and politically engaged work, particularly short, striking work that stretches boundaries."

Literary Magazines

☺ MISSISSIPPI REVIEW

University of Southern Mississippi, 118 College Dr. #5144, Hattiesburg MS 39406-0001. (601)266-4321. Fax: (601)266-5757. E-mail: rief@mississippireview.com. Website: www.mississippireview.com. **Contact:** Rie Fortenberry, managing editor. Semiannual. Estab. 1972. Circ. 1,500.

Needs Annual fiction and poetry competition. $1,000 awarded in each category plus publication of all winners and finalists. Fiction entries 5,000 words or less. Poetry entry equals 1-3 poems, page limit is 10. $15 entry fee includes copy of prize issue. No limit on number of entries. Deadline October 1. No manuscripts returned. Does not read mss in summer. **Publishes 10-20 new writers/year.**

How to Contact Sample copy for $8. Writer's guidelines online.

Payment/Terms Acquires first North American serial rights.

$☺ ☒ THE MISSOURI REVIEW

1507 Hillcrest Hall, University of Missouri, Columbia MO 65211. (573)882-4474. Fax: (573)884-4671. E-mail: question@missourireview.com. Website: www.missourireview.com. **Contact:** Speer Morgan, editor. Magazine: 6×9; 212 pages. "We publish contemporary fiction, poetry, interviews, personal essays, cartoons, special features—such as 'History as Literature' series and 'Found Text' series—for the literary and the general reader interested in a wide range of subjects." Estab. 1978. Circ. 5,500.

- This magazine had stories anthologized in the *Pushcart Prize Anthology, Best American Short Stories, O. Henry Awards, Best American Essays, Best American Erotica,* and *New Stories From the South.*

Needs Condensed novels, ethnic/multicultural, humor/satire, literary, mainstream, novel excerpts, literary. No genre fiction. Receives 400 unsolicited mss/month. Accepts 5-7 mss/issue; 16-20 mss/year. **Publishes 6-10 new writers/year.** Recently published work by Alice Hoffman, Peter Selgin, Emily Raboteau, Stephanie Watman and Cameron Walker. Also publishes literary essays, poetry. Often comments on rejected mss.

How to Contact Send complete ms. May include brief bio and list of publications. Send SASE for reply, return of ms or send disposable copy of ms. International submissions via website. Responds in 2 weeks to queries; 10 weeks to mss. Sample copy for $8 or online. Writer's guidelines online.

Payment/Terms Pays $30/printed page up to $750. Offers signed contract. Sponsors awards/contests.

☺ MOBIUS, The Journal of Social Change

505 Christianson, Madison WI 53714. (608)242-1009. E-mail: fmschep@charter.net. Website: www.mobiusmag azine.com. **Contact:** Fred Schepartz, editor. Magazine: 8½×11; 16-24 pages; 60 lb. paper; 60 lb. cover. "Looking for fiction which uses social change as either a primary or secondary theme. This is broader than most people think. Need social relevance in one way or another. For an artistically and politically aware and curious audience." Quarterly. Estab. 1989. Circ. 1,500.

Needs Ethnic/multicultural, experimental, fantasy, feminist, gay, historical, horror, humor/satire, lesbian, literary, mainstream, science fiction, contemporary, prose poem. "No porn, no racist, sexist or any other kind of ist. No Christian or spirituality proselytizing fiction." Wants to see more science fiction, erotica "assuming it relates to social change." Receives 15 unsolicited mss/month. Accepts 3-5 mss/issue. Publishes ms 3-9 months after acceptance. **Publishes 10 new writers/year.** Recently published work by Margaret Karmazin, Benjamin Reed, John Tuschen and Ken Byrnes. Length: 500-5,000 words; average length: 3,500 words. Publishes short shorts. Always comments on rejected mss.

How to Contact SASE. Responds in 4 months to mss. Accepts simultaneous and reprints, multiple submissions. Sample copy for $2, 9×12 SAE and 3 first class stamps. Writer's guidelines for SASE.

Payment/Terms Pays contributor's copies. Acquires one-time, electronic rights for www version.

Advice "Note that fiction and poetry may be simultaneously published in e-version of *Mobius*. Due to space constraints of print version, some works may be accepted in e-version, but not print version. We like high impact, we like plot and character-driven stories that function like theater of the mind. Looks for first and foremost, good writing. Prose must be crisp and polished; the story must pique my interest and make me care due to a certain intellectual, emotional aspect. Second, *Mobius* is about social change. We want stories that make some statement about the society we live in, either on a macro or micro level. Not that your story neeeds to preach from a soapbox (actually, we prefer that it doesn't), but your story needs to have *something* to say."

Ⓝ ◎ THE MUSING PLACE, The Literary & Arts Magazine of Chicago's Mental Health Community

The Thresholds, 2700 N. Lakeview, Chicago IL 60614. (773)281-3800, ext. 2465. Fax: (773)281—8790. **Contact:** Tim Collins, editor. Magazine: 8½×11; 36 pages; 60 lb. paper; glossy cover; illustrations. "We are mostly a poetry magazine by and for mental health consumers. We want to give a voice to those who are often not heard. All material is composed by mental health consumers. The only requirement for consideration of publication is having a history of mental illness." Semiannual. Estab. 1986. Circ. 1,000.

Needs Adventure, condensed novels, ethnic/multicultural, experimental, fantasy (science fantasy, sword and sorcery), feminist, gay, historical (general), horror, humor/satire, lesbian, literary, mainstream, mystery/suspense, regional, romance, science fiction, serialized novels. Publishes ms 6 months after acceptance. Recently published work by Allen McNair, Donna Willey and Mark Goniciarz. Length: 700 words; average length: 500 words.

How to Contact Send complete ms. Send a disposable copy of ms. Responds in 6 months to mss. Accepts simultaneous and reprints submissions. Sample copy for $3.

Payment/Terms Pays contributor's copies. Acquires one-time rights.

NASSAU REVIEW

Nassau Community College, State University of New York, 1 Education Dr., Garden City NY 11530-6793. (516)572-7792. **Contact:** Editorial Board. Magazine: $6^{1}/_{2} \times 9^{1}/_{2}$; 200 pages; heavey stock paper and cover; illustrations; photos. "Looking for high-level, professionally talented fiction on any subject matter except science fiction. Intended for a college and university faculty-level audience. Not geared to college students or others of that age who have not yet reached professional competency." Annual. Estab. 1964. Circ. 1,200. Member: Council of Literary Magazines & Presses.

Needs Historical (general), humor/satire, literary, mainstream, mystery/suspense (amateur sleuth, cozy). "No science fiction." Receives 200-400 unsolicited mss/month. Accepts 5-6 mss/year. Does not read mss April-October. Publishes ms 6 months after acceptance. **Publishes 1-2 new writers/year.** Recently published work by Louis Phillips, Dick Wimmer, Norbert Petsch and Mike Lipstock. Length: 2,000-6,000 words; average length: 3,000-4,000 words. Publishes short shorts. Also publishes literary essays, literary criticism, poetry.

How to Contact Send 3 disposable copies of ms and #10 SASE for reply only. Responds in 2 weeks to queries; 6 months to mss. No simultaneous submissions. Sample copy free.

Payment/Terms Pays contributor's copies. Acquires one-time rights. Sponsors awards/contests.

Advice "We look for narrative drive, perceptive characterization and professional competence. Write concretely. Do not over-elaborate details, and avoid digressions."

NATURAL BRIDGE

English Department, University of Missouri-St. Louis, One University Boulevard, St. Louis MO 63121-4400. (314)516-7327. Fax: (314)516-5781. E-mail: natural@umsl.edu. Website: www.umsl.edu/~natural. **Contact:** Steven Schreiner, editor. Magazine: 6×9; 250 pages; 60 lb. opaque recycled paper; 12 pt. coated glossy cover. "*Natural Bridge* is published by the UM-St. Louis MFA Program. Faculty and graduate students work together in selecting manuscripts, with a strong emphasis on originality, freshness, honesty, vitality, energy and linguistic skill." Semiannual. Estab. 1999. Circ. 400. CLMP.

Needs Literary. List of upcoming themes available for SASE or online. Receives 400 unsolicited mss/month. Accepts 35 mss/issue; 70 mss/year. Submit only July 1-August 31 and November 1-December 31. Publishes ms 9 months after acceptance. **Publishes 12 new writers/year.** Recently published work by A.E. Hotchner, Steve Stern, Brian Doyle, Lex Williford, Jennifer Haigh and Jim Ray Daniels. Also publishes literary essays, poetry. Sometimes comments on rejected mss.

How to Contact Send SASE for return of ms or send a disposable copy of ms and #10 SASE for reply only. Responds in 5 months to mss. Accepts simultaneous submissions. Sample copy for $8. Writer's guidelines for SASE, e-mail or on website.

Payment/Terms Pays 2 contributor's copies and a one-year subscription; additional copies $5. Acquires first North American serial rights.

Advice "We look for fresh stories, extremely well written, on any subject. We publish mainstream literary fiction. We want stories that work on first and subsequent readings—stories, in other words, that both entertain and resonate. Study the journal. Read all of the fiction in it, especially in a fiction-heavy issue like no. 4."

NEBO, A Literary Journal

Arkansas Tech University, Dept. of English, Russellville AR 72801. (501)968-0256. E-mail: nebo@mail.atu.edu. **Contact:** Dr. Michael Karl Ritchie, editor. Literary, fiction and poetry magazine: 5×8; 50-60 pages. For general, academic audience. Annual. Estab. 1983. Circ. 500.

Needs Literary, mainstream, reviews. Does not want science fiction, fantasy. Upcoming theme: pop icon fiction and poetry (fiction and poetry that plays with the roles of pop icons). Receives 20-30 unsolicited mss/month. Accepts 2 mss/issue; 6-10 mss/year. Does not read mss May 1-September 1. "Submission deadlines for all work are November 15 and January 15 of each year." Publishes ms 6 months after acceptance. **Publishes some new writers/year.** Recently published work by Jim Meinrose, R.T. Smith and Andrew Geyer. Also publishes literary essays, literary criticism, poetry. Occasionally comments on rejected mss.

How to Contact Responds in 3 months to mss. No simultaneous submissions. Sample copy for $6. Reviews fiction.

Payment/Terms Pays 1 contributor's copy. Acquires one-time rights.

Advice "A writer should carefully edit his short story before submitting it. Write from the heart and put

Literary Magazines

everything on the line. Don't write from a phony or fake perspective. Frankly, many of the manuscripts we recieve should be publishable with a little polishing. Manuscripts should *never* be submitted with misspelled words or on 'onion skin' or colored paper."

Ⓝ ⓓ ⓦ THE NEBRASKA REVIEW

The Nebraska Review, WFAB 212, University of Nebraska at Omaha, Omaha NE 68182-0324. (402)554-3159. E-mail: jreed@unomaha.edu. Website: http://www.unomaha.edu/ ~ fineart/wworkshop/submits.htm. **Contact:** James Reed, fiction editor. Magazine: 5½ × 8½; 108 pages; 60 lb. text paper; chrome coat cover stock. "*TNR* attempts to publish the finest available contemporary fiction, poetry and creative nonfiction for college and literary audiences." Publishes 2 issues/year. Estab. 1973. Circ. 1,000.

• Work published in *The Nebraska Review* was reprinted in *New Stories from the South* and the *Pushcart Prize Anthology*.

Needs Humor/satire, literary, mainstream, contemporary. "No genre fiction." Receives 40 unsolicited mss/month. Accepts 4-5 mss/issue; 8-10 mss/year. Reads for *The Nebraska Review* Awards in Fiction and Poetry and Creative Nonfiction September 1 through November 30. Open to submission January 1-April 30; does not read May 1-August 31. Publishes ms 6-12 months after acceptance. **Publishes 2-3 new writers/year.** Recently published work by Chris Mazza, Mark Wisniewski, Stewart O'Nan, Elaine Ford and Tom Franklin. Average length: 5,000-6,000 words. Also publishes poetry.

How to Contact Responds in 6 months to mss. Sample copy for $4.50.

Payment/Terms Pays 2 contributor's copies and 1 year subscription; additional copies $4. Acquires first North American serial rights.

Advice "Write stories in which the lives of your characters are the primary reason for writing and techniques of craft serve to illuminate, not overshadow, the textures of those lives. Sponsors a $500 award/year—write for rules."

ⓦ NERVE COWBOY

Liquid Paper Press, P.O. Box 4973, Austin TX 78765. Website: www.onr.com/user/jwhagins/nervecowboy.html. **Contact:** Joseph Shields or Jerry Hagins, editors. Magazine: 7 × 8½; 64 pages; 20 lb. paper; card stock cover; illustrations. "*Nerve Cowboy* publishes adventurous, comical, disturbing, thought-provoking, accessible poetry and fiction. We like to see work sensitive enough to make the hardest hard-ass cry, funny enough to make the most helpless brooder laugh and disturbing enough to make us all glad we're not the author of the piece." Semiannual. Estab. 1996. Circ. 350.

Needs Literary. No "racist, sexist or overly offensive work. Wants more unusual stories with rich description and enough twists and turns that leave the reader thinking." Receives 40 unsolicited mss/month. Accepts 2-3 mss/issue; 4-6 mss/year. Publishes ms 6-12 months after acceptance. **Publishes 5-10 new writers/year.** Recently published work by Lori Jakiele, Heather Cavanaugh, Dave Newman, Brad Kohler, Charlene Logan and L. Dale Van Auken. Length: 1,500 words; average length: 750-1,000 words. Publishes short shorts. Also publishes poetry.

How to Contact Send SASE for reply, return of ms or send a disposable copy of ms. Responds in 2 weeks to queries; 3 months to mss. Accepts reprints submissions. No simultaneous submissions. Sample copy for $5. Writer's guidelines for #10 SASE or online.

Payment/Terms Pays 1 contributor's copy. Acquires one-time rights.

Advice "We look for writing which is very direct and elicits a visceral reaction in the reader. Read magazines you submit to in order to get a feel for what the editors are looking for. Write simply and from the gut."

ⓓ ⓦ NEW DELTA REVIEW

Louisiana State University, Dept. of English, 214 Allen Hall, Baton Rouge LA 70803-5001. (225)578-4079. E-mail: new-delta@lsu.edu. Website: www.english.lsu.edu/journals/ndr. **Contact:** Editors change every year. Check website. Magazine: 6 × 9; 75-125 pages; high quality paper; glossy card cover; color artwork. "We seek vivid and exciting work from new and established writers. We have published fiction from writers such as Stacy Richter, Mark Poirier and George Singleton." Semiannual. Estab. 1984. Circ. 500.

• *New Delta Review* also sponsors the Matt Clark Prizes for fiction and poetry. Work from the magazine has been included in the *Pushcart Prize* anthology.

Needs Humor/satire, literary, mainstream, translations, contemporary, prose poem. "No Elvis stories, over-wrought 'Southern' fiction, or cancer stories." Receives 150 unsolicited mss/month. Accepts 3-4 mss/issue; 6-8 mss/year. Reads from August 15-April 15. **Publishes 1-3 new writers/year.** Length: 250 words; average length: 15 ms pages words. Publishes short shorts. Also publishes poetry. Rarely comments on rejected mss.

How to Contact SASE (or IRC). Responds in 3 weeks to queries; 3 months to mss. Accepts simultaneous submissions; only when stated in the cover letter. Sample copy for $7.

Payment/Terms Pays in contributor's copies. Charge for extras. Acquires first North American serial, electronic rights. Sponsors awards/contests.

Advice "Our staff is open-minded and youthful. We base decisions on merit, not reputation. The manuscript that's most enjoyable to read gets the nod. Be bold, take risks, surprise us."

$⬛ NEW ENGLAND REVIEW

Middlebury College, Middlebury VT 05753. (802)443-5075. Fax: (802)443-2088. E-mail: nereview@middlebury. edu. Website: www.middlebury.edu/~nereview/. **Contact:** Stephen Donadio, editor. Magazine: 7×10; 180 pages; 50 lb. paper; coated cover stock. Serious literary only. Reads September 1 to May 31 (postmarked dates). Quarterly. Estab. 1978. Circ. 2,000.

Needs Literary. Receives 250 unsolicited mss/month. Accepts 5 mss/issue; 20 mss/year. Does not read mss June-August. Publishes ms 6 months after acceptance. Agented fiction less than 5%. **Publishes 1-2 new writers/year.** Recently published work by Steve Almond, Padgett Powell, Peter Cameron and Joann Kobin. Publishes short shorts. Sometimes comments on rejected mss.

How to Contact "Send complete mss with cover letter. We don't want hype, or hard-sell, or summaries of the author's intentions. Will consider simultaneous submissions, but must be stated as such." SASE. Responds in 2 weeks to queries; 3 months to mss. Sample copy for $8. Writer's guidelines online.

Payment/Terms Pays $10/page ($20 minimum), and 2 copies. Pays on publication for first North American serial, first, second serial (reprint) rights. Sends galleys to author.

Advice "It's best to send one story at a time, and wait until you hear back from us to try again."

$⬛ ⬛ NEW LETTERS

University of Missouri-Kansas City, University House, 5101 Rockhill Rd., Kansas City MO 64110-2499. (816)235-1168. Fax: (816)235-2611. E-mail: newletters@umkc.edu. Website: www.newletters.org. **Contact:** Robert Stewart, editor. Magazine: 14 lb. cream paper; illustrations. "*New Letters* is intended for the general literate reader. We publish literary fiction, nonfiction, essays, poetry. We also publish art." Quarterly. Estab. 1934. Circ. 2,500.

● *New Letters Magazine* received a *Pushcart Prize* for fiction.

Needs Ethnic/multicultural, experimental, humor/satire, literary, mainstream, translations, contemporary. No genre fiction. Does not read mss May 15-October 15. Publishes ms 5 months after acceptance. Agented fiction 10%. Recently published work by Thomas E. Kennedy, Sheila Kohler, Charlotte Holmes, Rosellen Brown and Janet Burroway. Publishes short shorts.

How to Contact Send complete ms. Do not submit by e-mail. Responds in 1 month to queries; 3 months to mss. No simultaneous submissions. Sample copy for $7 or sample articles on website. Writer's guidelines online.

Payment/Terms Pays $30-75 for fiction and $15 for single poem. Pays on publication for first North American serial rights. Sends galleys to author.

Advice "Seek publication of representative chapters in high-quality magazines as a way to the book contract. Try literary magazines first."

$⬛ ⬛ NEW ORLEANS REVIEW

Box 195, Loyola University, New Orleans LA 70118. (504)865-2295. Fax: (504)865-2294. E-mail: noreview@loyno.edu. Website: www.loyno.edu/~noreview/. **Contact:** Christopher Chambers, editor. Journal: 6×9; perfect bound; 200 pages; photos. "Publishes poetry, fiction, translations, photographs, nonfiction on literature, art and film. Readership: those interested in contemporary literature and culture." Biannual. Estab. 1968. Circ. 1,500.

● Work from the *New Orleans Review* has been anthologized in *Best American Short Stories* and the *Pushcart Prize Anthology*.

Needs "Quality fiction from conventional to experimental." **Publishes 12 new writers/year.** Recently published work by Gordon Lish, Michael Martone, Marilyn Abidskov, Stephen Graham Jones, Carolyn Sanchez and Josh Russell.

How to Contact Responds in 4 months to mss. Accepts simultaneous submissions "if we are notified immediately upon acceptance elsewhere." Sample copy for $5. Reviews fiction.

Payment/Terms Pays $25-50 and 2 copies. Pays on publication for first North American serial rights.

Advice "We're looking for dynamic writing that demonstrates attention to the language and a sense of the medium, writing that engages, surprises, moves us. We're not looking for genre fiction or academic articles. We subscribe to the belief that in order to truly write well, one must first master the rudiments: grammar and syntax, punctuation, the sentence, the paragraph, the line, the stanza. We recieve about 3,000 manuscripts a year, and publish about 3% of them. Check out a recent issue, send us your best, proofread your work, be patient, be persistent."

🔀 🖉 📧 THE NEW ORPHIC REVIEW

New Orphic Publishers, 706 Mill St., Nelson BC V1L 4S5 Canada. (250)354-0494. Fax: (250)352-0743. **Contact:** Ernest Hekkanen, editor-in-chief. Magazine; 5½×8½; 120 pages; common paper; 100 lb. color cover. "In the traditional *Orphic* fashion, our magazine accepts a wide range of styles and approaches—from naturalism to the surreal, but, please, get to the essence of the narrative, emotion, conflict, state of being, whatever." Semiannual. Estab. 1998. Circ. 300.

• Margrith Schraner's story, "Dream Dig" was included in *The Journey Prize Anthology*, 2001.

Needs Ethnic/multicultural, experimental, fantasy, historical (general), literary, mainstream. "No detective or sword and sorcery stories." List of upcoming themes available for SASE. Receives 20 unsolicited mss/month. Accepts 10 mss/issue; 22 mss/year. Publishes ms 1 year after acceptance. **Publishes 6-8 new writers/year.** Recently published work by Eveline Hasler (Swiss), Leena Krohn (Finnish) and Pekka Salmi. Length: 2,000-10,000 words; average length: 3,500 words. Publishes short shorts. Also publishes literary essays, literary criticism, poetry. Sometimes comments on rejected mss.

How to Contact Send SASE (or IRC) for return of ms or send a disposable copy of ms and #10 SASE for reply only. Responds in 1 month to queries; 4 months to mss. Accepts simultaneous, multiple submissions. Sample copy for $15. Writer's guidelines for SASE. Reviews fiction.

Payment/Terms Pays 1 contributor's copy; additional copies $12. Pays on publication for first North American serial rights.

Advice "I like fiction that deals with issues, accounts for every motive, has conflict, is well written and tackles something that is substantive. Don't be mundane; try for more, not less."

🔀 $🖻 THE NEW QUARTERLY, Canadian Writers and Writing

St. Jerome's University, 290 University Ave. North, Waterloo ON N2L 3G3 Canada. (519)884-8111, ext. 290. E-mail: newquart@watarts.uwaterloo.ca. Website: www.newquarterly.uwaterloo.ca. **Contact:** Kim Jernigan, editor. "Emphasis on emerging writers and genres, but we publish more traditional work as well if the language and narrative structure are fresh." Quarterly. Estab. 1981. Circ. 1,000.

Needs Publishes ms 4 months after acceptance.

How to Contact Send complete ms. Accepts submissions by e-mail. Responds in 2 weeks to queries; 4 months to mss. Accepts simultaneoues submissions if indicated in cover letter. Sample copy for $15 (cover price, plus mailing). Writer's guidelines for #10 SASE or online.

Payment/Terms Pays $150/story, $25/poem. Pays on publication for first Canadian rights.

$ THE NEW RENAISSANCE, An international magazine of ideas & opinions, emphasizing literature and the arts

The Friends of "the new renaissance", 26 Heath Rd., #11, Arlington MA 02474-3645. **Contact:** Michal Anne Kucharski, co-editor. Magazine; 6×9; 144-182 pages; 70 lb. matte white paper; 4-color cover; illustrations; photos; artwork: 80 lb. dull glossy. "*tnr* is a diverse magazine, with a variety of styles, statements and tones for a literary sophisticated, but not specialized, audience. We publish assorted long & short fiction, including bilingual (Italian, German, French, Danish, Russian) and Indian fiction in translation." Semiannual. Estab. 1968. Circ. 1,300.

Needs Ethnic/multicultural (general), experimental, humor/satire, literary, regional (general), translations, pyschological. "We do not want to see formulaic or popular fiction. In the last couple of years we have received too many quasi-naturalistic stories and we like to see fewer, although we will still consider naturalistic fiction." Receives 440-470 mss (January-June) 25-45 mss (September 1-October 31. Accepts 3-5 mss/issue; 6-10 mss/year. Does not read mss in July-August or November-December. Publishes ms 10-18 months after acceptance. Agented fiction 3-4%. **Publishes 0-1 new writers/year.** Recently published work by B. Wongar, Gina Ochsner, Kathryn Kulpa and M.E. McMullen. Also publishes literary essays, literary criticism, poetry. Often comments on rejected mss.

How to Contact Send SASE (or IRC) for return of ms or send a disposable copy of ms and #10 SASE for reply. Accepts two stories if the mss are 4 pages or less. Responds in 1 month to queries; 5-7 months to mss. Sample copy not available. Writer's guidelines for SASE or by e-mail. Reviews fiction.

Payment/Terms Pays $48-80 and 1 contributor's copy (under 30 pages), 2 copies 31-36 pages. Offers discount for additional copies. Acquires all rights; after publication, rights returned to writer.

Advice "We're looking for the individual voice, in both style and vision. We prefer density in characterization and/or dialogue, atmosphere, etc. We're not interested in the 'Who Cares?' fiction. We like a story to be memorable; we leave the particulars of that to individual writers. We feel that first-person narration is becoming all too predictable and commonplace. We too often hear from writers who are not familiar with the lit magazine and who should be aware of, at least, what some independents are doing."

NEW WELSH REVIEW

P.O. Box 170, Aberystwyth, Ceredigion Wales SY23 1 WZ United Kingdom. 01970-626230. Fax: 01970-626230. E-mail: editor@newwelshreview.com. Website: www.newwelshreview.com. Editor: Francesca Rhydderch. **Contact:** Fiction Editor. *"NWR*, a literary quarterly ranked in the top five of British literary magazines, publishes stories, poems and critical essays. The best of Welsh writing in English, past and present, is celebrated, discussed and debated. We seek poems, short stories, reviews, special features/articles and commentary." Quarterly.
Needs Short fiction. Accepts 12 mss/year. **Publishes 20% new writers/year.** Recently published work by Peter Ho Davies.
How to Contact Send hard copy only with SASE or international money order for return.
Payment/Terms Pays "cheque on publication and one free copy."

THE NEW WRITER

P.O. Box 60, Cranbrook TN17 2ZR United Kingdom. 01580 212626. Fax: 01580 212041. E-mail: editor@the newwriter.com. Website: www.thenewwriter.com. **Contact:** Suzanne Ruthven, editor. Magazine: A4; 56 pages; illustrations; photos. Contemporary writing magazine which publishes "the best in fact, fiction and poetry." Publishes 6 issues per annum. Estab. 1996. Circ. 1,500.
Needs "We will consider most categories apart from stories written for children. No horror, erotic or cosy fiction." Accepts 4 mss/issue; 40 mss/year. Publishes ms 1 year after acceptance. Agented fiction 5%. **Publishes 12 new writers/year.** Recently published work by Alan Dunn, Alice Jolly, Kate Long, Annabel Lamb, Laureen Vonnegut and Stephen Finucan. Length: 2,000-5,000 words; average length: 3,500 words. Publishes short shorts. Also publishes literary essays, literary criticism, poetry. Often comments on rejected mss.
How to Contact Query with published clips. Accepts submissions by e-mail, fax. Send SASE (or IRC) for return of ms or send a disposable copy of ms and #10 SASE for reply only. "We consider short stories from subscribers only but we may also commission guest writers." Responds in 2 months to queries; 4 months to mss. Accepts simultaneous submissions. Sample copy for SASE and A4 SAE with IRCs only. Writer's guidelines for SASE. Reviews fiction.
Payment/Terms Pays £10 per story by credit voucher; additional copies for £1.50. Pays on publication for one-time rights. Sponsors awards/contests.
Advice "Hone it—always be prepared to improve the story. It's a competitive market."

$ NEW YORK STORIES

LaGuardia/CUNY, 31-10 Thomson Ave., Long Island City NY 11101. (718)482-5673. Website: www.newyorksto ries.org. **Contact:** Daniel Caplice Lynch, editor. Magazine: 9×11; 48 pages; photos. "Our purpose is to publish quality short fiction and New York-centered nonfiction. We look for fresh approaches, artistic daring, and story telling talent. We are especially interested in work that explores NYC's diversity—ethnic, social, sexual, psychological, economic and geographical." Estab. 1998. Circ. 1,500.
Needs Ethnic/multicultural, experimental, feminist, gay, humor/satire, lesbian, literary, mainstream, regional. Receives 300 unsolicited mss/month. Accepts 6-8 mss/issue; up to 24 mss/year. Publishes ms 3 months after acceptance. Agented fiction 5%. **Publishes 2 new writers/year.** Length: 300-6,000 words; average length: 2,500-3,000 words. Publishes short shorts. Also publishes literary essays. Sometimes comments on rejected mss.
How to Contact Send complete ms. Include 1-paragraph bio and e-mail address. Send SASE for return of ms or send disposable copy of ms. Responds in 2 weeks to queries; 6 months to mss. Accepts simultaneous submissions. Sample copy for $4. Writer's guidelines online.
Payment/Terms Pays $100-750. Pays on publication for first North American serial rights.
Advice "Fresh angles of vision, dark humor and psychological complexity are hallmarks of our short stories. Present characters who are 'alive.' Let them breathe. To achieve this, revise, revise, revise. Lately, the industry of publishing fiction seems to be playing it safe. We want your best—no matter what."

NIGHT TRAIN

Night Train Publications, Inc., P.O. Box 6250, Boston MA 02114. E-mail: submission@nighttrainmagazine.com. Website: www.nighttrainmagazine.com. **Contact:** Rusty Barnes, fiction editor. Magazine: 6×9; 200 pages; 60 lb. Glatfelter Natural paper; 12 pt. glossy laminated cover; photos. "We publish *Night Train* for anyone interested in the best available contemporary literature. We welcome all kinds of stories, but we strongly prefer those with an edge: fiction that leaves us gasping for breath, stories with people—real people—who are actors in their own lives and accept consequences for what they do. We honor the traditions of the short story but realize that to live, those traditions need new interpretations, new vision—a thrust forward. We provide a venue for writers to show us where the art will go and trust them to take us there." Semiannual. Estab. 2002. Circ. 3,000.
Needs Experimental, literary, mainstream. "A first-person, present-tense story would have to be remarkable for us to consider publishing it, but we rule out nothing. We also have a bias against stories about the pained

Literary Magazines

and tortured life of writers; we're writers too, but we don't find that interesting; again, it would have to be beyond excellent for us to consider.'' Receives 200-250 unsolicited mss/month. Accepts 20-25 mss/issue; 40-50 mss/year. Publishes ms 6 months after acceptance. **Publishes 5-10 new writers/year.** Recently published work by Terry Bain, Roy Kesey, Elaine Ford and Judd Hampton. Length: 250-10,000 words; average length: 3,000 words. Publishes short shorts. Often comments on rejected mss.

How to Contact Send a disposable copy of ms and #10 SASE for reply only. Responds in 2 months to queries; 3 months to mss. Accepts simultaneous submissions. Sample copy for $9.95. Writer's guidelines online.

Payment/Terms Pays 2 contributor's copies, a 1-year subscription and two 1-year gift subscriptions. Pays on publication for first North American serial, electronic, one-time anthology rights. Sends galleys to author. Sponsors awards/contests.

Advice ''We want to see characters who are active participants in their own lives, who recognize the impact they have on others, who think about the things they do and suffer (or not) as a result of those actions. *Night Train* is a place where blood, bone and nerve—the basic elements of stories—matter. Careless language, ethereal subject matter or lack of grounding in the 'whys' of human behavior will make us unhappy. Please read the guidelines and aesthetic statement on our website; and look at our editor's favorite pages. They're there for one reason: to help you understand what we like.''

NIMROD, International Journal of Prose and Poetry

University of Tulsa, 600 S. College Ave., Tulsa OK 74104-3189. (918)631-3080. Fax: (918)631-3033. E-mail: nimrod@utulsa.edu. Website: www.utulsa.edu/nimrod/. **Contact:** Gerry McLoud, fiction editor. Magazine: 6×9; 192 pages; 60 lb. white paper; illustrations; photos. ''We publish one thematic issue and one awards issue each year. A recent theme was ''The Celtic Fringe,'' a compilation of poetry and prose from all over the world. We seek vigorous, imaginative, quality writing. Our mission is to discover new writers and publish experimental writers who have not yet found a 'home' for their work.'' Semiannual. Estab. 1956. Circ. 3,000.

Needs ''We accept contemporary poetry and/or prose. May submit adventure, ethnic, experimental, prose poem or translations. No science fiction or romance.'' Receives 120 unsolicited mss/month. **Publishes 5-10 new writers/year.** Recently published work by Felicia Ward, Ellen Bass, Jeanette Turner Hospital and Kate Small. Also publishes poetry.

How to Contact SASE for return of ms. Accepts queries by e-mail. Does not accept submissions by e-mail unless the writer is living outside the U.S. Responds in 5 months to mss. Accepts simultaneous, multiple submissions.

Payment/Terms Pays 2 contributor's copies.

Advice ''We have not changed our fiction needs: quality, vigor, distinctive voice. We have, however, increased the number of stories we print. See current issues. We look for fiction that is fresh, vigorous, distinctive, serious and humorous, unflinchingly serious, ironic—whatever. Just so it is quality. Strongly encourage writers to send #10 SASE for brochure for annual literary contest with prizes of $1,000 and $2,000.''

NITE-WRITER'S INTERNATIONAL LITERARY ARTS JOURNAL

Nite Owl Press, 137 Pointview Rd., Suite 300, Pittsburgh PA 15227. (412)885-3798. E-mail: cexpression@msn.com. **Contact:** Fiction editor. Magazine: 8½×11; 30-50 pages; bond paper; illustrations. ''*Nite-Writer's International Literary Arts Journal* is dedicated to the emotional intellectual with a creative perception of life.'' Quarterly. Estab. 1993. Circ. 250.

Needs Adventure, erotica, historical, humor/satire, literary, mainstream, religious/inspirational, romance, young adult/teen (adventure), senior citizen/retirement, sports. Plans special fiction issue or anthology. Receives 3-5 unsolicited mss/month. Accepts 1-2 mss/issue; 5-8 mss/year. Publishes ms 1 year after acceptance. Recently published work by Julia Klatt Singer, Jean Oscarson Schoell, Lawrence Keough and S. Anthony Smith. Average length: 1,500 words. Publishes short shorts. Also publishes literary essays, literary criticism, poetry. Often comments on rejected mss.

How to Contact SASE for return of ms. Responds in 6 months to mss. Accepts simultaneous submissions. Sample copy for $6, 9×13 SAE and 6 first-class stamps. Writer's guidelines for legal size SASE.

Payment/Terms Does not pay. Copyright reverts to author upon publication.

Advice ''Read a lot of what you write, study the market; don't fear rejection, but use it as learning tool to strengthen your work before resubmitting. Express what the heart feels.''

N O NOON

1369 Madison Avenue PMB 298, New York New York 10128. **Contact:** Diane Williams, editor. Magazine: 5³/₁₆×8; 140 pages; illustrations; photographs. Annual. Estab. 2000. Circ. 5,000. Member: CLMP; AWP.

• Stories appearing in *Noon* have received a *Pushcart Prize*.

Needs Accepts 13-15 mss/year. **Publishes 2 new writers/year.** Recently published work by Gary Lutz, Lydia Davis, Christine Schutt, Karl Roloff and Adam Phillips. Publishes short shorts. Also publishes literary essays, literary criticism. Sometimes comments on rejected mss.

How to Contact Send SASE (or IRC) for return of the ms. Responds in 4 weeks to queries; 3 months to mss. Accepts simultaneous, multiple submissions. Sample copy for $9.
Payment/Terms Acquires first rights. Sends galleys to author.

$ ◎ ⬛ THE NORTH AMERICAN REVIEW

University of Northern Iowa, Cedar Falls IA 50614-0516. (319)273-6455. Fax: (319)273-4326. Website: www.we bdelsol.com/NorthAmReview/NAR/. **Contact:** Grant Tracey, fiction editor. *"The NAR* is the oldest literary magazine in America and one of the most respected; though we have no prejudices about the subject matter of material sent to us, our first concern is quality." Bimonthly. Estab. 1815. Circ. under 5,000.

 • Works published in *The North American Review* have won the *Pushcart Prize*.

Needs Open (literary). "No flat narrative stories where the inferiority of the character is the paramount concern." Wants to see more "well-crafted literary stories that emphasize family concerns. We'd also like to see more stories engaged with environmental concerns." Reads fiction mss from January 1 to April 1 only. Publishes ms 9 months after acceptance. **Publishes 2 new writers/year.** Recently published work by Rita Welty Bourke, Kurtus Davidson and Jonathan Wei.
How to Contact Accepts submissions by e-mail, fax, disk. Send complete ms with SASE. Responds in 3 months to queries; 3 months to mss. No simultaneous submissions. Sample copy for $5. Writer's guidelines online.
Payment/Terms $5/350 words; $20 minimum, $100 maximum. Pays on publication for first North American serial, first rights.
Advice "Stories that do not condescend to the reader or their character are always appealing to us. We also like stories that have characters doing things (acting upon the world instead of being acted upon). We also like a strong narrative arc. Stories that are mainly about language need not apply. Your first should be your second best line. Your last sentence should be your best. Everything in the middle should approach the two."

◎ NORTH CAROLINA LITERARY REVIEW, A Magazine of North Carolina Literature, Culture, and History

English Dept., East Carolina University, Greenville NC 27858-4353. (252)328-1537. Fax: (252)328-4889. E-mail: bauerm@mail.ecu.edu. Website: www.ecu.edu/nclr. "Articles should have a North Carolina slant. First consideration is always for quality of work. Although we treat academic and scholarly subjects, we do not wish to see jargon-laden prose; our readers, we hope, are found as often in bookstores and libraries as in academia. We seek to combine the best elements of magazine for serious readers with best of scholarly journal." Annual. Estab. 1992. Circ. 750.
Needs Regional (North Carolina). Must be North Carolina related—either by a North Carolina-connected writer or set in North Carolina. Publishes ms 1 year after acceptance.
How to Contact Query. Accepts submissions by e-mail. Responds in 1 month to queries; 6 months to mss. Sample copy for $10-25. Writer's guidelines online.
Payment/Terms Pays on publication for first North American serial rights. Rights returned to writer on request.

◪ ⬛ NORTH DAKOTA QUARTERLY

University of North Dakota, Box 7209, Grand Forks ND 58202. (701)777-3322. Fax: (701)777-2373. E-mail: ndq@und.nodak.edu. Website: www.und.nodak.edu/org/ndq. **Contact:** Robert W. Lewis, editor. Magazine: 6×9; 200 pages; bond paper; illustrations; photos. *"North Dakota Quarterly* is a literary journal publishing essays in the humanities; some short stories, some poetry. Occasional special topic issues." General audience. Quarterly. Estab. 1911. Circ. 700.

 • Work published in *North Dakota Quarterly* was selected for inclusion in *The O. Henry Awards* anthology, *The Pushcart Prize Series*, and *Best American Essays*.

Needs Ethnic/multicultural, experimental, feminist, historical, humor/satire, literary, Native American. Receives 100-120 unsolicited mss/month. Accepts 16 mss/issue; 16 mss/year. Publishes ms 1 year after acceptance. **Publishes 4-5 new writers/year.** Recently published work by Debra Marquart, Derek Walcott, Kim Chinquee, David W. Warfield, Peter Nabokov. Average length: 3,000-4,000 words. Also publishes literary essays, literary criticism, poetry. Sometimes comments on rejected mss.
How to Contact SASE. Responds in 3 months to mss. Sample copy for $8. Reviews fiction.
Payment/Terms Pays 2-4 contributor's copies; 30% discount for extras. Acquires one-time rights. Sends galleys to author.

◪ NORTHEAST ARTS MAGAZINE

P.O. Box 4363, Portland ME 04101. **Contact:** Mr. Leigh Donaldson, publisher. Magazine: 6½×9½; 32-40 pages; matte finish paper; card stock cover; illustrations; photos. Bimonthly. Estab. 1990. Circ. 750.
Needs Ethnic/multicultural, gay, historical, literary, mystery/suspense (private eye), prose poem (under 2,000 words). "No obscenity, racism, sexism, etc." Receives 50 unsolicited mss/month. Accepts 1-2 mss/issue; 5-7

Literary Magazines

mss/year. Publishes ms 2-4 months after acceptance. Agented fiction 20%. Publishes short shorts. Sometimes comments on rejected mss.

How to Contact SASE. Responds in 1 month to queries; 4-6 months to mss. Accepts simultaneous submissions. Sample copy for $4.50, SAE and 75¢ postage. Writer's guidelines free.

Payment/Terms Pays 2 contributor's copies. Acquires first North American serial rights.

Advice Looks for "creative/innovative use of language and style. Unusual themes and topics."

NORTHWEST REVIEW

369 PLC, University of Oregon, Eugene OR 97403. (541)346-3957. Website: darkwing.uoregon.edu/~nwreview. **Contact:** Janice MacCrae, fiction editor. Magazine: 6×9; 140-160 pages; high quality cover stock; illustrations; photos. "A general literary review featuring poems, stories, essays and reviews, circulated nationally and internationally. For a literate audience in avant-garde as well as traditional literary forms; interested in the important writers who have not yet achieved their readership." Triannual. Estab. 1957. Circ. 1,200.

Needs Experimental, feminist, literary, translations, contemporary. Receives 150 unsolicited mss/month. Accepts 4-5 mss/issue; 12-15 mss/year. **Publishes some new writers/year.** Recently published work by Diana Abu-Jaber, Madison Smartt Bell, Maria Flook and Charles Marvin. Also publishes literary essays, literary criticism, poetry. When there is time, comments on rejected mss.

How to Contact Responds in 4 months to mss. No simultaneous submissions. Sample copy for $4. Reviews fiction.

Payment/Terms Pays 3 contributor's copies and one-year subscription; 40% discount on extras. Acquires first rights.

$ NORTHWOODS JOURNAL, A Magazine for Writers

Conservatory of American Letters, P.O. Box 298, Thomaston ME 04861. (207)354-0998. Fax: (207)354-8953. E-mail: cal@americanletters.org. Website: www.americanletters.org. **Contact:** S.M. Hall, III fiction editor (submit fiction to S.M. Hall, III, 91A Bow St. Freeport ME 04032). Magazine: 5½×8½; 32-64 pages; white paper; 8 pt. glossy, full color cover; digital printing; some illustrations; photos. "No theme, no philosophy—for writers and for people who read for entertainment." Quarterly. Estab. 1993. Circ. 200.

Needs Adventure, experimental, fantasy (science fantasy, sword and sorcery), literary, mainstream, mystery/suspense (amateur sleuth, police procedural, private eye/hard-boiled, romantic suspense), psychic/supernatural/occult, regional, romance (gothic, historical), science fiction (hard science, soft/sociological), western (frontier, traditional), sports. "Would like to see more first-person adventure. No porn or evangelical." Publishes annual Northwoods Anthology. Receives 20 unsolicited mss/month. Accepts 12-15 mss/year. **Publishes 15 new writers/year.** Recently published work by J.F. Pytko, Richard Vaughn and Kelley Jean White. Also publishes literary criticism, poetry.

How to Contact Send SASE for reply, return of ms or send a disposable copy of ms. Responds in 2 days to queries; by next deadline plus 5 days to mss. No simultaneous submissions. Sample copy for $6.50 next issue, $9.75 current issue, $14.25 back issue, all postage paid. Or send 6×9 SASE with first-class postage affixed and $6.50. Writer's guidelines for #10 SASE. Reviews fiction.

Payment/Terms Varies, " but is generally 1 cent per word or more, based on experience with us." Pays on acceptance for first North American serial rights. 50/50 split of additional sales.

Advice "Read guidelines, read the things we've published. Know your market."

$ NOTRE DAME REVIEW

University of Notre Dame, 840 Flanner Hall, Notre Dame IN 46556. (574)631-6952. Fax: (574)631-8209. Website: www.nd.edu/~ndr/review.htm. **Contact:** William O'Rourke, fiction editor. Literary magazine: 6×9; 200 pages; 50 lb. smooth paper; illustrations; photos. "The *Notre Dame Review* is an indepenent, noncommercial magazine of contemporary American and international fiction, poetry, criticism and art. We are especially interested in work that takes on big issues by making the invisible seen, that gives voice to the voiceless. In addition to showcasing celebrated authors like Seamus Heaney and Czelaw Milosz, the *Notre Dame Review* introduces readers to authors they may have never encountered before but who are doing innovative and important work. In conjunction with the *Notre Dame Review*, the online companion to the printed magazine, the *Notre Dame Re-view* engages readers as a community centered in literary rather than commercial concerns, a community we reach out to through critique and commentary as well as aesthetic experience." Semiannual. Estab. 1995. Circ. 1,500.

● *Pushcart* prizes in fiction and poetry.

Needs No genre fiction. Upcoming theme issues planned. Receives 75 unsolicited mss/month. Accepts 4-5 mss/issue; 10 mss/year. Does not read mss November-January or May-August. Publishes ms 6 months after acceptance. **Publishes 1 new writer/year.** Recently published work by Ed Falco, Jarda Cerverka and David Green. Publishes short shorts. Also publishes literary criticism, poetry.

How to Contact Send complete ms with cover letter. Include 4-sentence bio. Send SASE for response, return of ms, or send a disposable copy of ms. Responds in 6 months to mss. Accepts simultaneous submissions. Sample copy for $6. Writer's guidelines online.

Payment/Terms Pays $5-25. Pays on publication for first North American serial rights.

Advice "We're looking for high quality work that takes on big issues in a literary way. Please read our back issues before submitting."

OASIS, A Literary Magazine

P.O. Box 626, Largo FL 33779-0626. (727)345-8505. E-mail: dasislit@aol.com. **Contact:** Neal Storrs, editor. Magazine: 70 pages. "The only criterion is high literary quality of writing." Quarterly. Estab. 1992. Circ. 300.

Needs High-quality writing. Also publishes translations. Receives 150 unsolicited mss/month. Accepts 6 mss/issue; 24 mss/year. Publishes ms 4 months after acceptance. **Publishes 2 new writers/year.** Recently published work by Wendell Mayo, Jim Meirose, Al Masarik and Mark Wisniewski. Also publishes literary essays, poetry. Occasionally comments on rejected mss.

How to Contact Send complete ms. Accepts submissions by e-mail, disk. Send SASE for reply, return of ms or send a disposable copy of ms. Responds in 1-3 days to mss. Accepts simultaneous and reprints, multiple submissions. Sample copy for $7.50. Writer's guidelines for #10 SASE.

Payment/Terms Pays in contributor's copies.

Advice "If you want to write good stories, read good stories. Cultivate the critical ability to recognize what makes a story original and true to itself."

OBSIDIAN III, Literature in the African Diaspora

Dept. of English, North Carolina State University, Raleigh NC 27695-8105. (919)515-4153. Fax: (919)515-1836. E-mail: obsidian@social.chass.ncsu.edu. Website: www.ncsu.edu/chass/obsidian/. **Contact:** Thomas Lisk, editor. Magazine: 6×9; 130 pages. "Creative works in English by black writers, scholarly critical studies by all writers on black literature in English." Published 2 times/year (spring/summer, fall/winter). Estab. 1975. Circ. 500.

Needs Ethnic/multicultural (Pan-African), feminist, literary. All writers on black topics. Accepts 7-9 mss/year. Publishes ms 4-6 months after acceptance. **Publishes 20 new writers/year.** Recently published work by Sean Henry, R. Flowers Rivera, Terrance Hayes, Eugene Kraft, Arlene McKanic, Pearl Bothe Williams and Kwane Dawes.

How to Contact Accepts submissions by e-mail (disk). Responds in 4 months to mss. Sample copy for $10.

Payment/Terms Pays in contributor's copies. Acquires one-time rights. Sponsors awards/contests.

Advice "Following proper format is essential. Your title must be intriguing and text clean. Never give up. Some of the writers we publish were rejected many times before we published them."

OHIO TEACHERS WRITE

Ohio Council of Teachers of English Language Arts, 644 Overlook Dr., Columbus OH 43214. E-mail: rmcclain@b right.net. **Contact:** Mark Jamison, editor. Editors change every 3 years. Magazine: 8½×11; 50 pages; 60 lb. white offset paper; 65 lb. blue cover stock; illustrations; photos. "The purpose of the magazine is three fold: (1) to provide a collection of fine literature for the reading pleasure of teachers and other adult readers; (2) to encourage teachers to compose literary works along with their students; (3) to provide the literate citizens of Ohio a window into the world of educators not often seen by those outside the teaching profession." Annual. Estab. 1995. Circ. 1,000. Submissions are limited to Ohio Educators.

Needs Adventure, ethnic/multicultural, experimental, fantasy (science fantasy), feminist, gay, historical, humor/satire, lesbian, literary, mainstream, regional, religious/inspirational, romance (contemporary), science fiction (hard science, soft/sociological), western (frontier, traditional), senior citizen/retirement, sports, teaching. Receives 2 unsolicited mss/month. Accepts 7 mss/issue. "We read only in May when editorial board meets." Recently published work by Lois Spencer, Harry R. Noden, Linda J. Rice and June Langford Berkley. Publishes short shorts. Also publishes poetry. Often comments on rejected mss.

How to Contact Send SASE with postage clipped for return of ms or send a disposable copy of ms. Accepts multiple submissions. Sample copy for $6.

Payment/Terms Pays 2 contributor's copies; additional copies $6. Acquires first rights.

$ ONE STORY

One Story, LLC, P.O. Box 1326, New York NY 10156. Website: www.one-story.com. **Contact:** Maribeth Batcha and Hannah Tinti, editors. "*One Story* is a literary magazine that contains, simply, one story. It is a subscription-only magazine. Every 3 weeks subscribers are sent *One Story* in the mail. *One Story* is artfully designed, lightweight, easy to carry, and ready to entertain on buses, in bed, in subways, in cars, in the park, in the bath, in the waiting rooms of doctors, on the couch, or in line at the supermarket. Subscribers also have access to a website, www.one-story.com, where they can learn more about *One Story* authors and hear about *One Story* readings and events. There is always time to read *One Story*." Estab. 2002. Circ. 3,500.

Needs Literary, literary short stories. *One Story* only accepts short stories. Do not send excerpts. Do not send more than 1 story at a time. Publishes ms 3-6 months after acceptance. Recently published work by John Hodgman, Melanie Rae Thon, Daniel Wallace and Judy Budnitz.

How to Contact Send complete ms. Accepts online submissions only. Responds in 2-6 months to mss. Accepts simultaneous submissions. Sample copy for $5. Writer's guidelines online.

Payment/Terms Pays $100. Pays on publication for first North American serial rights. Buys the rights to publish excerpts on website and in promotional materials.

OPEN SPACES

Open Spaces Publications, Inc., PMB 134, 6327-C SW Capitol Hwy., Portland OR 97239-1937. (503)227-5764. Fax: (503)227-3401. Website: www.open-spaces.com. **Contact:** Ellen Teicher, fiction editor. Magazine: 64 pages; illustrations; photos. "*Open Spaces* is a forum for informed writing and intelligent thought. Articles are written by experts in various fields. Audience is varied (CEOs and rock climbers, politicos and university presidents, etc.) but is highly educated and loves to read good writing." Quarterly. Estab. 1997.

Needs "Excellence is the issue—not subject matter." Accepts 2 mss/issue; 8 mss/year. Publishes ms 6 months after acceptance. **Publishes 5 new writers/year.** Recently published work by William Kittredge, Rick Bass, Pattiann Rogers and David James Duncan. Publishes short shorts. Also publishes literary essays, poetry. Sometimes comments on rejected mss.

How to Contact Accepts submissions by fax. Send complete ms with a cover letter. Include short bio, social security number and list of publications. SASE for return of ms or send a disposable copy of ms. Accepts simultaneous submissions. Sample copy for $10. Writer's guidelines online.

Payment/Terms Payment varies. Pays on publication. Rights purchased vary with author and material.

Advice "The surest way for a writer to determine whether his or her material is right for us is to read the magazine."

$ OTHER VOICES

University of Illinois at Chicago, 601 S. Morgan St., Chicago IL 60607. (312)413-2209. Website: www.othervoices magazine.org. **Contact:** Gina Frangello. Magazine: $5^7/8 \times 9$; 168-205 pages; 60 lb. paper; coated cover stock; occasional photos. "Original, fresh, diverse stories and novel excerpts" for literate adults. Semiannual. Estab. 1985. Circ. 1,800.

Needs Literary, contemporary, excerpted novel and one-act plays. Fiction only. "No taboos, except ineptitude and murkiness. No science fiction, romance, horror, fantasy." Receives 300 unsolicited mss/month. Accepts 17-20 mss/issue. **Publishes 6 new writers/year.** Recently published work by Wanda Coleman, Jeffery Renard Allen, Steve Almond and Dan Chaon. Length: 6,000 words; average length: 5,000 words.

How to Contact Send ms with SASE October 1-April 1 only. Mss received during non-reading period are returned unread. Cover letters "should be brief and list previous publications. Also, list title of submission. Most beginners' letters try to 'explain' the story—a big mistake." Responds in 10-12 weeks to mss. Accepts simultaneous submissions. Sample copy for $7 (includes postage). Writer's guidelines for #10 SASE.

Payment/Terms Pays $100 plus contributor's copies. Acquires one-time rights.

Advice "There are so *few* markets for *quality* fiction! By publishing up to 40 stories a year, we provide new and established writers a forum for their work. Send us your best voice, your best work, your best best."

OYSTER BOY REVIEW

P.O. Box 77842, San Francisco CA 94107-0842. E-mail: fiction@oysterboyreview.com. Website: www.oysterboy review.com. **Contact:** C. Earl Nelson, fiction editor. Electronic and print magazine. "We publish kick-ass, teeth-cracking stories." 4 times a year.

Needs No genre fiction. "Fiction the revolves around characters in conflict with themselves or each other; a plot that has a begining, a middle, and an end; a narrative with a strong moral center (not necessarily 'moralistic'); a story with a satisfying resolution to the conflict; and an ethereal something that contributes to the mystery of a question, but does not necessarily seek or contrive to answer it." Submissions accepted January-September. **Publishes 4 new writers/year.** Recently published work by Todd Goldberg, Ken Wainio, Elisha Porat and Kevin McGowan.

How to Contact Accepts multiple submissions. Sample copy not available.

Advice "Keep writing, keep submitting, keep revising."

PACIFIC COAST JOURNAL

French Bread Publications, P.O. Box 56, Carlsbad CA 92018. E-mail: paccoastj@frenchbreadpublications.com. Website: www.frenchbreadpublications.com/pcj. **Contact:** Stephanie Kylkis, fiction editor. Magazine:

$5^{1}/_{2} \times 8^{1}/_{2}$; 40 pages; 20 lb. paper; 67 lb. cover; illustrations; b&w photos. "Slight focus toward Western North America/Pacific Rim." Quarterly. Estab. 1992. Circ. 200.

Needs Ethnic/multicultural, experimental, feminist, historical, humor/satire, literary, science fiction (soft/sociological, magical realism). "No children's, religious or hard sci-fi." Receives 30-40 unsolicited mss/month. Accepts 3-4 mss/issue; 10-12 mss/year. Publishes ms 6-18 months after acceptance. Recently published work by Michael Onofrey and Francine Witte. Length: 4,000 words; average length: 2,500 words. Publishes short shorts. Also publishes literary essays, poetry. Sometimes comments on rejected mss.

How to Contact Send SASE for reply, return of ms or send a disposable copy of ms. Also accepts e-mail address for response instead of SASE. "More likely to comment if e-mail address is provided." Responds in 6-9 months to mss. Accepts simultaneous and reprints submissions. Sample copy for $2.50, 6×9 SASE and 3oz. postage. Reviews fiction.

Payment/Terms Pays 1 contributor's copy. Acquires one-time rights.

Advice "*PCJ* is an independent magazine and we have a limited amount of space and funding. We are looking for experiments in what can be done with the short fiction form. We don't want to see a story that you thought was okay for a mainstream litmag. We want to see something that you find you can't control through the writing process. The best stories will entertain as well as confuse."

pacific REVIEW

Dept. of English and Comparitive Lit., San Diego State University, 5500 Campanile Dr. MC8140, San Diego CA 92182-8140. E-mail: pacificREVIEW_sdsu@yahoo.com. Website: http://pacificREVIEW.sdsu.edu. **Contact:** Leon Lanzbom, editor-in-chief. Magazine: 6×9; 200 pages; book stock paper; paper back, extra heavy cover stock; b&w illustrations, b&w photos. "*pacific REVIEW* publishes the work of emergent literati, pairing their efforts with those of established artists. It is available at West Coast independent booksellers, university and college libraries, and is taught as text in numerous university literature and creative writing classes." Circ. 2,000.

Needs "We seek high-quality fiction and give preference to pieces that explore the themes of omnivore as a compass to a wider field of implication and reinvention." For information on theme issues see website. **Publishes 15 new writers/year.** Recently published work by Ai, Alurista, Susan Daitch, Lawrence Ferlinghetti and William T. Vollmann.

How to Contact Responds in 3 months to mss. Sample copy for $10.

Payment/Terms Pays 2 contributor's copies. Aquires first serial rights. All other rights revert to author.

Advice "We welcome all submissions, especially those created in or in the context of the West Coast/California and the space of our borders."

PALO ALTO REVIEW, A Journal of Ideas

Palo Alto College, 1400 W. Villaret, San Antonio TX 78224. (210)921-5021. Fax: (210)9215008. E-mail: eshull@accd.edu. **Contact:** Ellen Shull, editor. Magazine: $8^{1}/_{2} \times 11$; 64 pages; 60 lb. natural white paper (50% recycled); illustrations; photos. "Not too experimental nor excessively avant-garde, just good stories (for fiction). Ideas are what we are after. We are interested in connecting the interesting angles with which to investigate the length and breadth of the teaching/learning spectrum, life itself." Semiannual. Estab. 1992. Circ. 500.

● *Palo Alto Review* was awarded the *Pushcart Prize* for 2001.

Needs Adventure, ethnic/multicultural, experimental, fantasy, feminist, historical, humor/satire, literary, mainstream, mystery/suspense, regional, romance, science fiction, translations, western. Upcoming themes available for SASE. Receives 100-150 unsolicited mss/month. Accepts 2-4 mss/issue; 4-8 mss/year. Does not read mss March-April and October-November when putting out each issue. Publishes ms 2-15 months after acceptance. **Publishes 30 new writers/year.** Recently published work by Layle Silbert, Naomi Chase, Kenneth Emberly, C.J. Hannah, Tom Juvik, Kassie Fleisher and Paul Perry. Publishes short shorts. Also publishes poetry. Always comments on rejected mss.

How to Contact Send SASE for reply, return of ms or send a disposable copy of ms. "Request sample copy and guidelines." Accepts submissions by e-mail only if outside the US. Responds in 4 months to mss. Accepts simultaneous submissions. Sample copy for $5. Writer's guidelines for #10 SASE or e-mail to paloaltoreview@aol.com.

Payment/Terms Pays 2 contributor's copies; additional copies for $5. Acquires first North American serial rights.

Advice "Good short stories have interesting characters confronted by a dilemma working toward a solution. So often what we get is 'a moment in time,' not a story. Generally, characters are interesting because readers can identify with them. Edit judiciously. Cut out extraneous verbiage. Set up a choice that has to be made. Then create tension—who wants what and why they can't have it."

Literary Magazines

$ ☑ ☑ THE PARIS REVIEW

541 E. 72nd St., New York NY 10021. (212)861-0016. Fax: (212)861-4504. Website: www.theparisreview.com. Other Address: 541 E. 72nd St., New York NY 10021. **Contact:** Philip Gourevitch, editor. Magazine: $5\frac{1}{4} \times 8\frac{1}{2}$; about 260 pages; illustrations; photos (unsolicited artwork not accepted). "Fiction and poetry of superlative quality, whatever the genre, style or mode. Our contributors include prominent, as well as less well-known and previously unpublished writers. Writers at Work interview series includes important contemporary writers discussing their own work and the craft of writing." Quarterly.

• Work published in *The Paris Review* received five *Pushcart* awards.

Needs Literary. Receives 1,000 unsolicited mss/month. **Publishes 5 new writers/year.** Recently published work by Thomas Wolfe, Denis Johnson, Melissa Pritchard, Jim Shepard and Jonathan Safran Foer. Also publishes literary essays, poetry.

How to Contact Query. SASE. Responds in 4 months to mss. Accepts simultaneous, multiple submissions. Sample copy for $15 (includes postage). Writer's guidelines online.

Payment/Terms Payment varies depending on length. Pays on publication for first English-language rights. Sends galleys to author. Sponsors awards/contests.

☑ PARTING GIFTS

3413 Wilshire, Greensboro NC 27408-2923. E-mail: rbixby@aol.com. Website: www.marchstreetpress.com. **Contact:** Robert Bixby, editor. Magazine: 5×7; 72 pages. "*Parting Gifts* seeks good, powerful and short fiction that stands on its own and takes no prisoners." Semiannual. Estab. 1988.

Needs "Brevity is the second most important criterion behind literary quality." Publishes ms within one year after acceptance. Recently published work by Ray Miller, Katherine Taylor, Curtis Smith and William Snyder, Jr. Also publishes poetry. Sometimes comments on rejected mss.

How to Contact SASE. Responds in 1 day to queries; 1 week to mss. Accepts simultaneous, multiple submissions. Sample copy for $9. For a year subscription, $18.

Payment/Terms Pays in contributor's copies. Acquires one-time rights.

Advice "Read the works of Amy Hempel, Jim Harrison, Kelly Cherry, C.K. Williams and Janet Kaufman, all excellent writers who epitomize the writing *Parting Gifts* strives to promote. I look for original voice, original ideas, original setting and characters, language that makes one weep without knowing why, a deep understanding or keen observation of real people in real situations. The magazine is online, along with guidelines and feedback to authors; reading any one or all three will save a lot of postage."

☑ PASSAGES NORTH

Northern Michigan University, Department of English, Gries Hall, Rm 229, Marquette Mi 49855. (906)227-2711. Fax: (906)227-1096. E-mail: passages@nmu.edu. Website: http://myweb.nmu.edu/ ~ passages. **Contact:** Kate Myers Hanson, editor; John Smolens, fiction editor; Austin Hummell, poetry editor. Magazine: $8 \times 5\frac{1}{2}$; 80 lb. paper. "*Passages North* publishes quality fiction, poetry and creative nonfiction by emerging and established writers." Readership: General and literary. Annual. Estab. 1979. Circ. 1,000.

Needs Ethnic/multicultural, literary, mainstream, regional. No genre fiction, science fiction, "typical commercial press work." "Seeking more multicultural work." Receives 100-200 unsolicited mss/month. Accepts 20 mss/year. Reads mss September 1-April 15. **Publishes 25% new writers/year.** Recently published work by W.P. Kinsella, Jack Gantos, Lee Martin, Bonnie Campbell, Anthony Bukowski and Peter Orner. When there is time, comments on rejected mss.

How to Contact Responds in 2 months to mss. Accepts simultaneous submissions. Sample copy for $7.

Payment/Terms Pays 2 contributor's copies. Rights revert to author upon publication.

Advice "We look for voice, energetic prose, writers who take risks. Revise, revise. Read what we publish."

☑ ☑ THE PATERSON LITERARY REVIEW

Passaic County Community College, One College Blvd., Paterson NJ 07505. (973)684-6555. Fax: (973)523-6085. E-mail: mgillan@pccc.edu. Website: www.pccc.edu/poetry. **Contact:** Maria Mazziotti Gillan, editor. Magazine: 6×9; 336 pages; 60 lb. paper; 70 lb. cover; illustrations; photos. Annual.

• Work for *PLR* has been included in the *Pushcart Prize* anthology and *Best American Poetry*.

Needs Ethnic/multicultural, literary, contemporary. "We are interested in quality short stories, with no taboos on subject matter." Receives 60 unsolicited mss/month. Publishes ms 6-12 months after acceptance. **Publishes 5% new writers/year.** Recently published work by Robert Mooney and Abigail Stone. Also publishes literary essays, literary criticism, poetry.

How to Contact Send SASE for reply or return of ms. "Indicate whether you want story returned." Accepts simultaneous submissions. Sample copy for $13. Reviews fiction.

Payment/Terms Pays in contributor's copies. Acquires first North American serial rights.

Advice Looks for "clear, moving and specific work."

◨ ◎ PEARL, A Literary Magazine

3030 E. Second St., Long Beach CA 90803-5163. (562)434-4523. E-mail: pearlmag@aol.com. Website: www.pear lmag.com. **Contact:** Marilyn Johnson, editor. Magazine: $5^{1}/_{2} \times 8^{1}/_{2}$; 96 pages; 60 lb. recycled, acid-free paper; perfect bound; coated cover; b&w drawings and graphics. "We are primarily a poetry magazine, but we do publish some *very short* fiction and nonfiction. We are interested in lively, readable prose that speaks to *real* people in direct, living language; for a general literary audience." Biannual. Estab. 1974. Circ. 600.

Needs Humor/satire, literary, mainstream, contemporary, prose poem. "We will consider short-short stories up to 1,200 words. Longer stories (up to 4,000 words) may only be submitted to our short story contest. All contest entries are considered for publication. Although we have no taboos stylistically or subject-wise, obscure, predictable, sentimental or cliché-ridden stories are a turn-off." Publishes an all-fiction issue each year. Receives 10-20 unsolicited mss/month. Accepts 10-18 mss/issue; 12-15 mss/year. Submissions accepted September-May *only*. Publishes ms 6-12 months after acceptance. **Publishes 1-5 new writers/year.** Recently published work by Stephanie Dickinson, Linda Barnhart, Fred McGavran, Tim Foley and Lisa Glatt. Length: 500-1,200 words; average length: 1,000 words. Also publishes poetry.

How to Contact SASE. Responds in 2 months to mss. Accepts simultaneous, multiple submissions. Sample copy for $7 (postpaid). Writer's guidelines for #10 SASE.

Payment/Terms Pays 1 contributor's copy. Acquires first North American serial rights. Sends galleys to author. Sponsors awards/contests.

Advice "We look for vivid, *dramatized* situations and characters, stories written in an original 'voice' that make sense and follow a clear narrative line. What makes a manuscript stand out is more elusive, though—more to do with feeling and imagination than anything else."

$ PEEKS & VALLEYS, A Fiction Journal

Brink Publications, 702 Twyckenham Dr., South Bend IN 46615. E-mail: peeksandvalleys@earthlink.net. Website: www.peeksandvalleys.com. **Contact:** Meagan Church, editor. "*Peeks & Valleys* is a fiction journal that seeks quality writing and storytelling of various genres. We look for writing that leaves an impression—however tangible that may be. Our goal is to encourage and offer an outlet for both accomplished and new writers and to cause contemplation on the part of the reader." Quarterly. Estab. 1999.

Needs Please no sci-fi, fantasy, sex or obscenity. Receives 40 unsolicited mss/month. Accepts 7-8 mss/issue; 28-32 mss/year. Publishes ms 8 months after acceptance. **Publishes 80% new writers/year.** Length: 2,600 words; average length: 2,000 words. Also publishes poetry.

How to Contact Send complete ms. Accepts submissions by e-mail. Responds in 2 months to mss. Accepts simultaneous and reprints submissions. Sample copy for $5.75. Writer's guidelines online.

Payment/Terms Pays $5. Pays on publication for one-time, second serial (reprint) rights.

Advice "Follow submission guidelines, and don't exceed the recommended length. Study the journal to get a clear idea of what is needed. Be sure to check the website for information on the annual flash fiction contest."

◨ PENNSYLVANIA ENGLISH

Penn State DuBois, College Place, DuBois PA 15801. (814)375-4814. Fax: (814)375-4784. E-mail: ajv2@psu.edu "Mention Pennsylvania English in the subject line or at the beginning of the message." **Contact:** Antonio Vallone, editor. Magazine: $5^{1}/_{4} \times 8^{1}/_{4}$; up to 200 pages; perfect bound; full color cover featuring the artwork of a Pennsylvania artist. "Our philosophy is quality. We publish literary fiction (and poetry and nonfiction). Our intended audience is literate, college-educated people." Annual. Estab. 1985. Circ. 500.

Needs Literary, mainstream, contemporary. "No genre fiction or romance." Reads mss during the summer. Publishes ms 12-24 months after acceptance. **Publishes 4-6 new writers/year.** Recently published work by Dave Kress, Dan Leone and Paul West. Publishes short shorts. Also publishes literary essays, literary criticism, poetry. Sometimes comments on rejected mss.

How to Contact SASE. Does not normally accept electronic submissions. Responds in 9 months to mss. Accepts simultaneous submissions. Sample copy for $10.

Payment/Terms Pays in 2 contributor's copies. Acquires first North American serial rights.

Advice "Quality of the writing is our only measure. We're not impressed by long-winded cover letters detailing awards and publications we've never heard of. Beginners and professionals have the same chance with us. We receive stacks of competently written but boring fiction. For a story to rise out of the rejection pile, it takes more than the basic competence."

◨ PHANTASMAGORIA

Century College English Dept., 3300 Century Ave. N, White Bear Lake MN 55110. (651)779-3410. E-mail: allenabigail@hotmail.com. **Contact:** Abigail Allen, editor. Magazine: $5^{1}/_{2} \times 8^{1}/_{2}$; 140-200 pages. "We publish literary fiction, poetry and essays (no scholarly essays)." Semiannual. Estab. 2001. Circ. 1.000. CLMP.

Needs Experimental, literary, mainstream. "No children's stories or young adult/teen material." Receives 120 unsolicited mss/month. Accepts 20-40 mss/issue; 40-80 mss/year. Publishes ms 6 months after acceptance. **Publishes 5-10 new writers/year.** Recently published work by Greg Mulcahy, Hiram Goza, Simon Perchik and William Greenway. Length: 4,000 words; average length: 2,500 words. Publishes short shorts. Also publishes literary essays, poetry.

How to Contact Send SASE (or IRC) for return of ms or send a disposable copy of ms and #10 SASE for reply only. Responds in 2 weeks to queries. Sample copy for $9. Writer's guidelines for SASE. Reviews fiction.

Payment/Terms Pays 2 contributor's copies. Acquires first North American serial rights.

PHOEBE, A Journal of Literature and Art

George Mason University, MSN 2D6, 4400 University Dr., Fairfax VA 22030. (703)993-2915. E-mail: phoebe@gmu.edu. Website: www.gmu.edu/pubs/phoebe. **Contact:** Ryan Effgen, editor. Editors change every year. Magazine: 9×6; 112-120 pages; 80 lb. paper; 0-5 illustrations; 0-10 photos. ''We publish mainly fiction and poetry with occasional visual art.'' 2 times/year. Estab. 1972. Circ. 3,000.

Needs ''*Phoebe* prides itself on supporting up-and-coming writers, whose style, form, voice and subject matter demostrate a vigorous appeal to the senses, intellect and emotions of our readers. No romance, western, juvenile, erotica.'' Receives 100 unsolicited mss/month. Accepts 3-7 mss/issue. Does not read mss in summer. Publishes ms 3-6 months after acceptance. **Publishes 8-10 new writers/year.** Recently published work by Michelle Mounts, Tara Laskowski, Robert Drummond, Jessica Anthony, James Gish Jr., Karen Heuler, Matthew Norman and Bryn Chancellor.

How to Contact SASE. Accepts simultaneous submissions. Sample copy for $6.

Payment/Terms Pays 2 contributor's copies. Acquires one-time rights. All rights revert to author on publication.

Advice ''We are interested in a variety of fiction and poetry. We encourage writers and poets to experiment and stretch boundaries of genre. We suggest potential contributors study previous issues. Each year *Phoebe* sponsors fiction and poetry contests, with $1,000 awarded to the winning short story and poem. The deadline for both the Greg Grummer Award in Poetry and the Phoebe Fiction Prize is December 1. E-mail or send SASE for complete contest guidelines.''

$ PIG IRON PRESS

Pig Iron Series, P.O. Box 237, Youngstown OH 44501-0237. (330)747-6932. E-mail: jimv@cboss.com. **Contact:** Jim Villani. Annual series: 8½×11; 175 pages; 60 lb. offset paper; coated cover stock; b&w illustrations; b&w 120 line photos. Annual. Estab. 1975. Circ. 1,000.

• Now accepting freelance submissions.

Needs Literary, thematic. Receives 50 unsolicited mss/month. Accepts 60-70 mss/issue. Publishes ms 18 months after acceptance. Recently published work by Winona Baker, Joel Climenhaga, Joan Payne Kincaid, Lyn Lifshin, Dirk van Nouhuys, Mark Payne, J.A. Pollard and Arthur Schwartz. Also publishes poetry.

How to Contact Send complete ms. Responds in 3 weeks to queries; 3 months to mss. No simultaneous submissions. Sample copy for $6. Writer's guidelines and theme list for #10 SASE.

Payment/Terms Pays $5 minimum. Pays on publication for first North American serial, one-time rights.

Advice ''Looking for work that is polished, compelling and magical.''

PIKEVILLE REVIEW

Pikeville College, Sycamore St., Pikeville KY 41501. (606)218-5602. Fax: (606)218-5225. E-mail: sengland@pc.edu. Website: www.pc.edu. **Contact:** Sydney England. Magazine: 8½×6; 120 pages; illustrations; photos. ''Literate audience interested in well-crafted poetry, fiction, essays and reviews.'' Annual. Estab. 1987. Circ. 500.

Needs Ethnic/multicultural, experimental, feminist, humor/satire, literary, mainstream, regional, translations. Receives 60-80 unsolicited mss/month. Accepts 3-4 mss/issue. Does not read mss in the summer. Publishes ms 6-8 after acceptance. **Publishes 20 new writers/year.** Recently published work by Jim Wayne Miller, James Baker Hall, Robert Elkins and Robert Morgan. Length: 15,000 words; average length: 5,000 words. Publishes short shorts. Also publishes literary essays, poetry. Often comments on rejected mss.

How to Contact Accepts submissions by e-mail. Send SASE for reply, return of ms or send a disposable copy of ms. Sample copy for $4. Reviews fiction.

Payment/Terms Pays 5 contributor's copies; additional copies for $4. Acquires first rights. Sponsors awards/contests.

Advice ''Send a clean manuscript with well-developed characters.''

PINDELDYBOZ

Pindeldyboz, 23-55 38th St., Astoria NY 11105. E-mail: print@pindeldyboz.com. Website: www.pindeldyboz.com. **Contact:** Whitney Pastorek, executive editor. Literary magazine: 5½×8½; 272 pages; illustrations. ''*Pindeldyboz* is dedicated to publishing work that challenges what a short story can be. We don't ask for anything specific—we only ask that people take chances. We like heightened language, events, relationships—stories that paint the world a little differently, while still showing us the places we already know." Semiannual. Estab. 2001.

Needs Comics/graphic novels, experimental, literary, translations. Reads mss July 21-December 31 only. Publishes ms 3 months after acceptance. Recently published work by Carrie Hoffman, Matthew Derby, Amanda Eyre Ward, Dan Kennedy, Corey Mesler, Jason Wilson and Mike Magnuson. Length: 250+; average length: 2,000 words. Publishes short shorts. Also publishes literary essays, poetry. Always comments on rejected mss.

How to Contact Send complete copy of ms with cover letter. Accepts mss by e-mail and disk. Include brief bio and phone number with submission. Send SASE (or IRC) for return of the ms and disposable copy of ms and #10 SASE for reply only. Responds in 2 weeks to queries; 3 months to mss. Accepts simultaneous, multiple submissions. Sample copy for $12. Writer's guidelines online.

Payment/Terms Pays 2 contributor's copies; additional copies $10. Pays on publication for one-time rights.

Advice "Good grammar, spelling and sentence structure help, but what's more important is a willingness to take risks. Surprise us and we will love it."

$PLANET, The Welsh Internationalist

P.O. Box 44, Aberystwyth Ceredigion SY23 3ZZ, Cymru/Wales United Kingdom. 01970-611255. Fax: 01970-611197. Website: www.planetmagazine.org.uk. **Contact:** John Barnie, fiction editor. "A literary/cultural/political journal centered on Welsh affairs but with a strong interest in minority cultures in Europe and elsewhere." Bimonthly. Circ. 1,400.

Needs No magical realism, horror, science fiction. Recently published work by Harriet Richards, Katie O'Reilly and Guy Vanderhaeghe.

How to Contact No submissions returned unless accompanied by an SAE. Writers submitting from abroad should send at least 3 IRCs for return of typescript; 1 IRC for reply only. No e-mail queries. Sample copy for £4. Writer's guidelines online.

Payment/Terms Pays £50/1,000 words.

Advice "We do not look for fiction which necessarily has a 'Welsh' connection, which some writers assume from our title. We try to publish a broad range of fiction and our main criterion is quality. Try to read copies of any magazine you submit to. Don't write out of the blue to a magazine which might be completely inappropriate for your work. Recognize that you are likely to have a high rejection rate, as magazines tend to favor writers from their own countries."

$ PLEIADES

Pleiades Press, Department of English & Philosophy, Central Missouri State University, Martin 336, Warrensburg MO 64093. (660)543-4425. Fax: (660)543-8544. E-mail: ssteinberg@usfca.edu. Website: www.cmsu.edu/englp hil/pleiades. **Contact:** Susan Steinberg, fiction editor. Magazine: 5½×8½; 150 pages; 60 lb. paper; perfect-bound; 8 pt. color cover. "We publish contemporary fiction, poetry, interviews, literary essays, special-interest personal essays, reviews for a general and literary audience." Semiannual. Estab. 1991. Circ. 3,000.

● Work from *Pleiades* appears in recent volumes of *The Best American Poetry*, *The Pushcart Prize*, and *Best American Fantasy and Horror*.

Needs Ethnic/multicultural, experimental, feminist, gay, humor/satire, literary, mainstream, novel excerpts, regional, translations, magical realism. No science fiction, fantasy, confession, erotica. Receives 100 unsolicited mss/month. Accepts 8 mss/issue; 16 mss/year. "We're slower at reading manuscripts in the summer." Publishes ms 9 months after acceptance. **Publishes 4-5 new writers/year.** Recently published work by Sherman Alexie, Edith Pearlman, Joyce Carol Oates and James Tate. Length: 2,000-6,000 words; average length: 3,000-6,000 words. Also publishes literary essays, literary criticism, poetry. Sometimes comments on rejected mss.

How to Contact Send complete ms. Include 75-100 word bio and list of publications. Send SASE for reply, return of ms or send a disposable copy of ms. Responds in 2 months to queries; 2 months to mss. Accepts simultaneous submissions. Sample copy for $5 (back issue), $6 (current issue). Writer's guidelines for #10 SASE.

Payment/Terms Pays $10. Pays on publication for first North American serial, second serial (reprint) rights. Occasionally requests rights for TV, radio reading, website.

Advice Looks for "a blend of language and subject matter that entices from beginning to end. Send us your best work. Don't send us formula stories. While we appreciate and publish well-crafted traditional pieces, we constantly seek the story that risks, that breaks form and expectations and wins us over anyhow."

$ PLOUGHSHARES

Emerson College, Department M, 120 Boylston St., Boston MA 02116. Website: www.pshares.org. **Contact:** Fiction Editor. "Our mission is to present dynamic, contrasting views on what is valid and important in contemporary literature and to discover and advance significant literary talent. Each issue is guest-edited by a different writer. We no longer structure issues around preconceived themes." Estab. 1971. Circ. 6,000.

Literary Magazines

• Work published in *Ploughshares* has been selected regularly for inclusion in the *Best American Short Stories* and *O. Henry Prize* anthologies. In fact, the magazine has the honor of having the most stories selected from a single issue (three) to be included in *Best American Short Stories*. Guest editors have included Richard Ford, Tim O'Brien and Ann Beattie.

Needs Literary, mainstream. "No genre (science fiction, detective, gothic, adventure, etc.), popular formula or commerical fiction whose purpose is to entertain rather than to illuminate." Receives 1,000 unsolicited mss/ month. Accepts 30 mss/year. Reading period: postmarked August 1 to March 31. Publishes ms 6 months after acceptance. **Publishes some new writers/year.** Recently published work by ZZ Packer, Antonya Nelson and Stuart Dybek.

How to Contact Cover letter should include "previous pubs." SASE. Responds in 5 months to mss. Accepts simultaneous submissions. Sample copy for $9 (back issue). Writer's guidelines online.

Payment/Terms Pays $25/printed page, $50-250. Pays on publication for first North American serial rights.

Advice "Be familiar with our fiction issues, fiction by our writers and by our various editors (e.g., Sue Miller, Tobias Wolff, Rosellen Brown, Richard Ford, Jayne Anne Phillips, James Alan McPherson), and more generally acquaint yourself with the best short fiction currently appearing in the literary quarterlies and the annual prize anthologies (*Pushcart Prize, O. Henry Awards, Best American Short Stories*). Also realistically consider whether the work you are submitting is as good as or better than—in your own opinion—the work appearing in the magazine you're sending to. What is the level of competition? And what is its volume? Never send 'blindly' to a magazine, or without carefully weighing your prospect there against those elsewhere. Always keep a log and a copy of the work you submit."

POINTED CIRCLE

Portland Community College-Cascade, 705 N. Killingsworth St., Portland OR 97217. (503)978-5251. E-mail: ckimball@pcc.edu. **Contact:** Cynthia Kimball, English instructor, faculty advisor. Magazine: 80 pages; b&w illustrations; photos. "Anything of interest to educationally/culturally mixed audience." Annual. Estab. 1980.

Needs Ethnic/multicultural, literary, regional, contemporary, prose poem. "We will read whatever is sent but encourage writers to remember we are a quality literary/arts magazine intended to promote the arts in the community. No pornography. Be mindful of deadlines and length limits." Accepts submissions only October 1-March 1, for July 1 issue. Recently published work by Jack Maraglia, Hiroko Nelson and Kumaridevi Sivam.

How to Contact Accepts submissions by e-mail, fax. Submitted materials will not be returned; SASE for notification only. Accepts multiple submissions. Sample copy for $4.50 payable to PCC. Writer's guidelines for #10 SASE.

Payment/Terms Pays 1 copy. Acquires one-time rights.

Advice "Looks for quality—topicality—nothing trite. The author cares about language and acts responsibly toward the reader, honors the reader's investment of time and piques the reader's interest."

PORCUPINE LITERARY ARTS MAGAZINE

P.O. Box 259, Cedarburg WI 53012-0259. (262)375-3128. E-mail: ppine259@aol.com. Website: members.aol. com/ppine259. **Contact:** Chris Skoczynski, fiction editor. Magazine: $5 \times 8\frac{1}{2}$; 150 pages; glossy color cover stock; art work and photos. Publishes "primarily poetry and short fiction. Novel excerpts are acceptable if self-contained. No restrictions as to theme or style." Semiannual. Estab. 1996. Circ. 1,500.

Needs Condensed novels, ethnic/multicultural, literary, mainstream. "No pornographic or religious." Receives 40 unsolicited mss/month. Accepts 3 mss/issue; 6 mss/year. Publishes ms 6-12 months after acceptance. **Publishes 4-6 new writers/year.** Recently published work by Judith Ford, Colin Garrett, Ann Minoff, Halina Duraj, Holly Day and Jeffrey Perso. Length: 2,000-7,500 words; average length: 3,500 words. Also publishes literary essays, poetry. Sometimes comments on rejected mss.

How to Contact Accepts submissions by e-mail. Send SASE for reply, return of ms or send a disposable copy of ms. Responds in 2 weeks to queries; 2 months to mss. Sample copy for $5. Writer's guidelines for #10 SASE.

Payment/Terms Pays 1 contributor's copy; additional copies for $8.95. Pays on publication for one-time rights.

Advice Looks for "believable dialogue and a narrator I can see and hear and smell. Form or join a writers' group. Read aloud. Rewrite extensively."

POTOMAC REVIEW, The Journal for Arts & Humanities

Montgomery College, Paul Peck Humanities Institute, 51 Mannakee St., Rockville MD 20850. (301)251-7417. Fax: (301)738-1745. E-mail: wattrsedge@aol.com. Website: www.montgomerycollege.edu/potomacreview. **Contact:** Christa Watters. Magazine: $5\frac{1}{2} \times 8\frac{1}{2}$; 248 pages; 50 lb. paper; 65 lb. color cover; art; illustrations; photos. *Potomac Review* "explores the inner and outer terrain of the Mid-Atlantic and beyond via a challenging diversity of prose, poetry and b&w artwork." Biannual. Estab. 1994. Circ. 1,000.

Needs "Seeks stories with a vivid, individual quality that get at 'the concealed side' of life." Humor (plus essays, cogent nonfiction of all sorts) welcome. Special section opens each issue e.g., upcoming "Journeys"

for Spring/Summer 2005, "Discovery" for Fall/Winter 2005-06. Receives 200 + unsolicited mss/month. Accepts 50-60 mss/issue. Publishes ms within 1 year after acceptance. Agented fiction 2%. **Publishes 100 new writers/ year.** Recently published work by Clarissa Sligh, Herman Asarnow, Ivan Amato, Lyn Lifshin, Judith McCombs, J.D. Smith, Fay Picardi, E. Ethelbert Miller, Ann Knox and Hilary Tham. Length: 5,000 words; average length: 2,000 words. Publishes short shorts. Also publishes poetry.
How to Contact Send SASE for reply, return of ms or send a disposable copy of ms. Responds in 3 weeks to queries; 6 months to mss. Accepts simultaneous and reprints submissions. Sample copy for $10. Writer's guidelines for #10 SASE or on website. Reviews fiction.
Payment/Terms Pays 2 or more contributor's copies; additional copies for a 40% discount.
Advice "Have something to say in a original voice; check the magazine first; rewriting often trumps the original."

$ THE PRAIRIE JOURNAL, Journal of Canadian Literature
Prairie Journal Trust, P.O. Box 61203, Brentwood P.O., Calgary AB T2L 2K6 Canada. Website: www.geocities. com/prairiejournal. **Contact:** A.E. Burke, editor. Journal: 7×8½; 50-60 pages; white bond paper; Cadillac cover stock; cover illustrations. "The audience is literary, university, library, scholarly and creative readers/writers." Semiannual. Estab. 1983. Circ. 600.
Needs Literary, regional. No genre (romance, horror, western—sagebrush or cowboys), erotic, science fiction, or mystery. Receives 100 unsolicited mss/month. Accepts 10-15 mss/issue; 20-30 mss/year. Suggested deadlines: April 1 for spring/summer issue; October 1 for fall/winter. Publishes ms 4-6 months after acceptance. **Publishes 60 new writers/year.** Recently published work by Robert Clark, Sandy Campbell, Darcie Hasack and Christopher Blais. Length: 100-3,000 words; average length: 2,500 words. Also publishes literary essays, literary criticism, poetry. Sometimes comments on rejected mss.
How to Contact Send complete ms. SASE (IRC). Include cover letter of past credits, if any. Reply to queries for SAE with 55¢ for postage or IRC. No American stamps. Responds in 2 weeks to queries; 6 months to mss. No simultaneous submissions. Sample copy for $6. Writer's guidelines online. Reviews fiction.
Payment/Terms Pays $10-75. Pays on publication for first North American serial rights. In Canada, author retains copyright with acknowledgement appreciated.
Advice "We like character-driven rather than plot-centered fiction." Interested in "innovational work of quality. Beginning writers welcome! There is no point in simply republishing known authors or conventional, predictable plots. Of the genres we receive, fiction is most often of the highest calibre. It is a very competitive field. Be proud of what you send. You're worth it."

PRAIRIE SCHOONER
University of Nebraska, English Department, 201 Andrews Hall, P.O. Box 880334, Lincoln NE 68588-0334. (402)472-0911. Fax: (402)472-9771. Website: www.unl.edu/schooner/psmain.htm. **Contact:** Hilda Raz, editor. Magazine: 6×9; 200 pages; good stock paper; heavy cover stock. "A fine literary quarterly of stories, poems, essays and reviews for a general audience that reads for pleasure." Estab. 1926. Circ. 3,200.
• *Prairie Schooner*, one of the oldest publications in this book, has garnered several awards and honors over the years. Work appearing in the magazine has been selected for anthologies including *The Pushcart Prize* and *Best American Short Stories*.
Needs Good fiction (literary). Receives 500 unsolicited mss/month. Accepts 4-5 mss/issue. Mss are read September through May only. **Publishes 5-10 new writers/year.** Recently published work by Robert Olen Butler, Janet Burroway, Aimee Phan, Valerie Sayers and Daniel Stern. Also publishes poetry.
How to Contact Send complete ms with SASE and cover letter listing previous publications—where, when. Responds in 4 months to mss. Sample copy for $6. Writer's guidelines and excerpts online. Reviews fiction.
Payment/Terms Pays in contributor's copies and prize money awarded. Will reassign rights upon request after publication. Sponsors awards/contests.
Advice "*Prairie Schooner* is eager to see fiction from beginning and established writers. Be tenacious. Accept rejection as a temporary setback and send out rejected stories to other magazines. *Prairie Schooner* is not a magazine with a program. We look for good fiction in traditional narrative modes as well as experimental, meta-fiction or any other form or fashion a writer might try. Create striking detail, well-developed characters, fresh dialogue; let the images and the situations evoke the stories' themes. Too much explication kills a lot of otherwise good stories. Be persistent. Keep writing and sending out new work. Be familiar with the tastes of the magazines where you're sending. We are receiving record numbers of submissions. Prospective contributors must sometimes wait longer to receive our reply."

$ PRETEXT
Pen and Inc. Press, School of Literature & Creative Writing, University of East Anglia, Norwich Norfolk NR1-4HE United Kingdom. (+44)(0)1603592783. Fax: (+44)(0)1603507728. E-mail: info@penandinc.co.uk. Website:

Literary Magazines

www.inpressbooks.co.uk/penandinc/. **Contact:** Katri Skala, managing editor. Magazine: 210×148 mm; 170 pages; Albury 80qsm paper; 4-color 240qsm art board cover stock; illustrations; photos. Semiannual. Estab. 1999. Member of Inpress and Independent Publishers Guild.

Needs Ethnic/multicultural, feminist, gay, humor/satire, lesbian, literary, translations. No mass-market or non-literary work. Receives 70-80 unsolicited mss/month. Accepts 10 mss/issue; 20 mss/year. Publishes 6 months after acceptance. Agented fiction 30%. **Publishes 4 new writers/year.** Recently published work by Paul Bailey, J.G. Ballard, Maureen Duffy, Alison Fell, Tim Guest and William Luvass. Length: 6,000 words; average length: 3,000-4,000 words. Publishes short shorts. Also publishes literary essays, literary criticism, poetry. Often comments on rejected mss.

How to Contact Send complete ms. Send SASE (or IRC) for return of the ms. Responds in 2 days to queries; 3 months to mss. Accepts simultaneous, multiple submissions. Sample copy for £7.99(UK) £8.99(Europe) £9.99 (rest of world). Writer's guidelines for SASE, fax, e-mail or online.

Payment/Terms Pays £50 and 1 contributor's copy. Pays on publication. Sends galleys to author.

Advice "Looking for good writing with a sense of purpose and an awareness of literary context. Never send until you are sure it's the best it can be."

▣ ◎ PRIMAVERA

Box 37-7547, Chicago IL 60637-7547. (312)324-5920. **Contact:** Editorial Board. Magazine: 5½×8½; 128 pages; 60 lb. paper; glossy cover; illustrations; photos. Literature and graphics reflecting the experiences of women: poetry, short stories, photos, drawings. "We publish original fiction that reflects the experience of women. We select works that encompass the lives of women of different ages, races, sexual orientations and social class." Annual. Estab. 1975. Circ. 1,000.

• *Primavera* has won grants from the Illinois Arts Council, the Puffin Foundation and from Chicago Women in Publishing.

Needs Fantasy, feminist, gay, humor/satire, lesbian, literary, science fiction. "We dislike slick stories packaged for more traditional women's magazines. We publish only work reflecting the experiences of women, but also publish manuscripts by men." Receives 40 unsolicited mss/month. Accepts 6-10 mss/issue. Publishes ms 1 year after acceptance. **Publishes some new writers/year.** Recently published work by Elizabeth Keller Whitehurst, Gayle Whittier, Christine Stark, Robert Wallace and Alice Stern. Also publishes poetry. Sometimes comments on rejected mss.

How to Contact Send complete ms. Responds in 6 months to mss. No simultaneous submissions. Sample copy for $5; $10 for recent issues. Writer's guidelines for SASE.

Payment/Terms Pays 2 contributor's copies. Acquires first rights.

Advice "We're looking for artistry and deftness of untrendy, unhackneyed themes; an original slant on well-known themes, an original use of language, and the highest quality we can find."

▨ $▣ ▨ PRISM INTERNATIONAL

Department of Creative Writing, Buch E462-1866 Main Mall, University of British Columbia, Vancouver BC V6T 1Z1 Canada. (604)822-2514. Fax: (604)822-3616. E-mail: prism@interchange.ubc.ca. Website: prism.arts.ubc.ca. **Contact:** Marguerite Pigeon, editor. Magazine: 6×9; 72-80 pages; Zephyr book paper; Cornwall, coated one side cover; artwork on cover. "An international journal of contemporary writing—fiction, poetry, drama, creative nonfiction and translation." Readership: "public and university libraries, individual subscriptions, bookstores—a worldwide audience concerned with the contemporary in literature." Quarterly. Estab. 1959. Circ. 1,200.

• *Prism International* has won numerous magazine awards, and stories first published in *Prism International* have been included in the *Journey Prize Anthology* every year since 1991.

Needs Experimental, novel excerpts (up to 25 double-spaced pages), traditional. New writing that is contemporary and literary. Short stories and self-contained novel excerpts. Works of translation are eagerly sought and should be accompanied by a copy of the original. Would like to see more translations. "No gothic, confession, religious, romance, pornography or sci-fi." Also looking for creative nonfiction that is literary, not journalistic, in scope and tone. Receives over 100 unsolicited mss/month. Accepts 70 mss/year. "PRISM publishes both new and established writers; our contributors have included Franz Kafka, Gabriel Garcia Marquez, Michael Ondaatje, Margaret Laurence, Mark Anthony Jarman, Gail Anderson-Dargatz and Eden Robinson." Publishes ms 4 months after acceptance. **Publishes 7 new writers/year.** Recently published work by Micahel V. Smith, E.J. Levy, Adam Hosinger, Michael Kardos and Billie Livingston. Publishes short shorts. Also publishes poetry.

How to Contact Send complete ms. Accepts submissions by fax, disk. "Keep it simple. U.S. contributors take note: Do not send U.S. stamps, they are not valid in Canada. Send International Reply Coupons instead." Responds in 4 months to queries; 4 months to mss. Sample copy for $7 or on website. Writer's guidelines online.

Payment/Terms Pays $20/printed page and 1-year subscription. Pays on publication for first North American

serial rights. Selected authors are paid an additional $10/page for digital rights. Sponsors awards/contests.
Advice "Read several issues of our magazine before submitting. We are committed to publishing outstanding literary work. We look for strong, believeable characters; real voices; attention to language; interesting ideas and plots. Send us fresh, innovative work which also shows a mastery of the basics of good prose writing."

◙ PUCKERBRUSH REVIEW
Puckerbrush Press, 76 Maine St., Orono ME 04473. (207)866-4868/581-3832. **Contact:** Constance Hunting, editor/publisher. Magazine: 9×12; 80-100 pages; illustrations. "We publish interviews, fiction, reviews, poetry for a literary audience." Semiannual. Estab. 1979. Circ. 500.
Needs Experimental, gay (occasionally), literary, Belles-lettres. "Wants to see more original, quirky and well-written fiction. No genre fiction. Nothing cliché, nothing overly sensational exept in its human interest." Receives 30 unsolicited mss/month. Accepts 6 mss/issue; 12 mss/year. Publishes ms 1 year after acceptance. Recently published work by John Sullivan, Beth Thorpe, Chenoweth Hall, Merle Hillman and Wayne Burke. Publishes short shorts. Also publishes literary essays, literary criticism, poetry. Sometimes comments on rejected mss.
How to Contact SASE. Responds in 2 months to mss. Accepts simultaneous, multiple submissions. Sample copy for $2. Writer's guidelines for SASE. Reviews fiction.
Payment/Terms Pays in contributor's copies.
Advice "I don't want to see tired plots or treatments. I want to see respect for language—the right words, true views of human nature. Don't follow clichés, but don't be too outré either."

◘ PUERTO DEL SOL
New Mexico State University, Box 3E, Las Cruces NM 88003-0001. (505)646-2345. Fax: (505)646-7755. E-mail: PUERTO@nmsu.edu. Website: www.nmsu.edu/~puerto/welcome.html. **Contact:** Kevin McIlvoy, editor-in-chief and fiction editor. Kathleene West, poetry editor. Magazine: 6×9; 200 pages; 60 lb. paper; 70 lb. cover stock. "We publish quality material from anyone. Poetry, fiction, interviews, reviews, parts-of-novels, long poems." Semiannual. Estab. 1964. Circ. 2,000.
Needs Ethnic/multicultural, experimental, literary, mainstream, novel excerpts, translations, contemporary, prose poem. Accepts 8-10 mss/issue; 12-15 mss/year. Does not read mss March-August. **Publishes 8-10 new writers/year.** Recently published work by Dagoberto Gilb, Wendell Mayo and William H. Cobb. Also publishes literary essays, poetry. Always comments on rejected mss.
How to Contact Responds in 3-6 months to mss. Accepts simultaneous submissions. Sample copy for $8.
Payment/Terms Pays 2 contributor's copies. Acquires one-time rights. Rights revert to author after publication.
Advice "We are open to all forms of fiction, from the conventional to the wildly experimental and we are pleased to work with emerging writers."

Ⓝ Ⓔ ◙ QUALITY WOMEN'S FICTION, Extending the Boundaries of Women's Fiction
QWF, P.O. Box 1768, Rugby CV21 4ZA United Kingdom. E-mail: jo@qwfmagazine.co.uk. Website: www.qwfmagazine.co.uk. **Contact:** Sally Zigmond, assistant editor. Magazine: A5; 80 pages; glossy paper. "*QWF* gets under the skin of the female experience and exposes emotional truth." Bimonthly. Estab. 1994. Circ. 1,800.
Needs Experimental, feminist, literary. Receives 30 unsolicited mss/month. Accepts 12 mss/issue; 78 mss/year. Does not read mss June-August. Publishes ms 6-12 months after acceptance. **Publishes 15 new writers/year.** Recently published work by Kathryn Kulpa, Ruth Latta, Kirsten Marek. Length: 1,500-5,000 words; average length: 2,500 words. Publishes short shorts. Also publishes literary essays, literary criticism. Always comments on rejected mss.
How to Contact Send complete ms. Accepts submissions by e-mail. Send SASE (or IRC) for return of ms or send disposable copy of the ms and #10 SASE for reply only. Responds in 2 months to queries; 2 months to mss. Accepts reprints submissions. Sample copy for SASE. Writer's guidelines by e-mail. Reviews fiction.
Payment/Terms Pays 3 contributor's copies; additional copies $12. Pays on publication for First British Serial rights.
Advice "Study the stories published on the *QWF* website."

◙ ◎ QUARTER AFTER EIGHT, A Journal of Prose and Community
QAE, Ellis Hall, Ohio University, Atens OH 45701. (740)593-2827. E-mail: editor@quarteraftereight.org. Website: www.quarteraftereight.org. **Contact:** Hayley Haugen, co-editor-in-chief. Magazine: 6×9; 310 pages; 20 lb. glossy cover stock; photos. "We look to publish work which challenges boundaries of genre, style, idea and voice." Annual.
Needs Condensed novels, erotica, ethnic/multicultural, experimental, gay, humor/satire, lesbian, literary, mainstream, translations. "No traditional, conventional fiction." Send SASE for list of upcoming themes. Receives 150-200 unsolicited mss/month. Accepts 40-50 mss/issue. Does not read mss mid-March-mid-September.

Publishes ms 6-12 months after acceptance. **Publishes 20-30 new writers/year.** Recently published work by Virgil Suárez, Maureen Sexton, John Gallagher and Amy England. Length: 10,000 words; average length: 3,000 words. Publishes short shorts. Also publishes literary essays, literary criticism, poetry. Sometimes comments on rejected mss.

How to Contact Send SASE for return of ms or send a disposable copy of ms. Responds in 3 months to mss. Accepts simultaneous, multiple submissions. Sample copy for $10, 8×11 SAE and $1.60 postage. Writer's guidelines for #10 SASE. Reviews fiction.

Payment/Terms Pays 2 contributor's copies; additional copies $7. Acquires first North American serial rights. Rights revert to author upon publication. Sponsors awards/contests.

Advice "We look for fiction that is experimental, exploratory, devoted to and driven by language—that which succeeds in achieving the *QAE* aesthetic. Please subscribe to our journal and read what is published. We do not publish traditional lined poetry or straightforward conventional stories. We encourage writers to submit after they have gotten acquainted with the *QAE* aesthetic."

$ 🌀 📺 QUARTERLY WEST

University of Utah, 255 S. Central Campus Dr., Dept. of English, LNCO 3500, Salt Lake City UT 84112-9109. (801)581-3938. E-mail: dhawk@earthlink.net. Website: www.utah.edu/quarterlywest. **Contact:** Traci Oberg and Jennifer Colville. Magazine: 7×10; 50 lb. paper; 4-color cover stock; a selection of full color artwork is featured once a year; photos on occasion. "We publish fiction, poetry and nonfiction in long and short formats and will consider experimental as well as traditional works." Semiannual. Estab. 1976. Circ. 1,900.

• *Quarterly West* was awarded First Place for Editorial Content from the American Literary Magazine Awards. Work published in the magazine has been selected for inclusion in the *Pushcart Prize* anthology and *The Best American Short Stories* anthology.

Needs Ethnic/multicultural, experimental, humor/satire, literary, mainstream, novel excerpts, slice-of-life vignettes, short shorts, translations. No detective, science fiction or romance. Receives 300 unsolicited mss/month. Accepts 6-10 mss/issue; 12-20 mss/year. Reads mss between September 1 and May 1 only. "Submissions received between May 2 and August 31 will be returned unread." Publishes ms 6 months after acceptance. **Publishes 3 new writers/year.** Recently published work by Ann Pancake, David Shields, James Tate and Valerie Miner.

How to Contact Send complete ms. Brief cover letters welcome. Send SASE for reply or return of ms. Responds in 6 months to mss. Accepts simultaneous submissions if notified. Sample copy for $7.50. Writer's guidelines online.

Payment/Terms Pays $15-50, and 2 contributor's copies. Pays on publication for first North American serial rights.

Advice "We publish a special section of short shorts every issue, and we also sponsor a biennial novella contest. We are open to experimental work—potential contributors should read the magazine! We solicit occasionally, but tend more toward the surprises—unsolicited. Don't send more than one story per submission, and wait until you've heard about the first before submitting another."

🌀 RAINBOW CURVE

P.O. Box 93206, Las Vegas NV 89193-3206. E-mail: rainbowcurve@sbcglobal.net. Website: www.rainbowcurve .com. **Contact:** Daphne Young and Julianne Bonnet, editors. Magazine: 5½×8½; 100 pages; 60 lb. paper; coated cover. "*Rainbow Curve* publishes fiction and poetry that dabble at the edge; contemporary work that evokes emotion. Our audience is interested in exploring new worlds of experience and emotion; raw, visceral work is what we look for." Semiannual. Estab. 2002. Circ. 500.

Needs Ethnic/multicultural, experimental, feminist, gay, lesbian, literary. "No genre fiction (romance, western, fantasy, sci-fi)." Receives 60 unsolicited mss/month. Accepts 10-15 mss/issue; 20-30 mss/year. Publishes ms 6 months after acceptance. Agented fiction 1%. **Publishes 80% new writers/year.** Recently published work by Jonathan Barrett, Trent Busch, Rob Carney, Peter Fontaine, Bridget Hoida and Karen Toloui. Length: 500-10,000 words; average length: 7,500 words. Publishes short shorts. Sometimes comments on rejected mss.

How to Contact Send SASE for return of ms or send a disposable copy of ms and #10 SASE for reply only. Responds in 3 months to mss. Accepts simultaneous submissions. Sample copy for $6. Writer's guidelines for SASE or on website.

Payment/Terms Pays 1 contributor's copy; additional copies $5. Acquires one-time rights. Sends galleys to author.

Advice "Unusual rendering of usual subjects and strong narrative voice make a story stand out. Unique glimpses into the lives of others—make it new."

RAMBUNCTIOUS REVIEW

Rambunctious Press, Inc., 1221 W. Pratt Blvd., Chicago IL 60626-4329. **Contact:** Nancy Lennon, Richard Goldman and Elizabeth Hausler, editors. Magazine: 10×7; 48 pages; illustrations; photos. Annual. Estab. 1983. Circ. 300.

Needs Experimental, feminist, humor/satire, literary, mainstream. No mystery or drama. List of upcoming themes available for SASE. Receives 30 unsolicited mss/month. Accepts 4-5 mss/issue. Does not read May-August. Publishes ms 1 year after acceptance. **Publishes 4-5 new writers/year.** Recently published work by Pamela Miller, Maureen Flannery, Lynn Sadler, Ben Scott. Publishes short shorts. Also publishes poetry. Sometimes comments on rejected mss.

How to Contact Send complete ms. Send SASE for reply, return of ms or send a disposable copy of ms. Responds in 1 year to mss. Accepts simultaneous submissions. Sample copy for $4.

Payment/Terms Pays 2 contributor's copies. Acquires one-time rights. Sponsors awards/contests.

RATTAPALLAX

Rattapallax Press, 532 La Guardia Place, Suite 353, New York NJ 10012. (212)560-7459. E-mail: info@rattapallax.com. Website: www.rattapallax.com. **Contact:** Alan Cheuse, fiction editor. Literary magazine: 6×9; 128 pages; bound; some illustrations; photos. "General readership. Our stories must be character driven with strong conflict. All accepted stories are edited by our staff and the writer before publication to ensure a well-crafted and written work." Semiannual. Estab. 1999. Circ. 2,000.

Needs Literary. Receives 15 unsolicited mss/month. Accepts 3 mss/issue; 6 mss/year. Publishes ms 3-6 months after acceptance. Agented fiction 15%. **Publishes 3 new writers/year.** Recently published work by Stuart Dybek, Howard Norman, Dana Gioia and Williaim P.H. Root. Length: 1,000-10,000 words; average length: 5,000 words. Publishes short shorts. Also publishes poetry. Often comments on rejected mss.

How to Contact Send SASE for return of ms. Responds in 3 months to queries; 3 months to mss. Sample copy for $7.95. Writer's guidelines for SASE or on website.

Payment/Terms Pays 2 contributor's copies; additional copies for $7.95. Pays on publication for first North American serial rights. Sends galleys to author.

Advice "Character driven, well crafted, strong conflict."

RE:AL, The Journal of Liberal Arts

Stephen F. Austin State University, P.O. Box 13007-SFA Station, Nacogdoches TX 75962-3007. (936)468-2059. Website: http://libweb.sfasu.edu/real/default.htm. **Contact:** Dr. Christine Butterworth-McDermott, editor. Literary journal: 8×10; perfect-bound; 120-170 pages; "top" stock. Editorial content: 40% fiction, 40% poetry, 20% creative nonfiction. "Work is based on the intrinsic merit and its appeal to a sophisticated readership." Spring & Fall issues. Semiannual. Estab. 1968. Circ. 500.

Needs Realistic poetry and fiction. Open to well-crafted magical realism and exceptional genre work. No longer publishes scholarly articles. Receives 300 unsolicited mss/month. Accepts 10-20 mss/issue. Publishes ms 6-12 months after acceptance.

How to Contact SASE. Responds in 3-4 month to mss. Accepts simultaneous submissions. Sample copy for $12. Writer's guidelines for #10 SASE or online.

Payment/Terms Pays contributor copy; additional copies at reduced rate. Rights revert to author upon publication.

Advice "We are looking for the best work, whether you are established or not. Please submit a clean, neatly typed (or well-photocopied) manuscript. Please include all contact information in a cover letter. Please correspond with the editors in writing until your submission has been accepted."

N RED ROCK REVIEW

Community College of Southern Nevada, 3200 E. Cheyenne Ave. N., Las Vegas NV 89030. (702)651-4094. Fax: (702)651-4639. E-mail: richard_logsdon@ccsn.nevada.edu. Website: www.ccsn.nevada.edu/english/redrockreview/index.html. **Contact:** Dr. Richard Logsdon, senior editor. Magazine: 5×8; 125 pages. "We're looking for the very best literature. Stories need to be tightly crafted, strong is character development, built around conflict. Poems need to be tightly crafted, characterised by expert use of language." Semiannual. Estab. 1995. Circ. 250.

Needs Experimental, literary, mainstream. Receives 350 unsolicited mss/month. Accepts 40-60 mss/issue; 80-120 mss/year. Does not read mss during summer. Publishes ms 3-5 after acceptance. **Publishes 5-10 new writers/year.** Recently published work by Charles Harper Webb, Mary Sojourner and Mark Irwin. Length: 1,500-5,000 words; average length: 3,500 words. Publishes short shorts. Also publishes literary essays, literary criticism, poetry. Sometimes comments on rejected mss.

How to Contact Send SASE (or IRC) for return of ms. Responds in 2 weeks to queries; 3 months to mss. Accepts simultaneous, multiple submissions. Sample copy for $5.50. Writer's guidelines for SASE, by e-mail or on website.

Payment/Terms Pays 2 contributor's copies. Pays on acceptance for first rights.

Literary Magazines

Literary Magazines

🔘 RED WHEELBARROW

De Anza College, 21250 Stevens Creek Blvd., Cupertino CA 95014-5702. (408)864-8600. E-mail: splitterrandolph @fhda.edu. Website: www.deanza.edu/redwheelbarrow. **Contact:** Randolph Splitter, editor-in-chief. Magazine: 6×9; 140-216 pages; photos. "Contemporary poetry, fiction, creative nonfiction, b&w graphics, comics and photos." Annual. Estab. 1976 as *Bottomfish*; 2000 as *Red Wheelbarrow*. Circ. 250-500.

Needs "Thoughtful, personal writing. We welcome submissions of all kinds, and we seek to publish a diverse range of styles and voices from around the country and the world." Receives 100 unsolicited mss/month. Accepts 30-50 mss/issue. Reads mss September through February. Submission deadline: January 31; publication date: Spring or Summer. Publishes ms 2-4 months after acceptance. Agented fiction 1%. **Publishes 0-2 new writers/year.** Recently published work by Mark Brazaitis, Liesl Jobson and Virgil Suarez. Length: 4,000 words; average length: 2,500 words. Publishes short shorts. Also publishes poetry.

How to Contact Accepts submissions by e-mail. Responds in 2-4 months to mss. Accepts simultaneous submissions. Sample copy for $10; back issues $2.50. Writer's guidelines online.

Payment/Terms Pays 2 contributor's copies. Acquires first North American serial rights.

Advice "Write freely, rewrite carefully. Resist clichés and stereotypes. We are not affiliated with Red Wheelbarrow Press or any similarly named publication."

🔘 REFLECTIONS LITERARY JOURNAL

Piedmont Community College, P.O. Box 1197, Roxboro NC 27573. (336)599-1181. E-mail: reflect@piedmont.cc. nc.us. **Contact:** Ernest Avery, editor. Magazine: 100-150 pages. Annual. Estab. 1999. Circ. 250.

Needs Literary. Receives 30 unsolicited mss/month. Accepts 10-20 mss/issue. Publishes ms 4-6 months after acceptance. **Publishes 3-5 new writers/year.** Recently published work by Tim McLaurin, Peter Rennebohm, J. Dixon Hearne and Christopher Stanton. Length: 4,000 words; average length: 2,500 words. Publishes short shorts. Also publishes poetry.

How to Contact Send SASE for return of ms or #10 SASE for reply only. Sample copy for $6. Writer's guidelines for SASE or by e-mail.

Payment/Terms Pays 1 contributor's copy; additional copies $6 pre-publication; $7 post-publication. Acquires first North American serial rights. Sponsors awards/contests.

Advice "We look for good writing with a flair, which captivates an educated lay audience. Don't take rejection letters personally. We turn away many submissions simply because we don't have room for everything we like. For that reason, we're more likely to accept shorter well-written stories than longer stories of the same quality. Also, stories containing profanity that doesn't contribute to the plot, structure or intended tone are rejected immediately."

$🔘 THE REJECTED QUARTERLY, A Journal of Quality Literature Rejected at Least Five Times

Black Plankton Press, P.O. Box 1351, Cobb CA 95426. E-mail: bplankton@juno.com. **Contact:** Daniel Weiss, Jeff Ludecke, fiction editors. Magazine: 8½×11; 40 pages; 60 lb. paper; 10 pt. coated cover stock; illustrations. "We want the best literature possible, regardless of genre. We do, however, have a bias toward the unusual and toward speculative fiction. We aim for a literate, educated audience. *The Rejected Quarterly* believes in publishing the highest quality rejected fiction and other writing that doesn't fit anywhere else. We strive to be different but will go for quality every time, whether conventional or not." Semiannual. Estab. 1998.

Needs Experimental, fantasy, historical, humor/satire, literary, mainstream, mystery/suspense, romance (futuristic/time travel only), science fiction (soft/sociological), sports. Accepts poetry about being rejected. Receives 30 unsolicited mss/month. Accepts 4-6 mss/issue; 8-12 mss/year. Publishes ms 1-12 months after acceptance. **Publishes 1-2 new writers/year.** Recently published work by Vera Searles, RC Cooper and Stephen Jones. Length: 8,000 words; average length: 5,000 words. Publishes short shorts. Also publishes literary essays, literary criticism, poetry. Often comments on rejected mss.

How to Contact Accepts submissions by e-mail. Send SASE for reply, return of ms or send a disposable copy of ms. Responds in 2 weeks to queries; 9 months to mss. Accepts reprints submissions. Sample copy for $6 (IRCs for foreign requests). Reviews fiction.

Payment/Terms Pays $7.50 and 1 contributor's copy; additional copies, others $5. Pays on acceptance for first rights. Sends galleys to author.

Advice "We are looking for high-quality writing that tells a story or expresses a coherent idea. We want unique stories, original viewpoints and unusual slants. We are getting far too many inappropriate submissions. Please be familiar with the magazine. Be sure to include your rejection slips! Send out quality rather than quantity. Work on one piece until it is as close to a masterpiece in your own eyes as you can get it. Find the right place for it. Be selective in ordering samples, but do be familiar with where you're sending your work."

🔘 🔘 RIVER STYX

Big River Association, 634 N. Grand Blvd., 12th Floor, St. Louis MO 63103. (314)533-4541. Fax: (314)533-3345. Website: www.riverstyx.org. **Contact:** Richard Newman, editor. Magazine: 6×9; 100 pages; color card cover;

perfect-bound; b&w visual art. *"River Styx* publishes the highest quality fiction, poetry, interviews, essays and visual art. We are an internationally distributed multicultural literary magazine.'' Mss read May-November. Estab. 1975.

> ● *River Styx* has had stories appear in *New Stories from the South* and has been included in *Pushcart* anthologies.

Needs Ethnic/multicultural, experimental, feminist, gay, lesbian, literary, mainstream, novel excerpts, translations, short stories, literary. ''No genre fiction, less thinly veiled autobiography.'' Receives 350 unsolicited mss/ month. Accepts 2-6 mss/issue; 6-12 mss/year. Reads only May through November. Publishes ms 1 year after acceptance. **Publishes 20 new writers/year.** Recently published work by Julianna Baggott, Philip Graham, Katherine Min, Richard Burgin, Nancy Zafris and Eric Shade. Publishes short shorts. Also publishes poetry. Sometimes comments on rejected mss.

How to Contact Send complete ms. SASE required. Responds in 4 months to mss. Accepts simultaneous submissions ''if a note is enclosed with your work and if we are notified immediately upon acceptance elsewhere.'' Sample copy for $7. Writer's guidelines online.

Payment/Terms Pays 2 contributor copies, plus 1-year subscription; $8/page if funds are available. Pays on publication for first North American serial, one-time rights.

Advice ''We want high-powered stories with well-developed characters. We like strong plots, usually with at least three memorable scenes, and a subplot often helps. No thin, flimsy fiction with merely serviceable language. Short stories shouldn't be any different than poetry—every single word should count. One could argue every word counts more since we're being asked to read 10 to 30 pages.''

◙ RIVERWIND

Hocking College, 3301 Hocking Park Way, Nelsonville OH 45764. (740)753-3591. E-mail: williams_k@hocking.e du. **Contact:** Kristine Williams, co-editor. Magazine: 7×7; 125-150 pages; 60 lb. offset paper; illustrations; photos. *Riverwind* is an established magazine that prints fiction, poetry, black and white photos and prints, drawings, creative nonfiction, book reviews and plays. Special consideration is given to writers from the Appalachian region. Annual. Estab. 1976. Circ. 200-400.

Needs Adventure, ethnic/multicultural (Appalachian), humor/satire, literary, mainstream, regional. Does not want erotica, fantasy, horror, experimental, religious, children's/juvenile. Receives 25 unsolicited mss/month. Does not read mss June-September. Publishes ms 6-9 months after acceptance. **Publishes many new writers/ year.** Recently published work by Gerald Wheeler, Wendy McVicker, Roy Bentley, Perry A. White, Tom Montag and Beau Beadreaux. Length: 500-2,500 words; average length: 1,750 words. Publishes short shorts. Also publishes literary essays, literary criticism, poetry. Rarely comments on rejected mss.

How to Contact Send complete ms. Accepts submissions by e-mail, disk. Send disposable copy of the ms and #10 SASE for reply only. Responds in 4 weeks to queries; 8-16 weeks to mss. Accepts simultaneous, multiple submissions. Sample copy for $5. Writer's guidelines for #10 SASE or by e-mail.

Payment/Terms Pays 2 contributor's copies. Pays on publication for first North American serial rights.

Advice ''Avoid stereotypical plots and characters. We tend to favor realism but not sentimentality.''

$◙ ROANOKE REVIEW

Roanoke College, 221 College Lane, Salem VA 24153-3794. (540)375-2380. E-mail: review@roanoke.edu. **Contact:** Paul Hanstedt, editor. Magazine: 6×9; 200 pages; 60 lb. paper; 70 lb. cover. ''We're looking for fresh, thoughtful material that will appeal to a broader as well as literary audience. Humor encouraged.'' Annual. Estab. 1967. Circ. 500.

Needs Feminist, gay, humor/satire, lesbian, literary, mainstream, regional. No pornography, science fiction or horror. Receives 100 unsolicited mss/month. Accepts 5-10 mss/year. Does not read mss February 1-September 1. Publishes ms 6 months after acceptance. **Publishes 1-5 new writers/year.** Recently published work by Robert Morgan, Lucy Ferriss and Francine Witte. Length: 1,000-6,000 words; average length: 1,500 words. Publishes short shorts. Also publishes poetry. Sometimes comments on rejected mss.

How to Contact Send SASE for return of ms or send a disposable copy of ms and #10 SASE for reply only. Responds in 1 month to queries; 6 months to mss. Sample copy for 8×11 SAE with $2 postage. Writer's guidelines for SASE.

Payment/Terms Pays $10-50/story when budget allows and 2 contributor's copies; additional copies $5. Pays on publication for one-time rights.

Advice ''Pay attention to sentence-level writing—verbs, metaphors, concrete images. Don't forget, though, that plot and character keep us reading. We're looking for stuff that breaks the MFA story style.''

◙ THE ROCKFORD REVIEW

The Rockford Writers Guild, P.O. Box 858, Rockford IL 61105. E-mail: daveconnieross@aol.com. Website: http://writersguild1.tripod.com. **Contact:** David Ross, editor. Magazine: 5⅜×8½; 100 pages; perfect bound;

Literary Magazines

Literary Magazines

color illustrations; b&w photos. "We look for prose and poetry with a fresh approach to old themes or new insights into the human condition." Semiannual. Estab. 1971. Circ. 700.

Needs Ethnic/multicultural, experimental, fantasy, humor/satire, literary, regional, science fiction (hard science, soft/sociological). "No graphic sex, translations or overly academic work." Recently published work by James Bellarosa, Sean Michael Rice, John P. Kristofco and L.S. Sedishiro. Also publishes literary essays.

How to Contact SASE. Responds in 2 months to mss. Accepts simultaneous, multiple submissions. Sample copy for $6. Writer's guidelines for SASE or online.

Payment/Terms Pays contributor's copies. "Two $25 editor's choice cash prizes per issues." Acquires first North American serial rights.

Advice "We're wide open to new and established writers alike—particularly short satire."

⬛ � SALMAGUNDI

Skidmore College, 815 North Broadway, Saratoga Springs NY 12866. Fax: (518)580-5188. E-mail: pboyes@skid more.edu. **Contact:** Peg Boyers. Magazine: 8×5; 200-300 pages; illustrations; photos. "*Salmagundi* publishes an eclectic variety of materials, ranging from short short fiction to novellas and from the surreal to the realistic. Authors include Nadine Gordimer, Russell Banks, Steven Millhauser, Gordon Lish, Clark Blaise, Mary Gordon, Joyce Carol Oates and Cynthia Ozick. Our audience is a generally literate population of people who read for pleasure." Quarterly. Estab. 1965. Circ. 4,800. Member, CLMP.

  • *Salmagundi* authors are regularly represented in *Pushcart* collections and *Best American Short Story* collections.

Needs Ethnic/multicultural (multicultural), experimental, family saga, gay, historical (general), literary, poetry. Receives 50-70 unsolicited mss/month. Accepts 2 mss/year. Read mss October 1-May 1. Publishes ms up to 2 years after acceptance. Agented fiction 10%. Also publishes literary essays, literary criticism, poetry.

How to Contact Send complete ms. Accepts submissions by e-mail (pboyes@skidmore.edu). Only accepts submission by e-mail. Responds in 6 months to mss. Sample copy for $5. Writer's guidelines for #10 SASE.

Payment/Terms Pays 6-10 contributor's copies and subscription to magazine. Acquires first, electronic rights.

Advice "I look for excellence and a very unpredictable ability to appeal to the interests and tastes of the editors. Be brave. Don't be discouraged by rejection. Keep stories in circulation. Of course, it goes without saying: Work hard on the writing. Revise tirelessly. Study magazines and send only to those whose sensibility matches yours."

⬛ 🌠 SANSKRIT, Literary Arts Magazine of UNC Charlotte

University of North Carolina at Charlotte, 168 Conf. University Center, 9201 University City Blvd., Charlotte NC 28223-0001. (704)687-2326. Fax: (704)687-3394. E-mail: sanskrit@email.uncc.edu. Website: www.uncc.edu/ sanskrit. **Contact:** David M. Hill, editor-in-chief. Magazine: 10³/₄×10³/₄, 64 pages. "*Sanskrit* is an award-winning magazine produced with two goals in mind: service to the student staff and student body, and promotion of unpublished and beginning artists. Our intended audience is the literary/arts community of UNCC, Charlotte, other schools and contributors, and specifically individuals who might never have read a literary magazine before." Annual. Estab. 1968.

  • *Sanskrit* has received the Pacemaker Award, Associated College Press, Gold Crown Award and Columbia Scholastic Press Award.

Needs "Not looking for any specific category—just good writing." Receives 50 unsolicited mss/month. Accepts 2-3 mss/issue. Recently published work by Bayard. Publishes short shorts. Also publishes poetry. Rarely comments on rejected mss.

How to Contact Send complete ms. Accepts submissions by e-mail (sanskrit@email.uncc.edu), fax. Include complete manuscript with cover letter. Accepts simultaneous, multiple submissions. Sample copy for $10. Writer's guidelines for #10 SASE.

Payment/Terms Pays contributor's copy. Acquires one-time rights.

Advice "Remember that you are entering a market often saturated with mediocrity—an abundance of cute words and phrases held together by clichés simply will not do."

Ⓝ ⬛ THE SARANAC REVIEW

Suny Plattsburgh, Dept. of English, Champlain Valley Hall, Plattsburgh NY 12901. (518)564-2134. Fax: (518)564-2140. **Contact:** Fiction editor. Magazine: 5¹/₂×8¹/₂; 180-200 pages; 80 lb. cover/70 lb. paper; glossy cover stock; illustrations; photos. "*The Saranac Review* is committed to dissolving boundaries of all kinds, seeking to publish a diverse array of emerging and established writers from Canada and the U.S. *The Saranac Review* aims to be a textual clearing in which a space is opened for cross-pollination between American and Canadian writers. In this way, the magazine reflects the expansive bright spirit of the etymology of it's name, Saranac, meaning 'cluster of stars.'" Annual. Estab. 2004.

Needs Ethnic/multicultural, historical, literary. Publishes ms 8 months after acceptance. Publishes short shorts. Also publishes poetry. Sometimes comments on rejected mss.

How to Contact Send complete ms. Send SASE (or IRC) for return of ms or send disposable copy of the ms and #10 SASE for reply only. Responds in 4 months to mss. Accepts simultaneous submissions. Sample copy for $6. Writer's guidelines online or by e-mail.

Payment/Terms Pays 2 contributor's copies. Pays on publication for first North American serial, first rights.

Advice "We publish serious, generous fiction."

SCRIVENER, Creative Review

Scrivener Press, 853 Sherbrooke St. West, Montreal QC H3A 2T6 Canada. E-mail: scrivener.review@gmail.com. Website: www.arts.mcgill.ca/programs/english/scrivener. **Contact:** Fiction editor. "*Scrivener* is eclectic. We publish the best poetry, fiction and photography from Canada and abroad." Annual. Estab. 1981. Circ. 300. Member: CMPA.

Needs Comics/graphic novels, ethnic/multicultural, experimental, family saga, feminist, gay, glitz, historical, horror, humor/satire, literary, mainstream, military/war, regional (Montreal), thriller/espionage, translations, western. Receives 10 unsolicited mss/month. Accepts 2-6 mss/issue; 2-5 mss/year. Publishes ms 3 months after acceptance. **Publishes 1-3 new writers/year.** Recently published work by David Goldstein, Shane LaPorte, Magnus, Rosemary Mosco and Karen T. Miller. Length: 55-9,000 words; average length: 5,000 words. Publishes short shorts. Also publishes poetry. Rarely comments on rejected mss.

How to Contact Send complete ms. Accepts submissions by e-mail. Send SASE (or IRC) for return of the ms or send a disposable copy of the ms and #10 SASE for reply only. Responds in 6 weeks to queries; 5 months to mss. Accepts multiple submissions. Sample copy for $7 Canadian and $2 shipping. Writer's guidelines online.

Payment/Terms Pays 1 contributor's copy. Pays on publication. Writers retain all rights after publication.

Advice "Fiction must be well written, thoughtful (researched, if need be), and fresh."

THE SEATTLE REVIEW

Box 354330, University of Washington, Seattle WA 98195. (206)543-2302. E-mail: seaview@u.washington.edu. Website: depts.washington.edu/engl/seaview1.html. **Contact:** Colleen J. McElroy, editor. Magazine: 6×9; 150 pages; illustrations; photos. "Includes general fiction, poetry, craft essays on writing, and one interview per issue with a established writer." Semiannual. Estab. 1978. Circ. 1,000.

Needs Literary. Nothing in "bad taste (porn, racist, etc.)." Receives 200 unsolicited mss/month. Accepts 2-4 mss/issue; 4-8 mss/year. Does not read mss May 31-October 1. Publishes ms 1-2½ years after acceptance. **Publishes 1-2 new writers/year.** Recently published work by Rick Bass, Lauren Whitehurst and Martha Hurwitz. Length: 5,500 words; average length: 3,000 words. Publishes short shorts. Also publishes poetry.

How to Contact Send complete ms. Send SASE (or IRC) for return of the ms or send disposable copy of the ms and #10 SASE for reply only. Responds in 4-6 months to mss. Accepts simultaneous, multiple submissions. Sample copy for $7. Writer's guidelines for #10 SASE, online, or by e-mail.

Payment/Terms Pays 2 contributor's copies. Acquires first North American serial rights.

Advice "Know what we publish: no genre fiction; look at our magazine and decide if your work might be appreciated."

SENSATIONS MAGAZINE

P.O. Box 90, Glen Ridge NJ 07028. Website: www.sensationsmag.com. **Contact:** David Messineo. Magazine: 8½×11; 50-100 pages; 20 lb. paper; full color cover; color photography. "We publish short stories and poetry." Quarterly. Estab. 1987.

• *Sensations Magazne* is one of the few markets accepting longer work and is a 3-time winner in the American Literary Magazine Awards.

Needs **Publishes 4-8 new writers/year.** Recently published work by James Vance Elliott, Lynn Veach Sadler and Danalee Velie.

How to Contact Accepts submissions by e-mail. "Do not submit material before reading submission guidelines." Accepts simultaneous, multiple submissions. Writer's guidelines for SASE or online.

Payment/Terms Pays $100 for the story judged #1 by each of our three fiction editors.

Advice "Develop long-term relationships with five magazines whose editorial opinions you respect. As the last literary magazine in America to frequently publish stories up to 30 pages double-spaced, we believe we have earned the privilege of being one of those five."

$SHENANDOAH, The Washington and Lee University Review

Washington and Lee University, Mattingly House, 2 Lee Avenue, Washington and Lee University, Lexington VA 24450-0303. (540)458-8765. E-mail: lleech@wlu.edu. Website: http://shenandoah.wlu.edu. Quarterly. Estab. 1950. Circ. 2,000.

Literary Magazines

Needs Mainstream, novel excerpts. No sloppy, hasty, slight fiction. Publishes ms 10 months after acceptance.
How to Contact Send complete ms and SASE. Responds in 2 months to mss. Sample copy for $8. Writer's guidelines online.
Payment/Terms Pays $25/page and 1-year subscription. Pays on publication for first North American serial, one-time rights.

SHORT STUFF, For Grown-ups

Bowman Publications, 712 W. 10th St., Loveland CO 80537. (970)669-9139. ''We are perhaps an enigma in that we publish only clean stories in any genre. We'll tackle any subject but don't allow obscene language or pornographic description. Our magazine is for grown-ups, *not* X-rated 'adult' fare.'' Bimonthly. Estab. 1989. Circ. 10,400.
Needs Adventure, historical, humor/satire, mainstream, mystery/suspense, romance, science fiction (seldom), western. ''We want to see more humor—not essay format—real stories with humor; 1,000-word mysteries, modern lifestyles. The 1,000-word pieces have the best chance of publication.'' No erotica; nothing morbid or pornographic. Issues are Valentine (February/March); Easter (April/May); Mom's and Dad's (June/July); Americana (August/September); Halloween (October/November); and Holiday (December/January). Receives 500 unsolicited mss/month. Accepts 9-12 mss/issue; 76 mss/year. **Publishes 90% new writers/year.** Recently published work by Bill Hallstead, Dede Hammond and Skye Gibbons.
How to Contact Send complete ms. Responds in 6 months to mss. Sample copy for $1.50 and 9×12 SAE with 5 first-class stamps. Writer's guidelines for #10 SASE.
Payment/Terms Payment varies. Payment and contract upon publication. Acquires first North American serial rights.
Advice ''We seek a potpourri of subjects each issue. A new slant, a different approach, fresh viewpoints—all of these excite us. We don't like gore, salacious humor or perverted tales. Prefer third person, past tense. Be sure it is a story with a beginning, middle and end. It must have dialogue. Many beginners do not know an essay from a short story. Essays frequently used if *humorous.* We'd like to see more young (25 and over) humor; 'clean' humor is hard to come by. Length is a big factor. Writers who can tell a good story in a thousand words are true artists and their work is highly prized by our readers. Stick to the guidelines. We get manuscripts of up to 10,000 words because the story is 'unique and deserving.' We don't even read these. Too many writers fail to include SASE. These submissions are not considered.''

❏ ◎ SINISTER WISDOM, A Journal for the Lesbian Imagination in the Arts and Politics

Sinister Wisdom, Inc., Box 3252, Berkeley CA 94703. Website: www.sinisterwisdom.org. Magazine: 5½×8½; 128-144 pages; 55 lb. stock; 10 pt C1S cover; illustrations; photos. Lesbian-feminist journal, providing fiction, poetry, drama, essays, journals and artwork. Past issues included ''Lesbians of Color,'' ''Old Lesbians/Dykes'' and ''Lesbians and Religion.'' Triannual. Estab. 1976. Circ. 2,000.
Needs Lesbian (erotica, ethnic, experimental). No heterosexual or male-oriented fiction; no '70s amazon adventures; nothing that stereotypes or degrades women. List of upcoming themes available for SASE or on website. Receives 30 unsolicited mss/month. Accepts 6 mss/issue; 24 mss/year. Publishes ms 3-12 months after acceptance. **Publishes some new writers/year.** Recently published work by Jacqueline Miranda, Amananda Esteva and Sharon Bridgeforth. Length: 500-4,000 words; average length: 2,000 words. Publishes short shorts. Also publishes literary essays, literary criticism, poetry. Sometimes comments on rejected mss.
How to Contact Send complete ms. Accepts submissions by e-mail. SASE. Responds in 6 months to mss. Accepts simultaneous, multiple submissions. Sample copy for $7.50. Writer's guidelines for #10 SASE. Reviews fiction.
Payment/Terms Pays 2 contributor's copies. Acquires one-time rights.
Advice *Sinister Wisdom* is ''a multicultural lesbian journal reflecting the art, writing and politics of our communities.''

❏ ◎ SLIPSTREAM

P.O. Box 2071, New Market Station, Niagara Falls NY 14301. (716)282-2616. E-mail: editors@slipstreampress.org. Website: www.slipstreampress.org. **Contact:** Dan Sicoli, editor. Magazine: 7×8½; 80-100 pages; high quality paper; card cover; illustrations; photos. ''We use poetry and short fiction with a contemporary feel. Fifteen page manuscript limit.'' Annual. Estab. 1981. Circ. 600.
Needs Erotica, ethnic/multicultural, experimental, humor/satire, literary, mainstream, prose poem. ''No religious or romance.'' Wants to see more experimental fiction. Receives 25 unsolicited mss/month. Accepts 2-4 mss/issue; 6 mss/year. Publishes ms 6-18 months after acceptance. Recently published work by E.R. Baxter III and Greg Ames. Publishes short shorts. Rarely comments on rejected mss.
How to Contact Query. Send SASE for reply or return of ms. Include brief bio. Responds in 1 week to queries;

3 months to mss. Accepts simultaneous and reprints, multiple submissions. Sample copy for $7. Writer's guidelines for #10 SASE or online.

Payment/Terms 2 contributor copies. Acquires first North American serial rights.

Advice "Writing should be honest, fresh; develop your own style. Check out a sample issue first. Don't write for the sake of writing, write from the gut as if it were a biological need. Write from experience and mean what you say, but say it in the fewest number of words."

☑ SNAKE NATION REVIEW

Snake Nation Press, Inc., 110 West Force St., Valdosta GA 31601-3982. (912)244-0752. E-mail: jeana@snakenati onpress.org. Website: www.snakenationpress.org. **Contact:** Jean Arambula, editor. 6×9; 110 pages; acid free 70 lb. paper; 90 lb. cover; illustrations; photos. "We are interested in all types of stories for an educated, discerning, sophisticated audience." Triannual. Estab. 1989. Circ. 2,000.

• $100 Editor's Choice Award each issue in fiction and poetry.

Needs Condensed novels, erotica, ethnic/multicultural, experimental, fantasy, gay, horror, humor/satire, lesbian, literary, mainstream, mystery/suspense, psychic/supernatural/occult, regional, science fiction, contemporary, prose poem, senior citizen/retirement. Short stories of 5,000 words or less, poems (any length), art work will be returned after use. "We want our writers to have a voice, a story to tell, not a flat rendition of a slice of life." Plans annual anthology. Receives 200 unsolicited mss/month. Accepts 8-10 mss/issue; 40 mss/year. Publishes ms 6 months after acceptance. Agented fiction 1%. Recently published work by Robert Earl Price and O. Victor Miller. Length: 300-5,500 words; average length: 3,500 words. Publishes short shorts. Also publishes literary essays, poetry. Sometimes comments on rejected mss.

How to Contact Send complete ms with cover letter. SASE. Responds in 6-8 months to queries. Sample copy for $6, 8×10 SAE and 90¢ postage. Writer's guidelines for SASE. Reviews fiction.

Payment/Terms Pays 2 contributor's copies. $100 Editor's Choice Award each issue in fiction and poetry. Acquires one-time rights. Sends galleys to author.

$☑ SNOWY EGRET

The Fair Press, P.O. Box 29, Terre Haute IN 47808. **Contact:** Editors. Magazine: 8½×11; 60 pages; text paper; heavier cover; illustrations. "We publish works which celebrate the abundance and beauty of nature and examine the variety of ways in which human beings interact with landscapes and living things. Nature writing from literary, artistic, psychological, philosophical and historical perspectives." Semiannual. Estab. 1922. Circ. 400.

Needs "No genre fiction, e.g., horror, western, romance, etc." Receives 25 unsolicited mss/month. Accepts up to 6 mss/issue; up to 12 mss/year. Publishes ms 6 months after acceptance. **Publishes 20 new writers/year.** Recently published work by James Hinton, Ron Gielgun, Tom Noyes, Alice Cross and Maeve Mullin Ellis. Length: 500-10,000 words; average length: 1,000-3,000 words. Publishes short shorts. Sometimes comments on rejected mss.

How to Contact Send complete ms. Cover letter optional: do not query. SASE. Responds in 2 months to mss. Accepts simultaneous submissions if noted. Sample copy for 9×12 SASE and $8. Writer's guidelines for #10 SASE.

Payment/Terms Pays $2/page plus 2 contributor's copies. Pays on publication for first North American serial, one-time anthology rights, or reprints rights. Sends galleys to author.

Advice Looks for "honest, freshly detailed pieces with plenty of description and/or dialogue which will allow the reader to identify with the characters and step into the setting; fiction in which nature affects character development and the outcome of the story."

☑ ◎ SO TO SPEAK, A Feminist Journal of Language and Art

George Mason University, 4400 University Dr., MS 2D6, Fairfax VA 22030. (703)993-3625. E-mail: sts@gmu.edu. Website: www.gmu.edu/org/sts. **Contact:** Courtney Campbell, fiction editor. Magazine: 5½×8½; approximately 100 pages. "We are a feminist journal of language and art." Semiannual. Estab. 1993. Circ. 1,000.

Needs Ethnic/multicultural, experimental, feminist, lesbian, literary, mainstream, regional, translations. "No science fiction, mystery, genre romance." Receives 100 unsolicited mss/month. Accepts 3-5 mss/issue; 6-10 mss/year. Publishes ms 6 months after acceptance. **Publishes 5 new writers/year.** Length: For fiction up to 5,000 words; for poetry 3-5 pages per submission; average length: 4,000 words. Publishes short shorts. Also publishes literary essays, literary criticism, poetry.

How to Contact Send complete ms. Include bio (50 words maximum) and SASE. SASE for return of ms or send a disposable copy of ms. Responds in 6 months to mss. Accepts simultaneous submissions. Sample copy for $7. Reviews fiction.

Payment/Terms Pays contributor copies. Acquires first North American serial rights. Sponsors awards/contests.

Advice "We do not read between March 15 and August 15. Every writer has something they do exceptionally

Literary Magazines

well; do that and it will shine through in the work. We look for quality prose with a definite appeal to a feminist audience. We are trying to move away from strict genre lines. We want high quality fiction, nonfiction, poetry, art, innovative and risk-taking work.''

N ⦸ SONGS OF INNOCENCE

Pendragonian Publications, P.O. Box 719, New York NY 10101-0719. E-mail: mmpendragon@aol.com. **Contact:** Fiction Editor. Literary magazine/journal: 9×6; 175 pages; perfect bound; illustrations. ''A literary publication which celebrates the nobler aspects of humankind and the human experience. Along with sister publication Penny Dreadful, we seek to provide a forum for poetry and fiction in the 19th centure/Romance/Victorian tradition.'' Annual. Circ. 200.

Needs Fantasy, historical (19th century or earlier), literary, New Age, psychic/supernatural/occult. ''No children's, young adult, modern tales, Christian (or anything dogmatic).'' Receives 100 unsolicited mss/month. Accepts 15 mss/issue. Publishes ms up to 2 years after acceptance. Publishes short shorts. Also publishes literary essays, literary criticism, poetry. Rarely comments on rejected mss.

How to Contact Send complete ms. Accepts submissions by e-mail. Responds in 3 weeks to queries; 6-12 months to mss. Accepts reprints submissions. Sample copy for $10 and 9×6 SAE. Writer's guidelines for #10 SASE.

Payment/Terms Pays 1 contributor copy. Pays on publication for one-time rights. Sends galleys to author.

Advice ''We prefer tales set in 1910 or earlier—preferably earlier. We prefer prose in the 19th century/Victorian style. We do not like the terse, modern, post-Hemingway 'see Dick run' style. Also should transcend genres and include a spiritual/supernatural element without becoming fantasy. Avoid strong language, sex, etc. Include name and address on the title page. Include word count on the title page. We select stories that appeal to us and do not base selection on whether one has been published elsewhere.''

N ⦸ SONORA REVIEW

University of Arizona's Creative Writing MFA Program, University of Arizona, Dept. of English, Tucson AZ 85721. E-mail: sonora@email.arizona.edu. Website: www.coh.arizona.edu/sonora. **Contact:** Carol Test, fiction editor. Magazine: 6×9; approx. 100 pages; photos. ''We look for the highest quality poetry, fiction and nonfiction, with an emphasis on emerging writers. Our magazine has a long-standing tradition of publishing the best new literature and writers. Check out our website for a sample of what we publish and our submission guidelines, or write us for a sample back issue.'' Semiannual. Estab. 1980. Circ. 500.

Needs Ethnic/multicultural, experimental, literary, mainstream, novel excerpts. Receives 100 unsolicited mss/month. Accepts 2-3 mss/issue; 6-8 mss/year. Does not read in the Summer (June-August). Publishes ms 3-4 months after acceptance. **Publishes 1-3 new writers/year.** Recently published work by Meg Mullins, Dina Guidubaldi, Russell Tomlin, David Crouse. Also publishes literary essays, literary criticism, poetry. Sometimes comments on rejected mss.

How to Contact Send complete ms. Send disposable copy of the ms and #10 SASE for reply only. Responds in 2-5 weeks to queries; 3 months to mss. Accepts simultaneous, multiple submissions. Sample copy for $5. Writer's guidelines online. Reviews fiction.

Payment/Terms Pays 2 contributor's copies; additional copies for $4. Pays on publication for first North American serial, one-time, electronic rights.

Advice ''Send us your best stuff.''

⦸ SOUTH CAROLINA REVIEW

611 Strode Tower Box 340522, Clemson University, Clemson SC 29634-0522. (864)656-5399. Fax: (864)656-1345. E-mail: cwayne@clemson.edu. Website: www.clemson.edu/caah/cedp/scrintro.htm. **Contact:** Wayne Chapman, editor. Magazine: 6×9; 200 pages; 60 lb. cream white vellum paper; 65 lb. cream white vellum cover stock. Semiannual. Estab. 1967. Circ. 500.

Needs Literary, mainstream, poetry, essays, reviews. Does not read mss June-August or December. Receives 50-60 unsolicited mss/month. Recently published work by Joyce Carol Oates, Rosanne Coggeshal, Fred Chappell and Stephen Dixon. Rarely comments on rejected mss.

How to Contact Send complete ms. Requires text on disk upon acceptance in WordPerfect or Microsoft Word in PC format. Responds in 2 months to mss. Sample copy for $12 plus $1.50 postage. Reviews fiction.

Payment/Terms Pays in contributor's copies.

N ⦸ SOUTH DAKOTA REVIEW

University of South Dakota, Box 111, University Exchange, Vermillion SD 57069. (605)677-5184. Fax: (605)677-5298. E-mail: sdreview@usd.edu. Website: www.usd.edu/sdreview/. **Contact:** Fiction Editor. Magazine: 6×9; 140-170 pages; book paper; glossy cover stock; illustrations sometimes; photos on cover. ''Literary magazine for university and college audiences and their equivalent. Emphasis is often on the American West and its writers but will accept mss from anywhere. Issues are usually personal essay, fiction and poetry with some literary essays." Quarterly. Estab. 1963. Circ. 500.

• *Pushcart* and *Best American Essays* nominees.

Needs Ethnic/multicultural, literary, mainstream, regional. "We like very well-written, thematically ambitious, character-centered short fiction. Contemporary Western American setting appeals, but not necessary. No formula stories, horror, or adolescent 'I' narrator." Receives 40 unsolicited mss/month. Accepts 40 mss/year. Publishes ms 1-6 months after acceptance. **Publishes 3-5 new writers/year.** Recently published work by Nathan Whiting, Dan Tobin, Frederick Zydeck.

How to Contact Send complete ms. "We like cover letters that are not boastful and do not attempt to sell the stories, but rather provide some personal information about the writer which can be used for a contributor's note." Responds in 10 weeks to mss. Sample copy for $7.

Payment/Terms Acquires first, second serial (reprint) rights.

Advice Rejects mss because of "careless writing; often careless typing; stories too personal ('I' confessional); aimlessness of plot; unclear or unresolved conflicts; subject matter that editor finds cliched, senstationalized, pretentious or trivial. We are trying to use more fiction and more variety."

THE SOUTHEAST REVIEW

English Department, Florida State University, Tallahassee FL 32306-1036. (850)644-2773. E-mail: southeastreviw@english.fsu.edu. Website: www.english.fsu.edu/southeastreview. **Contact:** Ed Tarkington, senior editor. Magazine: 6×9; 160 pages; 70 lb. paper; 10 pt. Krome Kote cover; photos. "*The Southeast Review* is published for a literary audience with a sophisticated, intelligent knowledge of the fiction genre." Biannual. Estab. 1979. Circ. 1,000.

Needs "We want stories (under 6,000 words) with striking images, fresh language and a consistent voice." Would like to see more literary fiction. "No genre fiction. We receive approximately 400 submissions per month and we accept less than 1-2% of them. We will comment briefly on rejected mss when time permits." Publishes ms 2-6 months after acceptance. **Publishes 4-6 new writers/year.** Recently published work by Greg Johnson, D.C. Berry, Angela Ball, Tom Grimes, Michael Martone and Charles Wright.

How to Contact Send complete ms. Responds in 3-5 months to mss. Sample copy for $5.

Payment/Terms Pays 3 contributor's copies. Acquires first North American serial rights, which revert to author.

Advice "Avoid trendy experimentation for its own sake (present-tense narration, observation that isn't also revelation). Fresh stories, moving, interesting characters and a sensitivity to language are still fiction mainstays. Also publishes winner and runners-up of the World's Best Short Story Contest sponsored by the Florida State University English Department."

SOUTHERN CALIFORNIA ANTHOLOGY

University of Southern California, Waite Phillips Hall, Room 404, Los Angeles CA 90089-4034. (213)740-3252. Fax: (213)740-5775. E-mail: mpw@mizar.usc.edu. Website: www.usc.edu/dept/LAS/mpw/students/sca.html. **Contact:** Editor. Magazine: 5½×8½; 142 pages; semiglosss cover stock. "*The Southern California Anthology* is a literary review that contains an eclectic collection of previously unpublished, quality contemporary fiction, poetry and interviews with established literary people, published for adults of all professions; of particular interest to those interested in serious contemporary literature." Annual. Estab. 1983. Circ. 1,500.

Needs Ethnic/multicultural, experimental, feminist, historical, humor/satire, literary, mainstream, regional, serialized novels. "No juvenile, religious, confession, romance, science fiction or pornography." Receives 40 unsolicited mss/month. Accepts 1-2 mss/issue. Publishes ms 4 months after acceptance. **Publishes 1-2 new writers/year.** Recently published work by James Ragan, James Tate, Alice Fulton, John Updike, Joyce Carol Oates, Hubert Selby Jr., Marge Piercy, Stephen Dunn, Ruth Stone and Gay Talese. Publishes short shorts.

How to Contact Send complete ms. Cover letter should include list of previous publications. Responds in 4 months to mss. Sample copy for $4. Writer's guidelines for #10 SASE.

Payment/Terms Pays in contributor copies. Acquires first rights.

Advice "The *Anthology* pays particular attention to craft and style in its selection of narrative writing."

SOUTHERN HUMANITIES REVIEW

Auburn University, 9088 Haley Center, Auburn University AL 36849. Website: www.auburn.edu/english/shr/home.htm. **Contact:** Fiction Editor. Magazine: 6×9; 100 pages; 60 lb neutral pH, natural paper; 65 lb. neutral pH medium coated cover stock; occasional illustration; photos. "We publish essays, poetry, fiction and reviews. Our fiction has ranged from very traditional in form and content to very experimental. Literate, college-educated audience. We hope they read our journal for both enlightenment and pleasure." Quarterly. Estab. 1967. Circ. 800.

Needs Feminist, humor/satire, regional. Slower reading time in summer. Receives 25 unsolicited mss/month. Accepts 1-2 mss/issue; 4-6 mss/year. Recently published work by William Cobb, R.T. Smith, Heimito von

Doderer, Greg Johnson and Dieter Kuhn. Also publishes literary essays, literary criticism, poetry. Sometimes comments on rejected mss.

How to Contact Send complete ms. Cover letter with an explanation of the topic chosen—"special, certain book, etc., a little about the author if he/she has never submitted." No e-mail submissions. Responds in 3 months to mss.

Payment/Terms Pays in contributor copies. Rights revert to author on publication.

Advice "Send us the ms with SASE. If we like it, we'll take it or we'll recommend changes. If we don't like it, we'll send it back as promptly as possible. Read the journal. Send typewritten, clean copy, carefully proofread. We also award annual Hoepfner Prize of $100 for the best published essay or short story of the year. Let someone whose opinion you respect read your story and give you an honest appraisal. Rewrite, if necessary, to get the most from your story."

$ 🖉 💌 THE SOUTHERN REVIEW

43 Allen Hall, Louisiana State University, Baton Rouge LA 70803-5001. (225)578-5108. Fax: (225)578-5098. E-mail: perreaud@lsu.edu. Website: www.lsu.edu/thesouthernreview. **Contact:** Donna Perreault, associate editor. Magazine: 6¼×10; 240 pages; 50 lb. Glatfelter paper; 65 lb. #1 grade cover stock. No queries. Reading period: September-May. Quarterly. Estab. 1935. Circ. 3,100.

• Several stories published in *The Southern Review* were *Pushcart Prize* selections.

Needs Literary. "We emphasize style and substantial content. No mystery, fantasy or religious mss." Receives approximately 300 unsolicited mss/month. Accepts 4-5 mss/issue. Does not read mss June-August. Publishes ms 6 months after acceptance. Agented fiction 1%. **Publishes 4-6 new writers/year.** Recently published work by William Gay, Romulus Linney, Richard Bausch and Ingrid Hill. Also publishes literary essays, literary criticism, poetry.

How to Contact Send complete ms with cover letter and SASE. "Prefer brief letters giving information on author concerning where he/she has been published before, biographical info and what he/she is doing now." Responds in 2 months to mss. Sample copy for $8. Writer's guidelines online. Reviews fiction.

Payment/Terms Pays $30/page. Pays on publication for first North American serial rights. Sends galleys to author. Sponsors awards/contests.

Advice "Develop a careful, clear style. Although willing to publish experimental writing that appears to have a valid artistic purpose, *The Southern Review* avoids extremism and sensationalism."

$ 🖉 SOUTHWEST REVIEW

P.O. Box 750374, Dallas TX 75275-0374. (214)768-1037. Fax: (214)768-1408. E-mail: swr@mail.smu.edu. Website: www.southwestreview.org. **Contact:** Jennifer Cranfill, managing editor. Magazine: 6×9; 144 pages. "The majority of our readers are college-educated adults who wish to stay abreast of the latest and best in contemporary fiction, poetry, literary criticism and books in all but the most specialized disciplines." Quarterly. Estab. 1915. Circ. 1,600.

Needs "High literary quality; no specific requirements as to subject matter, but cannot use sentimental, religious, western, poor science fiction, pornographic, true confession, mystery, juvenile or serialized or condensed novels." Receives 200 unsolicited mss/month. Publishes ms 6-12 months after acceptance. Recently published work by Tracy Daugherty, Millicent Dillon and Mark Jacobs. Also publishes literary essays, poetry. Occasionally comments on rejected mss.

How to Contact Send complete ms. Responds in 6 months to mss. Accepts multiple submissions. Sample copy for $6. Writer's guidelines for #10 SASE or on website.

Payment/Terms Pays negotiable rate and 3 contributor copies. Acquires first North American serial rights. Sends galleys to author.

Advice "We have become less regional. A lot of time would be saved for us and for the writer if he or she looked at a copy of review before submitting. We like to receive a cover letter because it is some reassurance that the author has taken the time to check a current directory for the editor's name. When there isn't a cover letter, we wonder whether the same story is on 20 other desks around the country."

🖉 ◎ SOUTHWESTERN AMERICAN LITERATURE

Center for the Study of the Southwest, Texas State University-San Marcos, 601 University Drive, San Marcos TX 78666. (512)245-2224. Fax: (512)245-7462. E-mail: mb13@swt.edu. Website: swrhc.txstate.edu/cssw/publications/sal.php. **Contact:** Twister Marquiss, assistant editor; Mark Busby, co-editor; Dickie Maurice Heaberlin, co-editor. Magazine: 6×9; 125 pages; 80 lb. cover stock. "We publish fiction, nonfiction, poetry, literary criticism and book reviews. Generally speaking, we want material covering the Greater Southwest or material written by Southwest writers." Biannual. Estab. 1971. Circ. 300.

Needs Ethnic/multicultural, literary, mainstream, regional. "No science fiction or romance." Receives 10-15 unsolicited mss/month. Accepts 1-2 mss/issue; 4-5 mss/year. Publishes ms 6 months after acceptance. **Pub-**

lishes 1-2 new writers/year. Recently published work by Greg Garrett, Andrew Geyer, Susan Austin, Walt McDonald, Carol Hamilton and Larry D. Thomas. Length: 6,250 words; average length: 4,000 words. Also publishes literary essays, literary criticism, poetry. Sometimes comments on rejected mss.

How to Contact Send complete ms. Include cover letter, estimated word count, 2-5 line bio, and list of publications. Does not accept e-mail submissions. Responds in 3-6 months to mss. Accepts simultaneous submissions. Sample copy for $8. Writer's guidelines free.

Payment/Terms Pays 2 contributor copies. Acquires first rights.

Advice "We look for crisp language, an interesting approach to material; a regional approach is desired but not required. Read widely, write often, revise carefully. We are looking for stories that probe the relationship between the tradition of Southwestern American literature and the writer's own imagination in creative ways. We seek stories that move beyond stereotype and approach the larger defining elements and also ones that, as William Faulkner noted in his Nobel Prize acceptance speech, treat subjects central to good literature—the old verities of the human heart, such as honor and courage and pity and suffering, fear and humor, love and sorrow."

☐ ◎ SPEAK UP

Speak Up Press, P.O. Box 100506, Denver CO 80250. (303)715-0837. Fax: (303)715-0793. E-mail: SpeakUPres@aol.com. Website: www.speakuppress.org. **Contact:** Senior editor. Magazine: $5^1/_2 \times 8^1/_2$; 128 pages; 55 lb. Glat. Supple Opaque Recycled Natural paper; 12 CIS cover; illustrations; photos. "*Speak Up* features the original fiction, nonfiction, poetry, plays, photography and artwork of young people 13-19 years old. *Speak Up* provides a place for teens to be creative, honest and expressive in an uncensored environment." Annual. Estab. 1999. Circ. 2,900.

Needs Teen writers. Receives 30 unsolicited mss/month. Accepts 30 mss/issue; 30 mss/year. Publishes ms 3-12 months after acceptance. **Publishes 20 new writers/year.** Length: 5,000 words; average length: 500 words. Publishes short shorts. Also publishes literary essays, poetry.

How to Contact Send complete ms. Accepts submissions by e-mail, fax. Responds in 3 months to queries; 3 months to mss. Accepts simultaneous and reprints, multiple submissions. Sample copy free. Writer's guidelines for #10 SASE.

Payment/Terms Pays 2 contributor copies. Acquires first North American serial, one-time rights.

☑ ☒ SPINDRIFT

Shoreline Community College, 16101 Greenwood Ave. North, Seattle WA 98133. (206)546-5864. E-mail: spindrift@shoreline.edu. Website: http://success.shoreline.edu/spindrift/home.html. **Contact:** Literary Editor. Magazine: 125 pages; quality paper; photographs; b&w artwork. "We publish a variety of fiction, most of which would be considered literary. Authors are from all over the map, but we give priority to writers from our community." Annual. Estab. 1967. Circ. 500.

- *Spindrift* has received awards for "Best Literary Magazine" from the Community College Humanities Association both locally and nationally and awards from the Pacific Printing Industries.

Needs Ethnic/multicultural, experimental, historical, literary, mainstream, regional, serialized novels, translations, prose poem. "No detective, science fiction, romance, religious/inspirational. We look for fresh, original work that is not forced or 'straining' to be literary." Receives 300 unsolicited mss/month. Accepts 20 mss/issue. Publishes ms 3-4 months after acceptance. **Publishes 5-6 new writers/year.** Recently published work by Ed Harkness and Virgil Suarez.

How to Contact Send complete ms. Do not place name on ms, and please indicate multiple submissions in cover letter. Submit by Feb. 1. Responds by March 15 if SASE is included. Accepts multiple submissions. Sample copy for $8, 8×10 SAE and $1 postage; sample back issues for $2.

Payment/Terms Pays contributor's copies. Acquires first rights. Not copyrighted.

Advice "Let the story tell itself; don't force or overdo the language. Show the reader something new about people, situations, life itself."

Ⓝ ☑ SPIRE, The Future of Arts & Literature

532 La Guardia Pl. Ste. 298, New York NY 10012. E-mail: editor@spirepress.org. Website: www.spirepress.org. **Contact:** Shelly Reed. Magazine: $8^1/_2 \times 11$; 70 pages; color, laminated cover stock; illustrations; photos. "We are a nonprofit and encourage low-income and minority writers. We publish at least two poets and writers under 18 per issue." Semiannual. Estab. 2002. Circ. 800. Member: PMA.

Needs Historical, literary. No horror, romance or religious work. Accepts 4-6 mss/issue; 12 mss/year. Publishes ms 3 months after acceptance. **Publishes 20 new writers/year.** Recently published work by Sandra Kelly-Green, Yoon Choi, Lauren Maffeo, Sharon Wang and Derek Kannemeyer. Length: 500-3,000 words; average length: 1,600 words. Publishes short shorts. Also publishes literary essays, poetry. Rarely comments on rejected mss.

How to Contact Send complete ms. Accepts submissions by e-mail. Send disposable copy of the ms and #10 SASE for reply only. Responds in 3 months to mss. Accepts simultaneous submissions. Sample copy for $9. Writer's guidelines for #10 SASE, or online.

Payment/Terms Pays 1 contributor's copy. Pays on publication for one-time, electronic rights.

Advice "Write for a general audience. That means you should have someone read it first before submitting."

STAND MAGAZINE

Department of English, VCU, Richmond VA 23284-2005. (804)828-1331. E-mail: dlatane@vcu.edu. Website: www.standmagazine.org. "*Stand Magazine* is concerned with what happens when cultures and literatures meet, with translation in its many guises, with the mechanics of language, with the processes by which the policy receives or disables its cultural makers. *Stand* promotes debate of issues that are of radical concern to the intellectual community worldwide." Quarterly. Estab. 1952. Circ. 3,000 worldwide.

Needs Adventure, ethnic/multicultural, experimental, historical, mainstream. "No genre fiction." Publishes ms 10 months after acceptance.

How to Contact Send complete ms. Responds in 6 weeks to queries; 3 months to mss. Sample copy for $12. Writer's guidelines for #10 SASE with sufficient number of IRCs or online.

Payment/Terms Payment varies. Pays on publication. Aquires first world rights.

⋉ ▣ ◯ STAPLE MAGAZINE

Staple New Writing, 74 Rangeley Road, Walkley, Sheffield England S6 5DW. E-mail: e.barrett@shu.ac.uk. **Contact:** Elizabeth Barrett, editor. Magazines: A5; 100 pages; illustrations; photos. Quarterly. Estab. 1982. Circ. 500.

Needs Receives 1,000 unsolicited mss/month. Accepts 5 mss/issue; 15 mss/year. Publishes ms 10 weeks after acceptance. **Publishes 1 new writer/year.** Recently published work by Roy McRory, David Swann, Penny Feeny. Length: 5,000 words; average length: 3,000 words. Publishes short shorts. Also publishes literary essays, literary criticism, poetry. Sometimes comments on rejected mss.

How to Contact Send complete ms. Send SASE (or IRC) for return of ms. Responds in 8 weeks to queries; 12 weeks to mss. Accepts multiple submissions. Sample copy for $12. Writer's guidelines for SASE.

Payment/Terms Pays 2 contributor's copies; additional copies $12. Pays on publication for one-time rights.

$◯ ▣ ▣ STONE SOUP, The Magazine by Young Writers and Artists

Children's Art Foundation, P.O. Box 83, Santa Cruz CA 95063-0083. (831)426-5557. Fax: (831)426-1161. Website: www.stonesoup.com. **Contact:** Ms. Gerry Mandel, editor. Magazine: 7×10; 48 pages; high quality paper; photos. Audience is children, teachers, parents, writers, artists. "We have a preference for writing and art based on real-life experiences; no formula stories or poems." Bimonthly. Estab. 1973. Circ. 20,000.

- This is known as "the literary journal for children." *Stone Soup* has previously won the Ed Press Golden Lamp Honor Award and the Parent's Choice Award.

Needs Adventure, ethnic/multicultural, experimental, fantasy, historical, humor/satire, mystery/suspense, science fiction, slice-of-life vignettes, suspense. "We do not like assignments or formula stories of any kind." Receives 1,000 unsolicited mss/month. Accepts 10 mss/issue. Publishes ms 4 months after acceptance. **Publishes some new writers/year.** Also publishes literary essays, poetry.

How to Contact Send complete ms. "We like to learn a little about our young writers, why they like to write, and how they came to write the story they are submitting." Please do not include SASE. Do not send originals. Responds only to those submissions being considered for possible publication. "If you do not hear from us in 4 to 6 weeks it means we were not able to use your work. Don't be discouraged! Try again!" No simultaneous submissions. Sample copy for $5 or online. Writer's guidelines online.

Payment/Terms Pays $40 for stories. Authors also receive 2 copies, a certificate, and discounts on additional copies and on subscriptions. Pays on publication.

Advice Mss are rejected because they are "derivatives of movies, TV, comic books; or classroom assignments or other formulas. Go to our website, where you can see many examples of the kind of work we publish."

$▣ ▣ STORIE, All Write

Leconte, Via Suor Celestina Donati 13/E, Rome 00167 Italy. (+39)06 614 8777. Fax: (+39)06 614 8777. E-mail: storie@tiscali.it. Website: www.storie.it. **Contact:** Gianluca Bassi, editor; Barbara Pezzopane, assistant editor; George Lerner, foreign editor. Magazine: 186 pages; illustrations; photographs. "*Storie* is one of Italy's leading literary magazines. Committed to a truly crossover vision of writing, the bilingual (Italian/English) review publishes high quality fiction and poetry, interspersed with the work of alternative wordsmiths such as filmmakers and musicians. Through writings bordering on narratives and interviews with important contemporary writers, it explores the culture and craft of writing." Bimonthly. Estab. 1989. Circ. 20,000.

Needs Literary. Receives 150 unsolicited mss/month. Accepts 6-10 mss/issue; 30-50 mss/year. Does not read mss in August. Publishes ms 2 months after acceptance. **Publishes 20 new writers/year.** Recently published work by Joyce Carol Oates, Haruki Murakami, Robert Coover, Raymond Carver, André Brink, T.C. Boyle, Ariel Dorfman and Tess Gallagher. Length: 2,000-6,000 words; average length: 3,000 words. Publishes short shorts. Also publishes literary essays, literary criticism, poetry. Sometimes comments on rejected mss.

How to Contact Accepts submissions by e-mail (on disk; include brief bio). Send complete ms with cover letter. "Mss may be submitted directly by regular post without querying first; however, we do not accept unsolicited mss via e-mail. Please query via e-mail first. We only contact writers if their work has been accepted. We also arrange for and oversee a high-quality, professional translation of the piece." Responds in 1 month to queries; 6 months to mss. Accepts multiple submissions. Sample copy for $8. Writer's guidelines online.

Payment/Terms $30-600 and 2 contributor's copies. Pays on publication for first, (in English and Italian) rights.

Advice "More than erudite references or a virtuoso performance, we're interested in the recording of human experience in a genuine, original voice. *Storie* reserves the right to include a brief review of interesting submissions not selected for publication in a special column of the magazine."

STORYQUARTERLY

431 Sheridan Rd., Kenilworth IL 60043. (847)256-6998. Website: www.storyquarterly.com. **Contact:** Fiction Editors. Magazine: $5\frac{1}{2} \times 8\frac{1}{4}$; 550 pages; good quality paper; an all-story magazine, committed to a full range of styles and forms. "*StoryQuarterly*, an annual anthology of short stories, publishes contemporary American and international literature of high quality in a full range of styles and forms—outstanding writing and unusual insights." Annual. Estab. 1975. Circ. 6,000.

- *StoryQuarterly* received recognitions in *New Stories from the South*, *Best American Mystery Story*, *O. Henry Prize Stories*, *Best American Stories*, *Best American Essays* and *Pushcart Prize Collection* in the last 3 years. The publication also won Illinois Arts Council Awards, two apiece each of the last 5 years.

Needs "Well-written stories, serious or humorous, that get up and run from the first page. No genre fiction, light or slight stories, pornography or sentimental stories." Receives 1,500 unsolicited mss/month. Accepts 40-50 mss/issue. **Publishes 2-5 new writers/year.** Recently published work by Chris Abni, J.M. Coetzee, Robert Olen Butler, T.C. Boyle, Stuart Dybek, Stephen Dixon, Reginald Gibbons, Gail Godwin, Alice Hoffman, Mark Winegardner, Charles Johnson, Romulus Linney, Jim McManus and Askold Melnyczuk.

How to Contact Responds in 2-4 months to mss. Sample copy for $8. Writer's guidelines online at website.

Payment/Terms Pays 10 copies, plus lifetime subscription. Acquires first North American serial, one-time rights. Copyright reverts to author after publication. Electronic publishing agreement available.

Advice Subscribe to and study magazine and market. *SQ* fiction is selected for author control, subject matter, absence of cliché, originality of voice and subject matter.

STRUGGLE, A Magazine of Proletarian Revolutionary Literature

Box 13261, Detroit MI 48213-0261. (213)273-9039. E-mail: timhall11@yahoo.com. **Contact:** Tim Hall, editor. Magazine: $5\frac{1}{2} \times 8\frac{1}{2}$; 36-72 pages; 20 lb. white bond paper; colored cover; illustrations; occasional photos. Publishes material related to "the struggle of the working class and all progressive people against the rule of the rich—including their war policies, repression, racism, exploitation of the workers, oppression of women and general culture, etc." Quarterly. Estab. 1985.

Needs Ethnic/multicultural, experimental, feminist, historical, humor/satire, literary, regional, science fiction, translations, young adult/teen (10-18), prose poem, senior citizen/retirement. "The theme can be approached in many ways, including plenty of categories not listed here. Readers would like fiction about anti-globalization, the fight against racism, prison conditions, neo-conservatism and the Iraq War. Would also like to see more fiction that depicts life, work and struggle of the working class of every background; also the struggles of the 1930s and '60s illustrated and brought to life. No romance, psychic, mystery, western, erotica, religious." Receives 10-12 unsolicited mss/month. Recently published work by Gregory Alan Norton, G. Daglunis, Tim Hall, Kenneth Allen and T.D. Alexander. Length: 4,000 words; average length: 1,000-3,000 words. Publishes short shorts. Normally comments on rejected mss.

How to Contact Send complete ms. Accepts submissions by e-mail. "Tries to" report in 3-4 months to queries. Accepts simultaneous and reprints, multiple submissions. Sample copies for $3.00; subscriptions $10 for 4 issues; make checks payable to Tim Hall, Special Account, not to *Struggle*.

Payment/Terms Pays 1 contributor's copy. No rights acquired. Not copyrighted.

Advice "Write about the oppression of the working people, the poor, the minorities, women and, if possible, their rebellion against it—we are not interested in anything which accepts the status quo. We are not too worried about plot and advanced technique (fine if we get them!)—we would probably accept things others would call sketches, provided they have life and struggle. For new writers: just describe for us a situation in which some real people confront some problem of oppression, however seemingly minor. Observe and put down the real facts. Experienced writers: try your 'committed'/experimental fiction on us. We get poetry all the time. We have increased our fiction portion of our content in the last few years. The quality of fiction that

Literary Magazines

we have published has continued to improve. If your work raises an interesting issue of literature and politics, it may get discussed in letters and in my editorial. I suggest ordering a sample.''

$ subTERAIN, Strong words for a polite nation

P.O. Box 3008, MPO, Vancouver BC V6B 3X5 Canada. (604)876-8710. Fax: (604)879-2667. E-mail: subter@portal.com. Website: www.subterrain.ca. **Contact:** Fiction editor. Magazine: $8^{1}/_{4} \times 10^{7}/_{8}$; 46-52 pages; gloss stock paper; color gloss cover stock; illustrations; photos. "Looking for unique work and perspectives from Canada and beyond." Triannual. Estab. 1987. Circ. 3,000.

Needs Literary. Does not want genre fiction or children's fiction. Receives 100 unsolicited mss/month. Accepts 4 mss/issue; 10-15 mss/year. Publishes ms 4 months after acceptance. Recently published work by John Moore. Also publishes literary essays, literary criticism. Rarely comments on rejected mss.

How to Contact Send complete ms. Include disposable copy of the ms and #10 SASE for reply only. Responds in 3-4 months to queries; 4-6 months to mss. Accepts multiple submissions. Sample copy for $5. Writer's guidelines for #10 SASE or online.

Payment/Terms Pays $25-100. Pays on publication for first North American serial rights.

Advice "Read the magazine first. Get to know what kind of work we publish."

SULPHUR RIVER LITERARY REVIEW

P.O. Box 19228, Austin TX 78760-9228. (512)292-9456. **Contact:** James Michael Robbins, editor. Magazine: $5^{1}/_{2} \times 8^{1}/_{2}$; 145 pages; illustrations; photos. "*SRLR* publishes literature of quality—poetry and short fiction with appeal that transcends time. Audience includes a broad spectrum of readers, mostly educated, many of whom are writers, artists and educators." Semiannual. Estab. 1978. Circ. 350.

Needs Ethnic/multicultural, experimental, feminist, humor/satire, literary, mainstream, translations. "No religious, juvenile, teen, sports, romance or mystery. Wants to see more experimental, surreal and imaginative fiction." Receives 20 unsolicited mss/month. Accepts 4-5 mss/issue; 8-10 mss/year. Publishes ms 1-2 years after acceptance. Recently published work by William Jablonsky, Richard Vaughn and Frederic Boutet. Publishes short shorts. Also publishes literary essays, literary criticism, poetry.

How to Contact Send complete ms. Include short bio and list of publications. Send SASE for reply, return of ms, or send disposable copy of ms. Responds in 1 week to queries; 1 month to mss. Sample copy for $7.

Payment/Terms Pays 2 contributor copies. Additional copies $7. Acquires first North American serial rights.

Advice Looks for "quality. Imagination served perfectly by masterful control of language."

SWINK

244 Fifth Ave. #2722, New York NY 10001. (212) 591-1651. Fax: (212) 658-9995. Website: www.swinkmag.com. "*Swink* is a biannual print magazine dedicated to identifying and promoting literary talent in both established and emerging writers. We're interested in writing that pushes the boundaries of the traditional—writing that is new in concept, form or execution; that reflects a diversity of thought, experience or perspective; that provokes or entertains."

How to Contact Submissions must contain your name, address and a telephone number where you can be reached and must be accompanied by a self-addressed, stamped envelope. Accepts mss by mail only. Responds in 12 weeks to mss. Accepts simultaneous submissions.

Payment/Terms Payment varies depending on length and genre. Acquires first North American serial, electronic, non-exclusive, one-time anthology rights.

SYCAMORE REVIEW

Purdue University, Department of English, 500 Oval Drive, West Lafayette IN 47907. (765)494-3783. Fax: (765)494-3780. E-mail: sycamore@purdue.edu. Website: www.sla.purdue.edu/sycamore. **Contact:** Fiction Editor. Magazine: $5^{1}/_{2} \times 8^{1}/_{2}$; 150-200 pages; heavy, textured, uncoated paper; heavy laminated cover. "Journal devoted to contemporary literature. We publish both traditional and experimental fiction, personal essay, poetry, interviews, drama and graphic art. Novel excerpts welcome if they stand alone as a story." Semiannual. Estab. 1989. Circ. 1,000.

Needs Experimental, humor/satire, literary, mainstream, regional, translations. "We generally avoid genre literature but maintain no formal restrictions on style or subject matter. No romance, children's." Would like to see more experimental fiction. Publishes ms 11 months after acceptance. Recently published work by Lucia Perillo, June Armstrong, W.P. Osborn and William Giraldi. Also publishes poetry, "this list has included Billy Collins, Thomas Lux, Kathleen Pierce and Vandana Khanna." Sometimes comments on rejected mss.

How to Contact Send complete ms. Include with cover letter previous publications and address. SASE. Responds in 4 months to mss. Accepts simultaneous submissions. Sample copy for $7. Writer's guidelines for #10 SASE or online.

Payment/Terms Acquires one-time rights.

Advice "We publish both new and experienced authors but we're always looking for stories with strong emotional appeal, vivid characterization and a distinctive narrative voice; fiction that breaks new ground while still telling an interesting and significant story. Avoid gimmicks and trite, predictable outcomes. Write stories that have a ring of truth, the impact of felt emotion. Don't be afraid to submit; send your best."

⊕ $TAKAHE

P.O. Box 13-335, Christchurch 8001 New Zealand. (03)359-8133. **Contact:** Isa Moynihan, editor. "A literary magazine which appears three or four times a year and publishes short stories and poetry by both established and emerging writers. The publisher is Takahe Collective Trust, a charitable trust formed by established writers to help new writers and get them into print." The magazine is published in hard copy.

Needs "We are particularly losing interest in stories by 'victims' of various kinds, morbid stories. We would like to see more humorous and light-hearted stories." **Publishes 20 new writers/year.** Recently published work by Jenny Argante, Lyn McConchie, David Hill, Virgil Suarez, David Clarkson and Chrissie Ward.

How to Contact Send complete ms. Include e-mail address, brief bio and SASE (IRC for overseas submissions). Single spacing, indented paragraphs and double quotation marks for direct speech. Any use of foreign languages must be accompanied by English translation. Accepts multiple submissions.

Payment/Terms Pays $15 ($NZ30). Copyright reverts to author on publication.

Advice "We pay a flat rate to each writer/poet appearing in a particular issue regardless of the number/length of items. Amount is subject to change according to circumstances. Editorials and literary commentaries are by invitation only and, not being covered by our grant, are not paid for. All contributors receive two hard copies of the issue in which their work appears."

⊘ TALKING RIVER REVIEW

Lewis-Clark State College, Division of Literature and Languages, 500 8th Ave., Lewiston ID 83501. (208)792-2307. Fax: (208)792-2324. **Contact:** Mark Sanders, editor. Magazine: 6×9; 150 pages; 60 lb. paper; coated, color cover; illustrations; photos. "We look for new voices with something to say to a discerning general audience." Semiannual. Estab. 1994. Circ. 500.

Needs Condensed novels, ethnic/multicultural, feminist, historical, humor/satire, literary, mainstream, regional. "Wants more well-written, character-driven stories that surprise and delight the reader with fresh, arresting yet unself-conscious language, imagery, metaphor, revelation." No stories that are sexist, racist, homophobic, erotic for shock value, romance. Receives 200 unsolicited mss/month. Accepts 5-8 mss/issue; 10-15 mss/year. Reads mss September 1-May 1 only. Publishes ms up to 1 year after acceptance. Agented fiction 10%. **Publishes 10-15 new writers/year.** Recently published work by X.J. Kennedy and Clair Davis. Length: 7,500 words; average length: 3,000 words. Also publishes literary essays, poetry. Sometimes comments on rejected mss.

How to Contact Send complete manuscript with a cover letter. Include estimated word count, 2-sentence bio and list of publications. Send SASE for reply, return of ms or send disposable copy of ms. Responds in 3 months to mss. Accepts simultaneous submissions if indicated. Sample copy for $6. Writer's guidelines for #10 SASE.

Payment/Terms Pays 2 contributor's copies and a year's subscription; additional copies $4. Acquires one-time rights.

Advice "We look for the strong, the unique; we reject clichéd images and predictable climaxes."

$⊘ TAMPA REVIEW

University of Tampa Press, 401 W. Kennedy Blvd., Tampa FL 33606. (813)253-6266. Fax: (813)258-7593. Website: tampareview.ut.edu. **Contact:** Lisa Birnbaum and Kathleen Ochshorn, fiction editors. Magazine: 7½×10½; hardback; approximately 100 pages; acid-free paper; visual art; photos. An international literary journal publishing art and literature from Florida and Tampa Bay, as well as new work and translations from throughout the world. Semiannual. Estab. 1988. Circ. 500.

Needs Ethnic/multicultural, experimental, fantasy, historical, literary, mainstream, translations. "We are far more interested in quality than in genre. Nothing sentimental as opposed to genuinely moving, nor self-conscious style at the expense of human truth." Accepts 4-5 mss/issue. Reads September through December; reports January through May. Publishes ms 10 months after acceptance. Agented fiction 20%. Recently published work by Elizabeth Spencer, Lee K. Abbott, Lorrie Moore, Gordon Weaver and Tim O'Brien. Publishes short shorts. Also publishes literary essays, poetry.

How to Contact Send complete ms. Include brief bio. Responds in 5 months to mss. Accepts multiple submissions. Sample copy for $7. Writer's guidelines online.

Payment/Terms Pays $10/printed page. Pays on publication for first North American serial rights. Sends galleys to author.

Advice "There are more good writers publishing in magazines today than there have been in many decades. Unfortunately, there are even more bad ones. In T. Gertler's *Elbowing the Seducer*, an editor advises a young

Literary Magazines

writer that he wants to hear her voice completely, to tell (he means 'show') him in a story the truest thing she knows. We concur. Rather than a trendy workshop story or a minimalism that actually stems from not having much to say, we would like to see stories that make us believe they mattered to the writer and, more importantly, will matter to a reader. Trim until only the essential is left, and don't give up belief in yourself. And it might help to attend a good writers' conference, e.g. Wesleyan or Bennington.''

◙ TAPROOT LITERARY REVIEW

Taproot Writer's Workshop, Inc., Box 204, Ambridge PA 15003. (724)266-8476. E-mail: taproot10@aol.com. **Contact:** Tikvah Feinstein, editor. Magazine: 5½×8½; 93 pages; 20 lb. paper; hard cover; attractively printed; saddle-stitched. "We select on quality, not topic. Variety and quality are our appealing features." Annual. Estab. 1987. Circ. 500.

Needs Literary. "No pornography, religious, popular, romance fiction. Want more multicultural-displaced people living among others in new places." The majority of ms published are received through their annual contest. Receives 20 unsolicited mss/month. Accepts 6 mss/issue. **Publishes 2-4 new writers/year.** Recently published work by Alena Horowitz, Shirley Barasch, Rachel Mathies, Arlene Atwater and T. Anders Carson. Publishes short shorts. Also publishes poetry. Sometimes comments on rejected mss.

How to Contact Accepts submissions by e-mail. Send for guidelines first. Send complete ms with a cover letter. Include estimated word count and bio. Responds in 6 months to mss. No simultaneous submissions. Sample copy for $5, 6×12 SAE with 5 first-class stamps. Writer's guidelines for #10 SASE.

Payment/Terms Awards $25 in prize money for first place fiction and poetry winners each issue; certificate for 2nd and 3rd place; 1 contributor's copy. Acquires first rights. Sponsors awards/contests.

Advice "Taproot is getting more fiction submissions and every one is read entirely. This takes time, so response can be delayed at busy times of year. Our contest is a good way to start publishing. Send for a sample copy and read it through. Ask for a critique and follow suggestions. Don't be offended by any suggestions—just take them or leave them and keep writing. Looks for a story that speaks in its unique voice, told in a well-crafted and complete, memorable style, a style of signature to the author. Follow writer's guidelines. Research markets. Send cover letter. Don't give up.''

◙ THE TEXAS REVIEW

Texas Review Press at Sam Houston State University, P.O. Box 2146, Huntsville TX 77341-2146. (936)294-1992. Fax: (936)294-3070 (inquiries only). E-mail: eng_pdr@shsu.edu. Website: www.shsu.edu/~www_trp/. **Contact:** Paul Ruffin, editor. Magazine: 6×9; 148-190 pages; best quality paper; 70 lb. cover stock; illustrations; photos. "We publish top quality poetry, fiction articles, interviews and reviews for a general audience." Semiannual. Estab. 1976. Circ. 1,200. A member of the Texas A&M University Press consortium.

- See our Insider Report with Editor Paul Ruffin on page 274.

Needs Humor/satire, literary, mainstream, contemporary fiction. "We are eager enough to consider fiction of quality, no matter what its theme or subject matter. No juvenile fiction." Receives 40-60 unsolicited mss/month. Accepts 4 mss/issue; 6 mss/year. Does not read mss May-September. Publishes ms 6-12 months after acceptance. **Publishes some new writers/year.** Recently published work by George Garrett, Ellen Gilchrist and Fred Chappell. Also publishes literary essays, literary criticism, poetry. Sometimes comments on rejected mss.

How to Contact Send complete ms. No mss accepted via fax. Send disposable copy of the ms and #10 SASE for reply only. Responds in 2 weeks to queries; 3-6 months to mss. Accepts multiple submissions. Sample copy for $5. Writer's guidelines for SASE and on the website.

Payment/Terms Pays contributor's copies and one year subscription. Pays on publication for first North American serial, one-time rights. Sends galleys to author.

Advice "Submit often; be aware that we reject 90% of submissions due to overwhelming number of mss sent.''

◙ ⛉ THIRD COAST

Dept. of English, Western Michigan University, Kalamazoo MI 49008-5331. (269)387-2675. Fax: (269)387-2562. Website: www.wmich.edu/thirdcoast. Glenn Deutsch, editor. **Contact:** Peta Geye and Sean Mintus, fiction editors. Magazine: 6×9; 176 pages. "We will consider many different types of fiction and favor that exhibiting a freshness of vision and approach." Twice-yearly. Estab. 1995. Circ. 2,875.

- *Third Coast* has received *Pushcart Prize* nominations. The section editors of this publication change with the university year.

Needs Literary. "While we don't want to see formulaic genre fiction, we will consider material that plays with or challenges generic forms." Receives 100 unsolicited mss/month. Accepts 6-8 mss/issue; 15 mss/year. Recently published work by Keith Banner, Peter Ho Davies, Moira Crone, Lee Martin, John McNally and Peter Orner. Also publishes literary essays, poetry. Sometimes comments on rejected mss.

How to Contact Send complete ms. Send SASE for reply. Responds in 4 months to mss. Accepts simultaneous submissions. Sample copy for $8. Writer's guidelines online.
Payment/Terms Pays 2 contributor's copies as well as a 1-year subscription to the publication; additional copies for $4. Acquires first North American serial rights.
Advice "We seek superior fiction from short-shorts to 30-page stories."

☑ THORNY LOCUST

TL Press, P.O. Box 32631, Kansas City MO 64171-5631. (816)501-4178. E-mail: editors@thornylocust.com. **Contact:** Silvia Kofler. Magazine: 32 pages; illustrations; photos. "*Thorny Locust* is a literary journal produced in a dusty corner of the publisher's hermitage. We are interested in poetry, fiction and artwork with some 'bite'- e.g., satire, epigrams, well-structured tirades, black humor, and bleeding heart cynicism. Absolutely no natural or artificial sweeteners, unless they're the sugar-coating on a strychnine tablet. We are not interested in polemics, gratuitous grotesques, somber surrealism, weeping melancholy, or hate-mongering. To rewrite Jack Conroy, 'We prefer polished vigor to crude banality.'" Estab. 1993. Circ. 200.
Needs Ethnic/multicultural (general), experimental, humor/satire, literary. Receives 30-40 unsolicited mss/month. Accepts 1 mss/issue; 2-3 mss/year. Publishes ms 3-5 months after acceptance. Length: 250-1,500 words; average length: 1,500 words. Publishes short shorts. Also publishes poetry. Rarely comments on rejected mss.
How to Contact Send complete ms with a cover letter. Include brief bio. Send SASE (or IRC) for return of ms or send a disposable copy of ms and #10 SASE for reply only. Responds in 3 months to queries. No simultaneous submissions. Sample copy for $4. Writer's guidelines for SASE or by e-mail.
Payment/Terms Pays 1 contributor's copy. Acquires one-time rights.
Advice "We look for work that is witty and original. Edit your work carefully."

$ ☑ ☒ THE THREEPENNY REVIEW

P.O. Box 9131, Berkeley CA 94709. (510)849-4545. Website: www.threepennyreview.com. **Contact:** Wendy Lesser, editor. Tabloid: 10×17; 40 pages; Electrobrite paper; white book cover; illustrations. "We are a general interest, national literary magazine with coverage of politics, the visual arts, and the performing arts as well." Quarterly. Estab. 1980. Circ. 9,000.
- *The Threepenny Review* has received GE Writers Awards, CLMP Editor's Awards, NEA grants, Lila Wallace grants and inclusion of work in the *Pushcart Prize Anthology*.

Needs Literary. No fragmentary, sentimental fiction. Receives 300-400 unsolicited mss/month. Accepts 3 mss/issue; 12 mss/year. Does *not* read mss June through December. Publishes ms 1 year after acceptance. Agented fiction 5%. Recently published work by Sigrid Nunez, Dagoberto Gilb, Deborah Eisenberg and Tim Winston. Publishes short shorts. Also publishes literary essays, literary criticism, poetry.
How to Contact Send complete ms. Send SASE for reply, return of ms or send a disposable copy of the ms. Responds in 1 month to queries; 2 months to mss. No simultaneous submissions. Sample copy for $12 or online. Writer's guidelines online. Reviews fiction.
Payment/Terms Pays $400 per story and $200 per poem or Table Talk piece. Pays on acceptance for first North American serial rights. Sends galleys to author.

☒ ☐ TICKLED BY THUNDER, Helping Writers Get Published Since 1990

Tickled By Thunder Publishing Co., 14076 86A Ave., Surrey BC V3W 0V9 Canada. (604)591-6095. E-mail: info@tickledbythunder.com. Website: www.tickledbythunder.com. **Contact:** Larry Lindner, publisher. Magazine: digest-sized; 24 pages; bond paper; bond cover stock; illustrations; photos. "*Tickled By Thunder* is designed to encourage beginning writers of fiction, poetry and nonfiction." Quarterly. Estab. 1990. Circ. 1,000.
Needs Fantasy, humor/satire, literary, mainstream, mystery/suspense, science fiction, western. "No overly indulgent horror, sex, profanity or religious material." Receives 25 unsolicited mss/month. Accepts 3 mss/issue; 12 mss/year. Publishes ms 3-9 months after acceptance. **Publishes 10 new writers/year.** Recently published work by Rick Cook and Jerry Shane. Length: 2,000 words; average length: 1,500 words. Also publishes literary essays, literary criticism, poetry.
How to Contact Send complete ms. Include estimated word count and brief bio. Send SASE or IRC for return of ms; or send disposable copy of ms and #10 SASE for reply only. No e-mail submissions. Responds in 3 months to queries; 6 months to mss. Accepts simultaneous and reprints, multiple submissions. $2.50. Writer's guidelines online.
Payment/Terms Pays on publication for first, second serial (reprint) rights.
Advice "Make your characters breathe on their own. Use description with action."

$ ☑ TIMBER CREEK REVIEW

8969 UNCG Station, Greensboro NC 27413. E-mail: timber_creek_review@hoopsmail.com. **Contact:** John M. Freiermuth, editor. Newsletter: $5^{1}/_{2} \times 8^{1}/_{2}$; 80-88 pages; computer generated on copy paper; saddle-stapled with

Literary Magazines

Paul Ruffin

Keeping literary work alive at
The Texas Review

Photo courtesy of author

Literary Magazines

Paul Ruffin, general editor of the semiannual journal *The Texas Review* and The Texas Review Press, can tell you running both is extremely time-consuming. "I don't have a whole lot of time for my own writing," he says. "I teach a six-hour load, edit the review and direct the press. That just doesn't leave much time for personal projects, though over the past ten years I have managed an average of a book a year, but I don't know how long that can continue." To date, he's still keeping at it. Ruffin's novel, *Castle in the Gloom* (University Press of Mississippi), was published in 2004, and a latest book, *Here's to Noah, Bless His Ark* (Stone River Press), hit shelves in Spring of 2005.

For Ruffin, the challenge is well worth it, for there is one belief he holds as the key mission of both magazine and press: "There will *always* be a market for literary work, but that market is so small commercial presses will continue to shun it. This is where private and university presses play their greatest role: We will keep literary work alive in this country."

Doing so means ferreting out the best work *The Texas Review* staff can find from its huge slush pile. Like most literary magazines, the editors can only accept a small percentage of what they receive—1 to 2 percent of the 40 to 60 unsolicited submissions a month. To assure the highest quality, editorial decisions depend on "a network of readers, perhaps a dozen or so at any given time," Ruffin says. And it's an impressive staff. Those who winnow the stacks down include former winners of the Texas Review Press' annual contests for the George Garrett Fiction Prize and the Clay Reynolds Novella Prize, Ruffin's fellow authors and Sam Houston State University English Department colleagues, and Ruffin himself. From what remains of the slush pile, Ruffin redeems pieces for the "Finalists Box." Only a dozen stories from this box will be forwarded on to the fiction editor, George Garrett, with the top three or four stories actually making it into the magazine. "If George thinks five or six of them should be published, then I hold the next two or three over for the next issue. George always writes insightful notes to accompany these stories, and we usually send along his suggestions with rejected stories, hoping his suggestions will be of some benefit to the writer."

With such incredibly stiff competition, one might wonder if *The Texas Review* publishes the work of any new writers or if proven authors are the only ones whose words grace its pages. The fact is, like most literary magazines, *The Texas Review* is quite open to new, cutting-edge work. "We always have an eye out for talent. One thing that George Garrett and I do every chance we get is run a 'discovery story' in the journal from a writer who has never published fiction before. We average at least one a year."

If writers wish to beat the odds, Ruffin urges them to give great care to revision. Some writers hesitate to do much tinkering with their work beyond a certain point because they are concerned the original energy of the piece could be lost when the analytical mode takes over. But Ruffin believes otherwise. "It is nearly impossible to over-revise. It is a matter of finer and finer tuning until a story is about as perfect as it is likely to get." And in his own writing, he practices what he preaches: "I will sometimes go through 20 or 30 revisions of a story before I print it out the first time. When it is accepted by a journal, I may still revise until it actually goes to print. I will revise it again before it goes into an anthology or a collection of my stories. Even then, years later, I'll see little things that need addressing."

Assuming considerable attention has been given to craft, writers need to be aware, says Ruffin, of a couple of "terribly important" details when submitting their work: "One, make certain your manuscript looks good (good, clean copy, with name, address, e-mail address on the title page, and adequate margins); and two, be persistent and get a returned manuscript out again before it has even cooled off from the postman's hand."

Like most literary magazines, *The Texas Review* has a small circulation but still obtains "the very best" exposure for writers' work. "For one thing, libraries represent by far the bulk of our subscription base, so these writers end up being read by perhaps dozens of people in any number of libraries. More importantly, though, a lot of journals go to literary agents." Ruffin can't say exactly how many writers have found agents based on their work in *The Texas Review*, but he does have one memorable success story to offer—that of Tom Franklin, whose story "Poachers" was published in 1999 in *The Texas Review*.

"I heard Tom read from it at a conference and invited him to send the story to me. It was pretty long, but it was so damn good that I devoted a good portion of my fiction allotment that issue to the story," says Ruffin. "Agent Nat Sobel read the story, loved it and started showing it around in New York. Morrow expressed a real interest in the story, so Nat got in touch with Tom and had him put some more stories with 'Poachers' (which was novella length and took almost half the book), and then he parlayed that into a nice advance for Tom for the book of stories and the idea for a novel, *Hell at the Breach*, which ran red-hot on the book scene."

"Poachers" went on to win an Edgar Allen Poe Award in 1999 for Best Short Story. The eponymous collection was named a Distinguished First Book of Fiction by *Esquire* and a #1 Book Sense Pick by the independent booksellers of America. "Now, doubtless a writer of Tom's talent would have been a success anyway, but *The Texas Review* actually helped launch his literary career. Somebody had to—I'm just glad it was our good fortune to do it," says Ruffin. "As James Dickey said, 'Almost all of us begin right there, in the literary journals.' "

What is the key to getting one's work in *The Texas Review*, or even winning one of the fiction prizes in the annual contest? Here are some tips from Paul Ruffin on creating fiction that makes its mark.

No part of any story is more important than the opening scene. With the sheer number of unsolicited submissions the magazine receives, it is vital, says Ruffin, to "hook them with the opening scene" unless you want your story "on a fast freight back to you." A sluggish start? You might not get read past page one. "The best advice I can give any fiction writer is to work like hell on that opening scene—make it the best you can. And put a lot of effort into the conclusion, too. I sometimes read the opening scene and concluding scene. If either fails to please me, I'm not likely to read the whole thing."

Anyone who can write good dialogue can write a good story. Ruffin takes it a couple

Literary Magazines

steps further: "Good dialogue can redeem an otherwise insipid story. It's that simple."

Write fiction with good imagistic texture. This involves one's ability to create vivid word pictures with details that place the reader in a world of the five senses. Readers don't want to be distanced from characters and events. "Imagistic texture" pulls them right in. "This is my term for the presentation of story in such a way that the reader sees the story and doesn't simply hear it being told. All fiction is show-and-tell, but the best stories show more than tell."

Nothing beats the well-told story. Here's the bottom line at *The Texas Review*: "We really don't have any expectations, so far as style, tone, theme, subject matter, characters and setting go." For Ruffin, if the story has an "enticing opening scene, by far the most important part of any story," it's out of the gate with a great start. Then, it's a matter of good character development, convincing dialogue—and "an emphatic conclusion."

What about editorial tastes that are likely to vary, editor to editor—in the first-cut process, at least? It's true, Ruffin admits, one first-cut reader "might simply hate experimental forms," while another "might be bone-weary of traditional stories." But he does his best to choose readers who are "wide open" in their tastes. His watchwords: "good stories, period."

—*Jack Smith*

40 lb. colored paper cover; some illustrations. "Fiction, humor/satire, poetry and travel for a general audience." Quarterly. Estab. 1992. Circ. 140-160.

Needs Adventure, ethnic/multicultural, feminist, historical, humor/satire, literary, mainstream, mystery/suspense, regional, western, literary nonfiction. "No religious, children's, gay, modern romance, and no reprints please!" Receives 50 unsolicited mss/month. Accepts 30-40 mss/year. Publishes ms 2-6 months after acceptance. **Publishes 0-3 new writers/year.** Recently published work by Ben E. Campbell, Michelle Boyajian, Chris Waters, Gary Fincke, Steven J. McDermott and Kenneth W. Meyer.

How to Contact Cover letter required. Accepts simultaneous submissions. Sample copy for $4.75, subscription $16.

Payment/Terms Pays $10-35, plus subscription. Acquires first North American serial rights. Not copyrighted.

Advice "Stop watching TV and read that literary magazine where your last manuscript appeared. There are no automatons here, so don't treat us like machines. We may not recognize your name at the top of the manuscript. Include a statement that the mss have previously not been published on paper or on the Internet, nor have they been accepted by others. A few lines about yourself breaks the ice, the names of three or four magazines that have published you in the last year or two would show your reality, and a bio blurb of 27 words including the names of 2 or 3 of the magazines you send the occasional subscription check (where you aspire to be?) could help. If you are not sending a check to some little magazine that is supported by subscriptions and the blood, sweat and tears of the editors, why would you send your manuscript to any of them and expect to receive a warm welcome? No requirement to subscribe or buy a sample, but they're available and are encouraged. There are no phony contests and never a reading fee. We read all year long, but may take 1 to 6 months to respond."

☑ TOUCHSTONE LITERARY JOURNAL

P.O. Box 130233, Spring TX 77393-0233. E-mail: panthercreek3@hotmail.com. **Contact:** Julia Gomez-Rivas, fiction editor. Magazine: 5½×8½; 56 pages; linen paper; coated stock cover; perfect bound; b&w illustrations; occasional photos. "We publish literary and mainstream fiction but enjoy experimental and multicultural work as well. Our audience is middle-class, heavily academic. We are eclectic and given to whims—i.e., two years ago we devoted a 104-page issue to West African women writers." Annual. Estab. 1976. Circ. 1,000.

Needs Humor/satire, literary, translations. "No erotica, religious, juvenile, stories written in creative writing programs that all sound alike." List of upcoming themes available for SASE. Receives 20-30 unsolicited mss/month. Accepts 3-4 mss/issue. Publishes ms "within the year" after acceptance. Recently published work by Ann Alejandro, Lynn Bradley, Roy Fish and Julia Mercedes Castilla. Length: 250-5,000 words; average length: 2,500 words. Publishes short shorts. Also publishes literary essays, literary criticism, poetry.

How to Contact Send complete ms. Include estimated word count and three-sentence bio. Send SASE for return of ms. Responds in 6 weeks to mss. Accepts multiple submissions. Sample copy not available. Writer's guidelines for #10 SASE.

Payment/Terms Pays 2 contributor's copies. Acquires one-time rights. Sends galleys to author.

Advice "We like to see fiction that doesn't read as if it had been composed in a creative writing class. If you can entertain, edify or touch the reader, polish your story and send it in. Don't worry if it doesn't read like our other fiction.''

◨ ◎ ◪ TRANSITION, An International Review

69 Dunster St., Cambridge MA 02138. (617)496-2845. Fax: (617)496-2877. E-mail: transition@fas.harvard.edu. Website: www.transitionmagazine.com. **Contact:** Michael Vazquez, executive editor. Magazine: $9^1/_2 \times 6^1/_2$; 150-175 pages; 70 lb. Finch Opaque paper; 100 lb. White Warren Lustro dull cover; illustrations; photos. ''*Transition* magazine is a quarterly international review known for compelling and controversial writing on race, ethnicity, culture and politics. This prestigious magazine is edited at Harvard University, and editorial board members include such heavy-hitters as Toni Morrison, Jamaica Kincaid and bell hooks. The magazine also attracts famous contributors such as Spike Lee, Philip Gourevitch and Carolos Fuentes.'' Quarterly. Estab. 1961. Circ. 3,500.

- Four-time winner fo the Alternative Press Award for international reporting, (2001, 2000, 1999, 1995); finalist in the 2001 National Magazine Award in General Excellence category.

Needs Ethnic/multicultural, historical, humor/satire, literary, regional (African diaspora, Third World, etc.). Receives 40 unsolicited mss/month. Accepts 1-2 mss/year. Publishes ms 3-4 months after acceptance. Agented fiction 30-40%. **Publishes 5 new writers/year.** Recently published work by George Makana Clark, Paul Beatty and Victor D. LaValle. Length: 4,000-8,000 words; average length: 7,000 words. Also publishes literary essays, literary criticism. Sometimes comments on rejected mss.

How to Contact Query with published clips or send complete ms. Include brief bio and list of publications. Send disposable copy of ms and #10 SASE for reply only. Responds in 2 months to queries; 4 months to mss. Accepts simultaneous submissions. Sample copy not available. Writer's guidelines for #10 SASE.

Payment/Terms 3 contributor's copies. Sends galleys to author.

Advice ''We look for a non-white, alternative perspective, dealing with issues of race, ethnicity and identity in an upredictable, provocative way.''

◨ ◪ TRIQUARTERLY

629 Noyes St., Northwestern University, Evanston IL 60208-4170. (847)491-7614. Fax: (847)467-2096. Website: www.triquarterly.org. **Contact:** Susan Firestone Hahn, editor. Magazine: $6 \times 9^1/_4$; 240-272 pages; 60 lb. paper; heavy cover stock; illustration; photos. ''A general literary quarterly. We publish short stories, novellas or excerpts from novels, by American and foreign writers. Genre or style is not a primary consideration. We aim for the general but serious and sophisticated reader. Many of our readers are also writers.'' Triannual. Estab. 1964. Circ. 5,000.

- Stories from *Triquarterly* have been reprinted in *The Best American Short Stories*, *Pushcart Prizes* and *O. Henry Prize* Anthologies.

Needs Literary, translations, contemporary. ''No prejudices or preconceptions against anything *except* genre fiction (romance, science fiction, etc.).'' Receives 500 unsolicited mss/month. Accepts 10 mss/issue; 30 mss/year. Does not read or accept mss between April 1 and September 30. Publishes ms 1 year after acceptance. Agented fiction 10%. **Publishes 1-5 new writers/year.** Recently published work by John Barth, Chaim Potok, Joyce Carol Oates and Robert Girardi. Publishes short shorts.

How to Contact Send complete ms with SASE. Responds in 3 months to queries; 3 months to mss. No simultaneous submissions. Sample copy for $5. Writer's guidelines for #10 SASE.

Payment/Terms Payment varies depending on grant support. Pays on publication for first North American serial rights. Nonexclusive reprint rights. Sends galleys to author.

◨ UNBOUND

SUNY Potsdam Dept. of English and Communications, Morey Hall, SUNY Potsdam, Potsdam NY 13676. (315)267-2043. E-mail: unbound@potsdam.edu. Website: www2.potsdam.edu/henryrm/unbound.html. **Contact:** Rick Henry, editor. Magazine. ''*Unbound* seeks fiction that exceeds the page. We are interested in collage, avant-garde, experimental, new media, multi-media fiction that maintains a strong narrative thread.'' Annual. Estab. 2002.

Needs Experimental. ''No genre fiction.'' Publishes short shorts.

How to Contact Send complete ms. Include brief bio. Send SASE for return of ms or send a disposable copy of ms and #10 SASE for reply only. Responds in 2 months to queries; 10 weeks to mss. Accepts simultaneous submissions. Sample copy not available. Writer's guidelines by e-mail.

Payment/Terms Pays 1 contributor copy. Pays on publication for first North American serial rights.

Advice ''We look for an intelligent relationship between a fiction's form and content. Fiction need not be limited by the borders of $8^1/_2 \times 11$ sheets of paper.''

THE UNKNOWN WRITER

P.O. Box 698, Ramsey NJ 07446. E-mail: unknown_writer_2000@yahoo.com. Website: www.fyreflyjar.net/uw.html. Magazine: 6×9; 40 pages, saddle-stitched; cardstock cover; illustrations; photos. ''Please note that we are on hiatus until further notice and will not be able to read the submissions that have come in. Authors who send submissions via our postal box will receive their work back if return envelopes were provided. We will not be able to reply to e-mail submissions. We do plan to print pieces we accepted before our hiatus, and we will contact those authors about their pieces when we can. Please check our website periodically for news and status updates. We thank you for your patience and understanding." Bi-annual. Estab. 1995.

⊘ UNMUZZLED OX

Unmuzzled Ox Foundation Ltd., 105 Hudson St., New York NY 10013. (212)226-7170. E-mail: mandreox@aol.com. **Contact:** Michael Andre, editor. Magazine: 5½×8½. "Magazine about life of an intelligent audience." Irregular frequency. Estab. 1971. Circ. 7,000.

- Recent issues of this magazine have included art, poetry and essays only. Check before sending submissions.

Needs Literary, mainstream, translations, prose poetry. "No commercial fiction." Receives 20-25 unsolicited mss/month. Also publishes poetry. Sometimes comments on rejected mss.

How to Contact "Please no phone calls and no e-mail submissions. Correspondence by *mail* only. Cover letter is significant." Responds in 1 month to queries; 1 month to mss. Sample copy not available.

Payment/Terms Pays in contributor's copies.

Advice "You may want to check out a copy of the magazine before you submit."

$⊘ ⊻ VESTAL REVIEW, A flash fiction magazine

2609 Dartmouth Dr., Vestal NY 13850. E-mail: submissions@vestalreview.net. Website: www.vestalreview.net. **Contact:** Mark Budman, publisher/editor. Magazine: 8½×5½; 22 pages; heavy cover stock; illustrations. "*Vestal Review* is the magazine specializing in flash fiction (stories under 500 words). We accept only e-mail submissions." Quarterly. Circ. 1,500.

- Vestal Review received a Golden Web Award in 2002-2003.

Needs Ethnic/multicultural, horror, literary, mainstream, speculative fiction. Receives 60-100 unsolicited mss/month. Accepts 7-8 mss/issue; 28-32 mss/year. Does not read mss March, June, September and December. Publishes ms 2-3 months after acceptance. **Publishes 2-3 new writers/year.** Recently published work by Kir Nesset, Judith Cofer, Bruce Boston, Robert Boswell and Bruce Holland Rogers. Publishes short shorts. Sometimes comments on rejected mss.

How to Contact Send complete ms with a cover letter via e-mail only. Include estimated word count, brief bio and list of publications. Responds in 1 week to queries; 2 months to mss. Accepts simultaneous, multiple submissions. Sample copy for $5. Writer's guidelines online.

Payment/Terms Pays $0.03-0.1/word and 1 contributor's copy; additional copies $5. Pays on publication for first North American serial, electronic rights. Sends galleys to author.

Advice "We like literary fiction, with a plot, that doesn't waste words. Don't send jokes masked as stories."

⊘ WHISKEY ISLAND MAGAZINE

Dept. of English, Cleveland State University, Cleveland OH 44115-2440. (216)687-2056. Fax: (216)687-6943. E-mail: whiskeyisland@csuohio.edu. Website: www.csuohio.edu/whiskey_island. Editors change each year. Magazine of fiction and poetry. "We provide a forum for new writers and new work, for themes and points of view that are both meaningful and experimental, accessible and extreme." Semiannual. Estab. 1978. Circ. 2,500.

Needs "Would like to see more short shorts, flash fiction." Receives 100 unsolicited mss/month. Accepts 46 mss/issue. **Publishes 5-10 new writers/year.** Recently published work by Nin Andrews, Reginald Gibbons, Jim Daniels and Allison Luterman. Also publishes poetry.

How to Contact Send complete ms. Accepts submissions by e-mail. Responds in 4 months to queries; 4 months to mss. Sample copy for $6.

Payment/Terms Pays 2 contributor copies and one-year subscription. Acquires one-time rights. Sponsors awards/contests.

Advice "We read manuscripts year round. We seek engaging writing of any style."

Ⓝ ⊘ THE WILLIAM AND MARY REVIEW

The College of William and Mary, P.O. Box 8795, Williamsburg VA 23187. (757)221-3290. E-mail: review@wm.edu. Website: www.wm.edu/so/wmreview. **Contact:** Justin Fowler, prose editor. Magazine: 6×9; 96 pages; coated paper; 4-color card cover; photos. "We encourage good fiction and nonfiction that can be literary, though we are bound by tradition. Genre stories are acceptable only if the work transcends the genre. Our journal is read by a sophisticated audience of subscribers, professors and university students. Annual. Estab. 1962. Circ. 3,500.

Needs Experimental, family saga, historical, horror (psychological), humor/satire, literary, mainstream, science fiction, thriller/espionage, translations. "We do not want to see typical genre pieces. Do not bother sending fantasy or erotica." Receives 15 unsolicited mss/month. Accepts 6-8 mss/year. Does not read mss from March to August. Publishes ms 1-2 months after acceptance. **Publishes 1-2 new writers/year.** Length: 250-7,000 words; average length: 3,500 words. Publishes short shorts. Also publishes literary essays, poetry. Rarely comments on rejected mss.

How to Contact Send complete ms. Send SASE (or IRC) for return of the mss or send disposable copy of the ms and #10 SASE for reply only. Responds in 5-6 months to queries. Accepts simultaneous, multiple submissions. Sample copy for $5.50.

Payment/Terms Pays 5 contributor's copies; additional copies $5. Pays on publication for first North American serial rights.

Advice "We do not give much weight to prior publications; each piece is judged on its own merit. New writers should be bold and unafraid to submit unorthodox works that depart from textbook literary tradition."

ℕ ◑ WILLARD & MAPLE, The Literary Magazine of Champlain College

163 South Willard Street, Freeman 302, Box 34, Burlington VT 05401. (802)860-2700 ext.2462. E-mail: willardan dmaple@champlain.edu. **Contact:** Fiction editor. Magazine: perfect bound; 125 pages; illustrations; photos. "*Willard & Maple* is a student-run literary magazine from Champlain College that publishes a wide array of poems, short stories, creative essays, short plays, pen and ink drawings, black and white photos, and computer graphics. We now accept color." Annual. Estab. 1996.

Needs We accept all types of mss. Receives 20 unsolicited mss/month. Accepts 5 mss/year. Does not read mss September 1-March 31. Publishes ms within 1 year after acceptance. **Publishes 10 new writers/year.** Recently published work by Shannon Sevakian, Bill Mosler, Sandy Johnson, Bill Trippe and David Jacobs. Length: 5,000 words; average length: 2,500 words. Publishes short shorts. Also publishes literary essays, poetry. Sometimes comments on rejected mss.

How to Contact Send complete ms. Send SASE for return of ms or send disposable copy of mss and #10 SASE for reply only. Responds in 2 months to queries; 2 months to mss. Accepts simultaneous, multiple submissions. Sample copy for $8.50. Writer's guidelines for SASE or send e-mail. Reviews fiction.

Payment/Terms Pays 2 contributor's copies; additional copies $8.50. Pays on publication for one-time rights.

Advice "Work hard; be good; never surrender!"

ℕ ◯ WINDHOVER, A Journal of Christian Literature

University of Mary Hardin-Baylor, P.O. Box 8008, 900 College St., Belton TX 76513. (254)295-4561. E-mail: windhover@umhb.edu. **Contact:** D. Audell Shelburne, editor. Magazine: 6×9; white bond paper. "We accept poetry, short fiction, nonfiction, creative nonfiction. *Windhover* is devoted to promoting writers and literature with a Christian perspective and with a broad definition of that perspective." Annual. Estab. 1997. Circ. 500.

Needs Ethnic/multicultural, experimental, fantasy, historical, humor/satire, literary. No erotica. Receives 30 unsolicited mss/month. Accepts 5 mss/issue; 5 mss/year. Publishes ms 1 year after acceptance. **Publishes 5 new writers/year.** Recently published work by Walt McDonald, Cleatus Rattan, Greg Garrett and Barbara Crooker. Length: 1,500-4,000 words; average length: 3,000 words. Publishes short shorts. Also publishes literary essays, poetry. Sometimes comments on rejected mss.

How to Contact Send complete ms. Estimated word count, brief bio and list of publications. Include SASE postcard for acknowledgement. No submissions by e-mail. Responds in 4-6 weeks to queries; 4-6 months to mss. Accepts simultaneous submissions. Sample copy for $10. Writer's guidelines by e-mail.

Payment/Terms Pays 2 contributor copies. Pays on publication for first rights.

Advice "Be patient. We have an editorial board and sometimes take longer than I like. We particularly look for convincing plot and character development."

◑ ⚑ WISCONSIN REVIEW

University of Wisconsin-Oshkosh, 800 Algoma Blvd., Oshkosh WI 54902. (920)424-2267. E-mail: wireview@yah oo.com. Website: http://www.english.uwosh.edu/review.html. **Contact:** Andrew Osborne, senior editor. Magazine: 6×9; 60-100 pages; illustrations. "We seek literary prose and poetry. The publication is for an adult contemporary audience. Fiction including fantastic imagery and fresh voices is published. We seek to publish quality, not quantity." Triannual. Estab. 1966. Circ. 2,000.

 • *Wisconsin Review* won the Pippistrelle Best of the Small Press Award #13.

Needs Experimental, literary. Receives 30 unsolicited mss/month. Publishes ms 1-3 months after acceptance. **Publishes 3 new writers/year.** Recently published work by Brian Ames, Wendy Herbert, John Addiego and Silas Zobel. Publishes short shorts.

How to Contact Send complete ms. Sample copy for $4.

Payment/Terms Pays 2 contributor copies. Acquires first rights.

Advice "We accept fiction that displays strong characterization, dialogue that provides pertinent information and transports the story, vivid imagery, and unique plots and themes."

◙ THE WORCESTER REVIEW

Worcester County Poetry Association, Inc., 1 Ekman St., Worcester MA 01607. (508)797-4770. Website: www.ge ocities.com/Paris/LeftBank/6433. **Contact:** Fiction Editor. Magazine: 6×9; 100 pages; 60 lb. white offset paper; 10 pt. CS1 cover stock; illustrations; photos. "We like high quality, creative poetry, artwork and fiction. Critical articles should be connected to New England." Annual. Estab. 1972. Circ. 1,000.

Needs Literary, prose poem. "We encourage New England writers in the hopes we will publish at least 30 percent New England but want the other 70 percent to show the best of writing from across the US." Receives 20-30 unsolicited mss/month. Accepts 2-4 mss/issue. Publishes ms 11 months after acceptance. Agented fiction less than 10%. Recently published work by Robert Pinsky, Marge Piercy, Wes McNair and Ed Hirsch. Length: 1,000-4,000 words; average length: 2,000 words. Publishes short shorts. Also publishes literary essays, literary criticism, poetry. Sometimes comments on rejected mss.

How to Contact Send complete ms. Responds in 9 months to mss. Accepts simultaneous submissions only if other markets are clearly identified. Sample copy for $6. Writer's guidelines free.

Payment/Terms Pays 2 contributor copies and honorarium if possible. Acquires one-time rights.

Advice "Send only one short story—reading editors do not like to read two by the same author at the same time. We will use only one. We generally look for creative work with a blend of craftsmanship, insight and empathy. This does not exclude humor. We won't print work that is shoddy in any of these areas."

◙ WORDS OF WISDOM

8969 UNCG Station, Greensboro NC 27413. E-mail: wowmail@hoopsmail.com. **Contact:** Mikhammad Abdel-Ishara, editor. Newsletter: 5½×8½; 76-88 pages; computer-generated on copy paper; saddle-stapled with 40 lb. colored paper cover; some illustrations. "Fiction, satire/humor, poetry and travel for a general audience." Estab. 1981. Circ. 150-160.

Needs Adventure, ethnic/multicultural, feminist, historical, humor/satire, literary, mainstream, mystery/suspense (private eye, cozy), regional, western, one-act plays. "No religious, children, gay or romance." Receives 50 unsolicited mss/month. Accepts 65-75 mss/year. Publishes ms 2-6 months after acceptance. **Publishes 0-5 new writers/year.** Recently published work by Nancy Swallow, Roger L. Collins, Tom Pacheco, Clara Stites, Andrea Vojtko and Robert McGuill. Length: 1,200-6,000 words; average length: 3,000 words.

How to Contact Send complete ms. Accepts submissions by U.S. mail only. Responds in 1-6 months to mss. Accepts simultaneous submissions. Sample copy for $4.50.

Payment/Terms Offers subscription to magazine for first story published. Acquires first North American serial rights. Not copyrighted.

Advice "A few lines about yourself in the cover letter breaks the ice, the names of three or four magazines that have published your work in the last year would show your reality, and a bio blurb of about 27 words including the names of two or three magazines you send your subscription money to would show your dreams. No requirements to subscribe or buy a sample, but they are available at $16 and $4.50 and would be appreciated. There are no phony contests and never a reading fee. We read all year long, but it may take one to six months to respond."

$◙ THE WRITERS POST JOURNAL

Let's Be 'Frank', P.O. Box 7989, Pittsburgh PA 15216. (412)207-9120. E-mail: submissions@lbfbooks.com. Website: http://www.lbfbooks.com. Magazine: 8½×11; 70 pages; 100 bond cover stock; illustrations; photos. Monthly. Estab. 2004.

Needs Adventure, ethnic/multicultural, family saga, horror, humor/satire, literary, mainstream, military/war, mystery/suspense (cozy), religious/inspirational, romance (contemporary), science fiction (soft/sociological), thriller/espionage, young adult/teen. No pornography. Receives 200 unsolicited mss/month. Accepts 24 mss/issue; 250-300 mss/year. Publishes ms 3-6 months after acceptance. Agented fiction 5%. **Publishes 90 new writers/year.** Length: 1-2,000 words; average length: 1,500 words. Publishes short shorts. Also publishes literary essays, poetry. Often comments on rejected mss.

How to Contact Query. Accepts submissions by e-mail. Send SASE (or IRC) for return of the ms. Responds in 4-8 weeks to queries; 2-3 months to mss. Accepts simultaneous and reprints, multiple submissions. Sample copy free. Writer's guidelines online or by e-mail.

Payment/Terms Pays $5-25. Pays on publication for one-time rights.

Advice "We encourage new and unpublished authors. Be patient. Don't give up."

◙ XAVIER REVIEW

Xavier University, 1 Drexel Dr., New Orleans LA 70125-1098. (504)485-7944. Fax: (504)485-7197. E-mail: rcollin s@xula.edu (correspondence only—no mss). **Contact:** Richard Collins, editor. Mark Whitaker, associate editor.

Magazine: 6×9; 75 pages; 50 lb. paper; 12 pt. CS1 cover; photographs. Magazine of "poetry/fiction/nonfiction/ reviews (contemporary literature) for professional writers, libraries, colleges and universities. Semiannual. Estab. 1980. Circ. 500.

Needs Ethnic/multicultural, experimental, historical, literary, mainstream, regional (Southern, Latin American), religious/inspirational, serialized novels, translations. Receives 100 unsolicited mss/month. Accepts 2 mss/issue; 4 mss/year. **Publishes 2-3 new writers/year.** Recently published work by Andrei Codrescu, Terrance Hayes, Naton Leslie, Alvin Aubert. Also publishes literary essays, literary criticism. Occasionally comments on rejected mss.

How to Contact Send complete ms. Include 2-3 sentence bio. Sample copy for $5.

Payment/Terms 2 contributor copies.

$☑ XCONNECT

P.O. Box 2317, Philadelphia PA 19103. (215)898-5324. Fax: (215)898-9348. E-mail: editors@xconnect.org. Website: www.xconnect.org. **Contact:** David Deifer. Journal: 5½×8½; trade paper; 200 pages. "*Xconnect* publishes on the World Wide Web and annually in print, with the best of our Web issues. *Xconnect: writers of the information age* is a nationally distributed, full color, journal sized book."

Needs Experimental, literary. "Our mission—like our name—is one of connection. *Xconnect* seeks to promote and document the emergent creative artists as well as established artists who have made the transition to the new technologies of the Information Age." **Publishes 25 new writers/year.** Recently published work by Russell Banks, John Edgar Wideman and David Jauss. Rarely comments on rejected mss.

How to Contact Accepts simultaneous and reprints submissions. Sample copy not available.

Payment/Terms Pays 1 contributor's copy and $150-250 for stories used in print. Author retains all rights. Regularly sends prepublication galleys.

Advice "Persistence."

☑ THE YALOBUSHA REVIEW, The Literary Journal of the University of Mississippi

Dept. of English, P.O. Box 1848, University MS 38677. (662)915-3175. Fax: (662)915-7419. E-mail: yalobusha@o lemiss.edu. Magazine: 5×10; 125 pages; illustrations; photos. Annual. Estab. 1995. Circ. 1,000.

Needs Experimental, family saga, historical, humor/satire, literary, mainstream, genre. Receives 100 unsolicited mss/month. Accepts 6-8 mss/issue. Reading period: July 15-November 15. Publishes ms 6 months after acceptance. **Publishes 3-4 new writers/year.** Recently published work by Steve Almond, Shay Youngblood and Dan Chaon. Length: 1,000-5,000 words; average length: 4,000 words. Publishes short shorts. Also publishes poetry.

How to Contact Send complete ms. Include a brief bio. Send disposable copy of ms and #10 SASE for reply only. Responds in 3 months to mss. Sample copy for $5. Writer's guidelines for #10 SASE.

Payment/Terms Pays 2 contributor's copies. Acquires first North American serial rights.

Advice "We look for writers with a strong, distinct voice and good stories to tell. Thrill us."

Ⓝ ☑ Ⓨ YEMASSEE, The literary journal of the University of South Carolina

Department of English, University of South Carolina, Columbia SC 29208. (803)777-2085. Fax: (803)777-9064. E-mail: yemassee@gwm.sc.edu. Website: www.cas.sc.edu/ENGL/yemassee. **Contact:** Dawson Jones and Stacey Kikendall, editors. Magazine: 5½×8½; 70-90 pages; 60 lb. natural paper; 65 lb. cover; cover illustration. "We are open to a variety of subjects and writing styles. We publish primarily fiction and poetry, but we are also interested in one-act plays, brief excerpts of novels, and interviews with literary figures. Our essential consideration for acceptance is the quality of the work." Semiannual. Estab. 1993. Circ. 500.

• Stories from *Yemassee* have been selected for publication in *Best New Stories from the South*.

Needs Condensed novels, ethnic/multicultural, experimental, feminist, gay, historical, humor/satire, lesbian, literary, regional. "No romance, religious/inspirational, young adult/teen, children's/juvenile, erotica. Wants more experimental work." Receives 30 unsolicited mss/month. Accepts 1-3 mss/issue; 2-6 mss/year. "We read from August-May and hold ms over to the next year if they arrive in the summer." **Publishes 6 new writers/ year.** Recently published work by Robert Coover, Chris Railey, Virgil Suarez, Susan Ludvigson and Kwame Dawes. Publishes short shorts. Also publishes literary essays, poetry.

How to Contact Send complete ms. Include estimated word count, brief bio, and list of publications. Send SASE for reply, return of ms, or send disposable copy of ms. Responds in 2 weeks to queries; 4 months to mss. Accepts simultaneous submissions. Sample copy for $5. Writer's guidelines for #10 SASE.

Payment/Terms Acquires first rights.

Advice "Our criteria are based on what we perceive as quality. Generally that is work that is literary. We are interested in subtlety and originality, interesting or beautiful language, craft and precision. Read our journal and any other journal before you submit to see if your work seems appropriate. Send for guidelines and make sure you follow them."

$ ZOETROPE: ALL STORY

AZX Publications, The Sentinel Bldg., 916 Kearny St., San Francisco CA 94133. (415)788-7500. Website: www.all-story.com. **Contact:** Michael Ray, editor. Magazine specializing in the best of contemporary short fiction. "*Zoetrope: All Story* presents a new generation of classic stories." Quarterly. Estab. 1997. Circ. 20,000.

Needs Literary short stories, one-act plays. Accepts 25-35 mss/year. Publishes ms 5 months after acceptance.

How to Contact Send complete ms. Responds in 5 months (if SASE included) to mss. Accepts simultaneous submissions. Sample copy for $6.95. Writer's guidelines online.

Payment/Terms Pays $1,000. Acquires First serial rights.

$ ◎ ZYZZYVA, The Last Word: West Coast Writers & Artists

P.O. Box 590069, San Francisco CA 94159-0069. (415)752-4393. Fax: (415)752-4391. E-mail: editor@zyzzyva.org. Website: www.zyzzyva.org. **Contact:** Howard Junker, editor. "We feature work by writers currently living on the West Coast or in Alaska and Hawaii only. We are essentially a literary magazine, but of wide-ranging interests and a strong commitment to nonfiction." Estab. 1985. Circ. 3,500.

Needs Ethnic/multicultural, experimental, humor/satire, mainstream. Receives 300 unsolicited mss/month. Accepts 10 mss/issue; 30 mss/year. Publishes ms 3 months after acceptance. Agented fiction 5%. **Publishes 15 new writers/year.** Recently published work by Catherine Brady, Kate Braverman and Aimee Bender. Publishes short shorts. Also publishes literary essays, poetry.

How to Contact Send complete ms. Responds in 1 week to queries; 1 month to mss. Sample copy for $7 or online. Writer's guidelines online.

Payment/Terms Pays $50. Pays on acceptance. First North American serial and one-time anthology rights.

Small Circulation Magazines

This section of *Novel & Short Story Writer's Market* contains general interest, special interest, regional and genre magazines with circulations under 10,000. Although these magazines vary greatly in size, theme, format and management, the editors are all looking for short stories. Their specific fiction needs present writers of all degrees of expertise and interests with an abundance of publishing opportunities.

Although not as high-paying as the large-circulation consumer magazines, you'll find some of the publications listed here do pay writers 1-5¢/word or more. Also, unlike the big consumer magazines, these markets are very open to new writers and relatively easy to break into. Their only criteria is that your story be well written, well presented and suitable for their particular readership.

In this section you will also find listings for zines. Zines vary greatly in appearance as well as content. Some paper zines are photocopies published whenever the editor has material and money, while others feature offset printing and regular distribution schedules. A few have evolved into four-color, commercial-looking, very slick publications.

DIVERSITY IN OPPORTUNITY

Among the diverse publications in this section are magazines devoted to almost every topic, every level of writing, and every type of writer. Some of the markets listed here publish fiction about a particular geographic area or by authors who live in that locale.

SELECTING THE RIGHT MARKET

First, zero in on those markets most likely to be interested in your work. Begin by looking at the Category Index starting on page 581. If your work is more general—or conversely, very specialized—you may wish to browse through the listings, perhaps looking up those magazines published in your state or region. Also check the Online Markets section for other specialized and genre publications.

In addition to browsing through the listings and using the Category Index, check the openness icons at the beginning of listings to find those most likely to be receptive to your work. This is especially true for beginning writers, who should look for magazines that say they are especially open to new writers (❍) and for those giving equal weight to both new and established writers (◓). For more explanation about these icons, see the inside covers of this book.

Once you have a list of magazines you might like to try, read their listings carefully. Much of the material within each listing carries clues that tell you more about the magazine. You've Got a Story, starting on page 2, describes in detail the listing information common to all the markets in our book.

The physical description appearing near the beginning of the listings can give you clues about the size and financial commitment to the publication. This is not always an indication of quality, but chances are a publication with expensive paper and four-color artwork on the cover has more prestige than a photocopied publication featuring a clip-art cover. For more information on some of the paper, binding and printing terms used in these descriptions, see Printing and Production Terms Defined on page 551.

FURTHERING YOUR SEARCH

It cannot be stressed enough that reading the listing is only the first part of developing your marketing plan. The second part, equally important, is to obtain fiction guidelines and read the actual magazine. Reading copies of a magazine helps you determine the fine points of the magazine's publishing style and philosophy. There is no substitute for this type of hands-on research.

Unlike commercial magazines available at most newsstands and bookstores, it requires a little more effort to obtain some of the magazines listed here. You may need to send for a sample copy. We include sample copy prices in the listings whenever possible. See The Business of Fiction Writing on page 66 for the specific mechanics of manuscript submission. Above all, editors appreciate a professional presentation. Include a brief cover letter and send a self-addressed, stamped envelope for a reply. Be sure the envelope is large enough to accommodate your manuscript, if you would like it returned, and include enough stamps or International Reply Coupons (for replies from countries other than your own) to cover your manuscript's return. Many publishers today appreciate receiving a disposable manuscript, eliminating the cost to writers of return postage and saving editors the effort of repackaging manuscripts for return.

Most of the magazines listed here are published in the U.S. You will also find some English-speaking markets from around the world. These foreign publications are denoted with a 🌐 symbol at the beginning of listings. To make it easier to find Canadian markets, we include a 🍁 symbol at the start of those listings.

▨ ◎ 🌐 $ ALBEDO ONE, The Irish Magazine of Science Fiction, Fantasy and Horror
Albedo One, 2 Post Rd., Lusk, Co Dublin Ireland. (+353)1-8730177. E-mail: bobn@yellowbrickroad.ie. Website: homepage.tinet.ie/~goudriaan/. **Contact:** Editor, *Albedo One*. Magazine: A4; 44 pages. "We hope to publish interesting and unusual fiction by new and established writers. We will consider anything, as long as it is well written and entertaining, though our definitions of both may not be exactly mainstream. We like stories with plot and characters that live on the page. Most of our audience are probably committed genre fans, but we try to appeal to a broad spectrum of readers. The narrow focus of our readership is due to the public-at-large's unwillingness to experiment with their reading/magazine purchasing rather than any desire on our part to be exclusive." Triannual. Estab. 1993. Circ. 900.
Needs Comics/graphic novels, experimental, fantasy, horror, literary, science fiction. Receives more than 80 unsolicited mss/month. Accepts 15-18 mss/year. Publishes ms 1 year after acceptance. **Publishes 6-8 new writers/year.** Length: 2,000-5,000 words; average length: 4,000 words. Also publishes literary criticism. Sometimes comments on rejected mss.
How to Contact Responds in 4 months to mss. Sample copy not available. Guidelines available by e-mail or on website. Reviews fiction.
Payment/Terms Pays 100 Euro for best-in-issue story and 1 contributor's copy; additional copies $5 plus p&p. Pays on publication for first rights.
Advice "We look for good writing, good plot, good characters. Read the magazine, and don't give up."

Ⓝ ◯ ALEMBIC
Singularity Rising Press, P.O. Box 28416, Philadelphia PA 19149. E-mail: alembicmagazine@aol.com. **Contact:** Larry Farrell, editor. Magazine: 8½×11; 64 pages; bond paper; illustrations. "*Alembic* is a literary endeavor magically bordering intersecting continua." The magazine publishes poems, stories and art. Annual. Estab. 1999. Circ. 100.
Needs Fantasy (space fantasy, sword and sorcery), horror (dark fantasy, futuristic, psychological, supernatural), literary, mystery/suspense (amateur sleuth, cozy, police procedural, private eye/hard-boiled), science fiction (hard science/technological, soft/sociological), thriller/espionage. No children's, religious, romance. Would like to see more mystery. Receives 15 unsolicited mss/month. Accepts 6 mss/issue; 24 mss/year. Publishes ms

1-2 years after acceptance. **Publishes 15 new writers/year.** Recently published work by William S. Frankl and Bill Glose. Length: 1,000-5,000 words; average length: 3,000 words. Publishes short shorts. Also publishes poetry. Often comments on rejected mss.

How to Contact Sponosors contest. Send for guidelines. Responds in 9 months to mss. Accepts multiple submissions. Sample copy for $7.50. Guidelines for SASE or by e-mail. Reviews fiction.

Payment/Terms Pays 1 contributor's copy; additional copies $5. Pays on publication for first North American serial rights. Not copyrighted.

Advice "Fiction we publish has to grab me and make me care what will or won't happen to the characters. Write, rewrite and rewrite again. After all that, keep on submitting. A rejection never killed anyone."

$AMAZING JOURNEYS

Journey Books Publishing, 3205 Hwy. 431, Spring Hill TN 37174. (615)791-8006. Website: www.journeybooksp ublishing.com. "We are seeking the best in up-and-coming authors who produce great stories that appeal to a wide audience. Each issue will be packed with exciting, fresh material. *Amazing Journeys* will be a fun read, designed to stimulate the senses without offending them. With the introduction of *Amazing Journeys*, we intend to reintroduce the style of writing that made the Golden Age of science fiction "golden." If you are tired of 'shock culture' stories or stories written strictly to appeal to a commercial audience, then *Amazing Journeys* is the right magazine for you." Quarterly. Estab. 2003.

Needs Fantasy, science fiction. "Absolutely no sexual content will be accepted. Profanity is greatly restricted (none is preferred)." Publishes ms 6-12 months after acceptance.

How to Contact Send complete ms. Accepts submissions by e-mail. Responds in 1 week to queries; 2 months to mss. Sample copy for $4.99, plus 1 SAE with 3 First-Class stamps. Writer's guidelines for #10 SASE.

Payment/Terms Pays $10. Pays on acceptance for first North American serial rights.

$AMBITIONS MAGAZINE

P.O. Box 13486, St. Petersburg FL 33733. E-mail: ambitions@rembrandtandcompany.com. Website: http:// rembrandtandcompany.com. "*Ambitions* is a 10-page literary magazine photocopied at the local copy shop. Right now, *Ambitions* is growing and trying to reach everyone throughout America. This magazine is opening all doorways of free expression to bring out the artist within." Monthly. Estab. 2003. Circ. 100.

Needs Adventure, condensed novels, experimental, fantasy, historical, mystery/suspense, novel excerpts, science fiction, serialized novels, suspense. No pornography or anything offensive, no blood-shed stories, and nothing mainstream. Publishes ms 3 months after acceptance.

How to Contact Accepts submissions by e-mail (ambitionscoffee@hotmail.com). Responds in 3 weeks to mss. Accepts simultaneous submissions. Writer's guidelines by e-mail.

Payment/Terms Pays $4 and 1 contributor copy. Pays on publication for one-time rights.

ANY DREAM WILL DO REVIEW, Short Stories and Humor from the Secret Recesses of our Minds

Any Dream Will Do, Inc., 1830 Kirman Ave., C1, Reno NV 89502-3381. (775)786-0345. E-mail: cassjmb@iqe-mail.com. Website: www.willigocrazy.org/Ch08.htm. **Contact:** Dr. Jean M. Bradt, editor and publisher. Magazine: $5^{1}/_{2} \times 8^{1}/_{2}$; 52 pages; 20 lb. bond paper; 12pt. Carolina cover stock. "The 52-page *Any Dream Will Do Review* showcases a new literary genre, Psych-Inspirational Fiction, which attempts to fight the prejudice against consumers of mental-health services by touching hearts, that is, by exposing the consumers' deepest thoughts and emotions. In the *Review*'s stories, accomplished authors honestly reveal their most intimate secrets. See www.willigocrazy.org/Ch09a.htm for detailed instructions on how to write Psych-Inspirational Fiction." Annual. Estab. 2001. Circ. 200.

Needs Ethnic/multicultural, mainstream, psychic/supernatural/occult, romance (contemporary), science fiction (soft/sociological), Psych-Inspirational. No pornography, true life stories, black humor, political material, testimonials, experimental fiction, or depressing accounts of hopeless or perverted people. Accepts 10 mss/ issue; 20 mss/year. Publishes ms 6 months after acceptance. **Publishes 10 new writers/year.** Publishes short shorts. Often comments on rejected mss.

How to Contact Send complete ms. Accepts submissions by e-mail (cassjmb@iqe-mail.com). Please submit by e-mail, if possible. If you must submit by hardcopy, please send disposable copies. No queries, please. Responds in 8 weeks to mss. Sample copy for $10. Writer's guidelines online.

Payment/Terms Pays in contributor's copies; additional copies $10. Acquires first North American serial rights.

Advice "Read several stories on http://willigocrazy.org before starting to write. Proof your story many times before submitting. Make the readers think. Above all, present people (preferably diagnosed with mental illness) realistically rather than with prejudice."

$ ▣ ◎ ☑ ARTEMIS MAGAZINE, Science and Fiction for a Space-Faring Age

LRC Publications, Inc., 1380 E. 17th St., Suite 201, Brooklyn NY 11230-6011. E-mail: magazine@lrcpubs.com. Website: www.lrcpublications.com. **Contact:** Ian Randal Stock, editor. Magazine: 8½×11; 64 pages; glossy; illustrations. "As part of the Artemis Project, we present lunar and space development in a positive light. The magazine is an even mix of science and fiction. We are a proud sponsor of the Artemis Project, which is constructing a commercial, manned moon base. We publish science articles for the intelligent layman and near-term, near-Earth hard science fiction stories." Quarterly. Estab. 1999.

- Short stories published in *Artemis* have been nominated for Hugo and Nebula awards and have been named to the Year's Best Science Fiction 6.

Needs Adventure, science fiction, thriller/espionage. No fantasy, inspirational. Receives 200 unsolicited mss/month. Accepts 4-7 mss/issue. Publishes ms 3-12 months after acceptance. **Publishes 4 new writers/year.** Recently published work by Spider Robinson, Jerry Oltion, Allen M. Steele, Jack McDevitt, Stanley Schmidt and Jack Williamson. Length: 15,000 words maximum (shorter is better); average length: 2,000-8,000 words. Publishes short shorts. Also publishes poetry. Often comments on rejected mss.

How to Contact Send complete ms. Send a disposable copy of ms with SASE for reply. *Submissions sent without SASE will not be read.* Responds in 2 months to queries. Sample copy for $5 and a 9×12 SAE with 4 first-class stamps. Writer's guidelines for SASE or on website. Reviews fiction.

Payment/Terms Pays 3-5¢/word and 3 contributor's copies. Pays on acceptance. Buys first world English serial rights. Sends galleys to author.

Advice "Write the best possible story you can. Read a lot of fiction that you like, and reread it a few times. (If it doesn't hold up to rereading, it might not be so great. And don't give me any rip-offs of current television shows, video or role-playing games, or movies.) Then go over your story again, make it even better. Remember that neatness counts when you prepare your manuscript (also, knowledge of the English language and grammar, and the concepts of fiction). Then send it to the magazine that publishes fiction most like the story you've written. Remember that you're up against many hundreds of manuscripts for a very few slots in the magazine. Make your story absolutely fantastic. In my case, a science fiction story must contain both science and fiction. Remember that, to be interesting to the reader, your story will probably be about the most important moment or event in the character's life."

THE BINNACLE

University of Maine at Machias, 9 O'Brien Ave., Machias ME 04654. E-mail: ummbinnacle@maine.edu. Website: www.umm.maine.edu/binnacle. "We publish an alternative format journal of literary and visual art. We are restless about the ossification of literature and what to do about it." Semiannual. Estab. 1957. Circ. 300.

Needs Ethnic/multicultural, experimental, humor/satire, mainstream, slice-of-life vignettes. No extreme erotica, fantasy, horror or religious, but any genre attuned to a general audience can work. Publishes ms 3 months after acceptance.

How to Contact Send complete ms. Accepts submissions by e-mail (ummbinnacle@maine.edu). Responds in 1 month to queries; 3 months to mss. Accepts simultaneous submissions. Sample copy for $5. Writer's guidelines online at website or by e-mail.

Payment/Terms Acquires one-time rights.

$ ◎ BREAD FOR GOD'S CHILDREN

Bread Ministries, Inc., P.O. Box 1017, Arcadia FL 34265. (863)494-6214. Fax: (863)993-0154. E-mail: bread@sunline.net. "An interdenominational Christian teaching publication published 6-8 times/year written to aid children and youth in leading a Christian life." Estab. 1972. Circ. 10,000.

Needs No fantasy, science fiction, or non-Christian themes. Publishes ms 6 months after acceptance.

How to Contact Send complete ms. Responds in 6 months to mss. Accepts simultaneous submissions. Three sample copies for 9×12 SAE and 5 first-class stamps. Writer's guidelines for #10 SASE.

Payment/Terms Pays $40-50. Pays on publication for first rights.

Advice "We are looking for writers who have a solid knowledge of Biblical principles and are concerned for the youth of today living by those principles. Our stories must be well written, with the story itself getting the message across—no preaching, moralizing or tag endings."

$ BRUTARIAN, The Magazine of Brutiful Art

9405 Ulysses Ct., Burke VA 22015. E-mail: brutarian@msn.com. Website: www.brutarian.com. "A healthy knowledge of the great works of antiquity and an equally healthy contempt for most of what passes today as culture." Quarterly. Estab. 1991. Circ. 5,000.

Needs Adventure, confessions, erotica, experimental, fantasy, horror, humor/satire, mystery/suspense, novel excerpts. Publishes ms 3 months after acceptance.

How to Contact Send complete ms. Responds in 1 week to queries; 2 months to mss. Accepts simultaneous submissions. Sample copy for $6. Writer's guidelines online.

Payment/Terms Pays up to 10¢/word. Pays on publication for first, electronic rights.

N $◎ CHARACTERS, Kids Short Story & Poetry Outlet

Davis Publications, P.O. Box 708, Newport NH 03773. (603)864-5896. Fax: (603)863-8198. E-mail: hotdog@nhvt .net. **Contact:** Cindy Davis, editor. Magazine: $5^{1}/_{2} \times 8^{1}/_{2}$; 45 pages; saddle bound cover stock; illustrations. "We want to give kids a place to showcase their talents. Our subscribers are mostly schools and homeschoolers." Quarterly. Estab. 2003.

Needs "We accept all subjects of interest to kids. Particularly would like to see humor." Receives 45 unsolicited mss/month. Accepts 8-12 mss/issue; 36-48 mss/year. Publishes ms 1-6 months after acceptance. Publishes short shorts. Also publishes poetry. Sometimes comments on rejected mss.

How to Contact Send complete ms. Accepts submissions by e-mail, fax. Send disposable copy of the ms and #10 SASE or e-mail address for reply. Responds in 2-4 weeks to mss. Accepts simultaneous and reprints submissions. Sample copy for $5. Writer's guidelines for #10 SASE, or by e-mail.

Payment/Terms Pays $5 and contributor's copy; additional copies $4. Pays on publication for one-time rights. Not copyrighted.

Advice "We love to see a well-thought-out plot and interesting, different characters."

N $□ CIA—CITIZEN IN AMERICA

CIA—Citizen in America, Inc., 30 Ford St., Glen Cove, Long Island NY 11542. (516)671-4047. E-mail: ciamc@we btv.net. Website: www.citizeninamerica.com. **Contact:** John J. Maddox, magazine coordinator. Magazine: $8^{1}/_{4} \times 10^{1}/_{2}$; 40-80 pages; glossy cover stock; photos. "CIA—Citizen in America trys to strengthen democracy here and abroad by allowing the freedom of expression in all forms possible through the press. CIA does not shy away from controversy." Estab. 2002.

Needs Adventure, erotica, ethnic/multicultural, experimental, historical, humor/satire, mainstream, religious/ inspirational, romance, science fiction, slice-of-life vignettes, western, war stories. No screen or plays. No works that deliberately promote racism, prejudice or gender-oriented violence. Receives 150 unsolicited mss/month. Accepts 5-15 mss/issue. Publishes ms 3 months after acceptance. Length: 250-2,500 words; average length: 1,000 words. Publishes short shorts. Also publishes literary essays, literary criticism, poetry. Sometimes comments on rejected mss.

How to Contact Send complete ms. Accepts submissions by e-mail (ciamc@webtv.net), disk. Send SASE for return of the ms or send disposable copy of ms and #10 SASE for reply only. Responds in 2 weeks to queries; 1-2 months to mss. Accepts simultaneous and reprints submissions. Sample copy for $10. Writer's guidelines for #10 SASE, e-mail or on website.

Payment/Terms Pays $40-100. Pays on publication for first North American serial, first, one-time, simultaneous rights, makes work-for-hire assignments.

Advice "Feel free to submit all your work. State your age with all submissions."

□ THE CIRCLE MAGAZINE

Circle Publications, 173 Grandview Road, Wernersville PA 19565. (610)678-6550. E-mail: circlemag@aol.com. Website: www.circlemagazine.com. **Contact:** Penny Talbert, editor. Magazine: $5^{1}/_{2} \times 8^{1}/_{2}$; 48-52 pages; white offset paper; illustrations; photos. "The Circle is an eclectic mix of culture and subculture. Our goal is to provide the reader with thought-provoking reading that they will remember." Quarterly.

Needs Adventure, experimental, humor/satire, literary, mainstream, mystery/suspense, New Age, psychic/ supernatural/occult, romance, science fiction, thriller/espionage. No religious fiction. Receives 400 unsolicited mss/month. Accepts 3-5 mss/issue; 12-20 mss/year. Publishes ms 1-4 months after acceptance. Recently published work by David McDaniel, Bart Stewart, Ace Boggess and Stephen Forney. Length: 2,000-6,000 words; average length: 2,500 words. Publishes short shorts. Also publishes literary essays, literary criticism, poetry. Sometimes comments on rejected mss.

How to Contact Send complete ms. Accepts submissions by e-mail (circlemag@aol.com). Send complete ms with a cover letter. Include estimated word count, brief bio and list of publications. Responds in 1 month to queries; 4 months to mss. Accepts simultaneous and reprints, multiple submissions. Sample copy for $4. Writer's guidelines online.

Payment/Terms Pays 1 contributor's copy; additional copies $4. Pays on publication for one-time, electronic rights.

Advice "The most important thing is that submitted fiction keeps our attention and interest. The most typical reason for rejection: bad endings! Proofread your work, and send it in compliance with our guidelines."

◨ ◎ CITY SLAB, Urban Tales of the Grotesque

City Slab Publications, 1705 Summit Ave. #314, Seattle WA 98122. (206)568-4343. E-mail: dave@cityslab.com. Website: www.cityslab.com. **Contact:** Dave Lindschmidt, editor. Magazine: 8½×11; 60 pages; color covers; illustrations; photos. *"City Slab* presents the best in urban horror today. *City Slab* offers an intriguing mix of familiar voices with new discoveries. Each page is a cold, wet kiss to the genre."—Evan Wright, *Rolling Stone Magazine.* Quarterly. Estab. 2002.

Needs "We're looking for taunt, multi-leveled urban horror. Start the story with action. Capture the feel of your city whether it's real or imagined, and have a story to tell! We love crime fiction but there has to be a horror slant to it. Steer away from first person point of view." Publishes ms 3-6 months after acceptance. **Publishes 6 new writers/year.** Recently published work by Gerard Houarner, Christa Faust, Yvonne Navarro, Patricia Russo and Robert Dunbar.

How to Contact Accepts submissions by e-mail (submission@cityslab.com). Include estimated word count, brief bio and list of publications. Send disposable copy of ms and #10 SASE for reply only. Responds in 6 weeks to queries; 2 months to mss. Sample copy for $6. Writer's guidelines online.

Payment/Terms Pays on publication for first serial rights.

◨ COCHRAN'S CORNER

1003 Tyler Court, Waldorf MD 20602-2964. (301)870-1664. **Contact:** John Treasure, editor/art council. Magazine: 5½×11; 52 pages. "We publish fiction, nonfiction and poetry. Our only requirement is no strong language." For a "family" audience." Quarterly. Estab. 1986. Circ. 500.

Needs Adventure, children's/juvenile, historical, horror, humor/satire, mystery/suspense, religious/inspirational, romance, science fiction, young adult/teen. "Manuscripts must be free from language you wouldn't want your/our children to read." Would like to see more mystery and romance fiction. Plans a special fiction issue. Receives 50 unsolicited mss/month. Accepts 4 mss/issue; 8 mss/year. **Publishes 30 new writers/year.** Recently published work by James Hughes, Ellen Sandry, James Bennet, Susan Lee and Judy Demers. Length: 300-1,000 words; average length: 500 words. Also publishes literary essays, literary criticism, poetry.

How to Contact Send complete ms. "Right now we are forced to limit acceptance to *subscribers only.*" Send complete ms with cover letter. Responds in 3 weeks to queries; 6-8 weeks to mss. Accepts simultaneous and reprints submissions. Sample copy for $5, 9×12 SAE and 90¢ postage. Writer's guidelines for #10 SASE.

Payment/Terms Pays in contributor's copies. Acquires one-time rights.

Advice "I feel the quality of fiction is getting better. The public is demanding a good read, instead of having sex or violence carry the story. I predict that fiction has a good future. We like to print the story as the writer submits it if possible. This way writers can compare their work with their peers and take the necessary steps to improve and go on to sell to bigger magazines. Stories from the heart desire a place to be published. We try to fill that need. Be willing to edit yourself. Polish your manuscript before submitting to editors."

◨ COFFEE LOUNGE BOOK CLUB

Rembrandt and Co. Publishers International, P.O. Box 13486, St. Petersburg FL 33733. E-mail: ambitionscoffee@ hotmail.com. Website: rembrandtandcompany.com/Rembrandtandcompany18.html. "Give us your best work, your most outstanding philosophy on life. The Coffee Lounge wishes to separate certain authors from others so they can be recognized alone. The Coffee Lounge accepts one author per month, opening the door for just about anything. Of course, not all authors will be accepted, but the opportunity is there. Send stories and poetry, as many as you wish to be considered." Monthly. Estab. 2003. Circ. 100.

Needs Adventure, confessions, erotica, experimental, family saga, historical, horror, humor/satire, mainstream, mystery/suspense, romance, science fiction, serialized novels. Does not want pornography. Publishes ms 1 month after acceptance.

How to Contact Send complete ms. Accepts submissions by e-mail (ambitionscoffee@hotmail.com). Accepts simultaneous submissions. Writer's guidelines free.

Payment/Terms Pays on publication for first North American serial rights.

◨ $THE COUNTRY CONNECTION, Ontario's Green Magazine

Pinecone Publishing, P.O. Box 100, Boulter ON K0L 1G0 Canada. (613)332-3651. E-mail: editor@pinecone.on. ca. Website: www.pinecone.on.ca. *"The Country Connection* is a magazine for true nature lovers and the rural adventurer. Building on our commitment to heritage, cultural, artistic and environmental themes, we continually add new topics to illuminate the country experience of people living within nature. Our goal is to chronicle rural life in its many aspects, giving 'voice' to the countryside." Estab. 1989. Circ. 10,000.

Needs Adventure, fantasy, historical, humor/satire, slice-of-life vignettes, country living. Publishes ms 4 months after acceptance.

How to Contact Send complete ms. Accepts submissions by e-mail, disk. Sample copy for $4.55. Writer's guidelines online.

Payment/Terms Pays 10¢/word. Pays on publication for first rights.

☐ CREATIVE WITH WORDS PUBLICATIONS

Creative With Words Publications, P.O. Box 223226, Carmel CA 93922. Fax: (831)655-8627. E-mail: cwwpub@u sa.net. Website: members.tripod.com/CreativeWithWords. **Contact:** Brigitta Geltrich, general editor. Booklet: $5^{1}/_{2} \times 8^{1}/_{2}$; up to 50 pages; bond paper; illustrations/computer art work. 12 times/year. Estab. 1975. Circ. varies.
Needs Ethnic/multicultural, humor/satire, mystery/suspense (amateur sleuth, private eye), regional (folklore), young adult/teen (adventure, historical). "Do not submit essays." No violence or erotica, overly religious fiction or sensationalism. "Once a year we publish an anthology of the writings of young writers, titled, "We are Writers, Too!" List of upcoming themes available for SASE. Limit poetry to 20 lines or less, 46 characters per line or less. Receives 250-500 unsolicited mss/month. Accepts 50-80 mss/year. Publishes ms 1-2 months after acceptance. Recently published work by Najwa Salam Brax, June K. Silconas, William Bridge and David Napolin. Average length: 800 words. Publishes short shorts. Also publishes poetry. Sometimes comments on rejected mss.
How to Contact Send complete ms with a cover letter with SASE. Include estimated word count. Responds in 2 weeks to queries; 2 months to mss. Sample copy for $6. Writer's guidelines for #10 SASE.
Payment/Terms 20% reduction cost on 1-9 copies ordered, 30% reduction on each copy on order of 10 or more. Acquires one-time rights.
Advice "We offer a great variety of themes. We look for clean family-type fiction. Also, we ask the writer to look at the world from a different perspective, research topic thoroughly, be creative, apply brevity, tell the story from a character's viewpoint, tighten dialogue, be less descriptive, proofread before submitting, and be patient. We will not publish every manuscript we receive. It has to be in standard English, well written, proofread. We do not appreciate receiving manuscripts where we have to do the proofreading and the correcting of grammar."

ℕ ☐ ◎ CTHULHU SEX MAGAZINE, Blood, Sex and Tentacles

Cthulhu Sex, P.O. Box 3678, Grand Central Station, New York NY 10163. E-mail: stcthulhu@cthulhusex.com. Website: www.cthulhusex.com. **Contact:** Michael A. Morel, editor-in-chief. Magazine: $8^{1}/_{4} \times 10^{5}/_{8}$; 80 pages; 24 lb. white paper; 80 lb. glossy color cover stock; illustrations; photos. "We intend to corrupt the mainstream ideals of the apparent mutual exclusivity of beauty and horror. We generally publish poetry, short stories and artwork that evoke a dark and sensual atmosphere in the genre of erotic horror. We particularly look for edgy and experimental works that explore the dark side of sensuality and have a subtle yet powerful impact. We cater to mature readers and connoisseurs of sensual horror." Quarterly. Estab. 1998. Circ. 1,500. Horror Writers Association.
Needs Fantasy (dark), horror (dark fantasy, futuristic, psychological, supernatural, erotic), psychic/supernatural/occult, science fiction (dark). "We do not want to see explicit pornography, rape, rehashed vampire stories, erotica without a darker edge, serials." Receives 40-50 unsolicited mss/month. Accepts 5-7 mss/issue; 25-30 mss/year. Publishes ms 4 months after acceptance. **Publishes 5 new writers/year.** Recently published work by C.J. Henderson, Robert Masterson, Alex Severin and Mark McLaughlin. Length: 800-5,000 words; average length: 2,500 words. Publishes short shorts. Also publishes poetry. Sometimes comments on rejected mss.
How to Contact Send complete ms. Accepts submissions by e-mail. Send disposable copy of ms and #10 SASE for reply only. Responds in 1 month to queries; 3 months to mss. No simultaneous submissions. Sample copy for $4.95. Writer's guidelines for SASE, e-mail or on website.
Payment/Terms Pays 3 contributor's copies; additional copies $4. Pays on publication for one-time printing and promotional rights.
Advice "We look for work that explores at least one of the elements of the theme blood, sex and tentacles. Well-edited pieces are always appreciated. We want authors to use good writing to evoke a response instead of cheap TADA tactics. Have a unique plotline. We recommend prospective contributors read at least one copy of the magazine to get an idea of our content style. Do not try to sell your story; let it speak for itself."

◎ DAKOTA OUTDOORS, South Dakota

Hipple Publishing Co., P.O. Box 669 333 W. Dakota Ave., Pierre SD 57501-0669. (605)224-7301. Fax: (605)224-9210. E-mail: office@capjournal.com. Monthly. Estab. 1974. Circ. 7,000.
Needs Adventure, humor/satire. Does not want stories about vacations or subjects that don't include hunting and fishing. Receives 0-2 unsolicited mss/month. Publishes ms 1-2 months after acceptance. Agented fiction 90%. **Publishes 0-4 new writers/year.** Publishes short shorts.
How to Contact Send complete ms. Accepts submissions by e-mail. Responds in 3 months to queries. Accepts simultaneous submissions. Sample copy for $9 × 12$ SAE and 3 first-class stamps. Writer's guidelines by e-mail.
Payment/Terms Pays on publication.
Advice "Submit samples of manuscript or previous works for consideration; photos or illustrations with manuscript are helpful."

Small Circulation

◎ ⊕ DARK HORIZONS

104 Woodhouse Road, North Finchey London N12 ORL England. E-mail: darkhorizons@britishfantasysociety.or g.uk. Website: www.britishfantasysociety.org.uk. **Contact:** Marie O'Regan, editor. "We are a small press fantasy magazine. Our definition of fantasy knows no bounds, covering science, heroic, dark and light fantasy and horror fiction." Biannual. Circ. 500.

Needs No space opera, hard SF. Publishes short shorts. Also publishes poetry.

How to Contact Send complete ms. Send ms with brief cover letter and IRCs or e-mail address. Accepts submissions by mail.

Payment/Terms Pays contributor's copies.

Advice "We look for a good story with a beginning, middle, end, and point to it."

◪ ⊻ DESCANT, Ft. Worth's Journal of Fiction and Poetry

Texas Christian University, TCU Box 297270, Ft. Worth TX 76129. (817)257-6537. Fax: (817)257-6239. E-mail: descant@tcu.edu. Website: www.eng.tcu.edu./journals/descant. **Contact:** Dave Kuhne, editor. Magazine: 6×9; 120-150 pages; acid free paper; paper cover. "*descant* seeks high quality poems and stories in both traditional and innovative form." Annual. Estab. 1956. Circ. 500-750. Member, CLMP.

● Offers four cash awards: The $500 Frank O'Connor Award for the best story in an issue; the $250 Gary Wilson Award for an outstanding story in an issue; the $500 Betsy Colquitt Award for the best poem in an issue; the $250 Baskerville Publishers Award for outstanding poem in an issue. Several stories first published by *descant* have appeared in *Best American Short Stories.*

Needs Literary. "No horror, romance, fantasy, erotica." Receives 20-30 unsolicited mss/month. Accepts 25-35 mss/year. Publishes ms 1 year after acceptance. **Publishes 50% new writers/year.** Recently published work by William Harrison, Annette Sanford, Miller Williams, Patricia Chao, Vonesca Stroud and Walt McDonald. Length: 1,000-5,000 words; average length: 2,500 words. Publishes short shorts. Also publishes poetry.

How to Contact Send complete ms with cover letter. Include estimated word count and brief bio. Responds in 6-8 weeks to mss. Accepts simultaneous submissions. Sample copy for $10. SASE, e-mail or fax.

Payment/Terms Pays 2 contributor's copies, additional copies $6. Pays on publication for one-time rights. Sponsors awards/contests.

Advice "We look for character and quality of prose. Send your best short work."

Ⓝ ◯ DOWN IN THE DIRT, The Publication Revealing all your Dirty Little Secrets

Scars Publications and Design, 829 Brian Court, Gurnee IL 60031-3155. (847)281-9070. E-mail: alexrand@scars. tv. Website: scars.tv. **Contact:** Alexandria Rand, editor. Magazine: 5¹/₂×8¹/₂; 60 lb. paper; illustrations; photos. As material gathers. Estab. 2000.

Needs Adventure, ethnic/multicultural, experimental, fantasy, feminist, gay, historical, horror, lesbian, literary, mystery/suspense, New Age, psychic/supernatural/occult, science fiction. No religious or rhyming or family-oriented material. Publishes ms within 1 year after acceptance. Recently published work by Simon Perchik, Jim Dewitt, Jennifer Connelly, L.B. Sedlacek, Aeon Logan, Helena Wolfe. Average length: 1,000 words. Publishes short shorts. Also publishes poetry. Always, if asked, comments on rejected mss.

How to Contact Query with published clips or send complete ms. Accepts submissions by e-mail. Send SASE (or IRC) for return of the ms or disposable copy of the ms and #10 SASE for reply only. Responds in 1 month to queries; 1 month to mss. Accepts simultaneous and reprints, multiple submissions. Sample copy for $6. Writer's guidelines for SASE, e-mail or on the website. Reviews fiction.

◪ ◎ DREAM FANTASY INTERNATIONAL

#H-1, 411 14th Street, Ramona CA 92065-2769. **Contact:** Charles I. Jones, Editor-in-chief. Magazine: 8¹/₂×11; 143 pages; Xerox paper; parchment cover stock; some illustrations; photos. "Although we accept material from professional writers, we encourage "new" (unpublished) writers, as well. Our hope is to attract writers interested in dreams and the dream state. We hope to extend this interest to fantasy which is dream-related or inspired. We hope to attract readers (writers) with like interests." Estab. 1981.

Needs Confessions, erotica (soft), fantasy (dream), historical, horror, humor/satire, literary, psychic/supernatural/occult, science fiction, young adult/teen (10-18), prose poem. "No material that is not dream related or dream-related fantasy. Often we receive pieces with 'dream' or 'dreams' used in the title that we find are not dream-related. We would like to see submissions that deal with dreams that have an influence on the person's daily waking life. Suggestions for making dreams beneficial to the dreamer in his/her waking life. We would also like to see more submissions dealing with lucid dreaming." Receives 35-40 unsolicited mss/month. Accepts 20 mss/issue; 50-55 mss/year. Publishes ms 8 months to 3 years after acceptance. Agented fiction 1%. **Publishes 20-30 new writers/year.** Recently published work by Timothy Scott, Carmen M. Pursifull, Richard W. Sullivan and Robert Michael O'Hearn. Publishes short shorts. Also publishes literary essays, poetry.

How to Contact Send complete ms. Responds in 6 weeks to queries; 3 months to mss. Accepts simultaneous

and reprints submissions. Sample copy for $14. Writers guidelines for $2 and SAE with 2 first-class stamps.
Payment/Terms Pays contributor's copies. (Contributors must pay $4.50 for postage and handling.) Acquires first North American serial rights. Sends galleys to author.
Advice "Both poetry and prose submissions must be concise and free of ramblings and typographical errors. The material should be interesting and appealing and something that our readers can relate to. New and 'unique' material always grabs our attention. Write about what you know. Make the reader stand up and take notice. Avoid rambling and stay away from cliches in your writing unless, of course, it is of a humorous nature and is purposefully done to make a point."

$ DREAMS & VISIONS, Spiritual Fiction

Skysong Press, 35 Peter St. S., Orillia ON L3V 5A8 Canada. (705)329-1770. Fax: (705)329-1770. E-mail: skysong @bconnex.net. Website: www.bconnex.net/~skysong. **Contact:** Steve Stanton, editor. Magazine: 5¹/₂×8¹/₂; 56 pages; 20 lb. bond paper; glossy cover. "Innovative literary fiction for adult Christian readers." Semiannual. Estab. 1988. Circ. 200.
Needs Experimental, fantasy, humor/satire, literary, mainstream, mystery/suspense, novel excerpts, religious/ inspirational, science fiction (soft/sociological), slice-of-life vignettes. "We do not publish stories that glorify violence or perversity. All stories should portray a Christian worldview or expand upon Biblical themes or ethics in an entertaining or enlightening manner." Receives 20 unsolicited mss/month. Accepts 7 mss/issue; 14 mss/year. Publishes ms 4-8 months after acceptance. **Publishes 3 new writers/year.** Recently published work by Donna Farley, Michael Vance, Nina Munteanu and Kate Riedel. Length: 2,000-6,000 words; average length: 2,500 words.
How to Contact Send complete ms. Responds in 3 weeks to queries; 3 months to mss. Accepts simultaneous submissions. Sample copy for $4.95. Writer's guidelines online.
Payment/Terms Pays 1¢/word. Pays on publication for first North American serial, one-time, second serial (reprint) rights.
Advice "In general we look for work that has some literary value, that is in some way unique and relevant to Christian readers today. Our first priority is technical adequacy, though we will occasionally work with a beginning writer to polish a manuscript. Ultimately, we look for stories that glorify the Lord Jesus Christ, stories that build up rather than tear down, that exalt the sanctity of life, the holiness of God, and the value of the family."

ENIGMA

Audacious/Bottle Press, 402 South 25 Street, Philadelphia PA 19146. (215)545-8694. E-mail: sydx@att.net. **Contact:** Syd Bradford, publisher. Magazine: 8¹/₂×11; 100 pages; 24 lb. white paper; illustrations; photos. "Eclectic—I publish articles, fiction, poetry." Quarterly. Estab. 1989. Circ. 90.
Needs Adventure, experimental, fantasy, historical, humor/satire. Receives 30 unsolicited mss/month. Publishes ms 3 months after acceptance. **Publishes 20 new writers/year.** Recently published work by Richard A. Robbins, Eleanor Leslie and Diana K. Rubin. Length: 1,000-3,000 words; average length: 1,500 words. Also publishes literary essays, literary criticism, poetry.
How to Contact Send complete ms. Accepts submissions by e-mail (sydx@att.net). Send complete ms with cover letter. Sample copy for $6.
Payment/Terms Pays 1 contributor's copy; additional copies $6, plus $1.42 shipping and handling. Sends galleys to author.
Advice "I look for imaginative writing, excellent movement, fine imagery, stunning characters."

EYES

3610 North Doncaster Court, Apt. X7, Saginaw MI 48603-1862. (989)498-4112. E-mail: fjm3eyes@aol.com. Website: http://eyesonlinepublications.com. **Contact:** Frank J. Mueller III, editor. Magazine: 8¹/₂×11; 40+ pages. "No specific theme. Speculative fiction and surrealism most welcome. For a general, educated, not necessarily literary audience." Estab. 1991.
Needs Horror (psychological), mainstream, contemporary, ghost stories. No sword/sorcery, overt science fiction, pornography, preachiness or children's fiction. "Especially looking for speculative fiction and surrealism. Would like to see more ghost stories, student writing. Dark fantasy OK, but not preferred." Accepts 5-9 mss/ issue. Publishes ms 1 + years after acceptance. **Publishes 15-20 new writers/year.**
How to Contact Query first or send complete ms. A short bio is optional. No e-mail submissions. Responds in 12 + months to mss. No simultaneous submissions. Sample copy for $6, extras $4. Writer's guidelines for #10 SASE.
Payment/Terms Pays 1 contributor's copy. Acquires one-time rights.
Advice "Pay attention to character. A strong plot, while important, may not be enough alone to get you in the *Eyes*. Atmosphere and mood are also important. Please proofread. If you have a manuscript you like enough

to see in the *Eyes*, send it to me. Above all, don't let rejections discourage you. I would encourage the purchase of a sample to get an idea of what I'm looking for. Read stories by authors such as Algernon Blackwood, Nathaniel Hawthorne, Shirley Jackson, Henry James and Poe."

⊞ $⬛ THE FIRST LINE

Blue Cubicle Press, LLC, P.O. Box 250382, Plano TX 75025-0382. (972)824-0646. E-mail: submissions@thefirstline.com. Website: www.thefirstline.com. **Contact:** Robin LaBounty, manuscript coordinator. Magzine: 8×5; 56-60 pages; 20 lb. bond paper; 80 lb. cover stock. "We only publish stories that start with the first line provided. We are a collection of tales—of different directions writers can take when they start from the same place." Quarterly. Estab. 1999. Circ. 800.

Needs Adventure, ethnic/multicultural, fantasy, gay, humor/satire, lesbian, literary, mainstream, mystery/suspense, regional, romance, science fiction, western. Receives 100 unsolicited mss/month. Accepts 12 mss/issue; 48 mss/year. Publishes ms 1 month after acceptance. **Publishes 6 new writers/year.** Length: 300-3,000 words; average length: 1,500 words. Publishes short shorts. Also publishes literary essays, literary criticism. Often comments on rejected mss.

How to Contact Send complete ms. Accepts submissions by e-mail. Send SASE for return of ms or disposable copy of the ms and #10 SASE for reply only. Responds in 1 week to queries; 3 months to mss. Accepts multiple submissions. No simultaneous submissions. Sample copy for $3. Writer's guidelines for SASE, e-mail or on website. Reviews fiction.

Payment/Terms Pays $10 maximum and contributor's copy; additional copy $1.50. Pays on publication.

Advice "Don't just write the first story that comes to mind after you read the sentence. If it is obvious, chances are other people are writing about the same thing. Don't try so hard. Be willing to accept criticism."

$⬛ ◎ ⬛ FLESH AND BLOOD, Tales of Horror & Dark Fantasy

Flesh & Blood Press, 121 Joseph St., Bayville NJ 08721. E-mail: harrorjackf@aol.com. Website: http://zombie.horrorseek.com/horror/fleshnblood. **Contact:** Jack Fisher, editor-in-chief/publisher; Teri A. Jacobs, assistant editor. Magazine: full-sized; 52-60 pages; 60 lb. paper; thick/glossy, full-color cover; "fully and lavishly illustrated." "We publish fiction with heavy emphasis on the fantastic and bizarre." Quarterly. Estab. 1997. Circ. 1,000.

● The magazine recently won the 2001 Zine Publishing Competition Award in *Writer's Digest Magazine*, was a 2002 Bram Stoker Award nominee, and won The Best Magazine of the Year Award in the *Jobs In Hell* newsletter contest.

Needs Horror (dark fantasy, supernatural), slice-of-life vignettes, dark fantasy. "Nothing that isn't dark, strange, odd and/or offbeat." Receives 250 unsolicited mss/month. Accepts 7-10 mss/issue; 21-36 mss/year. Publishes ms 10 months after acceptance. Agented fiction 1%. **Publishes 4-6 new writers/year.** Recently published work by Wendy Rathbone, Teri Jacobs, Tim Piccirrilli, China Melville, Doug Clegg, Jay Bonansigna and Jack Ketchum. Length: 100-5,000 words; average length: 2,000 words. Publishes short shorts. Also publishes poetry. Often comments on rejected mss.

How to Contact Accepts submissions by e-mail. Send complete ms with a cover letter. Include brief bio and list of publications. Send SASE (or IRC) for return of ms. Responds in 2 weeks to queries; 1 month to mss. No simultaneous submissions. Sample copy for $6 (check payable to Jack Fisher). Writer's guidelines online.

Payment/Terms Pays 4-5¢/word. Pays on publication.

Advice "Stories that mix one or more of the following elements with a horrific/weird idea/plot have a good chance: the fantastical, whimsical, supernatural, bizarre; stories should have unique ideas and be strongly written; the weirder and more offbeat, the better."

⊞ ◯ FOLIATE OAK LITERARY MAGAZINE, Foliate Oak Online

University of Arkansas-Monticello, MCB 113, Monticello AR 71656. (870)460-1247. E-mail: foliate@uamont.edu. Website: www.uamont.edu/foliateoak. **Contact:** Diane Payne, faculty advisor. Magazine: 6×9; 80 pages. Monthly. Estab. 1980. Circ. 500.

Needs Adventure, comics/graphic novels, ethnic/multicultural, experimental, family saga, feminist, gay, historical, humor/satire, lesbian, literary, mainstream, science fiction (soft/sociological). No religious, sexist or homophobic work. Receives 30 unsolicited mss/month. Accepts 7 mss/issue; 50 mss/year. Does not read mss May-August. Publishes ms 1 month after acceptance. **Publishes 20 new writers/year.** Recently published work by David Barringer, Thom Didato, Joe Taylor, Molly Giles, Patricia Shevlin, Tony Hoagland. Length: 50-3,500 words; average length: 1,500 words. Publishes short shorts. Also publishes literary essays, literary criticism, poetry. Rarely comments on rejected mss.

How to Contact Send complete ms. Only send e-mail submissions. Responds in 1 week to queries; 2 months to mss. Accepts simultaneous and reprints, multiple submissions. Sample copy for SASE and 6×8 envelope. Writer's guidelines online. Reviews fiction.

Small Circulation

Payment/Terms Pays contributor's copy. Acquires electronic rights. Sends galleys to author. Not copyrighted.
Advice "We're open to honest experimental, offbeat, realistic and surprising fiction. We will *only* accept submissions via e-mail at foliateoak@uamont.edu. *Snail Mail submissions will not be returned*!!! Please use a text-only (not rich-text or html) format, and cut and paste your submission into the body of your message. No more than three submissions per person. Excessive poetry is not smiled upon! Artwork can be e-mailed as well, but please submit only gif's or jpg's. Please limit your photos to two per submission and wait until we respond before you send more."

$⊚ FOOTSTEPS, African American Heritage

Carus Publishing Company, 30 Grove Street, Suite C, Peterborough NH 03458. (603)924-7209. Fax: (603)924-7380. E-mail: cfbakeriii@meganet.net. Website: www.footstepsmagazine.com. Magazine: 7×9; 49 pages; glossy paper; heavy paper cover stock; illustrations; photos. *Footsteps* is a magazine on African-American heritage from middle school age children. Estab. 1998. Circ. 6,000.
Needs Historical (African-American history).
How to Contact Query with published clips. Sample copy for $4.95.
Payment/Terms Pays 20-25¢ per word. Pays on publication.

Ⓝ $⊘ FREE FOCUS/OSTENTATIOUS MIND

Wagner Press, Bowbridge Press, P.O. Box 7415, JAF Station, New York NY 10116-17415. **Contact:** Patricia Denise Coscia, editor. Editors change every year. Magazine: 8×14; 10 pages; recycled paper; illustrations; photos. "*Free Focus* is a small-press magazine which focuses on the educated women of today, and *Ostentatious Mind* is designed to encourage the intense writer, the cutting reality." Bimonthly. Estab. 1985 and 1987. Circ. 100.
Needs Experimental, feminist, humor/satire, mainstream, mystery/suspense (romantic), psychic/supernatural/occult, western, young adult/teen (adventure). "X-rated fiction is not accepted." List of upcoming themes available for SASE. Plans future special fiction issue or anthology. Receives 1,000 unsolicited mss/month. Does not read mss February to August. Publishes ms 3-6 months after acceptance. **Publishes 200 new writers/year.** Recently published work by Edward Janz, Carol S. Fowler, Beth Anne Wiggins. Length: 1,000 words; average length: 500 words. Publishes short shorts. Also publishes literary essays, literary criticism, poetry. Always comments on rejected mss.
How to Contact Query with published clips or send complete ms. Send SASE for reply. Responds in 3 months to mss. Accepts simultaneous submissions. Sample copy for $3, #10 SAE and $1 postage. Writer's guidelines for #10 SAE and $1 postage.
Payment/Terms Pays $2.50-5 and 2 contributor's copies; additional copies $2. Pays on publication. Sends galleys to author. Sponsors awards/contests.
Advice "This publication is for beginning writers. Do not get discouraged; submit your writing. We look for imagination and creativity; no x-rated writing."

$⊚ FUN FOR KIDZ

Bluffton News Publishing and Printing Company, P.O. Box 227, 103 N. Main Street, Bluffton OH 45817-0227. (419)358-4610. Fax: (419)358-5027. Website: www.funforkidz.com. **Contact:** Virginia Edwards, associate editor. Magazine: 7×8; 49 pages; illustrations; photographs. "*Fun for Kidz* focuses on activity. The children are encouraged to solve problems, explore and develop character. Target age: 6-13 years." Bimonthly. Estab. 2002. Circ. 6,000.
Needs Children's/juvenile (adventure, animal, easy-to-read, historical, mystery, preschool, series, sports). Bugs; Oceans; Animals; Camping; Fun with Stars; Healthy Fun; Summer Splash; In the Mountains; Fun with Words. List of upcoming themes for SASE. Accepts 10 mss/issue; 60 mss/year. Publishes short shorts. Also publishes poetry. Sometimes comments on rejected mss.
How to Contact Send complete ms with cover letter. Include estimated word count and brief bio. Responds in 6 weeks to queries; 6 months to mss. Accepts simultaneous, multiple submissions. Sample copy for $4. Writer's guidelines for #10 SASE.
Payment/Terms Pays 5¢ per word and 1 contributor's copy. Pays on publication for first rights.
Advice "Work needs to be appropriate for a children's publication ages 6-13 years. Request a theme list so story submitted will work into an upcoming issue."

◻ ⊚ THE FUNNY PAPER

F/J Writers Service, P.O. Box 455, Lee's MO 64063. E-mail: felixkcmo@aol.com. Website: www.angelfire.com/biz/funnypaper. **Contact:** F.H. Fellhauer, editor. Zine specializing in humor, contest and poetry: 8½×11; 8 pages. Published 4 times/year. No summer or Christmas. Estab. 1984.
Needs Children's/juvenile, humor/satire, literary. "No controversial fiction." Receives 10-20 unsolicited mss/

month. Accepts 1 mss/issue; 4-5 mss/year. Length: 1,000 words; average length: 295 words. Publishes short shorts. Also publishes poetry. Sometimes comments on rejected mss.

How to Contact Accepts submissions by e-mail. Send for guidelines. Include estimated word count with submission. Send disposable copy of ms and #10 SASE for reply only. Responds in 2 weeks to queries; 1-3 months to mss. Accepts simultaneous and reprints submissions. Sample copy for $3.

Payment/Terms Prizes for stories, jokes and poems for $5-100 (humor, inspirational, fillers). Additional copies $3. Pays on publication for first, one-time rights.

Advice "Do your best work, no trash. We try to keep abreast of online publishing and provide information."

$ 🖉 ◎ FUNNY TIMES, A Monthly Humor Review

Funny Times, Inc., P.O. Box 18530, Cleveland Heights OH 44118. (216)371-8600. Fax: (216)371-8696. Website: www.funnytimes.com. **Contact:** Ray Lesser and Susan Wolpert, editors. Zine specializing in humor: tabloid; 24 pages; newsprint; illustrations. "*Funny Times* is a monthly review of America's funniest cartoonists and writers. We are the *Reader's Digest* of modern American humor with a progressive/peace-oriented/environmental/politically activist slant." Monthly. Estab. 1985. Circ. 68,000.

Needs Humor/satire. "Anything funny." Receives hundreds unsolicited mss/month. Accepts 5 mss/issue; 60 mss/year. Publishes ms 3 months after acceptance. Agented fiction 10%. **Publishes 10 new writers/year.** Publishes short shorts.

How to Contact Query with published clips. Include list of publications. Send SASE for return of ms or disposable copy of ms. Responds in 3 months to mss. Accepts simultaneous and reprints submissions. Sample copy for $3 or 9×12 SAE with 4 first-class stamps (83¢ postage). Writer's guidelines online.

Payment/Terms Pays $50-150. Pays on publication for one-time, second serial (reprint) rights.

Advice "It must be funny."

Ⓝ $ 🖉 GRASSLIMB

Grasslimb, P.O. Box 420816, San Diego CA 92142. E-mail: valerie@grasslimb.com. Website: www.grasslimb.com/journal/. **Contact:** Valerie Polichar, editor. Magazine: 14×20; 8 pages; 60 lb. white paper; illustrations. "*Grasslimb* is sold in cafés as well as in bookstores. Our readers like some insight into both the pain and the strange joys of life along with their cups of coffee. Loss, alienation and grief are subjects which draw us. Conversely, we find the beauty of the natural world compelling. Fiction is best when it is short and avant-garde or otherwise experimental." Semiannual. Estab. 2002. Circ. 300.

Needs Comics/graphic novels, ethnic/multicultural, experimental, gay, literary, mystery/suspense (crime), regional, thriller/espionage, translations. Does not want romance or religious writings. Accepts 2-4 mss/issue; 4-8 mss/year. Does not read mss in December, January, June or July. Publishes ms 3 months after acceptance. **Publishes 2 new writers/year.** Recently published work by Leonard Crino, Josey Foo, Madeline Malan and James Sallis. Length: 500-2,000 words; average length: 1,500 words. Publishes short shorts. Also publishes poetry. Rarely comments on rejected mss.

How to Contact Send complete ms. Send SASE for return of ms or disposable copy of ms and #10 SASE for reply only. Responds in 2 months to mss. Accepts simultaneous and reprints, multiple submissions. Sample copy for $2.00. Writer's guidelines for SASE, e-mail or on website. Reviews fiction.

Payment/Terms Writers receive $5 minimum; $50 maximum, and 2 contributor's copies; additional copies $2. Pays on acceptance for first North American serial rights. Sends galleys to author.

Advice "We publish brief fiction work that can be read in a single sitting over a cup of coffee. Work can be serious or light, but is generally 'literary' in nature, rather than mainstream. Experimental work welcome. Remember to have your work proofread and to send short work."

$ 🖉 ◎ HARDBOILED

Gryphon Publications, P.O. Box 209, Brooklyn NY 11228. Website: www.gryphonbooks.com. **Contact:** Gary Lovisi, editor. Magazine: Digest-sized; 100 pages; offset paper; color cover; illustrations. "Hard-hitting crime fiction and private-eye stories—the newest and most cutting-edge work and classic reprints." Semiannual. Estab. 1988. Circ. 1,000.

Needs Mystery/suspense (private eye, police procedural, noir), hard-boiled crime, and private-eye stories, all on the cutting edge. No "pastiches, violence for the sake of violence." Wants to see more non-private-eye hard-boiled. Receives 40-60 unsolicited mss/month. Accepts 10-20 mss/issue. Publishes ms 18 months after acceptance. **Publishes 5-10 new writers/year.** Recently published work by Andrew Vachss, Stephen Solomita, Joe Hensley, Mike Black. Sometimes comments on rejected mss.

How to Contact Query with or without published clips or send complete ms. Accepts submissions by fax. Query with SASE only on anything over 3,000 words. All stories must be submitted in hard copy. If accepted, e-mail as an attachement in a word document. Responds in 2 weeks to queries; 1 month to mss. Accepts simultaneous

Small Circulation

and reprints submissions. Sample copy for $10 or double issue for $20 (add $1.50 book postage). Writer's guidelines for #10 SASE.

Payment/Terms Pays $5-50. Pays on publication for first North American serial, one-time rights.

Advice "By 'hard-boiled' the editor does not mean rehashing of pulp detective fiction from the 1940s and 1950s but rather realistic, gritty material. We look for good writing, memorable characters, intense situations. Lovisi could be called a pulp fiction 'afficionado,' however he also publishes *Paperback Parade* and holds an annual vintage paperback fiction convention each year."

$HORIZONS, The Jewish Family Journal

Targum Press, 22700 W. Eleven Mile Rd., Southfield MI 48034. Fax: (888)298-9992. E-mail: horizons@netvision. net.il. Website: www.targum.com. **Contact:** Miriam Zakon, chief editor. "We include fiction and nonfiction, memoirs, essays, historical and informational articles, all of interest to the Orthodox Jew." Quarterly. Estab. 1994. Circ. 5,000.

Needs Historical, humor/satire, mainstream, slice-of-life vignettes. Nothing not suitable to Orthodox Jewish values. Receives 4-6 unsolicited mss/month. Accepts 2-3 mss/issue; 10-12 mss/year. Publishes ms 6 months after acceptance. **Publishes 20-30 new writers/year.** Length: 300-3,000 words; average length: 1,500 words. Publishes short shorts. Also publishes poetry.

How to Contact Send complete ms. Accepts submissions by e-mail, fax. Responds in 1 week to queries; 2 months to mss. Accepts simultaneous submissions. Writer's guidelines available.

Payment/Terms Pays $20-100. Pays 4-6 weeks after publication. Acquires one-time rights.

Advice "Study our publication to make certain your submission is appropriate to our target market."

◙ ◎ HYBOLICS, Da Literature and Culture of Hawaii

Hybolics, Inc., P.O. Box 3016, Aiea HI 96701. (808)366-1272. E-mail: hybolics@lava.net. **Contact:** Lee Tonouchi, co-editor. Magazine: 8½×11; 80 pages; 80 lb. coated paper; cardstock cover; illustrations; photos. "We publish da kine creative and critical work dat get some kine connection to Hawaii." Annual. Estab. 1999. Circ. 1,000.

Needs Comics/graphic novels, ethnic/multicultural, experimental, humor/satire, literary. "No genre fiction. Wants to see more sudden fiction." Receives 50 unsolicited mss/month. Accepts 10 mss/year. Publishes ms 1 year after acceptance. **Publishes 3 new writers/year.** Recently published work by Darrell Lum, Rodney Morales, Lee Cataluna and Lisa Kanae. Length: 1,000-8,000 words; average length: 4,000 words. Publishes short shorts. Also publishes literary essays, literary criticism, poetry.

How to Contact Send complete ms with a cover letter. Include estimated word count, brief bio and list of publications. Responds in 5 weeks to queries; 5 months to mss. Sample copy for $13.35. Writer's guidelines for #10 SASE.

Payment/Terms 2 contributor's copies; additional copies $7.25. Pays on publication for first rights.

$◙ INK POT, a literary potpourri

Lit Pot Press, Inc., 3909 Reche Road Suite 132, Fallbrook CA 92028-3818. (760)731-3111. Fax: (760)731-3111. E-mail: _litpot@veryfast.biz. Website: www.inkpots.net. **Contact:** Beverly Jackson, editor-in-chief. Magazine: 5½×8½; 200 pages; 60 lb. paper; paperback and OPP cover stock; illustrations; photos. "*Ink Pot* has a simple mission: to publish literary work without abusing writers. We do not believe writers should have to wait for months to get a response for a submission. We welcome sim subs. We are unique inasmuch as we respond almost immediately, occasionally suggest other venues if the piece is not for us, and sometimes give feedback if the piece has potential. We like beginning writers with talent as well as seasoned professionals, and we'll give the outsider story a chance if it's well done. Our audience is a literary audience who appreciates the edgy, the innovative, and the solid plotted, emotive piece." Quarterly. Estab. 2003. Circ. 100. Member, CLMP.

Needs Ethnic/multicultural, humor/satire, literary, magical realism. Does not want children's, hard sci-fi, religious, romance. Receives 150 unsolicited mss/month. Accepts 10 mss/issue; 20 mss/year. Does not read mss in December. Publishes ms 6 months after acceptance. **Publishes 3-7 new writers/year.** Recently published work by Marc Phillips, Joseph Young, Richard Madelin, Mary McCluskey and Chimananda Ngozi Adichie. Length: 200-5,000 words; average length: 3,500 words. Publishes short shorts. Also publishes literary essays, poetry. Rarely comments on rejected mss.

How to Contact Accepts submissions by e-mail. Send disposable copy of the ms and #10 SASE for reply only. Responds in 2 days to queries; 1-2 weeks to mss. Accepts simultaneous submissions. Sample copy for $10. Writer's guidelines for e-mail or on the website.

Payment/Terms Pays $5-15 and 2 contributor's copies; additional copies $10. Pays on acceptance for first North American serial, electronic rights. Sends galleys to author.

Advice "We look for fresh fiction with a literary bent, work that uses language and imagery effectively and is not mainstream, simplistic storytelling. We like characterization and plot but also appreciate the abstract and absurd when well conceived. Humor and satire that move us are always appreciated. We don't want diatribes, rants, preachy or pedantic academic works.''

☑ ◎ ITALIAN AMERICANA

URI/CCE, 80 Washington Street, Providence RI 02903-1803. (401)277-5306. Fax: (401)277-5100. E-mail: bonom oal@etal.ui.edu. Website: www.uri.edu/prov/italian. **Contact:** C.B. Albright, editor. Magazine: 6×9; 240 pages; varnished cover; perfect bound; photos. *"Italian Americana* contains historical articles, fiction, poetry and memoirs, all concerning the Italian experience in the Americas.'' Semiannual. Estab. 1974. Circ. 1,200.
Needs Literary, Italian American. No nostalgia. Wants to see more fiction featuring "individualized characters.'' Receives 10 unsolicited mss/month. Accepts 3 mss/issue; 6-7 mss/year. Publishes ms up to 1 year after acceptance. Agented fiction 5%. **Publishes 2-4 new writers/year.** Recently published work by Mary Caponegro and Sal LaPuma. Publishes short shorts. Also publishes literary essays, literary criticism, poetry. Sometimes comments on rejected mss.
How to Contact Send complete ms (in triplicate) with a cover letter. Include 3-5 line bio, list of publications. Responds in 1 month to queries; 2 months to mss. No simultaneous submissions. Sample copy for $7. Writer's guidelines for #10 SASE. Reviews fiction.
Payment/Terms Pays 1 contributor's copy; additional copies $7. Acquires first North American serial rights.
Advice ''Please individualize characters, instead of presenting types (i.e., lovable uncle, etc.). No nostalgia.''

☑ JAW MAGAZINE, Just Another Writing Magazine

Jaw Press, P.O. Box 476, Caroga Lake NY 12032-0426. (518)835-2313. Fax: (518)835-2313. E-mail: jawmag@cap ital.net. Website: http://jawmag.blogspot.com. **Contact:** Richard Nilsen, editor. Magazine: 8½×5½; 60 pages; 20# acid free paper; card stock cover; illustrations; photos. Quarterly. Estab. 2002. Circ. 100.
Needs Experimental, fantasy, humor/satire, literary, mainstream, mystery/suspense, science fiction. Does not want grade B genre. Receives 3-4 unsolicited mss/month. Accepts 1-2 mss/issue; 8-12 mss/year. Publishes ms 3-9 months after acceptance. **Publishes 30 new writers/year.** Recently published work by Lyn Lifshin, Laura Stamps, Pam Selert, Claire Brouhard, Simon Perchik and Mat Dailey. Length: 300-2,000 words; average length: 1,000 words. Publishes short shorts. Also publishes literary essays, literary criticism, poetry. Sometimes comments on rejected mss.
How to Contact Send complete ms. Accepts submissions by e-mail. Send SASE (or IRC) for return of the ms or send a disposable copy of the ms and #10 SASE for reply only. Preference is given to e-mailed mss over hard copy mss. Responds in 1 week to queries; 3-6 months to mss. Accepts simultaneous and reprints, multiple submissions. Sample copy for $2.50. Writer's guidelines for #10 SASE, online, or by e-mail.
Payment/Terms Pays on publication for first North American serial rights.

◎ JEWISH CURRENTS MAGAZINE

22 E. 17th Street, New York NY 10003-1919. (845)626-2427. Fax: (212)414-2227. E-mail: babush@hvi.net. **Contact:** Lawrence Bush. Magazine: 8½×11; 40 pages. ''We are a secular, progressive, independent Jewish bimonthly, printing fiction, poetry articles and reviews on Jewish politics and history. Holocaust/Resistance; Mideast peace process, Black-Jewish relations; labor struggles, women's issues. Audience is secular, left/progressive, Jewish, mostly urban.'' Bimonthly. Estab. 1946. Circ. 16,000.
Needs Ethnic/multicultural, feminist, historical, humor/satire, translations, contemporary; senior citizen/retirement. ''No religious, sectarian; no porn or hard sex, no escapist stuff. Go easy on experimentation, but we're interested. Must be well written! We are interested in *authentic* experience and readable prose; humanistic orientation. Must have Jewish theme. Could use more humor; short, smart, emotional and intellectual impact.'' Upcoming Themes: (submit at least 6 months in advance): Black-Jewish Relations (January/February); International Women's Day, Holocaust/Resistance, Passover (March/April); Israel (May/June); Jews in the USSR and Ex-USSR (July/August); Jewish Book Month, Hanuka (November/December). Receives 6-10 unsolicited mss/month. Accepts 0-1 mss/issue; 8-10 mss/year. Publishes ms 2-24 months after acceptance. Recently published work by Lanny Lefkowitz, Esther Cohen, Paul Beckman, Shirley Adelman, Galena Vromen, Alex B. Stone. Length: 1,000-3,000 words; average length: 1,800 words. Publishes short shorts. Also publishes literary essays, literary criticism, poetry.
How to Contact Send complete ms with cover letter. ''Writers should include brief biographical information, especially their publishing histories.'' SASE. Responds in 2 months to mss. Sample copy for $3 with SAE and 3 first class stamps. Reviews fiction.
Payment/Terms Pays complimentary one-year subscription and 6 contributor's copies. ''We readily give reprint permission at no charge.'' Sends galleys to author.
Advice Noted for ''stories with Jewish content and personal Jewish experience—e.g., immigrant or Holocaust memories, assimilation dilemmas, dealing with Jewish conflicts OK. Space is increasingly a problem. Be intelli-

Small Circulation

gent, imaginative, intuitive and absolutely honest. Have a musical ear, and an ear for people: how they sound when they talk and also hear what they don't say."

◎ ⊕ KRAX MAGAZINE

63 Dixon Lane, Leeds Yorkshire Britain LS12 4RR United Kingdom. **Contact:** A. Robson, co-editor. "*Krax* publishes lighthearted, humorous and whimsical writing. It is for anyone seeking light relief at a gentle pace. Our audience has grown middle-aged along with us, especially now that we're annual and not able to provide the instant fix demanded by teens and twenties."

Needs "No war stories, horror, space bandits, boy-girl soap opera. We publish mostly poetry of a lighthearted nature but use comic or spoof fiction, witty and humorous essays. Would like to see more whimsical items, trivia ramblings or anything daft." Accepts 1 mss/issue. **Publishes 1 new writer/year.** Recently published work by Bill Glose, D. Warrender and Mary Knight.

How to Contact No specific guidelines but cover letter appreciated. Sample copy for $2.

Advice "Don't spend too long on scene-setting or character construction as this inevitably produces an anti-climax in a short piece. We look for original settings, distinctive pacing, description related to plot, i.e. only dress character in bow tie and gumboots if you're having a candlelight dinner in The Everglades. Look at what you enjoy in all forms of fiction from strip cartoons to novels, movies to music lyrics, then try to put some of this into your own writing. Send IRCs or currency notes for return postal costs."

$◢ LADY CHURCHILL'S ROSEBUD WRISTLET

Small Beer Press, 176 Prospect Ave., Northampton MA 01060. E-mail: info@lcrw.net. Website: www.lcrw.net/lcrw. **Contact:** Gavin Grant, editor. Zine: half legal size; 40 pages; 60 lb. paper; glossy cover; illustrations; photos. Semiannual. Estab. 1996. Circ. 700.

Needs Comics/graphic novels, experimental, fantasy, feminist, literary, science fiction, translations, short story collections. Receives 25 unsolicited mss/month. Accepts 4-6 mss/issue; 8-12 mss/year. Publishes ms 6-12 months after acceptance. **Publishes 2-4 new writers/year.** Recently published work by Amy Beth Forbes, Jeffrey Ford, Carol Emshwiller and Theodora Goss. Length: 200-7,000 words; average length: 3,500 words. Also publishes literary essays, poetry. Sometimes comments on rejected mss.

How to Contact Send complete ms with a cover letter. Include estimated word count. Send SASE (or IRC) for return of ms, or send a disposable copy of ms and #10 SASE for reply only. Responds in 2 weeks to queries; 1-3 months to mss. Sample copy for $5. Writer's guidelines online. Reviews fiction.

Payment/Terms Pays $.01/word, $20 minimum and 2 contributor's copies; additional copies contributor's discount 40%. Pays on publication for first, one-time rights.

Advice "I like fiction that tends toward the speculative."

$◎ LEADING EDGE, Magazine of Science Fiction and Fantasy

3146 JKHB, Provo UT 84602. (801)378-4455. E-mail: tle@byu.edu. Website: http://tle.byu.edu. **Contact:** Fiction director. Zine specializing in science fiction: $5^{1}/_2 \times 8^{1}/_2$; 170 pages; card stock; some illustrations. "*Leading Edge* is dedicated to helping new writers make their way into publishing. We send back critiques with every story. We don't print anything with heavy swearing, violence that is too graphic, or explicit sex." Semiannual. Estab. 1981. Circ. 500.

Needs Fantasy (space fantasy, sword/sorcery), science fiction (hard science/technological, soft/sociological). Receives 100 unsolicited mss/month. Accepts 8 mss/issue; 16 mss/year. Publishes ms 1-6 months after acceptance. **Publishes 9-10 new writers/year.** Recently published work by Orson Scott Card and Dave Wolverton. Length: 17,000; average length: 10,000 words. Publishes short shorts. Also publishes poetry. Always comments on rejected mss.

How to Contact Send complete ms with cover letter. Include estimated word count, brief bio and list of publications. Send disposable copy of ms and #10 SASE for reply only. Responds in 2 months to mss. Sample copy for $4.95. Writer's guidelines for SASE. Reviews fiction.

Payment/Terms Pays 1¢/word; $100 maximum and 2 contributor's copies; additional copies $4.95. Pays on publication for first North American serial rights. Sends galleys to author.

Advice "Don't base your story on your favorite TV show, book or game. Be original, creative and current. Base science fiction on recent science, not '50s horror flicks."

◎ LEFT CURVE

P.O. Box 472, Oakland CA 94604-0472. (510)763-7193. E-mail: editor@leftcurve.org. Website: www.leftcurve.org. **Contact:** Csaba Polony, editor. Magazine: $8^{1}/_2 \times 11$; 144 pages; 60 lb. paper; 100 pt. C1S gloss layflat lamination cover; illustrations; photos. "*Left Curve* is an artist-produced journal addressing the problem(s) of cultural forms emerging from the crises of modernity that strive to be independent from the control of dominant institutions, based on the recognition of the destructiveness of commodity (capitalist) systems to all life." Published irregularly. Estab. 1974. Circ. 2,000.

Needs Ethnic/multicultural, experimental, historical, literary, regional, science fiction, translations, contemporary, prose poem, political. "No topical satire, religion-based pieces, melodrama. We publish critical, open, social/political-conscious writing." Receives 35 unsolicited mss/month. Accepts 3-4 mss/issue. Publishes ms 6-12 months after acceptance. Recently published work by Mike Standaert, Susan Emerling, Paul E. Wolf. Length: 500-5,000 words; average length: 1,200 words. Publishes short shorts. Sometimes comments on rejected mss.

How to Contact Send complete ms with cover letter. Include "statement of writer's intent, brief bio and reason for submitting to *Left Curve*." Accepts electronic submissions; "prefer 3½ disk and hard copy though we do accept e-mail submissions." Responds in 6 months to mss. Sample copy for $10, 9×12 SAE and $1.42 postage. Writer's guidelines for 1 first-class stamp.

Payment/Terms Pays contributor's copies. Rights revert to author.

Advice "We look for continuity, adequate descriptive passages, endings that are not simply abandoned (in both meanings). Dig deep; no superficial personalisms, no corny satire. Be honest, realistic and gouge out the truth you wish to say. Understand yourself and the world. Have writing be a means to achieve or realize what is real."

$🖳 LIQUID OHIO, Voice of the Unheard

Grab Odd Dreams Press, P.O. Box 60265, Bakersfield CA 93386-0265. E-mail: amber@liquidohio.net. Website: www.liquidohio.net. **Contact:** Amber Goddard, editor; Suzanne Wigginton, art director. Magazine: 8½×11; 32 pages; newsprint; illustrations; photos. Quarterly. Estab. 1995. Circ. 500.

Needs Experimental, humor/satire, literary. Receives 15-20 unsolicited mss/month. Accepts 6 mss/issue; 24-30 mss/year. Publishes ms 6-12 months after acceptance. **Publishes 15 new writers/year.** Recently published work by Buddy Bell, Brent McKnight and Andy Senior. Length: 2,000-3,000 words; average length: 1,500-1,800 words. Publishes short shorts. Also publishes literary essays, literary criticism, poetry.

How to Contact Send complete ms with a cover letter. Should include estimated word count. Send SASE for reply, return of ms, or send a disposable copy of ms. Accepts simultaneous, multiple, reprint and electronic submissions. Responds in 1 month to queries; 3 months to mss. Sample copy for $4, 11×14 SAE and 3 first-class stamps. Writer's guidelines online.

Payment/Terms Pays 2 contributor's copies. Acquires one-time rights.

Advice "We like things that are different, but not too abstract or 'artsy' that one goes away saying, 'huh?' Write what you feel, not necessarily what sounds deep or meaningful—it will probably be that naturally if it's real. Send in anything you've got—live on the edge. Stories that are relatable, that deal with those of us trying to find a creative train in the world. We also love stories that are extremely unique, e.g., talking pickles, etc. Also, be sure to send us that SASE—we're poor, ya know!"

N $⊞ THE LONDON MAGAZINE, Review of Literature and the Arts

The London Magazine, 32 Addison Grove, London W4 1ER United Kingdom. (00)44 0208 400 5882. Fax: (00)44 0208 994 1713. E-mail: admin@thelondonmagazine.net. Website: www.thelondonmagazine.net. Bimonthly. Estab. 1732. Circ. 1,000.

Needs Adventure, confessions, erotica, ethnic/multicultural, experimental, fantasy, historical, humor/satire, mainstream, mystery/suspense, novel excerpts, religious/inspirational, romance, slice-of-life vignettes, suspense. Publishes ms 4 months after acceptance.

How to Contact Send complete ms. Include SASE. Responds in 1 month to queries; 4 months to mss. Accepts simultaneous submissions. Sample copy for £8.75. Writer's guidelines free.

Payment/Terms Pays minimum £20; maximum rate is negotiable. Pays on publication for first rights.

N 🖳 LOW BUDGET ADVENTURE STORIES

Cynic Press, P.O. Box 40691, Philadelphia PA 19107. **Contact:** Joseph Farley. Magazine: 8½×11; 28 pages; 20 lb. stock paper; 70 lb. cover stock; illustrations. Annual. Estab. 2004. Circ. 70.

Needs Adventure, military/war, mystery/suspense (amateur sleuth, cozy, police procedural, private eye/hardboiled). Receives 5 unsolicited mss/month. Accepts 4-6 mss/issue. Publishes ms 6 months to 2 years after acceptance. **Publishes some new writers/year.** Length: 1,000-15,000 words; average length: 4,000 words. Publishes short shorts. Sometimes comments on rejected mss.

How to Contact Send complete ms. Send SASE (or IRC) for return of the ms. Responds in 1 month to queries. Accepts simultaneous and reprints, multiple submissions. Sample copy for $7.

Payment/Terms Pays in 2 contributor's copies and free subscription to the magazine. Pays on publication for one-time rights.

◎ LOW BUDGET SCIENCE FICTION

Cynic Press, P.O. Box 40691, Philadelphia PA 19107. **Contact:** Joseph Farley, editor. Magazine specializing in science fiction: 8½×11; 24-40 pages; 20 lb. paper; 70 lb. cover; illustrations; photographs. "Quirky science fiction, horror and fantasy have a home here." Biannual. Estab. 2002. Circ. 100.

Needs Fantasy (space fantasy, sword and sorcery, cross-over), science fiction (erotica, experimental, hard science/technological, cross-genre). Receives 5 unsolicited mss/month. Accepts 4-10 mss/issue. Recently published work by Ernest Swallow, Joseph Farley and Brad Wells. Publishes short shorts. Sometimes comments on rejected mss.

How to Contact Send complete ms with cover letter. Include brief bio and list of publications. Send SASE for return of ms, or send disposable copy of ms with SASE for reply only. Responds in 4 months to mss. Accepts simultaneous and reprints, multiple submissions. Sample copy for $7. Reviews fiction.

Payment/Terms Pays 1 contributor's copy; additional copies $7. Pays on publication for one-time rights.

Advice "Finding a good manuscript is like falling in love: You may know it when you first see it, or you may need to get familiar with it for a while."

$◎ LULLABY HEARSE

26 Fifth St., Bangor ME 04401-6022. E-mail: editor@lullabyhearse.com. Website: www.lullabyhearse.com. "*Lullaby Hearse* seeks dark, literary fiction in which the protagonist never gets a free ride. Stories that are event- rather than character-driven or that utilize traditional horror themes will generally get the back door treatment. Stark imagery and powerful characterization are desirable." Quarterly. Estab. 2002. Circ. 200.

Needs Experimental, horror, science fiction. "Please don't send stories about writers, formulaic horror stories, or crime/mystery narratives that drag themselves down the beaten path. Fantasy and science fiction works are considered, but imagery must always be grounded in reality; miracles will be shot down." Publishes ms 3 months after acceptance.

How to Contact Send complete ms. Accepts submissions by e-mail (editor@lullabyhearse.com). Responds in 2 weeks to queries; 2 months to mss. Accepts simultaneous submissions. Sample copy for $6. Writer's guidelines online.

Payment/Terms Pays $10-20. Pays on acceptance for first rights.

Advice "We look for uniquely structured stories that ultimately cohere in a strong, decisive ending. Black humor is sometimes accepted, but humor alone isn't enough to take a story where it needs to go. Keenness of imagery and overall literary quality are important deciding factors. Crudity crosses the line when it insults the intelligence of the reader."

$◎ THE MIRACULOUS MEDAL

The Central Association of the Miraculous Medal, 475 E. Chelten Ave., Philadelphia PA 19144-5785. (215)848-1010. Website: www.cammonline.org. **Contact:** Charles Kelly, general manager. Magazine. Quarterly. Estab. 1915.

Needs Religious/inspirational. Should not be pious or sermon-like. Receives 25 unsolicited mss/month. Accepts 2 mss/issue; 8 mss/year. Publishes ms 2 years after acceptance.

How to Contact Responds in 3 months to queries. Sample copy for 6×9 SAE and 2 first-class stamps. Writer's guidelines free.

Payment/Terms Pays 3¢/word minimum. Pays on acceptance for first North American serial rights.

Ⓝ $◻ MONTHLY SHORT STORIES

David Hooper, P.O. Box 7044, Kansas City MO 64113. (816)509-8222. E-mail: dhooper@everestkc.net. Website: http://monthlyshortstories.com. **Contact:** David Hooper. Magazine: 8×11; 10-12 pages. "*Monthly Short Stories* is convenient. It is delivered by e-mail to most subscribers and they can choose to either read it online or print it out in an easy-to-read pdf format." Monthly. Estab. 2004. Circ. 2,500.

Needs Adventure, ethnic/multicultural, experimental, family saga, fantasy, horror, literary, mainstream, military/war, mystery/suspense, New Age, psychic/supernatural/occult, romance, science fiction. Receives 25 unsolicited mss/month. Accepts 2-5 mss/issue; 24-48 mss/year. Publishes ms 4-6 months after acceptance. Recently published work by B. Michelaard, Dr. Bob Rich, Paula Peters. Length: 1,000-5,000 words; average length: 3,500 words. Publishes short shorts. Sometimes comments on rejected mss.

How to Contact Accepts submissions by e-mail. Responds in 2-4 months to mss. Accepts simultaneous, multiple submissions. Writer's guidelines online.

Payment/Terms Pays $10-25. Pays on publication for one-time rights. Not copyrighted.

Advice "Get a free trial copy. I will work with writers who send me something that has merit."

◎ 🌐 MSLEXIA, For Women Who Write

Mslexia Publications Ltd., P.O. Box 656, Newcastle Upon Tyne NE99 1PZ United Kingdom. (00)44-191-2616656. Fax: (00)44-191-2616636. E-mail: postbag@mslexia.demon.co.uk. Website: www.mslexia.co.uk. **Contact:** Debbie Taylor, editor. Magazine: A4; 60 pages; some illustrations; photos. *"Mslexia* is for women who write, who want to write, who have a special interest in women's writing, or who teach creative writing. *Mslexia* is a blend of features, articles, advice, listings, and original prose and poetry. Many parts of the magazine are open to submission from any women. Please request contributor's guidelines prior to sending in work." Quarterly. Estab. 1999. Circ. 20,000.

Needs No work from men accepted. Each issue is to a specific theme. Send SAE for themes. Some themes have included fairy tales and interviews. Publishes ms 3-4 months after acceptance. **Publishes 40-50 new writers/ year.** Length:3,000 words; average length: 2,000 words. Publishes short shorts. Also publishes poetry.

How to Contact Accepts submissions by e-mail (postbag@mslexia.demon.co.uk). Query first. Responds in 3 months to mss. Guidelines for SAE, e-mail, fax or on website.

Payment/Terms Pays contributor's copies.

Advice "We look for an unusual slant on the theme. Well-structured, short pieces. Also intelligent, humorous, or with a strong sense of voice. Consider the theme and all obvious interpretations of it. Try to think of a new angle/slant. Dare to be different. Make sure the piece is strong on craft as well as content."

N 〇 MUDROCK: STORIES & TALES

MudRock Press, P.O. Box 31688, Dayton OH 45437. E-mail: mudrockpress@hotmail.com. Website: www.mudr ockpress.com. **Contact:** Brady Allen and Scott Geisel, editors. Magazine: $7 \times 8^{1}/_{2}$; 80-120 pages; bond paper; color cover; illustrations. *"MudRock* is an eclectic collection of stories, odd or not so, that people can follow, stories based in North America. We both like road stories, but we accept a wide range of genres from mainstream and realism to humor, horror and sci-fi." Triannual. Estab. 2003. Circ. 250-500.

Needs Ethnic/multicultural (North America), feminist, horror (dark fantasy, futuristic, psychological, supernatural), humor/satire, literary, mainstream, mystery/suspense (amateur sleuth, cozy, police procedural, private eye/hard-boiled), psychic/supernatural/occult, regional (North America), science fiction (hard science/technological, soft/sociological), thriller/espionage, western, road stories. We do not want experimental or postmodern fiction. Accepts 8-10 mss/issue; 25-30 mss/year. Publishes ms up to 12 months after acceptance. **Publishes 20-25 new writers/year.** Length: 8,000 words; average length: 3,000-6,000 words. Publishes short shorts. Always comments on rejected mss.

How to Contact Send disposable copy of the ms and #10 SASE for reply only. We do not return mss. Responds in 1 month to queries; 3 months to mss. Accepts simultaneous submissions. Sample copy for $5.00 (past issue), $6 current issue. Writer's guidelines for SASE or on website.

Payment/Terms Pays 2 contributor's copies; additional copies $4. Pays on publication for one-time rights. Sends galleys to author.

Advice "Stories first, style second. No post-modern or experimental fiction. We want vivid characters and setting and compelling action and storylines. If you have a story and aren't sure where it fits, try us. *MudRock* is an eclectic mix, so long as the stories relate somehow to the North American experience. Simply put: Something's gotta happen in your tale that readers will give a squat about. Check our editors' preferences and other info on our website, and send us something you think is as good as what we publish."

〇 NEW METHODS, The Journal of Animal Health Technology

713 S. Main St. C1, Willits CA 95490. (707)456-1262. E-mail: norwal13@yahoo.com. **Contact:** Ronald S. Lippert, publisher. Newsletter ("could become a magazine again"): $8^{1}/_{2} \times 11$; 2-4 pages; 20 lb. paper; illustrations; "rarely photos." Network service in the animal field, educating services for mostly professionals in the animal field; e.g., animal health technicians. Monthly. Estab. 1976. Circ. 5,608.

Needs Animals: contemporary, experimental, historical, mainstream, regional. No stories unrelated to animals. Receives 12 unsolicited mss/month. Accepts 1 mss/issue; 12 mss/year. Publishes short shorts. Occasionally comments on rejected mss.

How to Contact Query first with theme, length, expected time of completion, photos/illustrations, if any, biographical sketch of author, all necessary credits, or send complete ms. Responds in up to 4 months to queries. Accepts simultaneous, multiple submissions. Sample copy for $2.50. Writer's guidelines for SASE.

Payment/Terms Acquires one-time rights. Sponsors awards/contests.

Advice "Emotion, personal experiences—make the person feel it. We are growing."

N $〇 〇 NEW WITCH, not your mother's broomstick

B.B.I. Media, P.O. Box 641, Point Arena CA 95468. (707)882-2052. Fax: (707)882-2793. E-mail: info@bbimedia.com. Website: www.newwitch.com. **Contact:** Anne Niven, chief editor. Magazine: $8^{1}/_{2} \times 11$; 80 pages; 50 lb. recycled book paper; 80 lb. book cover stock; illustrations; photos. "We are the only magazine of this type. Dedicated to, featuring, and partially written by young or beginning Witches, Wiccans, Neo-Pagans and other earth-based, ethnic, pre-christian, shamanic and magical practitioners. Traditional Wiccans, potion-makers, Asatruar, eco-pagans all welcome." Quarterly. Estab. 2002. Circ. 15,000. Member: Independent Press Association.

Needs Fantasy, humor/satire, New Age, psychic/supernatural/occult, religious/inspirational, science fiction (hard science/technological, soft/sociological, pagan themes), Pagan/Wicca themes. No romance or juvenile. Receives 5-10 unsolicited mss/month. Accepts 10-12 mss/year. Publishes ms 6 months after acceptance. **Publishes many new writers/year.** Recently published work by Elizabeth Barette and Tamara Nelson. Also publishes poetry. Sometimes comments on rejected mss.

How to Contact Send complete ms. Accepts submissions by e-mail, fax, disk. Send SASE (or IRC) for return of the ms, or send disposable copy of the ms and #10 SASE for reply only. Responds in 3-6 weeks to mss. Accepts reprints submissions. No simultaneous submissions. Sample copy free. Writer's guidelines for #10 SASE, online, or by e-mail.

Payment/Terms Pays 2¢/word and 1-6 contributor's copies. Pays on publication. Aquires first worldwide periodical publications and non-exclusive e-rights.

Advice "Read the magazine! Must know who we are and what we like."

$☑ NEWN

(formerly New England Writers' Network), P.O. Box 483, Hudson MA 01749-0483. (978)562-2946. E-mail: NEWNmag@aol.com. **Contact:** Glenda Baker, fiction editor. Magazine: 8½×11; 24 pages; coated cover. "We are devoted to helping new writers get published and to teaching through example and content. We are looking for well-written stories that grab us from the opening paragraph." Quarterly. Estab. 1994. Circ. 300.

Needs Adventure, condensed novels, ethnic/multicultural, humor/satire, literary, mainstream, mystery/suspense, religious/inspirational, romance. "We will consider anything except pornography or extreme violence." Accepts 5 mss/issue; 20 mss/year. Publishes ms 4-12 months after acceptance. **Publishes 10-12 new writers/year.** Recently published work by Sandra McBride, Leslie Wheer and Judith Copek. Publishes short shorts. Also publishes poetry. Sometimes comments on rejected mss.

How to Contact Send complete ms with cover letter. Include estimated word count. Bio on acceptance. Reads mss only from June 1 to September 1. No simultaneous submissions. Sample copy for $5.50. Writer's guidelines free.

Payment/Terms Pays $10 for fiction, $5 for personal essays, $5 per poem and 1 contributor's copy. Pays on publication for first North American serial rights. Sponsors awards/contests.

Advice "We are devoted to helping new writers get published and to teaching through example and content. Give us a try! Please send for guidelines and a sample."

ℕ ✂ $NFG MAGAZINE, Writing with Attitude

NFG Media, Sheppard Centre, P.O. Box 43112, Toronto ON M2N 6N1 Canada. Fax: (1) 416-226-0994. E-mail: mrspeabody@nfg.ca. Website: www.nfg.ca. **Contact:** Shar O'Brien, publisher/editor-in-chief; J. Dale Hand-Humphries, managing editor. "We offer fiction without boundaries; content based on merit, not classification. From poetry to short stories, comics to art—if it titillates the mind, twists the subconscious or delivers an unexpected slap, we want to see it. Artists who submit to *NFG* log in as a member and may check the status of their work as it moves through the editorial process. Work accepted for review is read by a minimum of 5 editors, who leave constructive comments for the author." Triannual. Estab. October 2001; first issue January 2003. Circ. 5,000.

Needs Adventure, condensed novels, confessions, erotica, ethnic/multicultural, experimental, fantasy, historical, horror, humor/satire, mainstream, mystery/suspense, novel excerpts, religious/inspirational, romance, science fiction, serialized novels, slice-of-life vignettes, suspense, western. Publishes ms 6 months after acceptance.

How to Contact Sample copy for $11. Writer's guidelines online.

Payment/Terms Pays 5¢/word, up to 1,000 words, $15 minimum. Pays on acceptance for first, second serial (reprint) rights.

☑ ◎ ✂ NIGHT TERRORS

1202 W. Market Street, Orrville OH 44667-1710. (330)683-0338. E-mail: editor@night-terrors-publications.com. Website: www.night-terrors-publications.com. **Contact:** D.E. Davidson, editor/publisher. Magazine: 8½×11; 52 pages; 80 lb. glossy cover; illustrations; photos. "*Night Terrors* publishes quality, thought-provoking horror fiction for literate adults." Quarterly. Estab. 1996. Circ. 1,000.

- *Night Terrors* has had 24 stories listed in the Honorable Mention section of *The Year's Best Fantasy and Horror, Annual Colletions*.

Needs Horror, psychic/supernatural/occult. "*Night Terrors* does not accept stories involving abuse, sexual mutilation or stories with children as main characters. We publish traditional supernatural/psychological horror for a mature audience. Our emphasis is on literate work with a chill." Wants to see more psychological horror. Receives 50 unsolicited mss/month. Accepts 12 mss/issue; 46 mss/year. Publishes ms 6-12 months after acceptance. **Publishes 16 new writers/year.** Recently published work by John M. Clay, Ken Goldman and Barbara

Rosen. Length: 2,000-5,000 words; average length: 3,000 words. Often comments on rejected mss.

How to Contact Send complete ms with cover letter. Include estimated word count, 50-word bio and list of publications. Send a #10 SASE or larger SASE for reply or return of ms. Responds in 1 week to queries; 3 months to mss. Accepts simultaneous submissions. Sample copy for $6 (make checks payable to Night Terrors Publications). Writer's guidelines for #10 SASE.

Payment/Terms "Pays 2 contributor's copies for nonprofessional writers; additional copies for $4.50. Pays by arrangement with professional writers." Pays on publication for first North American serial rights. Sends galleys to author.

Advice "I publish what I like. I like stories which involve me with the viewpoint character and leave me with the feeling that his/her fate could have been or might be mine. Act professionally. Check your work for typos, spelling, grammar, punctuation, format. Send your work flat in a 9×12 envelopoe. And if you must, paper clip it, don't staple."

THE NOCTURNAL LYRIC, Journal of the Bizarre

The Nocturnal Lyric, P.O. Box 542, Astoria OR 97103. E-mail: nocturnallyric@melodymail.com. Website: www. angelfire.com/ca/nocturnallyric. **Contact:** Susan Moon, editor. Magazine: 8½×11; 40 pages; illustrations. "Fiction and poetry submitted should have a bizarre horror theme. Our audience encompasses people who stand proudly outside of the mainstream society." Annual. Estab. 1987. Circ. 400.

Needs Horror (dark fantasy, futuristic, psychological, supernatural, satirical). "No sexually graphic material—it's too overdone in the horror genre lately." Receives 25-30 unsolicited mss/month. Accepts 10-11 mss/issue; 10-11 mss/year. Publishes ms 1 year after acceptance. **Publishes 20 new writers/year.** Recently published work by Mary Blais, Brian Biswas, John Sunseri and J.A. Davidson. Length: 2,000 words maximum; average length: 1,500 words. Publishes short shorts. Also publishes literary essays, poetry. Rarely comments on rejected mss.

How to Contact Send complete ms with cover letter. Include estimated word count. Responds in 3 month to queries; 8 months to mss. Accepts simultaneous and reprints, multiple submissions. Sample copy for $2 (back issue); $3 (current issue). Writer's guidelines online.

Payment/Terms Pays with discounts on subscriptions and discounts on copies of issue. Pays on acceptance. Not copyrighted.

Advice "A manuscript stands out when the story has a very original theme and the ending is not predictable. Don't be afraid to be adventurous with your story. Mainstream horror can be boring. Surreal, satirical horror is what true nightmares are all about."

NTH DEGREE, The Fiction and Fandom 'Zine

Big Blind Productions, 77 Algrace Blvd., Stafford VA 22556. (540)720-6061. Fax: (540)720-7050. E-mail: editor@ nthzine.com. Website: www.nthzine.com. **Contact:** Michael Pederson, editor. Magazine: 8½×11; 32 pages; 50 lb. white off-set paper; 80 lb. glossy cover stock; illustrations; photos. "We print the best SF/Fantasy from the genre's newest writers and run artwork by the hottest new artists. Our goal is to help make it easier for new artists and writers to break into the field." Quarterly. Estab. 2002. Circ. 3,500.

Needs Fantasy (space fantasy, sword and sorcery), historical (alternate history), horror (dark fantasy, futuristic, psychological, supernatural), humor/satire, science fiction (hard science/technological), young adult/teen (fantasy/science fiction), comic strips. Receives 3 unsolicited mss/month. Accepts 4 mss/issue; 6 mss/year. Publishes ms 6 months after acceptance. **Publishes 6 new writers/year.** Recently published work by Michail Velichensky, James R. Stratton, C.J. Henderson, Robert Balder and Matt McIrvin. Length: 2,000-7,000 words; average length: 3,500 words. Publishes short shorts. Also publishes poetry. Always comments on rejected mss.

How to Contact Send complete ms. Accepts submissions by e-mail, disk. Send SASE (or IRC) for return of ms, or send disposable copy of the ms and #10 SASE for reply only. Responds in 2 weeks to queries; 2 months to mss. Accepts simultaneous, multiple submissions. Sample copy for $3. Writer's guidelines online or by e-mail.

Payment/Terms Pays 5 contributor's copies and free subscription to the magazine. Pays on publication for one-time rights.

Advice "Don't submit anything that you may be ashamed of ten years later."

NUTHOUSE, Your Place for Humor Therapy

Twin Rivers Press, P.O. Box 119, Ellenton FL 34222. E-mail: nuthous449@aol.com. Website: hometown.aol. com/nuthous499/index2.html. **Contact:** Dr. Ludwig "Needles" Von Quirk, chief of staff. Zine: digest-sized; 12-16 pages; bond paper; illustrations; photos. "Humor of all genres for an adult readership that is not easily offended." Published every 2-3 months. Estab. 1993. Circ. 100.

Needs Humor/satire (erotica, experimental, fantasy, feminist, historical [general], horror, literary, mainstream/contemporary, mystery/suspense, psychic/supernatural/occult, romance, science fiction and westerns). Receives 30-50 unsolicited mss/month. Accepts 5-10 mss/issue; 50-60 mss/year. Publishes ms 6-12 months after acceptance. **Publishes 10-15 new writers/year.** Recently published work by Michael Fowler, Dale Andrew White and Jim Sullivan. Length: 100-1,000 words; average length: 500 words. Publishes short shorts. Also publishes literary essays, literary criticism, poetry. Often comments on rejected mss.

How to Contact Send complete ms with a cover letter. Include estimated word count, bio (paragraph) and list of publications. SASE for return of ms or send disposable copy of ms. Sample copy for $1.25 (payable to Twin Rivers Press). Writer's guidelines for #10 SASE.

Payment/Terms Pays 1 contributor's copy. Acquires one-time rights. Not copyrighted.

Advice Looks for "laugh-out-loud prose. Strive for original ideas; read the great humorists—Saki, Woody Allen, Robert Benchley, Garrison Keillor, John Irving—and learn from them. We are turned off by sophomoric attempts at humor built on a single, tired, overworked gag or pun; give us a story with a beginning, middle and end."

☑ THE OAK

1530 Seventh Street, Rock Island IL 61201. (309)788-3980. **Contact:** Betty Mowery, editor. Magazine: 8½×11; 8-10 pages. "To provide a showcase for new authors while showing the work of established authors as well; to publish wholesome work, something with a message." Bimonthly. Estab. 1991. Circ. 300.

Needs Adventure, experimental, fantasy, humor/satire, mainstream, contemporary, prose poem. No erotica or love poetry. "Gray Squirrel" appears as a section in *Oak*, accepts poetry and fiction from seniors age 50 and up. Receives 25 unsolicited mss/month. Accepts 12 mss/issue. Publishes ms 3 months after acceptance. **Publishes 25 new writers/year.**

How to Contact Send complete ms. Responds in 1 week to mss. Accepts simultaneous and reprints, multiple submissions. Sample copy for $3; subscription $10. Writer's guidelines for #10 SASE.

Payment/Terms None, but not necessary to buy a copy in order to be published. Acquires first rights.

Advice "I do not want erotica, extreme violence or killing of humans or animals for the sake of killing. Just be yourself when you write. Also, write *tight*. Please include SASE, or manuscripts will be destroyed. Be sure name and address are on the manuscript. Study the markets for length of manuscript and what type of material is wanted."

⬚ ⬚ $⬚ ON SPEC

P.O. Box 4727, Station South, Edmonton AB T6E 5G6 Canada. (780)413-0215. Fax: (780)413-1538. E-mail: onspec@onspec.ca. Website: www.onspec.ca/. **Contact:** Diane L. Walton, editor. Magazine: 5¼×8; 112 pages; illustrations. "We publish speculative fiction by new and established writers, with a strong preference for Canadian authored works." Quarterly. Estab. 1989. Circ. 2,000.

Needs Fantasy, horror, science fiction, magical realism. No media tie-in or shaggy-alien stories. No condensed or excerpted novels, religious/inspirational stories, fairy tales. "We would like to see more horror, fantasy, science fiction—well-developed stories with complex characters and strong plots." Receives 100 unsolicited mss/month. Accepts 10 mss/issue; 40 mss/year. "We read manuscripts during the month after each deadline: February 28/May 31/August 31/November 30." Publishes ms 6-18 months after acceptance. **Publishes 10-15 new writers/year.** Recently published work by James Van Pelt, David Kirtle, Allen Weiss and Steve Mohn. Length: 1,000-6,000 words; average length: 4,000 words. Also publishes poetry. Often comments on rejected mss.

How to Contact Send complete ms. Accepts submissions by disk. SASE for return of ms or send a disposable copy of ms plus #10 SASE for response. Include Canadian postage or IRCs. No e-mail or fax submissions. Responds in 2 weeks to queries 4 months after deadline to mss. Accepts simultaneous submissions. Sample copy for $7. Writer's guidelines for #10 SASE or on website.

Payment/Terms Pays $50-180 for fiction. Short stories (under 1,000 words): $50 plus 1 contributor's copy. Pays on acceptance for first North American serial rights.

Advice "We're looking for original ideas with a strong SF element, excellent dialogue, and characters who are so believable, our readers will really care about them."

⬚ ☑ ◎ OPEN MINDS QUARTERLY, A Psychosocial Literary Journal

NISA/Northern Initiative for Social Action, 680 Kirkwood Dr., Bldg 1, Sudbury ON P3E 1X3 Canada. (705)675-9193 ext. 8286. Fax: (705)675-3501. E-mail: openmind@nisa.on.ca. Website: www.nisa.on.ca. **Contact:** Dinah Lapraine, editor. Magazine: 8½×11; 28 pages; illustrations; photos. "*Open Minds Quarterly* publishes quality, insightful writing from consumer/survivors of mental illness who have experiences to share and voices to be heard. We inform mental health professionals, family and friends, fellow consumer/survivors, and society at large of the strength, intelligence and creativity of our writers. The purpose is to reduce the stigma associated with mental illness." Quarterly. Estab. 1998. Circ. 750.

Needs Mental illness, mental health. Receives 5-10 unsolicited mss/month. Accepts 1-2 mss/issue; 4-8 mss/year. **Publishes many new writers/year.** Publishes short shorts. Also publishes literary essays, poetry. Sometimes comments on rejected mss.

Small Circulation

How to Contact Send complete ms. Accepts submissions by e-mail, fax, disk. Send disposable copy of the ms and #10 SASE for reply only. Responds in 1 week to queries; 16 weeks to mss. Accepts simultaneous and reprints, multiple submissions. Sample copy for $5. Writer's guidelines for #10 SASE, online, or by e-mail.

Payment/Terms Pays 2-3 contributor's copies. Acquires first, one-time rights.

ORACLE STORY & LETTERS

Rising Star Publishers, 7510 Lake Glen Drive, Glen Dale MD 20769. (301)352-233. Fax: (301)352-2529. E-mail: hekwonna@aol.com. **Contact:** Obi H. Ekwonna, publisher. Magazine: $5^{1}/_{2} \times 8^{1}/_{2}$; 60 lb. white bound paper. Quarterly. Estab. 1989. Circ. 1,000.

Needs Adventure, children's/juvenile (adventure, fantasy, historical, mystery, series), comics/graphic novels, ethnic/multicultural, family saga, fantasy (sword and sorcery), historical, literary, mainstream, military/war, romance (contemporary, historical, suspense), thriller/espionage, western (frontier saga), young adult/teen (adventure, historical). Does not want gay/lesbian or erotica works. Receives 10 unsolicited mss/month. Accepts 7 mss/issue. Publishes ms 4 months after acceptance. **Publishes 5 new writers/year.** Recently published work by Joseph Manco, I.B.S. Sesay. Publishes short shorts. Also publishes literary essays, literary criticism, poetry. Rarely comments on rejected mss.

How to Contact Send complete ms. Accepts submissions by disk. Send SASE (or IRC) for return of the ms, or send a disposable copy of the ms and #10 SASE for reply only. Responds in 1 month to mss. Accepts multiple submissions. Sample copy for $10. Writer's guidelines for #10 SASE or by e-mail.

Payment/Terms Pays 1 contributor's copy. Pays on publication for first North American serial rights.

Advice "Read anything you can lay your hands on."

OUTER DARKNESS, Where Nightmares Roam Unleashed

Outer Darkness Press, 1312 N. Delaware Place, Tulsa OK 74110. **Contact:** Dennis Kirk, editor. Zine: $8^{1}/_{2} \times 5^{1}/_{2}$; 60-80 pages; 20 lb. paper; 90 lb. glossy cover; illustrations. Specializes in imaginative literature. "Variety is something I strive for in *Outer Darkness*. In each issue we present readers with great tales of science fiction and horror along with poetry, cartoons and interviews/essays. I seek to provide readers with a magazine which, overall, is fun to read. My readers range in age from 16 to 70." Quarterly. Estab. 1994. Circ. 500.

- Fiction published in *Outer Darkness* has received honorable mention in *The Year's Best Fantasy and Horror*.

Needs Fantasy (science), horror, mystery/suspense (with horror slant), psychic/supernatural/occult, romance (gothic), science fiction (hard science, soft/sociological). No straight mystery, pure fantasy—works which do not incorporate elements of science fiction and/or horror. Also, no slasher horror with violence, gore, sex instead of plot. Wants more "character-driven tales—especially in the genre of science fiction and well-developed psychological horror. I do not publish works with children in sexual situations, and graphic language should be kept to a minimum." Receives 75-100 unsolicited mss/month. Accepts 7-9 mss/issue; 25-40 mss/year. **Publishes 2-5 new writers/year.** Recently published work by Tim Curran, Jim Lee, Erin McCole-Cupp and Steve Vertlieb. Length: 1,500-5,000 words; average length: 3,000 words. Also publishes poetry. Always comments on rejected mss.

How to Contact Send complete ms with a cover letter. Include estimated word count, 50- to 75-word bio, list of publications and "any awards, honors you have received." Send SASE for reply, return of ms, or send a disposable copy of ms. Responds in 2 weeks to queries; 4 months to mss. Accepts simultaneous, multiple submissions. Sample copy for $4.95. Writer's guidelines for #10 SASE.

Payment/Terms Pays 3 contributor's copies for fiction; 2 for poetry and 3 for art. Pays on publication for one-time rights.

Advice "I look for strong characters and well-developed plot. And I definitely look for suspense. I want stories which move—and carry the reader along with them. Be patient and persistent. Often it's simply a matter of linking the right story with the right editor. I've received many stories which were good but not what I wanted at the time. However, these stories worked well in another horror-sci-fi zine."

$ OVER THE BACK FENCE, Southern Ohio's Own Magazine

Panther Publishing, LLC, P.O. Box 756, Chillicothe OH 45601. (740)772-2165. Fax: (740)773-7626. Website: www.pantherpublishing.com. "We are a regional magazine serving 40 counties in Southern Ohio. *Over The Back Fence* has a wholesome, neighborly style. It appeals to readers from young adults to seniors, showcasing art and travel opportunities in the area." Quarterly. Estab. 1994. Circ. 15,000.

Needs Humor/satire. Receives 20 unsolicited mss/month. Accepts 2-3 mss/issue; 8-12 mss/year. Publishes ms 1 year after acceptance. **Publishes 4 new writers/year.** Recently published work by Debbie Farmer, Carol Lucas and Marcia Shonberg. Publishes short shorts. Also publishes poetry. Sometimes comments on rejected mss.

Small Circulation

How to Contact Query with published clips. Responds in 3 months to queries. Accepts simultaneous submissions. Sample copy for $4 or on website. Writer's guidelines online.

Payment/Terms Pays 10¢/word minimum, negotiable depending on experience. Pays on publication for one-time North American serial rights, makes work-for-hire assignments.

Advice "Submitted pieces should have a neighborly, friendly quality. Our publication is a positive piece on the good things in Ohio."

Ⓝ $⬚ ⓖ PANGAIA, A Pagan Journal for Thinking People

B.B.I. Media, P.O. Box 641, Point Arena CA 95468. (707)882-2052. Fax: (707)882-2793. Website: www.pangaia.com. **Contact:** Anne Niven, chief editor. Magazine: 8½×11; 80 pages; 50 lb. recycled book paper; 80 lb. book cover stock. "We are the only publication of this type. *PanGaia* explores Pagan and Gaian earth-based spirituality at home and around the world. We envision a world in which living in spirit and living on earth support and enrich each other; a spirituality that honors what is sacred in all life; a future in which ancient ritual and modern science both have a place. Intended audience: thinking adult Pagans of every sort, women and men of all earth-affirming spiritual paths." Quarterly. Estab. 1997. Circ. 7,000. Member: IPA.

• Nominated for the *Utne* Reader's Alternative Press Award for best spirituality coverage.

Needs Humor/satire, New Age, psychic/supernatural/occult, religious/inspirational (fantasy, mystery/suspense, thriller), science fiction (Pagan themes), Pagan/Gaian. No romance or juvenile stories. Receives 2-4 unsolicited mss/month. Accepts 1-4 mss/year. Publishes ms 6 months after acceptance. **Publishes some new writers/year.** Length: 500-5,000 words; average length: 3,500 words. Publishes short shorts. Also publishes poetry. Sometimes comments on rejected mss.

How to Contact Send complete ms. Accepts submissions by e-mail, fax, disk. Include SASE (or IRC) for return of ms, or send disposable copy of the ms and #10 SASE for reply only. Responds in 3-6 weeks to mss. Accepts reprints submissions. Sample copy free. Writer's guidelines for #10 SASE, online, or by e-mail.

Payment/Terms Pays 2¢/word. Pays on publication for first North American serial, electronic rights.

Advice "Read the magazine! Must know who we are and what we like."

ⓖ PARADOXISM

University of New Mexico, 200 College Rd., Gallup NM 87301. Fax: (503)863-7532. E-mail: smarand@unm.edu. Website: www.gallup.unm.edu/~smarandache/a/paradoxism.htm. **Contact:** Dr. Florentin Smarandache. Magazine: 8½×11; 100 pages; illustrations. "*Paradoxism* is an avant-garde movement based on excessive use of antinomies, antitheses, contradictions, paradoxes in the literary creations set up by the editor in the 1980s as an anti-totalitarian protest." Annual. Estab. 1993. Circ. 500.

Needs Experimental, literary. "Crazy, uncommon, experimental, avant-garde." Plans specific themes in the next year. Publishes annual special fiction issue or anthology. Receives 5 unsolicited mss/month. Accepts 10 mss/issue. Recently published work by Mirecea Monu, Doru Motoc and Patrick Pinard. Publishes short shorts. Also publishes literary essays, literary criticism, poetry. Sometimes comments on rejected mss.

How to Contact Send a disposable copy of ms. Responds in 2 months to mss. Accepts simultaneous submissions. Sample copy for $19.95 and 8½×11 SASE. Writer's guidelines online.

Payment/Terms Pays subscription. Pays on publication. Not copyrighted.

Advice "We look for work that refers to the paradoxism or is written in the paradoxist style. The Basic Thesis of the paradoxism: everything has a meaning and a non-meaning in a harmony with each other. The Essence of the paradoxism: a) the sense has a non-sense, and reciprocally B) the non-sense has a sense. The Motto of the paradoxism: 'All is possible, the impossible too!' The Symbol of the paradoxism: a spiral—optic illusion, or vicious circle."

⬚ ⓖ THE PEGASUS REVIEW

P.O. Box 88, Henderson MD 21640-0088. (410)482-6736. **Contact:** Art Bounds, editor. Magazine: 5½×8½; 6-8 pages; illustrations. "*The Pegasus Review* is a bimonthly, done in a calligraphic format and occasionally illustrated. Each issue is based on a specific theme." Estab. 1980. Circ. 120.

• Because *The Pegasus Review* is done is a calligraphic format, fiction submissions must be very short. Two pages, says the editor, are the ideal length.

Needs Humor/satire, literary, religious/inspirational, prose poem. Wants more short-shorts and theme-related fiction. Themes for 2005: Adventure (January/February); History (March/April); Imagination (May/June); Parents (July/August); Teaching (September/October); Music (November/December). Receives 35 unsolicited mss/month. Accepts 50 mss/issue. **Publishes 10 new writers/year.** Recently published work by Barbara Darr, Pearl Mary Wilshaw, Mike James, John Fitzpatrick and Kelley Jean White. Publishes short shorts. Sometimes comments on rejected mss.

How to Contact Send complete ms. Send brief cover letter with author's background, name and prior credits, if any. Responds in 2 months to mss. Accepts simultaneous submissions. Sample copy for $2.50. Writer's guidelines for #10 SASE.

Payment/Terms Pays 2 contributor's copies. Acquires one-time rights. Sponsors awards/contests.

Advice "Write and continue to read as well, especially what is being published today. Don't overlook the classics. They have achieved that status for a reason—quality. Seek every opportunity to have your work read at various organizations. The reading of a work can give you a new slant on it. Above all, believe in your craft and stick to it!"

☑ ◎ ☒ PENNY DREADFUL, Tales & Poems of Fantastic Terror

Pendragonian Publications, P.O. Box 719, New York NY 10101-0719. E-mail: mmpendragon@aol.com. Website: www.mpendragon.com. **Contact:** Michael Pendragon, editor. Zine specializing in horror: 9×6; 175 pages; illustrations; photos. Publication to "celebrate the darker aspects of man, the world and their creator. We seek to address a highly literate audience who appreciate horror as a literary art form." Biannual. Estab. 1996. Circ. 200.

• *Penny Dreadful* won several Honorable Mentions in St. Martin's Press's *The Year's Best Fantasy and Horror* competition.

Needs Fantasy (dark symbolist), horror, psychic/supernatural/occult. Wants more "tales set in and in the style of the 19th century." No modern settings "constantly referring to 20th century persons, events, products, etc." List of upcoming themes available for SASE. Receives 100 unsolicited mss/month. Accepts 10 mss/issue. *Penny Dreadful* reads all year until we have accepted enough submissions to fill more than one year's worth of issues."

Publishes 1-3 new writers/year. Recently published work by James S. Dorr, Scott Thomas, John B. Ford, Susan E. Abramski, Paul Bradshaw and John Light. Publishes short shorts. Also publishes poetry. Always comments on rejected mss.

How to Contact Send complete ms with a cover letter. Include estimated word count, bio and list of publications. Send SASE for reply, return of ms or send disposable copy of ms. Responds in up to 1 year to queries and mss. Accepts simultaneous and reprints submissions. Sample copy for $10. Subscription for $25. Writer's guidelines for #10 SASE.

Payment/Terms Pays 1 contributor's copy. Acquires one-time rights. Sends galleys to author. Not copyrighted.

Advice "Whenever possible, try to submit to independent zines specializing in your genre. Be prepared to spend significant amounts of time and money. Expect only one copy as payment. Over time—if you're exceptionally talented and/or lucky—you may begin to build a small following."

☑ ◎ THE PIPE SMOKER'S EPHEMERIS

The Universal Coterie of Pipe Smokers, 20-37 120 Street, College Point NY 11356-2128. **Contact:** Tom Dunn, editor. Magazine: $8^{1}/_{2} \times 11$; 84-116 pages; offset paper and cover; illustrations; photos. Pipe smoking and tobacco theme for general and professional audience. Irregular quarterly. Estab. 1964.

Needs Pipe smoking related: historical, humor/satire, literary. Publishes ms up to 1 year after acceptance. Length: 5,000 words; average length: 2,500 words. Publishes short shorts. Occasionally comments on rejected mss.

How to Contact Send complete ms with cover letter. Responds in 2 weeks to mss. Accepts simultaneous and reprints submissions. Sample copy for $8^{1}/_{2} \times 11$ SAE and 6 first-class stamps.

Payment/Terms Acquires one-time rights.

☒ ☒ ☑ THE PLOWMAN

Box 414, Whitby ON L1N 5S4 Canada. **Contact:** Tony Scavetta. Magazine: $8^{1}/_{2} \times 11$; 20-24 pages; bond paper; illustrations. Annual. Estab. 1988. Circ. 1,500.

Needs Humor/satire, religious/inspirational, romance. Receives 6-8 unsolicited mss/month. Publishes ms 4-8 months after acceptance. **Publishes 8-10 new writers/year.** Recently published work by Ken Harvey, Lois MacIssac and Martha Smith. Length: 100-1,500 words; average length: 1,500 words. Publishes short shorts. Also publishes poetry. Always comments on rejected mss.

How to Contact Send complete ms. Send disposable copy of the ms and #10 SASE for reply only. Responds in 1-2 weeks to queries; 4-6 weeks to mss. Accepts simultaneous and reprints, multiple submissions. Sample copy free. Writer's guidelines for #10 SASE.

Payment/Terms Pays 1 contributor's copy. Acquires one-time rights.

☑ ◎ POSKISNOLT PRESS

Yesterday's Press, JAF Station, Box 7415, New York NY 10116-4630. **Contact:** Patricia D. Coscia, editor. Magazine: $7 \times 8^{1}/_{2}$; 20 pages; regular typing paper. Estab. 1989. Circ. 100.

Needs Erotica, ethnic/multicultural, experimental, fantasy, feminist, gay, humor/satire, lesbian, literary, mainstream, psychic/supernatural/occult, romance, western, young adult/teen (10-18 years old), contemporary, prose poem, senior citizen/retirement. "X-rated material is not accepted!" Plans to publish a special fiction issue or anthology in the future. Receives 50 unsolicited mss/month. Accepts 30 mss/issue; 100 mss/year. Publishes ms 6 months after acceptance. Recently published work by Steve Swanbeck, Jenny D. Nasson, Carol S. Fowler. Length: 100-500 words; average length: 200 words. Publishes short shorts. Sometimes comments on rejected mss.

How to Contact Query with published clips or send complete ms. SASE. Responds in 1 week to queries; 6 months to mss. Accepts simultaneous submissions. Sample copy for $5 with #10 SAE and $2 postage. Writer's guidelines for #10 SAE and $2 postage.

Payment/Terms Pays with subscription to magazine or contributor's copies; charges for extras. Acquires first, one-time rights.

$⬚ THE POST

Publishers Syndication International, P.O. Box 6218, Charlottesville VA 22906-6218. E-mail: asamuels@publisherssyndication.com. Website: www.publisherssyndication.com. **Contact:** A.P. Samuels, editor. Magazine: 8½×11; 32 pages. Monthly. Estab. 1988.

Needs Adventure, mystery/suspense (private eye), romance (romantic suspense, historical, contemporary), western (traditional). "No explicit sex, gore, weird themes, extreme violence or bad language. Receives 35 unsolicited mss/month. Accepts 1 mss/issue; 12 mss/year. Agented fiction 10%. **Publishes 1-3 new writers/ year.** Average length: 10,000 words.

How to Contact Send complete ms with cover letter. Responds in 5 weeks to mss. Sample copy not available. Writer's guidelines for #10 SASE.

Payment/Terms 1-2¢/word. Pays on acceptance

Advice "Manuscripts must be for a general audience."

⬚ ◎ PRAYERWORKS, Encouraging God's people to do real work of ministry—intercessory prayer

The Master's Work, P.O. Box 301363, Portland OR 97294-9363. (503)761-2072. E-mail: vannm1@aol.com. **Contact:** V. Ann Mandeville, editor. Newsletter: 5½×8; 4 pages; bond paper. "Our intended audience is 70% retired Christians and 30% families. We publish 350-500 word devotional material—fiction, nonfiction, biographical, poetry, clean quips and quotes. Our philosophy is evangelical Christian, serving the body of Chirst in the area of prayer." Estab. 1988. Circ. 1,100.

Needs Religious/inspirational. "No nonevangelical Christian. Subject matter may include anything which will build relationship with the Lord—prayer, ways to pray, stories of answered prayer, teaching on a Scripture portion, articles that will build faith, or poems will all work. We even use a series occasionally." Publishes ms 2-6 months after acceptance. **Publishes 30 new writers/year.** Recently published work by Allen Audrey and Petey Prater. Length: 350-500 words; average length: 350-500 words. Publishes short shorts. Also publishes poetry. Often comments on rejected mss.

How to Contact Send complete ms with cover letter. Include estimated word count and a very short bio. Responds in 1 month to mss. Accepts simultaneous and reprints, multiple submissions. Writer's guidelines for #10 SASE.

Payment/Terms Pays free subscription to the magazine and contributor's copies. Pays on publication. Not copyrighted.

Advice Stories "must have a great take-away—no preaching; teach through action. Be thrifty with words— make them count."

⬚ PROSE AX, doses of prose, poetry, and visual art

P.O. Box 22643, Honolulu HI 96823-2643. E-mail: editor@proseax.com. Website: www.proseax.com. **Contact:** J.C. Salazar, editor. Zine and online magazine specializing in prose, poetry and art: 8½×5; 24-30 pages; 20 lb. paper; illustrations; photos. "We are a literary journal that publishes stimulating, fresh prose and poetry. We are committed to publishing new or ethnic writers or ethnic themes. The style of our website and print version is very visual, very stylish, and I think this makes our publication different. We present fresh voices in a fresh way." Triannual. Estab. 2000. Circ. 400-500 print; 50 unique visitors average per day to website.

Needs Ethnic/multicultural (general), experimental, literary, literary fantasy (fantastic realism), novel excerpts that work well alone, flash fiction. "No genre, especially romance and mystery." Receives 30-50 unsolicited mss/month. Accepts 7-15 mss/issue. Publishes ms 1-4 months after acceptance. **Publishes 10 new writers/ year.** Recently published work by Eric Paul Shafer, Ken Goldman, Suzanne Frischkorn, Jasmine Orr, Jason D. Smith, K.J. Stevens and Kenneth Champeon. Length: 50-5,000 words; average length: 1,000 words. Publishes short shorts. Also publishes literary essays, poetry. Often comments on rejected mss.

How to Contact Accepts submissions by e-mail. Send complete copy of ms with cover letter. Include estimated word count with submission. Send disposable copy of ms and #10 SASE for reply only. Responds in 1-2 months

Small Circulation

to mss. Accepts simultaneous and reprints, multiple submissions. Writer's guidelines for SASE, by e-mail or on website. Reviews fiction.

Payment/Terms Pays 2 contributor's copies. Pays on publication for one-time, electronic rights. Sends galleys to author. Sponsors awards/contests.

Advice "A good story has good details and descriptions. Read our zine first to see if what you write will fit in with the tone and style of *Prose Ax*. Write a little hello to us instead of sending only your mss."

$☑ PSI

P.O. Box 6218, Charlottesville VA 22906-6218. E-mail: asam@publisherssyndication.com. Website: www.publis herssyndication.com. **Contact:** A.P. Samuels, editor. Magazine: 8½×11; 32 pages; bond paper; self cover. "Mystery and romance." Bimonthly. Estab. 1987.

Needs Adventure, mystery/suspense (private eye), romance (contemporary, historical, young adult), western (traditional). No ghoulish, sex, violence. Wants to see more believable stories. Accepts 1-2 mss/issue. **Publishes 1-3 new writers/year.** Average length: 30,000 (novelettes) words. Publishes short shorts. Rarely comments on rejected mss.

How to Contact Send complete ms with cover letter. Responds in 2 weeks to queries; 6 weeks to mss.

Payment/Terms 1-4¢/word, plus royalty. Pays on acceptance.

Advice "Manuscripts must be for a general audience. Just good plain story telling (make it compelling). No explicit sex or ghoulish violence."

$☑ ◎ QUEEN OF ALL HEARTS

Montfort Missionaries, 26 S. Saxon Ave., Bay Shore NY 11706-8993. (631)665-0726. Fax: (631)665-4349. E-mail: montfort@optonline.net. Website: www.montfortmissionaries.com. **Contact:** Roger M. Charest, S.M.M., managing editor. Magazine: 7¾×10¾; 48 pages; self cover stock; illustrations; photos. Magazine of "stories, articles and features on the Mother of God by explaining the Scriptural basis and traditional teaching of the Catholic Church concerning the Mother of Jesus, her influence in fields of history, literature, art, music, poetry, etc." Bimonthly. Estab. 1950. Circ. 2,000.

Needs Religious/inspirational. "Wants mss only about Our Lady, the Mother of God, the Mother of Jesus." Publishes ms 6-12 months after acceptance. **Publishes 6 new writers/year.** Recently published work by Richard O'Donnell and Jackie Clements-Marenda. Sometimes comments on rejected mss.

How to Contact Send complete ms. Accepts submissions by e-mail, fax, disk. Accepts queries/mss by e-mail and fax (mss by permission only). Responds in 2 months to queries. Sample copy for $2.50 with 9×12 SAE.

Payment/Terms Pays $40-60. Pays on publication. Not copyrighted.

Advice "We are publishing stories with a Marian theme."

⬛ $▢ ◎ QUEEN'S QUARTERLY, A Canadian Review

Queen's University, Kingston ON K7L 3N6 Canada. (613)533-2667. Fax: (613)533-6822. E-mail: qquarter@post. queensu.ca. Website: info.queensu.ca/quarterly. **Contact:** Boris Castel, editor. Magazine: 6×9; 800 pgaes/year; illustrations. "A general interest intellectual review, featuring articles on science, politics, humanities, arts and letters. Book reviews, poetry and fiction." Quarterly. Estab. 1893. Circ. 3,000.

Needs Historical, literary, mainstream, novel excerpts, short stories, women's. "Special emphasis on work by Canadian writers." Accepts 2 mss/issue; 8 mss/year. Publishes ms 6-12 months after acceptance. **Publishes 5 new writers/year.** Recently published work by Gail Anderson-Dargatz, Tim Bowling, Emma Donohue, Viktor Carr, Mark Jarman, Rick Bowers and Dennis Bock. Also publishes literary essays, literary criticism, poetry.

How to Contact "Send complete ms with SASE and/or IRC. No reply with insufficient postage." Responds in 2-3 months to queries. Sample copy online. Writer's guidelines online. Reviews fiction.

Payment/Terms Pays $100-300 for fiction, 2 contributor's copies and 1-year subscription; additional copies $5. Pays on publication for first North American serial rights. Sends galleys to author.

☑ RHAPSOIDIA

40390 Rome Beauty Way, Cherry Valley CA 92223. E-mail: echo-7@earthlink.net. Website: http://rhapsoidia.c om. **Contact:** Dave Hora, fiction editor. Magazine: Digest size; 40-56 pages; illustrations; photos. "Our fiction tastes lean toward experimental fiction, magical realism, metafiction, or works of any genre told in innovative or different ways." Quarterly. Estab. 2002. Circ. 350.

Needs Experimental. No young adult/teen, children/juvenile. Receives 30 unsolicited mss/month. Accepts 10 mss/issue; 40 mss/year. Publishes ms 3 months after acceptance. **Publishes some new writers/year.** Recently published work by Debra Di Blasi, Stephanie Hammer, Lance Olsen and Steve Redwood. Length: 2,500-5,000 words; average length: 3,000 words. Also publishes poetry. Rarely comments on rejected mss.

How to Contact Send complete ms. Accepts submissions by e-mail. Responds in 1 month to queries; 4 months to mss. Sample copy for $2.95 plus $1.00 s&h. Writer's guidelines online.

Small Circulation

Payment/Terms Pays one contributor's copy. Pays on publication for first North American serial rights.
Advice "Visit our website for more detailed submission guidelines. We only accept online submissions. Please work long and hard on fine-tuning your pieces before sending them out."

$⊘ ROSEBUD, The Magazine For People Who Enjoy Good Writing

Rosebud, Inc., N3310 Asje Rd., Cambridge WI 53523. (608)423-9780. Fax: (608)423-9976. E-mail: jrodclark@sm allbytes.net. Website: www.rsbd.net. **Contact:** Roderick Clark, editor. Magazine: 7×10; 136 pages; 60 lb. matte; 100 lb. cover; illustrations. Quarterly. Estab. 1993. Circ. 9,000.
Needs Adventure, ethnic/multicultural, experimental, historical (general), literary, mainstream, novel excerpts, psychic/supernatural/occult, regional, romance (contemporary), science fiction (soft/sociological), slice-of-life vignettes, translations. "No formula pieces." Receives 1,200 unsolicited mss/month. Accepts 16 mss/issue; 64 mss/year. Publishes ms 1-3 months after acceptance. **Publishes 70% new writers/year.** Recently published work by Seamus Heany, Louis Simpson, Allen Ginsberg and Phillip Levine. Publishes short shorts. Also publishes literary essays. Often comments on rejected mss.
How to Contact Send complete ms. Include SASE for return of ms and $1 handling fee. Responds in 3 months to mss. Accepts simultaneous and reprints submissions. Sample copy for $6.95 or sample articles online. Writer's guidelines for SASE or on website.
Payment/Terms Pays $15 and 3 contributor's copies; additional copies $4.40. Pays on publication for first, one-time, second serial (reprint) rights.
Advice "Each issue will have six or seven flexible departments (selected from a total of sixteen departments that will rotate). We are seeking stories; articles; profiles; and poems of: love, alienation, travel, humor, nostalgia and unexpected revelation. Something has to 'happen' in the pieces we choose, but what happens inside characters is much more interesting to us than plot manipulation. We like good storytelling, real emotion and authentic voice."

▢ ◎ SLATE AND STYLE, Magazine of the National Federation of the Blind Writers Division

NFB Writer's Division, 2704 Beach Drive, Merrick NY 11566. (516)868-8718. Fax: (516)868-9076. E-mail: lorista y@aol.com. **Contact:** Lori Stayer, fiction editor. Newsletter: 8×10; 28 print/40 Braille pages; e-mail, cassette and large print. "Articles of interest to writers and resources for blind writers." Quarterly. Estab. 1982. Circ. 200.
Needs Adventure, fantasy, humor/satire, contemporary, blindness. No erotica. "Avoid theme of death." Does not read mss in June or July. **Publishes 2 new writers/year.** Recently published work by Bonnie Lannom, Jane Lansaw, Christina Oakes and Patricia Hubschman. Publishes short shorts. Also publishes literary criticism, poetry. Sometimes comments on rejected mss.
How to Contact Accepts submissions by e-mail. Responds in 3-6 weeks to queries; 3-6 weeks to mss. Sample copy for $2.50.
Payment/Terms Pays in contributor's copies. Acquires one-time rights. Not copyrighted. Sponsors awards/contests.
Advice "The best advice I can give is to send your work out; manuscripts left in a drawer have no chance at all."

Ⓝ ⊘ SQUARE LAKE

6041 Palatine Ave. N., Seattle WA 98103. (206)706-4169. E-mail: la@squarelake.com. Website: www.squarelak e.com. **Contact:** Fiction editor. Magazine: 5½×8½; 100 pages. "*Square Lake* wants to publish work that makes people stop and reconsider their whole lives." Semiannual. Estab. 2002. Circ. 600.
Needs Literary. Receives 100 unsolicited mss/month. Accepts 4 mss/issue; 8 mss/year. Publishes ms 6 months after acceptance. **Publishes 2 new writers/year.** Recently published work by Marge Piercy, Joe Taylor, Lassita Williams. Average length: 2,000 words. Also publishes poetry.
How to Contact Send complete ms. Accepts submissions by e-mail. Send SASE (or IRC) for return of the ms, or send disposable copy of the ms and #10 SASE for reply only. Responds in 6 months to mss. Accepts simultaneous, multiple submissions. Sample copy for $7. Writer's guidelines for #10 SASE, online, or by e-mail.
Payment/Terms Pays 2 contributor's copies. Acquires first North American serial rights. Sends galleys to author.
Advice "Read the publications you submit to."

▧ $⊘ STORYTELLER, Canada's Short Story Magazine

Tyo Communications, 858 Wingate Dr., Ottawa ON K1G 1S5 Canada. (613)521-9570. E-mail: info@storytellerm agazine.com. Website: www.storytellermagazine.com. **Contact:** Melanie Fogel, editor. Magazine: 8½×11; 44 pages; 140 lb. bond paper; 160m gloss cover stock; illustrations. *Storyteller* is Canada's only popular fiction magazine. "We focus on entertaining stories, preferably with a Canadian slant." Quarterly. Estab. 1994. Circ. 2000.

• Received the Arthur Ellis Award (1996) and honorable mention for the Journey Prize (1998).

Needs Adventure, ethnic/multicultural (general), fantasy (twilight zone), historical (general), horror (dark fantasy, futuristic, psychological, supernatural), humor/satire, mainstream, military/war, mystery/suspense (amateur sleuth, cozy, police procedural, private eye/hard-boiled), psychic/supernatural/occult, romance (contemporary, futuristic/time travel, gothic, historical, regency period, suspense), science fiction (soft/sociological), thriller/espionage, western (frontier saga, traditional). "No 'hardcore' genre. No 'American' stories; there are hundreds of American magazines for Canadian readers to read. No 'agenda' stories; write a letter to your newspaper instead. No novel excerpts, experimental writing or children's stories." Publishes annual Great Canadian Story Contest issue. Receives 200-400 unsolicited mss/month. Accepts 8-11 mss/issue; 40 mss/year. Publishes ms 6-10 weeks after acceptance. **Publishes 8-12 new writers/year.** Recently published work by Ken Goldman, Vicki Cameron, Edo van Belkom, Mary Jane Maffini, Matt Hughes, Barbara Fradkin, Rudy Kremberg, John Ballem. Length: 2,000-6,000 words; average length: 3,500 words. Sometimes comments on rejected mss.

How to Contact Send complete ms. Send SASE with Canadian postage. Responds in 2 months to mss. Accepts reprints, multiple submissions. No simultaneous submissions. Sample copy for $5 plus shipping and postage. Writer's guidelines for SASE or on website.

Payment/Terms Pays 1/2¢/word; 1/4¢ word for reprints; 2 contributor's copies; additional copies $5. Acquires first North American serial rights. Sponsors awards/contests.

Advice "We look for characters so real you can smell them, in situations that keep us asking: What happens next? A manuscript stands out when I'm still on the first page and I've forgotten I'm reading a manuscript. Don't be superficial. Short stories need all the depth of a good novel. If you don't know what kind of underwear your character prefers, or which brand of toothpaste, you don't know him/her well enough."

☐ THE STORYTELLER, A Writer's Magazine

2441 Washington Road, Maynard AR 72444. (870)647-2137. Fax: (870)647-2454. E-mail: storyteller1@cox-Internet.com. Website: http://freewebz.com/fossilcreek. **Contact:** Regina Cook Williams, editor. Tabloid: 8½×11; 72 pages; typing paper; glossy cover; illustrations. "This magazine is open to all new writers regardless of age. I will accept short stories in any genre and poetry in any type. Please keep in mind, this is a family publication." Quarterly. Estab. 1996.

• Offers *People's Choice Awards* and nominates for a *Pushcart Prize.*

Needs Adventure, historical, humor/satire, literary, mainstream, mystery/suspense, religious/inspirational, romance, western, young adult/teen, senior citizen/retirement, sports. "I will not accept pornography, erotica, science fiction, new age, foul language, graphic horror or graphic violence." Wants more well-plotted mysteries. Publishes ms 3-9 months after acceptance. **Publishes 30-50 new writers/year.** Recently published work by Mellie Justad, Rick Jankowski, Rick Magers, Barbara Deming, Dusty Richards and Tony Hillerman. Publishes short shorts. Also publishes literary essays, poetry. Sometimes comments on rejected mss.

How to Contact Send complete ms with cover letter. Include estimated word count and 5-line bio. Submission by mail only. Responds in 1 month to queries; 2 months to mss. Accepts simultaneous and reprints submissions. Sample copy for $6. Writer's guidelines for #10 SASE.

Payment/Terms Sponsors awards/contests.

Advice "Follow the guidelines. No matter how many times this has been said, writers still ignore this basic and most important rule." Looks for "professionalism, good plots and unique characters. Purchase a sample copy so you know the kind of material we look for. Even though this is for unpublished writers, don't send us something you would not send to paying markets." Would like more "well-plotted mysteries and suspense and a few traditional westerns. Avoid sending anything that children or young adults would not (or could not) read, such as really bad language."

$ ☑ ◎ THE STRAND MAGAZINE

P.O. Box 1418, Birmingham MI 48012-1418. (248)788-5948. Fax: (248)874-1046. E-mail: strandmag@strandmag.com. Website: www.strandmag.com. **Contact:** A.F. Gulli, editor. "After an absence of nearly half a century, the magazine known to millions for bringing Sir Arthur Conan Doyle's ingenious detective, Sherlock Holmes, to the world has once again appeared on the literary scene. First launched in 1891, *The Strand* included in its pages the works of some of the greatest writers of the 20th century: Agatha Christie, Dorothy Sayers, Margery Allingham, W. Somerset Maugham, Graham Greene, P.G. Wodehouse, H.G. Wells, Aldous Huxley and many others. In 1950, economic difficulties in England caused a drop in circulation which forced the magazine to cease publication." Quarterly. Estab. 1998. Circ. 50,000.

Needs Horror, humor/satire, mystery/suspense (detective stories), suspense, tales of the unexpected, tales of terror and the supernatural "written in the classic tradition of this century's great authror's. "We are NOT interested in submissions with any sexual content. Stories can be set in any time or place, provided they are well written and the plots interesting and well thought out." Publishes ms 4 months after acceptance.

How to Contact SASE (IRCs if outside the US). Responds in 1 month to queries; 4 months to mss. Sample copy not available. Writer's guidelines for #10 SASE.
Payment/Terms Pays $50-175. Pays on acceptance for first North American serial rights.

🖊 🌐 STUDIO, A Journal of Christians Writing

727 Peel Street, Albury 2640 Australia. (+61)26021-1135. E-mail: studio00@bigpond.net.au. **Contact:** Paul Grover, managing editor. Quarterly. Circ. 300.
Needs "*Studio* publishes prose and poetry of literary merit, offers a venue for new and aspiring writers, and seeks to create a sense of community among Christians writing." Accepts 30-40 mss/year. **Publishes 40 new writers/year.** Recently published work by Andrew Lansdown and Benjamin Gilmour.
How to Contact Accepts submissions by e-mail. Send SASE. "Overseas contributors must use international postal coupons in place of stamped envelope." Responds in 1 month to mss. Sample copy for $10 (Aus).
Payment/Terms Pays in copies; additional copies are discounted. Subscription $60 (Australian) for 4 issues (1 year). International draft in Australian dollars and IRC required, or Visa and Mastercard facilities available. "Copyright of individual published pieces remains with the author, while each colection is copyright to *Studio*."

$🖊 TALEBONES, Fiction on the Dark Edge

Fairwood Press, 5203 Quincy Avenue SE, Auburn WA 98092-8723. (253)735-6552. E-mail: info@talebones.com. **Contact:** Patrick and Honna Swenson, editors. Magazine: digest size; 88 pages; standard paper; glossy cover stock; illustrations; photos. "We like stories that have punch but still entertain. We like science fiction and dark fantasy, humor, psychological and experimental works." Quarterly. Estab. 1995. Circ. 800.
Needs Fantasy (dark), humor/satire, science fiction (hard science, soft/sociological, dark). "No straight slash and hack horror. No cat stories or stories told by young adults. Would like to see more science fiction." Receives 200 unsolicited mss/month. Accepts 6-7 mss/issue; 12-14 mss/year. Publishes ms 3-4 months after acceptance. **Publishes 2-3 new writers/year.** Recently published work by Jack Cady, Louise Marley, Tom Piccirilli, Kay Kenyon, Nina Kiriki Hoffman. Length: 1,000-6,000 words; average length: 3,000-4,000 words. Publishes short shorts. Also publishes poetry.
How to Contact Send complete ms with cover letter. Include estimated word count and 1-paragraph bio. Responds in 1 week to queries; 1-2 months to mss. Sample copy for $6. Writer's guidelines for #10 SASE. Reviews fiction.
Payment/Terms Pays 1-2¢ per word and 1 contributor's copy; additional copies $4.00. Pays on acceptance for first North American serial rights. Sends galleys to author.
Advice "The story must be entertaining but should blur the boundary between science fiction and horror. Most of our stories have a dark edge to them but often are humorous or psychological. Be polite and know how to properly present a manuscript. Include a cover letter, but keep it short and to the point."

$🖊 📖 📺 TALES OF THE TALISMAN

(formerly Hadrosaur Tales), Hadrosaur Productions, P.O. Box 2194, Mesilla Park NM 88047-2194. E-mail: hadrosaur@zianet.com. Website: www.hadrosaur.com. **Contact:** David L. Summers, editor. Zine specializing in science fiction: 8½×11; 84 pages; 50 lb. white stock; 80 lb. cover. "*Tales of the Talisman* is a literary science fiction and fantasy magazine published 4 times a year. We publish short stories, poetry and articles with themes related to science fiction and fantasy. Above all, we are looking for thought-provoking ideas and good writing. Speculative fiction set in the past, present and future is welcome. Likewise, contemporary or historical fiction is welcome as long as it has a mythic or science fictional element. Our target audience includes adult fans of the science fiction and fantasy genres along with anyone else who enjoys thought-provoking and entertaining writing." Quarterly. Estab. 1995. Circ. 150.
● Received an honorable mention in *The Year's Best Science Fiction 2004* edited by Gardner Dozois.
Needs Erotica, fantasy (space fantasy, sword and sorcery), horror, science fiction (hard science/technological, soft/sociological). "We do not want to see stories with graphic violence. Do not send 'mainstream' fiction with no science fictional or fantastic elements. Do not send stories with copyrighted characters, unless you're the copyright holder." Receives 15 unsolicited mss/month. Accepts 7-10 mss/issue; 21-30 mss/year. Only reads May 1-June 15 and November 1-December 15. Publishes ms 9 months after acceptance. **Publishes 8 new writers/year.** Recently published work by Tim Myers, Neal Asher, Ken Goldman, Sonya Taaffe, Mark Fewell, Christina Sng and Julie Shiel. Length: 1,000-6,000 words; average length: 4,000 words. Also publishes poetry. Often comments on rejected mss.
How to Contact Send complete ms. Accepts submissions by e-mail (hadrosaur@zianet.com). Include estimated word count, brief bio and list of publications. Send SASE (or IRC) for return of ms or send a disposable copy of ms and #10 SASE for reply only. Responds in 1 week to queries; 1 month to mss. Accepts reprints submissions. No simultaneous submissions. Sample copy for $6.95. Writer's guidelines online.
Payment/Terms Pays $6-10. Pays on acceptance for one-time rights.

Advice "First and foremost, I look for engaging drama and believable characters. With those characters and situations, I want you to take me someplace I've never been before. The story I'll buy is the one set in a new world or where the unexpected happens, yet I cannot help but believe in the situation because it feels real. Read absolutely everything you can get your hands on, especially stories and articles outside your genre of choice. This is a great source for original ideas."

$⊘ ◎ WEBER STUDIES, Vices and Viewpoints of the Contemporary West

1214 University Circle, Ogden UT 84408-1214. (801)626-6473. E-mail: blroghaar@weber.edu. Website: weberst udies.weber.edu. **Contact:** Brad L. Roghaar, editor. Magazine: $7\frac{1}{2} \times 10$; 120-140 pages; coated paper; 4-color cover; illustrations; photos. "We seek the following themes: preservation of and access to wilderness, environmental cooperation, insight derived from living in the West, cultural diversity, changing federal involvement in the region, women and the West, implications of population growth, a sense of place, etc. We love good writing that reveals human nature as well as natural environment." Triannual. Estab. 1984. Circ. 1,000.

Needs Adventure, comics/graphic novels, ethnic/multicultural, experimental, feminist, historical, humor/satire, literary, mainstream, military/war, mystery/suspense, New Age, psychic/supernatural/occult, regional (contemporary western US), translations, western (frontier sage, tradtional, contemporary), short story collections. No children's/juvenile, erotica, religious or young adult/teen. Receives 50 unsolicited mss/month. Accepts 3-6 mss/issue; 9-18 mss/year. Publishes ms up to 18 months after acceptance. **Publishes "few" new writers/year.** Recently published work by Gary Gildner, Ron McFarland and David Duncan. Publishes short shorts. Also publishes literary essays, poetry. Sometimes comments on rejected mss.

How to Contact Send complete ms with a cover letter. Include estimated word count, bio (if necessary), and list of publications (not necessary). Responds in 3 months to mss. Accepts multiple submissions. Sample copy for $10.

Payment/Terms Pays $100-$200. Pays on publication for first, electronic rights. Requests electronic archive permission. Sends galleys to author.

Advice "Is it true? Is it new? Is it interesting? Will the story appeal to educated readers who are concerned with the contemporary western United States? Declining public interest in reading generally is of concern. We publish both print media and electronic media because we believe the future will expect both options."

$⊘ ZAHIR, Unforgettable Tales

Zahir Publishing, 315 South Coast Hwy. 101, Suite U8, Encinitas CA 92024. E-mail: stempchin@zahirtales.com. Website: www.zahirtales.com. **Contact:** Sheryl Tempchin, editor. Magazine: Digest-size; 80 pages; heavy stock paper; glossy, full color cover stock; illustrations. "We publish quality speculative fiction for intelligent adult readers. Our goal is to bridge the gap between literary and genre fiction, and present a publication that is both entertaining and aesthetically pleasing." Triannual. Estab. 2003.

Needs Fantasy, literary, psychic/supernatural/occult, science fiction, surrealism, magical realism. No children's stories or stories that deal with excessive violence or anything pornographic. Accepts 6-8 mss/issue; 18-24 mss/year. Publishes ms 2-12 months after acceptance. **Publishes 6 new writers/year.** Sometimes comments on rejected mss.

How to Contact Send complete ms. Send SASE (or IRC) for return of ms, or send disposable copy of the ms and #10 SASE for reply only. E-mail queries okay. No e-mail mss except from writers living outside the U.S. Responds in 1-2 weeks to queries; 1-3 months to mss. Accepts reprints submissions. No simultaneous submissions. Sample copy for $5 (US), $6.50 elsewhere. Writer's guidelines for #10 SASE, by e-mail, or online.

Payment/Terms Pays $10 and 2 contributor's copies. Pays on publication for first, second serial (reprint) rights.

Advice "The stories we are most likely to buy are well written, have interesting, well-developed characters and/or ideas that fascinate, chill, thrill or amuse us. They must have some element of the fantastic or surreal."

Online Markets

As production and distribution costs go up the number of and subscribers falls, more and more magazines are giving up print publication and moving online. Relatively inexpensive to maintain and quicker to accept and post submissions, online fiction sites are growing fast in numbers and legitimacy. Says the editor of *EWGPresents*: "We have the means to reach a universal audience by the click of a mouse. Writers are gifted with a new medium of exposure and the future demands taking advantage of this format."

Writers exploring online opportunities for publication will find a rich and diverse community of voices. Genre sites are strong, in particular those for science fiction/fantasy and horror. (See the award-winning *Scifiction* and *Dargonzine*.) Mainstream short fiction markets are also growing exponentially. (See *American Feed Magazine* and *Paperplates*, among many others.) Online literary journals range from the traditional (*The Barcelona Review, Paumonok Review*) to those with a decidedly more quirky bent (*The Dead Mule School of Southern Literature, The Glut*). Writers will also find here more highly experimental work that could exist nowhere else than in cyberspace, such as the hypertext fiction found on Eastgate Systems' online journal *Tekka*.

Online journals are gaining respect for the writers who appear on their sites. As Jill Adams, publisher and editor of *The Barcelona Review*, says: "We see our Internet review, like the small independent publishing houses, as a means of counterbalancing the big-business mentality of the multi-national publishing houses. At the same time, we want to see our writers 'make it big.' Last year we heard from more and more big houses asking about some of our new writers, wanting contact information, etc. So I see a healthy trend in that big houses are, finally—after being skeptical and confused—looking at it seriously and scouting online."

While the medium of online publication is different, the traditional rules of publishing apply to submissions. Writers should research the sites and archives carefully, looking for a match in sensibility for their work. They should then follow submission guidelines exactly and submit courteously. True, these sites aren't bound by traditional print schedules, so your work theoretically may be published more quickly. But that doesn't mean online journals have a larger staff, so exercise patience with editors considering your manuscript.

Also, while reviewing the listings in this market section, notice they are grouped differently from other market listings. In our literary magazines section, for example, you'll find primarily only publications searching for literary short fiction. But Online Markets are grouped by medium, so you'll find publishers of mystery short stories listed next to those looking for horror next to those specializing in flash fiction, so review with care. In addition, online markets with print counterparts, such as *North American Review*, can be found listed in the print markets sections.

A final note about online publication: Like literary journals, the majority of these markets are either nonpaying or very low paying. In addition, writers will not receive print copies of the publications because of the medium. So in most cases, do not expect to be paid for your exposure.

$☑ THE ABSINTHE LITERARY REVIEW

P.O. Box 328, Spring Green WI 53588. E-mail: staff@absinthe-literary-review.com. Website: www.absinthe-literary-review.com. **Contact:** Charles Allen Wyman. Electronic literary magazine; print issue coming 2004-2005. "*ALR* publishes short stories, novel excerpts, poems, book reviews, and literary essays. Our target audience is the literate individual who enjoys creative language use, character-driven fiction, and the clashing of worlds—real and surreal, poetic and prosaic, sacred and transgressive."

Needs "Transgressive works dealing with sex, death, disease, madness and the like; the clash of archaic with modern-day; archetype, symbolism; surrealism, philosophy, physics; existential and post-modern flavoring; experimental or flagrantly textured (but not sloppy or casual) fiction; intense crafting of language from the writer's writer. See website for information on our annual Eros and Thanatos issue and the Absinthe Editors' Prize. Anathemas: mainstream storytellers, "Oprah" fiction, high school or beginner fiction, poetry or fiction that contains no capital letters or punctuation, "hot" trends, genre and utterly normal prose or poetry, first, second or third drafts, pieces that exceed our stated word count (5,000 max.) by thousands of words, writers who do not read and follow our onsite guidelines." **Publishes 3-6 new writers/year.** Recently published work by Bruce Holland Rogers, David Schneiderman, Virgil Suarez, John Tisdale, James Reidel and Dan Pope.

How to Contact Accepts submissions by e-mail. Read online guidelines, then send a single fiction submission per reading period to fiction@absinthe-literary-review.com; 3-7 poems to poetry@absinthe-literary-review.com; and single literary essays to essays@absinthe-literary-review.com. Prefers submissions by e-mail. Sample copy not available.

Payment/Terms Pays $2-10 for fiction and essays; $1-10 for poetry.

Advice "Be erudite and daring in your writing. Draw from the past to drag meaning from the present. Kill ego and cliché. Invest your work with layers of meaning that subtly reveal multiple realities. Do not submit pieces that are riddled with spelling errors and grammatical snafus. Above all, be professional. For those of you who don't understand exactly what this means, please send your manuscripts elsewhere until you have experienced the necessary epiphany."

Ⓝ $☑ ALIENSKIN MAGAZINE, An Online Science Fiction, Fantasy & Horror Magazine

Froggy Bottom Press, P.O. Box 495, Beaver PA 15009. E-mail: alienskin@alienskinmag.com. Website: www.alienskinmag.com. **Contact:** Feature fiction: K. A. Patterson; Flash fiction: Phil Adams. Online magazine. "Our magazine was created for, and strives to help, aspiring writers of SFFH. We endeavor to promote and educate genre writers, helping them learn and develop the skills they need to produce marketable short stories." Bimonthly. Estab. 2002. Circ. 1,000 + Internet.

Needs Fantasy (dark fantasy, sword and sorcery), horror (dark fantasy, futuristic, psychological, psychic/supernatural/occult), science fiction (hard science/technological, soft/sociological). "No excessive blood, gore, erotica or vulgarity. No experimental or speculative fiction that does not use basic story elements of character, conflict, action and resolution. No esoteric ruminations." Receives 100-200 unsolicited mss/month. Accepts 24-30 mss/issue; 144-180 mss/year. Publishes ms 30-60 days after acceptance. **Publishes 10-15 new writers/year.** Recently published work by Ricky D. Cooper, Ed Lynskey, Simon Owens and H.H. Morris. Length: 1,000-3,500 words; average length: 2,200 words. Publishes short shorts. Also publishes poetry. Always comments on rejected mss.

How to Contact Send complete ms. Accepts submissions by e-mail. Include estimated word count, brief bio, name, address, and e-mail address. Responds in 1-2 weeks to queries; 1-2 months to mss. Accepts multiple submissions. Sample copy online. Writer's guidelines online.

Payment/Terms 1/2¢/word for 1,001-3,500 words; $5 flat pay for 500-1,000 words. Pays on publication for first, electronic rights. Sponsors awards/contests.

Advice "We look for interesting stories that offer something unique; stories that use basic story elements of character, conflict, action and resolution. We like the dark, twisted side of SFFH genres. Read our guidelines and follow the rules, treating the submission process as a serious business transaction. Only send stories that have been spell-checked and proofread at least twice. Try to remember that editors who offer a critique on manuscripts do so to help you as a writer, not to hamper or dissuade you as a writer."

◙ THE ALSOP REVIEW

122 Broad Creek Road, Laurel DE 19956. E-mail: alsop@alsopreview.com. Website: www.alsopreview.com. **Contact:** Jaime Wasserman, editor. Web zine. "*The Alsop Review* is primarily a literary resource and as such does not solicit manuscripts. However, the review operates an e-zine which accepts manuscripts. *Octavo* is a

quarterly magazine that accepts short stories and poetry. Send submissions to Andrew Boobier at andrew@netst
ep.co.uk.''

Needs Experimental, literary. ''No genre work or humor for its own sake. No pornography. We would like to
see more experiemental and unconventional works. Surprise me.'' Recently published work by Kyle Jarrard,
Dennis Must, Kristy Nielsen, Bob Riche and Linda Sue Park.

How to Contact Accepts submissions by e-mail (jw@alsopreview.com). Accepts reprints submissions. Sample
copy not available.

Payment/Terms ''None. We offer a permanent 'home' on the Web for writers and will pull and add material
to their pages upon request.''

Advice ''Read, read, read. Treat submissions to Web zines as carefully as you would a print magazine. Research
the market first. For every great Web zine, there are a hundred mediocre ones. Remember that once your work
is on the Web, chances are it will be there for a very long time. Put your best stuff out there and take advantage
of the opportunities to re-publish work from print magazines.''

AMERICAN FEED MAGAZINE

American Feed Magazine, 35 Hinsdale Ave., Winsted CT 06098. (860)469-8060. E-mail: editor@americanfeedm
agazine.com. Website: www.americanfeedmagazine.com. **Contact:** Shaw Izikson, editor. Online magazine.
''We like to give a place for new voices to be heard, as well as established voices a place to get a wider audience
for their work.'' Estab. 1994.

Needs Adventure, ethnic/multicultural, experimental, family saga, fantasy, feminist, glitz, historical, horror,
humor/satire, literary, mainstream, mystery/suspense, New Age, psychic/supernatural/occult, science fiction,
thriller/espionage. Receives 100 unsolicited mss/month. Accepts 15 mss/issue. **Publishes 20 new writers/
year.** Recently published work by Richard Lind, Bill Glose, Angela Conrad, Ryan Miller, Joshua Farber and
Daniel LaFabvre. Average length: 1,500 words. Publishes short shorts. Also publishes literary essays, literary
criticism, poetry.

How to Contact Send complete ms. Include estimated word count and brief bio. Responds in 2 months to
queries; 2 months to mss. Accepts simultaneous and reprints, multiple submissions. Sample copy online. Writer's guidelines by e-mail. Reviews fiction.

Payment/Terms Acquires one-time rights.

Advice ''Make sure the story flows naturally, not in a forced way. You don't need a vivid imagination to write
fiction, poetry or anything. Just look around you, because life is usually the best inspiration.''

$ ANTI MUSE

502 S. Main St., Saint Joseph TN 38481. (931)845-4838. E-mail: antimuse@antimuse.org. Website: http://
antimuse.org. **Contact:** Michael Haislip, editor. *Anti Muse* appeals to readers with a somewhat jaded and cynical
outlook on life. Monthly. Estab. 2004. Circ. 10,000.

Needs Adventure, comics/graphic novels, erotica, ethnic/multicultural, experimental, fantasy, feminist, gay,
historical, horror, humor/satire, lesbian, literary, mainstream, military/war, New Age, psychic/supernatural/
occult, regional, science fiction, thriller/espionage, western. Receives 50 unsolicited mss/month. Accepts 2-5
mss/issue; 50 mss/year. Publishes ms 1 month after acceptance. **Publishes 50 new writers/year.** Recently
published work by Afica Fine, R. Thomas and J.D. Hallmark. Length: 200-10,000 words; average length: 1,000
words. Publishes short shorts. Also publishes literary essays, literary criticism, poetry. Sometimes comments
on rejected mss.

How to Contact Send complete ms. Accepts submissions by e-mail. Send SASE (or IRC) for return of the ms,
or send disposable copy of the ms and #10 SASE for reply only. Responds in 1 month to mss. Accepts simultaneous and reprints, multiple submissions. Sample copy free. Writer's guidelines online.

Payment/Terms Pays $5-20. Pays on publication for one-time rights.

Advice ''I want to be entertained by your submission. I want to feel as if I'd be foolish to put down your
manuscript.''

ASCENT, Aspirations for Artists

Ascent, 1560 Arbutus Dr., Nanoose Bay BC C9P 9C8 Canada. E-mail: ascent@bcsupernet.com. Website: www.b
csupernet.com/users/ascent. **Contact:** David Fraser, editor. E-zine specializing in short fiction (all genres) and
poetry, essays, visual art: 40 electronic pages; illustrations; photos. In the future, *Ascent* will be publishing one
additional issue in print each year starting with the premier print issue for poetry only, in 2005, followed by a
short fiction issue in 2006. ''*Ascent* is a quality electronic publication dedicated to promoting and encouraging
aspiring writers of any genre. The focus however is toward interesting experimental writing in dark mainstream,
literary, science fiction, fantasy and horror. Poetry can be on any theme. Essays need to be unique, current
and have social, philosophical commentary.'' Quarterly. Estab. 1997.

Needs Erotica, experimental, fantasy (space fantasy), feminist, horror (dark fantasy, futuristic, psychological, supernatural), literary, mainstream, mystery/suspense, New Age, psychic/supernatural/occult, science fiction (hard science/technological, soft/sociological). Receives 20-30 unsolicited mss/month. Accepts 5 mss/issue; 20 mss/year. Publishes ms 3 months after acceptance. **Publishes 5-10 new writers/year.** Recently published work by Taylor Graham, Janet Buck, Jim Manton, Steve Cartwright, Don Stockard, Margaret Karmazin, Bill Hughes. Length: 500-4,000 words; average length: 2,000 words. Publishes short shorts. Also publishes literary essays, literary criticism, poetry. Sometimes comments on rejected mss.

How to Contact "Query by e-mail with word attachment." Include estimated word count, brief bio and list of publications. If you have to submit by mail because it is your only avenue, provide a SASE with either International Coupons or Canadian stamps. Responds in 1 week to queries; 3 months to mss. Accepts simultaneous and reprints, multiple submissions. Guidelines by e-mail or on website. Reviews fiction.

Payment/Terms "No payment at this time. Rights remain with author."

Advice "Short fiction should first of all tell a good story, take the reader to new and interesting imaginary or real places. Short fiction should use language lyrically and effectively, be experimental in either form or content and take the reader into realms where they can analyze and think about the human condition. Write with passion for your material, be concise and economical and let the reader work to unravel your story. In terms of editing, always proofread to the point where what you submit is the best it possibly can be. Never be discouraged if your work is not accepted; it may just not be the right fit for a current publication."

BABEL, the Multi-lingual, Multicultural Online Journal and Community of Arts and Ideas

E-mail: malcolm@towerofbabel.com. Website: www.towerofbabel.com. **Contact:** Malcolm Lawrence, editor-in-chief. Electronic zine. "We publish regional reports from international stringers all over the planet, as well as feature roundtable discussions, fiction, columns, poetry, erotica, travelogues, reviews of all the arts and editorials. We are an online community involving an extensive group of over 100 artists, writers and programmers, and over 300 translators representing (so far) 75 of the world's languages."

Needs "There are no specific categories of fiction that we are not interested in. Possible exceptions: laywers/vampires, different genders hailing from different planets, cold war military scenarios and things that go bump in the suburban night." Recently published work by Neal Robbins, Jennifer Prado, Nicholas P. Snoek, Yves Jacques, Doug Williamson, A.L. Fern, Laura Feister, Denzel J. Hankinson, Pete Hanson and Malcolm Lawrence.

How to Contact Query. Accepts submissions by e-mail. Reviews fiction.

Advice "We would like to see more fiction with first-person male characters written by female authors as well as more fiction with first-person female characters written by male authors. The best advice we could give to writers wanting to be published is simply to know what you're writing about and to write passionately about it. We should also mention that the phrase 'dead white men' will only hurt your chances. The Internet is the most important invention since the printing press and will change the world in the same way. One look at *Babel* and you'll see our predictions for the future of electronic publishing."

🌐 📃 📺 THE BARCELONA REVIEW

Correu Vell 12 -2, 08002, Barcelona, Spain. (00) 34 93 319 15 96. E-mail: editor@barcelonareview.com. Website: www.barcelonareview.com. **Contact:** Jill Adams, editor. *"TBR* is an international review of contemporary, cutting-edge fiction published in English, Spanish and Catalan. Our aim is to bring both new and established writers to the attention of a larger audience. Well-known writers such as Alicia Erian in the U.S., Michel Faber in the U.K., Carlos Gardini in Argentina, and Nuria Amat in Spain, for example, were not known outside their countries until appearing in *TBR*. Our multilingual format increases the audience all the more. Internationally-known writers, such as Irvine Welsh and Douglas Coupland, have contributed stories that ran in small press anthologies available only in one country. We try to keep abreast of what's happening internationally and to present the best finds every two months. Our intended audience is anyone interested in high-quality contemporary fiction that often (but not always) veers from the mainstream; we assume that our readers are well read and familiar with contemporary fiction in general."

Needs Short fiction. "Our bias is towards potent and powerful cutting-edge material; given that general criteria we are open to all styles and techniques and all genres. No slice-of-life stories, vignettes or reworked fables, and nothing that does not measure up, in your opinion, to the quality of work in our review, which we expect submitters to be familiar with." **Publishes 20 new writers/year.** Recently published work by Louise Erdich, Adam Haslett, Mark Winegardner, Adam Johnson, Mary Wornov, Emily Carter, Jesse Shepard and Julie Orringer.

How to Contact Send submissions by e-mail as an attached file. Hard copies accepted but cannot be returned. No simultaneous submissions.

Payment/Terms "In lieu of pay we offer a highly professional Spanish translation to English language writers and vice versa to Spanish writers."

Advice "Send top drawer material that has been drafted two, three, four times—whatever it takes. Then sit on it for a while and look at it afresh. Keep the text tight (rewrite until every unnecessary word is eliminated).

Grab the reader in the first paragraph and don't let go. Keep in mind that a perfectly crafted story that lacks a punch of some sort won't cut it. Make it new, make it different. Surprise the reader in some way. Read the best of the short fiction available in your area of writing to see how yours measures up. Don't send anything off until you feel it's ready and then familiarize yourself with the content of the review/magazine to which you are submitting.''

☐ ▱ BIG COUNTRY PEACOCK CHRONICLE, Online Magazine

RR1, Box 89K-112, Aspermont TX 79502. (806)254-2322. E-mail: publisher@peacockchronicle.com. Website: www.peacockchronicle.com. **Contact:** Audrey Yoeckel, owner/publisher. Online magazine. "We publish articles, commentaries, reviews, interviews, short stories, serialized novels and novellas, poetry, essays, humor and anecdotes. Due to the nature of Internet publication, guidelines for length of written works are flexible and acceptance is based more on content. Content must be family friendly. Writings that promote hatred or violence will not be accepted. *The Big Country Peacock Chronicle* is dedicated to the preservation of community values and traditional folk cultures. In today's society, we are too often deprived of a solid feeling of community which is so vital to our security and well-being. It is our attempt to keep the best parts of our culture intact. Our goal is to build a place for individuals, no matter the skill level, to test their talents and get feedback from others in a non-threatening, friendly environment. The original concept for the magazine was to open the door to talented writers by providing not only a publishing medium for their work but support and feedback as well. It was created along the lines of a smalltown publication in order to remove some of the anxiety about submitting works for first-time publication." Quarterly. Estab. 2000.

Needs Adventure, children's/juvenile (adventure, easy-to-read, fantasy, historical, mystery, preschool, series, sports), ethnic/multicultural (general), family saga, fantasy (space fantasy, sword and sorcery), gay, historical (general), horror (futuristic, supernatural, psychological), humor/satire, literary, military/war, mystery/suspense (amateur sleuth, police procedural, private eye/hard-boiled), psychic/supernatural/occult, regional, religious/inspirational (children's religious), romance (gothic, historical, romantic suspense), science fiction (soft/sociological), thriller/espionage, translations (frontier saga, traditional), western. "While the genre of the writing or the style does not matter, excessive or gratuitous violence, foul language and sexually explicit material is not acceptable." Accepts 2-3 (depending on length) mss/issue. Publishes ms 3 months after acceptance. Average length: 2,500 words. Publishes short shorts. Also publishes literary essays, literary criticism, poetry. Always comments on rejected mss.

How to Contact Include estimated word count, brief bio, list of publications and Internet contact information; i.e. e-mail, website address. Responds in 3 weeks to queries; 6 weeks to mss. Accepts simultaneous and reprints, multiple submissions. Writer's guidelines online. Reviews fiction.

Payment/Terms Acquires electronic rights. Sends galleys to author.

Advice "We look for continuity and coherence. The work must be clean with a minimum of typographical errors. The advantage to submitting works to us is the feedback and support. We work closely with our writers, offering promotion, resource information, moral support and general help to achieve success as writers. While we recommend doing businesss with us via the Internet, we have also published writers who do not have access. For those new to the Internet, we also provide assistance with the best ways to use it as a medium for achieving success in the field."

$☐ BLACKBIRD, an online journal of literature and the arts

Virginia Commonwealth University Department of Fiction, P.O. Box 843082, Richmond VA 23284. (804)225-4729. E-mail: blackbird@vcu.edu. Website: www.blackbird.vcu.edu. **Contact:** Mary Flinn, Gregory Donovan, editors. Online journal: 80+ pages if printed; illustrations; photos. "We strive to maintain the highest quality of writing and design, bringing the best things about a print magazine to the outside world. We publish fiction that is carefully crafted, thoughtful and surprising." Semiannual. Estab. 2001. Circ. 10,000 readers per month.

Needs Adventure, comics/graphic novels, condensed novels, confessions, ethnic/multicultural, experimental, family saga, fantasy, feminist, gay, glitz, historical, horror, humor/satire, lesbian, literary, mainstream, military/war, mystery/suspense, New Age, novel excerpts, psychic/supernatural/occult, regional, religious/inspirational, serialized novels, slice-of-life vignettes, suspense, thriller/espionage, translations, western, young adult/teen. Does not want science fiction, romance, children's. Receives 50-100 unsolicited mss/month. Accepts 4-5 mss/issue; 8-10 mss/year. Does not read from May 15-August 15. Publishes ms 3-6 months after acceptance. **Publishes 1-2 new writers/year.** Length: 5,000-10,000 words; average length: 5,000-6,500 words. Also publishes literary essays, literary criticism, poetry. Sometimes comments on rejected mss.

How to Contact Send complete ms. Inlude cover letter, name, address, telephone number, brief biographical comment. Responds in 6 months to mss. Accepts simultaneous submissions. Sample copy online. Writer's guidelines online.

Payment/Terms Pays $200 for fiction, $40 for poetry. Pays on publication for first North American serial rights.

Advice "We like a story that invites us into its world, that engages our senses, soul and mind."

$ ⬚ ⬚ THE CAFE IRREAL, International Imagination

E-mail: editors@cafeirreal.com. **Website:** www.cafeirreal.com. **Contact:** Alice Whittenburg, G.S. Evans, editors. E-zine: illustrations. "*The Cafe Irreal* is a webzine focusing on short stories and short shorts of an irreal nature." Quarterly. Estab. 1998. Member, Council of Literary Magazine and Presses.

Needs Experimental, fantasy (literary), science fiction (literary), translations. "No horror or 'slice-of-life' stories; no genre or mainstream fiction or fantasy." Accepts 8-10 mss/issue; 30-40 mss/year. Recently published work by Istvan Orkeny, Jiri Kratochvil, Norman Lock and Ana Maria Shua. Publishes short shorts. Also publishes literary essays, literary criticism. Sometimes comments on rejected mss.

How to Contact Accepts submissions by e-mail. "No attachments, include submission in body of e-mail. Include estimated word count." Responds in 2-4 months to mss. No simultaneous submissions. Sample copy online. Writer's guidelines online.

Payment/Terms Pays 1 ¢ /word, $2 minimum. Pays on publication for first-time electronic rights. Sends galleys to author.

Advice "Forget formulas. Write about what you don't know, take me places I couldn't possibly go, don't try to make me care about the characters. Read short fiction by writers such as Franz Kafka, Kobo Abe, Donald Barthelme, Leonora Carrington and Stanislaw Lem. Also read our website and guidelines."

⬚ ⬚ CARVE MAGAZINE

P.O. Box 1573, Tallahassee FL 32302. E-mail: editor@carvezine.com. Website: www.carvezine.com. **Contact:** Melvin Sterne, editor. Bimonthly online journal with annual printed "best of" anthology. Bimonthly. Estab. 2000. Circ. 2,500. Member, CLMP.

- Fiction appearing in *Carve Magazine* has been nominated for the *Pushcart*, *O. Henry*, *Best American* and *e2ink* anthology series for best online fiction.

Needs Literary (fiction). No genre, poetry or nonfiction. Accepts 70+ mss/year. **Publishes 10-20 new writers/year.** Recently published work by Lynn Stegner, Clarinda Harriss, Sean Mackel, Vincent Lam, Yunny Chen and Bruce Taylor. Occasionally comments on rejected mss.

How to Contact Send complete ms. Accepts submissions by e-mail. Responds in 1-4 months to mss. Accepts simultaneous submissions "if identified, except for contest." Writer's guidelines online.

Payment/Terms Sponsors awards/contests.

Advice "We look for stories with strong characterization, conflict and tightly written prose. Do you know what a fictive moment is?"

⬚ $⬚ ⬚ CHALLENGING DESTINY, New Fantasy & Science Fiction

Crystalline Sphere Publishing, RR #6, St. Marys ON N4X 1C8 Canada. (519)885-6012. E-mail: csp@golden.net. Website: www.challengingdestiny.com. **Contact:** David M. Switzer, editor. "We publish all kinds of science fiction and fantasy short stories." Quarterly. Estab. 1997. Circ. 200.

Needs Fantasy, science fiction. No horror, short short stories. Receives 40 unsolicited mss/month. Accepts 6 mss/issue; 24 mss/year. Publishes ms 5 months after acceptance. **Publishes 6 new writers/year.** Recently published work by Uncle River, A.R. Morlan, Jay Lake and Ken Rand. Length: 2,000-10,000 words; average length: 6,000 words. Often comments on rejected mss.

How to Contact Send complete ms. Send SAE and IRC for reply, return of ms or send disposable copy of ms. Responds in 1 week to queries; 1 month to mss. Accepts simultaneous submissions. Writer's guidelines for #10 SASE, 1 IRC, or online. Reviews fiction.

Payment/Terms Pays 1¢/word (Canadian), plus 1 contributor's copy. Pays on publication for first North American serial, electronic rights. Sends galleys to author.

Advice "Manuscripts with a good story and interesting characters stand out. We look for fiction that entertains and makes you think. If you're going to write short fiction, you need to read lots of it. Don't reinvent the wheel. Use your own voice."

⬚ collectedstories.com, The Story on Short Stories

collectedstories.com, Columbia U. Station, P.O.Box 250626, New York NY 10025. (718)609-9454. E-mail: info@collectedstories.com. Website: www.collectedstories.com. **Contact:** Dara Albanese or Wendy Ball, co-publishers. Online magazine: photos. "An online magazine devoted exclusively to literary short fiction, *collectedstories.com* publishes original short stories but also reports on various aspects related to the short form, featuring upcoming releases, author interviews, news on short story book deals, etc. The founders strive to provide short fiction with a quality venue of its own." Quarterly. Estab. 2000.

Needs Literary. "No young adult or children's fiction." Receives 50-75 unsolicited mss/month. Accepts 4 mss/issue; 12 mss/year. Publishes ms 1 month after acceptance. **Publishes 7 new writers/year.** Recently published work by Penny Feeny, David Fickett, Linda Mannheim. Average length: 1,800 words. Publishes short shorts.

How to Contact Query with or without published clips or send complete ms. Include information from contact form. Accepts submission via online form or by e-mail with prior arrangement. Responds in 1 week to queries; 6 months to mss. Accepts multiple submissions. Sample copy online. Writer's guidelines online. Reviews fiction.

Payment/Terms Writers retain copyright.

Advice "Since stories are accepted on a revolving basis, criteria may vary in that a story is up against the best of only that particular batch under consideration for the next issue. We select the most readable stories, that is, stories that are original, compelling, or with a sense of character and evidence of talent with prose. Writers should become familiar with a publication before submission, develop a strong hold on grammar, and thereby submit only clean, finished works for consideration."

$ 🔲 CONVERSELY

Conversely, Inc., PMB #121, 3053 Fillmore St., San Francisco CA 94123-4009. E-mail: query@conversely.com. Website: www.conversely.com. **Contact:** Alejandro Gutierrez, editor. Online magazine specializing in relationships between men and women. Illustrations; photos. "*Conversely* is dedicated to exploring relationships between women and men, every stage, every aspect, through different forms of writing, essays, memoirs, and fiction. Our audience is both female and male, mostly between 18-35 age range. We look for writing that is intelligent, provocative and witty; we look for topics that are original and appealing to our readers." Quarterly, some sections are published biweekly. Estab. 2000.

Needs Literary, "must be about romantic relationships between women and men." No erotica, gothic, science fiction. Receives 300 unsolicited mss/month. Accepts 1-3 mss/issue; 8-12 mss/year. Publishes ms 3 months after acceptance. **Publishes 2-4 new writers/year.** Recently published work by Kirk Nesset, Sarah Arellano and Jon Boilard. Length: 500-3,000 words; average length: 2,500 words.

How to Contact "We only accept manuscript submissions through our online submissions system (no mail, no e-mail)." Go to http://conversly.com/Masth/submi.shtml to submit online. Queries by e-mail only. Responds in 2 weeks to queries; 3 months to mss. Accepts simultaneous submissions. Complete guidelines on website.

Payment/Terms Pays $50-200. Pays on publication. Aquires electronic rights (90 days exclusive, non-exclusive thereafter) Sends galleys to author.

Advice "We look for stories that hold attention from start to finish, that cover original topics or use a fresh approach, that have a compelling narrative voice. We prefer stories that deal with relationships in an insightful, honest way and that surprise by revealing more about a character than was expected. Keep in mind our target audience. Know when to start and know where to end, what to leave out and what it keep in."

◐ 🔲 THE COPPERFIELD REVIEW, A Journal for Readers and Writers of Historical Fiction

E-mail: info@copperfieldreview.com. Website: www.copperfieldreview.com. **Contact:** Meredith Allard, executive editor. "We are an online literary journal that publishes historical fiction and articles, reviews and interviews related to historical fiction. We believe that by understanding the lessons of the past through historical fiction we can gain better insight into the nature of our society today, as well as a better understanding of ourselves." Quarterly. Estab. 2000.

Needs Historical (general), romance (historical), western (frontier saga, traditional). "We will consider submissions in most fiction categories, but the setting must be historical in nature. We don't want to see anything not related to historical fiction." Receives 30 unsolicited mss/month. Accepts 7-10 mss/issue; 28-40 mss/year. Responds to mss during the months of January, April, July and October. **Publishes "between 30 and 40 percent" new writers/year.** Publishes short shorts. Also publishes literary essays, literary criticism, poetry. Seldom comments on rejected mss.

How to Contact Send complete ms. Accepts submissions by e-mail. Responds in 6 weeks to queries. Accepts simultaneous and reprints, multiple submissions. Sample copy online. Writer's guidelines online. Reviews fiction.

Payment/Terms Acquires one-time rights.

Advice "We wish to showcase the very best in literary historical fiction. Stories that use historical periods and details to illuminate universal truths will immediately stand out. We are thrilled to receive thoughtful work that is polished, poised and written from the heart. Be professional, and only submit your very best work. Be certain to adhere to a publication's submission guidelines, and always treat your e-mail submissions with the same care you would use with a traditional publisher. Above all, be strong and true to your calling as a writer. It is a difficult, frustrating but wonderful journey. It is important for writers to review our online submission guidelines prior to submitting."

🔲 CRIMSON

Night Terrors Publications, 1202 W. Market St., Orrville OH 44667-1710. (330)683-0338. E-mail: editor@night-terrors-publications.com. Website: www.night-terrors-publications.com. **Contact:** D.E. Davidson, editor/publisher. E-zine specializing in dark works: equivalent to 8½ × 5½; equivalent to 35-60 pages. "*Crimson* publishes stories submitted to *Night Terrors* magazine which the editor finds to have merit but which do not fit the concept for *Night Terrors*." Estab. 1999. Circ. 700.

Needs "We publish any story of sufficient quality which was submitted to *Night Terrors* but for various reasons was not appropriate for that publication. This could include science fiction, horror, religious, literary, erotica, fantasy or most other adult categories of fiction. No graphic sex or violence toward children and women. No stories written specifically for *Crimson*. Please read the *Night Terrors* guidelines and write with the goal of publication there." Receives 150 unsolicited mss/month. Accepts 4 mss/issue; 24 mss/year. Publishes ms 4 months after acceptance. **Publishes 10 new writers/year.** Recently published work by A.R. Morlan, Ezra Claverie, Vera Searles and Craig Maull. Length: 2,000-5,000 words; average length: 2,500 words. Sometimes comments on rejected mss.

How to Contact Send complete ms. Include estimated word count, brief bio and list of publications. Responds in 3 weeks to queries; 10 weeks to mss. Accepts simultaneous submissions. Sample copy online. Writer's guidelines online.

Payment/Terms Pays 1 (printed) contributor's copy or all back issues on CD. Pays on publication for one-time rights. Sends galleys to author.

Advice "Please read our guidelines before submitting. These are available on our website. Be professional. Do not submit stories which are less than 2,000 words or more than 5,000 words. Do not submit stories folded. Send stories only in a 9×12 envelope. Do not use small type. Please use 12 pt. Times New Roman or Courier or equivalent. Proof your work. Use appropriate ms format and always include SASE. Send only one story at a time."

$⌂ DANA LITERARY SOCIETY ONLINE JOURNAL

Dana Literary Society, P.O. Box 3362, Dana Point CA 92629-8362. E-mail: ward@danaliterary.org. Website: www.danaliterary.org. **Contact:** Robert L. Ward, director. Online journal. "Fiction we publish must be thought-provoking and well crafted. We prefer works that have a message or moral." Monthly. Estab. 2000. Circ. 8,000.

Needs Humor/satire, "also stories with a message or moral. Most categories are acceptable if work is mindful of a thinking audience." No romance, children's/juvenile, religious/inspirational, pornographic, excessively violent or profane work. Would like to see more humor/satire." Receives 120 unsolicited mss/month. Accepts 6 mss/issue; 72 mss/year. Publishes ms 3 months after acceptance. **Publishes 8 new writers/year.** Recently published work by A.B. Jacobs, Louis Winslow an Michael Fedo. Length: 800-2,500 words; average length: 2,000 words. Also publishes literary essays, poetry. Often comments on rejected mss.

How to Contact Send complete ms. Responds in 2 weeks to mss. Accepts simultaneous and reprints submissions. Sample copy online. Writer's guidelines online.

Payment/Terms Pays $50. Pays on publication for one-time rights. Not copyrighted.

Advice "Success requires two qualities: ability and tenacity. Perfect your technique through educational resources, expansion of your scope of interests and regular reevaluation and, as required, revision of your works. Profit by a wide exposure to the writings of others. Submit works systematically and persistently, keeping accurate records so you know what went where and when. Take to heart responses and suggestions and plan your follow-up accordingly."

⊚ DARGONZINE

E-mail: dargon@dargonzine.org. Website: dargonzine.org. **Contact:** Ornoth D.A. Liscomb, editor. Electronic zine specializing in fantasy. "*DargonZine* is an electronic magazine that prints original fantasy fiction by aspiring Internet writers. The Dargon Project is a collaborative anthology whose goal is to provide a way for aspiring fantasy writers on the Internet to meet and become better writers through mutual contact and collaboration as well as contact with a live readership via the Internet."

Needs Fantasy. "Our goal is to write fantasy fiction that is mature, emotionally compelling, and professional. Membership in the Dargon Project is a requirement for publication." **Publishes 4-12 new writers/year.**

How to Contact Guidelines available on website. Sample copy online.

Payment/Terms "As a strictly noncommercial magazine, our writers' only compensation is their growth and membership in a lively writing community. Authors retain all rights to their stories."

Advice "The Readers and Writers FAQs on our website provide much more detailed information about our mission, writing philosophy and the value of writing for *DargonZine*."

⊚ THE DEAD MULE, School of Southern Literature

P.O. Box 835, Winterville NC 28590. E-mail: contact@deadmule.com. Website: www.deadmule.com. **Contact:** Valerie MacEwan, editor, or Phoebe Kate Foster, associate editor. Online literary journal. "*The Dead Mule* is an online literary magazine featuring Southern fiction, articles, poetry and essays and is proud to claim a long heritage of Southern literary excellence. We consider any writing with a Southern slant. By that we mean the author needs either Southern roots or the writing must be Southern in subject matter. As the first online Southern literary journal, we've published almost 200 writers and are damn proud of it.'' Estab. 1996.

Needs Literary. "Also nonfiction articles about the South including festival critiques, Nascar worshipping diatribes and championship wrestling tributes. Always, always, stories about mules." Special poetry issue in September; special fiction issue published in the December/January *Dead Mule*. Does not read fiction from June-August.

How to Contact Send complete ms. Accepts submissions by e-mail (deadmulesubmissions@hotmail.com). Sample copy online. Writer's guidelines online.

Advice "What we want are writers. Pure and simple. Folks who write about the South. While long lists of previously published works are impressive, they don't matter much around here. That's why we don't include that type of information. We don't think anyone is less of a writer because their list is short. You're a writer because you say you are. Also, you've worked hard on whatever it is you wrote. Don't blow it all by not submitting correctly. If you're thinking about submitting, remember to tell us why, if it's not obvious from the content, you should be admitted to The Dead Mule School of Southern Literature. Before we read the submission, we need to know why you think you're 'Southern.' Remember, no good Southern fiction is complete without a dead mule.''

$ deathlings.com, Dark Fiction for the Discerning Reader

130 E. Willamette Ave., Colorado Springs CO 80903-1112. E-mail: cvgelvin@aol.com. Website: www.deathlings.com. **Contact:** CV Gelvin, editor. E-zine specializing in dark fiction. "Our wonderfully quirky themes for the short story contests have included "Frozen Smiles" (dolls), "Burbian Horrors," "Technology Run Amuck" and "Love Gone Bad." Quarterly. Estab. 2000.

Needs Horror (futuristic, psychological, supernatural). "No children's, fantasy, poetry or romance." List of upcoming themes available on website. Receives 20-30 unsolicited mss/month. Accepts 3-4 mss/issue. Publishes ms 1-2 months after acceptance. **Publishes 3-6 new writers/year.** Recently published work by David Ballard, Fiona Curnow, Denise Dumars, Jason Franks, dgk Golberg, Darren O. Godfrey and CV Gelvin. Length: 4,000 words; average length: 3,000 words. Publishes short shorts. Sometimes comments on rejected mss.

How to Contact E-mail story attached in RTF. Include estimated word count, brief bio and list of publications with submission. Responds in 1-3 months to mss. Accepts simultaneous and reprints, multiple submissions. Guidelines free by e-mail or on website.

Payment/Terms Pays 3¢/word. Pays on publication for electronic rights. Sponsors awards/contests.

DIAGRAM, A Magazine of Art, Text, and Schematic

New Michigan Press, 648 Crescent NE, Grand Rapids MI 49503. E-mail: prose@thediagram.com. Website: http://thediagram.com. **Contact:** Ander Monson, editor. "We specialize in work that pushes the boundaries of traditional genre or work that is in some way schematic. We do publish traditional fiction and poetry, too, but hybrid forms (short stories, prose-poems, indexes, tables of contents, etc.) are welcome! We also publish diagrams and schematics (original and found). Bimonthly. Estab. 2001. Circ. 100,000 hits/month. Member: CLMP.

Needs Experimental, literary. "We don't publish genre fiction, unless it's exceptional and transcends the genre boundaries." Receives 100 unsolicited mss/month. Accepts 2-3 mss/issue; 15 mss/year. **Publishes 15 new writers/year.** Average length: 250-1,000 words. Publishes short shorts. Also publishes literary essays, poetry. Often comments on rejected mss.

How to Contact Send complete ms. Accepts submissions by e-mail. Send SASE (or IRC) for return of the ms, or send disposable copy of the ms and #10 SASE for reply only. Responds in 2 weeks to queries; 1 month to mss. Accepts simultaneous submissions. Sample copy for $12 for print version. Writer's guidelines online.

Payment/Terms Acquires first, electronic rights.

Advice "We value invention, energy, experimentation and voice. When done very well, we like traditional fiction, too. Nearly all the work we select is propulsive and exciting."

DOTLIT, The Online Journal of Creative Writing

Creating Writing & Cultural Studies, Queensland University of Technology, Victoria Park Rd., Kelvin Grove Q 4059 Australia. E-mail: dotlit@qut.edu.au. Website: www.dotlit.qut.edu.au. Semiannual. Estab. 2000.

Needs Children's/juvenile (10 and above), literary, young adult/teen. Receives 400 unsolicited mss/month. Accepts 12-20 mss/issue; 24-40 mss/year. Publishes ms 6-12 months after acceptance. Recently published work by Ian McNeil, Olga Pavlinova and Lee Gutkind. Publishes short shorts. Also publishes literary essays, literary criticism, poetry.

How to Contact Send complete ms. Accepts submissions by e-mail. Send disposable copy of the ms and #10 SASE for reply only. Responds in 6-12 months to mss. Writer's guidelines online.

Payment/Terms Acquires electronic rights.

⊘ DUCTS

P.O. box 3203 Grand Central Station, New York New York 101163. (718)383-6728. E-mail: editor@ducts.org. Website: http://ducts.org. **Contact:** Jonathan Kravetz. *DUCTS* is a webzine of personal stories, fiction, essays, memoirs, poetry, humor, profiles, reviews and art. *"DUCTS* was founded in 1999 with the intent of giving emerging writers a venue to regularly publish their compelling, personal stories. The site has been expanded to include art and creative works of all genres. We believe that these genres must and do overlap. *DUCTS* publishes the best, most compelling stories and we hope to attract readers who are drawn to work that rises above. We hope to attract *readers."* Semiannual. Estab. 1999. Circ. 10,000. CLMP.

Needs Erotica, ethnic/multicultural, humor/satire, literary, mainstream. "Please do not send us genre work, unless it is extraordinarily unique." Receives 10 unsolicited mss/month. Accepts 5 mss/issue; 10 mss/year. Publishes ms 1-6 months after acceptance. **Publishes 10-12 new writers/year.** Recently published work by Charles Salzberg, Mark Goldbart, Richard Willis and Helen Zelon. Publishes short shorts. Also publishes literary essays, literary criticism, poetry. Sometimes comments on rejected mss.

How to Contact Send complete ms. Accepts submissions by e-mail. Responds in 1-4 weeks to queries; 1-6 months to mss. Accepts simultaneous and reprints submissions. Writer's guidelines by e-mail.

Payment/Terms Acquires one-time rights.

Advice "We prefer fiction that tells a compelling story with a strong narrative drive."

Ⓝ $⊘ EOTU, Ezine of Fiction, Art & Poetry

Clam City Publications, 2102 Hartman, Boise ID 83704. (208)322-3408. E-mail: editor@clamcity.com. Website: www.clamcity.com/eotu.html. **Contact:** Larry Dennis. "All fiction, art and poetry needs to be published to have meaning. We do what we can to make that happen. We are open to fiction, art and poetry of all genres, though we tend toward literary and speculative work, science fiction, fantasy and horror because that's where the editor's tastes lie." Bimonthly. Estab. 2000.

Needs Erotica, experimental, fantasy (space fantasy, sword and sorcery), horror (dark fantasy, futuristic, psychological, supernatural), humor/satire, literary, psychic/supernatural/occult, romance (futuristic/time travel, gothic, love stories), science fiction (hard science/technological, soft/sociological), thriller/espionage. Receives 150 unsolicited mss/month. Accepts 12-15 mss/issue; 75-90 mss/year. **Publishes 5-10 new writers/year.** Recently published work by Bruce Boston, Marge Simon, Randy Chandler, James Dorr, s.c virtes, Nancy Bennett, Chanya Weisman, Lida Broadhurst. Length: 1-3,000 words; average length: 1,500 words. Publishes short shorts. Also publishes poetry. Rarely comments on rejected mss.

How to Contact Send complete ms. Accepts submissions by e-mail. Send SASE for return of ms, or send a disposable copy of ms and #10 SASE for reply only. Responds in 2 weeks to queries; 2 months to mss. Accepts simultaneous and reprints, multiple submissions. Writer's guidelines online.

Payment/Terms Pays $5-$30. Pays on acceptance for electronic rights.

Advice "We go mostly on the editor's taste in fiction, art and poetry, which is for character-driven stories in speculative, literary, science fiction, fantasy and horror genres. Stories with a unique style and structure have an advantage."

⊘ ⓨ FAILBETTER.COM

Failbetter, 40 Montgomery Place, Suite #2, Brooklyn NY 11215. E-mail: submissions@failbetter.com. Website: www.failbetter.com. **Contact:** Thom Didato, editor. "We are a quarterly online magazine published in the spirit of a traditional literary journal—dedicated to publishing quality fiction, poetry and artwork. While the Web plays host to hundreds, if not thousands, of genre-related sites (many of which have merit), we are not one of them." Quarterly. Estab. 2000. Circ. 35,000. Member, Council of Literary Magazines and Presses.

Needs Literary, novel excerpts. "No genre fiction—romance, fantasy or science fiction." Always would like to see more "character-driven literary fiction where something happens!" Receives 50-75 unsolicited mss/month. Accepts 3-5 mss/issue; 12-20 mss/year. Publishes ms 4-8 months after acceptance. **Publishes 4-6 new writers/ year.** Recently published work by Susan Daitch, Geoffrey Becker, Frances Sherwook and Don Lee. Publishes short shorts. Often comments on rejected mss.

How to Contact Accepts submissions by e-mail. Responds in 8-12 weeks to queries; 4-6 month to mss. Accepts simultaneous submissions. Sample copy online. Writer's guidelines online.

Payment/Terms Acquires one-time rights.

Advice "Read an issue. Read our guidelines! We place a high degree of importance on originality, believing that even in this age of trends it is still possible. We are not looking for what is current or momentary. We are not concerned with length: One good sentence may find a home here, as the bulk of mediocrity will not. Most importantly, know that what you are saying could only come from you. When you are sure of this, please feel free to submit."

$ ◨ flashquake, An Online Journal of Flash Literature

River Road Studios, P.O. Box 2154, Albany NY 12220-0154. E-mail: dorton@flashquake.org. Website: www.flashquake.org. **Contact:** Debi Orton, publisher. E-zine specializing in flash literature. *"flashquake is a quarterly online literary journal specifically centered around flash literature—flash fiction, flash nonfiction, and short poetry. Our goal is to create a literary venue for all things flash. Send us your best flash works that leave your readers thinking. We define flash as works less than 1,000 words. Shorter pieces will impress us; poetry can be up to 35 lines. We want the best story you can tell us in the fewest words you need to do it! Move us, engage us, give us a complete story that only you could have written."*

Needs Ethnic/multicultural (general), experimental, literary, flash literature of all types: fiction, memoir, creative nonfiction, poetry and artwork. *"Not interested in romance, graphic sex, graphic violence, gore, vampires or work of a religious nature."* Receives 100-150 unsolicited mss/month. Accepts 30 mss/issue. Publishes ms 1-3 months after acceptance. Recently published work by Wayne Scheer, Margaret Frey and Barbara Jackson. Publishes short shorts. Sometimes comments on rejected mss.

How to Contact Accepts submissions by e-mail (submit@flashquake.org). No land mail. Include estimated word count, brief bio, mailing address and e-mail address. Guidelines and submission instructions on website.

Payment/Terms Pays $5-25. Pays on publication for electronic rights. Sponsors awards/contests.

Advice *"Read our submission guidelines before submitting. Proofread your work thoroughly! We will instantly reject your work for spelling and grammar errors. Save your document as plain text and paste it into an e-mail message. We will not open attachments. We want work that the reader will think about long after reading it, stories that compel the reader to continue reading them. We do like experimental work, but that should not be construed as a license to forget narrative clarity, plot, character development or reader satisfaction."*

N ◨ FLUENT ASCENSION

Fierce Concepts, P.O. Box 6407, Glendale AZ 85312. E-mail: submissions@fluentascension.com. Website: www.fluentascension.com. **Contact:** Warren Norgaard, editor. Online magazine. Quarterly. Estab. 2003.

Needs Comics/graphic novels, erotica, ethnic/multicultural, experimental, gay, humor/satire, lesbian, literary, translations. Receives 6-10 unsolicited mss/month. Accepts 1-3 mss/issue. Publishes short shorts. Also publishes literary essays, literary criticism, poetry. Sometimes comments on rejected mss.

How to Contact Send complete ms. Accepts submissions by e-mail. Include estimated word count, brief bio and list of publications. Send SASE (or IRC) for return of ms or send disposable copy of ms and #10 SASE for reply only. Responds in 4-8 weeks to queries; 4-8 weeks to mss. Accepts simultaneous, multiple submissions. Sample copy online. Writer's guidelines online.

Payment/Terms Acquires electronic rights. Sponsors awards/contests.

N ◻ THE FURNACE REVIEW

16909 N. Bay Rd. #305, Sunny Isles FL 33160. E-mail: editor@thefurnacereview.com. Website: www.thefurnacereview.com. **Contact:** Ciara LaVelle, editor. *"We reach out to a young, well-educated audience, bringing them new, unique, fresh work they won't find elsewhere."* Quarterly. Estab. 2004.

Needs Erotica, experimental, feminist, gay, historical, humor/satire, lesbian, literary, mainstream, military/war. Does not want children's, science fiction or religious submissions. Receives 20-30 unsolicited mss/month. Accepts 3-4 mss/issue; 9-12 mss/year. **Publishes 5 new writers/year.** Recently published work by Saul Nadata, Sarah Lynn Knowles, and Paul Calvert. Length: 7,000 words; average length: 4,000 words. Publishes short shorts. Also publishes poetry.

How to Contact Send complete ms. Accepts submissions by e-mail. Send disposable copy of the ms and #10 SASE for reply only. Online submissions are fine, submitted by mail: $2 per ms. Responds in 1 month to queries; 4 months to mss. Accepts simultaneous submissions.

Payment/Terms Acquires first North American serial rights.

N ◨ GIN BENDER POETRY REVIEW

P.O. Box 150932, Lufkin TX 75915. E-mail: ginbender@yahoo.com. Website: www.ginbender.com. **Contact:** T.A. Thompson, founder/chief editor. Online magazine. *"We publish a diverse group of writers including award-winning and debut authors."* Triannual. Estab. 2002.

Needs Historical, literary, mainstream, regional. *"No science fiction, horror."* Receives 20 unsolicited mss/month. Accepts 2-4 mss/issue; 6-12 mss/year. Publishes ms 4 months after acceptance. **Publishes 2-4 new writers/year.** Recently published work by Christopher Woods, Elizabeth Routen and Peggy Duffy. Length: 500-1,500 words; average length: 1,000 words. Publishes short shorts. Also publishes literary essays, poetry. Sometimes comments on rejected mss.

How to Contact Send complete ms. Accepts submissions by e-mail. Include estimated word count, brief bio and list of publications. Send disposable copy of ms and #10 SASE for reply only. Responds in 2 weeks to queries; 6 weeks to mss. Accepts reprints submissions. Sample copy online. Writer's guidelines online.

Payment/Terms Acquires first, electronic rights.

Advice "We look for fiction that grasps the soul momentarily. Read all the literary work you can. Study the masters and the new."

❑ ◎ THE GLUT, Online journal of prose and praise of gluttony

P.O. Box 362, Walnut Creek CA 94597. E-mail: calvin@theglut.com. Website: www.theglut.com. **Contact:** Calvin Liu, editor. "*The Glut* seeks all forms of prose, with a slight bias toward things related to food or gluttony—eating, overeating, cooking, overcooking, digesting, indigesting and so on. Irreverence is key. Also, please do not be fooled by our apparent meat-centrism; we like vegetables, too. Except peas. We hate peas." Bimonthly. Estab. 2003.

Needs Experimental, humor/satire, literary. Receives 30-40 unsolicited mss/month. Accepts 4-5 mss/issue. Publishes ms 1-2 months after acceptance. Recently published work by Blake Butler, Magdalen Powers, Avital Gad-Cykman, Jensen Whelan, Liz Tascio and Elizabeth Glixman. Length: 1,500 words; average length: 750 words. Publishes short shorts. Often comments on rejected mss.

How to Contact Send complete ms. Responds in 2 weeks to queries; 1 month to mss. Accepts simultaneous submissions. Writer's guidelines online.

Payment/Terms Acquires one-time rights.

Advice "Make us laugh, even if its nervous laughter from our inability to comprehend."

ℕ ❑ THE KING'S ENGLISH

3114 NE 47th Ave., Portland OR 97213. (503)709-1917. E-mail: thekingsenglish@comcast.net. Website: www.th ekingsenglish.org. **Contact:** Benjamin Chambers, editor. "We're an online publication only. Our focus is long literary fiction, especially if it's stuffed with strong imagery and gorgeous prose. Novellas 11,000 words-48,000 words (150 double-spaced pages). In very rare instances, we'll include detective fiction or sci-fi/fantasy, as long as there's a strong element of suspense, the setting is unusual, and the writing first-rate." Estab. 2003.

Needs Experimental, historical, literary, mainstream, mystery/suspense (private eye/hard-boiled), thriller/espionage, translations. No horror, religious or heartwarming tales of redemption. Accepts 3 mss/issue; 12 mss/year. Publishes short shorts. Also publishes literary essays, poetry. Sometimes comments on rejected mss.

How to Contact Send complete ms. Prefers electronic submissions but accepts submissions by mail. Responds in 2 weeks to queries; 1-2 months to mss. Accepts simultaneous, multiple submissions. Writer's guidelines for by e-mail or on the website.

Payment/Terms Aquires one-time, non-exclusive rights to anthologize.

Advice "Surprise us. With language, mostly, though concept and execution can do just as well or better. If your first page makes us long for a rainy day and a cozy armchair in which to curl up with your manuscript, you'll get our attention. Make sure your story deserves to be a long one. Write what you'd like to read. And pay no attention to advice from us—but save yourself some heartbreak and read our guidelines before submitting."

◎ ❑ MARGIN, Exploring Modern Magical Realism

321 High School Road, N.E., PMB #204, Bainbridge Island WA 98110. E-mail: magicalrealismmaven@yahoo.c om. Website: www.magical-realism.com. **Contact:** Tamara Kaye Sellman, editor. Electronic anthology specializing in literary magical realism. "*Margin* seeks, in a variety of ways, to answer the question 'what is magical realism?'" Estab. 2000. Circ. 30,000.

- *Margin* has received the Arete "Wave of a Site" award and the Point of Life Gold Award of Excellence. Member, CLMP, since 2001. Nominates for *Pushcart*.

Needs Translations, magical realism. "No magical realist knockoffs, no stock fantasy with elves or angels. Nothing gratuitous. If you are unsure what magical realism is, visit the website and look at our discussion of criteria before sending. Interested in academic writing; query first." Receives 100 unsolicited mss/month. Publishes ms 6 months after acceptance. Recently published work by Gayle Brandeis, Virgil Suarez and Brian Evenson. Also publishes literary essays, literary criticism. Sometimes comments on rejected mss.

How to Contact Send complete ms. Accepts submissions by e-mail. No attachments or surface mail. Please enclose SASE for return of mss or e-mail address for reply. Sample copy online. Writer's guidelines for SASE or online. Reviews fiction.

Payment/Terms Pay negotiable.

Advice "Technical strength, unique, engaging style, well-developed and inventive story. Surprise us by avoiding what has already been done. Manuscript must be magical realism. Do not send more than one submission at a time. You will not get a fair reading if you do. Always enclose SASE. Do not inquire before 3 months. Send us your A-list, no works in progress."

TIMOTHY MCSWEENEY'S INTERNET TENDENCY

826 Valencia Street, San Francisco CA 94110. E-mail: websubmissions@mcsweeneys.net. Website: www.mcsw eeneys.net. **Contact:** Dave Eggers, John Warner, editors. Online literary journal. *"Timothy McSweeney's Internet Tendency* is an offshoot of *Timothy McSweeney's Quarterly Concern*, a journal created by nervous people in relative obscurity and published four times a year."* Daily.

Needs Literate humor, sestinas. Sometimes comments on rejected mss.

How to Contact Accepts submissions by e-mail. "For submissions to the website, paste the entire piece into the body of an e-mail. Absolute length limit of 15,000 words, with a preference for pieces significantly shorter (700-1,000 words)." Sample copy online. Writer's guidelines online.

Advice "Do not submit your work to both the print submissions address and the Web submissions address, as seemingly hundreds of writers have been doing lately. If you submit a piece of writing intended for the magazine to the Web submissions address, you will confuse us, and if you confuse us, we will accidentally delete your work without reading it, and then we will laugh and never give it another moment's thought, and sleep the carefree sleep of young children. This is very, very serious."

🅽 ◨ ◉ THE MID-SOUTH REVIEW, A Journey into the Heart of the South

E-mail: midsouthreview@yahoo.com. Website: www.geocities.com/midsouthreview. **Contact:** Jeff Martindale, editor. Online magazine. "We are an online literary journal featuring fiction, essays and poetry with general interest in Southern culture and history. Our mission is to publish the best stories written by and about Mid-Southerners." Monthly. Estab. 2002.

Needs Humor/satire, literary, mainstream, "anything about the South. No gore, violence, hate, erotica or science fiction." List of upcoming themes available online. Accepts 3-5 mss/issue. Publishes ms 2-4 months after acceptance. Recently published work by Jeff Martindale and Scottie H. Freeman. Length: 2,500 words; average length: 1,500 words. Publishes short shorts. Also publishes literary essays, poetry. Sometimes comments on rejected mss.

How to Contact Send complete ms. Accepts submissions by e-mail. Include estimated word count and brief bio. No attachments. Place submission in the body of the e-mail. Responds in 3-4 months to queries; 3-4 months to mss. Accepts simultaneous and reprints submissions. Sample copy online. Writer's guidelines online.

Payment/Terms Pays free subscription to magazine.

Advice "Rewrite! Rewrite! Rewrite! Spend as much or more time rewriting your work than on your first draft. Follow submission guidelines to the letter. Incorrect submissions reduce your chance of getting published. Don't take rejection personally."

🅽 ◯ MIDNIGHT TIMES

1731 Shadwell Dr., Barnhart MO 63012. E-mail: tepes@midnighttimes.com. Website: www.midnighttimes.com. **Contact:** Jay Manning, editor. The intention of this online publication is to provide a forum for new writers to get exposure. The primary theme is darkness, but this doesn't necessarily mean evil. There can be a light at the end of the tunnel. Quarterly. Estab. 2003.

Needs Fantasy (sword and sorcery), horror (dark fantasy, futuristic, psychological, supernatural), literary, mainstream, psychic/supernatural/occult, science fiction, vampires. No pornography. Accepts 3-6 mss/issue; 12-24 mss/year. Publishes ms 3-9 months after acceptance. **Publishes many new writers/year.** Length: 500-10,000 words; average length: 4,000 words. Publishes short shorts. Also publishes poetry. Sometimes comments on rejected mss.

How to Contact Send complete ms. Accepts submissions by e-mail. Send SASE (or IRC) for return of the ms, or send disposable copy of the ms and #10 SASE for reply only. Responds in 2 weeks to queries; 1 month to mss. Accepts simultaneous and reprints submissions. Writer's guidelines for SASE or by e-mail or on website.

Payment/Terms No payment. Acquires one-time, electronic rights.

Advice "A good vampire story does not have to be a 'horror' story. Eternal darkness is a universal theme that transcends all genres."

◨ THE MOONWORT REVIEW

1160 Buckeye Rd., Elk Park NC 28622. Fax: (919)962-2388. E-mail: editor@moonwortreview.com. Website: www.themoonwortreview.com. **Contact:** RC Rutherford. Electronic zine specializing in fiction and poetry. Quarterly. Estab. 1999. Circ. 1,000. Member: HTML Writers Guild.

Needs Experimental, literary, mainstream, mystery/suspense (amateur sleuth, cozy, police procedural, private eye/hard-boiled), New Age. "No horror, erotic, fantasy or romance." Receives 20 unsolicited mss/month. Accepts 10-12 mss/issue; 60-80 mss/year. Publishes ms 2 months after acceptance. **Publishes 40-50 new writers/year.** Recently published work by Al Maginnes, Lee Upton, Janet Buck, Sara Claytor, Mark Smith-Sato and Ed Lynsky. Length: 500-3,000 words; average length: 2,000 words. Publishes short shorts. Also publishes literary essays, literary criticism, poetry. Sometimes comments on rejected mss.

How to Contact Send complete ms. Accepts submissions by e-mail. Include estimated word count, brief bio and list of publications. Responds in 3-4 months to queries; 4-6 months to mss. Sample copy online. Writer's guidelines online.

Payment/Terms Acquires one-time, electronic rights.

Advice "I look for strong characters and setting, original imagery and original voice."

$⬚ ◎ NOCTURNAL OOZE, an Online Horror Magazine

Froggy Bottom Press, P.O. Box 495, Beaver PA 15009-0495. E-mail: submit@nocturnalooze.com. Website: www.nocturnalooze.com. **Contact:** Katherine Patterson, Marty Hiller; senior editors. *Nocturnal Ooze* blends sight and sound in a themed enviroment, to create an atmosphere of the macabre that enhances the reading experience of visitors to the site. "We seek to promote dark fiction, tales that make our spines tingle." Monthly. Estab. 2003. Circ. 650+. Member: HWA.

Needs Horror (dark fantasy, psychological, supernatural), psychic/supernatural/occult. "No silly or humorous horror. No excessive blood and gore just for mere shock value. No child abuse or baby mutilation stories." Receives 40-80 unsolicited mss/month. Accepts 10-11 mss/issue; 132 mss/year. Publishes ms 1-2 months after acceptance. **Publishes 10% new writers/year.** Recently published work by Jason Brannon, Nancy Jackson, Charles Richard Laing, Michael Jessen and Mark Hodgett. Length: 750-3,500 words; average length: 1,250 words. Also publishes poetry. Always comments on rejected mss.

How to Contact Send complete ms. Accepts submissions by e-mail. Responds in 1 month to mss. Accepts multiple submissions. Writer's guidelines online.

Payment/Terms Pays $5-17.50. Pays on publication for first, electronic rights.

Advice "We look for a story that grabs us at the start and draws us into the darkness of the unknown. Stories that put us on the brink of peril and either save us in the end or shove us into the abyss."

⬚ ◻ THE ORACULAR TREE, A Transformational E-Zine

The Oracular Tree, 208-167 Morgan Ave., Kitchener ON N2A 2M4 Canada. E-mail: editor@oraculartree.com. Website: www.oraculartree.com. **Contact:** Teresa Hawkes, publisher. E-zine specializing in transformation. "The stories we tell ourselves and each other predict the outcome of our lives. We can affect gradual social change by transforming our deeply rooted cultural stories. The genre is not as important as the message and the high quality of the writing. We accept stories, poems, articles and essays which will reach well-educated, open-minded readers around the world. We offer a forum for those who see a need for change, who want to add their voices to a growing search for alternatives." Weekly. Estab. 1977. Circ. 75,000 hits/month.

Needs Fantasy, literary, New Age. "We'll look at any genre that is well written and can examine a new cultural paradigm. No tired dogma, no greeting card poetry, please." Receives 20-30 unsolicited mss/month. Accepts 80-100 mss/year. Publishes ms 3 months after acceptance. **Publishes 20-30 new writers/year.** Recently published work by Elisha Porat, Lyn Lyfshin, Rattan Mann and Dr. Elaine Hatfield. Publishes short shorts. Also publishes literary essays, poetry. Often comments on rejected mss.

How to Contact Send complete ms. Accepts submissions by e-mail. Responds in 2 weeks to queries; 2 months to mss. Accepts simultaneous and reprints, multiple submissions. Sample copy online. Writer's guidelines online.

Payment/Terms Author retains copyright; one-time archive posting.

Advice "The underlying idea must be clearly expressed. The language should be appropriate to the tale, using creative license and an awareness of rhythm. We look for a juxtaposition of ideas that creates resonance in the mind and heart of the reader. Write from your honest voice. Trust your writing to unfold."

⬚ ◎ OUTER ART, the worst possible art in world

The University of New Mexico, 200 College Road, Gallup NM 87301. (505)863-7647. Fax: (505)863-7532. E-mail: smarand@unm.edu. Website: www.gallup.unm.edu/~smarandache/a/outer-art.htm. **Contact:** Florentin Smarandache, editor. E-zine. Annual. Estab. 2000.

Needs Experimental, literary, outer-art. Publishes ms 1 month after acceptance. Publishes short shorts. Also publishes literary essays, literary criticism.

How to Contact Accepts submissions by e-mail. Send SASE (or IRC) for return of the ms. Responds in 1 month to mss. Accepts simultaneous and reprints submissions. Writer's guidelines online.

◻ OUTSIDER INK

Outsider Media, 201 W. 11th St., New York NY 10014. (646)373-3117. E-mail: editor@outsiderink.com. Website: www.outsiderink.com. **Contact:** Sean Meriwether, editor. E-zine specializing in alternative fiction, poetry and artwork. "We are an online quarterly only. Each issue contains an average of six short stories, one poet and one visual artist. A monthly feature spotlights an individual, normally an underpublished writer or poet. *Outsider Ink* has established an international readership by publishing new material with a diverse range of adult themes. We are all outsiders, artist and non-artist alike, but there are those brave enough to share their experiences with the world. Rattle my cage and demand my attention, tell me your story the way you want it to be told. I am looking for the harsh and sometimes ugly truths. Dark humor is especially appealing. We want to see more work by women.'' Quarterly. Estab. 1999. Circ. 50,000.

Needs Literary. ''No mainstream, genre fiction, children's or religious.'' Receives 200 unsolicited mss/month. Accepts 7 mss/issue; 28 mss/year. Publishes ms 3 months after acceptance. **Publishes 15 new writers/year.** Recently published work by Linda Boroff, Greg Wharton and Maryanne Stahl. Average length: 2,000 words. Publishes short shorts. Also publishes poetry. Often comments on rejected mss.

How to Contact Send complete ms. Accepts submissions by e-mail. Responds in 1 week to queries; 3 months to mss. Accepts simultaneous and reprints, multiple submissions. Sample copy online. Writer's guidelines online.

Payment/Terms Acquires electronic rights. Sends galleys to author. Not copyrighted.

Advice ''*Outsider Ink* publishes work that isn't afraid to cover unexplored territory, both emotionally and physically. Though we want work that pushes the envelope, it should maintain a literary foundation. We aren't looking for fiction or poetry that is weird for the sake of being weird; we want prose with a purpose. Please familiarize yourself with the e-zine before submitting. The bulk of submissions are not accepted because they are inappropriate to the venue. We encourage new writers and act as a launching pad to other venues. Trust your own voice when editing your own material. If you think it isn't ready yet, don't submit it—finish it first.''

☒ ☑ ☑ OXFORD MAGAZINE

Bachelor Hall, Miami University, Oxford OH 45056. (513)529-1279. E-mail: oxmag@muohio.edu. Website: www.oxfordmagazine.org. **Contact:** Fiction editor. Annual. Estab. 1985. Circ. 1,000.

● *Oxford* has been awarded two *Pushcart Prizes*.

Needs Wants quality fiction and prose, genre is not an issue but nothing sentimental. Receives 150 unsolicited mss/month. **Publishes some new writers/year.** Recently published work by Stephen Dixon, Andre Dubus and Stuart Dybek. Publishes short shorts. Also publishes poetry.

How to Contact SASE. Responds in 2 months, depending upon time of submissions; mss received after December 31 will be returned. Accepts simultaneous submissions if notified. Sample copy for $5.

Payment/Terms Acquires one-time rights.

Advice ''*Oxford Magazine* is dedicated to creating an online presence, a forum, establishing dialogue between text and reader. The fiction we publish (either print or electronic) is problematic: genre-jumping, frame-breaking, defying the pigeonholes that current publishing ideologies thrust in your face. Contextually traditional prose should be made self-aware of history; recharting familar territory or foraging in the cracks will produce lively work.''

☑ PAINTED BRIDE QUARTERLY

Rutgers University, 311 N. Fifth St., Camden NJ 08102-1519. (856)225-6129. Fax: (856)225-6117. E-mail: pbq@camden.rutgers.edu. Website: www.pbq.rutgers.edu. **Contact:** Kathleen Volk-Miller, managing editor. ''*PBQ* seeks literary fiction, experimental and traditional.'' Publishes online each quarter and a print annual each spring. Estab. 1973.

Needs Ethnic/multicultural, experimental, feminist, gay, lesbian, literary, translations. ''No genre fiction.'' ''Publishes theme-related work, check website; holds annual fiction contests. **Publishes 24 new writers/year.** Length: 5,000 words; average length: 3,000 words. Publishes short shorts. Also publishes literary essays, literary criticism, poetry. Occasionally comments on rejected mss.

How to Contact Send complete ms. No electronic submissions. Responds in 6 months to mss. Sample copy online. Writer's guidelines online. Reviews fiction.

Payment/Terms Acquires first North American serial rights.

Advice We look for ''freshness of idea incorporated with high-quality writing. We receive an awful lot of nicely written work with worn-out plots. We want quality in whatever—we hold experimental work to as strict standards as anything else. Many of our readers write fiction; most of them enjoy a good reading. We hope to be an outlet for quality. A good story gives, first, enjoyment to the reader. We've seen a good many of them lately, and we've published the best of them.''

☑ ☑ PAPERPLATES, a magazine for fifty readers

Perkolator Kommunikation, 19 Kenwood Ave., Toronto ON M6C 2R8 Canada. (416)651-2551. Fax: (416)651-2910. E-mail: magazine@paperplates.org. Website: www.paperplates.org. **Contact:** Bethany Gibson, fiction editor. Electronic magazine. Quarterly. Estab. 1990.

Needs Condensed novels, ethnic/multicultural, feminist, gay, lesbian, literary, mainstream, translations. ''No science fiction, fantasy or horror.'' Receives 12 unsolicited mss/month. Accepts 2-3 mss/issue; 6-9 mss/year. Publishes ms 6-8 months after acceptance. Recently published work by Celia Lottridge, C.J. Lockett, Deirdre

Kessler and Marvyne Jenoff. Length: 1,500-3,500 words; average length: 3,000 words. Publishes short shorts. Also publishes literary essays, literary criticism, poetry.
How to Contact Accepts submissions by e-mail. Responds in 6 weeks to queries; 3 months to mss. Accepts simultaneous submissions. Sample copy online. Writer's guidelines online.
Payment/Terms Pays 1 contributor's copy. Acquires first North American serial rights.

◪ THE PAUMANOK REVIEW

E-mail: submissions@paumanokreview.com. Website: www.paumanokreview.com. **Contact:** Katherine Arline, editor. Online literary magazine. *"TPR is dedicated to publishing and promoting the best in world art and literature."* Quarterly. Estab. 2000.
  • J.P. Maney's *Western Exposures* was selected for inclusion in the *E2INK Best of the Web Anthology*.
Needs Experimental, literary, mainstream. Receives 100 unsolicited mss/month. Accepts 6-8 mss/issue; 24-32 mss/year. Publishes ms 6 weeks after acceptance. **Publishes 4 new writers/year.** Recently published work by Patty Friedman, Elisha Porat, Barry Spacks and Walt McDonald. Length: 1,500-6,000 words; average length: 3,000 words. Publishes short shorts. Also publishes literary essays, poetry. Usually comments on rejected mss.
How to Contact Send complete ms. Accepts submissions by e-mail. Include estimated word count, brief bio, list of publications and where you discovered the publication. Responds in 1 week to queries; 1 month to mss. Accepts simultaneous and reprints submissions. Sample copy online. Writer's guidelines online.
Payment/Terms Free classified ads for the life of the magazine. Acquires one-time, anthology rights. Sends galleys to author.
Advice "Though this is an English-language publication, it is not US-or UK-centric. Please submit accordingly. *TPR* is a publication of Wind River Press, which also publishes *Critique* magazine and select print and electronic books."

◪ PBW

513 N. Central Ave., Fairborn OH 45324. (937)878-5184. E-mail: rianca@aol.com. Electronic disk zine; 700 pages, specializing in avant-garde fiction and poetry. *"PBW is an experimental floppy disk that prints strange and 'unpublishable' in an above-ground-sense writing."* Twice per year. Estab. 1988.
How to Contact "Manuscripts are only taken if they are submitted on disk or by e-mail." Send SASE for reply, return of ms. Sample copy not available.
Payment/Terms All rights revert back to author. Not copyrighted.

THE PINK CHAMELEON

E-mail: dpfreda@juno.com. Website: www.geocities.com/thepinkchameleon/index.html. **Contact:** Mrs. Dorothy Paula Freda, editor/publisher. Family-oriented electronic magazine. Annual. Estab. 2000.
Needs Adventure, family saga, fantasy, humor/satire, literary, mainstream, mystery/suspense, religious/inspirational, romance, science fiction, thriller/espionage, western, young adult/teen, psychic/supernatural. "No violence for the sake of violence." Receives 50 unsolicited mss/month. Publishes ms within 1 year after acceptance. **Publishes 50% new writers/year.** Recently published work by Deanne F. Purcell, Cenizas de Rosas, Martin Green, Albert J. Manachino, Don Stockard, James W. Collins and C.T. VanHoose. Length: 500-2,500 words; average length: 2,000 words. Publishes short shorts. Also publishes literary essays, poetry. Sometimes comments on rejected mss.
How to Contact Send complete ms. No attachments. Responds in 1 month to mss. Accepts reprints, multiple submissions. No simultaneous submissions. Sample copy online. Writer's guidelines online.
Payment/Terms "Nonprofit. Acquires one-time rights for one year but will return rights earlier on request."
Advice "Simple, honest, evocative emotion, upbeat submissions that give hope for the future; well-paced plots; stories, poetry, articles, essays that speak from the heart. Read guidelines carefully. Use a good, but not ostentatious, opening hook. Stories should have a beginning, middle and end that make the reader feel the story was worth his or her time. This also applies to articles and essays. In the latter two, wrap your comments and conclusions in a neatly packaged final paragraph. Turnoffs include violence, bad language. Simple, genuine and sensitive work does not need to shock with vulgarity to be interesting and enjoyable."

⊕ THE PLAZA, A Space for Global Human Relations

U-Kan, Inc., Yoyogi 2-32-1, Shibuya-ku, Tokyo 151-0053 Japan. E-mail: plaza@u-kan.co.jp. Website: www.u-kan.co.jp. **Contact:** Leo Shunji Nishida, publisher/fiction editor. Online literary magazine. *"The Plaza* is an intercultural and bilingual magazine (English and Japanese). Our focus is 'the essence of being human.' Some works are published in both Japanese and English (translations by our staff if necessary). The most important criteria is artistic level. We look for works that reflect simply 'being human.' Stories on intercultural (not international) relations are desired. *The Plaza* is devoted to offering a spiritual place where people around the world can share their creative work. We introduce contemporary writers and artists as our generation's contribution to the continuing human heritage.'' Annual.

Needs Wants to see more fiction ''of not human beings, but of being human. Of not international, but intercultural. Of not social, but human relationships.'' No political themes, religious evangalism, social commentary. Accepts 2 mss/issue. **Publishes 3 new writers/year.** Recently published work by Joe Kernac, Eleanor Lohse and Kikuzou Hidari.

How to Contact Send complete ms. Accepts submissions by e-mail, fax. Accepts multiple submissions. Sample copy online. Writer's guidelines online.

Advice ''The most important consideration is that the writer is motivated to write. If it is not moral but human, or if it is neither a wide knowledge nor a large computer-like memory, but rather a deep thinking like the quietness in the forest, it is acceptable. While the traditional culture of reading of some thousands of years may be destined to be extinct under the marvelous progress of civilization, we intend to present contemporary works as our global human heritage to readers of forthcoming generations.''

N ⊕ ◯ PREMONITIONS

Pigasus Press, 13 Hazely Combe, Arrenton Isle of Wight PO30 3AJ England. Website: www.pigasuspress.co.uk. **Contact:** Tony Lee, editor. ''A magazine of science fiction, horror stories, genre poetry and fantastic artwork.'' Biannual.

Needs Science fiction (hard, contemporary science fiction/fantasy). ''No sword and sorcery, supernatural horror.'' Accepts 12 mss/issue.

How to Contact ''Unsolicited submissions are always welcome, but writers must enclose SAE/IRC for reply, plus adequate postage to return ms if unsuitable. No fiction or poetry submissions accepted via e-mail.'' Sample copy online.

Advice ''Potential contributors are advised to study recent issues of the magazine.''

◢ REALPOETIK, A Little Magazine of the Internet

840 W. Nickerson #11, Seattle WA 98119. (206)282-3776. E-mail: salasin@scn.org. Website: www.scn.org/realpoetik. **Contact:** Fiction Editor. ''We publish the new, lively, exciting and unexpected in vernacular English. Any vernacular will do.'' Weekly. Estab. 1993.

Needs ''We do not want to see anything that fits neatly into categories. We subvert categories.'' Publishes ms 2-4 months after acceptance. **Publishes 20-30 new writers/year.** Average length: 250-500 words. Publishes short shorts. Also publishes literary essays, literary criticism, poetry. Sometimes comments on rejected mss.

How to Contact Query with or without published clips or send complete ms. Accepts submissions by e-mail. Responds in 1 month to queries. Sample copy online.

Payment/Terms Acquires one-time rights. Sponsors awards/contests.

Advice ''Be different but interesting. Humor and consciousness are always helpful. Write short. We're a post-modern e-zine.''

N ◯ REFLECTIONS EDGE

E-mail: editor@reflectionsedge.com. Website: www.reflectionsedge.com. **Contact:** Sharon Dodge, editor-in-chief. ''We're an ezine with a small staff; editor, staff writer/assistant, several tech members. Our focus is genre fiction. Estab. 2004.

Needs Adventure, erotica, fantasy, horror, mystery/suspense, psychic/supernatural/occult, science fiction (hard and soft), western, magical realism. Accepts 120 mss/year. Publishes ms 2 months after acceptance.

How to Contact Submit fiction with name, title, genre, length to fictionsubmissions@reflectionsedge.com. Accepts queries by e-mail only. No attachments. Responds in 1 week to queries; 2 months to mss. Accepts simultaneous submissions. Writer's guidelines online.

Payment/Terms Acquires electronic rights.

Advice ''We're drawn to great writing first, but great ideas are close behind. We're a zine for marginalized fiction. Don't send us anything mainstream!''

◢ RENAISSANCE ONLINE MAGAZINE

P.O. Box 3246, Pawtucket RI 02861-2331. E-mail: submit@renaissancemag.com. Website: www.renaissancemag.com. **Contact:** Kevin Ridolfi, editor. Electronic zine. ''We provide an open forum and exchange for an online community seeking diversity on the jumbled and stagnant Internet. Works should be well written and should deal with the effective resolution of a problem.''

Needs Humor/satire, serialized novels, young adult/teen. ''No lewd, adult fiction.'' **Publishes 6 new writers/year.** Recently published work by Sharon Suendsen, Rob Kerr and Steve Mueske.

How to Contact Query with or without published clips or send complete ms. Accepts submissions by e-mail. Sample copy online.

Advice "Browse through past issues for content tendencies and submission requirements. Don't be afraid to go out on a short limb, but please limit yourself to our already existing categories."

THE ROSE & THORN LITERARY E-ZINE, Showcasing Emerging and Established Writers and A Writer's Resource

E-mail: BAQuinn@aol.com. Website: www.theroseandthornezine.com. **Contact:** Barbara Quinn, fiction editor, publisher, managing editor. E-zine specializing in literary works of fiction, nonfiction, poetry and essays. "We created this publication for readers and writers alike. We provide a forum for emerging and established voices. We blend contemporary writing with traditional prose and poetry in an effort to promote the literary arts." Quarterly. Circ. 12,000.

Needs Adventure, ethnic/multicultural, experimental, fantasy, historical, horror (dark fantasy, futuristic, psychological, supernatural), humor/satire, literary, mainstream, mystery/suspense, New Age, regional, religious/inspirational, romance (contemporary, futuristic/time travel, gothic, historical, regency, romantic suspense), science fiction, thriller/espionage, western. Receives "several hundred" unsolicited mss/month. Accepts 8-10 mss/issue; 40-50 mss/year. **Publishes many new writers/year.** Publishes short shorts. Also publishes literary essays, poetry. Sometimes comments on rejected mss.

How to Contact Query with or without published clips or send complete ms. Accepts submissions by e-mail. Include estimated word count, 150-word bio, list of publications and author's byline. Responds in 1 week to queries; 1 month to mss. Accepts simultaneous and reprints submissions. Sample copy free. Writer's guidelines online.

Payment/Terms Writer retains all rights. Sends galleys to author.

Advice "Clarity, control of the language, evocative stories that tug at the heart and make their mark on the reader long after it's been read. We look for uniqueness in voice, style and characterization. New twists on old themes are always welcome. Use all aspects of good writing in your stories, including dynamic characters, strong narrative voice and a riveting original plot. We have eclectic tastes, so go ahead and give us a shot. Read the publication and other quality literary journals so you'll see what we look for. Always check your spelling and grammar before submitting. Reread your submission with a critical eye and ask yourself, 'Does it evoke an emotional response? Have I completely captured my reader?' Check your submission for 'it' and 'was' and see if you can come up with a better way to express yourself. Be unique."

RPPS/FULLOSIA PRESS

Rockaway Park Philosophical Society, P.O. Box 280, Ronkonkoma NY 11779. E-mail: deanofrpps@aol.com. Website: rpps_fullosia_press.tripod.com. **Contact:** J.D. Collins, editor. E-zine. "One-person, part-time. Publishes fiction and nonfiction. Our publication is right wing and conservative leaning to views of Patrick Buchanan but amenable to the opposition's point of view. We promote an independent America. We are anti-global, anti-UN. Collects unusual news from former British or American provinces. Fiction interests include military, police, private detective, courthouse stories." Monthly. Estab. 1999. Circ. 150.

Needs Historical (American), military/war, mystery/suspense, thriller/espionage. Christmas, St. Patrick's Day, Fourth of July. Publishes ms 1 week after acceptance. **Publishes 10 new writers/year.** Recently published work by Laura Stamps, John Meaney, John Grey, Dr. Kelly White, James Davies, Dave Waters, Andy Martin and Peter Vetrano's class. Length: 500-2,000 words; average length: 750 words. Publishes short shorts. Also publishes literary essays. Always comments on rejected mss.

How to Contact Query with or without published clips. Accepts submissions by e-mail. Include brief bio and list of publications. Mail submissions must be on 3¼ floppy disk. Responds in 1 month to mss. Accepts simultaneous and reprints, multiple submissions. Sample copy online. Reviews fiction.

Payment/Terms Acquires electronic rights.

Advice "Make your point quickly. If you haven't done so, after five pages, everybody hates you and your characters."

$ SCIFICTION

(formerly SCIFI.COM), PMB 391, 511 Avenue of the Americas, New York NY 10011-8436. (212)989-3742. E-mail: datlow@yahoo.com. Website: www.scifi.com/scifiction. **Contact:** Ellen Datlow, fiction editor. E-zine specializing in science fiction. "Largest and widest-ranging science fiction site on the Web. Affiliated with the Sci Fi Channel, *Science Fiction Weekly*, news, reviews, comics, movies and interviews." Weekly. Estab. 2000. Circ. 50,000/day.

- Linda Nagata's novella *Goddess*, first published on Scifi.com, was the first exclusively Net-published piece of fiction to ever win the Nebula Award from Science Fiction and Fantasy Writers of America. Andy Duncan's story "The Pottawatamie Giant" won the World Fantasy Award.

Needs Fantasy (urban fantasy), science fiction (hard science/technological, soft/sociological). "No space opera, sword and sorcery, poetry or high fantasy." Receives 100 unsolicited mss/month. Accepts 1 mss/issue; 40 mss/

year. Publishes ms within 6 months after acceptance. Agented fiction 2%. Recently published work by Carol Emshwiller, Paul Di Filippo, Lucius Sheppard, Kristine Kathryn Rusch, Robert Reed, Nancy Kress and Octavia Butler. Length: 2,000-17,500 words; average length: 7,500 words. Sometimes comments on rejected mss.

How to Contact Send complete ms. Send SASE for return of ms or send a disposable copy of the ms and #10 SASE for reply only. Responds in 2 months to mss. Writer's guidelines for SASE or on website.

Payment/Terms Pays 20¢/word up to $3,500. Pays on acceptance for first, electronic, and anthology rights.

Advice "We look for crisp, evocative writing, interesting characters, good storytelling. Check out the kinds of fiction we publish if you can. If you read one, then you know what I want."

SEED CAKE

1913 S. 262nd Place, Des Moines WA 98198. E-mail: seedcake@hotmail.com. Website: www.seedcake.com. **Contact:** Lisa Purdy, editor. Literary e-zine. "Each issue is a self-contained file and includes a cover with the contents arranged as an A and B side like old 78 or 45 rpm records." Estab. 1997. Circ. 5,000.

Needs Comics/graphic novels, experimental, feminist, gay, humor/satire, literary, short story collections. "We do not want to see genre fiction or fiction that is easily classified." Receives 20 unsolicited mss/month. Accepts 2 mss/issue; 10 mss/year. Publishes ms 1 month after acceptance. **Publishes 3 new writers/year.** Recently published work by Willie Smith, Diana George and Leonard Chang. Average length: 6,000 words. Also publishes literary essays. Often comments on rejected mss.

How to Contact Query with or without published clips or send complete ms. Accepts submissions by e-mail. Include bio. Responds in 1 week to queries; 1 month to mss. Accepts simultaneous and reprints, multiple submissions. Sample copy online. Writer's guidelines online. Reviews fiction.

Payment/Terms Pays magazine subscription. Acquires one-time, one-time anthology rights. Sends galleys to author.

Advice "We look for writing with a distinctive voice or subject matter that can be arranged into a pair of short stories."

THE SITE OF BIG SHOULDERS, Chicago Writing, Art and Photography

The Site of Big Shoulders, Chicago IL. E-mail: submissions@sobs.org. Website: sobs.org. **Contact:** Matt Wade, fiction editor; Justin Kerr, editor-in-chief. Online magazine. "*The Site of Big Shoulders* features original content with a connection to the greater Chicago area by virtue of authorship or subject matter. Founded on the idea that profit corrupts media, SOBS is a non-commercial community publishing effort that focuses on high editorial quality, aesthetics and production value without regard to commercial need or mass appeal." Estab. 1996. Circ. 20,000.

- This site has won the 2003 Community Arts Assistance Program Grant, the Bronze Trophy for Exceptional Creativity from the Chicago Internet Review (1998); the Artis Hot Site Award (1998) and the Juno Silver Award (1998).

Needs Regional (greater Chicago). "We do not publish fiction that does not have a connection to the greater Chicagoland region (northeast Illinois, northwest Indiana, southeast Wisconsin)." Receives 1-5 unsolicited mss/month. Accepts 4-8 mss/year. Publishes ms 2-12 months after acceptance. **Publishes 4-8 new writers/year.** Recently published work by Roger Marsh, Mike Beyer, Bob Nemtusak, Paul Barile and Jason Anthony Stavropoulos. Length: 200-3,000 words; average length: 1,000 words. Publishes short shorts. Also publishes literary essays, literary criticism, poetry.

How to Contact Send complete ms. Accepts submissions by e-mail. Include brief bio. Responds in 3 months to queries. Accepts simultaneous and reprints, multiple submissions. Sample copy online. Writer's guidelines online.

Payment/Terms Non-exclusive right to feature the submitted content within the Internet domain.

Advice "We are very open to the idea of publishing hypertext or other experimental fiction. Please submit clean, edited copy."

SKYLINE MAGAZINE

Skyline Publications, P.O. Box 295, Stormville NY 12582-5417. (845)227-5171. E-mail: skylineeditor@aol.com. Website: www.skylinemagazines.com. **Contact:** Victoria Valentine, publisher/editor. "*Skyline Magazine* publishes the excellent work of both established and new authors. Our readers and authors range in age from 17-100. We hope to bring the world together by presenting all forms of the arts through individual expression. We seek fiction and nonfiction stories, human-interest articles/essays, interviews about unique and/or accomplished everyday individuals, as well as celebrities. We feel everyone has something to say that would be of interest to others. Life holds many stories and we are open to all. We normally do not publish politics or religious material. In each issue we publish at least one student author and one student artist." Bimonthly. Estab. 2001.

Needs Adventure, ethnic/multicultural, experimental, fantasy, historical, horror (if tasteful), humor/satire, mainstream, mystery/suspense, novel excerpts, romance, science fiction, slice-of-life vignettes, suspense, thriller/espionage, western. No erotica. Nothing political or religious. Publishes ms 1-3 months after acceptance. Recently published work by Steve Manchester, Eric Tessier, Arthur Isaacson, David Evans Katz and Patricia Guthrie. Publishes short shorts. Also publishes literary essays, poetry.

How to Contact Accepts submissions by e-mail (admin@skylinemagazines.com). Responds in 6-8 weeks to queries; 2-4 months to mss. Accepts simultaneous submissions. Sample copy for $2.50, plus $1.50 postage. Writer's guidelines online or by e-mail.

Payment/Terms Pays in contributor copies. Acquires first North American serial, electronic rights.

Advice "Submit your cleanest edited work. Stories should include strong plot and characters and surprise or powerful conclusions. Much can be said in a few pages. Send interesting, compelling stories with rewarding conclusions. We support *Pushcart Prize* and submit nominations."

N ◪ SLOW TRAINS LITERARY JOURNAL

P.O. 4741, Denver CO 80155. (770)529-8540. E-mail: editor@slowtrains.com. Website: www.slowtrains.com. **Contact:** Susannah Indigo. Quarterly. Estab. 2000.

Needs Literary. No romance, sci-fi or other specific genre-writing. Receives 100+ unsolicited mss/month. Accepts 5-10 mss/issue; 20-40 mss/year. Publishes ms 3 months after acceptance. **Publishes 10-20 new writers/year.** Length: 1,000-5,000 words; average length: 3,500 words. Publishes short shorts. Also publishes literary essays, poetry. Rarely comments on rejected mss.

How to Contact Accepts submissions by e-mail. Responds in 4-8 weeks to mss. Accepts simultaneous and reprints submissions. Sample copy online. Writer's guidelines online.

Payment/Terms Pays 2 contributor's copies. Acquires one-time, electronic rights.

Advice "The first page must be able to pull the reader in immediately. Use your own fresh, poetic, compelling voice. Center your story around some emotional truth, and be sure of what you're trying to say."

N ◪ SMALL SPIRAL NOTEBOOK

E-mail: editor@smallspiralnotebook.com. Website: www.smallspiralnotebook.com. **Contact:** Felicia C. Sullivan, founder/editor-in-chief. Online magazine. Quarterly. Estab. 2001. Circ. 8,000. Member, CLMP.

Needs Experimental, family saga, feminist, gay, historical, humor/satire, lesbian, literary, translations. "No genre fiction." Receives 150 unsolicited mss/month. Accepts 10 mss/issue; 40 mss/year. Publishes ms 2-3 months after acceptance. **Publishes 25 new writers/year.** Recently published work by Judy Budnitz, Richard Grayson, Ken Foster, Lisa Glatt, Rachel Shetman and Lauren Grodstein. Average length: 3,500 words. Publishes short shorts. Also publishes literary essays, literary criticism, poetry.

How to Contact Send complete ms. Accepts submissions by e-mail (only). Include estimated word count, brief bio, list of publications. Send mss as attachment. Responds in 1 week to queries; 2-3 months to mss. Accepts simultaneous and reprints, multiple submissions. Sample copy online. Writer's guidelines online. Reviews fiction.

Payment/Terms Pays 2 contributor's copies. Sponsors awards/contests.

Advice "Send us your very best unpublished work. The only exception is if your work has been published in a *print* publication. One genre per submission: meaning either send fiction or poetry, not both. Send submissions as attachments. E-mail submissions with bio to submissions@smallspiralnotebook.com. Please spell check and proof your work. Surprise us! Give us fresh endings, a new way to tell a story, a great way to tell the story, engaging characters, shock us, piss us off, go for it!"

◪ SNREVIEW, Starry Night Review—A Literary E-Zine

197 Fairchild Ave., Fairfield CT 06825-4856. (203)366-5991. E-mail: editor@snreview.org. Website: www.snreview.org. **Contact:** Joseph Conlin, editor. E-zine specializing in literary short stories, essays and poetry. "We search for material that not only has strong characters and plot but also a devotion to imagery." Quarterly. Estab. 1999.

Needs Literary, mainstream. Receives 10 unsolicited mss/month. Accepts 5 mss/issue; 20 mss/year. Publishes ms 6 months after acceptance. **Publishes 20 new writers/year.** Recently published work by E. Lindsey Balkan, Marie Griffin and Jonathan Lerner. Length: 1,000-7,000 words; average length: 4,000 words. Also publishes literary essays, literary criticism, poetry.

How to Contact Accepts submissions by e-mail (only). Include 100 word bio and list of publications. Responds in 3 months to mss. Accepts simultaneous and reprints submissions. Sample copy online. Writer's guidelines online.

Payment/Terms Acquires first rights.

N ◪ ⊕ SPOILED INK MAGAZINE

Spoiledink.com, Dybbolsgade 14, Copenhagen 1721 Denmark. (0045) 35 81 81 02. E-mail: submissions@spoiledink.com. Website: www.spoiledink.com. **Contact:** Scott Dille, Alan Emmins, Christopher Lee, Sean Merrigan, editors. Print and online magazine. "We publish quality fiction, especially off-the-wall humour. Our goal is to act as a portal for great unpublished writers. We believe there are thousands of amazing writers that go unpublished. We want to fill the gap for those writers." Monthly. Estab. 2003. Circ. 10,000.

Needs Experimental, feminist, gay, horror, humor/satire, lesbian, mainstream, science fiction, thriller/espionage, modern voice. Receives 30-40 unsolicited mss/month. Accepts 5-7 mss/issue. Publishes ms 1-3 months after acceptance. Recently published work by Scotte Dille, Jim Muri, Rebekah Chen, Tariq Goddard, David Barringer, Steve Almond and Alan Emmins. Length: 1,000-25,000 words; average length: 6,000 words. Publishes short shorts. Also publishes literary essays, poetry. Rarely comments on rejected mss.

How to Contact Send complete ms. Accepts submissions by e-mail. Responds in 1 week to queries; 1 month to mss. Accepts simultaneous and reprints, multiple submissions. Sample copy online. Writer's guidelines online.

Payment/Terms Pays 1 contributor's copy. Acquires electronic rights. Sponsors awards/contests.

Advice "Follow instructions on the site. Original well-written stories always stand out. Write in your own true voice."

[N] [◑] STARK RAVING SANITY

IFP Studios, P.O. Box 44894, Columbus OH 43205. E-mail: info@ifpstudios.com. Website: www.starkravingsanity.com. **Contact:** Mike S. Dubose and H. Roger Baker II, editors. Electronic zine. "We have published short stories, poems, novel excerpts, prose poems, micro-fiction and everything in between. Our intended audience is anyone looking for an entertaining work of substance."

Needs "Anything goes, as long as it fits our eclectic, ever-changing tastes. We want works that illustrate a variant view of reality—but then all works do just that. So anything of quality is what we like. No hate prose or porn." **Publishes 2-3 new writers/year.** Recently published work by Joe Flowers, R.N. Friedland, Jonathan Lowe and Len Kruger.

How to Contact Accepts submissions by e-mail. Sample copy online. Writer's guidelines online.

Advice "In taking fiction, I like (and look for) characters who act as if they are real, situations that are interesting, and writing that sings. I will accept first-time writers if the writing does not look like it came from a first-timer. In other words, I want quality. Please be professional. Read the journal. Read and follow guidelines. And keep in mind also that we too are real people on schedules. Mutual respect, please."

[◑] STORY BYTES, Very Short Stories

E-mail: editor@storybytes.com. Website: www.storybytes.com. **Contact:** M. Stanley Bubien, editor. Electronic zine. "We are strictly an electronic publication, appearing on the Internet in three forms. First, the stories are sent to an electronic mailing list of readers. They also get placed on our website, both in PDF and HTML format."

Needs "Stories must be very short—having a length that is the power of 2, specifically: 2, 4, 8, 16, 32, etc." No sexually explicit material. "Would like to see more material dealing with religion—not necessarily 'inspirational' stories, but those that show the struggles of living a life of faith in a realistic manner." **Publishes 33 percent new writers/year.** Recently published work by Richard K. Weems, Joseph Lerner, Lisa Cote and Thomas Sennet.

How to Contact Query with or without published clips or send complete ms. Accepts submissions by e-mail. "I prefer plain text with story title, authorship and word count. Only accepts electronic submissions. See website for complete guidelines." Sample copy online. Writer's guidelines online.

Advice "In *Story Bytes* the very short stories themselves range in topic. Many explore a brief event—a vignette of something unusual, unique and at times something even commonplace. Some stories can be bizarre, while others quite lucid. Some are based on actual events, while others are entirely fictional. Try to develop conflict early on (in the first sentence if possible!), and illustrate or resolve this conflict through action rather than description. I believe we'll find an audience for electronic published works primarily in the short story realm."

[N] [$] STORY FRIENDS

Mennonite Publishing Network, 616 Walnut Ave., Scottdale PA 15683. (724)887-8500. Fax: (724)887-3111. Website: www.mph.org. **Contact:** Susan Reith, editor. "*Story Friends* is planned to nurture faith development in 4-9 year olds." Monthly. Estab. 1905. Circ. 7,000.

Needs Children's/juvenile. Stories of everyday experiences at home, in church, in school or at a play, which provide models of Christian values. "Wants to see more fiction set in African-American, Latino or Hispanic settings. No stories about children and their grandparents or children and their elderly neighbors. I have more than enough." Publishes ms 1 year after acceptance. **Publishes 10-12 new writers/year.** Recently published work by Virginia Kroll and Lisa Harkrader.

How to Contact Send complete ms. Responds in 2 months to queries. Accepts simultaneous submissions. Sample copy for $2, or for 9×12 SAE and 2 first-class stamps. Writer's guidelines for #10 SASE.

Payment/Terms Pays 3-5¢/word. Pays on acceptance for one-time, second serial (reprint) rights.

Advice "I am buying more 500-word stories since we switched to a new format. It is important to include relationships, patterns of forgiveness, respect, honesty, trust and caring. Prefer exciting yet plausible short stories which offer varied settings, introduce children to wide ranges of friends, and demonstrate joys, fears, temptations and successes of the readers. Read good children's literature, the classics, the Newberry winner and the Caldecott winners. Respect children you know and allow their resourcefulness and character to have a voice in your writing."

storySOUTH, The best from new south writers

898 Chelsea Ave., Columbus OH 43209. (614)545-0754. Website: www.storysouth.com. **Contact:** Jason Sanford, editor. "*storySouth* is interested in fiction, creative nonfiction and poetry by writers from the New South. The exact definition *New South* varies from person to person and we leave it up to the writer to define their own connection to the southern United States." Quarterly. Estab. 2001.

Needs Experimental, literary, regional (south), translations. Receives 70 unsolicited mss/month. Accepts 5 mss/issue; 20 mss/year. Publishes ms 1 month after acceptance. **Publishes 5-10 new writers/year.** Average length: 4,000 words. Publishes short shorts. Also publishes literary essays, literary criticism, poetry. Often comments on rejected mss.

How to Contact Send complete ms. Accepts submissions by e-mail. Responds in 2 months to mss. Accepts simultaneous, multiple submissions. Writer's guidelines online.

Payment/Terms Acquires one-time rights.

Advice "What really makes a story stand out is a strong voice and a sense of urgency—a need for the reader to keep reading the story and not put it down until it is finished."

THE SUMMERSET REVIEW

25 Summerset Dr., Smithtown NY 11787. E-mail: editor@summersetreview.org. Website: www.summersetrevi ew.org. **Contact:** Joseph Levens, editor. Magazine: illustrations and photographs. "Our goal is simply to publish the highest quality literary fiction and essays intended for a general audience. We love lighter pieces. We love romance and fantasy, as long as it isn't pure genre writing but rather something that might indeed teach us a thing or two. This a simple online literary journal of high quality material, so simple you can call it unique." Quarterly. Estab. 2002.

- Several editors-in-chief of very prominent literary publications have done interviews for *The Summerset Review*: M.M.M. Hayes of *StoryQuarterly*, Gina Frangello of *Other Voices*, Jennifer Spiegel of *Hayden's Ferry Review*.

Needs Fantasy, humor/satire, literary, romance. No sci-fi, horror, or graphic erotica. Receives 40 unsolicited mss/month. Accepts 4 mss/issue; 18 mss/year. Publishes ms 2-3 months after acceptance. **Publishes 5-10 new writers/year.** Length: 8,000 words; average length: 3,000 words. Publishes short shorts. Also publishes literary essays. Often comments on rejected mss.

How to Contact Send complete ms. Accepts submissions by e-mail. Responds in 1-2 weeks to queries; 4-12 weeks to mss. Accepts simultaneous and reprints submissions. Writer's guidelines online.

Payment/Terms Aquires no rights other than one-time publishing, although we request credit if first published in *The Summerset Review*. Sends galleys to author.

Advice "Style counts. We prefer innovative or at least very smooth, convincing voices. Even the dullest of premises or the complete lack of conflict make for an interesting story if it is told in the right voice and style. We like to find little, interesting facts and/or connections subtly sprinkled throughout the piece. Harsh language should be used only if/when necessary. If we are choosing between light and dark subjects, the light will usually win."

TATTOO HIGHWAY, a Journal of Prose, Poetry & Art

Tinamou Two. E-mail: smcaulay@scuhayward.edu. Website: www.tattoohighway.org. **Contact:** Sara McAulay, editor. *Tattoo Highway* publishes high quality literary prose, both experimental and mainstream, including hypertext and Flash media. Each issue has a theme, and subject matter generally spins off from that. The journal is visually handsome, with unusual graphics. "We have no taboos except weak, hackneyed writing. Intended audience: grown-ups who appreciate well-crafted fiction and don't mind an occasional touch of the absurd." Semiannual. Estab. 1998.

Needs Experimental, gay, lesbian, literary, mainstream. "Please no predictable 'formula' stories. No lectures, no tracts, no sermons (on the Mount or otherwise). Graphic sex and/or violence had better be absolutely necessary to the story and had better be exceptionally well written!" Accepts 5-8 mss/issue; 10-16 mss/year. Publishes ms 1 month after acceptance. Recently published work by D.S. Richardson, Susan Moon, Elizabeth Wray, Stephen D. Guitierrez, Daniel Olivas, Angela Costi, Stephen Newton, Yvonne Chism-Peace, Robert D.

Vivian and Richard Holeton. Length: 1,500 words; average length: 1,000 words. Publishes short shorts. Also publishes literary essays, poetry. Sometimes comments on rejected mss.

How to Contact Accepts submissions by e-mail (ONLY). Send complete ms with cover letter. Responds in 1 week to queries; 1-3 months to mss. Accepts simultaneous, multiple submissions. Sample copy online.

Payment/Terms Acquires first electronic rights rights. Sponsors awards/contests.

Advice "Three things: great writing, great writing and great writing. Look at past issues online, then bring us your best stuff."

🖸 TEKKA

Eastgate Systems, 134 Main St., Watertown MA 02472. (617)924-9044. Fax: (617)924-9051. E-mail: editor@tekka.net. Website: www.tekka.net. **Contact:** Elin Sjursen, assistant editor. "*Tekka* is about enjoying new media and creating beautiful software. The future of serious writing lies on the screen, we're interested in real ideas, catchy hyper texts, articles and reviews as well as sci-fi." Quarterly. Estab. 2003.

Needs Comics/graphic novels, fantasy (space fantasy), science fiction (hard science/technological, soft/sociological). Publishes short shorts. Also publishes literary essays, literary criticism, poetry. Often comments on rejected mss.

How to Contact Send complete ms. Accepts submissions by e-mail, disk. Accepts simultaneous submissions. Writer's guidelines online.

🖸 THE 13TH WARRIOR REVIEW

Asterius Press, P.O. Box 5122, Seabrook NJ 08302-3511. E-mail: theeditor@asteriuspress.com. Website: www.asteriuspress.com. **Contact:** John C. Erianne, publisher/editor. Online magazine. Estab. 2000.

Needs Erotica, experimental, humor/satire, literary, mainstream. Receives 200 unsolicited mss/month. Accepts 4-5 mss/issue; 10-15 mss/year. Publishes ms 6 months after acceptance. **Publishes 1-2 new writers/year.** Recently published work by Marjolyn Deurloo, Suzanne Nelson, Stoyan Valev, Paul A. Toth and D. Olsen. Length: 300-3,000 words; average length: 1,500 words. Publishes short shorts. Also publishes literary essays, literary criticism, poetry. Sometimes comments on rejected mss.

How to Contact Send complete ms. Include estimated word count, brief bio and address/e-mail. Send SASE or IRC for return of ms or send a disposable copy of ms and #10 SASE for reply only. Accepts submissions by e-mail (text in in message body only, no file attachements). Responds in 1 week to queries; 1-2 months to mss. Accepts simultaneous submissions. Sample copy online. Reviews fiction.

Payment/Terms Acquires first, electronic rights.

🖸 TOASTED CHEESE

E-mail: editors@toasted-cheese.com. Website: www.toasted-cheese.com. **Contact:** submit@toasted-cheese.com. E-zine specializing in fiction, creative nonfiction, poetry and flash fiction. "*Toasted Cheese* accepts submissions of previously unpublished fiction, flash fiction, creative nonfiction, and poetry. Our focus is on quality of work, not quantity. Some issues will therefore contain fewer/more pieces than previous issues. We don't restrict publication based on subject matter. We encourage submissions from innovative writers in all genres." Quarterly. Estab. 2001.

Needs Adventure, children's/juvenile, ethnic/multicultural, fantasy, feminist, gay, historical, horror, humor/satire, lesbian, literary, mainstream, mystery/suspense, New Age, psychic/supernatural/occult, romance, science fiction, thriller/espionage, western. "No fan fiction. No chapters or excerpts unless they read as a stand-alone story. No first drafts." Receives 70 unsolicited mss/month. Accepts 1-10 mss/issue; 5-30 mss/year. **Publishes 15 new writers/year.** Publishes short shorts. Also publishes poetry.

How to Contact Send complete ms. Accepts submissions by e-mail. Responds in 4 months to mss. Accepts simultaneous print submissions only; no simultaneous electronic submissions. Sample copy online. Writer's guidelines online.

Payment/Terms Acquires electronic rights. Sponsors awards/contests.

Advice "We are looking for clean, professional writing from writers of any level. Accepted stories will be concise and compelling. We are looking for writers who are serious about the craft: tomorrow's literary stars before they're famous. Take your submission seriously, yet remember that levity is appreciated. You are submitting not to traditional 'editors' but to fellow writers who appreciate the efforts of those in the trenches."

🅽 $🖸 UNDERSTANDING, The Magazine of the Alliance for Jewish Christian Muslim Understanding

20 Newton Street, Brookline MA 02445. (617)454-2736. E-mail: jflaska@bu.edu. Website: www.understanding-magazine.com. **Contact:** Jan R. Flaska, fiction editor. "In an effort to promote dialogue amongst people of all cultures, traditions and experiences, *Understanding* is a magazine intended to celebrate the gifts, talents and interests of all people instead of focusing on our differences. The magazine was inspired in part by the terrorist attacks of 9/11 and is open to all people for submissions. We accept all types of written submissions (poetry,

children's stories, fiction submissions, narratives, event reviews, editorial pieces, etc.). photographs of the human and natural world, photographs of architecture (concepts and completions), and photographs of all art mediums (sculpture, painting, drawings). Additionally, any types of submissions not mentioned previously will be considered as well." Quarterly. Estab. 2001.

Needs Adventure, children's/juvenile, ethnic/multicultural, family saga, feminist, historical, literary, mainstream, military/war, regional, religious/inspirational, translations, western, young adult/teen. Receives 15 unsolicited mss/month. Accepts 5 mss/issue; 30-50 mss/year. Publishes ms 1-2 months after acceptance. Publishes short shorts. Also publishes literary essays, literary criticism, poetry. Rarely comments on rejected mss.

How to Contact Send complete ms. Accepts submissions by e-mail, disk. Send disposable copy of ms and #10 SASE for reply only. Responds in 1-2 months to mss. Accepts simultaneous and reprints, multiple submissions. Sample copy online. Writer's guidelines online or by e-mail.

Payment/Terms Pays $5-100. Acquires one-time rights. Not copyrighted. Sponsors awards/contests.

Advice "Clearly, in the spirit of this magazine, submissions that promote religious dialogue will be provided with priority consideration. However submissions will be evaluated for their creative merits."

◩ ◎ VQ ONLINE, Web Quarterly

8009 18th Lane SE, Lacey WA 98503. (360)455-4607. E-mail: jmtanaka@webtv.net. Website: community.webtv .net/JMTanaka/VQ. **Contact:** Janet Tanaka, editor. "Our readers are professional and amateur volcanologists and other volcanophiles. It is not a journal, but an interesting e-zine that features fiction, poetry, nonfiction articles, book and movie reviews, and announcements of interest to volcano scientists." Quarterly.

Needs Serialized novels, short stories. Nothing pornographic. "Must have volcanoes as a central subject, not just window dressing." **Publishes 4-6 new writers/year.** Recently published work by Susan Mauer, Nolan Keating, Bill West and Wendall Duffield.

How to Contact Accepts submissions by e-mail. Sample copy online.

Payment/Terms Pays in contributor copies.

Advice "Material must be scientifically accurate."

◩ ◪ WEB DEL SOL

E-mail: submissions@webdelsol.com. Website: www.webdelsol.com. **Contact:** Michael Neff, editor-in-chief. Electronic magazine. "The goal of *Web Del Sol* is to use the medium of the Internet to bring the finest in contemporary literary arts to a larger audience. To that end, *WDS* not only webpublishes collections of work by accomplished writers and poets, but hosts over 25 literary arts publications on the WWW such as *Del Sol Review*, *North American Review*, *Global City Review*, *The Literary Review* and *The Prose Poem*." Estab. 1994.

Needs Literary. "*WDS* publishes work considered to be literary in nature, i.e. non-genre fiction. *WDS* also publishes poetry, prose poetry, essays and experimental types of writing." **Publishes 30-40 new writers/year.** Recently published work by Robert Olen Butler, Forrest Gander, Xue Di, Michael Buceja, Martine Billen and Robley Wilson. Publishes short shorts.

How to Contact "Submissions by e-mail from September through November and from January through March only. Submissions must contain some brief bio, list of prior publications (if any), and a short work or portion of that work, neither to exceed 1,000 words. Editors will contact if the balance of work is required." Sample copy online.

Advice "*WDS* wants fiction that is absolutely cutting edge, unique and/or at a minimum, accomplished with a crisp style and concerning subjects not usually considered the objects of literary scrutiny. Read works in such publications as *Conjunctions* (www.conjunctions.com) and *North American Review* (webdelsol.com/NorthAm-Review/NAR) to get an idea of what we are looking for."

◩ WILD VIOLET

Wild Violet, P.O. Box 39706, Philadelphia PA 19106-9706. E-mail: wildvioletmagazine@yahoo.com. Website: www.wildviolet.net. **Contact:** Alyce Wilson, editor. Online magazine: illustrations, photos. "Our goal is to democratize the arts: to make the arts more accessible and to serve as a creative forum for writers and artists. Our audience includes English-speaking readers from all over the world, who are interested in both 'high art' and pop culture." Quarterly. Estab. 2001.

Needs Comics/graphic novels, ethnic/multicultural, experimental, fantasy (space fantasy, sword and sorcery), feminist, gay, horror (dark fantasy, futuristic, psychological, supernatural), humor/satire, lesbian, literary, New Age, psychic/supernatural/occult, science fiction. "No stories where sexual or violent content is just used to shock the reader. No racist writings." Receives 15 unsolicited mss/month. Accepts 5 mss/issue; 20 mss/year. **Publishes 30 new writers/year.** Recently published work by Jessica DiMaio, Wayne Scheer, Jane McDonald and Eric Brown. Length: 500-6,000 words; average length: 3,000 words. Also publishes literary essays, literary criticism, poetry. Sometimes comments on rejected mss.

How to Contact Send complete ms. Accepts submissions by e-mail. Include estimated word count and brief bio. Send SASE for return of ms or send a disposable copy of ms and #10 SASE for reply only. Responds in 1 week to queries; 3-6 months to mss. Accepts simultaneous, multiple submissions. Sample copy online. Writer's guidelines by e-mail.

Payment/Terms Writers receive bio and links on contributor's page. All rights retained by author. Sponsors awards/contests.

Advice "We look for stories that are well paced and show character and plot development. Even short shorts should do more than simply paint a picture. Manuscripts stand out when the author's voice is fresh and engaging. Avoid muddying your story with too many characters and don't attempt to shock the reader with an ending you have not earned. Experiment with styles and structures, but don't resort to experimentation for its own sake."

N ◪ WORDS ON WALLS

3408 Whitfield Ave. Apt 4, Cincinnati OH 45220. (513)961-1475. E-mail: editor@wordsonwalls.net. Website: http://wordsonwalls.net. **Contact:** Kathrine Wright; Ariana-Sophia Kartsonis. Quarterly. Estab. 2003.

Needs Experimental, feminist, gay, literary. Receives 25-35 unsolicited mss/month. Accepts 2-3 mss/issue; 6-12 mss/year. Publishes ms 3-4 months after acceptance. Publishes short shorts. Also publishes literary essays, poetry. Often comments on rejected mss.

How to Contact Accepts submissions by e-mail. Accepts simultaneous and reprints, multiple submissions. Writer's guidelines online.

Payment/Terms Writer retains all rights.

Advice "We like work that is edgy, beautifully written with a strong sense of voice and music."

Consumer Magazines

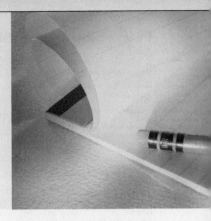

In this section of *Novel & Short Story Writer's Market* are consumer magazines with circulations of more than 10,000. Many have circulations in the hundreds of thousands or millions. Among the oldest magazines listed here are ones not only familiar to us but also to our parents, grandparents and even great-grandparents: *The Atlantic Monthly* (1857); *The New Yorker* (1925); *Esquire* (1933); and *Ellery Queen's Mystery Magazine* (1941).

Consumer periodicals make excellent markets for fiction in terms of exposure, prestige and payment. Because these magazines are well known, however, competition is great. Even the largest consumer publications buy only one or two stories an issue, yet thousands of writers submit to these popular magazines.

Despite the odds, it is possible for talented new writers to break into print in the magazines listed here. Your keys to breaking into these markets are careful research, professional presentation and, of course, top-quality fiction.

TYPES OF CONSUMER MAGAZINES

In this section you will find a number of popular publications, some for a broad-based, general-interest readership and others for large but select groups of readers—children, teenagers, women, men and seniors. There are also religious and church-affiliated magazines, publications devoted to the interests of particular cultures and outlooks, and top markets for genre fiction.

SELECTING THE RIGHT MARKET

Unlike smaller journals and publications, most of the magazines listed here are available at newsstands and bookstores. Many can also be found in the library, and guidelines and sample copies are almost always available by mail or online. Start your search by reviewing the listings, then familiarize yourself with the fiction included in the magazines that interest you.

Don't make the mistake of thinking that just because you are familiar with a magazine, their fiction is the same today as when you first saw it. Nothing could be further from the truth—consumer magazines, no matter how well established, are constantly revising their fiction needs as they strive to expand their audience base.

In a magazine that uses only one or two stories an issue, take a look at the nonfiction articles and features as well. These can give you a better idea of the audience for the publication and clues to the type of fiction that might appeal to them.

If you write genre fiction, look in the Category Index beginning on page 581. There you will find a list of markets that say they are looking for a particular subject.

FURTHERING YOUR SEARCH

See You've Got a Story (page 2) for information about the material common to all listings in this book. In this section in particular, pay close attention to the number of submissions a magazine receives in a given period and how many they publish in the same period. This will give you a clear picture of how stiff your competition can be.

While many of the magazines listed here publish one or two pieces of fiction in each issue, some also publish special fiction issues once or twice a year. When possible, we have indicated this in the listing information. We also note if the magazine is open to novel excerpts as well as short fiction, and we advise novelists to query first before submitting long work.

The Business of Fiction Writing, beginning on page 66, covers the basics of submitting your work. Professional presentation is a must for all markets listed. Editors at consumer magazines are especially busy, and anything you can do to make your manuscript easy to read and accessible will help your chances of being published. Most magazines want to see complete manuscripts, but watch for publications in this section that require a query first.

As in the previous section, we've included our own comments in many of the listings, set off by a bullet (●). Whenever possible, we list the publication's recent awards and honors. We've also included any special information we feel will help you in determining whether a particular publication interests you.

The maple leaf symbol (⬥) identifies our Canadian listings. You will also find some English-speaking markets from around the world. These foreign magazines are denoted with ⬛ at the beginning of the listings. Remember to use International Reply Coupons rather than stamps when you want a reply from a country other than your own.

Periodicals of Interest

For More Info

For more on consumer magazines, see issues of *Writer's Digest* (F+W Publications) and other industry trade publications available in larger libraries.

For news about some of the genre publications listed here and information about a particular field, there are a number of magazines devoted to genre topics, including *The Drood Review of Mystery*; *Locus* (for science fiction); *Science Fiction Chronicle*; and *Romance Writers' Report* (available to members of Romance Writers of America).

Consumer Magazines

⊘ ADVENTURES

WordAction Publications, 6401 The Paseo, Kansas City MO 64131-1213. (816)333-7000. **Contact:** Donna Fillmore, editor. Magazine: 8¼×11; 4 pages; self cover; color illustrations. "This weekly take-home paper connects Sunday school learning to life for first and second graders (ages 6-8)." Weekly. Circ. 45,000.

How to Contact *Adventures* is not accepting new submissions until September 2006.

$⊘ AFRICAN VOICES

African Voices Communications, Inc., 270 W. 96th St., New York NY 10025. (212)865-2982. Fax: (212)316-3335. Website: www.africanvoices.com. **Contact:** Kim Horne, fiction editor. Magazine: 52 pages; illustrations; photos. "*African Voices* is dedicated to highlighting the art, literature and history of people of color." Quarterly. Estab. 1992. Circ. 20,000.

Needs Adventure, children's/juvenile, condensed novels, erotica, ethnic/multicultural, experimental, fantasy, gay, historical (general), horror, humor/satire, literary, mainstream, mystery/suspense, novel excerpts, psychic/supernatural/occult, religious/inspirational, romance, science fiction, serialized novels, slice-of-life vignettes, suspense, young adult/teen (adventure, romance), African-American. List of upcoming themes available for SASE. Publishes special fiction issue. Receives 20-50 unsolicited mss/month. Accepts 20 mss/issue. Publishes ms 3-6 months after acceptance. Agented fiction 5%. **Publishes 30 new writers/year.** Recently published work by Junot Díaz, Michel Marriott and Carol Dixon. Length: 500-2,500 words; average length: 2,000 words. Publishes short shorts. Also publishes literary essays, poetry.

How to Contact Send complete ms. Include short bio. Send SASE for return of ms. Responds in 3 months to queries. Accepts simultaneous and reprints submissions. Sample copy for $5 or online. Writer's guidelines online. Reviews fiction.

Payment/Terms Pays $25-50. Pays on publication for first North American serial rights.

Advice "A manuscript stands out if it is neatly typed with a well-written and interesting story line or plot. Originality encouraged. We are interested in more horror, erotic and drama pieces. *AV* wants to highlight the diversity in our culture. Stories must touch the humanity in us all."

$⊘ AIM MAGAZINE

Aim Publishing Co., P.O. Box 1174, Maywood IL 60153. (708)344-4414. Fax: (206)543-2746. Website: aimmagazine.org. **Contact:** Ruth Apilado, associate editor. Magazine: 8½×11; 48 pages; slick paper; photos and illustrations. Publishes material "to purge racism from the human bloodstream through the written word—that is the purpose of *Aim Magazine.*" Quarterly. Estab. 1975. Circ. 10,000.

Needs Ethnic/multicultural, historical, mainstream, suspense. Open. No "religious" mss. Published special fiction issue last year; plans another. Receives 25 unsolicited mss/month. Accepts 15 mss/issue; 60 mss/year. Publishes ms 3 months after acceptance. **Publishes 40 new writers/year.** Recently published work by Christina Touregny, Thomas Lee Harris, Michael Williams and Jake Halpern. Publishes short shorts. Sometimes comments on rejected mss.

How to Contact Send complete ms. Accepts submissions by e-mail. Include SASE with cover letter and author's photograph. Responds in 2 months to queries; 1 month to mss. Accepts simultaneous submissions. Sample copy and writer's guidelines for $4 and 9×12 SAE with $1.70 postage or online.

Payment/Terms Pays $25-35. Pays on publication for first, one-time rights.

Advice "Search for those who are making unselfish contributions to their community and write about them. Write about your own experiences. Be familar with the background of your characters. Known for stories with social significance, proving that people from different ethnic, racial backgrounds are more alike than they are different."

$⊘ ◎ AMERICAN GIRL

Pleasant Co. Publications, 8400 Fairway Place, Middleton WI 53562. (608)836-4848. Website: www.americangirl.com. **Contact:** Magazine Department Assistant. Magazine: 8½×11; 52 pages; illustrations; photos. "Four-color bimonthly magazine for girls age 8-12. We want thoughtfully developed children's literature with good characters and plots." Bimonthly. Estab. 1992. Circ. 700,000.

Needs Adventure, children's/juvenile (girls 8-12 years), condensed novels, ethnic/multicultural, historical, humor/satire, slice-of-life vignettes. No romance, science fiction, fantasy. Receives 100 unsolicited mss/month. Accepts 6 mss/year. **Publishes 2-3 new writers/year.** Recently published work by Kay Thompson, Mavis Jukes and Susan Shreve. Publishes short shorts. Also publishes literary essays, poetry.

How to Contact Query with published clips. Include bio (1 paragraph). Send SASE for reply, return of ms or send a disposable copy of ms. Send SASE for guidelines. Responds in 3 months to queries. Accepts simultaneous and reprints submissions. Sample copy for $3.95 (check made out to *American Girl*) and 9×12 SAE with $1.98 postage. Writer's guidelines online.

Consumer Magazines

Payment/Terms Pays $500 minimum. Pays on acceptance for first North American serial rights. Sends galleys to author.

Advice "We're looking for excellent character development with an interesting plot."

$ ⬚ ⬚ ANALOG SCIENCE FICTION & FACT

Dell Magazine Fiction Group, 475 Park Ave. S., 11th Floor, New York NY 10016. (212)686-7188. Fax: (212)686-7414. E-mail: analog@dellmagazines.com. Website: www.analogsf.com. **Contact:** Stanley Schmidt, editor. Magazine: 144 pages; illustrations; photos. Monthly. Estab. 1930. Circ. 50,000.

• Fiction published in *Analog* has won numerous Nebula and Hugo Awards.

Needs Science fiction (hard science/technological, soft/sociological). "No fantasy or stories in which the scientific background is implausible or plays no essential role." Receives 500 unsolicited mss/month. Accepts 6 mss/issue; 70 mss/year. Publishes ms 10 months after acceptance. Agented fiction 5%. **Publishes 3-4 new writers/year.** Recently published work by Ben Bova, Stephen Baxter, Larry Niven, Michael F. Flynn, Timothy Zahn, Robert J. Sawyer and Joe Haldeman. Length: 2,000-80,000 words; average length: 10,000 words. Publishes short shorts. Sometimes comments on rejected mss.

How to Contact Send complete ms with a cover letter. Accepts queries for serials and fact articles only; query by mail. Include estimated word count. Send SASE for return of ms or send a disposable copy of ms and #10 SASE for reply only. Responds in 1 month to queries. Accepts multiple submissions. No simultaneous submissions. Sample copy for $5. Writer's guidelines online. Reviews fiction.

Payment/Terms Pays 4¢/word for novels; 5-6¢/word for novelettes; 6-8¢/word for shorts under 7,500 words; $450-600 for intermediate lengths. Pays on acceptance for first North American serial, nonexclusive foreign serial rights. Sends galleys to author. Not copyrighted.

Advice "I'm looking for irresistibly entertaining stories that make me think about things in ways I've never done before. Read several issues to get a broad feel for our tastes, but don't try to imitate what you read."

⬚ $ ⬚ ◎ THE ANNALS OF SAINT ANNE DE BEAUPRÉ

Redemptorist Fathers, P.O. Box 1000, St. Anne De Beaupré QC G0A 3C0 Canada. (418)827-4538. Fax: (418)827-4530. **Contact:** Father Roch Achard, C.Ss.R., editor. Magazine: 8×11; 32 pages; glossy paper; photos. "Our mission statement includes dedication to Christian family values and devotion to St. Anne." Releases 11 issues/year; July and August are one issue. Estab. 1885. Circ. 32,000.

Needs Religious/inspirational, inspirational. "No senseless mockery." Receives 50-60 unsolicited mss/month. Recently published work by Beverly Sheresh. Always comments on rejected mss.

How to Contact Send complete ms. Include estimated word count. Send SASE for reply or return of ms. Responds in 4-6 weeks to queries. No simultaneous submissions. Sample copy online. Writer's guidelines online.

Payment/Terms Pays 3-4¢/word. Pays on acceptance for first North American serial rights. Please state "rights" for sale.

$ ⬚ ART TIMES, Commentary and Resources for the Fine and Performing Arts

P.O. Box 730, Mount Marion NY 12456-0730. (914)246-6944. Fax: (914)246-6944. Website: www.arttimesjournal.com. **Contact:** Raymond J. Steiner, fiction editor. Magazine: 12×15; 24 pages; Jet paper and cover; illustrations; photos. "*Art Times* covers the art fields and is distributed in locations most frequented by those enjoying the arts. Our copies are distributed throughout the Northeast region as well as in most of the galleries of Soho, 57th Street and Madison Avenue in the metropolitan area; locations include theaters, galleries, museums, cultural centers and the like. Our readers are mostly over 40, affluent, art-conscious and sophisticated. Subscribers are located across U.S. and abroad (Italy, France, Germany, Greece, Russia, etc.)." Monthly. Estab. 1984. Circ. 27,000.

Needs Adventure, ethnic/multicultural, fantasy, feminist, gay, historical, humor/satire, lesbian, literary, mainstream, science fiction, contemporary. "We seek quality literary pieces. Nothing violent, sexist, erotic, juvenile, racist, romantic, political, etc." Receives 30-50 unsolicited mss/month. Accepts 1 mss/issue; 11 mss/year. Publishes ms 3 years after acceptance. **Publishes 6 new writers/year.** Publishes short shorts.

How to Contact Send complete ms. SASE. Responds in 6 months to mss. Accepts simultaneous, multiple submissions. Sample copy for 9×12 SAE and 6 first-class stamps. Writer's guidelines for #10 SASE or on website.

Payment/Terms Pays $25 maximum (honorarium) and 1 year's free subscription. Pays on publication for first North American serial, first rights.

Advice "Competition is greater (more submissions received), but keep trying. We print new as well as published writers."

Consumer Magazines

$ ⬚ ◎ ⬚ ASIMOV'S SCIENCE FICTION

Dell Magazine Fiction Group, 475 Park Ave. S., 11th Floor, New York NY 10016. (212)686-7188. Fax: (212)686-7414. E-mail: asimovs@dellmagazines.com. Website: www.asimovs.com. **Contact:** Sheila Williams, editor. Magazine: 5¼×8¼ (trim size); 144 pages; 30 lb. newspaper; 70 lb. to 8 pt. C1S cover stock; illustrations; rarely photos. Magazine consists of science fiction and fantasy stories for adults and young adults. Publishes "the best short science fiction available." Estab. 1977. Circ. 50,000.

• Named for a science fiction "legend," *Asimov's* regularly receives Hugo and Nebula Awards. Editor Gardner Dozois has received several awards for editing including Hugos and those from *Locus* magazine.

Needs Fantasy, science fiction (hard science, soft sociological). No horror or psychic/supernatural. Would like to see more hard science fiction. Receives approximately 800 unsolicited mss/month. Accepts 10 mss/issue. Publishes ms 6-12 months after acceptance. Agented fiction 10%. **Publishes 6 new writers/year.** Recently published work by Ursula LeGuin and Larry Niven. Publishes short shorts. Sometimes comments on rejected mss.

How to Contact Send complete ms with SASE. Responds in 2 months to queries; 3 months to mss. Accepts reprints submissions. No simultaneous submissions. Sample copy for $5. Writer's guidelines for #10 SASE or online. Reviews fiction.

Payment/Terms Pays 5-8¢/word. Pays on acceptance. Buys first North American serial, nonexclusive foreign serial rights; reprint rights occasionally. Sends galleys to author.

Advice "We are looking for character stories rather than those emphasizing technology or science. New writers will do best with a story under 10,000 words. Every new science fiction or fantasy film seems to 'inspire' writers—and this is not a desirable trend. Be sure to be familiar with our magazine and the type of story we like; workshops and lots of practice help. Try to stay away from trite, clichéd themes. Start in the middle of the action, starting as close to the end of the story as you possibly can. We like stories that extrapolate from up-to-date scientific research, but don't forget that we've been publishing clone stories for decades. Ideas must be fresh.'

$ THE ATLANTIC MONTHLY

77 N. Washington St., Boston MA 02114. (617)854-7749. Fax: (617)854-7877. Website: www.theatlantic.com. **Contact:** C. Michael Curtis, senior editor. General magazine for an educated readership with broad cultural interests. Monthly. Estab. 1857. Circ. 500,000.

• See our interview with C. Michael Curtis and other fiction editors in "Editors' Roundtable," starting on page 31. Also note that *The Atlantic* no longer publishes fiction monthly; instead, they produce an annual fiction issue.

Needs Literary and contemporary fiction. "Seeks fiction that is clear, tightly written with strong sense of 'story' and well-defined characters." Receives 1,000 unsolicited mss/month. **Publishes 3-4 new writers/year.** Recently published work by Mary Gordon, Donald Hall and Roxana Robinson.

How to Contact Send complete ms. Responds in 2 months to mss. Accepts multiple submissions. No simultaneous submissions. Writer's guidelines online.

Payment/Terms Pays $3,000. Pays on acceptance for first North American serial rights.

Advice When making first contract, "cover letters are sometimes helpful, particularly if they cite prior publications or involvement in writing programs. Common mistakes: melodrama, inconclusiveness, lack of development, unpersuasive characters and/or dialogue."

N $ BABYBUG

Carus Publishing Co., P.O. Box 300, Peru IL 61354. (815)224-5803, ext. 656. Website: www.cricketmag.com. "*Babybug* is 'the listening and looking magazine for infants and toddlers,' intended to be read aloud by a loving adult to foster a love of books and reading in young children ages 6 months-2 years." Estab. 1994. Circ. 45,000.

Needs Very simple stories for infants and toddlers.

How to Contact Send complete ms. Accepts simultaneous submissions. Sample copy for $5. Writer's guidelines online.

Payment/Terms Pays $25 and up. Pays on publication for variable rights.

Advice "*Babybug* is a board-book magazine. Study back issues before submitting."

$ ⬚ ◎ BALLOON LIFE

Balloon Life Magazine, Inc., 2336 47th Ave. SW, Seattle WA 98116-2331. (206)935-3649. Fax: (206)935-3326. E-mail: tom@balloonlife.com. Website: www.balloonlife.com. **Contact:** Tom Hamilton, editor. Magazine: 8½×11; 48 pages; color, b&w photos. Publishes material "about the sport of hot air ballooning. Readers participate as pilots, crew, official observers at events and spectators." Monthly. Estab. 1986. Circ. 4,000.

Needs Humor/satire, related to hot air ballooning. "Manuscripts should involve the sport of hot air ballooning in any aspect. Prefer humor based on actual events; fiction seldom published." Accepts 4-6 mss/year. Publishes ms 3-4 months after acceptance. Length: 800-1,500 words; average length: 1,200 words. Publishes short shorts. Sometimes comments on rejected mss.

How to Contact Send complete ms. Accepts submissions by e-mail, fax. SASE. Responds in 3 weeks to queries; 1 month to mss. Accepts simultaneous and reprints submissions. Sample copy for 9 × 12 SAE with $2 postage. Writer's guidelines for #10 SASE.

Payment/Terms Pays $25-75 and contributor's copies. Pays on publication for first North American serial, one-time rights. Buys nonexclusive, all rights.

Advice "Generally the magazine looks for humor pieces that can provide a light-hearted change of pace from the technical and current event articles. An example of a work we used was titled 'Balloon Astrology' and dealt with the character of a hot air balloon based on what sign it was born (made) under."

$⊘ THE BEAR DELUXE MAGAZINE

Orlo, P.O. Box 10342, Portland OR 97296. (503)242-1047. E-mail: bear@orlo.org. Website: www.orlo.org. **Contact:** Tom Webb, editor. Magazine: 9 × 12; 48 pages; newsprint paper; Kraft paper cover illustrations; photos. "*The Bear Deluxe Magazine* provides a fresh voice amid often strident and polarized environmental discourse. Street level, solution-oriented, and nondogmatic, *The Bear Deluxe* presents lively creative discussion to a diverse readership." Semiannual. Estab. 1993. Circ. 20,000.

- *The Bear Deluxe* has received publishing grants from the Oregon Council for the Humanities, Literary Arts, Regional Arts and Culture Council, Tides Foundation.

Needs Adventure, condensed novels, historical, humor/satire, mystery/suspense, novel excerpts, western. "No detective, children's or horror." Enviromentally focused: humor/satire, literary, science fiction. "We would like to see more nontraditional forms." List of upcoming themes available for SASE. Receives 20-30 unsolicited mss/month. Accepts 2-3 mss/issue; 8-12 mss/year. Publishes ms 3 months after acceptance. **Publishes 5-6 new writers/year.** Recently published work by Peter Houlahan, John Reed and Karen Hueler. Length: 750-4,500 words; average length: 2,500 words. Publishes short shorts. Also publishes literary essays, literary criticism, poetry. Sometimes comments on rejected mss.

How to Contact Query with or without published clips or send complete ms. Send disposable copy of mss. Responds in 3 months to queries; 6 months to mss. Accepts simultaneous and reprints submissions. Sample copy for $3. Writer's guidelines for #10 SASE or on website. Reviews fiction.

Payment/Terms Pays free subscription to the magazine, contributor's copies and 5¢/word; additional copies for postage. Pays on publication for first, one-time rights.

Advice "Keep sending work. Write actively and focus on the connections of man, nature, etc., not just flowery descriptions. Urban and suburban enviroments are grist for the mill as well. Have not seen enough quality humorous and ironic writing. Interview and artist profile ideas needed. Juxtaposition of place welcome. Action and hands-on great. Not all that interested in enviromental ranting and simple 'walks through the park.' Make it powerful, yet accessible to a wide audience."

$⊘ BOMB MAGAZINE

80 Hanson Place, Suite 703, Brooklyn NY 11217. (718)636-9100. Fax: (718)636-9200. E-mail: info@bombsite.com. Website: www.bombsite.com. Magazine: 11 × 14; 104 pages; 70 lb. glossy cover; illustrations; photos. Written, edited and produced by industry professionals and funded by those interested in the arts. Publishes "work which is unconventional and contains an edge, whether it be in style or subject matter." Quarterly. Estab. 1981. Circ. 36,000.

Needs Experimental, novel excerpts, contemporary. No genre: romance, science fiction, horror, western. Upcoming theme: "The Americas," featuring work by artists and writers from Central and South America (no unsolicited mss for theme issue, please). Receives 200 unsolicited mss/month. Accepts 6 mss/issue; 24 mss/year. Publishes ms 3-6 months after acceptance. Agented fiction 70%. **Publishes 2-3 new writers/year.** Recently published work by Melanie Rae Thon, Carole Maso, Molly McQuade and Mary Jo Bang.

How to Contact SASE. Responds in 3-5 months to mss. Accepts multiple submissions. Sample copy for $7, plus $1.42 postage and handling. Writer's guidelines by e-mail.

Payment/Terms Pays $100, and contributor's copies. Pays on publication for first, one-time rights. Sends galleys to author.

Advice "We are committed to publishing new work that commercial publishers often deem too dangerous or difficult. The problem is, a lot of young writers confuse difficult with dreadful. Read the magazine before you even think of submitting something."

$⊘ ▣ BOSTON REVIEW

E53-407, M.I.T., Cambridge MA 02139. (617)258-0805. Fax: (617)252-1549. E-mail: bostonreview@mit.edu. Website: www.bostonreview.net. **Contact:** Junot Diaz, fiction editor. Magazine: 10¾ × 14¾; 60 pages; newsprint. "The editors are committed to a society and culture that foster human diversity and a democracy in which we seek common grounds of principle amidst our many differences. In the hope of advancing these ideals, the *Review* acts as a forum that seeks to enrich the language of public debate." Bimonthly. Estab. 1975. Circ. 20,000.

• *Boston Review* is the recipient of a *Pushcart Prize* in poetry.

Needs Ethnic/multicultural, experimental, literary, regional, translations, contemporary, prose poem. "No romance, erotica, genre fiction." Receives 150 unsolicited mss/month. Accepts 4-6 mss/year. Publishes ms 4 months after acceptance. Recently published work by David Mamet, Rhonda Stamell, Jacob Appel, Elisha Porat and Diane Williams. Length: 1,200-5,000 words; average length: 2,000 words. Occasionally comments on rejected mss.

How to Contact Send complete ms. Responds in 4 months to queries. Accepts simultaneous submissions if noted. Sample copy for $5 or online. Writer's guidelines online. Reviews fiction.

Payment/Terms Pays $50-100, and 5 contributor's copies. Acquires first North American serial, first rights.

N $ ◎ BOWHUNTER, The Number One Bowhunting Magazine

Primedia Consumer Media & Magazine Group, 6405 Flank Dr., Harrisburg PA 17112. (717)657-9555. Fax: (717)657-9552. E-mail: bowhunter_magazine@primediamags.com. Website: www.bowhunter.com. **Contact:** Dwight Schuh, editor. Magazine: $7^3/_4 \times 10^1/_2$: 150 pages; 75 lb. glossy paper; 150 lb. glossy cover stock; illustrations; photos. "We are a special-interest publication, produced by bowhunters for bowhunters, covering all aspects of the sport. Material included in each issue is designed to entertain and inform readers, making them better bowhunters." Bimonthly. Estab. 1971. Circ. 158,446.

Needs Bowhunting, outdoor adventure. "Writers must expect a very limited market. We buy only one or two fiction pieces a year. Writers must know the market—bowhunting—and let that be the theme of their work. No 'me and my dog' types of stories; no stories by people who have obviously never held a bow in their hands." Receives 25 unsolicited mss/month. Accepts 30 mss/year. Publishes ms 3 months to 2 years after acceptance. **Publishes 3-4 new writers/year.** Length: 500-2,000 words; average length: 1,500 words. Publishes short shorts. Sometimes comments on rejected mss.

How to Contact Send complete ms. Accepts submissions by e-mail, fax. Responds in 2 weeks to queries; 1 month to mss. Sample copy for $2 and $8^1/_2 \times 11$ SAE with appropriate postage. Writer's guidelines for #10 SASE or on website.

Payment/Terms Pays $100-350. Pays on acceptance. Buys exclusive first, worldwide publication rights.

Advice "We have a resident humorist who supplies us with most of the 'fiction' we need. But if a story comes through the door which captures the essence of bowhunting and we feel it will reach out to our readers, we will buy it. Despite our macho outdoor magazine status, we are a bunch of English majors who love to read. You can't bull your way around real outdoor people—they can spot a phony at 20 paces. If you've never camped out under the stars and listened to an elk bugle and try to relate that experience without really experiencing it, someone's going to know. We are very specialized; we don't want stories about shooting apples off people's heads or of Cupid's arrow finding its mark. James Dickey's *Deliverance* used bowhunting metaphorically, very effectively . . . while we don't expect that type of writing from everyone, that's the kind of feeling that characterizes a good piece of outdoor fiction."

$ ◎ BOYS' LIFE

Boy Scouts of America, P.O. Box 152079, Irving TX 75015-2079. (972)580-2355. Fax: (972)580-2079. Website: www.boyslife.org. **Contact:** Rich Haddaway, associate editor. Magazine: 8×11; 68 pages; slick cover stock; illustrations; photos. "*Boys' Life* covers Boy Scout activities and general interest subjects for ages 8 to 18, Boy Scouts, Cub Scouts and others of that age group." Monthly. Estab. 1911. Circ. 1,300,000.

Needs Adventure, humor/satire, mystery/suspense (young adult), science fiction, western (young adult), young adult/teen, sports. "We publish short stories aimed at a young adult audience and frequently written from the viewpoint of a 10-to 16-year old boy protagonist." Receives 150 unsolicited mss/month. Accepts 12-18 mss/year. Publishes ms 1 year after acceptance. **Publishes 1 new writer/year.** Recently published work by Gary Paulsen, G. Clifton Wisler, Iain Lawrence and Walter Dean Myers. Length: 1,000-1,500 words; average length: 1,200 words. Rarely comments on rejected mss.

How to Contact Send complete ms. Send SASE. Responds in 2 months to queries. Sample copy for $3.60 and 9×12 SAE. Writer's guidelines for #10 SASE or online.

Payment/Terms Pays $750 minimum. Pays on acceptance for one-time rights.

Advice "*Boys' Life* writers understand the readers. They treat them as intelligent human beings with a thirst for knowledge and entertainment. We tend to use some of the same authors repeatedly because their characters, themes, etc., develop a following among our readers. Read at least a year's worth of the magazine. You will get a feeling for what our readers are interested in and what kind of fiction we buy."

Consumer Magazines

$🖉 🔲 BRAIN, CHILD, The Magazine for Thinking Mothers

March Press, P.O. Box 5566, Charlottesville VA 22905. (434)977-4151. E-mail: editor@brainchildmag.com. Website: www.brainchildmag.com. **Contact:** Jennifer Niesslein and Stephanie Wilkinson, co-editors. Magazine: 7¼×10; 60-100 pages; 80lb. matte cover; illustrations; photos. *"Brain, Child* reflects modern motherhood—the way it really is. We like to think of *Brain, Child* as a community, for and by mothers who like to think about what raising kids does for (and to) the mind and soul. *Brain, Child* isn't your typical parenting magazine. We couldn't cupcake-decorate our way out of a paper bag. We are more 'literary' than 'how-to,' more *New Yorker* than *Parents*. We shy away from expert advice on childrearing in favor of first-hand reflections by great writers (Jane Smiley, Barbara Ehrenreich, Anne Tyler) on life as a mother. Each quarterly issue is full of essays, features, humor, reviews, fiction, art, cartoons and our readers' own stories. Our philosophy is pretty simple: Motherhood is worthy of literature. And there are a lot of ways to mother, all of them interesting. We're proud to be publishing articles and essays that are smart, down to earth, sometimes funny, and sometimes poignant." Quarterly. Estab. 2000. Circ. 20,000. Member, IPA, ASME.

• *Brain, Child* has either won or been nominated for the *Utne* Independent Press Award each year it has been in existence.

Needs Literary, mainstream. No genre fiction. Receives 200 unsolicited mss/month. Accepts 1 mss/issue; 4 mss/year. Publishes ms 6 months after acceptance. Recently published work by Anne Tyler, Barbara Lucy Stevens and Jane Smiley. Length: 800-5,000 words; average length: 2,500 words. Also publishes literary essays. Sometimes comments on rejected mss.

How to Contact Send complete ms. Accepts submissions by e-mail (be sure to copy and paste the ms into the body of the e-mail). Include estimated word count, brief bio and list of publications. Send SASE (or IRC) for return of ms or send a disposable copy of ms and #10 SASE for reply only. Responds in 1 month to queries; 1-3 months to mss. Accepts simultaneous and reprints, multiple submissions. Sample copy online. Writer's guidelines online. Reviews fiction.

Payment/Terms Payment varies. Pays on publication for first North American serial, electronic rights, *Brain, Child* anthology rights. Sends galleys to author.

Advice "We only publish fiction with a strong motherhood theme. But, like every other publisher of literary fiction, we look for well-developed characters, a compelling story, and an ending that is as strong as the rest of the piece."

$🖉 ◎ BUGLE

Rocky Mountain Elk Foundation, P.O. Box 8249, 2291 W. Broadway, Missoula MT 59808. (406)523-4538. Fax: (406)543-7710. E-mail: bugle@rmef.org. Website: www.elkfoundation.org. **Contact:** Don Burgess, hunting/human interest editor (dburgess@rmef.org); Lee Cromrich, conservation editor (lcromrich@rmef.org.) Magazine: 8½×11; 114-172 pages; 55 lb. Escanaba paper; 80 lb. sterling cover, b&w, 4-color illustrations; photos. *Bugle* is the membership publication of the Rocky Mountain Elk Foundation, a nonprofit wildlife conservation group. "Our readers are predominantly hunters, many of them conservationists who care deeply about protecting wildlife habitat." Bimonthly. Estab. 1984. Circ. 132,000.

Needs Adventure, children's/juvenile, historical, humor/satire, novel excerpts, slice-of-life vignettes, western, human interest, natural history, conservation. "We accept fiction and nonfiction stories pertaining in some way to elk, other wildlife, hunting, habitat conservation, and related issues. We would like to see more humor." Upcoming themes: "Bowhunting"; "Odd Elk Behavior"; "Hunts from Hell," stories of elk hunting adventures gone bad; "The Long Haul," vignettes revealing essential experiences of nonresident hunters journeying to the Rockies each fall to hunt elk; "Bravehearts," stories of hunters overcoming severe physical handicaps to continue hunting. Receives 20-30 unsolicited mss/month. Accepts 3-4 mss/issue; 18-24 mss/year. Publishes ms 1-36 months after acceptance. **Publishes 12 new writers/year.** Recently published work by Rick Bass and Susan Ewing. Length: 1,500-4,500 words; average length: 2,500 words. Publishes short shorts. Also publishes literary essays, poetry.

How to Contact Query with or without published clips or send complete ms. Accepts submissions by e-mail, fax. Send SASE for reply, return of ms or send a disposable copy of ms. Responds in 1 month to queries; 3 months to mss. Accepts reprints, multiple submissions. Sample copy for $5. Writer's guidelines online.

Payment/Terms Pays 20¢/word. Pays on acceptance for one-time rights.

Advice "Hunting stories and essays should celebrate the hunting experience, demonstrating respect for wildlife, the land, and the hunt. Articles on elk behavior or elk habitat should include personal observations and entertain as well as educate. No freelance product reviews or formulaic how-to articles accepted. Straight action-adventure hunting stories are in short supply, as are 'Situation Ethics' manuscripts."

$🖉 ◎ CADET QUEST MAGAZINE

P.O. Box 7259, Grand Rapids MI 49510-7259. (616)241-5616. Fax: (616)241-5558. E-mail: submissions@calvinistcadets.org. Website: www.calvinistcadets.org. **Contact:** G. Richard Broene, editor. Magazine: 8½×11; 24

Consumer Magazines

pages; illustrations; photos. *"Cadet Quest Magazine* shows boys 9-14 how God is at work in their lives and in the world around them." Estab. 1958. Circ. 10,000.

Needs Adventure, children's/juvenile, religious/inspirational (Christian), spiritual, sports, comics. "Avoid preachiness. Avoid simplistic answers to complicated problems. Avoid long dialogue and little action." No fantasy, science fiction, fashion, horror or erotica. List of upcoming themes available for SASE or on website. Receives 60 unsolicited mss/month. Accepts 3 mss/issue; 18 mss/year. Publishes ms 4-11 months after acceptance. **Publishes 0-3 new writers/year.** Recently published work by Douglas DeVries and Betty Lou Mell. Length: 900-1,500 words; average length: 1,200 words. Publishes short shorts.

How to Contact Send complete ms by mail or send submissions in the body of the e-mail. Not as an attachment. Responds in 2 months to queries. Accepts simultaneous and reprints, multiple submissions. Sample copy for 9×12 SASE. Writer's guidelines for #10 SASE.

Payment/Terms Pays 4-6¢/word, and 1 contributor's copy. Pays on acceptance for first North American serial, one-time, second serial (reprint), simultaneous rights. Rights purchased vary with author and material.

Advice "On a cover sheet, list the point your story is trying to make. Our magazine has a theme for each issue, and we try to fit the fiction to the theme. All fiction should be about a young boy's interests—sports, outdoor activities, problems—with an emphasis on a Christian perspective. No simple moralisms."

$ ⊠ CALLIOPE, Exploring World History

Cobblestone Publishing Co., 30 Grove St., Suite C, Peterborough NH 03458-1454. (603)924-7209. Fax: (603)924-7380. Website: www.cobblestonepub.com. **Contact:** Rosalie Baker, editor. Magazine. *"Calliope* covers world history (east/west), and lively, original approaches to the subject are the primary concerns of the editors in choosing material. For 8-14 year olds." Estab. 1990. Circ. 11,000.

- Cobblestone Publishing also publishes the children's magazines *Appleseeds, Dig, Footsteps, Odyssey, Cobblestone* and *Faces*, some listed in this section. *Calliope* has received the Ed Press Golden Lamp and One-Theme Issue awards.

Needs Material must fit upcoming theme; write for themes and deadlines. Childrens/juvenile (8-14 years). "Authentic historical and biographical fiction, adventure, retold legends, folktales, etc. relating to the theme." Send SASE for guidelines and theme list. Published after theme deadline. **Publishes 5-10 new writers/year.** Recently published work by Diane Childress and Jackson Kuhle. Publishes short shorts.

How to Contact Query with or without published clips. Send SASE (or IRC) for reply. Responds in several months (if interested, responds 5 months before publication date) to mss. No simultaneous submissions. Sample copy for $4.95 and 7½×10½ SASE with 4 first-class stamps or online. Writer's guidelines for #10 SAE and 1 first-class stamp or on website.

Payment/Terms Pays 20-25¢/word. Pays on publication.

Advice "We primarily publish historical nonfiction. Fiction should be retold legends or folktales related to appropriate themes."

$ ▨ ◎ ⊠ CAMPUS LIFE

Christianity Today, Inc., 465 Gundersen Dr., Carol Stream IL 60188. (630)260-6200. Fax: (630)480-2004. E-mail: clmag@campuslife.net. Website: www.campuslife.net. **Contact:** Chris Lutes, editor. Magazine: 8¼×11¼; 72 pages; 4-color and b&w illustrations; 4-color and b&w photos. *"Campus Life* is a magazine for high-school and early college-age teenagers. Our editorial slant is not overtly religious. The indirect style is intended to create a safety zone with our readers and to reflect our philosophy that God is interested in all of life. Therefore, we publish 'message stories' side by side with general interest, humor, etc. We are also looking for stories that help high school students consider a Christian college education." Bimonthly. Estab. 1942. Circ. 100,000.

- *Campus Life* regularly receives awards from the Evangelical Press Association.

Needs "All fiction submissions must be contemporary, reflecting the teen experience in the new milllennium. We are a Christian magazine but are *not* interested in sappy, formulaic, sentimentally religious stories. We *are* interested in well-crafted stories that portray life realistically, stories high school and college youth relate to. Writing must reflect a Christian worldview. If you don't understand our market and style, don't submit." Accepts 5 mss/year. Reading and response time slower in summer. **Publishes 3-4 new writers/year.**

How to Contact Query. Responds in 8 weeks to queries. Sample copy for $3 and 9½×11 SAE with 3 first-class stamps. Writer's guidelines online.

Payment/Terms Pays 20-25¢/word, and 2 contributor's copies. Pays on acceptance for first, one-time rights.

Advice "We print finely-crafted fiction that carries a contemporary teen (older teen) theme. First person fiction often works best. Ask us for sample copy with fiction story. We want experienced fiction writers who have something to say to young people without getting propagandistic."

$CAPPER'S

Ogden Publications, Inc., 1503 SW 42nd St., Topeka KS 66609-1265. (785)274-4300. E-mail: tsmith@cappers.com. Website: www.cappers.com. "*Capper's* is upbeat, focusing on the homey feelings people like to share, as well as hopes and dreams." Biweekly. Estab. 1879. Circ. 240,000.

Needs Adventure, historical, humor/satire, mainstream, mystery/suspense, romance, serialized novels, western. No explicit sex, violence, profanity or alcohol use. Publishes ms 2-12 months after acceptance.

How to Contact Responds in 2-3 months to queries; 6 months to mss. No simultaneous submissions. Sample copy online. Writer's guidelines online.

Payment/Terms Pays $100-400. Pays for poetry and fiction on acceptance; articles on publication. Acquires first North American serial rights.

Advice "We buy very few fiction pieces—longer than short stories, shorter than novels."

$◙ CICADA MAGAZINE

Cricket Magazine Group, P.O. Box 300, Peru IL 61354. (815)224-5803 ext. 656. Fax: (815)224-6615. E-mail: mmiklavcic@caruspub.com. Website: www.cricketmag.com. **Contact:** Deborah Vetter, executive editor; Tracy C. Schoenle, senior editor. Literary magazine: 128 pages; some illustrations. "*Cicada*, for ages 14 and up, publishes original short stories, poems, and first-person essays written for teens and young adults." Bimonthly. Estab. 1998. Circ. 18,000.

Needs Adventure, fantasy, historical, humor/satire, mainstream, mystery/suspense, romance, science fiction, western, young adult/teen, sports. "Our readership is age 14-21. Submissions should be tailored for high school and college-age audience, not junior high or younger. We especially need humor and fantasy. We are also intersted in first-person, coming-of-age nonfiction (life in the Peace Corps, significant first jobs, etc.). We are currently receiving too many stories that deal with cancer." Accepts 10 mss/issue; 60 mss/year. Publishes ms 1 year after acceptance. Length: 3,000-15,000 words; average length: 5,000 words. Also publishes poetry. Sometimes comments on rejected mss.

How to Contact Send complete ms. Send SASE for return of ms or send a disposable copy of ms and #10 SASE for reply only. Responds in 3 months to mss. Accepts simultaneous and reprints submissions. Sample copy for $8.50. Writer's guidelines for SASE and on website. Reviews fiction.

Payment/Terms Pays 25¢/word, plus 6 contributor's copies. Pays on publication. Rights vary.

Advice "Quality writing, good literary style, genuine teen sensibility, depth, humor, good character development, avoidance of stereotypes. Read several issues to familiarize yourself with our style."

$◚ ◙ ◙ CRICKET

Carus Publishing Co., P.O. Box 300, Peru IL 61354-0300. (815)224-5803. Website: www.cricketmag.com. Marianne Carus, editor-in-chief. **Contact:** Submissions Editor. Magazine: 8×10; 64 pages; illustrations; photos. Magazine for children, ages 9-14. Monthly. Estab. 1973. Circ. 73,000.

- *Cricket* has received a Parents' Choice Award and awards from EdPress. Carus Corporation also publishes *Spider, the Magazine for Children*; *Ladybug, the Magazine for Young Children*; *Babybug*; and *Cicada*.

Needs Adventure, children's/juvenile, ethnic/multicultural, fantasy, historical, humor/satire, mystery/suspense, novel excerpts, science fiction, suspense, thriller/espionage, western, folk and fairy tales. No didactic, sex, religious or horror stories. All issues have different "mini-themes." Receives 1,100 unsolicited mss/month. Accepts 150 mss/year. Publishes ms 6-24 months after acceptance. Agented fiction 1-2%. **Publishes some new writers/year.** Recently published work by Aaron Shepard, Arnold Adoff and Nancy Springer.

How to Contact Send complete ms. Responds in 3 months to mss. Accepts reprints submissions. Sample copy for $5 and 9×12 SAE. Writer's guidelines for SASE and on website.

Payment/Terms Pays 25¢/word maximum, and 6 contributor's copies; $2.50 charge for extras. Pays on publication. Rights vary. Sponsors awards/contests.

Advice "Do not write *down* to children. Write about well-researched subjects you are familiar with and interested in, or about something that concerns you deeply. Children *need* fiction and fantasy. Carefully study several issues of *Cricket* before you submit your manuscript."

$◙ DISCIPLESWORLD, A Journal of News, Opinion, and Mission for the Christian Church

DisciplesWorld, Inc., P.O. Box 11469, Indianapolis IN 46201-0469. E-mail: editor@disciplesworld.com. Website: www.disciplesworld.com. "We are the journal of the Christian Church (Disciples of Christ) in North America. Our denomination numbers roughly 800,000. Disciples are a mainline Protestant group. Our readers are mostly laity, active in their churches, and interested in issues of faithful living, political and church news, ethics, and contemporary social issues." Monthly. Estab. 2002. Circ. 14,000.

Needs Ethnic/multicultural, mainstream, novel excerpts, religious/inspirational, serialized novels, slice-of-life vignettes. "We're a religious publication, so use common sense! Stories do not have to be overtly 'religious,' but they should be uplifting and positive." Publishes ms 6 months after acceptance.

Consumer Magazines

How to Contact Send complete ms. Accepts submissions by e-mail (editor@disciplesworld.com). Responds in 2 weeks to queries; 2 months to mss. Accepts simultaneous submissions. Sample copy for #10 SASE. Writer's guidelines online.
Payment/Terms Pays 16¢/word. Pays on publication for first North American serial rights.

$⬗ ◎ ⬙ ESQUIRE

Hearst, 1790 Broadway, 13th Floor, New York NY 10019. (212)649-4050. Website: www.esquire.com. **Contact:** Adrienne Miller, literary editor. Magazine. Monthly magazine for smart, well-off men. General readership is college educated and sophisticated, between ages 30 and 45. Written mostly by contributing editors on contract. Rarely accepts unsolicited manuscripts. Monthly. Estab. 1933. Circ. 750,000.

• *Esquire* is well-respected for its fiction and has received several National Magazine Awards. Work published in *Esquire* has been selected for inclusion in the *Best American Short Stories* and *O. Henry* anthologies. See our interview with Adrienne Miller in "Editors' Roundtable," starting on page 31.

Needs Novel excerpts, short stories, some poetry, memoirs and plays. No "pornography, science fiction or 'true romance' stories." Publishes special fiction issue in July. Receives 800 unsolicited mss/month. Rarely accepts unsolicited fiction. Publishes ms 2-6 months after acceptance. Recently published work by Russell Banks, Tim O'Brien, Richard Russo and David Means.
How to Contact Send complete ms. Accepts simultaneous, multiple submissions. Writer's guidelines for SASE.
Payment/Terms Pays in cash on acceptance, amount undisclosed. Retains first worldwide periodical publication rights for 90 days from cover date
Advice "Submit one story at a time. We receive over 10,000 stories a year, so worry a little less about publication, a little more about the work itself."

$⬗ ◎ EVANGEL

Free Methodist Publishing House, P.O. Box 535002, Indianapolis IN 46253-5002. (317)244-3660. Magazine: 5½×8½; 8 pages; 2 and 4-color illustrations; color and b&w photos. Sunday school take-home paper for distribution to adults who attend church. Fiction involves people coping with everday crises, making decisions that show spiritual growth. Weekly distribution. Printed quarterly. Estab. 1897. Circ. 10,000.
Needs Religious/inspirational. "No fiction without any semblance of Christian message or where the message clobbers the reader. Looking for more short pieces of devotional nature of 500 words or less." Receives 300 unsolicited mss/month. Accepts 3-4 mss/issue; 156-200 mss/year. Publishes ms 18-36 months after acceptance. **Publishes 7 new writers/year.** Recently published work by Karen Leet and Dennis Hensley.
How to Contact Send complete ms. Responds in 4-6 weeks to queries. Accepts multiple submissions. Sample copy and writer's guidelines for #10 SASE.
Payment/Terms Pays 4¢/word and 2 contributor's copies. Pays on publication for simultaneous, second serial (reprint) or one-time rights.
Advice "Choose a contemporary situation or conflict and create a good mix for the characters (not all-good or all-bad heroes and villians). Don't spell out everything in detail; let the reader fill in some blanks in the story. Keep him guessing." Rejects mss because of "unbelievable characters and predictable events in the story."

$◎ FIFTY SOMETHING MAGAZINE

Lude Graphics Co., 1168 S. Beachview Rd., Willoughby OH 44094. (440)951-2468. Fax: (440)951-1015. "We are focusing on the 50-and-better reader." Quarterly. Estab. 1990. Circ. 10,000.
Needs Adventure, confessions, ethnic/multicultural, experimental, fantasy, historical, humor/satire, mainstream, mystery/suspense, novel excerpts, romance, slice-of-life vignettes, suspense, western. No erotica or horror. Receives 150 unsolicited mss/month. Accepts 5 mss/issue. Publishes ms 6 months after acceptance. **Publishes 20 new writers/year.** Recently published work by Gail Morrisey, Sally Morrisey, Jenny Miller, J. Alan Witt and Sharon McGreagor. Length: 500-1,000 words; average length: 1,000 words. Publishes short shorts.
How to Contact Send complete ms. Responds in 3 months to queries; 3 months to mss. Accepts simultaneous and reprints submissions. Sample copy for 9×12 SAE and 4 first-class stamps. Writer's guidelines for #10 SASE.
Payment/Terms Pays $10-100. Pays on publication for one-time, second serial (reprint), simultaneous rights.

$◎ FIRST HAND, Experiences For Loving Men

Firsthand, Ltd., 310 Cedar Lane, Teaneck NJ 07666. (201)836-9177. Fax: (201)836-5055. **Contact:** Don Dooley, editor. Magazine: digest-size; 130 pages; illustrations. "Half of the magazine is made up of our readers' own gay sexual experience. Rest is fiction and video reviews." Monthly. Estab. 1980. Circ. 70,000.
Needs Erotica, gay. "Should be written in first person." No science fiction or fantasy. Erotica should detail experiences based in reality. Receives 75-100 unsolicited mss/month. Accepts 6 mss/issue; 72 mss/year. Pub-

lishes ms 9-18 months after acceptance. Length: 2,500-3,750 words; average length: 3,000 words. Sometimes comments on rejected mss.

How to Contact Send complete ms. Include name, address, telephone and Social Security number and "advise on use of a pseudonym if any. Also whether selling all rights or first North American rights." Responds in 2 months to queries; 4 months to mss. No simultaneous submissions. Sample copy for $5.99. Writer's guidelines for #10 SASE.

Payment/Terms Pays $75. Pays on publication. Aquires all rights (exceptions made) and second serial (reprint) rights.

Advice "Avoid the hackneyed situations. Be original. We like strong plots."

[N] $ GENERATIONXNATIONAL JOURNAL, Speaking for Our Generation

411 W. Front, Wayland IA 52654. (319)256-4221. E-mail: genxjournal2004@yahoo.com. Website: www.genxnatljounal.com. Estab. 2003.

Needs Adventure, confessions, ethnic/multicultural, experimental, fantasy, historical, humor/satire, mainstream, mystery/suspense, religious/inspirational, romance, slice-of-life vignettes, political pieces, success stories. No erotica or horror. Publishes ms 3 months after acceptance.

How to Contact Send complete ms. Accepts submissions by e-mail. Responds in 1 month to queries; 5 months to mss. Accepts simultaneous submissions.

Payment/Terms Pays $5-10. Pays on acceptance for one-time rights.

[icon] GRIT, American Life and Traditions

Ogden Publications, 1503 SW 42nd St., Topeka KS 66609-1265. (785)274-4300. Fax: (785)274-4305. E-mail: grit@grit.com. Website: www.grit.com. **Contact:** Fiction Department. Magazine: 64 pages; 30 lb. newsprint; illustrations; photos. "*Grit* is good news. As a wholesome, family-oriented magazine published for more than a century and distributed nationally, *Grit* features articles about family lifestyles, traditions, values and pastimes. *Grit* accents the best of American life and traditions—past and present. Our readers are ordinary people doing extraordinary things, with courage, heart, determination and imagination. Many of them live in small towns and rural areas across the country; others live in cities but share many of the values typical of small-town America." Monthly. Estab. 1882. Circ. 100,000.

• *Grit* is considered one of the leading family-oriented publications.

Needs Adventure, condensed novels, mainstream, mystery/suspense, religious/inspirational, romance (contemporary, historical), western (frontier, traditional), nostalgia. "No sex, violence, drugs, obscene words, abuse, alcohol or negative diatribes. Special Storytellers issue; 5-6 manuscripts needed; submit in June." Accepts 1-2 mss/issue; 30 mss/year. **Publishes 20-25 new writers/year.** Length: 1,200-6,000 words; average length: 1,500-3,000 words. Also publishes poetry.

How to Contact Send complete ms. Send SASE for return of ms. No e-mail submissions. No simultaneous submissions. Sample copy and writer's guidelines for $4 and 11×14 SASE with 4 first-class stamps. Sample articles on website.

Payment/Terms Pays on acceptance for first North American serial rights.

Advice "Keep trying and be patient."

$ [icons] HADASSAH MAGAZINE

50 W. 58th St., New York NY 10019. (212)688-0227. Fax: (212)446-9521. Website: www.hadassah.org. **Contact:** Zelda Shluker, managing editor. Jewish general interest magazine: 7⅞×10½; 64-80 pages; coated and uncoated paper; slick, medium weight coated cover; drawings and cartoons; photos. "*Hadassah* is a general interest Jewish feature and literary magazine. We speak to our readers on a vast array of subjects ranging from politics to parenting, from midlife crisis to Mideast crisis. Our readers want coverage on social and economic issues, Jewish women's (feminist) issues, the arts, travel and health." Monthly. Circ. 300,000.

• *Hadassah* has been nominated for a National Magazine Award and has received numerous Rockower Awards for Excellence in Jewish Journalism.

Needs Ethnic/multicultural (Jewish). No personal memoirs, "schmaltzy" or shelter magazine fiction. Receives 20-25 unsolicited mss/month. **Publishes some new writers/year.** Recently published work by Joanne Greenberg and Jennifer Traig.

How to Contact Must submit appropriate sized SASE. Responds in 4 months to mss. Sample copy and writer's guidelines for 9×12 SASE.

Payment/Terms Pays $700 minimum. Pays on acceptance for first North American serial, first rights.

Advice "Stories on a Jewish theme should be neither self-hating nor schmaltzy."

$ [icon] HARPER'S MAGAZINE

666 Broadway, 11th Floor, New York NY 10012. (212)420-5720. Fax: (212)228-5889. Website: www.harpers.org. **Contact:** Lewis H. Lapham, editor. Magazine: 8×10¾; 80 pages; illustrations. "*Harper's Magazine* encour-

ages national discussion on current and significant issues in a format that offers arresting facts and intelligent opinions. By means of its several shorter journalistic forms—Harper's Index, Readings, Forum, and Annotation—as well as with its acclaimed essays, fiction and reporting, *Harper's* continues the tradition begun with its first issue in 1850: to inform readers across the whole spectrum of political, literary, cultural and scientific affairs." Monthly. Estab. 1850. Circ. 230,000.

● See our interview with fiction editor Ben Metcalf in "Editors' Roundtable," starting on page 31.

Needs Humor/satire. Stories on contemporary life and its problems. Receives 50 unsolicited mss/month. Accepts 12 mss/year. Publishes ms 3 months after acceptance. **Publishes some new writers/year.** Recently published work by David Guterson, David Foster Wallace, Jonathan Franzen, Steven Millhauser, Lisa Rooney, Rick Moody and Steven Dixon.

How to Contact Query. Responds in 6 weeks to queries. Accepts reprints submissions. Sample copy for $3.95.

Payment/Terms Generally pays 50¢-$1/word. Pays on acceptance. Vary with author and material. Sends galleys to author.

$⚅◎ HIGH ADVENTURE

General Council of the Assemblies of God/Royal Rangers, 1445 N. Boonville Ave., Springfield MO 65802-1894. (417)862-2781, ext. 4177. Fax: (417)831-8230. E-mail: royalrangers@ag.org. Website: www.royalrangers.ag.org. **Contact:** Rev. Jerry Parks, editor. Magazine: 8×10¾; 16 pages; 50 lb. gloss paper; illustrations; photos. "*High Adventure* is a quarterly Royal Rangers magazine for boys. This 16-page, 4-color periodical is designed to provide boys with worthwhile leisure reading to challenge them to higher ideals and greater spiritual dedication; and to perpetuate the spirit of Royal Rangers ministry through stories, crafts, ideas and illustrations." Quarterly. Estab. 1971. Circ. 87,000.

Needs Adventure, children's/juvenile (adventure, historical, sports, ages 5-17), historical (general), humor/satire, religious/inspirational (children's religious), young adult/teen (adventure, historical, sports), camping. No objectionable language, innuendo, immoral, or non-Christian materials. Receives 50-60 unsolicited mss/month. Accepts 8-10 mss/issue; 32-40 mss/year. Publishes ms 6-12 months after acceptance. **Publishes 10-20 new writers/year.** Publishes short shorts.

How to Contact Send complete ms. Accepts submissions by e-mail (royalrangers@ag.org), fax. Send a disposable copy of ms and #10 SASE for reply only. Accepts simultaneous and reprints, multiple submissions. Sample copy and writer's guidelines for 9×12 SAE and 2 first-class stamps. Writer's guidelines for SASE, by e-mail or fax.

Payment/Terms Pays 6¢/word, plus 3 contributor's copies. Pays on publication for one-time, electronic rights. Buys first or all rights.

Advice "Stories must capture the interest of boys age 5-17 with a positive and encouraging message."

$⚅◎⚄ HIGHLIGHTS FOR CHILDREN

Manuscript Submissions, 803 Church St., Honesdale PA 18431-1824. (570)253-1080. Fax: (570)251-7847. Website: www.highlights.com. **Contact:** Marileta Robinson, senior editor. Magazine: 8½×11; 42 pages; uncoated paper; coated cover stock; illustrations; photos. "This book of wholesome fun is dedicated to helping children grow in basic skills and knowledge, in creativeness, in ability to think and reason, in sensitivity to others, in high ideals, and worthy ways of living—for children are the world's most important people. We publish stories for beginning and advanced readers. Up to 500 words for beginners (ages 3-7), up to 800 words for advanced (ages 8-12)." Monthly. Estab. 1946. Circ. 2,500,000.

● *Highlights* has won the Parent's Guide to Children's Media Award 2003, Parent's Choice Award, and Editorial Excellence Awards from the Association of Educational Publishers.

Needs Adventure, children's/juvenile (ages 2-12), fantasy, historical, humor/satire, animal, contemporary, folktales, multi-cultural, problem-solving, sports. "No war, crime or violence." Unusual stories appealing to both girls and boys; stories with good characterization, strong emotional appeal, vivid, full of action. "Needs stories that begin with action rather than description, have strong plot, believable setting, suspense from start to finish." Receives 600-800 unsolicited mss/month. **Publishes 30 new writers/year.** Recently published work by Eileen Spinelli, James M. Janik, Phillis Gershator, Teresa Bateman, Maryilyn Kratz and Ruskin Bond. Occasionally comments on rejected mss.

How to Contact Send complete ms. Responds in 2 months to queries. Accepts multiple submissions. Sample copy free. Writer's guidelines for SASE or on website.

Payment/Terms Pays $150 minimum, plus 2 contributor's copies. Pays on acceptance. Sends galleys to author.

Advice "We accept a story on its merit whether written by an unpublished or an experienced writer. Mss are rejected because of poor writing, lack of plot, trite or worn-out plot, or poor characterization. Children *like* stories and learn about life from stories. Children learn to become lifelong fiction readers by enjoying stories. Feel passion for your subject. Create vivid images. Write a child-centered story; leave adults in the background."

Consumer Magazines

$ ☑ ◎ ☒ ALFRED HITCHCOCK'S MYSTERY MAGAZINE

Dell Magazines, 475 Park Ave. S., 11th Floor, New York NY 10016. Website: www.themysteryplace.com. **Contact:** Linda Landrigan, editor. Mystery fiction magazine: $5\frac{1}{2} \times 8\frac{3}{8}$; 144 pages; 28 lb. newsprint paper; 70 lb. machine-coated cover stock; illustrations; photos. Monthly. Estab. 1956. Circ. 125,000.

• Stories published in *Alfred Hitchcock's Mystery Magazine* have won Edgar Awards for "Best Mystery Story of the Year," Shamus Awards for "Best Private Eye Story of the Year" and Robert L. Fish Awards for "Best First Mystery Short Story of the Year."

Needs Mystery/suspense (amateur slueth, private eye, police procedural, suspense, etc.). No sensationalism. Number of mss/issue varies with length of mss. Recently published work by Rhys Bowen, Doug Allyn, I.J. Parker and Kathy Lynn Emerson.

How to Contact Send complete ms. Responds in 3 months to mss. Sample copy for $5. Writer's guidelines for SASE or on website.

Payment/Terms Payment varies. Pays on publication for first, foreign rights.

$ ☑ ◎ HORIZONS, The Magazine of Presbyterian Women

100 Witherspoon St., Louisville KY 40202-1396. (502)569-5668. Fax: (502)569-8085. E-mail: sdunne@ctr.pcusa. org. Website: www.pcusa.org/horizons/. **Contact:** Sharon Dunne, associate editor. Magazine: 8×11; 40 pages; illustrations; photos. Magazine owned and operated by Presbyterian women offering "information and inspiration for Presbyterian women by addressing current issues facing the church and the world." Bimonthly. Estab. 1988. Circ. 21,000.

Needs Ethnic/multicultural, feminist, historical, humor/satire, literary, mainstream, religious/inspirational, translations, senior citizen/retirement. "No sex/violence or romance." List of upcoming themes available for SASE. Receives 50 unsolicited mss/month. Accepts 1 mss/issue. Publishes ms 4 months after acceptance. **Publishes 10 new writers/year.** Publishes short shorts. Also publishes literary essays, poetry. Sometimes comments on rejected mss.

How to Contact Send complete ms. Accepts submissions by e-mail, fax. SASE or disposable copy of ms. Responds in 4 weeks to queries; 6-8 weeks to mss. Accepts simultaneous, multiple submissions. Sample copy for $4. Reviews fiction.

Payment/Terms Pays $50/page and 2 contributor's copies; additional copies for $2.50. Pays on publication.

Advice "We are most interested in stories or articles that focus on current issues—family life, the mission of the church, and the challenges of culture and society—from the perspective of women committed to Christ."

$ ◎ INDY MEN'S MAGAZINE, The Guy's Guide to the Good Life

Table Moose Media, 8500 Keystone Crossing, Indianapolis IN 46240. (317)255-3850. E-mail: lou@indymensmag azine.com. Website: www.indymensmagazine.com. "Attitude and honesty are key. We never tell anything to our readers that we wouldn't tell our neighbor or brother-in-law. Query first for nonfiction." Monthly. Estab. 2002. Circ. 50,000.

Needs Adventure, fantasy, historical, horror, humor/satire, mainstream, mystery/suspense, science fiction.

How to Contact Send complete ms. Accepts submissions by e-mail (lou@indymensmagazine.com). Responds in 2 months to mss. Accepts simultaneous submissions. Sample copy for $5. Writer's guidelines by e-mail.

Payment/Terms Pays $50-250. Pays on publication for first North American serial rights.

$ ◎ KENTUCKY MONTHLY

Vested Interest Publications, 213 St. Clair St., Frankfort KY 40601. (502)227-0053. Fax: (502)227-5009. E-mail: membry@kentuckymonthly.com. Website: www.kentuckymonthly.com. **Contact:** Michael Embry, editor. "We publish stories about Kentucky and by Kentuckians, including those who live elsewhere." Monthly. Estab. 1998. Circ. 40,000.

Needs Adventure, historical, mainstream, novel excerpts. Publishes ms 3 months after acceptance.

How to Contact Query with published clips. Accepts submissions by e-mail, fax. Responds in 3 weeks to queries; 1 month to mss. Accepts simultaneous submissions. Sample copy online. Writer's guidelines online.

Payment/Terms Pays $50-100. Pays within 3 months of publication. Acquires first North American serial rights.

$ ☑ ◎ ☒ LADYBUG, The Magazine for Young Children

Carus Publishing Co., P.O. Box 300, Peru IL 61354-0300. (815)224-5803 ext. 656. **Contact:** Marianne Carus, editor-in-chief; Paula Morrow, editor. Magazine: 8×10; 36 pages plus 4-page pullout section; illustrations. "We look for quality writing—quality literature, no matter the subject. For young children, ages 2-6." Monthly. Estab. 1990. Circ. 134,000.

• *Ladybug* has received the Parents Choice Award; the Golden Lamp Honor Award and the Golden Lamp Award from Ed Press; and Magazine Merit awards from the Society of Children's Book Writers and Illustrators.

Needs "Looking for age-appropriate read-aloud stories for preschoolers."

How to Contact Send complete ms. SASE. Responds in 3 months to mss. Accepts reprints submissions. Sample copy for $5 and 9×12 SAE. Writer's guidelines online.

Payment/Terms Pays 25¢/word (less for reprints). Pays on publication. Rights purchased vary. For recurring features, pays flat fee and copyright becomes property of Cricket Magazine Group.

Advice Looks for "well-written stories for preschoolers: age-appropriate, not condescending. We look for rich, evocative language and sense of joy or wonder."

$⊚ LAKE SUPERIOR MAGAZINE

Lake Superior Port Cities, Inc., P.O. Box 16417, Duluth MN 55816-0417. (218)722-5002. Fax: (218)722-4096. E-mail: edit@lakesuperior.com. Website: www.lakesuperior.com. Bimonthly. Estab. 1979. Circ. 20,000.

Needs Ethnic/multicultural, historical, humor/satire, mainstream, novel excerpts, slice-of-life vignettes, ghost stories. "Wants stories that are Lake Superior related." Receives 5 unsolicited mss/month. Accepts 1-3 mss/year. Publishes ms 10 months after acceptance. **Publishes 1-6 new writers/year.** Length: 300-2,500 words; average length: 1,000 words. Publishes short shorts. Also publishes literary essays, poetry. Often comments on rejected mss.

How to Contact Query with published clips. Accepts submissions by e-mail. Responds in 3 months to queries. Sample copy for $3.95 and 5 first-class stamps. Writer's guidelines for #10 SASE.

Payment/Terms Pays $1-125. Pays on publication for first North American serial, second serial (reprint) rights.

$▢ ⊚ ▨ LIGUORIAN

One Liguori Dr., Liguori MO 63057-9999. (636)464-2500. Fax: (636)464-8449. E-mail: liguorianeditor@liguori.org. Website: www.liguorian.org. **Contact:** Fr. William Parker, C.S.R, editor-in-chief. Magazine: 10⅝×8; 40 pages; 4-color illustrations; photos. "Our purpose is to lead our readers to a fuller Christian life by helping them better understand the teachings of the gospel and the church and by illustrating how these teachings apply to life and the problems confronting them as members of families, the church, and society." Estab. 1913. Circ. 200,000.

- *Liguorian* received Catholic Press Association awards for 2002 including First Place for Best Short Story ("An August Night at St. Agnes," by David Nypaver).

Needs Religious/inspirational, young adult/teen, senior citizen/retirement. "Stories submitted to *Liguorian* must have as their goal the lifting up of the reader to a higher Christian view of values and goals. We are not interested in contemporary works that lack purpose or are of questionable moral value." Receives 25 unsolicited mss/month. Accepts 12 mss/year. **Publishes 8-10 new writers/year.** Recently published work by Darlene Takarsh, Mary Beth Teymaster and Maeve Mullen Ellis. Publishes short shorts. Occasionaly comments on rejected mss.

How to Contact Send complete ms. Accepts submissions by e-mail, fax, disk. Responds in 3 months to mss. Sample copy for 9×12 SAE with 3 first-class stamps or online. Writer's guidelines for #10 SASE and on website.

Payment/Terms Pays 10-12¢/word and 5 contributor's copies. Pays on acceptance. Buys all rights but will reassign rights to author after publication upon written request.

Advice "First read several issues containing short stories. We look for originality and creative input in each story we read. Since most editors must wade through mounds of manuscripts each month, consideration for the editor requires that the market be studied, the manuscript be carefully presented and polished before submitting. Our publication uses only one story a month. Compare this with the 25 or more we receive over the transom each month. Also, many fiction mss are written without a specific goal or thrust, i.e., an interesting incident that goes nowhere is *not a story*. We believe fiction is a highly effective mode for transmitting the Christian message and also provides a good balance in an unusually heavy issue."

$▨ ⊚ LIVE, A Weekly Journal of Practical Christian Living

Gospel Publishing House, 1445 N. Boonville Ave., Springfield MO 65802-1894. (417)862-2781. Fax: (417)862-6059. E-mail: rl-live@gph.org. Website: www.radiantlife.org. **Contact:** Paul W. Smith, editor. "*LIVE* is a take-home paper distributed weekly in young adult and adult Sunday school classes. We seek to encourage Christians in living for God through fiction and true stories which apply Biblical principles to everyday problems." Weekly. Estab. 1928. Circ. 60,000.

Needs Religious/inspirational, prose poem. No preachy fiction, fiction about Bible characters, or stories that refer to religious myths (e.g., Santa Claus, Easter Bunny, etc.). No science or Bible fiction. No controversial stories about such subjects as feminism, war or capital punishment. "Inner city, ethnic, racial settings." Accepts 2 mss/issue. Publishes ms 18 months after acceptance. **Publishes 75-100 new writers/year.** Recently published work by Judy Stoner, Ginger White, Lorie Ann Johnson and Amanda Jones.

How to Contact Send complete ms. Accepts submissions by e-mail, fax. Responds in 2 weeks to queries; 6 weeks to mss. Accepts simultaneous submissions. Sample copy for #10 SASE. Writer's guidelines for #10 SASE.

Consumer Magazines

Payment/Terms Pays 7-10¢/word. Pays on acceptance for first, second serial (reprint) rights.

Advice "Study our publication and write good, inspirational stories that will encourage people to become all they can be as Christians. Stories should go somewhere! Action, not just thought—life; interaction, not just insights. Heroes and heroines, suspense and conflict. Avoid simplistic, pietistic conclusions, preachy, critical or moralizing. We don't accept science or Bible fiction. Stories should be encouraging, challenging, humorous. Even problem-centered stories should be upbeat." Reserves the right to change the titles, abbreviate length and clarify flashbacks for publication.

⚡ $ 🖾 LIVING LIGHT NEWS

Living Light Ministries, 5306 89th St., #200, Edmonton AB T6E 5P9 Canada. (780)468-6872. Fax: (780)468-6872. Website: www.livinglightnews.org. **Contact:** Jeff Caporale. Newspaper: 11×17; 40 pages; newsprint; electrobrite cover; illustrations; photos. "Our publication is a seeker-sensitive evangelical outreach oriented newspaper focusing on glorifying God and promoting a personal relationship with Him." Bimonthly. Estab. 1995. Circ. 30,000. Member, Evangelical Press Association.

Needs Religious/inspirational. No Victorian-era or strongly American fiction. "We are a Northern Canadian publication interested in Christmas-related fiction focusing on the true meaning of Christmas, humorous Christmas pieces." Christmas deadline is November 1st. Receives 3-4 unsolicited mss/month. Accepts 5 mss/year. Publishes ms 2-6 months after acceptance. **Publishes 2-6 new writers/year.** Length: 300-1,250 words; average length: 700 words. Publishes short shorts. Always comments on rejected mss.

How to Contact Query with or without published clips or send complete ms. Accepts submissions by e-mail. Responds in 5 days to queries; 2 weeks to mss. Accepts simultaneous and reprints, multiple submissions. Sample copy for 9×13 SAE with $2.50 in IRCs or Canadian postage. Writer's guidelines for SASE, e-mail or on website.

Payment/Terms Pays $10-100. Pays on publication.

Advice "We are looking for lively, humorous, inviting heart-warming Christmas-related fiction that focuses on the non-materialistic side of Christmas or shares God's love and grace with others. Try to write with pizzazz. We get many bland submissions. Do not be afraid to use humor and have fun."

$ 🖾 THE LUTHERAN JOURNAL

Apostolic Publishing Co., Inc., P.O. Box 28158, Oakdale MN 55128. (651)702-0086. Fax: (651)702-0074. E-mail: lutheran2@msn.com. **Contact:** Vance E. Lichty. "A family magazine providing wholesome and inspirational reading material for the enjoyment and enrichment of Lutherans." Semiannual. Estab. 1938. Circ. 200,000.

Needs Literary, religious/inspirational, romance (historical), young adult/teen, senior citizen/retirement. Must be appropriate for distribution in the churches. Accepts 3-6 mss/issue.

How to Contact Send complete ms. Responds in 4 months to queries. Accepts simultaneous submissions. Sample copy for 9×12 SAE with 60¢ postage.

Payment/Terms Pays $10-50 and one contributor's copy. Pays on publication for first rights.

$ 🖉 🖾 🖾 THE MAGAZINE OF FANTASY & SCIENCE FICTION

Spilogale, Inc., P.O. Box 3447, Hoboken NJ 07030. E-mail: fsfmagf@fsmag.com. Website: www.fsfmag.com. **Contact:** Gordon Van Gelder, editor. Magazine: 5×8; 160 pages; groundwood paper; card stock cover; illustrations on cover only. "*The Magazine of Fantasy and Science Fiction* publishes various types of science fiction and fantasy short stories and novellas, making up about 80% of each issue. The balance of each issue is devoted to articles about science fiction, a science column, book and film reviews, cartoons and competitions." Monthly. Estab. 1949. Circ. 50,00.

- The *Magazine of Fantasy and Science Fiction* won a Nebula Award for Best Novella for "Bronte's Egg" by Richard Chwedyk and a Nebula Award for Best Short Story for "Creature" by Carol Emshwiller. Also won the 2002 World Fantasy Award for Best Short Story for "Queen for a Day" by Albert E. Cowdrey. Read our interview with Gordon Van Gelder, beginning on page 95.

Needs Adventure, fantasy (space fantasy, sword and sorcery), horror (dark fantasy, futuristic, psychological, supernatural), psychic/supernatural/occult, science fiction (hard science/technological, soft/sociological), young adult/teen (fantasy/science fiction, horror). No electronic submissions. "We're always looking for more science fiction." Receives 500-700 unsolicited mss/month. Accepts 5-8 mss/issue; 75-100 mss/year. Publishes ms 9-12 months after acceptance. **Publishes 1-5 new writers/year.** Recently published work by Ray Bradbury, Ursula K. Le Guin, Alex Irvine, Pat Murphy, Joyce Carol Oates and Robert Sheckley. Length: Up to 25,000 words; average length: 7,000 words. Publishes short shorts. Sometimes comments on rejected mss.

How to Contact Send complete ms. SASE (or IRC). Responds in 2 months to queries. Accepts reprints submissions. Sample copy for $5. Writer's guidelines for SASE, by e-mail or on website.

Payment/Terms Pays 6-9¢/word; additional copies $2.10. Pays on acceptance for first North American serial, foreign serial rights.

Consumer Magazines

Advice "A well-prepared manuscript stands out better that one with fancy doo-dads. Fiction that stands out tends to have well-developed characters and thinks through the implications of its fantasy elements. It has been said 100 times before, but read an issue of the magazine before submitting. In the wake of the recent films, we are seeing more fantasy stories about sorcerers than we can possibly publish."

$ 🖉 ◎ MATURE YEARS

The United Methodist Publishing House, 201 Eighth Ave. S., Nashville TN 37202-0801. (615)749-6292. Fax: (615)749-6512. E-mail: matureyears@umpublishing.org. **Contact:** Marvin Cropsey, editor. Magazine: 8½×11; 112 pages; illustrations; photos. Magazine "helps persons in and nearing retirement to appropriate the resources of the Christian faith as they seek to face the problems and opportunities related to aging." Quarterly. Estab. 1954. Circ. 55,000.

Needs Humor/satire, religious/inspirational, slice-of-life vignettes, retirement years nostalgia, intergenerational relationships. "We don't want anything poking fun at old age, saccharine stories, or anything not for older adults. Must show older adults (age 55 plus) in a positive manner." Accepts 1 mss/issue; 4 mss/year. Publishes ms 1 year after acceptance. **Publishes some new writers/year.** Recently published work by Rita Quinton, Raymond L. Paul and James Steimle.

How to Contact Send complete ms. Responds in 2 weeks to queries; 2 months to mss. No simultaneous submissions. Sample copy for $5.25 and 9×12 SAE. Writer's guidelines for #10 SASE or by e-mail.

Payment/Terms Pays $60-125. Pays on acceptance for first North American serial rights.

Advice "Practice writing dialogue! Listen to people talk; take notes; master dialogue writing! Not easy, but well worth it! Most inquiry letters are far too long. If you can't sell me an idea in a brief paragraph, you're not going to sell the reader on reading your finished article or story."

▤ $ 🖉 ◎ THE MESSENGER OF THE SACRED HEART

Apostleship of Prayer, 661 Greenwood Ave., Toronto ON M4J 4B3 Canada. (416)466-1195. **Contact:** Rev. F.J. Power, S.J. and Alfred DeManche, editors. Magazine: 7×10; 32 pages; coated paper; self-cover; illustrations; photos. Monthly magazine for "Canadian and U.S. Catholics interested in developing a life of prayer and spirituality; stresses the great value of our ordinary actions and lives." Estab. 1891. Circ. 11,000.

Needs Religious/inspirational, stories about people, adventure, heroism, humor, drama. No poetry. Accepts 1 mss/issue. Sometimes comments on rejected mss.

How to Contact Send complete ms. Responds in 1 month to queries. Sample copy for $1 and 7½×10½ SAE. Writer's guidelines for #10 SASE.

Payment/Terms Pays 8¢/word and 3 contributor's copies. Pays on acceptance for first North American serial, first rights.

Advice "Develop a story that sustains interest to the end. Do not preach, but use plot and characters to convey the message or theme. Aim to move the heart as well as the mind. If you can, add a light touch or a sense of humor to the story. Your ending should have impact, leaving a moral or faith message for the reader."

$ 🖉 ◎ MY FRIEND, The Catholic Magazine for Kids

Pauline Books & Media/Daughters of St. Paul, 50 Saint Pauls Ave., Jamaica Plain, Boston MA 02130-3491. (617)522-8911. Fax: (617)541-9805. E-mail: myfriend@pauline.org. Website: www.myfriendmagazine.org. **Contact:** Sister Maria Grace Dateno, editor. Magazine: 8½×11; 32 pages; smooth, glossy paper and cover stock; illustrations; photos. "*My Friend* is a 32-page monthly Catholic magazine for boys and girls. Its goal is to communicate religious truths and positive values in an enjoyable and attractive way." Theme list available. Send a SASE to the above address. Estab. 1979. Circ. 8,000.

Needs Children's/juvenile, religious/inspirational, sports, holidays. Receives 100 unsolicited mss/month. Accepts 3-4 mss/issue; 30-40 mss/year. Publishes ms 6 months after acceptance. **Publishes some new writers/year.** Recently published work by Diana Jenkins and Sandra Humphrey. Length: 600-1,200 words; average length: 850 words.

How to Contact Send complete ms. Responds in 2 months to mss. Sample copy for $2 and 9×12 SASE ($1.29). Writer's guidelines and theme list available at the website.

Payment/Terms Pays $75-150. Pays on acceptance. Buys worldwide publication rights.

Advice "We are particularly interested in fun and amusing stories with backbone. Good dialogue, realistic character development, current lingo are necessary. We have a need for each of these types at different times. We prefer child-centered stories in a real-world setting."

$ ◎ NA'AMAT WOMAN, Magazine of NA'AMAT USA, the Women's Labor Zionist Organization of America

NA'AMAT USA, 350 Fifth Ave., Suite 4700, New York NY 10118. (212)563-5222. Fax: (212)563-5710. **Contact:** Judith A. Sokoloff, editor. "Magazine covering a wide variety of subjects of interest to the Jewish community—

Consumer Magazines

including political and social issues, arts, profiles; many articles about Israel; and women's issues. Fiction must have a Jewish theme. Readers are the American Jewish community." Estab. 1926. Circ. 20,000.

Needs Ethnic/multicultural, historical, humor/satire, literary, novel excerpts, women-oriented. Receives 10 unsolicited mss/month. Accepts 3-5 mss/year.

How to Contact Query with published clips or send complete ms. Accepts submissions by fax. Responds in 3 months to queries; 3 months to mss. Sample copy for $9 \times 11\frac{1}{2}$ SAE and $1.20 postage. Writer's guidelines for #10 SASE.

Payment/Terms Pays 10¢/word and 2 contributor's copies. Pays on publication for first North American serial, first, one-time, second serial (reprint) rights, makes work-for-hire assignments.

Advice "No maudlin nostalgia or romance; no hackneyed Jewish humor and no poetry."

$◎ NEW MOON, The Magazine for Girls & Their Dreams

New Moon Publishing, Inc., 34 E. Superior St., #200, Duluth MN 55802. (218)728-5507. Fax: (218)728-0314. E-mail: girl@newmoon.org. Website: www.newmoon.org. "In general, all material should be pro-girl and feature girls and women as the primary focus. *New Moon* is for every girl who wants her voice heard and her dreams taken seriously. *New Moon* celebrates girls, explores the passage from girl to woman, and builds healthy resistance to gender inequities. The *New Moon* girl is true to herself and *New Moon* helps her as she pursues her unique path in life, moving confidently into the world." Bimonthly. Estab. 1992. Circ. 30,000.

Needs Adventure, fantasy, historical, humor/satire, slice-of-life vignettes. Publishes ms 6 months after acceptance.

How to Contact Send complete ms. Accepts submissions by e-mail, fax. Responds in 2 months to mss. Accepts simultaneous submissions. Sample copy for $6.75 or online. Writer's guidelines for SASE or online.

Payment/Terms Pays 6-12¢/word. Pays on publication.

$◙ THE NEW YORKER

The New Yorker, Inc., 4 Times Square, New York NY 10036. (212) 286-5900. E-mail: fiction@newyorker.com; poetry@newyorker.com. Website: www.newyorker.com. **Contact:** Deborah Treisman, fiction editor. A quality magazine of interesting, well-written stories, articles, essays and poems for a literate audience. Weekly. Estab. 1925. Circ. 750,000.

Needs Accepts 1 mss/issue.

How to Contact Send complete ms. Accepts submissions by e-mail. No more than 1 story or 6 poems should be submitted. No attachments. Responds in 3 months to mss. No simultaneous submissions. Writer's guidelines online.

Payment/Terms Payment varies. Pays on acceptance.

Advice "Be lively, original, not overly literary. Write what you want to write, not what you think the editor would like. Send poetry to Poetry Department."

$◎ PENTHOUSE VARIATIONS

General Media Communications, Inc., 11 Penn Plaza, 12th Floor, New York NY 10001. (212)702-6000. E-mail: variations@generalmedia.com. Monthly. Estab. 1978. Circ. 200,000.

Needs Erotica. Publishes ms 14 months after acceptance.

How to Contact Responds in 1 month to queries; 2 months to mss. Sample copy from (888)312-BACK. Writer's guidelines for #10 SASE or by e-mail.

Payment/Terms Pays $400 maximum. Pays on acceptance.

Advice "*Variations* publishes couple-oriented narratives in which a person fully describes his or her favorite sex scenes squarely focused within 1 of the magazine's usual categories, in highly explicit erotic detail, using the best possible language."

$◙ ⬛ PLAYBOY MAGAZINE

730 5th Avenue, New York NY 10019. (212)261-5000. Website: www.playboy.com. **Contact:** Fiction Department. "As the world's largest general interest lifestyle magazine for men, *Playboy* spans the spectrum of contemporary men's passions. From hard-hitting investigative journalism to light-hearted humor, the latest in fashion and personal technology to the cutting edge of the popular culture, *Playboy* is and always has been guidebook and dream book for generations of American men . . . the definitive source of information and ideas for over 10 million readers each month. In addition, *Playboy*'s 'Interview' and '20 Questions' present profiles of politicians, athletes and today's hottest personalities." Monthly. Estab. 1953. Circ. 3,283,000.

Needs Humor/satire, mainstream, mystery/suspense, science fiction. Does not consider poetry, plays, story outlines or novel-length mss. Writers should remember that the magazine's appeal is chiefly to a well-informed, young male audience. Fairy tales, extremely experimental fiction and out-right pornography all have their place, but it is not in *Playboy*. Handwritten submissions will be returned unread. Writers who submit mss without

Consumer Magazines

including a SASE will receive neither the ms nor a printed rejection. "We will not consider stories submitted electronically or by fax."

How to Contact Query. Responds in 1 month to queries. No simultaneous submissions. Writer's guidelines for #10 SASE or online at website.

Payment/Terms Acquires first North American serial rights.

Advice "*Playboy* does not consider poetry, plays, story outlines or novel-length manuscripts."

$⊚ POCKETS

The Upper Room, 1908 Grand Ave., P.O. Box 340004, Nashville TN 37203-0004. (615)340-7333. Fax: (615)340-7267. E-mail: pockets@upperroom.org. Website: www.pockets.org.; www.upperroom.org/pockets. **Contact:** Lynn W. Gilliam, editor. Magazine: 7×11; 48 pages; some photos. "We are a Christian, inter-denominational publication for children 6-11 years of age. Each issue reflects a specific theme." Estab. 1981. Circ. 96,000.

● *Pockets* has received honors from the Educational Press Association of America.

Needs Adventure, ethnic/multicultural, historical (general), religious/inspirational, slice-of-life vignettes. No fantasy, science fiction, talking animals. "All submissions should address the broad theme of the magazine. Each issue is built around one theme with material which can be used by children in a variety of ways. Scripture stories, fiction, poetry, prayers, art, graphics, puzzles and activities are included. Submissions do not need to be overtly religious. They should help children experience a Christian lifestyle that is not always a neatly-wrapped moral package, but is open to the continuing revelation of God's will. Seasonal material, both secular and liturgical, is desired. No violence, horror, sexual and racial stereotyping or fiction containing heavy moralizing." Receives 200 unsolicited mss/month. Accepts 4-5 mss/issue; 44-60 mss/year. Publishes ms 1 year to 18 months after acceptance. **Publishes 15 new writers/year.** Length: 600-1,400 words; average length: 1,200 words.

How to Contact Send complete ms. Responds in 6 weeks to mss. Accepts reprints, multiple submissions. 9×12 SASE with 4 first-class stamps. Writer's guidelines, themes and due dates avaialble online.

Payment/Terms Pays 14¢/word, plus 2-5 contributor's copies. Pays on acceptance for first North American serial rights. Sponsors awards/contests.

Advice "Listen to children as they talk with each other. Send for a sample copy. Study guidelines and themes before submitting. Many manuscripts we receive are simply inappropriate. Each issue is theme-related. Please send for list of themes. New themes published in December of each year. We strongly advise sending for themes or checking the website before submitting." Include SASE.

$⊘ ⊚ PORTLAND MAGAZINE, Maine's City Magazine

722 Congress St., Portland ME 041012. (207)775-4339. Fax: (207)775-2334. E-mail: editor@portlandmonthly.com. Website: www.portlandmagazine.com. **Contact:** Colin Sargent, editor. Magazine: 200 pages; 60 lb. paper; 100 lb. cover stock; illustrations; photos. "City lifestyle magazine—fiction, style, business, real estate, controversy, fashion, cuisine, interviews and art relating to the Maine area." Monthly. Estab. 1986. Circ. 100,000.

Needs Historical, literary (Maine connection). Query first. Receives 20 unsolicited mss/month. Accepts 1 mss/issue; 10 mss/year. **Publishes 50 new writers/year.** Recently published work by C.D.B. Bryan, Joan Connor, Mameve Medwed, Jason Brown and Sebastian Junger.

How to Contact Send complete ms. SASE.

Payment/Terms Pays on publication for first North American serial rights.

Advice "We publish ambitious short fiction featuring everyone from Frederick Barthelme to newly discovered fiction by Edna St. Vincent Millay."

$☐ PURPOSE

616 Walnut Ave., Scottdale PA 15683-1999. (724)887-8500. Fax: (724)887-3111. E-mail: horsch@mph.org. Website: www.mph.org. **Contact:** James E. Horsch, editor. Magazine: 5³/₈×8³/₈; 8 pages; illustrations; photos. Weekly. Estab. 1968. Circ. 9,000.

Needs Historical (related to discipleship theme), humor/satire, religious/inspirational. No militaristic, narrow patriotism, or racist themes. Receives 150 unsolicited mss/month. Accepts 3 mss/issue; 140 mss/year. Publishes ms 10 months after acceptance. **Publishes 15-25 new writers/year.** Length: 700 words; average length: 400 words. Occasionally comments on rejected mss.

How to Contact Send complete ms. Send all submissions by word attachment via e-mail. Responds in 3 months to queries. Accepts simultaneous and reprints, multiple submissions. Sample copy and writer's guidelines for $2, 6×9 SAE and 2 first-class stamps. Writer's guidelines online.

Payment/Terms Pays up to 6¢/word for stories, and 2 contributor's copies. Pays on acceptance for one-time rights.

Advice "Many stories are situational, how to respond to dilemmas. Looking for first-person storylines. Write crisp, action moving, personal style, focused upon an individual, a group of people, or an organization. The story form is an excellent literary device to help readers explore discipleship issues. The first two paragraphs are crucial in establishing the mood/issue to be resolved in the story. Work hard on the development of these.''

$ ◎ ⊠ ELLERY QUEEN'S MYSTERY MAGAZINE

Dell Magazines Fiction Group, 475 Park Ave. S., 11th Floor, New York NY 10016. (212)686-7188. Fax: (212)686-7414. E-mail: elleryqueen@dellmagazines.com. Website: www.themysteryplace.com. **Contact:** Janet Hutchings, editor. Magazine: $5^3/_8 \times 8^1/_2$; 144 pages with special 240-page combined March/April and September/October issues. *''Ellery Queen's Mystery Magazine* welcomes submissions from both new and established writers. We publish every kind of mystery short story: the psychological suspense tale, the deductive puzzle, the private eye case—the gamut of crime and detection from the realistic (including the policeman's lot and stories of police procedure) to the more imaginative (including ''locked rooms'' and ''impossible crimes''). EQMM has been in continuous publication since 1941. From the beginning, three general criteria have been employed in evaluating submissions: We look for strong writing, an original and exciting plot, and professional craftsmanship. We encourage writers whose work meets these general criteria to read an issue of EQMM before making a submission.''* Magazine for lovers of mystery fiction. Estab. 1941. Circ. 180,780 readers.

• *EQMM* has won numerous awards and sponsors its own award yearly for the best *EQMM* stories nominated by its readership.

Needs Mystery/suspense. No explicit sex or violence, no gore or horror. Seldom publishes parodies or pastiches. ''We accept only mystery, crime, suspense and detective fiction.'' 2,500-8,000 words is the preferred range. Also publishes minute mysteries of 250 words; novellas up to 20,000 words from established authors. Publishes ms 6-12 months after acceptance. Agented fiction 50%. **Publishes 10 new writers/year.** Recently published work by Jeffery Deaver, Joyce Carol Oates and Margaret Maron. Sometimes comments on rejected mss.

How to Contact Send complete ms. Responds in 3 months to mss. Accepts simultaneous, multiple submissions. Sample copy for $5. Writer's guidelines for SASE or online.

Payment/Terms Pays 5-8¢/word, occasionally higher for established authors. Pays on acceptance for first North American serial rights.

Advice ''We have a Department of First Stories and usually publish at least one first story an issue, i.e., the author's first published fiction. We select stories that are fresh and of the kind our readers have expressed a liking for. In writing a detective story, you must play fair with the reader, providing clues and necessary information. Otherwise you have a better chance of publishing if you avoid writing to formula.''

$ ◎ REDBOOK MAGAZINE

224 W. 57th St., New York NY 10019. (212)649-2000. Website: www.redbookmag.com. Magazine: $8 \times 10^3/_4$; 150-250 pages; 34 lb. paper; 70 lb. cover; illustrations; photos. *''Redbook* addresses young married women between the ages of 28 and 44. Most of our readers are married with children 10 and under; over 60 percent work outside the home. The articles entertain, educate and inspire our readers to confront challenging issues. Each article must be timely and relevant to *Redbook* readers' lives.''* Monthly. Estab. 1903. Circ. 3,200,000.

Needs Publishes ms 6 months after acceptance.

How to Contact *Redbook* was not accepting unsolicited mss at the time of publication. Responds in 3 months to queries; 3 months to mss. Sample copy not available. Writer's guidelines online.

Payment/Terms Pays on acceptance. Rights purchased vary with author and material.

Advice ''Read at least the last 6 issues of the magazine to get a better understanding of appropriate subject matter and treatment.''

N $ ◎ REFORM JUDAISM

Union of Reform Judaism, 633 Third Ave. 7th Floor, New York NY 10017-6778. (212)650-4240. Website: www.urj.org/rjmag/. Magazine: $8 \times 10^7/_8$; 80-112 pages; illustrations; photos. *''Reform Judaism* is the official voice of the Union for Reform Judaism, linking the institutions and affiliates of Reform Judaism with every Reform Jew. *RJ* covers developments within the Movement while interpreting events and Jewish tradition from a Reform perspective.''* Quarterly. Estab. 1972. Circ. 310,000.

• Recipient of The Simon Rockower Award for Excellence in Jewish Journalism for feature writing, graphic design and photography. The editor says they would publish more stories if they could find excellent, sophiticated, contemporary Jewish fiction.

Needs Humor/satire, religious/inspirational, sophisticated, cutting-edge, superb writing. Receives 75 unsolicited mss/month. Accepts 3 mss/year. Publishes ms 3 months after acceptance. Recently published work by Frederick Fastow and Bob Sloan. Length: 600-2,500 words; average length: 1,500 words.

How to Contact Send complete ms. SASE. Responds in 2 months to queries; 2 months to mss. Accepts simultaneous and reprints submissions. Sample copy for $3.50. Writer's guidelines online.

Payment/Terms Pays 30¢/word. Pays on publication for first North American serial rights.

Consumer Magazines

$ 🗓 ◎ SEEK

Standard Publishing, 8121 Hamilton Ave., Cincinnati OH 45231. (513)931-4050, ext. 351. Fax: (513)931-0950. E-mail: seek@standardpub.com. Website: www.standardpub.com. Magazine: 5½×8½; 8 pages; newsprint paper; art and photo in each issue. "Inspirational stories of faith-in-action for Christian adults; a Sunday School take-home paper." Quarterly. Estab. 1970. Circ. 27,000.

Needs Religious/inspirational, religious fiction and religiously slanted historical and humorous fiction. No poetry. List of upcoming themes available online. Accepts 150 mss/year. Publishes ms 1 year after acceptance.

How to Contact Send complete ms. Prefers submissions by e-mail. Sample copy for 6×9 SAE with 2 first-class stamps. Writer's guidelines online.

Payment/Terms Pays 5¢/word. Pays on acceptance for first North American serial, second serial (reprint) rights.

Advice "Write a credible story with a Christian slant—no preachments; avoid overworked themes such as joy in suffering, generation gaps, etc. Most manuscripts are rejected by us because of irrelevant topic or message, unrealistic story, or poor charater and/or plot development. We use fiction stories that are believable."

$ 🗓 ◎ 🖼 SHINE BRIGHTLY

GEMS Girls' Clubs, P.O. Box 7259, Grand Rapids MI 49510. (616)241-5616. Fax: (616)241-5558. E-mail: christina @gemsgc.org. Website: www.gemsgc.org. **Contact:** Christina Malone, managing editor. Magazine: 8½×11; 24 pages; 50 lb. paper; 50 lb. cover stock; illustrations; photos. "Our purpose is to lead girls into a living relationship with Jesus Christ and to help them see how God is at work in their lives and the world around them. Puzzles, crafts, stories and articles for girls ages 9-14." Monthly. Estab. 1971. Circ. 13,000.

• *Shine Brightly* has received awards for fiction and illustrations from the Evangelical Press Association.

Needs Adventure (that girls could experience in their hometowns or places they might realistically visit), children's/juvenile, ethnic/multicultural, historical, humor/satire, mystery/suspense (believable only), religious/inspirational (nothing too preachy), romance (stories that deal with awakening awareness of boys are appreciated), slice-of-life vignettes, suspense (can be serialized). Write for upcoming themes. Each year has an overall theme and each month has a theme to fit with yearly themes. Receives 50 unsolicited mss/month. Accepts 3 mss/issue; 30 mss/year. Publishes ms 1 year after acceptance. **Publishes some new writers/year.** Recently published work by A.J. Schut. Length: 400-1,000 words; average length: 800 words.

How to Contact Send complete ms. Responds in 2 months to queries. Accepts simultaneous and reprints submissions. Sample copy for 9×12 SAE with 3 first class stamps and $1. Writer's guidelines online.

Payment/Terms Pays 3¢/word. Pays on publication for first North American serial, second serial (reprint), simultaneous rights.

Advice "Try new and refreshing approaches. No fluffy fiction with Polyanna endings. We want stories dealing with real issues facing girls today. The one-parent, new girl at school is a bit overdone in our market. We have been dealing with issues like AIDS, abuse, drugs and family relationships in our stories—more awareness-type articles."

$ 🗓 ◎ SPIDER, The Magazine for Children

Cricket Magazine Group, P.O. Box 300, Peru IL 61354. (815)224-5803. Fax: (815)224-6615. Website: www.cricke tmag.com. **Contact:** Marianne Carus, editor-in-chief; Heather Delabre, editor. Magazine: 8×10; 33 pages; illustrations; photos. "*Spider* introduces 6- to 9-year-old children to the highest quality stories, poems, illustrations, articles and activities. It was created to foster in beginning readers a love of reading and discovery that will last a lifetime. We're looking for writers who respect children's intelligence." Monthly. Estab. 1994. Circ. 70,000.

• Carus Publishing also publishes *Cricket*, *Ladybug*, *Babybug* and *Cicada*.

Needs Adventure, children's/juvenile (6-9 years), ethnic/multicultural, fantasy (children's fantasy), historical, humor/satire, mystery/suspense, science fiction, realistic fiction, folk tales, fairy tales. No romance, horror, religious. Accepts 4 mss/issue. Publishes ms 2-3 years after acceptance. Agented fiction 2%. Recently published work by Polly Horvath, Katie Walker and Aaron Shepard. Length: 300-1,000 words; average length: 775 words. Also publishes poetry. Often comments on rejected mss.

How to Contact Send complete ms. Send SASE for return of ms. Responds in 4 months to mss. Accepts simultaneous and reprints submissions. Sample copy for $5. Writer's guidelines for #10 SASE or on website.

Payment/Terms Pays 25¢/word and 2 contributor's copies; additional copies $2. Pays on publication. Rights vary.

Advice "Read back issues of *Spider*." Look for "quality writing, good characterization, lively style, humor."

🖼 SPINNING JENNY

Black Dress Press, PO Box 1373, New York NY 10276. E-mail: submissions@blackdresspress.com. Website: www.blackdresspress.com. **Contact:** C.E. Harrison. Magazine: 112 pages; 60 lb. paper; offset printed; perfect bound; illustrations. Literary magazine publishing short stories and novel excerpts Estab. 1994. CLMP.

Needs Experimental, literary. Publishes ms 11 months after acceptance. **Publishes 3 new writers/year.**

How to Contact Send complete ms. Accepts submissions by e-mail. Send SASE for return of ms or send a disposable copy of ms and #10 SASE for reply only. Responds in 2 months to mss.

Payment/Terms 5 contributor copies.

$☑ ◎ ▣ ST. ANTHONY MESSENGER

28 W. Liberty St., Cincinnati OH 45202-6498. (513)241-5615. Fax: (513)241-0399. E-mail: stanthony@americanc atholic.org. Website: www.americancatholic.org. **Contact:** Father Pat McCloskey, O.F.M., editor. Magazine: 8×10¾; 60 pages; illustrations; photos. *"St. Anthony Messenger* is a Catholic family magazine which aims to help its readers lead more fully human and Christian lives. We publish articles which report on a changing church and world, opinion pieces written from the perspective of Christian faith and values, personality profiles, and fiction which entertains and informs." Estab. 1893. Circ. 308,884.

● This is a leading Catholic magazine, but has won awards for both religious and secular journalism and writing from the Catholic Press Association, the International Association of Business Communicators, the Society of Professional Journalists, and the Cincinnati Editors Association.

Needs Mainstream, religious/inspirational, senior citizen/retirement. "We do not want mawkishly sentimental or preachy fiction. Stories are most often rejected for poor plotting and characterization; bad dialogue—listen to how people talk; inadequate motivation. Many stories say nothing, are 'happenings' rather than stories." No fetal journals, no rewritten Bible stories. Receives 60-70 unsolicited mss/month. Accepts 1 mss/issue; 12 mss/year. Publishes ms 1 year after acceptance. **Publishes 3 new writers/year.** Recently published work by Geraldine Marshall Gutfreund, John Salustri, Beth Dotson, Miriam Pollikatsikis and Joseph Pici. Sometimes comments on rejected mss.

How to Contact Send complete ms. Accepts submissions by e-mail, fax. SASE for ms. "For quickest response send self-addressed stamped postcard with choices: "Yes, we're interested in publishing; Maybe, we'd like to hold for future consideration; No, we've decided to pass on the publication." Responds in 3 weeks to queries; 2 months to mss. No simultaneous submissions. Sample copy for 9×12 SAE with 4 first-class stamps. Writer's guidelines online. Reviews fiction.

Payment/Terms Pays 16¢/word maximum and 2 contributor's copies; $1 charge for extras. Pays on acceptance for first North American serial, electronic rights. Buys electronic, first worldwide serial rights.

Advice "We publish one story a month and we get up to 1,000 a year. Too many offer simplistic 'solutions' or answers. Pay attention to endings. Easy, simplistic, *deus ex machina* endings don't work. People have to feel characters in the stories are real and have a reason to care about them and what happens to them. Fiction entertains but can also convey a point and sound values."

$☑ ◎ STANDARD

Nazarene International Headquarters, 6401 The Paseo, Kansas City MO 64131. (816)333-7000. Fax: (816)333-4439. E-mail: cyourdon@nazarene.org. Website: www.nazarene.org. **Contact:** Everett Leadingham, editor; Charlie L. Yourdon, managing editor. Magazine: 8½×11; 8 pages; illustrations; photos. Inspirational reading for adults. *"In Standard* we want to show Christianity in action, and we prefer to do that through stories that hold the reader's attention." Weekly. Estab. 1936. Circ. 130,000.

Needs "Looking for stories that show Christianity in action." Accepts 200 mss/year. Publishes ms 14-18 months after acceptance. **Publishes some new writers/year.**

How to Contact Send complete ms. Accepts submissions by e-mail. SASE. Accepts simultaneous submissions; but pays at reprint rates. Writer's guidelines and sample copy for SAE with 2 first-class stamps.

Payment/Terms Pays 3½¢/word for first rights; 2¢/word for reprint rights, and contributor's copies. Pays on acceptance for one-time rights, whether first or reprint rights.

Advice "Be conscientious in your use of Scripture; don't overload your story with qoatations. When you quote the Bible, quote it exactly and cite chapter, verse, and version used. (We prefer NIV.) *Standard* will handle copyright matters for Scripture. Except for quotations from the Bible, written permission for the use of any other copyrighted material (especially song lyrics) is the responsibility of the writer. Keep in mind the international audience of *Standard* with regard to geographic refrences and holidays. We cannot use stories about cultural, national or secular holidays. Do not mention specific church affiliations. *Standard* is read in a variety of denominations. Do not submit any manuscript which has been submitted to or published in any of the following: *Vista, Wesleyan Advocate, Holiness Today, Preacher's Magazine, World Mission, Women Alive,* or various teen and children's publications produced by WordAction Publishing Company. These are overlapping markets."

$☑ THE SUN

The Sun Publishing Co., 107 N. Roberson St., Chapel Hill NC 27516. (919)942-5282. Fax: (919)932-3101. Website: www.thesunmagazine.org. **Contact:** Sy Safransky, editor. Magazine: 8½×11; 48 pages; offset paper; glossy cover stock; photos. "We are open to all kinds of writing, though we favor work of a personal nature." Monthly. Estab. 1974. Circ. 70,000.

Needs Literary. Open to all fiction. Receives 500 unsolicited mss/month. Accepts 2 mss/issue. Publishes ms 6-12 months after acceptance. Recently published work by Brian Buckbee, Theresa Williams, Tim Melley and Sybil Smith. Also publishes poetry.

How to Contact Send complete ms. Accepts reprints submissions. Sample copy for $5. Writer's guidelines online.

Payment/Terms Pays $300-750. Pays on publication for first, one-time rights.

Advice "We favor honest, personal writing with an intimate point of view."

$ ⬛ ◎ TRUE CONFESSIONS

Macfadden Women's Group, 333 Seventh Ave., New York NY 10001. (212)979-4898. Fax: (212)979-4825. E-mail: trueconfessionstales@yahoo.com. **Contact:** Pat Byrdsong, editorial director. Magazine: 8×10½; 112 pages; photos. *"True Confessions* is a women's magazine featuring true-to-life stories about working class women and their families. Monthly. Circ. 100,000.

Needs "Family problems, relationship issues, realistic romances, working woman and single mom, single woman problems, abuse, etc. Stories should help women lead better lives. Also stories about multicultural experience—Latino, African, Asian, Native American stories encouraged. Must be written in first-person. No science fiction or third-person stories. Wants to see more first-person inspirationals, thrillers, mysteries, romances with an edge." Publishes ms on average 4 months after acceptance. **Publishes 20 new writers/year.**

How to Contact Query. Accepts submissions by e-mail. Responds in 3 months to queries; 15 months to mss. Sample copy for $4.49.

Payment/Terms Pays 3¢/word or a flat $100 rate for mini-stories and 1 contributor's copy. Pays 1 month after publication.

Advice "Emotionally charged stories with a strong emphasis on characterization and well-defined plots are preferred. Stories should be intriguing, suspenseful, humorous, romantic or tragic. The plots and characters should reflect American life. I want stories that cover the wide spectrum of America. I want to feel as though I intimately know the narrator and his/her motivation. If your story is dramatically gripping and/or humorous, features three-dimensional characters, and a realistic conflict, you have an excellent chance of making a sale at *True Confessions*. I suggest writers read three to four issues of *True Confessions* before sending submissions. Do not talk down to our readers. Contemporary problems should be handled with insight and a fresh angle. Timely, first-person stories told by a sympathetic narrator are always needed as well as good romantic stories."

$ ⬛ ◎ U.S. CATHOLIC

Claretian Publications, 205 W. Monroe St., Chicago IL 60606. (312)236-7782. Fax: (312)236-8207. Website: www.uscatholic.org. **Contact:** Maureen Abood, literary editor. Magazine: 8½×11; 52 pages; photos. "*U.S. Catholic* is dedicated to the belief that it makes a difference whether you're Catholic. We invite and help our readers explore the wisdom of their faith tradition and apply their faith to the challenges of the 21st century." Monthly. Estab. 1935. Circ. 40,000. Member, Associated Church Press, Religious Communicators Council, Catholic Press Association.

Needs Ethnic/multicultural, family saga, mainstream, religious/inspirational, slice-of-life vignettes. Receives 100 unsolicited mss/month. Accepts 12 mss/year. Publishes ms 2-3 months after acceptance. **Publishes 20% new writers/year.** Publishes short shorts. Also publishes poetry.

How to Contact Send complete ms. Accepts submissions by e-mail, fax, disk. Send a disposable copy of ms and #10 SASE for reply only. Responds in 1 month to queries; 2 months to mss. Sample copy for large SASE. Guidelines by e-mail or on website. Reviews fiction.

Payment/Terms Pays $300. Pays on acceptance for first North American serial rights.

$ ⬛ ◎ THE WAR CRY

The Salvation Army, 615 Slaters Lane, Alexandria VA 22314. (703)684-5500. Fax: (703)684-5539. E-mail: war_cry@usn.salvationarmy.org. Website: www.salpubs.com. **Contact:** Lt. Colonel Marlene Chase, editor-in-chief. Magazine: 8½×11; 24 pages; glossy; illustrations; photos. Biweekly. Estab. 1881. Circ. 300,000. Member, Evangelical Press Association.

Needs Religious/inspirational. "Only 5% of all purchased material is fiction or poetry." Publishes ms 2 months-1 year after acceptance. Publishes short shorts. Also publishes poetry. Sometimes comments on rejected mss.

How to Contact Send complete ms. Send SASE for return of ms or disposable copy of ms. Maximum 5 poems/submission. Responds in 2 months to mss. Accepts simultaneous and reprints, multiple submissions.

Payment/Terms Pays up to 18-25¢/word; 15¢ for reprints, and 2 contributor's copies. Pays on acceptance for first, one-time rights.

$ ◎ 🖩 WOMAN'S DAY

54-58 Park St., Sydney NSW 2000 Australia. 9282 8000. Fax: 9267 4360. E-mail: womansday@acp.com.au. **Contact:** Julie Redlich, fiction editor. "Magazine for women of all ages (and the men in their lives enjoy it too)." Weekly.

Needs Publishes 25-30 new writers/year. Recently published work by Ian Rankin, James Patterson and Maeve Haran.

How to Contact Accepts submissions by e-mail, fax. "Manuscripts should be typed with double spacing and sufficient margins on either side of the text for notes and editing. They should be sent to the Fiction Editor with SAE and IRC. We accept unsolicited manuscripts, but must point out that we receive around 100 of these in the fiction department each week, and obiviously, are limited in the number we can accept." Accepts multiple submissions. Sample copy not available. Writer's guidelines online.

Payment/Terms Payment is usually $350 (Australian) for short fiction under 1,000 words; $450 for longer stories. Acquires the first Australian and New Zealand rights.

Advice "Study the market and submit manuscripts suitable for that publication."

N 🖩 $ WOMAN'S WEEKLY

IPC Magazines, King's Reach, Stamford St., London SE1 9LS England. **Contact:** Gaynor Davies. Publishes 1 serial and at least 2 short stories/week.

Needs "Short stories can be on any theme but must have warmth. No explicit sex or violence. Serials need not be written in installments. They are submitted as complete manuscripts and we split them up, or send first installment of serial (4,500 words) and synopsis of the rest."

How to Contact Writer's guidelines free.

Payment/Terms Short story payment starts at £100 and rises as writer becomes a more regular contributor. Serial payments start at around £600/installment. Writers also receive contributor's copies.

Advice "Read the magazine and try to understand who the publication is aimed at."

N $ ◻ 🖩 WRITERS' FORUM, Britain's Best Magazine for Writers

Writers International Ltd., P.O. Box 3229, Bournemouth Dorset BH1 1ZS United Kingdom. (44)1202 589828. Fax: (44)1202 587758. E-mail: editorial@writers-forum.com. Website: www.writers-forum.com. **Contact:** John Jenkins, editor. Monthly: A4; 64 pages; illustrations; photos. "In each issue *Writers' Forum* covers the *who, why, what, where, when* and *how* of writing. You will find the latest on markets, *how-to* articles, courses/holidays for writers and much more. There is also a short story competition in every issue—that means you have ten chances to get published and win some cash. Prizes range from £150 to £250 and there's £1,000 for the best story of the year. Monthly. Estab. 1995. Circ. 25,000.

Needs Erotica, historical, horror (psychological), literary, mainstream, mystery/suspense (cozy, private eye/hard-boiled), romance (contemporary, futuristic/time travel, historical, romantic suspense), science fiction (soft/sociological), thriller/espionage, western (frontier saga, traditional), young adult/teen (adventure, easy-to-read, historical, problem novels, romance). Receives hundreds unsolicited mss/month. Accepts 3-4 mss/issue; 20 mss/year. Publishes ms 2-3 months after acceptance. Length: 1,000-3,000 words; average length: 1,500 words. Also publishes literary essays, literary criticism, poetry. Always comments on rejected mss.

How to Contact Query. Accepts submissions by e-mail, fax. Send SASE (or IRC) for return of ms or send disposable copy of the ms and #10 SASE for reply only. Responds in 2-3 weeks to queries; 2-3 weeks to mss. Accepts simultaneous submissions. Sample copy online. Writer's guidelines online. Reviews fiction.

Payment/Terms Pays $120 maximum and 1 contributor's copy; additional copies $5. Pays 1 month following publication. Acquires first rights. Sponsors awards/contests.

Advice "A good introduction and an original slant on a common theme. Always read the competition rules and our guidelines."

$ WRITERS' JOURNAL, The Complete Writer's Magazine

Val-Tech Media, P.O. Box 394, Perham MN 56573-0394. (218)346-7921. Fax: (218)346-7924. E-mail: editor@writersjournal.com. Website: www.writersjournal.com. "*Writers' Journal* is read by thousands of aspiring writers whose love of writing has taken them to the next step: writing for money. We are an instructional manual giving writers the tools and information necessary to get their work published. We also print works by authors who have won our writing contests." Bimonthly. Estab. 1980. Circ. 26,000.

Needs "We only publish winners of our fiction contests—16 contests/year." Receives 200 contest entries/month. Accepts 5-7 mss/issue; 30-40 mss/year. Publishes ms 10 months after acceptance. Agented fiction 3%. **Publishes 100 new writers/year.** Also publishes poetry.

How to Contact Accepts submissions by e-mail (not as attachment). Responds in 6 weeks to queries; 6 months to mss. Accepts simultaneous submissions. Sample copy for $5.

Payment/Terms Pays on publication for one-time rights.

Book Publishers

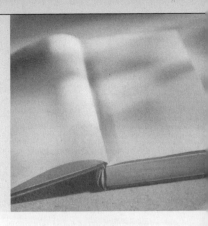

In this section, you will find many of the "big-name" book publishers. Many of these publishers remain tough markets for new writers or for those whose work might be considered literary or experimental. Indeed, some only accept work from established authors, and then often only through an author's agent. Although having your novel published by one of the big commercial publishers listed in this section is difficult, it is not impossible. The trade magazine *Publishers Weekly* regularly features interviews with writers whose first novels are being released by top publishers. Many editors at large publishing houses find great satisfaction in publishing a writer's first novel.

On page 545, you'll find the publishing industry's "family tree," which maps out each of the large book publishing conglomerates' divisions, subsidiaries and imprints. Remember, most manuscripts are acquired by imprints, not their parent company, so avoid submitting to the conglomerates themselves. (For example submit to Dutton or Berkley Books, not their parent Penguin.)

Also listed here are "small presses" publishing four or more titles annually. Included among them are small and mid-size independent presses, university presses and other non-profit publishers. Introducing new writers to the reading public has become an increasingly important role of these smaller presses at a time when the large conglomerates are taking fewer chances on unknown writers. Many of the successful small presses listed in this section have built their reputations and their businesses in this way and have become known for publishing prize-winning fiction.

These smaller presses also tend to keep books in print longer than larger houses. And, since small presses publish a smaller number of books, each title is equally important to the publisher, and each is promoted in much the same way and with the same commitment. Editors also stay at small presses longer because they have more of a stake in the business— often they own the business. Many smaller book publishers are writers themselves and know firsthand the importance of a close editor-author or publisher-author relationship.

TYPES OF BOOK PUBLISHERS

Large or small, the publishers in this section publish books "for the trade." That is, unlike textbook, technical or scholarly publishers, trade publishers publish books to be sold to the general consumer through bookstores, chain stores or other retail outlets. Within the trade book field, however, there are a number of different types of books.

The easiest way to categorize books is by their physical appearance and the way they are marketed. Hardcover books are the more expensive editions of a book, sold through bookstores and carrying a price tag of around $20 and up. Trade paperbacks are soft-bound books, also sold mostly in bookstores, that carry a more modest price tag of usually around $10 to $20. Today a lot of fiction is published in this form because it means a lower financial risk than hardcover.

Mass market paperbacks are another animal altogether. These are the smaller "pocket-size" books available at bookstores, grocery stores, drug stores, chain retail outlets, etc. Much genre or category fiction is published in this format. This area of the publishing industry is very open to the work of talented new writers who write in specific genres such as science fiction, romance and mystery.

At one time publishers could be easily identified and grouped by the type of books they produce. Today, however, the lines between hardcover and paperback books are blurred. Many publishers known for publishing hardcover books also publish trade paperbacks and have paperback imprints. This enables them to offer established authors (and a very few lucky newcomers) hard-soft deals in which their book comes out in both versions. Thanks to the mergers of the past decade, too, the same company may own several hardcover and paperback subsidiaries and imprints, even though their editorial focuses may remain separate.

CHOOSING A BOOK PUBLISHER

In addition to checking the bookstores and libraries for books by publishers that interest you, you may want to refer to the Category Index at the back of this book to find publishers divided by specific subject categories. The subjects listed in the Indexes are general. Read individual listings to find which subcategories interest a publisher. For example, you will find several romance publishers listed, but read the listings to find which type of romance is considered—gothic, contemporary, regency or futuristic. See You've Got a Story on page 2 for more on how to refine your list of potential markets.

The icons appearing before the names of the publishers will also help you in selecting a publisher. These codes are especially important in this section, because many of the publishing houses listed here require writers to submit through an agent. A ◙ icon identifies those that mostly publish established and agented authors, while a ◌ points to publishers most open to new writers. See the inside front cover of this book for a complete list and explanations of symbols used in this book.

IN THE LISTINGS

As with other sections in this book, we identify new listings with a 🅽 symbol. In this section, most with this symbol are not new publishers, but instead are established publishers who were unable or decided not to list last year and are therefore new to this edition.

In addition to the 🅽 symbol indicating new listings, we include other symbols to help you in narrowing your search. English-speaking foreign markets are denoted by a 🌐 . The maple leaf symbol 🍁 identifies Canadian presses. If you are not a Canadian writer but are interested in a Canadian press, check the listing carefully. Many small presses in Canada receive grants and other funds from their provincial or national government and are, therefore, restricted to publishing Canadian authors.

We also include editorial comments set off by a bullet (●) within listings. This is where we include information about any special requirements or circumstances that will help you know even more about the publisher's needs and policies. The star ⭐ signals that this market is an imprint or division of a larger publisher. The ▼ symbol identifies publishers who have recently received honors or awards for their books. And the Ⓐ symbol indicates that a publisher accepts agented submissions only.

Each listing includes a summary of the editorial mission of the house, an overarching principle that ties together what they publish. Under the heading **Contact** we list one or more editors, often with their specific area of expertise.

Book editors asked us again this year to emphasize the importance of paying close attention to the **Needs** and **How to Contact** subheads of listings for book publishers. Unlike magazine editors who want to see complete manuscripts of short stories, most of the book publishers listed here ask that writers send a query letter with an outline and/or synopsis and several chapters of their novel. The Business of Fiction Writing, beginning on page 66 of this book, outlines how to prepare work to submit directly to a publisher.

There are no subsidy book publishers listed in *Novel & Short Story Writer's Market*. By subsidy, we mean any arrangement in which the writer is expected to pay all or part of the cost of producing, distributing and marketing his book. We feel a writer should not be asked to share in any cost of turning his manuscript into a book. All the book publishers listed here told us that they *do not charge writers* for publishing their work. *If any of the publishers listed here ask you to pay any part of publishing or marketing your manuscript, please let us know.* See our Complaint Procedure on the copyright page of this book.

A NOTE ABOUT AGENTS

Some publishers are willing to look at unsolicited submissions, but most feel having an agent is in the writer's best interest. In this section more than any other, you'll find a number of publishers who prefer submissions from agents. That's why we've included a section of agents open to submissions from fiction writers (page 102).

Be wary of those agents who charge large sums of money for reading a manuscript. Reading fees do not guarantee representation. Think of an agent as a potential business partner and feel free to ask tough questions about his or her credentials, experience and business practices.

Periodicals of Interest

For More Info

Check out issues of *Publishers Weekly* for publishing industry trade news in the U.S. and around the world or *Quill & Quire* for book publishing news in the Canadian book industry.

For more small presses see the *International Directory of Little Magazines and Small Presses* published by Dustbooks. To keep up with changes in the industry throughout the year, check issues of two small press trade publications: *Small Press Review* (also published by Dustbooks) and *Independent Publisher* (Jenkins Group, Inc.).

Book Publishers

🌐 A&C BLACK PUBLISHERS, LTD.

Bloomsbury plc, 37 Soho Square, London W1D 3QZ England. +44 (020)7758-0200. E-mail: childrens@acblack.com. Website: www.acblack.com. **Contact:** Jon Appleton, editor (children's fiction). Publishes hardcover and trade paperback originals, trade paperback reprints. Averages 170 total titles/year.
Imprint(s) Adlard Coles Nautical (Janet Murphy, editor); Christopher Helm/Pica Press (Nigel Redman, editor); Herbert Press (Linda Lambert, editor).
Needs Juvenile.
How to Contact Submit 2 sample chapter(s), synopsis or submit complete ms. Responds in 1 month to queries; 2 months to mss. Accepts simultaneous submissions.
Terms Pays royalty on retail price or net receipts; makes outright purchase very occasionally on short children's books. Average advance: £1,500-6,000. Publishes ms 9 months after acceptance.

✖ HARRY N. ABRAMS, INC.

La Martiniere Groupe, Attn: Managing Editor, 100 Fifth Ave., New York NY 10011. (212)206-7715. Fax: (212)645-8437. Website: www.abramsbooks.com. **Contact:** Eric Himmel, editor-in-chief. Estab. 1949. Publishes hardcover and "a few" paperback originals. Averages 150 total titles/year.
How to Contact Responds in 6-8 weeks to queries. No simultaneous submissions, electronic submissions.
Terms Pays royalty. Average advance: variable. Publishes ms 2 years after acceptance. Book catalog for $5.

✦ ABSEY & CO.

23011 Northcrest Dr., Spring TX 77389. (281)257-2340. Fax: (281)251-4676. E-mail: abseyandco@aol.com. Website: www.absey.com. **Contact:** Edward E. Wilson, publisher. "We are interested in book-length fiction of literary merit with a firm intended audience." Publishes hardcover, trade paperback and mass market paperback originals. **Published 3-5 debut authors within the last year.** Averages 6-10 total titles, 6-10 fiction titles/year.
Needs Juvenile, mainstream/contemporary, short story collections. Published *Where I'm From*, by George Ella Lyon; *Blast Man Standing*, by Robert V. Spelleri.
How to Contact Accepts unsolicited mss. Query with SASE. Responds in 3 months to queries; 9 months to mss. No simultaneous submissions, electronic submissions.
Terms Royalty and advance vary. Publishes ms 1 year after acceptance. Ms guidelines online.
Advice "Since we are a small, new press looking for good manuscripts with a firm intended audience, we tend to work closely and attentively with our authors. Many established authors who have been with the large New York houses have come to us to publish their work because we work closely with them."

✦ ACADEMY CHICAGO PUBLISHERS

363 W. Erie St., Suite 7E., Chicago IL 60610-3125. (312)751-7300. Fax: (312)751-7306. E-mail: info@academychicago.com. Website: www.academychicago.com. **Contact:** Anita Miller, senior editor. Estab. 1975. Midsize independent publisher. Publishes hardcover originals and trade paperback reprints. Averages 15 total titles/year.
Needs Historical, mainstream/contemporary, military/war, mystery. "We look for quality work, but we do not publish experimental, avant-garde novels." Biography, history, academic and anthologies. Only the most unusual mysteries, no private-eyes or thrillers. No explicit sex or violence. Serious fiction, no romance/adventure. "We will consider historical fiction that is well researched. No science fiction/fantasy, no religious/inspirational, no how-to, no cookbooks. In general, we are very conscious of women's roles. We publish very few children's books." Published *Clean Start*, by Patricia Margaret Page (first fiction); *Cutter's Island: Caesar in Captivity*, by Vincent Panella (first fiction, historical); and *Murder at the Paniomic Games*, by Michael B. Edward.
How to Contact Accepts unsolicited mss. Submit 3 sample chapter(s), synopsis. Accepts queries by mail. Include cover letter briefly describing the content of your work. "Manuscripts without envelopes will be discarded. *Mailers* are a *must*, even from agents." Send SASE or IRC. Responds in 3 months to queries. No electronic submissions.
Terms Pays 7-10% royalty on wholesale price. Average advance: modest. Publishes ms 18 months after acceptance. Ms guidelines online.
Advice "At the moment we are swamped with manuscripts and anything under consideration can be under consideration for months."

✖ ✦ ◎ ACE SCIENCE FICTION AND FANTASY

The Berkley Publishing Group, Penguin Group (USA), Inc., 375 Hudson St., New York NY 10014. (212)366-2000. Website: www.penguin.com. **Contact:** Susan Allison, editor-in-chief; Anne Sowards, editor. Estab. 1953. Publishes hardcover, paperback and trade paperback originals and reprints. Averages 75 total titles, 72 fiction titles/year.

Needs Fantasy, science fiction. No other genre accepted. No short stories. Published *Iron Sunrise*, by Charles Stross; *Neuromancer*, by William Gibson; *King Kelson's Bride*, by Katherine Kurtz.

How to Contact Accepts unsolicited mss. Send SASE or IRC. Agented fiction 85-95%. Responds in 2 months to queries; 6 months to mss. No simultaneous submissions.

Terms Pays royalty. Offers advance. Publishes ms 1-2 years after acceptance. Ms guidelines for #10 SASE.

Advice "Good science fiction and fantasy are almost always written by people who have read and loved a lot of it. We are looking for knowledgeable science or magic, as well as sympathetic characters with recognizable motivation. We are looking for solid, well-plotted science fiction: good action adventure, well-researched hard science with good characterization, and books that emphasize characterization without sacrificing plot. In fantasy we are looking for all types of work, from high fantasy to sword and sorcery." Submit fantasy and science fiction to Anne Sowards.

AGELESS PRESS

3759 Collins St., Sarasota FL 34232. Website: http://irisforrest.com. **Contact:** Iris Forrest, editor. Estab. 1992. Independent publisher. Publishes paperback originals. Books: acid-free paper; notched perfect binding; no illustrations. Averages 1 total titles/year.

Needs Experimental, fantasy, humor, literary, mainstream/contemporary, mystery, new age/mystic, science fiction, short story collections, thriller/espionage. Looking for material "based on personal computer experiences." Stories selected by editor. Published *Computer Legends, Lies & Lore*, by various (anthology); and *Computer Tales of Fact and Fantasy*, by various (anthology).

How to Contact Does not accept unsolicited mss. Query with SASE. Accepts queries by e-mail, fax, mail. Responds in 1 week to queries; 1 week to mss. Accepts simultaneous submissions, electronic submissions, submissions on disk. Sometimes comments on rejected mss.

Terms Average advance: negotiable. Publishes ms 6-12 months after acceptance.

Advice "Query! Don't send work without a query!"

ALEF DESIGN GROUP

4423 Fruitland Ave., Los Angeles CA 90058. (800)238-6724. Fax: (323)585-0327. Website: www.alefdesign.com. Estab. 1990. Publishes hardcover and trade paperback originals. **Published 40% debut authors within the last year.** Averages 25 total titles/year.

Needs Juvenile, religious, young adult. "We publish books of Judaic interest only." Published *The Road to Exile*, by Didier Nebot (fiction).

How to Contact Query with SASE. Responds in 6 months to mss. Accepts simultaneous submissions.

Terms Pays 10% royalty. Offers advance. Publishes ms 3 years after acceptance. Ms guidelines for 9×12 SAE with 10 first-class stamps.

ALGONQUIN BOOKS OF CHAPEL HILL

Workman Publishing, P.O. Box 2225, Chapel Hill NC 27515-2225. (919)967-0108. Website: www.algonquin.com. **Contact:** Editorial Department. Publishes hardcover originals. Averages 24 total titles/year.

How to Contact Query by mail before submitting work. No phone, e-mail or fax queries or submissions. Visit our website for full submission policy to queries.

Terms Ms guidelines online.

ALLEN-AYERS BOOKS

4621 S. Atlantic Ave. #7603, Ponce Inlet FL 32127. E-mail: allen-ayers@cfl.rr.com. Website: http://home.att.net/~allen-ayers. Estab. 2000. Allen-Ayers Books is a two-person operation on a part-time basis. Publishes paperback originals. Distribute through Ingram Books.

• *Never by Blood*, by Noel Carroll, received Scribs World's Reviewers Choice Award.

Needs Humor, science fiction (hard science/technological), short story collections, thriller/espionage. Published *Broken Odyssey*, by Noel Carroll (thriller); *Never by Blood*, by Noel Carroll (thriller); *Hey, God; Got A Minute?*, by John Barr (humor/satire).

How to Contact Does not accept unsolicited mss. Never comments on rejected mss.

Terms Pays royalty. Ms guidelines for #10 SASE.

ALYSON PUBLICATIONS

6922 Hollywood Blvd., Suite 1000, Los Angeles CA 90028. (323)860-6065. Fax: (323)467-0152. E-mail: mail@alyson.com. Website: www.alyson.com. Estab. 1980. Medium-sized publisher specializing in lesbian- and gay-related material. Publishes hardcover and trade paperback originals and reprints. Books: paper and printing varies; trade paper, perfect-bound. **Published some debut authors within the last year.** Averages 50 total titles, 25 fiction titles/year.

Imprint(s) Alyson Wonderland, Advocate Books.

Needs "We are interested in all categories; *all* materials must be geared toward lesbian and/or gay readers." Publishes anthologies. Authors may submit to them directly.

How to Contact Query with SASE. Accepts queries by mail. Responds in 4 months to queries. Accepts simultaneous submissions.

Terms Pays 8-15% royalty on net receipts. Average advance: $1,500-5,000. Book catalog and ms guidelines for 6×9 SAE with 3 first-class stamps. Ms guidelines online.

AMBASSADOR BOOKS, INC.

91 Prescott St., Worcester MA 01605. (508)756-2893. Fax: (508)757-7055. Website: www.ambassadorbooks.com. **Contact:** Kathryn Conlan, acquisitions editor. Publishes hardcover and trade paperback originals. **Published 50% debut authors within the last year.** Averages 7 total titles/year.

Needs Juvenile, literary, picture books, religious, spiritual, sports, young adult, women's. Published *Survival Notes for Graduates,* by Robert Stofel (inspirational); *A Farewell to Glory,* by Wally Carew (sports); *The Man Who Met the King,* by Gerard Goggins (fiction); and *Spinner McClock and the Christmas Visit,* by Rick Dacey, illustrated by Hallie Gillett.

How to Contact Query with SASE or submit complete ms. Responds in 3-4 months to queries. Accepts simultaneous submissions.

Terms Pays 8-10% royalty on retail price. Publishes ms 1 year after acceptance. Book catalog free or online.

AMBER QUILL PRESS

P.O. Box 265, Indian Hills CO 80454. E-mail: business@amberquillpress.com. Website: www.amberquill.com. Trace Edward Zaber. Estab. 2002. "We are an Internet-based small press that offers high quality fiction of all genres." Publishes paperback originals and e-books. **Published 20 debut authors within the last year.**

Needs Adventure, erotica, family saga, fantasy (sword and sorcery), historical, horror, mainstream/contemporary, military/war, mystery (amateur sleuth, cozy, police procedural, private eye), psychic/supernatural, romance, science fiction, thriller/espionage, western, young adult. Published *Scent of the Wolf,* by Tracy Jones (paranormal gothic); *Killer Turtle,* by Alan M. Brooker (action/adventure).

How to Contact Does not accept unsolicited mss. Query with SASE. Accepts queries by mail. Include estimated word count, list of publishing credits. Send SASE or IRC. Responds in 4 months to queries; 6 months to mss. Accepts submissions on disk. No simultaneous submissions. Never comments on rejected mss.

Terms Pays royalty. Publishes ms 2 years after acceptance. Ms guidelines online.

Advice "Make certain that your work is really ready for publication. We see far too many submissions that are two or three drafts away from completion."

AMERICAN ATHEIST PRESS

P.O. Box 5733, Parsippany NJ 07054-6733. (908)276-7300. Fax: (908)276-7402. E-mail: info@atheists.org. Website: www.atheists.org. **Contact:** Frank Zindler, editor. Estab. 1963. Publishes trade paperback originals and reprints. Publishes quarterly journal, *American Atheist,* for which are needed articles of interest to atheists. **Published 40-50% debut authors within the last year.** Averages 12 total titles/year.

Imprint(s) Gustav Broukal Press.

Needs Humor (satire of religion or of current religious leaders), anything of particular interest to atheists. "We rarely publish any fiction. But we have occasionally released a humorous book. No mainstream. For our press to consider fiction, it would have to tie in with the general focus of our press, which is the promotion of atheism and free thought."

How to Contact Submit outline, sample chapter(s). Responds in 4 months to queries. Accepts simultaneous submissions.

Terms Pays 5-10% royalty on retail price. Publishes ms within 2 years after acceptance. Ms guidelines for 9×12 SAE.

Advice "We will need more how-to types of material—how to argue with creationists, how to fight for state/church separation. etc. We have an urgent need for literature for young atheists."

AMERICAN PRINTING HOUSE FOR THE BLIND

1839 Frankfort Ave. P.O. Box 6085, Louisville KY 40206-0085. (800)223-1839. Fax: (502)899-2274. E-mail: info@aph.org. Website: www.aph.org. Estab. 1858. "We publish braille and/or large print versions of books, primarily textbooks for individuals who are blind or visually impaired. We do not accept non-published works."

How to Contact Does not accept unsolicited mss.

AMERICANA PUBLISHING, INC.

303 San Mateo N.E., Suite 104 A, Albuquerque NM 87108. (505)265-6121. Fax: (505)255-6189. E-mail: editor@americanabooks.com. Website: www.americanabooks.com. **Contact:** Managing editor. Small, independent pub-

lisher of audio books and print books. Publishes audiobooks, most previously published in print, and a few trade paperbacks. Averages 150 total titles, 8 fiction titles/year.

Needs Adventure, fantasy (space fantasy), historical, military/war, mystery (amateur sleuth, police procedural, private eye/hard-boiled), science fiction, thriller/espionage, western (frontier). "Does not accept short stories. Prefer 30,000-60,000 words. Prefer series. Does not want nonfiction, children's, poetry, sexually explicit, autobiographies, juvenile, gratuitous violence." Published *Beloved Leah*, by Cynthia Davis, and *The Killings*, by Lon Campanozzi.

How to Contact Accepts unsolicited mss. Query with SASE or submit 2 sample chapter(s). Accepts queries by e-mail, mail. Include estimated word count, brief bio, list of publishing credits. Send copy of ms and SASE. Agented fiction 20%. Responds in 6 months to queries; 6 months to mss. Accepts simultaneous submissions.

Terms Publishes ms 1-2 years after acceptance. Ms guidelines for #10 SASE.

☑ ☒ ◎ ANNICK PRESS, LTD.

15 Patricia Ave., Toronto ON M2M 1H9 Canada. (416)221-4802. Fax: (416)221-8400. E-mail: annick@annickpress.com. Website: www.annickpress.com. Publisher of children's books. Publishes hardcover and trade paperback originals. Average print order: 9,000. First novel print order: 7,000. Plans 18 first novels this year. Averages 25 total titles/year. Distributes titles through Firefly Books Ltd.

Needs Juvenile, young adult.

How to Contact Query with SASE. Responds in 1 month to queries; 3 months to mss. No simultaneous submissions, electronic submissions. Sometimes comments on rejected mss.

Terms Publishes ms 2 years after acceptance. Ms guidelines online.

◎ ANTARCTIC PRESS

7272 Wurzbach, Suite 204, San Antonio TX 78240. (210)614-0396. Website: www.antarctic-press.com. "Antarctic Press is a Texas-based company that was started in 1984. Since then, we have grown to become one of the largest publishers of comics in the United States. Over the years we have produced over 850 titles with a total circulation of over 5 million. Among our titles are some of the most respected and longest-running independent series in comics today. Since our inception, our main goal has been to establish a series of titles that are unique, entertaining, and high in both quality and profitability. The titles we currently publish exhibit all these traits, and appeal to a wide audience." Publishes comic books, graphic novels.

Terms Pays royalty on net receipts. Ms guidelines online.

☒ ☑ ◎ ANVIL PRESS

278 East First Avenue, Vancouver BC V5T 1A6 Canada. (604)876-8710. Fax: (604)879-2667. E-mail: info@anvilpress.com. Website: www.anvilpress.com. **Contact:** Brian Kaufman, publisher. Estab. 1988. "3-person operation with volunteer editorial board." Publishes trade paperback originals. Canadian authors *only*. Books: offset or web printing; perfect bound. **Published some debut authors within the last year.** Averages 8-10 total titles/year.

Needs Experimental, literary, short story collections. Contemporary, modern literature—no formulaic or genre. Published *The Beautiful Dead End*, by Clint Hutzulack; *Knucklehead*, by W. Mark Giles (short stories); *Bogman's Music*, by Tammy Armstrong (poetry); *Shylock*, by Mark Leiren-Young (drama); and *Socket*, by David Zimmerman (winner of the 3-day Novel-Writing Contest).

How to Contact Accepts unsolicited mss. Query with SASE. Include estimated word count, brief bio. Send SASE for return of ms or send a disposable ms and SASE for reply only. Responds in 2 months to queries; 6 months to mss. Accepts simultaneous submissions.

Terms Pays 15% royalty on net receipts. Average advance: $500. Publishes ms 8 months after acceptance. Book catalog for 9×12 SAE with 2 first-class stamps. Ms guidelines online.

Advice "We are only interested in writing that is progressive in some way—form, content. We want contemporary fiction from serious writers who intend to be around for a while and be a name people will know in years to come. Read back titles, look through our catalog before submitting."

☒ ☒ ARCADE PUBLISHING

141 Fifth Ave., New York NY 10010. (212)475-2633. **Contact:** Richard Seaver, Jeannette Seaver, Cal Barksdale and Casey Ebro. Estab. 1988. Independent publisher. Publishes hardcover originals, trade paperback reprints. Books: 50-55 lb. paper; notch, perfect bound; illustrations. **Published some debut authors within the last year.** Averages 45 total titles, 12-15 fiction titles/year. Distributes titles through Time Warner Book Group.

Needs Ethnic, literary, mainstream/contemporary, mystery, short story collections. Published *Trying to Save Piggy Sneed*, by John Irving; *Judge Savage*, by Tim Parks; *Music of a Life*, by Andrei Makine; *The Stowaway*, by Norbert Hough; and *Bibliophilia*, by Michael Griffith.

Book Publishers

How to Contact Does not accept unsolicited mss. *Agented submissions only.* Agented fiction 100%. Responds in 2 weeks to queries; 4 months to mss.
Terms Pays royalty on retail price. 10 author's copies. Offers advance. Publishes ms within 18 months after acceptance. Ms guidelines for #10 SASE.

ARIEL STARR PRODUCTIONS, LTD.

P.O. Box 17, Demarest NJ 07627. E-mail: darkbird@aol.com. Cynthia Sorona, president. Estab. 1991. Publishes paperback originals. **Published 2 debut authors within the last year.**
How to Contact Submit outline, 1 sample chapter(s). Accepts queries by e-mail, mail. Include brief bio. Send SASE or IRC. Responds in 6 weeks to queries; 4 months to mss. Sometimes comments on rejected mss.
Terms Publishes ms one year after acceptance.

ARJUNA LIBRARY PRESS

Journal of Regional Criticism, 1025 Garner St., D, Space 18, Colorado Springs CO 80905-1774. E-mail: druphoff@aol.com. Website: http://hometown.aol.com/druphoff/myhomepage/newsletter.html. Count Joseph A. Uphoff, Jr. *The Journal of Regional Criticism* has now expressed the mission of studying distinguishments within the context of general surrealism as special surrealism to generate complex movement. This ideology presents such compounds as cultural surrealism, ethnic surrealism, or surrealist abstraction. Publishes trade paperback originals. Averages 3-6 total titles/year.
Needs Adventure, experimental, fantasy, historical, horror, literary, occult, science fiction, surrealism. "The focus being surrealism, the composition should embody principles of the theory in a spirit of experimental inquiry."
How to Contact Submit complete ms. Accepts simultaneous submissions.
Terms Publishes ms 6 months after acceptance. Book catalog for $2. Ms guidelines for #10 SASE.
Advice "Literature is not a process of commercial nature; distinguished and publishable work offers more than excellent writing. There must be a quality of relevance that serves audience needs and curiosity."

ARSENAL PULP PRESS

1014 Homer St., Suite 103, Vancouver BC V6B 2W9 Canada. (604)687-4233. Fax: (604)687-4283. Website: www.arsenalpulp.com. **Contact:** Linda Field, editor. Estab. 1980. Literary press. Publishes hardcover and trade paperback originals and trade paperback reprints. **Published some debut authors within the last year.** Plans 15 first novels this year. Averages 20 total titles/year. Distributes titles through Whitecap Books (Canada) and Consortium (U.S.). Promotes titles through reviews, excerpts and print advertising.
Needs Gay/lesbian, literary, multicultural, regional (British Columbia), cultural studies, pop culture, political/sociological issues. No poetry.
How to Contact Accepts unsolicited mss. Submit outline, 2-3 sample chapter(s), synopsis. Include list of publishing credits. Send copy of ms and SASE. Agented fiction 10%. Responds in 2 months to queries; 4 months to mss. Accepts simultaneous submissions. Sometimes comments on rejected mss.
Terms Publishes ms 1 year after acceptance. Book catalog for 9×12 SAE with 2 first-class stamps or online. Ms guidelines for #10 SASE or online.
Advice "We are not currently considering mss by non-Canadian writers."

ARTE PUBLICO PRESS

University of Houston, 452 Cullen Performance Hall, Houston TX 77204-2004. Fax: (713)743-3080. Website: www.artepublicopress.com. **Contact:** Dr. Nicolas Kanellos, editor. Estab. 1979. "Small press devoted to the publication of contemporary U.S.-Hispanic literature." Publishes hardcover originals, trade paperback originals and reprints. Plans 25-50 first novels this year. Averages 36 total titles/year.
- Arte Publico Press is the oldest and largest publisher of Hispanic literature for children and adults in the United States.
Imprint(s) Pinata Books featuring children's and young adult literature by U.S.-Hispanic writers.
Needs Ethnic, literary, mainstream/contemporary; written by U.S.-Hispanic authors. Published *Project Death*, by Richard Bertematti (novel, mystery); *A Perfect Silence*, by Alba Ambert; *Song of the Hummingbird*, by Graciela Limon; and *Little Havana Blues: A Cuban-American Literature Anthology*.
How to Contact Accepts unsolicited mss. Query with SASE or submit 2 sample chapter(s), synopsis or submit complete ms. Agented fiction 1%. Responds in 2-4 months to queries; 3-6 months to mss. Accepts simultaneous submissions. Sometimes comments on rejected mss.
Terms Pays 10% royalty on wholesale price. Provides 20 author's copies; 40% discount on subsequent copies. Average advance: $1,000-3,000. Publishes ms 2 years after acceptance. Ms guidelines online.
Advice "Include cover letter in which you 'sell' your book—why should we publish the book, who will want to read it, why does it matter, etc."

✴ ARTEMIS PRESS

A division of SRS Internet Publishing, 236 W. Portal Avenue #525, San Francisco CA 94127. (866)216-7333. E-mail: submissions@artemispress.com. Website: www.artemispress.com. **Contact:** Susan R. Skolnick, publisher and editor-in-chief; Kathryn Flynn, editor. Estab. 2000. "Small electronic publisher of fiction and nonfiction titles of interest to the worldwide women's community. We specialize in feminist and lesbian-related titles but are interested in all women-centered titles. We are open to working with new authors and provide extremely personalized services." Publishes electronic editions and paperback editions of original, out-of-print and previously published titles. **Published 3 debut authors within the last year.** Plans 6 first novels this year. Titles distributed and promoted online and offline to target market.

Needs Feminist, lesbian, literary, historical, gender studies, mystery, new age/mystic, psychic/supernatural, romance, science fiction. Published *Moon Madness and Other Stories*, by Liann Snow (short story collection); *Faith in Love*, by Liann Snow (humor/satire); *Luna Ascendings: Stories of Love*, by Renee Brown (short story collection); *Window Garden*, by Janet McClellan (romance); *Never Letting Go*, by Suzanne Hollo (humor/satire); *Clicking Stones*, by Nancy Tyler Glenn (new age/mystic); *Minding Therapy*, by Ros Johnson (humor/satire); *200 Gang Girls*, by Joan Arndt (science fiction); *Against a White Sky*, by Laurie Stapleton (gender studies).

How to Contact No unsolicited mss. Query with SASE. Accepts e-mail queries. Include estimated word count, brief bio. Agented fiction 10%. Responds in 3 months to queries; 6 months to mss. Accepts simultaneous submissions, electronic submissions, disk submissions. Often comments on rejected mss.

Terms Pays 30% royalty. Publishes ms 6 months after acceptance. Ms guidelines online.

Advice "We like to see clean manuscripts and an indication that the author has proofed and self-edited before submitting. We work collaboratively with our authors in all phases of publication and expect the same efforts of our authors in return."

◪ ARX PUBLISHING

10 Canal Street, Suite 231, Bristol PA 19007. E-mail: info@arxpub.com. Website: www.arxpub.com. **Contact:** Claudio Salvucci, editor. Estab. 2001. Small independent publisher committed to publishing high-quality literature in the classical style. Publishes hardcover and paperback originals and hardcover reprints. Books: library, paperback binding; b&w illustrations. **Published 1 debut author within the last year.** Plans 1 first novel this year. Averages 10 total titles, 1 fiction title/year.

Needs Fantasy (sword and sorcery), historical (pre-modern), humor, literary, religious (religious fantasy), science fiction, young adult (adventure, fantasy/science fiction). Recently published *Mask of Ollock*, by Robert F. Kauffman (fantasy/epic poetry); *Niamh and the Hermit*, by Emily C.A. Snyder (fantasy/fairy tale).

How to Contact Does not accept or return unsolicited mss. Query with SASE. Accepts queries by e-mail, mail. Include estimated word count. Send SASE for return of ms or send a disposable ms and SASE for reply only. Responds in 1 week to queries; 2 months to mss. Accepts simultaneous submissions, electronic submissions. Rarely comments on rejected mss.

Terms Pays 5-10% royalty. Publishes ms 1 year after acceptance. Book catalog for SASE or on website. Ms guidelines online.

Advice "Authors we publish are well grounded in the literary classics: Vergil, Shakespeare, Tolkien, Hawthorne, etc, and are able to write 'high prose' with a good mastery of language. The story's morals must be unimpeachable and consistent with Judaeo-Christian philosophy. We will NOT publish anything New Age, Wicca or atheistic."

✴ ◪ ◎ ▨ ATHENEUM BOOKS FOR YOUNG READERS

Simon & Schuster, 1230 Avenue of the Americas, New York NY 10020. (212)698-2715. Fax: (212)698-2796. Website: www.simonsayskids.com. **Contact:** Caitlyn Dlouhy, executive editor; Richard Jackson, editorial director, Richard Jackson Books; Anne Schwartz, vice president and editorial director; Anne Schwartz Books. Estab. 1960. Atheneum Books for Young Readers is a hardcover imprint with a focus on literary fiction and fine picture books for preschoolers through young adults. Publishes special interest first novels and new talent. Books: illustrations for picture books, some illustrated short novels. Averages 75 total titles/year.

● In the past year, three books by Atheneum have received awards: *House of the Scorpion*, by Nancy Farmer, National Book Award; *Clever Beatrice*, by Margaret Willey, Charlotte Zolotow Award; and *Silent Night*, by Sandy Turner, Ragazzi Award.

Needs Adventure, ethnic, experimental, fantasy, gothic, historical, horror, humor, mainstream/contemporary, mystery, science fiction, sports, suspense, western, animal. "We have few specific needs except for books that are fresh, interesting and well written. Fad topics are dangerous, as are works you haven't polished to the best of your ability. (The competition is fierce.) Other things we don't need at this time are safety pamphlets, ABC books, coloring books and board books. In writing picture book texts, avoid the coy and 'cutesy,' such as stories about characters with alliterative names. *Query letter only are best.* We do not accept unsolicited mss." Published *Ben Franklin's Almanac*, by Candace Fleming (nonfiction); *If I were a Lion*, by Sarah Weeks and Heather

Soloman; *Seadogs*, by Lisa Wheeler; *Friction*, by E.R. Frank (YA novel); and *Audrey and Barbara*, by Janet Lawson (picture book fiction; debut author).

How to Contact Does not accept unsolicited mss. Query with SASE. Accepts queries by mail. Send SASE or IRC. Agented fiction 70%. Responds in 3 months to queries. Accepts simultaneous submissions.

Terms Pays 10% royalty on retail price. Average advance: $5,000-6,500 average. Publishes ms 18 months after acceptance. Ms guidelines for #10 SASE.

Advice "Write about what you know best. We look for original stories, unique and flavor-filled voices, and strong, evocative characters with whom a reader will readily embark on a literary journey."

AUNT LUTE BOOKS

P.O. Box 410687, San Francisco CA 94141. (415)826-1300. Fax: (415)826-8300. E-mail: books@auntlute.com. Website: www.auntlute.com. **Contact:** Shahara Godfrey, first reader. Small feminist and women-of-color press. Publishes hardcover and paperback originals. Averages 4 total titles/year.

Needs Ethnic, feminist, lesbian.

How to Contact Accepts unsolicited mss. Query with SASE or submit outline, sample chapter(s), synopsis. Send SASE or IRC. Responds in 4 months to mss.

Terms Pays royalty.

Advice "We seek manuscripts, both fiction and nonfiction, by women from a variety of cultures, ethnic backgrounds and subcultures; women who are self-aware and who, in the face of all contradictory evidence, are still hopeful that the world can reserve a place of respect for each woman in it. We seek work that explores the specificities of the worlds from which we come, and which examines the intersections between the borders which we all inhabit."

AVALON BOOKS

Thomas Bouregy & Co., Inc., 160 Madison Ave., 5th Floor, New York NY 10016. (212)598-0222. Fax: (212)979-1862. E-mail: editorial@avalonbooks.com. Website: www.avalonbooks.com. **Contact:** Erin Cartwright-Niumata, editorial director; Abby Holcomb, assistant editor. Estab. 1950. Publishes hardcover originals. **Published some debut authors within the last year.** Averages 60 total titles/year. Distributes titles through Baker & Taylor, libraries, Barnes&Noble.com and Amazon.com. Promotes titles through *Library Journal*, *Booklist* and local papers.

Needs Historical (romance), mystery, romance, western. "We publish wholesome contemporary romances, mysteries, historical romances and westerns. Our books are read by adults as well as teenagers, and the characters are all adults. All mysteries are contemporary. We publish contemporary romances (four every two months), historical romances (two every two months), mysteries (two every two months) and westerns (two every two months). Submit first 3 sample chapters, a 2-3 page synopsis and SASE. The manuscripts should be between 40,000 to 70,000 words. Manuscripts that are too long will not be considered. Time period and setting are the author's preference. The historical romances will maintain the high level of reading expected by our readers. The books shall be wholesome fiction, without graphic sex, violence or strong language. We are actively looking for romantic comedy, chick lit." Published *Last One Down*, by Joyce and Jim Lavene (mystery); *The Bride Wore Blood*, by Vicky Hunnings (mystery); *Cruising for Love*, by Tami D. Cowden (romantic comedy); *Pickup Lines*, by Holly Jacobs (romantic comedy).

How to Contact Does not accept unsolicited mss. Query with SASE. Send SASE or IRC. Responds in 1 month to queries; 6-10 months to mss.

Terms Average advance: $1,000+. Publishes ms 8-12 months after acceptance. Ms guidelines online.

AVON BOOKS

HarperCollins Publishers, 10 E. 53 Street, New York NY 10022. Website: www.harpercollins.com. **Contact:** Michael Morrison, publisher. Estab. 1941. Publishes hardcover and paperback originals and reprints. Averages 400 total titles/year.

Imprint(s) Avon, EOS.

Needs Historical, literary, mystery, romance, science fiction, young adult, health, pop culture.

How to Contact Does not accept unsolicited mss. Query with SASE. Send SASE or IRC.

Terms Varies.

BAEN PUBLISHING ENTERPRISES

P.O. Box 1403, Riverdale NY 10471-0671. (718)548-3100. E-mail: slush@baen.com. Website: www.baen.com. **Contact:** Jim Baen, publisher and editor; Toni Weisskopf, executive editor. Estab. 1983. "We publish books at the heart of science fiction and fantasy." Publishes hardcover, trade paperback and mass market paperback originals and reprints. **Published some debut authors within the last year.** Plans 2-3 first novels this year. Averages 120 total titles, 120 fiction titles/year. Distributes titles through Simon and Schuster.

Imprint(s) Baen Science Fiction and Baen Fantasy.

Needs Fantasy, science fiction. Interested in science fiction novels (based on real science) and fantasy novels "that at least strive for originality." Published *A Civil Campaign*, by Lois McMaster Bujold; *Ashes of Victory*, by David Weber; *Sentry Peak*, by Harry Turtledove.

How to Contact Accepts unsolicited mss. Submit synopsis or submit complete ms. Include estimated word count, brief bio. Send SASE or IRC. Responds in 8 months to queries; 1 year to mss. No simultaneous submissions. Sometimes comments on rejected mss.

Terms Pays royalty on retail price. Offers advance. Ms guidelines online.

Advice "Keep an eye and a firm hand on the overall story you are telling. Style is important but less important than plot. Good style, like good breeding, never calls attention to itself. Read *Writing to the Point*, by Algis Budrys. We like to maintain long-term relationships with authors."

★ ∅ ◎ BAKER BOOKS

Baker Book House Company, P.O. Box 6287, Grand Rapids MI 49516-6287. (616)676-9185. Fax: (616)676-2315. Website: www.bakerbooks.com. **Contact:** Jeanette Thomason, special projects editor (mystery, literary, women's fiction); Lonnie Hull DuPont, editoral director (all genres); Vicki Crumpton, aquisitions editor (all genres). Estab. 1939. "Midsize publisher of work that interests Christians." Publishes hardcover and trade paperback originals and trade paperback reprints. Books: web offset print. Plans 50 first novels this year. Averages 200 total titles/year. Distributes titles through Ingram and Spring Arbor into both CBA and ABA markets worldwide.

Needs Literary, mainstream/contemporary, mystery, picture books, religious. "We are mainly seeking fiction of two genres: contemporary women's fiction and mystery." Published *Praise Jerusalem!* and *Resting in the Bosom of the Lamb*, by Augusta Trobaugh (contemporary women's fiction); *Touches the Sky*, by James Schaap (western, literary); and *Face to Face*, by Linda Dorrell (mystery); *Flabergasted*, by Ray Blackston; *The Fisherman*, by Larry Huntsberger.

How to Contact Does not accept unsolicited mss. Sometimes comments on rejected mss.

Terms Pays 14% royalty on net receipts. Offers advance. Publishes ms within 1 year after acceptance. Ms guidelines for #10 SASE.

Advice "We are not interested in historical fiction, romances, science fiction, biblical narratives or spiritual warfare novels. Do not call to 'pass by' your idea."

★ Ⓐ BALLANTINE BOOKS

Random House, Inc., 1745 Broadway, New York NY 10019. (212)782-9000. Website: www.randomhouse.com/BB. Estab. 1952. "Ballantine's list encompasses a large, diverse offering in a variety of formats." Publishes hardcover, trade paperback, mass market paperback originals.

Imprint(s) Ballantine Books; Del Ray; Fawcett (mystery line); Ivy (romance); Library of Contemporary Thought; Lucas Books; One World; Wellspring.

Needs Confession, ethnic, fantasy, feminist, gay/lesbian, historical, humor, literary, mainstream/contemporary (women's), military/war, multicultural, mystery, romance, short story collections, spiritual, suspense, general fiction.

How to Contact *Agented submissions only.*

Terms Pays 8-15% royalty. Average advance: variable. Ms guidelines online.

▼ Ⓐ ◑ BANCROFT PRESS

P.O. Box 65360, Baltimore MD 21209-9945. (410)358-0658. Fax: (410)764-1967. Website: www.bancroftpress.com. **Contact:** Bruce Bortz, publisher (health, investments, politics, history, humor); Fiction Editor (literary novels, mystery/thrillers, young adult). "Small independent press publishing literary and commercial fiction, often by journalists." Publishes hardcover and trade paperback originals. Also packages books for other publishers (no fee to authors). **Published 2 debut authors within the last year.** Plans several first novels this year. Averages 4 total titles, 2-4 fiction titles/year.

● *The Re-Appearance of Sam Webber*, by Scott Fugua is an ALEX Award winner.

Needs Ethnic (general), family saga, feminist, gay/lesbian, glitz, historical, humor, lesbian, literary, mainstream/contemporary, military/war, mystery (amateur sleuth, cozy, police procedural, private eye/harboiled), new age/mystic, regional, science fiction (hard science/technological, soft/sociological), thriller/espionage, young adult (historical, problem novels, series), thrillers. "Our No. 1 priority is publishing books appropriate for young adults, ages 10-18. All quality books on any subject that fit that category will be considered." Published *Those Who Trespass*, by Bill O'Reilly (thriller); *The Re-Appearance of Sam Webber*, by Scott Fugua (literary); and *Malicious Intent*, by Mike Walker (Hollywood).

How to Contact Accepts unsolicited mss. Query with SASE or submit outline, 2 sample chapter(s), synopsis, by mail or e-mail or submit complete ms. Accepts queries by e-mail, fax. Include brief bio, list of publishing

credits. Send SASE for return of ms or send a disposable ms and SASE for reply only. Agented fiction 100%. Responds in 6-12 months to mss. Accepts simultaneous submissions. Sometimes comments on rejected mss.
Terms Pays 6-8% royalty. Pays various royalties on retail price. Average advance: $750. Publishes ms up to 3 years after acceptance. Ms guidelines online.
Advice "Be patient, send a sample, know your book's audience."

✪ BANTAM DELL PUBLISHING GROUP

Random House, Inc., 1745 Broadway, New York NY 10019. (212)782-9000. Fax: (212)782-8890. Website: www. bantamdell.com. Estab. 1945. "In addition to being the nation's largest mass market paperback publisher, Bantam publishes a select yet diverse hardcover list." Publishes hardcover, trade paperback and mass market paperback originals; mass market paperback reprints. Averages 350 total titles/year.
Imprint(s) Bantam Hardcover; Bantam Trade Paperback; Bantam Mass-Market; Delacorte Press; The Dial Press; Delta; Dell.
Needs Adventure, fantasy, horror.
How to Contact Accepts simultaneous submissions.
Terms Offers advance. Publishes ms 1 year after acceptance.

✪ Ⓐ ⓨ BANTAM DOUBLEDAY DELL BOOKS FOR YOUNG READERS

Random House Children's Publishing, Random House, Inc., 1745 Broadway, New York NY 10019. (212)782-9000. Fax: (212)782-8234. Website: www.randomhouse.com/kids. **Contact:** Michelle Poplof, editorial director. Publishes hardcover, trade paperback and mass market paperback series originals, trade paperback reprints. Averages 300 total titles/year.
• *Bud, Not Buddy*, by Christopher Paul Curtis won the Newberry Medal and the Coretta Scott King Award.
Imprint(s) Delacorte Books for Young Readers; Doubleday Books for Young Readers; Laurel Leaf; Skylark; Starfire; Yearling Books.
Needs Adventure, fantasy, historical, humor, juvenile, mainstream/contemporary, mystery, picture books, suspense, chapter books, middle-grade. Published *Bud, Not Buddy*, by Christopher Paul Curtis; *The Sisterhood of the Traveling Pants*, by Ann Brashares.
How to Contact Does not accept unsolicited mss. *Agented submissions only.* Responds in 2 months to queries; 4 months to mss. No simultaneous submissions.
Terms Pays royalty. Average advance: varied. Publishes ms 2 years after acceptance. Book catalog for 9×12 SASE.

Ⓝ Ⓒ BAREFOOT BOOKS

2067 Massachusetts Avenue, Cambridge MA 02140. (617)576-0660. Website: www.barefootbooks.com. **Contact:** Submissions editor. Publishes hardcover and trade paperback originals. **Published 35% debut authors within the last year.** Averages 30 total titles/year.
Needs Juvenile. Barefoot Books only publishes children's picture books and anthologies of folktales. "We do not publish novels. We do accept query letters but prefer full manuscripts." *Daddy Island*, by Philip Wells (picture book); *Fiesta Femenina: Celebrating Women in Mexican Folktale*, by Mary-Joan Gerson (illustrated anthology).
How to Contact Query with SASE or submit first page of ms. Responds in 4 months to mss. Accepts simultaneous submissions.
Terms Pays 2½-5% royalty on retail price or makes outright purchase of $5.99-19.99. Offers advance. Publishes ms 2 years after acceptance. Book catalog for 9×12 SAE stamped with $1.80 postage. Ms guidelines online.
Advice "Our audience is made up of children and parents, teachers and students of many different ages and cultures. Since we are a small publisher and we definitely publish for a 'niche' market, it is helpful to look at our books and our website before submitting, to see if your book would fit into our list."

◻ Ⓒ BARKING DOG BOOKS

758 Peralta Avenue, Berkeley CA 94708. (510)527-6274. E-mail: barkingdogbooks@yahoo.com. Michael Mercer, editor. Estab. 1996. "Focuses on expatriate life, especially in Mexico, and America viewed from exile." Publishes paperback originals. Books: quality paper; offset printing; perfect bound. Average print order: 1,000. Titles distributed through Sunbelt Publications.
Needs Ethnic (Mexican), experimental, historical, humor, literary, regional (Mexico/Southwest), short story collections, expatriate life. Published *Bandidos*, by Michael Mercer.
How to Contact Accepts unsolicited mss. Submit outline, 3 sample chapter(s). Accepts queries by mail. Include brief bio, list of publishing credits. Send copy of ms and SASE. Responds in 2 months to queries; 6 months to mss. Accepts simultaneous submissions. No submissions on disk. Sometimes comments on rejected mss.
Terms Publishes ms 1 year after acceptance.

Advice "Don't try to write for a market; write for yourself, be authentic, and trust readers to gravitate to an authentic voice."

⚓ ◎ BEACH HOLME PUBLISHERS, LTD.

1010-409 Granville Street, Vancouver BC V6C 1T2 Canada. (604)733-4868. Fax: (604)733-4860. Website: www.b eachholme.bc.ca. **Contact:** Michael Carroll, publisher; Sarah Warren, publicity and marketing coordinator. Estab. 1971. Publishes trade paperback originals. **Published 6 debut authors within the last year.** Averages 10-14 total titles/year. Titles distributed through LitDistCo (Canada and U.S.).

Imprint(s) Sandcastle Books (YA novels); Porcepic Books (literary fiction/poetry); Prospect Books (literary nonfiction).

Needs Experimental, literary, young adult (Canada historical/regional), adult literary fiction from authors published in Canadian literary magazines. Interested in excellent quality, imaginative writing from writers published in Canadian literary magazines. Published *Kameleon Man*, by Kim Bamy Brunhuber (literary fiction); *The View from Tamischeira*, by Richard Cumyn (novella).

How to Contact Query with SASE or submit outline, 2 sample chapter(s). Responds in 4-6 months to queries. No simultaneous submissions.

Terms Pays 10% royalty on retail price. Average advance: $500. Publishes ms 1 year after acceptance. Ms guidelines online.

Advice "Make sure the manuscript is well written. We see so many that only the unique and excellent can't be put down. Prior publication is a must. This doesn't necessarily mean book-length manuscripts, but a writer should try to publish his or her short fiction."

◎ BEARPAW PUBLISHING

9120 Thorton Rd., #343, Stockton CA 95209. (800)books04. E-mail: stories@bearpawpublishing.com. Website: www.bearpawpublishing.com. Estab. 2002. Publishes trade paperback originals. Averages 5 total titles/year.

Needs Adventure, confession, erotica, ethnic, fantasy, gay/lesbian, gothic, historical, horror, humor, mainstream/contemporary, military/war, multicultural, mystery, occult, romance, science fiction, short story collections, spiritual, sports, suspense, western. All submissions should include gay characters as the main characters. Sex in the book is requested but not required.

How to Contact Query with SASE or submit complete ms. Accepts queries by e-mail. Responds in 1 month to queries; 2 months to mss. No simultaneous submissions.

Terms Pays 10% royalty on wholesale price. Publishes ms 10 months after acceptance. Ms guidelines online.

◪ FREDERIC C. BEIL, PUBLISHER, INC.

609 Whitaker St., Savannah GA 31401. (912)233-2446. Fax: (912)233-6456. Website: www.beil.com. **Contact:** Frederic C. Beil III, president; Mary Ann Bowman, editor. Estab. 1982. "Our objectives are (1) to offer to the reading public carefully selected texts of lasting value; (2) to adhere to high standards in the choice of materials and bookmarking craftsmanship; (3) to produce books that exemplify good taste in format and design; and (4) to maintain the lowest cost consistent with quality." Publishes hardcover originals and reprints. Books: acid-free paper; letterpress and offset printing; Smyth-sewn, hardcover binding; illustrations. Plans 10 first novels this year. Averages 13 total titles, 4 fiction titles/year.

Imprint(s) The Sandstone Press, Hypermedia, Inc.

Needs Historical, literary, regional, short story collections, biography. Published *The Dry Well*, by Marlin Barton; *Joseph Jefferson*, by Arthur Bloom (biography); and *Goya, Are You With Me Now?*, by H.E. Francis (fiction).

How to Contact Does not accept unsolicited mss. Query with SASE. Responds in 2 weeks to queries. Accepts simultaneous submissions.

Terms Pays 7½% royalty on retail price. Publishes ms 20 months after acceptance.

Advice "Write about what you love."

Ｎ ♥ BEN BELLA BOOKS

6440 N. Central Expy Suite 508, Dallas TX 75206. (214)750-3600. Fax: (214)750-3645. E-mail: shanna@benbella books.com. Website: www.benbellabooks.com. Shanna Caughey, editor; Leah Wilson, associate editor. Estab. 2001. Small, growing independent publisher specializing in popular culture, smart nonfiction and science fiction; our fiction is largely reprints or by established authors. Publishes harcover and paperback originals and paperback reprints. **Published 1 debut authors within the last year.** Averages 20 total titles, 5-10 fiction titles/year. Distributed through the Independent Publishers Group.

Needs Fantasy, science fiction (hard science/technological, soft/sociological), short story collections, thriller/espionage. Published *Blood and Fire*, by David Gerrold (science fiction); *The Listeners*, by James Gunn (science fiction); and *Those of My Blood*, by Jacqueline Lichtenberg (fantasy).

How to Contact Accepts unsolicited mss. Submit 1-3 sample chapter(s). Accepts queries by e-mail, mail. Include list of publishing credits. Send SASE for return of ms or send a disposable ms and SASE for reply only. Agented fiction 75%. Responds in 1 month to mss. Accepts simultaneous submissions, electronic submissions. Rarely comments on rejected mss.

Terms Pays royalty.

✸ Ⓐ THE BERKLEY PUBLISHING GROUP

Penguin Putnam, Inc., 375 Hudson St., New York NY 10014. (212)366-2000. E-mail: online@penguinputnam.com. Website: www.penguinputnam.com. Estab. 1954. "Berkley is proud to publish in paperback some of the country's most significant best-selling authors." Publishes paperback and mass market originals and reprints. Averages approximately 800 total titles/year.

Imprint(s) Ace Books, Berkley Books, HP Books, Perigee, Riverhead Books.

Needs Adventure, historical, literary, mystery, romance, spiritual, suspense, western, young adult.

How to Contact Query with SASE. Responds in 6 weeks to queries. No simultaneous submissions.

Terms Pays 4-15% royalty on retail price. Offers advance. Publishes ms 2 years after acceptance.

◨ ◉ BETHANY HOUSE PUBLISHERS

11400 Hampshire Ave. S., Minneapolis MN 55438. (952)829-2500. Fax: (952)829-2768. Website: www.bethanyhouse.com. Estab. 1956. "The purpose of Bethany House Publisher's publishing program is to relate biblical truth to all areas of life—whether in the framework of a well-told story, of a challenging book for spiritual growth, or of a Bible reference work." Publishes hardcover and trade paperback originals, mass market paperback reprints. Averages 90-100 total titles/year.

Needs Adventure, children's/juvenile, historical, juvenile, young adult. Published *The Still of Night*, by Kristen Heitzmann (fiction).

How to Contact Does not accept unsolicited mss. Accepts queries by fax. Accepts simultaneous submissions.

Terms Pays negotiable royalty on net price. Average advance: negotiable. Publishes ms 1 year after acceptance. Ms guidelines online.

◨ ◉ BILINGUAL PRESS

Hispanic Research Center, Arizona State University, P.O. Box 872702, Tempe AZ 85287-2702. (480)965-3867. Fax: (480)965-8309. E-mail: brp@asu.edu. Website: www.asu.edu/brp. **Contact:** Gary Keller, editor. Estab. 1973. "University affiliated." Publishes hardcover and paperback originals and reprints. Books: 60 lb. acid-free paper; single sheet or web press printing; perfect-bound. **Published several debut authors within the last year.**

Needs Ethnic, literary, short story collections. Always seeking Chicano, Puerto Rican, Cuban-American or other U.S. Hispanic themes with strong and serious literary qualities and distinctive and intellectually important themes. Does *not* publish children's literature or trade genres such as travelogues and adventure fiction. Novels set in a pre-Columbian past are not likely to be published. Published *Moving Target: A Memoir of Pursuit*, by Ron Arias; *Contemporary Chicano and Chicana Art: Artists, Works, Culture, and Education*, Gary Keller et al; *Assumption and Other Stories*, by Daniel A. Olivas; *Renaming Ecstasy: Latino Writings on the Sacred*, edited by Orlando Ricardo Menes.

How to Contact Accepts unsolicited mss. Query with SASE or submit 2-3 sample chapter(s). Accepts queries by e-mail, mail. Include brief bio, list of publishing credits. Send SASE or IRC. Responds in 6 weeks to queries; 2-6 months to mss.

Terms Pays 10% royalty. Average advance: $500. Publishes ms 2 years after acceptance. Ms guidelines by e-mail.

Advice "Writers should take the utmost care in assuring that their manuscripts are clean, grammatically impeccable, and have perfect spelling. This is true not only of the English but the Spanish as well. All accent marks need to be in place as well as other diacritical marks. When these are missing it's an immediate first indication that the author does not really know Hispanic culture and is not equipped to write about it. We are interested in publishing creative literature that treats the U.S Hispanic experience in a distinctive, creative, revealing way. The kind of books that we publish we keep in print for a very long time irrespective of sales. We are busy establishing and preserving a U.S. Hispanic canon of creative literature."

◉ BIRCH BROOK PRESS

P.O. Box 81, Delhi NY 13753. Fax: (607)746-7453. Website: www.birchbrookpress.info. **Contact:** Tom Tolnay, publisher. Estab. 1982. Small publisher of popular culture and literary titles in handcrafted letterpress editions. Specializes in fiction anthologies with specific theme, and an occasional novella. "Not a good market for full-length novels." Publishes hardcover and trade paperback originals. Books: 80 lb. vellum paper; letterpress printing; wood engraving illustrations. Averages 4 total titles, 2 fiction titles/year. Member, Small Press Center, Academy of American Poets. Distributes titles through Baker and Taylor, Barnes&Noble.com, Amazon.com,

Book Publishers

Gazelle Book Services in Europe. Promotes titles through website, catalogs, direct mail and group ads.

Imprint(s) Birch Brook Press; Persephone Press and Birch Brook Impressions.

Needs Literary, regional (Adirondacks), popular culture, special interest (fly-fishing, baseball, books about books, outdoors). "Mostly we do anthologies around a particular theme generated inhouse. We make specific calls for fiction when we are doing an anthology." Published *Magic and Madness in the Library*, edited by Eric Graeber (fiction collection); *Life & Death of a Book*, by William MacAdams; *Fateful Choices*, edited by Marshall Brooks and Stephanie Greene; *A Punk in Gallows America*, by P.W. Fox; *White Buffalo*, by Peter Skinner; *Cooperstown Chronicles*, by Peter Rutkoff; *The Suspense of Loneliness* (anthology).

How to Contact Query with SASE or submit sample chapter(s), synopsis. Responds in 1-2 months to queries. Accepts simultaneous submissions. Sometimes comments on rejected mss.

Terms Royalty varies. Average advance: modest. Publishes ms 1-2years after acceptance. Ms guidelines for #10 SASE.

Advice "Write well on subjects of interest to BBP such as outdoors, fly fishing, baseball, music, literary novellas, books about books, cultural history."

BKMK PRESS

University of Missouri-Kansas City, 5101 Rockhill Rd., Kansas City MO 64110-2499. (816)235-2558. Fax: (816)235-2611. E-mail: bkmk@umkc.edu. Website: www.umkc.edu/bkmk. Estab. 1971. Publishes trade paperback originals. Averages 5-6 total titles/year.

Needs Literary, short story collections.

How to Contact Query with SASE or submit 3 sample chapter(s). Responds in 8 months to mss. Accepts simultaneous submissions.

Terms Pays 10% royalty on wholesale price. Publishes ms 1 year after acceptance. Ms guidelines online.

BLACK LACE BOOKS

Virgin Books, Thames Wharf Studio, Rainville Road, London W6 9HA United Kingdom. +44 (0207) 386 3300. Fax: +44 (0207) 386 3360. E-mail: ksharp@virgin-books.co.uk. Website: www.blacklace-books.co.uk. **Contact:** Kerri Sharp, senior commissioning editor. Estab. 1993. Publishes paper originals.

Imprint(s) Nexus Fetish Erotic Fiction for Men (Paul Copperwaite, editor); Black Lace Erotic Fiction for Women (Kerri Sharp, editor). "Nexus and Black Lace are the leading imprints of erotic fiction in the UK."

Needs Erotica. "Female writers only for the Black Lace Series." Especially needs erotic fiction in contemporary settings. Publishes 2 erotic short story anthologies by women per year.

How to Contact Accepts unsolicited mss. Query with SASE. Include estimated word count. Agented fiction 25%. Responds in 1 month to queries; 8-12 months to mss. No simultaneous submissions. Always comments on rejected mss.

Terms Pays 7½% royalty. Average advance: £1,000. Publishes ms 7 months after acceptance. Ms guidelines online.

Advice "Contemporary settings are strongly preferred. Open to female authors only. Read the guidelines first."

JOHN F. BLAIR, PUBLISHER

1406 Plaza Dr., Winston-Salem NC 27103-1470. (336)768-1374. Fax: (336)768-9194. Website: www.blairpub.com. **Contact:** Carolyn Sakowski, president. Estab. 1954. Small, independent publisher. Publishes hardcover originals and trade paperbacks. Books: Acid-free paper; offset printing; illustrations. Averages 20 total titles/year.

Needs Prefers regional material dealing with southeastern U.S. "We publish one work of fiction per season relating to the Southeastern U.S. Our editorial focus concentrates mostly on nonfiction." Published *The Minotaur Takes a Cigarette Break*, by Steven Sherrill; *Lord Baltimore*, by Stephen Doster.

How to Contact Accepts unsolicited mss. Query with SASE or submit complete ms. Send SASE or IRC. Responds in 3 months to queries. Accepts simultaneous submissions.

Terms Royalty negotiable. Offers advance. Publishes ms 18 months after acceptance. Book catalog for 9×12 SAE with 5 first-class stamps. Ms guidelines online.

Advice "We are primarily interested in nonfiction titles. Most of our titles have a tie-in with North Carolina or the southeastern United States. Please enclose a cover letter and outline with the manuscript. We prefer to review queries before we are sent complete manuscripts. Queries should include an approximate word count."

BLEAK HOUSE BOOKS

953 E. Johnson Street, Madison WI 53703. (608)259-8370. E-mail: submissions@bleakhousebooks.com. Website: www.bleakhousebooks.com. Benjamin LeRoy, editor-in-chief. Estab. 1995. "We aren't afraid of longshot projects." Publishes hardcover and paperback originals. Books: 60 lb. offset paper; offset or digitally printed; perfect-bound. Average print order: 1,000. **Published 2-3 debut authors within the last year.** Averages 6-8

Book Publishers

total titles, 6 fiction titles/year. Member: PMA. Distributes titles through National Book Network, Baker & Taylor and Ingram.

Needs Literary, mystery (amateur sleuth, cozy, police procedural, private eye/hard-boiled), thriller/espionage, psychological. Needs "good psychological or suspense. Not formulaic, but well-thought-out plots and characters that get inside the reader's head." Published *The Nail Knot*, by John Galligan (mystery); *A Prayer for Dawn*, by Nathan Singer (literary); and *Blood of The Lamb*, by Michael Lister (mystery).

How to Contact Does not accept unsolicited mss. Query with SASE. Include estimated word count, brief bio, list of publishing credits. Agented fiction 35%. Responds in 2 weeks to queries; 2 months to mss. Accepts simultaneous submissions. No electronic submissions.

Terms Pays 6-15% royalty. Average advance: negotiable. Publishes ms 12-18 months after acceptance. Ms guidelines online.

Advice "We are growing and often very busy. Please have patience with publishers and agents. We will accept simultaneous submissions, but please note as such. We no longer accept unsolicited manuscripts. Our mission is to publish a wide range of dark fiction that goes from literary to mystery. Please, if you value your work, make sure it is well edited before sending it out."

THE BOOKS COLLECTIVE

214-21, 10405 Jasper Ave., Edmonton AB T5J 3S2 Canada. (780)448-0590. Fax: (780)448-0640. E-mail: admin@bookscollective.com. Website: www.bookscollective.com. **Contact:** Candas J. Dorsey or Timothy J. Anderson. Estab. 1992. "Small independent publisher of Canadian literary fiction, poetry, contemporary memoir and speculative." Publishes hardcover and trade paperback originals. Averages 4-8 total titles/year.

• *Tinka's New Dress*, by Ronnie Burkett won the Melbourne Age Critics Award.

Imprint(s) River/Slipstream Books (various non-genre); Dinosaur Soup Books (fiction for children); Partners in Design Books (architecture).

Needs Experimental, feminist, gay/lesbian, literary, mainstream/contemporary, multicultural, multimedia, regional, short story collections. River/Slipstream publishes a variety of work; Dinosaur Soup Books publishes books by Gerri Cook; Partners in Design Books has a focus on sustainable architecture. Published *Green Music*, by Ursula Pflug (speculative fiction); *Gypsy Messenger*, by Marijan Megla (poetry); and *Running Through the Devil's Club*, by Deborah Huford (nonfiction, debut author).

How to Contact Accepts unsolicited mss. Submit complete ms. Send SASE or IRC. Responds in 1 month to queries; 6 months to mss. No simultaneous submissions, electronic submissions. Sometimes comments on rejected mss.

Terms Pays 6-12% royalty on retail price. Average advance: $250-500 (Canadian). Publishes ms 1 year after acceptance. Ms guidelines online.

Advice "Only Canadian writers have their manuscripts read. All non-Canadian writers' manuscripts returned unread. Canadian writers living abroad must use Canadian stamps on SASEs. Most of our books are solicited by the press. Timelines for manuscript consideration are long."

BOOKS FOR ALL TIMES, INC.

Box 202, Warrenton VA 20188. Website: www.bfat.com. **Contact:** Joe David, publisher/editor. Estab. 1981. One-man operation. Publishes paperback originals.

Needs Literary, mainstream/contemporary, short story collections. "No novels at the moment; hopeful, though, of publishing a collection of quality short stories. No popular fiction or material easily published by the major or minor houses specializing in mindless entertainment. Only interested in stories of the Victor Hugo or Sinclair Lewis quality."

How to Contact Query with SASE. Responds in 1 month to queries. Sometimes comments on rejected mss.

Terms Pays negotiable advance. "Publishing/payment arrangement will depend on plans for the book."

Advice Interested in "controversial, honest stories which satisfy the reader's curiosity to know. Read Victor Hugo, Fyodor Dostoyevsky and Sinclair Lewis for example."

BOREALIS PRESS, LTD.

8 Mohawk Crescent, Nepean ON K2H 7G6 Canada. (613)829-0150. Fax: (613)798-9747. E-mail: drt@borealispress.com. Website: www.borealispress.com. **Contact:** Frank Tierney, editor; Glenn Clever, editor. Estab. 1972. "Publishes Canadiana, especially early works that have gone out of print, but also novels of today and shorter fiction for young readers." Publishes hardcover and paperback originals and reprints. Books: standard book-quality paper; offset printing; perfect bound. **Published some debut authors within the last year.** Averages 10-20 total titles/year. Promotes titles through website, catalogue distribution, fliers for titles, ads in media.

• Borealis Press has a "New Canadian Drama," with 7 books in print. The series won Ontario Arts Council and Canada Council grants.

Imprint(s) *Journal of Canadian Poetry*, Tecumseh Press Ltd., Canadian Critical Editions Series.

Needs Adventure, ethnic, historical, juvenile, literary, mainstream/contemporary, romance, short story collections, young adult. "Only material Canadian in content and dealing with significant aspects of the human situation." Published *Blue: Little Cat Come Home to Stay*, by Donna Richards (young adult); *Biography of a Beagle*, by Gail MacMillan (novel); *The Love of Women*, by Jennifer McVaugh (comic novel).

How to Contact Query with SASE or submit 1-2 sample chapter(s), synopsis. Accepts queries by e-mail, fax. Responds in 2 months to queries; 4 months to mss. No simultaneous submissions.

Terms Pays 10% royalty on net receipts. 3 free author's copies. Publishes ms 18 months after acceptance. Ms guidelines online.

Advice "Have your work professionally edited. Our greatest challenge is finding good authors, i.e., those who submit innovative and original material."

⊠ Ⓝ ◓ BOSON BOOKS

C & M Online Media, Inc., 3905 Meadow Field Lane, Raleigh NC 27606. (919)233-8164. Fax: (919)233-8578. E-mail: cm@cmonline.com. Website: www.cmonline.com. **Contact:** Aquisitions Editor. Estab. 1994. "We are an online book company with distribution through distributors such as CyberRead.com, powells.com, ebooks.com, mobipocket.com and Amazon.com." Publishes online originals and reprints. **Published 6 debut authors within the last year.** Member, Association of Online Publishers.

Needs "The quality of writing is our only consideration."

How to Contact Query with SASE. Accepts queries by e-mail.

Terms Pays 25% royalty.

Advice "We want to see only excellence in writing."

◉ ◎ BOYDS MILLS PRESS

Highlights for Children, 815 Church St., Honesdale PA 18431-1895. (570)253-1164. E-mail: contact@boydsmillspress.com. Website: www.boydsmillspress.com. **Contact:** Larry Rosler, editorial director. Estab. 1990. "Independent publisher of quality books for children of all ages." Publishes hardcover originals and trade paperback reprints. Books: coated paper; offset printing; case binding; 4-color illustrations. **Published 5 debut authors within the last year.** Averages 50 total titles, 4 fiction titles/year. Distributes titles through independent sales reps and via order line directly from Boyds Mills Press. Promotes titles through sales and professional conferences, sales reps, reviews.

Needs Adventure, ethnic, historical, humor, juvenile, mystery, picture books, young adult (adventure, animal, contemporary, ethnic, historical, humor, mystery, sports). "We look for imaginative stories or concepts with simple, lively language that employs a variety of literary devices, including rhythm, repitition, and when composed properly, rhyme. The stories may entertain or challenge, but the content must be age-appropriate for children. For middle and young adult fiction we look for stories told in strong, considered prose driven by well-imagined characters." Published *Sharks! Strange and Wonderful*, by Laurence Pringle; *Groover's Heart*, by Carole Crowe; and *Storm's Coming!*, by Audrey B. Baird.

How to Contact Accepts unsolicited mss. Query with SASE. Agented fiction 30%. Responds in 1 month to mss. Accepts simultaneous submissions.

Terms Pays royalty on retail price. Average advance: variable.

Advice "Read through our recently-published titles and review our catalogue. If your book is too different from what we publish, then it may not fit our list. Feel free to query us if you're not sure."

◉ BRANDEN PUBLISHING CO., INC.

P.O. Box 812094, Wellesley MA 02482. (781)235-3634. Fax: (781)790-1056. Website: www.branden.com. **Contact:** Adolph Caso, editor. Estab. 1909. Publishes hardcover and trade paperback originals, reprints and software. Books: 55-60 lb. acid-free paper; case—or perfect-bound; illustrations. Averages 15 total titles, 5 fiction titles/year.

Imprint(s) I.P.L; Dante University Press; Four Seas; Branden Publishing Co., Branden Books.

Needs Ethnic (histories, integration), historical, literary, military/war, religious (historical-reconstructive), short story collections. Looking for "contemporary, fast pace, modern society." Published *I, Morgain*, by Harry Robin; *The Bell Keeper*, by Marilyn Seguin; and *The Straw Obelisk*, by Adolph Caso.

How to Contact Does not accept unsolicited mss. Query with SASE. Responds in 1 month to queries.

Terms Pays 5-10% royalty on net receipts. 10 author's copies. Average advance: $1,000 maximum. Publishes ms 10 months after acceptance.

Advice "Publishing more fiction because of demand. *Do not make phone, fax or e-mail inquiries.* Do not oversubmit; single submissions only; do not procrastinate if contract is offered. Our audience is well-read general public, professionals, college students and some high school students. We like books by or about women."

▣ ▢ ◎ BREAKAWAY BOOKS

P.O. Box 24, Halcottsville NY 12438. (212)898-0408. Website: www.breakawaybooks.com. **Contact:** Garth Battista, publisher. Estab. 1994. "Small press specializing in fine literary books on sports. We have a new line of children's illustrated books (ages 3-7)—dealing with sports, especially running, cycling, triathlon, swimming and boating (canoes, kayaks, sailboats). Publishes hardcover and trade paperback originals. **Published 3 debut authors within the last year.** Averages 8-10 total titles, 5 fiction titles/year.

Needs Short story collections (sports stories).

How to Contact Accepts unsolicited mss. Query with SASE or submit complete ms. Accepts queries by e-mail. Include brief bio, list of publishing credits. Send SASE for return of ms or send a disposable ms and SASE for reply only. Agented fiction 50%. Responds in 1 month to queries; 2 months to mss. Accepts simultaneous submissions, electronic submissions. Rarely comments on rejected mss.

Terms Pays 6-15% royalty on retail price. Average advance: $2,000-3,000. Publishes ms 9 months after acceptance. Book catalog and ms guidelines free, ms guidelines online.

▢ BRITTON ROAD PRESS

P.O. Box 044618, Racine WI 53404-7013. (262)632-5339. Fax: (262)633-5503. E-mail: group500@execpc.com. Website: www.brittonroadpress.com. **Contact:** Jay E. Frances, editor; Lilo Solmsen, assistant editor. Estab. 1998. Brittton Road Press is a small, independent publisher. Publishes paperback and hardcover originals. Average print order: 2,000 copies. **Published 2 debut authors within the last year.** Member: SPAN.

Needs Children's/juvenile, literary, mainstream/contemporary, mystery, science fiction, young adult. Published *The Door in the Road*, by Genevieve Sesto (mainstream fiction); *The Pomelo Tree*, by Dominic J. Cibrario (mainstream fiction).

How to Contact Accepts unsolicited mss. Submit 3 sample chapter(s). Include brief bio, list of publishing credits. Send SASE or IRC. Agented fiction 20%. Responds in 4 weeks to queries; 4 months to mss. Accepts simultaneous submissions. Never comments on rejected mss.

Terms Pays 3% royalty. Publishes ms 12-18 months after acceptance.

▢ ◎ BROADMAN & HOLMAN

LifeWay Christian Resources, 127 Ninth Ave. N., Nashville TN 37234. (615)251-2392. Fax: (615)251-3752. Website: www.broadmanholman.com. **Contact:** Leonard G. Goss, editorial director (historical, romance, contemporary, suspense, western, thrillers, etc.). Estab. 1934. "Large, commericial, evangelical Christian publishing firm. We publish Christian fiction in all genres." Publishes hardcover and paperback originals. **Published 10 debut authors within the last year.** Averages 90 total titles, 25 fiction titles/year. Member: ECPA. Distributes and promotes titles "on a national and international scale through a large sales organization."

Needs Adventure, mystery, religious (general religious, inspirational, religious fantasy, religious mystery/suspense, religious thriller, religious romance), western. "We publish fiction in all the main genres. We want not only a very good story, but also one that sets forth Christian values. Nothing that lacks a positive Christian emphasis (but do NOT preach, however); nothing that fails to sustain reader interest." Published *Sea of Glory*, by Ken Wales and David Poling (historical, debut author); *The Third Dragon*, by Frank Simon (mystery/intrigue); and *Friends and Enemies*, by Steve Bly (western).

How to Contact Does not accept unsolicited mss. Query with SASE. Accepts queries by e-mail. Include estimated word count, brief bio, list of publishing credits. Send copy of ms and SASE. Agented fiction 50%. Responds in 3 months to queries. Accepts simultaneous submissions. No electronic submissions, submissions on disk. Sometimes comments on rejected mss.

Terms Pays negotiable royalty. Publishes ms 10 months after acceptance. Ms guidelines for #10 SASE.

▣ Ⓐ BROADWAY BOOKS

Doubleday Broadway Publishing Group, Random House, Inc., 1745 Broadway, New York NY 10019. (212)782-9000. Fax: (212)782-9411. E-mail: (first initial + last name)@randomhouse.com. Website: www.broadwaybooks.com. **Contact:** William Thomas, editor-in-chief. Estab. 1995. Broadway publishes general interest nonfiction and fiction for adults. Publishes hardcover and trade paperback originals and reprints.

Needs Publishes a limited list of commercial literary fiction. Published *Freedomland*, by Richard Price.

How to Contact *Agented submissions only.*

◎ ▦ BROWN SKIN BOOKS

Pentimento, Ltd., P.O. Box 46504, London N1 3NT United Kingdom. E-mail: info@brownskinbooks.co.uk. Website: www.brownskinbooks.co.uk. Estab. 2002. Publishes trade paperback originals. Averages 7 total titles/year.

Needs Erotica. "We are looking for erotic short stories or novels written by women of color."

How to Contact Submit proposal package including 2 sample chapter(s), synopsis. Responds in 1 month to queries; 2 months to mss. Accepts simultaneous submissions.
Terms Pays 5-50% royalty or makes outright purchase. Publishes ms 6 months after acceptance. Ms guidelines online.

⊘ ◎ CALYX BOOKS

P.O. Box B, Corvallis OR 97339-0539. (541)753-9384. Fax: (541)753-0515. **Contact:** M. Donnelly, director. Estab. 1986 for Calyx Books; 1976 for Calyx, Inc. "Calyx exists to publish women's literary and artistic work and is committed to publishing the works of all women, including women of color, older women, lesbians, working-class women, and other voices that need to be heard." Publishes fine literature by women—fiction, nonfiction and poetry. Publishes hardcover and paperback originals. Books: offset printing; paper and cloth binding. **Published 1 debut author within the last year.** Averages 1-2 total titles/year. Distributes titles through Consortium Book Sale and Distribution. Promotes titles through author reading tours, print advertising (trade and individuals), galley and review copy mailings, presence at trade shows, etc.
Needs Ethnic, experimental, feminist, lesbian, literary, mainstream/contemporary, short story collections. Published *Forbidden Stitch: An Asian American Women's Anthology; Women and Aging: Present Tense; Writing and Art by Young Women;* and *A Line of Cutting Women.*
How to Contact Responds in 1 year to queries.
Terms Pays 10-15% royalty on net receipts. Average advance: depends on grant support. Publishes ms 2 years after acceptance. Ms guidelines for #10 SASE.
Advice Closed for submissions until further notice.

◎ ✶ CANDLEWICK PRESS

2067 Massachusetts Ave., Cambridge MA 02140. (617)661-3330. Fax: (617)661-0565. E-mail: bigbear@candlewick.com. Website: www.candlewick.com. **Contact:** Joan Powers, editor-at-large; Liz Bicknell, editorial director/associate publisher (poetry, picture books, fiction); Mary Lee Donovan, executive editor (picture books, fiction); Kara LaReau, senior editor (picture books, fiction); Sarah Ketchersid, editor (board, toddler). Estab. 1991. "We are a truly child-centered publisher." Publishes hardcover originals, trade paperback originals and reprints. Averages 200 total titles/year.
- *The Tale of Despereaux,* by Kate DiCamillo won the 2004 Newbery Medal.

Needs Juvenile, picture books, young adult. Published *The Tale of Despereaux,* by Kate DiCamillo; *Judy Moody,* by Megan McDonald, illustrated by Peter Reynolds, *Feed,* by M.T. Anderson; *Fairie-ality,* by Eugenie Bird, photographs by David Ellwand, illustrations by David Downton.
How to Contact Does not accept unsolicited mss.

Ⓝ ◯ CAROLINA WREN PRESS

120 Morris St., Durham NC 27701. (919)560-2738. E-mail: carolina@carolinawrenpress.org. Website: www.carolinawrenpress.org. **Contact:** Andrea Selch, president. Estab. 1976. "We publish poetry, fiction, nonfiction, biography, autobiography, literary nonfiction work by and/or about people of color, women, gay/lesbian issues, health and mental health topics in children's literature." Books: 6×9 paper; typeset; various bindings; illustrations. **Published 1 debut authors within the last year.** Plans 15 first novels this year. Member: SPD. Distributes titles through Amazon.com, Barnes & Noble, Borders, Ingram and Baker & Taylor.
Needs "We read unsolicited manuscripts of fiction and nonfiction September-December."
How to Contact Accepts unsolicited mss. Accepts queries by e-mail, mail. Include brief bio. Send SASE or IRC. Responds in 3 months to queries; 6 months to mss.
Terms Publishes ms 1 year after acceptance. Ms guidelines online.
Advice "Please read our mission statement online before submitting."

✪ ⊘ ◎ CAROLRHODA BOOKS, INC.

Lerner Publishing Group, 241 First Ave. N., Minneapolis MN 55401. Fax: (612)332-7615. Website: www.lernerbooks.com. **Contact:** Rebecca Poole, submissions editor. Estab. 1969. Carolrhoda Books seeks creative picture books, middle-grade fiction, historical fiction and K-6 children's nonfiction. Publishes hardcover originals. Averages 50-60 total titles/year.
Needs Historical, juvenile, multicultural, picture books, young reader, middle grade and young adult fiction. "We continue to add fiction for middle grades and 8-10 picture books per year. Not looking for folktales or anthropomorphic animal stories." Recently published *The War,* by Anais Vaugelade; *Little Wolf's Haunted Hall for Small Horrors,* by Ian Whybrow.
How to Contact Submit complete ms. Responds in 8 months to queries. Accepts simultaneous submissions.
Terms Pays royalty on wholesale price or makes outright purchase. Negotiates payments of advance against royalty. Average advance: varied. Book catalog for 9×12 SAE with $3.50 postage. Ms guidelines online.

⬛ Ⓐ ☺ CARROLL & GRAF PUBLISHERS, INC.

Avalon Publishing Group, 245 W. 17th St. 11th floor, New York NY 10011. (212) 981-9919. Fax: (646)375-2571. Website: www.avalonpub.com. **Contact:** Will Balliett, publisher; Phillip Turner, editor-in-chief; Don Weine, editor. Estab. 1982. Publishes hardcover and trade paperback originals. Averages 120 total titles, 50 fiction titles/year.

Needs Literary, mainstream/contemporary, mystery, science fiction, suspense, thriller. Published *The Woman Who Wouldn't Talk*, by Susan McDougal.

How to Contact Does not accept unsolicited mss. *Agented submissions only.* Query with SASE. Send SASE or IRC. Responds in a timely fashion to queries. Sometimes comments on rejected mss.

Terms Pays 10-15% royalty on retail price for hardcover, 6-7½% for paperback. Offers advance commensurate with the work. Publishes ms 9-18 months after acceptance.

⬛ Ⓐ ◎ CARTWHEEL BOOKS

Scholastic, Inc., 557 Broadway, New York NY 10012. (212)343-6200. Website: www.scholastic.com. **Contact:** Grace Maccarone, executive editor; Sonia Black, senior editor; Jane Gerver, executive editor. Estab. 1991. "Cartwheel Books publishes innovative books for children, ages 3-9. We are looking for 'novelties' that are books first, play objects second. Even without its gimmick, a Cartwheel Book should stand alone as a valid piece of children's literature." Publishes novelty books, easy readers, board books, hardcover and trade paperback originals. Averages 85-100 total titles/year.

Needs Children's/juvenile (fantasy, horror, mystery, picture books, science fiction, holiday/seasonal), humor, mystery, picture books. "Again, the subject should have mass market appeal for very young children. Humor can be helpful, but not necessary. Mistakes writers make are a reading level that is too difficult, a topic of no interest or too narrow, or manuscripts that are too long." Published *Little Bill*, series, by Bill Cosby (picture book); *Dinofours*, series, by Steve Metzger (picture book); and *The Haunted House*, by Fiona Conboy (3-D puzzle storybook).

How to Contact Responds in 1-4 months to queries; 6 months to mss. Accepts simultaneous submissions.

Terms Pays royalty on retail price or flat fee. Offers advance. Publishes ms 2 years after acceptance. Book catalog for 9×12 SASE.

Advice Audience is young children, ages 3-9. "Know what types of books the publisher does. Some manuscripts that don't work for one house may be perfect for another. Check out bookstores or catalogs to see where your writing would 'fit' best."

◎ CAVE BOOKS

277 Clamer Rd., Trenton NJ 08628-3204. (609)530-9743. E-mail: pddb@juno.com. Website: www.cavebooks.com. **Contact:** Paul Steward, managing editor. Estab. 1980. Small press devoted to books on caves, karst and speleology. Fiction: novels about cave exploration only. Publishes hardcover and trade paperback originals and reprints. Books: acid-free paper; offset printing. **Published 2 debut authors within the last year.** Averages 2 total titles, 1 fiction titles/year.

Needs Adventure, historical, literary, caves, karst, speleology. Published *Hidden Beneath the Mountains: The Caves of Sequoia and Kings Canyon National Parks*, by Joel Despain; *Scary Stories of Mammoth Cave*, by Colleen O'Connor Olson and Charles Hanion.

How to Contact Accepts unsolicited mss. Query with SASE or submit complete ms. Accepts queries by e-mail. Send SASE for return of ms or send a disposable ms and SASE for reply only. Responds in 2 weeks to queries; 3 months to mss. Accepts simultaneous submissions, electronic submissions. Sometimes comments on rejected mss.

Terms Pays 10% royalty on retail price. Publishes ms 18 months after acceptance.

Advice "In the last 3 years we have received only 3 novels about caves, and we have published one of them. We get dozens of inappropriate submissions. We only print books about caves."

⬛ Ⓝ CHARLESBRIDGE PUBLISHING, School Division

85 Main St., Watertown MA 02472. Website: www.charlesbridge.com/school. Estab. 1980. Publishes educational curricula and hardcover and paperback nonfiction and fiction children's picture books. Averages 20 total titles/year.

Needs Multicultural, nature, science, social studies, bedtime, etc. Non-rhyming stories. Recently published *The Wedding*, by Eve Bunting; *Whale Snow*, by Debby Dahl Edwardson; and *Big Blue*, by Shelley Gill.

How to Contact Submit complete ms.

Terms Royalty and advance vary. Publishes ms 2 years after acceptance. Ms guidelines online.

⊕ CHRISTCHURCH PUBLISHERS LTD

2 Caversham Street, London SW3 4AH United Kingdom. Fax: 0044 171 351 4995. **Contact:** James Hughes, fiction editor.

Needs "Miscellaneous fiction, also poetry. More 'literary' style of fiction, but also thrillers, crime fiction, etc."
How to Contact Query with SASE.
Terms Pays royalty. Offers advance. "We have contacts and agents worldwide."

CHRONICLE BOOKS

85 Second St., 6th Floor, San Francisco CA 94105. (415)537-4200. Fax: (415)537-4440. Website: www.chronicleb ooks.com. Estab. 1966. Publishes hardcover and trade paperback originals. Averages 200 total titles/year.
How to Contact Submit complete ms. Responds in 3 months to mss. Accepts simultaneous submissions.
Terms Publishes ms 18 months after acceptance. Ms guidelines online.

★ ◎ CHRONICLE BOOKS FOR CHILDREN

85 Second St., 6th Floor, San Francisco CA 94105. (415)537-4200. Fax: (415)537-4460. E-mail: frontdesk@chroni clebooks.com. Website: www.chroniclekids.com. **Contact:** Victoria Rock, associate publisher; Beth Weber, publishing manager; Monique Stephens, editor; Susan Pearson, editor-at-large. Publishes hardcover and trade paperback originals. **Published 5% debut authors within the last year.** Averages 50-60 total titles/year.
Needs Mainstream/contemporary, multicultural, young adult, picture books; middle grade fiction; young adult projects. Published *The Man Who Went to the Far Side of the Moon*; *Just a Minute!*; *Mama, Do You Love Me?*.
How to Contact Query with SASE. Responds in 2-4 weeks to queries; 6 months to mss. Accepts simultaneous submissions. No electronic submissions, submissions on disk.
Terms Pays 8% royalty. Average advance: variable. Publishes ms 18-24 months after acceptance. Ms guidelines online.
Advice "We are interested in projects that have a unique bent to them—be it in subject matter, writing style, or illustrative technique. As a small list, we are looking for books that will lend our list a distinctive flavor. Primarily, we are interested in fiction and nonfiction picture books for children ages up to eight years, and nonfiction books for children ages up to twelve years. We publish board, pop-up, and other novelty formats as well as picture books. We are also interested in early chapter books, middle grade fiction, and young adult projects."

◎ ✦ CIRCLET PRESS, INC.

1770 Massachusetts Ave., #278, Cambridge MA 02140. (617)864-0492. E-mail: editorial@circlet.com. Website: www.circlet.com. **Contact:** Cecilia Tan, publisher. Estab. 1992. Small, independent specialty book publisher. "We are the only book publisher specializing in science fiction and fantasy of an erotic nature." Publishes hardcover and trade paperback originals. Books: perfect binding; illustrations sometimes. **Published 20 debut authors within the last year.** Averages 4-6 total titles/year. Distributes titles through SCB Distribution in the US/Canada, Turnaround UK in the UK and Bulldog Books in Australia. Promotes titles through reviews in book trade and general media, mentions in *Publishers Weekly*, *Bookselling This Week* and regional radio/TV.
● "Our titles were finalists in the Independent Publisher Awards in both science fiction and fantasy."
Imprint(s) The Ultra Violet Library (non-erotic lesbian/gay fantasy and science fiction).
Needs Ethnic, science fiction, short stories only. "Check online guidelines for annual anthology topics." "Fiction must combine both the erotic and the fantastic. The erotic content needs to be an integral part of a science fiction story, and vice versa. Writers should not assume that any sex is the same as erotica." All books are anthologies of short stories. Published *Nymph*, by Francesca Lia Block; *The Darker Passions*, by Amarantha Knight.
How to Contact Accepts unsolicited mss only between April 15 and August 31 annually. Query with SASE. Include estimated word count, brief bio, list of publishing credits. Send SASE for return of ms or send a disposable ms and SASE for reply only. Agented fiction 5%. Responds in 1 months to queries; 6-18 months to mss. Accepts simultaneous submissions, electronic submissions. Always comments on rejected mss.
Terms Pays 4-12% royalty on retail price or makes outright purchase. Also pays in books, if author prefers. Publishes ms 18 months after acceptance. Ms guidelines online or for SASE. Check guidelines annually for specific anthology topics.
Advice "Read what we publish, learn to use lyrical but concise language to portray sex positively. Make sex and erotic interaction integral to your plot. Stay away from genre stereotypes. Use depth of character, internal monologue and psychological introspection to draw me in."

Ⓝ CITY LIGHTS BOOKS

261 Columbus Ave., San Francisco CA 94133. (415)362-8193. Fax: (415)362-4921. E-mail: staff@citylights.com. Website: www.citylights.com. **Contact:** Robert Sharrard, editor. Estab. 1955. Publishes paperback originals. Plans 1-2 first novels this year. Averages 12 total titles, 4-5 fiction titles/year.
How to Contact Accepts unsolicited mss.

⊠ ◎ ☒ CLARION BOOKS

Houghton Mifflin Co., 215 Park Ave. S., New York NY 10003. Website: www.houghtonmifflinbooks.com. **Contact:** Dinah Stevenson, vice-president and associate publisher (YA, middle-grade, chapter book); Jennifer B. Greene, senior editor (YA, middle-grade, chapter book); Lynne Polvino, associate editor (YA, middle-grade, chapter book). Estab. 1965. "Clarion is a strong presence in the fiction market for young readers. We are highly selective in the areas of historical and contemporary fiction. We publish chapter books for children ages 7-10 and middle grade novels for ages 9-12, as well as picture books and nonfiction." Publishes hardcover originals for children. Averages 50 total titles/year.

• Clarion author Linda Sue Park received the 2002 Newbery Award for her book, *A Single Shard*. David Wiesner received the 2002 Caldecott Award for *The Three Pigs*.

Needs Adventure, historical, humor, mystery, suspense, strong character studies. Clarion is highly selective in the areas of historical fiction, fantasy and science fiction. A novel must be superlatively written in order to find a place on the list. Mss that arrive without an SASE of adequate size will *not* be responded to or returned. Accepts fiction translations. Published *The Great Blue Yonder*, by Alex Shearer (contemporary, middle-grade); *When My Name Was Keoko*, by Linda Sue Park (historical fiction); and *Dunk*, by David Lubar (contemporary YA).

How to Contact Submit complete ms. Responds in 2 months to queries. Prefers no multiple submissions.

Terms Pays 5-10% royalty on retail price. Average advance: minimum of $4,000. Publishes ms 2 years after acceptance. Ms guidelines for #10 SASE.

◪ CLEIS PRESS

P.O. Box 14697, San Francisco CA 94114. (415)575-4700. Fax: (415)575-4705. Website: www.cleispress.com. **Contact:** Frederique Delacoste, editor. Estab. 1980. Midsize independent publisher. Publishes trade paperback originals and reprints. **Published some debut authors within the last year.** Averages 20 total titles, 5 fiction titles/year.

Needs Feminist, gay/lesbian, literary. "We are looking for high quality fiction by women and men." *Black Like Us* (fiction); *Arts and Letters*, by Edmund White (essays); and *A Fragile Union*, by Joan Nestle (essays), which won a Lambda Literary Award.

How to Contact Accepts unsolicited mss. Submit complete ms. Accepts queries by e-mail. Include brief bio, list of publishing credits. Send SASE for return of ms or send a disposable ms and SASE for reply only. Agented fiction 10%. Responds in 1 month to queries.

Terms Pays variable royalty on retail price. Publishes ms 2 years after acceptance.

ℕ ◪ ☒ COFFEE HOUSE PRESS

27 N. Fourth St., Suite 400, Minneapolis MN 55401. Fax: (612)338-4004. **Contact:** Chris Fischbach, senior editor. Estab. 1984. "Nonprofit publisher with a small staff. We publish literary titles: fiction and poetry." Publishes hardcover and trade paperback originals. Books: acid-free paper; cover illustrations. **Published some debut authors within the last year.** Averages 12 total titles, 6 fiction titles/year.

• This successful nonprofit small press has received numerous grants from various organizations including the NEA, the Mellon Foundation and Lila Wallace/Readers Digest.

Needs Ethnic, experimental, literary, mainstream/contemporary, short story collections, novels. Publishes anthologies, but they are closed to unsolicited submissions. Published *Miniatures*, by Norah Labiner (novel); *Circle K Cycles*, by Karen Yamashita (stories); and *Little Casino*, by Gilber Sorrentino (novel).

How to Contact Accepts unsolicited mss. Query with SASE. Agented fiction 10%. Responds in 1 month to queries; up to 4 months to mss. No electronic submissions.

Terms Pays 8% royalty on retail price. Provides 15 author's copies. Publishes ms 18 months after acceptance. Book catalog and ms guidelines for #10 SASE with 2 first-class stamps. Ms guidelines for #10 SAE with 55¢ first-class stamps.

⊠ Ⓐ ⊕ CONSTABLE & ROBINSON, LTD.

(formerly Constable Publishers), Constable & Robinson, 3 The Lanchesters, 162 Fulham Palace Rd., London WG 9ER United Kingdom. 0208-741-3663. Fax: 0208-748-7562. **Contact:** Krystyna Green, editorial director (crime fiction). Publishes hardcover and trade paperback originals. Averages 160 total titles/year.

Needs Crime/whodunnit. Publishes "crime fiction (mysteries)." Length 80,000 words minimum; 130,000 words maximum. Recently published *The Judgement of Ceasar*, by Steven Saylor; *The Yeare's Midnight*, by Ed O'Connor; *The More Deceived*, by David Roberts.

How to Contact *Agented submissions only.* Submit 3 sample chapter(s), synopsis. Responds in 1 month to queries; 3 months to mss. Accepts simultaneous submissions.

Terms Pays royalty. Offers advance. Publishes ms 1 year after acceptance.

Book Publishers

Advice Constable & Robinson Ltd. is looking for "crime novles with good, strong identities. Think about what it is that makes your book(s) stand out from the others."

COPPER CANYON PRESS

P.O. Box 271, Building 313, Port Townsend WA 98368. (360)385-4925. Fax: (360)385-4985. E-mail: poetry@coppercanyonpress.org. Website: www.coppercanyonpress.org. **Contact:** Michael Wiegers. Estab. 1972. Publishes trade paperback originals and occasional clothbound editions. Averages 18 total titles/year.

Needs Poetry.

How to Contact Responds in 4 months to queries.

Terms Pays royalty. Publishes ms 2 years after acceptance. Ms guidelines online.

COTEAU BOOKS

Thunder Creek Publishing Co-operative Ltd., 2206 Dewdney Ave., Suite 401, Regina SK S4R 1H3 Canada. (306)777-0170. Fax: (306)522-5152. E-mail: coteau@coteaubooks.com. Website: www.coteaubooks.com. **Contact:** Nik L. Burton, managing editor. Estab. 1975. "Coteau Books publishes the finest Canadian fiction, poetry, drama and children's literature, with an emphasis on western writers." Publishes trade paperback originals and reprints. Books: 2 lb. offset or 60 lb. hi-bulk paper; offset printing; perfect bound; 4-color illustrations. Averages 20 total titles, 6-8 fiction titles/year. Distributes titles through Fitzhenry & Whiteside.

• 2003 Sask Book Award, Book of the Year for *Nobody Goes to Earth Anymore*, by Donald Ward.

Needs Ethnic, fantasy, feminist, gay/lesbian, historical, humor, juvenile, literary, mainstream/contemporary, multicultural, multimedia, mystery, regional, short story collections, spiritual, sports, young adult. Novels, short fiction, middle years. *Canadian authors only.* Published *Grasslands*, by Michael Hetherton (fiction); *Peacekeepers*, by Dianne Unden (young adult); and *Residual Desire*, by Jill Robinson (fiction).

How to Contact Accepts unsolicited mss. Submit 3-4 sample chapter(s), author bio. Accepts queries by e-mail. Send SASE or IRC. Responds in 2 months to queries; 6 months to mss. No simultaneous submissions. Sometimes comments on rejected mss.

Terms Pays 10% royalty on retail price. "We're a co-operative and receive subsidies from the Canadian, provincial and local governments. We do not accept payments from authors to publish their works." Publishes ms 1 year after acceptance. Ms guidelines online.

Advice "We publish short-story collections, novels, drama, nonfiction and poetry collections, as well as literary interviews and children's books. This is part of our mandate. The work speaks for itself! Be bold. Be creative. Be persistent!"

COUNTERPOINT

The Perseus Books Group, 387 Park Avenue South, 12th Fl, New York NY 10016. Website: www.counterpointpress.com. Estab. 1995. Publishes papback and hardcover originals.

Needs Literary, short story collections. Published *Appetites*, by Caroline Knapp (literary/nonfiction); *Why Did I Ever*, by Mary Robinson (novel).

How to Contact Accepts unsolicited mss. *Agented submissions only.* Submit outline, 1 sample chapter(s), author bio. Accepts queries by mail. Agented fiction 98%. Responds in 3 months to queries; 3 months to mss. Accepts simultaneous submissions. No electronic submissions, submissions on disk.

Terms Pays royalty. Average advance: negotiable. Publishes ms 24 months after acceptance.

COVENANT COMMUNICATIONS, INC.

920 E. State Rd., American Fork UT 84003-0416. (801)756-9966. E-mail: info@covenant-lds.com. Website: www.covenant-lds.com. Averages 50+ total titles/year.

Needs Adventure, historical, humor, juvenile, literary, mainstream/contemporary, mystery, picture books, regional, religious, romance, spiritual, suspense, young adult.

How to Contact Responds in 4 months to mss.

Terms Pays 6½-15% royalty on retail price. Publishes ms 6-12 months after acceptance. Ms guidelines online.

Advice Our audience is exclusively LDS (Latter-Day Saints, "Mormon").

CRICKET BOOKS

Carus Publishing, 140 South Dearborn Street, Suite 1450, Chicago IL 60604. E-mail: cricketbooks@caruspub.net. Website: www.cricketbooks.net. **Contact:** Submissions editor. Estab. 1999. "Small, independent publisher able to integrate publishing with related *Cricket* and *Cobblestone* magazine groups. We publish children's fiction and nonfiction, from picture books to high young adult." Publishes hardcover and paperback originals. Distributes titles through PGW. Promotes titles through in-house marketing.

• 2003 National Book Award finalist.

Imprint(s) Cricket Books, picture books to young adults.

Needs Children's/juvenile (adventure, animal, easy-to-read, fantasy, historical, mystery, preschool/picture book, sports), young adult (adventure, easy-to-read, fantasy/science fiction, historical, horror, mystery/suspense, problem novels, romance, sports, western), early chapter books and middle-grade fiction. Plans anthologies for Christmas, dragons, poetry and *Cricket Magazine*'s anniversary edition. Editors select stories. Published *Seek*, by Paul Fleischman (YA fiction); *Robert and the Weird and Wacky Facts*, by Barbara Seuling (chapter book); and *Scorpio's Child*, by Kezi Matthews (fiction, ages 11-14).

How to Contact Does not accept unsolicited mss. Submissions from agents are welcome. Include estimated word count, list of publishing credits. Send SASE for return of ms or send a disposable ms and SASE for reply only. Agented fiction 20%. Responds in 4 months to queries; 6 months to mss. Accepts simultaneous submissions. No electronic submissions, submissions on disk. Sometimes comments on rejected mss.

Terms Pays 10% royalty on net receipts. Pays up to 10% royalty on retail price. Average advance: $1,500 and up. Publishes ms 18 months after acceptance. Ms guidelines online.

CROSSQUARTER PUBLISHING GROUP

P.O. Box 8756, Santa Fe NM 87504. (505)438-9846. Website: www.crossquarter.com. **Contact:** Anthony Ravenscroft. Publishes case and trade paperback originals and reprints. **Published 90% debut authors within the last year.** Averages 5-10 total titles/year.

Needs Science fiction, visionary fiction.

How to Contact Query with SASE. Responds in 3 months to queries. Accepts simultaneous submissions.

Terms Pays 8-10% royalty on wholesale or retail price. Publishes ms 1 year after acceptance. Book catalog for $1.75. Ms guidelines online.

Advice "Audience is earth-conscious people looking to grow into balance of body, mind, heart and spirit."

CrossTIME

Crossquarter Publishing Group, P.O. Box 8756, Santa Fe NM 87504. (505)438-9846. Fax: (505)438-9846. E-mail: info@crossquarter.com. Website: www.crossquarter.com. **Contact:** Anthony Ravenscroft. Estab. 1985. Small Publisher. Publishes paperback originals. Books: recycled paper; docutech or offset printing; perfect-bound. **Published 2 debut authors within the last year.** Plans 2 first novels this year. Member, SPAN, PMA.

Needs Mystery (occult), new age/mystic, psychic/supernatural, romance (occult), science fiction, young adult (fantasy/science fiction). Plans an anthology of Paul B. Duquette Memorial Short Science Fiction contest winners. Guidelines on website. Recently published *The Shamrock and the Feather*, by Dori Dalton (debut author); *Shyla's Initiative*, by Barbara Casey (occult romance); *Emperor of Portland*, by Anthony Ravenscroft (occult mystery); and *CrossTIME SF Anthology Vol. II* (science fiction).

How to Contact Does not accept unsolicited mss. Query with SASE. Accepts queries by e-mail. Include estimated word count, brief bio, list of publishing credits. Send SASE for return of ms or send a disposable ms and SASE for reply only. Responds in 3 months to queries; 6 months to mss. Accepts simultaneous submissions, electronic submissions, submissions on disk.

Terms Pays 6-10% royalty. Publishes ms 6-9 months after acceptance. Ms guidelines online.

CROSSWAY BOOKS

Division of Good News Publishers, 1300 Crescent St., Wheaton IL 60187-5800. (630)682-4300. Fax: (630)682-4785. Website: www.crosswaybooks.org. **Contact:** Jill Carter. Estab. 1938. " 'Making a difference in people's lives for Christ' as its maxim, Crossway Books lists titles written from an evangelical Christian perspective." Midsize evangelical Christian publisher. Currently not accepting fiction manuscripts. Publishes hardcover and trade paperback originals. Averages 85 total titles, 5 fiction titles/year. Member, ECPA. Distributes titles through Christian bookstores and catalogs. Promotes titles through magazine ads, catalogues.

Needs Historical, literary, western, Christian. "We publish fiction that falls into these categories: (1) Christian realism, or novels set in modern, true-to-life settings as a means of telling stories about Christians today in an increasingly post-Christian era; (2) supernatural fiction, or stories typically set in the 'real world' but that bring supernatural reality into it in a way that heightens our spiritual dimension; (3) historical fiction, using historical characters, times and places of interest as a mirror for our own times; (4) some genre-technique fiction (mystery, western); and (5) children's fiction. We are not interested in romance novels, horror novels, biblical novels (i.e., stories set in Bible times that fictionalize events in the lives of prominent biblical characters), issues novels (i.e., fictionalized treatments of contemporary issues), and end times/prophecy novels. We do not accept full manuscripts or electronic submissions." Published *Freedom's Shadow*, by Marlo Schalesky (historical); *The Outlaw's Twin Sister*, by Stephen Bly (western/historical); *Picture Rock*, by Stephen Bly (western/historical).

How to Contact Does not accept unsolicited mss. Agented fiction 5%.

Terms Pays negotiable royalty. Average advance: negotiable. Publishes ms 18 months after acceptance. Ms guidelines online.

Advice "With so much Christian fiction on the market, we are carefully looking at our program to see the direction we wish to proceed. Be sure your project fits into our guidelines and is written from an evangelical Christain worldview. 'Religious' or 'Spiritual' viewpoints will not fit.''

☐ DAN RIVER PRESS

Conservatory of American Letters, P.O. Box 298, Thomaston ME 04861-0298. (207)354-0998. Fax: (207)354-0998. E-mail: cal@americanletters.org. Website: www.americanletters.org. **Contact:** Richard S. Danbury, fiction editor. Estab. 1977. ''Small press publisher of fiction and biographies owned by a non-profit foundation.'' Publishes hardcover and paperback originals. Books: paperback; offset printing; perfect and cloth binding; illustrations. Averages 8-10 total titles, 2-3 fiction titles/year. Promotes titles through the author's sphere of influence. Distributes titles by mail order to libraries and bookstores.

Needs Adventure, children's/juvenile, family saga, fantasy (space fantasy, sword and sorcery), historical (general), horror (dark fantasy, futuristic, psychological, supernatural), humor, literary, mainstream/contemporary, military/war, mystery (amateur sleuth, police procedural, private eye/hard-boiled), new age/mystic, psychic/supernatural, religious (general religious, inspirational, religious mystery/suspense, religious thriller, religious romance), romance (contemporary, futuristic/time travel, gothic, historical, romantic suspense), science fiction (hard science/technological, soft/sociological), short story collections, thriller/espionage, western (frontier saga, traditional), young adult, outdoors/fishing/hunting/camping/trapping. Accepts anything but porn, sedition, evangelical and children's literature. Publishes poetry and fiction anthology (submission guidelines to *Dan River Anthology* on the Web).

How to Contact Accepts unsolicited mss. Accepts queries by mail. Include estimated word count, brief bio, list of publishing credits. Send SASE for return of ms or send a disposable ms and SASE for reply only. Responds in 2-3 days to queries; 1-2 weeks to mss. Accepts simultaneous submissions. No electronic submissions.

Terms Pays 10-15% royalty. 10 author's copies. Average advance: occassional. Publishes ms 3-4 months after acceptance. Book catalog for 6×9 SAE with 60¢ postage affixed. Ms guidelines online.

Advice ''Spend some time developing a following.''

⚔ JOHN DANIEL AND CO.

Daniel & Daniel, Publishers, Inc., P.O. Box 2790, McKinleyville CA 95519. (707)839-3495. Fax: (707)839-3242. E-mail: dand@danielpublishing.com. Website: www.danielpublishing.com. **Contact:** John Daniel, publisher. Estab. 1980. ''We publish small books, usually in small editions, but we do so with pride.'' Publishes hardcover originals and trade paperback originals. Publishes poetry, fiction and nonfiction. Averages 4 total titles/year. Distributes through SCB Distributors. Promotes through direct mail, reviews.

Needs Literary, short story collections. Publishes poetry, fiction and nonfiction; specializes in belles lettres, literary memoir. Published *Cool Hand in a Hot Fire*, by Dave Diamond (novel); *When It Comes to Living*, by Salman Vendrof (stories); *Anya's Echoes*, by Esty Schachter (novel).

How to Contact Accepts unsolicited mss. Query with SASE or submit synopsis, 50 pages. Responds in 1 month to queries; 2 months to mss. Accepts simultaneous submissions.

Terms Pays 10% royalty on wholesale price. Average advance: $0-500. Publishes ms 1 year after acceptance. Ms guidelines online.

Advice ''Write for the joy of writing. That's as good as it gets.''

DARK HORSE COMICS, INC.

10956 SE Main St., Milwaukie OR 97222. (503)652-8815. Website: www.darkhorse.com. ''In addition to publishing comics from top talent like Frank Miller, Mike Mignola, Stan Sakai, and internationally-renowned humorist Sergio Aragonés, Dark Horse is recognized as the world's leading publisher of licensed comics.''

Needs Comic books, graphic novels. Published *Astro Boy Volume 10 TPB*, by Osamu Tezuka and Reid Fleming; *Flaming Carrot Crossover #1* by Bob Burden and David Boswell.

How to Contact Submit synopsis.

Advice ''If you're looking for constructive criticism, show your work to industry professionals at conventions.''

☐ ◎ MAY DAVENPORT, PUBLISHERS

26313 Purissima Rd., Los Altos Hills CA 94022. (650)947-1275. Fax: (650)947-1373. E-mail: mdbooks@earthlink .net. Website: www.maydavenportpublishers.com. **Contact:** May Davenport, editor/publisher. Estab. 1976. ''We prefer books which can be *used* in high schools as supplementary readings in English or creative writing courses. Reading skills have to be taught, and novels by humourous authors can be more pleasant to read than Hawthorne's or Melville's novels, war novels, or novels about past generations. Humor has a place in literature.'' Publishes hardcover and paperback originals. Averages 4 total titles/year. Distributes titles through direct mail order.

Imprint(s) md Books (nonfiction and fiction).

Needs Humor, literary. ''We want to focus on novels junior and senior high school teachers can share with their reluctant readers in their classrooms." Published *A Warm Familiar Feeling*, by Colby Farley; *Senioritis*, by Tate Thompson; *A Life on The Line*, by Michael Horton; *Making My Escape*, by David Lee Finkle.

How to Contact Query with SASE. Responds in 1 month to queries.

Terms Pays 15% royalty on retail price. Publishes ms 1 year after acceptance. Ms guidelines for #10 SASE.

Advice "Just write humorous novels about today's generation with youthful, admirable, believable characters to make young readers laugh. TV-oriented youth need role models in literature, and how a writer uses descriptive adjectives and similes enlightens youngsters who are so used to music, animation, special effects with stories."

DAW BOOKS, INC.

Penguin Putnam, Inc., 375 Hudson St., 3rd Floor, New York NY 10014-3658. (212)366-2096. Fax: (212)366-2090. E-mail: daw@penguinputnam.com. Website: www.dawbooks.com. **Contact:** Peter Stampfel, submissions editor. Estab. 1971. Publishes hardcover and paperback originals and reprints. Averages 60-80 total titles/year.

Needs Fantasy, science fiction. "We are interested in science fiction and fantasy novels. We need science fiction more than fantasy right now, but we're still looking for both. We like character-driven books with attractive characters. We accept both agented and unagented manuscripts. Long books are absolutely not a problem. We are not seeking collections of short stories or ideas for anthologies. We do not want any nonfiction manuscripts." Published *The War of the Flowers*, by Tad Williams (fantasy).

How to Contact Query with SASE or submit complete ms. Responds in 6 weeks to queries.

Terms Pays in royalties with an advance negotiable on a book-by-book basis. Ms guidelines online.

Advice "We strongly encourage new writers. Research your publishers and submit only appropriate work."

DEL REY BOOKS

The Random House Publishing Group, Random House, Inc., 1745 Broadway, 18th Floor, New York NY 10019. (212)782-9000. Website: www.delreybooks.com. **Contact:** Betsy Mitchell, editor-in-chief; Shelly Shapiro, editorial director; Steve Saffel, executive editor. Estab. 1977. "We are a long-established imprint with an eclectic frontlist. We're seeking interesting new voices to add to our bestselling backlist. Publishes hardcover, trade paperback, and mass market originals and mass market paperback reprints. Averages 120 total titles, 80 fiction titles/year.

Imprint(s) Imprints: Del Rey Manga, edited by Dallas Middaugh, publishes translations of Japanese comics.

Needs Fantasy (should have the practice of magic as an essential element of the plot), science fiction (well-plotted novels with good characterizations and interesting extrapolations), alternate history. Published *The Iron Council*, by China Mieville; *The Charnel Prince*, by Greg Keyes; *Marque and Reprisal*, by Elizabeth Moon; *Dragon's Kin*, by Ann McCaffrey and Todd McCaffrey; and *Star Wars: Yoda: Dark Rendezvous*, by Sean Stewart.

How to Contact Does not accept unsolicited mss. *Agented submissions only.* Responds in 6 months to queries. No simultaneous submissions. Sometimes comments on rejected mss.

Terms Pays royalty on retail price. Average advance: competitive. Publishes ms 1 year after acceptance. Ms guidelines online.

Advice Has been publishing "more fiction and hardcovers, because the market is there for them. Read a lot of science fiction and fantasy, such as works by Anne McCaffrey, David Eddings, China Mieville, Arthur C. Clarke, Terry Brooks, Richard K. Morgan, Elizabeth Moon. When writing, pay particular attention to plotting (and a satisfactory conclusion) and characters (sympathetic and well rounded) because those are what readers look for."

DELACORTE BOOKS FOR YOUNG READERS

Random House Children's Books, 1540 Broadway, New York NY 10036. (212)782-900. Website: www.randomhouse.com/kids. Distinguished literary fiction and commercial fiction for the middle grade and young adult categories.

Terms Ms guidelines online.

DENLINGER'S PUBLISHERS, LTD.

P.O. Box 1030, Edgewater FL 32132-1030. (386)416-0009. Fax: (386)238-0517. E-mail: editor@thebookden.com. Website: www.thebookden.com. **Contact:** Marcia Buckingham, acquisitions editor (fiction-all). Estab. 1926. Denlinger's Publishers has a small dedicated staff that is interested in new technology in the field of publishing, i.e. P.O.D. and electronic publication. Publishes paperback and hardcover originals. **Published 75% debut authors within the last year.** Plans 20 first novels this year. PMA. Distributes titles through Baker & Taylor, BN.com, direct mail, Amazon.com and company website.

- Delinger's Publishers won the Grand Prize Fiction Award at the 2000 Frankfurt International E-book Awards.

Needs Adventure, ethnic, family saga, feminist, historical, horror, military/war, mystery, new age/mystic, religious, romance, science fiction, short story collections, thriller/espionage, western, young adult. Published

The Power of The Shadow, by Darrell Pruitt (adventure/intrigue); *The Prodigal's Return*, by Dwight Geddes (multicultural); *Three Little Kings*, by David Schaafsma (adventure). Publishes the ongoing series *Wicked Witch of the West* (fantasy-teen).

How to Contact Accepts unsolicited mss. Include estimated word count, brief bio. Send SASE for return of ms or send a disposable ms and SASE for reply only. Agented fiction 5%. Responds in 3-6 weeks to queries. Accepts simultaneous submissions, electronic submissions, submissions on disk. Never comments on rejected mss.

Terms Pays 10% royalty. Plus six contributor's copies. Publishes ms 6-9 months after acceptance. Ms guidelines for SASE and on website.

Advice "Read the material on the website carefully. Do your research on questions regarding publishing *prior* to submission. We do not have time to explain the whole industry to each prospective submitter. Make sure you are comfortable with the publishing arrangement *prior* to submission. Our contract is online at www.theb-ookden.com/agree.html."

✪ ◎ DIAL BOOKS FOR YOUNG READERS

Penguin Group USA, 345 Hudson St., 14th Floor, New York NY 10014. (212)366-2000. Website: www.penguinpu tnam.com. **Contact:** Submissions Editor. Estab. 1961. Trade children's book publisher. Publishes hardcover originals. Averages 50 total titles/year.

Needs Adventure, fantasy, juvenile, picture books, young adult. Especially looking for "lively and well-written novels for middle grade and young adult children involving a convincing plot and believable characters. The subject matter or theme should not already be overworked in previously published books. The approach must not be demeaning to any minority group, nor should the roles of female characters (or others) be stereotyped, though we don't think books should be didactic, or in any way message-y. No topics inappropriate for the juvenile, young adult, and middle grade audiences. No plays." Published *A Year Down Yonder*, by Richard Peck; and *The Missing Mitten Mystery*, by Steven Kellog.

How to Contact Accepts unsolicited mss. Query with SASE. Responds in 4 months to queries. No simultaneous submissions. Sometimes comments on rejected mss.

Terms Pays royalty. Average advance: varies.

✪ Ⓐ DIAL PRESS

Bantam Dell Publishing Group, Random House, Inc., 1745 Broadway, New York NY 10019. (212)782-9000. Fax: (212)782-9523. Website: www.randomhouse.com/bantamdell/. **Contact:** Susan Kamil, vice president, editorial director. Estab. 1924. Averages 6-12 total titles/year.

Needs Literary (general). Published *Mary and O'Neil* (short story collection); and *Niagara Falls Over Again* (fiction).

How to Contact *Agented submissions only.* Accepts simultaneous submissions.

Terms Pays royalty on retail price. Offers advance. Publishes ms 18 months after acceptance.

DISCOVERY ENTERPRISES, LTD.

31 Laurelwood Dr., Carlisle MA 07141. (978)287-5401. Fax: (978)287-5402. E-mail: ushistorydocs@aol.com. Publishes trade paperback originals. Averages 10 total titles/year.

Needs Historical. "Wants short (80-100 pages double-spaced) historical fiction on U.S. history topics for grades 4-8, with 12-20 pages of primary source documents and graphics that complement the fiction."

How to Contact Query with SASE or submit complete ms. Responds in 1 month to queries. Accepts simultaneous submissions.

Terms Publishes ms 3 months after acceptance. Book catalog for 6×9 SAE with 3 first-class stamps.

Ⓝ ☐ ◎ DISKUS PUBLISHING

P.O. Box 43, Albany IN 47320. E-mail: books@diskuspublishing.com. Website: www.diskuspublishing.com. **Contact:** Marilyn Nesbitt, editor-in-chief; Joyce McLaughlin, inspirational and children's editor; Holly Janey, submissions editor. Estab. 1997. Publishes paperback originals and e-books. **Published 10 debut authors within the last year.** Averages 50 total titles, 50 fiction titles/year. Member, AEP, PMA.

● *Elrod McBugle On The Loose*, by Jeff Strand was the 2001 Eppie Finalist; *Camper of The Year*, by Ann Herrick was a 2003 Eppie Finalist.

Needs Adventure, children's/juvenile, ethnic (general), family saga, fantasy (space fantasy), historical, horror, humor, juvenile, literary, mainstream/contemporary, military/war, multicultural (general), mystery, psychic/supernatural, religious, romance, science fiction, short story collections, suspense, thriller/espionage, western, young adult. "We are actively seeking confessions for our Diskus Confessions line." *The Best Laid Plans*, by Leta Nolan Childers (romance); *Brazen*, by Lori Foster (adventure/romance); and *A Change of Destiny*, by Marilynn Mansfield (science fiction/futuristic)

How to Contact Accepts unsolicited mss. Submit publishing history, author bio, estimated word count and genre or submit complete ms. Send SASE for return of ms or send a disposable ms and SASE for reply only. Agented fiction 5%. Accepts simultaneous submissions, submissions on disk. Sometimes comments on rejected mss.

Terms Pays 40% royalty. Publishes ms usually within the year after acceptance. Ms guidelines online.

⭐ Ⓐ DOUBLEDAY

Doubleday Broadway Publishing Group, Random House, Inc., 1745 Broadway, New York NY 10019. (212)782-9000. Fax: (212)782-9700. Website: www.randomhouse.com. Estab. 1897. Publishes hardcover originals. Averages 70 total titles/year.

Needs Adventure, confession, ethnic, experimental, feminist, gay/lesbian, historical, humor, literary, mainstream/contemporary, religious, short story collections.

How to Contact *Agented submissions only.* No simultaneous submissions.

Terms Pays royalty on retail price. Offers advance. Publishes ms 1 year after acceptance.

⭐ Ⓞ DOUBLEDAY BOOKS FOR YOUNG READERS

Random House Children's Books, 1540 Broadway, New York NY 10036. (212)782-9000. Website: www.random house.com/kids.

⭐ Ⓐ ⭐ DOUBLEDAY CANADA

Random House of Canada, 1 Toronto Street, Suite 300, Toronto ON M5C 2V6 Canada. (416)364-4449. Website: www.randomhouse.ca. Publishes hardcover and paperback originals. Averages 50 total titles/year.

Imprint(s) Seal Books (mass market publisher); Anchor Canada (trade paperback publisher).

How to Contact Does not accept unsolicited mss. *Agented submissions only.*

⭐ Ⓐ Ⓞ DOUBLEDAY RELIGIOUS PUBLISHING

Doubleday Broadway Publishing Group, Random House, Inc., 1745 Broadway, New York NY 10019. (212)782-9000. Website: www.randomhouse.com. **Contact:** Eric Major, vice president, religious division; Trace Murphy, executive editor; Andrew Corbin, editor. Estab. 1897. Publishes hardcover and trade paperback originals and reprints. Averages 45-50 total titles/year.

Imprint(s) Image Books, Anchor Bible Commentary, Anchor Bible Reference, Galilee, New Jerusalem Bible.

Needs Religious.

How to Contact *Agented submissions only.* Accepts simultaneous submissions.

Terms Pays 7¹/₂-15% royalty. Offers advance. Publishes ms 1 year after acceptance. Book catalog for SAE with 3 first-class stamps.

⭐ Ⓛ Ⓞ DOWN EAST BOOKS

Down East Enterprise, Inc., P.O. Box 679, Camden ME 04843-0679. Fax: (207)594-7215. **Contact:** Chris Cornell, editor (Countrysport); Michael Steere, managing editor (general). Estab. 1967. "We are primarily a regional publisher concentrating on Maine or New England." Publishes hardcover and trade paperback originals, trade paperback reprints. First novel print order: 3,000. Averages 20-24 total titles/year.

Imprint(s) Countrysport Press, edited by Chris Cornell (fly fishing and wing-shooting nonfiction).

Needs Juvenile, mainstream/contemporary, regional. "We publish 1-2 juvenile titles/year (fiction and nonfiction), and 1-2 adult fiction titles/year." Published *The Boy Who Came Walking Home*, by Peter Scott (novel); *Allagash River Towboat*, by Jack Schneider (novel); and *Sarey By Lantern Light*, by Susan Beckhorn (young adult novel).

How to Contact Query with SASE. Responds in 3 months to queries. Accepts simultaneous submissions.

Terms Pays 10-15% royalty on net receipts. Average advance: $500. Publishes ms 1 year after acceptance. Ms guidelines for 9×12 SAE with 3 first-class stamps.

⭐ Ⓛ Ⓞ DOWN THERE PRESS

Subsidiary of Open Enterprises Cooperative, Inc., 938 Howard Street #101, San Francisco CA 94103-4100. E-mail: customerservice@goodvibes.com. Website: www.goodvibes.com/dtp/dtp.html. **Contact:** Leigh Davidson, managing editor. Estab. 1975. Small independent press with part-time staff; part of a large worker-owned cooperative. "Devoted exclusively to the publication of sexual health books for children and adults. We publish books that are innovative, lively and practical, providing realistic physiological information with nonjudgmental techniques for strengthing sexual communication." Publishes paperback originals. Books: Web offset printing; perfect binding; some illustrations. Average print order: 5,000; first novel print order: 3,000-5,000. Averages 1-2 total titles, 1 fiction title/year. Member, Publishers Marketing Association and Northern California Book Publicity and Marketing Association.

Imprint(s) Yes Press, Red Alder Books and Passion Press (audio division).

Needs Erotica, feminist, sex education/sex-positive nonfiction. Published *Herotica 6*, edited by Marcy Sheiner (anthology); *Sex Spoken Here: Erotic Reading Circle Stories*, edited by Carol Queen and Jack Davis (anthology); *Any 2 People Kissing*, by Kate Dominic (short stories, erotic); and *Sex Toy Tales*, edited by A. Semans and Cathy Weeks.

How to Contact Accepts unsolicited mss. Accepts queries by mail. Include estimated word count. Send SASE for return of ms or send a disposable ms and SASE for reply only. Responds in 9 months to mss. Accepts simultaneous submissions. No electronic submissions. Sometimes comments on rejected mss.

Terms Pays royalty. Publishes ms 18 months after acceptance. Ms guidelines for #10 SASE.

N ⬛ ▢ ◎ DRAGON MOON PRESS

Box 64312, 5512 Fourth St. NW, Calgary AB T2K 6J0 Canada. E-mail: publisher@dragonmoonpress.com. Website: www.dragonmoonpress.com. **Contact:** Gwen Gades, publisher. Estab. 1994. "Dragon Moon Press is dedicated to new and exciting voices in science fiction and fantasy." Publishes trade paperback and electronic originals. Books: 60 lb. offset paper; short run printing and offset printing. Average print order: 250-3,000. **Published several debut authors within the last year.** Plans 5 first novels this year. Averages 4-6 total titles, 4-5 fiction titles/year. Distributed through Baker & Taylor. Promoted locally, through authors, and promoted online at leading retail bookstores like Amazon, Barnes & Noble, Chapters, etc.

Imprint(s) Dragon Moon Press; Gwen Gades, Christine Mains, editors; fantasy and science fiction.

Needs Fantasy, science fiction (soft/sociological). No horror or children's fiction. "At Dragon Moon Press, continue to seek out quality manuscripts and authors who are eager to participate in the marketing of their book. We are receiving many high quality manuscripts that we feel deserve to be published." Published *The Magister's Mask*, by Deby Fredericks, *The Complete Guide to Writing Fantasy*, by Darin Park and Tom Dullemond; *The Dragon Reborn*, by Kathleen H. Nelson (fantasy).

How to Contact Accepts unsolicited mss. Query with SASE or submit outline, 3 sample chapter(s), synopsis. Include estimated word count, brief bio, list of publishing credits. Accepts simultaneous submissions. No submissions on disk.

Terms Pays 8-15% royalty on retail price. Publishes ms 2 years after acceptance. Ms guidelines online.

Advice "First, be patient. Read our guidelines at dragonmoonpress.com. Not following our submission guidelines can be grounds for automatic rejection. Second, we view publishing as a family affair. Be ready to participate in the process, and show some enthusiasm and understanding in what we do. Remember also, this is a business and not about egos, so keep yours on a leash! The reward with Dragon Moon Press is not so much in money as it is in the experience and the satisfaction in the final work. Show us a great story with well-developed characters and plot lines, show us that you are interested in participating in marketing and developing as an author, and show us your desire to create a great book and you may just find yourself published by Dragon Moon Press."

⬛ DRAWN & QUARTERLY

P.O. Box 48056, Montreal QU H2V 4S8 Canada. E-mail: chris@drawnandquarterly.com. Website: www.drawnandquarterly.com.

Needs Comic books.

How to Contact Accepts electronic submissions.

⬛ ▢ ◎ DREAMCATCHER BOOKS & PUBLISHING

105 Prince William St., Saint John New Brunswick E2L 2B2 Canada. (506)632-4008. E-mail: info@dreamcatcherbooks.ca. Website: www.dreamcatcherbooks.ca. **Contact:** Yvonne Wilson, aquisitions editor (trade books: novels, occasional collections of short stories); Joan Allison, editor (children's). Estab. 1998. "Dreamcatcher Publishing Inc. is small, independent and literary. We look for, but are not limited to, the work of writers from eastern Canada." Publishes paperback originals. Books: comutell coated paper; web printing; perfect binding; illustrations by artists with BFA. Average print order: 2-3,000; first novel print order: 1,000. **Published 2 debut authors within the last year.** Plans 1-2 first novels this year. Averages 4 total titles, 3 fiction titles/year. Self-Distribution.

Needs Children's/juvenile, humor, literary, mainstream/contemporary, romance (contemporary), short story collections, young adult (adventure, fantasy/science, mystery/suspense, problem novels), Regional (Atlantic Canada). Wants fiction with "Green" themes, "Hope" and children's stories. *Strange Lights at Midnight*, by Allison Mitchem (novel); *By Invitation Only*, by Gail Higgins (poetry); *The Ragged Believers*, by Robert M. Rayner (novel).

How to Contact Query with SASE. Accepts queries by e-mail, fax, phone. Include estimated word count, brief bio, list of publishing credits. Send SASE for return of ms or send a disposable ms and SASE for reply only. Responds in 2 weeks to queries; 2 months to mss. Often comments on rejected mss.

Terms Pays 7-12% royalty. Publishes ms 1-2 years after acceptance. Ms guidelines online.

Advice "Be businesslike. Phone first, but not until you have a well-prepared manuscript ready to show us. Our interests in fiction are eclectic, but we may say no. Never ask if we will look at an unfinished manuscript to see if it is worth finishing. Spelling and punctuation count."

🌢 ◎ DUFOUR EDITIONS

P.O. Box 7, Chester Springs PA 19425. (610)458-5005. Fax: (610)458-5005. E-mail: info@dufoureditions.com. Website: www.dufoureditions.com. **Contact:** Thomas Lavoie, associate publisher. Estab. 1948. Small independent publisher, tending toward literary fiction. Publishes hardcover originals, trade paperback originals and reprints. Averages 3-4 total titles, 1-2 fiction titles/year. Promotes titles through catalogs, reviews, direct mail, sales reps, Book Expo and wholesalers.

Needs Literary, short story collections. "We like books that are slightly off-beat, different and well written." Published *Tideland*, by Mitch Cullin; *The Case of the Pederast's Wife*, by Clare Elfman; *Last Love in Constantinople*, by Milorad Pavic; *Night Sounds and Other Stories*, by Karen Shoemaker; *From the Place in the Valley Deep in the Forest*, by Mitch Cullen (short stories); and *Beyond Faith and Other Stories*, by Tom Noyes.

How to Contact Query with SASE. Accepts queries by e-mail, fax. Include estimated word count, brief bio, list of publishing credits. Responds in 3 months to queries; 6 months to mss. Accepts simultaneous submissions.

Terms Pays 6-10% royalty on net receipts. Average advance: $100-500. Publishes ms 18 months after acceptance.

📭 🔁 ◎ DUNDURN PRESS, LTD.

8 Market St., Suite 200, Toronto ON M5E 1M6 Canada. (416)214-5544. Website: www.dundurn.com. **Contact:** Acquisitions Editor. Estab. 1972. Dundurn prefers work by Canadian authors. First-time authors are welcome. Publishes hardcover and trade paperback originals and reprints.

● *Shoulder the Sky*, by Lesley Choyce won the 2003 Ann Connor Brimer Children's Literature Prize.

Imprint(s) Simon & Pierre (literary fiction); Castle Street Mysteries (mystery); Boardwalk Books (young adult).

Needs Literary, mystery, young adult. Published *The Glenwood Treasure*, by Kim Moritugu (literary fiction); *A Year Less A Day*, by James Hawkins (mystery); *Nobody's Child*, by Marsha Forchuk Skrypuch (young adult).

How to Contact Query with SASE or submit 3 sample chapter(s), synopsis. Accepts queries by mail. Include estimated word count. Responds in 1-2 months to queries. Accepts simultaneous submissions. No electronic submissions.

Terms Pays 10% royalty on net receipts. Publishes ms an average of 1 year after acceptance. Ms guidelines online.

DURBAN HOUSE PUBLISHING CO.

7502 Greenville Ave., Suite 500, Dallas TX 75231. (214)890-4050. Fax: (214)890-9295. E-mail: info@durbanhouse.com. Website: www.durbanhouse.com. Estab. 2000. Publishes hardcover and trade paperback originals. Averages 8-12 total titles/year.

Needs Adventure, historical, horror, literary, mainstream/contemporary, mystery, suspense. "We are concentrating on mystery/thriller/suspense titles. Query only. No phone queries."

How to Contact Query with SASE. Accepts simultaneous submissions.

Terms Pays 8-15% royalty on wholesale price. Average advance: up to $2,000. Publishes ms 1 year-15 months after acceptance. Ms guidelines online.

🌟 Ⓐ 🌢 DUTTON (ADULT TRADE)

Penguin Putnam, Inc., 375 Hudson St., New York NY 10014. (212)366-2000. Website: www.penguinputnam.com. **Contact:** Editor-in-Chief: Brian Tart. Estab. 1852. Publishers hardcover originals. Averages 40 total titles/year.

Needs Adventure, historical, literary, mainstream/contemporary, mystery, short story collections, suspense. Published *The Darwin Awards II*, by Wendy Northcutt (humor); *Falling Angels*, by Tracy Chevalier (fiction); and *The Oath*, by John Lescroart (fiction).

How to Contact *Agented submissions only.* Responds in 6 months to queries. Accepts simultaneous submissions.

Terms Pays royalty. Average advance: negotiable. Publishes ms 12-18 months after acceptance.

Advice "Write the complete manuscript and submit it to an agent or agents. They will know exactly which editor will be interested in a project."

🌟 🌢 ◎ DUTTON CHILDREN'S BOOKS

Penguin Group, Inc., 345 Hudson St., New York NY 10014. (212)414-3700. Fax: (212)414-3397. Website: www.penguin.com. **Contact:** Stephanie Owens Lurie, president and publisher (picture books and fiction); Maureen Sullivan, executive editor (upper young adult, fiction and nonfiction); Lucia Monfried, senior editor (picture books, easy-to-read books, fiction); Mark McVeigh, editor (picture books and fiction); Julie Strauss-Gabel, editor (picture books and fiction); Meredith Mundy Wasinger, editor (picture books, fiction and nonfiction). Estab. 1852. Dutton Children's Books publishes fiction and nonfiction for readers ranging from preschoolers to young adults on a variety of subjects. Publishes hardcover originals as well as novelty formats. Averages 100 total titles/year.

Needs Dutton Children's Books has a diverse, general interest list that includes picture books; easy-to-read books; and fiction for all ages, from "first chapter" books to young adult readers. Published *My Teacher for President*, by Kay Winters, illustrated by Denise Brunkus (picture book); *The Best Pet of All*, by David LaRochelle, illustrated by Hanako Wakiyama (picture book); *The Schwa was Here*, by Neal Shulteman (novel); *Guitar Girl*, by Sara Manning (novel).

How to Contact Does not accept unsolicited mss. Query with SASE.

Terms Pays royalty on retail price. Offers advance.

◨ ◎ EAKIN PRESS/SUNBELT MEDIA, INC.

P.O. Box 90159, Austin TX 78709-0159. (512)288-1771. Fax: (512)288-1813. Website: www.eakinpress.com. **Contact:** Virginia Messer, publisher. Estab. 1978. Eakin specializes in Texana and Western Americana for juveniles and adults. Publishes hardcover and paperback originals and reprints. Averages 60 total titles/year.

Imprint(s) Nortex; Sunbelt/Eakin; Eakin Press, Penpoint Press.

Needs Historical, juvenile. Juvenile fiction for grades K-12, preferably relating to Texas and the Southwest or contemporary. Nonfiction adult with Texas or Southwest theme. *Inside Russia*, by Inez Jeffry.

How to Contact Accepts unsolicited mss. Agented fiction 5%. Responds in 3 months to queries. Accepts simultaneous submissions.

Terms Pays royalty. Pays 10-15% royalty on net sales. Publishes ms 18 months after acceptance. Book catalog for $1.25. Ms guidelines online.

Advice "Only fiction with strong Southwest theme. We receive around 1,200 queries or unsolicited mss a year."

✪ Ⓐ ◨ THE ECCO PRESS

HarperCollins, 10 E. 53rd St., New York NY 10022. (212)207-7000. Fax: (212)702-2460. Website: www.harpercollins.com. **Contact:** Daniel Halpern, editor-in-chief. Estab. 1970. Publishes hardcover and trade paperback originals and reprints. Books: acid-free paper; offset printing; Smythe-sewn binding; occasional illustrations. First novel print order: 3,000 copies. Averages 60 total titles, 20 fiction titles/year.

Needs Literary, short story collections. "We can publish possibly one or two original novels a year." Published *Blonde*, by Joyce Carol Oates; *Pitching Around Fidel*, by S.L. Price.

How to Contact Does not accept unsolicited mss. Query with SASE.

Terms Pays royalty. Average advance: negotiable. Publishes ms 1 year after acceptance.

Advice "We are always interested in first novels and feel it's important that they be brought to the attention of the reading public."

⬍ ◎ ECW PRESS

2120 Queen St. E., Suite 200, Toronto ON M4E 1E2 Canada. (416)694-3348. Fax: (416)698-9906. E-mail: info@ecwpress.com. Website: www.ecwpress.com. **Contact:** Jack David, publisher. Estab. 1979. Publishes hardcover and trade paperback originals. Averages 40 total titles/year.

Needs Literary, mystery, poetry, short story collections, suspense.

How to Contact Accepts simultaneous submissions.

Terms Pays 8-12% royalty on net receipts. Average advance: $300-5,000. Publishes ms 18 months after acceptance. Book catalog and ms guidelines free.

Advice "Make sure to include return postage (SASE, IRC if outside of Canada) it you wish your material to be returned."

⬍ ◎ EDGE SCIENCE FICTION AND FANTASY PUBLISHING

Box 1714, Calgary AB T2P 2L7 Canada. (403)254-0160. Fax: (403)254-0456. E-mail: publisher@hadespublications.com. Website: www.edgewebsite.com. **Contact:** Kimberly Gammon, editorial manager (science fiction/fantasy). Estab. 1996. "We are an independent publisher of science fiction and fantasy novels in hard cover or trade paperback format. We produce high-quality books with lots of attention to detail and lots of marketing effort. We want to encourage, produce and promote thought-provoking and fun-to-read science fiction and fantasy literature by 'bringing the magic alive: one world at a time' (as our motto says) with each new book released." Publishes hardcover and trade paperback originals. Books: natural offset paper; offset/web printing; HC/perfect binding; b&w illustration only. Average print order: 2,000-3,000. Plans 8 first novels this year. Averages 6-8 total titles/year. Member of Book Publishers Association of Alberta (BPAA), Independent Publishers Association of Canada (IPAC), Publisher's Marketing Association (PMA), Small Press Center.

Imprint(s) Edge, Alien Vistas, Riverbend.

Needs Fantasy (space fantasy, sword and sorcery), science fiction (hard science/technological, soft/sociological). "We are looking for all types of fantasy and science fiction, except juvenile/young adult, horror, erotica, religious fiction, short stories, dark/gruesome fantasy or poetry." Published *Throne Price*, by Lynda Williams and Alison Sinclair (science fantasy); *Keaen*, by Till Noever (fantasy); and *Orbital Burn*, by K.A. Bedford.
How to Contact Accepts unsolicited mss. Query with SASE or submit outline, 3 sample chapter(s), synopsis. Check website for guidelines or send SAE & IRCS for same. Include estimated word count. Responds in 1 month to queries; 4-5 months to mss. No simultaneous submissions, electronic submissions. Rarely comments on rejected mss.
Terms Pays 10% royalty on wholesale price. Average advance: negotiable. Publishes ms 18 months after acceptance. Ms guidelines online.
Advice "Send us your best, polished, completed manuscript. Use proper manuscript format. Take the time before you submit to get a critique from people who can offer you useful advice. When in doubt, visit our website for helpful resources, FAQs and other tips."

EERDMANS BOOKS FOR YOUNG READERS
William B. Eerdmans Publishing Co., 255 Jefferson Ave. SE, Grand Rapids MI 49503. (616)459-4591. Fax: (616)459-6540. **Contact:** Judy Zylstra, editor. Publishes picture books and middle reader and young adult fiction and nonfiction. Averages 12-15 total titles/year.
Needs Juvenile, picture books, young adult, middle reader. *The Enemy Has a Face*, by Gloria Miklowitz.
How to Contact Responds in 6 weeks to queries. Accepts simultaneous submissions.
Terms Pays 5-7½% royalty on retail price. Publishes middle reader and YA books in 1 year; publishes picture books in 2-3 years.

WILLIAM B. EERDMANS PUBLISHING CO.
255 Jefferson Ave. SE, Grand Rapids MI 49503. (616)459-4591. Fax: (616)459-6540. E-mail: sales@eerdmans.com. Website: www.eerdmans.com. **Contact:** Jon Pott, editor-in-chief, fiction editor (adult fiction); Judy Zylstra, fiction editor (children). Estab. 1911. "Although Eerdmans publishes some regional books and other nonreligious titles, it is essentially a religious publisher whose titles range from the academic to the semi-popular. We are a midsize independent publisher. We publish the occasional adult novel, and these tend to engage deep spiritual issues from a Christian perspective." Publishes hardcover and paperback originals and reprints. **Published some debut authors within the last year.** Averages 120-130 total titles, 6-8 (mostly for children) fiction titles/year.
 • Wm. B. Eerdmans Publishing Co.'s titles have won awards from the American Library Association and The American Bookseller's Association.
Imprint(s) Eerdmans Books for Young Readers.
Needs Religious (children's, general, fantasy). Published *I Wonder as I Wander*, by Gwenyth Swain, illustrated by Ronald Himler; *Gilgamesh the Hero*, by Geraldine McCaughrean, illustrated by David Parkins; and *The Enemy Has a Face*, by Gloria D. Miklowitz (young adult); *Down in the Piney Woods* and *Mariah's Pond*, by Ethel Footman Smothers.
How to Contact Accepts unsolicited mss. Submit outline, 2 sample chapter(s), synopsis. Include brief bio, list of publishing credits. Send SASE for return of ms or send a disposable ms and SASE for reply only. Agented fiction 5%. Responds in 6 weeks to queries. Accepts simultaneous submissions. Sometimes comments on rejected mss.
Terms Pays royalty. Average advance: occasional. Publishes ms usually within 1 year after acceptance.
Advice "Our readers are educated and fairly sophisticated, and we are looking for novels with literary merit."

THE EIGHTH MOUNTAIN PRESS
624 SE 29th Ave., Portland OR 97214. E-mail: eighthmt@pacifier.com. Estab. 1985. Publishes original trade paperbacks. Averages 1 total titles/year.
How to Contact Responds in 6 weeks to queries.
Terms Pays 7% royalty.

ELLORA'S CAVE PUBLISHING, INC.
1337 Commerce Dr. #113, Stow OH 44224. E-mail: submissions@ellorascave.com. Website: www.ellorascave.com. Estab. 2000. Publishes trade paperback and electronic originals and reprints. Averages 208 total titles/year.
Needs Erotica, fantasy, gay/lesbian, gothic, historical, horror, mainstream/contemporary, multicultural, mystery, romance, science fiction, suspense, western. All must be under genre romance. All must have erotic content or author be willing to add sex during editing.
How to Contact Submit proposal package including 3 sample chapter(s), synopsis. Responds in 2 months to mss. Accepts simultaneous submissions.
Terms Pays 8-40% royalty on net receipts. Publishes ms 9 months after acceptance. Ms guidelines online.

Book Publishers

⊘ ◎ EMPIRE PUBLISHING SERVICE

P.O. Box 1344, Studio City CA 91614-0344. Estab. 1960. Midsize publisher with related imprints. Publishes hardcover reprints and trade paperback originals and reprints. Book: paper varies; offset printing; binding varies. Average print order: 5,000-10,000. First novel print order: 2,500-5,000. **Published 4 debut authors within the last year.** Averages 40 total titles, 5 fiction titles/year. Sales & Marketing Distribution offices in five countries.

Imprint(s) Paul Mould Publishing, Paul Mould, editor (historical); Gaslight Publications (Sherlock Holmes); Collectors Publications (erotica).

Needs Historical (pre-18th century), mystery (Sherlock Holmes). Plans anthology of Sherlock Holmes short stories. Published *House Calls*, by Lawrence Brown (historical, debut author).

How to Contact Does not accept unsolicited mss. Query with SASE. Include estimated word count, brief bio, list of publishing credits, general background. Send SASE for return of ms or send a disposable ms and SASE for reply only. Agented fiction 2%. Responds in 1 month to queries; up to 1 year to mss. No simultaneous submissions, electronic submissions, submissions on disk.

Terms Pays 6-10% royalty on retail price. Average advance: variable. Publishes ms 6 months to 2 years after acceptance. Ms guidelines for $1 or #10 SASE.

Advice "Send query with SASE for only the type of material we publish, historical and Sherlock Holmes."

⊘ ◪ EMPYREAL PRESS

P.O. Box 1746, Place Du Parc, Montreal QC HZX 4A7 Canada. E-mail: empyrealpress@hotmail.com. Website: www.skarwood.com. **Contact:** Colleen B. McCool. "Our mission is the publishing of literature which doesn't fit into any standard 'mold'—writing which is experimental yet grounded in discipline, imagination." Empyreal Press is not currently accepting unsolicited manuscripts "due to extremely limited resources." Publishes trade paperback originals. **Published 50% debut authors within the last year.** Averages 1-2 total titles/year.

Needs Experimental, feminist, gay/lesbian, literary, short story collections.

✪ Ⓐ EOS

HarperCollins, 10 E. 53rd St., New York NY 10022. (212)207-7000. E-mail: eossubs@harpercollins.com. Website: www.eosbooks.com. **Contact:** Diana Gill, senior editor. Estab. 1998. Publishes hardcover originals, trade and mass market paperback originals and reprints. Averages 40-46 total titles, 40 fiction titles/year.

Needs Fantasy, science fiction. Published *The Isle of Battle*, by Sean Russell (fantasy); *Trapped*, by James Alan Gardner.

How to Contact *Agented submissions only.* Include list of publishing credits, brief synopsis. Agented fiction 99%. Responds in 6 months to queries. Never comments on rejected mss.

Terms Pays royalty on retail price. Average advance: variable. Publishes ms 18-24 months after acceptance. Ms guidelines for #10 SASE.

Advice "Know the field and our guidelines. Getting an agent is best. No unsolicited submissions. Query via e-mail only."

ETHOS PUBLISHING

HLMA, 2300 E. Mallory St., Pensacola FL 32503. (850)432-8478. Fax: (850)432-8478. E-mail: ethospub@worldn et.att.net. Website: www.ethospub.com. **Contact:** Jim Witherspoon. Publishes hardcover and paperback originals and paperback reprints. Books: offset paper; sheet fed printing; perfect bound; illustrations. Average print order: 3,000. Average first novel print order: 2,000. Distributes books through Biblio Distribution, Ingram, and the Internet.

Needs Historical (Morocco), literary, mainstream/contemporary, Middle East. Published *The Free Woman*, by Carol Malt; *Flicker in Morocco*, by Carol Malt.

How to Contact Does not accept unsolicited mss. Query with SASE. Accepts queries by e-mail, fax. Responds in 6 weeks to queries. Accepts simultaneous submissions, electronic submissions. No submissions on disk. Sometimes comments on rejected mss.

Terms Publishes ms 8 months after acceptance.

Ⓐ ⊘ M. EVANS AND CO., INC.

216 E. 49th St., New York NY 10017-1502. (212)688-2810. Fax: (212)688-2810. Website: www.mevans.com. **Contact:** Editor. Estab. 1960. Small, general trade publisher specializing in nonfiction titles on health, nutrition, diet, cookbooks, parenting, popular psychology. Publishes hardcover and trade paperback originals. Averages 30-40 total titles/year.

Needs "Our very small general fiction list represents an attempt to combine quality with commercial potential. We publish no more than one novel per season." Published *Dying Embers* and *Private Heat*, both by R. Bailey (mystery)..

How to Contact Does not accept unsolicited mss. Query with SASE. Agented fiction 100%. Responds in 2 months to queries.

Terms Pays negotiable royalty. Offers advance. Publishes ms 8 months after acceptance.

◪ FACTOR PRESS

P.O. Box 222, Salisbury MD 21803. (410)334-6111. E-mail: factorpress@earthlink.net. **Contact:** Robert Bahr. Estab. 1989. "We specialize in niche books, including religion and erotica, for which there is a clearly targetable audience. Subject is not as important as the niche the book can fill." Publishes hardcover and paperback originals. Books: 60 lb. white paper; web press; perfect, smyth bound; illustrations. Average print order: 1,500-6,000. **Published 4 debut authors within the last year.** Member: SPAN. Distributes titles by mail order, Quality Books, Marginal, Baker & Taylor.

Needs Erotica, family saga, gay/lesbian, historical, humor, literary, regional, religious, romance, young adult. Published *The Moralist*, by Rod Downey (contemporary sociology); *The Playing Tree*, by Mary Bird (historical); and *Indecent Exposures*, by Robert Bahr (sociology).

How to Contact Accepts unsolicited mss. Submit 1 sample chapter(s). Include estimated word count, brief bio, list of publishing credits. Send SASE for return of ms or send a disposable ms and SASE for reply only. Responds in 2 weeks to queries; 4 months to mss. Accepts simultaneous submissions. Often comments on rejected mss.

Terms Pays on net receipts. Publishes ms 6 months after acceptance.

Advice "Seek agent representation first. Agents can save you all sorts of time and get you a better deal than you're likely to get by yourself. They're worth the commission many times over. If you can't find an agent to represent your work, it may mean that your book isn't worth publishing. But if you still believe in it, try the smaller publishers yourself. You won't be the first to have a blockbuster that fell through the cracks of the big boys."

◪ ◳ FAITH KIDZ BOOKS

Cook Communications Ministries, 4050 Lee Vance View, Colorado Springs CO 80918. Fax: (719)536-3265. Website: www.cookministries.com. **Contact:** Heather Gemmen, senior editor. "Faith Kidz Books publishes works of children's inspirational titles, ages 1-12 , with a clear biblical value to influence children's spiritual growth." Publishes hardcover and paperback originals. Averages 40-50 total titles/year.

Needs Historical, juvenile, picture books, religious, toddler books. "Picture books, devotionals, Bible story-books, for an age range of 1-12. We're particularly interested in materials for beginning readers."

How to Contact Does not accept unsolicited mss. Query with SASE. Responds in 6 months to queries. Accepts simultaneous submissions.

Terms Pays one flat fee. Offers advance. Publishes ms 18 months after acceptance.

◪ FARRAR, STRAUS & GIROUX

19 Union Square West, New York NY 10003. (212)741-6900. Website: www.fsgbooks.com. Publishes hardcover and trade paperback books. Averages 180 total titles/year.

Needs Literary.

How to Contact Responds in 2 months to queries.

◪ ◻ ◉ ◳ FARRAR, STRAUS & GIROUX BOOKS FOR YOUNG READERS

Farrar Straus Giroux, Inc., 19 Union Square W., New York NY 10003. (212)741-6900. Fax: (212)633-2427. **Contact:** Wesley Adams, senior editor (children's); Beverly Reingold, executive editor (children's); Robert Mayes, editor (children's). Estab. 1946. "We publish original and well-written materials for all ages." Publishes hardcover originals and trade paperback reprints. **Published some debut authors within the last year.** Averages 75 total titles/year.

Imprint(s) Frances Foster Books, edited by Frances Foster (children's); Melanie Kroupa Books, edited by Melanie Kroupa (children's).

Needs Children's/juvenile, picture books, young adult, nonfiction. "Do not query picture books; just send manuscript. Do not fax queries or manuscripts." Published *The Tree of Life*, by Peter Sis; *Tadpole*, by Ruth White.

How to Contact Query with SASE. Include brief bio, list of publishing credits. Agented fiction 25%. Responds in 2 months to queries; 4 months to mss. Accepts simultaneous submissions. No electronic submissions, submissions on disk.

Terms Pays 2-6% royalty on retail price for paperbacks, 3-10% for hardcovers. Average advance: $3,000-25,000. Publishes ms 18 months after acceptance. Book catalog for 9×12 SAE with $1.87 postage. Ms guidelines for #10 SASE.

Advice "Study our list to avoid sending something inappropriate. Send query letters for long manuscripts; don't ask for editorial advice (just not possible, unfortunately); and send SASEs!"

✦ Ⓐ FARRAR, STRAUS & GIROUX PAPERBACKS

19 Union Square W., New York NY 10003. (212)741-6900. FSG Paperbacks emphasizes literary nonfiction and fiction, as well as poetry. Publishes hardcover and trade paperback originals and reprints. Averages 180 total titles/year.

Needs Literary. *The Corrections*, by Jonathon Franzen; and *The Haunting of L.*, by Howard Norman.

How to Contact Does not accept unsolicited mss.

FC2

Publications Unit, Campus Box 4241 Illinois University, Normal IL 61790. E-mail: fc2@english.fsu.edu. Website: http://fc2.org. **Contact:** R.M. Berry, publisher (fiction); Brenda L. Mills, managing editor. Estab. 1974. Publisher of innovative fiction. Publishes hardcover and paperback originals. Books: perfect/Smyth binding; illustrations. Average print order: 2,200. **Published some debut authors within the last year.** Plans 2 first novels this year. Averages 6 total titles, 6 fiction titles/year. Titles distributed through Northwestern U.P. $10 reader's fee. With your returned submission/notification, you will receive a coupon for 50% off your next purchase on the FC2 website.

Needs Experimental, feminist, gay/lesbian, innovative; modernist/postmodern; avant-garde; anarchist; minority; cyberpunk. Published *Book of Lazarus*, by Richard Grossman; *Is It Sexual Harassment Yet?*, by Cris Mazza; *Liberty's Excess*, by Lidia Yuknavitch; *Aunt Rachel's Fur*, by Raymond Federman.

How to Contact Accepts unsolicited mss. Query with SASE or submit outline, include publishing history, synopsis, author bio. Send copy of ms and SASE. Agented fiction 5%. Responds in 3 weeks to queries; 2-6 months to mss. Accepts simultaneous submissions. Often comments on rejected mss.

Terms Pays 10% royalty. Publishes ms 1-3 years after acceptance. Ms guidelines online.

Advice "Be familiar with our list."

◎ ◎ THE FEMINIST PRESS AT THE CITY UNIVERSITY OF NEW YORK

365 Fifth Ave., Suite 5406, New York NY 10016. (212)817-7917. Fax: (212)817-1593. E-mail: ltenzer@gc.cuny.edu. Website: www.feministpress.org. **Contact:** Jean Casella, publisher. Estab. 1970. Small, nonprofit literary and educational publisher. "The Feminist Press publishes only fiction reprints by classic American women authors and translations of distinguished international women writers." Publishes hardcover and trade paperback originals and reprints. Publishes no original fiction; exceptions are anthologies and international works. "We use an acid-free paper, perfect-bind our books, four color covers; and some cloth for library sales if the book has been out of print for some time; we shoot from the original text when possible. We always include a scholarly and literary afterword, since we are introducing a text to a new audience. Average print run: 2,500." Averages 15-20 total titles, 4-8 fiction titles/year. Member: CLMP, Small Press Association. Distributes titles through Consortium Book Sales and Distribution. Promotes titles through author tours, advertising, exhibits and conferences. Charges "permission fees (reimbursement)."

Needs Ethnic, feminist, gay/lesbian, literary, short story collections, women's. "The Feminist Press publishes only fiction reprints by classic American women authors and imports and translations of distinguished international women writers. Absolutely no original fiction is considered." Needs fiction by "U.S. women of color writers from 1920-1970 who have fallen out of print." Published *Apples From the Desert*, by Savyon Liebrecht (short stories, translation); *The Parish and the Hill*, by Mary Doyle Curran (fiction reprint); *Allegra Maud Goldman*, by Edith Konecky (fiction, reprint); and *Still Alive*, by Ruth Kluger (memoir).

How to Contact Does not accept unsolicited mss. Include estimated word count, brief bio, list of publishing credits. Responds in 1 month to queries. Accepts simultaneous submissions, electronic submissions.

Terms Pays 10% royalty on net receipts. Pays 5-10 author's copies. Average advance: $250-500. Publishes ms 18-24 months after acceptance. Ms guidelines online.

FLORIDA ACADEMIC PRESS

P.O. Box 540, Gainesville FL 32602. (352)332-5104. Fax: (352)331-6003. E-mail: fapress@worldnet.att.net. **Contact:** Max Vargas, CEO (nonfiction/self-help); Sam Decalo, managing editor (academic); Florence Dusek, assistant editor (fiction). Publishes hardcover and trade paperback originals. **Published 80% debut authors within the last year.** Averages 6 total titles/year.

Needs Literary criticism.

How to Contact Submit complete ms. Responds in 2-6 months to mss.

Terms Pays 5-8% royalty on retail price, depending if paperback or hardcover. Publishes ms 3-5 months after acceptance.

Advice Considers complete mss only. "Manuscripts we decide to publish must be re-submitted in camera-ready form."

Book Publishers

⬛ ⬛ ◨ FORGE AND TOR BOOKS

Tom Doherty Associates, LLC, 175 Fifth Ave. 14th Floor, New York NY 10010. (212)388-0100. Fax: (212)388-0191. Website: www.tor.com. **Contact:** Melissa Ann Singer, senior editor (general fiction, mysteries, thriller); Patrick Nielsen Hayden, senior editor (science fiction, fantasy). Estab. 1980. "Tor Books are science fiction, fantasy and horror and, occasionally, related nonfiction. Forge books are everything else—general fiction, historical fiction, mysteries and suspense, women's fiction, and nonfiction. Orb titles are trade paperback reprint editions of science fiction, fantasy and horror books." Publishes hardcover, trade paperback and mass market paperback originals, trade and mass market paperback reprints. **Published some debut authors within the last year.**

• Tor was named Best Publisher at the Locus Awards for the sixteenth consecutive year.

Imprint(s) Forge, Tor, Orb.

Needs Historical, horror, mainstream/contemporary, mystery (amateur sleuth, police procedural, private eye/hard-boiled), science fiction, suspense, thriller/espionage, western (frontier saga, traditional), thriller; general fiction and fantasy.

How to Contact Accepts unsolicited mss. Query with SASE. Include estimated word count, brief bio, list of publishing credits. Agented fiction 95%. Sometimes comments on rejected mss.

Terms Paperback: Pays 6-8% royalty for first-time authors, 8-10% royalty for established authors; Hardcover: Pays 10% first 5,000; 12½% second 5,000; 15% thereafter. Offers advance. Publishes ms 12-18 months after acceptance.

Advice "The writing must be outstanding for a new author to break into today's market."

◎ FORT ROSS INC. RUSSIAN-AMERICAN PUBLISHING PROJECTS

26 Arthur Place, Yonkers NY 10701. (914)375-6448. Fax: (914)375-6439. E-mail: fort.ross@verizon.net. Website: www.fortross.net. **Contact:** Dr. Vladimir P. Kartsev. Estab. 1992. "We welcome Russian-related manuscripts and books from well-established fantasy and romance novel writers who would like to have their novels translated in Russia and Eastern Europe by our publishing house in cooperation with the local publishers." Publishes paperback originals. **Published 3 debut authors within the last year.** Averages 10 total titles/year.

Needs Adventure, fantasy (space fantasy, sword and sorcery), horror, mainstream/contemporary, mystery (amateur sleuth, police procedural, private eye/hard-boiled), romance (contemporary, futuristic/time travel), science fiction (hard science/technological, soft/sociological), suspense, thriller/espionage.

How to Contact Does not accept unsolicited mss. Query with SASE. Include estimated word count, brief bio, list of publishing credits. Send SASE for return of ms or send a disposable ms and SASE for reply only. Responds in 1 month to queries; 3 months to mss. Accepts simultaneous submissions.

Terms Pays 5-10% royalty on wholesale price or makes outright purchase of $500-1,500. Average advance: $500-$1,000; negotiable.

⬛ FOUR WALLS EIGHT WINDOWS

245 West 17th Street, New York NY 10011. (212)206-8965. Fax: (212)206-8799. E-mail: edit@4w8w.com. Website: www.4w8w.com. **Contact:** Jofie Ferrari-Adler, editor. Estab. 1987. "We are a small independent publisher." Publishes hardcover originals, trade paperback originals and reprints. Books: quality paper; paper or cloth binding; illustrations sometimes. Average print order: 3,000-7,000. First novel print order: 3,000-5,000. **Published some debut authors within the last year.** Averages 35 total titles, 9 fiction titles/year. Distributes titles through Publisher's Group West, the largest independent distributor in the country. Promotes titles through author tours, bound galleys, select advertising, postcard mailing, etc.

• Four Walls Eight Windows' books have received mention from the *New York Times* as "Notable Books of the Year," and have been nominated for *L.A. Times* fiction and nonfiction prizes.

Needs Feminist, gay/lesbian, nonfiction.

How to Contact Does not accept unsolicited mss. Agented fiction 50%. Responds in 2 months to queries. Accepts simultaneous submissions.

Terms Pays royalty on retail or net price, depending on contract. Average advance: variable. Publishes ms 1-2 years after acceptance.

Advice "Please read our catalog and/or our website to be sure your work would be compatible with our list."

◨ ◎ ⬛ FRONT STREET

862 Haywood Rd., Asheville NC 28806. (828)236-3097. Fax: (828)221-2112. E-mail: contactus@frontstreetbooks.com. Website: www.frontstreetbooks.com. **Contact:** Stephen Roxburgh, president and publisher; Joy Neaves, editor. Estab. 1994. "Small independent publisher of high-quality picture books and literature for children and young adults." Publishes hardcover originals. Averages 10-15 total titles/year. Distributes titles through PGW. Titles promoted on the Internet, in catalog, by sales representatives, at library and education conferences.

Book Publishers

• *A Step from Heaven*, by An Na, won the Michael L. Printz Award for 2002. *Carver: A Life in Poems*, by Marilyn Nelson, won a Newberry Honor 2002 and a Coretta Scott King Honor.

Needs Adventure, historical, humor, juvenile, literary, picture books, young adult (adventure, fantasy/science fiction, historical, mystery/suspense, problem novels, sports). Published *Honeysuckle House*, by Andrea Cheng (YA); *Hunger Moon*, by Sarah Lamstein (YA); *Black Brothers*, by Liza Tetzner and Hans Binder (YA graphic novel).

How to Contact Accepts unsolicited mss. Query with SASE or submit complete ms. Accepts queries by e-mail, fax. Include brief bio, list of publishing credits. Send SASE for return of ms or send a disposable ms and SASE for reply only. Agented fiction 10%. Responds in 1 month to queries; 3 months to mss. Accepts simultaneous submissions. No electronic submissions.

Terms Pays royalty on retail price. Offers advance. Publishes ms 1 year after acceptance. Ms guidelines online.

FYOS ENTERTAINMENT, LLC

P.O. Box 25216, Philadelphia PA 19119. (215)972-8067. Fax: (215)438-0469. E-mail: info@fyos.com. Website: www.fyos.com. **Contact:** Tonya Marie Evans, editor-in-chief (poetry, African-America fiction); Susan Borden Evans, general manager (African-American fiction). Publishes hardcover originals and trade paperback originals. Averages 2-3 total titles/year.

Needs Multicultural, short story collections. "We concentrate acquisition efforts on poetry and fiction of interest primarily to the African-American reader. We are looking for thought-provoking, well-written work that offers a 'quick and entertaining' read." Published *Seasons of Her*, by T. Evans; *SHINE!*, by T. Evans.

How to Contact Query with SASE. Responds in 1-3 months to queries; 3-6 months to mss. Accepts simultaneous submissions.

Terms Pays 10-15% royalty on retail price. Pays a 60 (publisher)/40 (author) split of net receipts. Will also consider outright purchase opportunities. Publishes ms 1 year after acceptance. Ms guidelines online.

Advice "Neatness counts! Present yourself and your work in a highly professional manner."

GASLIGHT PUBLICATIONS

Empire Publishing Services, P.O. Box 1344, Studio City CA 91614. (818)784-8918. **Contact:** Simon Waters, fiction editor (Sherlock Holmes only). Estab. 1960. Publishes hardcover and paperback originals and reprints. Books: paper varies; offset printing; binding varies; illustrations. Average print order: 5,000. **Published 1 debut author within the last year.** Averages 4-12 total titles, 2-4 fiction titles/year. Promotes titles through sales reps, trade, library, etc.

Needs Sherlock Holmes only. Recently published *Puzzeling with Sherlock Holmes*, by David Williams; *Sherlock Holmes, The Complete Bagel Street Saga*, by Robert L. Fish; and *Subcutaneously: My Dear Watson*, by Jack Tracy (all Sherlock Holmes).

How to Contact Accepts unsolicited mss. Query with SASE. Include estimated word count, brief bio, list of publishing credits. Send SASE for return of ms or send a disposable ms and SASE for reply only. Agented fiction 10%. Responds in 2 weeks to queries; 1 year to mss.

Terms Pays 8-10% royalty. Royalty and advance dependent on the material. Publishes ms 1-6 months after acceptance.

Advice "Please send only Sherlock Holmes material. Other stuff just wastes time and money."

GAY SUNSHINE PRESS and LEYLAND PUBLICATIONS

P.O. Box 410690, San Francisco CA 94141-0690. Fax: (415)626-1802. Website: www.gaysunshine.com. **Contact:** Winston Leyland, editor. Estab. 1970. Midsize independent press. Publishes hardcover originals, trade paperback originals and reprints. Books: natural paper; perfect-bound; illustrations. Average print order: 5,000-10,000. Averages 3-4 total titles/year.

• Gay Sunshine Press has received a Lambda Book Award for *Gay Roots* (volume I), named "Best Book by a Gay or Lesbian Press," and received grants from the National Endowment for the Arts.

Needs Erotica, experimental, historical, literary, mystery, science fiction, all gay male material only. "We have a high literary standard for fiction. We desire fiction on gay themes of *high* literary quality and prefer writers who have already had work published in literary magazines. We also pubilsh erotica—short stories and novels." Recently published *Out in the Castro: Promise, Desire, Activism*, large anthology with 35+ writers, artists (2002).

How to Contact Does not accept unsolicited mss. Query with SASE. Responds in 6 weeks to queries; 2 months to mss.

Terms Pays royalty or makes outright purchase. Book catalog for $1.

Advice "We continue to be interested in receiving queries from authors who have book-length manuscripts of high literary quality. We feel it is important that an author know exactly what to expect from our press (promotion, distribution, etc.) before a contract is signed. Before submitting a query or manuscript to a particular press, obtain critical feedback on your manuscript from knowledgeable people. If you alienate a publisher by submitting a manuscript shoddily prepared/typed, or one needing very extensive rewriting, or one which is not in the area of the publisher's specialty, you will surely not get a second chance with that press."

GENESIS PRESS, INC.

1213 HWY 45 N., Columbus MS 39705. (662)329-9927. Fax: (662)329-9399. E-mail: books@genesis-press.com. Website: www.genesis-press.com. Publishes hardcover and trade paperback originals and reprints. **Published 50% debut authors within the last year.** Averages 30 total titles/year.

• *Tomorrow's Promise*, by Leslie Esdale won a Gold Pen Award.

Needs Erotica, ethnic, literary, multicultural, romance, women's. Published *Cherish the Flame*, by Beverly Clark; *No Apologies*, by Seressia Glass.

How to Contact Query with SASE or submit 3 sample chapter(s), synopsis. Responds in 2 months to queries; 4 months to mss.

Terms Pays 6-12% royalty on invoice price. Average advance: $750-5,000. Publishes ms 1 year after acceptance. Ms guidelines online.

Advice "Be professional. Always include a cover letter and SASE. Follow the submission guidelines posted on our website or send a SASE for a copy."

LAURA GERINGER BOOKS

HarperCollins Children's Books, 1350 Avenue of the Americas, New York NY 10019. (212)261-6500. Website: www.harperchildrens.com. **Contact:** Laura Geringer, senior vice president/publisher. "We look for books that are out of the ordinary, authors who have their own definite take, and artists that add a sense of humor to the text." Publishes hardcover originals. **Published some debut authors within the last year.** Averages 15-20 total titles/year.

Needs Adventure, fantasy, historical, humor, juvenile, literary, picture books, young adult. Recently published *Regular Guy*, by Sarah Weeks; and *Throwing Smoke*, by Bruce Brooks.

How to Contact Does not accept unsolicited mss. Query with SASE. Agented fiction 90%. Responds in 3 months to queries.

Terms Pays 10-12½% on retail price. Average advance: variable.

Advice "A mistake writers often make is failing to research the type of books an imprint publishes, therefore sending inappropriate material."

GIVAL PRESS

P.O. Box 3812, Arlington VA 22203. (703)351-0079. E-mail: givalpress@yahoo.com. Website: www.givalpress.com. **Contact:** Robert L. Giron, publisher. Estab. 1998. A small, independent publisher that publishes quality works by a variety of authors from an array of walks of life. Works are in English, Spanish and French and have a philosophical or social message. Publishes paperback originals and reprints and e-books. Books: perfect-bound. Average print order: 500. **Published 4 debut authors within the last year.** Plans 2 first novels this year. Member, AAP, PMA, Literary Council of Small Presses and Magazines. Distributes books through Ingram and BookMasters, Inc.

• Received a Silver Award, 2003 *Foreword Magazine* for fiction—translation.

Needs Ethnic, gay/lesbian, historical, literary, short story collections. "Looking for French books with English translation." The Gival Press Short Story Contest deadline is August 8, 2004. Guidelines on website. Recently published *A Change of Heart*, by David Garrett Izzo; *The Gay Herman Melville Reader*, by Ken Schellenberg (fiction); *The Smoke Week: Sept. 9-22, 2001*, by Ellis Avery (memoir).

How to Contact Does not accept unsolicited mss. Query with SASE or submit outline, 2 sample chapter(s). Reading period open from May to August. Accepts queries by e-mail, mail. Include estimated word count, brief bio, list of publishing credits. Send SASE for return of ms or send a disposable ms and SASE for reply only. Agented fiction 5%. Responds in 4 months to queries; 5 months to mss. Rarely comments on rejected mss.

Terms Pays 20 contributor's copies. Offers advance. Publishes ms 1 year after acceptance. Book catalog and ms guidelines for SASE and on website.

Advice "Study the types of books we have published—literary works with a message of high quality."

THE GLENCANNON PRESS

P.O. Box 633, Benicia CA 94510. (707)745-3933. Fax: (707)747-0311. E-mail: captjaff@pacbell.net. Website: www.glencannon.com. **Contact:** Bill Harris (maritime, maritime children's). Estab. 1993. "We publish quality books about ships and the sea." Publishes hardcover and paperback originals and hardcover reprints. Books: Smyth; perfect binding; illustrations. Average print order: 1,000. First novel print order: 750. **Published 1 debut authors within the last year.** Averages 4-5 total titles, 1 fiction titles/year. Member, PMA, BAIPA. Distributes titles through Quality Books, Baker & Taylor. Promotes titles through direct mail, magazine advertising and word of mouth.

Book Publishers

Imprint(s) Palo Alto Books (any except maritime); Glencannon Press (merchant marine and Navy).
Needs Adventure, children's/juvenile (adventure, fantasy, historical, mystery, preschool/picture book), ethnic (general), historical (maritime), humor, mainstream/contemporary, military/war, mystery, thriller/espionage, western (frontier saga, traditional maritime), young adult (adventure, historical, mystery/suspense, western). Currently emphasizing children's maritime, any age. Recently published *White Hats*, by Floyd Beaver (navy short stories); and *The Crafty Glencannon*, by Guy Gilpatric (merchant marine short stories).
How to Contact Accepts unsolicited mss. Submit complete ms. Include brief bio, list of publishing credits. Send SASE for return of ms or send a disposable ms and SASE for reply only. Responds in 1 month to queries; 2 months to mss. Accepts simultaneous submissions. Often comments on rejected mss.
Terms Pays 10-20% royalty. Publishes ms 6-24 months after acceptance.
Advice "Write a good story in a compelling style."

A DAVID R. GODINE, PUBLISHER, INC.

9 Hamilton Place, Boston MA 02108. (617)451-9600. Fax: (617)350-0250. E-mail: info@godine.com. Website: www.godine.com. **Contact:** President: David R. Godine. Estab. 1970. Small independent publisher (5-person staff). Publishes hardcover and trade paperback originals and reprints. Averages 35 total titles/year.
Imprint(s) Nonpareil Books (trade paperbacks), Verba Mundi (translations), Imago Mundi (photography).
Needs Children's/juvenile, historical, literary. *No unsolicited mss.*
How to Contact Does not accept unsolicited mss. Query with SASE.
Terms Pays royalty on retail price. Publishes ms 3 years after acceptance.
Advice "Have your agent contact us. Please no phone queries."

GOOSE LANE EDITIONS

469 King St., Fredericton, New Brunswick E3B 1E5 Canada. (506)450-4251. Fax: (506)459-4991. Website: www.gooselane.com. **Contact:** Laurel Boone, editorial director. Estab. 1954. Publishes hardcover and paperback originals and occasional reprints. Books: some illustrations. Average print order: 3,000. First novel print order: 1,500. Averages 16-18 total titles, 6-8 fiction titles/year. Distributes titles through University of Toronto Press (UTP).
• *Elle*, by Douglas Glover won the 2004 Governor General's Award for Fiction.
Needs Literary (novels), mainstream/contemporary, short story collections. "Our needs in fiction never change: substantial, character-centered literary fiction." Published *Tattycoram*, by Audrey Thomas.
How to Contact Accepts unsolicited mss. Query with SASE. Responds in 6 months to mss. No simultaneous submissions.
Terms Pays 8-10% royalty on retail price. Average advance: $200-1,000, negotiable. Ms guidelines online.
Advice "We do not consider submissions from outside Canada."

N GOTHIC CHAPBOOK SERIES

Gothic Press, 1701 Lobdell Avenue, No. 32, Baton Rouge LA 70806-8242. E-mail: gothicpt12@aol.com. Website: www.gothicpress.com. **Contact:** Gary W. Crawford, editor (horror, fiction, poetry and scholarship). Estab. 1979. "One person operation on a part-time basis." Publishes paperback originals. Books: printing or photocopying. Average print order: 150-200. Distributes titles through direct mail and book dealers.
Needs Horror (dark fantasy, psychological, supernatural). Need novellas and short stories.
How to Contact Accepts unsolicited mss. Query with SASE. Accepts queries by e-mail, phone. Include estimated word count, brief bio, list of publishing credits. Send SASE for return of ms or send a disposable ms and SASE for reply only. Responds in 2 weeks to queries; 2 months to mss. Sometimes comments on rejected mss.
Terms Pays 10% royalty. Ms guidelines for #10 SASE.
Advice "Know gothic and horror literature well."

GRAYWOLF PRESS

2402 University Ave., Suite 203, St. Paul MN 55114. E-mail: wolves@graywolfpress.org. Website: www.graywolfpress.org. **Contact:** Anne Czarniecki, executive editor; Katie Dublinski, editor. Estab. 1974. Growing small literary press, nonprofit corporation. Publishes trade cloth and paperback originals. Books: acid-free quality paper; offset printing; hardcover and soft binding. Average print order: 3,000-10,000. First novel print order: 3,000-7,500. Averages 22 total titles, 6-8 fiction titles/year. Distributes titles nationally through Farrar, Straus, & Giroux. "We have an in-house marketing staff and an advertising budget for all books we publish."
Needs Literary, short story collections. "Familiarize yourself with our list first." Published *One Vacant Chair*, by Joe Coomer; *The House on Eccles Road*, by Judith Kitchen; *Avoidance*, by Michael Lowenthal; *Operation Monsoon*, by Shona Ramaya.
How to Contact Query with SASE or submit 1 sample chapter(s). Include estimated word count, brief bio, list of publishing credits. Send SASE or IRC. Agented fiction 90%. Responds in 3 months to queries.

Terms Pays royalty on retail price, author's copies. Average advance: $2,500-15,000. Publishes ms 18-24 months after acceptance. Ms guidelines online.

Advice "Please review our catalog and submission guidelines before submitting your work. We rarely publish collections or novels by authors who have not published work previously in literary journals or magazines."

☑ ◎ GREENE BARK PRESS

P.O. Box 1108, Bridgeport CT 06601. (203)372-4861. Fax: (203)371-5856. Website: www.greenebarkpress.com. **Contact:** Michele Hofbauer, associate publisher. Estab. 1991. "We only publish children's fiction—all subjects, but in reading picture book format appealing to ages 3-9 or all ages." Publishes hardcover originals. **Published some debut authors within the last year.** Averages 1-6 total titles/year. Distributes titles through Baker & Taylor and Quality Books. Promotes titles through ads, trade shows (national and regional), direct mail campaigns.

Needs Juvenile. Published *Hey There's a Goblin Under My Throne*, by Rhett R. Pennell and *The Magical Trunk*, by GiGi Tegge.

How to Contact Submit complete ms. Responds in 2 months to queries; 6 months to mss. Accepts simultaneous submissions. No electronic submissions.

Terms Pays 10-15% royalty on wholesale price. Publishes ms 1 year after acceptance. Book catalog for $2. Ms guidelines for SASE.

Advice Audience is "children who read to themselves and others. Mothers, fathers, grandparents, godparents who read to their respective children, grandchildren. Include SASE, be prepared to wait, do NOT inquire by telephone, fax or e-mail."

✪ ☑ ◎ GREENWILLOW BOOKS

HarperCollins Publishers, 1350 Avenue of the Americas, New York NY 10019. (212)261-6500. Website: www.harperchildrens.com. **Contact:** Fiction Editor. Estab. 1974. Publishes hardcover originals and reprints. Averages 50-60 total titles/year.

Needs Fantasy, humor, literary, mystery, picture books. *The Queen of Attolia*, by Megan Whalen Turner; *Bo & Mzzz Mad*, by Sid Fleishman; *Whale Talk*, by Chris Crutcher; *Year of the Griffen*, by Diana Wynne Jones.

How to Contact Does not accept unsolicited mss.

Terms Pays 10% royalty on wholesale price for first-time authors. Average advance: variable. Publishes ms 2 years after acceptance.

☑ GREYCORE PRESS

2646 New Prospect Road, Pine Bush NY 12566. (845)744-5081. Fax: (845)744-8081. E-mail: joan123@frontiernet.net. Website: www.greycore.com. **Contact:** Joan Schweighandt, publisher. Estab. 1999. Small independent publisher of quality fiction and nonfiction titles. Established GreyCore Kids in 2003. Publishes hardcover and trade paperback originals. Books: cloth binding. Average print order: 7,000. **Published 1 debut author within the last year.** Averages 2 total titles, 2 fiction titles/year. Member, Dustbooks. Distributes titles through Client Distribution Services.

Needs Children's/juvenile, literary, mainstream/contemporary. Published *One Man's Leg*, by Paul Martin; *The Basket Maker*, by Kate Niles; *Buddha Wept*, by Rocco Lo Bosco; *When I Wished I Was Alone*, by Dave Cutler.

How to Contact Does not accept unsolicited mss. Query with SASE. Accepts queries by e-mail. Include estimated word count, list of publishing credits. Accepts simultaneous submissions. Sometimes comments on rejected mss.

Terms Payment varies. Publishes ms 18 months after acceptance.

Advice "We prefer to get cover letters that include author credentials and the ways in which writers are willing to help publicize their work. We are very small and can't keep up with the number of manuscripts we receive. Our preference is to receive a cover letter, synopsis and the author's credentials via snail mail. We will read e-mail queries too, of course, but as e-mails tend to get lost in the shuffle, our preference is snail mail, with SASE."

Ⓐ GROVE/ATLANTIC, INC.

841 Broadway 4th Floor, New York NY 10003. (212)614-7850. Fax: (212)614-7886. Website: www.groveatlantic.com. Estab. 1952. Publishes hardcover originals, trade paperback originals and reprints. Averages 60-70 total titles/year.

Imprint(s) Grove Press (estab. 1952), Atlantic Monthly Press (estab. 1917).

How to Contact Does not accept unsolicited mss. *Agented submissions only.* Accepts simultaneous submissions.

Terms Pays 7½-15% royalty on retail price. Average advance: varies. Publishes ms 1 year after acceptance.

☑ GRYPHON BOOKS

P.O. Box 209, Brooklyn NY 11228. (718)646-6126 (after 6 p.m. EST). Website: www.gryphonbooks.com. **Contact:** Gary Lovisi, owner/editor. Estab. 1983. Publishes paperback originals and trade paperback reprints. Books: bond paper; offset printing; perfect binding. Average print order: 500-1,000. **Published some debut authors within the last year.** Averages 10-15 total titles, 12 fiction titles/year.

Imprint(s) Gryphon Books, Gryphon Doubles, Gryphon SF Rediscovery Series.

Needs Mystery (private eye/hard-boiled, crime), science fiction (hard science/technological, soft/sociological). Published *The Dreaming Detective*, by Ralph Vaughn (mystery-fantasy-horror); *The Woman in the Dugout*, by Gary Lovisi and T. Arnone (baseball novel); and *A Mate for Murder*, by Bruno Fischer (hard-boiled pulp).

How to Contact "I am not looking for novels right now; *will only see a 1-2 page synopsis with SASE*." Include estimated word count, brief bio, list of publishing credits. Agented fiction 5-10%. Often comments on rejected mss.

Terms Publishes ms 1-3 years after acceptance. Ms guidelines for #10 SASE.

Advice "I am looking for better and better writing, more cutting-edge material with *impact*! Keep it lean and focused."

🍁 ☑ 🈯 GUERNICA EDITIONS

Box 117, Station P, Toronto, ON M5S 2S6 Canada. (416)658-9888. Fax: (416)657-8885. E-mail: guernicaeditions @cs.com. Website: www.guernicaeditions.com. **Contact:** Antonio D'Alfonso, fiction editor (novel and short story). Estab. 1978. "Guernica Editions is a small press that produces works of fiction and nonfiction on the viability of pluriculturalism." Publishes trade paperback originals, reprints and software. Books: various paper; offset printing; perfect binding. Average print order: 1,000. **Published 6 debut authors within the last year.** Averages 25 total titles, 18-20 fiction titles/year. Distributes titles through professional distributors.

• Two titles by Guernica Editions have won American Book Awards.

Imprint(s) Prose Series, Antonio D'Alfonso, editor, all; Picas Series, Antonio D'Alfonso, editor, reprints.

Needs Erotica, feminist, gay/lesbian, literary, multicultural. "We wish to open up into the fiction world and focus less on poetry. We specialize in European, especially Italian, translations." Publishes anthology of Arab women/Italian women writers. Published *A Demon in My View*, by Len Grasparin; *A Destroyer of Compasses*, by Wade Bell; *Voices in the Desert: An Anthology of Arab-Canadian Women Writers*, edited by Elizabeth Dahab.

How to Contact Accepts unsolicited mss. Query with SASE. Include estimated word count, brief bio, list of publishing credits. Responds in 1 month to queries; 1 year to mss. No simultaneous submissions.

Terms Pays 8-10% royalty on retail price. Or makes outright purchase of $200-5,000. Average advance: $200-2,000. Publishes ms 15 months after acceptance.

Advice "Know what publishers do, and send your works only to publishers whose writers you've read and enjoyed."

☑ ◎ HAMPTON ROADS PUBLISHING CO., INC.

1125 Stoney Ridge Rd., Charlottesville VA 22902. (434)296-2772. Fax: (434)296-5096. E-mail: editorial@hrpub.c om. Website: www.hrpub.com. **Contact:** Frank Demarco, chief editor. Estab. 1989. "We work as a team to produce the best books we are capable of producing which will impact, uplift and contribute to positive change in the world. We publish what defies or doesn't quite fit the usual genres. We are noted for visionary fiction." Publishes hardcover and trade paperback originals. Publishes and distributes hardcover and paperback originals on subjects including metaphysics, health, complementary medicine, visionary fiction and other related topics. Average print order: 3,000-5,000. **Published 6 debut authors within the last year.** Averages 24-30 total titles, 4 fiction titles/year. Distributes titles through distributors. Promotes titles through advertising, representatives, author signings and radio-TV interviews with authors.

Needs Literary, new age/mystic, psychic/supernatural, spiritual, visionary fiction, past-life fiction, based on actual memories. "Fiction should have one or more of the following themes: spiritual, inspirational, metaphysical, i.e., past life recall, out-of-body experiences, near death experience, paranormal." Published *Rogue Messiahs*, by Colin Wilson; *Spirit Matters*, by Michael Lerner; and *The Authenticator*, by William M. Valtos.

How to Contact Accepts unsolicited mss. Submit outline, 2 sample chapter(s), synopsis. Accepts queries by e-mail, fax. Send SASE for return of ms or send a disposable ms and SASE for reply only. Agented fiction 5%. Responds in 1-2 months to queries; 1-6 months to mss. Accepts simultaneous submissions.

Terms Pays royalty. Average advance: less than $10,000. Publishes ms 1 year after acceptance. Ms guidelines online.

Advice "Send us something new and different. Be patient. We take the time to give each submission the attention it deserves."

⊘ HARBOR HOUSE

111 Tenth St., Augusta GA 30901. (706)738-0354. Fax: (706)823-5999. E-mail: harborbook@bellsouth.net. Website: www.harborhousebooks.com. **Contact:** E. Randall Floyd, publisher. Estab. 1997. Harbor House seeks to publish the best in original fiction (mainstream, historical, horror). Publishes hardcover originals and paperback originals. Average print order: 5,000. **Published 3 debut authors within the last year.** Member: PMA. Distributes titles through the National Book Network; Ingram; Baker & Taylor.

• Received a Golden Eye Literary Award.

Imprint(s) Batwing Press.

Needs Historical (biography), horror (psychological, supernatural), mainstream/contemporary, military/war, new age/mystic, psychic/supernatural, romance (historical), young adult (horror, mystery/suspense), civil war. Published *Two Rivers*, by Naomi Williams (fiction).

How to Contact Accepts unsolicited mss. Submit outline, 3 sample chapter(s). Accepts queries by mail. Include estimated word count, brief bio, list of publishing credits, marketing plans. Send copy of ms and SASE. Agented fiction 10%. Responds in 4 weeks to queries; 2 months to mss. Accepts simultaneous submissions. Sometimes comments on rejected mss.

Terms Pays 10% royalty. Average advance: $5,000. Publishes ms 6-18 months after acceptance. Ms guidelines online.

Advice "We strongly encourage authors to consult our website before submitting material. We are particularly interested in developing unpublished authors."

⊠ Ⓐ HARCOURT, INC

Children's Books Division, 525 B St., Suite 1900, San Diego CA 92101. (619)281-6616. Fax: (619)699-6777. Website: www.harcourtbooks.com/htm/childrens_index.asp. Estab. 1919. "Harcourt Inc. owns some of the world's most prestigious publishing imprints—which distinguish quality products for the juvenile, educational, scientific, technical, medical, professional and trade markets worldwide." Publishes hardcover originals and trade paperback reprints.

Imprint(s) Harcourt Children's Books, Gulliver Books, Silver Whistle, Red Wagon, Odyssey Paperbacks, Magic Carpet, Voyager Books/Libros Viajeros and Green Light Readers.

Needs Children's/juvenile, young adult.

How to Contact Does not accept unsolicited mss.

⊠ ▢ ◎ HARLEQUIN AMERICAN ROMANCE

a Harlequin book line, 233 Broadway, Suite 1001, New York NY 10279. (212)553-4200. Website: www.eharlequin.com. **Contact:** Melissa Jeglinski, associate senior editor. "Upbeat and lively, fast-paced and well plotted, American Romance celebrates the pursuit of love in the backyards, big cities and wide-open spaces of America." Publishes paperback originals and reprints. Books: newspaper print paper; web printing; perfect-bound.

Needs Romance (contemporary, American). Needs "all-American stories with a range of emotional and sensual content and are supported by a sense of community within the plot's framework. In the confident and caring heroine, the tough but tender hero, and their dynamic relationship that is at the center of this series, real-life love is showcased as the best fantasy of all!"

How to Contact Accepts unsolicited mss. Query with SASE or submit complete ms. Send SASE for return of ms or send a disposable ms and SASE for reply only. No simultaneous submissions, electronic submissions, submissions on disk.

Terms Pays royalty. Offers advance. Ms guidelines online.

⊠ ⊠ ▢ ◎ HARLEQUIN BLAZE

a Harlequin book line, 225 Duncan Mill Road, Don Mills ON M3B 3K9 Canada. (416)445-5860. Website: www.eharlequin.com. **Contact:** Birgit Davis-Todd, executive editor. "Harlequin Blaze is a red-hot series. It is a vehicle to build and promote new authors who have a strong sexual edge to their stories. It is also *the* place to be for seasoned authors who want to create a sexy, sizzling, longer contemporary story." Publishes paperback originals and reprints. Books: newspaper print; web printing; perfect-bound. **Published some debut authors within the last year.**

Needs Romance (contemporary). "Sensuous, highly romantic, innovative plots that are sexy in premise and execution. The tone of the books can run from fun and flirtatious to dark and sensual. Submissions should have a very contemporary feel—what it's like to be young and single today. We are looking for heroes and heroines in their early 20s and up. There should be a a strong emphasis on the physical relationship between the couples. Fully described loves scenes along with a high level of fantasy and playfulness."

How to Contact No simultaneous submissions, electronic submissions, submissions on disk.

Terms Pays royalty. Offers advance. Ms guidelines online.

Advice "Are you a *Cosmo* girl at heart? A fan of *Sex and the City*? Or maybe you have a sexually adventurous spirit. If so, then Blaze is the series for you!"

⚡ ◻ ◎ 🌐 HARLEQUIN HISTORICALS

a Harlequin book line, Eton House, 18-24 Paradise Road, Richmond Surrey TW9 1SR United Kingdom. (212)553-4200. Website: www.eharlequin.com. **Contact:** Tracy Farrell, senior editor. "The primary element of a Harlequin Historical novel is romance. The story should focus on the heroine and how her love for one man changes her life forever. For this reason, it is very important that you have an appealing hero and heroine, and that their relationship is a compelling one. The conflicts they must overcome—and the situations they face—can be as varied as the setting you have chosen, but there must be romantic tension, some spark between your hero and heroine that keeps your reader interested." Publishes paperback originals and reprints. Books: newsprint paper; perfect-bound. **Published some debut authors within the last year.**

Needs Romance (historical). "We will not accept books set after 1900. We're looking primarily for books set in North America, England or France between 1100 and 1900 A.D. We do not buy many novels set during the American Civil War. We are, however, flexible, and will consider most periods and settings. We are not looking for gothics or family sagas, nor are we interested in the kind of comedy of manners typified by straight Regencies. Historical romances set during the Regency period, however, will definitely be considered."

How to Contact Accepts unsolicited mss. Query with SASE or submit complete ms. Send SASE for return of ms or send a disposable ms and SASE for reply only. No simultaneous submissions, electronic submissions, submissions on disk.

Terms Pays royalty. Offers advance. Ms guidelines online.

⚡ ◻ ◎ HARLEQUIN INTRIGUE

a Harlequin Book line, 233 Broadway, Suite 1001, New York NY 10279. (212)553-4200. Website: www.eharlequin.com. **Contact:** Denise O'Sullivan, associate senior editor. "These novels are taut, edge-of-the-seat, contemporary romantic suspense tales of intrigue and desire. Kidnappings, stalkings and women in jeopardy coupled with best-selling romantic themes are the examples of story lines we love most." Publishes paperback originals and reprints. Books: newspaper print; perfect-bound. **Published some debut authors within the last year.**

Needs Romance (romantic suspense). "Murder mystery, psychological suspense, or thriller; the love story must be inextricably bound to the resolution where all loose ends are tied up neatly—and shared dangers lead right to shared passions. As long as they're in jeopardy and falling in love, our heroes and heroines may traverse a landscape as wide as the world itself. Their lives are on the line—and so are their hearts!"

How to Contact Accepts unsolicited mss. Query with SASE or submit complete ms. Send SASE for return of ms or send a disposable ms and SASE for reply only. No simultaneous submissions, electronic submissions, submissions on disk.

Terms Pays royalty. Offers advance. Ms guidelines online.

⚡ Ⓝ 🌐 HARLEQUIN MILLS & BOON, LTD.

Harlequin Enterprises, Ltd., Eton House, 18-24 Paradise Rd., Richmond Surrey TW9 1SR United Kingdom. (44)0208-288-2800. Website: www.millsandboon.co.uk. **Contact:** K. Stoecker, editorial director; Tessa Shapcott, senior editor (Harlequin Presents); Samantha Bell, senior editor (Harlequin Romance); Linda Fildew, senior editor (Mills & Boon Historicals); Sheila Hodgson, senior editor (Mills & Boon Medicals). Estab. 1908-1909. Publishes mass market paperback originals. **Published some debut authors within the last year.** Plans 3-4 first novels this year.

Imprint(s) Harlequin Presents (Mills & Boon Presents); Harlequin Romance (Mills & Boon Tender Romance); Mills & Boon Historicals; Mills & Boon Medicals.

Needs Romance (contemporary, historical, regency period, medical).

How to Contact Submit 3 sample chapter(s), synopsis. Responds in 5 months to mss. No simultaneous submissions.

Terms Pays advance against royalty. Publishes ms 2 years after acceptance. Ms guidelines online.

⚡ ◻ ◎ 🌐 HARLEQUIN PRESENTS (MILLS & BOON)

a Harlequin book line, Eton House, 18-24 Paradise Road, Richmond Surrey TW9 1SR United Kingdom. (44)0208 288 2800. Website: www.millsandboon.co.uk. **Contact:** Tessa Shapcott, senior editor. Publishes paperback originals and reprints. Books: newspaper print; perfect-bound. **Published some debut authors within the last year.**

Needs Romance. Needs "novels written in the third person that feature spirited, independent heroines who aren't afraid to take the initiative, and breathtakingly attractive, larger-than-life heroes. The conflict between these characters should be lively and evenly matched, but always balanced by a developing romance that may include explicit lovemaking."

How to Contact Accepts unsolicited mss. Query with SASE or submit sample chapter(s), synopsis. Send SASE for return of ms or send a disposable ms and SASE for reply only. No simultaneous submissions, electronic submissions, submissions on disk.
Terms Pays royalty. Offers advance. Ms guidelines online.

✪ ◻ ◎ ⊕ HARLEQUIN ROMANCE (MILLS & BOON TENDER ROMANCE)
a Harlequin book line, Eton House, 18-24 Paradise Road, Richmond Surrey TW9 1SR United Kingdom. (44)208 288 2800. Website: www.millsandboon.co.uk. **Contact:** Bryony Green, associate senior editor. "Sparkling, fresh and emotionally fulfilling, these stories capture the rush of falling in love and deliver the ultimate in feel-good romantic fiction!" Publishes paperback originals and reprints. Books: newspaper print; perfect-bound. **Published some debut authors within the last year.**
Needs "Harlequin Romance celebrates women's experiences—in life, and especially in love—set against a variety of international settings. Although primarily written in third person, from the heroine's viewpoint, we do consider stories written from different perspectives. A strong, charismatic hero is essential; but most importantly, readers must be able to identify intimately with a believable, engaging heroine. Stories should capture the rush of excitement as the couple strive to overcome the emotional barriers keeping them apart. These conflicts should be contemporary and relevant to today's women. Whilst sexual description won't be explicit, there should be an edge of sensual tension. Above all, we're looking for novels with a fresh voice: sparkling, feel-good stories bursting with lively interaction and a guaranteed buzz of romantic excitement."
How to Contact Accepts unsolicited mss. Submit 3 sample chapter(s), synopsis. Send SASE for return of ms or send a disposable ms and SASE for reply only. No simultaneous submissions, electronic submissions, submissions on disk.
Terms Pays royalty. Offers advance. Ms guidelines online.

✪ ✪ ◻ ◎ HARLEQUIN SUPERROMANCE
a Harlequin book line, 225 Duncan Mill Road, Don Mills ON M3B 3K9 Canada. (416)445-5860. Website: www.eharlequin.com. **Contact:** Laura Shin, senior editor. "The aim of Superromance novels is to produce a contemporary, involving read with a mainstream tone in its situations and characters, using romance as the major theme. To achieve this, emphasis should be placed on individual writing styles and unique and topical ideas." Publishes paperback originals and reprints. Books: newspaper print; perfect-bound. **Published 3 debut authors within the last year.**
Needs Romance (contemporary). "The criteria for Superromance books are flexible. Aside from length, the determining factor for publication will always be quality. Authors should strive to break free of stereotypes, cliches and worn out plot devices to create strong, believable stories with depth and emotional intensity. Superromance novels are intended to appeal to a wide range of romance readers."
How to Contact Accepts unsolicited mss. Query with SASE or submit 3 sample chapter(s), synopsis. Send SASE for return of ms or send a disposable ms and SASE for reply only. No simultaneous submissions, electronic submissions, submissions on disk.
Terms Pays royalty. Offers advance. Ms guidelines online.
Advice "A general familiarity with current Superromance books is advisable to keep abreast of ever-changing treads and overall scope, but we don't want imitations and we are open to innovation. We look for sincere, heartfelt writing based on true-to-life experiences the reader can identify with."

✪ ◻ ◎ ⊕ HARLEQUIN TEMPTATION
a Harlequin book line, Eton House 10-24 Paradise Road, Richmond Surrey TW9 1SR United Kingdom. Website: www.eharlequin.com. **Contact:** Brenda Chin, senior editor. "Temptation is sexy, sassy and seductive! This is one of Harlequin's boldest, most sensuous series, focusing on men and women living and loving today!" Publishes paperback originals and reprints. Books: newspaper print; perfect-bound. **Published some debut authors within the last year.**
Needs Romance. "Almost anything goes in Temptation: the stories may be humorous, topical, adventurous or glitzy, but at heart they are pure romantic fantasy."
How to Contact Accepts unsolicited mss. Query with SASE or submit 3 sample chapter(s), synopsis. Send SASE for return of ms or send a disposable ms and SASE for reply only. No simultaneous submissions, electronic submissions, submissions on disk.
Terms Pays royalty. Offers advance. Ms guidelines online.
Advice "Think fast-paced, use the desire and language of women today, add a high level of sexual tension along with strong conflicts, and then throw in a good dash of 'what if.' The results should sizzle."

✪ Ⓐ ✪ ◎ HARPERCOLLINS CANADA LTD.
2 Bloor St. East, 20th Floor, Toronto ON M4W 1A8 Canada. (416)975-9334. Fax: (416)975-5223. Website: www.harpercanada.com. Harpercollins is not accepting unsolicited material at this time.

✪ Ⓐ HARPERCOLLINS CHILDREN'S BOOKS

HarperCollins Publishers, 1350 Avenue of the Americas, New York NY 10019. (212)261-6500. Fax: (212)261-6689. Website: www.harperchildrens.com. Publishes hardcover originals. Averages 350 total titles/year.
Imprint(s) Avon; Joanna Cotler; Greenwillow Books: Laura Geringer Books; HarperFestival; HarperTrophy; Avon & Tempest; HarperCollins Children's Books.
Needs Adventure, fantasy, historical, humor, juvenile, literary, picture books, young adult.
How to Contact *Agented submissions only.*
Terms Pays 10-12½% royalty on retail price. Average advance: variable. Publishes ms 1 year (novels) or 2 years (picture books) after acceptance.

✪ HARPERCOLLINS GENERAL BOOKS GROUP

Division of HarperCollins Publishers, 10 East 53 Street, New York NY 10022. (212)207-7000. Fax: (212)207-7633. Website: www.harpercollins.com. "HarperCollins, one of the largest English language publishers in the world, is a broad-based publisher with strengths in academic, business and professional, children's, educational, general interest, and religious and spiritual books, as well as multimedia titles." Publishes hardcover and paperback originals and paperback reprints.
Imprint(s) Access Press; Amistad Press; Avon; Ecco; Fourth Estate; HarperAudio; HarperBusiness; HarperCollins; HarperEntertainment; HarperLargePrint; HarperResource; HarperSanFranciso; HarperTorch; Perennial; PerfectBound; Quill; Rayo; ReganBooks; William Morrow.

✪ Ⓩ HARPERTORCH

(formerly HarperPaperbacks), Imprint of HarperCollins Publishers, 10 E. 53rd St., New York NY 10022. (212)207-7000. Fax: (212)207-7901. **Contact:** Michael Morrison, publisher. Publishes paperback originals and reprints. **Published some debut authors within the last year.**
Needs Mainstream/contemporary, mystery, romance (contemporary, historical, romantic suspense), suspense, thriller/espionage.
How to Contact Does not accept unsolicited mss. Query with SASE.
Terms Pays royalty. Offers advance.

Ⓐ Ⓩ HARVEST HOUSE PUBLISHERS

990 Owen Loop N., Eugene OR 97402. (541)343-0123. Fax: (541)302-0731. E-mail: manuscriptcoordinator@harvesthousepublishers.com. Website: www.harvesthousepublishers.com. **Contact:** Acquisitions. Estab. 1974. "Our mission is to glorify God by providing high-quality books and products that affirm biblical values, help people grow spiritually strong, and proclaim Jesus Christ as the answer to every human need." Publishes hardcover originals and reprints, trade paperback originals and reprints, and mass market paperback originals and reprints. Books: 40 lb. ground wood paper; offset printing; perfect binding. Average print order: 10,000. First novel print order: 10,000-15,000. **Published 5-6 debut authors within the last year.** Averages 160 total titles, 15-20 fiction titles/year.
Needs Harvest House no longer accepts unsolicited manuscripts, proposals or artwork.
How to Contact Does not accept unsolicited mss.
Advice "Attend a writer's conference where you have an opportunity to pitch your book idea to an editor face to face. We also look at fiction represented by a reputable agent."

Ⓩ HAWK PUBLISHING GROUP

7107 S. Yale Ave., #345, Tulsa OK 74136. (918)492-3677. Fax: (918)492-2120. Website: www.hawkpub.com. Estab. 1999. Independent publisher of general trade/commercial books, fiction and nonfiction. Publishes hardcover and trade paperback originals. **Published 4 debut authors within the last year.** Plans 2 first novels this year. Averages 6-8 total titles, 3 fiction titles/year. Member, PMA. Titles are distributed by NBN/Biblio Distribution.
Needs Looking for good books of all kinds. Not interested in juvenile, poetry or short story collections. Published *The Darkest Night*, by Jodie Larsen; *This Fair Land*, by K.D. Wentworth.
How to Contact Accepts unsolicited mss. Submit 3 sample chapter(s), synopsis, author bio, list of publishing credits. Accepts simultaneous submissions.
Terms Pays royalty. Publishes ms 1-2 years after acceptance. Ms guidelines online.
Advice "Prepare a professional submission and follow the guidelines. The simple things really do count; use 12 pt. pitch with 1" margins and only send what is requested."

Ⓩ HELICON NINE EDITIONS

Subsidiary of Midwest Center for the Literary Arts, Inc., P.O. Box 22412, Kansas City MO 64113. (816)753-1016. E-mail: helicon9@aol.com. Website: www.heliconnine.com. **Contact:** Gloria Vando Hickok. Estab. 1990.

Small not-for-profit press publishing poetry, fiction, creative nonfiction and anthologies. Publishes paperback originals. Also publishes one-story chapbooks called *feuillets*, which come with envelope, 250 print run. Books: 60 lb. paper; offset printing; perfect-bound; 4-color cover. Average print order: 1,000-5,000. **Published 1 debut author within the last year.** Distributes titles through Baker & Taylor, Brodart, Ingrams, Follet (library acquisitions), Midwest Library Service, all major distributors and booksellers. Promotes titles through reviews, readings, radio and television interviews.

How to Contact Does not accept unsolicited mss.

Terms Pays royalty. Author's copies. Offers advance. Publishes ms 6-12 months after acceptance.

Advice "We accept short story collections. We welcome new writers and first books. Submit a clean, readable copy in a folder or box—paginated with title and name on each page. Also, do not pre-design book, i.e., no illustrations. We'd like to see books that will be read 50-100 years from now."

HEMKUNT PRESS

Hemkunt Publishers (P) Ltd., A-78 Naraina Industrial Area Phase-I, New Delhi 110028 India. +91-11-2579-5079. E-mail: hemkunt1@ndf.vsnl.net.in. Website: www.hemkuntpublishers.com. **Contact:** Arvinder Singh, director. "We specialize in children's fiction and storybooks as well as novels and short stories." Distributes titles through direct sales, direct mailings and distributors.

Needs "We would be interested in novels and short stories, preferably by authors with a published work. Unpublished work is also considered. Would like to have distribution rights for US, Canada and UK, besides India."

How to Contact Query with SASE. Accepts queries by e-mail, fax. Accepts submissions on disk.

Terms By request.

Advice "Send interesting short stories and novels pertaining to the global point of view."

HENDRICK-LONG PUBLISHING CO., INC.

10635 Toweroaks D., Houston TX 77070. (832)912-7323. Fax: (832)912-7353. E-mail: hendrick-long@worldnet.att.net. Website: hendricklongpublishing.com. **Contact:** Vilma Long. Estab. 1969. Only considers manuscripts with Texas theme. Publishes hardcover and trade paperback originals and hardcover reprints. Averages 4 total titles/year.

Needs Juvenile, young adult.

How to Contact Submit outline, 2 sample chapter(s), synopsis. Responds in 3 months to queries. No simultaneous submissions.

Terms Pays royalty on selling price. Offers advance. Publishes ms 18 months after acceptance. Book catalog for $8^{1}/_{2} \times 11$ or 9×12 SASE with 4 first-class stamps. Ms guidelines online.

HERITAGE BOOKS, INC.

65 E. Main St., Westminster MD 21157. E-mail: submissions@heritagebooks.com. Website: www.heritagebooks.com. Estab. 1978. Publishes hardcover and paperback originals and reprints. Averages 200 total titles/year.

Needs Historical (relating to early American life, 1600-1900).

How to Contact Query with SASE. Responds in 1 month to queries. Accepts simultaneous submissions.

Terms Pays 10% royalty on list price.

HESPERUS PRESS

4 Rickett Street, London SW6 1RU United Kingdom. 44 20 7610 3331. Fax: 44 20 7610 3217. Website: www.hesperuspress.com. **Contact:** Alex Callenzi, publishing director (literary fiction). Estab. 2001. Hesperus is a small independent publisher mainly of classics and literary fiction. Publishes paperback originals. Books: munken paper; traditional printing; sewn binding. Average print order: 5,000. Distributes titles through Trafalgar Square in the US, Grantham Book Services in the UK.

Needs Literary. Published *Loveless Love*, by Luigi Pirandello (modern classic); *Portrait of Mr. W.H.*, by Oscar Wilde (modern classic); *Tragedy of the Korosko*, by Arthur Conan Doyle (modern classic).

How to Contact Does not accept unsolicited mss. *Agented submissions only.* Query with SASE. Accepts queries by mail. Include estimated word count, brief bio, list of publishing credits. Agented fiction 100%. Responds in 8-10 weeks to queries; 8-10 weeks to mss. Accepts simultaneous submissions. No electronic submissions, submissions on disk.

Advice Find an agent to represent you.

HIGH COUNTRY PUBLISHERS LTD.

197 New Market Center, #135, Boone NC 28607. (828)964-0590. Fax: (828)262-1973. E-mail: editor@highcountrypublishers.com. Website: www.highcountrypublishers.com. **Contact:** Judith Geary, senior editor. Estab. 2001. "We are a small regional house focusing on popular fiction and memoir. At present, we are most interested in

regional fiction, historical fiction and mystery fiction.'' Publishes hardcover orginals, paperback originals and paperback reprints. Books: 60 lb. paper; offset printing; b&w illustrations. Average print order: 1,500-5,000. First novel print order: 1,500-3,000. **Published 1 debut author within the last year.** Plans 3 first novels this year. Member: PMA, PAS, SEBA. Distributes titles through Biblio Distribution, sister company of NBN books.
Needs Ethnic, feminist, historical, mystery (amateur sleuth, cozy, police procedural, private eye/hard-boiled), regional (southern appalachian), romance (contemporary, historical, romantic suspense adventure), young adult (historical, mystery/suspense). Published *Dirty Deeds*, by Mark Terry (mystery); *Once Upon a Different Time*, by Marian Coe; *Gloria*, by Ann Chamberlin (historical fiction); and *Mount Doomsday*, by Don Berman (thriller).
How to Contact Accepts unsolicited mss. Query with SASE or submit outline, 3 sample chapter(s). Reading period open from July to October. Accepts queries by e-mail, mail. Include estimated word count, brief bio, list of publishing credits. Send copy of ms and SASE. Agented fiction 10%. Responds in 6 months to queries; 6 months to mss. Accepts simultaneous submissions, electronic submissions. No submissions on disk. Often comments on rejected mss.
Terms Pays 10% royalty. Publishes ms 6 months-2 years after acceptance. Ms guidelines online.

⭐ ☑ 🌐 HODDER & STOUGHTON/HEADLINE

Hodder Headline, 338 Euston Road, London NW1 3BH England. (020)7873-6000. **Contact:** Caroline Stofer, submissions editor, Headline (adult fiction). ''Big commercial, general book publishers of general fiction/nonfiction, thrillers, romance, sagas, contemporary, original, literary, crime.'' Publishes hardcover and paperback originals and paperback reprints.
Imprint(s) Sceptre, Hodder & Stoughton, LIR, Headline, Review, Feature.
Needs Family saga, historical (general), literary, mainstream/contemporary, mystery (amateur sleuth, cozy, police procedural, private eye/hard-boiled), romance (contemporary, romantic suspense), thriller/espionage. Published *Everything's Eventual*, by Stephen King (general); *Dinner for Two*, by Mike Gayle (general, romantic comedy); *The Rice Mother*, by Rani Manicka (literary).
How to Contact Accepts unsolicited mss. Query with SASE or submit outline, 1 sample chapter(s), synopsis. Accepts queries by e-mail. Include estimated word count, brief bio. Responds in 2 weeks to queries; 1 month to mss. Accepts simultaneous submissions.
Terms Book catalog for flat A4 SASE. Ms guidelines for #10 SASE.
Advice ''Minimum 80,000 words. For popular fiction titles (i.e. thrillers) we require around 120,000 words. Writing should be of good quality and commercial. No single short stories, horror or sci-fi/fantasy.''

◎ HOLIDAY HOUSE, INC.

425 Madison Ave., New York NY 10017. (212)688-0085. Fax: (212)421-6134. **Contact:** Aquisitions editor. Estab. 1935. ''Holiday House has a commitment to publishing first-time authors and illustrators.'' Independent publisher of children's books, picture books, nonfiction and novels for young readers. Publishes hardcover originals and paperback reprints. **Published some debut authors within the last year.** Averages 60 total titles/year.
Needs Adventure, children's/juvenile, historical, humor, literary, mainstream/contemporary, Judaica and holiday, animal stories for young readers. Children's books only. Published *There is a Frog in My Throat*, by Pat Street, illustrated by Loreen Leedy; *The Gorillas of Gill Park*, by Amy Gordon.
How to Contact Query with SASE. No simultaneous submissions.
Terms Pays royalty on list price, range varies. Average advance: flexible, depending on whether the book is illustrated. Publishes ms 18 months after acceptance. Ms guidelines for #10 SASE.
Advice ''We're not in a position to be too encouraging, as our list is tight, but we're always open to good writing. Please submit only one project at a time.''

⭐ ◎ HENRY HOLT & CO. BOOKS FOR YOUNG READERS

Henry Holt & Co., LLC, 115 W. 18th St., New York NY 10011. (212)886-9200. Website: www.henryholt.com. **Contact:** Submissions editor, Books for Young Readers. Estab. 1866 (Holt). Henry Holt Books for Young Readers publishes excellent books of all kinds (fiction, nonfiction, illustrated) for all ages, from the very young to the young adult. Publishes hardcover originals of picture books, chapter books, middle grade and young adult novels. Averages 70-80 total titles/year.
Needs Adventure, fantasy, historical, mainstream/contemporary, multicultural, picture books, young adult. Juvenile: adventure, animal, contemporary, fantasy, history, multicultural. Picture books: animal, concept, history, mulitcultural, sports. Young adult: contemporary, fantasy, history, multicultural, nature/environment, problem novels, sports. Published *When Zachary Beaver Came to Town*, by Kimberly Willie Holt (middle grade fiction); *The Gospel According to Larry*, by Janet Tashijian (YA fiction); *Visiting Langston*, by Willis Perdomo, illustrated by Bryan Collier (picture book); *Keeper of the Night*, by Kimberly Willis Holt; and *Alphabet Under Construction*, by Denise Fleming (picture book).

How to Contact Accepts unsolicited mss. Include estimated word count, brief bio, list of publishing credits. Send SASE or IRC. Responds in 4-5 months to queries. No simultaneous submissions.

Terms Pays royalty on retail price. Average advance: $3,000 and up. Publishes ms 18-36 months after acceptance. Book catalog for 8½×11 SAE with $1.75 postage. Ms guidelines online.

★ Ⓐ ♥ HENRY HOLT

Henry Holt and Company, 115 W. 18th Street, 6th Floor, New York NY 10011. (212)886-9200. **Contact:** Sara Bershtel, associate publisher (Metropolitan Books; literary fiction); Jennifer Barth, editor-in-chief (adult trade); Lisa Considine, senior editor (adult trade); Paul Golub, editorial director (Times Books). Publishes hardcover and paperback originals and reprints.

Imprint(s) John Macrae Books; Metropolitan Books; Times Books; Henry Holt & Company Books for Young Readers.

○ ◎ HOMA & SEKEY BOOKS

3rd Floor, North Tower, Mack-Cali Center III, 140 East Ridgewood Ave, Paramus NJ 07652. (201)261-8810. Fax: (201)261-8890. E-mail: info@homabooks.com. Website: www.homabooks.com. **Contact:** Shawn Ye, editor-in-chief. Estab. 1997. "We focus on publishing Asia-related titles. Both translations and original English manuscripts are welcome." Publishes hardcover and paperback originals. Books: natural paper; web press; perfect bound; illustrations. **Published 3 debut authors within the last year.** Averages 7 total titles, 3 fiction titles/ year. Member, PMA. Distributes titles through Ingram, Baker & Taylor, etc.

• Received the Notable Book Award for *Father & Son: A Novel.*

Needs Ethnic (Asian), literary, mystery, young adult (adventure, historical, mystery/suspense, romance). Wants China-related titles. Published *Father and Son*, by Sung-won Han (translation); *The General's Beard*, by Oyoung Lee (translation); *Reflections on a Mask*, by In-hun Choe (translation).

How to Contact Accepts unsolicited mss. Query with SASE or submit outline, 2 sample chapter(s). Accepts queries by e-mail, mail. Include estimated word count, brief bio, list of publishing credits. Send SASE for return of ms or send a disposable ms and SASE for reply only. Responds in 8 weeks to queries; 20 weeks to mss. Accepts simultaneous submissions, electronic submissions. Sometimes comments on rejected mss.

Terms Pays 5-10% royalty. Publishes ms 1 year after acceptance. Book catalog for 9×12 SASE. Ms guidelines online.

Advice "Authors should be willing and able to actively participate in the publicity and promotion of their books."

★ Ⓩ ◎ HOUGHTON MIFFLIN BOOKS FOR CHILDREN

Houghton Mifflin Company, 222 Berkeley St., Boston MA 02116. (617)351-5959. Fax: (617)351-1111. E-mail: children's_books@hmco.com. Website: www.houghtonmifflinbooks.com. **Contact:** Hannah Rodgers, submissions coordinator; Kate O'Sullivan, senior editor; Ann Rider, senior editor; Margaret Raymo, senior editor. "Houghton Mifflin gives shape to ideas that educate, inform, and above all, delight." Publishes hardcover originals and trade paperback originals and reprints. **Published 12 debut authors within the last year.** Averages 100 total titles/year. Promotes titles through author visits, advertising, reviews.

Imprint(s) Clarion Books, New York City; Walter Lorraine books.

Needs Adventure, ethnic, historical, humor, juvenile (early readers), literary, mystery, picture books, suspense, young adult, board books. *Gathering Blue*, by Lois Lowry; *The Circuit*, by Francisco Jimenez; and *When I Was Older*, by Garret Freymann-Weyr.

How to Contact Responds in 4 months to queries. Accepts simultaneous submissions. No electronic submissions.

Terms Pays 5-10% royalty on retail price. Average advance: variable. Publishes ms 18-24 months after acceptance. Book catalog for 9×12 SASE with 3 first-class stamps. Ms guidelines online.

Ⓐ HOUGHTON MIFFLIN CO.

222 Berkeley St., Boston MA 02116. (617)351-5000. Website: www.hmco.com. **Contact:** Submissions Editor. Estab. 1832. Publishes hardcover originals and trade paperback originals and reprints. **Published 5 debut authors within the last year.** Averages 250 total titles/year.

Needs Literary. "We are not a mass market publisher. Study the current list." Published *Extremely Loud and Incredibly Close*, by Jonathan Safran Foer; *The Plot Against America*, by Philip Roth; *Heir to the Glimmering World*, by Cynthia Ozick.

How to Contact Does not accept unsolicited mss. *Agented submissions only.* Accepts simultaneous submissions.

Terms Hardcover: pays 10-15% royalty on retail price, sliding scale or flat rate based on sales; paperback: 7½% flat rate, but negotiable. Average advance: variable. Publishes ms 3 years after acceptance.

✪ Ⓐ ⊘ HYPERION BOOKS FOR CHILDREN

Hyperion, 114 Fifth Ave., New York NY 10011. (212)633-440. Fax: (212)807-5880. Website: www.hyperionbook sforchildren.com. **Contact:** Editorial director. "The aim of Hyperion Books for Children is to create a dynamic children's program informed by Disney's creative vision, direct connection to children, and unparalleled marketing and distribution." Publishes hardcover and trade paperback originals. Averages 210 total titles/year.

Needs Juvenile, picture books, young adult. Published *McDuff*, by Roesmary Wells and Susan Jeffers (picture book); *Split Just Right*, by Adele Griffin (middle grade).

How to Contact *Agented submissions only.* Accepts simultaneous submissions.

Terms Pays royalty. Average advance: varies. Publishes ms 1 year after acceptance.

Advice "Hyperion Books for Children are meant to appeal to an upscale children's audience. Study your audience. Look at and research current children's books. Who publishes what you like? Approach them."

Ⓝ 🌐 ✪ ◯ IGNOTUS PRESS

BCM-Writer, London WC1N 3XX United Kingdom. E-mail: ignotuspress@aol.com. Website: www.ignotuspress. com. **Contact:** Suzanne Ruthuen. Estab. 1996. The aim of ignotus press is to provide a wide base of genuine information for all esoteric traditions. Publishes paperback originals, hardcover reprints, paperback reprints and e-books. Books: litho and digital printing; perfect binding; illustrations. Average first novel print order: 300. **Published 12 debut authors within the last year.** Averages 20 total titles/year.

Imprint(s) Moonraker.

Needs Horror (psychological, supernatural), humor, new age/mystic, psychic/supernatural, religious (religious mystery/suspense, religious thriller). "ignotus press hopes to fill the gap left by mainstream publishers who are moving away from traditional sources. What we don't want is New Age idealism, sword & sorcery, fantasy, 'mind, body & spirit', the white-light brand of modern Wicca, pseudo-spirituality or any form of neo-Hammer House of Horror fiction." Recently published *Wood Craft*, by Rupert Percy; *Velvet Vampire*, by Adam Thorne; *Hearth Fire*, by Fiona Walker-Craven.

How to Contact Does not accept unsolicited mss. Submit 2 sample chapter(s). Accepts queries by mail. Include estimated word count, brief bio, list of publishing credits. Send SASE for return of ms or send a disposable ms and SASE for reply only. Responds in 4 months to queries; 6 months to mss. Sometimes comments on rejected mss.

Terms Pays royalty. Pays 6 contributor's copies. Publishes ms 6-12 months after acceptance. Ms guidelines for SASE.

Advice "Seriously study the guidelines and back list."

✪ IMAGES SI, INC.

Images Publishing, 109 Woods of Arden Rd., Staten Island NY 10312. (718)966-3964. Fax: (718)966-3695. Website: www.imagesco.com. Estab. 1990. "We are currently looking for science fiction and fantasy stories and books more than anything else." Publishes hardcover originals, trade paperback originals and audio. Averages 5 total titles/year.

Needs Fantasy, science fiction. "We are looking for short stories as well as full-length novels."

How to Contact Query with SASE. Responds in 2 months to mss. Accepts simultaneous submissions.

Terms Pays 10-20% royalty on wholesale price. Average advance: $1,000-5,000. Publishes ms 6 months after acceptance.

◔ IMAJINN BOOKS

P.O. Box 545, Canon City CO 81212-0545. (719)275-0060. Fax: (719)276-0746. E-mail: editors@imajinnbooks.c om. Website: www.imajinnbooks.com. **Contact:** Linda J. Kichline, editor. Estab. 1998. "Imajinn Books is a small independent publishing house that specializes in romances with story lines involving ghosts, psychics or psychic phenomena, witches, vampires, werewolves, angels, space travel, the future." Publishes trade paperback originals. Books: 40 lb. text stock paper; camera ready and disk to film printing; perfect binding; illustrations; occasionally, but rare. Average print order: 2,500. First novel print order: 1,000. **Published 3 debut authors within the last year.** Member: SPAN and PMA. Distributes titles through Baker & Taylor, Amazon.com, BN.com and imajinnbooks.com. Promotes titles through advertising, review magazines.

Needs Fantasy (romance), horror (romance), psychic/supernatural, romance (futuristic/time travel), science fiction (romance). "We look for specific story lines based on what the readers are asking for and what story lines in which we're short. We post our current needs on our website." Published *Circle of Death*, by Keri Arthur (horror romance); and *Afterimage*, by Jeanette Roycraft (vampire romance).

How to Contact Query with SASE. Accepts queries by e-mail. Include estimated word count, brief bio, list of publishing credits. Send copy of ms and SASE. Agented fiction 20%. Responds in 3 months to queries; 9-12 months to mss. Often comments on rejected mss.

Terms Pays 6-10% royalty on retail price. Average advance: 25-100. Publishes ms 1-3 years after acceptance. Book catalog and ms guidelines for #10 SASE or online. Ms guidelines online.

Advice "Carefully read the author guidelines, and read books published by ImaJinn Books."

🖿 INSOMNIAC PRESS

192 Spadina Ave., Suite 403, Toronto ON M5T 2C2 Canada. (416)504-6270. Fax: (416)504-9313. E-mail: mike@insomniacpress.com. Website: www.insomniacpress.com. Estab. 1992. "Midsize independent publisher with a mandate to produce edgy experimental fiction." Publishes trade paperback originals and reprints, mass market paperback originals, and electronic originals and reprints. First novel print order: 3,000. **Published 15 debut authors within the last year.** Plans 4 first novels this year. Averages 20 total titles, 5 fiction titles/year.

Needs Comic books, ethnic, experimental, gay/lesbian, humor, literary, mainstream/contemporary, multicultural, mystery, suspense. We publish a mix of commercial (mysteries) and literary fiction. Published *Pray For Us Sinners*, by Patrick Taylor (novel).

How to Contact Accepts unsolicited mss. Accepts queries by e-mail. Include estimated word count, brief bio, list of publishing credits. Send SASE for return of ms or send a disposable ms and SASE for reply only. Agented fiction 5%. Responds in 1 week to queries; 2 months to mss. Accepts simultaneous submissions. Sometimes comments on rejected mss.

Terms Pays 10-15% royalty on retail price. Average advance: $500-1,000. Publishes ms 6 months after acceptance. Ms guidelines online.

Advice "Visit our website, read our writer's guidelines."

🖿 INTERLINK PUBLISHING GROUP, INC.

46 Crosby St., Northampton MA 01060. (413)582-7054. Fax: (413)582-7057. E-mail: editor@interlinkbooks.com. Website: www.interlinkbooks.com. **Contact:** Michel Moushabeck, publisher; Pam Thompson, editor. Estab. 1987. "Midsize independent publisher specializing in world travel, world literature, world history and politics." Publishes hardcover and trade paperback originals. Books: 55 lb. Warren Sebago Cream white paper; web offset printing; perfect binding. Average print order: 5,000. **Published new writers within the last year.** Averages 50 total titles, 2-4 fiction titles/year. Distributes titles through distributors such as Baker & Taylor. Promotes titles through book mailings to extensive, specialized lists of editors and reviews; authors read at bookstores and special events across the country.

Imprint(s) Interlink Books and Olive Branch Press.

Needs Ethnic, international. "Adult—We are looking for translated works relating to the Middle East, Africa or Latin America." Recently published *House of the Winds*, by Mia Yun (first novel); *The Gardens of Light*, by Amin Maalouf (novel translated from French); and *War in the Land of Egypt*, by Yusef Al-Qaid (novel translated from Arabic).

How to Contact Does not accept unsolicited mss. Query with SASE or submit outline, sample chapter(s). Responds in 3 months to queries. Accepts simultaneous submissions. No electronic submissions.

Terms Pays 6-8% royalty on retail price. Average advance: small. Publishes ms 18 months after acceptance. Ms guidelines online.

Advice "Our Interlink International Fiction Series is designed to bring to North America readers, writers who have achieved wide acclaim at home but have not been recognized beyond the borders of their native lands."

🖿 INVERTED-A

P.O. Box 267, Licking MO 65542. E-mail: amnfn@well.com. **Contact:** Aya Katz, chief editor (poetry, novels, political); Nets Katz, science editor (scientific, academic). Estab. 1985. Publishes paperback originals. Books: offset printing. Average print order: 1,000. Average first novel print order: 500. Distributes through Baker & Taylor, Amazon, Bowker.

Needs Utopian, political. Needs poetry submission for our newsletter, *Inverted-A Horn*.

How to Contact Does not accept unsolicited mss. Query with SASE. Reading period open from January 2 to March 15. Accepts queries by e-mail. Include estimated word count. Responds in 1 month to queries; 3 months to mss. Accepts simultaneous submissions. Sometimes comments on rejected mss.

Terms Pays in 10 author's copies. Publishes ms 1 year after acceptance. Ms guidelines for SASE.

Advice "Read our books. Read the *Inverted-A Horn*. We are different. We do not follow industry trends."

🖿 ION IMAGINATION PUBLISHING

Ion Imagination Entertainment, Inc., P.O. Box 210943, Nashville TN 37221-0943. Fax: (615)646-6276. E-mail: ionimagin@aol.com. Website: www.flumpa.com. **Contact:** Keith Frickey, editor. Estab. 1994. Small independent publisher of children's fiction, multimedia and audio products. Publishes hardcover and paperback originals. Average first novel print order: 10,000. Member: SPAN and PMA.

- Received the Parents Choice, National Parenting Centers Seal of Approval, Dr. Toy, Parent Council.
Needs Children's/juvenile (adventure, animal, preschool/picture book, science).
How to Contact Does not accept unsolicited mss. Query with SASE. Include brief bio, list of publishing credits. Send copy of ms and SASE. Responds in 1 month to queries; 1 month to mss. Accepts simultaneous submissions. Sometimes comments on rejected mss.
Terms Pays royalty.

IRONWEED PRESS
P.O. Box 754208, Parkside Station, Forest Hills NY 11375. (718)544-1120. Fax: (718)268-2394. Estab. 1996. Small independent publisher. "Annually we publish only one original title, selected through our Ironweed Press Fiction Prize. The deadline is in June. For guidelines, please send SASE." Publishes hardcover and paperback originals. Distributes titles through national wholesalers.

ITALICA PRESS
595 Main St., Suite 605, New York NY 10044-0047. (212)935-4230. Fax: (212)838-7812. E-mail: inquiries@italica press.com. Website: www.italicapress.com. **Contact:** Ronald G. Musto and Eileen Gardiner, publishers. Estab. 1985. Small independent publisher of Italian fiction in translation. "First-time translators published. We would like to see translations of Italian writers well known in Italy who are not yet translated for an American audience." Publishes trade paperback originals. Books: 50-60 lb. natural paper; offset printing; illustrations. Average print order: 1,500. Averages 6 total titles, 2 fiction titles/year. Distributes titles through website. Promotes titles through website.
Needs Translations of 20th century Italian fiction. Published *Eruptions*, by Monica Sarsini; *The Great Bear*, by Ginevra Bompianai; and *Sparrow*, by Giovanni Verga.
How to Contact Accepts unsolicited mss. Query with SASE. Accepts queries by e-mail, fax. Responds in 1 month to queries; 2 months to mss. Accepts simultaneous submissions, electronic submissions, submissions on disk.
Terms Pays 7-15% royalty on wholesale price. Pays author's copies. Publishes ms 1 year after acceptance. Ms guidelines online.
Advice "Remember we publish *only* fiction that has been previously published in Italian. A *brief* call saves a lot of postage. 90% of proposals we receive are completely off base—but we are very interested in things that are right on target. Please send return postage if you want your manuscript back."

JIREH PUBLISHING COMPANY
P.O. Box 42613, San Leandro CA 94579-0263. E-mail: jaholman@yahoo.com. Website: www.jirehpublishing.c om. Estab. 1995. Small independent publisher. "We have just begun our fiction line." Publishes hardcover, trade paperback and electronic originals. Books: paper varies; digital and offset printed; binding varies. Average print order: varies. First novel print order: varies. Plans 2 first novels this year. Averages 2-5 total titles, 1-2 fiction titles/year. Distributes titles through online bookstores and booksellers (retailers).
Needs Mystery, religious (Christian ebooks, general religious, mystery/suspense, thriller, romance), suspense. "We are looking for Christian values in the books that we publish."
How to Contact Accepts unsolicited mss. Query with SASE. Accepts queries by e-mail. Include brief bio, list of publishing credits. Send SASE for return of ms or send a disposable ms and SASE for reply only. Responds in 2-4 months to queries; 5-8 months to mss. Accepts simultaneous submissions, electronic submissions. No submissions on disk. Sometimes comments on rejected mss.
Terms Pays 10-12% royalty on wholesale price. Publishes ms 9-12 months after acceptance. Ms guidelines online.

JOURNEY BOOKS PUBLISHING
Journey Books, 3205 Hwy. 431, Spring Hill TN 37174. (615)791-8006. E-mail: journey@journeybookspublishing .com. Website: www.journeybookspublishing.com. Edward Knight (science fiction/fantasy). Estab. 1996. Publishes paperback originals. "Writers must be published in our magazine, *Amazing Journeys*, before being considered for book-length work." Distributes books through the Internet, Amazon and Ingram.
Needs Fantasy (space fantasy, sword and sorcery), science fiction (hard science/technological, soft/sociological), young adult (fantasy/science fiction).
How to Contact Accepts unsolicited mss. Query with SASE. Accepts queries by mail. Include estimated word count, brief bio, social security number, list of publishing credits. Send SASE for return of ms or send a disposable ms and SASE for reply only. Responds in 6 weeks to queries; 12 weeks to mss. No simultaneous submissions, electronic submissions, submissions on disk. Often comments on rejected mss.
Terms Negotiated on an individual basis. Ms guidelines online.

Advice "Read our guidelines before submitting. Authors must be published in our magazine, *Amazing Journeys Magazine*, before they are considered for anthologies or books."

☑ JUST US BOOKS, INC.

356 Glenwood Ave 3rd FL, East Orange NJ 07017. (973)672-7701. Fax: (973)677-7570. E-mail: justusbooks@aol. com. Website: www.justusbooks.com. Estab. 1988. Small independent publisher of children's books that focus on African-American experiences (fiction and nonfiction). Publishes hardcover originals, paperback originals, hardcover reprints and paperback reprints. Averages 4-8 total titles, 2-4 fiction titles/year. Member, Small Press Association; Children Book Council.

Needs Ethnic (African American), young adult (adventure, easy-to-read, historical, mystery/suspense, problem novels, series, sports). "Young adult fiction targeted to male readers." Published *A Blessing in Disguise*, by Eleanora Tate.

How to Contact Accepts unsolicited mss. Query with SASE or submit synopsis. Accepts queries by mail. Include brief bio, list of publishing credits. Send SASE for return of ms or send a disposable ms and SASE for reply only. Responds in 8-10 weeks to queries; 8-10 weeks to mss. Accepts simultaneous submissions. Rarely comments on rejected mss.

Terms Pays royalty. Ms guidelines for SASE or on website.

Advice "We are looking for realistic, contemporary characters; stories and interesting plots that introduce both conflict and resolution. We will consider various themes and story lines, but before an author submits a query we urge them to become familiar with our books."

Ⓝ ☑ ◎ KAEDEN BOOKS

P.O. Box 16190, Rocky River OH 44116-0190. (440)617-1400. Fax: (440)617-1403. E-mail: curmston@kaeden.c om. Website: www.kaeden.com. **Contact:** Craig Urmston, editor. Estab. 1990. "We are an educational publisher of early readers for use in the pre-K to 2nd grade market. Our materials are used by teachers in reading instruction in the classroom. These are fully illustrated books with kid-catching, interesting themes that are age appropriate." Publishes paperback originals. Books: offset printing; saddle binding; illustrations. Average print order: 5,000 **Published 6 debut authors within the last year.** Averages 8-16 total titles/year. Distributes titles through school sales representatives. Promotes titles in professional teacher and reading journals.

Needs Wants realistic fiction using simple vocabulary and sentence structure. Rhythm, rhyme, patterned text, and predictable text are key features for developing early readers. Themes need to relate to young readers including sports, family, animal and curriculum-related subjects. Published *When I Go to Grandma's House*, by Brian P. Cleary (fiction); *Sammy's Hamburger Caper*, by Kathleen and Craig Urmston (fiction); and *The Fishing Contest*, by Joe Yung Yukisgi.

How to Contact Accepts unsolicited mss. Query with SASE or submit outline, publishing history, synopsis, author bio. Send copy of ms and SASE.

Terms Pays royalty. Negotiable, either royalties or flat fee by individual arrangement with author depending on book. Publishes ms 6-24 months after acceptance. Ms guidelines online.

Advice "Our line is expanding with particular interest in fiction/nonfiction for grades K-2. Material must be suitable for use in the public school classroom, be multicultural and be high interest with appropriate word usage and a positive tone for the respective grade."

☑ KENSINGTON PUBLISHING CORP.

850 Third Ave., 16th Floor, New York NY 10022. (212)407-1500. Fax: (212)935-0699. Website: www.kensington books.com. **Contact:** Michaela Hamilton, editor in chief; Kate Duffy, editorial director (romance); John Scognamiglio, editorial director; Karen Thomas, editorial director (African American fiction, Dafina Books); Audrey LaFehr, editorial director. Estab. 1975. Full service trade commercial publisher, all formats. Publishes hardcover and trade paperback originals, mass market paperback originals and reprints. Averages over 500 total titles/year.

Imprint(s) Dafina (Karen Thomas, executive editor); Brava (Kate Duffy, editoral director); Kensington; Pinnacle; Zebra.

Needs Ethnic, gay/lesbian, historical, horror, mainstream/contemporary, multicultural, mystery, occult, romance (contemporary, historical, regency), suspense, thriller/espionage, western (epic), women's. Published *Sullivan's Law*, by Nancy Taylor Rosenberg.

How to Contact Does not accept unsolicited mss. *Agented submissions only.* Responds in 1 month to queries; 4 months to mss. Accepts simultaneous submissions.

Terms Pays 8-15% royalty on retail price or makes outright purchase. Average advance: $2,000 and up. Publishes ms 9-12 months after acceptance.

DENIS KITCHEN PUBLISHING

P.O. Box 9514, North Amherst MA 01059-9514. (413)259-1627. Fax: (413)259-1812. E-mail: publishing@deniski tchen.com. Website: www.deniskitchen.com. Publishes hardcover and trade paperback originals and reprints. Averages 4 total titles/year.

Needs Adventure, comic books, erotica, historical, horror, humor, literary, mystery, occult, picture books, science fiction. "We do not want pure fiction. We seek cartoonists or writer/illustrator teams who can tell compelling stories with a combination of words and pictures."

How to Contact Submit sample illustrations/comic pages or submit complete ms. Responds in 4-6 months to mss. Accepts simultaneous submissions.

Terms Pays 6-10% royalty on retail price. Occasionally makes deals based on percentage of wholesale if idea and/or bulk of work is done in-house. Average advance: $1-5,000. Publishes ms 9 months after acceptance. Book catalog and ms guidelines on website.

⭐ Ⓐ ALFRED A. KNOPF

Knopf Publishing Group, Random House, Inc., 1745 Broadway, 21st Floor, New York NY 10019. Website: www.aaknopf.com. **Contact:** Senior Editor. Estab. 1915. Publishes hardcover and paperback originals. **Published some debut authors within the last year.** Averages 200 total titles/year.

Needs Publishes book-length fiction of literary merit by known or unknown writers. Length: 40,000-150,000 words. Published *Gertrude and Claudius*, by John Updike; *The Emperor of Ocean Park*, by Stephen Carter; and *Balzac and the Little Chinese Seamstress*, by Dai Sijie.

How to Contact *Agented submissions only.* Query with SASE or submit sample chapter(s). Responds in 2-6 months to queries. Accepts simultaneous submissions.

Terms Pays 10-15% royalty. Royalty and advance vary. Must return advance if book is not completed or is unacceptable. Publishes ms 1 year after acceptance. Book catalog for $7\frac{1}{2} \times 10\frac{1}{2}$ SAE with 5 first-class stamps.

⭐ Ⓩ ◎ KREGEL PUBLICATIONS

Kregel, Inc., P.O. Box 2607, Grand Rapids MI 49501. (616)451-4775. Fax: (616)451-9330. Website: www.kregelp ublications.com. **Contact:** Acquisitions Editor. Estab. 1949. Midsize independent Christian publisher. Publishes hardcover and trade paperback originals and reprints. Averages 90 total titles, 10-15 fiction titles/year. Member, ECPA.

Imprint(s) Kregel Academic & Professional, Jim Weaver (academic/pastoral); Kregel Kid Zone, Steve Barclift (children).

Needs Adventure, children's/juvenile (adventure, historical, mystery, preschool/picture book, series, sports, Christian), historical, mystery, religious (children's, general, inspirational, fantasy/sci-fi, mystery/suspense, religious thriller, relationships), young adult (adventure). Fiction should be geared toward the evangelical Christian market. Wants "books with fast-paced, contemporary storylines—strong Christian message presented in engaging, entertaining style as well as books for juvenile and young adults, especially young women." Published *Divided Loyalties*, by L.K. Malone (action/thriller); *A Test of Love*, by Kathleen Scott (relationships); and *Jungle Hideout*, by Jeanette Windle (juvenile/adventure).

How to Contact Accepts unsolicited mss. Query with SASE. Accepts queries by e-mail. Include estimated word count, brief bio, summary of work. Responds in 3 months to queries. Accepts simultaneous submissions. No electronic submissions, submissions on disk.

Terms Pays 8-16% royalty on wholesale price. Average advance: $200-2,000. Publishes ms 14 months after acceptance. Book catalog for 9×12 SASE. Ms guidelines online.

Advice "Visit our website and review the titles listed under various subject categories. Does your proposed work duplicate existing titles? Does it address areas not covered by existing titles? Does it break new ground?"

LAST KNIGHT PUBLISHING COMPANY

P.O. Box 270006, Fort Collins Co 80527. (970)391-6857. Fax: (970)204-0935. E-mail: ckaine@lastknightpublishi ng.com. Website: www.LastKnightPublishing.com. **Contact:** Charles Kaine, publisher/owner. "Small independent publisher interested in various fictional forms. We are interested in books that have a niche market. We are interested in making high quality books, both by the words written and how it is printed." Publishes paperback originals. Books: 70 lb. Vellum opaque paper; offset-printed; perfect-bound. Average print order: 1,500-4,000. Average first novel print order: 1,500. **Published 1 debut author within the last year.** Plans 2-3 first novels this year.

Needs Fantasy (space fantasy, sword and sorcery), historical, horror (dark fantasy, futuristic, supernatural), literary, mainstream/contemporary, mystery (amateur sleuth, cozy), psychic/supernatural, thriller/espionage. Published *The Puppeteers*, by Ted Moss; *The Breach*, by Brian Kaufman (historical fiction).

How to Contact Accepts unsolicited mss. Query with SASE or submit 3 sample chapter(s), synopsis. Accepts queries by mail. Include estimated word count, brief bio, An explanation of "why people will want to read the work." Send SASE for return of ms or send a disposable ms and SASE for reply only. Responds in 6 weeks to queries; 2-3 months to mss. Accepts simultaneous submissions. Often comments on rejected mss.

Terms Pays royalty. Average advance: negotiable. Publishes ms 9 months after acceptance. Ms guidelines online.

LEAPFROG PRESS

P.O. Box 1495, 95 Commercial Street, Wellfleet MA 02667-1495. (508)349-1925. Fax: (508)349-1180. E-mail: leapfrog@c4.net. Website: www.leapfrogpress.com. **Contact:** Amy Gallo, acquisitions editor. Estab. 1996. "We search for beautifully written literary titles and market them aggressively to national trade and library accounts as well as to sell film, translation, foreign and book club rights." Publishes paperback originals and spoken word audio CD's. Books: acid-free paper; sewn binding. Average print order: 5,000. First novel print order: 4,000 (average). Member, Publishers Marketing Association, Bookbuilders of Boston and PEN. Distributes titles through Consortium Book Sales and Distribution, St. Paul, MN. Promotes titles through all national review media, bookstore readings, author tours, website, radio shows, chain store promotions, advertisements, book fairs.

• *The Devil and Daniel Silverman*, by Theodore Rosak, was nominated for the American Library Association Stonewall Award and it was a San Francisco Chronicle best-seller. *The German Money*, by Lev Raphael, was a Booksense 76 pick.

Needs "Genres often blur; we're interested in good writing. We are most interested in literary fiction." Published *The War at Home*, by Nora Eisenberg; *Junebug*, by Maureen McCoy; *Paradise Dance*, by Michael Lee; and *Waiting for Elvis*, by Toni Graham.

How to Contact Query with SASE. Accepts queries by e-mail. Send SASE for return of ms or send a disposable ms and SASE for reply only. Responds in 3-6 months to queries; 6 months to mss. No simultaneous submissions. Sometimes comments on rejected mss.

Terms Pays 4-8% royalty on net receipts. Average advance: negotiable. Publishes ms 1-2 years after acceptance.

Advice "Because editors have so little time, you had best send them your very best work. Editors don't have a lot of time to line edit. They love to work with you but they do not want to rewrite your book for you. In fact, if you send good material that is poorly written, they may wonder if you actually can do the revisions necessary. So don't be impatient. Send your work only when you feel it is as good as you can make it . . . and that means knowing what's out there in the market; knowing how to create characters and a dynamite beginning and a plot that doesn't meander all over the place because you don't know where the story is going. Learn your craft. Although we have been open to the work of novice writers, we have found that we have had much of our success recently from writers who were formerly published by large NYC presses and then came to us. For that reason, we're especially interested in knowing where you have published before and if the book has a history."

[N] LEAPING DOG PRESS

P.O. Box 3316, San Jose CA 95156-3316. (877)570-6873. Fax: (877)570-6873. E-mail: editor@leapingdogpress.com. Website: www.leapingdogpress.com. **Contact:** Jordan Jones, editor and publisher.

LEE & LOW BOOKS

95 Madison Ave., New York NY 10016. (212)779-4400. Fax: (212)532-6035. Website: www.leeandlow.com. **Contact:** Louise May, editor-in-chief. Estab. 1991. "Our goals are to meet a growing need for books that address children of color and to present literature that all children can identify with. We only consider multicultural children's fiction and nonfiction works. Of special interest are stories set in contemporary America." Publishes hardcover originals—picture books and middle-grade works only. Averages 12-16 total titles/year.

Imprint(s) Bebop Books.

Needs Children's/juvenile (historical, multicultural, books for children ages 5-12), ethnic, multicultural, illustrated. Published *The Pot that Juan Built*, by Nancy Andrews-Goebel; and *Everglades Forever*, by Trish Marx.

How to Contact Accepts unsolicited mss. Send SASE for return of ms or send a disposable ms and SASE for reply only. Agented fiction 30%. Responds in 2-4 months to queries; 2-4 months to mss. Accepts simultaneous submissions. Sometimes comments on rejected mss.

Terms Pays royalty. Offers advance. Book catalog for SASE with $1.98 postage. Ms guidelines online.

Advice "Writers should familarize themselves with the styles and formats of recently published children's books. Lee & Low Books is a multicultural children's book publisher. Animal stories and folktales are not considered at this time."

[⚡] LEISURE BOOKS

Dorchester Publishing Co., 200 Madison Ave., Suite 2000, New York NY 10016. (212)725-8811. Fax: (212)532-1054. Website: www.dorchesterpub.com. **Contact:** Micaela Bombard or Jessica McDonnell, editorial assistants.

Estab. 1970. Publishes mass market paperback originals and reprints. Publishes romances, westerns, horrors, young adult and thrillers only. Books: newsprint paper; offset printing; perfect-bound. Average print order: variable. First novel print order: variable. Plans 25 first novels this year. Averages 255 total titles/year. Promotes titles through national reviews, ads, author readings, promotional items, and on the website.

Imprint(s) Leisure Books (contact: Alicia Condon); Love Spell Books (contact: Christopher Keeslar); Smooch (contact: Kate Seaver).

Needs Historical (romance), horror, romance, western, thrillers. "We are strongly backing historical romance and young adult (90,000-100,000 words). All historical romance should be set pre-1900. Horrors and westerns are growing as well. No sweet romance, science fiction, erotica. New YA line, 45,000 words." Published *The Laird of Stonehaven*, by Connie Mason (historical romance); *Dark Melody*, by Christine Feehan (paranormal romance); and *To Wake the Dead*, by Richard Laymon (horror).

How to Contact Accepts unsolicited mss. Query with SASE or submit outline, first 3 sample chapter(s), synopsis. Agented fiction 70%. Responds in 6 months to queries. No simultaneous submissions, electronic submissions.

Terms Pays royalty on retail price. Average advance: negotiable. Publishes ms 18 months after acceptance. Book catalog for free, (800)481-9191. Ms guidelines online.

Advice Encourage first novelists "if they are talented and willing to take direction *and* write the kind of genre fiction we publish. Please include a brief synopsis if sample chapters are requested."

◩ ◪ ARTHUR A. LEVINE BOOKS

Scholastic Inc., 557 Broadway, New York NY 10012. (212)343-4436. Website: www.scholastic.com. **Contact:** Arthur Levine, editorial director. "Arthur A. Levine is looking for distinctive literature, for children and young adults, for whatever's extraordinary." Averages 10-14 total titles/year.

Needs Juvenile, picture books, young adult, middle-grade novels. Published *Frida*, by Jonah Winter, illustrated by Ana Juan; *Millicent Min, Girl Genius*, by Lisa Yee; *The Slightly True Story of Cedar B. Hartley*, by Martine Murray (middle-grade novel, debut author); and *At the Crossing-Places*, by Kevin Crossley-Holland (YA fantasy novel).

How to Contact Query with SASE.

Terms Pays variable royalty on retail price. Average advance: variable. Book catalog for 9×12 SASE.

◫ LIMITLESS DARE 2 DREAM PUBLISHING

100 Pin Oak Ct., Lexington SC 29073. (803)356-8231. Fax: (803)359-2881. E-mail: limitlessd2d@aol.com. Website: www.limitlessd2d.net. Estab. 2002. Publishes trade paperback originals, casebound and dust jacket hardbacks and reprints. Averages 40-80 total titles/year.

Needs Adventure, erotica, fantasy, feminist, gay/lesbian, historical, horror, humor, mainstream/contemporary, military/war, multimedia, mystery, occult, regional, romance, science fiction, short story collections, spiritual, suspense, western. "We do not do books that demean women in any way or books where women are helpless females waiting to be rescued. We also do not publish anything of a religious nature, so do not send it. Other than that, writers will find us quite open minded and willing to read and consider their manuscripts. The criteria at D2D is good stories, good writing, and hold the reader's interest."

How to Contact Query with SASE or submit complete ms. Responds in 1 month to queries; 3-5 months to mss. No simultaneous submissions.

Terms Pays 12-20% royalty on retail price. Publishes ms 6-8 months after acceptance. Ms guidelines for #10 SASE.

◪ ◪ LINTEL

24 Blake Lane, Middletown NY 10940. (845)342-5224. **Contact:** Editorial director. Estab. 1978. Two person organization on part-time basis. Publishes hardcover originals and reprints and trade paperback originals. Books: 90% opaque; photo offset printing; perfect binding; illustrations. Average print order: 1,000. First novel print order: 1,200.

How to Contact Does not accept unsolicited mss. Accepts simultaneous submissions. Sometimes comments on rejected mss.

Terms Pays royalty. Authors get 100 copies originally, plus royalties after expenses cleared. Offers advance. Publishes ms 6-8 months after acceptance.

◪ LIT POT PRESS, INC.

3909 Reche Road #96, Fallbrook CA 92028. (760)731-3111. Fax: (760)731-3111. E-mail: litpot@veryfast.biz. Website: http://litpotpress.com. Beverly Jackson, editor-in-chief. Estab. 2002. "Lit Pot Press, Inc. solicits virtuoso authors whose work has flown under the radar of the majors, or material too off beat or literary for mainstream press. We are a strictly literary, small independent press looking for edgy, contemporary and fresh work. We treat writers exceptionally well, which makes our house unique. We are noted for being excellent, fast and not abusing writers with neglect and unanswered mail.'' Books: 60 lb. paper; digital printing; perfect bound; illustrations. Average print order 100-500. Average first novel print order 250-500. Averages 5-6 total titles, 2-3 fiction titles/year. Member: CLMP. Distributes throught the website.

Needs Experimental, literary, short story collections. Published *The Carrington Monologues*, by Terri Brown-Davidson; *In the Shadow of the Globe*, by Michelle Cameron; and *This Rare Earth & Other Flights*, by Tom Sheehan.

How to Contact Does not accept unsolicited mss. Submit outline, 1 sample chapter(s). Accepts queries by e-mail. Include estimated word count, social security number, list of publishing credits. Responds in 2 weeks to mss. Accepts simultaneous submissions, electronic submissions. No submissions on disk. Sometimes comments on rejected mss.

Terms Pays royalty. Publishes ms 6 months after acceptance.

Advice ''First submit short work to *Ink Pot* and *Lit Pot*, via the Literarypotpourri.com website. If we accept your work and make known our interest in your body of work, you can query us with longer work, or we will solicit you if we have a sense that you are right for our press.''

★ Ⓐ LITTLE, BROWN AND CO. ADULT TRADE BOOKS

Division of AOL Time Warner Book Group, 1271 Avenue of the Americas, New York NY 10020. (212)522-8700. Fax: (212)522-2067. Website: www.twbookmark.com. Estab. 1837. ''The general editorial philosophy for all divisions continues to be broad and flexible, with high quality and the promise of commercial success as always the first considerations.'' Publishes hardcover originals and paperback originals and reprints.

Imprint(s) Arcade Books; Back Bay Books; Bulfinch Press.

How to Contact *Agented submissions only.*

★ Ⓐ LITTLE, BROWN AND CO. CHILDREN'S PUBLISHING

Division of AOL Time Warner Books Group, Time Life Building, 1271 Avenue of the Americas, 11th Floor, New York NY 10020. (212)522-8700. Website: www.twbookmark.com. Estab. 1837. ''We are looking for strong writing and presentation, but no predetermined topics.'' Publishes hardcover originals, trade paperback reprints. Averages 70-100 total titles/year.

Imprint(s) Back Bay Books.

Needs Adventure, ethnic, fantasy, feminist, gay/lesbian, historical, humor, juvenile, mystery, picture books, science fiction, suspense, young adult. ''We are looking for strong fiction for children of all ages in any area, including multicultural. We always prefer full manuscripts for fiction.''

How to Contact *Agented submissions only.* Responds in 1 month to queries; 2 months to mss. Accepts simultaneous submissions.

Terms Pays royalty on retail price. Average advance: negotiable. Publishes ms 2 years after acceptance. Ms guidelines online.

★ Ⓐ LITTLE, BROWN AND CO., INC.

Time Warner Inc., 1271 Avenue of the Americas, New York NY 10020. (212)522-8700. Website: twbookmark.com. **Contact:** Editorial Department. Estab. 1837. ''The general editorial philosophy for all divisions continues to be broad and flexible, with high quality and the promise of commercial success as always the first considerations.'' Medium-size house. Publishes adult and juvenile hardcover originals and paperback originals and reprints. Averages 100 total titles, varies fiction titles/year.

Imprint(s) Little, Brown; Back Bay; Bulfinch Press.

Needs Literary, mainstream/contemporary. Published *When the Wind Blows*, by James Patterson; *Angels Flight*, by Michael Connelly; *Sea Glass*, by Anita Shreve; and *City of Bones*, by Michael Connelly.

How to Contact Does not accept unsolicited mss. Query with SASE. No simultaneous submissions.

Terms Pays royalty. Average advance: varying. Ms guidelines online.

★ Ⓐ Ⓞ LITTLE, BROWN AND COMPANY CHILDREN'S BOOKS

Time Life Building, 1271 Avenue of the Americas, New York NY 10020. (212)5228700. Website: www.lbkids.com. **Contact:** Submission editor. Estab. 1837. Publishes hardcover originals and trade paperback reprints. Books: 70 lb. paper; sheet-fed printing; illustrations. Distributes titles through sales representatives. Promotes titles through author tours, book signings, posters, press kits, magazine and newspapers.

Imprint(s) Megan Tingley Books (Megan Tingley, associate publisher).

Needs Published *Gossip Girl* series, by Cecily von Ziegesar; and *Luna*, by Julie Anne Peters.

How to Contact *Agented submissions only.*

Terms Pays royalty. Average advance: negotiable. Publishes ms 1-2 after acceptance.

Advice ''Writers should avoid looking for the 'issue' they think publishers want to see, choosing instead topics they know best and are most enthusiastic about/inspired by.''

LIVINGSTON PRESS

University of West Alabama, Station 22, Livingston AL 35470. E-mail: jwt@uwa.edu. Website: www.livingstonp ress.uwa.edu. **Contact:** Joe Taylor, literary editor; Tina Jones, literary editor; Debbie Davis, literary editor. Estab. 1984. "Small university press specializing in offbeat and/or Southern literature." Publishes hardcover and trade paperback originals. Books: acid free; offset; some illustrations. Average print order: 2,500. First novel print order: 2,500. Plans 5 first novels this year. Averages 9 total titles, 10 fiction titles/year.

Imprint(s) Swallow's Tale Press.

Needs Experimental, literary, short story collections, off-beat or southern. "We are interested in form and, of course, style." Published *The Gin Girl*, by River Jordan (novel); *Pulpwood*, by Scott Ely (stories); *Live Cargo*, by Paul Toutonghi (stories).

How to Contact Query with SASE. Include estimated word count, brief bio, list of publishing credits. Send SASE for return of ms or send a disposable ms and SASE for reply only. Responds in 1 month to queries; 1 year to mss. Accepts simultaneous submissions.

Terms Pays 10% of 1,500 print run, 150 copies; thereafter pays a mix of royalties and books. Publishes ms 18 months after acceptance. Book catalog for SASE. Ms guidelines online.

LLEWELLYN PUBLICATIONS

Llewellyn Worldwide, Ltd., P.O. Box 64383, St. Paul MN 55164-0383. (651)291-1970. Fax: (651)291-1908. E-mail: lwlpc@llewellyn.com. Website: www.llewellyn.com. **Contact:** Nancy J. Mostad, acquisitions manager (New Age, metaphysical, occult); Barbara Moore, acquisitions editor (kits and decks, fiction and mystery); Ximena Ortiz Zamora (spanish); Natalie Harter (magic); Megan Atwood (YA and children's); Stephanie Clement (astrology). Estab. 1901. Publishes trade and mass market paperback originals. **Published 30% debut authors within the last year.** Averages 100 total titles/year.

Needs Occult, spiritual (metaphysical). "Authentic and educational, yet entertaining."

How to Contact Responds in 3 months to queries. Accepts simultaneous submissions.

Terms Pays 10% royalty on wholesale price or retail price. Book catalog for 9×12 SAE with 4 first-class stamps. Ms guidelines online.

LOST HORSE PRESS

105 Lost Horse Lane, Sandpoint ID 83864. (208)255-4410. Fax: (208)255-1560. E-mail: losthorsepress@mindspri ng.com. Website: http://losthorsepress.org. **Contact:** Christine Holbert, publisher. Estab. 1998. Publishes hardcover and paperback originals. Books: 60-70 lb. natural paper; offset printing; b&w illustration. Average print order: 1,000-2,500. First novel print order: 500. **Published 2 debut authors within the last year.** Averages 4 total titles/year. Distributed by Small Press Distribution.

• *Woman on the Cross*, by Pierre Delattre, won the *ForeWord Magazine's* 2001 Book of the Year Award for literary fiction.

Needs Literary, regional (Pacific NW), short story collections, poetry. Published *Tales of a Dalai Lama*, by Pierre Delattre (literary fiction); *Love*, by Valerie Martin (short stories); *Hiding From Salesmen*, by Scott Poole; and *Woman on the Cross*, by Pierre Delattre (literary).

Terms Publishes ms 1-2 years after acceptance.

LOVE SPELL

Dorchester Publishing Co., Inc., 200 Madison Ave., 20th Floor, New York NY 10016. (212)725-8811. Fax: (212)532-1054. Website: www.dorchesterpub.com. **Contact:** Kate Seaver, editor (romance, young adult). Love Spell publishes the quirky sub-genres of romance: time-travel, paranormal, futuristic. "Despite the exotic settings, we are still interested in character-driven plots." Publishes mass market paperback originals. Books: newsprint paper; offset printing; perfect-bound. Average print order: varies. First novel print order: varies. Plans 15 first novels this year. Averages 48 total titles/year.

Needs Romance (futuristic, time travel, paranormal, historical), whimsical contemporaries. "Books industry-wide are getting shorter; we're interested in 90,000 words." Published *Dark Melody*, by Chrisine Feehan (paranormal romance); and *The Laird of Stonehaven*, by Connie Mason (historical romance).

How to Contact Accepts unsolicited mss. Query with SASE or submit 3 sample chapter(s), synopsis. Send SASE or IRC. Agented fiction 70%. Responds in 6 months to mss. No simultaneous submissions.

Terms Pays 4% royalty on retail price. Average advance: varies. Publishes ms 1 year after acceptance. Book catalog for free, (800)481-9191. Ms guidelines online.

Advice "The best way to learn to write a Love Spell Romance is by reading several of our recent releases. The best-written stories are usually ones writers feel passionate about—so write from your heart! Also, the market is very tight these days so more than ever we are looking for refreshing, standout original fiction."

Book Publishers

N ☑ LOW FIDELITY PRESS

P.O. Box 21930, Brooklyn NY 11202. (917)254-1824. Fax: (205)918-0259. E-mail: info@lofipress.com. Website: www.lofipress.com. **Contact:** Brad Armstrong, Jeff Parker and Tobin O'Donnell. Estab. 2002. "Low Fidelity Press is a small independent publisher committed to publishing new, exceptional work regardless of the marketability of the work. We're willing to lose money on a title if it is essential that the work be published." Publishes paperback originals. Average print order: 1,000. **Published 1 debut author within the last year.** Averages 2-3 total titles, 1-2 fiction titles/year. Distributes books through Baker & Taylor.

Needs Experimental, literary, short story collections. Published *B*, by Jonathan Bambach.

How to Contact Does not accept or return unsolicited mss. Query with SASE. Accepts queries by e-mail, mail. Include list of publishing credits. Send copy of ms and SASE. Responds in 1 month to queries. Accepts simultaneous submissions. Rarely comments on rejected mss.

Terms Pays 10-20% royalty. Average advance: varies. Publishes ms 12-18 months after acceptance. Ms guidelines online.

Advice "We ignore trends. Trends are temporary, and we're interested in publishing books that transcend that."

☑ ☑ ☑ LTDBOOKS

200 N. Service Rd. West, Unit 1, Suite 301, Oakville ON L6M 2Y1 Canada. (905)847-6060. Fax: (905)847-6060. E-mail: publisher@ltdbooks.com. Website: www.ltdbooks.com. **Contact:** Dee Lloyd, editor. Estab. 1999. "LTDBooks, an energetic presence in the rapidly expanding e-book market, is a multi-genre, royalty-paying fiction publisher specializing in high quality stories with strong characters and great ideas." Publishes electronic originals by download as well as selected trade paperback titles. Books: as a download. **Published 14 debut authors within the last year.** Averages 15 total titles, 36 fiction titles/year. Member, Electronic Publishers Association. Distributes titles through the Internet, Baker and Taylor, Powells.com, Lightning Source, and Amazon.com.

Needs Adventure, fantasy (space fantasy, sword and sorcery), historical (general), horror (dark fantasy, futuristic, psychological, supernatural), mainstream/contemporary, mystery (amateur sleuth, cozy, police procedural, private eye/hard-boiled), romance (contemporary, futuristic/time travel, gothic, historical, regency period, romantic suspense), science fiction (hard science/technological, soft/sociological), suspense (amateur sleuth, cozy, police procedural, private eye/hard-boiled), thriller/espionage, western, young adult (adventure, fantasy/science fiction, historical, horror, mystery/suspense, problem novels, romance, series, sports, western). "Our new trade paperback program started June 2001." Published *Pilikia is my Business*, by Mark Troy (2002 Shamus Award Finalists) and *Beaudry's Ghost* (2002 Independent Publisher Award winner for best romance).

How to Contact Accepts unsolicited mss. Submit 3 sample chapter(s), synopsis. Include estimated word count, brief bio, list of publishing credits. Responds in 1-2 months to queries. Accepts simultaneous submissions, electronic submissions. No submissions on disk.

Terms Pays 30% royalty on electronic titles and flat rate on trade paperbacks. Publishes ms more than 1 year after acceptance. Ms guidelines online.

Advice "We publish only novel-length books. No short stories or novellas. Many of our books are electronic (as download) with ongoing additions to our new trade paperback program. Keep in mind that trade paperback publication is not guaranteed upon acceptance of electronic publication."

⊕ ☑ LUATH PRESS LTD.

54³/₂ Castlehill, The Royal Mile, Edinburgh Scotland EH1 2ND United Kingdom. 0044 (0)131 225 4326. Fax: 0044 (0)131 225 4324. E-mail: gavin.macdougall@luath.co.uk. Website: www.luath.co.uk. **Contact:** Gavin McDougall, editor. Estab. 1981. Committed to publishing well-written books worth reading. Publishes paperback and hardcover originals. **Published 5-10 debut authors within the last year.** Plans 5-10 first novels this year. Scottish Publishers Association.

Needs Published *Milk Reading*, by Nick Smith (fiction); *The Fundementals of New Caledonia*, by John MacKay (fiction).

How to Contact Accepts unsolicited mss. Query with SASE or submit complete ms. Accepts queries by e-mail, fax, phone, mail. Include estimated word count, brief bio, list of publishing credits. Send copy of ms and SASE. No submissions on disk. Never comments on rejected mss.

Terms Pays royalty.

Advice "Check out our website, buy lots of our books, read them—and then get in touch with us."

N ☑ ☑ ☑ JOHN MACRAE BOOKS

Henry Holt & Co., Inc., 115 W. 18th St., New York NY 10011. (212)886-9200. Estab. 1991. "We publish literary fiction and nonfiction. Our primary interest is in language; strong, compelling writing." Publishes hardcover originals. Averages 20-25 total titles/year.

Needs Literary, mainstream/contemporary. Recently published *Burning Their Boats*, by Angela Carter (novel).
How to Contact Does not accept unsolicited mss.
Terms Pays royalty. Average advance: varies. Publishes ms 9-12 months after acceptance.

⬛ ◻ MARCH STREET PRESS

3413 Wilshire, Greensboro NC 27408. E-mail: rbixby@aol.com. Website: www.marchstreetpress.com. Estab. 1988. "We are the smallest imaginable press. I could easily fit the entire thing in the back seat of a Corolla. Visualize the amount of copper remaining on your finger after pinching a penny, that's us." Publishes paperback originals.
How to Contact Accepts unsolicited mss. Submit complete ms. Accepts queries by e-mail, mail. Send SASE for return of ms or send a disposable ms and SASE for reply only.
Terms Ms guidelines online.
Advice "Don't forget Poland!"

◎ MARINE TECHNIQUES PUBLISHING, INC.

126 Western Ave., Suite 266, Augusta ME 04330-7252. (207)622-7984. Fax: (207)621-0821. E-mail: marinetechniques@midmaine.com. **Contact:** James L. Pelletier, president/CEO (commercial marine or maritime international); Christopher S. Pelletier, vice president operations (national and international maritime related properties). **Published 15% debut authors within the last year.** Averages 3-5 total titles/year.
Needs Must be commercial maritime/marine related.
How to Contact Submit complete ms. Responds in 2 months to queries; 6 months to mss. Accepts simultaneous submissions.
Terms Pays 25-43% royalty on wholesale or retail price. Publishes ms 6-12 months after acceptance.
Advice "Audience consists of commercial marine/maritime firms, persons employed in all aspects of the marine/maritime commercial and recreational fields, persons interested in seeking employment in the commercial marine industry; firms seeking to sell their products and services to vessel owners, operators and mangers in the commercial marine industry worldwide, etc."

◎ MARVEL COMICS

10 E. 40th St., New York NY 10016. (212)576-4000. Fax: (212)576-8547. Website: www.marvel.com. Publishes hardcover originals and reprints, trade paperback reprints, mass market comic book originals, electronic reprints. Averages 650 total titles/year.
Needs Adventure, comic books, fantasy, horror, humor, science fiction, young adult. "Our shared universe needs new heroes and villains; books for younger readers and teens needed."
How to Contact Query with SASE or submit synopsis. Responds in 2 months to queries; 3 months to mss. No simultaneous submissions.
Terms Pays on a per page, work-for-hire basis which is contracted. Ms guidelines online.

⬛ ◎ McBOOKS PRESS

10 Booth Building, 520 N. Meadow St., Ithaca NY 14850. (607)272-2114. Fax: (607)273-6068. E-mail: jackie@mcbooks.com. Website: www.mcbooks.com. **Contact:** Editorial director. Estab. 1979. "Small independent publisher; specializes in historical nautical fiction, American publisher of Alexander Kent's Richard Bolitho series, Dudley Pope's Ramage novels." Publishes trade paperback and hardcover originals and reprints. Averages 20 total titles, 17 fiction titles/year. Distributes titles through National Book Network.
Needs General historical, nautical (British and American naval), and military historical.
How to Contact Does not accept unsolicited mss. Query with SASE. Include list of publishing credits. Responds in 2 months to queries. Accepts simultaneous submissions.
Terms Pays 5-10% royalty on retail price. Average advance: $1,000-5,000.
Advice "We are small and do not take on many unpublished writers. Historical and military accuracy is a must. Our readers know their time periods as well as their guns and their ships. Especially looking for stories with at least one strong female character."

⬛ ⬛ ⬛ McCLELLAND & STEWART, LTD.

The Canadian Publishers, 481 University Ave., Suite 900, Toronto ON M5G 2E9 Canada. (416)598-1114. Fax: (416)598-7764. Website: www.mcclelland.com. Publishes hardcover, trade paperback and mass market paperback originals and reprints. Averages 80 total titles/year.
Needs Experimental, historical, humor, literary, mainstream/contemporary, mystery, short story collections. "We publish quality fiction by prize-winning authors."
How to Contact Query with SASE.
Terms Pays 10-15% royalty on retail price (hardcover rates). Offers advance. Publishes ms 1 year after acceptance.

⚡ ◎ MARGARET K. McELDERRY BOOKS

Simon & Schuster Children's Publishing Division, Simon & Schuster, 1230 Sixth Ave., New York NY 10020. (212)698-2761. Fax: (212)698-2797. Website: www.simonsayskids.com. **Contact:** Emma D. Dryden, vice president/editorial director. Estab. 1971. Publishes quality material for preschoolers to 18-year-olds. Publishes hardcover originals. Books: high quality paper; offset printing; three piece and POB bindings; illustrations. Average print order: 12,500. First novel print order: 7,500. **Published some debut authors within the last year.** Averages 35 total titles/year.

- Books published by Margaret K. McElderry Books have received numerous awards including the Newberry and the Caldecott Awards.

Needs Adventure, fantasy, historical, mainstream/contemporary, mystery, picture books, young adult (or middle grade); all categories (fiction and nonfiction) for juvenile and young adult. "We will consider any category. Results depend on the quality of the imagination, the artwork and the writing." Published *Bear Stays Up Late*, by Karma Wilson and illustrated by Jane Chapman (picture books); *On Pointe*, by Lori Ann Grover (middle grade fiction); and *The Legend of Buddy Bush*, by Sheila P. Moses (young adult fiction).

Terms Average print order is 5,000-10,000 for a first middle grade or young adult book; 7,500-20,000 for a first picture book. Pays royalty on hardcover retail price: 10% fiction; picture book, 5% author; 5% illustrator. Offers $5,000-8,000 advance for new authors. Publishes ms up to 3 years after acceptance. Ms guidelines for #10 SASE.

Advice "Imaginative writing of high quality is always in demand; also picture books that are original and unusual. Keep in mind that McElderry is a very small imprint, so we are very selective about the books we will undertake for publication. We try not to publish any 'trend' books. Be familiar with our list and with what is being published this year by all publishing houses."

MEDALLION PRESS, INC.

27825 N. Forest Garden Rd., Wauconda IL 60084. Website: www.medallionpress.com. **Contact:** Wenda Burbank, acquisitions editor. Estab. 2003. "We are an independent publisher looking for books that are outside-of-the-box. Please do not submit to us if you are looking for a large advance. We reserve our funds for marketing the books." Publishes paperback originals. Average print order: 5,000. **Published 10 debut authors within the last year.** Distributes books through Ingram, Baker & Taylor.

Imprint(s) Platinum/Hardcover; Gold/Mass Market; Silver/Trade Paper; Bronze/Young Adult; Jewel/Romance; Amethyst/Fantasy, Sci-Fi, Paranormal; Emerald/Suspense; Ruby/Contemporary; Sapphire/Historical.

Needs Adventure, ethnic, fantasy (space fantasy, sword and sorcery), glitz, historical, horror (dark fantasy, futuristic, psychological, supernatural), humor, literary, mainstream/contemporary, military/war, mystery (amateur slueth, police procedural, private eye/hard-boiled), romance, science fiction (hard science/technological, soft/sociological), thriller/espionage, western (frontier saga), young adult. Published *Dark Planet*, by Charles W.Sasser (military science fiction); *Men of Bronze*, by Scott Oden (historical fiction); *Big Hair and Flying Cows*, by Dolores J. Wilson (women's fiction).

How to Contact Does not accept unsolicited mss. Submit first 3 consecutive chapter(s). Also include a chapter-by-chapter synopsis. ("Without a synopsis, the submission will be rejected.") Accepts queries by mail. Include estimated word count, brief bio, list of publishing credits. Send SASE or IRC. Agented fiction 30%. Responds in 6-12 months to mss. Accepts simultaneous submissions. No electronic submissions. Sometimes comments on rejected mss.

Terms Pays 6-8% royalty. Offers advance. Publishes ms 1-2 years after acceptance. Ms guidelines online.

Advice "We are not affected by trends. We are simply looking for well-crafted, original, grammatically correct works of fiction. Please visit our website for the most current guidelines prior to submitting anything to us."

N: ○ MEISHA MERLIN PUBLISHING, INC.

P.O. Box 7, Decatur GA 30031. E-mail: email@meishamerlin.com. Website: www.meishamerlin.com. **Contact:** Stephen Pagel, senior editor. Estab. 1996. Midsize independent publisher devoted exclusively to science fiction, fantasy and horror. Publishes hardcover and paperback originals and reprints. Also publishes e-books. **Published 2 debut authors within the last year.**

Needs Fantasy (space fantasy, sword and sorcery), horror (dark fantasy, futuristic, psychological, supernatural), science fiction (hard science/technological, soft/sociological). Recently published *Traitor's Knot*, by Janny Wurts; *Crystal Soldier*, by Sharon Lee and Steve Miller.

How to Contact Accepts unsolicited mss. Query with SASE or submit first 75 pages. Accepts queries by e-mail, mail. Include estimated word count, brief bio, list of publishing credits. Send SASE for return of ms or send a disposable ms and SASE for reply only. Often comments on rejected mss.

Advice "We look for quality and originality first, specific genre or style second."

MERIWETHER PUBLISHING, LTD.

885 Elkton Dr., Colorado Springs CO 80907-3557. (719)594-4422. Fax: (719)594-9916. Website: www.meriwetherpublishing.com; www.contemporarydrama.com. **Contact:** Rhonda Wray, associate editor (church plays); Ted Zapel, editor (school plays, comedies, books). Estab. 1969. "Mid-size, independent publisher of plays. We publish plays for teens, mostly one-act comedies, holiday plays for churches and musical comedies. Our books are on the theatrical arts." Publishes paperback originals and reprints. Books: quality paper; printing house specialist; paperback binding. Average print order: 5,000-10,000. **Published 25-35 debut authors within the last year.**

Needs Mainstream/contemporary, religious (children's plays and religious Christmas and Easter plays), suspense, all in playscript format, comedy. Published *Murder in the Manor*, by Bill Hand (comic mystery play).

How to Contact Accepts unsolicited mss. Query with SASE. Accepts queries by e-mail. Include list of publishing credits. Send SASE for return of ms or send a disposable ms and SASE for reply only. Responds in 3 weeks to queries; 2 months to mss. Accepts simultaneous submissions. Sometimes comments on rejected mss.

Terms Pays 10% royalty on retail price or makes outright purchase. Publishes ms 6-12 months after acceptance. Book catalog and ms guidelines for $2 postage.

Advice "If you're interested in writing comedy/farce plays, we're your best publisher."

MID-LIST PRESS

4324 12th Ave S., Minneapolis MN 55407-3218. (612)432-8062. Fax: (612)823-8387. E-mail: guide@midlist.org. Website: www.midlist.org. **Contact:** James Cihlar, executive director. Estab. 1989. "We are a nonprofit literary press dedicated to the survival of the mid-list, those quality titles that are being neglected by the larger commercial houses. Our focus is on first-time writers, and we are probably best known for the Mid-List Press First Series Awards." Publishes hardcover and trade paperback originals. Books: acid-free paper; offset printing; perfect or Smyth-sewn binding. Average print order: 2,000. **Published 6 debut authors within the last year.** Averages 5 total titles, 2 fiction titles/year. Distributes titles through Small Press Distribution, Ingram, Baker & Taylor, Midwest Library Service, Brodart, Follett and Emery Pratt. Promotes titles through publicity, direct mail, catalogs, author's events and review and awards.

Needs General fiction. Published *The Trouble with You Is*, by Susan Jackson Rodgers (first fiction, short fiction); *Pleasant Drugs*, by Kathryn Kulpa; and *The Woman Who Never Cooked*, by Mary L. Tabor.

How to Contact Accepts unsolicited mss. Agented fiction less than 10%. Responds in 3 weeks to queries; 3 months to mss. Accepts simultaneous submissions.

Terms Pays 40-50% royalty on net receipts. Average advance: $1,000. Publishes ms 12-18 months after acceptance. Ms guidelines online.

Advice "Write first for guidelines or visit our website before submitting a query, proposal or manuscript. And take the time to read some of the titles we've published."

MIGHTYBOOK

10924 Grant Rd., #225, Houston TX 77070. (281)955-9855. Fax: (281)890-4818. E-mail: reaves@houston.rr.com. Website: www.mightybook.com. **Contact:** Richard Eaves, acquisitions editor. Estab. 1991. "Small independent publisher of electronic, read-aloud picture books for the Internet. Much of our marketing and sales are done on the Internet." Publishes only electronic books. **Published 10 debut authors within the last year.** Averages 30-50 total titles, 25 fiction titles/year.

Needs Very short children's picture books (100-200 words). Published *I Have No Tail*, by S.J. Arohalt; *Oliver's High Five*, by Beverly S. Brown; *How I Feel Happy*, by Marcia Leonard; *Purple Underwear* by Robin McKay Pimentel; and *Icky, Sticky, and Gooey*, by Kimberly Constant (debut fiction).

How to Contact Accepts unsolicited mss. Accepts queries by e-mail, fax, phone. Agented fiction 5%. Responds in 6 weeks to queries; 6 weeks to mss. Accepts simultaneous submissions, electronic submissions, submissions on disk.

Terms Publishes ms 3 months after acceptance.

Advice "Write short picture books with a good moral, but avoid references to violence and avoid controversial topics."

MILKWEED EDITIONS

1011 Washington Ave. S., Suite 300, Minneapolis MN 55415. (612)332-3192. Fax: (612)215-2550. E-mail: editor @milkweed.org. Website: www.milkweed.org and www.worldashome.org. **Contact:** H. Emerson Blake, publisher; Elisabeth Fitz, first reader. Estab. 1984. Nonprofit publisher. Publishes hardcover originals and paperback originals and reprints. Books: book text quality—acid-free paper; offset printing; perfect or hardcover binding. Average print order: 4,000. First novel print order depends on book. **Published some debut authors within the last year.** Averages 15 total titles/year. Distributes through Publisher's Group West. Each book has its own marketing plan involving print ads, tours, conferences, etc.

• Pattiann Rogers's *Song of the World Becoming* was a finalist for the 2001 *Los Angeles Times* Book Prize.

Needs Literary. Novels for adults and for readers 8-13. High literary quality. For adult readers: literary fiction, nonfiction, poetry, essays; for children (ages 8-13): literary novels. Translations welcome for both audiences. Published *Distant Music*, by Lee Langley; *Roofwalker*, by Susan Power (short stories); and *Hell's Bottom, Colorado*, by Laura Pritchett (first fiction, short stories).

How to Contact Submit complete ms. Responds in 2 months to queries; 6 months to mss. Accepts simultaneous submissions.

Terms Pays 7½% royalty on retail price. Average advance: varied. Publishes ms 1-2 years after acceptance. Book catalog for $1.50 postage. Ms guidelines online.

Advice "Read good contemporary literary fiction, find your own voice, and persist. Familiarize yourself with our list before submitting."

✪ ◎ ⚑ MILKWEEDS FOR YOUNG READERS

Milkweed Editions, 1011 Washington Ave. S., Suite 300, Minneapolis MN 55415. (612)332-3192. Fax: (612)215-2550. Website: www.milkweed.org. **Contact:** H. Emerson Blake, editor in chief; Elisabeth Fitz, children's reader. Estab. 1984. "Milkweeds for Young Readers are works that embody humane values and contribute to cultural understanding." Publishes hardcover and trade paperback originals. Averages 1-2 total titles/year. Distributes titles through Publishers Group West. Promotes titles individually through print advertising, website and author tours.

• *Perfect*, by Natasha Friend, was chosen as a Book Sense 76 Children's Book selection.

Needs Adventure, fantasy, historical, humor, mainstream/contemporary, animal, environmental. For ages 8-13. Published *Hard Times for Jake Smith*, by Aileen Kilgore Henderson; *A Bride for Anna's Papa*, by Isabel Marvin.

How to Contact Query with SASE. Agented fiction 30%. Responds in 2 months to queries. Accepts simultaneous submissions.

Terms Pays 7½% royalty on retail price. Average advance: variable. Publishes ms 1 year after acceptance. Book catalog for $1.50. Ms guidelines for #10 SASE or on the website.

Advice "Familiarize yourself with our books before submitting. You need not have a long list of credentials— excellent work speaks for itself."

✪ ◯ ◎ 🌐 MILLS & BOON HISTORICAL ROMANCE

a Harlequin book line, Eton House, 18-24 Paradise Rd., Richmond Surrey TW9 1SR United Kingdom. (44)0208 288 2800. Website: www.millsandboon.co.uk. "This series covers a wide range of British and European historical periods from ancient Greece up to and including the World War II." Publishes paperback orginals and reprints. Books: newspaper print; web printing; perfect-bound. **Published some debut authors within the last year.**

Needs Romance. "The romance should take priority, with all the emotional impact of a growing love and should be developed over a relatively short span of time; the historical detail should be accurate, without sounding like a textbook, and should help to create a true sense of the chosen setting, so the reader becomes immersed in that time." Manuscripts must be 75,000-90,000 words.

How to Contact Accepts unsolicited mss. Send SASE for return of ms or send a disposable ms and SASE for reply only. No simultaneous submissions, electronic submissions, submissions on disk.

Terms Pays royalty. Offers advance. Ms guidelines for SASE and on website.

✪ ◯ ◎ 🌐 MILLS & BOON MEDICAL ROMANCE

a Harlequin book line, Eton House, 18-24 Paradise Rd., Richmond Surrey TW9 1SR United Kingdom. (44)0208 288 2800. Website: www.millsandboon.co.uk. **Contact:** Sheila Hodgson, senior editor. "These are present-day romances in a medical setting." Publishes paperback originals and reprints. Books: newspaper print; web printing; perfect-bound. **Published some debut authors within the last year.**

Needs Romance (medical). Looking for writing with "a good balance between the romance, the medicine, and the underlying story. At least one of the main characters should be a medical professional, and developing the romance is easier if the hero and heroine work together. Medical detail should be accurate but preferably without using technical language. An exploration of patients and their illnesses is permitted, but not in such numbers as to overwhelm the growing love story. Settings can be anywhere in the world." Manuscripts must be 50,000-55,000 words.

How to Contact Accepts unsolicited mss. Query with SASE or submit complete ms. Send SASE for return of ms or send a disposable ms and SASE for reply only. No simultaneous submissions, electronic submissions, submissions on disk.

Terms Pays royalty. Offers advance. Ms guidelines for SASE and on website.

Advice "More detailed guidelines are available on request with a stamped, addressed envelope."

Book Publishers

🅰 🔀 ✖ MIRA BOOKS

an imprint of Harlequin, 225 Duncan Mill Rd., Don Mills ON M3B 3K9 Canada. Website: www.mirabooks.com. "MIRA Books is proud to publish outstanding mainstream women's fiction for readers around the world." Publishes paperback orginals.

Needs Family saga, historical (romance), mainstream/contemporary, suspense (romance), thriller/espionage, relationship novels. Published work by Penny Jordan, Debbie Macomber, Diana Palmer, Nan Ryan and Susan Wiggs.

How to Contact Does not accept unsolicited mss. *Agented submissions only.*

Terms Pays royalty. Offers advance.

Ⓝ ◑ ◎ MOODY PUBLISHERS

(formerly Moody Press), Moody Bible Institute, 820 N. LaSalle Blvd., Chicago IL 60610. (312)329-8047. Fax: (312)329-2019. E-mail: acquisitions@moody.edu. Website: www.moodypublishers.org. **Contact:** Acquistions Coordinator (all fiction). Estab. 1894. Small, evangelical Christian Publisher. "We publish only fiction that reflects and supports our evangelical worldview and mission." Publishes hardcover, trade and mass market paperback originals. Averages 60 total titles, 5-10 fiction titles/year. Member, CBA. Distributes and promotes titles through sales reps, print advertising, promotional events, Internet, etc.

Needs Children's/juvenile (series), fantasy, historical, mystery, religious (children's religious, inspirational, religious mystery/suspense), science fiction, young adult (adventure, fantasy/science fiction, historical, mystery/suspense, series). Recently published *Courage to Run*, by Wendy Lawton (YA, debut author); *Vinegar Boy*, by Alberta Hause (YA); and *Purity Reigns*, by Stephanie Perry Moore (YA). Publishes ongoing YA series, Daughters of the Faith.

How to Contact Accepts unsolicited mss. Query with SASE. Accepts queries by e-mail, fax. Include estimated word count, brief bio, list of publishing credits. Send SASE for return of ms or send a disposable ms and SASE for reply only. Agented fiction 90%. Responds in 2-3 months to queries. Accepts electronic submissions. No simultaneous submissions, submissions on disk.

Terms Royalty varies. Average advance: $1,000-10,000. Publishes ms 9-12 months after acceptance. Ms guidelines for SASE and on website.

Advice "Get to know Moody Publishers and understand what kinds of books we publish. We will decline all submissions that do not support our evangelical Christian beliefs and mission."

Ⓝ ✖ ◑ PAUL MOULD PUBLISHING

Empire Publishing, P.O. Box 1344, Studio City CA 91614. (818)784-8918. Paul Mould. Estab. 1960. Small independent publisher. Publishes paperback and hardcover originals and reprints. Book: 50 lb. bond paper; offset printing. Average print order: 2,000-5,000. **Published 3 debut authors within the last year.**

Imprint(s) Gaslight Publications; Collectors Publications.

Needs Children's/juvenile (Sherlock Holmes), erotica, historical (medieval), mystery (Sherlock Holmes), western, young adult (Sherlock Holmes).

How to Contact Does not accept unsolicited mss. Query with SASE. Accepts queries by mail. Include estimated word count, brief bio, list of publishing credits. Send SASE or IRC. Responds in 40-65 days to queries; 3-4 months to mss. Rarely comments on rejected mss.

Terms Pays royalty. Publishes ms 6 months to 2 years after acceptance. Ms guidelines for #10 SASE.

◎ MOUNTAIN STATE PRESS

2300 MacCorkle Ave. SE, Charleston WV 25304-1099. (304)357-4767. Fax: (304)357-4715. E-mail: msp1@neww ave.net. Website: www.mountainstatepress.com. **Contact:** Marshall Browning, fiction editor. Estab. 1978. "A small nonprofit press run by a board of 13 members who volunteer their time. We specialize in books about West Virginia or by authors from West Virginia. We strive to give a voice to Appalachia." Publishes paperback originals and reprints. **Published some debut authors within the last year.** Plans 1 first novel this year. Distributes titles through bookstores, distributors, gift shops and individual sales (Amazon.com and Barnes & Noble online carry our titles). Promotes titles through newspapers, radio, mailings and book signings.

Needs Family saga, historical (West Virginia), military/war, new age/mystic, religious. Currently compiling an anthology of West Virginia authors. Published *Peripheral Visions*, by Robert Flnagan; *Hears the Wind*, by Kate Dooley, *The Conversion of Big Jim Cane*, by Robert Elkins.

How to Contact Accepts unsolicited mss. Query with SASE or submit complete ms. Accepts queries by e-mail, fax. Include estimated word count, brief bio. Send SASE for return of ms or send a disposable ms and SASE for reply only. Responds in 6 months to mss. Often comments on rejected mss.

Terms Pays royalty.

Advice "Topic of West Virginia is the best choice for our press. Send your manuscript in and it will be read and reviewed by the members of the Board of Mountain State Press. We give helpful suggestions and critique the writing."

N MOYER BELL, LTD.

549 Old North Rd., Kingston RI 02881. (401)783-5480. Fax: (401)284-0959. E-mail: acomalliance@yahoo.com. Website: www.moyerbellbooks.com. Averages 15 total titles/year.

Imprint(s) Asphodel Press.

Needs Literary.

How to Contact Query with SASE.

Terms Pays 6-10% royalty on retail price.

MULTNOMAH PUBLISHERS, INC.

P.O. Box 1720, Sisters OR 97759. (541)549-1144. Fax: (541)549-8048. Website: www.multnomahbooks.com. **Contact:** Editorial department. Estab. 1987. Midsize independent publisher of evangelical fiction and nonfiction. Publishes hardcover and trade paperback originals Books: perfect binding. Average print order: 15,000. Averages 75 total titles/year.

• Multnomah Books has received several Gold Medallion Books Awards from the Evangelical Christian Publishers Association.

Imprint(s) Multnomah Books ("Christian living and popular theology books"); Multnomah Fiction ("Changing lives through the power of story"); Multnomah Gift ("Substantive topics with beautiful, lyrical writing").

Needs Adventure, historical, humor, literary, mystery, religious, romance, suspense, western. Published *The Rescuer*, by Dee Henderson (romance/suspense); *Diary Of a Teenage Girl* series, by Melody Carlson (YA); and *Sisterchicks Do the Hula*, by Robin Jones Gunn (contemporary).

How to Contact Does not accept unsolicited mss. *Agented submissions only.* Accepts simultaneous submissions.

Terms Pays royalty on wholesale price. Provides 100 author's copies. Offers advance. Publishes ms 1-2 years after acceptance. Ms guidelines online.

Advice "Looking for moral, uplifting fiction. We're particularly interested in contempoarary women's fiction, historical fiction, superior romance and mystery/suspense."

MY WEEKLY STORY COLLECTION

D.C. Thomson and Co., Ltd., 22 Meadowside, Dundee DD19QJ Scotland. **Contact:** Mrs. T. Steel, editor. "Paperback story library with full-colour cover. Material should not be violent, controversial or sexually explicit." Distributes titles through national retail outlets. Promotes titles through display cards in retail outlets and inhouse magazine adverts.

Needs Historical, mainstream/contemporary, romance. Length: approximately 30,000 words.

How to Contact Query with SASE or submit outline, 3 sample chapter(s), synopsis.

Terms Writers are paid on acceptance.

Advice "Avoid too many colloquialisms/Americanisms. Stories can be set anywhere but local colour not too 'local' as to be alien."

THE MYSTERIOUS PRESS

Warner Books, 1271 Avenue of the Americas, New York NY 10020. (212)522-7200. Fax: (212)522-7990. Website: www.mysteriouspress.com. **Contact:** Kristen Weber, editor. Estab. 1976. Publishes hardcover, trade paperback and mass market editions Books: hardcover and paperback binding; illustrations rarely. First novel print order: 10,000 copies minimum. **Published some debut authors within the last year.** Averages 20 total titles/year.

Needs Mystery, suspense, Crime/detective novels. Published *Open and Shut*, by David Rosenfelt; *Cyanide Wells*, by Marcia Mulle.

How to Contact *Agented submissions only.*

Terms Pays standard, but negotiable, royalty on retail price. Average advance: negotiable. Publishes ms an average of 1 year after acceptance. Ms guidelines online.

Advice "Write a strong and memorable novel, and with the help of a good literary agent, you'll find the right publishing house. Don't despair if your manuscript is rejected by several houses. All publishing houses are looking for new and exciting crime novels, but it may not be at the time your novel is submitted. Hang in there, keep the faith—and good luck."

NATURAL HERITAGE/NATURAL HISTORY, INC.

P.O. Box 95, Station O, Toronto ON M4A 2M8 Canada. (416)694-7907. Fax: (416)690-0819. E-mail: submissions @naturalheritagebooks.com. Website: www.naturalheritagebooks.com. **Contact:** Barry Penhale, publisher. Publishes trade paperback originals. **Published 50% debut authors within the last year.** Averages 10-12 total titles/year.

Imprint(s) Natural Heritage Books.

Needs Historical, children's (age 8-12). Published *Just a Little Later with Eevo and Sim*, by Henry Shykoff.

How to Contact Query with SASE. Responds in 4 months to queries; 6 months to mss. No simultaneous submissions.

Terms Pays 8% royalty on retail price. Offers advance. Publishes ms 2-3 years after acceptance. Ms guidelines online.

Advice ''We are a Canadian publisher in the natural heritage and history fields. We rarely publish fiction, the only exceptions being occasional historical fiction and children's chapter books.''

THOMAS NELSON, INC.

Box 141000, Nashville TN 37214-1000. (615)889-9000. Website: www.thomasnelson.com. **Contact:** Acquisitions Editor. ''Largest Christian book publishers.'' Publishes hardcover and paperback orginals. Averages 100-150 total titles/year.

Needs Publishes commercial fiction authors who write for adults from a Christian perspective. Published *Kingdom Come*, by Larry Burkett and T. Davis Bunn; *Dakota Moon*, series, by Stephanie Grace Whitson (romance); and *Empty Coffin*, by Robert Wise (mystery/suspense).

How to Contact Does not accept unsolicited mss. Responds in 3 months to queries. Accepts simultaneous submissions.

Terms Pays royalty on net receipts. Rates negotiated for each project. Offers advance. Publishes ms 1-2 years after acceptance. Ms guidelines online.

Advice ''We are a conservative publishing house and want material which is conservative in morals and in nature.''

THE NEW ENGLAND PRESS, INC.

P.O. Box 575, Shelburne VT 05482. (802)863-2520. Fax: (802)863-1510. E-mail: nep@together.net. Website: www.nepress.com. **Contact:** Christopher A. Bray, managing editor. Estab. 1978. Publishes hardcover and trade paperback originals. **Published 50% debut authors within the last year.** Averages 6-8 total titles/year.

Needs Historical (Vermont, New Hampshire, Maine). ''We look for very specific subject matters based on Vermont history and heritage, including historical novels for young adults set in Northern New England. We do not publish contemporary adult fiction of any kind.''

How to Contact Submit 2 sample chapter(s), synopsis. Agented fiction 10%. Responds in 6-9 months to queries. Accepts simultaneous submissions.

Terms Pays royalty on wholesale price. Publishes ms 15 months after acceptance. Ms guidelines online.

Advice ''Our readers are interested in all aspects of Vermont and northern New England, including hobbyists (railroad books) and students (young adult fiction and biography). No agent is needed, but our market is extremely specific and our volume is low, so send a query or outline and writing samples first. Sending the whole manuscript is discouraged. We will not accept projects that are still under development or give advances.''

NEW VICTORIA PUBLISHERS

P.O. Box 27, Norwich VT 05055-0027. (802)649-5297. Fax: (802)649-5297. E-mail: newvic@aol.com. Website: www.newvictoria.com. **Contact:** Claudia McKay, editor. Estab. 1976. ''Publishes mostly lesbian fiction—strong female protagonists. Most well known for Stoner McTavish mystery series.'' Small, three person operation. Publishes trade paperback originals. Averages 2-3 total titles/year. Distributes titles through Bookworld (Sarasota, FL) Words Distributing (Oakland, CA), Airlift (London) and Bulldog Books (Sydney, Australia). Promotes titles ''mostly through lesbian feminist media.''

● *Mommy Deadest*, by Jean Marcy, won the Lambda Literary Award for Mystery.

Needs Adventure, erotica, fantasy, feminist, historical, humor, lesbian, mystery (amateur sleuth), romance, science fiction, western. ''Looking for strong feminist characters, also strong plot and action. We will consider most anything if it is well written and appeals to lesbian/feminist audience. Hard copy only—no disks.'' Publishes anthologies or special editions. Published *Killing at the Cat*, by Carlene Miller (mystery); *Queer Japan*, by Barbara Summerhawk (anthology); *Skin to Skin*, by Martha Miller (erotic short fiction); *Talk Show*, by Melissa Hartman (novel); *Flight From Chador*, by Sigrid Brunel (adventure); and *Owl of the Desert*, by Ida Swearingen (novel).

How to Contact Accepts unsolicited mss. Submit outline, sample chapter(s), synopsis. Accepts queries by e-mail, fax. Send SASE or IRC. No simultaneous submissions.

Terms Pays 10% royalty. Publishes ms 1 year after acceptance. Ms guidelines for SASE.

Advice ''We are especially interested in lesbian or feminist mysteries, ideally with a character or characters who can evolve through a series of books. Mysteries should involve a complex plot, accurate legal and police procedural detail, and protagonists with full emotional lives. Pay attention to plot and character development. Read guidelines carefully.''

NEWEST PUBLISHERS LTD.

201, 8540-109 St., Edmonton AB T6G 1E6 Canada. (780)432-9427. Fax: (780)433-3179. E-mail: info@newestpress.com. Website: www.newestpress.com. **Contact:** Ruth Linka, general manager. Estab. 1977. Publishes trade paperback originals. **Published some debut authors within the last year.** Averages 13-16 total titles/year. Promotes titles through book launches, media interviews, review copy mailings and touring.

Imprint(s) Prairie Play Series (drama); Writer as Critic (literary criticisim); Nunatak New Fiction.

Needs Literary. "Our press is interested in Western Canadian writing." Published *Icefields*, by Thomas Wharton (novel); *Blood Relations and Other Plays*, by Sharon Pollock (drama); *A Thirst to Die For*, by Ian Waddell (mystery, debut author).

How to Contact Accepts unsolicited mss. Submit complete ms. Send SASE or IRC. Responds in 6 months to queries. Accepts simultaneous submissions.

Terms Pays 10% royalty. Publishes ms 24-30 months after acceptance. Book catalog for 9×12 SASE. Ms guidelines online.

Advice *"We publish western Canadian writers only or books about western Canada.* We are looking for excellent quality and originality."

W.W. NORTON CO., INC.

500 Fifth Ave., New York NY 10110. Fax: (212)869-0856. E-mail: manuscripts@wwnorton.com. Website: www.wwnorton.com. **Contact:** Midsize independent publisher of trade books and college textbooks. Publishes literary fiction. Estab. 1923. Publishes hardcover and paperback originals and reprints. Averages 300 total titles/year.

Needs Literary, poetry, poetry in translation, religious. High-qulity literary fiction. Published *Ship Fever*, by Andrea Barrett; *Oyster*, by Jannette Turner Hospital; and *Power*, by Linda Hogan.

How to Contact Does not accept unsolicited mss. Responds in 2 months to queries. No simultaneous submissions.

Terms Pays royalty. Offers advance. Ms guidelines online.

OMNIDAWN PUBLISHING

Omnidawn Corporation, P.O. Box 5224, Richmond CA 94805-5224. (510)237-5472. E-mail: submissions@omnidawn.com. Website: www.omnidawn.com. **Contact:** Rusty Morrison and Ken Keegan, editors (new wave fabulist). Estab. 1999. Omnidawn is a small independent publisher run by two part-time editors. "It specializes in new wave fabulist and fabulist fiction and innovative poetry. See website for further description." Publishes hardcover originals and paperback originals. Books: archival quality paper; offset printing; trade paperback and hardcover binding. Average print order: 3,000. **Published 1-2 debut authors within the last year.** Plans 2 first novels this year. Distributes titles through Small Press Distribution and Baker & Taylor.

Needs New wave fabulist and fabulist.

How to Contact Accepts unsolicited mss. Query with SASE. Accepts queries by e-mail, mail. Include estimated word count, brief bio, list of publishing credits. Send SASE for return of ms or send a disposable ms and SASE for reply only. Responds in 1 week to queries; 3-5 months to mss. Accepts simultaneous submissions. No electronic submissions, submissions on disk. Never comments on rejected mss.

Terms Publishes ms 6-12 months after acceptance. Ms guidelines online.

Advice "Check our website for latest information."

ONSTAGE PUBLISHING

214 E. Moulton St. NE, Decatur AL 35601. (256)308-2300. Website: www.onstagebooks.com. Estab. 1999. Publishes hardcover and mass market paperback originals. Averages 5 total titles/year.

Needs Adventure, children's/juvenile, fantasy, historical, humor, juvenile, literary, mainstream/contemporary, mystery, picture books, regional, romance, science fiction, short story collections, sports, suspense, young adult. "We pride ourselves in scouting out new talent and publishing works by new writers. We publish mainly children's titles."

How to Contact Submit proposal package including 3 sample chapter(s), synopsis. Responds in 1-2 months to queries; 2-4 months to mss. Accepts simultaneous submissions.

Terms Pays royalty on wholesale price. Average advance: variable. Publishes ms 1-2 years after acceptance. Book catalog for 9×12 SASE with 3 first-class stamps or online at website. Ms guidelines for #10 SASE or online at website.

ORCA BOOK PUBLISHERS

P.O. Box 5626, Victoria BC V8R 6S4 Canada. (250)380-1229. Fax: (250)380-1892. E-mail: orca@orcabook.com. Website: www.orcabook.com. **Contact:** Maggie deVries, children's book editor. Estab. 1984. Only publishes Canadian authors. Publishes hardcover and trade paperback originals, and mass market paperback originals and reprints. Books: quality 60 lb. book stock paper; illustrations. Average print order: 3,000-5,000. First novel print order: 3,000-5,000. Plans 3-4 first novels this year. Averages 50 total titles/year.

Needs Hi-lo, juvenile (5-9 years), literary, mainstream/contemporary, young adult (10-18 years). "Ask for guidelines, find out what we publish." Looking for "children's fiction."

How to Contact Query with SASE or submit proposal package including outline, 2-5 sample chapter(s), synopsis, SASE. Agented fiction 20%. Responds in 1 month to queries; 1-2 months to mss. No simultaneous submissions. Sometimes comments on rejected mss.

Terms Pays 10% royalty. Publishes ms 12-18 months after acceptance. Book catalog for $8^{1}/_{2} \times 11$ SASE. Ms guidelines online.

Advice "We are looking to promote and publish Canadians."

ORIENT PAPERBACKS

A Division of Vision Books Pvt Ltd., 1590 Madarsa Rd., Kashmere Gate Delhi 110 006 India. +911-11-2386-2267. Fax: +911-11-2386-2935. E-mail: orientpbk@vsnl.com. Website: www.orientpaperbacks.com. **Contact:** Sudhir Malhotra, editor. "We are one of the largest paperback publishers in S.E. Asia and publish English fiction by authors from this part of the world."

Needs Length: 40,000 words minimum.

Terms Pays royalty on copies sold.

OTHER PRESS

307 Seventh Ave., Suite 1807, New York NY 1001. (212)414-0054. Fax: (212)414-0939. E-mail: editor@otherpress.com. Website: www.otherpress.com. **Contact:** Stacey Hague and Blake Radcliffe, editors (literary and translations). Estab. 1998. The Other Press is a small independent publisher. Publishes hardcover originals and paperback reprints. **Published 1 debut author within the last year.** Plans 3 first novels this year.

Needs Literary. Published *San Remo Drive*, by Leslie Epstein (fiction); *Stories From the City of God*, by Pier Paolo Pasolini (fiction/translation); *Tigor*, by Peter Stephan Jungk (fiction).

How to Contact Accepts unsolicited mss. Query with SASE or submit outline, 2 sample chapter(s). Accepts queries by mail. Include brief bio, list of publishing credits. Agented fiction 50%. Responds in 3-4 weeks to queries; 3-4 months to mss. Accepts simultaneous submissions, electronic submissions. No submissions on disk. Rarely comments on rejected mss.

Terms Pays $7^{1}/_{2}$-10% royalty. Average advance: negotiable.

Advice "Please send us your absolute final draft of your completed manuscript and not a work in progress."

OUTRIDER PRESS, INC.

937 Patricia, Crete IL 60417. (708)672-6630. Fax: (708)672-5820. E-mail: outriderpr@aol.com. Website: www.outriderpress.com. **Contact:** Whitney Scott, editor. Estab. 1988. Small literary press and hand bindery; publishes many first-time authors. Publishes paperback originals. Books: 70 lb. paper; offset printing; perfect bound. Average print order: 2,000. **Published 25-30 debut authors within the last year.** Distributes titles through Baker & Taylor.

• Was a *Small Press Review* "Pick" for 2000.

Needs Ethnic, experimental, family saga, fantasy (space fantasy, sword and sorcery), feminist, gay/lesbian, historical, horror (psychological, supernatural), humor, lesbian, literary, mainstream/contemporary, mystery (amateur slueth, cozy, police procedural, private eye/hard-boiled), new age/mystic, psychic/supernatural, romance (contemporary, futuristic/time travel, gothic, historical, regency period, romantic suspense), science fiction (soft/sociological), short story collections, thriller/espionage, western (frontier saga, traditional). Published *Telling Time*, by Cherie Caswell Dost; *If Ever I Cease to Love*, by Robert Klein Engler.

How to Contact Accepts unsolicited mss. Query with SASE. Accepts queries by mail. Include estimated word count, brief bio, list of publishing credits. Agented fiction 10%. Responds in 3 weeks to queries; 4 months to mss. Accepts simultaneous submissions, electronic submissions, submissions on disk. Sometimes comments on rejected mss.

Terms Pays honorarium. Publishes ms 6 months after acceptance. Ms guidelines for SASE.

Advice "It's always best to familiarize yourself with our publications. We're especially fond of humor/irony."

RICHARD C. OWEN PUBLISHERS, INC.

P.O. Box 585, Katonah NY 10536. (914)232-3903. Website: www.rcowen.com. **Contact:** Janice Boland, director, children's books. Estab. 1982. "We believe children become enthusiastic, independent, life-long readers when supported and guided by skillful teachers who choose books with real and lasting value. The professional development work we do and the books we publish support these beliefs." Publishes hardcover and paperback originals. **Published 15 debut authors within the last year.** Averages 23 total titles/year. Distributes titles to schools via mail order. Promotes titles through website, database mailing, reputation, catalog, brochures and appropriate publications—magazines, etc.

Needs Picture books. "Brief, strong story line, believable characters, natural language, exciting—child-appealing stories with a twist. No lists books, alphabet or counting books." Seeking short, snappy stories and articles for 7-8-year-old children (2nd grade). Subjects include humor, careers, mysteries, science fiction, folktales, women, fashion trends, sports, music, mysteries, myths, journalism, history, inventions, planets, architecture, plays, adventure, technology, vehicles. Published *Mama Cut My Hair*, by Lisa Wilkinson (fiction, debut author); *Cool,* by Steven Morse (fiction, debut author); and *Author on My Street,* by Lisa Brodie Cook (fiction).

How to Contact Responds in 1 month to queries; 5 months to mss. Accepts simultaneous submissions.

Terms Pays 5% royalty on wholesale price. Books for Young Learners Anthologies: flat fee for all rights. Publishes ms 2-5 years after acceptance. Ms guidelines online.

Advice "Send entire ms. Write clear strong stories with memorable characters and end with a big wind up finish. Write for today's children—about real things that interest them. Read books that your public library features in their children's room to acquaint yourself with the best modern children's literature."

PETER OWEN PUBLISHERS

73 Kenway Rd., London SW5 0RE United Kingdom. 020-7373 5628. Fax: 020-7373 6760. E-mail: admin@peterow en.com. Website: www.peterowen.com. **Contact:** Antonia Owen, editorial director/fiction editor. "Independent publishing house from 1951. Publish literary fiction from around the world, from Russia to Japan. Publishers of Shusaku Endo, Paul and Jane Bowles, Hermann Hesse, Octavio Paz, Colette, etc." Publishes hardcover originals and trade paperback originals and reprints. Averages 20-30 total titles, 4 fiction titles/year. Titles distributed through Central Books, London and Dufour Editions, USA.

Needs Literary. "No first novels; authors should be aware that we publish very little new fiction these days." Does not accept short stories, only excerpts from novels of normal length. Published *Angels on the Head of a Pin*, by Yuri Druzhnikov (translated literary fiction); *Cassandra's Disk*, by Angela Green (literary); *Baudelaire in Chains*, by Frank Hilton (nonfiction, biography).

How to Contact Submit sample chapter(s), synopsis. Send SASE or IRC. Responds in 2 months to queries; 3 months to mss. Accepts simultaneous submissions.

Terms Pays 7$\frac{1}{2}$-10% royalty. Average advance: negotiable. Publishes ms 1 year after acceptance. Book catalog for SASE, SAE with IRC or on website.

Advice "Be concise. It helps if author is familiar with our list. Literary fiction is very hard to sell in the U.K; it is also hard to get it reviewed. At the moment we are publishing less fiction than nonfiction."

PALARI PUBLISHING

P.O. Box 9288, Richmond VA 23227-0288. (866)570-6724. Fax: (804)883-5234. E-mail: palaripub@aol.com. Website: www.palaribooks.com. **Contact:** David Smitherman, fiction editor. Estab. 1998. Small publisher specializing in southern mysteries and nonfiction. Publishes hardcover and trade paperback originals. **Published 2 debut authors within the last year.** Member, Publishers Marketing Association. Distributes titles through Baker & Taylor, Ingram, Amazon, mail order and website. Promotes titles through book signings, direct mail and the Internet.

Needs Adventure, ethnic, gay/lesbian, historical, literary, mainstream/contemporary, multicultural, mystery, suspense. "Tell why your idea is unique or interesting. Make sure we are interested in your genre before submitting." Published *We're Still Here* (cultural); and *In and Out in Hollywood* (Hollywood, gay); *The Guessing Game* (mystery).

How to Contact Does not accept unsolicited mss. Query with SASE. Accepts queries by e-mail, fax. Include estimated word count, brief bio, list of publishing credits. Send SASE for return of ms or send a disposable ms and SASE for reply only. Responds in 1 month to queries; 2-3 months to mss. Accepts electronic submissions. No simultaneous submissions. Often comments on rejected mss.

Terms Pays royalty. Publishes ms 1 year after acceptance. Ms guidelines online.

Advice "Send a good bio. I'm interested in a writer's experience and unique outlook on life."

PANTHER CREEK PRESS

P.O. Box 130233, Spring TX 77393-0233. E-mail: panthercreek3@hotmail.com. Website: www.panthercreekpre ss.com. **Contact:** Bobbi Sissel, editor (literary); Jerry Cooke, assistant editor (mystery); William Laufer, assistant editor (collections). Estab. 1999. "Mid-size publisher interested in Merchant-Ivory type fiction. Our production schedule is full for 2005 and we will be reading no new submissions until 2006." Publishes paperback originals. Books: 60 lb. white paper; docutech-printed; perfect-bound. Average print order: 1,500. **Published 4 debut authors within the last year.** Distributes titles through Baker & Taylor, Amazon.

Imprint(s) Enigma Books, Jerry Cooke, editor (mystery).

Needs Ethnic, experimental, humor, literary, mainstream/contemporary, multicultural, mystery (amateur

Book Publishers

sleuth), regional (Texana), short story collections. Published *The Caballeros of Ruby, Texas*, by Cynthia Leal Massey (literary); *Under a Riverbed Sky*, by Christopher Woods (literary collection); and *Killing Daddy: A Caprock Story*, by Sandra Gail Teichmann (literary experimental novel).

How to Contact Does not accept unsolicited mss. Query with SASE. Accepts queries by e-mail. Include estimated word count, brief bio, list of publishing credits. Send SASE for return of ms or send a disposable ms and SASE for reply only. Responds in 3 weeks to queries; 5 weeks to mss. Accepts simultaneous submissions.

Terms Pays 10% royalty, 5 author's copies. Publishes ms 1 year after acceptance. Guidelines and catalog available on website.

Advice "We would enjoy seeing more experimental work, but 'schock' narrative does not interest us. We don't want to see thrillers, fantasies, horror. The small, thoughtful literary story that large publishers don't want to take a chance on is the kind that gets our attention."

PARADISE CAY PUBLICATIONS
P.O. Box 29, Arcata CA 95518-0029. (707)822-9063. Fax: (707)822-9163. E-mail: mattm@humboldt1.com. Website: www.paracay.com. **Contact:** Matt Morehouse, publisher. Publishes hardcover and trade paperback originals and reprints. Books: 50 lb. paper; offset printing; perfect bound; illustrations. Average print order: 10,000. Average first novel print order: 3,000. **Published 3 debut authors within the last year.** Averages 5 total titles, 1 fiction titles/year.

Needs Adventure (nautical, sailing). All fiction must have a nautical theme. Published *Easing Sheets*, by L.M. Lawson.

How to Contact Query with SASE or submit 2-3 sample chapter(s), synopsis. Responds in 1 month to queries; 2 months to mss.

Terms Pays 10-15% royalty on wholesale price or makes outright purchase of $1,000-10,000. Average advance: $0-2,000. Publishes ms 4 months after acceptance. Book catalog and ms guidelines on website.

Advice "Must present in a professional manner. *Must* have a strong nautical theme."

PASSEGGIATA PRESS
420 West 14th St., Pueblo CO 81003-3404. (719)544-1038. Fax: (719)544-7911. E-mail: passegpress@cs.com. **Contact:** Donald Herdeck, publisher/editor-in-chief. Estab. 1973. "We search for books that will make clear the complexity and value of non-Western literature and culture." Small independent publisher with expanding list. Publishes hardcover and paperback originals. Books: library binding; illustrations. Average print order: 1,000-1,500. Averages 10-20 total titles, 6-8 fiction titles/year.

- Passeggiata, formerly Three Continents Press, has published three authors awarded the Nobel Prize in Literature."

Needs "We publish original fiction only by writers from Africa, the Caribbean, the Middle East, Asia and the Pacific. Published *Not Yet African*, by Kevin Gordon; and *Ghost Songs*; by Kathryn Abdul-Baki.

How to Contact Submit outline, table of contents. Accepts queries by e-mail, fax. Responds in 1 week to queries; 1 month to mss. Accepts simultaneous submissions. Sometimes comments on rejected mss.

Terms Pays 5-10% royalty. Foundation or institution receives 20-30 copies of book and at times royalty on first printing. We pay royalties once yearly (against advance) as a percentage of net paid receipts. Average advance: $300.

Advice "Submit professional work (within our parameters of interest) with well-worked-over language and clean manuscripts prepared to exacting standards."

PATHWISE PRESS
P.O. Box 2392, Bloomington IN 47402. (812)339-7298. E-mail: charter@bluemarble.net. Website: http://home.bluemarble.net/~charter/btgin.htm. **Contact:** Christopher Harter. Estab. 1997. Small independent publisher interested in work that is neither academic nor Bukowski. "We publish chapbooks only." Publishes paperback originals. Books: 20 lb. white linen paper; laser printing; saddle-stich bound; illustrations. Average print order: 200-300. **Published 5 debut authors within the last year.**

Needs Experimental, literary, short story collections.

How to Contact Accepts unsolicited mss. Accepts queries by e-mail. Include estimated word count, brief bio. Send SASE or IRC. Responds in 1 month to mss. Accepts simultaneous submissions. Sometimes comments on rejected mss.

Terms Pays 10-20% royalty. Publishes ms 6 months after acceptance. Ms guidelines online.

Advice "Proofread your work. Finished book should be 48-60 pages, including front and back matter, so consider length before submitting."

PAYCOCK PRESS
3819 No. 13th St., Arlington VA 22201. (703)525-9296. E-mail: hedgehogz@erols.com. Website: www.atticsbooks.com. **Contact:** Lucinda Ebersole and Richard Peabody. Estab. 1976. "Too academic for underground, to

Book Publishers

outlaw for the academic world. We want to be edgy and look for ultra literary work.'' Publishes paperback originals. Books: off-set printing. Average print order: 500. Averages 1 total title/year. Member: CLMP. Distributes through Amazon and website.

Needs Experimental, literary, short story collections.

How to Contact Accepts unsolicited mss. Reading period open from May 5 to September 4. Accepts queries by e-mail. Include brief bio. Send SASE for return of ms or send a disposable ms and SASE for reply only. Agented fiction 5%. Responds in 1 month to queries; 4 months to mss. Accepts simultaneous submissions, electronic submissions. Rarely comments on rejected mss.

Terms Publishes ms 8 months after acceptance.

Advice ''Check out our website, look at some back issues. Two of our favorite writers are Paul Bowles and Jeanette Winterson.''

PEACHTREE CHILDREN'S BOOKS

Peachtree Publishers, Ltd., 1700 Chattahoochee Avenue, Atlanta GA 30318-2112. (404)876-8761. Fax: (404)875-2578. E-mail: hello@peachtree-online.com. Website: www.peachtree-online.com. **Contact:** Helen Harriss, acquisitions editor. ''We publish a broad range of subjects and perspectives, with emphasis on innovative plots and strong writing.'' Publishes hardcover and trade paperback originals. Averages 30 total titles, 20-25 fiction titles/year.

Needs Juvenile, picture books, young adult. Looking for very well-written middle grade and young adult novels. No adult fiction. No short stories. Published *Sister Spider Knows All*; *Shadow of A Doubt*; *My Life and Death*, by Alexandra Canarsie.

How to Contact Submit 3 sample chapter(s) or submit complete ms. Responds in 6 months to queries; 6 months to mss. Accepts simultaneous submissions.

Terms Pays royalty on retail price; advance varies. Publishes ms 1 year or more after acceptance. Book catalog for 6 first-class stamps. Ms guidelines online.

PEACHTREE PUBLISHERS, LTD.

1700 Chattahoochee Ave., Atlanta GA 30318-2112. (404)876-8761. Fax: (404)875-2578. Website: www.peachtree-online.com. **Contact:** Helen Harriss, submissions editor. Estab. 1978. Independent publisher specializing in children's literature, nonfiction and regional guides. Publishes hardcover and trade paperback originals. First novel print run 5,000. **Published 2 debut authors within the last year.** Averages 20-25 total titles, 1-2 fiction titles/year. Promotes titles through review copies to appropriate publications, press kits and book signings at local bookstores.

Imprint(s) Peachtree Jr. and FreeStone.

Needs Juvenile, young adult. ''Absolutely no adult fiction! We are seeking YA and juvenile works including mystery and historical fiction, of high literary merit.''

How to Contact Accepts unsolicited mss. Query with SASE. Responds in 6 months to queries; 6 months to mss. Accepts simultaneous submissions. No electronic submissions.

Terms Pays royalty. Royalty varies. Offers advance. Publishes ms 1 year or more after acceptance. Ms guidelines online.

Advice ''Check out our website or catalog for the kinds of things we are interested in.''

PEDLAR PRESS

P.O. Box 26, Station P, Toronto ON M5S 2S6 Canada. (416)534-2011. Fax: (416)535-9677. E-mail: feralgrl@interlog.com. **Contact:** Beth Follett, editor (fiction, poetry). Publishes hardcover and trade paperback originals. **Published 50% debut authors within the last year.** Averages 4-6 total titles/year. Distributes in Canada through Harper Collins. In the US distributes directly for publisher.

Needs Erotica, experimental, feminist, gay/lesbian, humor, literary, picture books, short story collections. Published *Mouthing the Words*, by Camilla Gibb.

How to Contact Query with SASE or submit 5 sample chapter(s), synopsis. Responds in 1 month to queries; 6 months to mss. Accepts simultaneous submissions.

Terms Pays 10% royalty on retail price. Average advance: $200-400. Publishes ms 1 year after acceptance. Ms guidelines for #10 SASE.

Advice ''We select manuscripts according to our taste. Be familiar with some if not most of our recent titles.''

PELICAN PUBLISHING CO.

1000 Burmaster St., Gretna LA 70055. (504)368-1175. Website: www.pelicanpub.com. **Contact:** Nina Kooij, editor-in-chief. Estab. 1926. ''We seek writers on the cutting edge of ideas. We believe ideas have consequences. One of the consequences is that they lead to a best-selling book.'' Publishes hardcover, trade paperback and mass market paperback originals and reprints. Books: hardcover and paperback binding; illustrations sometimes. Buys juvenile mss with illustrations. Averages 65 total titles/year. Distributes titles internationally through distributors, bookstores, libraries. Promotes titles at reading and book conventions, in trade magazines, in radio interviews, print reviews and TV interviews.

• *The Warlord's Puzzle*, by Virginia Walton Pilegard was #2 on *Independent Bookseller's* Book Sense 76 list. *Dictionary of Literary Biography* lists *Unforgotten*, by D.J. Meador, as ''one of the best of 1999.''

Needs Historical, juvenile (regional or historical focus). ''We publish maybe one novel a year, usually by an author we already have. Almost all proposals are returned. We are most interested in historical Southern novels.'' Published *Jubal*, by Gary Penleytt (novel), and *Toby Belfer Visits Ellis Island*, by Gloria Teles Pushker (young reader).

How to Contact Does not accept unsolicited mss. Query with SASE or submit outline, 2 sample chapter(s), synopsis. Responds in 1 month to queries; 3 months to mss. No simultaneous submissions. Rarely comments on rejected mss.

Terms Pays royalty on actual receipts. Average advance: considered. Publishes ms 9-18 months after acceptance. Book catalog for SASE. Writer's guidelines for SASE or on website.

Advice ''Research the market carefully. Check our catalog to see if your work is consistent with our list. For ages 8 and up, story must be planned in chapters that will fill at least 90 double-spaced manuscript pages. Topic for ages 8-12 must be Louisiana-related and historical. We look for stories that illuminate a particular place and time in history and that are clean entertainment. The only original adult work we might consider is historical fiction, preferably Civil War (not romance). Please don't send three or more chapters unless solicited. Follow our guidelines listed under 'How to Contact.'''

PEMMICAN PUBLICATIONS

150 Henry Ave., Main Floor RM 12, Winnipeg MB R3B 0J7 Canada. (204)589-6346. Fax: (204)589-2063. E-mail: pemmican@pemmican.mbc.ca. Website: www.pemmican.mb.ca. **Contact:** Diane Ramsay, managing editor. Estab. 1980. Metis and Aboriginal children's books. Publishes paperback originals. Books: stapled binding and perfect-bound; 4-color illustrations. Average print order: 2,500. First novel print order: 1,000. **Published some debut authors within the last year.** Averages 9 total titles/year. Distributes titles through Pemmican Publications. Promotes titles through press releases, fax, catalogues and book displays.

Needs Preschool and young adult Metis stories. Recently published *Red Parka Mary*, by Peter Eyvindson (children's); *Nanabosho & Kitchie Odjig*, by Joe McLellan (native children's legend); and *Jack Pine Fish Camp*, by Tina Umpherville (children's).

How to Contact Accepts unsolicited mss. Submit complete ms. Send SASE for return of ms or send a disposable ms and SASE for reply only. Accepts simultaneous submissions.

Terms Pays 10% royalty. Provides 10 author's copies. Average advance: $350.

PENGUIN GROUP USA

375 Hudson St., New York NY 10014. (212)366-2000. Website: www.penguin.com. ''The company possesses perhaps the world's most prestigious list of best-selling authors and a backlist of unparalleled breadth, depth, and quality.'' General interest publisher of both fiction and nonfiction.

Imprint(s) Viking (hardcover); Dutton (hardcover); The Penguin Press (hardcover); Daw (hardcover and paperback); G P Putnam's Sons (hardcover and children's); Riverhead Books (hardcover and paperback); Tarcher (hardcover and paperback); Grosset/Putnam (hardcover); Putnam (hardcover); Avery; Viking Compass (hardcover); Penguin (paperback); Penguin Classics (paperback); Plume (paperback); Signet (paperback); Signet classics (paperback); Onyx (paperback); Roc (paperback); Topaz (paperback); Mentor (paperback); Meridian (paperback); Berkley Books (paperback); Jove (paperback); Ace (paperback); Prime Crime (paperback); HPBooks (paperback); Penguin Compass(paperback); Dial Books for Young Readers (children's); Dutton Children's Books (children's); Viking Children's Books (children's); Puffin (children's); Frederick Warne (children's); Philomel Books (children's); Grosset and Dunlap (children's); Wee Sing (children's); PaperStar (children's); Planet Dexter (children's); Berkely (hardcover); Gothom (hardcover and paperback); Portfolio (hard and paperback); NAL (hardcover).

Terms Ms guidelines online.

PERFECTION LEARNING CORP.

10520 New York Ave., Des Moines IA 50322-3775. (515)278-0133. Fax: (515)278-2980. Website: perfectionlearning.com. **Contact:** Sue Thies, editorial director. Estab. 1926. ''We are an educational publisher of hi/lo fiction and nonfiction with teacher support material.'' Publishes hardcover and trade paperback originals. **Publishes 50-100 fiction and informational; 25 workbooks titles/year. Published 10 debut authors within the last year.** Distributes titles through sales reps, direct mail and online catalog. Promotes titles through educational conferences, journals and catalogs.

Imprint(s) Cover-to Cover; Sue Thies, editorial director (all genres).

Needs "We are publishing hi-lo chapter books and novels as well as curriculum books, including workbooks, literature anthologies, teacher guides, literature tests, and niche textbooks for grades 3-12." Readability of ms should be at least two grade levels below interest level for hi-lo titles. "Please do not submit mss with fewer that 4,000 words or more than 30,000 words." Published *Tall Shadow*, by Bonnie Highsmith Taylor (Native American); *The Rattlesnack Necklace*, by Linda Baxter (historical fiction); and *Tales of Mark Twain*, by Peg Hall (retold short stories).

How to Contact Accepts unsolicited mss. Query with SASE or submit outline, 2-3 sample chapter(s), synopsis, SASE. Accepts queries by e-mail, fax. Include estimated word count, brief bio, list of publishing credits. Send SASE for return of ms or send a disposable ms and SASE for reply only. Responds in 3 months to mss. Accepts simultaneous submissions.

Terms Pays 5-7% royalty on net receipts. Average advance: $300-500. Publishes ms 6-8 months after acceptance. Book catalog for 9×12 SASE with $2.31 postage. Ms guidelines online.

Advice "We are an educational publisher. Check with educators to find out their needs, their students' needs and what's popular."

THE PERMANENT PRESS/SECOND CHANCE PRESS

4170 Noyac Rd., Sag Harbor NY 11963. (631)725-1101. Fax: (631)725-8215. Website: www.thepermanentpress. com. **Contact:** Judith and Martin Shepard, publishers. Estab. 1978. Mid-size, independent publisher of literary fiction. "We keep titles in print and are active in selling subsidiary rights." Publishes hardcover originals. Average print order: 1,500. **Published 4 debut authors within the last year.** Averages 12 total titles, 12 fiction titles/year. Distributes titles through Ingram, Baker & Taylor and Brodart. Promotes titles through reviews.

Needs Literary, mainstream/contemporary, mystery. Especially looking for high-line literary fiction, "artful, original and arresting." Accepts any fiction category as long as it is a "well-written, original full-length novel." Published *Hail to the Chiefs*, by Barbara Holland; *Angels in the Morning*, by Sasha Troyan; *All Honest Men*, by Claude and Michelle Stanush.

How to Contact Accepts unsolicited mss. Send SASE for return of ms or send a disposable ms and SASE for reply only. Responds in 4 weeks to queries; 6 months to mss. Accepts simultaneous submissions.

Terms Pays 10-15% royalty on wholesale price. Offers $1,000 advance for Permanent Press books; royalty only on Second Chance Press titles. Publishes ms 18 months after acceptance. Ms guidelines for #10 SASE.

Advice "We are looking for good books, be they 10th novels or first ones, it makes little difference. The fiction is more important than the track record. Send us the first 25 pages; it's impossible to judge something that begins on page 302. Also, no outlines—let the writing present itself."

DAVID PHILIP PUBLISHERS

P.O. Box 46962, Claremont 7702 South Africa. Fax: (21)6743358. Website: www.newafricabooks.co.za.

Needs "Fiction with Southern African concern or focus. Progressive, often suitable for school or university prescription, literary, serious."

How to Contact Submit 1 sample chapter(s), synopsis.

Terms Pays royalty. Write for guidelines.

Advice "Familiarize yourself with list of publishers to which you wish to submit work."

PHILOMEL BOOKS

Penguin Putnam Inc., 345 Hudson St., New York NY 10014. (212)414-3610. **Contact:** Patricia Lee Gauch, editorial director; Michael Green, senior editor. Estab. 1980. "A high-quality oriented imprint focused on stimulating pictue books, middle-grade novels and young adult novels." Publishes hardcover originals. Averages 20-25 total titles/year.

Needs Adventure, ethnic, family saga, fantasy, historical, juvenile (5-9 years), literary, picture books, regional, short story collections, western (young adult), young adult (10-18 years). Children's picture books (ages 3-8); middle-grade fiction and illustrated chapter books (ages 7-10); young adult novels (ages 10-15). Particularly interested in picture book mss with original stories and regional fiction with a distinct voice. Looking for "story-driven novels with a strong cultural voice but which speak universally." Published *Travel Team*, by Mike Lupica; *Olivia Kidney*, by Ellen Potter; and *Too Many Frogs*, by Sandy Asher.

How to Contact Does not accept unsolicited mss. Query with SASE or submit outline, 3 sample chapter(s), synopsis. Send SASE or IRC. Agented fiction 40%. Responds in 3 months to queries; 4 months to mss. Accepts simultaneous submissions. Sometimes comments on rejected mss.

Terms Pays royalty. Also gives complimentary author's copies. Average advance: negotiable. Publishes ms 1-2 years after acceptance. Ms guidelines for #10 SASE.

Advice "We are not a mass-market publisher and do not publish short stories independently. In addition, we do just a few novels a year."

☐ ⊞ PIATKUS BOOKS

5 Windmill Street, London W1T 2JA United Kingdom. 0207 631 0710. Fax: 0207 436 7137. E-mail: info@piatkus. co.uk. Website: www.piatkus.co.uk. **Contact:** Gillian Green, senior editor (literary); Emma Callagher, assistant editor (literary). Estab. 1979. Piatkus is a medium-sized independent publisher of nonfiction and fiction. The fiction list is highly commercial and includes women's fiction, crime and thriller as well as literary fiction. Publishes hardcover originals, paperback originals and paperback reprints. **Published 12 debut authors within the last year.** Plans 14 first novels this year. IPG

Imprint(s) Portrait (general/nonfiction).

Needs Adventure, erotica, family saga, historical, literary, mainstream/contemporary, mystery (amateur sleuth, cozy, police procedural, private eye/hard-boiled), regional, romance (contemporary, historical, regency period, romantic suspense), thriller/espionage. Published *Natural Selection*, by Bill Dare (general); *Dive From Clausen's Pier*, by Ann Packer (literary); *Three Fates*, Nora Roberts (romance/suspense).

How to Contact Accepts unsolicited mss. Query with SASE or submit first 3 sample chapter(s), synopsis. Accepts queries by mail. Include estimated word count, brief bio, list of publishing credits. Send SASE for return of ms or send a disposable ms and SASE for reply only. Agented fiction 80%. Responds in 12 weeks to mss. Accepts simultaneous submissions. No submissions on disk. Rarely comments on rejected mss.

Terms Pays royalty. Average advance: negotiable. Publishes ms 1 year after acceptance. Ms guidelines for SASE.

Advice "Study our list before submitting your work."

✦ ☑ PIÑATA BOOKS

Arte Publico Press, University of Houston, 452 Cullen Performance Hall, Houston TX 77204-2004. (713)743-2841. Fax: (713)743-3080. Website: www.artepublicopress.com. **Contact:** Nicolas Kanellos, director. Estab. 1994. Pinata Books is dedicated to the publication of children's and young adult literature focusing on US Hispanic culture by U.S. Hispanic authors. Publishes hardcover and trade paperback originals. **Published some debut authors within the last year.** Averages 10-15 total titles/year.

Needs Adventure, juvenile, picture books, young adult. Published *Trino's Choice*, by Diane Gonzales Bertrand (ages 11-up); *Delicious Hullabaloo/Pachanga Deliciosa*, by Pat Mora (picture book); and *The Year of Our Revolution*, by Judith Ortiz Cofer (young adult).

How to Contact Does not accept unsolicited mss. Query with SASE or submit 2 sample chapter(s), synopsis, SASE. Responds in 1 month to queries; 6 months to mss. Accepts simultaneous submissions.

Terms Pays 10% royalty on wholesale price. Average advance: $1,000-3,000. Publishes ms 2 years after acceptance. Book catalog and ms guidelines available via website or with #10 SASE.

Advice "Include cover letter with submission explaining why your manuscript is unique and important, why we should publish it, who will buy it, relevance to the U.S. Hispanic culture, etc."

☑ ◎ PINEAPPLE PRESS, INC.

P.O. Box 3889, Sarasota FL 34230. (941)359-0886. Fax: (941)351-9988. E-mail: info@pineapplepress.com. Website: www.pineapplepress.com. **Contact:** June Cussen, editor. Estab. 1982. Small independent trade publisher. Publishes hardcover and trade paperback originals. Books: quality paper; offset printing; Smyth-sewn or perfect-bound; illustrations occasionally. **Published some debut authors within the last year.** Averages 25 total titles/year. Distributes titles through Pineapple, Ingram and Baker & Taylor. Promotes titles through reviews, advertising in print media, direct mail, author signings and the World Wide Web.

Needs Historical, literary, mainstream/contemporary, regional (Florida). Published *Honorable Mention*, by Robert Macomber (novel).

How to Contact Does not accept unsolicited mss. Query with SASE. Responds in 3 months to queries. Accepts simultaneous submissions.

Terms Pays 6½-15% royalty on net receipts. Average advance: rare. Publishes ms 18 months after acceptance. Book catalog for 9×12 SAE with $1.25 postage.

Advice "Quality first novels will be published, though we usually only do one or two novels per year. We regard the author/editor relationship as a trusting relationship with communication open both ways. Learn all you can about the publishing process and about how to promote your book once it is published. A query on a novel without a brief sample seems useless."

ℕ ☐ ⊞ PIPERS' ASH, LTD.

Pipers' Ash, Church Rd., Christian Malford, Chippenham, Wiltshire SN15 4BW United Kingdom. +44(1249)720-563. Fax: 0870 0568917. E-mail: pipersash@supamasu.com. Website: www.supamasu.com. **Contact:** Manuscript Evaluation Desk. Estab. 1976. "Small press publisher. Considers all submitted manuscritps fairly—without bias or favor. This company is run by book-lovers, not by accountants." Publishes hardcover and electronic originals. **Published 12 debut authors within the last year.** Averages 12 total titles, 12 fiction titles/year. Distributes and promotes titles through direct mail and the Internet.

Needs Adventure, children's/juvenile (adventure), confession, feminist, historical, literary, mainstream/contemporary, military/war, regional, religious, romance (contemporary, romantic suspense), science fiction (hard science/technological, soft/sociological), short story collections, sports, suspense, young adult (adventure, fantasy/science fiction). "We publish 30,000-word novels and short story collections. Visit our website. Authors are invited to submit collections of short stories and poetry for consideration for our ongoing programs." Published *Tales out of Church*, by Rev. Andrew Sangster; *Cosmic Women*, by Margaret Karamazin; *Cross to Bear*, by Chris Spiller; *A Sailor's Song*, by Leslie Wilkie.

How to Contact Accepts unsolicited mss. Query with SASE or submit sample chapter(s), 25-word synopsis (that sorts out the writers from the wafflers). Accepts queries by e-mail, fax, phone. Include estimated word count. Send SASE for return of ms or send a disposable ms and SASE for reply only. Responds in 1 month to queries; 3 months to mss. Accepts electronic submissions, submissions on disk. No simultaneous submissions. Always comments on rejected mss.

Terms Pays 10% royalty on wholesale price. Also gives 5 author's copies. Publishes ms 6 months after acceptance. Book catalog for A5 SASE and on website. Ms guidelines online.

Advice "Study the market! Check your selected publisher's catalogue."

PLEXUS PUBLISHING, INC.
143 Old Marlton Pike, Medford NJ 08055-8750. (609)654-6500. Fax: (609)654-4309. E-mail: info@plexuspublishing.com. Website: www.plexuspublishing.com. **Contact:** John B. Bryans, editor-in-chief. Estab. 1977. Small regional publisher focusing on titles for New Jersey residents and visitors. Publishes hardcover and paperback originals and reprints. **Published 70% debut authors within the last year.** Averages 4-5 total titles/year.

Needs Regional (New Jersey). Mysteries and literary novels with a strong regional (southern NJ) angle. Published *Wrong Beach Island*, by Jane Kelly; *Welcome to the Motherhood*, M. Jarvis.

How to Contact Query with SASE. Accepts queries by mail. Include brief bio, list of publishing credits. Agented fiction 10%. Responds in 1 month to queries; 3 months to mss. Accepts simultaneous submissions. No submissions on disk.

Terms Pays 10-15% royalty on net receipts. Average advance: $500-1,000. Publishes ms 1 year after acceptance. Book catalog and ms guidelines for 10×13 SAE with 4 first-class stamps.

Advice "If it's not New Jersey focused, we are unlikely to publish it."

PLUME
(formerly Dutton Plume), Division of Penguin Putnam Inc., 375 Hudson St., New York NY 10014. (212)366-2000. Website: www.penguinputnam.com. **Contact:** Trena Keating, editor-in-chief (literary fiction). Estab. 1948. Publishes paperback originals and reprints. **Published some debut authors within the last year.**

Needs "All kinds of commercial and litearary fiction, including mainstream, historical, New Age, western, thriller, gay. Full-length novels and collections." Published *Girl with a Pearl Earring*, by Tracy Chevalier; *Liar's Moon*, by Phillip Kimball; and *The True History of Paradise*, by Margaret Cezain-Thompson.

How to Contact *Agented submissions only.* Query with SASE. Responds in 3 months to queries. Accepts simultaneous submissions.

Terms Pays in royalties and author's copies. Offers advance. Publishes ms 12-18 months after acceptance. Book catalog for SASE.

Advice "Write the complete manuscript and submit it to an agent or agents."

POCOL PRESS
6023 Pocol Drive, Clifton VA 20124. (703)830-5862. E-mail: chrisandtom@erols.com. Website: www.pocolpress.com. **Contact:** J. Thomas Hetrick, editor (baseball history and fiction). Pocol Press publishes first-time, unagented authors. Our fiction deals mainly with single author, short story anthologies from outstanding niche writers. Publishes paperback originals. Books: 50 lb. paper; offset printing; perfect binding. Average print order: 500. **Published 2 debut authors within the last year.** Averages 4 total titles, 3 fiction titles/year. Member: Small Press Publishers Association. Distributes titles through website, authors, e-mail, word-of-mouth and readings.

Needs Horror (psychological, supernatural), literary, mainstream/contemporary, short story collections, baseball. Published *Beast of Bengal*, by Elaine Pinkerton (historical fiction); *A Collection of Friends*, by Thomas Sheehan (memoir); *Double Play in Beantown*, by G.S. Rowe (baseball, mystery).

How to Contact Does not accept or return unsolicited mss. Query with SASE or submit 1 sample chapter(s). Accepts queries by mail. Include estimated word count, brief bio, list of publishing credits. Responds in 2 weeks to queries; 2 months to mss. No simultaneous submissions, submissions on disk. Sometimes comments on rejected mss.

Terms Pays 10-12% royalty. Publishes ms 1 year or less after acceptance. Book catalog for SASE or on website. Ms guidelines for SASE or on website.

Book Publishers

Advice "Pocol Press is unique; we publish good writing and great storytelling. Write the best stories you can. Read them to your friends/peers. Note their reaction."

☐ POISONED PEN PRESS

6962 E. 1st Ave. #103, Scottsdale AZ 85251. (480)945-3375. Fax: (480)949-1707. E-mail: info@poisonedpenpress .com. Website: www.poisonedpenpress.com. **Contact:** editor@poisonedpenpress.com (mystery, fiction). Estab. 1997. Publishes hardcover originals and paperback reprints. Books: 60 lb. paper; offset printing; hardcover binding. Average print order: 3,500. First novel print order: 3,000. **Published 6 debut authors within the last year.** Plans 8 first novels this year. Member: Publishers Marketing Associations, Arizona Book Publishers Associations, Publishers Association of West. Distributes through Ingram, Baker & Taylor, Brodart.
  • Was nominated in 2002 for the *LA Times* Book Prize. Also the recipient of several Edgar and Agatha nominations.
Needs Mystery (amateur sleuth, cozy, police procedural, private eye/hard-boiled, historical). Published *At Risk*, by Kit Ehrman (mystery/fiction); *Beat Until Stiff*, by Claire Johnson (mystery/fiction); *Beware the Solitary Drinker*, by Cornelius Lehane (mystery/fiction).
How to Contact Accepts unsolicited mss. Query with SASE. Accepts queries by e-mail. Responds in 1 week to queries; 6-9 months to mss. Accepts electronic submissions, submissions on disk. No simultaneous submissions. Often comments on rejected mss.
Terms Pays 7.5-15% royalty. Average advance: $500-1,000. Publishes ms 8-12 months after acceptance. Ms guidelines online.

Ⓝ ☐ PORT TOWN PUBLISHING

5909 Tower Avenue, Superior WI 54880. (715)392-6843. E-mail: porttownpublish@aol.com. Website: www.por ttownpublishing.bigstep.com. **Contact:** Jean Hackensmith, senior fiction editor. Estab. 1999. Port Town Publishing is a small publisher of paperback fiction novels. Publishes 24 titles per year, including 12 adult fiction titles ranging in genre from romance, to sci-fi, to mystery, to horror. "Our 'Little Ones' line is geared to childrent 4-7 years old, features 6 titles per year that will address sometimes 'difficult' issues." Publishes paperback originals. Books: 20 lb. stock paper; laser printing; perfect bound; color and pencil-sketch illustrations. Average print order: 400. **Published 6 debut authors within the last year.** Titles disributed by Ingram Book Group.
Imprint(s) Little Ones; Growing Years.
Needs Adventure, children's/juvenile (adventure, animal, easy-to-read, fantasy, historical, mystery, preschool/picture book, series), fantasy (space fantasy, sword and sorcery), historical, horror (dark fantasy, futuristic, psychological, supernatural), mainstream/contemporary, mystery (amateur sleuth, cozy, police procedural, private eye/hard-boiled), regional (Lake Superior area), romance (contemporary, futuristic/time travel, gothic, historical, regency period, romantic suspense), science fiction (hard science/technological, soft/sociological), thriller/espionage, young adult (adventure, easy-to-read, fantasy/science fiction, historical, horror, mystery/suspense, problem novels, romance, series, sports). Wants science fiction, thriller and mystery. Recently published *Exile's Journey*, by Ev Baldwin (fantasy); *Love and All That Jazz*, by Jeannine Van Eperen (contemporary romance); *Spliced*, by A.J. Russo (soft thriller).
How to Contact Does not accept unsolicited mss. Query with SASE. Accepts queries by e-mail, mail. Include estimated word count, brief bio, list of publishing credits. Send SASE for return of ms or send a disposable ms and SASE for reply only. Agented fiction 5%. Responds in 1 week to queries; 3-4 months to mss. Accepts simultaneous submissions.
Terms Publishes ms 1-2 years after acceptance. Ms guidelines online.
Advice "We are looking for a sellable, well-plotted story above all else. We are not afraid to take on a manuscript that needs work, but we always hope the author will grow during the editorial process."

☑ THE POST-APOLLO PRESS

35 Marie St., Sausalito CA 94965. (415)332-1458. Fax: (415)332-8045. E-mail: postapollo@earthlink.net. Website: www.postapollopress.com. **Contact:** Simone Fattal, publisher. Estab. 1982. Specializes in "woman writers published in Europe or the Middle East who have been translated into English for the first time." Publishes trade paperback originals and reprints. Books: acid-free paper; lithography printing; perfect-bound. Average print order: 1,000. **Published some debut authors within the last year.** Averages 4 total titles/year. Distributes titles through Small Press Distribution, Berkley, California. Promotes titles through advertising in selectted literary quarterlies, SPD catalog, ALA and ABA and SF Bay Area Book Festival participation.
Needs Experimental, literary (plays), spiritual. "Many of our books are first translations into English." Published *Some Life*, by Joanne Kyger; *In/somnia*, by Etel Adnan; *9:45*, by Kit Robinson; *Where the Rocks Started*, by Marc Atherton (debut author, novel); and *Happily*, by Lyn Hejinian.
How to Contact Submit 1 sample chapter(s). Responds in 3 months to queries.

Book Publishers

Terms Pays 5-7% royalty on wholesale price. Publishes ms 1½ years after acceptance. Book catalog and ms guidelines for #10 SASE.

Advice ''We want to see serious, literary quality, informed by an experimental aesthetic.''

⬛ ⬛ ◻ ◎ PRAIRIE JOURNAL PRESS

Prairie Journal Trust, P.O. Box 61203, Brentwood Postal Services, Calgary Alberta T2L 2K6 Canada. E-mail: prairiejournal@yahoo.com. Website: www.geocities.com/prairiejournal/. **Contact:** Anne Burke, literary editor. Estab. 1983. Small-press, noncommercial literary publisher. Publishes paperback originals. Books: bond paper; offset printing; stapled binding; b&w line drawings. **Published some debut authors within the last year.** Distributes titles by mail and in bookstores and libraries (public and university). Promotes titles through direct mail, reviews and in journals.

• Prairie Journal Press authors have been nominees for The Journey Prize in fiction and finalists and honorable mention for the National Magazine awards.

Needs Literary, short story collections. Published *Prairie Journal Fiction, Prairie Journal Fiction II* (anthologies of short stories); *Solstice* (short fiction on the theme of aging); and *Prairie Journal Prose.*

How to Contact Accepts unsolicited mss. Sometimes comments on rejected mss.

Terms Pays 1 author's copy; honorarium depends on grant/award provided by the government or private/corporate donations. SAE with IRC for individuals.

Advice ''We wish we had the means to promote more new writers. We look for something different each time and try not to repeat types of stories if possible. We receive fiction of very high quality. Short fiction is preferable although excerpts from novels are considered it they stand alone on their own merit.''

◻ PUBLISH AMERICA

P.O. Box 151, Frederick MO 21705. (301)695-1707. Fax: (301)631-9073. E-mail: acquisitions@publishamerica.com. Website: www.publishamerica.com. **Contact:** Melissa Crook, Jeni Watterson, Miranda Prather. Estab. 1999. Publish America is a traditional royalty-paying publisher. Publishes paperback originals and e-books. Books: print-on-demand; perfect bound; color and black and white illustrations. **Published 800 debut authors within the last year.** Member: PMA; AAP. Distributes titles through Ingram, Bowkers and promotes through press releases.

Needs Adventure, children's/juvenile, confession, erotica, ethnic, experimental, family saga, fantasy, feminist, gay/lesbian, glitz, gothic, hi-lo, historical, horror, humor, juvenile, literary, mainstream/contemporary, military/war, multicultural, mystery, new age/mystic, occult, psychic/supernatural, regional, religious, romance, science fiction, short story collections, suspense, thriller/espionage, western, young adult. Published *The Mind's Eye*, by Hilde Aardal; *I Eat Just One*, by Zaynab Armstrong-Jones; *I Can't Wait Any Longer*, by Shelby Barnhart.

How to Contact Accepts unsolicited mss. Query with SASE. Accepts queries by e-mail, fax, phone, mail. Include estimated word count, brief bio, list of publishing credits. Send SASE for return of ms or send a disposable ms and SASE for reply only. Agented fiction 5%. Responds in 1 week to queries; 2-4 weeks to mss. Accepts simultaneous submissions, electronic submissions, submissions on disk. Sometimes comments on rejected mss.

Terms Pays 8% royalty. Publishes ms within a year after acceptance. Ms guidelines for #10 SASE.

◻ PUBLISHERS SYNDICATION, INTERNATIONAL

P.O. Box 6218, Charlottesville VA 22906-6218. Website: www.publisherssyndication.com. **Contact:** A. Samuels. Estab. 1979.

Needs Adventure, mystery (amateur sleuth, police procedural), thriller/espionage, western (frontier saga).

How to Contact Accepts unsolicited mss. Submit complete ms. Include estimated word count. Send SASE or IRC. Responds in 1 month to mss.

Terms Pays .05-2% royalty. Average advance: negotiable. Ms guidelines for SASE.

Advice ''The type of manuscript we are looking for is devoid of references which might offend. Remember you are writing for a general audience.''

◻ PUCKERBRUSH PRESS

76 Main St., Orono ME 04473-1430. (207)581-3832. **Contact:** Constance Hunting, publisher/editor (fiction). Estab. 1971. ''Small independent trade publisher, unique because of editorial independent stance.'' Publishes trade paperback originals and reprints of literary fiction and poetry. Books: perfect-bound, illustrations. Average print order: 500. **Published 3 debut authors within the last year.** Averages 3-4 total titles, 1-2 fiction titles/year. Titles distributed through Amazon.com, Baker & Taylor, Barnes & Noble.

Needs Literary, short story collections. Published *Cora's Seduction*, by Mary Gray Hughes (short stories); *When Soft Was the Sun*, by Medle Hillman (fiction); *The Crow on the Spruce*, by C. Hall (Maine fiction); *Night-Sea Journey*, by M. Alpert (poetry).

How to Contact Accepts unsolicited mss. Submit complete ms. Accepts queries by phone. Include brief bio,

Book Publishers

list of publishing credits. Responds in 1 month to queries; 3 months to mss. No simultaneous submissions. Often comments on rejected mss.

Terms Pays 10-15% royalty on wholesale price. Book catalog for large SASE and 34¢. Ms guidelines for SASE.

Advice "Be true to your vision, not to fashion."

★ ✓ ◎ PUFFIN BOOKS

Penguin Putnam, Inc., 375 Hudson St., New York NY 10014. (212)366-2000. Website: www.penguinputnam.c om. **Contact:** Sharyn November, senior editor; Kristin Gilson, executive editor. Puffin Books publishes high-end trade paperbacks and paperback reprints for preschool children, beginning and middle readers, and young adults. Publishes trade paperback originals and reprints. Averages 175-200 total titles/year.

Needs Picture books, young adult, middle grade; easy-to-read grades 1-3. "We publish mostly paperback reprints. We do very few original titles. We do not publish original picture books." Published *A Gift for Mama*, by Esther Hautzig (Puffin chapter book).

How to Contact Does not accept unsolicited mss. Send SASE or IRC. Responds in 3 months to mss. No simultaneous submissions.

Terms Royalty varies. Average advance: varies. Publishes ms 1 year after acceptance. Book catalog for 9×12 SAE with 7 first-class stamps; send request to Marketing Department.

Advice "Our audience ranges from little children 'first books' to young adult (ages 14-16). An original idea has the best luck."

N ◯ ◎ ✓ PUREPLAY PRESS

11353 Missouri Ave., Los Angeles CA 90025. (310)479-8773. Fax: (310)473-9384. E-mail: editor@pureplaypress. com. Website: www.pureplaypress.com. **Contact:** David Landan. "We are a small, niche publisher devoted to Cuba's history and culture. We publish high-quality books that people will want to read for years to come. Books are in English, Spanish and bilingual formats. Publishes hardcover and paperback originals. **Published 3 debut authors within the last year.** Averages 6 total titles, 3-4 fiction titles/year.

● Best Poetry Book 2004, Latino Book Awards.

Imprint(s) Bumble Bee Books (popular fiction).

Needs Children's/juvenile, family saga, historical, literary, military/war, mystery, romance, young adult.

How to Contact Accepts unsolicited mss. Query with SASE. Accepts queries by e-mail, mail. Include brief bio. Send copy of ms and SASE. Responds in 8 weeks to queries; 16 weeks to mss. Accepts electronic submissions, submissions on disk. No simultaneous submissions. Sometimes comments on rejected mss.

Terms Pays 10% royalty. Offers advance. Ms guidelines online.

★ Ⓐ G.P. PUTNAM'S SONS

(Adult Trade), Penguin Putnam, Inc., 375 Hudson, New York NY 10014. (212)366-2000. Fax: (212)366-2664. Website: www.penguinputnam.com. **Contact:** Acquisition Editor. Publishes hardcover and trade paperback originals. **Published some debut authors within the last year.**

Imprint(s) Putnam, Riverhead, Jeremy P. Tarcher, Perigee.

Needs Adventure, literary, mainstream/contemporary, mystery, suspense, women's. Prefers agented submissions. Recently published *The Bear and the Dragon*, by Tom Clancy (adventure).

How to Contact *Agented submissions only.* Responds in 6 months to queries. Accepts simultaneous submissions.

Terms Pays variable royalties on retail price. Average advance: varies. Request book catalog through mail order department.

★ Ⓐ ✓ ◎ RANDOM HOUSE BOOKS FOR YOUNG READERS

Random House Children's Books, A Division of Random House, Inc., 1745 Broadway, New York NY 10019. (212)782-9000. Fax: (212)782-9698. Website: www.randomhouse.com/kids. **Contact:** Heidi Kilgras, editorial director (Step into Reading); Jennifer Dussling, senior director (Stepping Stones); Jim Thomas, senior editor (fantasy).

Needs "Random House publishes a select list of first chapter books and novels, with an emphasis on fantasy and historical fiction." Chapter books, middle-grade, young adult. Recently published *A to Z Mysteries*, by Ron Roy (chapter books); the Junie B. Jones series; the Magic Tree House series; and *Lady Knight*, by Tamora Pierce.

How to Contact Does not accept unsolicited mss. *Agented submissions only.* Responds in 4 months to queries. Accepts simultaneous submissions.

Advice "We look for orginal, unique stories. Do something that hasn't been done before."

★ Ⓐ ✓ RANDOM HOUSE CHILDREN'S BOOKS

Division of Random House, Inc., 1745 Broadway, New York NY 10019. (212)782-9000. Fax: (212)782-9452. Website: www.randomhouse.com/kids. **Contact:** Kate Klimo, editorial director of Random House Golden Books

Young Readers Group; Beverly Horowitz, editorial director for Knopf Delacorte Dell Young Readers Group. Estab. 1925. "Producing books for preschool children through young adult readers, in all formats from board to activity books to picture books and novels, Random House Children's Books brings together world-famous franchise characters, multimillion-copy series, and top-flight, award-winning authors and illustrators."
Imprint(s) *For Knopf Delacorte Dell Young Readers Group*—Doubleday, Alfred A. Knopf, Crown, Delacorte Press, Wendy Lamb Books, David Fickling Books, Dell Dragonfly, Dell Yearling, Dell Laurel-Leaf, Bantam. *For Random House Golden Books Young Readers Group*—Golden Books, Picturebacks, Beginner Books, Step Into Reading, Stepping Stones Books, Landmark Books.

⭐ Ⓐ Ⓞ RANDOM HOUSE TRADE PUBLISHING GROUP

Random House, Inc., 1745 Broadway, 17th Floor, New York NY 10019. (212)782-9000. Fax: (212)572-4960. Website: www.randomhouse.com. Estab. 1925. "The flagship imprint of Random House, Inc." Publishes hardcover and paperback trade books. Averages 120 total titles/year.
Imprint(s) The Modern Library; Random House Trade Books; Random House Trade Paperbacks; Villard Books; Strivers Row, Ballantine Books.
Needs Adventure, confession, experimental, fantasy, historical, horror, humor, mainstream/contemporary, mystery, suspense.
How to Contact *Agented submissions only.* Responds in 2 months to queries. Accepts simultaneous submissions.
Terms Pays royalty on retail price. Offers advance. Ms guidelines online.

⭐ Ⓐ Ⓞ RANDOM HOUSE, INC.

Division of Bertelsmann Book Group, 1745 Broadway, New York NY 10013. (212)782-9000. Fax: (212)302-7985. E-mail: editor@randomhouse.com. Website: www.randomhouse.com. Estab. 1925. "Random House has long been committed to publishing the best literature by writers both in the United States and abroad."
Imprint(s) Alfred A. Knopf; Anchor Books; Shaye Areheart Books; Ballantine Books; Bantam Hardcover; Bantam Mass Market; Bantam Trade Paperbacks; Bell Tower; Black Ink/Harlem Moon; Broadway; Clarkson Potter; Crown Books for Young Readers; Crown Publishers, Inc; Currency; Del Ray ; Del Ray/Lucas; Delacorte; Dell; Dell Dragonfly; Dell Laurel-Leaf; Dell Yearling; Delta; The Dial Press; Domain; Doubleday; Doubleday Religion; Doubleday Graphic Novels; DTP; Everyman's Library; Fanfare; Fawcett; David Fickling Books; First Choice Chapter Books; Fodor's; Grammercy Book; Harmony Books; Island; Ivy; Knopf Books for Young Readers; Knopf Paperbacks; Library of Contemporary Thought; Main Street Books; The Modern Library; Nan A. Talese; One World; Pantheon Books; Picture Yearling; Presidio Press; Random House Children's Publishing; Random House Large Print Publishing; Shocken Books; Spectra; Strivers Row; Three Rivers Press; Times Books; Villard Books; Vintage Books; Wings Books.
Terms Pays royalty. Offers advance. Ms guidelines online.

Ⓞ RAVENHAWKᶜ BOOKS

The 6DOF Group, 7739 Broadway Blvd., #95, Tucson AZ 85710. Website: www.ravenhawk.biz. **Contact:** Carl Lasky, publisher (all fiction). Estab. 1998. "Small, independent, literary press most interested in provocative and innovative works." Publishes hardcover and paperback originals. Books: 50 or 60 lb. paper; traditional, POD, e-book printing. First novel print order: 1,000. **Published 1 debut author within the last year.** Plans 3 first novels this year. Member: SPAN. Distibutes titles through Ingram, Baker & Taylor, Amazon, Borders, Barnes & Noble.
Needs Children's/juvenile (adventure, animal, easy-to-read, fantasy, mystery, series), fantasy (space fantasy, sword and sorcery), horror (dark fantasy, futuristic, psychological, supernatural), humor, literary, mainstream/contemporary, mystery (amateur sleuth, cozy, police procedural, private eye/hard-boiled), psychic/supernatural, religious (religious mystery/suspense, religious thriller), romance (contemporary, romantic suspense), science fiction (hard science/technological, soft/sociological), short story collections, thriller/espionage, young adult (adventure, easy-to-read, fantasy/science fiction, horror, mystery/suspense, problem novels, series). Planning anthology of Damon Shiller Mysteries. Published the Chaz Trenton Trilogy.
How to Contact Does not accept unsolicited mss. Agented fiction 10%. No simultaneous submissions, electronic submissions, submissions on disk. Sometimes comments on rejected mss.
Terms Pays 45-60% royalty. Publishes ms 18 months after acceptance. Ms guidelines for SASE; book catalog on website only.
Advice "Write dynamic prose utilizing a multi-dimensional edge (conflict). Although the majority of elitists that control the publishing industry won't admit it, it really is a crap shoot out there. Don't ever give up if you believe in yourself. Courage."

Ⓝ RECONCILIATION PRESS

10925 Milburn St., Fairfax VA 22030. (703)691-8416. Fax: (703)691-8466. E-mail: publisher@reconciliation.com. Website: www.reconciliation.com. **Contact:** John Jenkins, publisher. Estab. 1997. "Small publisher to home school and Christian school market. Online serial historical novels.'' Publishes paperback originals and online series. **Published 2 debut authors within the last year.** Plans 2 first novels this year.

Needs Historical (general, era: Christian American 19th and 20th century), young adult (historical). *Cry of the Blood*, by J.L. Jenkins (historical fiction); *The Gift*, by K. O'Hara (historical fiction); and *Fool's Gold*, by E. Stobbe (historical fiction).

How to Contact Query with SASE. Accepts queries by e-mail. Include estimated word count, brief bio, list of publishing credits. Send copy of ms and SASE. Responds in 2 weeks to queries; 2 months to mss. Accepts electronic submissions. Often comments on rejected mss.

Terms Pays 7-30% royalty. Publishes ms 3-6 months after acceptance.

RED DEER PRESS

813 MacKimmie Library Tower, 2500 University Dr., NW, Calgary AB T2N 1N4 Canada. (403)220-4334. Fax: (403)210-8191. E-mail: rdp@ucalgary.ca. Website: www.reddeerpress.com. **Contact:** Peter Carver, children's book editor. Estab. 1975. Publishes young adult and paperback originals "focusing on books by, about, or of interest to Canadian youth." Books: offset paper; offset printing; hardcover/perfect-bound. Average print order: 5,000. First novel print order: 2,500. Distributes titles in Canada, the US, the UK, Australia and New Zealand.

• Red Deer Press has received numerous honors and awards from the Book Publishers Association of Alberta, Canadian Children's Book Centre, the Governor General of Canada and the Writers Guild of Alberta.

Imprint(s) Northern Lights Books for Children, Northern Lights Young Novels, Roundup Books, Sirrocco Books.

Needs Young adult (juvenile and early reader), contemporary. No romance or horror. Published *A Fine Daughter*, by Catherine Simmons Niven (novel); *The Kappa Child*, by Hiromi Goto (novel); *The Dollinage*, by Martine Leavitt; and *The Game*, by Teresa Toten (nominated for the Governor General's Award).

How to Contact Accepts unsolicited mss. Query with SASE. Responds in 6 months to mss. Accepts simultaneous submissions. No submissions on disk.

Terms Pays 8-10% royalty. Advance is negotiable. Publishes ms 1 year after acceptance. Book catalog for 9 × 12 SASE.

Advice "We're very interested in young adult and children's fiction from Canadian writers with a proven track record (either published books or widely published in established magazines or journals) and for manuscripts with regional themes and/or a distinctive voice. We publish Canadian authors exclusively."

RED DRAGON PRESS

433 Old Town Court, Alexandria VA 22314-3545. Website: www.reddragonpress.com. Laura Qa, publisher. **Contact:** David Alan, editor. Estab. 1993. "Small independent publisher of innovative, progressive and experimental works. Short fiction only." Books: quality paper; offset printing; some illustrations. Average print order: 500. Member of Women's National Book Association. Distributes titles through Borders, Barnes & Noble, retail and wholesale, special order and direct mail order. Promotes titles through art reviews, journals, newsletters, special events, readings and signings.

Needs Experimental, horror (dark fantasy, futuristic, psychological, supernatural), literary, psychic/supernatural, short story collections. Published *True Stories: Fiction by Uncommon Women*, by Grace Cavalieri, Susan Cole, Jean Russell, Laura Qa and Dee Snyder.

How to Contact Accepts unsolicited mss. Query with SASE or submit 1-3 sample chapter(s). Accepts queries by fax. Include brief bio, list of publishing credits. Send SASE for return of ms or send a disposable ms and SASE for reply only. Responds in 6 weeks to mss. Accepts simultaneous submissions. Often comments on rejected mss.

Terms Publishes ms 6-12 months after acceptance. Ms guidelines for #10 SASE.

Advice "Be familiar with the work of one or more of our previously published authors."

RED DRESS INK

Harlequin Enterprises, Ltd., 233 Broadway, New York NY 10279. Website: www.eharlequin.com; www.reddressink.com. **Contact:** Margaret O'Neill Marbury, senior editor; Farrin Jacobs, associate editor. "We launched *Red Dress Ink* to provide women with unique and irreverent stories that reflect the lifestyles of today's modern women." Publishes hardcover, trade and mass market paperback originals.

Needs Adventure, confession, humor, literary, mainstream/contemporary, multicultural, regional, romance, short story collections, contemporary women's fiction. Red Dress Ink publishes "stories that reflect the lifestyles of today's urban, single women. They show life as it is, with a strong touch of humor, hipness and energy." Word length: 90,000-110,000 words. Point of view: first person/third person, as well as multiple viewpoints, if needed. Settings: urban locales in North America or well-known international settings, such as London or Paris. Tone: fun, up-to-the-minute, clever, appealing, realistic. Published *Fashionistas*, by Lynn Messina; *The Thin Pink Line*, by Lauren Baratz-Logsted; and *Engaging Men*, by Lynda Curnyn.

Book Publishers

How to Contact Accepts unsolicited mss. Query with SASE. Accepts queries by mail. Send SASE or IRC. No electronic submissions, submissions on disk.
Terms Pays 7¹/₂% royalty. Offers advance. Ms guidelines online.

RED HEN PRESS
P.O. Box 3537, Granada Hills CA 91394. (818)831-0649. Fax: (818)831-6659. E-mail: editor@redhen.org. Website: www.redhen.org. **Contact:** Mark E. Cull, publisher/editor (fiction); Katherine Gale, poetry editor (poetry, literary fiction). Estab. 1993. Publishes trade paperback originals. **Published 10% of books from debut authors within the last year.** Averages 10 total titles, 10 fiction titles/year.
Needs Ethnic, experimental, feminist, gay/lesbian, historical, literary, mainstream/contemporary, short story collections. "We prefer high-quality literary fiction." Published *The Misread City: New Literary Los Angeles*, edited by Dana Gioia and Scott Timberg; *Rebel*, by Tom Hayden.
How to Contact Query with SASE. Agented fiction 10%. Responds in 1 month to queries; 3 months to mss. Accepts simultaneous submissions.
Terms Publishes ms 1 year after acceptance. Book catalog and ms guidelines available via website or free.
Advice "Audience reads poetry, literary fiction, intelligent nonfiction. If you have an agent, we may be too small since we don't pay advances. Write well. Send queries first. Be willing to help promote your own book."

REVELL PUBLISHING
Subsidiary of Baker Book House, P.O. Box 6287, Grand Rapids MI 49516-6287. (616)676-9185. Fax: (616)676-9573. E-mail: lhdupont@bakerbooks.com or petersen@bakerbooks.com. Website: www.bakerbooks.com. **Contact:** Sheila Ingram, assistant to the editorial director; Jane Campbell, editorial director (Chosen Books). Estab. 1870. Midsize publisher. "Revell publishes to the heart (rather than to the head). For 125 years, Revell has been publishing evagelical books for personal enrichment and spiritual growth of general Christian readers." Publishes hardcover, trade paperback and mass market originals and reprints. Average print order: 7,500. **Published some debut authors within the last year.**
Imprint(s) Spire Books.
Needs Religious (general). Published *Triumph of the Soul*, by Michael R. Joens (contemporary); *Daughter of Joy*, by Kathleen Morgan (historical); and *Blue Mist on the Danube*, by Doris Elaine Fell (contemporary).
How to Contact Does not accept unsolicited mss.
Terms Pays royalty. Publishes ms 1 year after acceptance.

RISING MOON
Northland Publishing, LLC, 2900 N. Fort Valley Rd., P.O. Box 1389, Flagstaff AZ 86002-1389. (928)774-5251. Fax: (928)774-0592. E-mail: editorial@northlandpub.com. Website: www.northlandpub.com. **Contact:** Theresa Howell, kids editor. Estab. 1988. Rising Moon's objective is to provide children with entertaining and informative books that follow the heart and tickle the funny bone. Rising Moon is no longer publishing middle-grade children's fiction. Publishes hardcover and trade paperback originals. Averages 8-10 total titles/year.
Needs Picture books (broad subjects with wide appeal and universal themes). "We are also looking for exceptional bilingual stories (Spanish/English), activity books, fractured fairy tales and original stories with a Southwest flavor." Published *Kissing Coyotes*, by Monica Vaughan and Ken Spengler.
How to Contact Responds in 3 months to queries. Accepts simultaneous submissions.
Terms Pays royalty. Sometimes pays flat fee. Offers advance. Publishes ms 1-2 years after acceptance. Call for book catalog. Ms guidelines online.
Advice "Our audience is composed of regional Southwest interest readers."

RISING TIDE PRESS, NEW MEXICO
American-Canadian Publishers, INC., P.O. Box 136, Santa Fe NM 87502-6136. (505)983-8484. Estab. 1981. Rising Tide Press, New Mexico is a midsize publisher. Books: 8¹/₂×11; vellum bound; 140-150 pages; white trove paper.
Needs Wants innovative fiction. Recently published *Empire Sweets*, by Stanley Berne (fiction).
How to Contact Does not accept unsolicited mss.
Terms Pays royalty. Average advance: $10,000.

RIVER CITY PUBLISHING
River City Publishing, LLC, 1719 Mulberry St., Montgomery AL 36106. (334)265-6753. Fax: (334)265-8880. E-mail: gwaller@rivercitypublishing.com. Website: www.rivercitypublishing.com. **Contact:** Gail Waller, assistant editor. Estab. 1989. Midsize independent publisher (10-20 books per year). Our emphasis is on Southern literary fiction and nonfiction of national appeal. Publishes hardcover and trade paperback originals and reprints. **Published 2 debut authors within the last year.** Averages 12 total titles, 4 fiction titles/year.

● Had three nominess to *Foreword* fiction book of the year awards (2002). Their recent title *Course of the Waterman*, by Nancy Taylor Robson, was given The Fred Bonnie Award for Best First Novel.

Needs Historical, literary, regional (southern), short story collections. Published *Course of the Waterman*, by Nancy Taylor Robson (novel); *A Posturing of Fools*, by Brewster Milton Robertson (novel); *Love to the Spirits*, by Stephen Milton (short story collection).

How to Contact Accepts unsolicited mss. Submit 3 sample chapter(s), synopsis. Accepts queries by e-mail but does not accept submission of mss or portions of mss electronically. Aside from The Fred Bonnie Contest, accepts submissions of first novels only from authors who are represented by an agent. Include brief bio, list of publishing credits. Send SASE or IRC. Agented fiction 40%. Responds in 3 months to queries. Accepts simultaneous submissions. Rarely comments on rejected mss.

Terms Pays 10-15% royalty on retail price. Average advance: $500-5,000. Publishes ms 1 year after acceptance.

Advice "Only send your best work after you have received outside opinions. From approximately 1,000 submissions each year, we publish no more than 20 books and few of those come from unsolicited material. Competition is fierce, so follow the guidelines on our website exactly. In alternate years we sponsor The Fred Bonnie Memorial Award for Best First Novel. In odd-numbered years, we accept contest submissions and select the winner, whose manuscript is published in the fall of the following year. See our website for contest information and rules."

▨ Ⓐ ⬙ ◎ ROC BOOKS

New American Library, A Division of Penguin Putnam, Inc., 375 Hudson St., New York NY 10014. (212)366-2000. Website: www.penguinputnam.com. **Contact:** Liz Scheier, editor; Anne Sowards, editor; John Morgan, editor. "We're looking for books that are a good read, that people will want to pick up time and time again." Publishes mass market, trade and hardcover originals. Averages 48 total titles, 48 fiction titles/year.

Needs Fantasy, horror, science fiction. "Roc tries to strike a balance between fantasy and science fiction. We strongly discourage unsolicited submissions." Published *Dreams Made Flesh*, by Anne Bishop; *Days of Infamy*, by Harry Turtledove.

How to Contact Does not accept unsolicited mss. Submit 1-2 sample chapter(s), synopsis. Send SASE or IRC. Responds in 2-3 months to queries. Accepts simultaneous submissions.

Terms Pays royalty. Average advance: negotiable.

JAMES A. ROCK & CO., PUBLISHERS

9170 Traville Gateway Dr., #305, Rockville MD 20850. Fax: (301)294-1683. Website: www.rockpublishing.com. Estab. 1977. Publishes hardcover, trade paperback, and electronic originals and reprints. Averages 10-15 total titles, 5-10 fiction titles/year.

Needs Adventure, comic books, experimental, fantasy, gothic, horror, humor, juvenile, literary, mainstream/contemporary, multicultural, multimedia, mystery, picture books, plays, poetry, poetry in translation, regional, religious, romance, science fiction, short story collections, suspense, young adult, ghost.

How to Contact Query with SASE. Agented fiction 50%. Responds in 1 month to queries; 1 month to mss. No simultaneous submissions.

Terms Pays 5-15% royalty. Average advance: $0-2,000. Publishes ms 9 months after acceptance. Ms guidelines online.

▨ ◪ ◎ RONSDALE PRESS

3350 W. 21st Ave., Vancouver BC V6S 1G7 Canada. (604)738-4688. Fax: (604)731-4548. E-mail: ronsdale@shaw .ca. Website: www.ronsdalepress.com. **Contact:** Ronald B. Hatch, president/editor; Veronica Hatch, editor (YA historical). Estab. 1988. Ronsdale Press is "dedicated to publishing books that give Canadians new insights into themselves and their country." Publishes trade paperback originals. Books: 60 lb. paper; photo offset printing; perfect binding. Average print order: 1,500. **Published some debut authors within the last year.** Averages 10 total titles, 3 fiction titles/year. Sales representation: Literary Press Group. Distribution: Lit Distco. Promotes titles through ads in BC Bookworld and Globe & Mail, and interviews on radio.

Needs Literary, short story collections, novels. *Canadian authors only.* Published *The City in the Egg*, by Michel Tremblay (novel); *Jackrabbit Moon*, by Sheila McLeod Arnopoulos; and *When Eagles Call*, by Susan Dobbie.

How to Contact Accepts unsolicited mss. Accepts queries by e-mail. Send SASE or IRC. Responds in 2 weeks to queries; 2 months to mss. Accepts simultaneous submissions. Sometimes comments on rejected mss.

Terms Pays 10% royalty on retail price. Publishes ms 1 year after acceptance. Ms guidelines online.

Advice "We publish both fiction and poetry. Authors *must* be Canadian. We look for writing that shows the author has read widely in contemporary and earlier literature. Ronsdale, like other literary presses, is not interested in mass-market or pulp materials."

◎ ROYAL FIREWORKS PUBLISHING

1 First Ave., P.O. Box 399, Unionville NY 10988. (845)726-4444. Fax: (845)726-3824. E-mail: rfpress@frontiernet .net. Website: www.rfwp.com. **Contact:** William Neumann, editor (young adult); Dr. T.M. Kemnitz, editor (education). Estab. 1977. Publishes library binding and trade paperback originals, reprints and textbooks. **Published 30-50% debut authors within the last year.** Averages 75-140 total titles/year.

Needs Young adult. "We do novels for children from 8-16. We do a lot of historical fiction, science fiction, adventure, mystery, sports, etc. We are concerned about the values." Published *Hitler's Willing Warrior*, by H. Gutshe (young adult fiction); *Double Vision*, by Jerry Chris; *A Few Screws Loose*, by Mary Ann Easley (young adult fiction).

How to Contact Submit complete ms. Agented fiction 2%. Responds in 1 month to mss. No simultaneous submissions.

Terms Pays 5-10% royalty on wholesale price. Publishes ms 9 months after acceptance. Book catalog for $3.85. Ms guidelines for #10 SASE.

Advice Audience is comprised of gifted children, their parents and teachers, and children (8-18) who read.

RUMINATOR BOOKS

452 Selby Avenue, 2nd Fl West, St. Paul MN 55102. (651)224-7302. Fax: (651)699-7190. E-mail: susannah@rumi nator.com. Website: www.ruminator.com. **Contact:** Pearl Kilbride. Publishes hardcover originals, trade paperback originals and reprints. Averages 8-10 total titles, 4-6 fiction titles/year.

Needs Literary, adult fiction. Published *Facing the Congo*, by Jeffrey Tayler; *The Last Summer of Reason*, by Tahar Djaout; *An Algerian Childhood* (anthology).

How to Contact Query with SASE or submit outline, sample chapter(s). Agented fiction 40%. Accepts simultaneous submissions.

Terms Royalty varies. Average advance: varying. Publishes ms 12-18 months after acceptance. Ms guidelines for #10 SASE and on website.

◙ SALVO PRESS

61428 Elder Ridge St., Bend OR 97702. (541)330-9709. Fax: (541)330-8746. E-mail: query@salvopress.com. Website: www.salvopress.com. **Contact:** Scott Schmidt, publisher (mystery, suspense, thriller & espionage). Estab. 1998. "We are a small press specializing in mystery, suspense, espionage and thriller fiction. Our press publishes in trade paperback and e-book format." Publishes paperback originals and e-books in most formats. Books: 5½×8½; or 6×9 paper; offset printing; perfect binding. **Published 3 debut authors within the last year.** Averages 3 total titles, 3 fiction titles/year.

Needs Adventure, literary, mystery (amateur sleuth, police procedural, private/hard-boiled), science fiction (hard science/technological), suspense, thriller/espionage. "Our needs change. Check our website." Published *Fatal Network*, by Trevor Scott (mystery/thriller); *High Steaks*, by Rob Loughran (first fiction, mystery); and *Superior Position*, by Evan McNamara (first fiction, suspense thriller).

How to Contact Query with SASE. Include estimated word count, brief bio, list of publishing credits, "and something to intrigue me so I ask for more." Agented fiction 15%. Responds in 1 month to queries; 2 months to mss. No simultaneous submissions. Sometimes comments on rejected mss.

Terms Pays 10% royalty. Publishes ms 9 months after acceptance. Book catalog and ms guidelines online.

◪ ◙ ◎ SARABANDE BOOKS, INC.

2234 Dundee Rd., Suite 200, Louisville KY 40205. (502)458-4028. Fax: (502)458-4065. E-mail: info@sarabandeb ooks.org. Website: www.sarabandebooks.org. **Contact:** Sarah Gorham, editor-in-chief; Kirby Gann, managing editor. Estab. 1994. "Small literary press publishing poetry, short fiction and literary nonfiction." Publishes hardcover and trade paperback originals. **Published some debut authors within the last year.** Averages 10 total titles, 3-4 fiction titles/year. Distributes titles through Consortium Book Sales & Distribution. Promotes titles through advertising in national magazines, sales reps, brochures, newsletters, postcards, catalogs, press release mailings, sales conferences, book fairs, author tours and reviews.

● Marjorie Sander's story collection *Portrait of my Mother Who Posed Nude in Wartime* won the 2004 National Jewish Book Award.

Needs Literary, novellas, short novels, 250 pages maximum, 150 pages minimum. Submissions to Mary McCarthy Prize in Short Fiction accepted January thru February. Published *Where the Long Grass Bends*, by Neela Vaswani (fiction/short stories); *Bloody Mary*, by Sharon Solwitz.

How to Contact Send SASE or IRC. Responds in 3 months to queries; 6 months to mss. Accepts simultaneous submissions.

Terms Pays royalty, 10% on actual income received. Also pays in author's copies. Offers advance. Publishes ms 18 months after acceptance. Ms guidelines for #10 SASE.

Advice "Make sure you're not writing in a vacuum, that you've read and are conscious of contemporary literature. Have someone read your manuscript, checking it for ordering, coherence. Better a lean, consistently strong manuscript than one that is long and uneven. We like a story to have good narrative, and we like to be engaged by language, to find ourselves turning the pages with real interest.''

Ⓐ ⊘ ⛟ ◎ SCHOLASTIC CANADA, LTD.

175 Hillmount Rd., Markham ON L6C 1Z7 Canada. (905)887-7323. Fax: (905)887-3643. Website: www.scholastic.ca. Publishes hardcover and trade paperback originals. Averages 40 total titles/year.
Imprint(s) North Winds Press; Les Éditions Scholastic (contact Syvie Andrews, French editor).
Needs Children's/juvenile, juvenile (middle grade), young adult. Published *The Promise of the Unicorn*, by Vicki Blum (juvenile novel).
How to Contact *Agented submissions only*. Responds in 3 months to queries. No simultaneous submissions.
Terms Pays 5-10% royalty on retail price. Average advance: $1,000-5,000 (Canadian). Publishes ms 1 year after acceptance. Book catalog for 8½×11 SAE with 2 first-class stamps (IRC or Canadian stamps only).

✪ Ⓐ ◎ SCHOLASTIC PRESS

Scholastic Inc., 557 Broadway, New York NY 10012. (212)343-6100. Fax: (212)343-4713. Website: www.scholastic.com. **Contact:** Elizabeth Szabla, editorial director (picture books, middle grade, young adult); Dianne Hess, executive editor (picture books, middle grade, young adult); Tracy Mack, executive editor (picture books, middle grade, young adult); Lauren Thompson, senior editor (picture books, middle grade). Publishes hardcover originals. **Published some debut authors within the last year.** Averages 30 total titles/year. Promotes titles through trade and library channels.
Needs Juvenile, picture books, novels. Wants ''fresh, exciting picture books and novels—inspiring, new talent.'' Published *Chasing Vermeer*, by Blue Balliet; *Here Today*, by Ann M. Martin; *Detective LaRue*, by Mark Teague.
How to Contact Does not accept unsolicited mss. *Agented submissions only*. Responds in 2 months to queries; 6-8 months to mss. No simultaneous submissions.
Terms Pays royalty on retail price. Average advance: variable. Publishes ms 18-24 months after acceptance.
Advice ''Be a big reader of juvenile literature before you write and submit!''

SCIENCE & HUMANITIES PRESS

P.O. Box 7151, Chesterfield MO 63006-7151. (636)394-4950. E-mail: publisher@sciencehumanitiespress.com. Website: www.sciencehumanitiespress.com. **Contact:** Dr. Bud Banis, publisher. Publishes trade paperback originals and reprints, and electronic originals and reprints. **Published 25% of books from debut authors within the last year.** Averages 20-30 total titles/year.
Imprint(s) Science & Humanities Press; BeachHouse Books; MacroPrintBooks (large print editions); Heuristic Books; Early Editions Books.
Needs Adventure, historical, humor, literary, mainstream/contemporary, military/war, mystery, regional, romance, science fiction, short story collections, spiritual, sports, suspense, western, young adult. ''We prefer books with a theme that gives a market focus. Brief description by e-mail.''
How to Contact Responds in 2 months to queries; 3 months to mss. Accepts simultaneous submissions.
Terms Pays 8% royalty on retail price. Publishes ms 6-12 after acceptance. Ms guidelines online.
Advice Sales are primarily through the Internet, special orders, reviews in specialized media, direct sales to libraries, special organizations and use as textbooks. ''Our expertise is electronic publishing for continuous short-run-in-house production rather than mass distribution to retail outlets. This allows us to commit to books that might not be financially successful in conventional book store enviroments and to keep books in print and available for extended periods of time. Books should be types that would sell steadily over a long period of time, rather than those that require rapid rollout and bookstore shelf exposure for a short time. We consider the nurturing of new talent part of our mission but enjoy experienced writers as well. We are proud that many of our books are second, third and fourth books from authors who were once first-time authors. A good book is not a one-time accident.''

Ⓐ ◎ SERENDIPITY SYSTEMS

P.O. Box 140, San Simeon CA 93452. (805)927-5259. E-mail: bookware@thegrid.net. Website: www.s-e-r-e-n-d-i-p-i-t-y.com. **Contact:** John Galuszka, publisher. Estab. 1986. Electronic publishing for IBM-PC compatible systems. ''We publish on disks, the Internet and CD-ROMs, Adobe PDF format. Free sample e-books available at www.the-curiosity-shop.com.'' **Published some debut authors within the last year.** Averages 6-12 total titles, 15 fiction titles/year.
Imprint(s) Books-on-Disks; Bookware.
Needs ''We want to see *only* works which use (or have a high potential to use) hypertext, multimedia, interactivity or other computer-enhanced features. We cannot use on-paper manuscripts. We only publish book-length works, not individual stories.'' Published *The Blue-Eyed Muse*, by John Peter (novel).

How to Contact Submit complete ms. Accepts queries by e-mail. Send SASE or IRC. Responds in 1 month to mss. Accepts simultaneous submissions, submissions on disk. Often comments on rejected mss.

Terms Pays 33% royalty on wholesale price or on retail price, depending on how the books goes out. Publishes ms 2 months after acceptance. Ms guidelines online.

Advice "We are interested in seeing multimedia works suitable for Internet distribution. Would like to see: more works of serious literature—novels, short stories, etc. Would like to not see: right wing adventure fantasies from 'Tom Clancy' wanna-be's."

SEVEN STORIES PRESS

140 Watts St., New York NY 10013. (212)226-8760. Fax: (212)226-1411. E-mail: info@sevenstories.com. Website: www.sevenstories.com. **Contact:** Daniel Simon. Estab. 1995. "Publishers of a distinguished list of authors in fine literature, journalism and contemporary culture." Publishes hardcover and trade paperback originals. Average print order: 5,000. **Published some debut authors within the last year.** Averages 40-50 total titles, 10 fiction titles/year. Distibutes through Consortium Book Sales and Distribution.

Needs Literary. Plans anthologies. Ongoing series of short story collections for other cultures (e.g., Contemporary Fiction from Central America; from Vietnam, etc.). *A Place to Live and Other Selected Essays of Natalia Ginzburg; American Falls,* by Barry Gifford; and *The Incantation of Frida K.,* by Kate Braverman.

How to Contact Query with SASE. Include list of publishing credits. Send SASE or IRC. Agented fiction 60%. Accepts simultaneous submissions. Sometimes comments on rejected mss.

Terms Pays 7-15% royalty on retail price. Offers advance. Publishes ms 1-3 years after acceptance. Book catalog and ms guidelines free.

Advice "Writers should only send us their work after they have read some of the books we publish and find our editorial vision in sync with theirs."

⊕ Ⓐ SEVERN HOUSE PUBLISHERS

9-15 High St., Sutton, Surrey SM1 1DF United Kingdom. (0208)770-3930. Fax: (0208)770-3850. **Contact:** Amanda Stewart, editorial director. Publishes hardcover and trade paperback originals and reprints. Averages 150 total titles/year.

Needs Adventure, fantasy, historical, horror, mainstream/contemporary, mystery, romance, short story collections, suspense. Recently published *Future Scrolls,* by Fern Michaels (historical romance); *Weekend Warriors,* by Fern Michaels; *The Hampton Passion,* by Julie Ellis (romance); *Looking Glass Justice,* by Jeffrey Ashford (crime and mystery); and *Cold Tactics,* by Ted Allbeury (thriller).

How to Contact *Agented submissions only.* Accepts simultaneous submissions.

Terms Pays 7¹/₂-15% royalty on retail price. Average advance: $750-5,000.

SILHOUETTE BOOKS

233 Broadway, New York NY 10279. (212)553-4200. Fax: (212)227-8969. Website: www.eharlequin.com. Estab. 1979. Publishes mass market paperback originals. Averages over 350 total titles/year.

Needs Romance (contemporary and historical romance for adults). "We are interested in seeing submissions for all our lines. No manuscripts other than the types outlined. Manuscript should follow our general format, yet have an individuality and life of its own that will make them stand out in the readers' minds."

How to Contact No simultaneous submissions.

Terms Pays royalty. Offers advance. Publishes ms 1-3 years after acceptance. Ms guidelines online.

✖ ◻ ◎ SILHOUETTE DESIRE

a Harlequin book line, 233 Broadway, Suite 1001, New York NY 10279. (212)553-4200. Website: www.eharlequin.com. **Contact:** Joan Marlow Golan, senior editor. "Sensual, believable and compelling, these books are written for today's woman. Innocent or experienced, the heroine is someone we identify with; the hero is irresistible." Publishes paperback originals and reprints. Books: newspaper print; web printing; perfect-bound. **Published some debut authors within the last year.**

Needs Romance. Looking for novels in which "the conflict is an emotional one, springing naturally from the unique characters you've chosen. The focus is on the developing relationship, set in a believable plot. Sensuality is key, but lovemaking is never taken lightly. Secondary characters and subplots need to blend with the core story. Innovative new directions in storytelling and fresh approaches to classic romantic plots are welcome." Manuscripts must be 55,000-60,000 words.

How to Contact Accepts unsolicited mss. Query with SASE or submit complete ms. Send SASE for return of ms or send a disposable ms and SASE for reply only. No simultaneous submissions, submissions on disk.

Terms Pays royalty. Offers advance. Ms guidelines for SASE or on website.

★ ◻ ◎ SILHOUETTE INTIMATE MOMENTS

a Harlequin book line, 233 Broadway, Suite 1001, New York NY 10279. (212)553-4200. Website: www.eharlequin.com. **Contact:** Leslie Wagner, executive senior editor. "Believable characters swept into a world of larger-than-life romance are the hallmark of Silhouette Intimate Moment books. These books offer you the freedom to combine the universally appealing elements of a category romance with the flash and excitement of mainstream fiction." Publishes paperback originals and reprints. Books: newspaper print; web-printing; perfect-bound. **Published some debut authors within the last year.**

Needs Romance (contemporary). Looking for "novels that explore new directions in romantic fiction or classic plots in contemporary ways, always with the goal of tempting today's demanding reader. Adventure, suspense, melodrama, glamour—let your imagination be your guide as you blend old and new to create a novel with emotional depth and tantalizing complexity." Manuscripts must be approximately 80,000 words.

How to Contact Accepts unsolicited mss. Query with SASE or submit complete ms. Send SASE for return of ms or send a disposable ms and SASE for reply only. No simultaneous submissions, submissions on disk.

Terms Pays royalty. Offers advance. Ms guidelines for SASE or on website.

★ ◻ ◎ SILHOUETTE ROMANCE

a Harlequin book line, 233 Broadway, Suite 1001, New York NY 10279. (212)553-4200. Website: www.eharlequin.com. **Contact:** Mary-Theresa Hussey, senior editor. "Our ultimate goal is to give readers vibrant love stories with heightened emotional impact—books that touch readers' hearts and celebrate their values, including the traditional ideals of love, marriage and family." Publishes paperback originals and reprints. Books: newspaper print; web printing; perfect-bound. **Published some debut authors within the last year.**

Needs Romance (contemporary traditional). Looking for "talented authors able to portray modern relationships in the context of romantic love. Although the hero and heroine don't actually make love unless married, sexual tension is vitally important. Writers are encouraged to try creative new approaches to classic romantic and contemporary fairy tale plots." Manuscripts must be approximately 53,000-58,000 words.

How to Contact Accepts unsolicited mss. Query with SASE or submit complete ms. Send SASE for return of ms or send a disposable ms and SASE for reply only. No simultaneous submissions, submissions on disk.

Terms Pays royalty. Offers advance. Ms guidelines for SASE or on website.

★ ◻ ◎ SILHOUETTE SPECIAL EDITION

a Harlequin book line, 233 Broadway, Suite 1001, New York NY 10279. (212)553-4200. Website: www.eharlequin.com. **Contact:** Karen Taylor Richman, senior editor. "Whether the sensuality is sizzling or subtle, whether the plot is wildly innovative or satisfying traditional, the novel's emotional vividness, its depth and dimension, clearly label it a very special contemporary romance." Publishes paperback originals. Books: newspaper print; web printing; perfect-bound. **Published some debut authors within the last year.**

Needs Romance (contemporary). "Sophisticated, substantial and packed with emotions, Special Edition demands writers eager to probe characters deeply to explore issues that heighten the drama of living, loving and creating a family, to generate compelling romantic plots. Subplots are welcome, but must further or parallel the developing romantic relationship in a meaningful way." Manuscripts must be approximately 76,000-80,000 words.

How to Contact Does not accept unsolicited mss. Query with SASE. No simultaneous submissions, submissions on disk.

Terms Pays royalty. Offers advance. Ms guidelines for SASE or on website.

★ ∅ ◎ SILVER DAGGER MYSTERIES

The Overmountain Press, P.O. Box 1261, Johnson City TN 37605. (423)926-2691. Fax: (423)232-1252. E-mail: beth@overmtn.com. Website: www.silverdaggermysteries.com. **Contact:** Alex Foster, acquisitions editor (mystery). Estab. 1999. "Small imprint or a larger company. We publish Southern mysteries. Our house is unique in that we are a consortium of authors who communicate and work together to promote each other." Publishes hardcover and trade paperback originals and reprints. Books: 60 lb. offset paper; perfect/case binding. Average print order: 2,000-5,000; first novel print order: 2,000. **Published 6 debut authors within the last year.** Averages 30 total titles, 15 fiction titles/year. Member: PAS. Distributes titles through direct mail, Ingram, Baker & Taylor, Partners, trade shows.

● Julie Wray Herman was nominated for the Agatha Award for *Three Dirty Women & the Garden of Death*.

Needs Mystery (amateur sleuth, cozy, police procedural, private eye/hard-boiled), young adult (mystery). "We look for average-length books of 60-80,000 words." Publishes *Magnolias & Mayhem*, an anthology of Southern short mysteries. Published *Killer Looks*, by Laura Young; *Haunting Refrain*, by Ellis Vidler; and *Justice Betrayed*, by Daniel Bailey.

How to Contact Does not accept or return unsolicited mss. Query with SASE or submit outline, 3 sample chapter(s), synopsis, author bio. Accepts queries by mail. Include estimated word count, brief bio, list of publishing credits. Agented fiction 30%. Responds in 1 month to queries; 6 months to mss. Accepts simultaneous submissions.

Terms Pays 15% royalty on realized price. Publishes ms 2 years after acceptance. Book catalog and ms guidelines online.

Advice "We are very author friendly from editing to promotion. Make sure your book is 'Southern' or set in the South before taking the time to submit."

SIMON & SCHUSTER

1230 Avenue of the Americas, New York NY 10020. (212)698-7000. Website: www.simonsays.com.

Imprint(s) *Simon & Schuster Adult Publishing Group:* Simon & Schuster; Scribner (Scribner, Lisa Drew, Simple Abundance Press); The Free Press; Atria Books; Kaplan; Touchstone; Scribner Paperback Fiction; S&S Libros en Espanol; Simon & Schuster Source; Wall Street Journal Books; Pocket Books (Pocket Star; Washington Square Press; MTV Books; Sonnet Books; Star Trek; The New Fogler Shakespeare; VH-1 Books; WWF Books). *Simon & Schusters Children's Publishing:* Aladdin Paperbacks; Atheneum Books for Young Readers (Anne Schwartz Books; Richard Jackson Books); Little Simon (Simon Spotlight; Rabbit Ears Books & Audio); Margaret K. McElderry Books, (Archway Paperbacks; Minstreal Books); Simon & Schuster Books for Young Readers.

Terms Pays royalty. Offers advance. Ms guidelines online.

SIMON & SCHUSTER ADULT PUBLISHING GROUP

(formerly Simon & Schuster Trade Division, Division of Simon & Schuster), 1230 Avenue of the Americas, New York NY 10020. E-mail: ssonline@simonsays.com. Website: www.simonsays.com. Estab. 1924.

Imprint(s) Lisa Drew Books; Fireside; The Free Press; Pocket Book Press; Rawson Associates; Scribner; Scribner Classics; Scribner Paperback Fiction; Scribner Poetry; S&S—Libros en Espanol; Simon & Schuster; Simon & Schuster Source; Simple Abundance Press; Touchstone; Wall Street Journal Books.

How to Contact *Agented submissions only.*

SKYSONG PRESS

35 Peter St. S, Orillia ON L3V 5A8 Canada. (705)329-1770. E-mail: skysong@bconnex.net. Website: www.bconnex.net/~skysong/. Steve Stanton. Estab. 1988. Skysong Press is a small independent Christian publisher. Publishes paperback originals and reprints. **Published 3 debut authors within the last year.** Distributes titles through Raincoast Books and Amazon.

Imprint(s) Dreams & Visions.

Needs Ethnic, experimental, fantasy, literary, mainstream/contemporary, religious, romance, science fiction.

How to Contact Accepts unsolicited mss. Submit complete ms. Accepts queries by e-mail. Include estimated word count, list of publishing credits. Send copy of ms and SASE. Responds in 2-6 weeks to queries; 2-6 months to mss. Accepts simultaneous submissions. Rarely comments on rejected mss.

Terms Average advance: 1¢/word. Publishes ms 6-12 months after acceptance. Ms guidelines online.

SLIPSTREAM PUBLICATIONS

Box 2071, Niagara Falls NY 14301. (716)282-2616 after 5 PM E.S.T. E-mail: editors@slipstreampress.org. Website: www.slipstreampress.org. **Contact:** Dan Sicoli, editor. Estab. 1980. Small literary press which publishes 85% poetry and 15% fiction (under 15 pages) from writers whose work may go unnoticed by larger commercial presses. Use modern fiction with strong sense of place, fresh dialogue, and well-developed characters.

Needs Fiction. Holds annual Poetry Chapbook Contest.

How to Contact Accepts unsolicited mss. Accepts queries by mail. Include brief bio. Send SASE for return of ms or send a disposable ms and SASE for reply only. Responds in 2 weeks to queries; 3 months to mss. Accepts simultaneous submissions. No electronic submissions, submissions on disk. Rarely comments on rejected mss.

Terms Pays 2-3 contributor's copies. Publishes ms 6-12 months after acceptance. Ms guidelines for SASE or on website.

Advice "Read our magazine before submitting."

SOHO PRESS, INC.

853 Broadway, New York NY 10003. (212)260-1900. Fax: (212)260-1902. E-mail: soho@sohopress.com. Website: www.sohopress.com. **Contact:** Juris Jurjevics, editor (literary, mainstream novels); Laura Hruska, editor (literary fiction, literary mysteries); Bryan Devendorf, editor (literary fiction). Estab. 1986. "Independent publisher known for sophisticated fiction, mysteries set abroad, women's interest (no genre) novels and multicultural novels." Publishes hardcover and trade paperback originals. Books: acid free paper; perfect binding; halftone illustrations. First novel print order: 5,000. **Published 5 debut authors within the last year.** Averages 40 total titles, 34 fiction titles/year. Distributes titles through Consortium Book Sales & Distribution in the US, Hushion House in Canada, Turnaround in England.

Imprint(s) Soho Crime, edited by Laura Hruska: procedurals set abroad.

Needs Adventure, ethnic, feminist, historical, literary, mainstream/contemporary, mystery (police procedural), suspense. Published *Since the Layoffs*, by Iain Levinson; *A Loyal Character Dancer*, by Qiu Xialong; *Beemer*, by Glenn Gaslin; *We Can Still Be Friends*, by Kelly Cherry; *Maisie Dobbs*, by Jacqueline Winspear; and *Murder in the Bastille*, by Cara Black.

How to Contact Include estimated word count, brief bio, list of publishing credits. Send SASE for return of ms or send a disposable ms and SASE for reply only. Agented fiction 65%. Responds in 2 months to queries; 2 months to mss. Accepts simultaneous submissions. No electronic submissions, submissions on disk. Sometimes comments on rejected mss.

Terms Pays 10-15% royalty on retail price. Offers advance. Publishes ms within 1 year after acceptance. Ms guidelines online.

SOUTHERN METHODIST UNIVERSITY PRESS

P.O. Box 750415, Dallas TX 75275-0415. (214)768-1433. Fax: (214)768-1428. Website: www.tamu.edu/upress. **Contact:** Kathryn Lang, senior editor. Estab. 1937. "Small university press publishing in areas of film/theater, Southwest life and letters, medical ethics, sports, and contemporary fiction." Publishes hardcover and trade paperback originals and reprints. Books: acid-free paper; perfect bound; some illustrations. Average print order: 2,000. **Published 2 debut authors within the last year.** Averages 10-12 total titles, 3-4 fiction titles/year. Distibutes titles through Texas A&M University Press Consortium. Promotes titles through writers' publications.

Needs Literary, short story collections, novels. "We are willing to look at 'serious' or 'literary' fiction." No "mass market, science fiction, formula, thriller, romance." Published *In The River Province*, by Lisa Sandlin (a novella and stories), and *Shambles*, by Debra Monroe (novel).

How to Contact Accepts unsolicited mss. Query with SASE. Responds in 2 weeks to queries; up to 1 year to mss. No simultaneous submissions. Sometimes comments on rejected mss.

Terms Pays up to 10% royalty on wholesale price, 10 author's copies. Average advance: $500. Publishes ms 1 year after acceptance. Ms guidelines online.

Advice "We view encouraging first time authors as part of the mission of a university press. Send query describing the project and your own background. Research the press before you submit—don't send us the kinds of things we don't publish." Looks for "quality fiction from new or established writers."

SPECTRA BOOKS

Subsidiary of Random House, Inc., 1745 Broadway, New York NY 10019. (212)782-8632. Fax: (212)782-9174. Website: www.bantamdell.com. **Contact:** Anne Lesley Groell, senior editor. Estab. 1985. Large science fiction, fantasy and speculative line. Publishes hardcover originals, paperback originals and trade paperbacks.

● Many Bantam Spectra Books have recieved Hugos and Nebulas.

Needs Fantasy, literary, science fiction. Needs include novels that attempt to broaden the traditional range of science fiction and fantasy. Strong emphasis on characterization. Especially well-written traditional science fiction and fantasy will be considered. No fiction that doesn't have as least some element of speculation or the fantastic. Published *Storm of Swords*, by George R. Martin (medieval fantasy); *Fool's Fate*, by Robin Hobb (fantasy); and *The Years of Rice and Salt*, by Stanley Robinson (science fiction, alternative history).

How to Contact Send SASE or IRC. Agented fiction 90%. Responds in 6 months to mss. Accepts simultaneous submissions.

Terms Pays royalty. Average advance: negotiable. Ms guidelines for #10 SASE.

Advice "Please follow our guidelines carefully and type neatly."

SPOUT PRESS

P.O. Box 581067, Minneapolis MN 55458. (612)782-9629. E-mail: spoutpress@hotmail.com. Website: www.spoutpress.com. **Contact:** Chris Watercott, fiction editor. Estab. 1989. "Small independent publisher with a permanent staff of three—interested in experimental fiction for our magazine and books." Publishes paperback originals. Books: perfect bound; illustrations. Average print order: 1,000. **Published 1 debut author within the last year.** Distibutes and promotes books through the website, events and large Web-based stores such as Amazon.com.

Needs Ethnic, experimental, literary, short story collections. Published *I'm Right Here*, by Tony Rauch.

How to Contact Does not accept unsolicited mss. Query with SASE. Accepts queries by mail. Include estimated word count, brief bio, list of publishing credits. Send SASE for return of ms or send a disposable ms and SASE for reply only. Agented fiction 10%. Responds in 1 month to queries; 3-5 months to mss. Accepts simultaneous submissions. Rarely comments on rejected mss.

Terms Individual arrangement with author depending on the book. Publishes ms 12-15 months after acceptance. Ms guidelines for SASE or on website.

Advice "We tend to publish writers after we know their work via publication in our journal, *Spout Magazine*."

ⒶST. MARTIN'S PRESS

175 Fifth Ave., New York NY 10010. (212)674-5151. Fax: (212)420-9314. Website: www.stmartins.com. Estab. 1952. General interest publisher of both fiction and nonfiction. Publishes hardcover, trade paperback and mass market originals. Averages 1,500 total titles/year.

Imprint(s) Bedford Books; Buzz Books; Thomas Dunne Books; Forge; Minotaur; Picador USA; Stonewall Inn Editions; TOR Books; Griffin.

Needs Fantasy, historical, horror, literary, mainstream/contemporary, mystery, science fiction, suspense, western (contemporary), general fiction; thriller.

How to Contact *Agented submissions only.*

Terms Pays royalty. Offers advance. Ms guidelines online.

STARCHERONE BOOKS

P.O. Box 303, Buffalo NY 14201-0303. (716)885-2726. E-mail: publisher@starcherone.com. Website: www.starcherone.com. **Contact:** Ted Pelton, publisher. Estab. 2000. Non-profit publisher of literary and experimental fiction. Publishes paperback originals and reprints. Books: acid-free paper; perfect-bound; occasional illustrations. Average print order: 1,000. Average first novel print order: 1,000. **Published 2 debut authors within the last year.** Member: CLMP. Titles distributed through website, Small Press Distribution, Amazon, independent bookstores.

Needs Experimental, gay/lesbian, literary, short story collections. Published *Black Umbrella Stories*, by Nicolette de Csipkay (debut author, short stories); *The Voice in the Closet*, by Raymond Federman (experimental); *Endorsed by Jack Chapeau*, by Theodore Pelton (debut author, short stories); *Woman With Dark Horses*, by Aimee Parkinson (debut author, short stories).

How to Contact Accepts unsolicited mss. Accepts queries by e-mail. Include brief bio, list of publishing credits. Send copy of ms and SASE. Responds in 2 months to queries; 6-10 months to mss. Accepts simultaneous submissions.

Terms Pays 15% royalty. Publishes ms 9-18 months after acceptance. Guidelines and catalog available on website.

Advice "Become familiar with our interests in fiction. We are interested in new strategies for creating stories and fictive texts. Do not send genre fiction unless it is unconventional in approach."

⚡◯ STEEPLE HILL

Harlequin Enterprises, 233 Broadway, New York NY 10279. Website: www.eharlequin.com. **Contact:** Joan Marlow Golan, Krista Stroever, Diane Dietz, acquisition editors. Estab. 1997. Publishes mass market paperback originals.

Imprint(s) Love Inspired; Steeple Hill Woman's Fiction.

Needs Romance (Christian, 70,000 words). Wants all genres of inspirational women's fiction including contemporary and historical romance, chick/mom-lit, relationship novels, romantic suspense, mysteries, family sagas, and thrillers. Published *A Mother at Heart*, by Carolyne Aarsen.

How to Contact Accepts unsolicited mss. Query with SASE or submit 3 sample chapter(s), synopsis. No simultaneous submissions.

Terms Pays royalty. Offers advance. Ms guidelines online.

Advice "Drama, humor and even a touch of mystery all have a place in this series. Subplots are welcome and should further the story's main focus or intertwine in a meaningful way. Secondary characters (children, family, friends, neighbors, fellow church members, etc.) may all contribute to a substantial and satisfying story. These wholesome tales of romance include strong family values and high moral standards. While there is no permarital sex between characters, a vivid, exciting romance that is presented with a mature perspective is essential. Although the element of faith must clearly be present, it should be well integrated into the characterization and plot. The conflict between the main characters should be an emotional one, arising naturally from the well-developed personalities you've created. Suitable stories should also impart an important lesson about the powers of trust and faith."

◉▼ STONE BRIDGE PRESS

P.O. Box 8208, Berkeley CA 94707. (510)524-8732. Fax: (510)524-8711. Website: www.stonebridge.com. **Contact:** Peter Goodman, publisher. Estab. 1989. "Independent press focusing on books about Japan in English (business, language, culture, literature, animation,)." Publishes hardcover and trade paperback originals. Books: 60-70 lb. offset paper; web and sheet paper; perfect-bound; some illustrations. Averages 8 total titles/year. Distributes titles through Consortium. Promotes titles through Internet announcements, special-interest magazines and niche tie-ins to associations.

● Stone Bridge Press received a Japan-U.S. Friendship Prize for *Life in the Cul-de-Sac*, by Senji Kuroi.

Imprint(s) The Rock Spring Collection of Japanese Literature.

Needs Experimental, gay/lesbian, literary, Japan-themed. "Primarily looking at material relating to Japan. Translations only."

How to Contact Does not accept unsolicited mss. Query with SASE. Accepts queries by e-mail, fax. Agented fiction 25%. Responds in 4 months to queries; 8 months to mss. Accepts simultaneous submissions. Sometimes comments on rejected mss.

Terms Pays royalty on wholesale price. Average advance: variable. Publishes ms 2 years after acceptance. Book catalog for 2 first-class stamps and SASE. Ms guidelines online.

Advice "Fiction translations only for the time being. No poetry."

SYNERGEBOOKS

1235 Flat Shoals Rd., King NC 27021. (336)994-2405. Fax: (336)994-8403. E-mail: synergebooks@aol.com. Website: www.synergebooks.com. **Contact:** Debra Staples, editor. Estab. 1999. Small press publisher, specializing in quality ebooks from talented new writers in a myriad of genres, including print-on-demand. SynergEbooks "works together" with the author to edit and market each book. Publishes paperback originals and e-books. Books: 60 lb. paper; print-on-demand; perfect bound. Average first novel print order: 50. **Published 5-10 debut authors within the last year.** Averages 30 total titles, 15 fiction titles/year.

• Authors have received EPPIES and other awards for the past 3 years.

Needs Adventure, family saga, fantasy (space fantasy, sword and sorcery), historical, horror, humor, mainstream/contemporary, military/war, mystery, new age/mystic, religious (children's religious, inspirational, religious fantasy, religious mystery/suspense, religious thriller, religious romance), romance (contemporary, futuristic/time travel, historical, regency period, romantic suspense), science fiction, short story collections, western (frontier saga, traditional), young adult (adventure, fantasy/science fiction, historical, horror, mystery/suspense, romance), native american. Published *Mortar's Keep*, by Roxanne Smolen (Sci-Fi Series); *Red Earth*, by Harvey Mendez (fiction); *The Blue Mosaic Vase*, by Christie Shary (fiction).

How to Contact Accepts unsolicited mss. Query with SASE or submit outline, 3 sample chapter(s), synopsis. Accepts queries by e-mail. Include estimated word count, brief bio, list of publishing credits. Agented fiction 1%. Responds in 3 weeks to queries; 3 months to mss. Accepts simultaneous submissions, submissions on disk. Sometimes comments on rejected mss.

Terms Pays 15-40% royalty. Publishes ms 3-6 months after acceptance. Ms guidelines online.

Advice "We do not care if you've ever been published. If your work is unique in some way, and you are willling to work together to market your book, there is a good chance you will be accepted."

T N T CLASSIC BOOKS

360 West 36 St., #2NW, New York NY 10018-6412. (212)736-6279. Fax: (212)695-3219. E-mail: tntclassics@aol.com. **Contact:** Francine L. Trevens, publisher (novels, plays). Estab. 1994. T n T Classic Books keeps gay classics in print. Publishes paperback originals and reprints. Books: offset printing; perfect binding; illustrations. Average print order: 1,000. **Published 1 debut author within the last year.** Member of the Greater NY Independent Publishers Association.

Imprint(s) Happy Task (children); JH (gay plays).

Needs Children's/juvenile (easy-to-read), feminist, gay/lesbian, gay plays. Publishes a anthology of monologues for actors.

How to Contact Does not accept unsolicited mss. Query with SASE. Accepts queries by e-mail, fax. Include brief bio, list of publishing credits. Agented fiction 5%. Responds in 1 week to queries; 3 months to mss. Accepts simultaneous submissions. Often comments on rejected mss.

Terms Pays 10 contributors's copies. Publishes ms 9 months after acceptance.

Advice "Try us as a last resort. And remember to never stop writing creatively."

NAN A. TALESE

Random House, Inc., 1745 Broadway, New York NY 10019. (212)782-8918. Fax: (212)782-8448. Website: www.nantalese.com. **Contact:** Nan A. Talese, editorial director. "Nan A. Talese publishes nonfiction with a powerful guiding narrative and relevance to larger cultural trends and interests, and literary fiction of the highest quality." Publishes hardcover originals. Averages 15 total titles/year.

Needs Literary. "We want well-written narratives with a compelling story line, good characterization and use of language. We like stories with an edge." *Agented submissions only.* Published *The Blind Assassin*, by Margaret Atwood; *Atonement*, by Ian McEwan; and *Great Shame*, Thomas Keneally.

How to Contact Responds in 1 week to queries; 2 weeks to mss. Accepts simultaneous submissions.

Terms Pays variable royalty on retail price. Average advance: varying. Publishes ms 1 year after acceptance. Agented submissions only.

Advice "We're interested in literary narrative, fiction and nonfiction—we do not publish genre fiction. Our readers are highly literate people interested in good story-telling, intellectual and psychological signigicant. We want well-written material."

Book Publishers

◎ THIRD WORLD PRESS

P.O. Box 19730, 7822 S. Dobson Ave., Chicago IL 60619. (773)651-0700. Fax: (773)651-7286. E-mail: TWPress3 @aol.com. **Contact:** Gwendolyn Mitchell, editor. Estab. 1967. Black-owned an operated independent publisher of fiction and nonfiction books about the black experience throughout the Diaspora. Publishes hardcover and trade paperback originals and reprints. Averages 20 total titles/year. Distibutes titles through Partners, Baker & Taylor and bookstores. Promotes titles through direct mail, catalogs and newspapers.

Needs Ethnic, feminist, historical, juvenile (animal, easy-to-read, fantasy, historical, contemporary), literary, mainstream/contemporary, picture books, short story collections, young adult (easy-to-read/teen, folktales, historical), African-centered; African-American materials, preschool/picture book. "We primarily publish nonfiction, but will consider fiction by and about African Americans." Published *In the Shadow of the Sun*, by Michael Simanga; *Special Interest*, by Chris Benson.

How to Contact Accepts unsolicited mss. Submit outline, 5 sample chapter(s), synopsis. Responds in 6 weeks to queries; 5 months to mss. Accepts simultaneous submissions.

Terms Pays royalty on retail price. Individual arrangement with author depending on the book, etc. Offers advance. Publishes ms 18 months after acceptance. Ms guidelines for #10 SASE.

✪ ◎ TILBURY HOUSE, PUBLISHERS

imprint of Harpswell Press, Inc., 2 Mechanic St., Gardiner ME 04345. (207)582-1899. Fax: (207)582-8227. E-mail: tilbury@tilburyhouse.com. Website: www.tilburyhouse.com. **Contact:** Audrey Maynard, children's book editor. Estab. 1990. Publishes hardcover originals, trade paperback originals. Averages 10 total titles/year.

Needs Regional (New England adult). Recently published *Say Something*, by Peggy Moss; *The Goat Lady*, by Jane Bregoli.

Terms Pays royalty. Ms guidelines online.

❑ ⊕ TINDAL STREET PRESS, LTD.

217 The Custard Factory, Gibb Street, Birmingham B9 4AA United Kingdom. 0121 773 8157. Fax: 0121 693 5525. E-mail: info@tindalstreet.co.uk. Website: www.tindalstreet.co.uk. **Contact:** Emma Hargrave, managing editor. Estab. 1998. "Tindal Street is an independent, prize-winning publisher of strong contemporary fiction—novels and short stories—from the English regions. We are a small press—three members of staff—with a commitment to author development, diversity and excellence." Publishes paperback originals. Books: perfect bound. Average print order: 1,500-2,000. **Published 5 debut authors within the last year.** Averages 6 total titles, 6 fiction titles/year. Distributes in the UK through Turnaround and in the US through Dufour.

Needs Ethnic, feminist, literary, mainstream/contemporary, mystery (private eye/hard-boiled), regional (England), short story collections. Published *Birmingham Noir*, edited by Joel Land and Steve Bishop (fiction/short stories); *Astonishing Splashes of Colour*, by Clare Morrall (contemporary fiction); *What Goes Round*, by Maeve Clarke (contemporary fiction).

How to Contact Accepts unsolicited mss. Query with SASE or submit 3 sample chapter(s). Accepts queries by e-mail. Include brief bio, list of publishing credits. Send SASE for return of ms or send a disposable ms and SASE for reply only. Agented fiction 10-30%. Responds in 1-2 weeks to queries; 3-6 months to mss. No submissions on disk. Always comments on rejected mss.

Terms Average advance: negotiable. Publishes ms 6-18 months after acceptance.

Advice "Please check out our list of titles and judge how well your work might fit with the aims/standards/attitudes of Tindal Street Press."

Ⓝ ❑ TITAN PRESS

PMB 17897, Encino CA 91416. (818)377-4006. E-mail: titan91416@yahoo.com. Website: www.titanpress.com. **Contact:** Stephani Wilson, editor. Estab. 1981. Publishes hardcover originals and paperback originals. Books: recycled paper; offset printing; perfect bound. Average print order: 2,000. Average first novel print order: 1,000. **Published 3 debut authors within the last year.** Averages 12 total titles, 6 fiction titles/year. Distributed at book fairs and through the Internet and at Barnes & Noble.

Needs Literary, mainstream/contemporary, short story collections. Published *Orange Messiahs*, by Scott Alixander Sonders (fiction).

How to Contact Does not accept unsolicited mss. Query with SASE. Include brief bio, social security number, list of publishing credits. Agented fiction 50%. Responds in 3 months to mss. Accepts simultaneous submissions. Sometimes comments on rejected mss.

Terms Pays 20-40% royalty. Publishes ms 1 year after acceptance. Ms guidelines for #10 SASE.

Advice "Look, act, sound and *be* professional."

Book Publishers

TREBLE HEART BOOKS

1284 Overlook Dr., Sierra Vista AZ 85635. (520)458-5602. Fax: (520)458-5618. E-mail: submissions@trebleheart books.com. Website: www.trebleheartbooks.com. **Contact:** Lee Emory, publisher. Estab. 2001. Publishes trade paperback originals and reprints (limited), and electronic originals. **Published 9 debut authors within the last year.** Averages 48 total titles, 40 fiction titles/year.

Needs Adventure, fantasy, historical, horror, humor, mainstream/contemporary, mystery, occult, religious, romance, science fiction, short story collections, spiritual, suspense, western. "Follow our guidelines. Authors are encouraged to write outside of the box here, but traditional stories and plots are also accepted if handled with a fresh twist or approach." Published *Poisoned Again*, by Fred Woolverton; *Generous to a Fault*, by Lee Emory; *Combustion*, by Denise A. Agnew; *Death Rides a Pale Horse*, by Dusty Rhodes.

How to Contact Submit complete ms. Accepts queries by e-mail. Responds in 3 weeks to queries; 3-4 months to mss. No simultaneous submissions, submissions on disk.

Terms Pays 15-35% royalty on wholesale price. Publishes ms 6-8 months after acceptance. Ms guidelines online.

Advice "Study our guidelines before submitting."

🔲 🔽 TRICYCLE PRESS

P.O. Box 7123, Berkeley CA 94707. (510)559-1600. Website: www.tenspeed.com. **Contact:** Nicole Geiger, publisher. Estab. 1993. "Tricycle Press is a children's book publisher that publishes picture books, board books, chapter books, and middle grade novels. As an independent publisher, Tricycle Press brings to life kid-friendly books that address the universal truths of childhood in an off-beat way." Publishes hardcover and trade paperback originals. **Published 4 debut authors within the last year.** Averages 18-20 total titles, 15-17 fiction titles/year.

- ● Received a SCBWI Golden Kite Award: Best Picturebook text for *George Hogglesberry, Grade School Alien*, by Sarah Wilson, illustrated by Chad Cameron.

Needs Children's/juvenile (adventure, historical, board book, mystery, preschool/picture book), preteen. "One-off middle grade novels—quality fiction, 'tween fiction." Published *The Boss Queen*, by Sarah Jordan (middle grade); *Edgar & Ellen: Rare Beasts*, by Charles Ogden (middle grade series); and *Truth Is a Bright Star*, by Joan Price (middle grade adventure).

How to Contact Accepts unsolicited mss. Include brief bio, list of publishing credits, e-mail address. Send SASE for return of ms or send a disposable ms and SASE for reply only. Agented fiction 60%. Responds in 4-6 months to mss. Accepts simultaneous submissions.

Terms Pays 15-20% royalty on net receipts. Average advance: $0-9,000. Publishes ms 1-2 years after acceptance. Book catalog and ms guidelines for 9×12 SASE with 3 first-class stamps or visit the website.

🔲 ◎ TRIUMVIRATE PUBLICATIONS

497 West Avenue 44, Los Angeles CA 90065-3917. (818)340-6770. Fax: (818)3406770. E-mail: triumpub@aol.c om. Website: www.triumpub.com. Carolyn Porter, executive editor. Estab. 1985. Publishes hardcover and paperback originals. Books: Antique/natural paper; offset printing; case and perfect bound; illustrations. Average print order 5,000-10,000. Member: PMA (Publishers Marketing Assn.). Distributes books through wholesalers using direct mail, fax/e-mail/telephone, trade/consumer advertising, book exhibits, reviews, listings, and Internet.

Needs Adventure, fantasy, historical, horror, military/war, mystery, psychic/supernatural, science fiction, thriller/espionage. Published *A Continent Adrift*, by Vladimir Chernozemsky (science fiction), and *Life and Times of Ellmar Why*, by Vladimir Chernozemsky (supernatural).

How to Contact Does not accept unsolicited mss. Submit outline, 2 sample chapter(s). Accepts queries by fax, mail. Include brief bio, list of publishing credits. Send SASE for return of ms or send a disposable ms and SASE for reply only. Responds in 6 weeks to queries; 3 months to mss. Sometimes comments on rejected mss.

Terms Pays royalty. Publishes ms 6-12 months after acceptance.

Advice "Please query first. If interested, we will request the manuscript. Query should include: cover letter, short synopsis/description, 2-3 sample chapters, author bio and writing/publishing credits. Send by mail. Do not fax except for short, 1-2 page query letters only. Please do not submit by e-mail or phone. We will respond if interested."

⇆ 🔲 ◎ 🔽 TURNSTONE PRESS

607-100 Arthur St., Winnipeg MB R3B 1H3 Canada. (204)947-1555. Fax: (204)942-1555. E-mail: editor@turnsto nepress.mb.ca. Website: www.ravenstonebooks.com. **Contact:** Todd Besant, managing editor. Estab. 1976. "Turnstone Press is a literary press that publishes Canadian writers with an emphasis on writers from, and writing on, the Canadian west." Focuses on eclectic new writing, prairie writers, travel writing and regional mysteries. Publishes trade paperback originals, mass market for literary mystery imprint. Books: offset paper; perfect-bound. First novel print order: 1,500. **Published 5 debut authors within the last year.** Averages 10-

12 total titles/year. Distributes titles through Lit DistCo (Canada and US). Promotes titles through Canadian national and local print media and select US print advertising.

- Turnstone Press was a 2004 Nominee for Small Press Publisher of the Year. *Tatsea* won the McNally Robinson book of the Year and the Margaret Laurence Award for Fiction. *Kilter: 55 Fictions* was a finalist for The Giller Prize and the winner of the Mary Scorer Award.

Imprint(s) Ravenstone.

Needs Contemporary literary novels and short story collections and poetry. *Canadian authors only.* Published *Santiago* and *Leaving Wyoming* (novels) and *Korunukopia* (Ravenstone, action/thriller).

How to Contact Accepts unsolicited mss. Include list of publishing credits. Send SASE or IRC. Responds in 4 months to queries. No simultaneous submissions.

Terms Pays 10% royalty on retail price and 10 author's copies. Offers advance. Publishes ms 1 year after acceptance. Ms guidelines online.

Advice "As a Canadian literary press, we have a mandate to publish Canadian writers only. Do some homework before submitting works to make sure your subject matter/genre/writing style falls within the publisher's area of interest."

TURTLE BOOKS

866 United Nations Plaza, Suite #525, New York NY 10017. (212)644-2020. Fax: (212)223-4387. Website: www.turtl ebooks.com. "We are a independent publishing house. Our goal is to publish a small, select list of quality children's picture books in both English and Spanish editions. Publishes hardcover and trade paperback originals. Averages 6-8 total titles/year. Member: Association of American Publishers. Distrubed by Publshers Group West.

- Received the Willa Cather Award for Best Children's Book of the Year.

Needs Children's/juvenile. Subjects suitable for children's picture books. "We are looking for good stories which can be illustrated as children's picture books." Published *The Crab Man*, by Patricia Van West; *Keeper of The Swamp*, by Ann Garret; and *Prairie Dog Pioneers*, by Jo Harper.

How to Contact Accepts unsolicited mss. Submit complete ms. Include list of publishing credits. Send copy of ms and SASE. Accepts simultaneous submissions.

Terms Pays royalty on retail price. Offers advance. Publishes ms 12 months after acceptance.

Advice "We only publish children's books. Every book we've published has been under two-thousand words in length. Queries are a waste of time. Please send only complete manuscripts."

TWILIGHT TIMES BOOKS

P.O. Box 3340, Kingsport TN 37664. (423)323-0183. Fax: (423)323-2183. E-mail: publishes@twilighttimesbooks. com. Website: www.twilighttimesbooks.com. Ardy M. Scott, managing editor. Estab. 1999. "We publish compelling literary fiction by authors with a distinctive voice. Our cross-genre, intellectual and visionary works remain in print irregardless of sales." Publishes hardcover and paperback originals and paperback reprints and e-books. Book: 60 lb. paper; offset and digital printing; perfect bound. Average print order: 1500. **Published 5 debut authors within the last year.** Averages 18 total titles, 12 fiction titles/year. Member: AAP, PAS, SPAN, SLF. Nationally distributed by Midpoint Trade Books.

Needs Fantasy, historical, literary, mainstream/contemporary, military/war, mystery, new age/mystic, psychic/supernatural, regional, science fiction, thriller/espionage, young adult. Published *Monkey Trap*, by Lee Denning; *Sometimess There's a Dove*, by Cynthia Ward.

How to Contact Accepts unsolicited mss. Query with SASE or submit 2 sample chapter(s). Accepts queries by e-mail, mail. Include estimated word count, brief bio, list of publishing credits, marketing plan. Send copy of ms and SASE. Agented fiction 10%. Responds in 4 weeks to queries; 2 months to mss. Accepts electronic submissions, submissions on disk. Rarely comments on rejected mss.

Terms Pays 8-15% royalty. Ms guidelines online.

Advice "The only requirement for consideration at Twilight Times Books is that your novel must be entertaining and professionally written."

UNBRIDLED BOOKS

200 North 9th Street, Suite A, Columbia MO 65201. (573)256-4106. Fax: (573)256-5207. Website: www.unbridle dbooks.com. **Contact:** Greg Michalson and Fred Ramey, editors. Estab. 2004. "Unbridled Books aspires to become a premier publisher of works of rich literary quality that appeal to a broad audience." Publishes both fiction and creative nonfiction, hardcover and trade paperback originals. **Published 1 debut author within the last year.** Averages 4-8 total titles, 6 fiction titles/year.

- See our interview with editor Greg Michalson on page 454.

Needs Literary, nonfiction, memoir. *The Green Age of Asher Witherow*, by M. Allen Cunningham; *The Distance Between Us*, by Masha Hamilton; *Fear Itself*, by Candida Lawrence; *Lucky Strike*, by Nancy Zafris.

How to Contact Query with SASE. Accepts queries by mail. No electronic submissions.

Greg Michalson

Unbridled Books, like the novels they publish, seek to deliver everything

Photo courtesy of author

Book Publishers

Writers submitting to Unbridled Books need not be concerned about biases related to literary type or form of expression. "Beyond the necessity for great, strong writing, there isn't any one style or school of writing we subscribe to," says editor Greg Michalson. "The truth is, to be successful, a novel has to deliver everything." In a way, this philosophy of delivering everything describes the publishing goals of Michalson and founding partner Fred Ramey (both former Blue Hen Books editors); they want to reach the widest audience they possibly can.

The only kind of fiction that doesn't pass muster at Unbridled is straight, formula-driven genre work. As to any distinction between mainstream and literary, Michalson prefers the idea of quality fiction that can have its roots in any number of traditions. "I believe that high standards and a relatively broad readership are not mutually exclusive," he says. "On the contrary, we hope and believe enough people out there share our love of a good story, artfully told, to make our new venture successful."

For years, Michalson and Ramey have had an ongoing conversation about the kind of fiction that fully engages their hearts as well as their minds. "Between us," says Michalson, "we bring a fairly broad range of sensibilities to what we believe constitutes great fiction." As a result, Unbridled Books offers a broad range of books in any given season. Michalson realizes not every book will reach every reader, but he does believe, overall, readers will recognize and trust a consistency in quality in the various books Unbridled publishes from year to year.

While quality alone cannot be the deciding factor in editorial decisions since there's always the bottom line to reckon with, Michalson and Ramey's passionate pursuit of quality writing is what drives Unbridled Books. "Our egos, and that of everyone in the company, are behind every book we publish. The goal is to give the author a positive publishing experience, to have patience and to find ways to put each book in front of the right readers," says Michalson. "Our ambition is to find the best new talent we can and to stick with them over the course of their careers. We believe Unbridled Books gives us the best chance of doing that, and we're excited several of these authors have returned to us to publish their next book."

Finding new talent has been the mission of these two editors over their many years together in publishing. They've brought out such first novels as Steve Yarbrough's *Oxygen Man*, Susan Vreeland's *Girl in Hyacinth Blue*, William Gay's *The Long Home* and, most recently, *The Green Age of Asher Witherow*, by M. Allen Cunningham, a debut novel that earned the #1 Book Sense Pick selection when it first came out—along with a host of others, including debut work by Patricia Henley, Debra Earling, Mark Estrin, Susann Cokal,

Masha Hamilton, Rick Collignon and Nancy Zafris. "These authors represent a wide range of styles and themes. Some of them made best-seller lists, and many of them won a variety of regional and national book-of-the-year awards and major recognition."

Writers considering Unbridled should submit novels rich in storytelling that emphasize character over plot—yet this emphasis certainly doesn't mean a compelling plot isn't necessary. "We're interested in the kind of voice-driven, character-driven work that engages the reader on as many levels as possible while telling a story we haven't heard before. The story needs to be about something or someone, with something real at stake. We have to care what happens to the characters. There has to be a hook."

Since Unbridled puts out only eight to 12 books a year, the odds of getting a book accepted for publication are really tough, says Michalson. To beat these odds, he urges writers to read books Unbridled has published. "If you admire the work a particular house publishes, there's a good chance you will fit with them on at least some level."

Following standard submission protocol is also important. "Send a query first, and with any submission include a one-page cover letter that is succinct and includes any references, previous publications or personal background that might be relevant. But keep it professional and to the point; don't try to be cute or overly clever," says Michalson. "A separate one-page synopsis of your book can be helpful. Make sure whatever you send is clean and readable, include a SASE, and allow at least three months before you follow up. After that time, no one should mind your inquiry."

Writers, too, need to understand certain basic realities about the publishing business. "Remember most presses—small or large, for profit or nonprofit—are understaffed, and time to read manuscripts is at a premium, at times even a luxury. Remember, also, all good editors are in this business because they genuinely love to read, they admire writers and they hope every time they pick up a manuscript they'll be transported by it. This isn't an adversarial situation, though sometimes the distance and the long odds make it tempting to believe otherwise."

Authors submitting to Unbridled don't need agent representation. In fact, about half the books they receive are agented and the rest are submitted directly by the authors, usually through some connection Michalson and Ramey have made along the way.

Editorial decisions are made based on what Michalson calls a "champion system." Either he or Ramey will champion a manuscript as publishable. Then, both editors have to be convinced before they go with it; either of the two may veto it. "Fred and I have worked together for a long time. We have great respect for each other, and we both have to agree before we'll publish a given book. If I can't convince Fred about a certain book, how am I going to convince the booksellers and readers?"

For Michalson, being a small press is partly by necessity but also by design. As a small publisher, they can give their entire attention and enthusiasm to every book they nurture through the process of publication. Michalson believes writers are well served by the editorial process at Unbridled. He and Ramey are very hands-on editors. He sees this as an old-fashioned strength. "We often work closely with writers when we see something in their work but believe it isn't quite there. It's not unusual for us to go back and forth, even several times, reading a number of complete versions of a manuscript over time before we're finished. Oftentimes, that results in a publishable book, but sometimes it doesn't. There are no guarantees. And there has to be a meeting of the minds between editor and author. If not, that's fine and perfectly understandable, but then we'll have to move on to some other project."

Whatever project the pair devotes themselves to, they're counting on work that will gather the interest of as many readers as possible. "We like to say that Unbridled Books promises that rarest of pleasures: a good read. We hope to publish books that will be read for a long time to come. Really, Fred and I are in the business of publishing the books we love. And trusting that if we provide careful editing, the highest quality design and production values, savvy publicity and marketing, and long-term support for our books, we can reach enough like-minded readers to make this venture a success."

—*Jack Smith*

UNITY HOUSE
1901 NW Blue Parkway, Unity Village MO 64065-0001. (816)524-3559 ext. 3190. Fax: (816)251-3559. Website: www.unityonline.org. **Contact:** Adrianne Ford, product manager. Estab. 1903. "We are a bridge between traditional Christianity and New Age spirituality. Unity is based on metaphysical Christian principles, spiritual values and the healing power of prayer as a resource for daily living." Publishes hardcover and trade paperback originals and reprints. **Published 2 debut authors within the last year.** Averages 16 total titles/year.
Needs Spiritual, visionary fiction, inspirational, metaphysical.
How to Contact Query with SASE. Responds in 2 weeks to queries; 1 month to mss. No simultaneous submissions.
Terms Pays 10-15% royalty on net receipts. Offers advance. Publishes ms 13 months after acceptance. Ms guidelines online.

UNIVERSITY OF GEORGIA PRESS
330 Research Dr., Athens GA 30602-4901. (706)369-6130. E-mail: books@ugapress.uga.edu. Website: www.ugapress.org. Estab. 1938. University of Georgia Press is a midsized press that publishes fiction *only* through the Flannery O'Connor Award for Short Fiction competition. Publishes hardcover originals, trade paperback originals and reprints. Averages 75 total titles/year.
Needs Short story collections published in Flannery O'Connor Award Competition. Published *The Send-Away Girl*, by Barbara Sutton; *Curled in the Bed of Love*, by Catherine Brady; *Eyesores*, by Eric Shade.
How to Contact Responds in 2 months to queries. No simultaneous submissions.
Terms Pays 7-10% royalty on net receipts. Average advance: rare, varying. Publishes ms 1 year after acceptance. Book catalog and ms guidelines for #10 SASE. Ms guidelines online.
Advice "Please visit our website to view our book catalogs and for all manuscript submission guidelines."

UNIVERSITY OF IOWA PRESS
100 Kuhl House, Iowa City IA 52242-1000. (319)335-2000. Fax: (319)335-2055. Website: www.uiowapress.org. **Contact:** Holly Carver, director; Prasenjit Gupta, acquisitions editor. Estab. 1969. Publishes hardcover and paperback originals. Average print run for a first book is 1,000-1,500. Averages 35 total titles/year.
Needs Currently publishes the Iowa Short Fiction Award selections.
How to Contact Responds in 6 months to queries.
Terms Pays 7-10% royalty on net receipts. Publishes ms 1 year after acceptance. Ms guidelines online.

UNIVERSITY OF MICHIGAN PRESS
839 Greene St., Ann Arbor MI 48106. (734)764-4388. Fax: (734)615-1540. E-mail: ump.fiction@umich.edu. Website: www.press.umich.edu. **Contact:** Chris Hebert, editor (regional). Midsize university press. Publishes hardcover originals. Member: AAUP.
Imprint(s) Sweetwater Fiction Originals (literary/regional).
Needs Literary, short story collections, novels.
How to Contact Accepts unsolicited mss. Query with SASE or submit outline, 1 sample chapter(s). Accepts queries by mail. Include brief bio, list of publishing credits. Responds in 4-6 weeks to queries; 6-8 weeks to mss. Accepts simultaneous submissions. No electronic submissions, submissions on disk. Sometimes comments on rejected mss.
Terms Ms guidelines online.
Advice "Aside from work published through the Michigan Literary Fiction Awards, we seek only fiction set in the Great Lakes region."

UNIVERSITY OF MISSOURI PRESS
2910 LeMone Blvd., Columbia MO 65201. (573)882-7641. Fax: (573)884-4498. Website: www.system.missouri.edu/upress. **Contact:** Clair Willcox, acquisitions editor. Estab. 1958. "Mid-size university press." Publishes hardcover

and paperback originals and paperback reprints. **Published some debut authors within the last year.** Averages 65 total titles/year. Member: AAUP. Distributes titles through direct mail, bookstores, sales reps.

Needs Short story collections. Published *My Favorite Lies*, by Ruth Hamel (short story collection); *Boys Keep Being Born*, by Joan Frank (short story collections); *No Visible Means of Support*, by Dabney Stuart (short story collection).

How to Contact Query with SASE. Responds in 3 months to mss.

Terms Pays up to 10% royalty on net receipts. Publishes ms within 1 year after acceptance. Ms guidelines online.

🖉 ◎ 🔰 UNIVERSITY OF NEVADA PRESS

MS 166, Reno NV 89557. (775)784-6573. Fax: (775)784-6200. Website: www.nvbooks.nevada.edu. **Contact:** Joanne O'Hare, editor-in-chief. Estab. 1961. "Small university press. Publishes fiction that primarily focuses on the American West." Publishes hardcover and paperback originals and reprints. Averages 25 total titles, 2 fiction titles/year. Member: AAUP.

• *Strange White Male*, by Gerald Haslam won the WESTAF Award for Fiction in 2000 and *Foreword Magazine's* second place winner for Book of the Year.

Needs "We publish in Basque Studies, Gambling Studies, Western literature and Western history."

How to Contact Submit outline, 2-4 sample chapter(s), synopsis. Include estimated word count, brief bio, list of publishing credits. Send SASE or IRC. Responds in 2 months to queries. No simultaneous submissions.

Terms Publishes ms 18 months after acceptance. Book catalog and ms guidelines free.

Advice Publishes fiction in Western American Literature series only.

🖉 ◎ UNIVERSITY OF TEXAS PRESS

P.O. Box 7819, Austin TX 78713-7819. (512)471-7233. Fax: (512)232-7178. E-mail: utpress@uts.cc.utexas.edu. Website: www.utexas.edu/utpress/. **Contact:** Theresa May, assistant director/editor-in-chief (social sciences, Latin American studies); James Burr, sponsoring editor (humanities, classics); William Bishel, sponsoring editor (sciences; Texas history). Estab. 1952. Average print order for a first book is 1,000. **Published 50% debut authors within the last year.** Averages 90 total titles/year.

Needs "Latin American and Middle Eastern fiction only in translations. We do not publish original English-language fiction." Published *Whatever happened to Dulce Veiga?*, by Caio Fernando Abreu (novel).

How to Contact Query with SASE or submit outline, 2 sample chapter(s). Responds in 3 months to queries. No simultaneous submissions.

Terms Pays royalty on net receipts. Average advance: occasional. Publishes ms 18-24 months after acceptance. Book catalog and ms guidelines free.

VANDAMERE PRESS

P.O. Box 149, St. Petersburg FL 33731. **Contact:** Jerry Frank, senior acquistions editor. Estab. 1984. Publishes hardcover and trade paperback originals and reprints. **Published 25% debut authors within the last year.** Averages 8-15 total titles/year.

Needs Adventure, mystery, suspense. Recently published *Cry Me a River*, by Patricia Hagan (fiction).

How to Contact Submit 5-10 sample chapter(s), synopsis. Responds in 6 months to queries. Accepts simultaneous submissions.

Terms Pays royalty on revenues generated. Offers advance. Publishes ms 1-3 years after acceptance.

Advice "Authors who can provide endorsements from significant published writers, celebrities, etc., will *always* be given serious consideration. Clean, easy-to-read, *dark* copy is essential. Patience in waiting for replies is essential. All unsolicited work is looked at, but at certain times of the year our review schedule will stop. No response with SASE."

🔃 ◎ VEHICULE PRESS

Box 125, Place du Parc Station, Montreal QC H2X 4A3 Canada. (514)844-6073. Fax: (514)844-7543. Website: www.vehiculepress.com. **Contact:** Andrew Steinmetz, fiction editor. Estab. 1973. Small publisher of scholarly, literary and cultural books. Publishes trade paperback originals by *Canadian authors only*. Books: good quality paper; offset printing; perfect and cloth binding; illustrations. Average print order: 1,000-3,000. Averages 15 total titles/year.

Imprint(s) Signal Editions (poetry), Esplande Books (fiction).

Needs Literary, regional, short story collections. Published *A House by the Sea*, by Sikeena Karmali; *Seventeen Tomatoes: Tales from Kashmir*, by Jaspreet Singh; and *A Short Journey by Car*, by Liam Duran.

How to Contact Query with SASE. Responds in 4 months to queries.

Terms Pays 10-15% royalty on retail price. Average advance: $200-500. "Depends on press run and sales. Translators of fiction can receive Canada Council funding, which publisher applies for." Publishes ms 1 year after acceptance. Book catalog for 9×12 SAE with IRCs.

Advice "Quality in almost any style is acceptable. We believe in the editing process."

◨ VERNACULAR PRESS

560 Broadway Suite 509, New York NY 10012. (212)343-9074. Fax: (212)343-3895. E-mail: artistandwriters@ver nacularpress.com. Website: http://vernacularpress.com. Estab. 2002. Independent publisher. Publishes hardcover originals and paperback originals. Books: off-set printing; smythe sew binding. Average print order: 5,000. Average first novel print order: 7,000. **Published 2 debut authors within the last year.** Averages 4 total titles, 2 fiction titles/year. Distributes through Biblio/National Book Network.

How to Contact Accepts unsolicited mss. Submit outline, 1 sample chapter(s). Accepts queries by e-mail, mail. Include brief bio. Send copy of ms and SASE. Responds in 2 months to mss. Accepts simultaneous submissions. No electronic submissions, submissions on disk. Sometimes comments on rejected mss.

Terms Negotiable advance.

Advice ''The mission of Vernacular Press is to discover, preserve and promote the expression of original voices. Vernacular is a creative development and publishing company comprised of artists, printers, bookmakers and designers devoted to helping creative people make creative choices. We intend to bypass the commonly held axioms of deal making in the arts, and we look forward to producing works of beauty and purpose with artists who prefer experiences that are cooperative to ones that are hierarchial. Vernacular values the individual work over its potential to become a commodity, and it is this dedication to quality that we hope will help us attract projects of soul, resonance and creative merit.''

◨ ◨ VIKING

Penguin Putnam Inc., 375 Hudson St., New York NY 10014. (212)366-2000. **Contact:** Acquisitions Editor. Publishes a mix of literary and popular fiction and nonfiction. Publishes hardcover and originals.

Needs Literary, mainstream/contemporary, mystery, suspense. Published *Lake Wobegon Summer 1956*, by Garrison Keillor; *A Day Late and A Dollar Short*, by Terry McMillian; *A Common Life*, by Jan Karon; *In the Heart of the Sea*, by Nathaniel Philbrick.

How to Contact *Agented submissions only.* Responds in 6 months to queries. Accepts simultaneous submissions.

Terms Pays 10-15% royalty on retail price. Average advance: negotiable. Publishes ms 12-18 months after acceptance.

◨ ◨ ◎ VIKING CHILDREN'S BOOKS

A division of Penguin Young Readers Group, 345 Hudson St., New York NY 10014. (212)366-3600. Website: www.penguin.com. **Contact:** Catherine Frank, Tracy Gates and Joy Peskin. ''Viking Children's books publishes high quality trade hardcover books for children through young adults. These include fiction, nonfiction, and novelty books.'' Publishes hardcover originals. **Published some debut authors within the last year.** Averages 60 total titles/year. Promotes titles through press kits, institutional ads.

Needs Juvenile, picture books, young adult. Published *Prom*, by Laurie Halse Anderson (novel); *Science Verse*, by Jon Scieszka (picture book).

How to Contact Does not accept unsolicited mss. Submit complete ms. Send SASE or IRC. Responds in 6 months to queries.

Terms Pays 5-10% royalty on retail price. Average advance: negotiable. Publishes ms 1 year after acceptance. Does not accept unsolicited submissions.

Advice No ''cartoony'' or mass-market submissions for picture books.

◨ ◨ VILLARD BOOKS

Random House Publishing Group, 1745 Broadway 18th Fl., New York NY 10019. (212)572-2600. Website: www.atra ndom.com. Estab. 1983. Publishes hardcover and trade paperback originals. Averages 40-50 total titles/year.

Needs Commercial fiction.

How to Contact *Agented submissions only.* Agented fiction 95%. Accepts simultaneous submissions.

Terms Pays negotiable royalty. Average advance: negotiable.

◨ ◨ VINTAGE ANCHOR PUBLISHING

The Knopf Publishing Group, A Division of Random House, Inc., 1745 Broadway, New York NY 10019. Website: www.randomhouse.com. **Contact:** Submissions editor. Publishes trade paperback originals and reprints.

Needs Literary, mainstream/contemporary, short story collections. Published *Snow Falling on Cedars*, by Guterson (contemporary); and *Martin Dressler*, by Millhauser (literary).

How to Contact *Agented submissions only.* Query with SASE or submit 2-3 sample chapter(s), synopsis. Responds in 6 months to queries. Accepts simultaneous submissions. No electronic submissions.

Terms Pays 4-8% royalty on retail price. Average advance: $2,500 and up. Publishes ms 1 year after acceptance.

◨ ⌗ VISION BOOKS PVT LTD.

Madarsa Rd., Kashmere Gate Delhi 110006 India. (+91)11 23862267 or (+91)11 23862201. Fax: (+91)11 238862935. E-mail: orientpbk@vsnl.com. **Contact:** Sudhir Malhotra, fiction editor.

Imprint(s) Orient Paperbacks.
Needs ''We are a large multilingual publishing house publishing fiction and other trade books.''
Terms Pays royalty.

⚏ WALKER AND CO.

Walker Publishing Co., 104 Fifth Ave., New York NY 10011. Website: www.walkeryoungreaders.com. **Contact:** Emily Easton, publisher (picture books, middle grade & young adult novels); Timothy Travaglini, editor; Beth Marhoffer, assistant editor. Estab. 1959. Midsize independent publisher. Publishes hardcover trade originals. Average first novel print order: 2,500-3,500. Averages 25 total titles/year.
Needs Juvenile (fiction, nonfiction), picture books (juvenile). Published *Things Change*, by Patrick Jones; *The (Short) Story of My Life*, by Jennifer Jones.
How to Contact Accepts unsolicited mss. Query with SASE. Include ''a consice description of the story line, including its outcome, word length of story (we prefer 50,000 words maximum), writing experience, publishing credits, particular expertise on this subject and in this genre. Common mistake: not researching our publishing program and forgetting SASE.'' Agented fiction 50%. Responds in 3 months to queries. Sometimes comments on rejected mss.
Terms Pays 6% on paperback, 10% on hardcover. Average advance: competitive. Publishes ms 1 year after acceptance.

WALTSAN PUBLISHING, LLC

5000 Barnett St., Fort Worth TX 76103-2006. (817)492-0188. E-mail: sandra@waltsan.com. Website: www.waltsan.com. **Published 95% debut authors within the last year.** Averages 40-60 total titles/year.
Needs No queries accepted until January 2007 due to backlog of manuscripts. Published *The Last Knight of Camelot*, by Guy Ward.
How to Contact Query with SASE or submit 3 sample chapter(s), synopsis or submit complete ms. Agented fiction 5%. Responds in 2 months to queries; 4-6 months to mss. Accepts simultaneous submissions.
Terms Pays 20% royalty. Publishes ms 24-36 months after acceptance. Ms guidelines online.
Advice Audience is computer literate, generally higher income and intelligent. ''When possible, authors record their manuscripts to include audio on the CD. Check our website for guidelines and sample contract.'' Only publishes CDs and other removable media.

⚏ Ⓐ ◎ WARNER ASPECT

imprint of Warner Books, 1271 Avenue of the Americas, New York NY 10020. (212)522-7200. Website: www.twbookmark.com. **Contact:** Jaime Levine, editorial director. ''We're looking for 'epic' stories in both fantasy and science fiction.'' Publishes hardcover, trade paperback, mass market paperback originals and mass market paperback reprints. **Published 2 debut authors within the last year.** Averages 30 total titles/year. Distributes titles through nationwide sales force.
Needs Fantasy, science fiction. ''Mistake writers often make is hoping against hope that being unagented won't make a difference. We simply don't have the staff to look at unagented projects.'' Published *Burndive*, by Karin Lowachee (science fiction), *Parable of the Talents*, by Octavia Butler (fantasy); and *The Elder Gods*, by David and Leigh Eddings (fantasy).
How to Contact *Agented submissions only.* Responds in 3 months to mss.
Terms Pays royalty on retail price. Average advance: $5,000-up. Publishes ms 14 months after acceptance.
Advice ''Think epic! Our favorite stories are big-screen science fiction and fantasy, with plenty of characters and subplots. Sample our existing titles—we're a fairly new list and pretty strongly focused. Also seeking writers of color to add to what we've already published by Octavia E. Butler, Nalo Hopkinson, Walter Mosley, etc.''

⚏ Ⓐ WATERBROOK PRESS

Subsidiary of Random House, 2375 Telstar Dr., Suite 160, Colorado Springs CO 80920. (719)590-4999. Fax: (719)590-8977. Website: www.waterbrookpress.com. **Contact:** Dudley Delffs, editor. Estab. 1996. Publishes hardcover and trade paperback originals. Averages 70 total titles/year.
Needs Adventure, historical, literary, mainstream/contemporary, mystery, religious (inspirational, religious mystery/suspense, religious thriller, religious romance), romance (contemporary, historical), science fiction, spiritual, suspense. Published *A Name of Her Own*, by Jane Kirkpatrick (historical); *Women's Intuition*, by Lisa Samson (contemporary); *Thorn in My Heart*, by Liz Curtis Higgs (historical).
How to Contact Does not accept unsolicited mss. *Agented submissions only.* Responds in 1-2 months to queries; 1-2 months to mss. Accepts simultaneous submissions, electronic submissions.
Terms Pays royalty. Publishes ms 11 months after acceptance.

Book Publishers

✪ ◪ ◎ WHITE MANE KIDS

White Mane Publishing, P.O. Box 708, Shippensburg PA 17257. (717)532-2237. Fax: (717)532-6110. E-mail: marketing@whitemane.com. Website: www.whitemane.com. Publishes hardcover orginals and paperback originals.

Needs Children's/juvenile (historical), young adult (historical). Published *Anybody's Hero: Battle of Old Men & Young Boys*, by Phyllis Haslip; *Nowhere to Turn: Young Heroes of History #4*, by Alan Kay; *No Girls Allowed*, by Alan Kay.

How to Contact Accepts unsolicited mss. Query with SASE. Accepts queries by fax, mail. Include estimated word count, brief bio, summary of work and marketing ideas. Send SASE for return of ms or send a disposable ms and SASE for reply only. Responds in 1 month to queries; 3-4 months to mss. Accepts simultaneous submissions. Rarely comments on rejected mss.

Terms Pays royalty. Publishes ms 12-18 months after acceptance. Ms guidelines for #10 SASE.

Advice "Make your work historically accurate."

Ⓝ ◻ WILDE PUBLISHING

P.O. Box 4581, Alburquerque NM 87196. Fax: (419)715-1430. E-mail: wilde@unm.edu. Website: www.unm. edu/~wilde. **Contact:** Josiah Simon, Dusty McGowan, and David Wilde. Estab. 1989. Publishes hardcover and paperback originals. **Published 6 debut authors within the last year.**

Needs Children's/juvenile, fantasy (sword and sorcery), historical, literary, military/war, mystery, psychic/supernatural, romance, short story collections, thriller/espionage, western, young adult. Published *Scuttlebut*, by David Wilde (military) and *Harry The Magician*, byt Dusty McGowan (children).

How to Contact Does not accept unsolicited mss. Query with SASE. Accepts queries by e-mail, fax, mail. Include brief bio, list of publishing credits. Send SASE for return of ms or send a disposable ms and SASE for reply only. Accepts submissions on disk. No simultaneous submissions.

Terms Pay depends on grants/awards. Publishes ms 12 months after acceptance. Ms guidelines for #10 SASE.

Advice "Check spelling, write frequently, avoid excuses!"

WILLOWGATE PRESS

P.O. Box 6529, Holliston MA 01746. (508)429-8774. E-mail: willowgatepress@yahoo.com. Website: www.willowgatepress.com. **Contact:** Robert Tolins, editor. Publishes trade paperback and mass market paperback originals. **Published 50% debut authors within the last year.** Averages 3-5 total titles/year.

Needs Fantasy, gothic, historical, horror, humor, literary, mainstream/contemporary, military/war, mystery, occult, regional, science fiction, short story collections, sports. "We are not interested in children's, erotica or experimental."

How to Contact Query with SASE or submit outline, plus the first 10 pages and 10 pages of the author's choosing. Responds in 2 months to queries; 6 months to mss. Accepts simultaneous submissions.

Terms Pays 5-15% royalty on retail price. Average advance: $500. Publishes ms 6 months after acceptance. Book catalog and ms guidelines online.

Advice "If a manuscript is accepted for publication, we will make every effort to avoid lengthy delays in bringing the product to market. The writer will be given a voice in all aspects of publishing, promotion, advertising and marketing, including cover art, copy, promotional forums, etc. The writer will be expected to be an active and enthusiastic participant in all stages of the publication process. We hope to attract the finest writers of contemporary fiction and to help generate similar enthusiasm in them and in their readers. Please don't send cash or a check in lieu of stamps for return postage."

◪ WIND RIVER PRESS

E-mail: submissions@windriverpress.com. Website: www.windriverpress.com. **Contact:** Katherine Arline, editor (mainstream, travel, literary, historical, short story collections, translations). Estab. 2002. Publishes full and chapbook length paperback originals and reprints and electronic books. "Wind River Press works closely with the author to develop a cost-effective production, promotion and distribution strategy."

Needs Historical, literary, mainstream/contemporary, short story collections. Plans anthology of works selected from Wind River Press's magazines (*Critique* and *The Paumanok Review*). Recently published books by Elisha Porat, Gaither Stewart and Rochelle Mass.

How to Contact Accepts unsolicited mss. Accepts queries by e-mail. Include estimated word count, brief bio, list of publishing credits. Agented fiction 5%. Responds in 3 weeks to queries; 2 months to mss. Accepts simultaneous submissions. Always comments on rejected mss.

Terms Negotiable maximum depending on formats. Individual arrangement depending on book formats and target audience. Publishes ms 6 months after acceptance. Guidelines and book catalog available on website.

WINDRIVER PUBLISHING, INC.

72 N Windriver Lane, Silverton ID 83867-0446. (208)752-1836. Fax: (208)752-1876. E-mail: info@windriverpubl ishing.com. Website: www.windriverpublishing.com. Estab. 2003. Publishes hardcover originals and reprints, trade paperback originals, mass market originals. Averages 24 total titles/year.

Needs Adventure, fantasy, historical, humor, juvenile, literary, military/war, mystery, religious, science fiction, spiritual, suspense, young adult.

How to Contact Responds in 2 months to queries; 4 months to mss. Accepts simultaneous submissions.

Terms Pays 5-10% royalty on retail price. Publishes ms 9 months after acceptance. Ms guidelines online.

WORLDWIDE LIBRARY

Division of Harlequin Enterprises Limited, 225 Duncan Mill Rd., Don Mills ON M2B 3K9 Canada. (416)445-5860. Fax: (416)445-8655/8736. **Contact:** Feroze Mohammed, executive editor. Estab. 1979. Large commercial category line. Publishes paperback originals and reprints. "Mystery program is reprint; no originals please."

Imprint(s) Worldwide Mystery; Gold Eagle.

Needs "Action-adventure series and future fiction."

How to Contact Send SASE or IRC. Responds in 10 weeks to queries. Accepts simultaneous submissions.

Terms Advance and sometimes royalties; copyright buyout. Publishes ms 1-2 years after acceptance.

Advice "Publishing fiction in very selective areas."

YELLOW SHOE FICTION SERIES

Louisiana State University Press, P.O. Box 25053, Baton Rouge LA 70894-5053. Website: www.lsu.edu/lsupress. **Contact:** Michael Griffith. Estab. 2005. Literary fiction series. Averages 1 total title/year.

• See our Insider Report with Editor Michael Griffith on page 462.

Needs Literary. "Looking first and foremost for literary excellence, especially good manuscripts that have fallen through the cracks at the big commercial presses. I'll cast a wide net." Published *If the Sky Falls*, by Nicholas Montemarano.

How to Contact Does not accept unsolicited mss. Accepts queries by mail. No electronic submissions.

Terms Pays royalty. Offers advance. Ms guidelines online.

ZEBRA BOOKS

Kensington, 850 Third Ave., 16th Floor, New York NY 10022. (877)422-3665. Website: www.kensingtonbooks.c om. **Contact:** Michaela Hamilton, editor-in-chief; Ann La Farge, executive editor; Kate Duffy, editorial director (romance); John Scognamiglio, editorial director; Karen Thomas, editorial director (Dafina); Bruce Bender, managing director(Citadel); Margaret Wolf, editor; Richard Ember, editor; Bob Shuman, senior editor; Jeremie Ruby-Strauss, senior editor; Miles Lott, editor. Publishes hardcover originals, trade paperback and mass market paperback originals and reprints. Averages 600 total titles/year.

Needs Zebra books is dedicated to women's fiction, which includes, but is not limited to, romance.

How to Contact *Agented submissions only.* Accepts simultaneous submissions.

Terms Publishes ms 12-18 months after acceptance. Please no queries. Send synopsis and sample chapters with SASE.

ZONDERVAN

HarperCollins Publishers, 5300 Patterson Ave. SE, Grand Rapids MI 49530-0002. (616)698-6900. Fax: (616)698-3454. Website: www.zondervan.com. **Contact:** Manuscript Review Editor. Estab. 1931. "Our mission is to be the leading Christian communication company meeting the needs of people with resources that glorify Jesus Christ and promote biblical principles." Large evangelical Christian publishing house. Publishes hardcover and trade paperback originals and reprints. First novel print order: 5,000. **Published some debut authors within the last year.** Averages 120 total titles, 15-20 fiction titles/year.

Needs Some adult fiction (mainstream, biblical). "Inklings-style" fiction of high literary quality. Christian relevance in all cases. Will *not* consider collections of short stories. Published *Jacob's Way*, by Gilbert Morris; *The Prodigy*, by Alton Gansky; and *Times and Seasons*, by Terri Blackstock and Bev Lahaye.

How to Contact Does not accept unsolicited mss. Query with SASE or submit outline, 1 sample chapter(s), synopsis. Responds in 2 months to queries; 4 months to mss.

Terms Pays 14% royalty on net amount received on sales of cloth and softcover trade editions; 12% royalty on net amount received on sales of mass market paperbacks. Average advance: variable. Ms guidelines online.

Advice "Almost no unsolicited fiction is published. Send plot outline and one or two sample chapters. Editors will *not* read entire manuscripts. Your sample chapters will make or break you."

Michael Griffith

Original fiction returns to Louisiana State University Press

© Jon C. Hughes

Book Publishers

The Louisiana State University Press (LSUP) has accumulated an impressive trove of "firsts": In 1965, they established the first ongoing fiction program at a university press. They received much acclaim in 1980 for the original (though, sadly, posthumous) publication of John Kennedy Toole's *A Confederacy of Dunces*—making LSUP the first university press to produce a Pulitzer Prize winner in fiction. Just six years later, poet Henry Taylor's *The Flying Change* also won a Pulitzer Prize, earning the press the honor of being the first university press to have published both Pulitzer-winning fiction and poetry.

In addition to those distinctions, LSUP takes pride in its tradition of consistent quality and the cultivation of Southern literature. Over the span of almost 30 years, its fiction catalog has boasted titles by James Lee Burke, Lewis Nordan, Shirley Ann Grau, Madison Jones and Fred Chappell. From 1980-1994, the press published the annual winner of the Mobil Pegasus Prize, among these Martin Simecka's *L.A. Times* Book Award-winning novel *The Year of the Frog*. In 1994, it launched a paperback reprint series called Voices of the South, dedicated to keeping outstanding works of Southern fiction in print. But despite the press' unmatched accomplishments and venerable reputation, budget constraints forced a reluctant staff to pull the plug on its original fiction series that same year.

A decade later, under the new direction of MaryKatherine Callaway and with the help of Executive Editor John Easterly, LSUP made the revival of the original fiction series a priority. Callaway and Easterly tapped Michael Griffith, former associate editor of *The Southern Review* (itself an eminent literary force, established at Louisiana State University in the 1930s by Robert Penn Warren, Cleanth Brooks and Charles Pipkin), to steer the project. Griffith was a natural choice for series editor for several reasons. In addition to the decade he spent working at *The Southern Review*, he's the author of a novel, *Spikes* (Arcade, 2001), and a collection, *Bibliophilia* (2003), both lauded for their creative prowess and wry wit. Perhaps most apropos is the fact that Griffith copyedited Ana Teresa Torres' *Dona Ines v. Oblivion*, the very last book of original fiction LSUP published. In this way, Griffith serves as the bridge between LSUP's fiction history and its future.

When Easterly contacted Griffith, now an assistant professor of English at the University of Cincinnati, the latter was thrilled for the opportunity to edit the new series. "The decision was easy, instantaneous and ecstatic," Griffith recalls. "I was well aware of the press' rich history in publishing fiction and was deeply disappointed when they suspended the series during my first year or two at *The Southern Review*. I admit to having daydreamed—especially after the mid-1990s, when LSUP inaugurated Dave Smith's distinguished and successful Southern Messenger Poets line—about being at the helm should they ever establish another fiction series. But until John's call, I thought I had been doing my coveting quietly and futilely.''

With a strong literary foundation and an equally strong and capable editor, the only thing the new series lacked was the perfect name. Easterly suggested ''Yellow Shoe Fiction,'' and Callaway, Griffith and the official Press Committee embraced it. The name originated when the young niece of the poet Elizabeth Seydel Morgan heard the phrase ''the LSU poets''—pronounced with the proper regional drawl—and then later told Morgan that she was going to ''the yellow shoe football game'' that weekend. George Garrett also used the phrase as the title of his retrospective anthology *The Yellow Shoe Poets: Selected Poems, 1964-1999* (LSUP, 1999). ''We appropriated the phrase because it seemed to capture the whimsical, playful, unstuffy tone we wanted for the series,'' explains Griffith.

Griffith says the primary difference between the fiction that LSUP published in the past and the novels they hope to publish in their Yellow Shoe Fiction Series is ''a broader purview.'' While he welcomes books from the South, he will place no regional constraints on the manuscripts he receives. ''LSU is allowing me great flexibility,'' he says. ''The chief criterion for acceptance will be literary excellence.''

And what does that mean, exactly? ''The 'literary excellence' bit is essentially intentional vagueness so as to draw as wide a variety of work as possible,'' Griffith says. ''I want to consider all tones, modes, sensibilities, points of view and subject matter—but not formula romance, fantasy, erotica, etc.'' Griffith says the series is also open to both new and established writers, and he welcomes novels as well as story collections. LSUP is offering a small advance with publication, and the books will be high-quality trade paperbacks. The call for submissions is not a contest, so there's no reading fee.

LSU has committed to one book a year for four years. If both the critics and the market are receptive, expansion is possible. The inaugural volume is Nicholas Montemarano's *If the Sky Falls*, which Griffith describes as ''a dark and extraordinarily powerful collection of stories.'' Montemarano has already produced one highly acclaimed novel, *A Fine Place* (Context [NYC], 2001), and his stories have been published in many magazines, journals and anthologies, including *Esquire, Doubletake, Gettysburg Review, Zoetrope, Agni* and the 2003 *Pushcart Prize* volume. He was awarded a National Endowment for the Arts Fellowship in 2002. He is an assistant professor of English at Franklin & Marshall College in Lancaster, PA.

Griffith sees the series as the perfect conterpart to LSU's respected poetry program. ''I think part of the allure of establishing a new fiction series is that the press' poetry and fiction can compliment each other.''

—*Lauren Mosko*

Contests & Awards

In addition to honors and, quite often, cash prizes, contests and awards programs offer writers the opportunity to be judged on the basis of quality alone without the outside factors that sometimes influence publishing decisions. New writers who win contests may be published for the first time, while more experienced writers may gain public recognition of an entire body of work.

Listed here are contests for almost every type of fiction writing. Some focus on form, such as short stories, novels or novellas, while others feature writing on particular themes or topics. Still others are prestigious prizes or awards for work that must be nominated, such as the Pulitzer Prize in Fiction. Chances are no matter what type of fiction you write, there is a contest or award program that may interest you.

SELECTING AND SUBMITTING TO A CONTEST

Use the same care in submitting to contests as you would sending your manuscript to a publication or book publisher. Deadlines are very important, and where possible, we've included this information. At times contest deadlines were only approximate at our press deadline, so be sure to write, call or look online for complete information.

Follow the rules to the letter. If, for instance, contest rules require your name on a cover sheet only, you will be disqualified if you ignore this and put your name on every page. Find out how many copies to send. If you don't send the correct amount, by the time you are contacted to send more, it may be past the submission deadline. An increasing number of contests invite writers to query by e-mail, and many post contest information on their websites. Check listings for e-mail and website addresses.

One note of caution: Beware of contests that charge entry fees that are disproportionate to the amount of the prize. Contests offering a $10 prize, but charging $7 in entry fees, are a waste of your time and money.

If you are interested in a contest or award that requires your publisher to nominate your work, it's acceptable to make your interest known. Be sure to leave the publisher plenty of time, however, to make the nomination deadline.

☐ ◎ "BEST OF OHIO WRITER" CONTEST

Ohio Writer Magazine, 12200 Fairhill Rd., Townhouse #3A, Cleveland OH 44120. (216)421-0403. Fax: (216)421-8874. E-mail: pwlgc@yahoo.com. Website: www.pwlgc.com. **Contact:** Darlene Montonaro, executive director. Award "to promote and encourage the work of writers in Ohio." Prize: $150, $50. Judged by "a selected panel of prominent Ohio writers." Entry fee: $15, which includes 1-yr. subscription to the magazine. Deadline: July 31. Entries must be unpublished. Ohio residents only. Guidelines available after January 1 for SASE or e-mail. Accepts inquiries by e-mail and phone. Length: 2,500 words, "No cliché plots; we're looking for fresh unpublished voices." Results announced November 1. Winners notified by mail. For contest results, send SASE or e-mail after November 1.

Ⓝ AIM MAGAZINE SHORT STORY CONTEST

P.O. Box 1174, Maywood IL 60153-8174. (708)344-4414. E-mail: apiladoone@aol.com. Website: www.aimmagazine.org. **Contact:** Ruth Apilado, associate editor. $100 prize offered to contest winner for best unpublished short story (4,000 words maximum) "promoting brotherhood among people and cultures." Judged by staff members. No entry fee. Deadline: August 15. Competition receives 20 submissions per category. Guidelines available anytime. Accepts inquiries by e-mail and phone. Winners are announced in the autumn issue and notified by mail on September 1. List of winners available for SASE. Open to any writer.

ALABAMA STATE COUNCIL ON THE ARTS INDIVIDUAL ARTIST FELLOWSHIP

201 Monroe St., Montgomery AL 36130-1800. (334)242-4076, ext. 224. Fax: (334)240-3269. E-mail: randyshoults @arts.alabama.gov. Website: www.arts.state.al.us. **Contact:** Randy Shoults, literature program manager. "To recognize the achievements and potential of Alabama writers." Judged by independent peer panel. Guidelines available in January. For guidelines, fax, e-mail, visit website. Accepts inquiries by fax, e-mail and phone. "Two copies of the following should be submitted: a résumé and a list of published works with reviews, if available. A minimum of 10 pages of poetry or prose, but no more than 20 pages. Please label each page with title, artist's name and date. If published, indicate where and the date of publication." Winners announced in June and notified by mail. List of winners available for SASE, fax, e-mail or visit website. No entry fee. Deadline: March. Competition receives 25 submissions annually. Two-year residency required. Open to any writer.

NELSON ALGREN SHORT FICTION CONTEST

Chicago Tribune, Nelson Algren Awards, 1717 N. Penny Lane, #200, Schaumburg IL 60173. E-mail: akostovski@ tribune.com. Website: about.chicagotribune.com/community/literaryawards.htm. **Contact:** Aleksandra Kostovski, events producer. "Honors excellence in short story writing by previously unpublished authors." Prize: $5,000 grand prize, $1,500 runners-up prizes (3). Judged by a group of *Chicago Tribune* editors and contributors. No entry fee. Cover letter should include name, address, phone, e-mail, word count, title. "No info on manuscript besides title and page numbers." Results announced October 2005. Winners notified by mail or phone in September. For contest results, visit website or in the *Chicago Tribune*. Deadline: March 18. Entries must be unpublished. Competition for short stories. Open to any writer. Guidelines also available by e-mail and on website. Accepts inquiries by e-mail, phone.

Ⓝ ◎ AMERICAN ASSOCIATION OF UNIVERSITY WOMEN AWARD IN JUVENILE LITERATURE

North Carolina Literary and Historical Association, 4610 Mail Service Center, Raleigh NC 27699-4610. (919)733-9375. Fax: (919)733-8807. E-mail: michael.hill@ncmail.net. **Contact:** Michael Hill, awards coordinator. Award's purpose is to "select the year's best work of literature for young people by a North Carolina writer." Annual award for published books. Award: cup. Competition receives 10-15 submissions per category. Judged by three-judge panel. No entry fee. Deadline: July 15. Entries must be previously published. Contest open to "residents of North Carolina (three-year minimum)." Guidelines available July 15. For guidelines, send SASE, fax, e-mail or call. Accepts inquiries by fax, e-mail, phone. Winners announced October 15. Winners notified by mail. List of winners available for SASE, fax, e-mail.

AMERICAN LITERARY REVIEW SHORT FICTION AWARD

American Literary Review, P.O. Box 311307, University of North Texas, Denton TX 76203-1307. (940)565-2755. Website: www.engl.unt.edu/alr. "This award for short stories is meant to award excellence in short fiction." Prize: $1,000 and publication. Judged by rotating outside writer. Past judges have included Marly Swick, Antonya Nelson and Jonis Agee. Entry fee: $10. For guidelines, send SASE or visit website. Accepts inquiries by fax and phone. Deadline: November 1. Entries must be unpublished. Contest open to anyone not affiliated with the University of North Texas. "Only solidly crafted, character-driven stories will have the best chance for success." Winners announced and notified by mail and phone in February. List of winners available for SASE.

AMERICAN MARKETS NEWSLETTER SHORT STORY COMPETITION

American Markets Newsletter, 1974 46th Ave., San Francisco CA 94116. E-mail: sheila.oconnor@juno.com. Award is "to give short story writers more exposure." Accepts fiction and nonfiction up to 2,000 words. Entries are eligible for cash prizes and all entries are eligible for worldwide syndication whether they win or not. Send double-spaced manuscripts with your story/article title, byline, word count and address on the first page above your article/story's first paragraph (no need for separate cover page). There is no limit to the number of entries you may send. Prize: 1st Place: $300; 2nd Place: $100; 3rd Place: $50. Judged by a panel of independent judges. Entry fee: $10 per entry; $15 for 2; $20 for 3; $23 for 4; $4 each entry thereafter. For guidelines, send SASE, fax or e-mail. Deadline: June 30 and December 31. Contest offered biannually. Published and unpublished stories are actively encouraged. Add a note of where and when previously published. Open to any writer. "All kinds of fiction are considered. We especially want women's pieces—romance, with a twist in the tale—but all will be considered." Results announced within 3 months of deadlines. Winners notified by mail if they include SASE.

⊚ AMERICAN SCANDINAVIAN FOUNDATION TRANSLATION PRIZE

American Scandinavian Foundation, 58 Park Ave., New York NY 10016. (212)879-9779. Fax: (212)686-2115. E-mail: info@amscan.org. Website: www.amscan.org. **Contact:** Andrey Henkin. Award to recognize excellence in fiction, poetry and drama translations of Scandinavian writers after 1800. Prize: $2,000 grand prize; $1,000 prize. No entry fee. Cover letter should include name, address, phone, e-mail and title. Deadline: June 1. Entries must be unpublished. Length: no more than 50 pages for drama, fiction; no more than 35 pages for poetry. Open to any writer. Guidelines available in January for SASE, by fax, phone, e-mail or on website. Accepts inquiries by fax, e-mail, phone. Results announced in November. Winners notified by mail. Results available for SASE or by fax, e-mail, website.

THE SHERWOOD ANDERSON FOUNDATION FICTION AWARD

The Sherwood Anderson Foundation, 216 College Rd., Richmond VA 23229. (804)289-8324. Fax: (804)287-6052. E-mail: mspear@richmond.edu. Website: richmond.edu/~mspear/sahome.html. **Contact:** Michael M. Spear, foundation co-president. Contest is "to honor, preserve and celebrate the memory and literary work of Sherwood Anderson, American realist for the first half of the 20th century." Annual award for short stories and chapters of novels to "encourage and support developing writers." Entrants must have published at least 1 book of fiction or have had several short stories published in major literary and/or commercial publications. Do not send your work by e-mail. Only mss in English will be accepted. Prize: Award for 2003 was $15,000. Judged by a committee established by the foundation. Entry fee: $20 application fee (payable to The Sherwood Anderson Foundation). Deadline: April 1. Send a detailed résumé that provides a bibliography of your publications. Self-published stories do not qualify. Include a cover letter that provides a history of your writing experience and your future plans for writing projects. Also, submit 2 or 3 examples of what you consider to be your best work. Open to any writer. Accepts inquiries by e-mail. Mail your application to the above address. No mss or publications will be returned. "Send in your best, most vivid prose that clearly shows talent."

✱ ANNUAL FICTION CONTEST

Women in the Arts, PO Box 2907, Decatur IL 62524. (217)872-0811. **Contact:** Vice President. Annual competition for essays, fiction, fiction for children, plays, rhymed poetry, unrhymed poetry. Prize: $50, $35, $15 in all categories. Categories: Essay (up to 1,500 words); fiction (up to 1,500 words); fiction for children (up to 1,500 words); play (one act, 10-page limit); rhymed and unrhymed poetry (up to 32 lines). Judged by published, professional writers who live outside the state of Illinois. All entries will be subject to blind judging. Entry fee: $2 per entry, unlimited entries. Deadline: November 1. Do not submit drawings for any category. Double-space prose. Entries must be typed on $8\frac{1}{2} \times 11$ paper and must be titled. Do not put your name on any page of the ms. Do put your name, address, telephone number, e-mail and titles of your entries on a cover sheet. Submit one cover sheet and one check, with all entries mailed flat in one envelope. Do not staple. No entries published by WITA, author retains rights. Open to any writer. Results announced March 15 annually. Winners notified by mail. "Send a perfect manuscript—no typos, Liquid Paper or holes from 3-ring binders."

⊚ ANNUAL JUVENILE FICTION CONTEST

Women in the Arts, P.O. Box 2907, Decatur IL 62524. (217)872-0811. **Contact:** Vice President. Annual competition for essays, fiction, fiction for children, plays, rhymed poetry, unrhymed poetry. Prize: $15-$50. Judged by anonymous judges who are published, professional writers who live outside Illinois. Entry fee: $2 per entry. Word length: 1,500 maximum for fiction, essay, fiction for children; one act for plays; up to 32 lines for poetry. Deadline: November 1. Entries must be original work of the author. Entries must be typed on $8\frac{1}{2} \times 11$ white paper and must be titled. Do not put your name on any page of the entry. Instead, put your name, address, telephone number, e-mail and titles of your entries on a cover sheet. Submit one cover sheet and one check.

Mail all entries flat in a single envelope. Do not staple. Open to any writer. "Entrants must send for contest rules and follow the specific format requirements."

ANNUAL POETRY/FICTION CONTEST
Rambunctious Press, Inc., 1221 Pratt Blvd., Chicago IL 60626. (773)338-2439. **Contact:** E. Hausler, editor. Annual competition for short stories. Prize: $100, $75, $50. Entry fee: $4 per story or $15 subscription. For guidelines send SASE. Deadline: December 31. Entries must be unpublished. Length: 12 pages. Open to any writer. "Follow the theme with creativity. Each contest has a theme. Examples: Courage, Color and Milestones." Winners announced three months after contest deadline. "All contestants will receive a list of winners."

ANTIETAM REVIEW ANNUAL LITERARY AWARD
Antietam Review, 41 S. Potomac St., Hagerstown MD 21740. (301)791-3132. Fax: (240)420-1754. E-mail: antietamreview@washingtoncountyarts.com (for queries only). Website: www.washingtoncountyarts.com. **Contact:** Mary Jo Vincent, managing editor. Review estab. 1982. Circ. 1,000. To encourage and give recognition to excellence in short fiction. Prize: $150 for selected prose and $100 for selected poem. Both categories receive two copies of magazine. Categories: "Fiction: Contributors may submit only 1 entry with fewer than 5,000 words. Editors seek high quality, well-crafted work with significant character development and shift. A manuscript stands out because of its energy and flow. Short stories are preferred; however, novel excerpts are considered if they work as independent pieces. Poetry: Up to three poems with no more than 30 lines. No haiku, religious or rhyme." Entry fee: $15 for fiction (three poems considered one fee); check, credit card and money orders accepted. Entries must be unpublished. Open to any writer.

ARROWHEAD REGIONAL ARTS COUNCIL INDIVIDUAL ARTIST CAREER DEVELOPMENT GRANT
Arrowhead Regional Arts Council, 1301 Rice Lake Rd., Suite 111, Duluth MN 55811. (218)722-0952 or (800)569-8134. Fax: (218)722-4459. E-mail: aracouncil@aol.com. Website: www.aracouncil.org. Award to "provide financial support to regional artists wishing to take advantage of impending, concrete opportunities that will advance their work or careers." Prize: up to $1,000. Categories: novels, short stories, story collections and translations. Judged by ARAC Board. No entry fee. Guidelines available by phone, e-mail or on website. Deadline: was April 29 in 2005. See website for 2006 dates. Entries must be unpublished. Award is offered 3 times per year. Applicants must live in the seven-county region of Northeastern Minnesota. Results announced approximately 6 weeks after deadline. Winners notified by mail. List of winners available by phone.

THE ART OF MUSIC ANNUAL WRITING CONTEST
Piano Press, P.O. Box 85, Del Mar CA 92014-0085. (619)884-1401. Fax: (858)755-1104. E-mail: eaxford@aol.com. Website: www.pianopress.com. **Contact:** Elizabeth C. Axford. Offered annually. Categories are: essay, short story, poetry and song lyrics. All writings must be on music-related topics. The purpose of the contest is to promote the art of music through writing. Acquires one-time rights. All entries must be accompanied by an entry form indicating category and age; parent signature is required of all writers under age 18. Poems may be of any length and in any style; essays and short stories should not exceed five double-spaced, typewritten pages. All entries shall be previously unpublished (except poems and song lyrics) and the original work of the author. Guidelines and entry form for SASE, on website or by e-mail. Prize: Cash, medal, certificate, publication in the biannual anthology/chapbook titled *The Art of Music: A Collection of Writings,* and copies of the book. Judged by a panel of published poets, authors and songwriters. Entry fee: $20 fee. Inquiries accepted by fax, e-mail, phone. Deadline: June 30. Short stories should be no longer than five pages typed and double spaced. Open to any writer. "Make sure all work is fresh and original. Music-related topics only." Results announced October 31. Winners notified by mail. For contest results, send SASE or visit website.

ASTED/GRAND PRIX DE LITTERATURE JEUNESSE DU QUEBEC-ALVINE-BELISLE
Association pour l'avancement des sciences et des techniques de la documentation, 3414 Avenue du Parc, Bureau 202, Montreal QC H2X 2H5, Canada. (514)281-5012. Fax: (514)281-8219. E-mail: info@asted.org. Website: www.asted.org. **Contact:** Marie-Helene Parent, president. "Prize granted for the best work in youth literature edited in French in the Quebec Province. Authors and editors can participate in the contest." Prize: $1,000. No entry fee. Deadline: June 1. Entries must be previously published. Open to editors and authors with books published during the preceding year.

THE ATHENAEUM LITERARY AWARD
The Athenaeum of Philadelphia, 219 S. Sixth St., Philadelphia PA 19106-3794. (215)925-2688. Fax: (215)925-3755. E-mail: erose@PhilaAthenaeum.org. Website: www.PhilaAthenaeum.org. **Contact:** Ellen L. Rose, circulation director. Annual award to recognize and encourage outstanding literary achievement in Philadelphia and its vicinity. Prize: a certificate bearing the name of the award, the seal of the Athenaeum, the title of the book,

the name of the author and the year. Categories: The Athenaeum Literary Award is granted for a work of general literature, not exclusively for fiction. Judged by a committee appointed by the Board of Directors. No entry fee. Deadline: December. Entries must be previously published. Nominations shall be made in writing to the Literary Award Committee by the author, the publisher, or a member of the Athenaeum, accompanied by a copy of the book. Open to work by residents of Philadelphia and its vicinity. Guidelines available for SASE, by fax, by e-mail and on website. Accepts inquiries by fax, e-mail and phone. Juvenile fiction is not included. Results announced in Spring. Winners notified by mail. For contest results, see website.

AWP AWARD SERIES IN THE NOVEL, CREATIVE NONFICTION AND SHORT FICTION

The Association of Writers & Writing Programs, Mail Stop 1E3, George Mason University, Fairfax VA 22030. (703)993-4301. Fax: (703)993-4302. E-mail: awp@awpwriter.org. Website: www.awpwriter.org. **Contact:** Supriya Bhatnagar, director of publications. The AWP Award Series was established in cooperation with several university presses in order to publish and make fine fiction and nonfiction available to a wide audience. Offered annually to foster new literary talent. Guidelines for SASE and on website. Categories: novel ($2,000), Donald Hall Prize in Poetry ($4,000), Grace Paley Prize in Short Fiction ($4,000), and creative nonfiction. Entry fee: $20 for nonmembers, $10 for members. Entries must be unpublished. Mss must be postmarked between January 1-February 28. Cover letter should include name, address, phone number, e-mail and title. "This information should appear in cover letter only." Open to any writer. Guidelines available on website in November. No phone calls, please. Manuscripts published previously in their entirety, including self-publishing, are not eligible. No mss returned. Results announced in August. Winners notified by mail or phone. For contest results send SASE, or visit website. No phone calls, please.

AWP INTRO JOURNALS PROJECT

The Association of Writers & Writing Programs, Mail Stop 1E3, George Mason University, Fairfax VA 22030. (703)993-4301. Fax: (703)993-4302. E-mail: awp@gmu.edu. Website: www.awpwriter.org. **Contact:** Supriya Bhatnagar, director of publications. "This is a prize for students in AWP member university creative writing programs only. Authors are nominated by the head of the creative writing department. Each school may nominate no more than one work of nonfiction, one work of short fiction and three poems." Prize: $50 plus publication in participating journal. 2004 journals included *Puerto del Sol, Quarterly West, Mid-American Review, Willow Springs, Shenandoah, Tampa Review, Controlled Burn, Artful Dodge* and *Hayden's Ferry Review.* Categories: Short stories, nonfiction and poetry. Judged by AWP. No entry fee. Deadline: December 1. Entries must be unpublished. Open to students in AWP Member University Creative Writing Programs only. Accepts inquiries by e-mail, fax and phone. Guidelines available for SASE or on website. Results announced in Spring. Winners notified by mail in Spring. For contest results, send SASE or visit website.

EMILY CLARK BALCH AWARD

Virginia Quarterly Review, 1 West Range, P.O. Box 400223, Charlottesville VA 22904-4233. (434)924-3124. Fax: (434)924-1397. Website: www.virginia.edu/vqr. **Contact:** Ted Genoways. Annual award for the best short story/poetry accepted and published by the *Virginia Quarterly Review* during a calendar year. No deadline. Prize: $1,000. No entry fee.

BARD FICTION PRIZE

Bard College, P.O. Box 5000, Annandale-on-Hudson NY 12504-5000. (845)758-7087. Fax: (845)758-7043. E-mail: bfp@bard.edu. Website: www.bard.edu/bfp. **Contact:** Irene Zedlacher. The Bard Fiction Prize is intended to encourage and support young writers of fiction to pursue their creative goals and to provide an opportunity to work in a fertile and intellectual environment. Prize: $30,000 cash award and appointment as writer-in-residence at Bard College for 1 semester. Judged by committee of 5 judges (authors associated with Bard College). No entry fee. Cover letter should include name, address, phone, e-mail and name of publisher where book was previously published. Guidelines available by SASE, fax, phone, e-mail or on website. Deadline: July 15. Entries must be previously published. Open to US citizens aged 39 and below. Accepts inquiries by fax, e-mail and phone. Results announced by October 15. Winners notified by phone. For contest results, e-mail or visit website.

MILDRED L. BATCHELDER AWARD

Association for Library Service to Children, 50 E. Huron St., Chicago IL 60611. (800)545-2433 ext. 2163. Fax: (312)944-7671. E-mail: alsc@ala.org. Website: www.ala.org/alsc. **Contact:** ALSC, attn: Batchelder Award. Award is to "encourage international exchange of quality children's books by recognizing US publishers of such books in translation." Prize: Citation. Judged by Batchelder Award selection committee. No entry fee. Deadline: December 31. Books should be US trade publications for which children, up to and including age 14, are the potential audience. Previously published translations only. Accepts inquiries by fax, e-mail and phone.

Guidelines available in February for SASE, by fax, phone, e-mail or on website. Results announced at ALA Midwinter Meeting. Winners notified by phone. Contest results by phone, fax, for SASE or visit website.

◎ THE BEACON CONTEST

First Coast Romance Writers, % Maria Connor, 11567 Kelvyn Grove Place, Jacksonville FL 32225. E-mail: theconnorfamily@msn.com. **Contact:** Maria Connor, contest coordinator. Award "to provide published authors with a chance for greater success." Prize: Beacon lapel pin. Categories: Historical, Traditional Regency, Long Contemporary (over 70,000 words), Short Contemporary (up to 70,000 words), Inspirational, Paranormal/ Fantasy/Sci Fi, Single Title Mainstream, Romantic Suspense Chick Lit, First Book. Judged by finalists are read by book retailers. Entry fee: $25 per category (make checks payable to FCRW). 2006 entries should be published (romance genre; send 3 autographed copies of the entry novel). Deadline: March 1. Entries must be previously published. Must be copyright 2005. Open to writers of all romance categories. Guidelines available on website, for SASE or by e-mail. Accepts inquiries by e-mail. Results announced in June. Winners notified by mail. For contest results, send SASE. "Make certain to autograph the 3 copies sent in, as well as verify publication year."

◻ GEORGE BENNETT FELLOWSHIP

Phillips Exeter Academy, 20 Main St., Exeter NH 03833-2460. Website: www.exeter.edu. Annual award for fellow and family "to provide time and freedom from material considerations to a person seriously contemplating or pursuing a career as a writer. Applicants should have a manuscript in progress which they intend to complete during the fellowship period." Duties: To be in residency for the academic year; to make oneself available informally to students interested in writing. Guidelines for SASE or on website. The committee favors writers who have not yet published a book with a major publisher. Residence at the Academy during the fellowship period required. Prize: $10,000 stipend, room and board. Judged by committee of the English department. No entry fee. Application form and guidelines for SASE and on website. Deadline: December 1. Results announced in March. Winners notified by letter or phone. List of winners available in March. All entrants will receive an announcement of the winner. "Stay within a few pages of the limit. (We won't read more anyway.) Trust us to recognize that what you are sending is a work in progress. (You have the chance to talk about that in your statement.) Hope, but don't expect anything. If you don't win, some well-known writers have been in your shoes—at least as many as have won the fellowship."

◎ BERTELSMANN FOUNDATION'S WORLD OF EXPRESSION SCHOLARSHIP PROGRAM

Bertelsmann USA, 1745 Broadway, New York NY 10019. (212)782-8319. Fax: (212)940-7590. E-mail: worldofexp ression@randomhouse.com. Website: www.worldofexpression.org. **Contact:** Melanie Fallon Hauska, director. Offered annually for unpublished work to NYC public high school seniors. Three categories: poetry, fiction/ drama and personal essay. Prize: 72 awards given in literary (3) and nonliterary (2) categories. Awards range from $500-10,000. Categories: short stories and poems. Judged by various city officials, executives, authors, editors. No entry fee. Guidelines available in October on website and in publication. Deadline: February 1. Entries must be unpublished. Word length: 2,500 words or less. Applicants must be seniors (under age 21) at a New York high school. No college essays or class assignments will be accepted. Results announced mid-May. Winners notified by mail and phone. For contest results, send SASE, fax, e-mail or visit website.

BINGHAMTON UNIVERSITY JOHN GARDNER FICTION BOOK AWARD

Binghamton University Creative Writing Program, PO Box 6000, Binghamton NY 13902. (607)777-2713. Fax: (607)777-2408. E-mail: cwpro@binghamton.edu. Website: english.binghamton.edu/cwpro. **Contact:** Maria Mazzioni Gillan, director. Award's purpose is "to serve the literary community by calling attention to outstanding books of fiction." Prize: $1,000. Categories: novels and short story collections. Judged by "rotating outside judges." No entry fee. Entry must have been published in book form with a minimum press run of 500. Each book submitted must be accompanied by an application form. Submit three copies of the book; copies will not be returned. Publishers may submit more than one book for prize consideration. Deadline: March 1. Entries must have appeared in print between January 1 and December 31 of the year preceding the award. Open to any writer. Results announced in Summer. Winners notified by e-mail or phone. For contest results, send SASE or visit website.

◪ IRMA S. AND JAMES H. BLACK AWARD

Bank Street College of Education, 610 W. 112th St., New York NY 10025. (212)875-4450. Fax: (212)875-4558. E-mail: lindag@bnkst.edu. Website: streetcat.bnkst.edu/html/isb.html. **Contact:** Linda Greengrass, award director. Offered annually for a book for young children, for excellence of both text and illustrations. Entries must have been published during the previous calendar year. Prize: press function and scroll and seals by Maurice Sendak for attaching to award winner's book run. Judged by adult children's literature experts and children 6-10 years old. No entry fee. Guidelines for SASE, fax, e-mail or on website. Accepts inquiries by phone, fax, e-

Contests & Awards

mail. Deadline: December 15. Entries must be previously published. "Write to address above. Usually publishers submit books they want considered, but individuals can too. No entries are returned." Winners notified by phone in April and announced in May. A list of winners will be available on website.

⬇ 🌐 JAMES TAIT BLACK MEMORIAL PRIZES

Department of English Literature, University of Edinburgh, David Hume Tower, George Square, Edinburgh EH8 9JX Scotland. (44-13) 1650-3619. Fax: (44-13) 1650-6898. E-mail: s.strathdee@ed.ac.uk. Website: www.englit.ed.ac.uk/jtbinf.htm. **Contact:** Sheila Strathdee, Department of English Literature. "Two prizes are awarded: one for the best work of fiction, one for the best biography or work of that nature, published during the calendar year October 1 to September 30." Judged by the professor of English Literature. No entry fee. Guidelines available September 30. Accepts inquiries by fax, e-mail, phone. Deadline: September 30 Entries must be previously published. "Eligible works are those written in English and first published or co-published in Britain in the year of the award. Works should be submitted by publishers." Open to any writer. Winners notified by phone, via publisher. Contact department of English Literature for list of winners or check website.

ℕ BLACK WARRIOR REVIEW FICTION CONTEST

Black Warrior Review, P.O. Box 862936, Tuscaloosa AL 35486. Website: www.webdelsol.com/bwr. **Contact:** Fiction Contest. Prize: $1,000 and publication in Spring issue. All entrants receive 1-yr subscription to journal. Entry fee: $15 per short story. Make checks payable to the University of Alabama. Send name, phone number, e-mail, SASE and reading fee with ms. Deadline: October 1. Entries must be unpublished. Open to any writer. Winners announced in December.

⬇ ◎ 🌐 THE BOARDMAN TASKER AWARD FOR MOUNTAIN LITERATURE

The Boardman Tasker Charitable Trust, Pound House, Llangennith, Swansea Wales SA3 1JQ United Kingdom. Phone/fax: (44-17) 9238-6215. E-mail: margaretbody@lineone.net. Website: www.boardmantasker.com. **Contact:** Margaret Body. "The award is to honor Peter Boardman and Joe Tasker, who disappeared on Everest in 1982." Offered annually to reward a work of nonfiction or fiction, in English or in translation, which has made an outstanding contribution to mountain literature. Books must be published in the UK between November 1 of previous year and October 31 of year of the prize. Writers may obtain information, but entry is by publishers only. "No restriction of nationality, but work must be published or distributed in the UK." Prize: £2,000. Judged by a panel of 3 judges elected by trustees. No entry fee. "May be fiction, nonfiction, poetry or drama. Not an anthology. Subject must be concerned with a mountain environment. Previous winners have been books on expeditions, climbing experiences, a biography of a mountaineer, novels." Guidelines available in January for SASE, by fax, e-mail or on website. Deadline: August 1. Entries must be previously published. Publisher's entry only. Open to any writer. Results announced in October. Winners notified by phone or e-mail. For contest results, send SASE, fax, e-mail or visit website. "The winning book needs to be well written to reflect a knowledge of and a respect and appreciation for the mountain environment."

BOULEVARD SHORT FICTION CONTEST FOR EMERGING WRITERS

Boulevard Magazine, 6614 Clayton Rd., PMB #325, Richmond Heights MO 63117. (314)862-2643. Fax: (314)781-7250. E-mail: ballymon@hotmail.com. Website: www.richardburgin.com. **Contact:** Richard Burgin, editor. Offered annually for unpublished short fiction to award a writer who has not yet published a book of fiction, poetry or creative nonfiction with a nationally distributed press. "We hold first North American rights on anything not previously published." Open to any writer with no previous publication by a nationally known press. Guidelines for SASE or on website. Prize: $1,500, and publication in 1 of the next year's issues. Judged by editors of *Boulevard*. Entry fee: $15 fee/story; includes 1-year subscription to *Boulevard*. Guidelines available in April for SASE, e-mail, on website and in publication. Accepts inquiries by e-mail, phone. Deadline: December 15. Entries must be unpublished. Length: 9,000 words. Open to any writer. Author's name, address, phone, e-mail, story title, word count and "Boulevard Emerging Writers Contest" should appear on page 1; last name on each page is helpful. Include a 3×5 index card with your name, address and title of your submission(s). Results announced in Spring issue. Winners notified by mail or phone usually during February/March, only through Spring issue.

THE BRIAR CLIFF POETRY, FICTION & CREATIVE NONFICTION COMPETITION

The Briar Cliff Review, Briar Cliff University, 3303 Rebecca St., Sioux City IA 51104-0100. (712)279-5321. Fax: (712)279-5410. E-mail: curranst@briarcliff.edu. Website: www.briarcliff.edu/bcreview. **Contact:** Tricia Currans-Sheehan, editor. Award "to reward good writers and showcase quality writing." Offered annually for unpublished poem, story and essay. Prize: $500, and publication in Spring issue. All entrants receive a copy of the magazine with winning entries. Judged by editors. "We guarantee a considerate reading." Entry fee: $15. Guidelines available in August for SASE. Inquiries accepted by e-mail. Deadline: Submissions between August

1 and November 1. No mss returned. Entries must be unpublished. Length: 6,000 words maximum. Open to any writer. Results announced in December or January. Winners notified by phone or letter around December 20. For contest results, send SASE with submission. "Send us your best. We want stories with a plot."

THE BRIDPORT PRIZE

Bridport Arts Centre, South Street, Dorset DT6 3NR United Kingdom. (01308) 485064. Fax: (01308) 485120. E-mail: frances@poorton.demon.co.uk. Website: www.bridportprize.org.uk. **Contact:** Frances Everitt, administrator. Award to "promote literary excellence, discover new talent." Prize: £3,000 sterling; £1,000 sterling; £500 sterling, plus various runners-up prizes and publication of approximately 10 best stories in anthology. Categories: short stories and poetry. Judged by 1 judge for fiction (in 2005, Maggie Gee) and 1 judge for poetry (in 2005, Andrew Motion, poet laureate). Entry fee: £6 sterling for each entry. Deadline: June 30. Entries must be unpublished. Length: 5,000 maximum for short stories; 42 lines for poetry. Open to any writer. Guidelines available in January for SASE or visit website. Accepts inquiries by fax, e-mail, phone. Results announced in November of year of contest. Winners notified by phone or mail in September. For contest results, send SASE.

BURNABY WRITERS' SOCIETY CONTEST

Burnaby Writers' Society, 6584 Deer Lake Ave., Burnaby BC V5G 3T7, Canada. E-mail: info@bws.bc.ca. Website: www.bws.bc.ca. Offered annually for unpublished work. Open to all residents of British Columbia. Categories vary from year to year. Send SASE for current rules. Purpose is to encourage talented writers in all genres. Prize: 1st Place: $200; 2nd Place: $100; 3rd Place: $50; and public reading. Entry fee: $5. Guidelines available by e-mail, for SASE or on website. Accepts inquiries by e-mail. Deadline: May 31. Results announced in September. Winners notified by mail, phone, e-mail. Results available for SASE or on website.

BUSH ARTIST FELLOWS PROGRAM

Bush Foundation, 332 Minnesota St., Suite E-900, St. Paul MN 55101. Fax: (651)297-6485. E-mail: kpolley@bush foundation.org. Website: www.bushfoundation.org. **Contact:** Kathi Polley, program assistant. Award to "provide artists with significant financial support that enables them to further their work and their contributions to their communities. Fellows may decide to take time for solitary work or reflection, engage in collaborative or community projects, or embark on travel or research." Prize: $44,000 for 12-24 months. Categories: fiction, creative nonfiction, poetry. Judged by a panel of artists and arts professionals who reside outside of Minnesota, South Dakota, North Dakota or Wisconsin. No entry fee. Applications available in August. Accepts inquiries by fax and e-mail. Applicants must be at least 25 years old, U.S. citizens or permanent residents of Minnesota, South Dakota, North Dakota or Western Wisconsin. Students not eligible. Open to any writer. Must meet certain publication requirements. Results announced in Spring. Winners notified by letter. List of winners available in May and sent to all applicants.

BYLINE MAGAZINE AWARDS

P.O. Box 5240, Edmond OK 73083-5240. (405)348-5591. E-mail: mpreston@bylinemag.com. Website: www.bylinemag.com. **Contact:** Marcia Preston, award director. Several monthly contests, open to anyone, in various categories that include fiction, nonfiction, poetry and children's literature; an annual poetry chapbook award which is open to any poet; and an annual *ByLine* Short Fiction and Poetry Award open only to our subscribers. For chapbook award and subscriber awards, publication constitutes part of the prize; winners grant first North American rights to *ByLine*. Prize: **Monthly contests:** Cash and listing in magazine; **Chapbook Award:** Publication of chapbook, 50 copies and $200; *ByLine* Short Fiction and Poetry Award: $250 in each category, plus publication in the magazine. Entry fee: $3-5 for monthly contests and $15 for chapbook contest. Deadline: varies. Entries must be unpublished. Open to any writer.

THE CAINE PRIZE FOR AFRICAN WRITING

51a Southwark St., London SE1 1RU England. E-mail: info@caineprize.com. Website: www.caineprize.com. **Contact:** Nick Elam, administrator. Annual award for a short story (3,000-15,000 words) by an African writer. "An 'African writer' is normally taken to mean someone who was born in Africa, who is a national of an African country, or whose parents are African, and whose work has reflected African sensibilities." Entries must have appeared for the first time in the 5 years prior to the closing date for submissions, which is January 31 each year. Publishers should submit 12 copies of the published original with a brief cover note (no pro forma application). Prize: $15,000 (£10,000). Judged by a panel of judges appointed each year. No entry fee. Cover letter should include name, address, phone, e-mail, title and publication where story was previously published. Deadline: January 31. Entries must be previously published. Word length: 3,000-15,000 words. "Manuscripts not accepted. Entries must be submitted in published form." Writer's work is submitted by publisher. Writing must reflect its "African-ness." Results announced in mid-July. Winners notified at event/banquet. For contest results, send fax, e-mail or visit our website.

Contests & Awards

◎ CALIFORNIA BOOK AWARDS

Commonwealth Club of California, 595 Market St., San Francisco CA 94118. (415)597-4846. Fax: (415)597-6729. E-mail: blane@commonwealthclub.org. Website: www.commonwealthclub.org. **Contact:** Barbara Lane, literary director. Award to honor excellence in literature written by California residents. Prize: $2,000, gold medal; $300, silver medal. Categories: fiction, first work of fiction, nonfiction, juvenile, poetry. Judged by jury. No entry fee. Deadline: December 31. Entries must be previously published. California residents only. Writer or publisher may nominate work. Guidelines available in January on website. Results announced in Spring. Winners notified by phone. For contest results, send e-mail.

◉ JOHN W. CAMPBELL MEMORIAL AWARD FOR BEST SCIENCE FICTION NOVEL OF THE YEAR

Center for the Study of Science Fiction, English Department, University of Kansas, Lawrence KS 66045. (785)864-3380. Fax: (785)864-1159. E-mail: jgunn@ku.edu. Website: www.ku.edu/~sfcenter. **Contact:** James Gunn, professer and director. Award to "honor the best science fiction novel of the year." Prize: Certificate. Winners receive tropies and an expense-paid trip to the university to receive their award. Their names are also engraved on a permanent trophy. Categories: novels. Judged by a jury. No entry fee. Deadline: see website. Entries must be previously published. Open to any writer. Accepts inquiries by e-mail and fax. "Ordinarily publishers should submit work, but authors have done so when publishers would not. Send for list of jurors." Results announced in July. For contest results, send SASE.

CAPTIVATING BEGINNINGS CONTEST

Lynx Eye, 581 Woodland Dr., Los Osos CA 93402. (805)528-8146. E-mail: pamccully@aol.com. **Contact:** Pam McCully, co-editor. Annual award for unpublished stories "with engrossing beginnings, stories that will enthrall and absorb readers." Prize: $100, plus publication; $10 each for 4 honorable mentions, plus publication. Judged by *Lynx Eye* editors. Entry fee: $5/story. Guidelines available year round for SASE. Accepts inquiries by e-mail and phone. Deadline: January 31. Entries must be unpublished. Length: 7,500 words or less. "Stories will be judged on the first 500 words." Open to any writer. Results announced March 15. Winners notified by mail. For contest results, send SASE after March 31.

◙ THE CHELSEA AWARD FOR POETRY AND SHORT FICTION

P.O. Box 773, Cooper Station, New York NY 10276-0773. E-mail: chelseaassoc@aol.com. **Contact:** Alfredo de Palchi. Prize: $1,000, winning entries published in *Chelsea*, 2 free copies and discount on additional copies. Judged by the editors. Entry fee: $10 (includes free subscription to *Chelsea*). Guidelines available for SASE. Deadline: June 15. Entries must be unpublished. Mss must not exceed 30 typed pages, or about 7,500 words. The stories must not be under consideration elsewhere or scheduled for book publication within 8 months of the competition deadline. Absolutely no simultaneous submissions. Open to any writer. Include separate cover sheet with entrant's name; no name on ms. Mss will not be returned; include SASE for notification of results. Results announced August 15. Winners notified by phone. "Read first what kind of fiction is published in *Chelsea*. No submissions, notification or guidelines will be sent or responded to by e-mail. Read and follow contest guidelines. Manuscripts on which the author's name appears will be destroyed unread."

Ⓝ ◙ CITY OF TORONTO BOOK AWARDS

City of Toronto, 100 Queem St. West, City Hall, 10th Floor, West Tower, Toronto ON M9W 3X3 Canada. (416)392-8191. Fax: (416)392-1247. Website: www.toronto.ca/book_awards. **Contact:** Bev Kurmey, protocol officer. "The Toronto Book Awards honour authors of books of literary or artistic merit that are evocative of Toronto." Categories: short stories, novels, story collections, translations. Generally receives 75-100 books/year per category. Judged by committee. No entry fee. Guidelines available by e-mail, on website and in libraries. Accepts inquiries by phone, fax, e-mail. Writers may submit their own fiction. Cover letter should include name, address, phone, e-mail, title. Deadline: Feb. 28. Entries must be previously published. Books must have been published during the year prior to the award (i.e. in 2005 for the 2006 deadline). Open to any writer. Results announced in Sept., short list in June. Winners notified by mail, e-mail. Results available on website.

CNW/FFWA ANNUAL FLORIDA STATE WRITING COMPETITION

% CNW Publishing, Florida Freelance Writers Association, P.O. Box A, North Stratford NH 03590-0167. E-mail: contest@writers-editors.com. Website: www.writers-editors.com. **Contact:** Dana K. Cassell, executive director. Annual award "to recognize publishable talent." Divisions & Categories: Nonfiction (previously published article/essay/column/nonfiction book chapter; unpublished or self-published article/essay/column/nonfiction book chapter); Fiction (unpublished or self-published short story or novel chapter); Children's Literature (unpublished or self-published short story/nonfiction article/book chapter/poem); Poetry (unpublished or self-published free verse/traditional). Prize: 1st Place: $100, plus certificate; 2nd Place: $75, plus certificate; 3rd Place: $50, plus certificate. Honorable Mention certificates will be awarded in each category as warranted.

Judged by editors, librarians and writers. Entry fee: $5 (active or new CNW/FFWA members) or $10 (nonmembers) for each fiction/nonfiction entry under 3,000 words; $10 (members) or $20 (nonmembers) for each entry of 3,000 words or longer; and $3 (members) or $5 (nonmembers) for each poem. Guidelines for SASE or on website. Accepts inquiries by fax, e-mail, phone and mail. Deadline: March 15. Open to any writer. Results announced May 31. Winners notified by mail and posted on website. Results available for SASE or visit website.

⬛ ◎ CONSEIL DE LA VIE FRANCAISE EN AMERIQUE/PRIX CHAMPLAIN

Conseil de la Vie Francaise en Amerique, Maison de la Francophonie, 39 rue Dalhousie, Quebec City G1K 8R8 Canada. (418)646-9117. Fax: (418)644-7670. E-mail: cvfa@cvfa.ca. Website: www.cvfa.ca. **Contact:** Director General. Award to encourage literary work in novel or short story in French by Francophiles living outside Quebec, in the US or Canada. Prize: $1,500 Canadian. Judged by 3 different judges each year. No entry fee. Deadline: December 31. Entries must be previously published. "There is no restriction as to the subject matter. If the author lives in Quebec, the subject matter must be related to French-speaking people living outside of Quebec." Submissions must have been published no more than 3 years before award. Open to any writer. Guidelines for SASE or IRC or on website. Author must furnish 4 examples of work, curriculum vitae, address and phone number.

Ⓝ ☐ CRAZYHORSE FICTION PRIZE

College of Charleston/*Crazyhorse*, College of Charleston, Dept. of English, 66 George St., Charleston SC 29424. (843)953-7740. E-mail: crazyhorse@cofc.edu. Website: crazyhorse.cofc.edu. **Contact:** Editors. Prize: $1,000 and publication in *Crazyhorse*. Judged by anonymous writer whose identity is disclosed when the winners are announced in April. Past judges: Charles Baxter (2001), Michael Martone (2002), Diana Abu-Jaber (2003). Entry fee: $15 (covers 1-yr subscription to *Crazyhorse*; make checks payable to *Crazyhorse*). To enter, please send up to 25 pages of prose. Include a detachable cover sheet with your name, address and telephone number; please do not include this information on the ms itself. Send SASE or see website for additional details. Deadline: see website. Open to any writer.

Ⓝ ☐ ◎ CROSSTIME SHORT SCIENCE FICTION CONTEST

Crossquarter Publishing Group, P.O. Box 23749, Santa Fe NM 87502. (505)438-9846. Website: www.crossquarter.com. **Contact:** Therese Francis, Owner. Original short (up to 10,000 words) science fiction stories that demonstrate the best of the human spirit. Stories may be science fiction, fantasy or urban fantasy. No horror. No dystopia. Prize: 1st place: $250 plus publication in next volume of *CrossTIME Anthology*; 2nd place: $125 plus publication in the anthology; 3rd place: $75 plus publication in the anthology; 4th place: $50 plus publication in the anthology; 5th through 15th places: a distinctive certificate honoring their accomplishment plus publication in the anthology. Judges are not required to award all 15 positions; ties are possible. Each entrant will receive one copy of the resulting anthology highlighting the 1st through 15th place winners. Entry fee: $15 for first submission, $10 for each additional submission. The official entry form is required (available online), along with entry fee (check, money order, Visa, Mastercard, American Express). If you are entering more than one ms, you may mail all entries in the same envelope and write one check for the total entry fee. Submission should be typewritten on 8½×11" white paper. Your name, address, phone number and word count must appear in the upper left-hand corner of the first page. Staple or paperclip the pages together. Team writing is acceptable, but only one copy of the anthology will be sent. The "team leader" should complete the official entry form. Deadline: January 15. Entries must be unpublished. "Your entry must be original, unpublished and unproduced, not accepted by any other publisher or producer at the time of submission. However, stories previously printed for copies only or for less than $25 are acceptable, provided all copyrights have reverted to you. (Example would be school newspapers. Include information on where and when previously published.) Open to any writer. Byline given. Publisher buys all rights for five years (early buy-out negotiable). To receive notification of the receipt of your ms, include self-addressed, stamped postcard.

Ⓝ THE CRUCIBLE POETRY AND FICTION COMPETITION

Crucible, Barton College, College Station, Wilson NC 27893. (252)399-6456. E-mail: tgrimes@barton.edu. **Contact:** Terrence L. Grimes, editor. Offered annually for unpublished short stories. Prize: $150 (1st Prize); $100 (2nd Prize) and publication in *Crucible*. Competition receives 300 entries. Categories: Fiction should be 8,000 words or less. Judged by in-house editorial board. No entry fee. Guidelines available in January for SASE, e-mail or in publication. Deadline: April. Open to any writer. "The best time to submit is December through April." Results announced in July. Winners notified by mail. For contest rules, send e-mail.

DOROTHY DANIELS ANNUAL HONORARY WRITING AWARD

Simi Valley Branch of the National League of American Pen Women, Inc., P.O. Box 1485, Simi Valley CA 93062. E-mail: cdoering@adelphia.net. **Contact:** Carol E. Doering, vice president and contest chairperson. Award for short stories. Prize: $100. Judged by NLAPW members. Entry fee: $5 per entry; make checks payable to NLAPW-SV Branch. Guidelines available in January for SASE. Accepts inquiries by e-mail. Deadline: July 31. Entries must be unpublished. Length: 2,000 words maximum. Open to any writer. Cover letter should include name, address, phone, word count, title and category; name and address must not appear on ms, entry must be titled. Results announced November 5. Winners notified by mail. For contest results, send SASE.

◻ DEAD OF WINTER

Toasted Cheese, E-mail: editors@toasted-cheese.com. Website: www.toasted-cheese.com. **Contact:** Stephanie Lenz, editor. The contest is a winter-themed short fiction contest with a new topic each year. Topic and word limit announced Nov. 1. The topic is usually geared toward a supernatural theme. Prize: Amazon gift certificates in the amount of $25, $15 and $10; publication in *Toasted Cheese*. Also offers honorable mention. Categories: short stories. Judged by two *Toasted Cheese* editors who blind judge each contest. Each judge uses her own criteria to rate entries. No entry fee. Cover letter should include name, address, e-mail, word count and title. Deadline: December 21. Entries must be unpublished. Word limit varies each year. Open to any writer. Guidelines available in November on website. Accepts inquiries by e-mail. "Follow guidelines. Write a smart, original story. We have further guidelines at the website." Results announced January 31. Winners notified by e-mail. List of winners on website.

◻ ◎ DELAWARE DIVISION OF THE ARTS

820 N. French St., Wilmington DE 19801. (302)577-8278. Fax: (302)577-6561. Website: www.artsdel.org. **Contact:** Kristin Pleasanton, art & artist services coordinator. Award "to help further careers of emerging and established professional artists." For Delaware residents only. Prize: $10,000 for masters; $5,000 for established professionals; $2,000 for emerging professionals. Judged by out-of-state, nationally recognized professionals in each artistic discipline. No entry fee. Guidelines available after January 1 on website. Accepts inquiries by e-mail, phone. Expects to receive 25 fiction entries. Deadline: August 15. Open to any writer. Results announced in December. Winners notified by mail. Results available on website. "Follow all instructions and choose your best work sample."

◎ DOBIE/PAISANO FELLOWSHIPS

Dobie House, 702 E. Dean Keeton St., Austin TX 78705. (512)471-8542. Fax: (512)471-9997. E-mail: aslate@mail.utexas.edu. Website: www.utexas.edu/ogs/Paisano. **Contact:** Audrey N. Slate, director. Award to "honor the achievement and promise of two writers." Prize: $2,000/month for six months and rent-free stay at Paisano ranch southwest of Austin, TX. Judged by committee from Texas Institute of Letters and the University of Texas. Entry fee: $10. Accepts inquiries by fax, e-mail and phone. Deadline: January 28. Entries must be unpublished. "Open to writers with a Texas connection—native Texans, people who have lived in Texas at least three years, or writers with published work on Texas." Winners announced April 15. List of winners available at website.

◻ JACK DYER FICTION PRIZE

Crab Orchard Review, Dept. of English, Faner Hall, Southern Illinois University Carbondale, Carbondale IL 62901-4503. Website: www.siu.edu/~crborchd. **Contact:** Jon Tribble, managing editor. Offered annually for unpublished short fiction. *Crab Orchard Review* acquires first North American serial rights to all submitted work. Open to any writer. Prize: $1,500 and publication. Judged by editorial staff (pre-screening); winner chosen by genre editor. Entry fee: $15/entry (can enter up to 3 stories, each story submitted requires a separate fee and can be up to 6,000 words), which includes a 1-year subscription to *Crab Orchard Review*. Guidelines available after January for SASE or on website. Deadline: Reading period for entries is Feb. 1 through April 1 Entries must be unpublished. Length: 6,000 words maximum. U.S. citizens only. "Please note that no stories will be returned." Results announced by end of October. Winners notified by mail. Contest results on website or send SASE. "Carefully read directions for entering and follow them exactly. Send us your best work. Note that simultaneous submissions are accepted for this prize, but the winning entry must NOT be accepted elsewhere. No electronic submissions."

EATON LITERARY AGENCY'S ANNUAL AWARDS PROGRAM

Eaton Literary Agency, P.O. Box 49795, Sarasota FL 34230. (941)366-6589. Fax: (941)365-4679. E-mail: eatonlit@aol.com. Website: www.eatonliterary.com. **Contact:** Richard Lawrence, vice president. Offered biannually for unpublished mss. Prize: $2,500 (over 10,000 words); $500 (under 10,000 words). Judged by an independent agency in conjunction with some members of Eaton's staff. No entry fee. Guidelines available for SASE, by fax, e-mail, or on website. Accepts inquiries by fax, phone and e-mail. Deadline: March 31 (mss under 10,000 words); August 31 (mss over 10,000 words). Entries must be unpublished. Open to any writer. Results announced in April and September. Winners notified by mail. For contest results, send SASE, fax, e-mail or visit website.

◎ THE EMILY CONTEST

West Houston Chapter Romance Writers of America, 5603 Chantilly Lane, Houston TX 77092. E-mail: ellen_watkins@juno.com. Website: www.whrwa.com. **Contact:** Ellen Watkins, Emily Contest chair. Award "to help people writing romance novels learn to write better books and to help them make contacts in the publishing world." Prize: first place entry in each category receives the Emily brooch; all finalists receive certificates. Judged by authors and experienced critiquers in the first round; final round judges are editors at a major romance publishing house. Entry fee: $20 for WHRWA members; $30 for non-members. Deadline: October 1. Entries must be unpublished. Length: first 35 pages of a novel. Open to all unpublished romance writers. Guidelines available in July for SASE, by e-mail or on website. Accepts inquiries by e-mail. "We look for dynamic, interesting romance stories with a hero and heroine readers can relate to and love. Hook us from the beginning and keep the level of excitement high." Results announced in February. Winners notified by mail or phone. For contest results, send SASE or visit website.

◪ ◎ THE VIRGINIA FAULKNER AWARD FOR EXCELLENCE IN WRITING

Prairie Schooner, 201 Andrews Hall, P.O. Box 880334, Lincoln NE 68588-0334. (402)472-0911. Fax: (402)472-9771. E-mail: kgrey2@unl.edu. Website: www.unl.edu/schooner/psmain.htm. **Contact:** Hilda Raz, editor. Offered annually for work published in *Prairie Schooner* in the previous year. Prize: $1,000. Categories: short stories, essays, novel excerpts and translations. Judged by Editorial Board. No entry fee. Guidelines for SASE or on website. Accepts inquiries by fax and e-mail. "We only read mss from September 1 through May 1." Winning entry must have been published in *Prairie Schooner* in the year preceeding the award. Results announced in the Spring issue. Winners notified by mail in February or March.

▦ FISH SHORT STORY PRIZE

Fish Publishing, Durrus, Bantry, Co. Cork, Ireland. 353 (0)27 55645. E-mail: info@fishpublishing.com. Website: www.fishpublishing.com. **Contact:** Clem Cairns, editor. Purpose is to "find and publish new and exciting short fiction from all over the world; to support the short story and those who practice it." Offered annually for unpublished fiction mss. Prize: 1st Prize: 10,000 Euros (approx. $13,000); 2nd Prize: 1 week at Anam Cara Writers' Retreat in the west of Ireland plus 250 Euros; third prize is 250 Euros. The top 15 stories will be published in Fish's anthology, which is launched at the West Cork Literary Festival in June, and will be read by literary agents, including Shirley Stewart, Merric Davidson and others. Judged by a panel of international judges which changes every year. Entry fee: $30 per story. Guidelines available in July by e-mail, on website or in publication. Enter online at www.fishpublishing.com. Accepts inquiries by mail, phone. Deadline: November 30. Length: 5,000 words maximum. Open to any writer except those who have won before or who have been a runner up twice. "Don't be afraid to write with your own voice. We value originality. Do make sure that your story is as good as you can get it. Don't try to please a judge or judges. Make sure it is neat and easy to read." Results announced March 17 every year. Winners notified by mail, phone or e-mail and at prize ceremony book launch in Bantry, County Cork, last Saturday in June. For contest results, send SASE, e-mail, or visit website. See website for additional contests, including "One Page Story Prize," "Historical Short Fiction Prize," and "Unpublished Novel Award."

▦ FISH VERY SHORT STORY PRIZE

Fish Publishing, Durrus, Bantry, County Cork, Ireland. E-mail: vssp@fishpublishing.com. Website: www.fishpublishing.com. **Contact:** Clem Cairns, editor. Prize: 1st prize: 1,000 Euro (approx. $1,300). Nine runners up get 100 Euro (approx. $130). The authors of the 10 best works of short short fiction will be published in the Fish Short Story Prize Anthology. Entry fee: $15 per story. Enter online. Deadline: March 4. Entries must be unpublished. Stories must be no longer than 250 words. Entries can be in any style or format and can be on any subject. The competition is open to writers from all countries, but entries must be written in English. Open to any writer. Guidelines on website or by e-mail.

FLORIDA FIRST COAST WRITERS' FESTIVAL NOVEL, SHORT FICTION, PLAYWRITING & POETRY AWARDS

Writers' Festival & Florida Community College at Jacksonville, FCCJ North Campus, 4501 Capper Road, Jacksonville FL 32218-4499. (904)766-6559. Fax: (904)766-6654. E-mail: dathomas@fccj.edu or hshepard@fccj.edu. Website: opencampus.fccj.org/WF/. **Contact:** Hershel Shepard and Paul Stark, festival contest directors. Conference and contest "to create a healthy writing environment, honor writers of merit and find a novel manuscript to recommend to New York publishers for 'serious consideration.'" Judged by university faculty and freelance and professional writers. Entry fee: $40 (novels); $20 (plays); $10 (short fiction); $5 (poetry). Deadline: December 1 for novels; February 28 for plays; February 1 for poetry and short fiction. Entries must be unpublished. Word length: no limit for novel; 6,000 words for short fiction; 30 lines for poetry. Open to any writer. Guidelines available on the website or in the fall for SASE. Accepts inquiries by fax and e-mail. "For stories and novels, make the opening pages sparkle. For plays, make them at least two acts and captivating. For poems, blow us over with imagery and insight and avoid clichés and wordiness.'' Results announced on the website and at the Florida First Coast Writers' Festival held in May.

◯ FLORIDA STATE WRITING COMPETITION

Florida Freelance Writers Association, P.O. Box A, Stratford NH 03590-0167. (603)922-8338. E-mail: contest@writers-editors.com. Website: www.writers-editors.com. **Contact:** Dana K. Cassell, executive director. Award ''to offer additional opportunities for writers to earn income and recognition from their writing efforts.'' Prize: varies from $50-100. Categories: novels and short stories. Judged by authors, editors and teachers. Entry fee: $5-20. Deadline: March 15. Entries must be unpublished. Open to any writer. Guidelines are revised each year and are subject to change. New guidelines are available in Summer of each year. Accepts inquiries by e-mail. Results announced May 31. Winners notified by mail. For contest results, send SASE marked ''winners'' or visit website.

H.E. FRANCIS SHORT STORY AWARD

The Ruth Hindman Foundation, University of Alabama English Dept., Department of English, Huntsville AL 35899. E-mail: MaryH71997@aol.com. Website: www.uah.edu/colleges/liberal/english/whatnewcontest.html. **Contact:** Patricia Sammon. Offered annually for unpublished work not to exceed 5,000 words. Acquires first time publication rights. Prize: $1,000. Judged by a panel of nationally recognized, award-winning authors, directors of creative writing programs, and editors of literary journals. Entry fee: $15 reading fee (make check payable to the Ruth Hindman Foundation). Deadline: December 31.

Ⓝ ◯ THE GLASGOW PRIZE FOR EMERGING WRITERS

Washington and Lee University/Shenandoah, Mattingly House, 2 Lee Ave., Lexington VA 24450-0303. (540)458-8765. Fax: (540)458-8461. E-mail: lleech@wlu.edu. Website: shenandoah.wlu.edu. **Contact:** Lynn Leech, managing editor. Award for writer with only one published book in genre being considered. (Genre rotates: 2005, creative nonfiction; 2006, short story; 2007, poetry; 2008, creative nonfiction . . . etc.) Prize: $2,500, publication of new work in *Shenandoah*, and a reading at Washington and Lee University. Judged by anonymous writer/editor, announced after prize winner is selected. Entry fee: $22 (includes 1-yr subscription to *Shenandoah*; send credit card information or make checks payable to *Shenandoah*). To apply, send first book, one unpublished piece of work (short story for 2006), SASE, and vita, along with check for $22 (from either author or publisher). Cover letter should include name, address, phone and e-mail. Guidelines available on website. Accepts inquiries by e-mail. Results announced on website and winners notified by mail or e-mail in May. Deadline: March 15-31. Open to any writer.

◯ GLIMMER TRAIN'S FALL SHORT-STORY AWARD FOR NEW WRITERS

Glimmer Train Press, Inc., 1211 NW Glisan St., Suite 207, Portland OR 97209. (503)221-0836. Fax: (503)221-0837. Website: www.glimmertrain.com. **Contact:** Linda Swanson-Davies, contest director. Offered for any writer whose fiction hasn't appeared in a nationally-distributed publication with a circulation over 5,000. Word limit: 1,200-10,000 words. **Open August 1-September 30.** Follow online submission procedure on website. Notification on January 2. Prize: Winner receives $1,200, publication in *Glimmer Train Stories*, and 20 copies of that issue. First/second runners-up receive $500/$300, respectively, and consideration for publication. Entry fee: $12 fee/story. Entries must be unpublished. Length: 1,200-10,000 words maximum. Open to any writer.

◯ GLIMMER TRAIN'S SPRING SHORT-STORY AWARD FOR NEW WRITERS

Glimmer Train Press, Inc., 1211 NW Glisan St., Suite 207, Portland OR 97209. (503)221-0836. Fax: (503)221-0837. Website: www.glimmertrain.com. Offered for any writer whose fiction hasn't appeared in a nationally-distributed publication with a circulation over 5,000. Word limit: 1,200-10,000 words. **Contest open February 1-March 31.** Follow online submission procedure at www.glimmertrain.com. Notification on July 1. Prize: Winner receives $1,200, publication in *Glimmer Train Stories* and 20 copies of that issue. First/second runners-up receive $500/$300, respectively, and consideration for publication. Entry fee: $12 fee/story. Open to any writer.

◯ GLIMMER TRAIN'S SUMMER FICTION OPEN

Glimmer Train Press, Inc., 1211 NW Glisan St., Suite 207, Portland OR 97209. (503)221-0836. Fax: (503)221-0837. Website: www.glimmertrain.com. Offered annually for unpublished stories as ''a platform for all themes, all lengths, all writers.'' Open to any writer. Follow online submission procedure on website. Prize: 1st Place: $2,000, publication in *Glimmer Train Stories*, and 20 copies of that issue; 2nd Place: $1,000, and possible publication in *Glimmer Train Stories*; 3rd Place: $600, and possible publication in *Glimmer Train Stories*. Entry fee: $15 fee/story. Deadline: June 30. Make your submissions online at www.glimmertrain.com. Winners will be notified and results posted posted by October 15.

⬤ GLIMMER TRAIN'S WINTER FICTION OPEN

Glimmer Train, Inc., 1211 NW Glisan St., Suite 207, Portland OR 97209. (503)221-0836. Fax: (503)221-0837. Website: www.glimmertrain.com. Offered annually for unpublished work as "a platform for all themes, all lengths, and all writers." Follow online submission procedure on website. Prize: 1st Place: $2,000, publication in *Glimmer Train Stories*, and 20 copies of that issue; 2nd Place: $1,000, possible publication in *Glimmer Train Stories*; 3rd Place: $600, possible publication in *Glimmer Train Stories*. Entry fee: $15/story. Deadline: January 11. Open to any writer. Make your submissions online (www.glimmertrain.com). Winners will be notified and results will be posted April 15.

Ⓝ THE GOODHEART PRIZE FOR FICTION

Shenandoah: The Washington and Lee University Review, Mattingly House, 2 Lee Ave., Lexington VA 24450-0303. (540)458-8765. Fax: (540)458-8461. E-mail: lleech@wlu.edu. Website: shenandoah.wlu.edu. **Contact:** Lynn Leech, managing editor. Awarded to best story published in *Shenandoah* during a volume year. Prize: $1,000. Judged by writer whose identity is revealed after the prize winner has been selected. No entry fee. In order to be eligible for The Goodheart Prize, your work needs to be submitted and accepted by *Shenandoah* first. (See website for submission guidelines.) All stories published in the review are automatically considered for the prize. Winners are notified by mail or e-mail each Spring. Results are available on website. Work MUST be published in *Shenandoah* before it is considered for the prize. All writers published in *Shenandoah* during the volume year. "Read *Shenandoah* to familiarize yourself with the work we publish."

⬤ THE GREAT BLUE BEACON SHORT-SHORT STORY CONTEST

The Great Blue Beacon: The Newsletter for Writers of All Genres and Skill Levels, 1425 Patriot Drive, Melbourne FL 32940-6881. (321)253-5869. E-mail: ajircc@juno.com. **Contact:** A.J. Byers, editor/publisher. Award to "recognize outstanding short-short stories." Prize: $50 (first prize), $25 (second prize), $10 (third prize) and publication of winning entry in *The Great Blue Beacon*. Judged by outside panel of judges. Entry fee: $5 ($4 for subscribers). Make checks out to A.J. Byers. Guidelines available periodically when announced. Length: 1,000 words or fewer. Cover letter and first page of ms should include name, address, phone, e-mail, word count and title. Deadline: TBA. Entries must be unpublished. Open to any writer. Two-three contests a year for short-short stories. Receives 50-75 entries per contest. For guidelines, send SASE or e-mail. Accepts inquiries by e-mail and phone. Results announced two months after contest deadline. Winners notified by SASE or e-mail. For contest results, send SASE or e-mail.

🍁 🔘 GREAT CANADIAN STORY CONTEST

Storyteller, Canada's Short Story Magazine, 858 Wingate Dr., Ottawa ON K1G 1S5 Canada. (613)521-9570. E-mail: info@storytellermagazine.com. Website: www.storytellermagazine.com. **Contact:** Terry Tyo, publisher/managing editor. "Purpose of competition is to publish great Canadian stories. Stories must have a uniquely Canadian element (theme, setting, history, institution, politics, social phenomenon, etc.)." Prize: Varies from year to year. Judged by short list determined by editors; judges choose from short list. Entry fee: $5 Canadian (make cheque or money order payable to TYO Communications). Deadline: sometime in mid-April every year. Entries must be unpublished. Canadian citizens or residents only. Guidelines available in February by SASE or on website. Length: 2,000-6,000 words. No simultaneous submissions or e-mail submissions. *Storyteller* cannot return mss unless accompanied by SASE. "Read the magazine. The short list comprises our summer issue, so all stories must be suitable for publication in *Storyteller* to qualify. Results announced in May. Winners notified by phone or e-mail. For contest results, send SASE or visit website.

GREAT LAKES COLLEGES ASSOCIATION NEW WRITERS AWARD

Great Lakes Colleges Association Inc., 535 W. William, Suite 301, Ann Arbor MI 48103. (734)761-4833. Fax: (734)761-3939. E-mail: shackelford@glca.org. **Contact:** Dr. Mark Andrew Clark. Award for first publication in fiction or poetry. Writer must be nominated by publisher. Prize: Winners are invited to tour the GLCA colleges. An honorarium of $300 will be guaranteed the author by each GLCA member college they visit. Judged by professors from member colleges. No entry fee. Deadline: February 28. Open to any writer. Submit 4 copies of the book to Dr. Mark Andrew Clark, Faculty of Writing, Literature & Education, Great Lakes Colleges Association, Director, New Writers Awards, The Philadelphia Center, North American Bldg., 121 S. Broad St., 7th Floor, Philadelphia PA 19107. Guidelines available after November 1. Accepts inquiries by fax and e-mail. Results announced in May. Letters go to publishers who have submitted.

Contests & Awards

THE GREENSBORO REVIEW LITERARY AWARD IN FICTION AND POETRY

The Greensboro Review, English Department, 134 McIver Bldg., P.O. Box 26170, Greensboro NC 27402-6170. (336)334-5459. E-mail: tlkenned@uncg.edu. Website: www.uncg.edu/eng/mfa. **Contact:** Terry Kennedy, assistant editor. Offered annually for fiction (7,500 word limit) and poetry recognizing the best work published in the Spring issue of *The Greensboro Review*. Sample issue for $5. Prize: $500 each for best short story and poem. Judged by editors of *The Greensboro Review*. No entry fee. Guidelines for SASE or on website. Deadline: September 15. Entries must be unpublished. Open to any writer. Winners notified by mail, phone or e-mail. List of winners published in Spring issue. "All manuscripts meeting literary award guidelines will be considered for cash award as well as for publication in the Spring issue of *The Greensboro Review*."

GSU REVIEW WRITING CONTEST

The GSU Review, Georgia State University, Campus Box 1894, MSC 8R0322, Unit 8, Atlanta GA 30303-3083. (404)651-4804. E-mail: martah@mindspring.com. Website: www2.gsu.edu/~wwwrev. **Contact:** Dan Marshall, editor. To promote quality work of emerging writers. Prize: Publication for finalists (up to 10 stories). $1,000 first prize; $250 second prize. Categories: fiction, poetry; receives more than 250 entries each. Judged by staff at *The Review* (finalists); 2004 winners picked by Cris Mazza (fiction) and C.K. Williams (poetry). Entry fee: $15, includes copy of Spring issue with contest results. Make checks payable to The GSU Review. Deadline: February 2. Entries must be unpublished. Length: should not exceed 7,500 words. Address fiction submissions to Jody Brooks, Fiction Editor. Mss must be typed or letter-quality printed. On the first page of the ms include name, address, phone, e-mail, word count. Limit each submission to one short story. Guidelines available in December by SASE, on website, by e-mail or by phone. Accepts inquiries by e-mail, phone. Contest open to all except faculty, staff, students of Georgia State University. Results announced March 25. Winners notified by phone. All entrants receive contest issue. "We look for engagement with language and characters we care about."

◎ HAMMETT PRIZE

Internatonal Association of Crime Writers/North American Branch, P.O. Box 8674, New York NY 10116-8674. Fax: (815)361-1477. E-mail: mfrisque@igc.org. Website: www.crimewritersna.org. **Contact:** Mary A. Frisque, executive director, North American Branch. Award established "to honor a work of literary excellence in the field of crime writing by a U.S. or Canadian author." Award for novels, story collections by one author and also nonfiction. Prize: trophy. Judged by committee. "Our reading committee seeks suggestions from publishers and they also ask the membership for recommendations. Eligible books are read by a committee of members of the organization. The committee chooses five nominated books, which are then sent to three outside judges for a final selection. Judges are outside the crime writing field." No entry fee. For guidelines, send SASE or e-mail. Accepts inquiries by e-mail. Deadline: December 1. Entries must be previously published. To be eligible "the book must have been published in the U.S. or Canada during the calendar year." The author must be a U.S. or Canadian citizen or permanent resident. Nominations announced in January, winners announced in Fall. Winners notified by mail, phone and recognized at awards ceremony in October. For contest results, send SASE or e-mail.

◪ DRUE HEINZ LITERATURE PRIZE

University of Pittsburgh Press, 13400 Forbes Ave., 5th Floor, Eureka Building, Pittsburgh PA 15260. (412)383-2492. Fax: (412)383-2466. E-mail: susief@pitt.edu. Website: www.pitt.edu/~press. **Contact:** Christine Pollock, assistant to the director. Award to "support the writer of short fiction at a time when the economics of commercial publishing make it more and more difficult for the serious literary artist working in the short story and novella to find publication." Prize: $15,000 and publication by the University of Pittsburgh Press. No entry fee. "It is imperative that entrants request complete rules of the competition by sending an SASE before submitting a manuscript." Deadline: Submissions received only during the months of May and June. Competition for story collections. No previously published collections. Manuscripts must be unpublished in book form. Length: 150-300 typed pages. The award is open to writers who have publshed a book-length collection of fiction or three short stories or novellas in commmercial magazines or literary journals of national distribution. Cover letter should include name, address, phone, e-mail, title, name of publications where work was originally published. This information should not appear on the ms. Results announced in February. Winners notified by phone. For contest results, send SASE with manuscript.

◖ LORIAN HEMINGWAY SHORT STORY COMPETITION

P.O. Box 993, Key West FL 33041-0993. (305)294-0320. E-mail: calico2419@aol.com. Website: www.shortstory competition.com. **Contact:** Carol Shaughnessy, co-director. Award to "encourage literary excellence and the efforts of writers who have not yet had major-market success." Competition for short stories. Prize: $1,000 (first prize), $500 (second prize), $500 (third prize), honorable mentions. Judged by a panel of writers, editors and literary scholars selected by author Lorian Hemingway. Entry fee: $10-15. Guidelines available in January for SASE, by e-mail or on website. Accepts inquiries by SASE, e-mail, or visit website. Deadline: May 1-15. Entries must be unpublished. Length: 3,000 words maximum. "Open to all writers whose work has not appeared in a nationally distributed publication with a circulation of 5,000 or more." Entry fee is $10 for each story postmarked by May 1, and $15 for stories postmarked between May 1 and May 15. "We look for excellence, pure and simple—no genre restrictions, no theme restrictions. We seek a writer's voice that cannot be ignored." Results announced at the end of July during Hemingway Days festival. Winners notified by phone prior to announcement. For contest results, send e-mail or visit website. "All entrants will receive a letter from Lorian Hemingway and a list of winners by October 1."

◯ ◎ HIGHLIGHTS FOR CHILDREN FICTION CONTEST

Highlights for Children, 803 Church St., Honesdale PA 18431-1824. (570)253-1080. Fax: (570)251-7847. E-mail: eds@highlights-corp.com. Website: www.highlights.com. **Contact:** Marileta Robinson, senior editor. Award "to honor quality stories (previously unpublished) for young readers and to encourage children's writers." Offered for stories for children ages 2-12; category varies each year. No crime or violence, please. Specify that ms is a contest entry. Prize: $1,000 to 3 winners, plus publication in *Highlights*. Categories: Short stories. Judged by *Highlights* editors, with input given by outside readers. No entry fee. "There is a different contest theme each year. We generally receive about 1,400 entries." Cover letter should include name, address, phone, e-mail, word count and title. "We prefer that these things appear on the first page of the manuscript as well." Deadline: January 1-February 28 (postmarked). Entries must be unpublished. Length: 500 words maximum for stories for beginning readers (to age 8) and 800 words for more advanced readers (ages 9-12). No minimum word count. Open to anyone 16 years of age or older. Results announced in June. Winners notified by mail or phone. For contest results, send SASE. See www.highlights.com for current theme and guidelines.

◯ ◎ L. RON HUBBARD'S WRITERS OF THE FUTURE CONTEST

Author Services Inc., P.O. Box 1630, Los Angeles CA 90078. (323)466-3310. Fax: (323)466-6474. E-mail: contests @authorservicesinc.com. Website: www.writersofthefuture.com. **Contact:** Ria Rutten, contest administrator. Established in 1983. Foremost competition for new and amateur writers of unpublished science fiction or fantasy short stories or novelettes. Offered "to find, reward and publicize new speculative fiction writers so they may more easily attain professional writing careers." Open to new and amateur writers who have not professionally published a novel or short novel, more than 1 novelette, or more than 3 short stories. Eligible entries are previously unpublished short stories or novelettes (under 17,000 words) of science fiction or fantasy. Guidelines for SASE or on website. Accepts inquiries by fax, e-mail, phone. Prize: awards quarterly: 1st place: $1,000; 2nd place: $750; and 3rd place: $500. Annual grand prize: $4,000. "Contest has four quarters. There shall be 3 cash prizes in each quarter. In addition, at the end of the year, the 4 first-place, quarterly winners will have their entries rejudged, and a grand prize winner shall be determined." Judged by K.D. Wentworth (initial judge), then by a panel of 4 professional authors. No entry fee. Deadline: December 31, March 31, June 30, September 30. Entries must be unpublished. Limit one entry per quarter. No entry fee and entrants retain all rights to their stories. Open to any writer. Manuscripts: white paper, black ink; double-spaced; typed; each page appropriately numbered with title, no author name. Include cover page with author's name, address, phone number, e-mail address (if available), as well as estimated word count and the title of the work. Results announced quarterly in e-newsletter. Winners notified by phone.

INDIANA REVIEW ½ K (SHORT-SHORT/PROSE-POEM) CONTEST

Indiana Review, BH 465/Indiana University, 1020 E. Kirkwood Ave., Bloomington IN 47405-7103. (812)855-3439. Fax: (812)855-4253. E-mail: inreview@indiana.edu. Website: www.indiana.edu/ ~ inreview. **Contact:** Grady Jaynes, editor. Competition for fiction and prose poems no longer than 500 words. Prize: $1,000 plus publication, contributor's copies and a year's subscription. All entries considered for publication. Judged by *Indiana Review* staff and outside judges. Entry fee: $15 fee for no more than 3 pieces (includes a year's subscription, two issues). Make checks payable to *Indiana Review*. Deadline: June 13. Entries must be unpublished. Guidelines available in March for SASE, by phone, e-mail, on website, or in publication. Length: 500 words, 3 mss per entry. Open to any writer. Cover letter should include name, address, phone, e-mail, word count and title. No identifying information on ms. "We look for command of language and form." Results announced in August. Winners notified by mail. For contest results, send SASE or visit website.

◯ INDIANA REVIEW FICTION CONTEST

Indiana Review, BH 465/Indiana University, 1020 E. Kirkwood Ave., Bloomington IN 47405-7103. (812)855-3439. Fax: (812)855-4253. E-mail: inreview@indiana.edu. Website: www.indiana.edu/ ~ inreview. **Contact:** Grady Jaynes, editor. Contest for fiction in any style and on any subject. Prize: $1,000, publication in the *Indiana Review* and contributor's copies. Judged by *Indiana Review* staff and outside judges. Entry fee: $15 fee

Contests & Awards

(includes a year's subscription). Deadline: October 17. Entries must be unpublished. Mss will not be returned. No previously published work, or works forthcoming elsewhere, are eligible. Simultaneous submissions accepted, but in the event of entrant withdrawal, contest fee will not be refunded. Length: 15,000 words (about 40 pages) maximum, double spaced. Open to any writer. Cover letter must include name, address, phone number and title of story. Entrant's name should appear only in the cover letter, as all entries will be considered anonymously. Results announced January. Winners notified by mail. For contest results, send SASE. "We look for a command of language and structure, as well as a facility with compelling and unusual subject matter. It's a good idea to obtain copies of issues featuring past winners to get a more concrete idea of what we are looking for."

⋈ INTERNATIONAL READING ASSOCIATION CHILDREN'S BOOK AWARDS

International Reading Association, P.O. Box 8139, 800 Barksdale Rd., Newark DE 19714-8139. (302)731-1600, ext. 221. E-mail: exec@reading.com. "This award is intended for newly published authors of children's books who show unusual promise in the children's book field." Offered annually for an author's first or second published book in fiction and nonfiction in 3 categories: primary (preschool-age 8), intermediate (ages 9-13), and young adult (ages 14-17). Guidelines and deadlines for SASE. Prize: 6 awards of $500 each, and a medal for each category. Categories: fiction and nonfiction. No entry fee. Entries in a language other than English must include a one-page abstract in English and a translation into English of one chapter or similar selection that in the submitter's estimation is representative of the book. Deadline: November 1. Entries must be previously published. Books from any country and in any language copyrighted during the 2005 calendar year will be considered. For guidelines with specific information write to Executive Office, International Reading Association, P.O. Box 8139, Newark DE 19714-8139.

⋈ The Iowa Short Fiction Award

Iowa Writers' Workshop, 102 Dey House, 507 N. Clinton St., Iowa City IA 52242-1000. (319)335-2000. Fax: (319)335-2055. Website: www.uiowapress.org. **Contact:** Holly Carver, director. Award "to give exposure to promising writers who have not yet published a book of prose." Prize: publication by University of Iowa Press. Judged by Senior Iowa Writers' Workshop members who screen manuscripts; published fiction author of note makes final selections. No entry fee. Deadline: Aug. 1-Sept. 30. Entries must be unpublished. "The manuscript must be a collection of short stories of at least 150 word-processed, double-spaced pages." Open to any writer. No application forms are necessary. Do not send original ms. Include SASE for return of ms. Announcement of winners made early in year following competition. Winners notified by phone.

▢ ◎ JOSEPH HENRY JACKSON AWARD

The San Francisco Foundation, Administered by Intersection for the Arts, 446 Valencia St., San Francisco CA 94103. (415)626-2787. Fax: (415)626-1636. Website: www.theintersection.org. **Contact:** Kevin B. Chen, program director. Award "to encourage young, unpublished writers." Offered annually for unpublished, work-in-progress fiction (novel or short story), nonfiction or poetry by an author age 20-35, with 3-year consecutive residency in northern California or Nevada prior to submission. Prize: $2,000 and certificate. Categories: short stories, novels and short story collections. No entry fee. Deadline: January 31. Entries must be unpublished. Work cannot exceed 50 double-spaced, typed pages. Entry form and rules available in mid-October for SASE. "Submit a serious, ambitious portion of a book-length manuscript." Results announced June 15. Winners notified by mail. Winners will be announced in letter mailed to all applicants.

▣ JAMES JONES FIRST NOVEL FELLOWSHIP

Wilkes University, English Department, Kirby Hall, Wilkes-Barre PA 18766. (570)408-4530. Fax: (570)408-7829. E-mail: english@wilkes.edu. Website: www.wilkes.edu/humanities/jones.asp. **Contact:** J. Michael Lennon, English department professor. Offered annually for unpublished novels, novellas and closely-linked short stories (all works in progress). "The award is intended to honor the spirit of unblinking honesty, determination and insight into modern culture exemplified by the late James Jones." The competition is open to all American writers who have not previously published novels. Prize: $10,000; $250 honorarium (runner-up). Categories: novel, novella, collected short stories. Entry fee: $20 fee. Make checks payable to Wilkes University. Deadline: March 1. Entries must be unpublished. Open to any previously unpublished writer. Guidelines available after June 1 by e-mail, for SASE and on website. Accepts inquiries by e-mail. Word length: 50 double-spaced pages and a two-page thematic outline. Title page should include name, address, phone and e-mail address if available. Results announced on or near September 30. For contest results see website, e-mail or send SASE marked 'winner's list.'

▣ ◎ EZRA JACK KEATS/KERLAN COLLECTION MEMORIAL FELLOWSHIP

Ezra Jack Keats Foundation, University of Minnesota, 113 Andersen Library, 222 21st Ave. S., Minneapolis MN 55455. (612)624-4576. Fax: (612)625-5525. E-mail: clrc@tc.umn.edu. Website: special.lib.umn.edu/clrc/.

Competition for books of children's literature. Purpose is "to award a talented writer and/or illustrator of children's books who wishes to use Kerlan Collection for the furtherance of his or her artistic development. Special consideration will be given to someone who would find it difficult to finance the visit to the Kerlan Collection." Open to any writer and illustrator. Prize: $1,500 for travel to study at Kerlan Collection. Judged by panel of non-Kerlan Collection staff, area professionals, educators, etc. No entry fee. Deadline: May 1. Accepts unpublished and previously published entries. Guidelines available after November for 55-cent SASE. Accepts inquiries by fax, phone and e-mail. Results announced mid-June. Winners notified by phone and letter. For contest results, visit website or send SASE.

THE KIRIYAMA PACIFIC RIM BOOK PRIZE
Kiriyama Pacific Rim Institute, 650 Delancey St., Suite 101, San Francisco CA 94107. (415)777-1628. Fax: (415)777-1646. Website: www.kiriyamaprize.org. Offered for work published during the previous year to promote books that will contribute to greater mutual understanding and increased cooperation throughout all areas of the Pacific Rim and South Asia. Guidelines and entry form on request or may be downloaded from the prize website. Books must be submitted for entry by the publisher. Proper entry forms must be submitted. Contact the administrators of the prize for complete rules and entry forms. Prize: $30,000 to be divided equally between the author of 1 fiction and of 1 nonfiction book. No entry fee. Deadline: March.

E.M. KOEPPEL SHORT FICTION AWARD
Writecorner Press, P.O. Box 140310, Gainesville FL 32614-0310. Website: www.writecorner.com. **Contact:** Mary Sue Koeppel, editor. Award for short stories. Prize: $1,100 first prize, and $100 for Editors' Choices. Judged by award-winning writers. Entry fee: $15 first story, $10 each additional story. Make checks payable to Writecorner Press. Send 2 title pages: One with title only and one with title, name, address, phone, e-mail, short bio. Place no other identification of the author on the ms that will be used in the judging. Guidelines available in January for SASE or on website. Accepts inquiries by e-mail and phone. Expects 300+ entries. Deadline: October 1- April 30. Entries must be unpublished. Open to any writer. Results announced in Summer. Winners notified by mail, phone in July (or earlier). For results, send SASE or check website. "Send well-crafted stories."

THE LAWRENCE FOUNDATION AWARD
Prairie Schooner, 201 Andrews Hall, P.O. Box 880334, Lincoln NE 68588-0334. (402)472-0911. Fax: (402)472-9771. E-mail: kgrey2@unl.edu. Website: www.unl.edu/schooner/psmain.htm. **Contact:** Hilda Raz, editor-in-chief. Offered annually for the best short story published in *Prairie Schooner* in the previous year. Prize: $1,000. Judged by editorial staff of *Praire Schooner*. No entry fee. Only work published in *Prairie Schooner* in the previous year is considered. Work is nominated by editorial staff. Results announced in the Spring issue. Winners notified by mail in February or March.

LAWRENCE FOUNDATION PRIZE
Michigan Quarterly Review, 3574 Rackham Building, Ann Arbor MI 48109-1070. (734)764-9265. E-mail: mqr@umich.edu. Website: www.umich.edu/~mqr. **Contact:** Vicki Lawrence, managing editor. Competition for short stories. Prize: $1,000. Judged by editorial board. No entry fee. Deadline: September. "An annual cash prize awarded to the author of the best short story published in *Michigan Quarterly Review* each year. Stories must be already published in *Michigan Quarterly Review*. This is not a competition in which manuscripts are read outside of the normal submission process." Guidelines available in December for SASE or on website. Accepts inquires by e-mail and phone. Results announced in December. Winners notified by phone or mail.

STEPHEN LEACOCK MEMORIAL MEDAL FOR HUMOUR
Stephen Leacock Association, Box 854, Orrillia ON L3V 6K8 Canada. (705)835-3218 or (705)835-3408. Fax: (705)835-5171 or (705)835-3689. E-mail: drapson@encode.com or moonwood@sympatico.ca. Website: www.leacock.com. **Contact:** Judith Rapson, award chair. Award for humorous Canadian writing, given in memory of Stephen B. Leacock, Canada's best-known writer of humorous fiction. Prize: silver medal and $10,000. Categories: novels, short story collections, drama, poetry, translations. Judged by five judges from across Canada, plus a local reading committee which has one vote. Entry fee: $75; make checks payable to Stephen Leacock Association. Entry must be a book published in the year prior to the presentation of the award and must be accompanied by a short biographical sketch and photograph of the author. Cover letter should include publisher's name, address, e-mail and name of contact person. Deadline: December 31. Authors must be Canadian citizens or landed immigrants; no more than two authors permitted for any given entry. Guidelines available in August for fax or on website. Book may be nominated by author or publisher. Books are judged primarily on humorous content but also on literary merit and general appeal. Results announced in April at luncheon in

Orillia; winner required to attend Award Dinner in Orillia in June and deliver address. Results available for SASE, by fax, e-mail or on website.

◎ LEAGUE OF UTAH WRITERS CONTEST

League of Utah Writers, P.O. Box 460562, Leeds UT 84746. (435)313-4459. Fax: (435)879-8190. E-mail: justwrite @numucom.com or reelsweetjustwrite@juno.com. Website: www.luwrite.com. **Contact:** Dorothy Crofts, membership chair. ''The LUW Contest has been held since 1935 to give Utah writers an opportunity to get their works read and critiqued. It also encourages writers to keep writing in an effort to get published.'' Competition for short stories and novels. Prize: $30/$20/$10 in children's book category; $50/$25/$15 full-length teen book category; $100/$50/$25 full-lentgh book category. Categories: 34 total categories. ''We do have separate categories for speculative fiction, children's and teens' besides our full-length book category on any subject.'' Judged by professional judges who are paid for their services. Entry fee: $3-6, short story; $5-20 full-length book. Guidelines available after February for SASE or on website. Accepts inquiries by fax, e-mail and phone. Deadline: June 15. Entries must be unpublished. Open to any writer. ''Read the contest rules and guidelines. Don't skim over them. Rules change and are revised from year to year. Don't forget to enclose your entry fee when mailing your entries.'' Winners announced at the Annual Writers Round-Up in September. List of winners available at Round-Up or for SASE.

LITERAL LATTÉ FICTION AWARD

Literal Latté, 200 East 10th Street Suite 240, New York NY 10003. (212)260-5532. E-mail: litlatte@aol.com. Website: www.literal-latte.com. **Contact:** Edward Estlin, contributing editor. Award ''to provide talented writers with three essential tools for continued success: money, publication and recognition.'' Offered annually for unpublished fiction. Guidelines for SASE or on website. Open to any writer. Prize: $1,000 and publication in *Literal Latté* (first prize), $300 (second prize), $200 (third prize), up to 7 honorable mentions. Judged by the editors. Entry fee: $10/story. Guidelines available for SASE, by e-mail or on website. Accepts inquiries by e-mail. Deadline: January 15. Entries must be unpublished. Length: 6,000 words maximum. Guidelines available for SASE, by e-mail or on website. Accepts inquiries by e-mail or on website. ''The first prize story in the first annual *Literal Latté* Fiction Awards has been honored with a Pushcart Prize.'' Winners notified by phone. List of winners available in late April for SASE or by e-mail.

◖ ▦ LONG FICTION CONTEST INTERNATIONAL

(formerly Long Fiction Contest), White Eagle Coffee Store Press, P.O. Box 383, Fox River Grove IL 60021. (847)639-9200. E-mail: wecspress@aol.com. Website: http://members.aol.com/wecspress. **Contact:** Frank E. Smith, publisher. Offered annually since 1993 for unpublished work to recognize and promote long short stories of 8,000-14,000 words (about 30-50 pages). Sample of previous winner: $5.95, including postage. Open to any writer, no restrictions on materials. Prize: (A.E. Coppard Prize) $500 and publication, plus 25 copies of chapbook; 40 additional copies sent to agents; and 10 press kits. Categories: No limits on style or subject matter. Entry fee: $15 fee, $10 for second story in same envelope. Guidelines available in April by SASE, e-mail or on website. Accepts inquiries by e-mail. Length: 8,000-14,000 words (30-50 pages double-spaced) single story; may have multiparts or be a self-contained novel segment. Deadline: December 15. Accepts previously unpublished submissions, but previous publication of small parts with acknowledgment is okay. Simultaneous submissions okay. Send cover with name, address, phone; second title page with title only. Submissions are not returned; they are recycled. ''SASE for most current information.'' Results announced in late Spring. Winners notified by phone. For contest results, send SASE or visit website in late Spring. ''Write with richness and depth.''

◎ THE HUGH J. LUKE AWARD

Prairie Schooner, 201 Andrews Hall, P.O. Box 880334, Lincoln NE 68588-0334. (402)472-0911. Fax: (402)472-9771. E-mail: kgrey2@unl.edu. Website: prairieschooner.unl.edu/. **Contact:** Hilda Raz, editor-in-chief. Offered annually for work published in *Prairie Schooner* in the previous year. Prize: $250. Judged by editorial staff of *Prairie Schooner*. No entry fee. Only work published in *Prairie Schooner* in the previous year is considered. Work is nominated by the editorial staff. Guidelines for SASE or on website. Results announced in the Spring issue. Winners notified by mail in February or March.

◎ ▦ THE MAN BOOKER PRIZE

The Man Group, Middlesex House, 34-42 Cleveland Street, London W1T 4JE England. 020 7631 2666. Fax: 020 7631 2699. Website: www.themanbookerprize.com. ''The Booker Prize for Fiction was set up in 1968 as a result of discussions between Booker plc and the Publishers Association about the need for a signifiant literary award in Britain, along the lines of the Prix Goncourt and similar awards in France. In 2002 the sponsorship of the Prize was awarded to The Man Group, and the prize is now known as The Man Booker Prize.'' Books are only accepted through UK publishers. However, publication outside the UK does not disqualify a book once it is published in the UK. Open to any full-length novel written by a citizen of the Commonwealth or the Republic of Ireland. No novellas, collections of short stories, translations, or self-published books. Prize: The winner receives £50,000, and the short-listed authors receive £2,500. Judged by Ireland's finest critics, writers and academics. No entry fee. Deadline: July Open to citizens of the Commonwealth or Republic of Ireland.

◎ ⊕ MARSH AWARD FOR CHILDREN'S LITERATURE IN TRANSLATION

Marsh Christian Trust, Roehampton University, Froebel College, Roehampton Lane, London SW15 5PJ England. E-mail: G.Lathey@roehampton.ac.uk. **Contact:** Dr. Gillian Lathey. Award "to promote the publication of translated children's books in the UK." Biennial award for children's book translations. Judged by Patricia Crampton, Anthea Bell, Wendy Cooling, Elizabeth Hammill. No entry fee. Entries must be previously published. Entries should be translations into English first published in the UK. Entries must be nominated by publishers. Open to any writer. Guidelines available for SASE. Cover letter should include name, address, phone, e-mail and title. Accepts inquiries by e-mail. Results announced in January. Winners notified by mail and at presentation event.

◻ ◎ WALTER RUMSEY MARVIN GRANT

Ohioana Library Association, 274 E. First Ave., Suite 300, Columbus OH 43201. (614)466-3831. Fax: (614)728-6974. E-mail: ohioana@sloma.state.oh.us. Website: www.ohioana.org. **Contact:** Linda Hengst. Award "to encourage young, unpublished writers 30 years of age or younger." Competition for short stories. Prize: $1,000. No entry fee. Up to 6 pieces of prose may be submitted; maximum 60 pages, minimum 10 pages double-spaced, 12-point type. Deadline: January 31. Entries must be unpublished. Open to unpublished authors born in Ohio or who have lived in Ohio for a minimum of five years. Must be 30 years of age or younger. Guidelines for SASE. Winner notified in May or June. Award given in October.

◻ MASTERS LITERARY AWARDS

Titan Press, P.O. Box 17897, Encino CA 91416-7897. Website: www.titanpress.info. Offered annually and quarterly for work published within 2 years (preferred) and unpublished work (accepted). Fiction, 15-page maximum; poetry, 5 pages or 150-lines maximum; and nonfiction, 10 pages maximum. "A selection of winning entries may appear in our national literary publication." Winners may also appear on the Internet. Titan Press retains one-time publishing rights to selected winners. Prize: $1,000, and possible publication in the *Titan Press Internet* journal. Judged by 3 literary professionals. Entry fee: $15. Deadline: Ongoing (nominations made March 15, June 15, September 15, December 15). Any submission received prior to an award date is eligible for the subsequent award. Submissions accepted throughout the year. All entries must be in the English language. Guidelines for #10 SASE. "Be persistent, be consistent, be professional."

◻ ◎ THE JOHN H. McGINNIS MEMORIAL AWARD

Southwest Review, P.O. Box 750374, Dallas TX 75275-0374. (214)768-1037. Fax: (214)768-1408. E-mail: swr@mail.smu.edu. Website: www.southwestreview.org. **Contact:** Jennifer Cranfill, managing editor. Award for short fiction and nonfiction. Prize: $500. Judged by *Southwest Review*'s editor in chief and managing editor. No entry fee. Stories or essays must have been published in the *Southwest Review* prior to the announcement of the award. Pieces are not submitted directly for the award but for publication in the magazine. Open to any writer. Guidelines available for SASE and on website. Results announced in first issue of the year. Winners notified in January by mail, phone and e-mail.

◎ MICHIGAN LITERARY FICTION AWARDS

University of Michigan Press, 839 Greene St., Ann Arbor MI 48104. Fax: (734)615-1540. E-mail: ump.fiction@umich.edu. Website: www.press.umich.edu/fiction/index.html. Award to "provide an outlet for writers whose previous works have not yet met with great commercial success." Prize: $1,000 and publication. Categories: novels and short story collections. No entry fee. Guidelines for SASE or on website. Accepts inquiries by e-mail. Deadline: July 1. Entries must be unpublished. Contest open to writers who have previously published at least one book-length work of literary fiction. Cover letter should include name, address, phone, e-mail and title; title only on every page of ms. Results announced in November. Winners notified by mail. For contest results, send SASE or visit website.

◪ MID-LIST PRESS FIRST SERIES AWARD FOR SHORT FICTION

Mid-List Press, 4324 12th Ave. S., Minneapolis MN 55407-3218. (612)822-3733. E-mail: cihlar@midlist.org. Website: www.midlist.org. **Contact:** James Cihlar, executive director. Open to any writer who has never published a book-length collection of short fiction (short stories, novellas); minimum 50,000 words. Accepts simultaneous submissions. Guidelines and entry form for SASE or on website. Prize: $1,000 advance and publication. Judged by manuscript readers and the editors of Mid-List Press. Entry fee: $30 (US dollars). Guidelines available in February for SASE or on website. Deadline: July 1. Submissions may be previously published or unpublished. Length: 50,000 words minimum. Open to any writer who has never published a collection of fiction. Results announced in January. Winners notified by phone and mail in January. Winners' list published in *Poets & Writers* and *AWP Chronicle*; also available for SASE, by e-mail or phone.

MID-LIST PRESS FIRST SERIES AWARD FOR THE NOVEL

Mid-List Press, 4324-12th Ave. S., Minneapolis MN 55407-3218. (612)822-3733. Fax: (612)823-8387. E-mail: chilar@midlist.org. Website: www.midlist.org. **Contact:** James Chilar, executive director. Offered annually for unpublished novels to locate and publish quality mss by first-time writers, particularly those mid-list titles that major publishers may be rejecting. Guidelines for SASE or on website. Open to any writer who has never published a novel. Prize: $1,000 advance against royalties, plus publication. Judged by manuscript readers and the editors of Mid-List Press. Entry fee: $30 (US dollars). Length: minimum 50,000 words. Deadline: February 1. Guidelines available in July for SASE or on website. Results announced in July. Winners notified by phone and mail. Winners' list published in *Poets & Writers* and *AWP Chronicle*; also available for SASE, e-mail, or on website.

N ◯ ◎ A MIDSUMMER TALE

Toasted Cheese, E-mail: editors@toasted-cheese.com. Website: www.toasted-cheese.com. **Contact:** Stephanie Lenz, Editor. A Midsummer Tale is a summer-themed creative nonfiction contest. Topic changes each year. Check website for current focus and word limit. "We usually receive around 15 entries." Prize: First prize: $20 Amazon gift certificate, publication; Second prize: $15 Amazon gift certificate, publication; Third prize: $10 Amazon gift certificate, publication. Some feedback is often given to entrants. Categories: creative nonfiction. Judged by two Toasted Cheese editors who blind-judge each contest. Each judge has her own criteria for selecting winners. No entry fee. Guidelines, including the e-mail address to which you should send your entry and instructions for what to include and how to format, are available in May on website. Accepts inquiries by e-mail. Deadline: June 21. Entries must be unpublished. Open to any writer. Results announced July 31 on website. Winners notified by e-mail.

◎ MILLION WRITERS AWARD

StorySouth, 898 Chelsea Ave., Columbus OH 43209. (614)545-0754. E-mail: storysouth@yahoo.com. Website: www.storysouth.com. **Contact:** Jason Sanford, editor. Contest "to honor and promote the best fiction published annually in online journals and magazines. The reason for the Million Writers Award is that most of the major literary prizes for short fiction (such as the O. Henry Awards) ignore Web-published fiction. This award aims to show that world-class fiction is being published online and to promote this fiction to the larger reading and literary community." Prize: publicity for the author and story. Categories: short stories. Judged by *StorySouth* judges. No entry fee. Cover letter should include e-mail address, word count, title and publication where story was previously published. Guidelines available in December on website. Deadline: January. Entries must be previously published. All stories must be 1,000 words or longer. Open to any writer. Results announced in March on website. Winners notified by e-mail.

THE MILTON CENTER POSTGRADUATE FELLOWSHIP

The Milton Center at *Image*, 3307 Third Ave. West, Seattle WA 98119. (206)281-2988. E-mail: miltoncenter@imagejournal.org. Website: www.imagejournal.org/milton. **Contact:** Gregory Wolfe, director. Award "to bring emerging writers of Christian commitment to the Center, where their primary goal is to complete their first book-length manuscript in fiction, poetry or creative nonfiction." No entry fee. Guidelines on website. Deadline: March 15. Open to any writer.

MISSISSIPPI REVIEW PRIZE

Mississippi Review, 118 College Dr., #5144, Hattiesburg MS 39406. (601)266-4321. Fax: (601)266-5757. E-mail: reif@mississippireview.com. Website: www.mississippireview.com. **Contact:** Rie Fortenberry, managing editor. Award "to reward excellence in new fiction and poetry and to find new writers who are just beginning their careers." Offered annually for unpublished fiction and poetry. Guidelines available online. Accepts inquiries by e-mail or phone. Prize: $1,000 plus publication for fiction and poetry winners; publication for all runners up. Entry fee: $15. Deadline: October 1. Entries must be unpublished. Length: 50,000 words or less. Cover letter should include author's name, address, phone, e-mail, word count and title of story. No mss returned. Winners notified in January. For contest results, send SASE or visit website.

THE MISSOURI REVIEW EDITORS' PRIZE CONTEST

Missouri Review, 1507 Hillcrest Hall, Columbia MO 65211. (573)882-4474. Fax: (573)884-4671. Website: www.missourireview.org. **Contact:** Richard Sowienski, managing editor. Prize: $2,000 for fiction and poetry; $2,000 for essay; and publication in *The Missouri Review*. Judged by *The Missouri Review* editors. Entry fee: $15; make checks payable to *Missouri Review*. Each fee entitles entrant to a one-year subscription to the journal, an extension of a current subscription, or a gift subscription. Guidelines and inquiries accepted on website. Expects to receive 1,800 entries. Deadline: October 15. Entries must be unpublished. Page length restrictions: 25 typed, double-spaced for fiction and essays; 10 for poetry. Open to any writer. Guidelines available in June for SASE. Outside of envelope should be marked "fiction" or "essay" or "poetry." Enclose an index card with the author's name, address and telephone number in the upper left corner and, for fiction and essay entries only, the work's title in the center. Results announced in January. Winners notified by phone and mail. For contest results, send SASE. "Send only fully realized work with a distinctive voice, style and subject."

◎ ⊕ BRIAN MOORE SHORT STORY AWARDS

Creative Writers Network, 109-113 Royal Ave., Belfast 6T1 1FF Ireland. E-mail: info@creativewritersnetwork.org. Website: www.creativewritersnetwork.org. **Contact:** Administrator. Award to promote the short story form. Prize: $500. Judged by established Irish fiction writer. No entry fee. Deadline: January. Entries must be unpublished. Open to writers born in Northern Ireland. Guidelines available in August/September by e-mail, on website. Accepts inquiries by e-mail. Results announced in April/May. Winners notified by mail in March. List of winners available on website.

ℕ ⬍ ◎ MUNICIPAL CHAPTER OF TORONTO IODE BOOK AWARD

Municipal Chapter of Toronto IODE (Imperial Order of the Daughters of the Empire), 40 St. Clair Ave., Suite 205, Toronto ON M4T 1M9 Canada. (416)925-5078. Fax: (416)925-5127. **Contact:** Mary K. Anderson, education officer. To acknowledge authors and/or illustrators in the Greater Toronto Area. Prize: $1,000 to author and/or illustrator. Categories: short stories, novels, story collections. Judged by committee comprised of IODE education officer, president and other officers (approx. 5). No entry fee. Guidelines available by fax. Accepts inquiries by fax, phone. Cover letter should include name, address, phone, e-mail, title, place of original publication. Deadline: Nov. 1. Entries must be previously published. Open to books geared toward 6-12 year olds. Must be Canadian citizens. Authors/illustrators may submit their own work. "Submit books directly to the attention of Theo Heras at the Lillian Smith Library, Toronto. She compiles submissions and short lists them." Results announced in January and available by fax. Award given at annual dinner meeting in March. Winners notified by mail in December.

◎ NATIONAL READERS' CHOICE AWARDS

Oklahoma Romance Writers of America, E-mail: NRCAcontest@hotmail.com. Website: www.okrwa.com. **Contact:** Donnell Epperson, coordinator. Contest "to provide writers of romance fiction with a competition where their published novels are judged by readers." Prize: "There is no monetary award; just an awards banquet hosted at the Annual National Romance Writers Convention." Categories: The 12 categories include traditional series (50-60,000 words); short contemporary series (fewer than 70,000 words); long contemporary series (more than 70,000 words); single title contemporary (novel or novella of at least 25,000 words); historical (25,000+ words); Regency (25,000+ words); romantic suspense (25,000+ words); inspirational (25,000+ words); young adult (25,000+ words); paranormal (25,000+ words); romantica (erotic novel or novella of 25,000+ words); mainstream with romantic elements (25,000+ words). Entry fee: $25; make checks payable to NRCA. See website for entry address and contact information. All entries must have an original copyright date the current contest year. (See website for details.) Entries will be accepted from authors, editors, publishers, agents, readers, whoever wants to fill out the entry form, pay the fee and supply the books. Deadline: Fee deadline: November; book deadline: January. (See website for exact dates.) No limit to the number of entries, but each title may be entered only in one category. Open to any writer. For guidelines, send SASE, e-mail or visit website. Entry form required—available on website. Deadline for entry forms is November 20 (send to above address). Five copies of each entry must be mailed to the category coordinator; contact information for coordinator will be provided by December 1. Results announced in July. Winners notified by phone, if not at the awards ceremony, in July. List of winners will be mailed; also available by e-mail.

◻ NATIONAL WRITERS ASSOCIATION NOVEL WRITING CONTEST

The National Writers Association, 10940 S. Parker Rd #508, Parker CO 80134. (303)841-0246. Fax: (303)841-2607. E-mail: contests@nationalwriters.com. Website: www.nationalwriters.com. **Contact:** Sandy Whelchel, director. Annual contest "to help develop creative skills, to recognize and reward outstanding ability, and to increase the opportunity for the marketing and subsequent publication of novel manuscripts." Prize: 1st place: $500; 2nd place: $300; 3rd place: $200. Judges' evaluation sheets sent to each entry with SASE. Categories: Open to any genre or category. Judged by editors and agents. Entry fee: $35. Deadline: April 1. Entries must be unpublished. Length: 20,000-100,000 words. Open to any writer. Entry form and information available on Benefits section of website.

☐ ◎ NATIONAL WRITERS ASSOCIATION SHORT STORY CONTEST

The National Writers Association, 10940 S. Parker Rd. #508, Parker CO 80134. (303)841-0246. Fax: (303)841-2607. E-mail: contests@nationalwriters.com. Website: www.nationalwriters.com. **Contact:** Sandy Whelchel, director. Annual contest "to encourage writers in this creative form and to recognize those who excel in fiction writing." Prize: 1st place: $200; 2nd place: $100; 3rd place: $50. Entry fee: $15. Deadline: postmarked by July 1. Entries must be unpublished. Length: 5,000 words maximum. Entry form and information available in January on Benefits section of website. Accepts inquiries by fax, phone and e-mail. Evaluation sheets sent to each entrant if SASE is provided. Results announced at the NWAF Summer Conference in June. Winners notified by phone or e-mail. List of winners available in *Authorship* or on website.

☐ ◎ NEVADA ARTS COUNCIL ARTIST FELLOWSHIPS

716 N. Carson St., Suite A, Carson City NV 89701. (702)687-6680. Fax: (775)687-6688. Website: www.nevadaartscouncil.org. **Contact:** Fran Morrow, artist service coordinator. Award "to honor Nevada individual artists and their artistic achievements and to support artists' efforts in advancing their careers." Prize: $5,000 ($4,500 immediately and $500 after public service event completed). Categories: fiction, nonfiction, poetry, playwriting and writing for children. Judged by peer panels of professional artists. No entry fee. Deadline: April. Open to Nevada residents only. Guidelines available by phone, e-mail or on website. Results announced in June. Winners notified by mail and phone. Entrants receive list of recipients. "Inquire about jackpot grants for Nevada residents' projects, up to $1,000."

☑ NEW ENGLAND WRITERS SHORT FICTION CONTEST

New England Writers, P.O. Box 5, Windsor VT 05089-0005. (802)674-2315. E-mail: newvtpoet@aol.com. Website: www.newenglandwriters.org. **Contact:** Frank or Susan Anthony, co-directors. Annual competition for short stories for publication in *The Anthology of New England Writers*. Prize: $300 Marjory Bartlett Sanger Award; five honorable mentions of $30 each. Final judges are published writers and usually creative writing professors. Entry fee: $5/story (unlimited entries allowed). Send disposable mss. Length: 1,000 word limit. Deadline: postmarked by June 15. Entries must be unpublished. Open to any writer. Guidelines available for SASE or on website by November. Please send a 3×5 card with name, address and title(s) of fiction pieces with entry. Accepts inquiries by e-mail, phone. Results announced at annual New England Writers Conference in July. Winners notified right after conference. For contest results, visit website. "Strive for originality taken from your own life experience. We look for creative, concise work with an unexpected ending."

☐ NEW LETTERS LITERARY AWARDS

New Letters, 5101 Rockhill Rd., Kansas City MO 64110-2499. (816)235-1168. Fax: (816)235-2611. **Contact:** newletters@umkc.edu. Award to "find and reward good writing from writers who need the recognition and support." Award has 3 categories (fiction, poetry and creative nonfiction) with 1 winner in each. Offered annually for previously unpublished work. Prize: 1st place: $1,000, plus publication; all entries are considered for publication. Judged by 2 rounds of regional writers (preliminary judging). Winners picked by an anonymous judge of national repute. Entry fee: $15/entry (includes year's subscription). Make checks payable to *New Letters* or send credit card information. Deadline: May 18. Entries must be unpublished. Open to any writer. Guidelines available in January for SASE, e-mail, on website and in publication. Cover letter should include name, address, phone, e-mail and title. Results announced in September. Winners notified by phone. For contest results, send SASE, e-mail or visit website.

NEW MILLENNIUM WRITING AWARDS

New Millennium Writings, Room M2, P.O. Box 2463, Knoxville TN 37901. (423)428-0389. Fax: (865)428-2302. E-mail: DonWilliams7@charter.net. Website: www.newmillenniumwritings.com/awards.html. **Contact:** Don Williams, editor. Award "to promote literary excellence in contemporary fiction." Offered twice annually for unpublished fiction, poetry, essays or nonfiction prose to encourage new fiction writers, poets and essaysists and bring them to attention of publishing industry. Entrants receive an issue of *NMW* in which winners appear. Prize: fiction: $1,000; poetry: $1,000; nonfiction: $1,000; winners published in *NMW* and on website. Judged by novelists and short story writers. Entry fee: $17 for each submission. Deadline: November 17 and June 17. Entries must be unpublished. Biannual competition. Length: 1,000-6,000 words. Guidelines available year round for SASE and on website. "Provide a bold, yet organic opening line, sustain the voice and mood throughout, tell an entertaining and vital story with a strong ending. *New Millennium Writings* is a forward-looking periodical for writers and lovers of good reading. It is filled with outstanding poetry, fiction, essays and other speculations on subjects both topical and timeless about life in our astonishing times. Our pages brim with prize-winning essays, humor, full-page illustration, writing advice and poetry from writers at all stages of their careers. First-timers find their work displayed alongside such well-known writers as John Updike, Sharyn McCrumb, Lee Smith, Norman Mailer, Madison Smartt Bell and Cormac McCarthy." Results announced October and April.

Winners notified by mail and phone. All entrants will receive a list of winners, plus a copy of the annual anthology. Send letter-sized SASE with entry for list.

NEW YORK STORIES FICTION PRIZE

New York Stories, English Department, E-103, LaGuardia Community College/CUNY, 31-10 Thomson Ave., Long Island City NY 11101. E-mail: nystories@lagcc.cuny.edu. Website: www.newyorkstories.org. **Contact:** Daniel Caplice Lynch, editor-in-chief. Offered annually for unpublished work to showcase new, quality short fiction. Stories must not exceed 6,000 words. Prize: 1st place: $500 and publication; 2nd place: $250 and consideration for publication. Judged by the editor. Entry fee: $15. Each submission should be accompanied by a separate, non-refundable check for $15, payable to *New York Stories*. Mss are not returned. Please write "New York Stories Fiction Prize" on the outer envelope and the title page. Deadline: September 15. Entries must be unpublished. Open to any writer. Guidelines on website and in publication. Accepts inquires by e-mail. Cover letter should include name, address, phone, e-mail, word count and title. "Also include this information on the manuscript." Winners notified by phone or e-mail. For contest results, send SASE or visit website.

JOHN NEWBERY AWARD

American Library Association (ALA), Association for Library Service to Children, 50 E. Huron St., Chicago IL 60611. (312)280-2163. Fax: (312)944-7671. E-mail: alsc@ala.org. Website: www.ala.org/alsc. **Contact:** ALSC, Attn: Newbery Medal. Prize: Medal. Judged by Newbery Award Selection Committee. No entry fee. Deadline: December 31. Entries must be previously published. Only books for children published in the US during the preceeding year are eligible. Entry restricted to US citizens, residents. Guidelines available on website, by fax, phone or e-mail. Accepts inquiries by fax and e-mail. Results announced at the ALA Midwinter Meeting. Winners notified by phone. For contest results, visit website in February or contact via phone, fax, e-mail or SASE.

THE NOMA AWARD FOR PUBLISHING IN AFRICA

P.O. Box 128, Witney, Oxon 0X8 5XU United Kingdom. E-mail: maryljay@aol.com. Website: www.nomaaward.org. **Contact:** Mary Jay. Sponsored by Kodansha Ltd. Award "to encourage publication of works by African writers and scholars in Africa, instead of abroad as is still too often the case at present." Categories: scholarly or academic; books for children; literature and creative writing, including fiction, drama and poetry. Judged by a committee of African scholars and book experts and representatives of the international book community. Chairman: Walter Bgoya. No entry fee. Deadline: February 28. Entries must be previously published. Guidelines and entry forms available in December by fax, e-mail or on website. Submissions are through publishers only. "Publisher must complete entry form and supply six copies of the published work." Maximum number of entries per author is three. Results announced in October. Winners notified through publisher. List of winners available from Secretariat or on website. "The award is for an outstanding book. Content is the overriding criterion, but standards of publication are also taken into account."

NORTH CAROLINA ARTS COUNCIL WRITERS' RESIDENCIES

221 E. Lane St., Raleigh NC 27699-4632. (919)715-1519. Fax: (919)733-4834. E-mail: debbie.mcgill@ncmail.net. Website: www.ncarts.org. **Contact:** Deborah McGill, literature director. Award "to encourage and recognize North Carolina's finest creative writers. Every year we offer a two-month residency for one writer at Headlands Center for the Arts (California) and a one-month residency for 1 writer at Vermont Studio Center. Judged by panels of writers and editors convened by the residency centers. No entry fee. Deadline: early June. Writers must be over 18 years old, not currently enrolled in a degree-granting program on undergraduate or graduate level, and must have been a resident of North Carolina for 1 full year as of application deadline. Please see website for other eligibility requirements. Guidelines available after March 1 by phone or online. Accepts inquiries by fax and e-mail. Results announced in the Fall. Winners notified by phone. Other applicants notified by mail.

NOVEL MANUSCRIPT CONTEST

Writers' League of Texas, 1501 W. 5th St., #E-2, Austin TX 78703. (512)499-8914. Fax: (512)499-0441. E-mail: wlt@writersleague.org. Website: www.writersleague.org. **Contact:** Terri Schexnayder. Prize: First place winners meet individually with an agent at the Writers' League of Texas Agents Conference in June. Categories: mainstream fiction, mystery/thriller/action adventure, romance, science fiction/fantasy/horror, historical/western and children's long and short works. Judged by preliminary judges (first round), then published authors (advancing entries); agent or editor reads finalists' ms. Entry fee: $50 for score sheet with comments. Send credit card information or make check payable to Writer's League of Texas. Cover letter should include name, address, phone, e-mail, title. Entries must be unpublished. Submit first 10 pages of novel, double-spaced. Open to any writer. Guidelines available in January for SASE, by e-mail or on website. Accepts inquiries by e-mail. Results announced at the June conference. Winners notified after conference. Results available on website.

Contests & Awards

⬤ ◎ THE FLANNERY O'CONNOR AWARD FOR SHORT FICTION

The University of Georgia Press, 330 Research Dr., Athens GA 30602-4901. Website: www.ugapress.uga.edu. **Contact:** Andrew Berzanskis, coordinator. Does not return mss. Manuscripts must be 200-275 pages long. Authors do not have to be previously published. Prize: $1,000, and publication under standard book contract; selects two prize winners a year. Categories: Wants collections of short stories. Stories that have previously appeared in magazines or in anthologies may be included. Collections that include long stories or novellas (50-150 pages) are acceptable. However, novels or single novellas will not be considered. Stories previously published in a book-length collection of the author's own work may not be included. Entry fee: $20; checks payable to University of Georgia Press. Complete submission guidelines online. Deadline: Submission Period: April 1-May 31. Open to all writers in English. "Manuscripts under consideration for this competition may be submitted elsewhere at the same time. Please notify us immediately, however, if your manuscript is accepted by another publisher while it is under review with our press. Authors may submit more than one manuscript to the competition as long as each submission is accompanied by a $20 entry fee, meets all eligibility requirements, and does not duplicate material sent to us in another manuscript." Winners are usually notified before the end of November. Entrants who have enclosed an SASE will receive a letter announcing the winners.

⬜ ◎ FRANK O'CONNOR FICTION AWARD

descant, Texas Christian University, TCU Box 297270, Fort Worth TX 76129. (817)257-6537. Fax: (817)257-6239. E-mail: descant@tcu.edu. Website: www.eng.tcu.edu/journals/descant/index.htm. **Contact:** David Kuhne, editor. Annual award to honor the best published fiction in *descant* for its current volume. Prize: $500. No entry fee. Guidelines available for SASE or on website. Deadline: April 1. Entries must be previously published. Results announced in August. Winners notified by phone in July. For contest results, send SASE. Also offers the Gary Wilson Award for short fiction. Prize: $250. Send SASE for guidelines.

THE OHIO STATE UNIVERSITY PRIZE IN SHORT FICTION

The Ohio State University Press and the MFA Program in Creative Writing at The Ohio State University, 1070 Carmack Rd., Columbus OH 43210-1002. (614)292-1462. Fax: (614)292-2065. Website: ohiostatepress.org. Offered annually to published and unpublished writers. Submissions may include short stories, novellas or a combination of both. Manuscripts must be 150-300 typed pages; novellas must not exceed 125 pages. No employee or student of The Ohio State University is eligible. Prize: $1,500, publication under a standard book contract. Entry fee: $20. Deadline: Must be postmarked during the month of November.

◎ (ALICE WOOD MEMORIAL) OHIOANA AWARD FOR CHILDREN'S LITERATURE

Ohioana Library Association, 274 E. First Ave., Suite 300, Columbus OH 43201. (614)466-3831. Fax: (614)728-6974. E-mail: ohioana@sloma.state.oh.us. Website: www.ohioana.org. **Contact:** Linda Hengst, executive director. Offered to an author whose body of work has made, and continues to make, a significant contribution to literature for children or young adults and through their work as a writer, teacher, or administrator, or through their community service, interest in children's literature has been encouraged and children have become involved with reading. Nomination forms for SASE. Recipient must have been born in Ohio or lived in Ohio at least 5 years. Prize: $1,000. No entry fee. Deadline: December 31. Open to any writer. Guidelines for SASE. Accepts inquiries by fax and e-mail. Results announced in August or September. Winners notified by letter in May. For contest results, call or e-mail.

⬤ ◎ OHIOANA BOOK AWARDS

Ohioana Library Association, 274 E. 1st Ave., Suite 300, Columbus OH 43201-3673. (614)466-3831. Fax: (614)728-6974. E-mail: ohioana@sloma.state.oh.us. Website: www.ohioana.org. **Contact:** Linda Hengst, executive director. Offered annually to bring national attention to Ohio authors and their books, published in the last 2 years. (Books can only be considered once.) Categories: Fiction, nonfiction, juvenile, poetry, and books about Ohio or an Ohioan. Books about Ohio or an Ohioan need not be written by an Ohioan. Writers must have been born in Ohio or lived in Ohio for at least 5 years. Prize: certificate and glass sculpture. Judged by a jury selected by librarians, book reviewers, writers and other knowledgeable people. Each Spring the jury considers all books received since the previous jury. No entry fee. Deadline: December 31. Two copies of the book must be received by the Ohioana Library by December 31 prior to the year the award is given; literary quality of the book must be outstanding. No entry forms are needed, but they are available July 1 of each year. "We will be glad to answer letters asking specific questions." Results announced in August or September. Winners notified by mail in May.

Ⓝ ⬜ OPEN WINDOWS

Ghost Road Press, 10200 E. Girard Ave., Bldg. C, Suite 145, Denver CO 80231. (303)842-5161. Fax: (303)671-5664. E-mail: info@ghostroadpress.com. Website: www.ghostroadpress.com. **Contact:** Matthew Davis, president. To showcase new voices in poetry, fiction and nonfiction. Prize: 1st place: $200; 2nd place: $150; 3rd place: $50. Categories: short stories. Contest is open to all genres, including fiction, poetry and essays. Judged by published writers, journalists and creative writing professors from local colleges. All entries will be judged on literary merit and/or well-argued themes. Entry fee: $10 per short story or essay and $10 for up three poems. Send credit card information, make checks payable to Ghost Road Press, or pay by Pay Pal on our website. Your cover letter should include your name, address, phone number, e-mail address, word count, title. Only your name should appear on the ms. Please read and follow submission guidelines on website. Ms should be clean and error free. Accepts inquiries by fax, e-mail, phone. Deadline: February 1. Entries must be unpublished. Word length: 3,000-5,500 for short stories; no flash fiction, please. Open to any writer. Contest results announced March 15 on website. Winners notified by mail, e-mail.

◖ ORANGE BLOSSOM FICTION CONTEST

The Oak, 1530 Seventh St., Rock Island IL 61201. (309)788-3980. **Contact:** Betty Mowery, editor. Award "to build up circulation of publication and give new authors a chance for competition and publication along with seasoned writers." Prize: subscription to *The Oak*. Categories: short fiction. Judged by published authors. Entry fee: six 37-cent stamps. Deadline: October. "May be on any subject, but avoid gore and killing of humans or animals." Open to any writer. Guidelines available in January for SASE. Prefers name, address, contest deadline and title on ms; no cover letter. Guidelines for other contests available for SASE. "No reply will be made without SASE." Results announced a week after deadline. Winners notified by mail. "Material is judged on content and tightness of writing as well as word lengths, since there is a 500-word limit. Always include a SASE with submissions. Entries without six 37-cent stamps will not be judged."

◎ OREGON BOOK AWARDS

Literary Arts, 224 NW 13th Ave., Ste. 306, #219, Portland OR 97209. (503)227-2583. E-mail: kristy@literary-arts.org. Website: www.literary-arts.org. **Contact:** Kristy Athens, program coordinator. The annual Oregon Book Awards celebrate Oregon authors in the areas of poetry, fiction, nonfiction, drama and young readers' literature published between April 1, 2005 and March 31, 2006. Prize: Finalists are invited on a statewide reading tour and are promoted in bookstores and libraries across the state. Judged by writers who are selected from outside Oregon for their expertise in a genre. Past judges include Dorothy Allison, Chris Offutt and Maxine Kumin. Entry fee. Deadline: last Friday in May. Entries must be previously published. Oregon residents only. Guidelines available in February for SASE and on website. Accepts inquiries by phone and e-mail. Finalists announced in October. Winners announced at an awards ceremony in November. List of winners available in November.

◎ OREGON LITERARY FELLOWSHIPS

Literary Arts, Inc., 224 NW 13th Ave., Suite 306, Portland OR 97209. (503)227-2583. Fax: (503)243-1167. E-mail: la@literary-arts.org. Website: www.literary-arts.org. **Contact:** Kristy Athens, program coordinator. Annual fellowships for writers of fiction, poetry, literary nonfiction, young readers and drama. Prize: amount varies; $500-$3,000 for approximately 18 writers. Judged by out-of-state experts. No entry fee. Guidelines available in February for SASE. Accepts inquiries by e-mail, phone. Deadline: last Friday in June. Oregon residents only. Recipients announced in December.

PATERSON FICTION PRIZE

The Poetry Center at Passaic County Community College, One College Blvd., Paterson NJ 07505-1179. (973)684-6555. Fax: (973)523-6085. E-mail: mgillan@pccc.edu. Website: www.pccc.edu/poetry. **Contact:** Maria Mazziotti Gillan, executive director. Award "to encourage recognition of high-quality writing." Offered annually for a novel or collection of short fiction published the previous calendar year. Prize: $1,000. Judges rotate each year. No entry fee. Deadline: Submissions accepted after January 10. Open to any writer. Guidelines available for SASE, e-mail or on website. Accepts inquiries by e-mail or phone. Results announced in July. Winners notified by mail. For contest results, send SASE or visit website.

◖ PEARL SHORT STORY PRIZE

Pearl Magazine, 3030 E. Second St., Long Beach CA 90803-5163. (562)434-4523. E-mail: Pearlmag@aol.com. Website: www.pearlmag.com. **Contact:** Marilyn Johnson, fiction editor. Award to "provide a larger forum and help widen publishing opportunities for fiction writers in the small press and to help support the continuing publication of *Pearl*." Prize: $250, publication in *Pearl* and 10 copies of the journal. Judged by the editors of *Pearl*: Marilyn Johnson, Joan Jobe Smith, Barbara Hauk. Entry fee: $10/story. Include a brief bio and SASE for reply or return of mss. Accepts simultaneous submissions, but asks to be notified if story is accepted elsewhere. Deadline: May 31. Entries must be unpublished. "Although we are open to all types of fiction, we look most favorably on coherent, well-crafted narratives containing interesting, believable characters in meaningful situations." Length: 4,000 words maximum. Open to any writer. Guidelines for SASE or on website. Accepts queries

Contests & Awards

by e-mail or fax. Results announced in September. Winners notified by mail. For contest results, send SASE, e-mail or visit website.

☐ ◎ WILLIAM PEDEN PRIZE IN FICTION

The Missouri Review, 1507 Hillcrest Hall, Columbia MO 65211. (573)882-4474. Fax: (573)884-4671. Website: www.missourireview.com. **Contact:** Speer Morgan. Offered annually "for the best story published in the past volume year of the magazine. All stories published in *The Missouri Review* are automatically considered." Prize: $1,000, and reading/reception. No entry fee. Submissions must have been previously published in the volume year for which the prize is awarded. No application process: All fiction published in *The Missouri Review* is automatically entered.

◢ ◎ PEN CENTER USA ANNUAL LITERARY AWARDS

PEN Center USA, 672 S. Lafayette Park Place, #42, Los Angeles CA 90057. (213)365-8500. Fax: (213)365-9616. E-mail: awards@penusa.org. Website: www.penusa.org. Offered annually for fiction, nonfiction, poetry, children's literature or translation published January 1-December 31 of the current year. Prize: $1,000, plaque and honored at a ceremony in Los Angeles. Judged by panel of writers, booksellers, editors. Entry fee: $35. Guidelines available in July for SASE, fax, e-mail or on website. Accepts inquiries by fax, phone and e-mail. All entries must include 4 non-returnable copies of each submission and a completed entry form. Deadline: December 16. Entries must be previously published. Open to authors west of the Mississippi River, including all of Minnesota and Louisiana. Results announced in May. Winners notified by phone and mail. For contest results, send SASE or visit website.

◖ ◎ PEN/FAULKNER AWARDS FOR FICTION

PEN/Faulkner Foundation, % The Folger Shakespeare Library, 201 E. Capitol St., Washington DC 20003. (202)675-0345. Fax: (202)608-1719. E-mail: delaney@folger.edu. Website: www.penfaulkner.org. **Contact:** Janice Delaney, PEN/Faulkner Foundation Executive Director. Offered annually for best book-length work of fiction by an American citizen published in a calendar year. Prize: $15,000 (one winner); $5,000 (4 nominees). Judged by three writers chosen by the Trustees of the Award. No entry fee. Deadline: October 31. Open to US citizens only, but they need not be US residents. Writers and publishers submit four copies of eligible titles published during the current year. No juvenile or self-published books.

☐ ◎ PHOEBE WINTER FICTION CONTEST

Phoebe, George Mason University, 4400 University Dr., Fairfax VA 22030-4444. (703)993-2915. Website: www.gmu.edu/pubs/phoebe/. **Contact:** John Copenhaver, editor. To recognize new and exciting short fiction. Offered annually for unpublished work. Prize: $1,000 and publication. All entrants receive a free issue. Judged by outside judge—recognized fiction writer hired by *Phoebe*—who changes each year. The 2005 judge was Tom Franklin. Entry fee: $12/story. Send ms and cover letter, which should contain name, address, title of story and brief bio. Name and address should not appear on actual ms. Enclose SASE for contest results. Additional guidelines available after September for SASE or on website. Mss not returned. Deadline: December 1. Entries must be unpublished. Word length: 25 pages maximum. Open to any writer. Results announced in the Fall. Winners notified by mail. List of winners available. "*Phoebe* encourages experimental writing."

Ⓝ ◎ PLAYBOY COLLEGE FICTION CONTEST

Playboy, 730 Fifth Ave., New York NY 10019. Website: www.playboy.com/on-campus/collegefiction/. **Contact:** Contest director. Prize: 1st prize: $3,000 US and publication in magazine; 2nd prize: $500 and year's subscription; 3rd prize: $200 and year's subscription. Categories: short stories. No entry fee. Guidelines available online and in magazine. Length: 25 double-spaced pages (max). Include 3×5 card with name, age, college affiliation, home address, phone, e-mail, title. Deadline: Feb. 15. Entries must be unpublished. Open to college students (including graduate students). No age limit. Closed to employees of *Playboy* and their families, agents, affiliates. Winners will be notified by mail. Results available for SASE.

☐ ◎ POCKETS FICTION-WRITING CONTEST

Upper Room Publications, 1908 Grand Ave. AV, P.O. Box 340004, Nashville TN 37203-0004. (615)340-7333. Fax: (615)340-7267. E-mail: pockets@upperroom.org. Website: www.pockets.org. *Pockets* is a devotional magazine for children of elementary school age. Contest offered annually for unpublished work to discover new children's writers. Prize: $1,000 and publication in *Pockets*. Categories: short stories. Judged by *Pockets* staff and staff of other Upper Room Publications. No entry fee. Guidelines available for #10 SASE or on website. Deadline: Must be postmarked between March 1-August 15. Entries must be unpublished. Because the purpose of the contest is to discover new writers, previous winners are not eligible. No violence, science fiction, romance, fantasy or talking animal stories. Word length 1,000-1,600 words. Open to any writer. Winner announced

November 1 and notified by US mail. Contest submissions accompanied by SASE will be returned Nov. 1. "Send SASE with 4 first-class stamps to request guidelines and a past issue, or go to www.pockets.org."

☐ THE KATHERINE ANNE PORTER PRIZE FOR FICTION
Nimrod International Journal, 600 S. College Ave., University of Tulsa, Tulsa OK 74104. (918)631-3080. Fax: (918)631-3033. E-mail: nimrod@utulsa.edu. Website: www.utulsa.edu/nimrod. **Contact:** Francine Ringold, editor-in-chief. This annual award was established to discover new, unpublished writers of vigor and talent. Prize: 1st place: $2,000 and publication; 2nd place: $1,000 and publication. Categories: short stories. Judged by the *Nimrod* editors (finalists), and a recognized author selects the winners. Past judges include Ron Carlson, Anita Shreve, Mark Doty, Gordon Lish, George Garrett and John Leonard. Entry fee: $20 (includes a 1-year subscription to *Nimrod*). Guidelines available after January for #10 SASE or by e-mail. Accepts inquiries by e-mail or phone. Deadline: April 30. Entries must be unpublished. Must be typed, double-spaced. Our contest is judged anonymously, so we ask that writers take their names off their mss. Include a cover sheet containing your name, full address and phone and the title of your work. Include SASE for notification of the results. Length: 7,500 words maximum. Open to US residents only. "We encourage writers to read *Nimrod* before submission to discern whether or not their work is compatible with the style of our journal. Single issues are $10 (book rate postage included)." Results announced in July. Winners notified by mail. For contest results, send SASE with entry or visit website.

◎ PRAIRIE SCHOONER READERS' CHOICE AWARDS
Prairie Schooner, 201 Andrews Hall, P.O. Box 880334, Lincoln NE 68588-0334. (402)472-0911. Fax: (402)472-9771. E-mail: kgrey@unl.edu. Website: www.unl.edu/schooner/psmain.htm. **Contact:** Hilda Raz, editor-in-chief. Awards to honor work published the previous year in *Prairie Schooner*, including poetry, essays and fiction. Prize: $250 in each category. Judged by editorial staff of *Prairie Schooner*. No entry fee. For guidelines, send SASE or visit website. Entries must be previously published. "Only work published in *Prairie Schooner* in the previous year is considered." Work nominated by the editorial staff. Results announced in the Spring issue. Winners notified by mail in February or March.

◎ PUSHCART PRIZE
Pushcart Press, P.O. Box 380, Wainscott NY 11975. (516)324-9300. Website: www.pushcartprize.com. **Contact:** Bill Henderson, president. Award to "publish and recognize the best of small press literary work." Prize: Publication in *Pushcart Prize: Best of the Small Presses* anthology. Categories: short stories, poetry, essays on any subject. No entry fee. Deadline: December 1. Entries must be previously published. Must have been published during the current calendar year. Open to any writer. Nomination by small press publishers/editors only.

DAVID RAFFELOCK AWARD FOR PUBLISHING EXCELLENCE
National Writers Association, 10940 S. Parker Rd. #508, Parker CO 80134. (303)841-0246. Fax: (303)841-2607. E-mail: contests@nationalwriters.com. Website: www.nationalwriters.com. **Contact:** Sandy Whelchel, executive director. Award to "assist published authors in marketing their work and promoting them." Prize: publicity tour, including airfare,and services of a publicist (valued at $5,000). Categories: novels and short story collections. Judged by publishers and agents. Entry fee: $100. Deadline: May 1. Entries must be unpublished. Open to any writer. Guidelines for SASE, by e-mail or on website. Winners announced in June at the NWAF conference and notified by mail or phone. List of winners available for SASE or visit website.

◢ ◎ SIR WALTER RALEIGH AWARD
North Carolina Literary and Historical Association, 4610 Mail Service Center, Raleigh NC 27699-4610. (919)807-7290. **Contact:** Michael Hill, awards coordinator. "To promote among the people of North Carolina an interest in their own literature." Prize: statue of Sir Walter Raleigh. Categories: novels and short story collections. Judged by university English and history professors. No entry fee. Guidelines available in August for SASE. Accepts inquiries by fax. Deadline: July 15. Entries must be previously published. Book must be an original work published during the 12 months ending June 30 of the year for which the award is given. Writer must be a legal or physical resident of North Carolina for the 3 years preceeding the close of the contest period. Authors or publishers may submit 3 copies of their book to the above address. Results announced in October. Winners notified by mail. For contest results, send SASE.

Ⓝ RAMBUNCTIOUS REVIEW FICTION CONTEST
Rambunctious Review, 1221 W. Pratt Blvd., Chicago IL 60626. **Contact:** N. Lennon, Editor. Annual themed contest for unpublished stories. Acquires one-time publication rights. Open to any writer. "There are no stylistic limitations, but the story should reflect the writer's philosophy on the theme of the next issue." Last year's theme: Signs & Symbols. Prize: 1st prize: $100; 2nd prize: $75; 3rd prize: $50; all winning stories will be

published in future issues of *Rambunctious Review*. Judged by previous contest winners. Entry fee: $4/story. The writer's name and address must be on each page. Stories will not be returned. Entrants will be notified of contest results the following February. Guidelines available for SASE or in publication in September. Deadline: December 31. Entries must be unpublished. Looking for "originality; short, clear exposition; character-driven" stories.

THE REA AWARD FOR THE SHORT STORY

Dungannon Foundation, 53 W. Church Hill Rd., Washington CT 06794. Website: www.reaaward.org. **Contact:** Elizabeth Rea, president. "Sponsored by the Dungannon Foundation, the Rea Award was established in 1986 by Michael M. Rea to honor a living U.S. or Canadian writer who has made a significant contribution to the short story form." Prize: $30,000. Categories: short stories Judged by 3 jurors (2004 judges were Edwidge Danticat, Adam Haslett, Amy Hempel). No entry fee. Award cannot be applied for. The recipient is selected by an annually appointed jury. Open to any writer. Award announced in Fall annually. List of winners available on website. 2004 winner was Lorrie Moore.

REAL WRITERS SHORT STORY AWARDS

REAL Writers Support & Appraisal Service, P.O. Box 170, Chesterfield Derbyshire S40 IFE United Kingdom. E-mail: info@real-writers.com. Website: www.real-writers.com. **Contact:** Lynne Patrick. Annual contest for unpublished short stories to provide an outlet for writers of short fiction and to open up opportunities for development. We have a good working relationship with a major publisher. Prize: £2500 sterling and category prizes of £100 each. Judged by an experienced team of readers who select a shortlist from which prize winners are chosen by a smaller team of literary agents and editors, led by a senior editor from a major publishing house. Entry fee: £5 sterling (payable by credit card, so converted to dollars of current exchange rate). Guidelines available in June for SASE, by e-mail or visit website. Accepts inquiries by e-mail, phone. Deadline: November 30. Entries must be unpublished. Length: 5,000 words maximum. Open to any writer. Entry form or cover sheet should include name, address, phone, e-mail, word count and title. Results announced in April. Winners notified by phone or mail. For contest results, visit website.

THE RED HOUSE CHILDREN'S BOOK AWARD

(formerly The Children's Book Award), Federation of Children's Book Groups, The Old Malt House, Aldbourne, Marlborough, Wiltshire SN8 2DW England. E-mail: marianneadey@aol.com. Website: www.redhousechildrens bookaward.co.uk. **Contact:** Marianne Adey, national coordinator. Purpose of award is "to find out what children choose among books of fiction published in the United Kingdom." Prize: silver bowl, portfolio of children's letters and pictures. Categories: Books for Younger Children, Books for Younger Readers, Books for Older Children. No entry fee. Deadline: Closing date is Dec. 31. Entries must be previously published. UK authors only. Either author or publisher may nominate title. Guidelines available on website. Accepts inquiries by fax, e-mail and phone. Results announced in June for books published the previous year. Winners notified at event/banquet and via the publisher. For contest results, visit website.

HAROLD U. RIBALOW AWARD

Hadassah Magazine, 50 W. 58th St., New York NY 10019. (212)451-6289. Fax: (212)451-6257. E-mail: imarks@h adassah.org. **Contact:** Ian Marks, Ribalow Prize Coordinator. Offered annually for English-language books of fiction (novel or short stories) on a Jewish theme published the previous calendar year. Books should be submitted by the publisher. "Harold U. Ribalow was a noted writer and editor who devoted his time to the discovery and encouragement of young Jewish writers." Prize: $3,000 and excerpt of book in *Hadassah Magazine*. No entry fee. Deadline: March 1. Book should have been published the year preceding the award.

MARY ROBERTS RINEHART FUND

Mailstop Number 3E4, English Department, George Mason University Creative Writing Program, Fairfax VA 22030-4444. (703)993-1185. E-mail: wmiller@gmu.edu. Website: www.gmu.edu/departments/writing/rinehar t.htm. **Contact:** William Miller, director. **Editors' note (taken from award's website):** *"The Rinehart Awards have been suspended for 2005 and 2006 due to the investments profile of the endowment that supports the award series. We deeply regret having to take this action but we are doing it to protect the awards series over the long term. We will not accept entries in the fall of 2004 or in the fall of 2005, but will résumé receiving entries in the fall of 2006."* Offered annually for unpublished authors "who, in order to finish projected work, need financial assistance otherwise unavailable." Grants by nomination to unpublished creative writers for fiction, poetry and nonfiction with a strong narrative quality. Submissions must include nominating letter from person in appropriate field. Prize: 3 grants worth $2,000 each. No entry fee. Deadline: November 30. Entries must be unpublished. Writers must be nominated by a sponsoring writer, writing teacher, editor or agent. Guidelines for SASE or by e-mail. Accepts inquires by e-mail and phone. Results announced in Spring. Winners notified by mail. For contest results, send SASE.

THE SCARS/CC&D EDITOR'S CHOICE AWARDS

Scars Publications and Design/*Children, Churches & Daddies* Magazine, 829 Brian Court, Gurnee IL 60031-3155. E-mail: ccandd96@scars.tv. Website: http://scars.tv. **Contact:** Janet Kuypers, editor/publisher. Award "to showcase good writing in an annual book." Prize: publication of story/essay and 1 copy of the book. Categories: short stories. Entry fee: $15/short story. Deadline: revolves for appearing in different upcoming books as winners. Entries may be unpublished or previously published. Open to any writer. For guidelines, visit website. Accepts inquiries by e-mail. Length: "We appreciate shorter works. Shorter stories, more vivid and more real storylines in writing have a good chance." Results announced at book publication, online. Winners notified by mail when book is printed. For contest results, send SASE or e-mail. "See website for magazine guidelines, and look at past accepted writing to see what we look for and accept."

SCIENCE FICTION WRITERS OF EARTH (SFWoE) SHORT STORY CONTEST

Science Fiction Writers of Earth, P.O. Box 121293, Fort Worth TX 76121-1293. E-mail: sfwoe@flash.net. Website: www.flash.net/~sfwoe. **Contact:** Gilbert Gordon Reis, SFWoE administrator. Award to "promote the art of science fiction/fantasy short story writing." Prize: $200, $100, $50, $25. Categories: short story. Judged by author Edward Bryant. Entry fee: $5 for membership and first entry; $2 each for additional entries (make checks payable to SFWoE). Cover letter should include name, address, phone, e-mail address, word count and title. Same information should appear on ms title page. Deadline: October 30. Entries must be unpublished. The author must not have received payment for a published piece of fiction. Stories should be science fiction or fantasy, 2,000-7,500 words. Open to any writer. Guidelines available after November for SASE, e-mail or on website. Accepts inquiries by e-mail and mail. "Visit our website and read the winning story. Read our online newsletter to know what the judge looks for in a good story. Contestants enjoy international competition." Results announced January 31. Winners notified by mail, phone or e-mail. "Each contestant is mailed the contest results, judge's report, and a listing of the top 10 contestants." Send separate SASE for complete list of the contest stories and contestants (or print from website).

SCRIPTAPALOOZA TELEVISION WRITING COMPETITION

Supported by Writers Guild of America West, 7775 Sunset Blvd., PMB #200, Hollywood CA 90046. (323)654-5809. E-mail: info@scriptapalooza.com. Website: www.scriptapaloozatv.com. Award to "discover talented writers who have an interest in American television writing." Prize: $500 to top winner in each category (total $1,500), production company consideration. Categories: sitcoms, pilots and one-hour dramas. Entry fee: $40; accepts Paypal credit card or make checks payable to Scriptapalooza. Deadline: May 15 and November 15 of each year. Entries must be unpublished. Length: standard television format whether one hour, one-half hour or pilot. Open to any writer 18 or older. Guidelines available now for SASE or on website. Accepts inquiries by e-mail, phone. "Pilots should be fresh and new and easy to visualize. Spec scripts should stay current with the shows, up-to-date story lines, characters, etc." Winners announced February 15 and August 15. For contest results, visit website.

SHORT GRAIN WRITING CONTEST

Grain Magazine, Box 67, Saskatoon SK S7K 3K1 Canada. (306)244-2828. Fax: (306)244-0255. E-mail: grainmag@sasktel.net. Website: www.grainmagazine.ca. **Contact:** Bobbi Clackson-Walker. Competition for postcard (flash) fiction, prose poems, dramatic monologues. Prize: 4 prizes of $500 in each category. Entry fee: $28 fee for 2 entries, plus $8 for additional entries; US and international entries $28, and $6 postage in US funds (non-Canadian). Guidelines available in June by fax, e-mail, on website or for SASE. Deadline: January 31. Contest entries must be either an original postcard story (narrative fiction in 500 words or less); prose poem (lyric poem written as a prose paragraph or paragraphs in 500 words or less); dramatic monologue (a self-contained speech given by a single character in 500 words or less). Cover letter should include name, address, phone, e-mail, word count and title; title only on ms. Results announced in May. Winners notified by phone, e-mail, fax or mail. For contest results, send SASE, e-mail, fax or visit website.

SIDE SHOW SHORT STORY CONTEST

Somersault Press, 404 Vista Heights Rd., El Cerrito CA 94530. Website: www.somersaultpress.com. **Contact:** Shelley Anderson and Jean Schiffman, editors. Award "to attract quality writers for our 300-odd page paperback fiction anthology." Prize: $100; $75; $50; $5 payment per printed page to each accepted writer (on publication). Entry fee: $12.50; covers all submissions mailed in same envelope and includes sample copy of *Side Show*; make checks payable to Somersault Press. Please include your contact info (and e-mail address, if you have one) with submission. No guidelines or restrictions on length and style. For informational leaflet, send SASE

Contests & Awards

or check website. Accepts inquiries by e-mail. Will critique if requested. Prefers previously unpublished submissions but previous publication is okay; must have permission from previous publisher. Open to any writer. *Side Show* is published on no particular schedule. Thus there is no fixed deadline and editors continue to read ms entries year round. Multiple submissions (in the same mailing envelope) are encouraged; only one entry fee required for each writer. Winners notified by mail before printing and announced upon publication. "We look for original, dramatic, literary stories."

JOHN SIMMONS SHORT FICTION AWARD

University of Iowa Press, 102 Dey House, 507 N. Clinton St., Iowa City IA 52242-1000. (319)335-2000. Fax: (319)335-2055. Website: www.uiowapress.org. **Contact:** Holly Carver, director. Award "to give exposure to promising writers who have not yet published a book of prose." Offered annually for a collection of short stories. Anyone who has not published a book of prose fiction is eligible to apply. Prize: Publication by the University of Iowa Press. Judged by Senior Iowa Writers' Workshops members who screen manuscripts; published fiction author of note makes final two selections. No entry fee. For guidelines, send SASE or visit website. Accepts inquiries by fax, phone. No application forms are necessary. A SASE must be included for return of ms. Deadline: August 1-September 30. "Individual stories can have been previously published (as in journals), but never in *book* form." Stories must be in English. Length: "at least 150 word-processed, double-spaced pages; 8-10 stories on average for ms." Open to any writer. Results announced early in year following competition. Winners notified by phone.

SKIPPING STONES HONOR AWARDS

P.O. Box 3939, Eugene OR 97403-0939. Phone/fax: (541)342-4956. E-mail: editor@skippingstones.org. Website: www.skippingstones.org. **Contact:** Arun N. Toké, executive editor. Award to "promote multicultural and/or nature awareness through creative writings for children and teens." Prize: honor certificates; seals; reviews; press release/publicity. Categories: short stories, novels, story collections, poetry and nonfiction. Judged by "a multicultural committee of teachers, librarians, parents, students and editors." Entry fee: $50 ($25 for small, low-income publishers/self-publishers). Deadline: January 20. Entries must be previously published. Open to previously published books and resources that appeared in print between January 2005 and January 2006. Open to any writer and publisher. Guidelines for SASE or e-mail and on website. Accepts inquiries by e-mail, fax, phone. "We seek authentic, exceptional, child/youth friendly books that promote intercultural, international, intergenerational harmony and understanding through creative ways. Writings that come out of your own experiences and cultural understanding seem to have an edge." Results announced in May. Winners notified through personal notifications, press release and by publishing reviews of winning titles. For contest results, send SASE, e-mail or visit website.

SKIPPING STONES YOUTH AWARDS

Skipping Stones Magazine, P.O. Box 3939, Eugene OR 97403-0903. Phone/fax: (541)342-4956. E-mail: editor@skippingstones.org. Website: www.skippingstones.org. **Contact:** Arun N. Toké, executive editor. Award to "promote creativity and multicultural and nature awareness in youth." Prize: publication in Autumn issue, honor certificate, subscription to magazine, plus 5 multicultural or nature books. Categories: short stories. Entry fee: $3/entry, make checks payable to *Skipping Stones*. Cover letter should include name, address, phone and e-mail. Deadline: June 20. Entries must be unpublished. Length: 750 words maximum. Open to any writer between 7 and 17. Guidelines available by SASE, e-mail or on website. Accepts inquiries by e-mail, phone. "Be imaginative in your approach. Be creative. Do not use stereotypes or excessive violent language or plots. Be sensitive to cultural diversity." Results announced in the September-October issue. Winners notified by mail. For contest results, visit website. Everyone who enters receives the issue which features the award winners.

THE BERNICE SLOTE AWARD

Prairie Schooner, 201 Andrews Hall, P.O. Box 880334, Lincoln NE 68588-0334. (402)472-0911. Fax: (402)472-9771. E-mail: kgrey2@unl.edu. Website: www.unl.edu/schooner/psmain.htm. **Contact:** Hilda Raz, editor-in-chief. Offered annually for the best work by a beginning writer published in *Prairie Schooner* in the previous year. Prize: $500. Categories: short stories, essays and poetry. Judged by editorial staff of *Prairie Schooner*. No entry fee. For guidelines, send SASE or visit website. Entries must be previously published. "Only work published in the journal during the previous year will be considered." Work is nominated by the editorial staff. Results announced in the Spring issue. Winners notified by mail in February or March.

KAY SNOW WRITING AWARDS

Willamette Writers, 9045 SW Barbur Blvd., Suite 5A, Portland OR 97219. (503)452-1592. Fax: (503)452-0372. E-mail: wilwrite@teleport.com. Website: www.willamettewriters.com. **Contact:** Marlene Moore. Contest offered annually to "offer encouragement and recognition to writers with unpublished submissions." Acquires right to publish excerpts from winning pieces 1 time in their newsletter. Prize: 1st place: $300; 2nd place: $150; 3rd place: $50; excerpts published in Willamette Writers newsletter, and winners acknowledged at banquet during writing conference. Student writers win $50 in categories for grades 1-5, 6-8, and 9-12. $500 Liam Callen Memorial Award goes to best overall entry. Entry fee: $15 fee; no fee for student writers. Deadline: May 15. Guidelines for #10 SASE, fax, by e-mail or on website. Accepts inquires by fax, phone and e-mail. Winners notified by mail and phone. For contest results, send SASE. Prize winners will be honored at the two-day August Willamette Writers' Conference. Press releases will be sent to local and national media announcing the winners, and excerpts from winning entries may appear in our newsletter.

SOUTH DAKOTA ARTS COUNCIL

800 Governors Drive, Pierre SD 57501-2294. (605)773-3131. E-mail: sdac@state.sd.us. Website: www.sdarts.org. **Contact:** Dennis Holub, executive director. "Individual Artist Grants (up to $3,000) and Artist Collaboration Grants (up to $6,000) are planned for fiscal 2006." No entry fee. Deadline: March 1. Open to South Dakota residents only. Students pursuing an undergraduate or graduate degree are ineligible. Guidelines and application available on website or by mail. Applicants must submit application form with an original signature; current résumé no longer than 5 pages; appropriate samples of artistic work (see guidelines); up to 5 pages additional documentation; SASE with adequate postage for return of ms (if desired).

THE SOUTHERN REVIEW/LOUISIANA STATE UNIVERSITY SHORT FICTION AWARD

Louisiana State University, 43 Allen Hall, Baton Rouge LA 70803. (225)578-5108. Fax: (225)578-5098. E-mail: perreaud@lsu.edu. Website: www.lsu.edu/thesouthernreview. **Contact:** Donna Perreault, associate editor. Offered for first collections of short stories by Americans published in the US during the previous year. Publisher or author may enter by mailing 2 copies of the collection. Prize: $500 and possible paid reading invitation. Judged by committee of editors and faculty members. No entry fee. Guidelines available for SASE, by fax, phone, e-mail and on website. Accepts inquiries by fax, e-mail and phone. Deadline: January 31. Entries must be previously published. Winner announced in Summer and notified by mail. For results, send SASE.

SOUTHWEST WRITERS (SWW) CONTEST

SouthWest Writers (SWW), 3721 Morris St. NE, Suite A, Albuquerque NM 87111-3611. (505)265-9485. Fax: (505)265-9483. E-mail: SWriters@aol.com. Website: www.southwestwriters.org. **Contact:** David J. Corwell, chair, or Joanne Marsh, co-chair. The SouthWest Writers (SWW) Contest encourages and honors excellence in writing. There are 18 catagories in which writers may enter their work. (Please see Category Specific Guidelines on website for more details.) Prize: Finalists in all categories are notified by mail and are listed on the SWW website with the title of their entry. First, second and third place winners in each category also receive cash prizes of $150, $100, and $50 (respectively), as well as a certificate of achievement. First place winners also compete for the $1,000 Storyteller Award. Winners will be honored at a contest awards banquet (date and time TBA). Categories: Eleven categories—broken down by genre—are for short story and novel writers. For novels: Mainstream and Literary; Mystery, Suspense, Thriller, or Adventure; Romance; Science Fiction, Fantasy, or Horror; Historical or American Frontier/Western; Middle Grade (4th-6th grade) or Young Adult (7th grade and up). For short stories: Science Fiction, Fantasy, or Horror; Mainstream and Literary; Mystery or Romance; Other Genres: Historical, Western, etc; Middle Grade (4th-6th grade) or Young Adult (7th grade and up). Judged by editors and agents (most from New York publishing houses) who are chosen by the contest chairs. Judges critique the top three entries in each category. All entries also receive a written critique by a qualified consultant (usually, but not always, a published author). Entry fee: $29 for members, $44 for nonmembers (make checks payable to SouthWest Writers). No cover letter is required; send signed copy of the SWW Contest Entry Form. Personal information should not appear anywhere else on ms. NOVELS: The first 20 pages or less, beginning with the prologue and/or first chapter, plus a 1-page synopsis. SHORT STORIES: 5,000 words or less. (For all children's writing, you must type *Middle Grade* or *Young Adult* in the top right corner of the first page.) Please follow detailed instructions for submission in Category Specific Guidelines on website. Deadline: May 1. Entries must be unpublished. Open to all writers from around the world. All entries should be submitted in English and follow standard ms format. "Entrants should read the SWW Contest Entry Form, General Contest Rules and the Category Specific Guidelines for complete information. A Tips & Resources page (as well as all contest info/entry form) is also available on the SWW website." Guidelines available in January by SASE, fax, e-mail, on website or in SouthWest Sage SWW newsletter. Accepts inquiries by fax, e-mail, phone.

SPUR AWARDS

Western Writers of America, Inc., 1012 Fair St., Franklin TN 37064. (615)791-1444. E-mail: tncrutch@aol.com. Website: www.westernwriters.org. **Contact:** Awards Coordinator. Purpose of award is "to reward quality in the fields of western fiction and nonfiction." Prize: Trophy. Categories: short stories, novels, poetry and nonfiction. No entry fee. Deadline: December 31. Entries must be published during the contest year. Open to any writer. Guidelines available in Sept./Oct. for SASE or by phone. Inquiries accepted by e-mail or phone. Results announced annually in Summer. Winners notified by mail. For contest results, send SASE.

STONY BROOK SHORT FICTION PRIZE

Department of English, State University of New York, Stony Brook NY 11794-5350. (631)632-7400. Website: www.stonybrook.edu/fictionprize. **Contact:** John Westermann. Award "to recognize excellent undergraduate fiction." Prize: $1,000 and publication on website. Categories: Short stories. Judged by faculty of the Department of English & Creative Writing Program. No entry fee. Guidelines available on website. Inquiries accepted by e-mail. Expects 300 entries. Deadline: March 1. Word length: 7,500 words or less. "Only undergraduates enrolled full time in American or Canadian colleges and universities for the 2004-2005 academic year are eligible. Proof required. Students of all races and backgrounds are encouraged to enter. Guidelines for SASE or on website. Ms should include name, permanent address, phone, e-mail, word count and title. Winners notified by phone; results posted on website by June.

THEODORE STURGEON MEMORIAL AWARD FOR BEST SCIENCE FICTION SHORT FICTION

Center for the Study of Science Fiction, English Department, University of Kansas, Lawrence KS 66045. (785)864-3380. Fax: (785)864-1159. E-mail: jgunn@ku.edu. Website: www.ku.edu/~sfcenter. **Contact:** James Gunn, professor and director. Award to "honor the best science fiction short story of the year." Prize: certificate. Winners receive trophy and have their names engraved on permanent trophy. Categories: short stories. Judged by jury. No entry fee. Entries must be previously published. Open to any writer. Guidelines available in December by phone, e-mail or on website. Accepts inquiries by e-mail and fax. Entrants for the Sturgeon Award are by nomination only. Results announced in July. For contest results, send SASE.

subTERRAIN ANNUAL LITERARY AWARDS COMPETITION: THE LUSH TRIUMPHANT

subTERRAIN Magazine, P.O. Box 3008 MPO, Vancouver, British Columbia V6B 3X5 Canada. (604)876-8710. Fax: (604)879-2667. E-mail: subter@portal.ca. Website: www.anvilpress.com. **Contact:** Jenn Farrell, managing editor. Award to "inspire writers to get down to it and struggle with a form that is condensed and difficult. To encourage clean, powerful writing." Offered annually to foster new and upcoming writers. Prize: $500 (Canadian), publication in summer issue, and 1-year subscription to *subTERRAIN*. Runners up also receive publication. Categories: short stories. Judged by an editorial collective. Entry fee: $20. Guidelines available in November for SASE. "Contest kicks off in November." Deadline: May 15. Entries must be unpublished. Length: 3,000 words maximum. Results announced in July issue. Winners notified by phone call and in press release. "All entries must be previously unpublished material. Submissions will not be returned, so do not send originals. If you would like to receive information regarding the outcome of the contest prior to their publication in the magazine, please include a regular letter-size SASE with your entry. If submitting from outside Canada, please include International Reply Coupons to cover return postage."

TALL GRASS WRITERS GUILD LITERARY ANTHOLOGY/CONTEST

Outrider Press, 937 Patricia, Crete IL 60417. (708)672-6630. Fax: (708)672-5820. E-mail: outriderpr@aol.com. Website: www.outriderpress.com. **Contact:** Whitney Scott, senior editor. Competition to collect diverse writings by authors of all ages and backgrounds on the theme of "Vacations" (spiritual as well as physical). Prize: publication in anthology, free copy to all published authors, $1,000 in cash prizes. Categories: short stories, poetry and creative nonfiction. Entry fee: $16; $12 for members (make check payable to Tallgrass Writers Guild). Deadline: February 28, 2006. Word length: 2,500 words or less. Previously published and unpublished submissions accepted. Maximum two prose, 8 poetry entries per person. Send SASE. Open to any writer. Guidelines and entry form available for SASE, by fax, e-mail and on website. Accepts inquiries by e-mail. Cover letter and ms should include name, address, phone, e-mail, word count and title. Results announced in May. "Must include e-mail address and SASE for response." For contest results, send e-mail.

SYDNEY TAYLOR MANUSCRIPT COMPETITION

Association of Jewish Libraries, 315 Maitland Ave., Teaneck NJ 07666. (201)862-0312. Fax: (201)862-0362. E-mail: rkglasser@aol.com. Website: www.jewishlibraries.org. **Contact:** Rachel Glasser, coordinator. Award "to identify and encourage writers of fiction for ages 8-11 with universal appeal of Jewish content; story should deepen the understanding of Judaism for all children, Jewish and non-Jewish, and reveal positive aspects of Jewish life. No short stories or plays. Length: 64-200 pages." Judged by 5 AJL member librarians. Prize: $1,000. No entry fee. Guidelines available by SASE, e-mail or on website. Deadline: December 30. Entries must be unpublished. Cover letter should include name, address, phone, e-mail and title. Results announced April 15. Winners notified by phone or e-mail. For contest information, send e-mail or visit website. Check website for more specific details and to download release forms which must accompany entry.

⚙ THE PETER TAYLOR PRIZE FOR THE NOVEL

Knoxville Writers' Guild and University of Tennessee Press, 100 S. Gay Street, Suite 101, Knoxville TN 37902. Website: www.knoxvillewritersguild.org. Offered annually for unpublished work to discover and publish novels of high literary quality. Guidelines for SASE or on website. Only full-length, unpublished novels will be considered. Short story collections, translations, or nonfiction cannot be considered. Prize: $1,000, publication by University of Tennessee Press (a standard royalty contract). Judged by a widely published novelist who chooses the winner from a pool of finalists. 2005 judge: Jill McCorkle; 2004 judge: Barry Hannah. Entry fee: $25 fee, payable to KWG. Multiple and simultaneous submissions okay. Manuscripts should be a minimum of 40,000 words and should be of letter-quality print on standard white paper. Text should be double-spaced, paginated and printed on one side of the page only. Please do not use a binder; use two rubber bands instead. Please use a padded mailer for shipping. The mss should be accompanied by two title pages: one with the title only; the other with the title and author's name, address and phone number. The author's name or other identifying information should not appear anywhere else on the ms. Manuscripts will not be returned. Each ms must be accompanied by a self-addressed, stamped postcard for confirmation of receipt, along with an SASE for contest results. No FedEx or UPS, please. Deadline: February 1-April 30. Entries must be unpublished. The contest is open to any U.S. resident writing in English. Members of the Knoxville Writers' Guild, current or former students of the judge, and employees and students of the University of Tennessee system are not eligible. Contest results will be announced in November.

⚙ TEDDY CHILDREN'S BOOK AWARD

Writers' League of Texas, 1501 W. 5th St., Suite E-2, Austin TX 78703-5155. (512)499-8914. Fax: (512)499-0441. E-mail: wlt@writersleague.org. Website: www.writersleague.org. **Contact:** Helen Ginger, executive director. Award established to "honor an outstanding book for children published by a member of the Writers' League of Texas." Prize: $1,000. Categories: long works and short works. Entry fee: $25. Deadline: May 31. Entries should be previously published children's books (during the period of June 1 to May 31) by Writers' League of Texas members. Open to Writers' League of Texas members. Guidelines available in January for SASE, fax, e-mail or visit website. Results announced in September. Winners notified at ceremony.

◻ THREE CHEERS AND A TIGER

Toasted Cheese, E-mail: editors@toasted-cheese.com. Website: www.toasted-cheese.com. **Contact:** Stephanie Lenz, editor. Purpose of contest is to write a short story (following a specific theme) within 48 hours. Prize: A tiger-themed prize and publication. Also a few lines of feedback and judges' comments are often provided on entries. Categories: short stories. Judged by two *Toasted Cheese* editors. The entries are presented to the judges by a third editor who removes author info for blind judging. Each judge uses her own criteria to choose entries. No entry fee. Cover letter should include name, address, phone, e-mail, word count and title. Information should be in the body of the e-mail. It will be removed before the judging begins. Entries must be unpublished. Contest offered biannually. Word limit announced at the start of the contest. Contest-specific information is announced 48 hours before the contest submission deadline. Open to any writer. Accepts inquiries by e-mail. "Follow the theme, word count and other contest rules. We have more suggestions at our website." Results announced in April and October. Winners notified by e-mail. List of winners at website.

THREE OAKS PRIZE FOR FICTION

Story Line Press, P.O. Box 1240, Ashland OR 97520-0055. (541)482-9363. E-mail: mail@storylinepress.com. Website: www.storylinepress.com. **Contact:** Three Oaks Competition. Offered annually to find and publish the best work of fiction (novels or short story collections). Open to any writer. Prize: $1,500 advance and book publication by Story Line Press. Entry fee: $25. Guidelines for SASE or on website. Deadline: April 30. Entries must be unpublished. Results announced 6-8 weeks after deadline. Winners notified by phone. "A press release announcing the winner along with a letter from the publisher is sent to all entrants who supply SASE for contest results. If for some reason a contestant doesn't receive this, they may contact us by phone, e-mail or mail."

◖ ⊕ THE THURBER PRIZE FOR AMERICAN HUMOR

Thurber House, 77 Jefferson Ave., Columbus OH 43215. (614)464-1032. Fax: (614)280-3645. E-mail: eswartzlander@thurberhouse.org. Website: www.thurberhouse.org. **Contact:** Emily Schwartzlander, marketing manager. Award "to give the nation's highest recognition of the art of humor writing." Prize: $5,000. Judged by well-known members of the national arts community. Entry fee: $50 per title. Deadline: April 1. Published submissions or accepted for publication in US for the first time. Primarily pictorial works such as cartoon collections are not considered. Word length: no requirement. Work must be nominated by publisher. Open to any writer. Guidelines available for SASE. Accepts inquiries by phone and e-mail. Results announced in November. Winners notified in person at the Algonquin Hotel in New York City. For contest results, visit website.

DeWitt Henry

How a contest win 'saved my writing life'

© Karen Couture

Contests & Awards

A s the founding editor of *Ploughshares*, the editor of several literary anthologies, and an award-winning short story writer, one would assume that DeWitt Henry would have no problem finding a commercial publisher for his first novel, *The Marriage of Anna Maye Potts*. With such an impressive publishing background and valuable connections in the literary world, he should be able to land a big book contract without much trouble. Not so.

Henry went through a lengthy, rigorous process in order to find a home for his novel. First, it took him 15 tries to find an agent. That agent submitted the manuscript to 13 publishers. Henry submitted to 19 publishers on his own, followed by 10 submissions by a second agent, and then 10 more tries on his own. Little did he know that *Anna Maye's* knight in shining armor was not an agent or acquisitions editor, but the University of Tennessee's inaugural Peter Taylor Prize for the Novel contest. "The realm of contests and merit-driven literary presses and magazines has been my best hope all along. By education, by nature, and by choice, I think I write deliberately against established market appeal, at least in the present."

Early on, at the suggestions of fellow writers Richard Yates, Dan Wakefield, George Garrett, and others, Henry began a long process of revision in an effort to find a commercial press for *The Marriage of Anna Maye Potts*. Meanwhile, excerpts were published in several literary magazines, including *Agni* and *The Texas Review*, and in 1979 he won a National Endowment for the Arts fellowship in fiction. The future of his novel at a major commercial press looked quite promising. Indeed, Henry's high-powered agent declared the novel "a property" and simultaneously submitted it to several New York houses, hoping for an auction. Publishers were quick to turn it down, noting vaguely that they couldn't market it.

More revision followed, and with a tightened story structure, Henry again felt optimistic. His new agent, a former editor who had championed it unsuccessfully at David Godine Publishers, now proclaimed that "a new generation of editors" was at hand. Again, however, publication failed to materialize—no luck but "warm regrets." Still more revision.

In 1998, Henry confided in a writer friend, Margot Livesey, that he had "the best unpublished novel in America, if not the best unpublishable novel in America," and, at her quick invitation, he sent her the novel. Encouraged by her advice to send it out again, Henry submitted it to the Peter Taylor Prize contest. In the Spring of 1999, he received a phone call from Brian Griffin, prize committee chairman, informing him that out of over 400 submissions, his was one of three finalists to be forwarded on to George Garrett, the contest judge. "Stoic at this point, I tried not to think about it, but then a week later came the call that *Anna Maye* had won. There is no overstating the heartache of having an unpublished novel.

Anna Maye had always felt like my life's unfinished business. When that call came I was speechless. I wrote my thanks to Garrett, saying that he had saved my writing life.''

At the award ceremony in Knoxville in October 2000, Henry told those who gathered that he hoped the story of the long process of seeing *The Marriage of Anna Maye Potts* into print ''might deepen their commitment to their dreams.''

Henry cautions committed fiction writers preparing to send out their work to distinguish between legitimate contests and gimmicks. Legitimate contests are usually hosted by literary presses and magazines as well as national organizations like the National Endowment for the Arts. Reputable contests include the Associated Writing Program contest, the Peter Taylor Prize for the Novel, the Drue Heinz, and prizes from the University of Nebraska, University of Illinois, Carnegie Mellon University, University of Massachusetts, and University of Iowa. (For more information on these contests, check out their listings in this section.)

As a whole, judging of contests is eminently fair, Henry believes. ''Most contests are judged 'blind,' that is on the merits of the manuscript without any indication of the author's name or status,'' says Henry. ''Of course, there are usually pre-screeners working on the 300-500 novels submitted in a given cycle, each with his or her own taste and sophistication, and there is no guarantee your work will reach the named judge for finalists.'' But outside of individual taste, which is always a factor in judging literary work, the playing field is a level one.

Henry also values contests for being open to beginners. Writers don't have to worry about being represented by agents. In addition, writers can keep entering, from year to year, without being concerned about their work having gotten negative responses in the past. The judge is often not the usual publication editor. ''In the case of AWP, for instance, the judges change each year, so you can resubmit annually.''

Winning a prestigious contest gives an author real clout. For instance, says Henry, one's work gathers interest from reviewers and buyers—and the contest-winning book has a chance of going into a paperback edition or even being made into a movie. Even if the book isn't a top seller, the author has a ''credential that can stand in place of actual sales figures.'' If a university press sponsors the contest, most likely the book will remain in print indefinitely.

''I don't know if we can count on contests and a handful of small literary and university presses to serve book manuscripts like mine,'' Henry says, ''but they do seem to be proliferating. There is no disadvantage to entering contests that I am aware of, although in time the panache of 'award winning' may become less meaningful.''

For Henry, those seeking success in their writing must, above all, be prepared for the long haul, with unflinching commitment to their work. ''Don't get petulant, locked in a mindset of 'I've given my best and nobody cares.' As with a broken heart, there's no therapy but going forward.'' How does one do this? Look to the imagination as the wellspring of your literary work: ''Keep coming back to your manuscript, rediscover your belief in its essence as you become a more seasoned human being and artist, and keep looking for ways to make the essence of your story more vivid.''

—*Jack Smith*

Contests & Awards

⚡ TICKLED BY THUNDER ANNUAL FICTION CONTEST

Tickled By Thunder, 14076-86A Ave., Surrey BC V3W 0V9 Canada. E-mail: info@tickledbythunder.com. Website: www.tickledbythunder.com. **Contact:** Larry Lindner, editor. Award to encourage new writers. Prize: $150 Canadian, 4-issue subscription (one year) plus publication. Categories: short stories. Judged by the editor and other writers. Entry fee: $10 Canadian (free for subscribers but more than one story requires $5 per entry). Deadline: February 15. Entries must be unpublished. Word length: 2,000 words or less. Open to any writer. Guidelines available for SASE, e-mail, on website. Accepts inquiries by e-mail. Results announced in May. Winners notified by mail. For contest results, send SASE.

⚡ ◎ TORONTO BOOK AWARDS

Toronto Protocol, City Clerk's Office, 100 Queen St. West, City Hall, 10th Floor, West Tower, Toronto M5H 2N2 Canada. (416)392-8191. Fax: (416)392-1247. E-mail: bkurmey@toronto.ca. Website: www.toronto.ca/book_awards. **Contact:** Bev Kurmey, protocol officer. The Toronto Book Awards honor authors of books of literary or artistic merit that are evocative of Toronto. Annual award for short stories, novels, poetry or short story collections. Prize: $15,000. Each short-listed author (usually 4-6) receives $1,000 and the winner receives the remainder. Categories: No separate categories—novels, short story collections, books of poetry, biographies, history, books about sports, children's books—all are judged together. Judged by jury of five who have demonstrated interest and/or experience in literature, literacy, books and book publishing. No entry fee. Cover letter should include name, address, phone, e-mail and title of entry. Six copies of the entry book are also required. Deadline: February 28. Entries must be previously published. Open to any writer. Guidelines available in September on website. Accepts inquires by fax, e-mail, phone. Finalists announced in June; winners notified in September at a gala reception. More information and results available on website.

◎ 🌐 THE TROLLOPE SOCIETY SHORT STORY PRIZE

The Trollope Society, 9A North St., London SW4 OHN England. E-mail: pamela@tvdox.com. Website: www.trollopestoryprize.org. **Contact:** Pamela Neville-Sington. Competition to "encourage interest in the novels of Anthony Trollope among young people; the emphasis is on reading and writing—for fun." Prize: $1,400 to the winner; story published in the Society's quarterly journal *Trollopiana* and on website; occasionally a runner up prize of $140. Categories: short stories. Judged by a panel of writers and academics. No entry fee. Guidelines available on website. Deadline: January 15. Length: 3,500 words maximum. Open to students worldwide, 21 and under. Guidelines available in May on website. Accepts inquiries by fax, e-mail, phone. Cover letter should include name, address, phone, e-mail, word count and title. Results announced in March each year. Winners notified by e-mail.

▢ ◎ 🌐 UPC SCIENCE FICTION AWARD

Technical University of Catalonia, Board of Trustees, Gran Capita 2-4, Edifici NEXUS 08034 Barcelona Spain. E-mail: consell.social@upc.edu. Website: www.upc.edu/sciencefiction. **Contact:** Anna Serra Hombravella, secretary. "The award is based on the desire for integral education at UPC, since it unifies the concepts of science and literature." Prize: 6,000£ (about $16,000 US). Judged by professors of the university and science fiction writers. No entry fee. Submissions may be made in Spanish, English, Catalan or French. The author must sign his work with a pseudonym and enclose a sealed envelope with full name, personal ID number, address and phone. The pseudonym and title of work must appear on the envelope. Deadline: September 15. Entries must be unpublished. Length: 70-115 pages, double-spaced, 30 lines/page, 70 characters/line. Open to any writer. Guidelines available in January for SASE, e-mail, phone, or on website. Results announced in December. Winners notified by phone in November. List of winners sent to all entrants; also available for SASE and on website.

VERY SHORT FICTION SUMMER AWARD

Glimmer Train, 1211 NW Glisan St., Suite 207, Portland OR 97209. (503)221-0836. Fax: (503)221-0837. Website: www.glimmertrain.com. **Contact:** Linda Swanson-Davies, editor. Award to encourage the art of the very short story. "We want to read your original, unpublished, very short story (2,000 words or less)." Prize: $1,200 and publication in *Glimmer Train Stories* and 20 author's copies (1st place); $500; $300. Entry fee: $10 reading fee. Deadline: July 31. Entries must be unpublished. Submit online at website. Open to any writer. Winners will be notified, and top 25 places will be posted by November 1.

VERY SHORT FICTION WINTER AWARD

Glimmer Train, 1211 NW Glisan St., Suite 207, Portland OR 97209. (503)221-0836. Fax: (503)221-0837. Website: www.glimmertrain.com. **Contact:** Linda Swanson-Davies. Award offered to encourage the art of the very short story. "We want to read your original, unpublished, very short story (2,000 words or less)." Prize: $1,200 and publication in *Glimmer Train Stories* and 20 author's copies (1st place); $500; $300. Entry fee: $10 reading fee.

Deadline: January 31. Entries must be unpublished. Open to any writer. Make your submissions online at www.glimmertrain.com. Winners will be notified, and top 25 places will be posted by November 1.

☐ ◎ VIOLET CROWN BOOK AWARD

Writers' League of Texas, 1501 W. Fifth St., Suite E-2, Austin TX 78703-5155. (512)499-8914. Fax: (512)499-0441. E-mail: wlt@writersleague.org. Website: www.writersleague.org. **Contact:** Helen Ginger, executive director. Award "to recognize the best books published by Writers' League of Texas members from June 1 to May 31 in fiction, nonfiction, literary poetry and literary prose categories." Prize: three $1,000 cash awards and 3 trophies. Judged by a panel of judges who are not affiliated with the League. Entry fee: $25. Send credit card information or make checks payable to Writers' League of Texas. "Anthologies that include the work of several authors are not eligible." Deadline: May 31. Entries must be previously published. "Entrants must be Writers' League of Texas members. League members reside all over the US and in some foreign countries. Persons may join the League when they send in their entries." Publisher may also submit entry in author's name. Open to any writer. Guidelines available after January for SASE, fax, e-mail or on website. Accepts inquiries by fax, e-mail or on phone. Results announced in September. Winners notified by phone and mail. For contest results, send SASE or visit website. "Special citations are presented to finalists."

Ⓝ ☐ KURT VONNEGUT FICTION PRIZE

North American Review, University of Northern Iowa, 1222 W. 27th St., Cedar Falls IA 50614-0516. (319)273-6455. Fax: (319)273-4326. E-mail: nar@uni.edu. Website: webdelsol.com/NorthAmReview/NAR/HTMLpages/NARToday.htm. Prize: 1st: $1,000; 2nd: $100; 3rd: $50. All winners and finalists will be published. Judged by acclaimed writer. 2004 judge was Richard Russo. Entry fee: $18.00 (includes a 1-yr subscription). Send two copies of one story (7,000 words max). No names on mss. Include cover letter with name, address, phone, e-mail, title. Stories will not be returned, so do not send SASE for return. For acknowledgement of receipt, please include a SAS postcard. Make your check or money order out to *North American Review*. If you are outside the US, please make sure the entry fee is in US currency and routed through a US bank. Deadline: Dec. 31. Entries must be unpublished. Simultaneous submission is not allowed. Stories entered must not be under consideration for publication elsewhere. Open to any writer. For list of winners, send business-sized SASE. Winners will be announced on website and in writers' trade magazines.

Ⓝ ◎ EDWARD LEWIS WALLANT BOOK AWARD

Irving and Fran Waltman, 3 Brighton Rd., West Hartford CT 06117. (860)232-1421. **Contact:** Mrs. Fran Waltman, co-sponsor. To recognize an American writer whose creative work of fiction has significance for the American Jew. Prize: $500 and a scroll. Judged by panel of 3 judges. No entry fee. Accepts inquiries by phone. Writers may submit their own work. Deadline: Dec. 31. Entries must be previously published. Open to novels or story collections. Open to all American writers. Winner announced in Jan./Feb. and notified by phone.

◭ ◎ WISCONSIN INSTITUTE FOR CREATIVE WRITING FELLOWSHIP

University of Wisconsin—Creative Writing/English Department, 6195B H.C. White Hall, 600 N. Park St., Madison WI 53706. (608)263-3374. E-mail: rfkuka@wisc.edu. Website: www.wisc.edu/english/cw. **Contact:** Ron Kuka, program coordinator. Competition "to provide time, space and an intellectual community for writers working on first books." Receives approximately 300 applicants a year. Prize: $25,000 for a 9-month appointment. Judged by English Department faculty. Entry fee: $20, payable to the Department of English. Applicants should submit up to 10 pages of poetry or one story of up to 30 pages and a résumé or vita directly to the program during the month of February. An applicant's name must not appear on the writing sample (which must be in ms form) but rather on a separate sheet along with address, social security number, phone number, e-mail address and title(s) of submission(s). Candidates should also supply the names and phone numbers of two recommendations. Accepts inquiries by e-mail and phone. Deadline: February. Entries must be unpublished. Open to any writer. Please enclose a SASE for notification of results. Results announced by May 1. "Send your best work. Stories seem to have a small advantage over novel excerpts."

☐ TOBIAS WOLFF AWARD IN FICTION

Bellingham Review, Mail Stop 9053, Western Washington University, Bellingham WA 98225. (360)650-4863. E-mail: bhreview@cc.wwu.edu. Website: www.wwu.edu/~bhreview. **Contact:** Fiction Editor. Offered annually for unpublished work. Guidelines for SASE or online. Prize: $1,000, plus publication and subscription. Categories: novel excerpts and short stories. Entry fee: $15 for 1st entry; $10 each additional entry. Guidelines available in August for SASE or on website. Deadline: Contest runs: Dec. 1-March15. Entries must be unpublished. Length: 8,000 words or less per story or chapter. Open to any writer. Winner announced in August and notified by mail. For contest results, send SASE.

JOHN WOOD COMMUNITY COLLEGE ADULT CREATIVE WRITING CONTEST

1301 S. 48th St., Quincy IL 62305. (217)224-6500. Fax: (214)228-9483. E-mail: ssparks@jwcc.edu. Website: www.jwcc.edu. **Contact:** Sherry L. Sparks, director of continuing and community education. Award to "promote new writing." Prize: Cash prizes dictated by the number of entries received. Categories: traditional rhyming poetry, limerick or haiku, light or humerous poetry, nonfiction, fiction. Entry fee: $5/poem; $7/fiction or nonfiction. "No identification should appear on manuscripts, but send a separate 3×5 card for each entry with name, social security number (in order to print checks for cash prizes), address, phone number, e-mail address, word count, title of work and category in which each work should be entered. You may use one check or money order and place all entries in the same envelope." Guidelines available after July for SASE, fax, e-mail, phone or on website. Entries must be unpublished. Open to any writer. Winners notified by mail in late June. For contest results, send SASE, fax, e-mail or visit website.

WORLD FANTASY AWARDS

World Fantasy Awards Association, P.O. Box 43, Mukilteo WA 98275-0043. E-mail: sfexecsec@aol.com. Website: www.worldfantasy.org. **Contact:** Peter Dennis Pautz, president. Award "to recognize excellence in fantasy literature worldwide." Offered annually for previously published work in several categories, including life achievement, novel, novella, short story, anthology, collection, artist, special award-pro and special award-nonpro. Works are recommended by attendees of current and previous 2 years' conventions and a panel of judges. Prize: Bust of HP Lovecraft. Judged by panel. No entry fee. Guidelines available in December for SASE or on website. Deadline: June 1. Entries must be previously published. Published submissions from previous calendar year. Word length: 10,000-40,000 for novella, 10,000 for short story. "All fantasy is eligible, from supernatural horror to Tolkien-esque to sword and sorcery to the occult, and beyond." Cover letter should include name, address, phone, e-mail, word count, title and publications where submission was previously published. Results announced November 1 at annual convention. For contest results, visit website.

THE WRITERS BUREAU POETRY AND SHORT STORY COMPETITION

The Writers Bureau, Sevendale House, 7 Dale St., Manchester M1 1JB England. E-mail: comp@writersbureau.com. Website: www.writersbureau.com/resources.htm. **Contact:** Angela Cox, competition secretary. Annual competition for short stories and poems. Prize: £1,000; £400; £200; £100 and 6 prizes of £50. Judged by Alison Chisolm and Iain Pattison. Entry fee: £8 per entry. Guidelines available in April for SASE, by fax, e-mail, phone or at website. Accepts inquiries by fax, e-mail, phone. Deadline: July 31. Entries must be unpublished. Length: 2,000 words. Open to any writer. Results announced September 30. Winners notified by mail. For contest results, send SASE or visit website.

WRITERS' FELLOWSHIP

NC Arts Council, Department of Cultural Resources, Raleigh NC 27699-4632. (919)715-1519. Fax: (919)733-4834. E-mail: debbie.mcgill@ncmail.net. Website: www.ncarts.org. **Contact:** Deborah McGill, literature director. Fellowships are awarded to support the creative development of NC writers and to stimulate the creation of new work. Prize: $8,000. Categories: short stories, novels, literary nonfiction, literary translation, spoken word. Work for children also invited. Judged by a panel of literary professionals appointed by the NC Arts Council, a state agency. No entry fee. Deadline: November 1, 2006. Entries must be unpublished. Mss must not be in published form. We receive approximately 300 applications. Word length: 20 double-spaced pages (max). The work must have been written within the past 5 years. Only writers who have been full-time residents of NC for at least 1 year as of the application deadline may apply. North Carolina writers only. Guidelines available in March on website. Accepts inquiries by fax, e-mail, phone. Results announced in late summer. All applicants notified by mail.

WRITERS' FORUM SHORT STORY COMPETITION

Writers International Ltd., P.O. Box 3229, Bournemouth BH1 1ZS United Kingdom. E-mail: editorial@writers-forum.com. Website: www.writers-forum.com. **Contact:** Zena O'Toole, editorial assistant. "The competition aims to promote the art of short story writing." Prize: Prizes are £300 for 1st place, £150 for 2nd place and £100 for 3rd place, with an annual trophy and a cheque for £1,000 for the best story of the year. Categories: short stories. Judged by a panel who provides a short list to the editor. Entry fee: £10 or £6 for subscribers to *Writers' Forum*. Cover letter should include name, address, phone, e-mail, word count and title. Entries must be unpublished. "The competition is open to all nationalities, but entries must be in English." Length: 1,500-3,000 words. Open to any writer. Guidelines available for e-mail, on website and in publication. Accepts inquiries by fax, e-mail, phone. Make entry fee cheques payable to Writers International Ltd., or send credit card information. Winners notified by mail. List of winners available in magazine.

◘ WRITERS' JOURNAL ANNUAL FICTION CONTEST

Val-Tech Media, P.O. Box 394, Perham MN 56573. (218)346-7921. Fax: (218)346-7924. E-mail: writersjournal@ writersjournal.com. Website: www.writersjournal.com. **Contact:** Leon Ogroske, editor (editor@writersjournal.com). Offered annually for previously unpublished fiction. Open to any writer. Prize: 1st Place: $500; 2nd Place: $200; 3rd Place: $100, plus honorable mentions. Prize-winning stories and selected honorable mentions published in *Writers' Journal*. Entry fee: $15 reading fee. Guidelines and entry forms available for SASE and on website. Accepts inquiries by fax, e-mail and phone. Deadline: January 30. "Writer's name must not appear on submission. A separate cover sheet must include name of contest, title, word count and writer's name, address, phone and e-mail (if available)." Results announced in July. Winners notified by mail. A list of winners is published in July/August issue and posted on website or available for SASE.

◉ WRITERS' JOURNAL ANNUAL HORROR/GHOST CONTEST

Val-Tech Media, P.O. Box 394, Perham MN 56573. (218)346-7921. Fax: (218)346-7924. E-mail: writersjournal@ writersjournal.com. Website: www.writersjournal.com. **Contact:** Leon Ogroske, editor. Offered annually for previously unpublished works. Open to any writer. Prize: 1st place: $50; 2nd place: $25; 3rd place: $15, plus honorable mentions. Prize-winning stories and selected honorable mentions published in *Writers' Journal*. Entry fee: $5. Guidelines available for SASE, by fax, phone, e-mail, on website and in publication. Accepts inquiries by e-mail, phone, fax. Deadline: March 30. Entries must be unpublished. Length: 2,000 words. Cover letter should include name, address, phone, e-mail, word count and title; just title on ms. Results announced in September annually. Winners notified by mail. For contest results, send SASE, fax, e-mail or visit website.

◘ ◉ WRITERS' JOURNAL ANNUAL ROMANCE CONTEST

Val-Tech Media, P.O. Box 394, Perham MN 56573. (218)346-7921. Fax: (218)346-7924. E-mail: writersjournal@ writersjournal.com. Website: www.writersjournal.com. **Contact:** Leon Ogroske, editor. Offered annually for previously unpublished works. Open to any writer. Prize: 1st place: $50; 2nd place: $25; 3rd place: $15, plus honorable mentions. Prize-winning stories and selected honorable mentions published in *Writers' Journal*. Entry fee: $5 fee. No limit on entries per person. Guidelines for SASE, by fax, phone, e-mail, on website and in publication. Accepts inquiries by fax, e-mail, phone. Deadline: July 30. Entries must be unpublished. Length: 2,000 words maximum. Open to any writer. Cover letter should include name, address, phone, e-mail, word count and title; just title on ms. Results announced in January/February issue. Winners notified by mail. Winners list published in *Writer's Journal* and on website. Enclose SASE for winner's list or send fax or e-mail.

WRITERS' JOURNAL ANNUAL SHORT STORY CONTEST

Val-Tech Media, P.O. Box 394, Perham MN 56573. (218)346-7921. Fax: (218)346-7924. E-mail: writersjournal@ writersjournal.com. Website: www.writersjournal.com. **Contact:** Leon Ogroske. Offered annually for previously unpublished short stories less than 2,000 words. Open to any writer. Guidelines for SASE and online. Prize: 1st place: $300; 2nd place: $100; 3rd place: $50, plus honorable mentions. Prize-winning stories and selected honorable mentions published in *Writers' Journal*. Entry fee: $7 reading fee. Deadline: May 30.

◘ ZOETROPE SHORT STORY CONTEST

Zoetrope: All-Story, 916 Kearny St., San Francisco CA 94133. (415)788-7500. Fax: (415)989-7910. E-mail: contests@all-story.com. Website: www.all-story.com. **Contact:** Francis Ford Coppola, publisher. Annual contest for unpublished short stories. Prize: 1st place: $1,000; 2nd place: $500, 3rd place: $250; plus 10 honorable mentions. Judged by Susan Straight in 2004. Entry fee: $15 fee. Guidelines for SASE, by fax and e-mail, in publication, or on website. Deadline: October 1. Entries must be unpublished. Word length: 5,000 words maximumm. Open to any writer. "Please mark envelope clearly 'short fiction contest'." Winners notified by phone or e-mail in November. Results announced December 1. A list of winners will be posted on website and published in Spring issue.

Conferences & Workshops

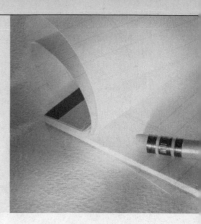

Why are conferences so popular? Writers and conference directors alike tell us it's because writing can be such a lonely business—at conferences writers have the opportunity to meet (and commiserate) with fellow writers, as well as meet and network with publishers, editors and agents. Conferences and workshops provide some of the best opportunities for writers to make publishing contacts and pick up valuable information on the business, as well as the craft, of writing.

The bulk of the listings in this section are for conferences. Most conferences last from one day to one week and offer a combination of workshop-type writing sessions, panel discussions and a variety of guest speakers. Topics may include all aspects of writing from fiction to poetry to scriptwriting, or they may focus on a specific type of writing, such as those conferences sponsored by the Romance Writers of America for writers of romance or by SCBWI for writers of children's books.

Workshops, however, tend to run longer—usually one to two weeks. Designed to operate like writing classes, most require writers to be prepared to work on and discuss their fiction while attending. An important benefit of workshops is the opportunity they provide writers for an intensive critique of their work, often by professional writing teachers and established writers.

Each of the listings here includes information on the specific focus of an event as well as planned panels, guest speakers and workshop topics. It is important to note, however, some conference directors were still in the planning stages for 2006 when we contacted them. If it was not possible to include 2006 dates, fees or topics, we have provided information from 2005 so you can get an idea of what to expect. For the most current information, it's best to send a self-addressed, stamped envelope to the director in question about three months before the date(s) listed or check the conference website.

FINDING A CONFERENCE

Many writers try to make it to at least one conference a year, but cost and location count as much as subject matter or other considerations when determining which conference to attend. There are conferences in almost every state and province and even some in Europe open to North Americans.

To make it easier for you to find a conference close to home—or to find one in an exotic locale to fit into your vacation plans—we've divided this section into geographic regions. The conferences appear in alphabetical order under the appropriate regional heading.

Note that conferences appear under the regional heading according to where they will be held, which is sometimes different from the address given as the place to register or send for information. The regions are as follows:

To find a conference based on the month in which it occurs, check out our Conference Index by Date at the back of this book.

LEARNING AND NETWORKING

Besides learning from workshop leaders and panelists in formal sessions, writers at conferences also benefit from conversations with other attendees. Writers on all levels enjoy sharing insights. Often, a conversation over lunch can reveal a new market for your work or let you know which editors are most receptive to the work of new writers. You can find out about recent editor changes and about specific agents. A casual chat could lead to a new contact or resource in your area.

Many editors and agents make visiting conferences a part of their regular search for new writers. A cover letter or query that starts with ''I met you at the Green Mountain Writers Conference,'' or ''I found your talk on your company's new romance line at the Moonlight and Magnolias Writer's Conference most interesting . . .'' may give you a small leg up on the competition.

While a few writers have been successful in selling their manuscripts at a conference, the availability of editors and agents does not usually mean these folks will have the time there to read your novel or six best short stories (unless, of course, you've scheduled an individual meeting with them ahead of time). While editors and agents are glad to meet writers and discuss work in general terms, usually they don't have the time (or energy) to give an extensive critique during a conference. In other words, use the conference as a way to make a first, brief contact.

SELECTING A CONFERENCE

Besides the obvious considerations of time, place and cost, choose your conference based on your writing goals. If, for example, your goal is to improve the quality of your writing, it will be more helpful to you to choose a hands-on craft workshop rather than a conference offering a series of panels on marketing and promotion. If, on the other hand, you are a science fiction novelist who would like to meet your fans, try one of the many science fiction conferences or ''cons'' held throughout the country and the world.

Look for panelists and workshop instructors whose work you admire and who seem to be writing in your general area. Check for specific panels or discussions of topics relevant to what you are writing now. Think about the size—would you feel more comfortable with a small workshop of eight people or a large group of 100 or more attendees?

If your funds are limited, start by looking for conferences close to home, but you may want to explore those that offer contests with cash prizes—and a chance to recoup your

Conferences

expenses. A few conferences and workshops also offer scholarships, but the competition is stiff and writers interested in these should find out the requirements early. Finally, students may want to look for conferences and workshops that offer college credit. You will find these options included in the listings here. Again, send a self-addressed, stamped envelope for the most current details.

NORTHEAST (CT, MA, ME, NH, NY, RI, VT)

Ⓝ THE "WHY IT'S GREAT" WRITING WORKSHOP & RETREAT
21 Aviation Road, Albany NY 12205. (518)453-0890; (800)720-1170. E-mail: workshop@whyitsgreat.com. Website: www.whyitsgreat.com. **Contact:** David Vigoda, director. Estab. 2003. Annual. Conference held in July. Conference duration: 4 days. Average attendance: 25. The fundemental activity is the appreciation and understanding of what makes great writing great. The key insight is realizing that no analysis of technique alone can be sufficient. Great writing is the melding of great technique with great heart and each must be able to get out of the way of the other even as they complete each other. Technique without heart is meaningless; heart without technique is incoherent. There are workshops about one and workshops about the other, but this is the one about cultivating and resolving the struggle between them. Fiction and nonfiction are emphasized, but poets and playwrights also benefit. Issues include thematic material, narration and voice. Examples are drawn from all types of writing. Site: World Fellowship Center is a secular non-profit organization founded in 1941 to promote peace, justice and freedom. The vacation resort is situated on 450 undeveloped acres of beautiful woods, wetlands and a large "forever wild" sanctuary pond in the New Hampshire Whithe Mountains. It is perfect for a writer's retreat and attracts singles, couples and families. There are always interesting conversations to join and lots of recreational choices, including swimming, boating and hiking. Themes are determined by particpants, according to their preferences. David Vidoda, award-winning novelist, playwright and poet, conducts the workshop. In 2005, Marge Piercy and Ira Wood gave workshops as writers in residence.
Costs The workshop fee for 2005 was $145. The cost to stay at the World Fellowship Center ranges from $42-$81 per day per adult (less for children), including all meals, facilities and programs. Weekly rates are available.
Accommodations Guests arrange their own transportation. Shuttle service is available for those arriving by bus. Carpools may be available from Massachusetts and metro New York/New Jersey.
Additional Information Brochure available by phone, e-mail or on the website. "No proof of ability is required. It doesn't matter if someone has written three novels or is still trying to get the first one started—or wrote 30 pages and froze. The workshop is non-competitive so all participants can feel safe in a group setting as they share their own work, insights and experience."

BREAD LOAF WRITERS' CONFERENCE
Middlebury College, Middlebury VT 05753. (802)443-5286. Fax: (802)443-2087. E-mail: blwc@middlebury.edu. Website: www.middlebury.edu/~blwc. **Contact:** Noreen Cargill, administrative manager. Estab. 1926. Annual. Last conference held August 17-28, 2005. Conference duration: 11 days. Average attendance: 230. For fiction, nonfiction, poetry. Site: Held at the summer campus in Ripton, Vermont (belongs to Middlebury College).
Costs In 2005, $2,081 (included room and board).
Accommodations Accommodations are at Ripton. Onsite accommodations included in fee.
Additional Information 2006 conference information available December 2005 on website. Accepts inquiries by fax, e-mail and phone.

GOTHAM WRITERS' WORKSHOP
WritingClasses.com (online division), 1841 Broadway, Suite 809, New York NY 10023-7603. (212)974-8377. Fax: (212)307-6325. E-mail: dana@write.org. Website: www.writingclasses.com. **Contact:** Dana Miller, director of student affairs. Estab. 1993. "Classes held throughout the year. There are four terms, beginning in January, April, June/July, September/October." Conference duration: 10-week, 1-day, and online courses offered. Average attendance: approximately 1,300 students per term, 5,000 students per year. Offers craft-oriented creative writing courses in fiction writing, screenwriting, nonfiction writing, memoir writing, novel writing, children's book writing, playwriting, poetry, songwriting, mystery writing, science fiction writing, romance writing, television writing, sketch comedy, travel writing and business writing. Also, Gotham Writers' Workshop offers a teen program, private instruction and classes on selling your work. Site: Classes are held at various schools in New York City as well as online at www.writingclasses.com. View a sample online class on the website.
Costs 10-week and online courses—$420 (includes $25 registration fee); 1-day courses—$150 (includes $25 registration fee). Meals and lodging not included.
Additional Information "Participants do not need to submit workshop material prior to their first class." Sponsors a contest for a free 10-week online creative writing course (value = $420) offered each term. Students

should fill out a form online at www.writingclasses.com to participate in the contest. The winner is randomly selected. For brochure send e-mail, visit website, call or fax. Accepts inquiries by SASE, e-mail, phone, fax. Agents and editors participate in some workshops.

GREEN MOUNTAIN WRITERS CONFERENCE

47 Hazel St., Rutland VT 05701. (802)775-5326. E-mail: ydaley@sbcglobal.net. Website: www.vermontwriters.com. **Contact:** Yvonne Daley, director. Estab. 1999. Annual. Check website for 2006 conference dates. Conference duration: 5 days. Average attendance: 40. "The conference is an opportunity for writers at all stages of their development to hone their skills in a beautiful, lakeside environment where published writers across genres share tips and give feedback." Site: Conference held at an old dance pavillion on a 5-acre site on a remote pond in Tinmouth, VT. Past features include Place in story: The Importance of Environment; Creating Character through Description, Dialogue, Action, Reaction, and Thought; The Collision of Real Events and Imagination. Previous staff has included Yvonne Daley, Ruth Stone, Verandah Porche, Grace Paley, David Huddle, Sydney Lea, Joan Connor, Tom Smith and Howard Frank Mosher.
Costs $500 (including lunch, snacks, beverages, readings).
Accommodations Offers list of area hotels and lodging.
Additional Information Participants' mss can be read and commented on at a cost. Sponsors contests. Conference publishes a literary magazine featuring work of participants. Brochures available in January on website or for SASE, e-mail. Accepts inquiries by SASE, e-mail, phone. "We aim to create a community of writers who support one another and serve as audience/mentors for one another. Participants often continue to correspond and share work after conferences." Further information available on website, by e-mail or by phone.

IWWG MEET THE AGENTS AND EDITORS: THE BIG APPLE WORKSHOPS

% International Women's Writing Guild, P.O. Box 810, Gracie Station, New York NY 10028-0082. (212)737-7536. Fax: (212)737-9469. E-mail: iwwg@iwwg.com. Website: www.iwwg.com. **Contact:** Hannelore Hahn, executive director. Estab. 1976. Biannual. Workshops held the second weekend in April and the second weekend in October. Average attendance: 200. Workshops to promote creative writing and professional success. Site: Private meeting space of Scandinavia House, mid-town New York City. Saturday: 1-day writing workshop. Sunday afternoon: open house/meet the agents, independent presses and editors.
Costs $130 for the weekend.
Accommodations Information on transportation arrangements and overnight accommodations available.
Additional Information Accepts inquiries by fax, e-mail.

N IWWG SUMMER CONFERENCE

% International Women's Writing Guild, P.O. Box 810, Gracie Station, New York NY 10028-0082. (212)737-7536. Fax: (212)737-9469. E-mail: iwwg@iwwg.org. Website: www.iwwg.org. **Contact:** Hannelore Hahn, executive director. Estab. 1977. Annual. Conference held for one week in June. Average attendance: 450, including international attendees. Conference to promote writing in all genres, personal growth and professional success. Conference is held "on the tranquil campus of Skidmore College in Saratoga Springs, NY, where the serene Hudson Valley meets the North Country of the Adirondacks." 70 different workshops are offered every day. Overall theme: "Writing Towards Personal and Professional Growth."
Costs $945 single/$810 double (members); $975 single/$840 double (non-members) for weeklong program, includes room and board.
Accommodations Conference attendees stay on campus. Transportation by air to Albany, NY, or Amtrak train available from New York City.
Additional Information Conference information available with SASE. Accepts inquiries by fax, e-mail.

THE MACDOWELL COLONY

100 High St., Peterborough NH 03458. (603)924-3886. Fax: (603)924-9142. E-mail: admissions@macdowellcolony.org. Website: www.macdowellcolony.org. **Contact:** Admissions Coordinator. Estab. 1907. Open to writers, composers, visual artists, film/video artists, interdisciplinary artists and architects. Site: includes main building, library, 3 residence halls and 32 individual studios on over 450 mostly wooded acres, 1 mile from center of small town in southern New Hampshire. Available up to 8 weeks year-round. Provisions for the writer include meals, private sleeping room, individual secluded studio. Accommodates variable number of writers, 10 to 20 at a time.
Costs "There are no residency fees. Grants for travel to and from the Colony are available based on need. The MacDowell Colony is pleased to offer grants up to $1,000 for writers in need of financial assistance during a residency at MacDowell. At the present time, only artists reviewed and accepted by the literature panel are eligible for this grant." Application forms available. Application deadline: January 15 for summer (June-Sept.), April 15 for fall (Oct.-Jan.), September 15 for winter/spring (Feb.-May). Writing sample required. For novel,

send a chapter or section. For short stories, send 2-3. Send 6 copies. Brochure/guidelines available; SASE appreciated.

🅽 MARYMOUNT MANHATTAN COLLEGE WRITERS' CONFERENCE

Marymount Manhattan College, 221 E. 71st St., New York NY 10021. (212)774-4810. Fax: (212) 774-4814. E-mail: lfrumkes@mmm.edu. **Contact:** Lauren Kivlen and Dana Thompson. Estab. 1993. Annual. June. Conference duration: "Actual conference is one day, and there is a three-day intensive preceeding." Average attendance: 200. "We present workshops on several different writing genres and panels on publicity, editing and literary agents." Site: College/auditorium setting. 2003 conference featured 2 fiction panels, a children's book writing panel, a mystery/thriller panel and a panel focusing on how to start a book. 2003 3-day intensive included fiction writer Erica Jong, magazine writer and editor Pamela Fiori, and memoir writer Malachy Mc-Court. The conference itself included more than 50 authors.

Costs $165, includes lunch and reception.

Accommodations Provides list of area lodging.

Additional Information 2006 conference information will be available in March by fax or phone. Also accepts inquiries by e-mail. Editors and agents sometimes attend conference.

NEW ENGLAND WRITERS CONFERENCE

P.O. Box 5, 151 Main St., Windsor VT 05089-0483. (802)674-2315. E-mail: newvtpoet@aol.com. Website: www.newenglandwriters.org. **Contact:** Dr. Frank or Susan Anthony, co-directors. Estab. 1986. Annual. Conference held third Saturday in July. Conference duration: 1 day. Average attendance: 150. The purpose is "to bring an affordable literary conference to any writers who can get there and to exposé them to emerging excellence in the craft." Site: The Old South Church on Main St. in Windsor, VT. Offers panel and seminars by prominent authors, agents, editors or publishers; open readings, contest awards and book sales/signings. Featured guest speakers have included Reeve Lindbergh, Rosanna Warren and John Kenneth Galbraith.

Costs $20 (includes refreshments). No pre-registration required.

Accommodations Provides a list of area hotels or lodging options.

Additional Information Sponsors poetry and fiction contests as part of conference (award announced at conference). Conference information available in May. For brochure send SASE or visit website. Accepts inquiries by SASE, e-mail, phone. "Be prepared to listen to the speakers carefully and to network among participants."

🅽 NEW-CUE WRITERS' CONFERENCE AND WORKSHOP

in honor of Rachel Carson, % St. Thomas Aquinas College, 125 Route 340, Sparkill NY 10976. (845)398-4247. Fax: (845)398-4224. E-mail: info@new-cue.org. Website: www.new-cue.org. **Contact:** Barbara Ward Klein, President. Estab. 1999. Biennial (on the "even" year). Conference held June 13-16, 2006. Conference duration: Tuesday-Friday. Average attendance: 100. Participants can expect to hear award-winning authors, to enjoy guided outdoor activities and (if selected) to read from their own work at morning sessions. Site: The 2006 New-Cue Conference and Workshop will be held once again at The Spruce Point Inn in Boothbay Harbor, Maine. The Inn is one of the finest in New England and Boothbay Harbor is the largest boating harbor north of Boston. A call for submissions will be posted with registration information in early September, 2005. In addition, there will be featured speakers each day of the Conference/Workshop. 2002 and 2004 speakers were Bill McKibben, Carl Safina, Robert Finch, Jean Craighead George, Joe Bruchac, Deborah Cramer, Andrea Cohen and Tom Horton. In addition, there were 15 concurrent sessions led by college/university faculty and published authors.

Costs Registration costs for 2006 have not been posted. In 2004, registration was $398 and included all meals, program events and speakers but did *not* include accomodations and travel.

Accommodations Rooms at the Spruce Point Inn are $95-150/night (dbl. ocupancy); rooms nearby are $70-125/night (dbl. ocupancy).

Additional Information Participants need to submit workshop material prior to arrival only if they wish to be considered for presentation during a morning session. Readings limited to 15 minutes. Deadline for submissions January 15, 2006. "The events are interdisciplinary, encouraging participants from colleges and universities, governmental agencies, public and private organizations as well as amateur and published writers. This is an opportunity to participate and to enjoy the company of like-minded individuals in one of the most beautiful coastal locations on the eastern seaboard."

🔘 ODYSSEY FANTASY WRITING WORKSHOP

P.O. Box 75, Mont Vernon NH 03057-1420. Phone/fax: (603)673-6234. E-mail: jcavelos@sff.net. Website: www.sff.net/odyssey. **Contact:** Jeanne Cavelos, director. Estab. 1996. Annual. Last workshop held June 13 to July 22, 2005. Conference duration: 6 weeks. Average attendance: limited to 20. "A workshop for fantasy, science fiction and horror writers that combines an intensive learning and writing experience with in-depth feedback on students' manuscripts. The only workshop to combine the overall guidance of a single instructor with the varied perspectives of guest lecturers. Also, the only such workshop run by a former New York City book editor." Site: conference held at Saint Anselm College in Manchester, New Hampshire. Previous guest lecturers included: George R.R. Martin, Harlan Ellison, Ben Bova, Dan Simmons, Jane Yolen, Elizabeth Hand, Terry Brooks, Craig Shaw Gardner, Patricia McKillip and John Crowley.

Costs In 2005: $1,500 tuition, $625 housing (double room), $1250 (single room); $25 application fee, $500-600 food (approximate), $120 processing fee to receive college credit.

Accommodations "Workshop students stay at Saint Anselm College Apartments and eat at college."

Additional Information Students must apply and include a writing sample. Students' works are critiqued throughout the 6 weeks. Workshop information available in October. For brochure/guidelines send SASE, e-mail, visit website, call or fax. Accepts inquiries by SASE, e-mail, fax, phone.

THE PUBLISHING GAME

Peanut Butter and Jelly Press, P.O. Box 590239, Newton MA 02459. E-mail: conference@publishinggame.com. Website: www.publishinggame.com. **Contact:** Alyza Harris, manager. Estab. 1998. Monthly. Conference held monthly, in different locales across North America: Boston, New York City, Philadelphia, Washington DC, Boca Raton, San Francisco, Los Angeles, Toronto, Seattle, Chicago. Conference duration: 9 a.m. to 4 p.m. Maximum attendance: 18 writers. "A one-day workshop on finding a literary agent, self-publishing your book, creating a publishing house and promoting your book to bestsellerdom!" Site: "Elegant hotels across the country. Boston locations alternate between the Four Seasons Hotel in downtown Boston and The Inn at Harvard in historic Harvard Square, Cambridge." Fiction panels in 2005 included Propel Your Novel from Idea to Finished Manuscript; How to Self-Publish Your Novel; Craft the Perfect Book Package; How to Promote Your Novel; Selling Your Novel to Bookstores and Libraries. Workshop led by Fern Reiss, author and publisher of The Publishing Game series.

Costs $195.

Accommodations "All locations are easily accessible by public transportation." Offers discounted conference rates for participants who choose to arrive early. Offers list of area lodging.

Additional Information Brochures available for SASE. Accepts inquiries by SASE, e-mail, phone, fax, but e-mail preferred. Agents and editors attend conference. "If you're considering finding a literary agent, self-publishing your novel or just selling more copies, this conference will teach you everything you need to know to successfully publish and promote your work."

ROBERT QUACKENBUSH'S CHILDREN'S BOOK WRITING & ILLUSTRATING WORKSHOPS

460 E. 79th St., New York NY 10021-1443. (212)744-3822. Fax: (212)861-2761. E-mail: rqstudios@aol.com. Website: www.rquackenbush.com. **Contact:** Robert Quackenbush, director. Estab. 1982. Annual. Workshop to be held during second week of July. Conference duration: Four days. Average attendance: 10. Workshops to promote writing and illustrating books for children. "Focus is generally on picture books, easy-to-read and early chapter books. Come prepared with stories and/or illustrations to be developed or in a finished state ready to present to a publisher. And be ready to meet a lot of nice people to help you." Site: Held at the Manhattan studio of Robert Quackenbush, author and illustrator of more than 180 books for children. All classes led by Robert Quackenbush.

Costs $650 tuition covers all the costs of the workshop but does not include housing and meals. A $100 nonrefundable deposit is required with the $550 balance due two weeks prior to attendance.

Accommodations A list of recommended hotels and restaurants is sent upon receipt of deposit.

Additional Information Class is for beginners and professionals. Critiques during workshop. Private consultations also available at an hourly rate. "Programs suited to your needs; individualized schedules can be designed. Write or phone to discuss your goals and you will receive a prompt reply." Conference information available 1 year prior to conference. For brochure, send SASE, e-mail, visit website, call or fax. Accepts inquiries by fax, e-mail, phone, SASE.

REMEMBER THE MAGIC IWWG ANNUAL SUMMER CONFERENCE

International Women's Writing Guild, P.O. Box 810, Gracie Station, New York NY 10028-0082. (212)737-7536. Fax: (212)737-9469. E-mail: dirhahn@aol.com. Website: www.iwwg.com. **Contact:** Hannelore Hahn. Estab. 1978. Annual. Conference held in the summer. Conference duration: 1 week. Average attendance: 500. The conference features 70 workshops held every day on every aspect of writing and the arts. Site: Saratoga Springs, 30 minutes from Albany, NY, and 4 hours from New York City. Conference is held "on the tranquil campus of Skidmore College in Saratoga Springs, where the serene Hudson Valley meets the North Country of the Adirondacks."

Costs $945 single, $810 double (members); $975 single, $840 double (nonmembers). Includes meals and lodging.

Accommodations Modern, air-conditioned and non-air-conditioned dormitories—single and/or double occupancy. Equipped with spacious desks and window seats for gazing out onto nature. Meals served cafeteria-style with choice of dishes. Variety of fresh fruits, vegetables and salads have been found plentiful, even by vegetarians. Conference information is available in January. For brochure send SASE, e-mail, visit website or fax. Accepts inquiries by SASE, e-mail, phone or fax. "The conference is for women only."

◎ SCBWI WINTER CONFERENCE, NYC

(formerly SCBWI Midyear Conference), 8271 Beverly Blvd., Los Angeles CA 90048. (323)782-1010. Fax: (323)782-1892. E-mail: conference@scbwi.org. Website: www.scbwi.org. **Contact:** Stephen Mooser. Estab. 2000. Annual. Conference held in February. Average attendance: 700. Conference is to promote writing and illustrationg for children: picture books; fiction; nonfiction; middle grade and young adult; meet an editor; meet an agent; financial planning for writers; marketing your book; art exhibition; etc. Site: Manhattan.
Costs See website for current cost and conference information.

◎ SCBWI/HOFSTRA CHILDREN'S LITERATURE CONFERENCE

University College of Continuing Education, Hofstra University, Hempstead NY 11549. (516)463-5016. Website: www.hofstra.edu/writers. **Contact:** Connie C. Epstein, Adrienne Betz and Marion Flomenhaft, co-organizers. Estab. 1985. Annual. Average attendance: 200. Conference to encourage good writing for children. "Purpose is to bring together various professional groups—writers, illustrators, librarians, teachers—who are interested in writing for children." Site: The conference takes place at the Student Center Building of Hofstra University, located in Hempstead, Long Island. "Each year we organize the program around a theme. Last year it was Finding Your Voice. We have two general sessions, an editorial panel and five break-out groups held in rooms in the Center or nearby classrooms." Previous agents/speakers have included: Paula Danziger and Anne M. Martin and a panel of children's book editors who critique randomly selected first-manuscript pages submitted by registrants. Special interest groups are offered in picture books, nonfiction and submission procedures, with others in fiction.
Costs $77 (previous year) for SCBWI members; $82 for nonmembers. Lunch included.

SEACOAST WRITERS ASSOCIATION SPRING AND FALL CONFERENCES

59 River Road, Stratham NH 03885-2358. E-mail: patparnell@comcast.net. **Contact:** Pat Parnell, conference coordinator. Annual. Conferences held in May and October. Conference duration: 1 day. Average attendance: 60. "Our conferences offer workshops covering various aspects of fiction, nonfiction and poetry." Site: Chester College of New England in Chester, New Hampshire.
Costs Appr. $50.
Additional Information "We sometimes include critiques. It is up to the speaker." Spring meeting includes a contest. Categories are fiction, nonfiction (essays) and poetry. Judges vary from year to year. Conference information available for SASE April 1 and September 1. Accepts inquiries by SASE, e-mail and phone.

THE SOUTHAMPTON COLLEGE WRITERS CONFERENCE

239 Montauk Highway, Southampton NY 11968. (631)287-8175. Fax: (631)287-8253. E-mail: writers@southampton.liu.edu. Website: www.southampton.liu.edu/summer. **Contact:** Carla Cagliati, summer director. Estab. 1975. Annual. Conference held in July. Conference duration: 12 days. Average attendance: 95. The primary work of the conference is conducted in writing workshops in the novel, short story, poem, play, literary essay and memoir. Site: The seaside campus of Southampton College is located in the heart of the Hamptons, a renowned resort area only 70 miles from New York City. During free time, participants can draw inspiration from Atlantic beaches or explore the charming seaside towns. Faculty has included Frank McCourt, Billy Collins, Bharati Mukherjee, Roger Rosenblatt, Bruce Jay Friedman, Melissa Bank and Matt Klam.
Costs application fee: $25; tuition, room and board: $2,320; tuition only: $1,890 (includes breakfast and lunch); program pass: $660 (to attend morning, afternoon and evening readings/lectures, no housing or workshops).
Accommodations On-campus housing—doubles and small singles with shared baths—is modest but comfortable. Housing assignment is by lottery. A limited number of single supplements are available at additional cost on a first-come basis. Supplies list of lodging alternatives.
Additional Information Applicants must complete an application form and submit a writing sample of unpublished, original work up to 20 pages (15 pages for poetry). See website for details. Brochures available in December by fax, phone, e-mail and on website. Accepts inquiries by SASE, e-mail, phone and fax. Editors and agents attend this conference.

◎ VERMONT COLLEGE POSTGRADUATE WRITERS' CONFERENCE

36 College St., Montpelier VT 05602. (802)223-2133. Fax: (802)828-8585. E-mail: roger.weingarten@tui.edu. Website: www.tui.edu/conferences. **Contact:** Roger Weingarten, director. Estab. 1995. Annual. August. Confer-

ence duration: 6 days. Average attendance: 65. This workshop covers the following areas of writing: novels, short stories, creative nonfiction, poetry, poetry manuscript and translation. Site: Union Institute & University's historic Vermont College campus in Montpelier. Workshops are centered on craft and often include exercises. 2005 facutly included Rikki DuCornet, Antonya Nelson, Michael Martone, Ellen Lesser, Robin Hemley and Roger Weingarter.
Costs Tuition is $800-875; private dorm room is $270; shared dorm room is $150; meals are $135.
Accommodations Shuttles from airport available.
Additional Information Workshop material must be submitted 6 weeks prior to conference. Submit 25 pages of prose, 6 pages of poetry, 50 pages of poetry ms. Brochures available in January for SASE, by e-mail, on website or in publication. "This conference is for advanced writers with postgraduate degrees or equivalent experience. Workshops are limited to 5-7 participants."

VERMONT STUDIO CENTER
P.O. Box 613, Johnson VT 05656. (802)635-2727. Fax: (802)635-2730. E-mail: writing@vermontstudiocenter.org. Website: www.vermontstudiocenter.org. **Contact:** Ryan Walsh, writing program coordinator. Estab. 1984. Ongoing residencies. Conference duration: From 2-12 weeks. "Most residents stay for 1 month." Average attendance: 53 writers and visual artists/month. "The Vermont Studio Center is an international creative community located in Johnson, Vermont, and serving more than 500 American and international artists and writers each year (50 per month). A Studio Center Residency features secluded, uninterrupted writing time, the companionship of dedicated and talented peers, and access to a roster of two distinguished Visiting Writers each month. All VSC Residents receive three meals a day, private, comfortable housing and the company of an international community of painters, sculptors, poets, printmakers and writers. Writers attending residencies at the Studio Center may work on whatever they choose—no matter what month of the year they attend." Visiting writers have included Alexander Theroux, John Keeble Creeley, Brigit Pegeen Kelly, Amy Hempel, Maureen Howard, Dean Young and Jane Hirshfeld.
Costs "The cost of a 4-week residency is $3,500. Many applicants receive financial aid."
Accommodations Provided.
Additional Information Conferences may be arranged with visiting writers of the resident's genre. If conference scheduled, resident may submit up to 15 pages of ms. "We have competitions for full fellowships three times a year. The deadlines are February 15, June 15 and October 1. Writers should submit manuscripts of 15 pages. Application fee is $25." Writers encouraged to visit website for more information. May also e-mail, call, fax.

WESLEYAN WRITERS CONFERENCE
Wesleyan University, Middletown CT 06459. (860)685-3604. Fax: (860)685-2441. E-mail: agreene@wesleyan.edu. Website: www.wesleyan.edu/writers. **Contact:** Anne Greene, director. Estab. 1956. Annual. Conference held the third week of June. Average attendance: 100. For fiction techniques, novel, short story, poetry, screenwriting, nonfiction, literary journalism, memoir. Site: The conference is held on the campus of Wesleyan University, in the hills overlooking the Connecticut River. Meals and lodging are provided on campus. Features daily seminars, readings of new fiction, poetry and nonfiction, optional ms consultations and guest speakers on a range of topics including publishing. "Both new and experienced writers are welcome."
Costs In 2004, day students' rate $725 (included tuition and meals); boarding students' rate of $910 (included tuition, meals and room for 5 nights).
Accommodations "Participants can fly to Hartford or take Amtrak to Meriden, CT. We are happy to help participants make travel arrangements." Overnight participants stay on campus or in hotels.
Additional Information "Award-winning faculty. Fiction writers are welcome to attend the poetry and nonfiction sessions if they are interested. Scholarships and teaching fellowships are available, including the Jakobson Scholarships for new writers of fiction, poetry and nonfiction and the Jon Davidoff Scholarships for journalists. Accepts inquiries by e-mail, phone, fax.

N WRITER'S VOICE OF THE WEST SIDE YMCA
5 West 63rd Street, New York NY 10023. (212)875-4124. Fax: (212)875-4184. E-mail: graucher@ymcanyc.org. **Contact:** Glenn Raucher. Estab. 1981. Workshop held 4 times/year (Summer, Spring, Winter and Fall). Conference duration: 10 weeks (8 weeks in summer); 2 hours, one night/week. Average attendance: 12. Workshop on "fiction, poetry, writing for performance, nonfiction, multi-genre, playwriting and memoir." Special one-day intensives throughout the year. Frequent Visiting Author readings, which are free and open to the public. Site: Workshop held at the Westside YMCA.
Costs $400/workshop, free for West Side Y members.
Additional Information For workshop brochures/guidelines send SASE, e-mail, visit website, call or fax. Accepts inquiries by SASE, e-mail, fax, phone. "The Writer's Voice of the Westside Y is the largest non-academic literary arts center in the U.S."

◎ WRITING, CREATIVITY AND RITUAL: A WOMAN'S RETREAT

995 Chapman Road, Yorktown Heights NY 10598. (914)926-4432. E-mail: emily@emilyhanlon.com. Website: www.awritersretreat.com. **Contact:** Emily Hanlon. Estab. 1998. Annual. Last retreat held in Glastonbury, England, July 14-22, 2005, with an additional post-retreat trip to London, July 22-27, 2005. The retreat goes to Costa Rica Sept. 24-Oct. 5, 2006. Average attendance: 20 is the limit. Women only. Retreat for all kinds of creative writing. Site: "Held at the Glastonbury Abbey, Glastonbury, England. Glastonbury is thought to be the ancient isle of Avalon and, in the morning, the mists still hover over the gently rolling landscape. At night, moonlight splays across the cathedral ruins and the hills of Sommerset. Indeed, there is no finer place for a writer's retreat, no better place to inspire the imagination and nourish the writer's soul. An ideal site for a gathering of women passionate about their writing and anxious to connect with others of like mind and heart. With every need attended to, we open doorways to new stories, characters, techniques and friendships with each other as well as ourselves. We explore the deeper passions behind our writing, including what drives us to write and what stops us from being as creative as we might be."

Costs In 2005: $2,350-2,550, depending on choice of room. Includes workshop and all meals. Save $200 if you pay in full by May 15. Optional trip to London, 5 nights.

Additional Information Conference information free and available. Accepts inquiries by e-mail, phone. "More than just a writing workshop or conference, the retreat is an exploration of the creative process through writing, 3-hour writing workshops daily, plus creativity workshops and time to write and explore." Please e-mail or call if you would like to be put on the Costa Rica mailing list.

YADDO

Box 395, Saratoga Springs NY 12866-0395. (518)584-0746. Fax: (518)584-1312. E-mail: yaddo@yaddo.org. Website: www.yaddo.org. **Contact:** Candace Wait, program director. Estab. 1900. Two seasons: large season is in mid-May-August; small season is late September-May (stays from 2 weeks to 2 months; average stay is 5 weeks). Average attendance: Accommodates approximately 34 artists in large season, 12-15 in the small season. "Those qualified for invitations to Yaddo are highly qualified writers, visual artists, composers, choreographers, performance artists and film and video artists who are working at the professional level in their fields. Artists who wish to work collaboratively are encouraged to apply. An abiding principle at Yaddo is that applications for residencies are judged on the quality of the artists' work and professional promise." Site: includes four small lakes, a rose garden, woodland.

Costs No fee is charged; residency includes room, board and studio space. Limited travel expenses are available to artists accepted for residencies at Yaddo.

Accommodations Provisions include room, board and studio space. No stipends are offered.

Additional Information To apply: Filing fee is $20 (checks payable to Corporation of Yaddo). Two letters of recommendation are requested. Applications are considered by the Admissions Committee and invitations are issued by March 15 (deadline: January 1) and October 1 (deadline: August 1). Information available for SASE (60¢ postage), by e-mail, fax or phone and on website. Accepts inquiries by e-mail, fax, SASE, phone.

MIDATLANTIC (DC, DE, MD, NJ, PA)

GREATER LEHIGH VALLEY WRITERS GROUP 'THE WRITE STUFF' WRITERS CONFERENCE

Four Points Sheraton, 3400 Airport Rd., Allentown PA 18109. (908)479-6581. Fax: (908)479-6744. E-mail: juswrite@earthlink.net. Website: www.glvwg.org. **Contact:** JoAnn Dahan, chair. Estab. 1993. Annual. Last conference was April 1-2, 2005. Conference duration: 1 day. Average attendance: 140. This conference features workshops in all genres. Site: "The Four Points Sheraton is located in the beautiful Lehigh Valley. The spacious hotel has an indoor swimming pool where our keynote will address the conference over a wonderful, three-course meal. The hotel rooms are very inviting after a long day's drive. We try to offer a little bit of everything to satisfy all our attendees." 2005 keynote speaker was Nancy Kress, who gained prominence as a writing coach through her two books, *Dynamic Characters* and *Beginnings, Middles and Ends* (Elements of Fiction Series), and through her monthly stint as fiction columnist for *Writer's Digest Magazine*.

Costs In 2005, for members, $95, which includes all workshops, 2 meals and a chance to pitch your work to an editor or agent. Also a book fair with book signing. For non-members, cost is $115. Late registration: $130.

Additional Information For more information, see the website. Sponsors contest for conferees. The Writer's Flash contest is judged by conference participants. Write 100 words or less in fiction, creative nonfiction or poetry. Brochures available in March for SASE, or by phone, e-mail or on website. Accepts inquiries by SASE, e-mail, phone, fax. Agents and editors attend conference. "Be sure to refer to the website, as often with conferences things change. Greater Lehigh Valley Writers Group has remained one of the most friendly conferences and we give the most for your money. Breakout rooms offer craft topics, editor and agent panels, a 'chick lit' panel and more."

HIGHLIGHTS FOUNDATION FOUNDERS WORKSHOPS

814 Court St., Honesdale PA 18431. (570)253-1192. Fax: (570)253-0179. E-mail: contact@highlightsfoundation. org. Website: www.highlightsfoundation.org. **Contact:** Kent L. Brown, Jr., executive director. Estab. 2000. Workshops held seasonally in March, April, May, June, September, October, November. Conference duration: 3-7 days. Average attendance: limited to 10-15. Conference focuses on children's writing: fiction, nonfiction, poetry, promotions. "Our goal is to improve, over time, the quality of literature for children by educating future generations of children's authors." Site: Highlights Founders' home in Boyds Mills, PA. Faculty/speakers in 2004 included Joy Cowley, Patricia Lee Gauch, Carolyn Yoder, Sandy Asher, Rebecca Dotlich, Rich Wallace, Neil Waldman, Kent L. Brown, Jr. and Peter Jacobi.

Costs 2004 costs ranged from $495-995, including meals, lodging, materials.

Accommodations Coordinates pickup at local airport. "Participants stay in guest cabins on the wooded grounds surrounding Highlights Founders' home adjacent to the house/conference center."

Additional Information "Some workshops require pre-workshop assignment." Brochure available for SASE, by e-mail, on website, by phone, by fax. Accepts inquiries by phone, fax, e-mail, SASE. Editors attend conference. "Applications will be reviewed and accepted on a first-come, first-served basis, applicants must demonstrate specific experience in writing area of workshop they are applying for—writing samples are required for many of the workshops."

HIGHLIGHTS FOUNDATION WRITING FOR CHILDREN

814 Court St., Honesdale PA 18431. (570)253-1192. Fax: (570)253-0179. E-mail: contact@highlightsfoundation. org. Website: www.highlightsfoundation.org. **Contact:** Kent L. Brown. Estab. 1985. Annual. Conference held July 16-23, 2005; July 15-22, 2006. Average attendance: 100. Focuses on all genres of children's writing. Site: Chautauqua Institution. "Few cars are allowed on the grounds making for peaceful, idyllic surroundings. Architecture reflects the charm of the late 19th century." Panels planned included Characterization, Writing Dialogue, Point of View, Developing a Plot, Think Pictures, etc. 2005 speakers included Larry Dane Brimner, Carolyn Coman, Joy Cowley, Heather Harrison, Peter P. Jacobi, Yolanda Leroy, Fredrick and Patricia McKissack, Susan Pearson, Stephen Roxburgh, Pam Muñoz Ryan and more.

Costs In 2004, $2,100 with meals, gate pass, conference supplies included. Lodging and transportation extra.

Accommodations Coordinates pickup from local airports: Jamestown, PA; Erie, PA; and Buffalo, NY. Coordinates locating lodging. "Accommodations available on the grounds: inns, hotels, guesthouses." $350-1,000 per week.

Additional Information Participants must submit ms if participating in ms program. Brochures available in December by SASE, e-mail, phone, fax or on website. Accepts inquiries by SASE, e-mail, phone, fax. Agents and editors attend conference.

MONTROSE CHRISTIAN WRITER'S CONFERENCE

5 Locust Street, Montrose Bible Conference, Montrose PA 18801-1112. (570)278-1001 or (800)598-5030. Fax: (570)278-3061. E-mail: mbc@montrosebible.org. Website: www.montrosebible.org. **Contact:** Donna Kosik, MBC Secretary/Registrar. Estab. 1990. Annual. Conference held in July 2006. Average attendance: 75. "We try to meet a cross-section of writing needs, for beginners and advanced, covering fiction, poetry and writing for children. It is small enough to allow personal interaction between conferees and faculty. We meet in the beautiful village of Montrose, Pennsylvania, situated in the mountains. The Bible Conference provides hotel/motel-like accommodation and good food. The main sessions are held in the chapel with rooms available for other classes. Fiction writing has been taught each year."

Costs In 2004 registration (tuition) was $135.

Accommodations Will meet planes in Binghamton, NY and Scranton, PA. On-site accomodations: room and board $225-270/conference; $50-60/day including food (2004 rates). RV court available.

Additional Information "Writers can send work ahead of time and have it critiqued for a small fee." The attendees are usually church related. The writing has a Christian emphasis. Conference information available April 2005. For brochure send SASE, visit website, e-mail, call or fax. Accepts inquiries by SASE, e-mail, fax, phone.

OUTDOOR WRITERS ASSOCIATION OF AMERICA ANNUAL CONFERENCE

158 Lower Georges Valley Rd., Spring Mills PA 16875. (814)364-9557. Fax: (814)364-9558. E-mail: eking4owaa @cs.com. Website: www.owaa.org. **Contact:** Eileen King, meeting planner. Estab. 1927. Annual. Conference held June 17-21, 2006, in Lake Charles, Louisiana. Average attendance: 700-750. Conference concentrates on outdoor communications (all forms of media). Featured speakers have included Don Ranley, University of Missouri, Columbia; Brig. General Chuck Yeager; Nina Leopold Bradley (daughter of Aldo Leopold); Secretary of the Interior, Gail Norton; Bill Irwin, the only blind man to hike the Appalachian Trail.

Costs $325 for nonmembers; "applicants must have prior approval from the Executive Director." Registration fee includes cost of most meals.

Accommodations List of accommodations available after February. Special room rates for attendees.

Additional Information Sponsors contests, "but all is done prior to the conference and you must be a member to enter them." Conference information available February 2006. For brochure visit website, send e-mail, call or fax. Accepts inquiries by e-mail, fax.

PENN WRITERS CONFERENCE

3440 Market St., Suite 100, Philadelphia PA 19104. (215)898-6493. Fax: (215)573-2053. E-mail: writconf@sas.up enn.edu. Website: www.pennwritersconference.org. **Contact:** Nadia Daniel, manager, non-credit programs. Estab. 1995. Annual. 2005 conference held in October. Conference duration: Two days. Average attendance: 300. Upcoming themes and speakers to be announced.

Costs Check website for 2006 costs.

Additional Information Brochures available in September.

N ⓒ SANDY COVE CHRISTIAN WRITERS CONFERENCE AND MENTORING RETREAT

60 Sandy Cove Rd., North East MD 21901-5436. (800)234-2683. Fax: (410)287-3196. E-mail: info@sandycove. org or sandycove@jameswatkins.com. Website: www.sandycove.org. **Contact:** Jim Watkins, director of conference. Estab. 1982. Annual. Last conference held October 2-5, 2005. Average attendance: 130. Focus is on "all areas of writing from a Christian perspective such as: periodicals, devotionals, fiction, juvenile fiction, Sunday School curriculum, screenwriting, self-publishing, Internet writing, etc." Site: "Sandy Cove is conveniently located mid-way between Baltimore and Philadelphia, just off I-95." Located on 220 acres of Maryland woodland, near headwaters of the Chesapeake Bay. Past faculty included Christy Allen Scannel, Bonnie Brechbill, Michael Davis, Sharon Ewell Foster, Lisa Halls Johnson, Curtis Lundgren, Doug Newton, Kristi Rector, John Riddle, Kathy Scott, Olivia Seaton, Brian Taylor, Claudia Tynes, Jim Watkins, Carol Wedeven.

Costs In 2004, costs were full package: $692 per person (single room occupancy) or $558 per person (double room occupancy)—includes lodging, meals, materials, seminars, sessions, private appointments and 2 ms evaluations; day guest package: $424 per person, excluding lodging.

Accommodations No arrangements for transportation. "Hotel-style rooms, bay view available. Suites available for additional fee."

Additional Information "For manuscript evaluations, participants may submit their manuscripts between six and two weeks prior to the conference. One copy should be sent in a 9×12 manila envelope. Include a self-addressed, stamped postcard if you want confirmation that it arrived safely." Accepts inquiries by e-mail, phone, fax. Editors and publishers participate in conference. Also offers 1-day student training for high school and college age as well as a writer's retreat—24 hours of uninterrupted writing and mentoring.

N WASHINGTON INDEPENDENT WRITERS (WIW) WASHINGTON WRITERS CONFERENCE

733 15th St. NW, Suite 220, Washington DC 20005-2112. (202)737-9500. Fax: (202)638-7800. E-mail: info@was hwriter.org. Website: www.washwriter.org. **Contact:** Donald Graul, Jr., executive director. Estab. 1975. Annual. Conference held in May. Conference duration: Friday and Saturday. Average attendance: 450. "Gives participants a chance to hear from and talk with dozens of experts on book and magazine publishing as well as meet one-on-one with literary agents." Site: George Washington University Cafritz Center. Past keynote speakers included Erica Jong, Diana Rehm, Kitty Kelley, Lawrence Block, John Barth, Stephen Hunter.

Additional Information Send inquiries to info@washwriter.org.

WILLIAM PATERSON UNIVERSITY SPRING WRITER'S CONFERENCE

English Dept., Atrium 250, 300 Pompton Rd., Wayne NJ 07470-2103. (973)720-3567. Fax: (973)720-2189. E-mail: liut@wpunj.edu. Website: http://euphrates.wpunj.edu/WritersConference. **Contact:** Timothy Liu, associate professor. Annual. Conference held in April. Conference duration: 1 day. Average attendance: 100-125. The 2005 conference focused on "writing the world." Several hands-on workshops were offered in many genres of creative writing, critical writing and literature. Included reading by nationally recognized author. Site: William Paterson University campus. 2005 keynote speaker: poet Linda Gregg. Past faculty has included Yusef Komunyakaa, Joyce Carol Oates, Susan Sontag and Jimmy Santiago Braca.

Costs $40 (2005) includes 2 workshops, plenary readings, meals.

Additional Information Conference information is available November/December. For brochure send e-mail, visit website, call or fax. Accepts inquiries by SASE, e-mail, phone and fax. Agents and editors participate in conference.

WINTER POETRY & PROSE GETAWAY IN CAPE MAY

18 North Richards Ave., Ventnor NJ 08406. (609)823-5076. E-mail: info@wintergetaway.com. Website: www.w intergetaway.com. **Contact:** Peter E. Murphy, founder/director. Estab. 1994. Annual. 2006 dates: January 13-

16. Conference duration: Four-day event. Average attendance: 200. "Open to all writers, beginners and experienced over the age of 18. Workshops offered include Writing New Stories, Revising a Short Story Toward Publication, Focusing Your Fiction, Finishing Your Novel, as well as workshops in Creative Nonfiction and Turning Memory into Memoir. Workshops meet from 9-4 Saturday & Sunday and 9-12 on Monday. The Getaway also features workshops in poetry writing, song writing, writing for children, painting and photography. Other special features include extra-supportive sessions for beginners. There are usually 10 or fewer participants in each workshop and fewer than 7 in each of the prose workshops. Previous staff have included Renée Ashley, Christian Bauman, Anndee Hochman, Laura McCullough, Joyce McDonald, Carol Plum-Ucci.

Costs Cost for 2005 was $495, which included breakfast and lunch for 3 days, all sessions and a double room. Participants responsible for dinners only. Participants may choose a single room at an additional cost. A $25 "early bard" discount is available if full payment is made by November 15.

Accommodations "The Grand Hotel on the Oceanfront in Historic Cape May, NJ. Participants stay in comfortable rooms, most with an ocean view, perfect for thawing out the muse. Hotel facilities include a pool, sauna, and whirlpool, as well as a lounge and disco for late evening dancing for night people."

Additional Information "Individual critiques available." Brochure and registration form available by mail or on website. "The Winter Getaway is known for its challenging and supportive workshops that encourage imaginative risk-taking and promote freedom and transformation in the participants' writing."

MIDSOUTH (NC, SC, TN, VA, WV)

AMERICAN CHRISTIAN WRITERS CONFERENCES
P.O. Box 110390, Nashville TN 37222. (800)21-WRITE. Fax: (615)834-7736. E-mail: ACWriters@aol.com. Website: www.ACWriters.com. **Contact:** Reg Forder, director. Estab. 1988. Annual. Conferences held throughout the year in over 2 dozen cities. Conference duration: 2 days. Average attendance: 30-80. Conference's purpose is to promote all forms of Christian writing. Site: Usually located at a major hotel chain like Holiday Inn.
Costs $99 for 1 day; $189 for 2 days. Plus meals and accommodations.
Accommodations Special rates available at host hotel.
Additional Information Conference information available for SASE, e-mail, phone or fax. Accepts inquiries by fax, e-mail, phone, SASE.

◎ BLUE RIDGE MOUNTAINS CHRISTIAN WRITERS CONFERENCE
(800)588-7222. E-mail: ylehman@bellsouth.net. Website: www.lifeway.com/christianwriters. **Contact:** Yvonne Lehman, director. Estab. 1999. Annual. Conference held April 17-21, 2006. Average attendance: 240. All areas of Christian writing, including fiction, nonfiction, scriptwriting, devotionals, greeting cards, etc. For beginning and advanced writers. Site: LifeWay Ridgecrest Conference Center, 18 miles east of Asheville NC. "Companies represented this year include AMG Publications, Broadman and Holman, Focus on the Family, Howard Publishers, Upper Room, LifeWay Christian Resources, Lawson Falle Greeting Cards & Gift Books, Christian Film & TV, Crosswalk, Evangel, Christian Writers Guild, Light and Life, Living Ink Books, NavPress, WestBow Press, MovieGuide, Hartline Literary Agency, Les Stobbe Agency." Faculty includes professional authors, agents and editors.
Accommodations LifeWay Ridgecrest Conference Center.
Additional Information Sponsors contests for unpublished in categories for poetry and lyrics, articles and short stories, novels and novellas, nonfiction, greeting cards, and scripts. Awards include trophy and $200 scholarship toward next year's conference. See website for critique service and daily schedule—offering keynote sessions, continuing classes and workshops.

Ⓝ THE COMPLETE WRITER INTENSIVE WRITERS' CAMP
Jones Brehony Seminars in partnership with Island Path Seminars, P.O. Box 878, Ocracoke Island NC 27960. (877)708-7284. E-mail: islandpath@ocracokenc.net. Website: www.jonesbrehony.com. **Contact:** Ruth Fordon or Ken DeBarth. Estab. July 2001. Last conference held Sept. 25-Oct. 1, 2005. Conference duration: 6 days. Average attendance: under 20. Conference focuses on fiction, nonfiction, publishing. Site: Ocracoke Island, NC. Panels include Understanding the Publishing Industry and How to Make it Work for You, Letting the Muse Flow: Exploring and Manifesting Your Creativity as a Writer, Building the Container: Strategies and Discipline to Capture Your Creative Flow, Techniques of Fiction.
Costs Workshop and all breakfasts, all lunches, 2 dinners—$1,625; workshop and all breakfasts, all lunches, 2 dinners and lodging—$1,875. Discounts for early registration. Fees include "16 hours of structured class time, 14 hours of intensive writing exercises with 1:1 mentoring, evening speakers—published authors and a publisher/editor, all handout materials, two post-workshop conference calls to report on your goals, T'ai chi

at sunrise by the ocean, 50% off one bicycle rental for the week, 50% off one massage from a certified massage therapist.''
Accommodations Those not staying in the guest house receive 10% off other accommodations.
Additional Information Brochure available by e-mail for SASE. Accepts inquiries by SASE, e-mail and phone. Agents and editors attend conference.

◎ GALACTICON

5465 Hwy. 58, #502, Chattanooga TN 37416-1659. (423)326-0339. E-mail: galacticon@vei.net. Website: www.g alacticoninc.com. **Contact:** Clara Miller, programming director. Estab. 1999. Annual. Conference held in March. Average attendance: 200-250. Conference focuses on ''science fiction/fantasy: novels, short stories, poetry (when we have poets for panels), music (filk and folk).'' Site: Comfort Inn. 2006 schedule TBA. ''In the past we have had panels on Novel vs. Short Story; Writing for Special Markets; Building Your World and/or Universe; Alternate Worlds; Choosing a Publisher; Preparing a Manuscript; Writing With Another Author; Self-Publishing; Comparative Religions.''
Costs See website for 2006 rates.
Accommodations E-mail Galacticon for details.

HIGHLAND SUMMER CONFERENCE

Box 7014, Radford University, Radford VA 24142-7014. (540)831-5366. Fax: (540)831-5951. E-mail: jasbury@ra dford.edu. Website: www.radford.edu/~arsc. **Contact:** Jo Ann Asbury, assistant to director. Estab. 1978. Annual. Conference held first 2 weeks of June. Conference duration: 2 weeks. Average attendance: 25. Three hours graduate or undergraduate credits. Site: The Highland Summer Conference is held at Radford University, a school of about 9,000 students. Radford is in the Blue Ridge Mountains of southwest Virginia, about 45 miles south of Roanoke, VA. ''The HSC features one (two weeks) or two (one week each) guest leaders each year. As a rule, our leaders are well-known writers who have connections, either thematic or personal or both, to the Appalachian region. The genre emphasis depends upon the workshop leader(s). In the past we have had as guest lecturers Nikki Giovanni, Sharyn McCrumb, Gurney Norman, Denise Giardinia, George Ella Lyon, Jim Wayne Miller, Wilma Dykeman and Robert Morgan.''
Costs ''The cost is based on current Radford tuition for 3 credit hours plus an addidtional conference fee. On-campus meals and housing are available at additional cost. 2004 conference tuition was $519 for in-state undergraduates, $670 for graduate students.''
Accommodations ''We do not have special rate arrangements with local hotels. We do offer accommodations on the Radford University Campus in a recently refurbished residence hall. (In 2004 cost was $24.04-33.44 per night.)''
Additional Information ''Conference leaders typically critique work done during the two-week conference, but do not ask to have any writing sumbitted prior to the conference beginning.'' Conference information available after February for SASE. Accepts inquiries by e-mail, fax.

HILTON HEAD ISLAND WRITERS RETREAT

40 Governors Lane, Hilton Head Island SC 29928. Phone/fax: (843)671-5118. E-mail: bob@bobmayer.org. Website: www.bobmayer.org. **Contact:** Bob Mayer. Estab. 2002. Every 3 months. Last conferences: March, June, September, December 2005. Conference duration: 4 days. Site: Held at the Marriott Beach & Golf Resort, oceanside, Hilton Head Island.
Costs $550 in 2005.
Accommodations at Marriott.
Additional Information Participants should submit cover letter, one-page synopsis, and first 15 pages of ms.

MID-MISSISSIPPI WRITERS CONFERENCE

John Wood Community College, 1301 S. 48th St., Quincy IL 62305. (217)641-4903. Fax: (217)641-4900. E-mail: ssparks@jwcc.edu. **Contact:** Sherry Sparks. Estab. 2001. Conference in June. Conference duration: 1 weekend. Average attendance: 30-50. Workshop/conference covers all areas of writing, for beginners and more advanced. ''We encourage and invite beginning-level writers.'' Site: John Wood Community College.
Costs $35-$50; some meals included.
Accommodations List of area hotels available.
Additional Information Sponsors contest. Brochures/registration forms available in February; send SASE, visit website, e-mail, fax or call. ''Come ready to make new friends, see a beautiful city and be inspired to write!''

NORTH CAROLINA WRITERS' NETWORK FALL CONFERENCE

P.O. Box 954, Carrboro NC 27510-0954. (919)967-9540. Fax: (919)929-0535. E-mail: mail@ncwriters.org. Website: www.ncwriters.org. **Contact:** Cynthia Barrett, executive director. Estab. 1985. Annual. Average attendance:

450. "The conference is a weekend full of classes, panels, readings and informal gatherings. The Network serves writers at all stages of development from beginning, to emerging, to established. We also encourage readers who might be considering writing. We have several genres represented. In the past we have offered fiction, nonfiction, poetry, screenwriting, writing for children, journalism and more. We always invite New York editors and agents and offer craft classes in editing, pitching and marketing." Site: "We hold the conference at a conference center with hotel rooms available."
Costs "Conference registration fee for NCWN members is approximately $250 and includes at least two meals."
Accommodations "Special conference hotel rates are available, but the individual makes his/her own reservations."
Additional Information Conference information available September 1. For brochure, e-mail us or visit our website. Online secure registration available at www.ncwriters.org.

SEWANEE WRITERS' CONFERENCE

735 University Ave., Sewanee TN 37383-1000. (931)598-1141. E-mail: cpeters@sewanee.edu. Website: www.sewaneewriters.org. **Contact:** Cheri B. Peters, creative writing programs manager. Estab. 1990. Annual. 2006 conference held in July. Average attendance: 110. "We offer genre-based workshops in fiction, poetry and playwriting and a full schedule of readings, craft lectures, panel discussions, talks, Q&A sessions and the like." Site: "The Sewanee Writers' Conference uses the facilities of the University of the South. Physically, the University is a collection of ivy-covered Gothic-style buildings, located on the Cumberland Plateau in mid-Tennessee." Invited editors, publishers and agents structure their own presentations, but there is always opportunity for questions from the audience." 2005 faculty included Richard Bausch, John Casey, Tony Earley, Daisy Foote, John Hollander, Randall Kenan, X.J. Kennedy, Romulus Linney, Jill McCorkle, Brad Leithauser, Margot Livesey, Alice McDermott, Mary Jo Salter and Mark Winegardner.
Costs Full conference fee (tuition, board and basic room) is $1,470; a single room costs an additional $75.
Accommodations Participants are housed in university dormitory rooms. Motel or B&B housing is available but not abundantly so. Dormitory shared housing costs are included in the full conference fee. Complimentary chartered bus service is available—on a limited basis—on the first and last days of the conference.
Additional Information "We offer each participant (excepting auditors) the opportunity for a private manuscript conference with a member of the faculty. These manuscripts are due one month before the conference begins." Conference information available after February. For brochure send address and phone number, e-mail, visit website or call. "The conference has available a limited number of fellowships and scholarships; these are awarded on a competitive basis." Accepts inquiries by website, e-mail, phone, regular mail (send address and phone number).

SOUTH CAROLINA WRITERS WORKSHOP ANNUAL CONFERENCE

P.O. Box 7104, Columbia SC 29202. (803)794-0832. Website: www.scwriters.com. Estab. 1990. Annual. Conference held in October. Conference duration: 3 days. Average attendance: 150. Conference theme varies each year. Hands-on and lecture-style sessions in both craft and the business of writing are featured for all major genres.
Additional Information Please check website for more information. Accepts inquiries by e-mail. Agents and editors attend this conference.

STELLARCON

Box I-1, Elliott University Center, UNCG, Greensboro NC 27412. (336)294-8041. E-mail: info@stellarcon.org. Website: www.stellarcon.org. **Contact:** James Fulbright, convention manager. Estab. 1976. Annual. Last conference held March 11-13, 2005. Average attendance: 500. Conference focuses on "general science fiction and fantasy (horror also) with an emphasis on literature." Site: Downtown Marriott, Greensboro, NC. See website for 2006 speakers.
Costs See website for 2006 rates.
Accommodations "Lodging is available at the Marriott."
Additional Information Accepts inquiries by e-mail. Agents and editors participate in conference.

VIRGINIA FESTIVAL OF THE BOOK

145 Ednam Dr., Charlottesville VA 22903. (434)924-6890. Fax: (434)296-4714. E-mail: vabook@virginia.edu. Website: www.vabook.org. **Contact:** Nancy Damon, programs director. Estab. 1995. Annual. Festival held in March. Average attendance: 22,000. Festival held to celebrate books and promote reading and literacy. Site: Held throughout the Charlottesville/Albemarle area.
Costs See website for 2006 rates.
Accommodations Overnight accomodations available.
Additional Information "Authors must 'apply' to the festival to be included on a panel." Conference information

Conferences

is available on the website, e-mail, fax or phone. For brochure visit website. Accepts inquiries by e-mail, fax, phone. Authors, agents and editors participate in conference. "The festival is a five-day event featuring authors, illustrators and publishing professionals. The featured authors are invited to convene for discussions and readings or write and inquire to participate. All attendees welcome."

SOUTHEAST (AL, AR, FL, GA, LA, MS, PR [PUERTO RICO])

ALABAMA WRITERS' CONCLAVE

107 Twentieth Street South, Birmingham AL 35233. (205)326-4460. E-mail: jim@jimreedbooks.com. Website: www.alabamawritersconclave.org. **Contact:** Jim Reed, president. Estab. 1923. July. Average attendance: 80-100. Conference to promote "all phases" of writing. Site: Four Points Sheraton at the University of Alabama, Tuscaloosa, Alabama.

Costs Fees for 3 days are $120, including 3 meals.

Accommodations $80 per night at Sheraton.

Additional Information "We have major speakers and faculty members who conduct intensive, energetic workshops. Our annual writing contest guidelines and all other information is available at www.alabamawritersconclave.org."

ARKANSAS WRITERS' CONFERENCE

AR Penwomen Pioneer Branch of the National League of American Penwomen, 6817 Gingerbread Lane, Little Rock AR 72204. (501)565-8889. Fax: (501)565-7220. E-mail: pvining@aristotle.net. Website: http://groups.yahoo.com/group/arpenwomen. **Contact:** Clouita Rice, registrar/treasurer. Estab. 1944. Annual. Conference held first weekend in June. Average attendance: 175. "We have a variety of subjects related to writing. We have some general sessions, some more specific, but we try to vary each year's subjects."

Costs Registration: $10; luncheon: $15; banquet: $17.50; contest entry $5 (2004 rates).

Accommodations "We meet at a Holiday Inn Select—rooms available at reasonable rate." Holiday Inn has a bus to bring anyone from the airport. Rooms average $70.

Additional Information "We have 36 contest categories. Some are open only to Arkansans, most are open to all writers. Our judges are not announced before conference but are qualified, many from out of state." Conference information available February 15. For brochures or inquiries send SASE (include full mailing address), call or fax. "We have had 226 people attending from 12 states—over 2,000 contest entries from 40 states and New Zealand, Mexico and Canada."

FLORIDA FIRST COAST WRITERS' FESTIVAL

9911 Old Baymeadows Rd., FCCJ Deerwood Center, Jacksonville FL 32256-8117. (904)997-2726. Fax: (904)997-2746. E-mail: kclower@fccj.edu. Website: opencampus.fccj.org/WF/. **Contact:** Kathleen Clower, conference coordinator. Estab. 1985. Annual. Last festival held in May 19-22, 2005. Average attendance: 300-350. All areas; mainstream plus genre. Site: Held at Sea Turtle Inn on Atlantic Beach.

Costs Early bird special $225 for 2 days (including lunch and banquet) or $190 for 2 days (including lunch) or $95 for each day; pre-conference workshops and agents & editors day on Sunday are extra.

Accommodations Sea Turtle Inn, (904)249-7402 or (800)874-6000, has a special festival rate.

Additional Information Sponsors contests for short fiction, poetry and novels. Novel judges are David Poyer and Lenore Hart. Entry fees: $30, novels; $10, short fiction; $5, poetry. Deadline: December 1 for novels, short fiction, poems. New playwriting contest was added in 2005. Conference information available in January. For brochures/guidelines visit website, e-mail, fax, call. Accepts inquiries by e-mail, phone, fax. E-mail contest inquiries to hdenson@fccj.edu.

GEORGIA WRITERS SPRING FESTIVAL OF WORKSHOPS

1071 Steeple Run, Lawrenceville GA 30043. (678)407-0703. Fax: (678)407-9917. E-mail: festival@georgiawriters.org. Website: www.georgiawriters.org; www.georgiawriters.org/Festival-2006.htm. **Contact:** Geri Taran, executive director. Estab. 1995. Annual. Last conference held May 21, 2005. Conference duration: 1 day. Average attendance: 200. Conference is comprehensive—all genres and business aspects of a writing career. Site: Smyrna Community Center, large main area, separate rooms for sessions. Presenters/speakers have included Bobbie Christmas, Michael Lucker, Eric Haney, Barbara Lebey, David Fulmer and many others.

Costs 2005: $75 at the door; $65 in advance; $75 with new or renewed membership ($40 annual).

HOW TO BE PUBLISHED WORKSHOPS

P.O. Box 100031, Birmingham AL 35210-3006. (205)907-0140. E-mail: mike@writing2sell.com. Website: www.writing2sell.com. **Contact:** Michael Garrett. Estab. 1986. Workshops are offered continuously year-round at various locations. Conference duration: 1 session. Average attendance: 10-15. Workshops to "move writers of category fiction closer to publication." Focus is not on how to write, but what publishers want to buy. Site: Workshops held at college campuses and universities. Themes include marketing, idea development and manuscript critique.

Costs $49-79.

Additional Information "Special critique is offered, but advance submission is not required." Workshop information available on website. Accepts inquiries by e-mail.

ⓝ MOONLIGHT AND MAGNOLIAS WRITER'S CONFERENCE

Georgia Romance Writers, 2173 Indian Shoals Drive, Loganville GA 30052. E-mail: info@georgiaromancewriters .org. Website: www.georgiaromancewriters.org. **Contact:** Pam Mantovani. Estab. 1982. Annual. Last conference held Sept. 30-Oct. 2, 2005, in the Westin Atlanta North Hotel in Atlanta, GA . Average attendance: 175. "Conference focuses on writing of women's fiction with emphasis on romance. Includes agents and editors from major publishing houses. Previous workshops have included: beginning writer sessions, research topics, writng basics and professional issues for the published author; plus specialty sessions on writing young adult, multi-cultural, inspirational and Regency. Speakers have included experts in law enforcement, screenwriting and research. Literary raffle and advertised speaker and GRW member autographing open to the public. Published authors make up 25-30% of attendees." Brochures available for SASE in June.

Costs $170 GRW member/$180 nonmember for conference registration. Check website for current conference fees, hotel rates and registration forms.

Additional Information Maggie Awards for excellence are presented to unpublished writers. The Maggie Award for published writers is limited to Region 3 members of Romance Writers of America. Deadline for published Maggie is May 2. Deadline for unpublished Maggies is June 1. Entry forms and guidelines available on website. Published authors judge first round, category editors judge finals. Guidelines available for SASE in Spring.

NATCHEZ LITERARY AND CINEMA CELEBRATION

P.O. Box 1307, Natchez MS 39121-1307. (601)446-1208. Fax: (601)446-1214. E-mail: carolyn.smith@colin.edu. Website: www.colin.edu/NLCC. **Contact:** Carolyn Vance Smith, co-chairman. Estab. 1990. Annual. Conference held February 22-26, 2006. Average attendance: 3,000. Conference focuses on "all literature, including film scripts." Site: 500-seat auditorium, various sizes of break-out rooms. Theme will be "Biscuits, Gumbo, Sweet Tea and Bourbon Balls: Food and Drink in the Deep South." Scholars will speak on food and drink in history, literature, film and real life.

Costs "About $100, includes a meal, receptions, book signings, workshops. Lectures/panel discussions are free."

Accommodations "Groups can ask for special assistance. Usually they can be accommodated." Call 866-296-6522.

Additional Information "Participants need to read selected materials prior to attending writing workshops. Thus, pre-enrollment is advised." Conference information is available in Fall 2005. For brochure send SASE, e-mail, visit website, call or fax. Accepts inquiries by SASE, e-mail, phone and fax. Agents and editors participate in conference.

OXFORD CONFERENCE FOR THE BOOK

Center for the Study of Southern Culture, The University of Mississippi, University MS 38677-1848. (662)915-5993. Fax: (662)915-5814. E-mail: aabadie@olemiss.edu. Website: www.olemiss.edu/depts/south. **Contact:** Ann J. Abadie, associate director. Estab. 1993. Annual. Conference held in April. Average attendance: 300. "The conference celebrates books, writing and reading and deals with practical concerns on which the literary arts depend, including literacy, freedom of expression and the book trade itself. Each year's program consists of readings, lectures and discussions. Areas of focus are fiction, poetry, nonfiction and—occasionally—drama. We have, on occasion, looked at science fiction and mysteries. We always pay attention to children's literature." Site: University of Mississippi campus. Annual topics include Submitting Manuscripts/Working One's Way into Print; Finding a Voice/Reaching an Audience; The Endangered Species: Readers Today and Tomorrow. In 2004, among the more than 50 speakers were fiction writers Tom Bissell, Roy Blount Jr., Kaye Gibbons, Barry Hannah, Beverly Lowry and Margaret McMullan. Also on the program were publisher Jonathan Galassi and editor Gary Fisketjon.

Costs "The conference is open to participants without charge."

Accommodations Provides list of area hotels.

Additional Information Brochures available in February by e-mail, on website, by phone, by fax. Accepts inquiries by e-mail, phone, fax. Agents and editors participate in conference.

Conferences

MARJORIE KINNAN RAWLINGS: WRITING THE REGION

P.O. Box 12246, Gainesville FL 32604. (888)917-7001. Fax: (352)373-8854. E-mail: shakes@ufl.edu. Website: www.writingtheregion.com. **Contact:** Norma M. Homan, executive director. Estab. 1997. Annual. Last conference held July 20-24, 2005. Conference duration: 5 days. Average attendance: 100. Conference concentrates on fiction, writing for children, poetry, nonfiction, drama, screenwriting, writing with humor, setting, character, etc. Site: Conference held at historic building, formerly the Thomas Hotel.

Costs $365 for 5 days including meals; $340 "early bird" registration (breakfast and lunch); $125 single day; $75 half day.

Accommodations Special conference rates at area hotels available.

Additional Information Optional trip and dinner at Rawlings Home at Crosscreek offered. Evening activities and banquets also planned. Manuscript consultation on an individual basis by application only and $100 additional fee. Sponsors essay contest for registrants on a topic dealing with Marjorie Kinnan Rawlings. Call for brochures/guidelines. Accepts inquiries by fax, e-mail.

SCBWI SOUTHERN BREEZE FALL CONFERENCE

Writing and Illustrating for Kids, P.O. Box 26282, Birmingham AL 35260. E-mail: jskittinger@bellsouth.net. Website: www.southern-breeze.org. **Contact:** Jo Kittinger, co-regional advisor. Estab. 1992. Annual. Conference held in October (usually the third Saturday). Conference duration: One-day Saturday conference. Average attendance: 125. "All Southern Breeze SCBWI conferences are geared to the production and support of quality children's literature." Keynote speakers TBA.

Costs About $75 for SCBWI members, $80 for non-members.

Accommodations "We have a room block with a conference rate. The conference is held at a nearby school."

Additional Information "The fall conference offers approximately 28 workshops on craft and the business of writing, including a basic workshop for those new to the children's field." Ms critiques are offered; mss must be sent by deadline. Conference information is included in the Southern Breeze newsletter, mailed in September. Brochure is available for SASE, by e-mail or visit website for details. Accepts inquiries by SASE or e-mail. Agents and editors attend/participate in conference. "Familiarize yourself with the works of the speakers before the event."

SCBWI SOUTHERN BREEZE SPRING CONFERENCE

Springmingle06, P.O. Box 26282, Birmingham AL 35260. E-mail: jskittinger@bellsouth.net. Website: www.southern-breeze.org. **Contact:** Jo Kittinger, co-regional advisor. Estab. 1992. Annual. Conference held in February or March each year. Average attendance: 60. "All Southern Breeze SCBWI conferences are geared to the production and support of quality children's literature." Site: Event is held "in a hotel in one of the 3 states which compose our region: Alabama, Georgia or Mississippi. The 2006 conference will be held in Alabama." Speakers generally include editors, agents, authors, art directors and/or illustrators of children's books.

Costs "About $200; SCBWI non-members pay $10-15 more. Some meals are included."

Accommodations "We have a room block with a conference rate in the hotel conference site. Individuals make their own reservations. If we can get an airline discount, we publish this in our newsletter and on our website."

Additional Information There will be ms critiques available this year for an additional fee. Manuscripts must be sent ahead of time. Conference information is included in the Southern Breeze newsletter, mailed in January. Brochure is available for SASE, by e-mail or visit website in January for details. Accepts inquiries by SASE, e-mail.

SILKEN SANDS CONFERENCE

Gulf Coast Chapter RWA,. (228)875-3864. E-mail: mcnabbf@bellsouth.net. Website: www.gccrwa.com. **Contact:** Fran McNabb, conference chair. Estab. 1995. Annual. Conference is April 21-23, 2006, in Pensacola Beach, FL. Average attendance: 150. Focuses on romance fiction including paranormal, inspirational, romantic suspense, category. 2004 panelists included Maggie Shayne (keynote speaker), Vicki Hinze (kickoff speaker), Robin Wells, Sherry Cobb South, Elizabeth Smith, Beth White, Jane Porter, Joanna Wayne.

Costs To be announced.

Additional Information Accepts inquiries by e-mail, phone. Agents and editors participate in conference. "The conference is noted for its relaxed, enjoyable atmosphere where participants can immerse themselves in the total writing experience from the moment they arrive. Get up close and personal with professionals in the publishing field."

SOUTHEASTERN WRITERS ASSOCIATION

P.O. Box 20161, St. Simons Island GA 31522. E-mail: purple@southeasternwriters.com. Website: www.southeasternwriters.com. **Contact:** Marilyn Marsh, treasurer. Estab. 1975. Annual. Conference held third week of June every year. Average attendance: 75 (limited to 100). Conference offers classes in fiction, nonfiction, juvenile, inspirational writing, poetry, etc. Site: Epworth-by-the-Sea, St. Simons Island, GA.

Costs 2005 costs: $265 early bird tuition, $305 after April 15, $85 daily tuition.

Accommodations Offers overnight accommodations. 2005 rates were approximately $650/single to $425/double and included motel-style room and 3 meals/day per person.

Additional Information Sponsors numerous contests in several genres and up to 3 free ms evaluation conferences with instructors. Agents and editors participate in conference panels and/or private appointments. Complete information is available on the website in March of each year, including registration forms. E-mail or send SASE for brochure.

TENNESSEE WILLIAMS/NEW ORLEANS LITERARY FESTIVAL

938 Lafayette St., Suite 328, New Orleans LA 70113. (504)581-1144. E-mail: info@tennesseewilliams.net. Website: www.tennesseewilliams.net. **Contact:** Paul J. Willis, executive director. Estab. 1987. Annual. Conference held in late March. Average attendance: "10,000 audience seats filled." Conferences focus on "all aspects of the literary arts including editing, publishing and the artistic process. Other humanities areas are also featured, including theater and music." Site: "The festival is based at historic Le Petit Theatre du Vieux Carré and continues at other sites throughout the French Quarter."

Costs "Ticket prices range from $5 for a single event to $50 for a special event. Master classes are $35 per class. Theatre events are sold separately and range from $10-25."

Accommodations "Host hotel is the Monteleone Hotel."

Additional Information "In conjunction with the University of New Orleans, we sponsor a one-act play competition. Entries are accepted from September 1 through December 1. There is a $15 fee which must be submitted with the application form. There is a $1,000 cash prize and a staged reading at the festival, as well as a full production of the work at the following year's festival." Conference information is available in late January. For brochure send e-mail, visit website or call. Accepts inquiries by e-mail and phone. Agents and editors participate in conference.

ℕ WRITE IT OUT

P.O. Box 704, Sarasota FL 34230-0704. (941)359-3824. E-mail: rmillerwio@aol.com. Website: www.writeitout.com. **Contact:** Ronni Miller, director. Estab. 1997. Workshops held 2-3 times/year in March, June, July and August. Conference duration: 5-10 days. Average attendance: 4-10. Workshops on "fiction, poetry, memoirs. We also offer intimate, motivational, in-depth free private conferences with instructors." Site: Workshops held across the United States as well as in Italy in a Tuscan villa, in Sarasota at a hotel, or in Cape Cod at an inn. Theme: "Feel It! Write It!" Past speakers included Arturo Vivante, novelist.

Costs 2005 fees: Italy, $1,695; Sarasota, $495; Cape Cod, $610. Price includes tution, room and board in Italy, all other locations just tuition. Airfare not included.

Additional Information "Critiques on work are given at the workshops." Conference information available year round. For brochures/guidelines e-mail, call or visit website. Accepts inquiries by phone, e-mail. Workshops have "small groups, option to spend time writing and not attend classes, with personal appointments with instructors for feedback."

ℕ ◎ WRITING STRATEGIES FOR THE CHRISTIAN MARKET

2712 S. Peninsula Dr., Daytona Beach FL 32118-5706. (386)322-1111. Fax: (386)322-1111. E-mail: rupton@cfl.rr.com. Website: www.ruptonbooks.com. **Contact:** Rosemary Upton. Estab. 1991. Independent studies with manual. Includes Basics I, Marketing II, Business III, Building the Novel. Critique by mail with SASE. Question and answer session via e-mail or U.S. mail. Critique shop included once a month, except summer (July and August). Instructor: Rosemary Upton, novelist.

Costs $30 for manual and ongoing support.

Additional Information "Designed for correspondence students as well as the classroom experience, the courses are economical and include all materials, as well as the evaluation assignments." Those who have taken Writing Strategies instruction are able to attend an on-going monthly critiqueshop where their peers critique their work. Manual provided. For brochures/guidelines send SASE, e-mail, fax or call. Accepts inquiries by fax, e-mail. Independent study by mail only offered at this time.

MIDWEST (IL, IN, KY, MI, OH)

ℕ ANTIOCH WRITERS' WORKSHOP

P.O. Box 494, Yellow Springs OH 45387. (937)475-7357. E-mail: info@antiochwritersworkshop.com. Website: www.antiochwritersworkshop.com. **Contact:** Laura Carlson, director. Estab. 1984. Annual. Conference held in early July (9-15 in 2005). Conference duration: 1 week. Average attendance: 80. Workshop concentration: poetry, nonfiction, fiction, personal essay, memoir, mystery. Site: Workshop located in the idyllic Glen Helen Nature Preserve and in locations around the charming village of Yellow Springs. Faculty in 2005 included Sue Grafton (keynote), Imogene Bolls, Jeff Gundy, Sharon Short, Ralph Keyes and Crystal Wilson-Harris.

Costs Tuition is $610 (regular) or $550 (alumni and local participants), plus meals.

Accommodations Accomodations are available in local homes through the village host program ($150 for the week) or at area hotels and B&Bs.

Additional Information Intensive sessions for beginning and experienced writers, small group lunches with faculty, optional ms critiques.

COLUMBUS WRITERS CONFERENCE

P.O. Box 20548, Columbus OH 43220. (614)451-3075. Fax: (614)451-0174. E-mail: AngelaPL28@aol.com. Website: www.creativevista.com. **Contact:** Angela Palazzolo, director. Estab. 1993. Annual. Conference held in August. Average attendance: 350+. "In addition to consultations, the conference covers a variety of fiction and nonfiction topics presented by writers, editors and literary agents. Writing topics have included novel, short story, children's, young adult, poetry, historical fiction, science fiction, fantasy, humor, mystery, playwriting, screenwriting, magazine writing, travel, humor, cookbook, technical, queries, book proposals and freelance writing. Other topics have included finding and working with an agent/author/editor, targeting markets, time management, obtaining grants, sparking creativity and networking." Previous agents, writers, editors have included Lee K. Abbott, Sarah Willis, Lee Martin, Donald Maass, Rita Rosenkrantz, Sheree Bykofsky, Jack Heffron and Patrick Lobrutto, as well as many other professionals in the writing field.

Costs TBA.

Additional Information Call, write, e-mail or send fax to obtain a conference brochure, available mid-summer.

FESTIVAL OF FAITH AND WRITING

Calvin College/Department of English, 1795 Knollcrest Circle SE, Grand Rapids MI 49546. (616)526-6770. Fax: (616)526-8508. E-mail: ffw@calvin.edu. Website: www.calvin.edu/academic/engl/festival.htm. **Contact:** English Dept. Estab. 1990. Biennial. Conference usually held in April of even years (April 20-22, 2006). Conference duration: 3 days. Average attendance: 1,800. The Festival of Faith and Writing encourages serious, imaginative writing by all writers interested in the intersections of literature and belief. Site: The festival is held at Calvin College in Grand Rapids, MI, 180 miles north of Chicago. Focus is on fiction, nonfiction, memoir, poetry, drama, children's, young adult, literary criticism, film and song lyrics. Past speakers have included Annie Dillard, John Updike, Katherine Paterson, Elie Wiesel, Joyce Carol Oates and Leif Enger.

Costs Registration: consult website. Registration includes all sessions during the 3-day event but does not include meals, lodging or evening concerts.

Accommodations Shuttles are available to and from local hotels. Shuttles are also available for overflow parking lots. Consult festival website for a list of hotels with special conference rates.

Additional Information Brochures available in October of the year prior to the festival. Also accepts inquiries by e-mail, phone and fax. Agents and editors attend the festival and consult with prospective writers.

GREEN RIVER NOVELS-IN-PROGRESS WORKSHOP

2011 Lauderdale Rd., Louisville KY 40205. (502)417-5514. E-mail: novelsinprogress@bellsouth.net. Website: www.greenriverwriters.org/nipw.html. **Contact:** Jeff Yocom, workshop director. Estab. 1991. Annual. Conference usually held in March. Conference duration: 1 week. Average attendance: 50. Conference covers fiction writing in various genres. Site: Held on the urban campus of Spalding University; small dormitories and class rooms/meeting rooms. Features faculty-led breakout sessions on subjects such as character development, plot, contacting agents, etc. Includes individual mentoring and opportunities to pitch to editors and agents. 2005 speakers included Liz Beverly, William Cobb, Jeanne M. Dams, J. Ardian (Julianne) Lee and Elaine Fowler Palencia.

Costs $449 with personal instruction option, $299 without.

Accommodations $17 per night for private dorm room.

Additional Information Brochures available in December for SASE, by phone, e-mail or on website. 2005 agents in attendance included PMA Literary and Film Agency and Serendipity Literary Agency. Editors in attendance from Echelon Press.

INDIANA UNIVERSITY WRITERS' CONFERENCE

464 Ballantine Hall, Bloomington IN 47405-7103. (812)855-1877. Fax: (812)855-9535. E-mail: writecon@indiana.edu. Website: www.indiana.edu/~writecon. **Contact:** Amy Locklin, director. Estab. 1940. Annual. Conference/workshops held in June (June 5-10 in 2005). Average attendance: 115. "The Indiana University Writers' Conference believes in a craft-based teaching of writing. We emphasize an exploration of creativity through a

variety of approaches, offering workshop-based craft discussions, classes focusing on technique, and talks about the careers and concerns of a writing life." Site: Located on the campus of Indiana University, Bloomington. Participants in the week-long conference join faculty-led workshops in fiction, poetry and creative nonfiction; take classes on various aspects of writing; engage in one-on-one consultation with faculty members; and attend a variety of readings and social events. Previous faculty include: Raymond Carver, Gwendolyn Brooks, Andre Dubus, Kurt Vonnegut Jr., Mark Doty, Robert Olen Butler, Aimee Bender, Jean Thompson, Brenda Hillman, Li-Young Lee and Brigit Pegeen Kelly.

Costs Approximately $350 for all classes and $500 for all classes and a workshop; does not include food or housing. Scholarships and college credit options are available.

Additional Information "In order to be accepted in a workshop, the writer must submit the work they would like critiqued. Work is evaluated before accepting applicant. Scholarship awards are based on the quality of the manuscript and are determined by an outside judge." For brochures/guidelines send SASE, visit our website, e-mail or call. Deadline for scholarship application is April 1. Apply early, as workshops fill up quickly.

KENTUCKY WRITER'S WORKSHOP

1050 State Park Rd., Pineville KY 40977. (606)337-3066. Fax: (606)337-7250. E-mail: dean.henson@ky.gov. Website: parks.ky.gov/pinemtn2.htm. **Contact:** Dean Henson, event coordinator. Estab. 1995. Annual. Workshop held each March. Average attendance: 50-65. "Focuses on writing in various genres, including fiction, mystery, poetry, novels, short stories, essays, etc." Site: Pine Mountain State Resort Park (a Kentucky State Park). Previous panels included Writing for 16 and Under; Grist for the Mill (transforming personal experience into fiction); The Writing Commitment; Adult Novel Writing. Past panelists included Martha Bennett Stiles, children's author; James Baker Hall, former poet laureate of Kentucky; Jenny Davis, novelist.

Costs Registration fee is $30 for non-package participants.

Accommodations Special all-inclusive event packages available. Call for information.

Additional Information Brochures available 2 months in advance by e-mail or phone. Accepts inquiries by SASE, e-mail, phone, fax. "Our conference features Kentucky authors of note speaking and instructing on various topics of the writing endeavor. This workshop is designed to help developing authors improve their writing craft."

ON THE WRITE PATH

Seventh Annual Writers' Conference, Elgin Community College, 1700 Spartan Drive, Elgin IL 60123. (847)622-3036. Fax: (847)214-7815. E-mail: dnewberg@elgin.edu. Website: www.elgin.edu. **Contact:** Donna Newberg. Estab. 1997. Annual. Conference usually held in March. Conference duration: 1 day. Average attendance: 60-80. Event focus changes every year. 2004 conference focused on publishing. Site: Held at Elgin Community College; keynote speaker presents in auditorium, smaller sessions held in breakout rooms, lunch buffet. 2004 topics included How Characters Converse and Planning the Storyline. Speakers for 2004 were Judy Snyder, Pat DiPrima, Rick Holinger and Dianne Helm.

Costs $109 includes full cost, including lunch.

Additional Information Participants need to register with social security number, name, address, birthdate and year, and pay in advance. Brochure with registration form available in January by phone, e-mail and on website. Accepts inquiries by SASE, e-mail, phone and fax. Agents and editors attend conference.

OPEN WRITING WORKSHOPS

Creative Writing Program, Department of English, Bowling Green State University, Bowling Green OH 43403. (419)372-8370. Fax: (419)372-6805. E-mail: mmcgowa@bgnet.bgsu.edu. Website: www.bgsu.edu/departments/creative-writing/. "Check our website for next workshop dates." Conference duration: 1 day. Average attendance: 10-15. Workshop covers fiction and poetry. Site: Workshops are held in a conference room, roundtable setting, on the campus of Bowling Green State University. Provides close reading and ms critique. 2005 faculty included fiction writer Wendell Mayo and poet/editor Karen Craigo.

Costs $50 for workshop; does not include lodging or other services; $35 for alums and students.

Accommodations Parking provided on campus.

Additional Information Participants need to submit workshop material prior to conference. Fiction or nonfiction: 1 story, 15 pages double-spaced maximum; send 2 copies. Poetry: 3 poems, a total of 100 lines for all 3; send 2 copies. "Deadlines are set about 3 weeks before the workshop. This gives us time to copy all the manuscripts and mail to all participants with detailed instructions." For brochure or inquiries, e-mail, visit website, call or fax. "These are no-nonsense workshops whose purpose is to 'open' doors for writers who are writing in comparative isolation. We provide guidance on preparation of manuscripts for publication as well."

READERS AND WRITERS HOLIDAY CONFERENCE

Central Ohio Fiction Writers (COFW), P.O. Box 1981, Westerville OH 43086-1981. E-mail: mollygbg@columbus.rr.com. Website: www.cofw.org. **Contact:** Molly Greenberg, president. Estab. 1990. Annual. Conference held

October 2006 in Columbus, OH. Dates TBA. Average attendance: 120. COFW is a chapter of Romance Writers of America. The conference focuses on all romance subgenres and welcomes published writers, pre-published writers and readers. Conference theme: connecting with the romance market. "As always, a popular romance writer will be the keynote speaker. Past speakers were Stella Cameron, Sherrilyn Kenyon, Jennifer Cruisie and Mary Jo Putney. Two national editors and one agent will speak and take short appointments. Appointments to early registrants."
Costs Price will include Saturday lunch. Friday night dinner and workshop extra and optional.
Accommodations See www.cofw.org for exact location. There will be a special conference rate for hotel rooms.
Additional Information Registration form and information available on website or by e-mail.

WALLOON WRITERS' RETREAT
P.O. Box 304, Royal Oak MI 48068-0304. (248)589-3913. Fax: (248)589-9981. E-mail: johndlamb@ameritech.net. Website: www.springfed.org. **Contact:** John D. Lamb, director. Estab. 1999. Annual. Last conference held September 22-25, 2005. Average attendance: 75. Focus includes fiction, poetry, creative nonfiction. Site: Michigania is owned and operated by the University of Michigan Alumni Association. Located on Walloon Lake. Attendees stay in spruce-paneled cabins, and seminars are held in a large conference lodge wtih fieldstone fireplaces and dining area. Past faculty included Billy Collins, Jacquelyn Mitchard, Jane Hamilton, Thomas Lux, Joyce Maynard, Craig Holden, Laurel Blossom.
Costs Single occupancy is $600, $535 (3 nights, 2 nights, all meals included). $360 non-lodging.
Accommodations Shuttle rides from Traverse City Airport or Pellston Airport. Offers overnight accommodations. Provides list of area lodging options.
Additional Information Optional: Attendees may submit 3 poems or 5 pages of prose for conference with a staff member. Brochures available mid-June by e-mail, on website or by phone. Accepts inquiries by SASE, e-mail, phone. Editors participate in conference. "Walloon Lake in Northern Michigan is the same lake at which Ernest Hemingway spent the first 19 years of his life at his family's Windemere Cottage. The area plays a role in some of his early short stories. Notably in a couple Nick Adams stories."

WESTERN RESERVE WRITERS & FREELANCE CONFERENCE
Lakeland Community College, 7700 Clocktower Dr., Kirtland OH 44094. (440) 525-7000. E-mail: deencr@aol.com. **Contact:** Deanna Adams or Nancy Piazza, co-coordinators. Estab. 1983. Biannual. Last conference held March 19, 2005. Conference duration: One day. Average attendance: 120. "The Western Reserve Writers Conferences are designed for all writers, aspiring and professional, and offer presentations in all genres—nonfiction, fiction, poetry, essays and the business of writing." Site: Located in the main building of Lakeland Community College, the conference is easy to find and just off the I-90 freeway. The Fall 2003 conference featured "some of Ohio's best writers presenting on mystery, children's and women's fiction, with a focus on characterization and plotting. The Fall 2005 conference featured performance poet/author Michael Salinger as keynote speaker. Also featured renowned mystery writer Les Roberts, biographer Ted Schwarz and award-winning romance writer Sarah Willis. Also featured presentations on book proposals and research."
Costs Fall conference, including lunch: $69. Spring conference, no lunch: $45.
Additional Information Brochures for the 2007 conferences will be available in January 2006 with SASE or by fax. Also accepts inquiries by e-mail and phone, or see website. Editors and agents often attend the conferences.

◎ WRITE-TO-PUBLISH CONFERENCE
9731 N. Fox Glen Dr., Suite 6F, Niles IL 60714-4222. (847)299-4755. Fax: (847)296-0754. E-mail: lin@writetopublish.com. Website: www.writetopublish.com. **Contact:** Lin Johnson, director. Estab. 1971. Annual. Conference held June 7-10, 2006. Average attendance: 275. Conference on "writing all types of manuscripts for the Christian market." Site: Wheaton College, Wheaton, IL.
Costs $410.
Accommodations In campus residence halls or discounted hotel rates. Cost $210-290.
Additional Information Optional ms evaluation available. College credit available. Conference information available in January. For brochures/ guidelines, visit website, e-mail, fax or call. Accepts inquiries by e-mail, fax, phone.

WRITERS ONLINE WORKSHOPS
4700 E. Galbraith Rd., Cincinnati OH 45236. (800)759-0963. Fax: (513)531-0798. E-mail: wdwowadmin@fwpubs.com. Website: www.writersonlineworkshops.com. **Contact:** Lynn Beirl, Manager of Educational Services. Estab. 2000. Online workshop; ongoing. Conference duration: From 4-28 weeks. Average attendance: 10-15 per class. "We have workshops in fiction, nonfiction, memoir, poetry, proposal writing and more." Site: Internet-based, operated entirely on the website. Current fiction-related courses include Fundamentals of Fiction, Focus on the Novel, Focus on the Short Story, Advanced Novel Writing, Advanced Story Writing, Creating Dynamic

Characters, Writing Effective Dialogue, Writing the Novel Proposal and others. New in 2005: Writing the Query Letter, Essentials of Mystery Writing, Essentials of Science Fiction Writing, Marketing Short Stories, and Mastering Point of View.

Costs $170-579.

Additional Information Additional information always available on website. Accepts inquiries by e-mail and phone.

NORTH CENTRAL (IA, MN, NE, ND, SD, WI)

N INTERNATIONAL MUSIC CAMP CREATIVE WRITING WORKSHOP

1930 23rd Ave. SE, Minot ND 58701. Phone/fax: (701)838-8472. E-mail: joe@internationalmusiccamp.com. Website: www.internationalmusiccamp.com. **Contact:** Joseph T. Alme, executive director. Estab. 1956. Annual. Last conference held June 26-July 2, 2005. Average attendance: 35. "The workshop offers students the opportunity to refine their skills in thinking, composing and writing in an environment that is conducive to positive reinforcement. In addition to writing poems, essays and stories, individuals are encourgaged to work on their own area of interest with conferencing and feedback from the course instructor." Site: International Peace Garden on the border between the US and Canada. "Similar to a university campus, several dormitories, classrooms, lecture halls and cafeteria provide the perfect site for such a workshop. The beautiful and picturesque International Peace Garden provides additional inspiration to creative thinking." 2005 instructor was Bonnie Robinson from Minot State University.

Costs The cost including meals and housing is $275.

Accommodations Airline and depot shuttles are available upon request. Housing is included in the $275 fee.

Additional Information Conference information is available in September. For brochure visit website, e-mail, call or fax. Accepts inquiries by e-mail, phone and fax. Agents and editors participate in conference.

IOWA SUMMER WRITING FESTIVAL

100 Oakdale Campus, W310, University of Iowa, Iowa City IA 52242-1802. (319)335-4160. E-mail: iswfestival@u iowa.edu. Website: www.uiowa.edu/ ~ iswfest. **Contact:** Amy Margolis, director. Estab. 1987. Annual. Festival held in June and July. Workshops are one week or a weekend. Average attendance: limited to 12/class—over 1,500 participants throughout the summer. "We offer workshops across the genres, including novel, short story, poetry, essay, memoir, humor, travel, playwriting, screenwriting, writing for children and more. All are welcome. You need only have the desire to write." Site: University of Iowa campus. Guest speakers are undetermined at this time. Readers and instructors have included Lee K. Abbott, Susan Power, Joy Harjo, Gish Jen, Abraham Verghese, Robert Olen Butler, Ethan Canin, Clark Blaise, Gerald Stern, Donald Justice, Michael Dennis Browne, Marvin Bell, Hope Edelman, Lan Samantha Chang.

Costs $475-500 for full week; $225 for weekend workshop. Discounts available for early registration. Housing and meals are separate.

Accommodations "We offer participants a choice of accommodations: dormitory, $35/night; Iowa House, $74/night; Sheraton, $85/night (rates subject to change)."

Additional Information Conference information available in February. Accepts inquiries by fax, e-mail, phone. "Register early. Classes fill quickly."

N MINNEAPOLIS WRITERS' CONFERENCE

Zurah Shrine Center, 2450 Park Ave., Minneapolis MN 55404. (612)869-8902. E-mail: dfingerman1@mn.rr.com. Website: www.minneapoliswriters.net. **Contact:** David Fingerman, president. Estab. 1984. Annual. Conference held in August. Conference duration: 1 day. Average attendance: 100. The conference helps writers find markets for their books by providing resources, publishing contacts, motivational support and guidance from successful authors of fiction and nonfiction. 2003 speakers: Lorna Landvik, M.D. Lake, Joel Turnipseed, Ellen Hart and Dr. Roger McDonald.

Costs $75; includes luncheon and continental breakfast.

N WISCONSIN REGIONAL WRITERS' ASSOCIATION CONFERENCES

N 4549 Cty Rd Y, Montello WI 53949. (608)297-9746. E-mail: registration@wrwa.net. Website: www.wrwa.net. **Contact:** Kathleen McGwin, president. Estab. 1948. Annual. Conferences held in May and September "are dedicated to self-improvement through speakers, workshops and presentations. Topics and speakers vary with each event." Average attendance: 100-150. "We honor all genres of writing. Fall conference is a two-day event featuring the Jade Ring Banquet and awards for six genre categories. Spring conference is a one-day event."

Costs $40-75.

Accommodations Provides a list of area hotels or lodging options. "We negotiate special rates at each facility. A block of rooms is set aside for a specific time period."

Additional Information Award winners receive a certificate and a cash prize. First place winners of the Jade Ring contest receive a jade ring. Must be a member to enter contests. For brochure, call, e-mail or visit website in March/July.

WRITERS INSTITUTE
610 Langdon St., Room 621, Madison WI 53703. (608)262-3447. Fax: (608)265-2475. Website: www.dcs.wisc. edu/lsa/writing. **Contact:** Christine DeSmet. Estab. 1989. Annual. Conference usually held in July. Site: Pyle Center. Average attendance: 200. 2004 keynote speakers were Chitra Divakaruni and Richard Lederer.
Costs $205 includes materials, breaks.
Accommodations Provides a list of area hotels or lodging options.
Additional Information Sponsors contest. Submit 1-page writing sample and $10 entry fee. Conference speakers are judges. Conference information is available in April. For brochure send e-mail, visit website, call, fax. Accepts inquiries by SASE, e-mail, phone, fax. Agents and editors participate in conference.

ⓝ WRITING WORKSHOP
P.O. Box 65, Ellison Bay WI 54210. (920)854-4088. E-mail: clearing@theclearing.org. Website: www.theclearing .org. **Contact:** Kathy Vanderhoof, registrar. Estab. 1935. Annual. Average attendance: 16. "General writing, journal, poetry as well as fiction and nonfiction." Held in a "quiet, residential setting in deep woods on the shore of Green Bay."
Costs $725 for double (2005); includes lodging, meals, tuition.
Accommodations "Two to a room with private bath in rustic log and stone buildings with meals served family-style."

SOUTH CENTRAL (CO, KS, MO, NM, OK, TX)

ⓒ THE AFRICAN AMERICAN BOOK CLUB SUMMIT
PMB 120, 2951 Marina Bay Dr., Suite 130, League City TX 77573. (866)875-1044. E-mail: pwsquare@pageturner. net. Website: www.summitatsea.com. **Contact:** Pamela Walker Williams, literary events chairman. Estab. 2000. Annual. Conference held each October on board a Carnival cruise ship; the last event was scheduled for October 16-23, 2005, on board the Carnival ship Pride. (Check website for 2006 dates and prices.) Average attendance: 200. "The purpose of the conference is to bring authors and readers together. Aspiring writers will have an opportunity to discuss and obtain information on self-publishing, marketing and writing fiction." Site: on board cruise ship. Includes pool, jacuzzi, restaurant, bar, spa, room service, wheelchair accessible, fitness center, children's facilities, air conditioning.
Costs 2005 fees: for inside cabin, $887; for ocean view, $1,027-$1,147. Includes cruise, conference, on-board meals, port charges and gratuities.
Accommodations "Participants have the option to add airfare and/or shuttle service." Provides a list of area accommodations for people who choose to arrive early.
Additional Information Brochures available on website. Accepts inquiries by e-mail, phone, fax. Agents and editors attend conference.

AGENTS & EDITORS CONFERENCE
(formerly Agents! Agents! Agents! & Editors Too!), Writers' League of Texas, 1501 W. Fifth St., Suite E-2, Austin TX 78703. (512)499-8914. Fax: (512)499-0441. E-mail: wlt@writersleague.org. Website: www.writerslea gue.org. **Contact:** Helen Ginger, executive director. Estab. 1982. Conference held in Summer. Conference duration: Friday-Sunday. Average attendance: 300. "Each Summer the League holds its annual Agents & Editors Conference, which provides writers with the opportunity to meet top literary agents and editors from New York and the West Coast." Open to writers of both fiction and nonfiction. Topics include: Finding and working with agents and publishers; writing and marketing fiction and nonfiction; dialogue; characterization; voice; research; basic and advanced fiction writing/focus on the novel; business of writing; also workshops for genres. Agents/ speakers have included Malaika Adero, Stacey Barney, Sha-Shana Crichton, Jessica Faust, Dena Fischer, Mickey Freiberg, Jill Grosjean, Anne Hawkins, Jim Hornfischer, Jennifer Joel, David Hale Smith and Elisabeth Weed. Agents and editors will be speaking and available for meetings with attendees.
Costs $220-275. Contests and awards programs are offered separately.
Additional Information Brochures/guidelines are available on request.

ANNUAL RETREATS, WORKSHOPS AND CLASSES

(formerly Spring and Fall Workshops and Classes), 1501 W. Fifth St., Suite E-2, Austin TX 78703-5155. (512)499-8914. Fax: (512)499-0441. E-mail: wlt@writersleague.org. Website: www.writersleague.org. **Contact:** Helen Ginger, executive director. All year long, except for the month of December. ''Classes and workshops provide practical advice and guidance on various aspects of fiction, creative nonfiction and screenwriting.'' Site: Writers' League of Texas resource center or as indicated on website. Some classes are by e-mail. ''Topics for workshops and classes have included E-publishing; Creative Nonfiction; Screenwriting Basics; Novel in Progress; Basics of Short Fiction; Technique; Writing Scenes; Journaling; Manuscript Feedback; Essays; Newspaper Columns.'' Instructors include Suzy Spencer, Barbara Burnett Smith, Scott Wiggerman, Diane Fanning, Marion Winik, Emily Vander Veer, Annie Reid, Bonnie Orr, Jan Epton Seale, Susan Wade, Lila Guzman, Laurie Lynn Drummond, David Wilkinson, John Pipkin, Ann McCutchan and Dao Strom.
Costs $45-$250.
Additional Information Available on our website.

ASPEN SUMMER WORDS INTERNATIONAL LITERARY FESTIVAL & WRITING RETREAT

110 E. Hallam St., #116, Aspen CO 81611. (970)925-3122. Fax: (970)925-5700. E-mail: info@aspenwriters.org. Website: www.aspenwriters.org. **Contact:** Lisa Consiglio, executive director. Estab. 1976. Annual. Conference held in late June. Conference duration: 5 days. Average attendance: Writing retreat, 96; literary festival, 200 passholders, 1,800 visitors. For fiction, creative nonfiction, poetry, personal essay, screenwriting, literature, author readings and agent/editor meetings, and industry panels. 2005 festival featured Seamus Heaney, Edna O'Brien, Joe O'Connor, Elinor Lipman and more.
Costs $375/retreat; $200/festival; $525/both; $35/private meetings with agents and editors.
Accommodations On-campus housing in 2005 was $110/night single; $55/night double. Off-campus rates vary. Free shuttle.
Additional Information New application deadline: April 1. Mss must be submitted prior to conference for review by faculty. Brochures available for SASE, by e-mail and phone request, and on website.

N O EAST TEXAS CHRISTIAN WRITER'S CONFERENCE

East Texas Baptist University, School of Humanities, 1209 N. Grove, Marshall TX 75670. (903)923-2269. E-mail: jhopkins@etbu.edu or dgribble@etbu.edu. Website: www.etbu.edu. **Contact:** Donna Gribble. Estab. 2002. Annual. Conference held first Saturday of June each year. Conference duration: 1 day (Saturday). Average attendance: 60. ''Primarily we are interested in promoting quality Christian writing that would be accepted in mainstream publishing.'' Site: ''We use the classrooms, cafeterias, etc. of East Texas Baptist University. 2005 conference themes were: 10 Commandments of Powerful Writers; Editor's Perspective Do's and Don'ts; The Writer's Life; 7 Effective Habits for Christian Writers; Writing for Youth/Children; Scholarly Publications; E-Publishing and Publishing on Demand; Creative Nonfiction; Writing Grants; Inspirational Writing. 2005 conference speakers were: David Jenkins, Chris Collins, Carolyn Pedison, Kathy Holdway, Jim Pence, Archie McDonald, Faye Field, Fredna Stuckey, Marv Knox and Marcia Preston.
Costs $50 for individual; $40 student. Price includes a meal.
Additional Information ''Would like to expand to an opportunity to meet with agents or an editor.''

O EMINENCE AREA ARTS COUNCIL SHORT STORY WORKSHOP

P.O. Box 551, Eminence MO 65466-0551. (573)226-5655. E-mail: hilma@socket.net. **Contact:** Hilma Hughes, administrator. Estab. 1989. Annual. Last workshop held April 14-16, 2005. Conference duration: 3 days. Average attendance: 12. ''The Short Story Workshop focuses on fiction of any genre.'' Workshop centers on the process of writing; participants leave with a finished short story. Site: Museum and Art Gallery conference room. We have large tables with chairs for participants. There is already a large-screen TV and VCR for the leaders to use. The museum is accessible to the physically challenged. Workshop led by Dr. Tom Nordgren.
Costs $45.
Accommodations EAAC provides list of area lodging.
Additional Information Accepts inquiries by e-mail or phone. ''We are a small rural community on the scenic Riverways. The workshops are an excellent opportunity to rest, relax and get away from the rush of daily life. Many participants have valued this part of the experience as much as the learning and writing process.''

N FORT BEND WRITERS GUILD WORKSHOP

12523 Folkcrest Way, Stafford TX 77477-3529. E-mail: rogerpaulding@earthlink.net. **Contact:** Roger Paulding. Estab. 1997. Annual. Last conference held April 2, 2005. Conference duration: 1 day. Average attendance: 75. Focuses on fiction (novels) and screenwriting. Site: Held at Holiday Inn Southwest.
Costs $50 (including buffet lunch).
Additional Information Sponsors a contest. Submit for novel competition first 15 pages plus one page synopsis,

entry fee $15; for short story competition 10 pages complete, $10 each. "Judges are published novelists." First prize: $300 if attending workshop, otherwise $200. For brochure send SASE or e-mail.

◎ GLORIETA CHRISTIAN WRITERS' CONFERENCE

Glorieta Conference Center, P.O. Box 66810, Albuquerque NM 87193-6810. (800)433-6633. Fax: (505)899-9282. E-mail: info@classervices.com. Website: www.glorietacwc.com or www.lifeway.com. **Contact:** Marita Littauer, director. Estab. 1997. Annual. Last conference held October 26-30, 2005. Conference duration: 5 days. Average attendance: 330. For "beginners, professionals, fiction, poetry, writing for children, drama, magazine writing, nonfiction books." To train Christian writers in their craft, provide them with an understanding of the industry, and give opportunities to meet with publishers. Site: "Located just north of historic Santa Fe, NM, conference center with hotels and dining hall with buffet-style meals." Plans "continuing course for fiction writers and numerous one-hour workshops."

Costs 2005 rates were $350 for early registration or $390 regular registration; meals and lodging were additional and ranged from $200-400 depending on housing and meal plans.

Additional Information "The craft of writing is universal, but attendees should be aware this conference has a Christian emphasis."

◎ TONY HILLERMAN WRITERS CONFERENCE

304 Calle Oso, Santa FE NM 87501. (505)471-1565. E-mail: wordharvest@yahoo.com. Website: http://sfworkshops.com. **Contact:** Jean Schaumberg, co-director. Estab. 2004. Annual. November. Conference duration: 4 days. Average attendance: 160. Site: Albuquerque Hilton hotel, mid-town Albuquerque. Previous faculty included Tony Hillerman, David Morrell, Michael McGarrity, and Jonathan and Faye Kellerman.

Costs Previous year's costs: $395.

Accommodations $69 per night at the Albuquerque Hilton.

Additional Information Sponsors on-site contest for an opening paragraph and short-story contest with *Cowboys & Indians Magazine*. Judged by the faculty. Brochures available in July for SASE, by phone, e-mail, fax and on website. Accepts inquiries by SASE, phone, e-mail.

NATIONAL WRITERS ASSOCIATION FOUNDATION CONFERENCE

10940 S. Parker Rd. #508, Parker CO 80138. (303)841-0246. Fax: (303)841-2607. E-mail: conference@nationalwriters.com. Website: www.nationalwriters.com. **Contact:** Sandy Whelchel, executive director. Estab. 1926. Annual. Conference held in June. Conference duration: 3 days. Average attendance: 200-300. For general writing and marketing.

Costs $200 (approximately).

Additional Information Awards for previous contests will be presented at the conference. Conference information available annually in December. For brochures/guidelines send SASE, visit website, e-mail, fax or call.

NIMROD ANNUAL WRITERS' WORKSHOP

University of Tulsa, 600 S. College Ave., Tulsa OK 74104. (918)631-3080. Fax: (918)631-3033. E-mail: nimrod@utulsa.edu. Website: www.utulsa.edu/nimrod. **Contact:** Eilis O'Neal, managing editor. Estab. 1978. Annual. Conference held in October. Conference duration: 1 day. Average attendance: 100-150. Workshop in fiction and poetry. "Prize winners (*Nimrod*/Hardman Prizes) conduct workshops as do contest judges." Past judges: Rosellen Brown, Stanley Kunitz, Toby Olson, Lucille Clifton, W.S. Merwin, Ron Carlson, Mark Doty, Anita Shreve and Francine Prose.

Costs Approximately $50. Lunch provided. Scholarships available for students.

Additional Information *Nimrod International Journal* sponsors *Nimrod*/Hardman Literary Awards: The Katherine Anne Porter Prize for fiction and The Pablo Neruda Prize for poetry. Poetry and fiction prizes: $2,000 each and publication (1st prize); $1,000 each and publication (2nd prize). Deadline: must be postmarked no later than April 30.

◎ ROMANCE WRITERS OF AMERICA NATIONAL CONFERENCE

3707 FM 1960 West, Suite 555, Houston TX 77068. (281)440-6885, ext. 27. Fax: (281)440-7510. E-mail: info@rwanational.com. Website: www.rwanational.com. **Contact:** Jane Detloff, office manager. Estab. 1981. Annual. Conference held July 26-29, 2006, in Atlanta. Average attendance: 1,500. Over 100 workshops on writing, researching and the business side of being a working writer. Publishing professionals attend and accept appointments. Site: Conference will be held in Atlanta in 2006, Dallas in 2007, and San Francisco in 2008. Keynote speaker is renowned romance writer.

Costs In 2005, early registration $340 for RWA members/$415 nonmembers; late registration, $390 for RWA members/$465 nonmembers.

Additional Information Annual RTA awards are presented for romance authors. Annual Golden Heart awards are presented for unpublished writers. Conference brochures/guidelines and registration forms are available for SASE and on website in May. Accepts inquiries by SASE, e-mail, fax, phone.

SAN JUAN WRITERS WORKSHOP
P.O. Box 841, Ridgeway CO 81432. (806)438-2385. E-mail: inkwellliterary@mac.com. Website: http://homepag e.mac.com/inkwellliterary. **Contact:** Jill Patterson, director. Estab. 2002. Annual. Workshop held July or August each year. Last conference was July 16-23, 2005. Conference duration: up to 10 days. Average attendance: 40 per session. Focuses on "fiction, poetry, creative nonfiction in each session. Sessions focus on generating new material, workshopping manuscripts, revising and submitting for publication. "The goal of the San Juan Workshops is to remove writers from the hectic pace of everyday life and give them the inspiration, space and quiet to attend to their writing." Site: "The Workshops are held for one week, each summer, in Ouray, CO, Switzerland of America. In this cozy mountain village, everything is within walking-distance, including the Ouray Hot Springs Pool, Cascade Falls, the local movie theater in the historical Wright Opera House, several fine restaurants, lodging and the Community Center where workshop events take place." 2005 panels included Generating New Material, Craft and Critique, Revising and Submitting for Publication. Panelists in 2005 included Melanie Rae Thon, Pam Houston, Dorothy Allison, Phillip Lopate, Brenda Miller, Maura Stanton, Andrew Hudgins, Stephen Dunn. .
Costs $350-475, includes workshop instruction, faculty readings, breakfast each day and admission to all receptions. "All sessions will require an additional, non-refundable application fee of $25. There are substantial discounts for attending multiple sessions. There are also $100 scholarships available." .
Accommodations Offers shuttle to/from airport in Montrose, CO. Provides a list of hotels.
Additional Information Accepts inquiries by SASE, e-mail, phone. "There are social activities, including mountain cookout, concerts in the local park, the annual pub crawl, champagne brunch and readings." See website for more information.

SMALL PUBLISHERS CONFERENCE/WORKSHOP
(formerly Book Publish 2004), Small Publishers Association of North America, P.O. Box 1306, Buena Vista CO 81211. (719)395-4790. Fax: (719)395-8374. E-mail: span@spannet.org. Website: www.spannet.org. **Contact:** Jennifer Quintana, coordinator. Estab. 1996. Annual. Last conference was October 2005. Conference duration: 3 days. Average attendance: 85. Conference/workshop and trade show for the self-publisher or independent/small press. Attendees learn how to sell more books, increase profits, create a more effective message and boost their professional standing. Site: Denver, CO.
Costs TBA. Meals are included in registration fee. Lodging is available for an additional charge.
Additional Information Brochures available in June by fax, e-mail and on website. Accepts inquiries for SASE and by e-mail, phone and fax.

SOUTHWEST LITERARY CENTER OF RECURSOS DE SANTA FE
826 Camino de Monte Rey, Santa Fe NM 87505. (505)577-1125. Fax: (505)982-7125. E-mail: litcenter@recursos. org. Website: www.recursos.org or www.santafewritersconference.com. **Contact:** Literary Center director. Estab. 1984. Annual. 2005 conference was held June 14-19. Conference duration: 5 days. Average attendance: 65. "This year's conference is titled Crossing Borders: From Poetry and Fiction to Creative Nonfiction." Site: Downtown Santa Fe. Previous speakers included C. Michael Curtis, Natalie Goldberg, Pagan Kennedy, Christopher Merrill and Lauren Slater.
Costs $675-1,125. Some meals included. Scholarships may be available.
Additional Information Brochure available by e-mail, fax, phone and on website.

SOUTHWEST WRITERS CONFERENCE
3271 Morris NE, Albuquerque NM 87111. (505)265-9485. Fax: (505)265-9483. E-mail: swriters@aol.com. Website: www.southwestwriters.org. **Contact:** Conference Chair. Estab. 1983. Annual. Conferences held throughout the year. Average attendance: 400. "Conferences concentrate on all areas of writing and include appointments and networking." Workshops and speakers include writers, editors and agents of all genres for all levels from beginners to advanced.
Costs $99 and up (members); $159 and up (nonmembers); includes conference sessions and lunch.
Accommodations Usually have official airline and discount rates. Special conference rates are available at hotel. A list of other area hotels and motels is available.
Additional Information Sponsors an annual contest judged by authors, editors and agents from New York, Los Angeles, etc., and from other major publishing houses. Eighteen categories. Deadline: See website. Entry fee is $29 (members) or $44 (nonmembers). For brochures/guidelines send SASE, visit website, e-mail, fax, call. "An appointment (10 minutes, one-on-one) may be set up at the conference with the editor/agent of your choice on a first-registered/first-served basis."

Conferences

STEAMBOAT SPRINGS WRITERS GROUP

Steamboat Arts Council, P.O. Box 774284, Steamboat Springs CO 80477. (970)879-8079. E-mail: sswriters@cs.com. Website: www.steamboatwriters.com. **Contact:** Harriet Freiberger, director. Estab. 1982. Annual. Group meets year-round on Thursdays, 12:00 to 2:00 at Arts Depot; guests welcome. Conference held in July. Conference duration: 1 day. Average attendance: 30. "Our conference emphasizes instruction within the seminar format. Novices and polished professionals benefit from the individual attention and camaraderie which can be established within small groups. A pleasurable and memorable learning experience is guaranteed by the relaxed and friendly atmosphere of the old train depot. Registration is limited." Site: Restored train depot.

Costs $35 before June 1, $45 after. Fee covers all conference activities, including lunch.

Accommodations Lodging available at Steamboat Resorts.

Additional Information Optional dinner and activities during evening preceding conference. Accepts inquiries by e-mail, phone, mail.

N ◎ TEXAS CHRISTIAN WRITERS' CONFERENCE

First Baptist Church, 6038 Greenmont, Houston TX 77092. (713)686-7209. E-mail: marthalrogers@sbcglobal.net. **Contact:** Martha Rogers. Estab. 1990. Annual. Conference held in August. Conference duration: 1 day. Average attendance: 60-65. "Focus on all genres." Site: Held at the First Baptist Church fellowship center and classrooms. Previous faculty: Jim Stafford, Rebecca Germany, Eva Marie Everson, Jeanette Littleton, Debra White-Smith, Cecil Murphy, Diann Mills and Kathy Ide.

Costs $60 for members of IWA, $75 nonmembers, discounts for seniors (60+) and couples, meal at noon, continental breakfast and breaks.

Accommodations Offers list of area hotels or lodging options.

Additional Information Open conference for all interested writers. Sponsors a contest for short fiction; categories include articles, devotionals, poetry, short story, book proposals, drama. Fees: $8 member, $10 nonmember. Conference information available with SASE or e-mail. Agents participate in conference. Senior discounts available.

N THUNDER WRITER'S RETREATS

Durango CO 81301-3408. (970)385-5884. Fax: (970)247-5327. E-mail: thunder@thunderforwriters.com. Website: www.thunderforwriters.com. **Contact:** Michael Thunder. Estab. 2000. On demand, per client's need. Conference duration: 1-2 weeks. Average attendance: 1 individual/session. Focus is on fiction and scriptwriting. Site: Durango, Colorado, "beautiful mountain environment."

Costs $1,000/week coaching fee. Meals and lodging are dependent on the writer's taste and budget.

Accommodations Provides a list of area hotels or lodging options.

Additional Information "These writer's retreats are geared toward concepting a project or project development. Usually writers stay one week and receive 10 hours of one-on-one coaching. The rest of their time is spent writing. One and sometimes two interviews are required to design a course of action adapted to the writer's needs." Please call, e-mail, fax or send SASE for more information.

N MARK TWAIN CREATIVE WRITING WORKSHOPS

University House, 5101 Rockhill Rd., Kansas City MO 64110-2499. (816)235-1168. Fax: (816)235-2611. E-mail: BeasleyM@umkc.edu. Website: www.newletters.org. **Contact:** Betsy Beasley, adminstrative associate. Estab. 1990. Annual. Held first 3 weeks of June, from 9:30 to 12:30 each weekday morning. Conference duration: 3 weeks. Average attendance: 40. "Focus is on fiction, poetry and literary nonfiction." Site: University of Missouri-Kansas City Campus. Panels planned for next conference include the full range of craft essentials. Staff includes Robert Stewart, editor-in-chief of *New Letters* and BkMk Press.

Costs Fees for regular and noncredit courses.

Accommodations Offers list of area hotels or lodging options.

Additional Information Submit for workshop 6 poems/one short story prior to arrival. Conference information is available in March by SASE, e-mail or on website. Editors participate in conference.

UNIVERSITY OF NEW MEXICO'S TAOS SUMMER WRITERS' CONFERENCE

Department of English Language and Literature MSC03 2170, 1 University of New Mexico, Albuquerque NM 87131-0001. (505)277-6248. Fax: (505)277-2950. E-mail: taosconf@unm.edu. Website: www.unm.edu/~taosconf. **Contact:** Sharon Oard Warner, director. Estab. 1999. Annual. Held each year in mid-July. Average attendance: 180. Workshops in novel writing, short story writing, screenwriting, poetry, creative nonfiction, travel writing and in special topics such as historical fiction, memoir and revision. Master classes in novel and poetry. For beginning and experienced writers. "Taos itself makes our conference unique. We also offer daily visits to the D.H. Lawrence Ranch, the Harwood Museum and other local historical sites." Site: Workshops and readings are all held at the Sagebrush Inn Conference Center, part of the Sagebrush Inn, an historic hotel and Taos landmark since 1929.

Costs Weeklong workshop tuition is $525, includes a Sunday evening Mexican buffet dinner, a Friday evening barbecue and other special events. Weekend workshop tuition is $250.

Accommodations We offer a discounted car rental rate through the Sagebrush Inn or the adjacent Comfort Suites. Conference participants receive special discounted rates $59-99/night. Room rates at both hotels include a full, hot breakfast.

Additional Information "We offer three Merit Scholarships, the Taos Resident Writer Award, the Hispanic Writer Award and one D.H. Lawrence Fellowship. Scholarship awards are based on submissions of poetry, fiction and creative nonfiction." They provide tuition remission; transportation and lodging not provided. To apply, submit 10 pages of poetry or fiction along with registration and deposit. Applicants should be registered for the conference. The Fellowship is for emerging writers with one book in print, provides tuition remission and cost of lodging. Brochures available late January-early February 2006. "The conference offers a balance of special events and free time. If participants take a morning workshop, they'll have the afternoons free and vice versa. We've also included several outings, including a tour of the Harwood Arts Center and a visit to historic D.H. Lawrence Ranch outside Taos."

◎ WRITERS WORKSHOP IN SCIENCE FICTION

English Department/University of Kansas, Lawrence KS 66045-2115. (785)864-3380. Fax: (785)864-1159. E-mail: jgunn@ku.edu. Website: www.ku.edu/~sfcenter. **Contact:** James Gunn, professor. Estab. 1984. Annual. Workshop held in late June to early July. Conference duration: 2 weeks. Average attendance: 10-14. The workshop is "small, informal and aimed at writers on the edge of publication or regular publication." For writing and marketing science fiction. Site: "Housing is provided and classes meet in university housing on the University of Kansas campus. Workshop sessions operate informally in a lounge." Past guests included Frederik Pohl, SF writer and former editor and agent; John Ordover, writer and editor; and Kij Johnson and Christopher McKittrick, writers.

Costs $400 tuition. Housing and meals are additional.

Accommodations Several airport shuttle services offer reasonable transportation from the Kansas City International Airport to Lawrence. During past conferences, students were housed in a student dormitory at $13.50/day double, $27/day single.

Additional Information "Admission to the workshop is by submission of an acceptable story. Two additional stories should be submitted by the end of May. These three stories are copied and distributed to other participants for critquing and are the basis for the first week of the workshop; one story is rewritten for the second week. The workshop offers a 3-hour session manuscript critiquing each morning. The rest of the day is free for writing, study, consultation and recreation." Information available in December. For brochures/guidelines send SASE, visit website, e-mail, fax, call. "The Writers Workshop in Science Fiction is intended for writers who have just started to sell their work or need that extra bit of understanding or skill to become a published writer."

WEST (AZ, CA, HI, NV, UT)

Ⓝ AWP ANNUAL CONFERENCE AND BOOKFAIR

MS 1E3, George Mason University, Fairfax VA 22030. (703)993-4303. Fax: (703)993-4302. E-mail: awpconf@gmu.edu. Website: www.awpwriter.org. **Contact:** Matt Scanlon, director of conferences. Estab. 1967. Annual. Conference held March 8-11, 2006, in Austin, TX. Conference duration: 4 days. Average attendance: 3,000. The annual conference is a gathering of 3,000+ students, teachers, writers, readers and publishers. All genres are represented. Site: This year the conference will be held at Hilton Austin. "We will offer 175 panels on everything from writing to teaching to critical analysis. In 2005 Deborah Eisenberg, Ursula K. Le Guin, Alistair MacLeod, Michael Ondaatje and Guy Vanderhaeghe were special speakers.

Costs Early registration fees: $35/student; $135/AWP member; $155/non-member.

Accommodations Provide airline discounts and rental-car discounts. Special rate Hilton.

Additional Information Check website for more information.

Ⓝ BIG BEAR WRITER'S RETREAT

P.O. Box 1441, Big Bear Lake CA 92315-1441. (909)585-0059. Fax: (909)266-0710. E-mail: info@writers-review.com. **Contact:** Mike Foley, director. Estab. 1995. Biannual. Last conferences held July, October 2005. Conference duration: 3 days. Average attendance: 15-25. Past themes included Finding New Creativity, Character and Setting, Avoiding Common Errors, Character Depth, Embracing Yourself as a Writer. Site: "A small, intimate lodge in Big Bear, San Bernardino mountains of Southern California." Retreat is hosted annually by Mike Foley, editor of *Dream Merchant Magazine*, and Tom Foley, Ph.D., artistic psychologist.

Conferences

Costs $499, includes meals and lodging.

Accommodations Offers overnight accommodations. On-site facilites included in retreat fee.

Additional Information Prior to arrival, submit a fiction or nonfiction sample, 10 double-spaced pages maximum. 2007 conference information is available March 2006. For brochure send SASE, e-mail, call or fax. Accepts inquiries by SASE, e-mail, phone and fax. Editors participate in conference. "This is unlike the standard writer's conference. Participants will live as writers for a weekend. Retreat includes workshop sessions, open writing time and private counseling with retreat hosts. A weekend of focused writing, fun and friendship. This is a small group retreat, known for its individual attention to writers, intimate setting and strong bonding among participants."

BLOCKBUSTER PLOT INTENSIVE WRITING WORKSHOPS

708 Blossom Hill Rd. #146, Los Gatos CA 95032. Fax: (408)356-1798. E-mail: martha@blockbusterplots.com. Website: www.blockbusterplots.com. **Contact:** Martha Alderson, instructor. Estab. 2000. Held four times per year. Conference duration: 2 days. Average attendance: 6-8. Workshop is intended to help writers create an action, character and thematic plotline for a memoir, short story, novel or creative nonfiction. Site: a house. Martha Alderson.

Costs $135 per day.

Accommodations Provides list of area hotels and lodging options.

Additional Information Brochures available by fax, e-mail or on website. Accepts inquiries by SASE, e-mail and fax.

JAMES BONNET'S STORYMAKING: THE MASTER CLASS

P.O. Box 841, Burbank CA 91503-0841. (818)567-0521. Fax: (818)567-0038. E-mail: bonnet@storymaking.com. Website: www.storymaking.com. **Contact:** James Bonnet. Estab. 1990. Conference held February, May, June, November. Conference duration: 2 days. Average attendance: 40. Conferences focus on fiction, mystery and screenwriting. Site: In 2005, Sportsmen's Lodge, Studio City, California and Hilton Resort, Palm Springs, California. Panels for next conference include High Concept, Anatomy of A Great Idea, the Creative Process, Metaphor, The Hook, The Fundamentals of Plot, Structure, Genre, Character, Complications, Crisis, Climax, Conflict, Suspense and more. James Bonnet (author) is scheduled to participate as speaker.

Costs $350 per weekend.

Accommodations Provides a list of area hotels or lodging options.

Additional Information For brochure send SASE, e-mail, visit website, call or fax. Accepts inquiries by SASE, e-mail, phone and fax. "James Bonnet, author of *Stealing Fire From the Gods*, teaches a story structure and storymaking seminar that guides writers from inspiration to final draft."

◎ BOUCHERCON

507 S. 8th Street, Philadelphia PA 19147. (215)923-0211. Fax: (215)923-1789. E-mail: registration@bouchercon2 004. Website: www.bouchercon.com. Conference held September 28-October 1, 2006, in Madison, WI. The Bouchercon is "the world mystery and detective fiction event." Site: See website for details. Past speakers and panelists included Dennis Lehane, Marcia Muller and Jonathan Gash.

Costs $175 registration fee covers writing workshops, panels, reception, etc.

Additional Information Sponsors Anthony Award for published mystery novel; ballots due prior to conference. Information available on website.

◎ BYU WRITING FOR YOUNG READERS WORKSHOP

348 HCEB, Brigham Young University, Provo UT 84602. (801)422-2568. E-mail: cw348@byu.edu. Website: http://wfyr.byu.edu. **Contact:** Bill Kelly. Estab. 2000. Annual. Workshop held June or July each year. Average attendance: 150. Conference focuses on "all genres for children and teens." Site: Brigham Young University's Conference Center. Mornings feature small group workshop sessions with a published author. Afternoon break-out sessions on a variety of topics of interest to writers. Sessions for picture book, novel, illustration, fantasy, beginners, general writing. Two editors and an agent are in attendance. Past faculty has included Eve Bunting, Tony Johnston, Tim Wynne-Jones, John H. Ritter, Alane Ferguson, Lael Little, Laura Torres, Cloria Skurzynski and Claudia Mills.

Costs $399 conference fee and closing banquet.

Accommodations Provides list of area hotels.

Additional Information Brochures available in March by phone and on website. Accepts inquiries by SASE, e-mail, phone. Agents and editors participate in conference. "Bring the manuscript you are currently working on."

COMMUNITY OF WRITERS AT SQUAW VALLEY

(formerly Squaw Valley Community of Writers), P.O. Box 1416, Nevada City CA 95959-1416. (530)470-8440. Fax: (530)470-8446. E-mail: info@squawvalleywriters.org. Website: www.squawvalleywriters.org. **Contact:** Brett Hall Jones, executive director. Estab. 1969. Annual. Conference held in August. Conference duration: 7 days. Average attendance: 132. "The writers workshops in fiction, nonfiction and memoir assist talented writers by exploring the art and craft as well as the business of writing." Offerings include daily morning workshops led by writer-teachers, editors, or agents of the staff, limited to 12-13 participants; seminars; panel discussions of editing and publishing; craft colloquies; lectures; and staff readings. Past themes and panels included "Personal History in Fiction," "Narrative Structure," "Roots" and "Anatomy of a Short Story." Past faculty and speakers included Michael Chabon, Mark Childress, Janet Finch, Richard Ford, Karen Joy Fowler, Lynn Freed, Molly Giles, Glen David Gold, Sands Hall, James D. Houston, Louis B. Jones, Alice Sebold, Al Young.
Costs Tuition is $695, which includes 6 dinners.
Accommodations The Community of Writers rents houses and condominiums in the Valley for participants to live in during the week of the conference. Single room (one participant): $550/week. Double room (twin beds, room shared by conference participant of the same sex): $350/week. Multiple room (bunk beds, room shared with 2 or more participants of the same sex): $200/week. All room subject to availability; early requests are recommended. Can arrange airport shuttle pick-ups for a fee.
Additional Information Admissions are based on submitted ms (unpublished fiction, a couple of stories or novel chapters); requiries $25 reading fee. Submit ms to Brett Hall Jones, Squaw Valley Community of Writers, P.O. Box 1416, Nevada City, CA 95959. Deadline: May 10. Notification: June 10. Brochure/guidelines available February by phone, e-mail or visit website. Accepts inquiries by SASE, e-mail, phone. Agents and editors attend/participate in conferences.

DESERT DREAMS CONFERENCE: REALIZING THE DREAM

1066 E. Hope Street, Mesa AZ 85203. (623)910-0524. E-mail: desertdreams@desertroserwa.org. Website: www.desertroserwa.org. **Contact:** Carrie Weaver, conference coordinator. Estab. 1986. Biennial. Conference held April 21-23, 2006. Next conference Spring 2008. Average attendance: 250. Conference focuses on romance fiction. Site: Chaparral Suites Resort in Scottsdale, AZ. Past panels included: Plotting, Dialogue, Manuscript Preparation, Website Design, Synopsis, Help for the Sagging Middle. Keynote speakers in 2006 are Debbie Macomber and Debra Dixon. Guest editors/agents from St. Martin's Press, Harlequin, Irene Goodman Literary Agency, Borders Group, Ellora's Cave, Spectrum Literary Agency and more.
Costs For RWA members: $160 before January 1; $180 January 1-March 15; $225 late registration or on-site. For non-members: $180 before January 1; $200 January 1-March 15; $225 late registration or on-site. Debra Dixon workshop extra. "Full conference price includes workshops, mixers, events on Friday (beginning mid-afternoon), all day Saturday events and events through noon on Sunday; dinner on Friday, lunch on Saturday and full breakfast for those staying at the hotel."
Accommodations Hotel provides shuttle service from airport. $130/night at Chaparral Suites Resort. Mention conference to receive special rate. Price includes full breakfast each morning, afternoon appetizers and happy hour. For more information about transportation, see website or e-mail transportation@desertroserwa.org.
Additional Information Sponsors contest as part of conference. For brochure, inquiries, contact by e-mail, phone, fax, mail or visit website. Agents and editors participate in conference.

IWWG EARLY SPRING IN CALIFORNIA CONFERENCE

International Women's Writing Guild, P.O. Box 810, Gracie Station NY 10028-0082. (212)737-7536. Fax: (212)737-7536. E-mail: iwwg@iwwg.com. Website: www.iwwg.com. **Contact:** Hannelore Hahn, executive editor. Estab. 1982. Annual. Conference held second week in March. Average attendance: 80. Conference to promote "creative writing, personal growth and empowerment." Site: Bosch Bahai School, a redwood forest mountain retreat in Santa Cruz, CA.
Costs $345 for weekend program with room and board ($325 for members); $90 per day for commuters ($80 for members); $170 for weekend program without room and board ($150 for members).
Accommodations Accommodations are all at conference site.
Additional Information Conference information is available after August. For brochures/guidelines, send SASE. Accepts inquiries by e-mail, fax.

LA JOLLA WRITERS CONFERENCE

P.O. Box 178122, San Diego CA 92177. (858)467-1978. Fax: (858)467-1971. E-mail: akurtz@lajollawritersconference.com. Website: www.lajollawritersconference.com. **Contact:** Antoinette Kurtz, founder. Estab. 2001. Annual. Conference held October 7-9. Conference duration: 3 days. Average attendance: 175-200. "With seminars in both fiction and nonfiction, the La Jolla Writers Conference focuses on the art, craft and business of writing. We hope to engender a sense of community, encourage self-confidence, and inspire new levels of creativity in our attendees." Site: The Hilton Resort on Mission Bay in San Diego is an extremely ambiant setting. Located in the park surrounding Mission Bay, the hotel benefits from the walking, biking and jogging paths as well as access to the Bay for boating and watersports. Speakers for 2005; Lorenzo Carcaterra, Michael Connelly, and many more.

Costs $315, includes 2 meals. Double rooms approximately $150 per night with conference discount. Less expensive hotels nearby.

Additional Information For individual read & critiques, send 10 double-spaced pages one month prior to conference.

LEAGUE OF UTAH WRITERS ROUND-UP

P.O. Box 460562, Leeds UT 84746. (435)313-4459 or (801)450-7310. E-mail: reelsweetjustwrite@juno.com. Website: www.luwrite.com. **Contact:** Dorothy Crofts, membership chairman. Estab. 1935. Annual. Last conference held September 16-17, 2005. Conference duration: 2 days, Friday and Saturday. Average attendance: 200. "The purpose of the conference is to award the winners of our annual contest as well as offer instruction in all areas of writing. Speakers cover subjects from generating ideas to writing a novel to working with a publisher. We have something for everyone." Site: Conference held at hotel conference rooms and ballroom facilities. 2005 themes included: Essays, Mystery, Writing for Magazines, Children's Nonfiction, Poetry, General Fiction. 2005 keynote speaker was Mary Higgins Clark.

Costs $125 for LUW members; $160 for nonmembers (fee includes 4 meals).

Accommodations St. George Hilton Garden Inn, 1731 Convention Center Drive, St. George, UT. Special hotel rate for conferees: $89/night.

Additional Information Opportunity for writers to meet one-on-one with literary agents from New York. Sponsors contests for 8 fiction categories, 3 open to nonmembers of League. Word limits vary from 1,500 to 90,000. Conference brochures/guidelines available for SASE, by fax and on website. Accepts inquiries by phone, fax, e-mail, SASE.

MENDOCINO COAST WRITERS CONFERENCE

College of the Redwoods, 1211 Del Mar Drive, Fort Bragg CA 95437. (707)964-6810. E-mail: info@mcwc.org. Website: http://mcwc.org. **Contact:** Stephen Garber, registrar. Estab. 1989. Annual. Last conference held August 11-13, 2005. Average attendance: 100. "We hope to encourage the developing writer by inviting presenters who are both fine writers and excellent teachers." Site: College of the Redwoods is a small community college located on the gorgeous northern California coast. Focuses are fiction, poetry, creative nonfiction—special areas have included children's (2003), mystery (2002), social awareness. In 2005 faculty included Bonnie Hearn Hiu, Les Standiford, Carolyn Cooke, Diane Theil, David Weitzman, Dorianne Laux, David Godine, Sheree Petree, Ronnie Gilbert.

Costs Before June 10, 2005: $300 (2 days); $375 (3 days). After June 20, 2005: $375 (2 days); $410 (3 days).

Additional Information Brochures for the conference will be available in March by SASE, phone, e-mail or on the website. Agents and editors participate in the conference. "The conference is small, friendly and fills up fast with many returnees."

MORMON WRITERS' CONFERENCE

Association for Mormon Letters, P.O. Box 51364, Provo UT 84605-1364. (801)582-2090. E-mail: aml@aml-online.org. Website: www.aml-online.org. **Contact:** conference chair. Estab. 1999. Annual. Conference held November. Conference duration: one day, usually first Saturday of the month. Average attendance: 150. The conference will cover anything to do with writing by, for or about Mormons, including fiction, nonfiction, theater, film, children's literature. Site: Provo, UT. "Plenary speeches, panels and instructional presentations by prominent authors and artists in the LDS artistic community."

Costs $55, includes catered lunch with pre-registration. AML member and student discounts available.

Additional Information For brochures/guidelines send SASE, e-mail, visit website. Accepts inquiries by SASE, e-mail.

MOUNT HERMON CHRISTIAN WRITERS CONFERENCE

P.O. Box 413, Mount Hermon CA 95041-0413. (831)335-4466. Fax: (831)335-9413. E-mail: info@mhcamps.org. Website: www.mounthermon.org/writers. **Contact:** David R. Talbott, director of adult ministries. Estab. 1970. Annual. Conference held April 7-11, 2006. Average attendance: 450. "We are a broad-ranging conference for all areas of Christian writing, including fiction, children's, poetry, nonfiction, magazines, books, educational curriculum and radio and TV scriptwriting. This is a working, how-to conference, with many workshops within the conference involving on-site writing assignments." Site: "The conference is sponsored by and held at the 440-acre Mount Hermon Christian Conference Center near San Jose, California, in the heart of the coastal redwoods. Registrants stay in hotel-style accommodations, and full board is provided as part of the conference fees. Meals are taken family style, with faculty joining registrants. The faculty/student ratio is about 1:6 or 7. The bulk of our faculty are editors and publisher representatives from major Christian publishing houses nationwide.''

Costs Registration fees include tution, conference sessions, resource notebook, refreshment breaks, room and board and vary from $675 (economy) to $995 (deluxe), double occupancy (2005 rates).

Accommodations Airport shuttles are available from the San Jose International Airport. Housing is not required of registrants, but about 95% of our registrants use Mount Hermon's own housing facilites (hotel-style double-occupancy rooms). Meals with the conference are required and are included in all fees.

Additional Information Registrants may submit 2 works for critique in advance of the conference. No advance work is required, however. Conference brochures/guidelines are available online only in December. Accepts inquiries by e-mail, fax. ''The residential nature of our conference makes this a unique setting for one-on-one interaction with faculty/staff. There is also a decided inspirational flavor to the conference, and general sessions with well-known speakers are a highlight. Come rested, with plenty of business cards and samples of works in progress or just completed.''

PIMA WRITERS' WORKSHOP

Pima Community College, 2202 W. Anklam Road, Tucson AZ 85709-0170. (520)206-6084. Fax: (520)206-6020. E-mail: mfiles@pima.edu. **Contact:** Meg Files, director. Estab. 1988. Annual. Conference held in May. Average attendance: 300. ''For anyone interested in writing—beginning or experienced writer. The workshop offers sessions on writing short stories, novels, nonfiction articles and books, children's and juvenile stories, poetry, screenplays.'' Site: Sessions are held in the Center for the Arts on Pima Community College's West campus. Past speakers include Michael Blake, Ron Carlson, Gregg Levoy, Nancy Mairs, Linda McCarriston, Jerome Stern, Connie Willis, Larry McMurtry, Barbara Kingsolver and Robert Morgan.

Costs $70 (can include ms critique). Participants may attend for college credit, in which case fees are $104 for Arizona residents and $164 for out-of-state residents. Meals and accommodations not included.

Accommodations Information on local accommodations is made available and special workshop rates are available at a specified motel close to the workshop site (about $70/night).

Additional Information Participants may have up to 20 pages critiqued by the author of their choice. Manuscripts must be submitted 3 weeks before the workshop. Conference brochure/guidelines available for SASE. Accepts inquiries by e-mail. ''The workshop atmosphere is casual, friendly and supportive, and guest authors are very accessible. Readings, films and panel discussions are offered as well as talks and manuscript sessions.''

◎ SCBWI/SUMMER CONFERENCE ON WRITING & ILLUSTRATING FOR CHILDREN

(formerly SCBWI/International Conference on Writing & Illustrating for Children), 8271 Beverly Blvd., Los Angeles CA 90048. (323)782-1010. Fax: (323)782-1892. E-mail: conference@scbwi.org. Website: www.scbwi.o rg. **Contact:** Lin Oliver, executive director. Estab. 1972. Annual. Conference held in August. Conference duration: 4 days. Average attendance: 800. Writer and illustrator workshops geared toward all levels. Covers all aspects of children's magazine and book publishing.

Costs Approximately $400; includes all 4 days and one banquet meal. Does not include hotel room.

Accommodations Information on overnight accommodations made available.

Additional Information Ms and illustration critiques are available. Brochure/guidelines available on website.

TMCC WRITERS' CONFERENCE

TMCC Workforce Development and Continuing Education Division, 5270 Neil Road Rm 216, Reno NV 89502. (775)829-9010. Fax: (775)829-9032. E-mail: asefchick@tmcc.edu or mikedcroft@aol.com. Website: www.tmcc. edu/wdce/ or www.tmccwriters.com. Estab. 1990. Annual. 2005 conference held in April. Average attendance: 125. Conference focuses on fiction (literary and mainstream), poetry, memoirs, screenwriting, marketing to agents, publishers. Site: John Ascuaga's Nugget Hotel/Casino Resort—facilites include indoor pool, spa, numerous restaurants, celebrity showrooms, casino, sportsbook, wireless Internet. ''We strive to provide a well-rounded event for fiction writers and poets.''

Costs 4-day Track A $389; 2-day Track B $109 before February 28, $119 after. ''Scholarships based on merit and financial need are awarded every December.''

Accommodations Hotel shuttle service from Reno airport available. Overnight accommodations available at site for conference rate of $85/night.

Additional Information If participating in Track A, attendees should submit first chapter (5,000 words maximum) by January 21. Brochures available November by e-mail, phone, mail, fax or on website. Accepts inquires by e-mail or phone. Agent will participate in conference. ''This conference features an informal, friendly atmosphere where questions are encouraged. A Writers' Reception session allows for participants to mix with event speakers. No-host lunches with presenters (limited to first 9 sign-ups per lunch) will also be held. The 4-day Track A keeps each critique group small.''

ⓝ UCLA EXTENSION WRITERS' PROGRAM

10995 Le Conte Avenue, #440, Los Angeles CA 90024-2883. (310)825-9415 or (800)388-UCLA. Fax: (310)206-7382. E-mail: writers@UCLAextension.edu. Website: www.uclaextension.edu/writers. **Contact:** Cindy Lieberman, program manager. Courses held year-round with one-day or intensive weekend workshops to 12-week courses. Writers Studio held in February. A 9-month master class is also offered every fall. "The diverse offerings span introductory seminars to professional novel and script completion workshops. The annual Writers Studio and a number of 1-, 2- and 4-day intensive workshops are popular with out-of-town students due to their specific focus and the chance to work with industry professionals. The most comprehensive and diverse continuing education writing program in the country, offering over 500 courses a year including: screenwriting, fiction, writing for young people, poetry, nonfiction, playwriting and publishing. Adult learners in the UCLA Extension Writers' Program study with professional screenwriters, fiction writers, playwrights, poets and nonfiction writers, who bring practical experience, theoretical knowledge and a wide variety of teaching styles and philosophies to their classes." Site: Courses are offered in Los Angeles on the UCLA campus and in the 1010 Westwood Center in Westwood Village, as well as online.
Costs Vary from $90 for one-day workshops to $3,000 for the 9-month master class.
Accommodations Students make own arrangements. The program can provide assistance in locating local accommodations.
Additional Information Writers Studio information available October. For brochures/guidelines/guide to course offerings, visit website, e-mail, fax or call. Accepts inquiries by e-mail, fax, phone. "Some advanced level classes have manuscript submittal requirements; instructions are always detailed in the quarterly UCLA Extension course catalog. An annual fiction prize, The James Kirkwood Prize in Creative Writing, has been established and is given annually to one ficion writer who has produced outstanding work in a Writers' Program course."

WILD WRITING WOMEN WRITING WORKSHOP

110 Forrest Ave., Fairfax CA 94930. (415)454-1754. E-mail: writing@lisaalpine.com. Website: www.wildwritingwomen.com. **Contact:** Lisa Alpine. Estab. 2003. Annual. January 2006. Conference duration: 2 days. Average attendance: 50. Designed for serious and would-be serious writers, the conference includes classes on travel writing, chronicling your family legacy, the writer's voice, personal essay, real-time travelogues, food writing, understanding contracts, self publishing and more. Site: Historic Fort Mason on San Francisco Bay, featuring breathtaking views of the Golden Gate Bridge. "We've arranged a panel discussion with magazine and book editors, a panel with the WWW on how to run a successful writing group, a travel photography discussion and slide show presentation, creativity exercises and more." Classes will be taught by members of the Wild Writing Women, LCC, the acclaimed San Francisco writing group and authors of *Wild Writing Women: Stories of World Travel*, an award-winning anthology of travelogues and the 2004 winners of Natja's Best Travel Ezine.
Costs $350 by Dec. 15; $400 after that date. Includes all classes and panels, lunch and a wine mixer.
Accommodations Provides list of hotels and lodging options.
Additional Information Brochures for the 2006 conference will be available in November 2005 by phone, e-mail and on website. Accepts inquiries by e-mail and phone. Agents and editors attend the conference.

ⓝ WRITERS STUDIO AT UCLA EXTENTION

(formerly Los Angeles Writer's Conference), 1010 Westwood Blvd., Los Angeles CA 90024. (310)825-9415. E-mail: writers@uclaextension.edu. Website: www.uclaextension.edu/writers. **Contact:** Mae Respicto. Estab. 1997. Annual. Last conference was February 3-6, 2005. Conference duration: 4 days; 10 a.m. to 6 p.m. Average attendance: 150-200. Conference on creative writing, screenwriting and memoir writing. Site: Conducted at UCLA Extension's 1010 Westwood Center.
Accommodations Information on overnight accommodations is available.
Additional Information For more information, call number above.

ⓝ WRITING FOR YOUNG READERS WORKSHOP

348 HCEB, BYU, Provo UT 84602-1532. (801)422-2568. Fax: (801)422-0745. E-mail: cw348@byu.edu. Website: http://wfyr.byu.edu. **Contact:** Conferences & Workshops. Estab. 2000. Annual. Workshop held June of each year. Average attendance: limited to 175. Workshop focuses on fiction for young readers: picture books, book-length fiction, illustration and general writing. "Mornings are spent in small group workshop sessions with published author." Site: Conference Center at Brigham Young University in the foothills of the Wasatch Mountain range. Previous faculty have included Eve Bunting, Lael Littke, Claudia Mills, Tim Wynne-Jones and Alane Ferguson.
Costs $399, includes final banquet.
Accommodations Local lodging, airport shuttle. Lodging rates: $55-85/night.
Additional Information Participants who are not registered in the beginning writing section must bring at least one manuscript in progress to the workshop. Conference information is available April of each year. For brochure visit website, call or fax. Accepts inquiries by e-mail, phone and fax. Editors particpate in conference.

NORTHWEST (AK, ID, MT, OR, WA, WY)

CENTRUM'S PORT TOWNSEND WRITERS' CONFERENCE
P.O. Box 1158, Port Townsend WA 98368-0958. (360)385-3102. Fax: (360)385-2470. E-mail: info@centrum.org. Website: www.centrum.org. **Contact:** Rebecca Brown, creative director. Estab. 1974. Annual. Conference held mid-July. Average attendance: 180. Conference to promote poetry, fiction, creative nonfiction "featuring many of the nation's leading writers." Two different workshop options: critiqued (limit 16 participants) and open enrollment. Site: The conference is held at Fort Worden State Park on the Strait of Juan de Fuca. "The site is a Victorian-era military fort with miles of beaches, wooded trails and recreation facilities. The park is within the limits of Port Townsend, a historic seaport and arts community, approximately 80 miles northwest of Seattle, on the Olympic Peninsula." Guest speakers participate in addition to full-time faculty.
Costs Tuition for critiqued workshop is $525, for open-enrollment workshops $425. Room and board ranges from $285-$540, depending on the option you choose.
Accommodations "Modest room and board facilities on site." Also list of hotels/motels/inns/bed & breakfasts/ private rentals available.
Additional Information Brochures/guidelines available for SASE or on website. "The conference focus is on the craft of writing and the writing life, not on marketing."

◎ CLARION WEST WRITERS' WORKSHOP
340 15th Avenue E, Suite 350, Seattle WA 98112-5156. (206)322-9083. E-mail: info@clarionwest.org. Website: www.clarionwest.org. **Contact:** Leslie Howle, executive director. Estab. 1983. Annual. Workshop usually held in June or July. Average attendance: 18. "Conference to prepare students for professional careers in science fiction and fantasy writing." Deadline for applications: April 1. Site: Conference held in Seattle's University district, an urban site close to restaurants and cafes, but not too far from downtown. Faculty: 6 teachers (professional writers and editors established in the field). "Every week a new instructor—each a well-known writer chosen for the quality of his or her work and for professional stature—teaches the class, bringing a unique perspective on speculative fiction. During the fifth week, the workshop is taught by a professional editor."
Costs Workshop tuition: $1,700 ($125 discount if application received by March 1). Dormitory housing: $1,200, some meals included.
Accommodations Students are strongly encouraged to stay on-site in workshop housing at one of the University of Washington's sorority houses.
Additional Information "Students write their own stories every week while preparing critiques of all the other students' work for classroom sessions. This gives participants a more focused, professional approach to their writing. The core of the workshop remains science fiction, and short stories (not novels) are the focus." Conference information available in Fall 2005. For brochure/guidelines send SASE, visit website, e-mail or call. Accepts inquiries by e-mail, phone, SASE. Limited scholarships are available, based on financial need. Students must submit 20-30 pages of ms with $25 application fee by mail to qualify for admission.

FLATHEAD RIVER WRITERS CONFERENCE
P.O. Box 7711, Kalispell MT 59904. E-mail: hows@centurytel.net. **Contact:** Jake How, director. Estab. 1990. Annual. Last conference: October 7-9, 2005. Conference duration: 3 days. Average attendance: 100 (max). Deals with all aspects of writing, including short and long fiction and nonfiction. Site: Grouse Mountain Lodge in Whitefish, MT. Recent speakers: Bill Brooks (fiction), Bharti Kirchner (fiction/nonfiction), Jacky Sach (agent), Linda McFall (editor), Gary Ferguson (nonfiction), Gordon Kirkland (humor).
Costs $150 general weekend conference; includes breakfast and lunch, not lodging. $460 for both 3-day workshop preceeding general conference and general conference.
Accommodations Lodging at Grouse Mountain Lodge. Approximately 50% discount (around $100 a night).
Additional Information "We limit attendance to 100 in order to assure friendly, easy access to presentations."

◎ THE GLEN WORKSHOP
Image, 3307 Third Avenue W, Seattle WA 98119. (206)281-2988. Fax: (206)281-2335. E-mail: glenworkshop@i magejournal.org. Website: www.imagejournal.org. Estab. 1991. Annual. Workshop held in August. Conference duration: 1 week. Average attendance: 140-150. Workshop focuses on "fiction, poetry and spiritual writing, essay, memoir. Run by *Image*, a literary journal with a religious focus. The Glen welcomes writers who practice or grapple with religious faith." Site: 2005 conference held in Santa Fe, NM in the first week of August and features "presentations and readings by the faculty." Faculty has included Erin McGraw (fiction), Lauren F. Winner (spiritual writing), Paul Mariani and Andrew Hudgins (poetry) and Jeanne Murray Walker (playwriting).
Costs $630-855, including room and board; $230 for commuters (lunch only).

Accommodations Arrange transportation by shuttle. Accommodations included in conference cost.

Additional Information Prior to arrival, participants may need to submit workshop material depending on the teacher. "Usually 10-25 pages." Conference information is available in February. For brochure send SASE, e-mail, visit website, call or fax. "Like *Image*, the Glen is grounded in a Christian perspective, but its tone is informal and hospitable to all spiritual wayfarers."

HAYSTACK WRITING PROGRAM

Portland State University, P.O. Box 1491, Portland OR 97207-1491. (503)725-4186. Fax: (503)725-4840. E-mail: snydere@pdx.edu. Website: www.haystack.pdx.edu. **Contact:** Elizabeth Snyder, director. Estab. 1968. Annual. Program runs July 12 through August 6. Average attendance: 10-15/workshop; total program 200. Offers weekend and weeklong workshops in fiction, nonfiction, nature writing, memoir, regional fiction, screenwriting, publishing, dangerous writing, poetry and essay. Site: Classes are held at the Cannon Beach Elementary School in Cannon Beach, OR, a small coastal community. Speakers have included Diana Abu-Jaber, Judith Barrington, Ursula Le Guin and others.

Costs Non-credit. Approximately $415/course (weeklong); $225 (weekend). 2 quarter credits: $505. Does not include lodging.

Accommodations Various accommodations available including B&B, motel, hotel, private rooms, camping, private homes.

Additional Information Free brochure available after March. Accepts inquiries by e-mail and fax. University credit (graduate or undergraduate) is available. Classes are held in the local school with supplemental activities at the beach, community lecture hall, galleries and other areas of the resort town.

HEART TALK

Women's Center for Ministry, Western Seminary, 5511 SE Hawthorne Blvd., Portland OR 97215-3367. (503)517-1931 or (877)517-1800, ext. 1931. Fax: (503)517-1889. E-mail: wcm@westernseminary.edu. Website: www.westernseminary.edu/women/. **Contact:** Kenine Stein, administrative assistant. Estab. 1998. Every other year (alternates with speaker's conferences). Conference held in March. (2005 date was March 12.) Conference duration: writing, 1 day; speaking, 3-4 days. Average attendance: 100+. "Heart Talk provides inspirational training for women desiring to write for publication and/or speak publicly." Site: "Western Seminary has a chapel plus small and large classrooms to accommodate various size groups. The campus has a park-like atmosphere with beautiful lawns, trees and flowers. The squirrels are at home in this peaceful setting." Topics in 2005 ranged from writing fiction, nonfiction, gift books, book proposals, and greating cards to editing, steps to getting published, ministering to people in pain, writing for children and more. 2005 keynote speaker was Patricia Rushford. 14 workshops by Marion Duckworth, Kimberly Schumate, Jeannie St. John Taylor, Karla Dornacher, Liz Heaney, Doris Sanford and Patricia Rushford.

Costs $55 in 2005; box lunch can be ordered.

Additional Information Conference information available in January by e-mail, phone, fax and on website. For inquiries, contact by mail, e-mail, phone. Conference "is open to Christian women who desire to begin to write for publication."

JACKSON HOLE WRITERS CONFERENCE

Jackson WY . (307)766-2938. Fax: (307)766-3914. E-mail: jrieman@uwyo.edu. Website: www.jacksonholewriters.org. **Contact:** Jerimiah Rieman, coordinator. Annual. Last conference held June 23-26, 2005. Conference duration: 4 days. Average attendance: 100. The Jackson Hole Writers Conference draws a wide range of participants, from beginners to published writers. Site: Snow King Resort. The conference is directed toward fiction, screen writing and creative nonfiction, offering programs relevant to all 3 disciplines: story structure, character development, narrative thrust, work habits and business techniques. In addition, separate sessions deal with skills particular to each specialty.

Costs $325 conference pre-registration; $300 conference pre-registration for past participants; $75 spouse/guest registration; $50 ms evaluation; $75 extended ms evaluation. "You must register for conference to be eligible for manuscript evaluation."

Accommodations $135/night for single or double; $145/night triple; $155/night quadruple.

Additional Information The conference faculty's goal is to help our writers get published. Agent and editor roundtable discussions are geared specifically to teach you how your writing can be crafted, shaped and packaged for sale. Ms evaluations are also available. See website for details.

NATURE WRITERS RETREAT WITH NORTH CASCADES INSTITUTE

North Cascades Institute, 810 Highway 20, Sedro-Wooley WA 98284-9394. (360)856-5700 ext. 209. Fax: (360)859-1934. E-mail: nci@ncascades.org. Website: www.ncascades.org. **Contact:** Deb Martin, registrar. Estab. 1999. Annual. 2005 conference was held August 24-28. Conference duration: 4 days. Average attendance:

32. Led by three outstanding authors and poets, the NCI Nature Writing Retreat engages amateur and professional writers alike—lectures, discussions, readings and writing exercises centered on the natural world. "Nature writing, at its simplest, strives to explore basic principles at work in nature and to convey these in language that introduces readers to the facility and wonder of their own place in the world." Site: The 2005 conference was held at the new learning center in North Cascades National Park. 2005 faculty was Gary Ferguson, Tim McNulty and Scott Russell Sanders, PhD.

Costs 2005 costs were $575 (double occupancy), $495 (commuter), $725 (single). All options include meals.
Additional Information For conference information, visit website, e-mail or call.

PACIFIC NORTHWEST WRITERS CONFERENCE

P.O. Box 2016, Edmonds WA 98020-9516. (425)673-2665. Fax: (425)771-9588. E-mail: pnwa@pnwa.org. Website: www.pnwa.org. **Contact:** Dana Murphy-Love, association executive. Annual. Last conference held July 7-10, 2005. Average attendance: 450.

Accommodations Hotel shuttle to and from airport available. Offers discounted rate for overnight lodging; $129/night in 2005.

Additional Information Offers contest with 10 fiction categories: The Stella Cameron Romance Genre Contest, screenwriting, adult genre novel, Jean M. Auel Mainstream Novel, Judine and Terry Brooks Juvenile/YA Novel, adult short story, juvenile short story/picture book, poetry, nonfiction book/memoir, adult article/essay/short memoir. Entry requirements vary with category. Guidelines for contest available on website; brochure for conference available on website in late February. Accepts inquiries by e-mail, phone, fax. Agents and editors participate in conference.

SAGEBRUSH WRITERS WORKSHOP

P.O. Box 1255, Big Timber MT 59011-1255. (406)932-4227. E-mail: sagebrsh@ttc-cmc.net. **Contact:** Gwen Petersen, director. Estab. 1997. Annual. Workshop usually held in April or May. Conference duration: 2½ days. Average attendance: 25-30. "Each year, the workshop has a different focus." Conference features "intensive personal instruction, good food, advance critiques, well-published authors/instructors, agents/editors, book sales and signings, readings." Site: American Legion, Carnegie Library or other venue, Big Timber, MT. Faculty consists of one writer/instructor and 2 guest speakers.

Costs $190 (2005), included Friday evening banquet dinner with guest speakers, all snacks at breaks.
Accommodations Offers shuttle from airport by arrangement with Sagebrush. Provides a list of area hotels and/or lodging options.

Additional Information "Submissions optional but encouraged—up to 10 pages." Workshop information is available February. For brochure send SASE, e-mail, call or fax. Accepts inquiries by SASE, e-mail, phone and fax. Agents and editors participate in conference.

N SITKA SYMPOSIUM

P.O. Box 2420, Sitka AK 99835-2420. (907)747-3794. Fax: (907)747-6554. E-mail: island@ak.net. Website: www.islandinstitutealaska.org. **Contact:** Carolyn Servid, director. Estab. 1984. Annual. Conference held in July. Conference duration: 1 week. Average attendance: 60. Conference "to consider the relationship between writing and the ideas of selected theme focusing on social and cultural issues." Site: The Symposium is held in downtown Sitka. Many points of visitor interest are within walking distance. The town looks out over surrounding water and mountains. Guest speakers have included Alison Deming, Scott Russell Sanders, Rina Swentzell, Barry Lopez, William Kittredge, Gary Synder, Margaret Atwood, Terry Tempest Williams, Robert Hass, Richard Nelson and Linda Hogan.

Costs $365.
Accommodations Accommodation info is listed on Symposium brochure.
Additional Information Conference brochures/guidelines are available for SASE or online. Accepts inquiries by e-mail and fax.

N SOUTH COAST WRITERS CONFERENCE

P.O. Box 590, 29392 Ellensburg Avenue, Gold Beach OR 97444. (541)247-2741. Fax: (541)247-6247. E-mail: scwc@socc.edu. Website: www.socc.edu/scwriters. **Contact:** Janet Pretti, coordinator. Estab. 1996. Annual. Conference held President's Day weekend. Workshops held Friday and Saturday. Average attendance: 100. "We try to cover a broad spectrum: fiction, historical, poetry, children's, nature." Site: "Friday workshops are held at The Event Center on the Beach. Saturday workshops are held at the high school." 2005 keynote speaker was Bob Welch. Other presenters were Larry Colton, Shannon Applegate, Dr. Al Siebert, William Sullivan, Jackie Moyer-Fischer, Gerry Frank, Linda Berry, Ross Browne, Jerry Kimble Holcomb, Robert McDowell.

Costs $50 before January 31; $60 after. Friday workshops are an additional $35. No meals or lodging included.
Accommodations Provides list of area hotels.

Additional Information Sponsors contest. "Southwestern scholarship open to anyone. This year's scholarship topic is 'Breaking Rules.' Contact SCWC for details."

WILLAMETTE WRITERS CONFERENCE
9045 SW Barbur Blvd., Suite 5-A, Portland OR 97219-4027. (503)452-1592. Fax: (503)452-0372. E-mail: wilwrite @willamettewriters.com. Website: www.willamettewriters.com. **Contact:** Bill Johnson, office manager. Estab. 1981. Annual. Conference held in August. Conference duration: 3 days. Average attendance: 600. "Williamette Writers is open to all writers, and we plan our conference accordingly. We offer workshops on all aspects of fiction, nonfiction, marketing, the creative process, screenwriting, etc. Also we invite top notch inspirational speakers for keynote addresses. Recent theme was 'The Writers Way.' We always include at least one agent or editor panel and offer a variety of topics of interest to both fiction and nonfiction writers and screenwriters." Recent editors, agents and film producers in attendance have included: Donald Maass, Donald Maass Literary Agency; Angela Rinaldi; Kim Cameron.
Costs Cost for 2-day conference including meals is $325 members; $375 nonmembers.
Accommodations If necessary, these can be made on an individual basis. Some years special rates are available.
Additional Information Conference brochure/guidelines are available in May for catalog-size SASE, e-mail, fax, phone or on website. Accepts inquiries by fax, e-mail, phone, SASE.

N WRITE ON THE SOUND WRITERS' CONFERENCE
Edmonds Arts Commission, 700 Main Street, Edmonds WA 98020. (425)771-0228. Fax: (425)771-0253. E-mail: wots@ci.edmonds.wa.us. **Contact:** Kris Gillespie, conference coordinator. Estab. 1986. Annual. Last conference held October 1-2, 2005. Conference duration: 2 days. Average attendance: 180. "Conference is small—good for networking—and focuses on the craft of writing rather than publishers and editors." Site: "Edmonds is a beautiful community on the shores of Puget Sound, just north of Seattle."
Costs $104 by Sept. 19, $125 after Sept. 19 for 2 days, $68 for 1 day (2005); includes registration, morning refreshments and 1 ticket to keynote lecture.
Additional Information Brochures available August 1. Accepts inquiries by e-mail, fax.

N WRITERS STUDIO
P.O. Box 820141, Portland OR 97282-1141. E-mail: jesswrites@juno.com or jessica@inspirationnotebook.com. Website: www.writing-life.com or www.inspirationnotebook.com. **Contact:** Jessica P. Morrell. Estab. 1991. "Every year I teach a variety of one-day and weekend workshops in Portland and Eugene, OR; Seattle, WA; and at the Oregon Coast. Subjects include Fiction Middles; The First 50 Pages; Show, Don't Tell; Secondary Characters; Literary Nonfiction; Between the Lines: the Subtler Aspects of Fiction. At this time my schedule for 2006 is not finalized because I will be a guest speaker at a number of writing conferences, including PNWA in July, Willamette Writers Conference in August, and the Surrey International Writing Conference in October. I generally teach workshops the last weekend of each month except in November and December." *Writing Out the Storm* author Jessica Morrell is scheduled to participate as faculty.
Costs Price ranges from $70-225. Accomodations and meals sometimes included.
Accommodations Provides a list of area hotels or lodging options.
Additional Information Available via e-mail or mail inquiries.

CANADA

N ⚟ ◎ BLOODY WORDS MYSTERY CONFERENCE
12 Roundwood Court, Toronto ON M1W 1Z2 Canada. Phone/fax: (416)497-5293. E-mail: soles@sff.net. Website: www.bloodywords.com. **Contact:** Caro Soles, chair. Estab. 1999. Annual. Last conference held June 10-12, 2005. Average attendance: 300. Focus: Mystery/true crime/forensics, with Canadian slant. Purpose: To bring readers and writers of the mystery genre together in a Canadian setting. Site: Marriott Eaton Centre Hotel, Bay St., Toronto. Conference includes two workshops and two tracks of panels, one on factual information such as forensics, agents, scene of the crime procedures, etc. and one on fiction, such as "Death in a Cold Climate," "Murder on the Menu," "Elementary, My Dear Watson," and a First Novelists Panel. Guests of honor in 2005 were Maureen Jennings and Anne Perry.
Costs 2005 fee: $175 (included the banquet and all panels, readings, dealers' room and workshop).
Accommodations Offers hotel shuttle from the airport. Offers block of rooms in hotel; list of optional lodging available. Call Marriott Eaton Centre Hotel for special conference rates ($169).
Additional Information Sponsors short mystery story contest—4,000 word limit; judges are experienced editors of anthologies; fee is $5 (entrants must be registered). Conference information is available now. For brochure visit website. Accepts inquiries by e-mail and phone. Agents and editors participate in conference. "This is a

conference for both readers and writers of mysteries, the only one of its kind in Canada. We also run 'The Mystery Cafe,' a chance to get to know 15 authors, hear them read and ask questions (half hour each)."

◨ BOOMING GROUND

Buch E-462, 1866 Main Mall, Creative Writing Program, UBC, Vancouver BC V6T 121 Canada. (604)822-2469. Fax: (604)822-3616. E-mail: bg@arts.ubc.ca. Website: bg.arts.ubc.ca. **Contact:** Andrew Gray, director. Estab. 1998. Annual. Last conference held July 9-15, 2005. Average attendance: 70. Conference on "fiction, poetry, nonfiction, children's writing. We offer two sessions: online-only mentorships and summer workshops. Online mentorships offer 16 weeks of work with an instructor, allowing up to 120 pages of material to be created. Summer workshops have two class options: regular one-week workshops or regular one-week workshops followed by a 16-week online correspondence course." Site: "Green College, a residential college at the University of Columbia, overlooking the ocean." Past panels included "The Writing Life" and "Paths to Publication." **Costs** 2005 fees were $775 (Canadian) for online-only mentorship; $695 (Canadian) for one-week workshop; and $1,375 for one-week workshop plus correspondence course. Meals and accommodations separate. Some scholarships available.
Accommodations "Information on overnight accommodations is available and students are encouraged to stay onsite at Green College." On-site accommodations: inquire about cost.
Additional Information Workshops are based on works-in-progress. Writers must submit ms with application for jury selection. Conference information available February of each year. For brochures/guidelines send SASE, visit website, e-mail, fax or call. Accepts inquiries by SASE, phone, fax, e-mail. "Classes are offered for writers at all levels—from early career to mid-career. All student work is evaluated by a jury. New correspondence classes are ideal for novelists."

◨ ◨ HUMBER SCHOOL FOR WRITERS SUMMER WORKSHOP

Humber Institute of Technology and Advanced Learning, 3199 Lake Shore Blvd. West, Toronto ON M8V 1K8 Canada. (416)675-6622 ext. 3448. Fax: (416)251-7167. E-mail: antanas.sileika@humber.ca. Website: www.humber.ca/creativeandperformingarts. **Contact:** Antanas Sileika, director. Annual. Workshop held July. Conference duration: 1 week. Average attendance: 100. Focuses on fiction, poetry, creative nonfiction. Site: Humber College's north campus in Toronto. Panels cover success stories, small presses, large presses, agents. Faculty: Stevie Cameron, Wayson Choy, Bruce Jay Friedman, Isabel Huggan, John Metcalf, Kim Moritsugu, Tim O'Brien, Olive Senior.
Costs Workshop fee is $950 Canadian ($491 US).
Accommodations Provides lodging. Residence fee is $350 Canadian ($204 US).
Additional Information Participants "must submit sample writing no longer than 15 pages approximately 3 weeks before workshop begins." Brochures available mid-December for e-mail, phone, fax. Accepts inquiries by e-mail, phone, fax. Agents and editors participate in conference.

◨ MARITIME WRITERS' WORKSHOP

Extension & Summer Session, UNB Arts Centre, P.O. Box 4400, Fredericton NB E3B 5A3 Canada. Phone/fax: (506)474-1144. E-mail: k4jc@unb.ca. Website: www.unb.ca/extend/writers/. **Contact:** Rhona Sawlor, coordinator. Estab. 1976. Workshop held annually in July. Average attendance: 50. "We offer small groups of 10, practical manuscript focus. Novice writers welcome. Workshops in four areas: fiction, poetry, nonfiction, writing for children. The annual Maritimes Writers' Workshop is a practical, wide-ranging program designed to help writers develop and refine their creative writing skills. This weeklong program will involve you in small group workshops, lectures and discussions, public readings and special events, all in a supportive community of writers who share a commitment to excellence. Workshop groups consist of a maximum of 10 writers each. Instructors are established Canadian authors and experienced teachers with a genuine interest in facilitating the writing process of others. For over a quarter century, Maritmes Writers' Workshop has provided counsel, encouragement and direction for hundreds of developing writers." Site: University of New Brunswick, Fredericton campus.
Costs 2005: $395 tuition.
Accommodations On-campus accommodations and meals.
Additional Information "Participants must submit 10-20 manuscript pages which form a focus for workshop discussions." Brochures available after March. No SASE necessary. Accepts inquiries by e-mail and fax.

◨ SAGE HILL WRITING EXPERIENCE

Box 1731, Saskatoon SK S7K 3S1 Canada. Phone/fax: (306)652-7395. E-mail: sage.hill@sasktel.net. Website: www.sagehillwriting.ca. **Contact:** Steven Ross Smith. Annual. Workshops held in August and November. Conference duration: 10-14 days. Average attendance: Summer, 30-40; Fall, 6-8. "Sage Hill Writing Experience offers a special working and learning opportunity to writers at different stages of development. Top quality instruction, low instructor-student ratio and the beautiful Sage Hill setting offer conditions ideal for the pursuit of excellence in the arts of fiction, poetry and playwriting.'' Site: The Sage Hill location features ''individual accommodation, in-room writing area, lounges, meeting rooms, healthy meals, walking woods and vistas in several directions.'' Various classes are held: Introduction to Writing Fiction & Poetry; Fiction Workshop; Nonfiction Workshop; Writing Young Adult Fiction Workshop; Poetry Workshop; Poetry Colloquium; Novel Colloquium; Playwriting Lab.

Costs Summer program, $895 (Canadian) includes instruction, accommodation, meals, and all facilities. Fall Poetry Colloquium: $1,195 (Canadian).

Accommodations On-site individual accommodations for Summer and Fall programs located at Lumsden, 45 kilometers outside Regina.

Additional Information Application requirements for Introduction to Creative Writing: A 5-page sample of your writing or a statement of your interest in creative writing; list of courses taken required. For workshop and colloquium programs: A résumé of your writing career and a 12-page sample of your work-in-progress, plus 5 pages of published work required. Application deadline is April 25. Guidelines are available after January for SASE, e-mail, fax, phone or on website. Scholarships and bursaries are available.

⊠ THE VICTORIA SCHOOL OF WRITING

Suite 306-620 View St., Victoria BC V8W 1J6 Canada. (250)595-3000. E-mail: info@victoriaschoolofwriting.org. Website: www.victoriaschoolofwriting.org. **Contact:** Jill Margo, director. Conference held the third week in July annually. ''Five-day intensive workshop on beautiful Vancouver Island with outstanding author-instructors in fiction, poetry, nonfiction and other genres.''

Costs $585 (Canadian).

Accommodations On site .

Additional Information Workshop brochures available. Accepts inquiries by e-mail, phone or website.

Ⓝ ⊠ THE WRITERS RETREAT

15 Canusa St., Stanstead, QC J0B 3E5 Canada. (819) 876-2065. E-mail: info@writersretreat.com. Website: www.writersretreat.com. **Contact:** Anthony Lanza, program director, and Micheline Cote, executive director. Estab. 1998. Year-round. Conference duration: 2-5 days. Any length of stay for residency. The Writers Retreat workshops feature instruction in fiction writing, nonfiction writing and screenwriting. ''Our sole purpose is to provide an ambiance conducive to creativity for career and emerging writers. Residency includes a private studio and breakfast, a library with reference tools, Internet access, complimentary critique. The Writers Retreat is a full literary service retreat including residency, private mentoring, workshops, editing (exclusively for our writers [workshop participants and residents]) and submission to publishers.'' Site: Quebec headquarters are located on the Vermont/Quebec border with a satellite facility in Zihuatanejo, Mexico. Workshops include Self-Editing for Publication, Story Realization, Dynamics of Dramatic Structure, Screenwriting Dynamics and more.

Costs Most workshops are conducted at the retreat in Quebec and Mexico and in the USA. Residency starts at $525/week. Private mentoring starts at $1495. Workshop tuition varies from $150-$1120, depending on the format.

Additional Information Accepts inquiries by SASE, e-mail and phone.

INTERNATIONAL

ANNUAL WRITERS' CONFERENCE

University College Winchester, Chinook, Southdown Road, Winchester, Hampshire, England. 44 (0) 1962 712307. E-mail: writerconf@aol.com. Website: writers-conference.com. **Contact:** Mrs. Barbara Large, conference director. Last conference: June 24-26, 2005, followed by weeklong workshops June 27-July 1. Conference duration: 8 days. Average attendance: 500. This conference offers all writers the opportunity to harness their creative ideas and to develop their technical and marketing skills under the guidance of 62 published authors and poets, playwrights and producers, literary agents and publishers, during 15 mini-courses, 20 workshops, 6 seminars, 60 lectures and 300 one-on-one appointments. Benefit too from the weeklong workshops, an opportunity to work in small groups to structure your fiction, nonfiction, children's stories and film scripts. Site: The conference is held at University College Winchester easily reached within an hour by train or flight from London. Delegates stay in college accommodations. Themes will include writing effectively for children, developing characters in your novels, turning ideas into plausible plots and more. Past speakers included Dame Beryl Bainbridge (Honorary Patron), Margaret Graham, Hugh Graham, Judy Waite, Helene Wiggins, Fay Weldon, Simon Brett, Andrew Taylor, Ursula Fanthorpe and more.

Costs £225 to include accommodations and all meals.

Accommodations Offers overnight accommodations at the college and provides list of area hotels and lodging options.

Additional Information Also features 15 writing competitions that are adjudicated and 63 prizes and trophies awarded during the conference. Brochures available in March for SASE and on website. Accepts inquiries by SASE, e-mail, phone. Editors and agents attend the conference.

ART WORKSHOPS IN GUATEMALA

4758 Lyndale Ave. S, Minneapolis MN 55419-5304. (612)825-0747. Fax: (612)825-6637. E-mail: info@artguat.org. Website: www.artguat.org. **Contact:** Liza Fourre, director. Estab. 1995. Annual. Workshops held year-round. Maximim class size: 10 students per class. Workshop titles include: Fiction Writing: Shaping and Structuring Your Story with Gladys Swan; New Directions in Travel Writing with Richard Harris; Poetry: Snapshots in Words with Rosanne Lloyd; and Creative Writing: Journey of the Soul with Sharon Doubiago.

Costs $1,945 (includes tuition, air fare to Guatemala from USA, lodging and ground transportation).

Accommodations All transportation and accommodations included in price of conference.

Additional Information Conference information available now. For brochure/guidelines visit website, e-mail, fax or call. Accepts inquiries by e-mail, phone, fax.

DINGLE WRITING COURSES

Ballintlea, Ventry, Co Kerry, Ireland. 353 66 9159815. Fax: 00 353 66 9154992. E-mail: info@dinglewritingcourses.ie. Website: www.dinglewritingcourses.ie. **Contact:** Abigail Joffe and Nicholas McLachlan. Estab. 1996. Annual. Conference held 3 or 4 weekends per year. Average attendance: 14. Creative writing weekends for fiction, poetry, memoir, novel, etc. Site: "Residential centre at Inch on the Dingle Peninsula." 2004 faculty included Clare Boylan, Brian Leydan, Eva Salzman and Andrew O'Hagan.

Costs $340 for a weekend (Friday evening to Sunday evening) includes all meals, accommodation, tuition.

Accommodations "We arrange taxis on request; cost not included in fee." Provides overnight accommodations. "Large communal eating facility and workroom; snug; all rooms with individual tables and lamps." Also provides list of area lodging.

Additional Information Some workshops require material submitted in advance. Brochures available in May by e-mail, phone, fax or on website. Accepts inquiries by e-mail, phone, fax.

N INTERNATIONAL READERS THEATRE WORKSHOPS

P.O. Box 17193, San Diego CA 92177. (619)276-1948. Fax: (858)581-3289. E-mail: wadams1@san.rr.com. Website: www.readerstheatreinstitute.com. **Contact:** Bill Adams, director. Estab. 1974. Last workshop held July 10-23, 2005. Average attendance: 50-70. Workshop on "all aspects of Readers Theatre with emphasis on scriptmaking." Site: Workshop held at Britannia Hotel in London.

Costs "$1,795 includes housing for two weeks (twin accommodations), continental breakfast, complimentary mid-morning coffee break on class days, textbook (a $45 value) and all Institute fees."

Additional Information "One-on-one critiques available between writer and faculty (if members)." Conference information available December. For brochures/guidelines visit website, e-mail, fax, call, send SASE. Conference offers "up to 12 credits in theatre, theatre (speech) and/or education (6 credits) from the University of Southern Maine at $154/unit (subject to legislative change for 2006)."

N KILLALOE HEDGE-SCHOOL OF WRITING

4 Riverview, Killaloe Co. Clare, Ireland. (+353)61 375 217. Fax: (+353)61 375 487. E-mail: khs@killaloe.ie. Website: www.killaloe.ie/khs. **Contact:** K. Thorne, secretary. Estab. 1999. Held every second weekend between October and April. Conference duration: 10 a.m. Saturday till 4 p.m. Sunday. Average attendance: 15-20. Holds workshops on 6 different topics: Get Started Writing; Start Your Novel; Writing a Nonfiction Book; Write for Magazines and Papers; Write Your Memoirs; Get Started Writing-Level Two. Speakers include David Rice, Catherine Thorne and others yet to be invited.

Costs 185 EURO per workshop. Includes midday meal each day. Does not include lodging.

Accommodations Runs a shuttle from Shannon Airport.

Additional Information "Please check out our website."

N PARIS WRITERS WORKSHOP/WICE

20, Bd. du Montparnasse, Paris 75015, France. (331)45.66.75.50. Fax: (331)40.65.96.53. E-mail: pww@wice-paris.org. Website: www.wice-paris.org. **Contact:** Rose Burke and Marcia Lebre, directors. Estab. 1987. Annual. Conference held June-July. Average attendance: 40-50. "Conference concentrates on fiction, nonfiction and poetry. Visiting lecturers speak on a variety of issues important to beginning and advanced writers. 2005 writers in residence are Elizabeth Cox (novel), C. Michael Curtis (short fiction), Honor Moore (poetry), Floyd Skloot (creative nonfiction), Katharine Weber (writing intensive tutorial). Located in the heart of Paris on the Bd. du

Montparnasse, the stomping grounds of such famous American writers as Ernest Hemingway, Henry Miller and F. Scott Fitzgerald. The site consists of four classrooms, a resource center/library and private terrace.'' **Costs** 380 Euros—tuition only.
Additional Information ''Students submit 1 copy of complete manuscript or work-in-progress which is sent in advance to writer-in-residence. Each student has a one-on-one consultation with writer-in-residence.'' Conference information available late Fall. For brochures/guidelines visit website, e-mail, call or fax. Accepts inquiries by SASE, phone, e-mail, fax. ''Workshop attracts many expatriate Americans and other English-language writers from all over Europe and North America. We are an intimate workshop with an exciting mix of more experienced, published writers and enthusiastic beginners.''

TY NEWYDD WRITERS' CENTRE

Llanystumdwy, Cricieth Gwynedd LL52 0LW, United Kingdom. Phone: 01766-522811. Fax: 01766 523095. E-mail: post@tynewydd.org. Website: www.tynewydd.org. **Contact:** Sally Baker, director. Estab. 1990. Year-round. Regular courses held throughout the year. Every course held Monday-Saturday. Average attendance: 14. ''To give people the opportunity to work side-by-side with professional writers, in an informal atmosphere.'' Site: Ty Newydd, large manor house, last home of the prime minister, David Lloyd George. Situated in North Wales, Great Britain—between mountains and sea. Past featured tutors include novelists Beryl Bainbridge and Bernice Rubens.
Costs Single room, £360, shared room, £335 for Monday-Saturday (includes full board, tuition).
Accommodations Transportation from railway stations arranged. Accommodation in Ty Newydd (onsite).
Additional Information Conference information available by mail, phone, e-mail, fax or visit website. Accepts inquiries by SASE, e-mail, fax, phone. ''More and more people come to us from the U.S. often combining a writing course with a tour of Wales.''

ZOETROPE: ALL-STORY SHORT STORY WRITERS' WORKSHOP

916 Kearny St., San Francisco CA 94133. (415)788-7500. E-mail: info@all-story.com. Website: www.all-story.com. **Contact:** Michael Ray, senior editor. Estab. 1997. Annual. Last workshop was September 16-23, 2005. Conference duration: 1 week. Average attendance: 20. Workshop focuses on fiction, specifically short stories. Site: Francis Ford Coppola's gorgeous Blancaneaux Lodge in Belize, on the banks of the Privassion River. Guests stay in luxurious private cabanas and villas, all with spa baths and decks with hammocks and river views. Past instructors include New Yorker staff writer Philip Gourevitch, National Book Award finalist Susan Straight, and Terry McMillan.
Costs range from $2,500 to $3,550, depending on accommodations. That fee is all-inclusive, including accommodations, food, workshop, day excursions, all transfers to and from Belize city, and a camp T-shirt.
Additional Information Please submit a completed application and an original work of short fiction less than 5,000 words by August 15. Application forms are available on the website. Brochures available now for SASE, by fax, phone, e-mail, and on website. Accepts inquiries by phone, fax, e-mail and for SASE. Editors attend the conference.

Publishers and Their Imprints

The publishing world is constantly changing and evolving. With all of the buying, selling, reorganizing, consolidating and dissolving, it's hard to keep publishers and their imprints straight. To help you make sense of these changes, we offer this breakdown of major publishers (and their divisions)—who owns whom and which imprints are under each company umbrella. Keep in mind that this information is constantly changing. We have provided the websites of each of the publishers so you can continue to keep an eye on this ever-evolving business.

HARPERCOLLINS

www.harpercollins.com

HarperCollins Australia/New Zealand
Angus & Robertson
Flamingo
Fourth Estate
HarperBusiness
HarperCollins
HarperPerennial
HarperReligious
HarperSports
Voyager

HarperCollins Canada
HarperFlamingoCanada
PerennialCanada

HarperCollins Children's Books Group
Amistad
Julie Andrews Collection
Avon
Joanna Cotler books
Eos
Laura Geringer Books
Greenwillow Books

HarperCollins Children's Books
HarperFestival
HarperKidsEntertainment
HarperTempest
HarperTrophy
Rayo
Katherine Tegen Books

HarperCollins General Books Group
Access
Amistad
Avon
Caedmon
Dark Alley
Ecco
Eos
Fourth Estate
Harper Design
HarperAudio
HarperBusiness
HarperCollins
HarperEntertainment
HarperLargePrint

Resources

HarperResource
HarperSanFrancisco
HarperTorch
Perennial
Perennial Currents
PerfectBound
Rayo
ReganBooks
William Morrow

HarperCollins UK
Collins
Collins Crime & Thrillers

HarperCollins Children's Books
HarperCollins Freedom to Teach
Thorsons/Element
Voyager Books

Zondervan
Inspirio
Vida
Zonderkidz
Zondervan

HOLTZBRINCK PUBLISHERS

www.holtzbrinck.com

Farrar, Straus & Giroux
Books for Young Readers
Faber & Faber
Hill & Wang (division)
North Point Press

Henry Holt and Co. LLC
Books for Young Readers
Metropolitan Books
Owl Books
Times Books

The MacMillan Group
MacMillan Education
Nature Publishing Group
Palgrave MacMillan
Pan MacMillan
  Boxtree
  Campbell Books
  MacMillan
  MacMillan Childrens
  Pan
  Picador
  Sidgwick & Jackson
  Young Picador

PENGUIN GROUP (USA), INC.

www.penguingroup.com

Penguin Adult Division
Ace Books
Alpha Books
Avery
Berkley Books
Chamberlain Bros.
Dutton
Gotham Books
HPBooks
Hudson Street Press
Jove
New American Library
Penguin
Perigree
Plume

Portfolio
G.P. Putnam's Sons
Riverhead Books
Sentinel
Jeremy P. Tarcher
Viking
Fredrick Warne

Penguin Children's Division
Dial Books for Young Readers
Dutton Children's Books
Firebird
Grosset & Dunlap
Philomel

Price Stern Sloan
Puffin Books
G.P. Putnam's Sons
Speak

Viking Children's Books
Frederick Warne

RANDOM HOUSE, INC.
www.randomhouse.com

Ballantine Publishing Group
Ballantine Books
Ballantine Reader's Circle
Del Rey
Del Rey/Lucas Books
Fawcett
Ivy
One World
Wellspring

Bantam Dell Publishing Group
Bantam Hardcover
Bantam Mass Market
Bantam Trade Paperback
Crimeline
Delacorte Press
Dell
Delta
The Dial Press
Domain
DTP
Fanfare
Island
Spectra

Crown Publishing Group
Shaye Arehart Books
Bell Tower
Clarkson Potter
Crown Business
Crown Forum
Crown Publishers, Inc.
Harmony Books
Three Rivers Press

Doubleday Broadway Publishing Group
Broadway Books
Currency
Doubleday
Doubleday Image

Doubleday Religious Publishing
Main Street Books
Nan A. Talese

Knopf Publishing Group
Anchor Books
Alfred A. Knopf
Everyman's Library
Pantheon Books
Schocken Books
Vintage Books

Random House Audio Publishing Group
Listening Library
Random House Audible
Random House Audio
Random House Audio Assets
Random House Audio Dimensions
Random House Audio Roads
Random House Audio Voices
Random House Price-less

Random House Children's Books
BooksReportsNow.com
GoldenBooks.com
Junie B. Jones
Kids@Random

Knopf/Delacorte/Dell Young Readers Group
Alfred A. Knopf
Bantam
Crown
David Fickling Books
Delacorte Press
Dell Dragonfly
Dell Laurel-Leaf
Dell Yearling Books
Doubleday
Wendy Lamb Books

Resources

Random House Young Readers Group

Akiko
Arthur
Barbie
Beginner Books
The Berenstain Bears
Bob the Builder
Disney
Dragon Tales
First Time Books
Golden Books
Landmark Books
Little Golden Books
Lucas Books
Mercer Mayer
Nickelodeon
Nick, Jr.
pat the bunny
Picturebacks
Precious Moments
Richard Scarry
Sesame Street Books
Step Into Reading
Stepping Stones
Star Wars
Thomas the Tank Engine and Friends

Seussville
Teachers@Random
Teens@Random

Random House Information Group

Fodor's Travel Publications
Living Language
Prima Games
The Princeton Review
Random House Español
Random House Puzzles & Games
Random House Reference Publishing

Random House International

Arete
McClelland & Stewart Ltd.
Plaza & Janes
Random House Australia
Random House of Canada Ltd.
Random House of Mondadori
Random House South Africa
Random House South America
Random House United Kingdom
Transworld UK
Verlagsgruppe Random House

Random House Value Publishing

Children's Classics
Crescent
Derrydale
Gramercy
Testament
Wings

Waterbrook Press

Fisherman Bible Study Guides
Shaw Books
Waterbrook Press

SIMON & SCHUSTER

www.simonsays.com

Simon & Schuster Adult Publishing

Atria Books
Washington Square Press

The Free Press
Simon & Schuster Source
Wall Street Journal Books

Kaplan

Pocket Books
Downtown Press
MTV Books
Paraview Pocket

Pocket Star
Star Trek
VH-1 Books
World Wrestling Entertainment

Scribner
Lisa Drew Books
Scribner Classics
Scribner Paperback Fiction

Simon & Schuster
Simon & Schuster Classic Editions

The Touchstone & Fireside Group

Simon & Schuster Audio
Pimsleur
Simon & Schuster Audioworks
Simon & Schuster Sound Ideas

Simon & Schuster Children's Publishing
Aladdin Paperbacks

> **Atheneum Books for Young Readers**
> Richard Jackson Books
> Anne Schwartz Books

Little Simon
Margaret K. McElderry Books

> **Simon & Schuster Books for Young Readers**
> Paula Wiseman Books

Simon Pulse
Simon Spotlight

Simon & Schuster International
Simon & Schuster Australia
Simon & Schuster Canada
Simon & Schuster UK

TIME WARNER BOOK GROUP

www.twbookmark.com

Warner Books
Aspect
Bulfinch Press

> **Little, Brown, and Co.**
> **Adult Trade Division**
> Back Bay Books

Little, Brown, and Co. Books for Young
 Readers
Mysterious Press
Time Warner Audio Books
Warner Business Books
Warner Faith
Warner Forever
Warner Vision

Canadian Writers Take Note

While much of the information contained in this section applies to all writers, here are some specifics of interest to Canadian writers:

Postage: When sending an SASE from Canada, you will need an International Reply Coupon. Also be aware, a GST tax is required on postage in Canada and for mail with postage under $5 going to destinations outside the country. Since Canadian postage rates are voted on in January of each year (after we go to press), contact a Canada Post Corporation Customer Service Division (located in most cities in Canada) or visit www.canadapost.ca for the most current rates.

Copyright: For information on copyrighting your work and to obtain forms, write Canadian Intellectual Property Office, Industry Canada, Place du Portage I, 50 Victoria St., 2nd Floor, Gatineau, Quebec K1A 0C9 or call (819)997-1936. Website: www.cipo.gc.ca.

The public lending right: The Public Lending Right Commission has established that eligible Canadian authors are entitled to payments when a book is available through a library. Payments are determined by a sampling of the holdings of a representative number of libraries. To find out more about the program and to learn if you are eligible, write to the Public Lending Right Commission at 350 Albert St., P.O. Box 1047, Ottawa, Ontario K1P 5V8 or call (613)566-4378 or (800)521-5721 for information. Website: www.plr-dpp.ca/. The Commission, which is part of The Canada Council, produces a helpful pamphlet, *How the PLR System Works,* on the program.

Grants available to Canadian writers: Most province art councils or departments of culture provide grants to resident writers. Some of these, as well as contests for Canadian writers, are listed in our Contests and Awards section. For national programs, contact The Canada Council, Writing and Publishing Section, 350 Alberta St., P.O. Box 1047, Ottawa, Ontario K1P 5V8 or call (613)566-4414 or (800)263-5588 for information. Fax: (613)566-4410. Website: www.canadacouncil.ca.

For more information: See the Resources section of *Novel & Short Story Writer's Market* for listings of writers' organizations in Canada. Also contact The Writer's Union of Canada, 90 Richmond St. E, Suite 200, Toronto, Ontario M5C 1P1; call them at (416)703-8982 or fax them at (416)504-9090. E-mail: info@writersunion.ca. Website: www.writersunion.ca. This organization provides a wealth of information (as well as strong support) for Canadian writers, including specialized publications on publishing contracts; contract negotiations; the author/editor relationship; author awards, competitions and grants; agents; taxes for writers, libel issues and access to archives in Canada.

Printing & Production

Terms Defined

I n most of the magazine listings in this book, you will find a brief physical description of each publication. This material usually includes the number of pages, type of paper, type of binding and whether or not the magazine uses photographs and/or illustrations.

Although it is important to look at a copy of the magazine to which you are submitting, these descriptions can give you a general idea of what the publication looks like. This material can provide you with a feel for the magazine's financial resources and prestige. Do not, however, rule out small, simply produced publications, as these may be the most receptive to new writers. Watch for publications that have increased their page count or improved their production from year to year. This is a sign the publication is doing well and may be accepting more fiction.

You will notice a wide variety of printing terms used within these descriptions. We explain here some of the more common terms used in our listing descriptions. We do not include explanations of terms such as Mohawk and Karma which are brand names and refer to the paper manufacturer.

PAPER

acid-free: Paper that has low or no acid content. This type of paper resists deterioration from exposure to the elements. More expensive than many other types of paper, publications done on acid-free paper can last a long time.

bond: Bond paper is often used for stationery and is more transparent than text paper. It can be made of either sulphite (wood) or cotton fiber. Some bonds have a mixture of both wood and cotton (such as "25 percent cotton" paper). This is the type of paper most often used in photocopying or as standard typing paper.

coated/uncoated stock: Coated and uncoated are terms usually used when referring to book or text paper. More opaque than bond, it is the paper most used for offset printing. As the name implies, uncoated paper has no coating. Coated paper is coated with a layer of clay, varnish or other chemicals. It comes in various sheens and surfaces depending on the type of coating, but the most common are dull, matte and gloss.

cover stock: Cover stock is heavier book or text paper used to cover a publication. It comes in a variety of colors and textures and can be coated on one or both sides.

CS1/CS2: Most often used when referring to cover stock, CS1 means paper that is coated only on one side; CS2 is paper coated on both sides.

newsprint: Inexpensive absorbent pulp wood paper often used in newspapers and tabloids.

text: Text paper is similar to book paper (a smooth paper used in offset printing), but it has been given some texture by using rollers or other methods to apply a pattern to the paper.

vellum: Vellum is a text paper that is fairly porous and soft.

Some notes about paper weight and thickness: Often you will see paper thickness described in terms of pounds such as 80 lb. or 60 lb. paper. The weight is determined by figuring how many pounds in a ream of a particular paper (a ream is 500 sheets). This can be confusing, however, because this figure is based on a standard sheet size and standard sheet sizes vary depending on the type of paper used. This information is most helpful when comparing papers of the same type. For example, 80 lb. book paper versus 60 lb. book paper. Since the size of the paper is the same it would follow that 80 lb. paper is the thicker, heavier paper.

Some paper, especially cover stock, is described by the actual thickness of the paper. This is expressed in a system of points. Typical paper thicknesses range from 8 points to 14 points thick.

PRINTING

letterpress: Letterpress printing is printing that uses a raised surface such as type. The type is inked and then pressed against the paper. Unlike offset printing, only a limited number of impressions can be made, as the surface of the type can wear down.

offset: Offset is a printing method in which ink is transferred from an image-bearing plate to a "blanket" and from the blanket to the paper.

sheet-fed offset: Offset printing in which the paper is fed one piece at a time.

web offset: Offset printing in which a roll of paper is printed and then cut apart to make individual sheets.

There are many other printing methods but these are the ones most commonly referred to in our listings.

BINDING

case binding: In case binding, signatures (groups of pages) are stitched together with thread rather than glued together. The stitched pages are then trimmed on three sides and glued into a hardcover or board "case" or cover. Most hardcover books and thicker magazines are done this way.

comb binding: A comb is a plastic spine used to hold pages together with bent tabs that are fed through punched holes in the edge of the paper.

perfect binding: Used for paperback books and heavier magazines, perfect binding involves gathering signatures (groups of pages) into a stack, trimming off the folds so the edge is flat and gluing a cover to that edge.

saddle stitched: Publications in which the pages are stitched together using metal staples. This fairly inexpensive type of binding is usually used with books or magazines that are under 80 pages.

Smythe-sewn: Binding in which the pages are sewn together with thread. Smythe is the name of the most common machine used for this purpose.

spiral binding: A wire spiral that is wound through holes punched in pages is a spiral bind. This is the binding used in spiral notebooks.

Glossary

Advance. Payment by a publisher to an author prior to the publication of a book, to be deducted from the author's future royalties.

All rights. The rights contracted to a publisher permitting a manuscript's use anywhere and in any form, including movie and book club sales, without additional payment to the writer.

Amateur sleuth. The character in a mystery, usually the protagonist, who does the detection but is not a professional private investigator or police detective.

Anthology. A collection of selected writings by various authors.

Association of Authors' Representatives (AAR). An organization for literary agents committed to maintaining excellence in literary representation.

Auction. Publishers sometimes bid against each other for the acquisition of a manuscript that has excellent sales prospects.

Backlist. A publisher's books not published during the current season but still in print.

Book producer/packager. An organization that may develop a book for a publisher based upon the publisher's idea or may plan all elements of a book, from its initial concept to writing and marketing strategies, and then sell the package to a book publisher and/or movie producer.

Cliffhanger. Fictional event in which the reader is left in suspense at the end of a chapter or episode, so that interest in the story's outcome will be sustained.

Clip. Sample, usually from a newspaper or magazine, of a writer's published work.

Cloak-and-dagger. A melodramatic, romantic type of fiction dealing with espionage and intrigue.

Commercial. Publishers whose concern is salability, profit and success with a large readership.

Contemporary. Material dealing with popular current trends, themes or topics.

Contributor's copy. Copy of an issue of a magazine or published book sent to an author whose work is included.

Copublishing. An arrangement in which the author and publisher share costs and profits.

Copyediting. Editing a manuscript for writing style, grammar, punctuation and factual accuracy.

Copyright. The legal right to exclusive publication, sale or distribution of a literary work.

Cover letter. A brief letter sent with a complete manuscript submitted to an editor.

"Cozy" (or "teacup") mystery. Mystery usually set in a small British town, in a bygone era, featuring a somewhat genteel, intellectual protagonist.

Resources

Cyberpunk. Type of science fiction, usually concerned with computer networks and human-computer combinations, involving young, sophisticated protagonists.

Electronic rights. The right to publish material electronically, either in book or short story form.

E-zine. A magazine that is published electronically.

Electronic submission. A submission of material by e-mail or on computer disk.

Experimental fiction. Fiction that is innovative in subject matter and style; avant-garde, non-formulaic, usually literary material.

Exposition. The portion of the storyline, usually the beginning, where background information about character and setting is related.

Fair use. A provision in the copyright law that says short passages from copyrighted material may be used without infringing on the owner's rights.

Fanzine. A noncommercial, small-circulation magazine usually dealing with fantasy, horror or science-fiction literature and art.

First North American serial rights. The right to publish material in a periodical before it appears in book form, for the first time, in the United States or Canada.

Flash fiction. See short short stories.

Galleys. The first typeset version of a manuscript that has not yet been divided into pages.

Genre. A formulaic type of fiction such as romance, western or horror.

Gothic. A genre in which the central character is usually a beautiful young woman and the setting an old mansion or castle, involving a handsome hero and real danger, either natural or supernatural.

Graphic novel. A book (original or adapted) that takes the form of a long comic strip or heavily illustrated story of 40 pages or more, produced in paperback. Though called a novel, these can also be works of nonfiction.

Hard science fiction. Science fiction with an emphasis on science and technology.

Hard-boiled detective novel. Mystery novel featuring a private eye or police detective as the protagonist; usually involves a murder. The emphasis is on the details of the crime.

High fantasy. Fantasy with a medieval setting and a heavy emphasis on chivalry and the quest.

Horror. A genre stressing fear, death and other aspects of the macabre.

Hypertext fiction. A fictional form, read electronically, which incorporates traditional elements of storytelling with a nonlinear plot line, in which the reader determines the direction of the story by opting for one of many author-supplied links.

Imprint. Name applied to a publisher's specific line (e.g. Owl, an imprint of Henry Holt).

Interactive fiction. Fiction in book or computer-software format where the reader determines the path the story will take by choosing from several alternatives at the end of each chapter or episode.

International Reply Coupon (IRC). A form purchased at a post office and enclosed with a letter or manuscript to a international publisher, to cover return postage costs.

Juvenile. Fiction intended for children 2-12.

Libel. Written or printed words that defame, malign or damagingly misrepresent a living person.

Literary fiction. The general category of fiction which employs more sophisticated technique, driven as much or more by character evolution than action in the plot.

Literary agent. A person who acts for an author in finding a publisher or arranging contract terms on a literary project.

Mainstream fiction. Fiction which appeals to a more general reading audience, versus literary or genre fiction. Mainstream is more plot-driven than literary fiction and less formulaic than genre fiction.

Malice domestic novel. A mystery featuring a murder among family members, such as the murder of a spouse or a parent.

Manuscript. The author's unpublished copy of a work, usually typewritten, used as the basis for typesetting.

Mass market paperback. Softcover book on a popular subject, usually around 4×7, directed to a general audience and sold in drugstores and groceries as well as in bookstores.

Middle reader. Juvenile fiction for readers aged 8-13, featuring heavier text than picture books and some light illustration.

Ms(s). Abbreviation for manuscript(s).

Multiple submission. Submission of more than one short story at a time to the same editor. Do not make a multiple submission unless requested.

Narration. The account of events in a story's plot as related by the speaker or the voice of the author.

Narrator. The person who tells the story, either someone involved in the action or the voice of an observer.

New Age. A term including categories such as astrology, psychic phenomena, spiritual healing, UFOs, mysticism and other aspects of the occult.

Noir. A style of mystery involving hard-boiled detectives and bleak settings.

Nom de plume. French for "pen name"; a pseudonym.

Novella (also novelette). A short novel or long story, approximately 7,000-15,000 words.

#10 envelope. 4×9½ envelope, used for queries and other business letters.

Offprint. Copy of a story taken from a magazine before it is bound.

One-time rights. Permission to publish a story in periodical or book form one time only.

Outline. A summary of a book's contents, often in the form of chapter headings with a few sentences outlining the action of the story under each one; sometimes part of a book proposal.

Over the transom. A phrase referring to unsolicited manuscripts, or those that come in "over the transom."

Payment on acceptance. Payment from the magazine or publishing house as soon as the decision to print a manuscript is made.

Payment on publication. Payment from the publisher after a manuscript is printed.

Pen name. A pseudonym used to conceal a writer's real name.

Periodical. A magazine or journal published at regular intervals.

Plot. The carefully devised series of events through which the characters progress in a work of fiction.

Police procedural. A mystery featuring a police detective or officer who uses standard professional police practices to solve a crime.

Print on demand (POD). Novels produced digitally one at a time, as ordered. Self-publishing through print on demand technology typically involves some fees for the author. Some authors use POD to create a manuscript in book form to send to prospective traditional publishers.

Proofreading. Close reading and correction of a manuscript's typographical errors.

Proofs. A typeset version of a manuscript used for correcting errors and making changes, often a photocopy of the galleys.

Proposal. An offer to write a specific work, usually consisting of an outline of the work and one or two completed chapters.

Protagonist. The principal or leading character in a literary work.

Public domain. Material that either was never copyrighted or whose copyright term has expired.

Pulp magazine. A periodical printed on inexpensive paper, usually containing lurid, sensational stories or articles.

Query. A letter written to an editor to elicit interest in a story the writer wants to submit.

Reader. A person hired by a publisher to read unsolicited manuscripts.

Reading fee. An arbitrary amount of money charged by some agents and publishers to read a submitted manuscript.

Regency romance. A subgenre of romance, usually set in England between 1811-1820.

Remainders. Leftover copies of an out-of-print book, sold by the publisher at a reduced price.

Reporting time. The number of weeks or months it takes an editor to report back on an author's query or manuscript.

Reprint rights. Permission to print an already published work whose rights have been sold to another magazine or book publisher.

Roman à clef. French "novel with a key." A novel that represents actual living or historical characters and events in fictionalized form.

Romance. The genre relating accounts of passionate love and fictional heroic achievements.

Royalties. A percentage of the retail price paid to an author for each copy of the book that is sold.

SAE. Self-addressed envelope.

SASE. Self-addressed stamped envelope.

Science fiction. Genre in which scientific facts and hypotheses form the basis of actions and events.

Second serial (reprint) rights. Permission for the reprinting of a work in another periodical after its first publication in book or magazine form.

Self-publishing. In this arrangement, the author keeps all income derived from the book, but he pays for its manufacturing, production and marketing.

Sequel. A literary work that continues the narrative of a previous, related story or novel.

Serial rights. The rights given by an author to a publisher to print a piece in one or more periodicals.

Serialized novel. A book-length work of fiction published in sequential issues of a periodical.

Setting. The environment and time period during which the action of a story takes place.

Short short story. A condensed piece of fiction, usually under 700 words.

Simultaneous submission. The practice of sending copies of the same manuscript to several editors or publishers at the same time. Some editors refuse to consider such submissions.

Slant. A story's particular approach or style, designed to appeal to the readers of a specific magazine.

Slice of life. A presentation of characters in a seemingly mundane situation which offers the reader a flash of illumination about the characters or their situation.

Slush pile. A stack of unsolicited manuscripts in the editorial offices of a publisher.

Social fiction. Fiction written with the purpose of bringing about positive changes in society.

Soft/sociological science fiction. Science fiction with an emphasis on society and culture versus scientific accuracy.

Space opera. Epic science fiction with an emphasis on good guys versus bad guys.

Speculation (or Spec). An editor's agreement to look at an author's manuscript with no promise to purchase.

Speculative fiction (SpecFic). The all-inclusive term for science fiction, fantasy and horror.

Splatterpunk. Type of horror fiction known for its very violent and graphic content.

Subsidiary. An incorporated branch of a company or conglomerate (e.g. Alfred Knopf, Inc., a subsidiary of Random House, Inc.).

Subsidiary rights. All rights other than book publishing rights included in a book contract, such as paperback, book club and movie rights.

Subsidy publisher. A book publisher who charges the author for the cost of typesetting, printing and promoting a book. Also called a vanity publisher.

Subterficial fiction. Innovative, challenging, nonconventional fiction in which what seems to be happening is the result of things not so easily perceived.

Suspense. A genre of fiction where the plot's primary function is to build a feeling of anticipation and fear in the reader over its possible outcome.

Synopsis. A brief summary of a story, novel or play. As part of a book proposal, it is a comprehensive summary condensed in a page or page and a half.

Tabloid. Publication printed on paper about half the size of a regular newspaper page (e.g. *The National Enquirer*).

Tearsheet. Page from a magazine containing a published story.

Theme. The dominant or central idea in a literary work; its message, moral or main thread.

Trade paperback. A softbound volume, usually around 5×8, published and designed for the general public, available mainly in bookstores.

Traditional fantasy. Fantasy with an emphasis on magic, using characters with the ability to practice magic, such as wizards, witches, dragons, elves and unicorns.

Unsolicited manuscript. A story or novel manuscript that an editor did not specifically ask to see.

Urban fantasy. Fantasy that takes magical characters such as elves, fairies, vampires or wizards and places them in modern-day settings, often in the inner city.

Vanity publisher. See Subsidy publisher.

Viewpoint. The position or attitude of the first- or third-person narrator or multiple narrators, which determines how a story's action is seen and evaluated.

Western. Genre with a setting in the West, usually between 1860-1890, with a formula plot about cowboys or other aspects of frontier life.

Whodunit. Genre dealing with murder, suspense and the detection of criminals.

Work-for-hire. Work that another party commissions you to do, generally for a flat fee. The creator does not own the copyright and therefore cannot sell any rights.

Young adult. The general classification of books written for readers 12-18.

Zine. Often one- or two-person operations run from the home of the publisher/editor. Themes tend to be specialized, personal, experimental and often controversial.

Literary Agents
Category Index

Agents listed in this edition of *Novel & Short Story Writer's Market* are indexed below according to the categories of fiction they represent. Use this index to find agents who handle the specific kind of fiction you write. Then turn to those listings in the alphabetical Literary Agents section for complete contact and submission information.

Action/Adventure

Detective/Police/Crime

Literary

Mainstream/Contemporary

Agents Category Index

Russell and Volkening 161
Schiavone Literary Agency, Inc. 162
Schulman, A Literary Agency, Susan 163
Scribe Agency, LLC 164
Sedgeband Literary Associates, Inc. 165
Seligman, Literary Agent, Lynn 165
Simmons Literary Agency, Jeffrey 167
Spectrum Literary Agency 168
Spencerhill Associates 168
Steele-Perkins Literary Agency 169
Teal Literary Agency, Patricia 170
Van Der Leun & Associates 170
Vines Agency, Inc., The 171
Wald Associates, Inc., Mary Jack 171
Weiner Literary Agency, Cherry 173
Weingel-Fidel Agency, The 173
Wieser & Elwell, Inc. 174
Writers House 174
Zachary Shuster Harmsworth 176
Zeckendorf Assoc., Inc., Susan 176

Military/War
Brown, Ltd., Curtis 112
Goodman Associates 131
Hamilburg Agency, The Mitchell J. 134
Hawkins & Associates, Inc., John 135
Lazear Agency, Inc. 142
Writers House 174

Multimedia
Brown, Ltd., Curtis 112
Goodman Associates 131
Harris Literary Agency, Inc., The Joy 134
Hawkins & Associates, Inc., John 135
Lazear Agency, Inc. 142
Van Der Leun & Associates 170

Mystery/Suspense
Acacia House Publishing Services, Ltd. 103
Ahearn Agency, Inc., The 103
Alive Communications, Inc. 104
Amster Literary Enterprises, Betsy 105
Amsterdam Agency, Marcia 105
Appleseeds Management 106

Authentic Creations Literary Agency 106
Axelrod Agency, The 106
Barrett Books, Inc., Loretta 107
Bernstein Literary Agency, Meredith 107
Bleecker Street Associates, Inc. 108
Blumer Literary Agency, Inc., The 109
BookEnds, LLC 110
Bova Literary Agency, The Barbara 111
Brandt & Hochman Literary Agents, Inc. 111
Broadhead & Associates Literary Agency, Rick 111
Brown, Ltd., Curtis 112
Browne & Miller Literary Associates 113
Browne, Ltd., Pema 113
Bykofsky Associates, Inc., Sheree 114
Carvainis Agency, Inc., Maria 114
Castiglia Literary Agency 115
Congdon Associates Inc., Don 116
Cornerstone Literary, Inc. 118
Crawford Literary Agency 118
Creative Media Agency, Inc. 118
Dawson Associates, Liza 120
DeFiore & Co. 120
DHS Literary, Inc. 120
Dijkstra Literary Agency, Sandra 121
Donovan Literary, Jim 124
Dupree/Miller and Associates Inc. Literary 125
Dystel & Goderich Literary Management 125
English, Elaine P. 127
Farber Literary Agency, Inc. 127
Farris Literary Agency, Inc. 127
Fort Ross, Inc., Russian-American Publishing Projects 129
Gelfman, Schneider, Literary Agents, Inc. 130
Gislason Agency, The 130
Goodman Associates 131
Greenburger Associates, Inc., Sanford J. 132
Grosjean Literary Agency, Jill 133
Grosvenor Literary Agency, The 133
Halsey North, Reece 133

Occult

Picture Books

Conference Index by Date

Our conference index organizes all conferences listed in this edition by the month in which they are held. If a conference bridges two months, you will find its name and page number under both monthly headings. If a conference occurs multiple times during the year (seasonally, for example), it will appear under each appropriate monthly heading. Turn to the listing's page number for exact dates and more detailed information.

Category Index

Our category index makes it easy for you to identify magazines and book publishers who are looking for a specific type of fiction. Publishers who are not listed under a fiction category either accept all types of fiction or have not indicated specific subject preferences. Also not appearing here are listings that need very specific types of fiction, e.g., "fiction about fly fishing only."

To use this index to find markets for your work, go to the category title that best describes the type of fiction you write and look under either Magazines or Book Publishers (depending on whom you're targeting). Finally, read individual listings *carefully* to determine the publishers best suited to your work.

For a listing of agents and the types of fiction they represent, see the Literary Agents Category Index beginning on page 558.

Book Publishers

CHILDRENS/JUVENILE
Magazines

Book Publishers

ETHNIC/MULTICULTURAL

Magazines

EXPERIMENTAL
Magazines

Book Publishers

Book Publishers

FEMINIST

Magazines

Book Publishers

Book Publishers

Category Index

Category Index

HUMOR/SATIRE

Magazines

LESBIAN
Magazines

Book Publishers

LITERARY
Magazines
ACM 179
Advocate, PKA's Publication 179
African American Review 179
African Voices 340
Alaska Quarterly Review 180
Albedo One 284
Alembic 284
Allegheny Review, The 181
Alsop Review, The 314
American Feed Magazine 315
American Literary Review 181
Ancient Paths 182
Anthology Magazine 182
Anti Muse 315
Antietam Review 182
Antigonish Review, The 183
Antioch Review 183
Appalachian Heritage 183
Aquarius 183
Arable 184
Arkansas Review 184
Art Times 341
Artful Dodge 185
Arts & Letters 185
Ascent 315
Axe Factory Review 185
Baltimore Review, The 186
Barbaric Yawp 186
Bathtub Gin 186
Beginnings Publishing Inc. 187
Bellevue Literary Review 187
Bellingham Review 187
Bellowing Ark 188
Beloit Fiction Journal 188
Berkeley Fiction Review 189
Bibliophilos 189
Big Country Peacock Chronicle 317
Big Muddy: A Journal of the Mississippi
    River Valley 189
BIGnews 190
Black Mountain Review, The 191
Black Warrior Review 191
Blackbird 317

Blue Mesa Review 191
Blueline 192
Boston Review 343
Boulevard 193
Brain, Child 345
Briar Cliff Review, The 193
Brillant Corners 193
Bryant Literary Review 194
Byline 194
Callaloo 194
Caribbean Writer, The 195
Carolina Quarterly 195
Carve Magazine 318
Center 196
Chaffin Journal 196
Chapman 196
Chariton Review, The 196
Chicago Quarterly Review 197
Chicago Review 197
Circle Magazine, The 287
collectedstories.com 318
Colorado Review 198
Columbia, A Journal of Literature and Art
    199
Concho River Review 199
Confluence 199
Confrontation, A Literary Journal 200
Connecticut Review 200
Convergence 200
Crab Orchard Review 201
Crucible 202
Dalhousie Review, The 203
Dan River Anthology 203
Dead Mule, The 320
Delmar 203
descant 290
Desert Voices 203
Diagram 321
Dicey Brown Magazine 204
DotLit 321
Down in the Dirt 290
Downstate Story 204
Dream Fantasy International 290
Dreams & Visions 291
Ducts 322

Category Index

Book Publishers

MAINSTREAM/ CONTEMPORARY

Magazines

MILITARY/WAR
Magazines

Book Publishers

MYSTERY/SUSPENSE

Magazines

NEW AGE/MYSTIC/SPIRITUAL

Magazines

Book Publishers

PSYCHIC/SUPERNATURAL/OCCULT

Magazines

REGIONAL

Magazines

Book Publishers

RELIGIOUS/INSPIRATIONAL
Magazines

Book Publishers

Writer's Digest

WRITE BETTER
GET PUBLISHED

DISCOVER A WORLD OF WRITING SUCCESS!

Are you ready to be praised, published, and paid for your writing? It's time to invest in your future with *Writer's Digest!* Beginners and experienced writers alike have been relying on *Writer's Digest*, the world's leading magazine for writers, for more than 80 years — and it keeps getting better! Each issue is brimming with:

- Technique articles geared toward specific genres, including fiction, nonfiction, business writing and more

- Business information specifically for writers, such as organizational advice, tax tips, and setting fees

- Tips and tricks for rekindling your creative fire

- The latest and greatest markets for print, online and e-publishing

- And much more!

That's a lot to look forward to every month. Let *Writer's Digest* put you on the road to writing success!

Get 2 FREE ISSUES of Writer's Digest!

NO RISK!
Send No Money Now!

☐ **Yes!** Please rush me my 2 FREE issues of *Writer's Digest* — the world's leading magazine for writers. If I like what I read, I'll get a full year's subscription (12 issues, including the 2 free issues) for only $19.96. That's 72% off the newsstand rate! If I'm not completely satisfied, I'll write "cancel" on your invoice, return it and owe nothing. The 2 FREE issues are mine to keep, no matter what!

Name _____

Address_____

City _____

State_____ZIP _____

E-mail _____

☐ You may contact me about my subscription via e-mail.
   (We won't use your address for any other purpose.)

Subscribers in Canada will be charged an additional US$10 (includes GST/HST) and invoiced. Outside the U.S. and Canada, add US$10 and remit payment in U.S. funds with this order. Annual newsstand rate: $71.88. Please allow 4-6 weeks for first-issue delivery.

Writer's Digest   www.writersdigest.com

J5FNMK

Get 2 FREE TRIAL ISSUES of

Writer's Digest

**WRITE BETTER
GET PUBLISHED**

Packed with creative inspiration, advice, and tips to guide you on the road to success, *Writer's Digest* offers everything you need to take your writing to the next level! You'll discover how to:

- Create dynamic characters and page-turning plots
- Submit query letters that publishers won't be able to refuse
- Find the right agent or editor
- Make it out of the slush-pile and into the hands of publishers
- Write award-winning contest entries
- And more!

See for yourself — order your 2 FREE trial issues today!

RUSH! 2 Free Issues!

**NO POSTAGE
NECESSARY
IF MAILED
IN THE
UNITED STATES**

BUSINESS REPLY MAIL
FIRST-CLASS MAIL   PERMIT NO. 340   FLAGLER BEACH FL

POSTAGE WILL BE PAID BY ADDRESSEE

Writer's Digest
PO BOX 421365
PALM COAST FL 32142-7104

SCIENCE FICTION

Magazines

Book Publishers

SHORT STORY COLLECTIONS
Book Publishers

THRILLER/ESPIONAGE

Magazines

Book Publishers

TRANSLATIONS
Magazines

Category Index

YOUNG ADULT/TEEN

Magazines

Book Publishers

General Index

O

General Index